30 *Romantic* We have Weekends for Two

WIN a *Romantic weekend for* 2

to be won in the AA Lifestyle Guide Free Prize Draw with the Virgin Hotel Collection

The Virgin Hotel Collection offers you an unbeatable experience of the highest standards of service, the friendliest welcome, adventurous, award-winning cuisine complemented by the finest wines and immaculate attention to detail to make your stay that little bit special. Splendid architecture reflecting past centuries houses luxurious interiors that enhance the ambience and individual style of each property. Beautiful scenery in secluded surroundings will ensure that your stay is peaceful, relaxing and one to remember.

A bouquet of flowers for every winner courtesy of Interflora

A total of 6 Prize Draws throughout the year, with 5 winners per draw.

Draws will be made on the last day of December 96 and then February, April, June, August and October 97.

For more information on the Virgin Hotel Collection, please call 0800 716 919

HOW TO ENTER
Just complete (in capitals, please) and ⸻ .ame and
address on a **stamped** postcard to the ⸻ :s limited to
one per household and to residents of ⸻ ll require a
stamp if posted in the Republic of Ire

GW00504622

MR/MRS/MISS/MS/OTHER, PLEASE ST.

NAME:

ADDRESS:

POSTCODE:

TEL.NOS:

Are you an AA Member ?   Yes/No

Have you bought this or any other AA Lifestyle Guide before?   Yes/No
If yes, please indicate the year of the last edition you bought:

The AA Hotel Guide	19____
AA Best Restaurants	19____
AA Bed and Breakfast Guide	19____
AA Camping and Caravanning (Britain & Ireland)	19____
AA Camping and Caravanning (W. Country & S. England)	19____
AA Camping and Caravanning (Europe)	19____

If you do not wish to receive further information or special offers on
AA Publishing ☐   Virgin Hotel Collection ☐ please tick the box

CCE97

Terms and Conditions

1. Five winners will be drawn for each of six prize draws to take place on 31 December, 1996, 28 February, 30 April, 30 June, 29 August, 31 October, 1997.

2. Closing date for receipt of entries is 1 day prior to the relevant draw date. Final close date for receipt of entries is 30 October 1997.

3. Entries received after any draw date except the final one will go forward into the next available draw. Entries will be placed in one draw only. Only one entry per household accepted.

4. Winners will be notified by post within 14 days of the relevant draw date. Prizes will be valid for 3 months from the relevant draw date. Prizes are not transferable and there will be no cash alternative.

5. Each prize is comprised of two nights with dinner, bed and a champagne breakfast on one morning, offered by Virgin Hotels. The package will be for two people sharing a double/twin room at any

of the UK hotels in the Virgin Hotel Collection. Dates subject to availability. The prize does not include other meals and drinks (except as stated), special activities such as golf etc. (these will be charged as taken), or travelling expenses.

6. All hotel accommodation, services and facilities are provided by Virgin Hotels and AA Publishing is not party to your agreement with Virgin Hotels in this regard.

7. The prize draw is open to anyone resident in the UK or the Republic of Ireland over the age of 18 other than employees of the Automobile Association or Virgin Hotels, their subsidiary companies, their families or agents

8. For a list of winners, please send a stamped, self-addressed envelope to AA Lifestyle Guide winners, Publishing Admin, Fanum House, Basing View, Basingstoke, Hants RG21 4EA.

9. If this card is posted in the Republic of Ireland it must have a stamp.

AA Lifestyle Guide Prize Draw

AA PUBLISHING

FANUM HOUSE

BASING VIEW

BASINGSTOKE

HANTS RG21 4EA

CAMPING
AND
CARAVANNING
EUROPE
1997

This edition published March 1997
© The Automobile Association 1997. The Automobile Association retains
the copyright in the current edition © 1997 and in all subsequent
editions, reprints and amendments to editions

Mapping is produced by the Cartographic Department of the Automobile
Association from the Automaps database using electronic and computer
technology. Maps © The Automobile Association 1997

The directory is compiled by the AA's Hotels and Touring Services
Department and generated from the AA's establishment database

Filmset by Avonset, 1 Palace Yard Mews, Monmouth Street, Bath
Printed and bound in Great Britain by Bemrose Security Printing, Derby
Advertisement Sales
Head of Advertisement Sales: Christopher Heard, telephone 01256 20123
ext. 21544
Advertisement Production: Karen Weeks, telephone 01256 20123
ext. 21545

The cover photograph was supplied by ZEFA Pictures Ltd.

A CIP catalogue record for this book is available from the British Library
ISBN 0 7495 1388 8   AA Ref. 57875

Published by AA Publishing, a trading name of
Automobile Association Developments Limited, whose registered office is
Norfolk House, Priestley Road, Basingstoke, Hampshire RG24 9NY.
Registered number 1878835

CONTENTS

SYMBOLS AND ABBREVIATIONS

For a more detailed explanation refer to About the Book (see contents page).

• ENGLISH •

A	adult
V	car
pp	per person
🚐	caravan or motor caravan
🛖	tent
☎	telephone
HEC	1 hectare (equals approx 2 acres)
▨	grass
⋮⋮	sand
⬦	stone
⇘	little shade
⌾	partly shaded
♠	mainly shaded
☂	shower
⚱	shop
✕	cafe/restaurant
⚲	bar
⊘	no dogs
☉	electric points for razors
⚡	electric points for caravans
⊘	Camping Gaz International
⚙	gas other than Camping Gaz
🏠	bungalows for hire
🚐	caravans for hire
⛺	tents for hire
⚓	swimming:
	L lake
	P pool
	R river
	S sea
🅿	parking by tents permitted
🅿	compulsory separate car park
♦	facilities not on site, but within 2km
⊞	first-aid facilities
⚑	site belongs to 'Castels & Camping Caravanning' chain (France only)
CM	camping municipal, parque munici pal de campismo, or parque de la camara municipal (local authority site)
KC	Kommunens Campingplads (local authority site)
lau	laundry
pitch	pitch charge per night for car with tent or caravan (there is usually a charge per adult

charge per night (applies to A, V, pp, caravan, tent)

in addition to this)

☞ Entry continued overleaf

Entries in italics indicate that particulars have not been confirmed by management.

Pour plus amples informations veuillez vous referer a About the Book (voir la table de matieres).

• FRANCAIS •

A	Adulte
V	Voiture
pp	par personne
🚐	Caravane ou camping car
🛖	Tente
☎	Telephone
HEC	1 hectare (correspond a environ 2 acres (mesures imperiales))
▨	Gazon
⋮⋮	Sable
⬦	Pierres
⇘	Peu ombrage
⌾	En partie ombrage
♠	Surtout ombrage
☂	Douches
⚱	Magasin
✕	Cafe/restaurant
⚲	Bar
⊘	Chiens non admis
☉	Prises de courant pour rasoirs electriques
⚡	Branchements electriques pour caravanes
⊘	Camping Gaz International
⚙	Gaz autre que Camping Gaz
🏠	Bungalows a louer
🚐	Caravanes a louer
⛺	Tentes a louer
⚓	Natation:
	L Lac
	P Piscine
	R Rivere
	S Mer
🅿	Stationnement voiture pres des tentes autorise
🅿	Utilisation des parkings voitures obligatoire
♦	Amenities pas sur le terrain, mais au plus, a 2km
⊞	Poste de premiers-secours
⚑	Terrain fait partie de la chaine

tarif pour une nuit (applies to A, V, pp, Caravane, Tente)

'Castels & Camping Caravanning' (en France seulement)

CM	Camping municipal
KC	Kommunens Campingplads (camping municipal)
lau	Blanchisserie
pitch	Tarif d'un emplacement pour une nuit pour voiture avec tente ou caravane (en general s'ajoute un tarif par adulte)

☞ Suite au verso

Une insertion imprime en italiques indique que la direction de l'etablissement n'a pas confirme les precisions.

Fur weitere Angaben beziehen Sie sich auf About the Book (siehe Inhaltsverzeichnis).

• DEUTSCH •

A	Erwachsene (r)
V	Auto
pp	Pro person
🚐	Caravan bzw. Campingbus
🛖	Zelt
☎	Telefon
HEC	1 Hektar (ca 2 acres)
▨	Grasboden
⋮⋮	Sandgelande
⬦	Steiniges Gelande
⇘	Wenig Schatten
⌾	Teilsschattig
♠	Grosstenteilsschattig
☂	Dusche
⚱	Laden
✕	Imbiss/Restaurant
⚲	Bar
⊘	Hundeverbot
☉	Stromanschlusse fur Rasierapparate
⚡	Stromanschlusse fur Caravans
⊘	Camping Gaz International
⚙	Gas ausser Camping Gaz International
🏠	Mietbungalows
🚐	Mietcaravans
⛺	Mietzelte
⚓	Schwimmen
	L See
	P Schwimmbad

Preis pro nacht (applies to A, V, pp, Caravan, Zelt)

● 4 ●

R Fluss
S Meer
⌂ Abstellen des PKWs neben dem Zelt gestattet
🅿 Separates Abstellen des PKWs obligatorisch
➡ Einrichtungen nicht an Ort und Stelle aber nicht weiter als 2 Kilometer entfernt
⊞ Unfallstation
🏰 Platz gehort der 'Castels & Camping Caravanning' (nur Frankreich)
CM Stadischer Campingplatz
KC Kommunens Campingplads (stadis cher Campingplatz)
lau Wascherei
pitch Stellplatzpreis pro Nacht fur Auto mit Zelt bzw. Caravan (normaler weise eine zusatzliche Berechnung pro Erwachsener)
☞ siehe umseitig

Eine kursiv gedruckte Eintragung zeigt an, dass die entsprechenden Angaben nicht von der Direktion bestatigt worden sind.

Per una spiegazione piu dettagliata, consultare la sezione About the Book (vedi indice).

──── ● **ITALIANO** ● ────

A Adulto ⎫
V Vettura ⎪
pp a persona ⎬ Prezzo per notte
🚐 Roulotte o camper ⎪
⎭
🔺 Tenda
☎ Telefono
HEC 1 ettaro (pari a 2 acri circa)
▤ Erba
∵ Sabbia
⬧ Pietra
⚲ Poca ombra
♧ Ombreggiato in parte
♠ Ombreggiato in gran parte
☂ Doccia
🏪 Negozio
✕ Caffe ristorante
🍸 Bar
🐕 Proibito ai cani
⊙ Prese elettriche rasoi
⊠ Prese elettriche roulotte
⊘ Camping Gaz Internatioal
🛢 Altri tipi di gas che non siano il Camping Gaz
🏨 Alfittansi bungalows
🚐 Affittansi roulotte
⚠ Affittansi tende
⚓ Nuoto

L Lago
P Piscina
R Fiume
S Mare
⌂ E permesso parcheggiare vicino alle tende
🅿 E obbligatorio parcheggiare nel posteggio apposito
➡ Le attrezzature non sono nel campeggio, bensi in un raggio di 2km
⊞ Proto soccorso
🏰 If campeggio appartienne alla cate na 'Castels & Camping Caravanning' (per la Francia sola mente)
CM Camping municipal (campeggio municipale)
KC Kommunens Campingplads (Campeggio municipale)
lau Lavanderia
pitch Prezzo pe notte di un posto macchina e tenda o roulotte (di solito ciascun adulto paga un extra oltre al posto macchina)
☞ La lista delle voci continua a tergo

Le voci in corsivo stanno a indicare che i particolari non sono stati confermati dalla Direzione.

Para una explicacion mas detallada, consultese la section About the Book (vease el indice de materias).

──── ● **ESPANOL** ● ────

A Adulto ⎫
V Automovil ⎪
pp Por persona ⎬ Precio por noche
🚐 Rulota o coche-rulota ⎪
⎭
🔺 Tienda
☎ Telefono
HEC 1 hectarea (igual a 2 acres aproximadamente)
▤ Hierba
∵ Arena
⬧ Piedra
⚲ Poca sombra
♧ Sombreado en parte
♠ Sombreado en su mayor parte
☂ Ducha
🏪 Almacen
✕ Cafe/restaurante
🍸 Bar
🐕 Se prohiben los perros
⊙ Tomas de corriente para maquini las electricas
⊠ Tomas de corriente para rulotas
⊘ Camping Gaz International

🛢 Otros tipos de gas que no sean el Gaz International
🏨 Se alquilan bungalows
🚐 Se alquiln rulotas
⚠ Se alquin tiendas
⚓ Natacion:
L Lago
P Piscina
R Rio
S Mar
⌂ Se permite estacionar el coche junto a las tiendas
🅿 Prohibido estacionarse fuera del aparacamiento
➡ Los servicios no estan en el camping, sino en un radio de 2km
⊞ Puesto de socorro
🏰 Este camping pertenece al grupo 'Castle & Camping Caravanning' (para Francia solamente)
CM Camping municipal
KC Kommunens Campingplads (camping municipal)
lau Lavanderia
pitch Precio por noche de un puesto para coche y tienda o ruleta (cada adulto pagara un suplemento ade mas del precio susodicho)
☞ La lista de simbolos continua a la vuelta

Los articulos en bastardilla indican que los detalles no han sido confirmados por la Direccion.

HOW TO USE THE GUIDE

Each COUNTRY IN THIS guide is divided into regions, so that you can easily find all the sites in your chosen holiday area. Within the regions, place names are listed in alphabetical order, and details of regional boundaries and site locations can be found on the country maps at the back of this book. If you need overnight stops on the way to your destination, the country maps should help you find something in the right place. Please remember that these maps are for site location purposes only and not for finding your way around. For route planning and use on the road, you should have a road atlas, such as the AA Big Road Atlas of Europe. Individual atlases of France, Germany and Italy are also available in the series.

• ADVANCE BOOKING •
Despite the carefree nature of a camping or caravanning holiday, it is best to book well in advance for peak holiday seasons, or for your first and last stop close to a ferry crossing point. However, we do find that some sites will not accept reservations. Although the AA cannot undertake to find sites or make reservations for you, we do include in this guide specimen booking letters in English, French, German, Italian and Spanish.

Please note that, although it is not common practice, some campsites may regard your deposit as a booking fee which is not deductible from the final account.

• ON ARRIVAL •
Look over the site if possible before you decide to stay. The information for any publication must be collected some time in advance, and ownership and standards may well have changed since our research was done. Even where standards are of the expected quality, the site may be very crowded and you may prefer to look elsewhere for more space and less noise.

When you look over a site, consider the following:

- Pleasant general situation, clean and tidy with plenty of refuse bins, site fenced and guarded.

- Sufficient and clean lavatories, washing facilities and showers with hot water. Well defined roads on site, preferably lit at night.

- Pitches should not be cramped.

- If you have a tent, make sure the surface is suitable for pegs; if you have a caravan, make sure the ground is firm enough.

- In hot weather there should be suitable shade, and if the weather is damp the ground should appear well drained.

- A good supply of safe drinking water.

- If you need the following facilities, confirm that they exist on the site: electric point for razors, Camping Gaz, a well stocked shop, laundry facilities, restaurant serving reason ably priced food, ice for sale.

Although most of the sites in this guide have been selected for the high standards they maintain, we have included, at the request of AA members, a number of sites along touring routes and others near the Channel ports which are suitable for overnight stops. These transit sites tend to become crowded at the height of the season, but provide the necessary amenities.

If you require information on additional sites, lists are free from most national tourist offices. In the introductions for each country we give details of local organisations which either publish a camping guide or provide more detailed information.

• CAMPSITE ENTRIES •
In order to update our information we send out questionnaires each year to every campsite. Inevitably a number of the questionnaires are not returned to us in time for publication, and where this is the case the campsite name is printed in italics.

• PRICES •
Prices are given in local currencies and are

detailed per night, per adult, car, caravan and tent. We do not give charges relating to children, as these vary, but generally a 50 per cent reduction is made for children aged 3-14. To determine the cost of one night, simply add up the prices that apply to your party.

Some campsites do have different ways of structuring their prices. Whatever the variations may be, all will be reflected in the entry. Exceptions are:

pp Campsite charges per person. The charge for the vehicle and caravan/tent is included in the price for each person. For a party of four people, multiply the **pp** price by four for the total cost per night.

pitch This is the price per pitch, regardless of whether it is a caravan or a tent. Where the word pitch follows the 'A' for adult price, you should multiply the 'A' price by the number of adults in the party, then add the pitch price to that total tobtain the cost per night for your party.

● **OPENING TIMES** ●
Dates shown are inclusive of opening dates. If the site is open all year, then 'All year' is written in the entry. All information was correct at the time of going to press, but we recommend you to check with the site before arriving. Changes of date often occur because of demand and/or weather. Sometimes only restricted facilities are available between October and April.

● **COMPLAINTS** ●
If you have any complaint about a site, do discuss the problem with the site proprietor immediately so that the matter can be dealt with promptly. If a personal approach fails, inform the AA when you return home.
We regret, however, that the AA cannot act as intermediary in any dispute, or attempt to gain refunds or compensation. Your comments, however, help us to prepare new editions.

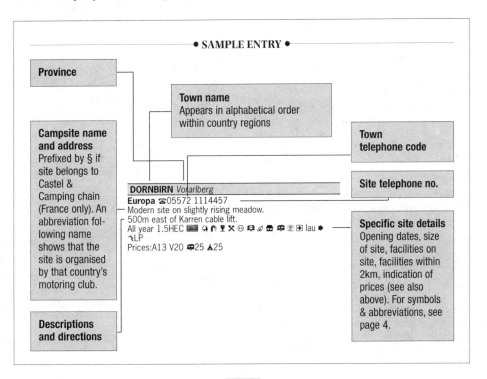

● SAMPLE ENTRY ●

Province

Town name
Appears in alphabetical order within country regions

Campsite name and address
Prefixed by § if site belongs to Castel & Camping chain (France only). An abbreviation following name shows that the site is organised by that country's motoring club.

Town telephone code

Site telephone no.

DORNBIRN *Vorarlberg*
Europa ☎05572 1114457
Modern site on slightly rising meadow.
500m east of Karren cable lift.
All year 1.5HEC ▦ ⊕ ♁ ⬆ ✗ ⊙ ⬆ ∅ ☎ ⬆ ⬆ ☎ ⊞ lau ➡ ↘LP
Prices:A13 V20 ⬆25 ▲25

Specific site details
Opening dates, size of site, facilities on site, facilities within 2km, indication of prices (see also above). For symbols & abbreviations, see page 4.

Descriptions and directions

PREPARING FOR YOUR JOURNEY

BEFORE SETTING OFF ON YOUR CONTINENTAL HOLIDAY, THERE
ARE CERTAIN PREPARATIONS YOU SHOULD MAKE AND SOME
REGULATIONS YOU SHOULD KNOW ABOUT. EXPERIENCED CAMPERS
AND CARAVANNERS WILL, OF COURSE, BE FAMILIAR WITH MOST OF
THIS, BUT WE HOPE IT WILL BE A USEFUL
CHAPTER FOR NEWCOMERS.

• PREPARING YOUR CARAVAN •

Your caravan should of course be regularly serviced, but the following tips should be useful, specially for the first trip after winter storage.

Just before your trip give the caravan a good airing and, if you have a water pump fitted, check the flow and flush with clean water to get rid of any staleness. Make sure that there are no leaks and replace any doubtful washers. Examine all potential leak spots, especially around window rubbers, rear light clusters and roof lights, applying sealing compound as necessary. Test all window, cupboard and locker catches to make sure that they shut firmly. Outside, clean rain gutters and make sure down-spouts and window channel drainpipes are clear.

Brakes

Check that the caravan braking mechanism is correctly adjusted. If it has a breakaway safety mechanism, the cable between car and caravan must be firmly anchored so that the trailer brakes act immediately if the two part company.

Lights

Make sure that all the lights are working - rear lights, stop lights, number-plate lights, rear fog guard lamps and flashers (check that the flasher rate is correct: 60-120 times a minute).

Tyres

Both tyres on the caravan should be of the same size and type. Make sure that the tread depth is well above the legal minimum (see Continental ABC) and that there is no uneven wear. Look also for cuts and for cracks that might have developed during the winter. Replace any suspect tyres and any tyres over five years old, irrespective of the amount of tread remaining. Remember, caravan tyres rarely wear out but do deteriorate with age.

If the caravan tyres are not going to be used for a long period, inflate them and take the weight off them by jacking the axle on wood blocks. Leave in an airy place where they will not be exposed to the sun, and cover if possible.

• PREPARING YOUR TENT •

Some weeks before your holiday, choose a fine day, spread the tent on the lawn or some other space so that you can make a close inspection of all potential stress points: where guylines attach, where the ground sheet meets tent walls, and where the frame poles come into contact with fabric. The fabric of the tent can be damaged by branches or sharp objects and by mildew if it has not been stored correctly. Additionally, it can lose its proofing through long exposure to the weather, as a result of being splashed by cooking fat or by washing-up water containing detergent. If your tent is damaged in this way, consult a specialist camping supplier. Patch kits of different colours and materials are available, as are proofing preparations and sprays.

• PREPARING YOUR CAMPING EQUIPMENT •

Use this camping equipment check list when you are planning what to take:

- Air mattress and pump, or camp beds
- All-purpose knife
- Bucket
- Camp stove and fuel
- Clothes-line and pegs
- Cutlery, including cooking utensils
- Dishcloths, scouring pad, and tea towels

- First-aid kit
- Folding chairs or stools
- Folding table
- Food containers
- Ground sheet
- Icebox (portable)
- Kettle
- Mallet
- Matches
- Plastic bags or bags for litter
- Plates, cups and saucers, or mugs
- Rope
- Saucepans, frying pan
- Sleeping bags
- Small brush (useful when camping on sand)
- Teapot
- Tent, poles, tent pegs (spares), sand pegs and discs
- Tent-tidy (for scissors, string, needles, thread, etc.)
- Tin-opener, bottle-opener, and corkscrew
- Torch and batteries
- Washing powder
- Washing-up bowl and washing-up liquid
- Water and milk containers
- Water-purifying tablets
- Windshield

● HOW TO ENSURE GOOD ROAD HANDLING ●

Before you load all your luggage and equipment into the caravan,check on the weight restrictions that apply to it and to the towing vehicle. The laden weight of the caravan should always be less than, and ideally no more than 85 per cent of the kerbside weight of the towing vehicle.

This kerbside weight is defined as: the weight of the vehicle, inclusive of any towing bracket with which it is normally equipped, a supply of fuel and of other necessary liquids (e.g. water, oil, brake fluid, etc.) but with no passengers and no load other than normal tools and equipment.

The weight of the caravan is normally specified in the purchase literature, and usually refers to the weight 'ex works' or 'delivered'. This can be misleading because it is normally based on the standard model and may not take into account any fitted extras; one way to be certain is to take the unladen caravan to your local public weighbridge. Once you have the accurate unladen weight, subtract that from the manufacturer's

recommended gross weight, and the figure you arrive at will be the amount of equipment you can safely load into the caravan.Remember that this weight should not exceed 85 per cent of the kerbside weight of your car as given in the manufacturer's handbook.

Loading can greatly affect the stability of the car-caravan combination on the road. Keep as much weight as possible near the trailer axle, and store heavy equipment on the caravan floor. Never store heavy items at the rear of the caravan in an attempt to counterbalance an excessive nose weight - this causes instability and can be very dangerous. Keep the roof lockers free of luggage if possible and ensure lockers, drawers and cupboards are securely closed so there are no loose items that could roll about.

After loading, check that the caravan, when coupled to the car, is level with the ground, or slightly nose down. If the nose is up, this can be corrected by a hitch height adjuster, available from caravan manufacturers or dealers. An adapter plate can be used to lower the tow-ball mounting, but it does put extra pressure on the bracket.

Check that the nose weight of the trailer complies with the car manufacturer's recommendations. As a guide, the nose weight should be heavier than the rear by about 40-50kg (90-119lbs). Check the nose weight of the laden caravan with bathroom scales and blocks of wood or a spring balance. A twin-axle trailer must be weighed when the coupling is at the exact towing height.

Obtaining the ideal weight and weight distribution of the car-trailer combination helps prevent pitching and snaking. Pitching can also be prevented by stiffening the towing car's rear suspension - either fit a supplementary rubber or air spring unit to the rear spring, or use heavier duty shock absorbers. (more expensive) but always ensure first that the car's front and rear shock absorbers are in good condition.

Excessive pitching and/or bad weight distribution can lead to snaking as the vertical movement sways the caravan sideways. This can be particularly dangerous, since the first instinct is to steer against the movement, which only makes matters worse. The best course is to steer straight and gently decelerate. Stabilisers are available, but it is far better to cure the cause.

When choosing a car with which you intend to tow a caravan or trailer, remember that the amount of overhang - the distance between the car's rear axle and the towing ball - has an effect on the handling. The greater the overhang the more difficult handling will be.

• **A FEW FINAL CHECKS** •

● corner steadies are fully wound up and the brace is handy for when you arrive on site;

● windows, vents and doors are firmly shut;

● any fires or flames are extinguished and the tap on the gas cylinder is turned off;

● the coupling is firmly in position;

● the over-run brake is working correctly;

● both car wing mirrors give good visibility ;

● all the car and caravan lights are working;

● the safety catch on the hitch is on;

● the jockey wheel is raised and secured, the handbrake is released, and the fire extinguishers are operational and close at hand.

Much of the art of towing comes with experience, but many of the problems can be eliminated by being aware:

● Know your car well before attempting to tow.

● Stop before you get tired.

● Plan to use roads suitable for towing.

● Have the appropriate mirrors and use them.

● If traffic builds up behind you, pull up safely and let it pass.

● Keep a safe stopping distance between you and the vehicle in front.

● Switch on your headlights whenever visibility becomes poor.

● Make good use of the gears on hills.

● Allow plenty of time when overtaking or pulling across a main road.

● Never stop on narrow roads, bends, crests of hills, or anywhere that could be dangerous

● In case of breakdown or accident, use hazard flashers and warning triangle(s).

Off-road handling
On site you may encounter difficult ground. Try to avoid pitches liable to be waterlogged; sand that will not take the force of a driving wheel; and stone and shingle that provide no grip.
    If you have to drive over difficult ground, keep moving slowly with a very light throttle. If you stop, do not accelerate hard or the wheels will spin and dig in. Move gently backwards and forwards to get out of a dip. If the driving wheels do dig in, put brushwood or sacks in front of and behind the wheels. To move the trailer manually, pull sideways on the drawbar and then work the trailer forwards by chocking alternate wheels.

• **CAMPING FUELS** •
Gas in cylinders or bottles, as used in caravans, is mainly of two types, butane and propane. Both are kept as liquid under pressure and become a combustible gas once the pressure is released. They are available on the Continent, but propane is more widely distributed in countries with low winter temperatures. Propane has a higher pressure than butane. See pages 11-12.

Carriage of gas by car ferries
Vehicles carrying unsealed cylinders of liquefied petroleum gas (LPG) must report at both United Kingdom and European ports for a leakage test at least 30 minutes before the published reporting time. A maximum of three Home Office approved cylinders, not exceeding 35lb net weight each, or up to 12 small expendable cartridges, sealed and packed in an outer container, are allowed for each caravan. Cylinders should be securely fixed in or on the caravan as intended by the caravan manufacturer.
    New users of LPG particularly should follow safety instructions and experienced people sometimes need reminding of the safety rules:

● change cylinders with care
● provide fresh air for safe combustion
● don't improvise or tamper with equipment
● have regular maintenance carried out by ●
qualified engineers

Gas safety rules

1 Always use the right type and length of hose for connections If in doubt, ask the dealer's advice.
2 Replace worn hose. Never try repairs.
3 When fitting the hose, where applicable use worm-drive clips and ensure they are tight.
4 Always use a spanner when fitting connections - finger tightness is not enough. Before fitting a regulator or other screwed connec tion to a butane cylinder, always ensure that the sealing washer is there and in good condition. When fitting to switch-on or clip-on valves, refer to the manufacturer's or supplier's instructions.
5 Check for leaks by applying soapy water. Any leaks will be shown by bubbles.
6 NEVER check for leaks with a naked flame.
7 Always keep containers away from excessive heat or naked flames.
8 When starting,.open container valve slowly.
9 If the container is not to be used for a while close the valve, remove the pressure regulator and replace the valve cover if fitted.
10 When changing a cartridge or container, keep away from any naked light, flame or source of ignition. Ensure good ventilation. With cartridge appliances, check that the sealing washer, usually housed in the appliance inlet connection, is in position and in good condition. Make sure that the valve on the container, where fitted, and the tap on the regulator are fully closed. Never try to change a pierceable cartridge (such as the Camping Gaz type) until you are sure all the gas has been expended. You can usually hear any gas remaining by gently shaking.
11 Once the pressure regulators are set they should not be tampered with. Adjustments or repairs should be left to a dealer.
12 Containers must always stand upright, valves uppermost, whether in use or not. Carry them upright, but not by the valve.
13 Whether full or empty, never store the containers below ground or near drains, as all

these gases are heavier than air and will collect at the lowest point in the event of a leak.
14 Good ventilation is essential where gas burning appliances are used. Un-flued appliances must not be installed in sleeping areas. Only room-sealed appliances should be installed in bath or shower rooms.
15 When moving, turn off all appliances and cylinder valves.
16 Do not sleep in a room where gas cylinders are in use.
17 Permanent storage must always be outdoors.
18 When fitting cylinders, always check that the cylinder valve is fully closed in a clock wise direction before removing the valve-sealing cap or plug.

● BRANDED GASES ●

Shell Gas BUTANE This product is marketed in 5.5kg, 7kg, 13kg and 15kg cylinders, with a variety of connecting systems, by eight local subsidiary companies operating in England and Wales. Details of these companies, who will also advise on the location of stockists, can be obtained by ringing Freephone Shell Gas. However, because of differing official standards and regulations to which cylinders must conform, butane cylinders cannot be exchanged for Continental ones, nor can they be refilled abroad. Foreign cylinders must not be brought back to the United Kingdom, nor British cylinders left on the Continent. For these reasons it is wise to take enough gas to last throughout the holiday.

A list of main agents can be obtained from Shell Gas, West Riverside, Immingham, Humberside DN40 1AA telephone 01496 578076.Main agents will be able to give you names and addresses of local sub-agents.

Butane is, however, marketed by Shell in France, the Netherlands, Switzerland, Belgium, Portugal and Luxembourg, usually in cylinders of 13kg capacity (approximately 29lb). British butane regulators will not connect directly with cylinders obtained in these countries because of differing connections. A regulator must be obtained on loan. Deposits on cylinders are payable on purchase; you must ensure that you obtain a receipt in order to get your deposit refunded. If your burner is specifically designed for use with butane gas it is inadvisable to use it with any other gas, such as propane or a propane-butane mixture.

Shell Gas (PROPANE): Marketed by Shell Gas in 3.9kg, 11kg, 18.5kg and 46kg cylinders in Britain.

Calor Gas (BUTANE): Marketed by Calor Gas Ltd, Appleton Park, Datchet, Slough, Berks SL3 9JG tel 0800 626626. Although Calor Gas refills are not available abroad, You can take sufficient with you to last for a short holiday, as follows:

Camping: Single-burner picnic set or double-burner camp stove with 4.5kg butane cylinder

Motor Caravan: Two-burner hotplate or two-burner hotplate grill with 4.5kg butane cylinder

Caravan: Two-burner hotplate or small cooker, with 4.5kg butane cylinder with screw-on connections or 15kg butane cylinder or 7kg butane cylinder which will both accept the switch-on regulator. Take two 4.5kg or two 7kg.

If you follow the instructions a 4.5kg cylinder will last a month on either single or double-burner units.

If you cannot take enough Calor Gas cylinders in your outfit, you are advised to buy a Camping Gaz connecting tap before leaving this country. This enables a Calor Gas regulator or flow-control valve (or just the Calor Gas connecting nut in the case of appliances not using regulating equipment) to be connected to a Camping Gaz 904 or 907 cylinder (the exception to this is the quick-boiling ring or single burner, which fits directly to the 4.5kg cylinder shroud). The connecting tap is available fromCalor Gas dealers.

Calor Gas (PROPANE): Marketed by Calor Gas Ltd, in 3.9kg, 6kg, 13kg and 19kg cylinders. This is suitable for those undertaking all-year-round camping and caravanning.

Primus (PROPANE): Primus cylinders are available in three sizes - 2000 (0.34kg), 2005 (0.8kg) and 2012 (1.98kg) - to complement the company's extensive range of leisure, DIY and industrial appliances. Cylinders are filled and distributed

in this country by Calor Gas Ltd, and are available from most Calor Dealers.

Primus (BUTANE): Cartridges nos. 2201 (200g), 2202 (420g) and the new 2207 (220g) low profile, are widely available in Britain and on the Continent (except in Spain and Eastern Europe). French legislation makes it advisable to carry enough cartridges for passage through France.

Camping Gaz International (BUTANE): Marketed in the United Kingdom by Camping Gaz (GB) Ltd, 9 Albert Street, Slough, Berks SL1 2BH tel 0753 691707. This product is widely marketed throughout the Continent (see below) but prices can vary considerably in different countries. A list of their general agents is available from the company. Please contact them direct.

The cartridges are expendable, but cylinders are fully interchangeable for use with cooking, lighting and heater units. A special connecting tap unit is available to fit Shell Gas or Calor Gas regulators to Camping Gaz 904 or 907 cylinders. Gas is available in the following European countries: Andorra, Austria, Belgium, France, Germany, Italy, Luxembourg, Netherlands, Portugal, Spain including Majorca and Ibiza (cartridge 206 and 901 and 907 only), Switzerland and the United Kingdom.

Paraffin
Paraffin (pétrole or kerosene) is not easily obtainable in country districts in Europe and you are advised to get supplies on arrival in large towns. Methylated spirit (alcoöl à brûler) is easier to get.

Safety
●
Always make sure you have the right size and type of gas cartridge for the appliance.
●
Never put a cartridge in a cartridge holder unless the upper part of the appliance has been unscrewed and completely removed.
●
A cartridge with gas in it must never be removed from an appliance nor must the upper part of the appliance be unscrewed.

CONTINENTAL ABC
MOTORING AND GENERAL
INFORMATION

THIS ABC PROVIDES A GENERAL BACKGROUND OF MOTORING REGULATIONS AND GENERAL INFORMATION, AND IS DESIGNED TO BE READ IN CONJUNCTION WITH THE RELEVANT COUNTRY INTRODUCTIONS.

MOTORING LAWS ON THE Continent should cause little difficulty to British motorists, but drivers should take more care and extend greater courtesy then they would normally do at home, and bear in mind the essentials of good motoring - avoiding any action likely to obstruct traffic, endanger persons or cause damage to property.

Road signs are mainly the familiar international ones, but in every country there are a few exceptions; watch especially for signs showing crossings and speed limits. Probably the most unfamiliar aspect of motoring abroad to British motorists is the rule giving priority to traffic coming from the right, and unless this priority is varied by signs, it must be strictly observed.

A tourist driving abroad should always carry a current passport, a full valid national driving licence (even when an International Driving Permit is held), the registration document of the car and evidence of insurance. The proper international distinguishing sign should be displayed on the rear of the vehicle and caravan or trailer. The appropriate papers must be carried at all times. The practice of spot checks on foreign cars is widespread; to avoid inconvenience or a police fine, be sure that your papers are in order and that the international distinguishing sign is of the approved standard design.

Make sure that you have clear all-round vision. See that your seat belts are securely mounted and undamaged, and remember that in most Continental countries their use is compulsory. If you carry skis remember that their tips should point to the rear. You must be sure that your vehicle complies with the regulations concerning dimensions for all the countries you intend to pass through (see below and relevant country introductions). This is particularly necessary if you are towing a trailer of any sort.

Mechanical repairs and replacement parts can be very expensive abroad and many occur because the vehicle has not been properly prepared before the journey, which may involve many miles of hard driving over unfamiliar roads.

We recommend a major service by a franchised dealer before you go abroad. You should also check yourself for any obvious defects. It is not practicable to provide a complete check list, but consult the ABC below under the following headings:

Automatic gearboxes
Automatic transmission fluid
Brakes
Cold-weather touring
Direction indicators
Electrical
Engine and mechanical
Lights
Spares
Tyres
Warm-climate touring

Also consult your manufacturer's handbook. AA members can arrange a thorough check of their car by one of the AA's experienced engineers; any AA shop can arrange this at a few days' notice. Our engineer will submit a written report, complete with a list of repairs required. There is a fee for this service; for more information please ask for our leaflet Tech 8.

Accidents
The country introductions give telephone numbers for the fire, police and ambulance services.

International regulations are similar to those in the UK; the following action is usually required or advisable:

If you are involved in an accident you must stop. A warning triangle should be placed on the road at a suitable distance to warn following traffic of the obstruction. The use of hazard warning lights in no way affects the regulations governing the use of warning triangles. Get medical assistance for anyone injured in the accident. If the accident necessitates calling the police, leave the vehicle in the position in which it came to rest. If it seriously obstructs other traffic, mark the position of the vehicle on the road and get the details confirmed by independent witnesses before moving it.

The accident must be reported to the police in the following circumstances: if it is required by law, if the accident has caused death or bodily injury, or if an unoccupied vehicle or property has been damaged and there is no one present to represent the interests of the party suffering damage.

Be sure to notify your insurance company (by letter if possible), within 24 hours of the accident (see the conditions of your policy). If a third party is injured,contact your insurers for advice or, if you have a Green Card, notify the company-or bureau, given on the back of your Green Card; this company or bureau will deal with any compensation claim from the injured party. AA policy holders should refer to 'AA Policy Holders Driving Abroad' statement for advice.

Make sure that all essential particulars are noted, especially details concerning third parties, and co-operate with police or other officials taking on-the-spot notes by supplying your name, address or other personal details as required. It is also a good idea to take photographs of the scene. Try to get good shots of other vehicles involved, their registration plates and any background which might help later enquiries. This record may be useful when completing the insurance company's accident form.

Automatic gearboxes

The fluid in an automatic gearbox does more work when it has to cope with the extra weight of a caravan. It becomes hotter and thinner, so there is more slip and more heat generated in the gearbox. Many manufacturers recommend the fitting of a gearbox oil cooler. Check with the manufacturer as to what is suitable for your car.

Automatic transmission fluid

Automatic transmission fluid is not always readily available, especially in some of the more remote areas of Western Europe, and tourists are advised to carry an emergency supply.

•B•

BBC World Service

World Service is the international radio arm of the BBC. It broadcasts in more than 40 languages, including a 24-hour-a-day English Service. English programmes can be heard throughout Europe. There is world news on the hour and regular bulletins of British news. People in north-west Europe can listen on medium or long wave at these times:

kHz	Metres	Summer broadcasting times - GMT
198	1515	2345-0500
648	463	0000-0800;
		0830-1200;1215-1530;
		1600-1730; 1800-2400

BBC World Service also transmits on short wave. Full details are available in the free programme guide. To obtain a copy, write to BBC World Service, PO Box 76, Bush House, London WC2B 4PH. If you are buying a new radio receiver to listen to the BBC overseas, World Service recommends that you choose a digitally tuned one because it makes finding frequencies easier.. Make sure your short-wave set can receive some of the key European frequencies such as 9410, 12095 and 15070kHz. A monthly magazine, BBC On Air, provides details of all World Service programmes and frequencies, with background information about features and personalities. It costs £2.00 per copy or an annual subscription of £18.00. For information, call. 0171 257 2211.

Boats

The completion of the Single Market on 1 January 1993 abolished temporary importation, permitting free movement of privately owned boats between member states provided VAT has been paid. Boat owners are now able to use their boats throughout the year in all EU countries, instead of being limited to a specified period of, for example, only six months of the year.

However all boats taken abroad by road should be registered in the UK, except for very small craft to be used close inshore in France. In France such craft are exempt from registration and the dividing line falls approximately between a Laser dinghy (which should be registered) and a Topper (which need not be); however, to avoid any confusion, registration is recommended. See also Identification Plate. Registration is carried out by the Small Ships Register at the DVLA at a current fee of £10. The original Certificate of Registry is required, not a photocopy. Application forms for Small Ships Registration, accompanied by notes on the purpose of the Register, eligibility for registration, and on completion of the form, are available from the DVLA, Swansea SA99 1BX telephone 01792 783355

Application forms are also available from each of the Department of Transport's Vehicle Registration Offices; from most yacht/boat clubs, marinas and shipyards

Of the countries in this guide, an International Certificate of Competence (ICC) is required for Germany, Portugal, Spain and some parts of Italy; it is also required on French inland waters for vessels with an engine of more than 6HP and on Belgian and Dutch inland waters for vessels over 15 metres in length or capable of more than 20km per hour. The ICC is only acceptable for vessels on lakes, rivers and canals. For vessels over 15 metres in length or capable of more than 20 km per hour using the Schelde estuary, Ijsselmeer or Waddersee, an RYA (shore-based) day skipper course is required as well as the ICC. For further information, contact the Royal Yachting Association, RYA House, Romsey Road, Eastleigh, Hampshire SO50 9YA telephone 01703 627400

Third party insurance is compulsory for boats in Italy and Switzerland (see country introductions) and advisable elsewhere on the Continent.

Brakes

Car brakes must always be in peak condition. Check both the level in the brake fluid reservoir and the thickness of the brake lining/pad material. The brake fluid should be completely changed according to the manufacturer's instructions or at intervals of not more than 18 months or

18,000 miles. However, it is always advisable to change the brake fluid before starting a Continental holiday, particularly if the journey includes travelling through a hilly or mountainous area.

Breakdown

If your car breaks down, try to move it to the side of the road, or to a position where it will obstruct the traffic flow as little as possible. Place a warning triangle at the appropriate distance on the road behind the obstruction. Bear in mind road conditions and, if near or on a bend, the triangle should be placed where it is clearly visible to following traffic. If the car is fitted with hazard warning lights these may only be effective on straight roads, and will have no effect at bends or rises in the road. If the fault is electrical, the lights may not operate, which is why they cannot take the place of a triangle.

Motorists are advised to take out AA Five Star Europe, the overseas motoring emergency service. You can purchase breakdown and accident benefits, and personal travel insurance. It is available to all motorists travelling in Europe, although non-AA members pay a small additional premium. The AA and/or the insurer may also ask for an indemnity or guarantee if the proposer is under 18 or not permanently resident within the British Isles. Details/brochures are available from AA shops or phone 0345 555577.

NOTE: Members who have not purchased AA Five Star Europe prior to departure and who subsequently need assistance will have to provide a deposit to cover estimated costs and a service fee. All expenses must be reimbursed to the AA in addition to the service fee.

British Embassies/Consulates (See also country introductions)

In most Continental countries there is usually more than one British Consulate. The functions and office hours of Vice-Consulates and Honorary Consuls can be more restricted than those of full Consulates.

Consulates (and consular sections of the embassy) are ready to help British travellers overseas, but there are limits to what they can do. A consulate cannot pay your hotel, medical or any other bills, nor will they do the work of travel agents, information bureaux or police. Any loss or theft should first be reported to the local police, not the consulate, and a statement obtained confirming the loss or theft. If you still need help, such as the issue of an emergency passport or guidance on how to transfer funds, contact the consulate. See respective country introductions for addresses and locations of British Embassies and British Consulates.

•C•

Camping Card International
A Camping Card International may be purchased from the AA by anyone over 18 who has taken out AA Five Star Europe and/or is a member of the AA or other motoring organisation affiliated to the Alliance Internationale de Tourisme (AIT). Recognised at most campsites in Europe, the camping card is essential in some cases and you will not be allowed to camp without it. At certain campsites a reduction to the advertised charge may be allowed on presentation of the camping card. An application form may be obtained from any AA shop.

The camping card provides third-party insurance cover for up to 11 people camping away from home or staying in rented accommodation or at a hotel. Although valid for 12 months from date of issue, expiry of your Five Star Europe cover or club membership invalidates the card. Each card purchased is accompanied by a summary of the third-party insurance cover, conditions of use and details of the campers' code. A CCI Information and Discount booklet will also be provided.

On arrival at the campsite, report to the campsite manager who will tell you where you may pitch your tent or caravan. You may be asked to pay in advance, or alternatively, to give into charge the camping card for the length of your stay. Some campsite managers may also insist upon the retention of all passports.

Caravan and luggage trailers
Take a list of contents, especially if any valuable or unusual equipment is being carried, as this may be required at a frontier. A towed vehicle should be readily identifiable by a plate in an accessible position showing the name of the maker of the vehicle and the production or serial number. See Identification plate and also Principal mountain passes.

Channel Tunnel
Eurotunnel's Le Shuttle car passenger service provides fast, frequent, reliable travel between Folkestone and Calais, 24 hours a day. With up to four departures an hour at peak times, reservations are not necessary. The journey takes only 35 minutes from platform to platform, and just over an hour from the M20 motorway in Britain to the A16 motorway in France.

Motorists leave the M20 at Exit 11a (clearly signposted to the Channel Tunnel) and buy a ticket on arrival at the tollbooths by cash, cheque or credit card - or in advance from the Le Shuttle Customer Service Centre, travel agents or motoring organisations. Prices are charged per vehicle, and not by the number of passengers.

Passengers can then follow the clearly signposted routes to take the next available departure, or visit the Passenger Terminal which has a selection of shops, restaurants and cafes, with toilets, telephones, duty free and bureau de change facilities. Before boarding Le Shuttle, passengers pass through frontier controls for both Britain and France, so there are no delays on arrival.

The shuttles are spacious, air-conditioned and well lit. Passengers stay with their vehicles for the short journey, although they can get out and walk around, and use the toilet facilities situated in every third carriage. Le Shuttle Radio and visual display screens keep passengers informed of the journey's progress, and traffic and weather conditions.

On arrival in France, unloading Le Shuttle takes about 8 minutes and - with no further frontier controls - motorists drive straight on to the A16 autoroute with the minimum of fuss.

For further information, telephone Le Shuttle Customer Service Centre on 0990 353535, or write to: PO Box 300, Folkestone, Kent CT19 4QW.

Claims against third parties
The law and levels of damages in foreign countries are different to our own. Some types of claim present difficulties, the most common

relating to recovery of car hire charges. Rarely are they fully recoverable, and in some countries they may be drastically reduced or not recoverable at all. General damages for pain and suffering are not recoverable in certain countries but even in countries where they are, the level of damages is usually lower than that expected in the UK.

The negotiation of claims against foreign insurers is extremely protracted and translation of documents slows the process. A delay of three months between sending a letter and getting a reply is not uncommon.

Legal costs and expenses are not recoverable in many Continental countries. AA Five Star Europe includes a discretionary service in certain matters arising abroad requiring legal assistance, including pursuit of uninsured loss claims against third parties arising from an accident involving the insured vehicle. Policy holders should seek assistance from the AA.

Cold-weather touring
If you are planning a winter tour, fit a high-temperature (winter) thermostat and make sure that the strength of your antifreeze mixture is correct for low temperatures.

If travelling through snow-bound regions, it is important to remember that for many resorts and passes the authorities insist on wheel chains or spiked or studded tyres. However, as these can damage bare road surfaces, they can only be used during limited periods, and in certain countries the use of spiked or studded tyres is illegal. Signposts usually indicate if wheel chains or spiked or studded tyres are compulsory.

In fair weather, wheel chains or spiked or studded tyres are only necessary on the higher passes, but (as a rough guide) in severe weather you will probably need them at altitudes exceeding 610 metres (2000ft).

Wheel chains fit over the driving wheels to enable them to grip on snow or icy surfaces. They are sometimes called snow chains or anti-skid chains. Full-length chains which fit tightly round a tyre are the most satisfactory, but they must be fitted correctly. Check that they do not foul your vehicle bodywork; if your vehicle has front-wheel drive put the steering on full lock while checking. It is essential that you also check the vehicle's handbook for the manufacturer's

recommendations on snow chains. On some vehicles there is insufficient clearance between the tyre and bodywork and they cannot be used. Chains should only be used when compulsory or necessary, as prolonged use on hard surface will damage the tyres.

Spiked or studded tyres are sometimes called snow tyres. They are tyres with rugged treads on to which spikes or studs have been fitted. For the best grip they should be fitted to all wheels. The correct type of spiked or studded winter tyres will generally be more effective than chains.

NOTE: The above guidelines do not apply where extreme winter conditions prevail. For extreme conditions it is doubtful whether the cost of preparing a car normally used in the UK would be justified for a short period. However, the AA's Technical Services Department can advise on specific enquiries.

Compulsory equipment
All countries have differing regulations as to how vehicles circulating on their roads should be equipped, but generally domestic laws are not enforced on visiting foreigners. However, where a country considers aspects of safety or other factors are involved, they will impose some regulations on visitors and these will be mentioned in the country introductions.

Crash (safety) helmets
All countries in this guide require visiting motorcyclists and their passengers to wear crash, or safety, helmets except Belgium where they are currently a recommendation and may become compulsory in the course of 1997.

Credit and charge cards
See under Payment Cards.

Currency notes (See also country introductions)
There is no limit to the amount of sterling notes you may take abroad. It is better, however, to take enough currency notes of the country you are visiting for immediate expenses. Some countries have regulations controlling the import and export of their currency. You are advised to consult your bank for information before making final arrangements.

Customs regulations for Continental countries
The completion of the European single market on 1 January 1993 abolished temporary importation, permitting free movement between member states. Consequently, persons travelling from one member state to another will be free to take not only their personal belongings, but a motor vehicle, boat (see also Boats), caravan or trailer across the internal frontiers without being subject to any Customs control or formality. Bona fide visitors to non-EU countries may generally assume that they may temporarily import personal articles duty free, providing the following conditions are met:

● that the articles are for personal use, and are not to be sold or otherwise disposed of;

● that they may be considered as being in use, and in keeping with the personal status of the importer;

● that they are taken out when the importer leaves the country;

● that the goods stay for no more than 6 months in any 12 month period, whichever is the earlier.

All dutiable articles must be declared when you enter a country, or you will be liable to penalties. If you will be taking a large number of personal effects with you, it would be wise to prepare an inventory to present to the Customs authorities on entry. Customs officers may withhold concessions at any time and ask travellers to deposit enough money to cover possible duty, especially on portable items of apparent high value such as television sets, radios, cassette recorders, portable computers, musical instruments, etc., all of which must be declared. Any deposit paid (for which a receipt must be obtained) is likely to be high; it is recoverable on leaving the country and exporting the item but only at the entry point at which it was paid. Alternatively the Customs may enter the item in the traveller's passport; if this happens it is important to get the entry cancelled when the item is exported. Duty and tax-free allowances may not apply if travellers enter the country more than once a month, or are under 17 years of age (other ages may apply in some countries). Residents of the Channel Islands and the Isle of Man do not benefit from EU allowances because of their fiscal policies.

A temporarily imported motor vehicle, boat, caravan, or any other type of trailer is subject to strict control on entering a country, attracting Customs duty and a variety of taxes: much depends upon the circumstances and the period of the import, and also upon the status of the importer. Non-residents entering a country with a private vehicle for holiday or recreational purposes who intend to export the vehicle within a short period enjoy special privileges, and minimal formalities in the interests of tourism.
A temporarily imported vehicle, etc., should not:

● be left in the country after the importer has left;

● be put at the disposal of a resident of the country;

● be retained in the country longer than the permitted period; or

● be lent, sold, hired, given away, exchanged or otherwise disposed of.

Generally, people entering a country with a motor vehicle to stay for a period of more than six months (see also Visa), or who intend to take up residence, employment, any commercial activity or who intend to dispose of the vehicle should seek advice concerning their position well in advance of their departure. The AA Information Centre can give advice to members; for assistance, telephone 0990 500600.

Customs regulations for the United Kingdom
If, when leaving Britain, you take any items bought in the UK which look very new, for example, watches, jewellery, cameras etc., particularly of foreign manufacture, it is a good idea to carry the retailer's receipts with you. In the absence of such receipts, you may be asked for a written declaration of where the goods were obtained.

There are prohibitions or restrictions on taking certain goods out of the UK. These include controlled drugs, some animals, birds and plants;

firearms and ammunition; strategic and techno-logical equipment (including computers); and items manufactured more than 50 years before the date of exportation, including motor vehicles temporarily imported for a period of more than three months).

When you enter the United Kingdom, you will pass through Customs. You must declare everything in excess of the duty and tax free allowances (see below) which you have obtained outside the EU or on the journey, and everything previously obtained free of duty or tax in the United Kingdom. Additionally, although the limits on duty and tax-paid goods purchased within the EU ended on 31 December 1992, the import of tobacco goods and wines and spirits have the following guide levels to differentiate between personal and commercial importation:

a Tobacco goods: 800 cigarettes and 400 cigar illos and 200 cigars and 1kg of pipe and hand-rolling tobacco;
b Wines and spirits: 10 litres of spirits and 20 litres of fortified wines and 90 litres of wine (of which not more than 60 litres are sparkling) and 110 litres of beer.

You must also declare any prohibited or restrict-ed goods, and goods for commercial purposes. Do not be tempted to hide anything or to mislead the Customs. The penalties are severe and articles not properly declared may be forfeit. If articles are hidden in a vehicle, that too becomes liable to forfeiture. Customs officers are legally entitled to examine your luggage. You are responsible for opening, unpacking and repacking it.

The importation of certain goods from other EU countries into the United Kingdom is prohibited or restricted. These include:

a Controlled drugs: under the Misuse of Drugs Act 1971 the importation and exportation of certain drugs such as diamorphine (heroin), cocaine, cannabis, lysergide (LSD), opium, barbiturates and amphetamine are prohibit ed. Only controlled drugs covered by an appropriate Home Office licence may be brought into or taken out of the UK. However, the Home Office has issued an Open General Licence (OGL) which allows ordinary trav ellers to import small quantities of certain

controlled drugs, when in medicinal form, for the personal use of themselves or a member of household travelling with them. The OGL also allows doctors to import and export a dif ferent range of drugs for administration to a patient under their care. Full details of the OGL can be obtained from Prohibitions and Restrictions Division, Branch 1, New King's Beam House, Upper Ground, London SE1 9PJ, telephone 0171-865 4904. It is a serious matter to smuggle controlled drugs as the offence carries very heavy penalties on con viction. Where passengers are unaware as to whether or not the drugs they intend to bring into or take out of the UK are controlled under the Misuse of Drugs Act, they should contact a Customs Officer. You should be aware that possession of drugs controlled under the Misuse of Drugs Act 1971 is an absolute offence, in other words liability for prosecution is not dependent on knowledge of the Act. You should therefore be on your guard if anyone asks you to carry anything through Customs control for him/her.
b Firearms, ammunition, certain weapons, for example, swordsticks, knuckle-dusters, flick knives, explosives, electric-shock devices, stun-guns, CS-gas canisters, self-defence sprays.

c Obscene material, indecent and obscene material featuring children.

d Unlicensed animals, such as cats and dogs, susceptible to rabies.

The importation of certain goods from outside the EU into the United Kingdom is prohibited or restricted. These include:

a Prohibited Goods (goods which are banned completely):
i Unlicensed Drugs: for example, heroin, mor phine, cocaine, cannabis, amphetamines, bar biturates and LSD (see (a) above).
ii Offensive Weapons: for example, certain knives, swordsticks, knuckledusters and some martial arts equipment.
iii Obscene Material.
iv Indecent and Obscene Material featuring Children: for example, books, magazines, films,

videotapes, laser discs, computer software and other articles.
v Counterfeit and Pirated Goods: for example, watches, garments and CDs.

b Restricted Goods (goods which cannot be imported without prior authority, such as a licence)
i Firearms, explosives and ammunition (1)
ii Dogs, cats and other animals: including rabbits, mice, rats and gerbils. These must not be landed unless a British import licence (Rabies) has been previously issued. (2)
iii Live birds: including family pets unless covered by a British health import licence. (2)
iv Endangered species: (including birds and plants) whether live or dead, and many goods derived from protected species such as some fur-skins, ivory, reptile leather and/or goods made from them. (3)
v Meat and poultry: including most of their products including bacon, ham, sausages, pâté, eggs, milk and cream (except 1Kg per person of fully cooked meats in hermetically sealed containers). (2)
vi Certain plants and associated produce: including trees and shrubs, potatoes, certain fruit, bulbs and seeds. (4)
vii Radio transmitters (CB radios, cordless telephones, etc.) of a type not approved for use in the UK. (5)

For more information please telephone:
1 Excise and Inland Customs Advice Centre (under Customs and Excise in the telephone directory).
2 0181-330 4411 Ministry of Agriculture, Fisheries and Food.
3 0117 9218202 Department of the Environment.
4 01904 641000 Ministry of Agriculture, Fisheries and Food
5 0171-215 2297 Radio Communications Agency.

Customs Notice No. 1, A Guide for Travellers, is available to all travellers at UK points of entry and exit. A copy may also be obtained from any Excise and Inland Customs Advice Centre (see Customs and Excise in the telephone directory.) These are the duty and tax-free allowances for goods obtained duty-free, or obtained outside the EU (for each journey between EU member states travellers may buy the quantities shown below from duty-free and tax-free shops):

TOBACCO PRODUCTS
Cigarettes 200
or
Cigarillos 100
or
Cigars 50
or
Tobacco 250g

ALCOHOLIC DRINKS
Still table wine 2 litres
Over 22% vol. (e.g. spirits and strong liqueurs) 1 litre
or
Not over 22% vol. (e.g. low strength liqueurs or fortified wines or sparkling wines) 2 litres

PERFUME
50g/60cc
Toilet water
250cc

OTHER GOODS
£145 when arriving from outside the EU, or £75 for goods bought from duty-free and tax-free shops

NOTE: Persons under 17 are not entitled to tobacco and drinks allowances.

Cycle carriers
If you intend taking your bicycles on a rear-mounted cycle rack, make sure that they do not obstruct rear lights and/or number plate, or you risk an on-the-spot fine. The AA recommends roof-mounted racks.

•D•

Dimensions and weight restrictions
For an ordinary private car, a height limit of 4 metres and a width limit of 2.50 metres are generally imposed. However, see country introduc-

tions for full details. Apart from a laden-weight limit imposed on commercial vehicles, every vehicle has an individual weight limit. See Overloading and also Major road and rail tunnels as some dimensions are restricted by the shape of the tunnels.

Direction indicators
All direction indicators should be working at between 60 and 120 flashes per minute. Most standard car-flasher units will be overloaded by the extra lamps of a caravan or trailer, and a special heavy duty unit or relay device should be fitted.

Drinking and driving
There is only one safe rule - if you drink, don't drive. The laws are strict and the penalties severe.

Driving licence and International Driving Permit
You should carry your national driving licence with you even when you hold an International Driving Permit. A driving licence issued in the UK or Republic of Ireland is generally acceptable, subject to the minimum age requirements of the country concerned, but see also individual country introductions. If you wish to drive a hired or borrowed car in the country you are visiting, make local enquiries. If your licence is due to expire before your return, renew it in good time prior to your departure. The Driver and Vehicle Licensing Agency (in Northern Ireland, Driver and Vehicle Licensing Northern Ireland, DVLNI) will accept an application two months before the expiry of your old licence; in the Republic of Ireland, one month before expiry.

An International Driving Permit (IDP) is an internationally recognised document which enables the holder to drive for a limited period in countries where their national licences are not recognised (see Italy and Spain country introductions under Driving licence). The permit, for which a statutory charge is made, is issued by the AA to an applicant who holds a valid full British driving licence and who is over 18. Any AA shop will advise you on the procedure for personal or postal applications. The permit cannot be issued to holders of foreign licences.

Holders of driving licences issued in the Republic of Ireland, Channel Islands or Isle of Man should apply to their local AA shops.

•E•

Electrical
General: The public electricity supply in Europe is predominantly 220 volts (50 cycles) AC (alternating current), but can be as low as 110 volts. In some isolated areas, low voltage DC (direct current) is provided. Continental circular two-pin plugs and screw-type bulbs are usually the rule.

Electrical adapters (not voltage transformers) which can be used in Continental power sockets, shaver points and light bulb sockets are available in the United Kingdom from electrical retailers.
Vehicle: Check that all connections are sound, and wiring is in good condition. If problems arise with the charging system, you must obtain the services of a qualified auto-electrician.

Emergency messages to tourists
In emergencies, the AA will assist in the passing on of messages to tourists whenever possible. Members wishing to use this service should telephone the AA Information Centre on 0990 500600.

The AA can arrange for messages to be published in overseas editions of the Daily Mail, and in an extreme emergency (death or serious illness of next-of-kin) undertake to pass on messages to the appropriate authorities so that they can be broadcast on overseas radio networks. Obviously the AA cannot guarantee that messages will be broadcast, nor can the AA or the Daily Mail accept any responsibility for the authenticity of messages.

If you have any reason to expect a message from home, it is best to contact the tourist office or the motoring club of the country in which you are staying. They will be able to advise you on appropriate radio frequencies, and at what time messages are normally broadcast. Before you leave home, make sure your relatives understand what to do if an emergency occurs.

Emergency 'SOS' messages about dangerous illness of a close relative may be broadcast on BBC Radio 4's long wave transmitters on 1515m/198Hz at 06.59 and 17.59hrs BST (see BBC World Service). These should be arranged through the local police or hospital authorities.

Engine and mechanical
Consult your vehicle handbook for servicing intervals. Unless the engine oil has been changed recently, drain and refill it with fresh oil and fit a new filter. Deal with any significant leaks.

Brands and grades of engine oil familiar to the British motorist are usually available in Western Europe, but may be difficult to find in remote country areas. When available, they will be much more expensive than in the UK and are generally packed in 2-litre cans (3.5 pints). Motorists are strongly advised to carry a sufficient supply of oil

If you suspect that there is anything wrong with the engine - even if it seems insignificant - it should be dealt with immediately. And do not neglect such common-sense precautions as checking valve clearances, sparking plugs, and contact breaker points where fitted, and make sure that the distributor cap is sound, and all drive belts in good condition.

Any obvious mechanical defects should be attended to at once. Look particularly for play in steering connections and wheel bearings and, where applicable, ensure that they are adequately greased. A car that has covered many miles will have absorbed a certain amount of dirt into the fuel system, and as breakdowns are often caused by dirt, it is essential that all filters (fuel and air) should be cleaned or renewed.

The cooling system should be checked for leaks and the correct proportion of anti-freeze, and any perished hoses or suspect parts replaced. Owners should seriously reconsider towing a caravan with a car that has already given appreciable service. Hard driving on motorways and in mountainous country puts an extra strain on ageing parts, and items such as a burnt-out clutch can be very expensive.

Eurocheques
The Eurocheque scheme is a flexible money-transfer system operated by a network of European banks. All the major UK banks are part of the Eurocheque scheme and they can provide a chequebook enabling you to write cheques in the local currency. Most European banks will cash Eurocheques * and retailer acceptance is widespread. Some UK banks issue cards which allow access to over 55,000 automatic cash dispensers in 20 countries. A Personal Identification Number (PIN) is required. This can be obtained from the account-holding branch of your bank.
* Note: Most French banks are no longer encashing Eurocheques. However, retail acceptance is unaffected and cash can be withdrawn from a network of about 15,000 automatic cash dispensers.

Eurotunnel
See under Channel Tunnel.

Ferry crossings
Before making ferry bookings, remember that the shortest sea crossing from a southern port to the Continent is not always the best choice; consider the roads and ease of travel from your home to a British port (an eastern British port might be easier if you are starting from the north of the country). Similarly consider the roads and travel from the Continental port to your final destination. Motorail services may be worth considering to save time and possibly an overnight stop.

The AA can book your crossing (ferry, hovercraft or catamaran). For advice on booking and instant confirmation visit your local AA shop.

Fire extinguisher
It is a wise precaution to take a fire extinguisher when motoring abroad. Fire extinguishers may be purchased from most AA shops.

First-aid kit
It is a wise precaution (compulsory in Austria) to carry a first-aid kit when motoring abroad. First-aid kits can be purchased from most AA shops. See also Motoring abroad kit.

Foods (See also country introductions)
Countries do have regulations governing the types and quantities of foodstuffs which may be imported. Although they are usually not strictly applied, visitors should know that they exist and only take reasonable quantities of food with them. Where specific regulations exist they are listed under the country introductions. Tinned, frozen and dehydrated foods offer great variety and are useful for camping. It is best to take only as much as you need until you can

shop locally. Good value for money will be found in supermarkets or in the open markets in towns, but the golden rule is to shop where you see locals shopping - a sure sign of good quality.

Horn
In built-up areas, the general rule is that you should not use it unless safety demands it: in many large towns and resorts, and in areas indicated by the international sign (a horn inside a red circle, crossed through) use of the horn is totally banned.

Identification plate
If a boat, caravan or trailer is taken abroad, it must have a unique chassis number for identification purposes. If yours does not have a number, you can buy an identification plate from the AA. Boats registered on the Small Ships Register (see Boats) have a unique number which must be permanently displayed.

Insurance, including caravan insurance
See under Motor Insurancer

International distinguishing sign
An international distinguishing sign of the approved pattern, and size (oval with black letters on a white background; GB at least 6.9in by 4.5in), must be displayed on a vertical surface at the rear of your vehicle (and caravan or trailer if you are towing one). These signs indicate the country of registration of the vehicle. On the Continent, fines are imposed for failing to display a nationality plate, or for not displaying the correct nationality plate. See also Motoring abroad kit and Police fines.

Level crossings
Practically all level crossings are indicated by international signs. Most guarded ones are the lifting barrier type, sometimes with bells or flashing lights to warn of an approaching train.

Lights (See also country introductions)
For driving abroad headlights should be altered so that the dipped beam does not dazzle oncoming drivers. You can easily fit headlamp converters (kit on sale at AA shops). However, don't forget to remove them as soon as you return to the UK. Remember to have the lamps set to compensate for the load being carried.

Dipped headlights should also be used in fog, snowfall, heavy rain and in a tunnel, irrespective of its length and lighting. Police may wait at the end of a tunnel to check vehicles.

Headlight flashing is used only to signal approach or as an overtaking signal at night. In other circumstances, it is taken as a sign of irritation, and could lead to misunderstandings. It is a wise precaution (compulsory in Spain and recommended in France, Germany and Italy) to carry a set of replacement bulbs. AA Emergency Auto Bulb Kits, suitable for most cars, can be purchased from AA shops. See also Motoring abroad kit.

Luggage or roof racks
Only use equipment suitable for your vehicle, i.e., approved by the vehicle manufacturer. Distribute the load evenly, taking care not to exceed the vehicle manufacturer's roof rack load limit. A roof rack laden with luggage increases fuel consumption, so remember this when calculating mileage per gallon, and it also reduces stability, especially when cornering.

Medical treatment
Travellers who normally take certain medicines should ensure they have a sufficient supply since they may be very difficult to get abroad.

Those with certain medical conditions (diabetes or coronary artery diseases, for example) should get a letter from their doctor giving treatment details. Some Continental doctors will understand a letter written in English, but it is better to have it translated into the language of the country you intend to visit. The AA cannot make translations.

Travellers who, for legitimate health reasons, carry drugs (see also Customs regulations for the United Kingdom) or appliances (e.g., a hypodermic syringe), may have difficulty with Customs or other authorities. They should carry translations which describe their special condition and appropriate treatment in the language of the country they intend to visit to present to Customs. Similarly, people with special dietary requirements may find translations helpful in hotels and restaurants.

The National Health Service is available in the UK only, and medical expenses incurred overseas cannot generally be reimbursed by the UK Government. There are reciprocal health agreements with most of the countriesin this guide, but you should not rely exclusively on these arrangements, as the cover provided under the respective national schemes is not always comprehensive. (For instance, the cost of bringing a person back to the UK in the event of illness or death is never covered). The full costs of medical care must be paid in Andorra and Switzerland. Therefore, you are strongly advised to take out adequate insurance cover before leaving the UK, such as the AA's Personal Travel Insurance.

Urgent medical treatment in the event of an accident or unforeseen illness is available for most visitors, free of charge or at reduced costs, from the health care schemes of those countries with whom the UK has health-care arrangements. Details are in the Department of Health booklet T5 which also gives advice about health precautions and vaccinations. Free copies are available from main post offices or by ringing the Health Literature Line on 0800 555 777 any time, free of charge. In some of these countries, visitors can obtain urgently needed treatment by showing their UK passport, but in some an NHS medical card must be produced, and in most European Economic Area countries a certificate of entitlement (E111) is necessary. The E111 can be obtained over the counter of the post office on completion of the forms incorporated in booklet T5. However, the E111 must be stamped and signed by the post office clerk to be valid. Residents of the Republic of Ireland must apply to their Regional Health Board for an E111.

Minibus

A minibus constructed and equipped to carry 10 or more persons (including the driver) and used outside the UK is subject to the regulations governing international bus and coach journeys. Such vehicles must be fitted with a tachograph (except for journeys between UK and Republic of Ireland) and carry documentation to show the type of journey being made. This is determined by whether the vehicle is owned or hired and countries to be visited, as follows:

a **Outside EU (except Norway and Switzerland)**- model control document and ASOR waybill for closed door tours (round trips carrying same group of passengers throughout). For other kinds of tours or journeys to countries outside the EU contact
The Department of Transport, Freight Road Haulage Division, Gt. Minster House, 76 Marsham Street, London SW1P 4DR, phone 0171-271 4532 for advice.

b **Inside EU** - own account certificate (owned vehicle); EU passenger waybill (hired vehicle).

For vehicles registered and driven by holders of licences issued in England, Scotland and Wales, contact:

a Confederation of Passenger Transport UK, Imperial House, 15-19 Kingsway, London WC2B 6UN, phone 0171-240 3131 for model control document and waybills.

b Department of Transport, International Road Freight Office, Westgate House, Westgate Road, Newcastle-upon-Tyne NE1 1TW, phone 0191-201 4090 for own account certificate.

For vehicles registered and driven by holders of licences issued in Northern Ireland, contact the Transport Licensing and Enforcement Branch, 148-58 Corporation Street, Belfast BT1 3DH, telephone (01232) 254100 for information.

To drive a minibus with up to 16 passenger seats not for hire or reward, a minibus driver must be at least 21 years old and, if visiting other EU countries, have at least one year's experience of driving a minibus. A certificate INTP 5 may be obtained from the local Department of Transport Traffic Area Office to certify this, although it is not a legal requirement to carry one. Alternatively, if the driver does not have a year's experience of driving minibuses, a year's experience of driving a goods vehicle over 3.5 tonnes is acceptable. The minibus driver must hold a full UK car driving licence.(Category D1 or A).

NOTES

i From 1 January 1997 there have been changes in the regulations covering the driving of minbuses by holders of car driving licenses. Details of these changes were not available when this guide went to press.

ii From 1 October 1992 it has been necessary for drivers of vehicles with more than 16 passenger seats to hold a valid PCV licence (Northern Ireland PSV) or pink and green licence (Northern Ireland pink and blue) indicating entitlement to category D.

For vehicles registered in the Republic of Ireland, contact the Department of Transport, Road Haulage Section, Setanta Centre, South Frederick Street, Dublin 2 for details about tachographs, and the Government Publications Sales Office, Molesworth Street, Dublin 2 for information about documentation.

Mirrors

When driving or towing on the Continent on the right, it is essential to have clear all-round vision. Ideally, external rear-view mirrors should be fitted to both sides of your vehicle, but certainly on the left, to allow for driving on the right.

When towing a caravan it is essential to fit mirror accessories for better rear vision. The accessories available include clip-on extensions, arms to extend wing mirrors; long-arm wing or door mirror, and periscopes fitted on the car roof to reflect the rear view through the caravan window. A periscope and wing mirrors used together are best. The longer the mirror arm is, the more rigid its mounting has to be. Some mirrors have supporting legs or extra brackets to minimise vibration. A mirror mounted on the door pillar gives a wide field of vision because it is close to the driver, but it is at a greater angle to the forward line of sight. Convex mirrors give an even wider field of vision, but practice is needed in judging distance due to the diminished image.

Motor insurance

When driving abroad you must carry your certificate of motor insurance with you at all times.

Third-party is the minimum legal requirement in most countries. Therefore, before taking a motor vehicle, caravan or trailer abroad, contact your motor insurer or broker to notify them of your intentions and ask their advice. Some insurers will extend your UK or Republic of Ireland motor policy to apply in the countries you plan to visit free of charge, others may charge an additional premium. It is most important to know the level of cover you will actually have and what documents you will need to prove it. If visiting Spain, see also the country introduction under 'Bail Bond'.

Of the countries covered by this guide, a Green Card is compulsory in Andorra. This document is issued by your motor insurer and provides internationally recognised proof of insurance. The Green Card must be signed on receipt as it will not be accepted without the signature of the insured.

Motorists can obtain expert advice through AA Insurance Services for all types of insurance. Several special schemes have been arranged with leading insurers at economic premiums. More information is available from any AA shop or direct from AA Insurance Services Ltd, PO Box 2AA, Newcastle upon Tyne NE99 2AA.

Finally, do check to make sure that you are covered against damage in transit (e.g. on the ferry) when the vehicle is not being driven.

Motoring abroad kit

A motoring abroad kit has all the essential motoring accessories you require for safe and legal motoring in the countries covered by this guide. The kit, which may be purchased from most AA shops, comprises a nylon holdall with bulb kit, first-aid kit, GB sticker, headlamp converters and warning triangle.

Motoring clubs on the Continent

The Alliance Internationale de Tourisme (AIT) is the largest confederation of touring and motoring associations in the world, and it is through this network that the AA is able to offer its members the widest possible touring information service. Tourists visiting a country where there is an AIT club may use its touring advisory services on proof of membership of their home AIT club. AA members should seek the advice of the AA before setting out overseas and should approach the overseas AIT club for information on arrival.

•O•

Off-site camping

Off-site camping may contravene local regulations. You are strongly advised never to camp by the roadside and in isolated areas.

Orange badge scheme for drivers with disabilities and passengers

Some European countries which operate national schemes of parking concessions for the disabled have reciprocal arrangements whereby visitors with disabilities get the same concessions by displaying their national badge. In some countries responsibility for the concessions rests with individual local authorities and in some cases they may not be generally available. You will have to enquire locally to find out about specific requirements.

As in the UK, these arrangements apply only to badge-holders themselves, and the concessions are not for the benefit of able-bodied companions. Wrongful display of the orange badge may incur whatever local penalties are imposed.

Overloading

This can create risks, and in most countries the offence can involve on-the-spot fines (see Police fines). You would also be made to reduce the load to an acceptable level before being allowed to continue your journey.

The maximum loaded weight, and its distribution between front and rear axles, is decided by the vehicle manufacturer, and if your owner's handbook does not give these facts, contact the manufacturer direct. There is a public weighbridge in all districts, and when the car is fully loaded (including driver and passengers) use this to check that the vehicle is within the limits.

Load your vehicle carefully so that no lights, reflectors, or number plates are masked, and the driver's view is not impaired. All luggage loaded on a roof-rack must be tightly secured, and should not exceed the vehicle manufacturer's recommended maximum limit. Any projections beyond the front, rear, or sides of a vehicle, that may not be noticed by other drivers, must be clearly marked. Specific limits apply to projections and may vary from country to country.

Overtaking

When overtaking on roads with two lanes or more in each direction, signal in good time, and also signal your return to the inside lane. Do not remain in any other lane. Failure to comply with this regulation, particularly in France, will incur an on-the-spot fine (immediate deposit in France) - see Police fines.

Always overtake on the left and use your horn to warn the driver (except where the use of a horn is banned). Do check the vehicles behind before overtaking. Do not overtake at level crossings,intersections, the crest of a hill or pedestrian crossings. When being overtaken, keep to the right and reduce speed if necessary.

•P•

Parking

Parking is a problem everywhere in Europe, and the police are extremely strict with offenders. Heavy fines are imposed and unaccompanied offending cars can be towed away. Besides being inconvenient, heavy charges are imposed for the recovery of impounded vehicles. Find out about local parking regulations and make sure you understand all relative signs. As a rule, always park on the right-hand side of the road or at an authorised place. As far as possible, park off the main carriageway, but not in cycle or bus lanes.

Passengers

It is an offence in all countries to carry more passengers in a car than the vehicle is constructed to seat, and some have regulations as to how the passengers should be seated. For information about regulations applied to visiting foreigners, see country introductions.

Special regulations (see Minibus) apply to passenger-carrying vehicles constructed and equipped to carry more than 10 passengers, including the driver.

Passports

Each person must hold, or be named on, a valid passport. Carry your passport at all times and, as an extra precaution, a separate note of the number, date and place of issue. There is now only one type of passport, the standard 10-year passport.

Standard UK passports are issued to British nationals, i.e. British citizens, British Dependent Territories citizens, British Overseas citizens, British nationals (Overseas), British subjects, and British protected persons. A standard UK passport is valid for travel to all countries in the world - but you must check whether a visa is also required. Children under the age of 16 may be included in the passport of an accompanying British relative, or have their own passport, issued initially for 5 years, to take into account changes in appearance, and renewable free of charge for a further 5 years from expiry date.

Full information and application forms are available, on the UK mainland, from main Post Offices, branches of Lloyds Bank, Artac World Choice Travel Agents, or from one of the Passport Offices in Belfast, Douglas (Isle of Man), Glasgow, Liverpool, London, Newport (Gwent), Peterborough, St Helier (Jersey) and St Peter Port (Guernsey). Application for a standard passport should be made to the appropriate area Passport Office. Allow 15 working days Apr-Aug,when demand is at its highest, and 10 working days for the rest of the year.

Irish citizens who require an Irish Passport, and who are resident either in the Dublin metropolitan area or in Northern Ireland should apply to the Passport Office, Dublin; if, however, they are resident elsewhere in the Irish Republic, they should apply through the nearest Garda station. Irish citizens resident in Britain should apply to the Irish Embassy in London.

Payment Cards
Credit, debit and charge cards are as convenient to use abroad as they are at home. Their use is subject to the conditions set out by the issuing company which, on request, will provide full information. Establishments display the symbols of cards which they accept.

Petrol/Diesel
You will find comparable grades of petrol in all of the countries in this guide, with familiar brands available along the main routes. You will normally have to buy a minimum of 5 litres (just over a gallon) but it is wise to keep the tank topped up, particularly in more remote areas. Remember when calculating mileage per gallon that the extra weight of a caravan or roof rack

increases petrol consumption. It is best to use a locking filler cap. Some garages may close between 12.00hrs and 15.00hrs, but petrol is generally available, with 24-hour service on motorways. Prices for petrol on motorways will normally be higher than elsewhere; self-service pumps will be slightly cheaper. The current position on petrol prices can be checked with the AA. Make sure you know the fuel requirement of the vehicle before you go (leaded petrol, unleaded premium, unleaded super or diesel) and whether or not the car has an exhaust catalyst. Catalyst-equipped petrol cars will usually have a small fuel filler neck, to prevent the use of the standard sized nozzle dispensing leaded petrol. If in doubt, check with a franchised dealer, or with the AA.

On the Continent both unleaded and leaded petrol is graded as 'normal' and 'super' and the local definitions are generally recognisable. Some countries are supplying 98 octane unleaded petrol either in addition to, or instead of, 95 octane. The name may be 'super plus' or 'premium' but look for the octane rating 98. You should be careful to use the recommended type of fuel, particularly if your car has a catalytic converter, and the octane grade should be the same or higher. If you accidentally fill the tank of a catalyst-equipped car with leaded fuel, the best course, to avoid any possible reduction in the effectiveness of the catalyst, will be to have the tank drained and refilled with unleaded. However, if your car doesn't have a catalyst but is designed or converted for unleaded petrol, an accidental filling with leaded fuel will do no harm; simply go back to unleaded at the next fill. If your car requires leaded fuel and you fill with unleaded, avoid hard use of the engine until about half the tank is used, then fill with leaded.

Diesel fuel is generally known as 'diesel' or 'gas-oil'. Although readily available it is probably more inconvenient to run out of diesel, and it is wise to keep the tank topped up. If more than about a gallon of petrol is put into the tank of a diesel car (or vice versa) you must drain the tank and refill with the correct fuel before the engine is started.
NOTE: **Importing fuel** Whilst it is usually a good idea to carry a reserve supply of fuel in a can, remember that all operators (ferry, motorail etc.) will either forbid the carriage of fuel in spare cans or insist that spare cans must be empty. In

Italy and Luxembourg motorists are forbidden to carry petrol in cans in the vehicle.

Police fines

Some countries impose on-the-spot fines for minor traffic offences, which vary in amount according to the offence and the country concerned. Others (e.g. France) impose an immediate deposit, and subsequently levy a fine which may be the same as, or greater or lesser than, this sum. Fines are normally paid in cash in the local currency, either to the police or at a local post office against a ticket issued by the police. The amount can exceed the equivalent of £1000 for the most serious offences. The reason for the fines is to penalise, and to keep minor motoring offences out of the law courts.

Disputing the fine usually leads to a court appearance, delays and extra expense. If the fine is not paid, legal proceedings will usually follow. Some countries immobilise vehicles until a fine is paid, and may sell it to pay the penalty imposed.

Once paid, a fine cannot be recovered, but a receipt should always be obtained as proof of payment. AA members who need assistance in any motoring matter involving local police should apply to the legal department of the relevant national motoring organisation.

Pollution

Pollution of seawater at certain Continental coastal resorts, including the Mediterranean, may still represent a health hazard, although the general situation is improving. Countries of the European Union publish detailed information on the quality of their bathing beaches, including maps, which are available from national authorities and the European Union. In many (though not all) popular resorts where the water quality may present risk, signs (generally small) are erected which forbid bathing:

FRENCH
No bathing Défense de se baigner
Bathing prohibited Il est défendu de se baigner

ITALIAN
No bathing Vietato bagnarsi
Bathing prohibited Evietato bagnarsi

SPANISH
No bathing Prohibido bañarse
Bathing prohibited Se prohibe bañarse

Poste restante

If you are uncertain of having a precise address, you can be contacted through the local poste restante. Before leaving the UK notify your approximate whereabouts abroad at given times. If you expect mail, call with your passport at the main post office of the town where you are staying. To ensure that the arrival of correspondence will coincide with your stay, your correspondent should check with the post office before posting, as delivery times differ throughout Europe, and appropriate allowances must be made. It is important that the recipient's name be written in full: Mr John Smith, Poste Restante, Sintra, Portugal. Do not use 'Esq'.

The Italian equivalent of 'Poste Restante' is 'Fermo in Posta' plus the name of the town or village and the province or region, if necessary. The Spanish equivalent is 'Lista de Correos'. Correspondence will be lodged at the main post office, and you will need proof of identity (e.g., a passport) to collect it.

For all other countries, correspondence should be addressed as in the 'Mr John Smith' example.

Priority including roundabouts (See also country introductions)

The general rule is to give way to traffic entering a junction from the right, but this is sometimes varied at roundabouts (see below). This is one aspect of Continental driving which may cause British drivers the most confusion. Road signs indicate priority or loss of priority, and tourists must be sure that they understand such signs.

Great care should be taken at intersections, and tourists should never rely on being ceded the right of way, particularly in small towns and villages where local, often slow moving, traffic - farm tractors etc., will assume right of way regardless of oncoming traffic. Always give way to public services and military vehicles, blind and disabled people, funerals and marching columns. Vehicles such as buses and coaches will expect, and should be allowed, priority.

Generally, priority at roundabouts is given to vehicles entering the roundabout unless sign-posted to the contrary (see France). This is a reversal of the UK and Republic of Ireland rule, and particular care should be exercised when circulating in an anti-clockwise direction on a roundabout. It is advisable to keep to the outside lane if possible, to make your exit easier.

•R•

Radio telephone/citizens' band radios, transmitters and detection devices

Many countries control the temporary importation and use of radio telephones and radio transmitters. If your vehicle contains such equipment, whether fitted or portable, approach the AA for guidance before departure.

The use or even possession of devices, whether inside or outside vehicles, to detect police radar speed traps is illegal in most countries. Penalties are severe, including confiscation of the equipment, payment of an immediate deposit to serve as collateral against any fine subsequently levied, and/or a driving ban. Finally, if the case is viewed sufficiently seriously, confiscation of vehicle and even imprisonment may result.

Registration document

You must take the registration document, which should be in your name, with you and keep it with you. If you do not have a registration document, apply to a Vehicle Registration Office (in Northern Ireland, a Local Vehicle Licensing Office) for a temporary certificate of registration (V379) to cover the period away. The address of your nearest Vehicle Registration Office is in the local telephone directory or in leaflet V100, available from post offices. You should apply well in advance of your journey, as there could be delays of up to two weeks in issuing the certificate if you are not already recorded as the vehicle keeper. Proof of identity (e.g. driving licence) and proof of ownership (e.g. bill of sale), should be produced for the Vehicle Registration Office.

If you plan to use a borrowed, hired or leased vehicle, you should be aware that:

a for a borrowed vehicle, the registration document must be accompanied by a letter of authority to use the vehicle from the registered keeper, and

b for a UK registered hired or leased vehicle, the registration document will normally be retained by the hiring company. Under these circumstances, a Hired/Leased Vehicle Certificate (VE103A), which may be purchased from the AA, should be used.

Road signs

Most road signs throughout Europe conform to international standards and most will be familiar. Watch for road markings - do not cross a solid white or yellow line marked on the road centre. In Belgium there are two official languages, and signs will be in Flemish or French, see the country introduction for Belgium for further information. In the Basque and Catalonian areas of Spain local and national place names appear on signposts, see the country introduction for Spain for further information.

Rule of the road

In all countries in this guide, drive on the right and overtake on the left.

•S•

Seat belts

All countries in this guide require wearing of seat belts.

Spares

The spares you should carry depend on the vehicle and how long you are likely to be away. Useful items include a pair of windscreen wiper blades, a length of electrical cable and a torch.

Remember that when ordering spare parts for dispatch abroad, you must be able to identify them clearly - by the manufacturer's part numbers if known. Always quote your engine and chassis numbers. See also Lights.

Speed limits

It is important to observe speed limits at all times. Remember that it can be an offence to travel so slowly as to obstruct traffic flow without good reason. Offenders may be fined, and driving licences confiscated on the spot, causing great inconvenience and possible expense.

The standard legal limits are given in the appropriate country introductions for private cars and for car-caravan-trailer combinations, but these may be varied by road signs, and where such signs are displayed the lower limit applies. At certain times, limits may also be temporarily varied, so watch out for the appropriate signs.

•T•

Tolls
Tolls are payable on most motorways in France, Italy, Portugal, Spain and on sections in Austria. Over long distances, the toll charges can be quite considerable. Compare the cost against time and convenience (e.g., overnight stops), particularly as some of the all-purpose roads are often fast.

Always have some local currency ready to pay the tolls, as travellers cheques etc. are not acceptable at toll booths. Credit cards are accepted at toll booths in France and Spain.
In Austria and Switzerland authorities levy a tax for use of motorway networks. See under Motorway tax in the respective country introduction for further information.

Tourist information
National tourist offices are well equipped to deal with enquiries relating to their countries. They are particularly useful for information on current events, tourist attractions, car hire, equipment hire and specific activities such as skin-diving, gliding, horse-riding, etc. The offices in London (see country introductions for addresses) are helpful, but the local offices overseas merit a visit when you arrive at your destination for information not available elsewhere.

Traffic lights
In principal cities and towns, traffic lights operate in a way similar to those in the United Kingdom, although they are sometimes suspended over the roadway. The density of the light may be so poor that lights could be missed - especially those overhead. There is usually only one set on the right-hand side of the road some distance before the road junction, and if you stop too close to the corner the lights will not be visible. Look out for 'filter' lights enabling you to turn right at a junction against the main lights. If you wish to go straight ahead, do not enter a lane leading to 'filter' lights or you may obstruct traffic trying to turn right.

Trams
Trams take priority over other vehicles. Always give way to passengers boarding and alighting. Never position a vehicle so that it impedes the free passage of a tram. Trams must be overtaken on the right, except in one-way streets.

Travellers cheques
We recommend that you take travellers cheques. Local currency cheques can often be used like cash. Sterling cheques may be changed for local currency notes at banks. Your bank will be able to recommend currency travellers cheques for the countries your are visiting.

Tyres
Inspect your tyres carefully: if you think they are likely to be more than three-quarters worn before you get back, replace them before you leave. If you notice uneven wear, scuffed treads, or damaged walls, get expert advice on whether the tyres are suitable for further use.

The regulations in the UK governing tyres requires a minimum tread depth of 1.6mm over the central three-quarters of the tyre around the whole circumference. As many countries have similar requirements, the AA recommends at least 2mm of tread.

Check the car handbook for recommended tyre pressures. Different tyre pressures will be recommended for a fully loaded car travelling at motorway speeds. Remember pressures can only be checked accurately when the tyres are cold, and don't forget the spare wheel.

If towing a caravan find out the recommended tyre pressures from the caravan manufacturer. These will vary with the type and size of tyre.

•V•

Vehicle excise licence

When taking a vehicle out of the UK for a temporary visit remember that the vehicle excise licence (tax disc) needs to be valid on your return*. Therefore, if it will expire while you are abroad, you can apply by post to a Head Post Office for a tax disc up to 42 days in advance of the expiry date of your present disc. You should explain why you want it in advance, and ask for it to be posted to you before you leave, or to your address abroad. However, your application form must always be completed with your UK address.

To find out which post office in your area offers this service, you should contact the Post Office Customer Service Unit listed in your local telephone directory. Residents of the Republic of Ireland should contact their local Tax Office.

Residents of Northern Ireland must apply to Driving and Vehicle Licensing Northern Ireland, Vehicle Licensing Division, County Hall, Coleraine BT51 3HS.

*Agreement within the EU provides for the temporary use of foreign-registered vehicles within the member states. A vehicle which is properly registered and taxed in its home country should not be subject to the domestic taxation and registration laws of the host country during a temporary stay.

Visa
EU citizens travelling within the EU do not require visas. A visa is not normally required by United Kingdom and Republic of Ireland passport holders when visiting non-EU countries within Western Europe for periods of three months or less. However, if you hold a passport of any other nationality, a UK passport not issued in this country, or if you are in any doubt at al,l check with the embassies or consulates of the countries you intend to visit.

Visitors' registration
In most countries registration formalities are to be undertaken by visitors spending up to three months. However, this formality is usually satisfied by completing a card or certificate when booking into a hotel, campsite or other accommodation. If you are staying with friends or relatives it is usually the responsibility of the host to seek advice from the police within 24 hours of the arrival of guests.

If you intend visiting a country for longer than three months and/or the circumstances are not as described above, then you should make the appropriate enquiries before your departure from the UK.

•W•

Warm-climate touring
In hot weather, and at high altitudes excessive heat in the engine compartment can cause carburation problems. If you are towing a caravan consult the manufacturers of your towing vehicle about the limitations of the cooling system, and the operating temperature of the gearbox fluid if automatic transmission is fitted (see Automatic gearboxes).

Warning triangles/Hazard warning lights
The use of a warning triangle is compulsory in most Continental countries. It should be placed on the road behind a stopped vehicle to warn traffic approaching from the rear of an obstruction ahead. The triangle should be used when a vehicle has stopped for any reason - not just breakdowns. It should be placed in such a position as to be clearly visible up to 100m (110yds) by day and night, about 60cm (2ft) from the edge of the road, but not in such a position as to present a danger to oncoming traffic. It should be set up about 30m (33yds) behind the obstruction, but this distance should be increased to 100m (110yds) on motorways. A warning triangle is not required for two-wheeled vehicles.

An AA warning triangle, which complies with the latest international and European standards, can be purchased from AA shops. See also Motoring abroad kit.

Although four flashing indicators are allowed in the countries covered by this guide, they in no way affect the regulations governing the use of warning triangles. Generally, hazard warning lights should not be used in place of a triangle, although they may complement it. See the country introductions for France, Netherlands and Switzerland. See also Breakdown.

Weather information
UK regional weather reports are provided direct from the Met. Office by the AA Weatherwatch recorded information service. By calling the following premium rate numbers you will hear the weather report for your chosen area followed by

a report for the next four days:

National Forecast	* 0336 401 130
London & SE England	0336 401 131
West Country	0336 401 132
Wales	0336 401 133
Midlands	0336 401 134
East Anglia	0336 401 135
NW England ·	0336 401 136
NE England	0336 401 137
Scotland	0336 401 138
Northern Ireland	0336 401 139

For weather reports for crossing the Channel and northern France, call 0336 401 361, whilst Continental Roadwatch on 0336 401 904 provides information on traffic conditions to and from ferry ports, ferry news and details of major European events. A world-wide, city-by-city six-day weather forecast is also available on 0336 411 212.

For other weather information for the UK and the Continent (but not road conditions) please contact:

> The Met Office
> Enquiries Officer
> London Road
> Bracknell
> Berkshire RG12 2SZ

or telephone 01344 854455 during normal office hours.

* Calls are charged at 50p per minute daytime, 45p per minute evenings and weekends.

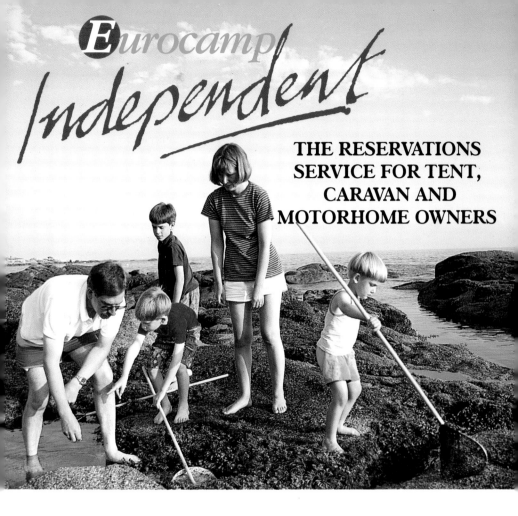

Eurocamp Independent

THE RESERVATIONS SERVICE FOR TENT, CARAVAN AND MOTORHOME OWNERS

Eurocamp Independent
FREEPOST ALM1584
KNUTSFORD
Cheshire
WA16 0BR

THE RESERVATIONS SERVICE FOR
TENT, CARAVAN AND MOTORHOME OWNERS

Are you taking your own tent, caravan or motorhome abroad this year?

Do you want to be sure of staying on the best sites in Europe?

Do you want to save time and avoid the worry of making your own arrangements?

Would you appreciate the help and reassurance that comes from booking with a friendly and professional company?

Do you want to pay a competitive price for your holiday?

Would you like a copy of the 1997 Eurocamp Independent brochure with details of over 100 of Europe's best sites and our comprehensive reservations service?

If you have answered yes to the above questions please complete the card below (no stamp required) or call 01565 625544.

A B T A

V2310

A|TO
THE ASSOCIATION
OF INDEPENDENT
TOUR OPERATORS

MR/MRS/MISS _____

INITIAL _____

SURNAME _____

ADDRESS _____

_____

_____

_____

_____

POSTCODE _____

Have you ever taken your own tent, caravan or motorhome abroad before?   YES ☐ NO ☐

If Yes how many times? _____

Do you have:
tent ☐   caravan ☐   motorhome ☐

How many adults are in your party? ☐

If applicable what are the ages of your children? _____

Would you be interested in pursuing any of the following interests whilst on holiday, with your own equipment?

Golf ☐   Birdwatching ☐   Fishing ☐

Wine ☐   Cooking ☐

Tick if you do not wish to receive direct mail from other carefully screened companies whose products or services we feel may be of interest. ☐

AA

Driving to Europe for your holiday this year

YOU NEED A ROUTE FROM European Routes Services

For more details
tel: 0117 9308242

Hotels in France 1997

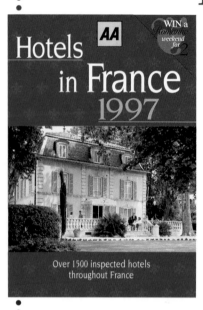

◆ Produced with the co-operation of the French Tourist Office

◆ Over 1500 inspected hotels from luxury to family-run are described and many colour photographs are included

◆ Colour maps and Paris plans

◆ How-to-book letter in French plus helpful French words and phrases

◆ Travel information for the traveller

Bed & Breakfast in France 1997

◆ Description of over 1500 delightful French guest houses, farmhouses and inns

◆ Colour photographs of many establishments plus colour maps

◆ French ABC of practical information

◆ Sample accommodation booking letter in French and everyday words and phrases

Both published March 1997
Price £9.99 and £8.99

AA **Lifestyle Guides**

Sail away to the sites and delights of Denmark, Norway, Sweden and Holland.

Camping Holidays in Scandinavia and Holland are perfect for the outdoor life and great value when you sail away, in style, with Scandinavian Seaways.

One, all-inclusive price covers transportation for you, your family and your car aboard one of our sleek white liners plus camping vouchers to any one of a large selection of superb sites all over Sweden, Norway, Denmark or Holland. You get a lot more than you imagine, for a lot less than you think.

See your travel agent or call our 24-hour Brochure Line on 0990 333 666 (quote ref 97/PN1017) for the Motoring Holidays Brochure.

From £80 per person

SCANDINAVIAN SEAWAYS
A BETTER WAY OF TRAVELLING

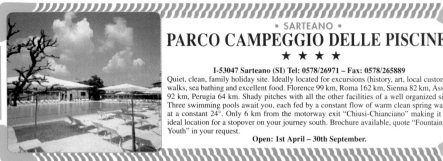

• SARTEANO •

PARCO CAMPEGGIO DELLE PISCINE
★ ★ ★ ★

I-53047 Sarteano (SI) Tel: 0578/26971 – Fax: 0578/265889

Quiet, clean, family holiday site. Ideally located for excursions (history, art, local customs, walks, sea bathing and excellent food. Florence 99 km, Roma 162 km, Sienna 82 km, Assisi 92 km, Perugia 64 km. Shady pitches with all the other facilities of a well organized site. Three swimming pools await you, each fed by a constant flow of warm clean spring water at a constant 24°. Only 6 km from the motorway exit "Chiusi-Chianciano" making it an ideal location for a stopover on your journey south. Brochure available, quote "Fountain of Youth" in your request.

Open: 1st April – 30th September.

Well located in the north of the city. Exit 5 from "Grande Raccordo Annulare" (Rome orbital motorway). Direct underground service every 10 minutes to city centre. Modern facilities, all electricity and hot water free. Washing machines – bar – supermarket – restaurant – swimming pools.

I-00123 ROMA
Tel: 0039/6/33626401-3320270 Tel. and Fax 33613800
SS. Casia bei Veientana – Exit 5 G.R.A.

Discount from 5th day on presentation of this Publication and discount for young people under 30 during April, May, June, September and October. Discount for AA members and ICC.

★ ★ ★ ★
Mare Pineta
International Camping - Bungalow - Appartamenti

- ◆ Right by the sea
- ◆ Natural pine wood
- ◆ Right in the town centre
- ◆ 4 swimming pools
- ◆ Sporting events
- ◆ Entertainment
- ◆ Water sports
- ◆ Mobile homes sleeping 6/4/2
- ◆ Caravans sleeping 4
- ◆ Bungalows and apartments
- ◆ Excursions organized

International Camping
MARE PINETA
44024 Lido degli Estensi
Comacchio (FE)
Tel: 0533/330194-330110
Telex: 511498 Fax 0533/330052
Tel: in winter 0544/971753
Fax in winter 0544/30388

CAMPING AND CARAVANNING HOLIDAYS IN EUROPE

Carefree TRAVEL SERVICE

FROM BOULOGNE TO BUDAPEST WE'RE WITH YOU ALL THE WAY.

From a simple ferry booking to an all-inclusive holiday anywhere in Europe - no one does it better than The Camping and Caravanning Club's Carefree Travel Service. You can pick and choose the service you require to fit in with your own personal holiday requirements.

La Vendée, France from £31.00 per night for the family*
Includes: Ferry Tickets ✔ Sites Fees ✔ Holiday Insurance ✔ Maps & Guides ✔ Camping Card International ✔

The Club's Carefree Travel Service offers members a choice of 110 sites in 14 countries - including sites near Disneyland Paris, Parc Asterix and Futuroscope. The cost of membership is just £26.50 (plus a £4 joining fee†). As a Club member you can enjoy all kinds of benefits throughout the year: the pick of over 84 Club sites in the UK at members' rates - which means you can recoup your membership fee in just 9 camping nights - our famous "Your Big Sites Book", free monthly magazine, low cost insurance and much more.

HOTLINE
01203 422 024
For your free Carefree colour brochure call now quoting Ref. 9406

The Camping and Caravanning Club
The friendly Club

*Camping Domaine des Renardieres Notre Dame de Riez Price based on 2 adults, 2 children for 10 nights on site, taking your own caravan, motor caravan, trailer tent or tent.
†Waived if you pay by direct debit or continuous credit card transaction. All prices are correct at time of printing

BTA
/3987

Via Magone 13
25080 Moniga del Garda (BS) Italia
tel. 0039 365 502079
fax 0039 365 503324
eMail : scavazza@gardanet.it
Open 1997: 25.04 / 28.09
A peaceful location on the shores of Lake Garda. The campsite covers an area of 40,000 sq.mt. well shaded by olive trees with a 450 mt. beach. All the facilities are newly modernised, offering free hot water, washing machines and dryers. Bungalows are also available for rent. Equipped with Pizzeria and Bar, shop, large swimming pool, tennis, childrens play area and a slipway for boats. A friendly campsite with English speaking staff. Bookings accepted from November.

CAMPING

fontanelle

An idyllic setting, nestled amongst the olive groves on the banks of Lake Garda. Stretching over 70.000 sq mt. with a 500 mt long beach, the pitches are spacious and well shaded. All our facilities are first class, modern and well maintained, offering free hot water, washing machines and dryers. Luxurious chalets and mobile homes furnished with every comfort are also available. Fully equipped with large pool, childrens play area, Restaurant, Pizzeria and Bar with panoramic views. Fornella is a family run campsite.

Fornella Camping

Via Fornella, 1
25010 S.Felice del Benaco (BS) Italia
tel. 0039 365 62294   Fax 0039 365 62200 / 559418
eMail : scavazza@gardanet. it

TUSCANY
Holiday in unspoilt country

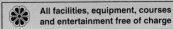

ARGENTARIO
INTERNATIONAL CAMPING VILLAGE

I-58010 Albinia (GR) – Tel: (0564) 87 03 02
Fax (0564) 87 13 80

Right next to the beautiful bay of Santo Stefano, famous for its clear water and rock pools full of fish. The holiday village is located in a centuries old pine forest adjacent to the W.W.F. oasis, rich in wildlife. Site of a historic Hispanic palace. Ideal for nature lovers.

Private beach with parasols and sun beds. Bar, restaurant and pizzeria on the beach. Boat moorings available. One and two room bungalows with bath, kitchen and veranda. Caravan hire.

Open from Easter to 30th September
booking (also for pitches) (0564) 87 00 68
Fax: (0564) 87 04 70

Camping il Gabbiano

T. ..MONE
INTERNATIONAL CAMPING VILLAGE

I-58010 Talamone (GR) – Tel. (0564) 88 70 26
Fax (0564) 88 71 70

Set in the enchanting and unspoiled countryside of the Maremma National Park. Because of its extraordinary position, the Talamone holiday village has a unique view of the entire Bay of Talamone and Porto Santo Stefano.

Open from Easter to 30th September
booking (also for pitches): (0564) 87 00 68 ;4) 87 04 70
Fax: (0564) 87 04 70

I-58010 Albinia (GR) – S.S. Aurelia km 154.200
Tel and Fax (0564) 87 02 02

IL GABBIANO Campsite – right by the sea – on the silver coast between the ports of Porto Santo Stefano and Talamone and set beneath a dense covering of pines.

Open from Easter to 30th September
booking (also for pitches) (0564) 87 00 68
Fax: (0564) 87 04 70

Lauterbrunnen "Jungfrau"

The ideal family campsite for both summer and winter, at the foot of those mountain giants the Eiger, Mönch and Jungfrau. Set in the heart of the "Jungfrau" region, famous throughout the world for its walking and skiing. Open throughout the year. Ticket sales for all cable cars. We shall be pleased to provide information on reduced-rate excursions (eg Jungfraujoch, Schilthorn). Modern facilities with separate facilities for the disabled. Restaurant, large grocery shop/kiosk and children's playground. Mountain bikes for hire. Ideal for touring caravans (disposal facilities). Bungalows, caravans and inexpensive rooms for rent. During the winter free practice ski lift and cross-country loipe on the site plus free ski bus to cable car valley stations. Winter season sites. Ask for our brochure.
Important!!! Turn right 100m before the church
Families von Allmen, Nolan and Fuchs
Tel: 0041 33 856 20 10, Fax 33 856 20 20

CAMPING
VILANOVA PARK
Apartado, 64 • Telf.: (34-3) 893 34 02
E-08800 Vilanova i la Geltrú
(Prov. Barcelona)

An elegant site with country club atmosphere 50 km south of Barcelona, in the wine and champagne centre of Catalonia. New and very quiet. Very modern sanitary installations with an abundance of hot water. 1000 m² swimming pool and children's pool with big colour fountain (lighted in the evening). Excellent restaurant "Chaine des Rôtisseurs" in old Catalonian mansion. Supermarket, shops. English newspapers, children's programme, organised leisure. Large sites 70-100 m² with electrical connections. 40 ha park and forest for beautiful walks and picnics (with more than 600 palm trees!). Ideal climate. Bus service to beach – private ecological park.
Access: Motorway A7, coming from Barcelona exit 29 coming from Tarragona, exits 30 & 31; follow indications Vilanova i la Geltrú/Stiges.
Open throughout the year. We speak English.

LES TOURNELS ★★★★
Camping Caravanning

Provençale charm and Mediterranean sun on the deep blue background of the Gulf of St. Tropez.
In the middle of a pine forest and vineyard, no more than 1,000 metres from the sea, in the enchanting Provençale countryside, the peaceful Les Tournels camping park offers you its 3-star facilities on shaded, marked pitches. Sanitary facilities heated in the cooler seasons. **On site:** a shopping centre, restaurant, newspapers, children's playground, tennis, mini golf, caravans for hire. **New:** sports activities park, heated SWIMMING POOL. **Nearby:** yachting, surfing, water skiing, underwater fishing, St. Tropez. Ideal touring base.
Route de Camarat, 83350 Ramatuelle, Tel: 04.94.55.90.90 Fax: 04.94.55.90.99

CAMPING STRANDBAD WÖRTHERSEE KLAGENFURT

Camping Strandbad
A-9020 Klagenfurt,
Tel: 0463/21169
Fax: 0463/21169-93
From Great Britain
dial 0043/463/21169

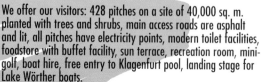

We offer our visitors: 428 pitches on a site of 40,000 sq. m. planted with trees and shrubs, main access roads are asphalt and lit, all pitches have electricity points, modern toilet facilities, foodstore with buffet facility, sun terrace, recreation room, mini-golf, boat hire, free entry to Klagenfurt pool, landing stage for Lake Wörther boats.
Reservations prior to 5.7 and after 11.8 are unrestricted there is no reservation fee. From 6.7 to 10.8 only a limited number of sites can be restricted each day and during this period the reservation fee ATS 200 per pitch.
Hot water is included in the site fee.

KLAGENFURT
Die Stadt vom Wörthersee

► KT 17

n't be afraid;
n only in the
advert !!

la ballena alegre 2

SANT PERE PESCADOR
GIRONA

Because in your language, which we also speak, I'm called "**THE MERRY WHALE**". Situated next to the natural park of "The Aiguamolls de l'Empurdà" and the Roman remains of Empuries, you will find the ideal spot to spend a good time with your family. The camp is situated along a 1.700 m long, large, sandy beach (where by the way, you won't find any whales). We offer a fantastic animation program and all facilities you need for a restful holiday.

53% discount per pich (15/5 a 22/6 y 25/8 a 28/9)

Our best recommendation are happy guests,

Adress in summer: (15/5-30/9)
LA BALLENA ALEGRE 2 / Inf.B2-AA
E-17470 Sant Pere Pescador (Girona) Spain
Tel. 34 / 72 / 52 03 02 - 34 / 72 / 52 03 26
Fax 34 / 72 / 52 03 32

Tel. office in winter:
34 / 3 / 226 13 02

Access: A-7, exit (sortida) 5, direction L'Escala and turn of at St. Marti d'Empuries.

Internet Adress:
http://webs.adam.es/ballena
E-mail: ballena@adam.es

1ª
★★★

- *Now tell me Ducky, how come you know your way so well?*

- *Well, this is not the first, and certainly not the last time we're taking this route.*

The winter has been hard.
We're all looking forward impatiently for the summer to come. But holidays are unfortunately very short.
So we have to make our choice very carefully: a sunny spot, near to an enormous sandy beach, a perfectly equipped site where rest and comfort are garanteed.
So that's why, for generations, so many friends came to make their nests near to us, on the campsite La Ballena Alegre. Don't you think so, Ducky? Ain't it true, Ducky?

At the camp site La Ballena Alegre, you will find the perfect combination: a quiet and sunny beach, exceptionel equipment and, which is most important, a team of professionals who are totally devoted to assure the comfort of their guests. This is why all leading Camping & Automobile Associations give Ballena Alegre top marks!
Now than, have a jolly good holiday, Ducky!

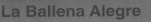

La Ballena Alegre

45% reduction
(1.4-22.6 & 25.8-30.9)

At 10 minutes south of **BARCELONA.**
C-246 Autovia Castelldefels km 12,5 (Before arriving in Barcelona, follow signs direction Aeropuerto).
Tel. (34-3) 658 05 04 - Fax (34-3) 658 05 75 (summer)
Tel. (34-3) 226 13 02 - Fax (34-3) 226 65 28 (winter)

Camping Caravaning
el delfin verde

CASTELL MONTGRI

1ª CAMPING CARAVANING

E-17258 ESTARTIT (COSTA BRAVA)

An exclusive holiday site in beautiful surroundings, in midst woods, with terraced sites on slope of mountain and on flat ground.

It's our guests who promote us.

We offer you, among other services:
— Panorama-swimming pool (70 × 40 metres, the largest in the Costa Brava).
— 2 Children's pools.
— Another 20 × 20m swimming pool.
— 2 bars. Pub. Sound-proof, underground disco with air-conditioning. Restaurant with air-conditioning. Piano-Bar with air-conditioning. 2 take-aways Barbecue.
— 2000 square metres of panorama terraces. 600 sq.m. free-covered terraces. 10,000 sq.m. of grass covered solarium.
— Folklore and shows daily.
— Minigolf, tennis, football, table tennis, trampoline. Children's castle. Children's playground. Free water slide.
— Supermarket. Souvenirs gift shop. Newspapers.
— Excursions. Money exchange. Car rental.
— Public Relations office.
— Daily doctor's visit.
— Car wash. Washing machines. Ironing room.
— Free hot water. Modern ablution blocks.
— 200,000 sq.m. tree covered square.
— Dogs only on lead.
— TV and Video Jumbo Screen. (4 × 3m)
— Mobile Homes and Bungalows to rent

Just come and see us. We are sure you will want to stay.

Open: 10.5 - 12.10

SITE FEE REDUCTION

10.5 - 15.6
31.8 - 12.10 **40%**

Road Torroella-Estartit, km 4,7.
Tel: (34-72) 75.16 30
Fax: (34-72) 75.09.06

Special prices in low season.

Free bottle of Spanish champagne per family on showing this advertisement.

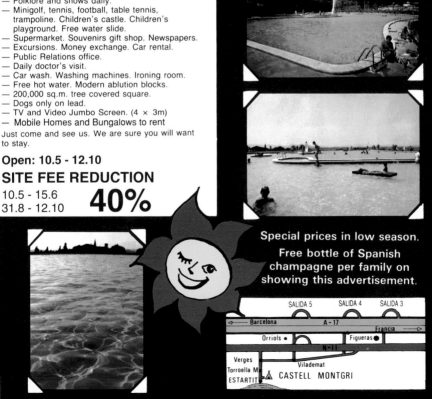

PRINCIPAL MOUNTAIN PASSES *

I t is best not to attempt to cross mountain passes at night, and daily schedules should make allowances for the comparatively slow speeds inevitable in mountainous areas.

Gravel surfaces (such as dirt and stone chips) vary considerably; they are dusty when dry, slippery when wet. Where known to exist, this type of surface has been noted. Road repairs can be carried out only during the summer, and may interrupt traffic. Precipitous road sides are rarely, if ever, totally unguarded; on the older roads, stone pillars are placed at close intervals. Gradient figures take the mean figure on hairpin bends, and may be steeper on the inside of the curves, particularly on the older roads.

● **CONVERSION TABLE GRADIENTS** ●
All steep hill signs show the grade in percentage terms. The following conversion table may be used as a guide:

30% 1 in 3	14% 1 in 7
25% 1 in 4	12% 1 in 8
20% 1 in 5	11% 1 in 9
16% 1 in 6	10% 1 in 10

Before attempting late evening or early morning journeys across frontier passes, check the times of opening of the frontier controls. A number close at night; for example the Timmelsjoch border is closed between 20.00 and 07.00hrs and throughout the winter.

Always engage a low gear before either ascending or descending steep gradients, and keep well to the right-hand side of the road and avoid cutting corners. Avoid excessive use of brakes. If the engine overheats, pull off the road, making sure that you do not cause an obstruction, leave the engine idling, and put the heater controls (including the fan) into the maximum heat position. Under no circumstances should you remove the radiator cap until the engine has cooled down. Do not fill the coolant system of a hot engine with cold water.

Always engage a lower gear before taking a hairpin bend, give priority to vehicles ascending and remember that as your altitude increases, so your engine power decreases. Always give priority to postal coaches travelling in either direction. Their route is usually signposted.

● CARAVANS ●
Passes suitable for caravans are indicated in the table on the following pages. Those shown to be negotiable by caravans are best used only by experienced drivers in cars with ample power; the rest are probably best avoided. A correct power-to-load ratio is always essential.

Where there is a reference to tunnels in the table, please consult the Contents Page under Road and Rail Tunnels for the appropriate chapter.

● CONDITIONS IN WINTER ●
Winter conditions are given in italics in the last column. *UO* means usually open, although a severe fall of snow may temporarily obstruct the road for 24 to 48 hours, and wheel chains are often necessary; *OC* means occasionally closed, *UC*, usually closed, between the dates stated. Dates for opening and closing the passes are approximate only. Warning notices are usually posted at the foot of a pass if it is closed, or if chains or snow tyres should or must be used.

Wheel chains may be needed early and late in the season, and between short spells (a few hours) of obstruction. At these times, conditions are usually more difficult for caravans.

In fair weather, wheel chains or snow tyres are only necessary on the higher passes, but in severe weather you will probably need to use them (as a rough guide) at altitudes exceeding 610 metres (2000ft)

* Please note that heights and distances in the table which follows are approximations only.

Pass and height	From To	Distances from summit and max gradient	Min width of road	Conditions (see previous page for key to abbreviations)
*Albula 2312 metres (7585ft) Switzerland	Tiefencastel 851 metres (2792ft) La Punt 1687 metres (5535ft)	30km 1 in 10 18.6 miles 9km 1 in 10 5.6 miles	11ft 6in 3.5 metres	UC Nov - early Jun. An inferior alternative to the Julier; tar and gravel, fine scenery. Alternative rail tunnel.
Allos 2250 metres (7382ft) France	Barcelonnette 1132 metres (3714ft) Colmars 1235 metres (4052ft)	20km 1 in 10 12.4 miles 24km 1 in 12 14.9 miles	13ft 4.0 metres	UC Early Nov - early Jun. Very winding, narrow mostly unguarded but not difficult otherwise; passing bays on southern slope, poor surface (maximum width vehicles 1.8 metres, 5ft 11in).
Aprica 1176 metres (3858ft) Italy	Tresenda 375 metres(1230ft) Edolo 699 metres (2293ft)	14km 1 in 11 8.7 miles 15km 1 in 16 9.3 miles	13ft 4.0 metres	UO Fine scenery, good surface, well graded; suitable for caravans.
Aravis 1498 metres (4915ft) France	La Clusaz 1041 metres (3412ft) Flumet 917 metres (3008ft)	8km 1 in 11 5.0 miles 12km 1 in 11 7.4 miles	13ft 4.0 metres	OC Dec - Mar. Outstanding scenery, and a fairly easy road.
Arlberg 1802 metres (5912ft) Austria	Bludenz 581 metres (1905ft) Landeck 816 metres (2677ft)	35km 1 in 8 21.7 miles 32km 1 in 7.5 20 miles	19ft 8in 6 metres	OC Dec - Apr. Modern road; short, steep stretch from west easing towards the summit; heavy traffic; parallel toll road tunnel available. Suitable for caravans; using tunnel (see note on p. 49). Pass road closed to vehicles towing trailers.
Aubisque 1710 metres (5610ft) France	Eaux Bonnes 751 metres (2461ft) Argelés-Gazost 463 metres (1519ft)	12km 1 in 10 6.7 miles 30km 1 in 10 19 miles	11ft 6in 3.5 metres	UC Mid Oct - Jun. A very winding road; continuous but easy ascent; the descent incorporates the Col de Soulor (1451 metres, 4757ft); 8km (5 miles) of very narrow, rough unguarded road, with a steep drop.
Ballon d'Alsace 1178 metres (3865ft) France	Giromagny 476metres (1562ft) St-Maurice-sur-Moselle 549 metres (1800ft)	17km 1 in 9 10.6 miles 9km 1 in 9 5.6 miles	13ft 4.0 metres	OC Dec - Mar. A fairly straightforward ascent and descent, but numerous bends; negotiable by caravans.
Bayard 1248 metres (4094ft) France	Chauffayer 911 metres (2988ft) Gap 733 metres (2405ft)	18km 1 in 12 11.2 miles 8km 1 in 7 5.0 miles	19ft 8in 6 metres	UO Part of the Route Napoléon. Fairly easy, steepest on the southern side with several hairpin bends; negotiable by caravans from north to south.
*Bernina 2330 metres (7644ft) Switzerland	Pontresina 1804 metres (5915ft) Poschiavo 1019 metres (3343ft)	15.5km 1 in 10 10.5 miles 18.5km 1 in 8 11.5 miles	16ft 5in 5 metres	OC Dec - Mar. A good road on both sides; negotiable by caravans.
Bonaigua 2072 metres (6797ft) Spain	Viella 974 metres (3195ft) Esterri d'Aneu 958 metres (3140ft)	23km 1 in 12 14.3 miles 23km 1 in 12 14.3 miles	14ft 4.3 metres	UC Nov - Apr. A sinuous and narrow road with many hairpin bends and some precipitous drops; the alternative route to Lleida (Lérida) through the Viella tunnel is open in winter.
Bracco 613 metres (2011ft) Italy	Riva Trigoso 43 metres (141ft) Borghetto di Vara 104metres (341ft)	15km 1 in 7 9.3 miles 18km 1 in 7 11.2 miles	16ft 5in 5 metres	UO A two-lane road with continuous bends; passing usually difficult; negotiable by caravans; alternative toll motorway available.
Brenner 1374 metres (4508ft) Austria - Italy	Innsbruck 574 metres (1883ft) Vipiteno 949 metres (3110ft)	36km 1 in 12 22miles 15km 1 in 7 9.3 miles	19ft 8in 6 metres	UO Parallel toll motorway open; heavy traffic; suitable for caravans using toll motorway. Pass road closed to vehicles towing trailers.
+Brünig 1007 metres (3304ft) Switzerland	Brienzwiler Station 575 metres (1886ft) Giswil 485 metres (1591ft)	6km 1 in 12 3.7 miles 13km 1 in 12 8.1 miles	19ft 8in 6 metres	UO An easy but winding road, heavy traffic at weekends; suitable for caravans.

* Permitted maximum width of vehicles 7ft 6in + Permitted maximum width of vehicles 8ft 2.5in ++ Maximum length of vehicle 30ft

Pass and height	From To	Distances from summit and max gradient	Min width of road	Conditions (see page 49 for key to abbreviations)
Bussang 721 metres (2365ft) France	Thann 340 metres (1115ft) St Maurice-sur-Moselle 549 metres (1800ft)	24km 1 in 14 15 miles 8km 1 in 14 5.0 miles	13ft 4metres	UO A very easy road over the Vosges; beautiful scenery; suitable for caravans.
Cabre 1180 metres (3871ft) France	Luc-en-Diois 580 metres (1903ft) Aspres sur Buëch 764 metres (2507ft)	24km 1 in 11 15 miles 17km 1 in 14 10.6 miles	18ft 5.5 metres	UO An easy pleasant road; suitable for caravans.
Campolongo 1875 metres (6152ft) Italy	Corvara in Badia 1568 metres (5144ft) Arabba 1602 metres (5256ft)	6km 1 in 8 3.7 miles 4km 1 in 8 2.5 miles	16ft 5in 5metres	OC Dec - Mar. A winding but easy ascent; long level stretch on summit followed by easy descent; good surface; suitable for caravans.
Cayolle 2326 metres (7631ft) France	Barcelonnette 1132 metres (3714ft) Guillaumes 820 metres (2687ft)	30km 1 in 10 19 miles 33km 1 in 10 20.5 miles	13ft 4 metres	UC early Nov - early Jun. Narrow and winding road with hairpin bends; poor surface and broken edges; steep drops. Long stretches of single-track road with passing places.
Costalunga (Karer) 1753 metres (5751ft) Italy	Cardano 282 metres (925ft) Pozza 1291 metres (4232ft)	24km 1 in 6 14.9 miles 11km 1 in 8 7 miles	16ft 5in 5 metres	OC Dec - Apr. A good well-engineered road but mostly winding; caravans prohibited.
Croix 1778 metres (5833ft) Switzerland	Villars-sur-Ollon 1254 metres (4111ft) Les Diablerets 1156 metres (3789ft)	8km 1 in 7.5 5.0 miles 9km 1 in 11 5.6 miles	11ft 6in 3.5 metres	UC Nov - May. A narrow and winding route but extremely picturesque.
Croix-Haute 1179 metres (3868ft) France	Monestier-de-Clermont 832 metres (2730ft) Aspres-sur-Buëch 764 metres (2507ft)	34km 1 in 14 21 miles 29km 1 in 14 18 miles	18ft 5.5 metres	UO Well engineered; several hairpin bends on the north side; suitable for caravans.
Envalira 2407 metres (7897ft) Andorra	Pas de la Casa 2091 metres (6860ft) Andorra 1029 metres (3375ft)	5km 1 in 10 3.1 miles 25km 1 in 8 16 miles	19ft 8in 6 metres	OC Nov - Apr. A good road with wide bends on ascent and descent; fine views; negotiable by caravans (maximum height vehicles 3.5 metres, 11ft 6in on northern approach near L'Hospitalet).
Falzárego 2117 metres (6945ft) Italy	Cortina d'Ampezzo 1224 metres (4016ft) Andraz 1428 metres (4685ft)	17km 1 in 12 10.6 miles 9km 1 in 12 5.6 miles	16ft 5in 5 metres	OC Dec - Apr. Well engineered bitumen surface; many hairpin bends on both sides; negotiable by caravans.
Faucille 1323 metres (4341ft) France	Gex 628 metres (2060ft) Morez 702 metres (2303ft)	11km 1 in 10 6.8 miles 27km 1 in 12 17miles	16ft 5in 5 metres	UO Fairly wide, winding road across the Jura mountains; negotiable by caravans, but it is probably better to follow La Cure-St-Cergue-Nyon.
Fern 1209 metres (3967ft) Austria	Nassereith 844 metres (2766ft) Lermoos 995 metres (3264ft)	10km 1 in 10 6 miles 10km 1 in 10 6 miles	19ft 8 in 6 metres	UO An easy pass, but slippery when wet; heavy traffic at summer weekends; suitable for caravans.
Flexen 1784 metres (5853ft) Austria	Lech 1448 metres (4747ft) Rauzalpe (near Arlberg Pass) 1629 metres (5341ft)	6.5km 1 in 10 4 miles 3.5km 1 in 10 2.2 miles	18ft 5.5 metres	UO The magnificent 'Flexenstrasse', a well engineered mountain road with tunnels and galleries. The road from Lech to Warth, north of the pass, is usually closed between November and April due to danger of avalanches.

* **Permitted maximum width of vehicles** 7ft 6in + **Permitted maximum width of vehicles** 8ft 2.5in ++ **Maximum length of vehicle** 30ft

Pass and height	From To	Distances from summit and max gradient	Min width of road	Conditions (see page 49 for key to abbreviations)
*Flüela 2383 metres (7818ft) Switzerland	Davos-Dorf 1564 metres (5128ft) Susch 1439 metres (4718ft)	14km 1 in 10 9 miles 14km 1 in 8 9 miles	16ft 5in 5metres	OC Nov - May. Easy ascent from Davos; some acute hairpin bends on the eastern side; bitumen surface; negotiable by caravans.
+Forclaz 1527 metres (5010ft) Switzerland France	Martigny 476 metres (1562ft) Argentière 1254 metres (4111ft)	13km 1 in 12 8.1 miles 19km 1 in 12 11.8 miles	16ft 5in 5 metres	UO Forclaz; OC Montets Dec - early Apr. A good road over the pass and to the frontier; in France, narrow and rough over Col des Montets (1461 metres, 4793ft); negotiable by caravans.
Foscagno 2291 metres (7516ft) Italy	Bormio 1226 metres (4019ft) Livigno 1817 metres (5958ft)	24km 1 in 8 14.9 miles 14km 1 in 8 8.7 miles	10ft 10in 3.3 metres	OC Nov - May. Narrow and winding through lonely mountains, generally poor surface. Long winding ascent with many blind bends; not always well guarded. The descent includes winding rise and fall over the Passo d'Eira (2200 metres, 7218ft).
Fugazze 1159 metres (3802ft) Italy	Rovereto 201 metres (660ft) Valli del Pasubio 350 metres (1148ft)	27km 1 in 7 16.4 miles 12km 1 in 7 7.4 miles	11ft 6 in 3.5 metres	UO Very winding with some narrow sections, particularly on northern side. The many blind bends and several hairpin bends call for extra care.
*Furka 2431 metres (7976ft) Switzerland	Gletsch 1757 metres (5764ft) Realp 1538 metres (5046ft)	10km 1 in 9 6.2 miles 13km 1 in 10 8.1 miles	13ft 4 metres	UC Oct - Jun. A well graded road, with narrow sections and several sharp hairpin bends on both ascent and descent. Fine views of the Rhône glacier. Alternative rail tunnel available.
Galibier 2645 metres (8678ft) France	Lautaret Pass 2059 metres (6752ft) St-Michel-de-Maurienne 712 metres (2336ft)	7km 1 in 9 4.4 miles 34km 1 in 8 21.1 miles	9ft 10in 3 metres	UC Oct - Jun. Mainly wide, well surfaced but unguarded. Ten hairpin bends on descent then 5km (3.1 miles) narrow and rough. Rise over the Col du Télégraphe (1600 metres, 5249ft), then 11 more hairpin bends. (The tunnel under the Galibier summit is closed.)
Gardena (Grödner-Joch) 2121 metres (6959ft) Italy	Val Gardena 1863 metres (6109ft) Corvara in Badia 1568 metres (5144ft)	6km 1 in 8 3.7 miles 10km 1 in 8 6.2 miles	16ft 5in 5metres	OC Dec - Jun. A well engineered road, very winding on descent.
Gavia 2621 metres (8599ft) Italy	Bormio 1226 metres (4019ft) Ponte di Legno 1258 metres (4127ft)	25km 1 in 5.5 15.5 miles 18km 1 in 5.5 11 miles	9ft 10in 3 metres	UC Oct - Jul. Steep and narrow, but with frequent passing bays; many hairpin bends and a gravel surface; not for the faint-hearted; extra care necessary. (Maximum width for vehicles 1.8 metres, 5ft 11in.)
Gerlos 1628 metres (5341ft) Austria	Zell am Ziller 575 metres (1886ft) Wald 886 metres (2904ft)	29km 1 in 12 18 miles 15km 1 in 11 9.3 miles	13ft 4 metres	UO Hairpin ascent out of Zell to modern toll road; the old, steep, narrow, and winding route with passing bays and 1-in-7 gradient is not recommended, but is negotiable with care; caravans prohibited.
+Grand St Bernard 2473 metres (8114ft) Switzerland - Italy	Martigny 476 metres (1562ft) Aosta 583 metres (1913ft)	46km 1 in 9 29 miles 34km 1 in 9 21 miles	13ft 4 metres	UC Oct - Jun. Modern road to entrance of road tunnel (usually open; see note p. 49) then narrow but bitumen surface over summit to frontier; also good in Italy; suitable for caravans using tunnel. Pass road closed to vehicles towing trailers.
*Grimsel 2164 metres (7100ft) Switzerland	Innerkirchen 630 metres (2067ft) Gletsch 1757 metres (5764ft)	26km 1 in 10 16.1 miles 6km 1 in 10 3.7 miles	16ft 5in 5 metres	UC mid Oct - late Jun. A fairly easy, modern road, but heavy traffic at weekends. A long winding ascent, finally hairpin bends; then a terraced descent with six hairpins into the Rhône valley.
Grossglockner 2503 metres (8212ft) Austria	Bruck an der Glocknerstrasse 755 metres (2477ft) Heiligenblut 1301 metres (4268ft)	34km 1 in 8 21 miles 15m 1 in 8 9.3 miles	18ft 5.5 metres	UC late Oct - early May. Numerous well engineered hairpin bends; moderate but very long ascent, toll road; very fine scenery; heavy tourist traffic; negotiable preferably from south to north, by caravans. Road closed at night, 22.00 to 05.00 hrs.

* **Permitted maximum width of vehicles** 7ft 6in   + **Permitted maximum width of vehicles** 8ft 2.5in   ++ **Maximum length of vehicle** 30ft

● PRINCIPAL MOUNTAIN PASSES ●

Pass and height	From To	Distances from summit and max gradient	Min width of road	Conditions (see page 49 for key to abbreviations)
Hochtannberg 1679 metres (5509ft) Austria	Schröcken 1270 metres(4163ft) Warth (near Lech) 1501 metres (4921ft)	5.5km 1 in 7 3.4 miles 4.5km 1 in 11 2.8 miles	13ft 4 metres	OC Jan - Mar. A reconstructed modern road.
Ibañeta (Roncesvalles) 1057 metres (3468ft) France - Spain	St-Jean-Pied-de-Port 163 metres (535ft) Pamplona 421 metres (1380ft)	26km 1 in 10 17 miles 52km 1 in 10 32.2 miles	13ft 4 metres	UO A slow and winding, scenic route; negotiable by caravans.
Iseran 2770 metres (9088ft) France	Bourg-St-Maurice 841 metres (2756ft) Lanslebourg 1399 metres (4590ft)	47km 1 in 12 29 miles 33km 1 in 9 20.5 miles	13ft 4.metres	UC Mid Oct - late Jun. The second highest pass in the Alps. Well graded with reasonable bends, average surface; several unlit tunnels on northern approach.
Izoard 2360 metres (7743ft) France	Guillestre 1000 metres (3281ft) Briançon 1321 metres (4334ft)	32km 1 in 8 13.6 miles 20km 1 in 10 12.4 miles	16ft 5 in 5 metres	UC Late Oct - mid Jun. A winding and sometimes narrow road with many hairpin bends. Care is required at several unlit tunnels near Guillestre.
*Jaun 1509 metres (4951ft) Switzerland	Broc 718 metres (2356ft) Reidenbach 845 metres (2772ft)	25km 1 in 10 15.5 miles 8km 1 in 10 5.miles	13ft 4 metres	UO A modernised but generally narrow road; some poor sections on ascent, and several hairpin bends on descent; negotiable by caravans.
+Julier 2284 metres (7493ft) Switzerland	Tiefencastel 852 metres (2792ft) Silvaplana 1816 metres (5955ft)	35km 1 in 10 22miles 7km 1 in 7.5 4.4 miles	13ft 4 metres	UO Well engineered road, approached from Chur by Lenzerheide Pass (1549 metres, 5082ft); negotiable by caravans, preferably from north to south.
Katschberg 1641 metres (5384ft) Austria	Spittal 554 metres (1818ft) St Michael 1068 metres (3504ft)	37km 1 in 5 23 miles 6km 1 in 6 3.7 miles	19ft 8in 6metres	UO Steep though not particularly difficult, parallel toll motorway, including tunnel available; negotiable by light caravans, using tunnel (see note p. 49, Tauern Autobahn)
*Klausen 1948 metres (6391ft) Switzerland	Altdorf 458 metres (1503ft) Linthal 662 metres (2172ft)	25km 1 in 10 15.5 miles 23km 1 in 11 14.3 miles	16ft 5in 5 metres	UC Late Oct - early Jun. Narrow and winding in places, but generally easy, in spite of a number of sharp bends; no through route for caravans as they are prohibited from using the road between Unterschächen and Linthal.
Larche (della Maddalena) 1994 metres (6542ft) France - Italy	Condamine Châtelard 1309 metres (4291ft) Vinadio 911 metres (2986ft)	19km 1 in 12 11.8 miles 32km 1 in 12 19.8 miles	11ft 6in 3.5 metres	OC Dec - Mar. An easy, well graded road; narrow and rough on ascent, wider with better surface on descent; suitable for caravans.
Lautaret 2058 metres (6752ft) France	Le Bourg-d'Oisans 719 metres (2359ft) Briançon 1321 metres (4334ft)	38km 1 in 8 23.6 miles 28km 1 in 10 17.4 miles	13ft 4 metres	OC Dec - Mar. Modern, evenly graded, but winding, and unguarded in places; very fine scenery; suitable for caravans.
Loibl (Ljubelj) 1067 metres (3500ft) Austria - Slovenia	Unterloibl 518 metres (1699ft) Kranj 385 metres (1263ft)	10km 1 in 5.5 6.2 miles 26km 1 in 8 16miles	19ft 8in 6.metres	UO Steep rise and fall over Little Loibl pass to tunnel (1.6km, 1 mile long) under summit. The old road over the summit is closed to through traffic.
*Lukmanier (Lucomagno) 1916 metres (6286ft) Switzerland	Olivone 894 metres (2930ft) Disentis 1134 metres (3717ft)	20km 1 in 11 12 miles 20km 1 in 11 12 miles	16ft 5in 5metres	UC early Nov - late May. Rebuilt, modern road; suitable for caravans.

* Permitted maximum width of vehicles 7ft 6in   + Permitted maximum width of vehicles 8ft 2.5in   ++ Maximum length of vehicle 30ft

● 53 ●

● PRINCIPAL MOUNTAIN PASSES ●

Pass and height	From To	Distances from summit and max gradient	Min width of road	Conditions (see page 49 for key to abbreviations)
+Maloja 1815 metres (5955ft) Switzerland	Silvaplana 1816 metres (5955ft) Chiavenna 333 metres (1093ft)	11km level 6.8 miles 32km 1 in 11 19.8 miles	13ft 4metres	UO Escarpment facing south; fairly easy, but many hairpin bends on descent; negotiable by caravans, possibly difficult on ascent.
Mauria 1298 metres (4285ft) Italy	Lozzo Cadore 753 metres (2470ft) Ampezzo 560 metres (1837ft)	13km 1 in 14 8 miles 31km 1 in 14 19.2 miles	16ft 5in 5 metres	UO A well designed road with easy, winding ascent and descent; suitable for caravans.
Mendola 1363 metres (4472ft) Italy	Appiano (Eppan) 411 metres (1348ft) Sarnonico 978 metres (3208ft)	15km 1 in 8 9.3 miles 9km 1 in 10 6 miles	16ft 5in 5 metres	UO A fairly straightforward but winding road, well guarded; suitable for caravans.
Mont Cenis 2083 metres (6834ft) France - Italy	Lanslebourg 1399 metres (4590ft) Susa 503 metres (1650ft)	11km 1 in 10 6.8 miles 28km 1 in 8 17.4 miles	16ft 5in 5 metres	UC Nov - May. Approach by industrial valley. An easy broad highway, but with poor surface in places; suitable for caravans. Alternative Fréjus road tunnel available (see note p.49).
Monte Croce di Comélico (Kreuzberg) 1636 metres (5368ft) Italy	San Candido 1174metres (3852ft) Santo Stefano di Cadore 908 metres (2979ft)	15km 1 in 12 9.3 miles 21km 1 in 12 13miles	16ft 5in 5metres	UO A winding road with moderate gradients, beautiful scenery; suitable for caravans.
Montgenèvre 1850m (6070ft) France - Italy	Briançon 1321 metres (4334ft) Cesana Torinese 1344 metres (4409ft)	12km 1 in 14 7.4 miles 8km 1 in 11 5miles	16ft 5in 5metres	UO An easy, modern road; suitable for caravans.
Monte Giovo (Jaufen) 2094 metres (6870ft) Italy	Merano 324 metres (1063ft) Vipiteno 949 metres (3110ft)	40km 1 in 8 24.8 miles 19km 1 in 11 11.8 miles	13ft 4metres	UC Nov - May. Many well engineered hairpin bends; caravans prohibited.
Montets (see Forclaz)				
Morgins 1369 metres (4491ft) France - Switzerland	Abondance 931 metres (3051ft) Monthey 424 metres (1391ft)	14km 1 in 11 8.7 miles 15km 1 in 7 9.3 miles	13ft 4metres	UO A lesser used route through pleasant, forested countryside crossing the French-Swiss border.
*Mosses 1445m (4740ft) Switzerland	Aigle 417 metres (1368ft) Château d'Oex 962 metres (3153ft)	16km 1 in 12 11.2 miles 15km 1 in 12 9.3 miles	13ft 4metres	UO A modern road; suitable for caravans.
Nassfeld (Pramollo) 1530m (5020ft) Austria - Italy	Tröpolach 601 metres (1972ft) Pontebba 568 metres (1864ft)	10km 1 in 5 6.2 miles 10km 1 in 10 6.2 miles	13ft 4metres	OC Late Nov - Mar. The winding descent in Italy has been improved.
*Nufenen (Novena) 2478 metres (8130ft) Switzerland	Ulrichen 1347 metres (4416ft) Airolo 1143 metres (3747ft)	13km 1 in 10 8.1 miles 24km 1 in 10 14.9 miles	13ft 4.0 metres	UC Mid Oct - mid Jun. The approach roads are narrow, with tight bends, but the road over the pass is good; negotiable by caravans.
*Oberalp 2044 metres (6706ft) Switzerland	Andermatt 1448 metres (4747ft) Disentis 1134 metres (3717ft)	10km 1 in 10 6.2 miles 21km 1 in 10 13miles	16ft 5in 5 metres	UC Nov - late May. A much improved and widened road with a modern surface; many hairpin bends, but long level stretch on summit; negotiable by caravans. Alternative rail runnel during the winter (see note p49).

* Permitted maximum width of vehicles 7ft 6in   + Permitted maximum width of vehicles 8ft 2.5in   ++ Maximum length of vehicle 30ft

Pass and height	From To	Distances from summit and max gradient	Min width of road	Conditions (see page 49 for key to abbreviations)
*Ofen (Fuorn) 2149 metres (7051ft) Switzerland	Zernez 1474 metres (4836ft) Santa Maria im Münstertal 1375 metres (4511ft)	22km 1 in 10 13.6 miles 14km 1 in 8 8.7 miles	13ft 4 metres	UO Good, fairly easy road through the Swiss National Park; negotiable by caravans.
Petit St Bernard 2188 metres (7178ft) France - Italy	Bourg-St-Maurice 841 metres (2756ft) Pré St-Didier 1000 metres (3281ft)	30km 1 in 16 19 miles 23km 1 in 12 14.3 miles	16ft 5in 5 metres	UC Mid Oct - Jun. Outstanding scenery; a fairly easy approach, but poor surface and unguarded broken edges near the summit; good on the descent in Italy; negotiable by light caravans.
Peyresourde 1563 metres (5128ft) France	Arreau 705 metres (2310ft) Luchon 630 metres (2067ft)	18km 1 in 10 11.2 miles 14km 1 in 10 8.7 miles	13ft 4metres	UO Somewhat narrow with several hairpin bends, though not difficult.
*Pillon 1546 metres (5072ft) Switzerland	Le Sépey 974 metres (3196ft) Gsteig 1184 metres (3885ft)	15km 1 in 11 9 miles 7km 1 in 11 4.4 miles	13ft 4metres	OC Jan - Feb. A comparatively easy modern road; suitable for caravans.
Plöcken (Monte Croce-Carnico) 1362 metres (4468ft) Austria - Italy	Kötschach 706 metres (2316ft) Paluzza 600 metres (1968ft)	16km 1 in 7 10 miles 17km 1 in 14 10.6 miles	16ft 5in 5metres	OC Dec - Apr. A modern road with long, reconstructed sections; heavy traffic at summer weekends; delay likely at the frontier; negotiable by caravans, best used only by experienced drivers in cars with ample power.
Pordoi 2239 metres (7346ft) Italy	Arabba 1602 metres (5256ft) Canazei 1465 metres (4806ft)	9km 1 in 10 5.6 miles 12km 1 in 10 7.4 miles	16ft 5in 5 metres	OC Dec - Apr. An excellent modern road with numerous hairpin bends; negotiable by caravans.
Port 1249 metres (4098ft) France	Tarascon 474 metres (1555ft) Massat 650 metres (2133ft)	18km 1 in 10 11.2 miles 12km 1 in 10 7.4 miles	13ft 4metres	OC Nov - Mar. A fairly easy road, but narrow on some bends; negotiable by caravans.
Portet-d'Aspet 1069 metres (3507ft) France	Audressein 508 metres (1667ft) Fronsac 472 metres (1548ft)	18km 1 in 7 11.2 miles 29km 1 in 7 18miles	11ft 6in 3.5 metres	UO Approached from the west by the easy Col des Ares (797 metres, 2615ft) and Col de Buret (599 metres, 1965ft); well engineered road, but calls for particular care on hairpin bends; rather narrow.
Pötschen 982 metres (3221ft) Austria	Bad Ischl 469 metres (1539ft) Bad Aussee 651 metres (2133ft)	19km 1 in 11 11.8 miles 9 km 1 in 11 5.6 miles	23ft 7 metres	UO A modern road; suitable for caravans.
Pourtalet 1792 metres (5879ft) France - Spain	Eaux-Chaudes 656 metres (2152ft) Biescas 860 metres (2822ft)	23km 1 in 10 14.3 miles 34km 1 in 10 21.1 miles	11ft 6in 3.5metres	UC late Oct - early Jun. A fairly easy, unguarded road, but narrow in places.
Puymorens 1915 metres (6283ft) France	Ax-les-Thermes 720 metres (2362ft) Bourg-Madame 1131 metres (3707ft)	28km 1 in 10 17.4 miles 27km 1 in 10 16.8 miles	18ft 5.5 metres	OC Nov - Apr. A generally easy, modern tarmac road, but narrow, winding and with a poor surface in places; not suitable for night driving; suitable for caravans (max height vehicles 3.5 metres, 11ft 6in). Parallel toll road tunnel available.
Quillane 1714 metres (5623ft) France	Quillan 291 metres (955ft) Mont-Louis 1600 metres (5249ft)	63km 1 in 12 39.1 miles 6 km 1 in 12 3.5 miles	16ft 5in 5 metres	OC Nov - Mar. An easy, straightforward ascent and descent; suitable for caravans.

* Permitted maximum width of vehicles 7ft 6in   **+ Permitted maximum width of vehicles** 8ft 2.5in   **++ Maximum length of vehicle** 30ft

Pass and height	From To	Distances from summit and max gradient	Min width of road	Conditions (see page 49 for key to abbreviations)
Radstädter-Tauern 1739 metres (5702ft) Austria	Radstadt 862 metres (2828ft) Mauterndorf 1123 metres (3681ft)	21km 1 in 6 13.0 miles 17km 1 in 7 10.6 miles	16ft 5in 5 metres	OC Jan - Mar. Northern ascent steep, but not difficult otherwise; parallel toll motorway including tunnel available; negotiable by light caravans, using tunnel (see note p.49).
Résia (Reschen) 1504 metres (4934ft) Italy - Austria	Spondigna 885 metres (2903ft) Pfunds 971 metres (3182ft)	29km 1 in 10 18 miles 21km 1 in 10 13miles	19ft 8in 6metres	UO A good, straightforward alternative to the Brenner Pass; suitable for caravans.
Restefond (La Bonette) 2802 metres (9193ft) France	Jausiers (near Barcelonnette) 1220 metres (40036ft) St-Etienne-de-Tinée 1144 metres (3753ft)	23km 1 in 8 14.3 miles 27km 1 in 6 16.8 miles	9ft 10in 3metres	UC Oct - Jun. The highest pass in the Alps, completed in 1962. Narrow, rough, unguarded ascent with many blind bends, and nine hairpins. Descent easier, winding with 12 hairpin bends. Not for the faint-hearted; extra care required.
Rolle 1970 metres (6463ft) Italy	Predazzo 1019 metres (3340ft) Mezzano 637 metres (2090ft)	21km 1 in 11 13.0 miles 27km 1 in 14 17 miles	16ft 5in 5metres	OC Dec - Mar. A well engineered road with many hairpin bends on both sides; very beautiful scenery; good surface; negotiable by caravans.
Rombo (see Timmelsjoch)				
Routes des Crêtes 1283 metres (4210ft) France	St-Dié 343 metres (1125ft) Cernay 296 metres (971ft)	- 1 in 8 - 1 in 8	13ft 4 metres	UC Nov - Apr. A renowned scenic route crossing seven ridges, with the highest point at 'Hôtel du Grand Ballon'.
+St Gotthard (San Gottardo) 2108 metres (6916ft) Switzerland	Göschenen 1106 metres (3629ft) Airolo 1143 metres (3747ft)	18km 1 in 10 11miles 15km 1 in 10 9.3 miles	19ft 8in 6 metres	UC Mid Oct - early Jun. Modern, fairly easy two to three-lane road. Heavy traffic; negotiable by caravans. Alternative road tunnel available (see note p. 49).
*San Bernardino 2066 metres (6778ft) Switzerland	Mesocco 790 metres (2592ft) Hinterrhein 1625 metres (5328ft)	21km 1 in 10 13miles 9.5km 1 in 10 5.9 miles	13ft 4metres	UC Oct - late Jun. Easy, modern roads on northern and southern approaches to tunnel (see note p. 49); narrow and winding over summit, via tunnel suitable for caravans.
Schlucht 1139 metres (3737ft) France	Gérardmer 666 metres (2182ft) Munster 381 metres (1250ft)	15km 1 in 14 9.3 miles 18km 1 in 14 11miles	16ft 5in 5 metres	UO An extremely picturesque route crossing the Vosges mountains, with easy, wide bends on the descent; suitable for caravans.
Seeberg (Jezersko) 1218 metres (3996ft) Austria - Slovenia	Eisenkappel 555 metres (1821ft) Kranj 385 metres (1263ft)	14km 1 in 8 8.7 miles 33km 1 in 10 20.5 miles	16ft 5in 5metres	UO An alternative to the steeper Loibl and Wurzen passes; moderate climb with winding, hairpin ascent and descent.
Sella 2240 metres (7349ft) Italy	Plan 1607 metres (5269ft) Canazei 1466 metres (4806ft)	9km 1 in 9 5.6 miles 12km 1 in 9 7 miles	16ft 5in 5metres	OC Dec - Jun. A finely engineered, winding road; exceptional views of the Dolomites.
Semmering 985 metres (3232ft) Austria	Mürzzuschlag im Mürztal 673 metres (2205ft) Gloggnitz 457 metres (1499ft)	14km 1 in 16 8.7 miles 17km 1 in 16 10.6 miles	19ft 8in 6metres	UO A fine, well engineered highway; suitable for caravans.
Sestriere 2033 metres (6670ft) Italy	Cesana Torinese 1344 metres (4409ft) Pinerolo 376 metres (1234ft)	12km 1 in 10 7.4 miles 55km 1 in 10 34.2 miles	19ft 8in 6metres	UO Mostly bitumen surface; negotiable by caravans.

* Permitted maximum width of vehicles 7ft 6in **+ Permitted maximum width of vehicles** 8ft 2.5in **++ Maximum length of vehicle** 30ft

Pass and height	From To	Distances from summit and max gradient	Min width of road	Conditions (see page 49 for key to abbreviations)
Silvretta (Bielerhöhe) 2032 metres (6666ft) Austria	Partenen 1052 metres (3448ft) Galtür 1585 metres (5197ft)	16km 1 in 9 9.9 miles 10km 1 in 9 6.2 miles	16ft 5in 5metres	UC Late Oct - early Jun. For the most part reconstructed; 32 easy hairpin bends on western ascent; eastern side more straightforward. Toll road; caravans prohibited.
+Simplon 2005 metres (6578ft) Switzerland - Italy	Brig 681 metres (2234ft) Domodóssola 280 metres (919ft)	22km 1 in 9 13.6 miles 41km 1 in 11 25.5 miles	23ft 7metres	OC Nov - Apr. An easy, reconstructed modern road, but 13 miles long, continuous ascent to summit; suitable for caravans.
Somport 1632 metres (5354ft) France - Spain	Bedous 416 metres (1365ft) Jaca 820 metres (2690ft)	31km 1 in 10 19.2 miles 32km 1 in 10 20miles	11ft 6in 3.5 metres	UO A favoured, old-established route; generally easy, but in parts narrow and unguarded; fairly well surfaced road; suitable for caravans.
*Splügen 2113 metres (6932ft) Switzerland - Italy	Splügen 1458 metres (4780ft) Chiavenna 330 metres (1083ft)	9km 1 in 9 5.6 miles 30km 1 in 7.5 18.6 miles	11ft 6in 3.5 metres	UC Nov - Jun. Mostly narrow and winding, with many hairpin bends, and not well guarded; care is also required at many tunnels and galleries (max height vehicles 9ft 2in).
++Stelvio 2757 metres (9045ft) Italy	Bormio 1226 metres (4019ft) Spondigna 885 metres (2903ft)	22km 1 in 8 13.6 miles 28km 1 in 8 12.9 miles	13ft 4metres	UC Oct - late Jun. the third highest pass in the Alps; the number of acute hairpin bends, all well engineered; is exceptional - from 40 to 50 on either side; the surface is good, the traffic heavy. Hairpin bends are too acute for long vehicles.
+Susten 2224 metres (7297ft) Switzerland	Innertkirchen 630 metres (2067ft) Wassen 917 metres (3005ft)	28km 1 in 11 12.9 miles 19km 1 in 11 11.8 miles	19ft 8in 6 metres	UC Nov - Jun. A very scenic and well guarded mountain road; easy gradients and turns; heavy traffic at weekends; caravans prohibited.
Tenda (Tende) 1321 metres (4334ft) Italy - France	Borgo S Dalmazzo 641 metres (2103ft) La Giandola 308 metres (1010ft)	24km 1 in 11 14.9 miles 29km 1 in 11 18miles	19ft 8in 6metres	UO Well guarded, modern road with several hairpin bends; road tunnel at summit; suitable for caravans; but prohibited during the winter.
+Thurn 1274 metres (4180ft) Austria	Kitzbühel 762 metres (2500ft) Mittersill 789 metres (2588ft)	19km 1 in 12 11.8 miles 10km 1 in 16 6.2 miles	16ft 5in 5metres	UO A good road with narrow stretches; northern approach rebuilt; suitable for caravans.
Timmelsjoch (Rombo) 2509 metres (8232ft) Austria - Italy	Obergurgl 1910 metres (6266ft) Moso 1007 metres (3304ft)	14km 1 in 7 8.7 miles 23km 1 in 8 14miles	11ft 6 in 3.5 metres	UC mid Oct - late Jun. Pass open to private cars (without trailers) only as some tunnels on the Italian side are too narrow for larger vehicles; toll road. Border closed at night 20.00 -07.00 hrs.
Tonale 1883 metres (6178ft) Italy	Edolo 699 metres (2293ft) Dimaro 766 metres (2513ft)	30km 1 in 12 18.6 miles 27km 1 in 10 16.7 miles	16ft 5in 5metres	UO A relatively easy road; suitable for caravans.
Toses (Tosas) 1800 metres (5906ft) Spain	Puigcerdá 1152 metres (3780ft) Ribes de Freser 920 metres (3018ft)	26km 1 in 10 16miles 25km 1 in 10 15.5 miles	16ft 5in 5metres	UO Now a fairly straightforward, but continuously winding, two-lane road with many sharp bends; negotiable by caravans.
Tourmalet 2114 metres (6936ft) France	Luz 712 metres (2333ft) Ste-Marie-de-Campan 857 metres (2811ft)	18km 1 in 8 11miles 17km 1 in 8 10.6 miles	13ft 4metres	UC Oct - mid Jun. The highest of the French Pyrenean routes; the approaches are good, though winding and exacting over summit; sufficiently guarded.
Tre Croci 1809 metres (5935ft) Italy	Cortina d'Ampezzo 1224 metres (4016ft) Auronzo di Cadore 865 metres (2835ft).	7km 1 in 9 4.4 miles 26 km 1 in 9 16 miles	19ft 8in 6metres	OC Dec - Mar. An easy pass; very fine scenery; suitable for caravans.

* Permitted maximum width of vehicles 7ft 6in   + Permitted maximum width of vehicles 8ft 2.5in   ++ Maximum length of vehicle 30ft

Pass and height	From To	Distances from summit and max gradient	Min width of road	Conditions (see page 49 for key to abbreviations)
Turracher Höhe 1763 metres (5784ft) Austria	Predlitz 922 metres (3024ft) Ebene-Reichenau 1086 metres (3563ft)	20km 1 in 5.5 12.4 miles 8km 1 in 4.5 5miles	13ft 4metres	UO Formerly one of the steepest mountain roads in Austria; now much improved. A steep, fairly straightforward ascent is followed by a very steep descent; good surface and mainly two-lane width; fine scenery.
*Umbrail 2501 metres (8205ft) Switzerland - Italy	Santa Maria im Münstertal 1375 metres (4511ft) Bormio 1226 metres (4019ft)	14km 1 in 11 9 miles 19km 1 in 11 11.8 miles	14ft 4.3 metres	UC Early Nov - early Jun. Highest of the Swiss passes; narrow; mostly gravel surfaced with 34 hairpin bends, but not too difficult.
Vars 2109 metres (6919ft) France	St-Paul-sur-Ubaye 1470 metres (4823ft) Guillestre 1000 metres (3281ft)	8km 1 in 10 5miles 20km 1 in 10 12.4 miles	16ft 5in 5metres	OC Dec - Mar. Easy winding ascent with seven hairpin bends; gradual winding descent with another seven hairpin bends; good surface; negotiable by caravans.
Wurzen (Koren) 1073 metres (3520ft) Austria - Slovenia	Riegersdorf 541 metres (1775ft) Kranjska Gora 810 metres (2657ft)	7km 1 in 5.5 4.5miles 6km 1 in 5.5 3.5 miles	13ft 4metres	UO A steep two-lane road, which otherwise is not particularly difficult; heavy traffic at summer weekends; delay likely at the frontier; caravans prohibited.
Zirler Berg 1009 metres (3310ft) Austria	Seefeld 1180 metres (3871ft) Zirl 622 metres (2041ft)	6km 1 in 7 3.5 miles 5km 1 in 6 3.1 miles	23ft 7 metres	UO An escarpment facing south, part of the route from Garmisch to Innsbruck; a good, modern road, but heavy tourist traffic and a long steep descent, with one hairpin bend, into the Inn Valley. Steepest section from the hairpin bend down to Zirl; caravans prohibited northbound.

* **Permitted maximum width of vehicles** 7ft 6in **+ Permitted maximum width of vehicles** 8ft 2.5in **++ Maximum length of vehicle** 30ft

In late 1996, as we went to press a new telephone numbering system was introduced in France to cope with the anticipated increase in telecommunications traffic.

As of this date, to call all numbers in France, you must dial a 9-digit number after the international access code for France, which remains 33.
Paris and Paris region: no change.
Provinces (other regions): one digit to add.

How to call all numbers in France

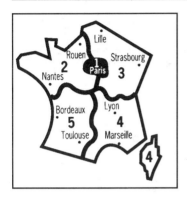

For numbers in the provinces (other regions):
Simply dial either 2,3,4 or 5 depending on the location, before the current 8-digit number.
For example: + 33 20 .. .. .. will now be +33 3 20 .. .. ..

Add:	To the current numbers beginning with	Add:	To the current numbers beginning with	Add:	To the current numbers beginning with
3	20	2	48	4	76
3	21	5	49	4	77
3	22	4	50	4	78
3	23	2	51	4	79
3	24	5	53	3	80
3	25	2	54	3	81
3	26	5	55	3	82
3	27	5	56	3	83
3	28	5	57	3	84
3	29	5	58	3	85
2	31	5	59	3	86
2	32	3	60	3	87
2	33	5	61	3	88
5	34	5	62	3	89
2	35	5	63	4	90
2	37	5	65	4	91
2	38	4	66	4	92
2	39	4	67	4	93
2	40	4	68	4	94
2	41	4	69	4	95
4	42	4	70	2	96
2	43	4	71	2	97
3	44	4	72	2	98
5	45	4	73	2	99
5	46	4	74		
2	47	4	75		

• **For Paris and the Paris region:**
There are no changes. You continue to dial the 9-digit number, beginning with 1.
For example: +33 1 .. .. ..

Numbers with the following first three digits remain the same:		
1 30	1 42	1 47
1 34	1 43	1 48
1 39	1 44	1 49
1 40	1 45	1 53
1 41	1 46	1 55

• **Mobile services:**
Dial 6 before the current 8-digit number.
For example: + 33 6 .. ..

Dialling procedures when you call from France

For all calls inside France
dial 0 before the 9-digit number.
e.g. Paris 01 .. .. ..   Marseille 04 .. .. ..

To call abroad from France
dial 00

For information and directory assistance
dial 12

KEY TO
COUNTRY REGIONS

THE COUNTRY DIRECTORIES, with the exception of Andorra and Luxembourg, are divided into regions, each introduced by a brief description, to help people to plan their touring holidays. Below is a list of the regional headings used in each country directory, followed by a list of the departments, districts or administrative areas that may be included within each region. See also the country maps at the end of the book.

• AUSTRIA •

TIROL
CARINTHIA = Kärnten
STYRIA = Steiermark
LOWER AUSTRIA - Niederösterreich, Burgenland
UPPER AUSTRIA - Oberösterreich, Salzburg
VORARLBERG
VIENNA = Wien

• BELGIUM •

SOUTH WEST/COAST - Hainaut, West-Vlaanderen
NORTH/CENTRAL - Brabant, Oost-Vlaanderen
NORTH EAST - Antwerpen, Limburg
SOUTH EAST - Liège, Luxembourg, Namur

• FRANCE •

ALPS/EAST - Ain, Doubs, Hautes-Alpes, Haute Saône, Haute Savoie, Jura, Isère, Savoie, Territoire-de-Belfort
ALSACE/LORRAINE - Bas-Rhin, Haut-Rhin, Meurthe-et-Moselle, Meuse, Moselle, Vosges
BURGUNDY/CHAMPAGNE - Aube, Ardennes, Côte-d'Or, Haute-Marne, Marne, Nièvre, Saône-et-Loire, Yonne
SOUTH WEST/ PYRENEES - Ariège, Dordogne, Gers, Gironde, Haute-Garonne, Hautes-Pyrénées, Landes, Lot, Lot-et-Garonne, Pyrénées-Atlantiques, Tarn, Tarn-et-Garonne
LOIRE/CENTRAL - Charente, Charente-Maritime, Cher, Corrèze, Creuse, Deux-Sèvres, Eure-et-Loir, Haute-Vienne, Indre, Indre-et-

Loire, Loire-Atlantique, Loiret, Loir-et-Cher, Maine-et-Loire, Mayenne, Sarthe, Vendée, Vienne
BRITTANY/NORMANDY - Calvados, Côtes-d'Armor, Eure, Finistère, Ille-et-Vilaine, Manche, Morbihan, Orne, Seine-Maritime
PARIS/NORTH - Aisne, Essonne, Hauts-de-Seine, Nord, Oise, Paris, Pas-de-Calais, Seine-et-Marne, Seine-St-Denis, Somme, Val-de-Marne, Val d'Oise, Yvelines
AUVERGNE - Allier, Aveyron, Cantal, Haute-Loire, Loire, Lozère, Puy-de-Dôme, Rhône
SOUTH COAST/RIVIERA - Alpes-Maritimes, Alpes-de-Haute-Provence, Ardèche, Aude, Bouches-du-Rhône, Drôme, Gard, Hérault, Monaco, Pyrénées-Orientales, Var, Vaucluse
CORSICA - Corse-du-Sud, Haute-Corse

• GERMANY •

SOUTH EAST - Bayern
SOUTH WEST - Baden-Württemberg
BERLIN AND EASTERN PROVINCES - Brandenburg, Sachsen, Thüringen
CENTRAL - Hessen, Nordrhein-Westfalen, Rheinland-Pfalz, Saarland
NORTH - Bremen, Hamburg, Niedersachsen, Schleswig-Holstein

• ITALY •

NORTH WEST/ALPS/LAKES - Aosta, Alessandria, Asti, Beramo, Bolzano, Brescia, Como, Cremona, Cuneo, Mantova, Milano, Novara, Pavia, Sondrio, Trento, Torino, Varese, Vercelli
VENICE/NORTH - Belluno, Gorizia, Padova, Pordenone, Rovigo, Treviso, Trieste, Udine, Venezia, Verona, Vicenza,
NORTH WEST/MED COAST - Arezzo, Firenze, Genova, Grosseto, Imperia, Livorno, Lucca, Massa Carrara, Pisa, Pistoia, Savona, Siena, La Spezia
NORTH EAST/ADRIATIC - Ancona, L'Aquila, Ascoli Piceno, Bologna, Campobasso, Chieti, Ferrara, Forli, Iserina, Macerata, Modena,

Parma, Perugia, Pescara, Pesaro & Urbino,
Piacenza, Ravenna, Reggio nell'Emilia, Teramo,
Terni
ROME - Frosinone, Latina, Roma, Rieti, Viterbo
SOUTH - Avellino, Bari, Benevento, Brindisi,
Caserta, Catanzaro, Cosenza, Foggia, Lecce,
Matera, Napoli, Potenza, Reggio di Calabria,
Salerno, Taranto
SARDINIA - Cagliari, Nuoro, Oristano, Sassari
SICILY - Agrigento, Caltanissetta, Catania,
Enna, Messina, Palermo, Ragusa, Siracusa,
Trapani

● NETHERLANDS ●

NORTH - Ameland, Drenthe, Friesland,
Groningen
CENTRAL - Flevoland, Gelderland, Noord-
Holland, Overijssel, Utrecht
SOUTH - Limburg, Noord-Brabant, Zeeland,
Zuid-Holland

● PORTUGAL ●

SOUTH - Algarve, Baixo-Alentejo
NORTH - Costa Verde, Douro Litoral, Minho,
Tras os Montes, Alto Douro
CENTRAL - Alto Alentejo, Beira Alta, Beira
Baixo, Beira Litoral, Costa de Prata,
Estremadura, Ribatejo

● SPAIN ●

NORTH EAST COAST - Barcelona, Girona
CENTRAL - Albacete, Avila, Badajoz, Cáceres,
Ciudad Real, Cuenca, Guadalajara, Madrid,
Salamanca, Segovia, Soria, Teruel, Toledo
SOUTH EAST COAST - Alicante, Castellón,
Tarragona, Valencia
NORTH COAST - Asturias, Cantabria,
Guipúzcoa, La Coruña, Lugo, Vizcaya
NORTH EAST - Alava, Burgos, Huesca, Lleida,
La Rioja, Navarra, Zaragoza
NORTH WEST - Léon, Logrono Orense,
Palencia, Pontevedra, Valladolid, Zamora
SOUTH - Almeria, Cádiz, Cordoba, Granada,
Huelva, Jaén, Málaga, Murcia, Sevilla
ISLANDS - Ibiza, Mallorca Menorca

● SWITZERLAND ●

NORTH - Aargau, Basel, Solothurn
NORTH EAST - Appenzell, Liechtenstein, St
Gallen, Schaffhausen, Thurgau, Zürich
NORTH WEST/CENTRAL - Bern, Jura, Luzern,
Neuchâtel, Nidwalden, Obwalden, Schwyz, Uri,
Zug
EAST - Glarus, Graubünden
SOUTH - Ticino
SOUTH WEST - Fribourg, Genève, Valais, Vaud

AUSTRIA

Austria is a land of chalet villages and beautiful cities bordered by eight countries: the Czech Republic, Germany, Hungary, Italy, Liechtenstein, Switzerland, Slovak Republic and Slovenia.

The scenery is predominantly Alpine, an inspiring mix of mountains, lakes and pine forests. The splendour of the mountains is seen in the imposing Dachstein region of upper Austria and the massive Tyrolean peaks. The lakes of Burgenland and Salzkammergut, the river Danube, the forests and woods of Styria and the world-famous city of Wien (Vienna) are outstanding features of the landscape.

Most of the country enjoys a moderate climate during the summer, although eastern areas are sometimes very hot. The heaviest rainfall occurs in midsummer. The language of Austria is German, and English is not widely spoken.

Austria offers a variety of outdoor activities to suit everyone and there are numerous campsites throughout the country. Most are open from May to September, although a number remain open all year. *Off-site camping or caravanning* is generally prohibited. In areas with no campsites contact local police to find out whether an overnight stay is possible. If permission is granted, no camping activity must be seen from outside, eg chairs, awnings etc. Open fires are generally prohibited in woodland areas. Campers not on an official site, eg private property, staying in Austria for more than three days should report to the police as soon as possible, and also inform them of subsequent changes of location. Within Wien (Vienna) any form of off-site camping or caravanning is prohibited.

HOW TO GET THERE

Apart from the crossing via the Channel Tunnel, the usual Continental Channel ports for this journey are Calais, Dunkerque (Dunkirk) or Oostende (Ostend). From Calais drive through eastern France to Strasbourg, then via Karlsruhe and Stuttgart, crossing into Austria at Füsen for **Innsbruck and the Tirol**, and beyond München (Munich) for **Salzburg and central Austria**.

From the other ports mentioned above, drive through Belgium to Aachen, then via Köln (Cologne) Frankfurt, Nürnberg and München (Munich).

As an alternative, you could cross to Dieppe, Le Havre, Caen or Cherbourg and drive through northern France via **Strasbourg** and **Stuttgart**, or via **Basel** and northern Switzerland. But see 'Motorway tax' in this and the Swiss section. For details of the *AA European Routes Service* please consult the Contents Page.

Distance
From the Continental Channel ports, Salzburg is about 1140km (708 miles) and Vienna is about 1320km (820 miles), and you would normally need one overnight stop on the way.

Car sleeper trains
Services are available in summer from Brussels in Belgium to Salzburg and Villach.

MOTORING AND GENERAL INFORMATION
The information given here is specific to Austria. It **must** be read in conjunction with the European ABC at the front of the book, which covers those regulations which are common to many countries.

Air pollution alarm
In certain areas there are restrictions on the circulation of tourist vehicles when the level of air pollution exceeds certain limits. However, these restrictions do not apply to tourists using non-polluting vehicles, ie, those fitted with a catalytic converter system or low-pollution vehicles, ie all diesel-engine vehicles put on the road after 1 January 1990. Drivers of exempt vehicles must purchase a permit from the ÖAMTC and display a white test plaque on the windscreen in the event of a pollution alarm.

Boats*
Motorboats are not allowed on most of Austria's lakes. It is advisable to check with the Tourist Office before taking a boat into Austria (see *Tourist information* above for address).

British Embassy /Consulates*
The British Embassy is located at 1030 Wien, Jaurèsgasse 12 ☎ (0222) 716130; consular section, Jaurèsgasse 10 ☎ (0222) 71613 5151. There are British Consulates with Honorary Consuls in Bregenz, Graz, Innsbruck and Salzburg.

Children in cars
Child under 12 and/or 1.50 metres in height not permitted to travel as front or rear seat passenger unless using suitable restraint system.

Currency
There are no restrictions on the amount of foreign or Austrian currency that a *bona fide* tourist can take into or out of the country. The bank counter at the **Österreichischer Automobil,-Motorrad-und Touring Club** (ÖAMTC) head office is open during office hours (see *Motoring Club*); exchange offices at some main railway stations are open Saturdays, Sundays and public holidays.

Dimension and weight restrictions
Private **cars** and towed **trailers** or **caravans** are restricted to the following dimensions – height, 4 metres; width, 2.50 metres; length, 12 metres. The maximum permitted overall length of vehicle/trailer or caravan combination is 18 metres.

Trailers without brakes may weigh up to 750kg and may have a total weight of up to 50% of the towing vehicle.

Driving licence
A valid UK or Republic of Ireland licence is acceptable in Austria. However, those licences which do not incorporate a photograph will not be recognised unless accompanied by photographic proof of identity, e.g., a passport. The minimum age at which a visitor may use a temporarily imported motorcycle (exceeding 50cc) or car is 18 years.

First-aid kit*
In Austria all vehicles (including motorcycles) must be equipped with a first-aid kit by law and visitors are expected to comply. This item will not be checked at the frontier, but motorists can be stopped at the scene of an accident and their first-aid kit demanded; if this is not forthcoming the police may take action.

Foodstuffs*
Visitors may import tea, coffee and foodstuffs for their own personal use but raw meat (fresh or frozen) from hooved animals (*eg* beef, pork) and shell-fish (*eg* mussels, crab) cannot be imported.

Motoring club*
The **Österreichischer Automobil-, Motorrad-und Touring Club** (ÖAMTC) which has its

headquarters at 1010 Wien, Schubertring 1-3 ☎ (0222) 71199-0 has offices at the major frontier crossings, and is represented in most towns either direct or through provincial motoring clubs. The offices are usually open between 09.00 and 18.00hrs weekdays, 09.00 to 12.00hrs on Saturday and are closed on Sundays and public holidays.

Motorway Tax
From 1 January 1997 all vehicles using Austrian motorways must display a motorway tax sticker (vignette). Stickers may be purchased at the frontier and from ÖAMTC offices, post offices and petrol stations for periods of 10 days, 2 months or 1 year. The cost of a 10-day sticker (i.e. Friday to Sunday) for vehicles up to 3.5 tonnes in weight, with or without a trailer is öS70.

Roads
The motorist crossing into Austria from any frontier enters a network of well-engineered roads.

The main traffic artery runs from Bregenz in the west to Wien (Vienna) in the east, via the Arlberg Tunnel (Toll: see *Major Road and Rail Tunnels*), Innsbruck, Salzburg, and Linz. Most of the major alpine roads are excellent, and a comprehensive tour can be made through the Tirol, Salzkammergut and Carinthia without difficulty. Service stations are fairly frequent, even on mountain roads.

In July and August, several roads across the frontier become congested. The main points are on the Lindau-Bregenz road; at the Brenner Pass (possible alternative - the Résia (Reschen) Pass); at Kufstein; on the München (Munich)-Salzburg *Autobahn* and on the Villach-Tarvisio road. Additionally, because of increasing traffic from Germany, Klingenbach and Nickelsdorf on the Austro/Hungarian border are very busy. For details of mountain passes consult the Contents page.

Austria has some 1000 miles of motorway *(autobahn)* with addditional tolls payable on the Brenner, Karawanken Tunnel, Tauern, Pyhrn (Gleinalm and Bosruck Tunnels). Triangles marked on motorway posts indicate the nearest emergency telephone (every 2km). A flashing orange/yellow light at the top of telephone posts indicates danger ahead.

Speed limits*
Car
Built-up areas 50kph (31mph)
Other roads 100kph (62mph)
Motorways 130kph (80mph)
Car towing caravan not exceeding 750kg (1,650lb)†
Built-up areas 50kph (31mph)
Other roads 100kph (62mph)
Motorways 100kph (62mph)
Car towing caravan exceeding 750kg (1,650lb)†
Built-up areas 50kph (31mph)
Other roads 80kph (49mph)
Motorways 100kph (62mph)
†If the total weight of the two vehicles exceeds 3,500kg the following speed limits apply:
Built-up areas 50kph (31mph)
Other roads 70kph (43mph)
Motorways 80kph (49mph)
Notes
i. The total weight of a caravan/trailer equipped with overrun brakes must not exceed the weight of the towing vehicle.
ii. When the total weight of the two vehicles exceeds 3,500kg, it is not permissible to tow with a motor-car driving licence.

Warning triangle*
The use of a warning triangle is compulsory in the event of an accident or breakdown. The triangle must be placed 30 metres (33yds) behind the vehicle on ordinary roads and 100 metres (110yds) on motorways to warn following traffic of any obstruction; it must be visible at a distance of 50 metres (55yds).

*Additional information will be found in the Continental ABC at the front of the book.

A-Z DIRECTORY

Prices are in Austrian Schillings. Abbreviation: str strasse.
Each placename preceded by 'Bad' is listed under the name that follows it.

Tirol

Magnificent lofty peaks, crystal-clear mountain lakes, peaceful forests and tranquil valleys characterise this internationally-amous corner of Austria. The high mountain regions, reaching altitudes of over 10,000ft (4,000 metres), are accessible by mountain road passes and dozens of cable-cars and chair lifts, and for the climbing and walking enthusiast this is a wonderland of opportunity. The Tirol has a long architectural heritage; even the trim little provincial towns and villages have dignified burgher houses with impressive façades; there are mosaics on public buildings and private houses, and medieval castles and castle ruins command some of the finest settings in the Tirol. The cheerful hospitality of the region is renowned, and folk festivals, dancing and yodelling are colourful local traditions. Innsbruck, the capital of the region, still boasts its medieval old town, with handsome houses facing narrow, irregular streets. Highlights here include the Golden Roof (Goldenes Dachl), with its gilded copper tiles; the Cathedral (Dom), with its imposing west front and rich interior; and the fascinating and extensive displays in the Museum of Folk Art (Tiroler Volkskunstmuseum).

ASCHAU Tirol
Aufenfeld Distelberg ☎05282 2916
Level meadowland on forest slope.
Signposted.
4 Nov-2 Dec 4HEC ▦ ◖ ⋔ ቈ ✕ ⊙ ⬛ ∅ ᄆ ⊞ ⤳ ₹ PR ⊉ lau ➡ ⊞
Prices: A55-66 pitch 80-110

EHRWALD Tirol
International Dr-Ing E Lauth Zugspitzstr 34 ☎05673 2666
On undulating grassland, surrounded by high conifers, below the Wetterstein mountain range.
To the right of the access road to the Zugspitz funicular.
All year 1HEC ▦ ◖ ⋔ ቈ ✕ ⊙ ⬛ ∅ ᄆ ⊉ lau ➡ ⿔ ₹LP ⊞ Prices: A79.50-92.50 V10 ◪60-70 ▲60

Tiroler Zugspitzcamp Obermoos ☎05673 2254 & 2309
Several grassy terraces. Modern sanitary installations with bathrooms.
Near the Zugspitz funicular station.
All year 5HEC ▦ ◊ ◖ ⋔ ቈ ✕ ⊙ ⬛ ᄆ ₹ P ⊉ ⊞

FERNSTEINSEE Tirol
Schloss Fernsteinsee ☎05265 5210-157
A shady wooded meadowland site.
Approx. 3km from Nassereith towards the Fernpass. Signposted.
Mar-Oct 8HEC ▦ ➡ ◖ ቈ ✕ ⊙ ⬛ ∅ ₹ LR ⊉ ⊞ lau ➡ ⿔ ✕ ᄆ ₹P
Prices: A53 V33 ▲31

FIEBERBRUNN Tirol
Tirol-Camp ☎05354 6666
All year 4.7HEC ▦ ◖ ⋔ ቈ �️ ✕ ⊙ ⬛ ∅ ᄆ ₹ P ⊉ ⊞ ➡ ₹L

FÜGEN Tirol
Zillertal-Hell ☎05288 2203
In a meadow surrounding a farm.
1km N of Fügen on the B169.
All year 1.5HEC ▦ ◖ ⋔ ◖ ⊙ ⬛ ∅ ᄆ ⊉ ⊞ ⊞ ✎ ➡ ቈ ✕ ₹LPR

GRÄN Tirol
Tannheimer Tal ☎05675 6570
Dogs allowed summer only.
1km N of the village centre on the Pfronten-Tannheimer Tal road.
Closed 3 Nov-15 Dec 3HEC ▦ ⠇ ᄽ ◖ ⋔ ቈ ✕ ⊙ ⬛ ∅ ᄆ ⊞
◪ ⊉ ⊞ lau ➡ ₹LPR

HAIMING Tirol
Center Oberland Bundestr 9 ☎05266 88294
On a sloping meadow behind the BP garage.
Off B171 at Km485.
All year 4HEC ▦ ◖ ⋔ ቈ ✕ ⊙ ⬛ ∅ ᄆ ₹ P ⊉ ⊞ lau Prices: A55 V40 ◪40 ▲40

HÄSELGEHR Tirol
Rudi Luxnach 122 ☎05634 6425
Camping Card Compulsory.
By the church. Approach from B198.
All year 1HEC ▦ ◖ ⋔ ⊙ ⬛ ∅ ᄆ ₹ R ⊉ ⊞ lau ➡ ቈ ✕ ₹PR

HEITERWANG Tirol
Heiterwangersee ☎05674 5116
In a quiet situation in a meadow beside lake.
By Hotel Fischer am See.
All year 1HEC ▦ ◖ ➡ ⋔ ◖ ✕ ⊙ ⬛ ∅ ᄆ ₹ L ⊉ ⊞ lau ➡ ቈ Prices: A90 pitch 60

HOPFGARTEN Tirol
Reiterhof Penninberg 90 ☎05335 3512
Take B170 towards Kitzbühel and branch off in Kelschauer Tal.
All year 2HEC ▦ ◖ ⋔ ◖ ⊙ ⬛ ∅ ᄆ ₹ R ⊉ lau ➡ ቈ ✕

Schlossberg-Itter ☎05335 2181
In terraced meadowland below Schloss Itter on the Brixental Ache.
2km W on B170.
All year 4HEC ▦ ⠇ ᄽ ◖ ⋔ ቈ ✕ ⊙ ⬛ ∅ ᄆ ◪ ₹ PR ⊉ ⊞ lau
Prices: A68 pitch 45-90

HUBEN Tirol
Ötztaler Naturcamping ☎05253 5855
S of the town. Signposted from Km27 on B186.
All year ▦ ◖ ⋔ ◖ ⊙ ⬛ ᄆ ⊉ ⊞ lau ➡ ቈ ✕ ∅ ₹LP Prices: A57-59 V27 ◪51 ▲35-51

IMST Tirol
Imst-West Langgasse 62 ☎05412 66293
On open meadowland in the Langgasse area.
Off the bypass near the turn for the Pitztal.
All year 1HEC ▦ ◖ ⋔ ቈ ⊙ ⬛ ∅ ᄆ ⊉ lau ➡ ✕ ₹LPR ⊞ Prices: A55 pitch 70

INNSBRUCK Tirol
Innsbruck-Kranebitten Kranebitter Allee 214 ☎0512 284180
Signposted from A12/E60 (Innsbruck-Arlberg).
Apr-Oct 2.2HEC ▦ ᄽ ◖ ⋔ ቈ ✕ ⊙ ⬛ ∅ ᄆ ◪ ▲ ⊉ ⊞ lau ➡ ₹R Prices: A66 ◪40 ▲40

KITZBÜHEL Tirol
Schwarzsee Reitherstr 24 ☎05356 2806
In meadowland on the edge of a wood behind a large restaurant.
2km from town on B170 towards Wörgl turn right, 400m after Schwarzsee railway station.
All year 6.5HEC ▦ ➡ ◖ ⋔ ቈ ✕ ⊙ ⬛ ∅ ᄆ ₹ L ⊉ ⊞ lau Prices: A85-88 pitch 92

KÖSSEN Tirol
Wilder Kaiser Kranebittau 18 ☎05375 6444
Situated in a lovely position below Unterberg, this level site is adjoined on three sides by woodland.For access follow road to

Unterberg Lift, then turn right and continue for 200m.
All year 5HEC ▥ ⏚ ⋔ ⚡ ✕ ⊙ ⊘ ⚓ Å �ᕔ P ☎ ⊞ lau

KRAMSACH *Tirol*

Ferien Comfort Seeblick Toni Brantlhof ☎05337 63544
Rural site near the Brantlhof above Lake Reintaler.
Camping Card Compulsory.
From Inntal Motorway (Rattenberg/Kramsach exit) follow signs 'Zu den Seen' for about 3km, then drive through Seehof site.
All year 3HEC ▥ ⏚ ⋔ ⚡ ✕ ⊙ ⊘ ⚓ ᕔ L ☎ ⊞ lau

Stadlerhof ☎05337 63371
A pleasant, year-round site on the Reintaler See.
Access via A12.
All year 3HEC ▥ ⏚ ⋔ ⚡ ✕ ⊙ ⊘ ⚓ ☎ ⚑ ᕔ LP ☎ ⊞ lau Prices:
A56-79 pitch 69-104

KUFSTEIN *Tirol*

Hager Langkampfen 326 ☎05372 64170
Site situated on level meadowland.
All year 0.8HEC ▥ ⏚ ⋔ ⚡ ✕ ⊙ ⊘ ⚓ ☎ ⊞ lau ➡ ᕔLPR Prices:
pitch 160 (incl 2 persons)

Kufstein Salurnerstr 36 ☎05372 65066
Site has sporting facilities.
1km W of Kufstein between River Inn and B171.
May-Oct 1.5HEC ▥ ⏚ ⋔ ⚡ ✕ ⊙ ⊘ ⚓ ☎ ⊞ lau ➡ ᕔLPR Prices:
A48 V32 ⊞34 ▲31

LANDECK *Tirol*

See also ZAMS

Riffler ☎05442 624774
Site on meadowland between residential housing and banks of Sanna.
Closed May 0.3HEC ⏚ ⋔ ⚡ ✕ ⊙ ⚓ ᕔ R ☎ ⊞ lau ➡ ⊘ Prices:
A50 V25 ⊞80-100 ▲55-90

Sport Camp Tirol Mühlkanal 1 ☎05442 64636
Meadowland site with many fruit trees.
On B316.
All year 1HEC ▥ ⏚ ⋔ ⚡ ✕ ⊙ ⊘ ⚓ ᕔ R ☎ ⊞ lau ➡ ⚓ ᕔP
Prices: A55 V35 ⊞90-105 ▲37-90

LÄNGENFELD *Tirol*

Ötztal ☎05253 5348
In meadowland with some tall trees on the edge of woodland.
Turn right off E186 at fire station.
All year 3HEC ▥ ⏚ ⋔ ⚡ ✕ ⊙ ⊘ ⚓ ☎ ⚑ ☎ ⊞ lau ➡ ᕔP Prices:
A59-61 V28 ⊞51-52 ▲30-51

LERMOOS *Tirol*

Happy Camp Hofherr Garmischer Str 21 ☎05673 2980
15 Dec-Apr & Jun-Oct 0.7HEC ▥ ⏚ ⋔ ✕ ⊙ ⊘ ☎ ➡ ⚓ ⚓ ᕔP ⊞
Prices: A64.50-76.50 pitch 80-96

LEUTASCH *Tirol*

Holiday ☎05214 6570
A modern site on level grassland screened by trees on the Leutascher Ache.
Turn off B313 (Mittenwald-Scharnitz) towards Leutasch.
5 May-30 Oct & 10 Dec-10 Apr 2.8HEC ▥ ⏚ ⋔ ⚡ ✕ ⊙ ⊘ ⚓
⚓ ᕔ PR ☎ ⊞ lau Prices: pitch 240-310 (incl 2 persons)

LIENZ *Tirol*

Falken Eichholz 7 ☎04852 64022
Closed 21 Nov-15 Dec 1.5HEC ▥ ⋔ ⏚ ⋔ ⚡ ✕ ⊙ ⊘ ⚓ ☎ lau ➡ ⊞
Prices: A45-60 pitch 65-80

MAURACH *Tirol*

Karwendel ☎05243 6116
In town turn off the B181 and follow the Pertisau road.
All year 1HEC ▥ ⏚ ⋔ ✕ ⊙ ⊘ ⚓ ☎ ⊞ lau ➡ ⚓ ᕔLP Prices:
A50-60 V30 ⊞60 ▲40-50

MAYRHOFEN *Tirol*

Laubichl ☎05285 2580
On a gently sloping meadow near a farm at N entrance to village.
All year 2HEC ▥ ⋔ ⏚ ⋔ ✕ ⊙ ⊘ ⚓ ☎ ⊞ lau ➡ ᕔP

NASSEREITH *Tirol*

Rossbach ☎05265
All year 1HEC ▥ ➡ ⏚ ⋔ ✕ ⊙ ⊘ ⚓ ⚓ ᕔ P ☎ ⊞ Prices: A45-50 V30-34 ⊞30-34 ▲30-34

NATTERS *Tirol*

Natterer See Natterer see 1 ☎0512 546732
A terraced site beautifully situated amidst woodland and mountains on the shore of Nattersee.
Approach via Brenner Motorway, exit 'Innsbruck Süd', via Natters, onto B182 and follow signs.
Closed Oct-15 Dec 7HEC ⏚ ⋔ ⚡ ✕ ⊙ ⊘ ⚓ ☎ ⚑ ⚓ Å ᕔ L ☎
P ⊞ lau Prices: A72-93 pitch 88-125

NAUDERS *Tirol*

Alpencamping Nauders ☎05473 266
Closed Nov-16 Dec ▥ ⏚ ⋔ ✕ ⊙ ⊘ ⊘ ☎ lau

NEUSTIFT *Tirol*

Hochstubai ☎05226 3484
On slightly sloping meadowland.
Near the Geier Alm approximately 5km S of town on the road towards the Gletscher bahn.
All year 2.7HEC ▥ ⏚ ⋔ ✕ ⊙ ⊘ ⚓ ⚓ ᕔ R ☎ ⊞ lau ➡ ᕔLP Prices:
A62 V20 ⊞30 ▲30

PFUNDS *Tirol*

Sonnen ☎05474 5232
Site in meadowland with some fruit trees.
On road B315 between SHELL Garage and Gasthof Sonne.
All year 1HEC ▥ ⏚ ⋔ ⚡ ✕ ⊙ ⊘ ⚓ ☎ ⊞ ➡ ᕔLP Prices: A40 V25
⊞30-50 ▲25-45

PILL *Tirol*

Plankenhof ☎05242 64195
Site in meadow.
On B171 near Gasthof Plankenhof.
May-Sep 0.6HEC ▥ ⏚ ⋔ ⊙ ⚓ ᕔ P ⊞ lau ➡ ⏚ ✕ ⊘ Prices: A40
pitch 90

PRUTZ *Tirol*

Prutz ☎05472 6825
All year 2.5HEC ▥ ⏚ ⋔ ⚡ ✕ ⊙ ⊘ ⚓ ᕔ R ☎ ⊞ lau ➡ ᕔLP Prices:
A80-88 pitch 95-115

REUTTE *Tirol*

Reutte Ehrenbergstr 53 ☎05672 2809
Well kept site on a meadow on the edge of a forest near the sports centre. Modern swimming pool in town.
Turn right towards Waldrast.
Closed May 2.2HEC ⋔ ⏚ ⋔ ⚡ ✕ ⊙ ⊘ ⚓ ᕔ P ☎ ⊞ lau Prices:
A64 pitch 73

Seespitze ☎05672 78121
May-15 Oct 2HEC ▥ ⏚ ⋔ ⚡ ✕ ⊙ ⊘ ⚓ ᕔ L ☎ ⊞ lau ➡ ✕ Prices:
A45 V20 ⊞50-55 ▲30-50

Sennalpe ☎05672 78115
In a quiet situation next to the lake.
On Reutte-Oberammergau road 200m from the Hotel Forelle.
Closed 16 Oct-14 Dec 3HEC ▥ ⏚ ⋔ ⊙ ⊘ ⚓ ᕔ L ☎ ⊞ lau ➡ ⚡
✕ Prices: A45 V20 ⊞50-55 ▲30-50

RIED BEI LANDECK *Tirol*

Dreiländereck ☎05472 6571
Level site in centre of village.
All year 1HEC ▥ ⏚ ⋔ ⚡ ✕ ⊙ ⊘ ⚓ ☎ ⚑ ☎ ⊞ lau ➡ ✕ ᕔLPR
Prices: A50-55 V31.50-35 ⊞50-55 ▲30-55

RINN *Tirol*

Judenstein ☎05223 8620
Apr-15 Oct 0.6HEC ▥ ⏚ ⋔ ⊙ ⊘ ⚓ ☎ ⊞ lau ➡ ⏚ ⚡ ✕ Prices: A40
V25 ⊞40 ▲30-40

ST JOHANN *Tirol*
Michelnhof Weiberndorf 6 ☎05352 62584
1.5km S via B161 (St-Johann-Kitzbühel).
All year 1.8HEC ▥ ⊖ ⋒ ☚ ✕ ⊙ ◘ ∅ 菜 ☲ ⊞ lau ♦ ♟ ⭐R

SCHARNITZ *Tirol*
Alm
On level, open grassland. Near B177.
Access from S outskirts.
Nov-15 Dec & 15 Apr-30 Apr 0.7HEC ▥ ⊖ ⋒ ✕ ⊙ ◘ ∅ 菜 ◘ ☲
lau ♦ ☚ ✕ ⭐R ⊞ Prices: A52-57 pitch 40-50

SCHWAZ *Tirol*
At **WEER**(6km W)
Alpencamping Mark Maholmhof ☎05224 68146
Situated on meadowland by a farm on the edge of a forest.
Off B171.
Apr-30 Oct 2HEC ▥ ♦ ⋒ ☚ ♟ ✕ ⊙ ◘ ∅ ◘ ▲ ⭐ P ☲ ⊞ lau Prices:
A60 pitch 65

SÖLDEN *Tirol*
Sölden ☎05254 2672
Situated on meadowland on left bank of Ötztaler tributary. Beautiful
views of the surrounding mountains.
By Grauer Bär Inn at Km36 on the B186.
Closed May-15 Jun 1.2HEC ▥ ⇘✔ ⋒ ⊖ ◘ ∅ 菜 ☲ ⊞ lau ♦ ☚ ♟ ✕
⭐P Prices: A80-110 pitch 100-145

STAMS *Tirol*
Eichenwald Schiessstand weg 10 ☎05263 6159
Well managed terraced site in oak wood.
Turn off B171 at ESSO filling station in direction of abbey, onto a
steep, narrow access road.
May-Sep 2HEC ▥ ⊖ ⋒ ☚ ✕ ⊙ ◘ ∅ 菜 ◘ ◘ ▲ ⭐ P ☲ ⊞ lau ♦
⭐R Prices: pitch 72 (incl 2 persons)

Schlosscamping VOLDERS
near Innsbruck

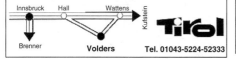

Near motorway (WATTENS exit 2km and
SOLBAD HALL exit 5km). Favourable holiday
and touring site (Innsbruck 15km). Hot
showers free of charge, mini golf – alpine bath
Wattens 2km. Own heated swimming pool and
paddling pool. Apartments in the castle.

Innsbruck Hall Wattens
Kufstein
Brenner **Volders** **Tel. 01043-5224-52333**

THIERSEE *Tirol*
Rueppenhof Seebauern 8 ☎05376 5694
Site made up of several meadows surrounding a farm that lies on the
banks of a lake.
Apr-Oct 1HEC ▥ ⊖ ⋒ ☚ ∅ ⊙ ◘ ⭐ L ☲ ⊞ ♦ ♟ ✕ ∅ 菜 Prices: A50
V20 ◘35 ▲10-30

UMHAUSEN *Tirol*
Ötztal Arena Camp Krismer ☎05255 5390
Signposted from B186.
All year 1HEC ▥ ⊖ ⋒ ⊙ ◘ ∅ ∅ ⭐ R ☲ ⊞ lau ♦ ☚ ♟ ✕ Prices: A65
pitch 50

UNTERPERFUSS *Tirol*
Farm ☎05232 2209
Modern site on gently sloping meadow.
W end of village near Amberg railway and main road.
All year 2.5HEC ▥ ⊖ ⋒ ☚ ✕ ⊙ ◘ ∅ 菜 ⭐ P ☲ ♦ ☚

VOLDERS *Tirol*
Schloss ☎05224 52333
A pleasant site in the grounds of a castle surrounded by thick
woods.
Camping Card Compulsory.
Access from the B171 by ARAL filling station or from motorway exit
Schwaz or Wattens.
15 May-15 Oct 2.5HEC ⋒ ☚ ♟ ✕ ⊙ ◘ ∅ ▲ ⭐ P ☲ ⊞ lau

VÖLS *Tirol*
Völs ☎0512 303533
May-Sep 0.4HEC ▥ ⊖ ⋒ ☚ ♟ ✕ ⊙ ◘ ☲ ⊞ lau ♦ ⭐PR

WAIDRING *Tirol*
Steinplatte Unterwasser 43 ☎05353 5345
All year 4HEC ▥ ⊖ ⋒ ☚ ♟ ✕ ⊙ ◘ ∅ ◘ ⭐ L ☲ ⊞ ♦ ⭐P Prices:
A60 pitch 55-80

WALCHSEE *Tirol*
Seespitz Wassersportzentrum ☎05374 5359
Site made up of several plots of land.
Between B172 and bank of lake.
All year 2HEC ▥ ⇘✔ ⋒ ☚ ✕ ⊙ ◘ ∅ ⭐ L ☲ ⊞ ♦ ♟
Terrassencamping Süd-See Seestr 78 ☎05374 5339
Extensively terraced site, the lowest are reserved for tourers.
500m W on B172 turn into 'no through road' and continue for
1500m.
All year 10HEC ▥ ♦ ⊖ ⋒ ☚ ♟ ✕ ⊙ ◘ ∅ 菜 ⭐ L ☲ ⊞ lau Prices:
A60-65 pitch 70-80

WESTENDORF *Tirol*
Panorama Mühltal 26 ☎05334 6166
W towards Wörgl via B170.
All year 2.2HEC ▥ ⊖ ⋒ ☚ ♟ ✕ ⊙ ◘ ∅ 菜 ◘ ◘ ☲ ⊞ lau ♦ ⭐P
Prices: A59-85 V42-66 ◘42-66 ▲42

ZAMS *Tirol*
See also LANDECK
Zams Magdalenaweg 1 ☎05442 63289
2km NE of Landeck. Access via A12 and B171.
Jun-25 Sep 0.2HEC ▥ ⊖ ⋒ ⊙ ◘ ◘ ⊞ ♦ ☚ ✕ ∅ 菜 ⭐LPR Prices:
A42 V18 ◘48 ▲48

ZELL AM ZILLER *Tirol*
Hofer Gerlossasstr 33 ☎05282 2248
On meadowland with some fruit trees.
Site lies to the end of Zillertal off the road leading to the Gerlos
Pass.
All year 2HEC ▥ ⊖ ⋒ ☚ ✕ ⊙ ◘ ∅ 菜 ☲ ⊞ lau ♦ ⭐PR Prices:
A50-55 pitch 60

ZIRL *Tirol*
Alpenfrieden Eigenhofen 11 ☎05238 3520
Near the B171.
May-Sep 1HEC ▥ ⊖ ⋒ ✕ ⊙ ◘ ∅ ⭐ P ☲ ⊞ ♦ ☚ ♟ ✕ 菜 ⭐R Prices:
A45 pitch 80

Carinthia

High mountains on all sides tumble down to this sunny, southern, gentle land of soft light and over a thousand warm, clear lakes. The climate is kind to holiday-makers - most of the weather troughs are broken up by the surrounding mountains, so this province gets many more sunny days than the rest of the country. The lakes provide a wealth of water sports in the summer, frequently reaching temperatures of over 75 degrees F (24 degrees C) - ideal for swimmers, wind-surfers and sailors. Anglers can fish for pike, whitefish and carp, and hot springs in the region have been channelled into waterpark complexes with chutes and whirling currents, or health spas offering the 'gift of youth'. But the mild summers are complemented by sharp winters, making Nassfeld and the Nock district popular areas for winter sports.
There is a relaxed Mediterranean atmosphere in this region, and a substantial Slovene minority, dating back to the 6th century, adds its own distinct character and language to southern parts. The capital of Carinthia is Klagenfurt which, according to legend, was built on a swamp once dominated by a dragon. The centre of the town now is the Dragon Fountain (Lindwurmbrunnen), with its huge grim 16th-century sculpture of the town's heraldic emblem. Now an important junction and commercial centre, Klagenfurt's old quarter has many handsome baroque buildings set in attractive lanes and passageways.

ANNENHEIM Kärnten
Bad Ossiacher See ☎04248 2757
An extensive level site with adjoining meadow.
Situated on B94 Villach-Wien road.
15 May-15 Sep 5.4HEC ▥ ❑♠♣❑✗⊙❑∅↝L❑⊞✿ lau

DELLACH Kärnten
Neubauer ☎04766 2530
Access from B100, Leinz-Spittal road. The turn-off is well signposted in the village.
15 Apr-15 Oct 1.5HEC ▥ ❑♠♣❑✗⊙❑↝L❑ lau ♣∅

DELLACH IM DRAUTAL Kärnten
Waldbad ☎04714 288 & 234
Leave A10 at Spittal & turn onto B100.
May-Sep 2HEC ▥ ❑♠❑✗⊙❑∅↝P❑⊞ lau ♣♣↝R

DÖBRIACH Kärnten
Brunner am See Glanzerstr 108 ☎04246 7189
Tidily arranged with poplar trees. Private bathing area.
The access road is at the E end of Lake Millstatt.
All year 2.5HEC ▥ ⠿ ❑♠♣❑✗⊙❑∅⌸❑❑↝L❑⊞ lau
Prices: A65-95 pitch 85-140 (incl 2 persons)

Burgstaller Seefeldstr 16 ☎04246 7774
A quiet site situated 100m from the lake, with good modern facilities.At SE end of lake. From B98 continue towards Lake Millstatt for 1km.
All year 7.5HEC ▥ ❑♠❑♣❑✗⊙❑∅⌸❑❑↝LP❑⊞ lau Prices: A65-95 pitch 50-120

Ebner's Seefeldstr 1 ☎04246 7735
On either side of the Seefeldstr, beyond Camping Burgstaller, at E end of Lake Millstatt.
1HEC ▥ ❑♠♣❑✗⊙❑∅⌸❑↝P❑⊞ lau ♣↝L

Winkler Strandweg 26 ☎04246 7187
On level ground, divided into sections.
Approx. 200m E of the lake.
15 Apr-15 Oct 2HEC ▥ ❑♠❑♣❑✗⊙❑∅⌸❑❑↝LP❑⊞ lau ♣↝LPR

DÖLLACH Kärnten
Zirknitzer ☎04825 451
Beside the River Möu.
Between Km8 and Km9 on the Glocknerstr (B107).

A naturist campsite holiday = a holiday of natural freedom with real relaxation and an all-over suntan. At the RUTAR LIDO, a naturist holiday centre with apartment hotel, holiday apartments and FKK camping (with indoor pool) it is easy to sample and experience a naturist holiday.

Take the liberty – to spend holiday in RUTAR LIDO

For further information and brochure including extract from walking map:

RUTAR LIDO
A-9141 Eberndorf/Carinthia
Tel: 0043/4236/2262-0, Fax: /2220

All year 0.6HEC ▥ ❑♠♣❑✗⊙❑↝R❑⊞ lau ♣♣∅↝P Prices: A39-50 V20-28 ❑24-28 ▲14-28

DROBOLLACH Kärnten
Mittewald Fuchsbichlweg 9 ☎04242 27392
In a hollow on slightly rising ground surrounded by trees and divided into pitches. Large children's playground.
Off Villach-Faaker See road. Signposted 'Serai'.
All year 2.5HEC ▥ ❑♠♣❑✗⊙❑❑↝P❑ lau ♣♣ Prices: A51 V25 ❑45 ▲45

EBERNDORF Kärnten
Rutar Lido ☎04236 22620
Shop open April to September only.
All year 15HEC ▥ ❑♠♣❑✗⊙❑∅❑❑↝LP❑⊞ lau ♣♣
Prices: A55-80 pitch 50-140

FELDKIRCHEN Kärnten
Maltschach Briefelsdorf 7 ☎04277 2644
Near the lake, next to Sotour Holiday Village.
On B95 take exit 'Radweg', then follow signposts.
May-Sep 7HEC ▥ ❑♠♣❑❑⊞❑ lau ♣♣♣✗∅↝LP

GNESAU Kärnten
Hobitsch Sonnleiten 24 ☎04278 368
From B95, drive N towards Sonnleiten.
31 May-Sep 0.6HEC ▥ ❑♠✗⊙❑↝P❑⊞ lau ♣♣✗∅

HEILIGENBLUT Kärnten
Grossglockner Hadergasse 11 ☎04824 2048
Signposted.
May-Sep & 10 Dec-20 Apr 2.5HEC ▥ ♣↝♠♣✗⊙❑∅↝♣↝R ❑ lau ♣↝P⊞ Prices: A60-70 V30 ❑30

HERMAGOR Kärnten
Flaschberger ☎(04282) 2020
Camping Card Compulsory
2km E via B111.
All year 2HEC ▥ ❑♠✗⊙❑∅⌸❑↝LP❑⊞ lau ♣♣♣✗

Schluga ☎04282 2051
6km E.
All year 5HEC ▥ ❑♠♣❑♣✗⊙❑∅⌸❑❑▲↝P❑⊞ Prices: A41-81 pitch 47-93

Schluga Seecamping ☎04282 2051
Approx. 300m N of lake in meadowland with some terraces and fine views.
6km E of Hermagor.
20 May-20 Sep 7HEC ▥ ❑♠♣❑♣✗⊙❑∅⌸❑▲❑⊞♣↝L
Prices: A56-81 pitch 56-93

KEUTSCHACH Kärnten
Reautschnighof Reautz 4 ☎0463 281106
May-Sep 0.5HEC ▥ ❑♠⊙❑↝L❑♣✗

Strandcamping Süd ☎04273 2773
South side of the Keutschachersee.

May-Sep 2HEC ▦ ⌕ ⋔ ✕ ⊙ ◙ ⇡ L ☎ ⊞ lau ➡ ⅏ ⌀ Prices: A50-60 V20-25 ⊕60-65

KLAGENFURT Kärnten
Strandbad Metnitzstrand 4 ☎0463 21169
Large site divided into sections by trees and bushes.
From town centre take B83 towards Velden. Turn left just outside town in direction of bathing area.
May-Sep 4HEC ▦ ➡ ⌕ ⅀ ✕ ⊙ ◙ ⬛ ⊞ ⇡ L ☎ ⊞ lau ➡ ✕ ⌀
Prices: A50-80 pitch 100

KÖTSCHACH-MAUTHEN Kärnten
Alpen ☎04715 429
In meadowland beside River Gail.Turn off B110 in the S part of the village on the road to the Plöcken Pass and drive 800m towards Lesachtal.
May-15 Oct 1.4HEC ▦ ➡ ⌕ ⅀ ⅋ ✕ ⊙ ◙ ⌀ ⬛ ⬛ ⇡ PR ☎ ⊞ lau ➡ ✕
Prices: A40-62 pitch 70-97

MALTA Kärnten
Maltatal ☎04733 234
On a gently rising alpine meadow.
In Gmünd turn off B99 and drive 5.5km through Malta valley.
Apr-Oct 3.5HEC ▦ ➡ ⌕ ⅀ ⅋ ✕ ⊙ ◙ ⌀ ◙ ⬛ ⇡ P ☎ ⊞ lau ➡ ⇡R
Prices: A65-85 pitch 60-130

MÖLLBRÜCKE Kärnten
Rheingold Mölltalstr 65 ☎04769 2338
Site on main road from Spittal to Mallnitz, next to swimming pool.
All year 1.5HEC ▦ ⌕ ⌕ ⅋ ✕ ⊙ ◙ ⇡ PR ☎ ➡ ⅏ Prices: A60 V15 ⊕15 ▲15

OBERVELLACH Kärnten
Sport Erlebnis ☎04782 2727
May-Sep ▦ ⌕ ⌕ ⅋ ✕ ◙ ▲ ⇡ R lau ➡ ⌀ ⇡L ⊞ Prices: pp60

OSSIACH Kärnten
Ossiach ☎04243 436
Divided into pitches with generally well-situated terraces.
Off B94 on E bank of Kale Ossiacher.
May-1 Oct 8.5HEC ▦ ➡ ⌕ ⅀ ⅋ ✕ ⊙ ◙ ⌀ ⅄ ⬛ ◙ ▲ ⇡ L ☎ ⊞ ⊘ lau

Parth Ostriach 10 ☎04243 2744
On hilly ground on S shore of the lake. Steep, but there are some terraces.
Off B94 on S bank of Lake Ossiach.
May-Sep 1.8HEC ▦ ⌕ ⌕ ⅀ ⅋ ✕ ⊙ ◙ ⌀ ⅄ ◙ ⇡ L ☎ ⊞ ⊘ lau

At HEILIGEN GESTADE(5km SW)
Seecamping Berghof Ossiachersee-Süduferstr 241
☎04242 41133
Terraced meadowland in attractive setting. 800m long promenade with bathing areas. Dogs not allowed Jul-Aug
E shore of Lake Ossiacher.
20 Apr-15 Oct 10HEC ▦ ⋮⋮⋮ ⌕ ⌕ ⅀ ⅋ ✕ ⊙ ◙ ⌀ ⅄ ⬛ ⇡ L ☎
Prices: A58-90 pitch 90-160

SCHIEFLING Kärnten
Weisses Rössl Auen bei Velden am Wörthersee ☎04274 28984
May-Sep 2.5HEC ▦ ⌕ ⌕ ⅀ ✕ ⊙ ◙ ⌀ ⅄ ⬛ ⬛ ⇡ L ☎ ⊞ lau Prices: A70-80 V20 ⊕30-40 ▲30-40

SEEBODEN Kärnten
Ferienpark Lieseregg Lieseregg ☎04762 2723
On large level meadows; some terraces and asphalt drives.
B99 from Spittal north to B98, then left for 1.5km.
May-Oct 4HEC ▦ ⌕ ⌕ ⅀ ✕ ⊙ ◙ ⌀ ⅄ ⬛ ◙ ▲ ⇡ P ☎ ⊞ lau Prices: A70-90 pitch 90

Seecamping Penker ☎04762 81267
Site situated on meadowland and divided into fields on both sides of the lakeside promenade. There are some rows of poplars and the lower part of the site is terraced.
For access turn off opposite ADEG store and continue for 300m.
May-Oct 1.2HEC ▦ ⇘ ⌕ ⅀ ⅋ ✕ ⊙ ◙ ⌀ ⇡ LP ☎ ⊞

SPITTAL AN DER DRAU Kärnten
Draufluss ☎04762 2466
A long, narrow riverside site, partly surrounded by a hedge.
From town centre follow road to river towards Goldeckbahn.
Apr-Oct 0.8HEC ▦ ⌕ ⌕ ⊙ ◙ ◙ ⇡ PR ◙ ⊞ lau ➡ ⅏ ⌀ Prices: A60 V30-40 ⊕30-40 ▲30-40

STOCKENBOI Kärnten
Ronacher ☎04761 256
Situated on meadow between forest slopes, gently sloping to the shore of Lake Weissensee.
Approach for caravans via Weissensee.
May-Sep 1.8HEC ▦ ⌕ ⌕ ⅀ ✕ ⊙ ◙ ⌀ ⅄ ⇡ L ☎ ⊞ lau

TECHENDORF Kärnten
Strandcamping Knaller ☎04713 2234
From B87, drive towards Weissensee.
May-Oct 1.5HEC ▦ ⌕ ⌕ ⅀ ✕ ⊙ ◙ ⌀ ⇡ L ☎ ⊞ ➡ ⅋ ✕ Prices: A70-90 V45 ⊕25-35 ▲5-20

UNTERNARRACH Kärnten
Strandcamping Turner See St Primus ☎04239 2350
27 Apr-5 Oct 6.8HEC ▦ ➡ ⌕ ⅀ ⅋ ✕ ⊙ ◙ ⌀ ⅄ ⬛ ◙ ⇡ L ☎ ➡ ⊞
Prices: A48-79 pitch 70-115

VILLACH Kärnten
Gerli St Georgenerstr 140 ☎04242 57402
Level, quiet, isolated site, with heated swimming pool annexed to it which is open to the public.
From Spittal/Drau turn off B100, turn right just before Villach and continue for 2km.
All year 2.2HEC ▦ ⌕ ⌕ ⅀ ✕ ⊙ ◙ ⌀ ⅄ ⬛ ◙ ⇡ P ☎ ⊞ lau ➡ ⅋ ⇡R
Prices: A45-55 pitch 45-55

At FAAK AM SEE(10km SE)
Komfortcamping Poglitsch ☎04254 2718
Mar-Oct 7HEC ▦ ⌕ ⌕ ⅀ ⅋ ✕ ⊙ ◙ ⌀ ⅄ ⇡ L ☎ ⊞ lau Prices: A65-85 pitch 80-110

Strandcamping Arneitz ☎04254 2137
24 Apr-1 Oct 6HEC ▦ ⋮⋮⋮ ⌕ ⌕ ⅀ ⅋ ✕ ⊙ ◙ ⌀ ⅄ ◙ ⇡ L ☎ ⊞ lau
Prices: A88-91 pitch 120-150

Strandcamping Florian Badweg 3 ☎04254 2261
A partially shaded site between the lakeside and the road.
Access from road by Hotel Fürst.
May-25 Sep 3.5HEC ▦ ⌕ ⌕ ⅀ ✕ ⊙ ◙ ⌀ ⬛ ◙ ⇡ L ☎ ⊞ lau ➡ ⅏ ⅄
Prices: A60-80 V30 ⊕50-60

Strandcamping Gruber ☎04254 2298
May-Sep 3.5HEC ▦ ⋮⋮⋮ ⌕ ⌕ ⅀ ✕ ⊙ ◙ ⇡ L ☎ ⊞ lau ➡ ⌀ ⅄

WERTSCHACH Kärnten
Alpenfreude ☎04256 2708
May-Sep 5HEC ▦ ⌕ ⌕ ⅀ ✕ ⊙ ◙ ⌀ ⅄ ⬛ ◙ ⇡ P ☎ ⊞ lau Prices: A55 pitch 75

Styria

Styria is a mosaic; soft hills in the southern wine-growing area, wide forest areas which have given the province the name of the 'green march', and the grand rocky massifs of the upper Styria. Between the high Alps, crossed by dramatic mountain passes, nd the lowland regions, is a spectrum of beautiful scenery, with pleasant summer resorts as well as winter sports areas. The region is rich in beautiful gorges and waterfalls, the largest and the best known of which is the Gesause, where the River Enns has carved its way through the mountains. Caves are a feature of Styria - the large Lurgrotten at Peggau is well equipped for visitors - and some caves have revealed evidence of prehistoric occupation. Austria's second largest city and Styria's capital, the lively city of Graz is in the south-east corner of the province. A major industrial and university town, Graz boasts many interesting historic buildings, and above the attractive old town, a funicular leads to the 1,552ft (473 metres) Schlossberg which is dominated by the town's distinctive landmark, the 92ft (28 metre) clock tower (Uhrturm).

AIGEN Steiermark

Hohenberg ☎03682 8130
Lakeside site on terraced hillside with some fruit trees.
Turn right in Wiler Ketten after the Military Airfield and right again after the ARAL petrol station and follow narrow road to site.
Apr-Oct 1.5HEC ▦ � ౬⊙♀∅▦ ⚏ ⚓ L ⚐⊞ lau ♦ ♀ ✕

AUSSEE, BAD Steiermark

Traun Grundlseer Str 21 ☎03622 54565
In pleasant wooded surroundings.
2.5km from Bad Aussee towards Grundlsee.
All year 0.4HEC ▦ ⚀⚏✕⊙♀♀ ⚓ PR ⚐♦ ᝒ∅⚏⚓L⊞
Prices: A55 pitch 40

GRAZ Steiermark

S C Central Martinhofstr 3 ☎0316 281831
A site with many lawns separated by asphalt paths and partly divided into pitches.
Turn off the B70 in Strassgang S of Graz and continue for 300m.
Mar-Nov 2.5HEC ▦ ♦⚀౬♀✕♀∅⚏▲⚓ P ⚐⊞ lau Prices: pitch 180-220

At MANTSCHA

Tenniscamping Reiderhof ☎0316 284380
A peaceful, terraced site surrounded by woodlands.
From Graz take Reininghausstr and Steinbergstr towards Mantscha signposted from railway station.
All year 5HEC ▦ ⚀⚏౬♀✕⊙♀⚐lau ♦ ⚓PR

HARTBERG Steiermark

Hartberg Gartengasse 6 ☎03332 62250
In quiet situation surrounded by trees and hedges in meadowland next to an open-air pool.
Turn off B54 towards swimming pool and continue 300m.
Apr-Sep 1HEC ▦ ⚀⚀⊙♀⚐lau ♦ ౬♀✕ ⚓P

HIRSCHEGG Steiermark

Hirschegg ☎03141 2201
All year 2HEC ▦ ⚀⚀౬♀✕⊙♀∅⚏▦⚓ PR⚐lau ♦ ⚓L

KATSCH Steiermark

Katschtal Peterdorf 24 ☎03536 310
May-Sep 4HEC ▦ ౹⚘⚀౬♀✕⊙♀⚏⚓P ⚐⊞lau

LANGENWANG-MÜRTZAL Steiermark

Europa Siglstr 5 ☎03854 2950
On level meadow with some trees, surrounded by hedges.
The B306 (E7) by-passes the town, so be careful not to miss the exit 6km S of Mürzzuschlag.
All year 0.6HEC ▦ ⚀⚀⊙♀∅⚏⚐⊞lau ♦ ౬♀✕ Prices: A40 V35 ⚘35-52 ▲35

LEIBNITZ Steiermark

Leibnitz R-H-Bartsch-Gasse 33 ☎03452 82463
W of town. Signposted.
May-Sep 0.7HEC ▦ ♦⚀✕⊙♀⚓ PR⚐⊞♦౬♀∅⚏

LIEBOCH Steiermark

Graz-Lieboch ☎03136 61797
Access via A2, exit Lieboch.
May-Oct 0.3HEC ▦ ⚀⚀⊙♀∅⚏▦⚓P⚐⊞lau ♦ ౬♀✕∅⚏
Prices: A50 V50 ⚘50 ▲50

MÜHLEN Steiermark

Badsee Hitzmannsdorf 2 ☎03586 2418
N via B92.
May-15 Oct 1.5HEC ▦ ⚀⚀♀✕⊙♀▦ ⚓ L ⚐lau ♦ ✕ Prices: A45 V40 ⚘40 ▲40

OBERWÖLZ Steiermark

Schloss Rothenfels ☎03581 208
Apr-Oct 8HEC ▦ ⚀⚀⊙♀▦⚏ ⚓ LR ⚐⊞ lau ♦ ౬♀✕∅⚓P Prices: A50 V40 ⚘40 ▲30

ST GEORGEN Steiermark

Olachgut ☎03532 2162
Camping Card Compulsory.
Signposted.
All year 10HEC ▦ ⚀⚀✕⊙♀∅⚏▦▲⚓ L ⚐⊞ lau Prices: pitch 140-180

ST SEBASTIAN Steiermark

Erlaufsee Erlaufseestr 3 ☎03882 4937
Signposted.
May-15 Sep 0.5HEC ▦ ♦⚀⊙♀⚐lau ♦ ౬♀✕ ⚓L

SCHLADMING Steiermark

Zirngast Linke Ennsau 633 ☎03687 23195
Site in meadow on left bank of River Enns next to railway. Turn off B308 towards town as far as the MOBIL filling station.
All year 1.5HEC ▦ ⚀⚀౬♀✕⊙♀∅⚏⚓ R ⚐ lau ♦ ⚓P⊞
Prices: pitch 190-260 (incl 2 persons)

STUBENBERG Steiermark

Steinmann ☎03176 8390
5km towards Hirnsdorf towards the lake.
All year 4HEC ▦ ♦⚀౬♀✕⊙♀∅⚏⚓ L ⚐⊞ Prices: A60 V45 ⚘60 ▲40

UNGERSDORF BEI FROHNLEITEN Steiermark

Lanzmaierhof ☎03126 2360
Signposted 2km S of Frohnleiten on the Graz road.
Apr-15 Oct 0.5HEC ▦ ⚀⚀♀✕⊙♀∅⚏⊞♦ ⚓LPR Prices: A43 V25 ⚘25 ▲14-28

WILDALPEN Steiermark

Wildalpen ☎03636 342 & 341
Apr-Oct 0.8HEC ▦ ∷⚀⚀⊙♀∅⚓ R ⚐ lau ♦ ౬♀✕ ⚓P⊞
Prices: A30-35 V22 ⚘22-39 ▲14-33

Lower Austria

Lower Austria, by far the largest of the nine provinces, wraps itself around the federal capital of Vienna, itself a separate province. The Danube divides Lower Austria roughly in half, and has been central to the development of the area for centuries: prehistoric and Roman remains have been found, castles and fortified churches testify to the Romanesque and Gothic periods and great monasteries and pilgrimage churches celebrate the Baroque. North of the river the countryside, flat in the west, becomes hilly towards the Czechoslovak border; south of the river the land rises into wooded hills (including the well-known Vienna Woods - Wienerwald), and climbs to over 6,560ft (2,000 metres) in the Schneeberg and Rax regions - popular holiday areas for the Viennese.

Good communications have promoted industrial development in the Vienna basin and it is now the largest industrial area in the country. But agriculture is also important in the province, and vineyards around Krems and Weinviertel produce excellent wines. The south of the province, Burgenland the 'land of castles', has many monuments to a valiant past in what was for centuries a frontier area, occupied by the Romans and later vulnerable to attack from the Huns and the Turks. It is now a peaceful landscape of wooded hills, pastures, fruit orchards and vineyards. In dramatic contrast is the impressive expanse of the 'paszta' plain in the north east, and the vast Neusiedler See - the only steppe lake in central Europe, and well known for unique flora and fauna - providing good opportunities for bathing and yachting. Eisenstadt, the provincial capital is dominated by the Schloss Esterhazy, where this aristocratic family had its seat in the 17th and 18th centuries. There is an attractive old town, a cathedral, and the Haydnhaus (now a museum) where Haydn lived during the 30 years he was Kapellmeister here.

ANDAU Burgenland
Pusstasse ☎02176 3512 & 2301
A family site with good modern sanitary installations. Access via A4, exit Mönchhof/Halbturn/Andau towards Tadten.
15 Apr-15 Oct 1HEC ▦ ⚶ 𝕏 ⊙ ᵿ ⤳ L 🏊 lau ♦ ᵿ ♥ 𝕏 ᵿ ᵿ

BREITENBRUNN Burgenland
Seebad ☎02683 5252
Apr-Oct 10HEC ▦ ⚶ ⍨ 𝕏 ⊙ ᵿ ⤳ L 🏊 ⊞ ⍻ lau

DONNERSKIRCHEN Burgenland
Sonnenwaldbad ☎02683 8670
Grassy site with wide terraces beside a wood. View of the lake.
May-Oct 10HEC ▦ ⚶ ⍨ 𝕏 ⊙ ᵿ ⤳ P 🏊 ⊞ lau ♦ ♥ ᵿ

GMÜND Niederösterreich
Assangteich Albrechtser St 10 ☎02852 52506
Signposted from B41.
Apr-Oct 0.5HEC ▦ ⚶ ⍨ ⍨ 𝕏 ⊙ ᵿ ᵿ ⤳ LP 🏊 lau ♦ ♥ Prices: A55.50 pitch 70

HIRTENBERG Niederösterreich
Hirtenberg ☎02256 81111
Take exit Leobersdorf on A2/E59 and continue W on B18 for approx. 0.8km.
1 Jun-15 Sep 1HEC ▦ ⚶ ⍨ ⊙ ᵿ 🏊 ⍻ ♦ ♥ 𝕏 ᵿ ⤳PR ⊞ Prices: A40 pitch 50

INPRUGG Niederösterreich
Finsterhof ☎02772 52130
N towards Tulln.
All year 2HEC ▦ ⚶ ⍨ ⊙ ᵿ ᵿ 🏊 🏊 ⊞ lau ♦ 𝕏

JENNERSDORF Burgenland
Jennersdorf Freizeitzentrum 3 ☎03329 46133
15 Mar-31 Oct 1HEC ▦ ⚶ ⍨ ⊙ ᵿ ⤳ P 🏊 ⊞ ⍻ lau ♦ ♥ ♥ 𝕏 ᵿ
Prices: A58 pitch 50

KREMS Niederösterreich
Donau (ÖAMTC) Wiedengasse 7 ☎02732 84455
By river opposite SHELL filling station.
May-Sep 1HEC ▦ ⚶⚶ ⍨ 𝕏 ⊙ ᵿ 🏊 ⤳ R 🏊 ⍻

LAXENBURG Niederösterreich
Schlosspark Laxenburg Münchendorfer Str ☎02236 71333
On level meadowland with surfaced roads. The site lies in a recreation centre within the grounds of the historic Laxenburg Castle.
Access 600m S on the road leading to the B16.
Apr-Oct 2.4HEC ▦ ⚶ ⍨ ♥ 𝕏 ⊙ ᵿ ᵿ ⤳ P 🏊 ⊞ lau Prices: pitch 58-64

MARBACH Niederösterreich
Marbach ☎07413 466
Apr-Oct 0.5HEC ▦ ⚶ ⍨ ♥ 𝕏 ⊙ ᵿ ⤳ R 🏊 ⊞ lau ♦ ♥ 𝕏 ᵿ 🏊 ⤳P
Prices: A45 V30 ᵿ45 ᵿ45

MARKT ST MARTIN Burgenland
Markt St Martin Mühlweg 2 ☎02618 2239
May-Sep 0.5HEC ▦ ♦ ♥ 𝕏 ⊙ ᵿ ⤳ PR ⍻ ♦ ♥ ♥ 𝕏 ⊞

OBERRETZBACH Niederösterreich
Hubertus ☎02942 3238
Camping Card Compulsory.
Signposted.
All year 1HEC ▦ ⚶ ⍨ 𝕏 ⊙ ᵿ 🏊 ⊞ lau ♦ ♥ ♥

PODERSDORF Burgenland
Strandcamping Podersdorf am See Strandpl ☎02177 2279-0
Apr-Oct 7.5HEC ▦ ⦂⦂⦂ ⚶ ⚶ ⍨ 𝕏 ⊙ ᵿ ᵿ ⤳ L 🏊 lau ♦ ᵿ ⊞
Prices: A80 V62 ᵿ70 ᵿ52

PURGSTALL Niederösterreich
Erlauftal-Camp Purgstall Augasse 8-12 ☎07489 2015
All year 1.5HEC ▦ ⚶ ⍨ ⍨ ♥ 𝕏 ⊙ ᵿ ᵿ ᵿ ⤳ L 🏊 ⊞ lau ♦ ᵿ ᵿ ⤳P
Prices: A65 pitch 85-115

RAPPOLTENKIRCHEN Niederösterreich
Rappoltenkirchen Kreuthstr 5 ☎02274 8422
Turn off B1 at Sieghartskirchen and continue S for 3km.
Mar-Dec 2.2HEC ▦ ⚶ ⍨ ♥ ♥ 𝕏 ⊙ ᵿ ᵿ 🏊 🏊 ⊞ lau ♦ 𝕏 ⤳LP Prices: pitch 160 (incl 2 persons)

RECHNITZ Niederösterreich
GC Hauptpl 10 ☎03363 79202
Jun-Aug 1HEC ▦ ⚶⚶ ⍨ 𝕏 ⊙ ᵿ ⤳ L 🏊 ⊞ ♦ ♥ ♥ 𝕏 ᵿ 🏊 Prices: A35
V20 ᵿ70 ᵿ40

RUST Burgenland
Rust ☎02685 595
Situated on level meadowland with young trees.
From Rust follow the lake road.
Apr-Oct 57HEC ▦ ⚶ ⍨ ♥ 𝕏 ⊙ ᵿ ᵿ ⤳ L 🏊 ⊞ lau ♦ ᵿ 🏊 ⤳P
Prices: A44-55 V38-44 ᵿ44-55 ᵿ24-33

SCHÖNBÜHEL Niederösterreich
Stumpfer Schönbühel 7 ☎02752 8510
SW of town.
Apr-Oct 1HEC ▦ ♦ ♥ ♥ 𝕏 ⊙ ᵿ ᵿ ⤳ R 🏊 ⊞ lau Prices: A50 pitch 50-70

TRAISEN Niederösterreich
Kulmhof Kulmhof 1 ☎02762 52900
0.6km W via B20.
All year 1.7HEC ▦ ⚶ ⍨ ♥ ⊙ ᵿ ᵿ 🏊 🏊 ⤳ P 🏊 ⊞ lau ♦ ♥ 𝕏 Prices: A50 pitch 50

TULLN Niederösterreich
Donaupark-Camping Tulln Hafenstr ☎02272 65200
May-Sep 10HEC ▦ ⚶ ⍨ ♥ 𝕏 ⊙ ᵿ ᵿ 🏊 🏊 ᵿ ⤳ L 🏊 ⊞ lau ♦ ⤳PR
Prices: A60 pitch 130

TÜRNITZ Niederösterreich
Gravogl Pichlrotte 16 ☎02769 201
All year 0.9HEC ▦ ⚶ ⍨ 𝕏 ⊙ ᵿ 🏊 ⊞ lau ♦ ⤳P

Upper Austria/Salzburg

The province of Salzburg is wonderfully diverse: in the north mighty massifs fall away to rolling uplands and plains, and to the east the hills of the Salzkammergut merge into the Alpine landscape of Upper Austria. Visitors are drawn to the province by the natural landscape; dozens of attractive summer resorts, from smart cosmopolitan spas to picturesque mountain hamlets; and facilities for winter sports in almost every part of the province. A magnificent setting and a wealth of beautiful buildings and attractive streets have given Salzburg an international reputation as one of the most beautiful cities in the world. It contains a rich heritage of architecture and the arts, and Mozart was born here in 1756. The city is still a major musical centre, and hosts an annual music festival every summer, with performances of the highest quality.

The scenic facets of Upper Austria (Oberösterreich) stretch from the wooded Mühlviertel area north of the Danube to the lake-studded Salzkammergut and the glacier region of the Dachstein - all dotted with lively holiday centres, peaceful villages and idyllic spas and health resorts.

The provincial capital Linz, Austria's third-largest city, spans both banks of the Danube in the Linz basin. The old town's original market square is flanked by impressive buildings, and the city has many attractive streets and arcaded courtyards.

ABERSEE Salzburg
Wolfgangblick ☎06138 2475
Camping Card Compulsory.
May-Sep 2.2HEC ▦ ♠ ⚐ ♠ ⚡ ✕ ⊙ ◓ ∅ ⍨ LR ☎ ⊞ lau ♦ ♨ ⍨R ⊞
Prices: A52 pitch 70

ABTENAU Salzburg
Oberwötzhof Erlfeld 37 ☎06243 2698
All year 2HEC ⚐ ♠ ⚡ ✕ ⊙ ◓ ◍ ⍨ P ☎ ♦ ⍨R

ALTENMARKT Salzburg
Götschl-Au Palfen 386 ☎06452 7821
S towards the Zauchensee
All year 10HEC ▦ ♦ ♠ ⚐ ⚡ ✕ ⊙ ◓ ∅ ♨ ☎ lau ♦ ⍨P

ALTMÜNSTER Oberösterreich
Schweizerhof Haupstr 14 ☎07612 89313
A modern site on the shore of Lake Traunsee.
May-Sep 6HEC ▦ ∷ ♦ ♠ ✕ ⊙ ◓ ⍨ L ☎ ⊞ lau ♦ ♨ Prices: A60
V28 ⊞80-125

BADGASTEIN Salzburg
Kurcamping 'Erlengrund' ☎06434 2790
On meadowland below the road leading to the Tauern railway tunnel.
From Hofgastein turn left off B167 and descend for 100m.
All year 3.5HEC ▦ ⚐ ♠ ⚡ ⚐ ⊙ ◓ ∅ ⍨ P ☎ ⊞ lau ♦ ♨ ✕ ⍨LR

BRUCK AN DER GROSSGLOCKNERSTRASSE Salzburg
Woferlgut Kroessenbach 40 ☎06545 7303-0
Access via Bruck-Süd or Grossglockner on B311
All year 2.8HEC ▦ ⚐ ♠ ⚐ ⚡ ✕ ⊙ ◓ ∅ ♨ ⬢ ◓ ▲ ⍨ LP ☎ lau
Prices: A47-60 V42-55 ⊞52-65 ▲37-65

BURGAU Salzburg
Burgau ☎07663 266
Mainly level site surrounded by trees between the road and the
Attersee at Weissenbach.
On B152 at Km 27.6 opposite Hotel Burgau.
May-Oct 100HEC ▦ ⚐ ♠ ♨ ✕ ⊙ ◓ ∅ ⍨ LR ☎ ⊞

Eitzinger Burgau 4 ☎07663 769
In a fine situation directly on the Attersee with good recreational
facilities.
Access from 'Mondsee' exit on Autobahn.
Apr-Sep ▦ ⚐ ♠ ♨ ⊙ ◓ ⚡ ⍨ L ☎ ⊞ Prices: A50 V25 ⊞35 ▲35

ESTERNBERG Oberösterreich
Pyrawang ☎07714 504
At Km45.5 on B130 (Passau-Linz).
Apr-Sep 0.3HEC ▦ ⚐ ♠ ⊙ ◓ ☎ ⊞ ♦ ✕ ⍨LR

GLEINKERAU Oberösterreich
Air Pyhrn Priel ☎07562 7066
Signposted from Windischgarsten towards Gleinkersee.
All year 1HEC ▦ ♥ ⟵ ♠ ✕ ⊙ ◓ ∅ lau ♦ ♨ ✕ ∅ ♨ ⍨LP ⊞ Prices:
A50 V20 ⊞60 ▲35

GOLLING Salzburg
Torrener Hof ☎06244 5522
On the outskirts of the village on the B159.
Nov 2HEC ▦ ∷ ⚐ ♠ ♨ ⚡ ✕ ⊙ ◓ ☎ ☎ lau ♦ ⍨LPR Prices: A50
V30 ⊞30 ▲30

HAIBACH Oberösterreich
Schlögen ☎0043 72788241
In wooded surroundings on the shore of the marina.
Camping Card Compulsory.
Access via B139.
All year 2.2HEC ▦ ⚐ ♠ ✕ ⊙ ◓ ⍨ L ☎ ⊞ lau ♦ ♨

KAPRUN Salzburg
Mühle ☎06547 8254
On long stretch of meadow by the Kapruner Ache. S end of village
towards cable lift.
All year 1.5HEC ▦ ⚐ ♠ ⚡ ✕ ◓ ⚐ ⍨ P ☎ ⊞ lau ♦ ♨ ⍨L Prices:
A65-70 pitch 90-100

MAISHOFEN Salzburg
Kammerlander Oberreith 120 ☎06542 8755
On B168.
15 Apr-1 Oct ▦ ⚐ ♠ ⚡ ✕ ⊙ ◓ ☎ ♦ ∅ ♨ ⍨LP Prices: A30 V20
⊞20 ▲20

NEUSTIFT Oberösterreich
Gasthof Weiss Puhret 5 ☎07284 8104
Leave the motorway at Passau-Nord and take B388.
Apr-Nov 0.7HEC ▦ ♦ ♠ ♨ ✕ ⊙ ◓ ∅ ∅ ⍨ LPR ☎ ⊞ lau ♦ ⍨LPR
Prices: A40 V40 ⊞40 ▲30-40

NUSSDORF Oberösterreich
See Camping Gruber Dortstr 63 ☎07666 80450
On fairly long meadow parallel to the promenade.
S of village, access is at Km19.7. Turn off B151 towards the lake
(Attersee).
15 Apr-15 Oct 2.6HEC ▦ ♦ ♠ ♨ ⚡ ✕ ⊙ ◓ ⍨ LP ☎ ⊞ lau ♦ ∅ ♨
Prices: A50-69 pitch 75-110

Strandcamping Graus Dorfstr 55 ☎07666 8008
Site on long meadow with fruit trees, sloping towards lake and
bathing area. Access is within the village.
Turn off main road B151 at Km19.5 towards the lake (Attersee).
May-Sep 2.7HEC ▦ ♦ ♠ ⚡ ✕ ⊙ ◓ ∅ ♨ ♨ ⍨ L ☎ ⊞ ⊞ ⊘ lau ♦ ♨

PERWANG AM GRABENSEE Oberösterreich
Perwang ☎06217 8288
Site beside lake.
May-Oct 1.5HEC ▦ ⚐ ♠ ♨ ✕ ⊙ ◓ ☎ ☎ ⊘ lau ♦ ♨ ⍨L Prices: A54
pitch 70

PETTENBACH Oberösterreich
Almtal ☎07586 8627
Leave A1/E55/E60 at Sattledt exit and continue towards Graz.
All year 3HEC ▦ ⚐ ♠ ♨ ✕ ⊙ ◓ ∅ ♨ ⍨ P ☎ ⊞ lau

RADSTADT Salzburg
Forellencamp ☎06452 7861
Flat meadowland near town
SW via B99.
All year 1HEC ▦ ∷ ⚐ ♠ ♨ ✕ ⊙ ◓ ♨ ☎ lau ♦ ♨ ⍨P Prices: A50
V30 ⊞50 ▲25

ST JOHANN IM PONGAU Salzburg
Hirschenwirt Bundesstr 1 ☎06412 6012
Access via Bischofshofen and B311.
Dec-May & 15 Jun-Oct 0.8HEC ▦ ⚐ ♠ ♨ ✕ ⊙ ◓ ∅ ♨ ⍨ P lau ♦ ⍨R

Wieshof Wieshofgasse 8 ☎06412 8292
On gently sloping meadow behind pension and farmhouse. Modern
facilities. Big spa house with sauna, massage facilities and health
bars, adjacent to site.
Off B311 towards Zell am Zee.
All year 1.2HEC ▦ ⚐ ♠ ⊙ ◓ ∅ ♨ lau ♦ ♨ ✕ ⍨P ⊞ Prices: A60
pitch 60

ST LORENZ Oberösterreich
Alten Ischler Bahn St Lorenz 88 ☎06232 2902
Clean orderly site, easily accessible in the beautiful Mondsee Valley.
All year 1HEC ▦ ♦ ♠ ♨ ✕ ⊙ ◓ ∅ ♨ ⍨L

Austria-Camp St Lorenz 229 ☎06232 2927
Level site on grassland bordered by trees and hedges and divided
into fields by internal roads. Separate field for young people.
4km from Mondsee, beside the lake.
May-Sep 3.7HEC ▦ ♦ ♠ ♨ ⚡ ✕ ⊙ ◓ ▲ ⍨ L ☎ lau Prices: A40 V40
⊞55 ▲40

ST MARTIN BEI LOFER Salzburg
Park Grubhof ☎06588 237
Situated in meadowland on the banks of the River Saalach. Separate
sections for dog owners, families, teenagers and groups.
1.5km S of Lofer turn off B311.
May-Sep 10HEC ▦ ⚐ ♠ ♨ ✕ ⊙ ◓ ∅ ♨ ▲ ◓ ♨ ⍨R ☎ ⊞ ♦ ♨ ⍨P
Prices: A58 V29 ⊞41-52 ▲29-41

Park Camping Grubhof-Family
Mory-A-5092 St. Martin b. Lofer
Tel. 010 43 6588/237 or 405
(from April '97 Tel. & Fax 8237 or 8405)

The camping Park Grubhof is located in magnificent mountain scenery between Berchtesgaden, Tyrol and the Grossglocker, 100,000 square metre park and meadow site with old trees, avenues of chestnuts, trees and bushes. On the bank of the Saalach is a large playing field and young persons' sports field. The surrounding area offers many miles of easy footpaths through woods and meadows and also mountain tours to the high summits. For motorists there are many interesting places to visit and circular tours. In addition nearby and easy to reach are lakes and swimming pools. Tennis courts, mini golf and cable car in the immediate vicinity. Full services for motor-caravans

English spoken

ST WOLFGANG *Oberösterreich*
Appesbach Au 99 ☎06138 2206
On sloping meadow facing lake with no shade at upper end. 0.8km E of St Wolfgang between lake and Strobl road.
Apr-Oct 2HEC ▦ ⅃⌁ ⌂ ⚍ ⚎ 🍴 ⚌ ⊙ ⚑ ∅ ⌁ ⊥ L 🕭 ⊞ lau ✦ ⊞

Berau Schwarzenbach 16 ☎06138 2543
Site lies between lake and road from Strobl, N of lake. 1.3km E of entrance to St Wolfgang.
All year 2HEC ▦ ✦ ⌁ ⊙ ⚑ ∅ ⌁ L 🕭 ⊞ lau ✦ ⚌ ⚎ 🍴 ⚌ ⌁P Prices: A57-61 pitch 83-160

Ried 18 ☎06138 2521
Signposted towards Ried.
15 May-Sep 0.4HEC ▦ ⚍ ⌂ 🍴 ⊙ ⚑ ⌁ L 🕭 ⊞ lau ✦ ⚌ ⚎ ∅ ⌁P

SALZBURG *Salzburg*
Kasern Carl-Zuckmayer str 26 ☎0662 450576
Access via exit 'Salzburg-Nord' on the A1.
Closed Jan & Feb 1.1HEC ▦ ✦ ⌁⌂🍴⚍⚌⊙⚑∅⚎⚌⚍A🕭 lau ✦⚎🍴 Prices: A60 V35 ⚐35 ▲35

Nord Sam Samstr 22A ☎0662 660611
Site divided into pitches.
400m from Salzburg Nord Autobahn Exit.
22 Mar-Oct 2HEC ▦ ⁚⁚⁚ ⚍⌂🍴⚌⚎🍴⊙⚑∅⚎⌁P⊞ lau
Prices: A43-53 pitch 79-99

Schloss Aigen ☎0662 622079
Site divided into pitches in partial clearing on mountain slope. From Salzburg-Süd motorway exit through Anif and Glasenbach.
May-Sep 25HEC ▦ ⚍⌂🍴⚌⚎🍴⊙⚑∅⚎🕭⊞ lau Prices: A50 pitch 60

Stadtblick Rauchenbichlerstr 21 ☎0662 450652
Leave motorway at exit Salzburg-Nord and follow signs.
20 Mar-Oct 0.8HEC ▦ ⁚⁚⁚ ⚍⌂🍴⚌⚎🍴⊙⚑∅⚎🕭A🕭⊞ lau
Prices: A60-65 V20 ⚐40 ▲20

SCHLÖGEN *Oberösterreich*
Terrassencamping Pension Schlögen ☎07279 8241
Apr-Oct 1.8HEC ▦ ⚍⌂🍴⚌⚎🍴⊙⚑⚎⌁PR🕭 lau

SEEKIRCHEN *Salzburg*
Strand Seestr 2 ☎06212 4088
Beside the Wallersee in beautiful meadow.
Apr-Oct 2HEC ▦ ⚍⌂🍴⚌⚎🍴⊙⚑∅⌁LP🕭⊞ lau ✦⚌ Prices: A45 pitch 90

Zell am Wallersee ☎06212 4080
Level meadowland separated from the lake by the Lido. Access from A1 exit Wallersee then via Seekirchen to Zell.
May-Oct 2.5HEC ▦ ⚍⌂🍴⚎🍴⊙⚑⌁L🕭⊞ lau ✦⚌⚎∅⚍ Prices: A60 pitch 120

STEINBACH *Oberösterreich*
Seefeld ☎07663 342
On meadowland sloping gently towards lake, behind Gasthof Föttinger.
Near MOBIL garage on B152 at Km13.6.
May-Oct 1.2HEC ▦ ⚍⌂🍴⚌⚎🍴⊙⚑⚎⌁LP🕭⊞ lau ✦∅

STEYR-MÜNICHOLZ *Oberösterreich*
Forelle ☎07252 68008
N in Münicholz.
Apr-Oct ▦ ✦⌁⌁R🕭⚎⚑⊞ lau

TIEFGRABEN *Oberösterreich*
Fohlenhof Hof 17 ☎06232 2600
From Mondsee exit on A1/E55/E60 take B154 towards Strasswalden for 1.5km, then take Haider-Mühle road for 2km.
Apr-10 Oct 2.5HEC ▦ ⚍⌂🍴⚌⚎🍴⊙⚑∅⚎⚌⌁P🕭 lau ✦⌁L⊞
Prices: A43 pitch 64

UNTERACH *Oberösterreich*
Insel ☎07665 8311
Quiet site on shore of Lake Attersee; divided into two sections by River Seeache. Family site.
Entrance below B152 towards Steinbach at Km24.5; about 300m from fork with B151.
15 May-15 Sep 1.8HEC ▦ ⚍⌂🍴⚎🍴⊙⚑⌁LR🕭 lau ✦⚎🍴∅⊞
Prices: A58 V25 ⚐35 ▲30

WALD *Salzburg*
S.N.P Lahn 65 ☎06565 8446
W of town.
All year 7HEC ▦ ⚍⌂🍴⚎🍴⊙⚑∅⚎🕭⊞ lau ✦⚌⌁P

WESENUFER *Oberösterreich*
Nibelungen ☎07718 589
Camping Card Compulsory
Beside the River Donau, 500m from B130.
Apr-Sep 12HEC ▦ ⚍⌂🍴⚎🍴⚎🕭⊞ lau ✦⚌⚎🍴⚎⌁R

ZELL AM SEE *Salzburg*
Seecamp Zell am See Thumersbacherstr 34 ☎06542 2115
Access via B311, N of lake towards Thumersbach. Signposted.
All year 2.8HEC ▦ ⚍⚍⌂🍴⚌⚎🍴⊙⚑∅⚎⚌⚍⚎⌁L🕭⊞ lau ✦⌁P Prices: A76-85 pitch 50-120

Südufer Seeuferstr 196 ☎06542 56228
Level site close to lake.
S via B311 towards Thumersbach.
All year 0.6HEC ▦ ✦⌁⌂🍴⊙⚑∅⚎🕭 lau ✦⚎🍴⚎ Prices: A55-60 V25 ⚐70-75 ▲50-70

Vorarlberg

Austria's most western province, Vorarlberg is small but very beautiful. The gardens and orchards in the Rhine valley and on the shores of Lake Constance give way to a forested upland region, and finally to the peaks and glaciers of the Silvretta, rising to over 9,800ft (3,000 metres). With its lovely old towns and villages, clear mountain lakes and rivers, quiet bays on Lake Constance, pastures and meadowlands, steep-sided valleys and peaks, Vorarlberg is a province of special charm. Watersports are popular on Lake Constance, but there is good access to the mountainous regions, making them popular in the summer with walkers and climbers, as well as in winter for skiers.

The onion-domed St Martin's tower (Martinstrum), dating back from 1602, distinguishes the skyline of Bregenz, the provincial capital. The newer districts of the town, on the shores of Lake Constance, have modern well-equipped tourist facilities - an open air-pool, lakeside gardens, a floating stage and a Festspielhaus for festivals and conferences.

AU Vorarlberg

Au ☎05515 2331
On B200 (Dornbirn-Wath)
Closed 7 Apr-8 May & 22 Sep-Oct 0.3HEC ▦ ꝸ✓ ⋔✕☉ ⬤ ⌀ ☎ ⊞ ⬇ lau ◆ ⚏ ⚲ ✕ ⅂PR

BEZAU Vorarlberg

Bezau Ach 206 ☎05514 2964
S via B200 (Dornbirn-Warth).
All year 4HEC ▦ ꝸ ⋔☉ ⬤ ⌀ ⛌ ⊞ ◆ ⚏ ⚲ ✕ ⅂PR Prices: A50 ⬛80-90 ▲70-90

BLUDENZ Vorarlberg

At **BRAZ**(7km SE)

Traube ☎05552 8103
On sloping grassland.
7km SE of Bludenz via E17, S16 (Bludenz-Arlberg-Innsbruck).
Signposted. Near railway.
All year 2HEC ▦ ꝸ ⋔☉ ⬤ ⌀ ⛌ ⅂ P ☎ ⊞ ⅂R

At **NÜZIDERS**(2.5km NW)

Sonnenberg Hinterferst 12 ☎05552 64035
Clean site with modern facilities in gently sloping meadowland and splendid mountain scenery.
Access from Bludenz-Nüziders road, at first fork follow up hill.
17 May-5 Oct 1.8HEC ▦ ꝸ✓ ⋔☉ ⬤ ⌀ ⛌ ☎ ☎ ⊞ ꝸ lau ◆ ⚏ ✕ ⅂R Prices: A50 pitch 110-150

BREGENZ Vorarlberg

See Bodangasse 7 ☎05574 71895
Quiet site on level meadow beside lake.
From town centre (Bahnhofplatz) follow signs towards 'Seecamping'.
15 May-15 Sep 8HEC ▦ ꝸ ⚏ ⚲ ✕☉ ⬤ ⬛ ⅂ L ☎ ⊞ lau ◆ ⌀ ⅂P

DALAAS Vorarlberg

Erne ☎05585 223
In the town, next to the swimming pool. Access via S16, exit 'Dalass'.
All year 0.6HEC ▦ ꝸ ⋔☉ ⬤ ⌀ ⛌ ⅂ PR ☎ ⊞ ◆ ⚏ ✕ ⅂P ⊞ Prices: pitch 220-240

DORNBIRN Vorarlberg

In der Enz ☎05572 29119
A municipal site beside a public park, some 100m beyond the Karren cable lift.
May-Sep 10HEC ▦ ꝸ ⋔ ⚏ ⚲ ✕☉ ⬤ ⌀ ☎ ⊞ lau ◆ ⅂PR ⊞

LANGEN Vorarlberg

At **KLÖSTERLE**(2km W)

Alpencamping ☎05582 269
Well signposted.
All year 1.5HEC ▦ ꝸ ⋔ ⚏ ⚲ ✕☉ ⬤ ⌀ ⅂ R ⊞ lau ◆ ⅂P. Prices: A73 pitch 50

LINGENAU Vorarlberg

Feurstein Haidach 185 ☎05513 6114
All year 1HEC ▦ ꝸ ⋔☉ ⬤ ⌀ ⛌ ☎ ☎ ⊞ lau ◆ ⚏ ⚲ ✕ ⅂PR Prices: A60 V15 ⬛35 ▲25-35

NENZING Vorarlberg

Alpencamping Nenzing Garfrenga 1 ☎05525 62491
Signposted from B190 from Nenzing-2km towards Gurtis.
All year 3HEC ▦ ꝸ ⋔ ⚏ ⚲ ✕☉ ⬤ ⌀ ⛌ ☎ ☎ ⅂ P ☎ ⊞ lau Prices: pitch 230 (incl 2 persons)

RAGGAL-PLAZERA Vorarlberg

Grosswalsertal ☎05553 209
Situated in a quiet location on gently sloping terrain, with pleasant views.
15 May-Sep 0.8HEC ▦ ꝸ✓ ⋔☉ ⬤ ⌀ ☎ ⅂ P ☎ lau ◆ ⚏ ⚲ ✕ ⊞ Prices: A40-45 pitch 50-60

TSCHAGGUNS Vorarlberg

Zelfen ☎05556 72326
Partly uneven, grassy site beside River Ill.
All year 2HEC ▦ ꝸ ⋔ ⚏ ⚲ ✕☉ ⬤ ⌀ ⅂ R ☎ ⊞ lau ◆ ⛌ ⅂P Prices: A52 pitch 75

Vienna (Wien)

For hundreds of years Vienna was the heart of a vast empire and cultural focus of central Europe. Today Vienna is very much one of the world's great modern tourist cities with a confident and cosmopolitan atmosphere, but it still keeps a distinctive charm and native flair. The mighty facades of the buildings and palaces of the city bear witness to the tall, grand Baroque buildings that earn it the name 'Vienna gloriosa'. And it retains and builds on its traditions of the finest music; many of the world's great composers lived and worked here, and the Opera House (Staatsoper) plays a prominent part in the social, cultural and political life of the city.

Vienna's cultural district is encircled by the wide boulevard, the Ringstrasse, on which many of the city's main buildings stand: the Opera House, the Burg Theatre, the Hofburg, the Parliament, and the neo-Gothic City Hall (Rathaus), as well as churches, museums and lovely parks, gardens and squares.

There is a full programme of events in the city - everything from operas and concerts to sporting events. For more casual entertainment, though, the Viennese cafés are a famous and historic institution - popular meeting places for the Viennese and a delight for the tourists - with tables outside in the summer, newspapers and magazines always available, and of course, the traditional strong, aromatic Viennese coffee.

WIEN (VIENNA) Wien

Donaupark Klosterneuburg In der Au ☎02243 85877
A modern site in delightful wooded surroundings with fine recreational facilities and within easy reach of the city centre.
Signposted from A1.
All year 2HEC ▦ ꝸ✓ ⋔ ✕☉ ⬤ ⌀ ⛌ ☎ ▲ ☎ lau ◆ ⅂PR ⊞ Prices: A60 ⬛140

Neue Donau Am Kleehaufl ☎1 2024010
May-Sep ▦ ⬇ ꝸ ⋔ ⚏ ⚲ ✕☉ ⬤ ⌀ ⛌ lau ◆ ⅂R Prices: A68 pitch 64

Wien-West 2 Hüttelbergstr 80 ☎0222 9142314
On slightly rising meadow with asphalt paths.
From end of A1/E5 (Linz-Wien) to Bräuhausbrücke, then turn left and across road to Linz, continue for approx. 1.8km.
Closed Feb 2HEC ▦ ◆ ⋔ ⚏ ⚲ ✕☉ ⬤ ⌀ ☎ ☎ lau ◆ ✕

At **RODAUN**(4km SW)

Schwimmbad Camping Rodaun An der Au 2 ☎0222 884154
Between An der Austr and Leising River dam. Access from Breitenfürter Str N492.
16 Mar-16 Nov 1.2HEC ▦ ꝸ ⋔ ⚏ ⚲ ✕☉ ⬤ ⌀ ⅂ P ☎ ⊞ lau

BELGIUM

Belgium is a small, densely populated country bordered by France, Germany, Luxembourg and The Netherlands.

Despite the fact that it is heavily industrialised, it possesses some beautiful scenery, notably the great forest of the Ardennes. The resorts in the Oostende (Ostend) area offer a selection of wide, safe, sandy beaches and cover about forty miles of coastline.

The climate is temperate and similar to that of Britain: the variation between summer and winter lessened by the effects of the Gulf Stream. French is spoken in the south, Dutch in the north and German in the eastern part of the province of Liège.

Belgium is a varied, charming country in which to spend a camping holiday - the rivers and gorges of the Ardennes contrasting sharply with the rolling plains which make up the rest of the countryside. There are now over 800 campsites officially authorised by local authorities. They are normally open from April to October, but many are open throughout the year. Coastal sites tend to be very crowded at the height of the season.

Off-site camping (including sleeping) is prohibited beside public roads for more than 24 consecutive hours; on seashores; within a 100-metre radius of a main water point; or on a site classified for the conservation of monuments. Elsewhere, camping is permitted free of charge, as long as the stay does not exceed 24 hours and the camper has obtained authorisation from the landowner.

HOW TO GET THERE

There are direct ferry services to Belgium:
To **Oostende** (Ostend) from **Ramsgate** takes 4hrs.

FACTS AND FIGURES

Capital: Bruxelles (Brussel, Brussels)
Language: French, Dutch, German
IDD code: 32. To call the UK dial 00 44
Currency: Belgian Franc (*BFr*1 = 100 centimes)
At the time of going to press £1 = *BFr*46.40
Local time: GMT + 1 (summer GMT + 2)
Emergency Services: Police 101; Fire 100; Ambulance 100
Business hours-
Banks: Mon-Fri 09.00-12.00, 14.00-16.00
Shops: Mon-Sat 09.00-18.00

Average daily temperatures:
Bruxelles (Brussel, Brussels)
Jan 3°C	Jul 17°C
Mar 5°C	Sep 14°C
May 13°C	Nov 5°C

Tourist Information: Belgian National Tourist Office
UK 29 Princes Street London W1R 7RG
☎ 0891 887799 (premium rate information line)
USA 745 Fifth Avenue New York, NY 10151
☎ (212) 758 8130
Camping Card recommended; some reductions on site fees.

To **Zeebrugge** from **Hull** takes 13 hrs 45 mins
Alternatively, you could use the Channel Tunnel, or take a shorter crossing by ferry or Hoverspeed to Calais, France, and drive along the coast road to Belgium.

For details of the *AA European Routes Service* please consult the Contents Page.

MOTORING & GENERAL INFORMATION

The information given here is specific to Belgium. It **must** be read in conjunction with the Continental ABC at the front of the book, which covers those regulations which are common to many countries.

Accidents

The police must also be called if an unoccupied, stationary vehicle is damaged, or if injuries are caused to persons; in the latter case, the car must not be moved; see recommendations under *Accidents* (also *Warning triangle*) in the European ABC.

British Embassy/Consulates*

The British Embassy is located at 1040 Bruxelles, rue d'Arlon 85 ☎ (02) 2876211. There are British Consulates with Honorary Consuls in Antwerpen (Antwerp) and Liège.

Children in cars

Child under 3 not permitted to travel as front seat passenger unless using suitable child restraint system. Children under 3 in rear must use suitable restraint system if fitted. Children over 3 and under 12 seated in front or rear must use seat-belt or child restraint appropriate to their size and weight.

Currency

There are no restrictions on the amount of Belgian or foreign currency which may be taken into or out of Belgium.

Dimensions and weight restrictions

Private **cars** and towed **trailers** or **caravans** are restricted to the following dimensions: height, 4 metres; width, 2.5 metres; length (including any coupling device) **car** 12 metres, **trailer/caravan with one axle** up to 3,500kg 8 metres; between 3,500kg and 8,000kg 10 metres, over 8,000kg 11 metres; trailer/caravan with 2 axles or more 12 metres.The maximum permitted overall length of vehicle/trailer or caravan combination is 18 metres. Trailers without brakes may have a total maximum weight of 750kg.

Driving Licence*

A valid UK or Republic of Ireland licence is acceptable in Belgium. The minimum age at which visitors from UK or Republic of Ireland may use a temporarily imported car or motorcycle is 18 years.

Foodstuffs*

There are no limits on the importation of foodstuffs obtained duty and tax paid within the EC. Up to 500g of coffee (200g of coffee extract) and 100g of tea (40g of tea extract) purchased duty free or outside the EC may be imported free of duty and tax. However, coffee bought duty free or outside the EC cannot be imported by visitors under 15 years of age.

Language

There are *three* official languages in Belgium - *Dutch, French* and *German*. Dutch is spoken in the north, French in the south and, in the eastern provinces, German. Both Dutch and French are spoken in Brussels. These divisions are administrative but act as a rough guide to the areas in which the various languages are spoken.

Some of the town names in the directory are shown in both Dutch and French, and that shown first is the one used locally. However, Brussels (Bruxelles-Brussel) is officially bi-lingual.

Motoring club*

The **Touring Club Royal de Belgique** (TCB) has its head office at 1040 Bruxelles, 44 rue de la Loi ☎(02) 2332211 and branch offices in most towns. The Bruxelles (Brussels) head office is open weekly 08.30-17.30hrs; Saturday 09.00-12.00hrs. Regional offices are open weekdays 09.00-12.30hrs (Monday from 09.30hrs) and 14.00-18.00hrs; Saturday 09.00-12.00hrs. All offices are closed on Saturday afternoons and Sundays.

Roads

A good road system is available. However, one international route that has given more cause for complaints than any other is, without doubt, that from Calais (France) through Belgium to Köln/Cologne (Germany). The problem is aggravated by the fact that there are two official languages in Belgium; in the Flemish part of Belgium all signs are in Dutch only, while in Wallonia (the French-speaking half of the country), the signs are all in French. Brussels (Bruxelles-Brussel) seems to be the only neutral ground where the signs show the two alternative spellings of placenames (Antwerpen-Anvers; Gent-Gand; Liège-Luik; Mons-Bergen; Namur-Namen; Oostende-Ostende; Tournai-Doornik.) From the Flemish part of the country, Dunkirk (Dunkerque) in France is signposted *Duinkerke* and Lille is referred to as *Rijsel*, and even Paris is shown as *Parijs*.

Belgium has a comprehensive system of toll-free motorways linking major towns and adjoining countries. Generally, signposts leading to and on motorways show foreign destination place-names in the language of the country concerned. The exceptions to this are on the E40 and E314 where cities such as Aachen and Köln may be given as Aken (Dutch) and Cologne (French).

Speed limits*
Car/caravan/trailer
Built-up areas 50kph (31mph)
Other roads 90kph (56pmh)
Motorways and 4-lane roads separated by central reservation 120kph (74mph)†. Minimum speed on motorways on straight level stretches is 70kph (43mph).

Vehicles being towed due to accident or breakdown are limited to 25kph (15mph) on all roads and, if on a motorway, must leave at the first exit.
†On dual carriageways separated only by road markings the limit is 90kph (55mph).

Warning triangle*
The use of a warning triangle is compulsory in the event of accident or breakdown. The triangle must be placed 30 metres (33yds) behind the vehicle on ordinary roads and 100 metres (110yds) on motorways to warn following traffic of any obstruction; it must be visible at a distance of 50 metres (55yds).
*Additional information will be found in the Continental ABC at the front of the book.

A-Z DIRECTORY

Prices are in Belgian Francs Abbreviations: av avenue rte route r rue str straat T C B Touring Club de Belgique.
Belgium is divided into the Dutch-speaking region in the north and the French-speaking Walloon region in the south. Some of the town names in the gazetteer show both languages, and that shown first is the one used locally. Brussels (Bruxelles/Brussel) is officially bi-lingual. Each name preceded by 'De' or 'La' is listed under the name that follows it.

South West/Coast

The coastline of Belgium is one of fine sandy beaches backed by dunes, with few openings to the sea. The coast is lined with resorts: De Panne; Niewpoort; Ostende, with its port, is also a fashionable resort; Blankenberge; Zeebrugge; and popular Knokke-Heist. Bruges, once connected to the sea by an inlet, was a great medieval port. When the inlet silted up, the city declined, preserving a city whose architecture and unique atmosphere has survived until today, to the delight of the increasing number of visitors.
Ypres is historically an important textile centre. Reduced to rubble in World War I, the town has been almost completely restored, and now has its lovely Cloth Hall and cathedral. There are hundreds of war cemeteries and memorials near by, recalling the massive war casualties suffered in the area. Tournai is one of the oldest cities in Belgium and an important ecclesiastical centre, evidenced by the remarkable Cathedral of Notre Dame, with its rich interior and wealth of treasures.

BELOEIL Hainaut
Orangerie r du Major 3 ☎069 689190
Behind the Château de Beloeil.
Apr-Oct 3HEC ▦ ⅃⅃ 🐾 ⅂ ✕ ⊙ ⊟ ♨ 🏕 ⊞ lau ✦ ✕ Prices: pitch 300

BLANKENBERGE West-Vlaanderen
Bonanza I & III Zeebruggelaan 137 ☎050 416658
Mar-Sep 5HEC ▦ ⅃ ⅂ ✕ ⊙ ⊟ ♨ ✦ P ⊞ lau ✦ ⅃LS

Dallas Ruzettelaan 191 ☎050 418157
Mar-Oct 3HEC ▦ 🐾 ⊙ ⊟ ♨ 🏕 ⊞ lau ✦ ✕ ⅃LPS Prices:
A150 V150 ♨150 ▲100-150

BRUGELETTE Hainaut
Parc et Loisirs r de Bollignies 20 ☎068 455422
All year 6HEC ▦ ⅃ 🐾 ⊙ ⊟ ⅃ LPR ⊞ lau ✦ ⅃ ✕ Prices: pitch 300

HAAN, DE West-Vlaanderen
Tropical Bredeweg 76A ☎050 236341
Signposted from A10/E40.
Apr-Sep 2.6HEC ▦ ⅃↙ ⅂ ⊙ ⊟ ♨ 🏕 ⊞ lau ✦ 🐾 ✕ ⅃ Prices:
A110-120 V40-60 ♨280-330 ▲280-330

KNOKKE-HEIST West-Vlaanderen
Vuurtoren Heistlaan 168 ☎050 511782
On level meadow with tarred roads.
Turn S off Knokke-Ostende road 4km from Knokke and follow signposts.
15 Mar-15 Oct 6.6HEC ▦ ⅃ 🐾 ⅂ ✕ ⊙ ⊟ 🏕 ⊞ lau ✦ ♨ ⅃LPŚ
Prices: A105 ♨260-560 ▲220-460

Zilvermeeuw Heistlaan 166 ☎050 512726
Level site in wooded surroundings.
SW via N300.
Mar-Nov 7HEC ▦ ⅃↙ 🐾 ✕ ⊙ ⊟ ♨ 🟰 ♨ ⊟ ⊞ lau ✦ ⅃ ✕ ⅃LS
Prices: pitch 375-575 (incl 2 persons)

At **WESTKAPELLE**(3km S)
Holiday Natienlaan 70-72 ☎050 601203
Apr-Sep 1.7HEC ▦ ⅃ 🐾 ⊙ ⊟ ♨ 🏕 ⊞ ⅋ lau ✦ ♨ 🐾 ⅂ ✕ ⅃PS Prices:
A150 pitch 250
KOKSIJDE West-Vlaanderen
Blekker & Blekkerdal Jachtwakerstr 12 ☎058 511633

In a peaceful location, surrounded by trees, with good modern facilities. Situated between Dunkerque and Oostende, 5km from the Belgian frontier.
All year 3HEC ▦ ⚲ ⋔ ✕ ⊙ ♥ ⌀ ☎ 🅿 ⊞ lau ➧ ♨ ♊ ⁀P Prices: pitch 620-850

LOMBARDSIJDE West-Vlaanderen
Lombarde Elisabethlaan 4 ☎058 236839
All year 8.5HEC ▦ ⥤ ⋔ ♨ ♊ ✕ ⊙ ♥ ⌀ ⊞ ♨ 🅿 ⊞ lau ➧ ⁀PS
Prices: pitch 385-795 (incl 6 persons)

Zomerzon Elisabethlaan 1 ☎058 237396
All year 10HEC ▦ ⥤ ⋔ ⊙ ♥ ♨ ⚶ ☎ ☎ ⊞ ✻ lau ➧ ♨ ✕ ⌀ ⁀PS
Prices: pitch 225-420

LOPPEM West-Vlaanderen
Lac Loppem ☎050 822264
Leave A10/E40 at Torhout exit and turn right by the ESSO service station.
All year 9HEC ▦ ⚲ ⋔ ♨ ♊ ✕ ⊙ ♥ ⌀ ⁀ L ☎ 🅿 ⊞

MIDDELKERKE West-Vlaanderen
Myn Plezier Duinenweg 489 ☎059 300279
In wooded surroundings close to the castle. The camp shop only operates during high season.
Apr-10 Sep 3HEC ▦ ⥤ ⋔ ♨ ♊ ✕ ⊙ ♥ ⌀ ☎ lau ➧ ⁀S
Prices: A110 pitch 250

MONS Hainaut
Waux-Hall av St-Pierre 17 ☎065 337923
In a secluded position with direct access to the Parc du Waux-Hall.
All year 1.4HEC ▦ ⚲ ⋔ ⊙ ♥ ☎ ⊞ lau ➧ ♨ ♊ ✕ ⌀ ⚶ ⁀P
Prices: A80 V28 ♥28 ▲28

NIEUWPOORT West-Vlaanderen
Info Brugsesteenweg 49 ☎058 236037
A family site. Facilities for watersports.
On N67 between St Joris and Nieuwpoort.
28 Mar-12 Nov 24HEC ▦ ⚲ ⋔ ♨ ✕ ⊙ ♥ ♨ ⚶ ☎ ⁀ P ☎ ⊞ lau
Prices: pitch 655-920

OOSTENDE (OSTENDE) West-Vlaanderen
At BREDENE(5km NE)
Asterix Duinenstr 200 ☎059 331000
Camping Card Compulsory
All year 3HEC ⠿ ⚲ ⋔ ♨ ✕ ⊙ ♥ ♨ ☎ ♥ ⌀ ☎ 🅿 ⊞ lau ➧ ⌀
⁀LPS Prices: A100 ♥500

KACB Kon Astridlaan 53 ☎059 322475
Only Camping Card holders admitted.
Level grassland site on outskirts of village between other sites.
Off the N72 Oostende/Blankenberge road. Signposted.
All year 6.4HEC ▦ ⚲ ⋔ ♨ ⊙ ♥ ♨ ⁀ ⁀ S ☎ ⊞

ST SAUVEUR Hainaut
Hauts r des Vertes Feuilles 13 ☎069 768748
In a secluded, wooded situation within the Flemish Ardennes with fine facilities.
Signposted from Renaix.
All year 1HEC ▦ ⋔ ⊙ ♥ ⌀ ⚶ ☎ ⊞ lau ➧ ♨ ♊ ✕ ⁀P Prices: pitch 300

TOURNAI Hainaut
Orient Vieux Chemin de Mons 8 ☎069 222635
A pleasant site with good recreational facilities.
From motorway exit 'Tournai Est' head towards the town centre. Turn left at first crossroads and follow signs.
All year 20HEC ▦ ⚲ ⋔ ♨ ♊ ⊙ ♥ ☎ ⊞ lau ➧ ⌀ ⚶
Prices: A70 V70 ♥90 ▲70

WAREGEM West-Vlaanderen
Gemeentelijk Sportstadion Zuiderlaan 15 ☎056 609532
Access via E17 (Kortrijk-Gent).
Apr-Sep 1HEC ▦ ⚲ ⋔ ⊙ ♥ ♨ ⁀ P ☎ ⊞ ➧ ♨ ♊ ✕ ⌀ ⚶ ⁀R
Prices: A60 V45 ♥55 ▲55

WAUDREZ Hainaut
Gloriettes r de la Résistance 92 ☎064 332611
Apr-Oct 3HEC ▦ ⚲ ⋔ ♨ ♊ ✕ ⊙ ♥ ♨ ☎ ⊞ lau Prices: A90 V90
♥90 ▲90

WESTENDE West-Vlaanderen
KACB Bassevillestr 81 ☎058 237343
Situated between Westende and Lombardsijde towards the sea.
Camping Card Compulsory.
All year 6.5HEC ▦ ⚲ ⋔ ♨ ♊ ✕ ⊙ ♥ ⌀ ⌀ ☎ ☎ ⊞ lau ➧ ⚶ ⁀PS
Prices: pitch 610-750 (incl 5 persons)

WIERS Hainaut
Château du Biez r du Prince d'Espinoy 11
☎069 772126
All year 5HEC ▦ ⚲ ⋔ ♊ ✕ ⊙ ♥ ⌀ ⌀ ⚶ ☎ ⊞ ➧ ♨
Prices: pitch 200

North/Central

Most of this central region of Belgium is intensely agricultural, vast open plains are covered in crops, with large, compact villages in the valleys. Gent is the capital of the province of East Flanders - one of the most beautiful of Belgian cities with a wonderful medieval heart. Rivers and canals dissect the city, and it buzzes with commerce and industry, lively shopping streets and markets. Imposing buildings are reminders of a colourful past: the view from St Michael's Bridge takes in the towers of St Nicholas' Church (13th to 15th century), the Belfry (13th to 14th century) and the Cathedral of St Bavo (dating from the 10th century). Also in East Flanders, Oodenaarde is historically a textile centre; its tapestries are still renowned, and the town has many beautiful buildings dating from the late Middle Ages.
The centre of the south of this region, and capital of Belgium, is Brussels. Although some parts of the old Brussels remain intact, today it is essentially a modern cosmopolitan centre, the cultural and educational capital of Belgium, headquarters of the EC and NATO and many other international organisations. The city exudes vitality and prosperity, in keeping with its position as an international centre.

BACHTE-MARIA-LEERNE Oost-Vlaanderen
Groeneveld Groenevelddreef ☎09 3801014
23 Mar-11 Nov 2HEC ▦ ⚲ ⋔ ♨ ♊ ✕ ⊙ ♥ ⌀ ⌀ ☎ ☎ ⊞ lau
Prices: pitch 430-545

BEAUVECHAIN Brabant
Arpents Verts r Longue 115 ☎010 866993
Access via E411 exit 8 towards Louvain or E40 exit 23 towards Bevekom.
May-Aug 1HEC ▦ ⚲ ⋔ ♨ ♊ ✕ ⊙ ♥ ⌀ ⌀ ☎ ☎ ⊞ ✻ lau ➧ ✕ ⁀P
Prices: pitch 420-840 (incl 2 persons)

BEGYNENDYK Brabant
Roygaerden Betekomsesteenweg 75 ☎016 531087
Pitches are in wooded surroundings beside a lake.
All year 5HEC ▦ ⚲ ⋔ ⊙ ♥ ⌀ ⌀ ☎ ☎ 🅿 ⊞ lau ➧ ♨ ♊ ✕ ⁀LP
Prices: A150 ♥350 ▲100

BEVERE Oost-Vlaanderen
Vlaamse Ardennen Kortrijkstr 342 ☎055 315473
20 Mar-11 Nov 2HEC ▦ ➧ ⋔ ⊙ ♥ ♨ ⁀ LP ☎ lau ➧ ⌀ ⚶ ⁀R
Prices: pitch 520-820

GENT (GAND) Oost-Vlaanderen
Blaarmeersen Zuiderlaan 12 ☎09 2215399
Mar-15 Oct 6.5HEC ▦ ⚲ ⋔ ♨ ♊ ✕ ⊙ ♥ ⌀ ⌀ ☎ ⊞ lau ➧ ⚶ ⁀P
Prices: A110-120 V60-65 ♥120-130 ▲120-130

GRIMBERGEN Brabant
Grimbergen Veldkanstr 64 ☎02 2709597
Access via exit 7 on Bruxelles ringroad.
Apr-Oct 1.5HEC ▦ ⌾ ฅ ⊙ ⊟ ◿ ☲ ⊞ ⌂ lau ➧ ⅄ ⅄ ✕ ♨ ⇃P Prices:
A100 V50 ⊕100 ▲100

HEVERLEE Brabant
Ter Munck Kampingweg ☎016 238668
15 Jun-14 Sep 2.5HEC ▦ ⌾ ฅ ⅄ ✕ ⊙ ⊟ ⊡ ⊞ lau ➧ ⅄ Prices: pitch
360 (incl 2 persons)

HUIZINGEN Brabant
Provinvie Domein Provincie Domein 6 ☎02 3830026
500m from exit 15 on Brussels-Paris autoroute.
Camping Card Compulsory.
15 Mar-Sep 1.5HEC ▦ ⌴ ฅ ⊙ ⊟ ☲ ⊞ ➧ ⅄ ✕ ♨ ⇃P

LOONBEEK Brabant
Bergendal Biezen Str 81 ☎016 403904 & 470169
Camping Card Compulsory.
Access via E411 and RN253.
Mar-Oct 9HEC ▦ ◬ ⌾ ฅ ⊙ ⊟ ☲ ⊞ lau ➧ ⅄ ✕ ♨ ⅄ ⇃P Prices: pitch
300-440

ONKERZELE Oost-Vlaanderen
Gavers Onkerzelestr 280 ☎054 416324
All year 12HEC ▦ ⌾ ฅ ⅄ ✕ ⊙ ⊟ ♨ ⇃ LP ☲ ⊞ lau

STEKENE Oost-Vlaanderen
Eurocamping Baudeloo Heirweg 159 ☎03 7890663
All year 4.5HEC ▦ ➧ ฅ ⅄ ✕ ⊙ ⊟ ⅄ ⇃ P ☲ ⊞ lau ➧ ⅄ ✕ ♨ Prices:
A70 V70 ⊕70 ▲70

Reinaert Lunterbergstr 4 ☎03 7798525
All year 2HEC ▦ ⌾ ฅ ⅄ ✕ ⊙ ⊟ ⅄ ☲ ⊞ lau ➧ ⅄ ♨ Prices: A70 V60
⊕60 ▲60

WACHTEBEKE Oost-Vlaanderen
Puyenbroeck Puyenbrug 1A ☎09 3557607
Apr-Sep 8HEC ▦ ⌴ ฅ ⊙ ⊟ ☲ ⊞ ⌂ lau ➧ ⅄ ✕ ⇃LPR

North East

The natural entrance to this region is Antwerp. One of the great ports of Europe and a fascinating city to visit, it is dominated by the elegant tower of its cathedral. The cathedral's graceful exterior is complemented by a spacious and rich interior, with some fine Rubens masterpieces. Near the cathedral is the Grote Markt, with an impressive town hall, and several guildhalls with wonderful façades. The extensive old city contains many fine old buildings and some fascinating museums, including the Plantin Moretus Museum, and Rubens' House.
Other interesting towns in this region include Turnhout, a commercial centre with a modern town hall and lovely church in the market place; Mechelen - an ecclesiastical centre with a particularly well preserved old town; Tongeren, known as the oldest town in Belgium and containing many interesting reminders of the past; The quiet picturesque town of Zoutleeuw, with its lovely 13th-century church; Lier, with its attractive market place; and the old abbey town of Averbode.

ANTWERPEN (ANVERS) Antwerpen
De Molen Thonetlaan ☎03 2196090
Apr-Sep 1.3HEC ▦ ⌾ ฅ ⊙ ⊟ ⊞ ☲ ⊞ lau ➧ ⅄ ⅄ ✕ ⇃PR Prices:
A35 V35 ⊕35 ▲35

BRECHT Antwerpen
Floreal Het Veen Eekhoornlaan 1, St-Job In't Goor ☎03 6361327
Leave Autoroute E19 at exit St Job In't Goor.
Apr-Sep 7.5HEC ▦ ⌾ ฅ ⅄ ✕ ⊙ ⊟ ⊞ ⇃ R ☲ ⊞ lau ➧ ⅄ ♨ Prices:
A90 pitch 250

EKSEL Limburg
Lage Kempen Kiefhoeki str 19 ☎011 402243
Etr-2 Nov 3.5HEC ▦ ⌾ ฅ ⅄ ✕ ⊙ ⊟ ◿ ☲ ⊞ ⇃ P ☲ lau Prices:
A110 V70 ⊕100 ▲110

GIERLE Antwerpen
Lilse Bergen Strandweg 6 ☎014 557901
E39 exit 22.
All year 6HEC ➧ ฅ ⅄ ⅄ ✕ ⊙ ⊟ ◿ ☲ ⊞ ⇃ L ⊡ ⊞ lau ➧ ⇃P Prices:
pitch 370-550

HOUTHALEN Limburg
Hengelhoef ☎089 382500
Apr-Nov 15HEC ▦ ➧ ฅ ⅄ ✕ ⊙ ⊟ ◿ ⊞ ☲ ⊞ ⌂ lau ➧ ⇃LP

KASTERLEE Antwerpen
Houtum Houtum 51 ☎014 852365
All year 9HEC ▦ ⌾ ฅ ⊙ ⊟ ◿ ⊞ ⇃ R ☲ lau ➧ ⅄ ⅄ ✕ ⇃P ⊞ Prices:
A99 pitch 177

LOMMEL Limburg
Luna Strand Luikersteenweg 313a ☎011 643708
On Leopoldsburg road (N446).
Apr-Sep 52HEC ▦ ⌾ ฅ ⅄ ✕ ⊙ ⊟ ◿ ☲ ⇃ LPR ☲ ⊞

MOL Antwerpen
Zilvermeer Zilvermeerlaan 2 ☎014 816021
A pleasant lakeside site with good recreational facilities.
All year 145HEC ▦ ⸪ ⌾ ฅ ⅄ ✕ ⊙ ⊟ ◿ ☲ ⇃ L ☲ ⊡ ⊞ lau
Prices: pitch 300-440 (incl 4 persons)

OPGLABBEEK Limburg
Jeugdparadijs Speeltuinstr 8 ☎089 854347
Apr-Sep 8HEC ▦ ⌾ ฅ ⅄ ✕ ⊙ ⊟ ⇃ P ☲ ➧ ♨ Prices: A75 pitch
240

REKEM Limburg
Sonnevijer Heidestr 103 ☎089 713048
4km S of Autoroute E39, exit 'Lanaken'.
All year 30HEC ▦ ➧ ฅ ⅄ ✕ ⊙ ⊟ ◿ ☲ ⇃ LP ☲ ⊞ lau

RETIE Antwerpen
Berkenstrand Brand 76-78 ☎014 377590
3km NE on road to Postel.
Apr-Sep 10HEC ▦ ⌾ ฅ ⅄ ✕ ⊙ ⊟ ◿ ☲ ☲ ⇃ L ☲ Prices: A75
V75 ⊕75 ▲75

VORST-LAAKDAL Antwerpen
Kasteel Meerlaer Verboekt 105 ☎013 661420
E313 exit 24 towards Hosselt or exit 24 towards Antwerp.
All year 6HEC ▦ ⸪ ➧ ฅ ⅄ ✕ ⊙ ⊟ ☲ ☲ ⊞ lau ➧ ⅄ ✕ ♨ Prices:
A67 V67 ⊕67 ▲67

ZONHOVEN Limburg
Berkenhof Teutseweg 33 ☎011 814439
Apr-Oct 3.5HEC ▦ ⌾ ฅ ⅄ ✕ ⊙ ⊟ ◿ ☲ ☲ ☲ Prices: A70 pitch
150

Holsteenbron Hengelhoelseweg 9 ☎011 817140
Apr-15 Nov 6HEC ▦ ⌾ ➧ ฅ ✕ ⊙ ⊟ ◿ ☲ ☲ ⊞ lau ➧ ⇃P

South East

This region is known as the great garden of the Ardennes - dense forests, hills rising to over 2,000ft, imposing chalk cliffs, deep, wide valleys and serene reservoirs. Small villages, ancient monasteries, high fortress citadels and picturesque towns - with imposing civic buildings and half-timbered dwellings, dot the countryside. The graceful Meuse flows through the north of this area; historically an important north-south artery. Today barges frequent its waters, and the 'castles of Namur' adorn its banks. There are a number of impressive caves in the region - the caves at Han-sur-Lesse are remarkable, stretching some miles underground, with fantastic formations.

Towns set on the River Meuse include Dinant, overlooked by the mass of its castle; picturesque Namur, between the banks of the Meuse and the Sambre, also dominated by its castle; and cosmopolitan Liège, a bustling mix of culture and industry. La Roche-en-Ardenne is beautifully set in its deep valley on a loop of the Ourthe, and Spa is a traditional resort with thermal springs.

AISCHE-EN-REFAIL Namur
Manoir de lá Bas rte de Gembloux 180 ☎081 655353
5km W of Eghezée.
Apr-Oct 12HEC ▦ ⊶ ⋔ ⅃ ⅂ ✕ ⊙ ⊟ ⌂ ⃗ P ☎ ⊞ ➧ ⌀ Prices: A80 pitch 130-185

AMBERLOUP Luxembourg
Tonny r Tonny 35-36 ☎061 688285
In a pleasant valley beside the River Ourthe with fine sporting facilities.
All year 3HEC ▦ ⅃ ⋔ ⅃ ⅂ ✕ ⊙ ⊟ ⌀ ⌂ ⊞ ⋔ ⃗ R ₽ ⊞ lau Prices: A75 pitch 250

AMONINES Luxembourg
Val de l'Aisne Blier ☎086 477053
All year 15HEC ▦ ⊶ ⋔ ⅃ ✕ ⊙ ⊟ ⌂ ⃗ R ☎ ⊞ lau Prices: pitch 60

AVE-ET-AUFFE Namur
Roptai r Roptai 34 ☎084 388319
The site is located in a hilly situation in pretty clearings amidst a large forest about 1km from the village.
Feb-Dec 10HEC ▦ ⅃ ⋔ ⅃ ⅂ ✕ ⊙ ⊟ ⌀ ⌂ ⊞ ⋔ P ☎ ⊞ lau
Prices: pitch 540-680 (incl 4 persons)

BARVAUX-SUR-OURTHE Luxembourg
Hazalles Chainrue 77a ☎086 211642
Apr-Oct 0.3HEC ▦ ⅃ ⋔ ⊙ ⊟ ⌂ ⊞ ⊞ lau ➧ ⅃ ⅂ ✕ ⌀ ⋔PR
Prices: A55 V40 ⊞85

Rives de l'Ourthe r Inzespres 70 ☎086 211730
Apr-Sep 1.5HEC ▦ ⅃ ⋔ ⅂ ✕ ⊙ ⊟ ⌂ ⋔ R ☎ ⊞ ➧ ⅃ ✕ ⌀ ⋔LP
Prices: A70 pitch 140

BERTRIX Luxembourg
Info rte de Mortehan ☎061 412281
S of town beyond the church. Signposted from N884.
16 Feb-13 Nov 14HEC ▦ ⅃ ⋔ ⅃ ⅂ ✕ ⊙ ⊟ ⌀ ⌂ ⋔ P ☎ ⊞ lau
Prices: pitch 283-850

BONNERT Luxembourg
Officiel rte de Bastogne 373 ☎063 226582
E of E9-N4.
All year 1.4HEC ▦ ⅃ ⋔ ⅂ ✕ ⊙ ⊟ ⌀ ⌂ ⌂ ⋔ P ☎ ₽ ⊞ lau ➧ ⋔LP

BÜLLINGEN (BULLANGE) Liège
Hêtraie Rotheck 264 ☎080 642413
This site is situated on a sloping meadow near a fish pond and is surrounded by groups of beautiful beech trees and conifers. Leave village in direction of Amel then left and continue for 2km. Signposted.
15 Apr-10 Nov 3HEC ▦ ⅃ ➧ ⋔ ⅂ ✕ ⊙ ⊟ ⌂ ⋔ P ☎ ⊞ lau ➧ ⅃ ✕ ⌀ ⌂ ⋔L Prices: A70 V45 ⊞45 ▲45

BURE Luxembourg
Parc la Clusure 30 chemin de la Clusure ☎084 366080
Pleasant site with good facilities in the centre of the Ardennes.
Access from E411 and N846 via Tellin.
All year 12HEC ▦ ⅃ ⋔ ⅃ ⅂ ✕ ⊙ ⊟ ⌀ ⌂ ⌂ ⋔ PR ☎ ⊞ lau
Prices: pitch 490-900 (incl 2 persons)

BURG-REULAND Liège
Hohenbusch Grüfflingen ☎080 227523
All year 5HEC ▦ ⅃ ⋔ ✕ ⊙ ⊟ ⌀ ⌂ ⌂ ⋔ P lau Prices: A125 V100 ⊞175 ▲100

BÜTGENBACH Liège
Worriken Worriken-Centre 1 ☎080 446358
Situated on the shores of a lake.
Closed 12 Nov-9 Dec 8HEC ▦ ⅃ ⋔ ⅂ ✕ ⊙ ⊟ ⋔ LP ☎ ⊞ lau ➧ ⅃ ✕ ⌀ ⌂ ⋔R Prices: pitch 560 (incl 4 persons)

CHEVETOGNE Namur
Domaine Provincial ☎083 688821
All year 0.5HEC ▦ ⅃ ⋔ ⅃ ⅂ ✕ ⊙ ⊟ ⌂ ⋔ P ☎ ₽ ⊞ ➧ ⌀ ⌂ Prices: pitch 464-545 (incl 4 persons)

COO-STAVELOT Liège
Cascade Chemin des Faravennes 5 ☎080 684312
Apr-Oct 0.7HEC ▦ ⊶ ⋔ ✕ ⊙ ⊟ ⋔ R ☎ ⊞ ➧ ✕ ⌀ ⌂ ⋔LP Prices: A70 pitch 200-260

DOCHAMPS Luxembourg
Petite Suisse r du Panorama ☎084 444030
All year 6.5HEC ▦ ⅃ ⋔ ⅃ ⅂ ✕ ⊙ ⊟ ⌀ ⋔ P ☎ ⊞ lau

EUPEN Liège
'An der Hill' Hutte 46 ☎087 744617
SW of town via N67 towards Monschau.
All year 0.6HEC ▦ ⅃ ⋔ ⅂ ✕ ⊙ ⊟ ⌀ ☎ ₽ ⊞ lau ➧ ⅃ ⋔P Prices: A100 V120 ⊞160 ▲130

FLORENVILLE Luxembourg
Rosière Rive Gauche de la Semois ☎061 311937
In wooded surroundings close to the town centre.
Apr-Oct 8HEC ▦ ⅃ ⋔ ⅃ ⅂ ✕ ⊙ ⊟ ⌂ ⋔ PR ☎ ⊞ lau Prices: A70 V30 ⊞250 ▲200

FORRIÈRES Luxembourg
Pré du Blason r de la Ramée 30 ☎084 212867
This well-kept site lies on a meadow surrounded by wooded hills and is completely divided into pitches and crossed by rough gravel drives.Off N49 Masbourg road.
Apr-Sep 3HEC ▦ ➧ ⋔ ⅃ ⅂ ✕ ⊙ ⌀ ⌂ ⋔ R ☎ ⊞ lau ➧ ✕ Prices: A78 ⊞250 ▲180

GEDINNE Namur
Melezes rte Dinant-Bouillon ☎061 588560
All year 2HEC ▦ ⅃ ⋔ ⅃ ⅂ ✕ ⊙ ⊟ ⌂ ⌂ ₽ ⊞ lau

GEMMENICH Liège
Kon Tiki Terstraeten 141 ☎087 785973
All year 12HEC ▦ ⅃ ⋔ ⅃ ⅂ ✕ ⊙ ⊟ ⌀ ⌂ ⋔ PR ☎ ⊞ lau Prices: pitch 350-520 (incl 5 persons)

GOUVY Luxembourg
Lac de Cherapont Cherapont 2 ☎080 517082
Apr-Oct 10HEC ▦ ⅃ ⋔ ⅃ ⅂ ✕ ⊙ ⊟ ⌂ ⌂ ⋔ LR ☎ ⊞ lau ➧ ⌀ Prices: A60 V50 ⊞60 ▲60

HABAY-LA-NEUVE Luxembourg
Portail de la Forêt r du Bon-Bois 3 ☎063 422312
Parklike, terraced site on a hill surrounded by woodland.
Turn off N48 and follow signs.
Closed 15 Dec-Jan 4HEC ▦ ⅃ ⋔ ⅃ ⅂ ✕ ⊙ ⊟ ⌀ ⌂ ⋔ P ☎ ⊞ lau ➧ ⋔R Prices: pitch 500-550 (incl 4 persons)

HAMOIR-SUR-OURTHE Liège
Dessous Hamoir r de Moulin 31 ☎086 388925
15 Mar-15 Nov 3.5HEC ▦ ⊶ ⋔ ⊙ ⊟ ⋔ R ☎ ⊞ lau ➧ ⅃ ⅂ ✕ ⌀ ⌂ ⋔LPRS Prices: A80 V50 ⊞100 ▲90

HOGNE Namur
Relais 16 r de Serinchamps ☎084 311580
Take N4 from Courriere to Hogne via Marche.
Closed 15 Jan-15 Feb 10HEC ▦ ⊶ ⋔ ⅃ ✕ ⊙ ⊟ ⌀ ⌂ ⌂ ⋔ L ☎ ⊞ lau ➧ ⅃

HOUFFALIZE Luxembourg
Chasse et Pêche r de la Roche 63 ☎061 288314
3km NW off E25.
All year 2HEC ▦ ➧ ⋔ ⅂ ✕ ⊙ ⊟ ⌀ ⌀ ⋔ R ☎ ⊞ lau ➧ ⅃ ⋔P Prices: A100 V85 ⊞85 ▲70-85

Moulin de Rensiwez Moulin de Rensiwez 1 ☎061 289027
Isolated terraced site by the River Ourthe around an old water-mill.
Shop open July and August only.
All year 8HEC ▦ 🚰 🏕 🛎 🍴 ✕ ⊙ 🚱 🔌 🐟 ⚡ R 🅿 ⊞ ≋ lau Prices:
pitch 440 (incl 4 persons)

JAMOIGNE *Luxembourg*

Faing ☎061 330272
A municipal camp on a meadow situated behind a sports ground
which separates the site from the road.
400m W on N44.
Jan 3.5HEC 🚰 🏕 🍴 ✕ ⊙ 🚱 ⚡ R 🔔 lau ✦ 🛒 🔌 🚿 ⚡P ⊞ Prices:
A88 pitch 166-240

LOUVEIGNÉ *Liège*

Moulin du Rouge-Thier Rouge-Thier 8 ☎014 608341
Apr-Oct 7HEC 🏃 🏕 🍴 ✕ ⊙ 🚱 🔌 🚿 ⚡ P 🔔 lau Prices: pitch 410 (incl
4 persons)

MALONNE *Namur*

Trieux r des Três 99 ☎081 445583
Apr-Oct 2HEC ▦ 🚰 🏕 🛎 ⊙ 🚱 🔌 🐟 🚿 🔔 ⊞ lau ✦ 🛒 ✕ Prices: A85
V100 🚐100 ▲100

MARCHE-EN-FAMENNE *Luxembourg*

Euro Camping Paola r du Panorama 10 ☎084 311704
A long site on a hill with a beautiful view. The only noise comes from
a railway line, which passes right by the site.
Take road towards Hotton, turn right after cemetery and continue
1km.
All year 13HEC ▦ 🔥 🚰 🏕 🍴 ✕ ⊙ 🚱 🚿 🔔 ⊞ ✦ 🛒 ✕ 🔌 Prices: A65
pitch 330

NEUFCHÂTEAU *Luxembourg*

International Spineuse rte de Florenville ☎061 277320
Camp shop operates July-Aug only.
Situated 2km from Florenville in the direction of Neufchâteau.

15 Feb-15 Dec 2HEC ▦ 🚰 🏃 🛎 🍴 ✕ ⊙ 🚱 🔌 🚿 ⚡ R 🔔 ⊞ lau Prices:
A85 pitch 250-300

Lac rte de Florenville ☎061 277615
All year 0.7HEC ▦ 🚰 🏃 🍴 ✕ ⊙ 🚱 🚿 🔔 ⚡ LPR 🔔 ⊞ lau ✦ 🛒

OLLOY-SUR-VIROIN *Namur*

Try des Baudets r de la Champagne ☎060 390108
In a peaceful situation on the edge of a forest.
All year 12HEC ▦ 🚰 🏃 🍴 ✕ ⊙ 🚱 🚿 🔔 lau ✦ 🛒 ✕ 🔌 ⚡LPRS
Prices: A20 pitch 416

OTEPPE *Liège*

Hirondelle Château d'Oteppe ☎085 711131
Ideal family site with modern facilities.
N of town between E40 and E42. Signposted.
Apr-Oct 60HEC 🚰 🏃 🏕 🍴 ✕ ⊙ 🚱 🔌 🐟 ⚡ P 🔔 ⊞ lau Prices:
A90-110 pitch 180-260

POLLEUR *Liège*

Polleur r de Congrès 90 ☎087 541033
Signposted from A27/E42.
Apr-1 Nov 3.7HEC ▦ 🏃 🏕 🛎 🍴 ✕ ⊙ 🚱 🔌 🐟 ⚡ PR 🔔 ⊞ lau Prices:
A101-116 V101-116 🚐101-116 ▲101-116

PURNODE *Namur*

Bocq av de la Vallée ☎082 612269
Apr-Sep 2HEC ▦ 🚰 🏃 🍴 ✕ ⊙ 🚱 ⚡ R 🔔 ⊞ ✦ 🛒 🔌 ⚡P Prices: A90
V90 🚐90 ▲90

REMOUCHAMPS *Liège*

Eden r de Trois Ponts 92 ☎041 844165
Apr-Oct 3.5HEC ▦ 🚰 ✦ 🏃 🍴 ✕ ⊙ 🚱 🔌 🚿 🔔 ⚡ R 🔔 ⊞ Prices: A70
pitch 150-300

RENDEUX *Luxembourg*

Festival rte de la Roche 89 ☎032 84477371
In unspoiled surroundings beside the River Ourthe.
Mar-Sep 12HEC ▦ 🚰 🏃 🛎 🍴 ✕ ⊙ 🚱 🔌 🐟 🚿 🔔 ⚡ R 🔔 ⊞ lau Prices:
pitch 600-670 (incl 4 persons)

RIVIÈRE *Namur*

7 Meuses r des Cortils 43 ☎081 412822
All year 1.5HEC ▦ 🚰 🏃 ✕ ⊙ 🚱 🔌 🚐 ⚡ P 🔔 ⊞ ✦ ⚡R

ROBERTVILLE *Liège*

Plage 33 rte des Bains ☎080 446658
All year 1.8HEC ▦ 🚰 🏃 🛎 🍴 ✕ ⊙ 🚱 🚿 🚐 ⚡ LPR 🔔 ⊞

ROCHE-EN-ARDENNE, LA *Luxembourg*

Grillon r des Echarées ☎084 412062
Etr-Oct 3.5HEC 🚰 🏃 🛎 ⊙ 🚱 🔌 🚿 ⚡ R 🔔 ⊞ lau ✦ ✕ ⚡P Prices:
A75 pitch 220

Lohan 20a rte de Houffalize ☎084 411545
In a park, on N bank of the River Ourthe.
Apr-Oct 4HEC ▦ 🚰 🏃 🛎 🍴 ✕ ⊙ 🚱 🔌 🐟 ⚡ R 🔔 ⊞ ≋ lau Prices:
A75 pitch 220-250

Ourthe ☎084 411459
Well kept site, beside the River Ourthe.
On SW bank of the Ourthe below the N34.
15 Mar-15 Oct 3HEC ▦ ✦ 🏃 🛎 ⊙ 🚱 🔌 🐟 ⚡ R 🔔 ⊞ lau ✦ ✕

ROCHEHAUT *Luxembourg*

Laviot r Laviot 6 ☎061 466314
Apr-15 Oct 6HEC ▦ 🏃 🏃 🛎 🍴 ✕ ⊙ 🚱 🔌 🚐 ⚡ R 🔔 lau ✦ ✕ 🚿

SART-LEZ-SPA *Liège*

Touring Club Stockay 17 ☎087 474400
Signposted from the E of Spa.
All year 5.5HEC ▦ 🚰 🏃 🛎 🍴 ✕ ⊙ 🚱 🚿 🔔 ⊞ lau ✦ 🔌 ⚡LP

SCHÖNBERG *Liège*

Waldecho Weberbach 28A ☎080 542222
Spread over two valleys in wooded surroundings.
Turn W off N26 at Km11.1 and continue for 0.5km.
Apr-15 Nov 3.8HEC 🚰 🏃 ✕ ⊙ 🚱 🔌 ⚡ P 🔔 ⊞ lau ✦ 🛒 ✕ 🔌 🚿

SIPPENAEKEN *Liège*

Vieux Moulin 114 Zebruggen ☎087 784255
Apr-Sep 8HEC ▥ ⌕ ♠ ⚡ ✕ ⊙ ⊟ ⚑ ⊞ ⚓ PR ☎ ⊞ lau

SPA *Liège*

Parc des Sources av de la Sauvenière 141 ☎087 772311
S of town centre on N32.
Apr-Oct 2.5HEC ▥ ⌕ ♠ ⚡ ✕ ⊙ ⊟ ⚑ ⊞ lau ➡ ⚡ ✕ ⚓P ⊞
Prices: A9500 V70 ⚑135 ▲135

SPRIMONT *Liège*

Tultay r de Tultay 22 ☎041 3821162
All year 1.5HEC ▥ ⌕ ♠ ⚡ ✕ ⊙ ⊟ ☎ ⊞ ⚲ lau ➡ ⚡ ✕ ⚑ ⚓PR
Prices: A100 pitch 150

STAVELOT *Liège*

Domaine de l'Eau Rouge Cheneux 25 ☎080 863075
All year 3.8HEC ▥ ⌕ ♠ ⚡ ✕ ⊙ ⊟ ⚑ ⚪ ⚓ R ☎ ⊞ lau

STER *Liège*

Francopole ☎087 275099
In a secluded position beside the Eau Ronge River.
Off N32 in Francorchamps to Ster and Verviers, then turn right.
All year 10HEC ▥ ⌕ ♠ ♠ ⚡ ✕ ⊙ ⊟ ⚪ ☎ ⚓ R ☎ ⊞ lau

TENNEVILLE *Luxembourg*

Pont de Berguème r Berguème 9 ☎084 455443
Turn off E40/N4 towards Berguème then turn right.
All year 3HEC ▥ ⌕ ♠ ⚡ ✕ ⊙ ⊟ ⚑ ⚪ ☎ ☎ ⚓ PR ⏚ ⊞ lau ➡ ✕
Prices: A80 pitch 130

THOMMEN-REULAND *Liège*

Hohenbusch Luxemburgstr 44 ☎080 227523
All year 5HEC ▥ ⌕ ♠ ⚡ ✕ ⊙ ⊟ ⚪ ☎ ⚓ P ☎ lau

TINTIGNY *Luxembourg*

Chênefleur ☎063 444078
Apr-15 Oct 7HEC ▥ ⌕ ♠ ⚡ ✕ ⊙ ⊟ ⚪ ⚑ ☎ ⚓ PR ☎ ⊞ lau ➡ ⚡ ✕

VIELSALM *Luxembourg*

Salm chemin de la Vallée ☎080 216241
All year 2.5HEC ▥ ➡ ⚡ ✕ ⊙ ⊟ ⚑ ☎ ⚓ R ☎ lau ➡ ⚡ ✕ ⚑ ⚓LP

VIRTON *Luxembourg*

Vallée de Rabais r du Bonlieu ☎063 570144
All year 5HEC ▥ ⌕ ♠ ⊙ ⊟ ☎ ⚓ L ☎ ⊞ lau ➡ ⚡ ✕ ⚑ ⚑ Prices:
pitch 400-630

WAIMES *Liège*

Anderegg Bruyerès 4 ☎080 679393
All year 1.5HEC ▥ ⌕ ♠ ⚡ ✕ ⊙ ⊟ ⚪ ☎ ➡ ✕ Prices: A70 pitch
140

FRANCE

France, rich in history and natural beauty, is bordered by six countries: Belgium, Germany, Italy, Luxembourg, Spain and Switzerland.

The country offers a great variety of scenery from the mountain ranges of the Alps and the Pyrénées to the attractive river valleys of the Loire, Rhône and Dordogne. And with some 1,800 miles of coastline, which includes the golden sands of the Côte-d'Azur, there is a landscape appealing to everyone's taste.

The climate of France is temperate but varies considerably. The Mediterranean coast enjoys a sub-tropical climate with hot summers, whilst along the coast of Brittany the climate is very similar to that of Devon and Cornwall. The language is, of course, French and this is spoken throughout the country, although there are many local dialects and variations.

France has an enormous number of campsites, over 10,000 of them under the auspices of the *French Federation of Camping and Caravanning.*

There are *castels et camping* caravanning sites in the grounds of châteaux (castles) and many are included in this guide. On sites in state forests, *forêts domaniales,* it is necessary to apply to the *garde forestier* for permission to camp and evidence of insurance must be produced (such as the *camping card*). Opening periods vary widely and some sites are open all year. Local information offices (see *Tourist information* above) can supply detailed information about sites in their locality.

Camping information can also be obtained from

FACTS AND FIGURES

Capital: Paris
Language: French
IDD code: 33.
Please note that all French telephone numbers have changed since our press date. Consult the Contents page for instructions on the new system.
To call the UK dial 00 44
Currency: Franc (*Fr*1 = 100 centimes). At the time of going to press £1 = *Frs*7.79.
Local time: GMT + 1 (summer GMT + 2)
Emergency Services: Police 17; Fire 18; Ambulance - dial number given in callbox, or, if no number given, the police.
Business hours-
Banks: Mon-Fri 09.00-12.00 & 14.00-16.00
Shops: Mon-Sat 09.00-18.00 (times may vary for food shops)
Average daily temperature:
Paris

Jan 3°C	Jul 18°C
Mar 6°C	Sep 15°C
May 13°C	Nov 6°C

Tourist Information:
UK French Government Tourist Office
178 Piccadilly
London W1V 0AL
☎0891 244123 (premium rate information line; 08.30 - 21.30 weekdays, 09.00 - 17.00 Saturdays)
Monaco Government Tourist and Convention Office
3-18 Chelsea Garden Market
Chelsea Harbour
London SW10 0XE
☎0171-352 9962
USA French Government Tourist Office
610 First Ave
New York, NY 10020
☎(212) 757 1125
Camping Card: not compulsory, but advisable when using *Castels et Camping* caravanning sites and also the *forts domaniales*.

500 *Total* petrol service stations which have been equipped with information offices. During July and August there is over-demand around the French coasts, particularly on the Mediterranean.

All graded sites must display their official classification, site regulations, capacity and current charges at the site entrance. Some sites have inclusive charges per pitch, others show basic prices per person, vehicle and space, with extra facilities like showers, swimming pools and ironing incurring additional charges. In practice, most campsites charge from midday to midday, with each part day being counted as a full day. Reductions for children are usually allowed up to 7 years of age; there is generally no charge for children under 3.

Off-site camping in the South of France is restricted because of the danger of fire; in other parts, camping is possible, provided that permission has been obtained, although camping is seldom allowed near the water's edge, or at a large seaside resort. Casual camping is prohibited in state forests, national parks in the Landes and Gironde *départements* and in the Camargue. Camping in an unauthorised place renders offenders liable to prosecution or confiscation of equipment, or both, especially in the South. However, an overnight stop on parking areas of some motorways is tolerated, but make sure you do not contravene local regulations; overnight stops in a lay-by are not permitted. Camping is not permitted in *Monaco*. Caravans in transit are allowed but it is forbidden to park them.

HOW TO GET THERE

For details of the *AA European Routes Service* please consult the Contents page.

Apart from the direct crossing by the Channel Tunnel (Folkestone-Calais, 35mins), the following ferry services are available:

Short ferry crossings

From **Dover** to **Calais** takes 75-90min or 45 mins by Lynx catamaran.

Longer ferry crossings

From **Ramsgate** to **Dunkerque** (Dunkirk) takes 2hrs 30mins.

From **Newhaven** to **Dieppe** takes 4hrs or 2hrs 15 mins by Lynx catermaran.

From **Portsmouth** to **Le Havre** takes 5hrs 30mins (day) - 7hrs 30mins/8hrs (night); to **Caen** takes 6hrs; to **Cherbourg** takes 5hrs (day) - 7hrs/8hrs 15mins (night); to **St Malo** takes 8hrs 45mins/11hrs 30mins (night)

From **Poole** to **Cherbourg** takes 4hrs 15mins; to **St Malo**† 8hrs

From **Plymouth** to **Roscoff** takes 6hrs

From **Southampton** to **Cherbourg** takes 5hrs

†Summer service only

Fast Hoverspeed services

Hoverspeed/Hovercraft from Dover to Calais takes 35 mins. Hoverspeed/Seacat catamaran from Folkestone to Boulogne takes 55 mins.

Car sleeper trains

A daily service operates from Calais to the south of the country.

MOTORING & GENERAL INFORMATION

The information given here is specific to France. It **must** be read in conjunction with the European ABC at the front of the book, which covers those regulations which are common to many countries.

British Embassy/Consulates*

The British Embassy is located at 75383 Paris Cedex 08, 35 rue du Faubourg St-Honoré ☎0144513100; consular section 16 rue d'Anjou ☎0142663810. There are British Consulates in Bordeaux, Lille, Lyon and Marseille; there are British Consulates with Honorary Consuls in Biarritz, Boulogne-sur-Mer, Calais, Cherbourg, Dunkerque (Dunkirk), Le Havre, Nantes, Nice, St Malo-Dinard and Toulouse.

Childen in cars

Child under 10 not permitted to travel as front seat passenger, with the exception of baby - up to 9 months and less than 9kg weight - in rear-facing seat. Childern under 10 in rear must use restraint system appropriate to age and weight. **Note**: Under no circumstances should a rear facing restraint be used in a front seat with an airbag.

Currency

There are no restrictions on the amount of French or foreign currency that can be taken in or out of France. However, amounts over Fr50,000 should be declared if re-exportation likely.

Banks close at midday on the day prior to a national holiday, and all day on Monday if the holiday falls on a Tuesday.

Dimensions and weight restrictions

Private **cars** and towed **trailers** or **caravans** are restricted to the following dimensions - height, no

restrictions, but 4 metres is a recommended maximum; width, 2.50 metres; length, 12 metres (excluding towing device). The maximum permitted overall length of vehicle/trailer or caravan combination is 18 metres.
If the weight of the trailer exceeds that of the towing vehicle, see also *Speed limits* below.

Driving licence*

(see also *Speed limits* below)
A valid UK or Republic of Ireland licence is acceptable in France. The minimum age at which visitors from UK or Republic of Ireland may use a temporarily imported motorcycle (over 80cc) or car is 18. Visitors may use temporarily imported motorcycles of up to 80cc at 16.

Foodstuffs*

There are no limits on the importation of foodstuffs obtained duty and tax paid within the EC. Up to 500g of coffee (200g of coffee extract) and 100g of tea (40g of tea extract) purchased duty free or outside the EC may be imported free of duty and tax. However, coffee bought duty-free outside the EC cannot be imported by visitors under 15 years of age. Visitors may also import up to 10kg of fully cooked meat and meat products including poultry (if from EC) for personal consumption and not for resale. Meat and meat products from Africa are prohibited

Lights*

It is obligatory to use headlights, as driving on sidelights only is not permitted. In fog, mist or poor visibility during the day, either two fog lamps or two dipped headlights must be switched on in addition to two sidelights. It is also compulsory for motorcyclists riding machines exceeding 125cc to use dipped headlights during the day. Failure to comply with these regulations will lead to an on-the-spot deposit(see *Police fines* in the Continental ABC).
It is recommended that visiting motorists equip their vehicles with a set of replacement bulbs. Drivers able to replace a faulty bulb when requested to do so by the police will not avoid a fine, but may avoid the cost and inconvenience of a garage call out. Yellow tinted headlights are no longer necessary in France.

Motoring club*

The AA is affiliated to the **Automobile Club National (ACN)** whose office is at 75009 Paris, 5 rue Auber ☎44515399.

Parking*

In Paris it is absolutely forbidden to stop or park on a *red route*. The east-west route includes the left bank of the Seine and the Quai de la Megisserie; the north-south route includes the Avenue du Général Leclerc, part of the Boulevard St Michel, the Rue de Rivoli, the Boulevards Sébastopol, Strasbourg, Barbès and Ornano, Rue Lafayette and Avenue Jean Jaurès. Cars towing caravans are prohibited from the *blue zone* between 14.00 and 20.30hrs. Cars towing trailers with an overall surface of 10sq metres or more may neither circulate nor park in the central *green zone* between 14.00-20.30hrs, except on Sundays and Public Holidays. Vehicle combinations with an overall surface exceeding 16sq metres may neither circulate nor park in the *green zone* between 08.00-20.30hrs. Those wishing to cross Paris during these hours with vehicle/trailer combinations, can use the *Boulevard Périphérique*, although the route is heavily congested, except during Public holiday periods. In some parts of the *green zone*, parking is completely forbidden. It is prohibited to park caravans, even for a limited period, not only in the *green zone* but in almost all areas of Paris.

Priority including Roundabouts*

In built-up areas, you must give way to traffic coming from the right - *priorit droite*. However, at roundabouts with signs bearing the words *"Vous n'avez pas la priorité" or "Cédez le passage"* traffic **on** the roundabout has priority; Where no such sign exists, traffic **entering** the roundabout has priority. Outside built-up areas, all main roads of any importance have right of way. This is indicated by a red-bordered triangle showing a black cross on a white background with the words *"Passage Protégé"* underneath; or a red-bordered triangle showing a pointed black upright with horizontal bar on a white background; or a yellow square within a white square with points vertical.

Roads

France has a very comprehensive network of roads, and surfaces are generally good; exceptions are usually signposted *Chauseé deformeé*. The camber is often severe and the edges rough.

During July and August, and especially at weekends, traffic on main roads is likely to be very heavy. Special signs are erected to indicate alternative routes with the least traffic congestion. Wherever they appear, it is usually advantageous to follow them, although you cannot be absolutely sure of gaining time. The alternative routes are quiet, but they are not as wide as the main roads. They are **not** suitable for caravans.

A free road map showing the marked alternative routes, plus information centres and petrol stations open 24 hours, is available from service stations displaying the *Bison Futé* poster (a Red Indian chief in full war bonnet). These maps are also available from *Syndicats d'Initiative* and information offices.

Speed limits*

Built-up areas 50kph (31mph)
Outside built-up areas on normal roads 90kph (55mph); on dual-carriageways separated by a central reservation 110kph (69mph).
On Motorways 130kph (80mph). **Note** The minimum speed in the fast lane on a level stretch of motorway during good daytime visibility is 80kph (49mph), and drivers travelling below this speed are liable to be fined. The maximum speed on the Paris ring road is 80kph (49mph) and, on other urban stretches of motorway, 110kph (69mph).

In **fog**, when visibility is reduced to 50 metres (55yds), the speed limit on all roads is 50kph (31mph). In **wet weather** speed limits outside built-up areas are reduced to 80kph (49mph), 100kph (62mph) and 110kph (69mph) on motorways.

These limits also apply to private cars towing a trailer or caravan, if the latter's weight does not exceed that of the car and the total weight is less than 3.5 tonnes. However, if the weight of the trailer exceeds that of the car by less than 30%, the speed limit is 65kph (40mph), if more than 30% the speed limit is 45kph (28mph). Additionally these combinations must:

i Display a disc at the rear of the caravan/trailer showing the maximum speed.

ii Not be driven in the fast lane of a 3-lane motorway.

Both French residents and visitors to France, who have held a driving licence for less than two years, must not exceed 80kph (49mph) outside built-up areas, 100kph (62mph) on dual carriageways separated by a central reservation and 110kph (69mph) on motorways.

Warning triangle/Hazard warning lights*

The use of a warning triangle or hazard warning lights† is compulsory in the event of accident or breakdown. As hazard warning lights may be damaged or inoperative, it is recommended that a warning triangle be carried. The triangle must be placed on the road 30 metres (33yds) behind the vehicle and clearly visible from 100 metres (110yds).
†If your vehicle is equipped with hazard warning lights, it is also complusory to use them if you are forced to drive temporarily at a greatly reduced speed. However, when slow moving traffic is established in an uninterrupted lane or lanes, this only applies to the last vehicle in the lane(s).

*Additional information will be found in the Continental ABC at the front of the book.

A-Z DIRECTORY

Prices are in French Francs Abbreviations: av avenue bd boulevard espl esplanade fbg faubourg Gl Général Ml Maréchal pl place Prés President r rue rte route Sgt Sergent sq square CM Camping Municipal (local authority site).
Each placename preceded by 'La', 'Le' or 'Les' is listed under the name that follows it.
All telephone numbers in France have been increased to ten digits. The two extra digits will precede the old number and you are advised to check the current position before using telephone numbers quoted in our Directory. Please refer to Contents page for the explanation.

Alps/East

Within the French Alps is the old Duchy of Savoie, which only became part of France in the middle of the last century, and which still retains a distinctive character. The Alps is a region of clear air, majestic mountain peaks, peaceful valleys and meadows. Good roads link the valleys; steep winding mountain roads lead to delightful villages and spectacular viewpoints, but cable cars offer a unique alternative. A cable car goes up to the 12,000ft Aiguille du Midi, and a funicular railway leads to the spectacular 'Mer de Glace'. Annecy has a delightful, bustling medieval centre, and Lake Annecy, with its backdrop of mountains, provides opportunities for watersports and cruising. There are a number of attractive Alpine resorts - La Clusaz, Morzine, and the sophisticated Chamonix, and Savoy's ancient capital, Chambéry, has a fascinating old town and castle.
A well-kept secret is the Jura - a land of thickly wooded hills and plateaux and lush meadows grazed by sheep, goats and cattle. The rivers Rhône, Doubs and Ain flow through the region, and the many smaller rivers and lakes make this a fisherman's paradise.

ABRETS, LES Isère

Coin Tranquille ☎76321348
Completely divided into pitches with attractive flower beds in rural surroundings.
2 km E of village, 500m off N6.
Apr-Oct 5HEC ▦ ⏚ ⋒ ⅀ ♥ ✕ ⊙ ⋒ ⌀ ⛺ ⊞ lau Prices: pitch 75-115 (incl 2 persons)

ALBENS Savoie

Beauséjour ☎79541520
SW via rte de la Chambotte. Signposted
10 Jun-15 Sep 2HEC ▦ ⋒ ⊙ ⋒ ⌀ ⌘ ⊞ lau ♥ ⅀ ♥ ✕ ⚊ ⇗R Prices: A8.50 V10 ⊞10

ALLEVARD Isère

Clair Matin ☎76975519
Gently sloping terraced area divided into pitches.
S of village, 300m off D525.
15 May-Sep 3.5HEC ▦ ⏚ ⋒ ⊙ ⋒ ⌀ ⚊ ⌘ ⊞ lau ♥ ⅀ ♥ ✕ ⇗LP

ANNECY Haute-Savoie

Belvédère 8 rte du Semnoz ☎50454830
On S outskirts, on the Semnoz road.
Closed 16 Oct-19 Dec 2.7HEC ▦ ⏚ ⋒ ⅀ ✕ ⊙ ⋒ ⌀ ⊞ lau ♥ ♥ ✕ ⇗LP

ANTHY-SUR-LÉMAN Haute-Savoie

Pays Léman rte des Pêcheurs ☎50760195
In a quiet situation 200m from the beach on Lake Geneva.
Apr-20 Oct 1.5HEC ▦ ⏚ ⋒ ⅀ ⊙ ⋒ ⌀ ⌘ ⅀ ⊞ lau ♥ ♥ ✕ ⚊ ⇗LP Prices: A18-22 pitch 10-20

ARBOIS Jura

CM Vignes av Gl-Leclerc ☎84661412

Terraced site. Shop open Jul-Aug only.
E on D107 Mesnay road at stadium.
Apr-Sep 5HEC ▦ ⏚ ⋒ ⊙ ⋒ ⌀ ⅀ ⊞ lau ♥ ♥ ⇗P

ARGENTIÈRE Haute-Savoie

Glacier d'Argentière ☎50541736
Clean site on sloping meadowland in beautiful quiet situation at the foot of the Mont Blanc Massif.
Access is 1km S of Argentière, turn off N506 towards Cableway Lognan et de Grandes Montets, then a further 200m to site.
Jun-Sep 1.1HEC ▦ ꜱ⟋ ⋒ ⊙ ⋒ ⌀ ⅀ ⊞ lau ♥ ⅀ ♥ ✕

ARS-SUR-FORMANS Ain

Bois de la Dame Chemin du Bois de la Dame ☎74007723
Camping Card Compulsory.
Access from A6, exit Villefranche. Continue E via D904.
May-Sep 1.5HEC ▦ ⏚ ⋒ ⊙ ⋒ ⅀ ⅀ ⌘ lau ♥ ⅀ ♥ ✕ ⇗P

AUTRANS Isère

Caravaneige du Vercors les Gaillards ☎76953188
0.6km S via D106c towards Méaudre
All year 1HEC ▦ ꜱ⟋ ⋒ ⊙ ⋒ ⌀ ⇗ P ⅀ ⊞ lau ♥ ⅀ ♥ ✕ ⚊ ⇗R
Prices: pitch 61 (incl 2 persons)

Joyeux Réveil ☎76953344
Dry woody site.
NE of town via rte de Montaud.
All year 1.5HEC ▦ ꜱ⟋ ⋒ ⊙ ⋒ ⅀ ⌘ ⌘ ⇗ P ⅀ ⊞ lau ♥ ⅀ ♥ ✕ ⌀

BARATIER Hautes-Alpes

Verger ☎92431587
Terraced site in plantation of fruit trees with fine views of Alps.
Divided into pitches. Rest room.
From N94 drive 2.5km S of Embrun, 1.5km E on D40.
All year 2.5HEC ▦ ꜱ⟋ ⋒ ⊙ ⋒ ⅀ ⌘ ⌘ ⇗ P ⅀ ⊞ lau ♥ ♥ ✕ ⇗LR

BELLEGARDE-SUR-VALSERINE Ain

Crêt d'Eau 2 av de Lattre-de-Tassigny ☎50566081
3km N of town, 200m from N84.
Jul-Aug 5.2HEC ▦ ⏚ ⋒ ⊙ ⋒ ⌘ ⇗ P ⅀ ⊞ lau ♥ ⅀ ♥ ✕ ⌀ ⚊ ⇗R

BOURG-D'OISANS, LE Isère

Caravaneige le Vernis ☎76800268
Well-kept site with modern sanitary facilities. At foot of mountain in summer ski-ing area.
2.5km of N91, rte de Briançon.
Closed Sep-Dec 1.2HEC ▦ ⏚ ⋒ ⊙ ⋒ ⅀ ⊞ ⊞ ⊘ ♥ ⅀ ♥ ✕ ⌀ ⚊ ⇗R

Cascade rte de l'Alpe-d'Huez ☎76800242
Completely divided into pitches at the foot of a mountain with a waterfall and modern, very well-kept sanitary arrangements.
Television lounge with library, open fireplace. Booking essential.
15 Dec-30 Sep 2.5HEC ▦ ⏚ ⋒ ⅀ ✕ ⊙ ⋒ ⌀ ⌘ ⌘ ⇗ PR ⅀ ⊞ lau ♥ ⅀ ✕ Prices: pitch 90-122 (incl 3 persons)

Rencontre du Soleil rte de l'Alpe-d'Huez ☎76800033
Charming site in a lovely setting in the Dauphiny Alps at the foot of a mountain. Fine rustic common room with open fireplace. TV, playroom for children.
At the foot of the hairpin road to L'Alp-d'Huez, leave N91 (Grenoble-Briançon road) in Le Bourg d'Osians.
20 May-10 Sep 1HEC ▦ ⏚ ⋒ ⅀ ✕ ⊙ ⋒ ⇗ P ⅀ ⊞ lau ♥ ⅀ ✕ ⌀ ⇗L
Prices: pitch 84-122 (incl 2 persons)

At VENOSC(10km SE on N91 and D530)

Champ de Moulin ☎76800738
15 May-15 Jul & 15 Dec-30 Apr 1.5HEC ▦ ꜱ⟋ ⋒ ⅀ ✕ ⊙ ⋒ ⌀ ⚊ ⌘ ⇗ P ⅀ ⊞ lau Prices: pitch 97 (incl 2 persons)

BOURG-EN-BRESSE Ain

CM de Challes av de Bad Kreuznach ☎74453721

Camping municipal
★★★★
F-01000 Bourg en Bresse

120 peaceful, shady pitches. Free swimming pool, children's playground, snack bar. Open from 1st April till 15th October.

A6 Lyon Paris — Chalon sur Saône — Sortie A40 Bourg Nord — Lons le Saunier Strasbourg — Sortie A40 Bourg Est — D975 — N83 — **Bourg en Bresse** — A40 — N83 — N75 — Nantua — Sortie A40 Bourg Sud — Genève Grenoble

A40 sortie Bourg Est (Tanvol), direction Lons Le Saunier

© **04 74 45 37 21**
and **04 74 45 71 38**

In football ground near swimming pool.
Well signposted from outskirts of town.
Apr-15 Oct 2.7HEC ▦ ⌕ ♠ 🅰 ⚫ ▦ ⊕ ▦ ⊞ lau ♦ ⌀ 🅰 ⁀P ⊞

BOURGET-DU-LAC, LE Savoie
CM Ile aux Cygnes ☎79250176
May-24 Sep 4.3HEC ▦ ♠ 🅰 🅰 ⚫ ▦ ⁀ LR ⊞ ⊞ lau ♦ ⌀ 🅰

BOURG-ST-MAURICE Savoie
Versoyen rte des Arcs ☎79070345
Two communal sanitary blocks - one heated. Ski-ing facilities. Many secluded pitches in a wood.
On S outskirts of town. Access via N90.
Closed mid Nov-mid Dec 3.5HEC ▦ ⌕ 🅰 ⚫ ▦ ⌀ 🅰 ▦ ⊞ lau ♦ 🅰 ⁀
✕ ⁀PR ⊞ Prices: A21-24 pitch 21

BOUT-DU-LAC Haute-Savoie
International du Lac Bleu rte d'Albertville ☎50443018
Modern, well-kept site. Overflow area with own sanitary blocks.
On the southern shores of Lake Annecy via the N508, opposite ANTAR Garage.
Apr-10 Oct 3.3HEC ♠ 🅰 ✕ ⚫ ▦ 🅰 ⁀ L ⊞ ⊞ lau ♦ 🅰 ⌀ 🅰

Nublière ☎50443344
Extensive site divided into pitches in attractive surroundings.
150m off N508 at S end of Lac d'Annecy.
Jun-Sep 9HEC ▦ ♠ 🅰 ⚫ ▦ ⌀ 🅰 🅰 ⊞ lau ♦ ⌀ ✕ 🅰 ⁀LR
Prices: pitch 59-77 (incl 2 persons)

CHAMONIX-MONT-BLANC Haute-Savoie
Mer de Glace chemin de la Bagna ☎50530863
2km NE to Les Praz. On approach to village (from Chamonix) turn right under railway bridge.
27 Apr-Sep 2.2HEC ▦ ∷∷ ⌕ 🅰 ⌀ ✕ ⚫ ▦ ⊞ ⊞ lau ♦ 🅰 ✕ ⌀ ⁀P

Rosières 121 Clos des Rosières ☎50531042
1.2km NE via N506

Closed 13 Oct-15 Dec 1.6HEC ▦ ∷∷ ♠ 🅰 ⚫ ▦ ⌀ 🅰 ▦ ⊞ lau ♦
✕ ⁀P Prices: A24-27 pitch 22-28

At **BOSSONS, LES**(3km W)
Cimes 28 rte des Tissieres ☎50535893
In a wooded meadow at the foot of Mont Blanc Massif. Ideal for hiking and mountain tours.
Jun-Sep 1HEC ▦ ⌕ 🅰 ⚫ ▦ ⌀ 🅰 ⁀ R ⊞ lau ♦ 🅰 ✕ 🅰 ⁀LP ⊞

Deux Glaciers 80 rte des Tissières ☎50531584
A glacial stream runs through the site. Pitches shaded by trees, very modern, well-kept sanitary installations. Rustic common room with open fires.
Leave N506 towards road underpass. 250m to site.
All year 16HEC ▦ ⌕ 🅰 ⚫ 🅰 ✕ ⚫ ▦ ⌀ 🅰 🅰 ⊞ lau ♦ 🅰 🅰

CHAMPAGNOLE Jura
CM Boyse r G-Vallery ☎84520032
Clean and tidy site with asphalt drives and completely divided into pitches. In grounds of municipal swimming pool.
Turn onto D5 just before town and continue 1.3km to site.
15 Jun-15 Sep 7HEC ▦ ♠ 🅰 🅰 🅰 ✕ ⚫ ▦ ⌀ 🅰 ⁀ PR ⊞ lau

CHÂTEAUROUX-LES-ALPES Hautes-Alpes
Cariamas ☎92432263
On a meadow in an attractive mountain setting beside the River Durance.
1.5km SE.
Jul-Aug 10HEC ▦ 🅰⌀ ♠ 🅰 🅰 ⚫ ▦ 🅰 🅰 ⁀ P ⊞ lau ♦ 🅰 ✕ ⌀ 🅰
⁀LR ⊞

CHOISY Haute-Savoie
Chez Langin ☎50774165
In pleasant wooded surroundings.
1.3km NE via D3.
15 Apr-15 Oct 2HEC ▦ ⌕ 🅰 🅰 ✕ 🅰 ⚫ ▦ ⌀ 🅰 ⁀ P ⊞ ⊞ lau Prices:
pitch 80 (incl 2 persons)

CHORGES Hautes-Alpes
Prévalière ☎92506758 or 92506042
Clean site, on meadowland, partly terraced.
From village follow D3 south for 500m. Also direct access from Gap by N94.
15 Jun-Aug 2HEC ▦ ⌕ 🅰 ⚫ ▦ ⌀ 🅰 ⊞ lau ♦ 🅰 ✕ 🅰 ⊞ Prices: A15 pitch 16

CLAIRVAUX-LES-LACS Jura
Fayolan ☎84252619
1.2km SE via D118 beside the lake.
May-Sep 17HEC ▦ ⌕ 🅰 🅰 ✕ 🅰 ⚫ ▦ ⌀ 🅰 ⁀ LP ⊞ lau ♦ 🅰 ⁀R ⊞

Grisière et Europe Vacances chemin du Langard ☎84258048
Fenced in meadowland with some trees, sloping down to the Grand Lac. The site is guarded during July and August.
From village centre turn off N78, follow D118 towards Châtel-de-Joux for 800m to the site.
May-Sep 11HEC ▦ ⌕ 🅰 🅰 ✕ 🅰 ⚫ ▦ ⌀ 🅰 ⁀ L ⊞ ⊞ lau ♦ ⁀R
Prices: A16 pitch 28

CLUSAZ, LA Haute-Savoie
Plan du Fernuy rte des Confins ☎0450024475
Airing rooms. 30 ski-lifts nearby. Several cable cars. Well-situated for skiing or walking.
At the road fork E of La Clusaz leave N50 the Col des Aravis road, and drive towards Les Confins from road fork 2km to site.
15 Jun-15 Sep 1.3HEC ▦ ⌕ 🅰 🅰 ✕ 🅰 ⚫ ▦ 🅰 ⁀ P ⊞ lau ♦ ✕
⌀ ⁀LR ⊞ Prices: pitch 70-91 (incl 3 persons)

DIVONNE-LES-BAINS Ain
Fleutron Quartier Villard ☎50200195
3 km N.
29 Mar-2 Nov 8HEC ▦ ⌕ 🅰 🅰 ✕ 🅰 ⚫ ▦ 🅰 🅰 ⁀ P ⊞ lau Prices:
A22-27 pitch 23-39

DOLE Jura
Pasquier 18 Chemin Theremot ☎84720261
Clean meadow site near River Doubs.

900m SE of town centre.
1.5 Mar-15 Oct 2HEC ▦ ♦ ↑ ⚍ ⚑ ⊙ ⊝ ⌀ ⚐ ⚏ ⊞ lau ♦ ✕ 🚿
⚡PR Prices: pitch 60 (incl 2 persons)

DOUCIER *Jura*

Domaine de Chalain ☎84242900
A large site beside Lake Chalain.
3km NE.
May-19 Sep 30HEC ▦ ♦ ↑ ⚍ ⚑ ⚡ ✕ ⊙ ⊝ ⌀ ⚏ ⚐ ⚋ L ⚍ ⊞ lau ♦ 🚿

DOUSSARD *Haute-Savoie*

Serraz r de la Poste ☎50443068
Modern site divided into pitches. Cosy bar in rustic style.
At E end of village 500m from N508 on D181.
15 May-Sep 3HEC ▦ ♦ ↑ ⚍ ⚑ ⚡ ✕ ⊙ ⊝ ⌀ ⚏ ⚋ P ⚍ ⊞ lau ♦ 🚿 ⚋L

EGATS, LES *Isère*

Belvédère de l'Obiou ☎76304080
Situated in beautiful scenery; modern sanitary installations.
May-Sep 1HEC ▦ ⚍ ⊝ ✕ ⊙ ⊝ ⌀ ⚏ 🚿 ⚋ P ⚍ ⊞ lau ♦ 🚍 ⚡ ✕
Prices: A25 pitch 20

EMBRUN *Hautes-Alpes*

CM Clapière Av du Lac ☎92430183
Well-managed site with shaded pitches on stony ground, on N shore
of lake. Site shop open during summer only.
2.5km SW on N94.
10 Apr-Sep 6HEC ▦ ⚍ ↑ ⊙ ⚡ ⊞ lau ♦ 🚍 ⚡ ✕ ⌀ 🚿 ⚋LP

ENTRE-DEUX-GUIERS *Isère*

Arc en Ciel ☎76660697
On D520 300m from N6.
Mar-Oct 1.2HEC ▦ ♦ ↑ ⚍ ⊙ ⚡ ⌀ ⚏ ⚐ ⚋ R ⊞ lau ♦ ⚡ ✕ ⚋P

ÉVIAN-LES-BAINS *Haute-Savoie*

At **AMPHION-LES-BAINS**(3.5km W on N5)

Plage ☎50700046
NW of town on N5, 150m from lake.
Apr-Nov 1.5HEC ▦ ⚍ ↑ ⚡ ✕ ⊙ ⊝ ⚡ ⚐ ⚋ ⚋LP ⚍ ⊞ lau ♦ ✕ ⌀ 🚿

At **MAXILLY**(2.5km E on N5)

Clos Savoyard ☎50752584
Very clean and tidy site.
Turn onto D21 in town 1200m after Hôtel le Maximillien and continue
uphill.
Apr-Sep 2HEC ▦ ♦ ↑ ⚍ ⊙ ⚡ ⚏ ⚐ ⚏ ⊞ lau ♦ ⚡ ✕ ⌀ 🚿 ⚋L Prices:
pitch 35 (incl 2 persons)

GRESSE-EN-VERCORS *Isère*

4 Saisons ☎76343027
1.3km SW
26 Dec-Apr & 25 May-8 Sep 2.2HEC ▦ ⚍ ⚍ ↑ ⊙ ⌀ ⚋ ⚋ PR ⚍
lau ♦ ⚡ ✕ ⚋L ⊞ Prices: pitch 65 (incl 2 persons)

GUILLESTRE *Hautes-Alpes*

Villard ☎92450654
2km W via D902A and N4, rte de Gap.
All year 3HEC ▦ ⚍ ↑ ⚍ ⚡ ✕ ⊙ ⊝ ⌀ ⚏ 🚿 ⚋ PR ⚍ ⊞ lau Prices:
pitch 105 (incl 2 persons)

HOUCHES, LES *Haute-Savoie*

Bourgeat 1146 av des Alpages ☎50544214
1.5 km NE.
15 Jun-15 Sep 1HEC ▦ ⚍ ⚍ ↑ ⊙ ⚡ ⚍ ⊞ lau ♦ 🚍 ⚡ ✕ 🚿

HUANNE-MONTMARTIN *Doubs*

Étangs du Bois de Reveuge ☎81843860
A terraced site in a 20 hectare park with good recreational facilities.
Access via A36 exit 'Baumes-les-Dames'.
May-Sep 20HEC ▦ ░░░ ♦ ↑ ⚍ ⚡ ✕ ⊙ ⊝ ⌀ 🚿 ⚋ ⚋LP ⚍ ⊞ lau
Prices: pitch 110-160 (incl 2 persons)

ISLE-SUR-LE-DOUBS, L' *Doubs*

CM Lumes ☎81927305
The site lies close to the town. Common room with TV.
Off N83. Entrance near bridge over the Doubs.
15 May-15 Sep 1HEC ▦ ⚍ ↑ ⊙ ⚡ ⚋ R ⚍ ⊞ lau

LONS-LE-SAUNIER *Jura*

Majorie 640 bd de l'Europe ☎84242694
Clean, tidy site with tent and caravan sections separated by a
stream. Caravan pitches (80 sq m) are gravelled and surrounded by
hedges. Heated common room with TV, reading area, kitchen.
Swimming pool free to campers.
Near swimming stadium on outskirts of town.
Apr-15 Oct 7.5HEC ▦ ⚍ ↑ ⚍ ⚡ ✕ ⊙ ⊝ ⌀ ⚏ ⚐ ⚍ ⊞ lau ♦ ✕ 🚿 ⚋P
Prices: pitch 66-79 (incl 2 persons)

LUGRIN *Haute-Savoie*

Myosotis 28 chemin du Grand Tronc ☎50760759
W of town. Signposted.
20 Apr-Sep 0.9HEC ▦ ⚍ ↑ ⊙ ⌀ ⚏ ⚐ ⚍ ⊞ lau ♦ 🚍 ⚡ ✕ 🚿 ⚋LP
Prices: A14-17 V3-4 ⚑6-7 ▲6-7

Rys Route le Rys ☎50760575
W of town. Signposted.
Apr-15 Oct 1.5HEC ▦ ♦ ↑ ⊙ ⌀ ⚏ ⚐ ⚍ ⊞ lau ♦ 🚍 ⚡ ✕ ⚋L
Prices: A16 V10 pitch 22

Vieille Église ☎50760195
On rising meadow with good views.
Apr-20 Oct 1.5HEC ▦ ♦ ↑ ⚍ ⊙ ⚡ ⚐ ⚏ ⚐ ⚋ P ⚍ ⊞ lau ♦ ⚡ ✕ 🚿
⚋L Prices: pitch 75 (incl 2 persons)

MALBUISSON *Doubs*

Fuvettes ☎81693150
Mainly level site with some terraces, gently sloping towards lake.
500m S on D437.
Apr-Nov 6HEC ▦ ⚍ ↑ ⚍ ⚡ ✕ ⊙ ⊝ ⌀ 🚿 ⚏ ⚋ L ⚍ ⊞ lau ♦ ⚋PR
Prices: pitch 81 (incl 2 persons)

MARIGNY *Jura*

Pergola ☎84257003
Terraced site.
S of Marigny off D27.
May-Sep 12HEC ▦ ⚍ ↑ ⚍ ⚡ ✕ ⊙ ⊝ ⌀ ⚏ ⚋ ⚋ LP ⚍ ⊞ lau ♦ ⚋R
Prices: pitch 90-207.50 (incl 2 persons)

MÉAUDRE *Isère*

Buissonnets ☎76952104
200m from village centre.
All year 2HEC ▦ ⚍ ↑ ⊙ ⌀ 🚿 ⚏ ⚐ ⚍ ⊞ lau ♦ 🚍 ⚡ ✕ ⚋R Prices:
pitch 57 (incl 2 persons)

MEGÈVE *Haute-Savoie*

Ripaille 395 rte de Vauray ☎50214724
Facing Mont-Blanc.
On N212, 800m from Pont d'Arbon.
All year 0.9HEC ▦ ⚍ ↑ ⚡ ✕ ⊙ ⊝ ⌀ 🚿 ⚏ ⚐ ⚋ P ⚍ ⊞ lau

MESSERY *Haute-Savoie*

Relais du Léman ☎50947111
1.5km SW via D25
Apr-Oct 3HEC ▦ ♦ ↑ ⚍ ✕ ⊙ ⊝ ⌀ ⚏ ⚐ ⚋ P ⚍ ⊞ lau ♦ 🚍 ⚋L
Prices: A26 pitch 35

MIRIBEL-LES-ÉCHELLES *Isère*

Bourdons ☎76552853
400m from village centre.
Feb-Nov 2HEC ▦ ♦ ↑ ⚍ ⚡ ✕ ⊙ ⊝ ⌀ 🚿 ⚏ ⚐ ⚏ ⚋ P ⚍ ⊞ lau Prices:
A20-22 V8.20 ⚑13.40 ▲13.40

MONTMAUR *Hautes-Alpes*

Mon Repos ☎92580314
Generally well-kept site on wooded terrain with shaded pitches.
1km E on D937 and D994.
Etr-Oct 10HEC ▦ ♦ ↑ ⊙ ⌀ ⚏ ⚐ ▲ ⚍ ⊞ lau ♦ 🚍 ⚡ ✕ ⚋LPR

MONTMÉLIAN *Savoie*

Manoir av du Prés E-Herriot ☎0479652238
Situated close to the historical area of the town with 90 pitches
divided by hedges.
Closed 25 Oct-Nov 2.8HEC ▦ ♦ ↑ ⊙ ⚡ ⚍ ⊞ ♦ 🚍 ⚡ ✕ ⌀ 🚿 Prices:
A15 V5 ⚑20 ▲20

MONTREVEL-EN-BRESSE *Ain*
Plaine Tonique Base de Plein Air ☎74308052
Entrance closed between 22.00 & 07.00 hrs.
0.5km E on D28.
May-Sep 15HEC ▨ ♦♣ ﬡ ♀ × ⊙ ◙ ∅ ⌸ ⌂ ⌐ ⤳ L 🗢 ⊞ lau Prices:
A18-22 pitch 40-55

MOUCHARD *Jura*
Halte Jurassienne Bel Air ☎84378392
Camping Card Compulsory.
NE, near the service station.
15 Apr-15 Oct 0.5HEC ▨ ◔ ﬡ ⊙ ◙ ∅ ⌸ 🗢 ⊞ lau ♦ ♣ ♀ ×

NANTUA *Ain*
Signal ☎74750209
The site is within a sports ground.
SW opposite Nantua railway station.
15 Jun-15 Sep 5HEC ♦ ﬡ ♣ ♀ × ⊙ ◙ 🗢 ◲ lau ♦ ⤳L ⊞

NEYDENS *Haute-Savoie*
Colombière ☎50351314
A pleasant, friendly site with good recreational facilities.Access via A40.
Apr-Sep 2.2HEC ▨ ♠ ◔ ﬡ ♀ × ⊙ ◙ ∅ ⌂ ⌐ ⤳ P 🗢 ⊞ lau ♦ ♣
Prices: pitch 90 (incl 2 persons)

NOVALAISE *Savoie*
Charmilles Lac d'Aiguebelette ☎79360467
150m from the lake
25 Jun-5 Sep 2.3HEC ▨ ⋮⋮ ◔ ﬡ ♣ ⊙ ◙ ∅ ⌐ 🗢 ⊞ lau ♦ ♀ × ⤳L
Prices: pitch 76.30-94.30 (incl 3 persons)

ORNANS *Doubs*
Chanet rte de Chassagne ☎81622344
1.5km SW on D241. Follow green signs.
Mar-15 Nov 1.5HEC ▨ ♦ ﬡ ♣ ⊙ ◙ ∅ ⌐ 🗢 ⊞ lau ♦ ♀ × ⤳PR
Prices: A19 pitch 20-21

ORPIERRE *Hautes-Alpes*
Princes d'Orange ☎92662253
The site lies on a meadow with terraces.
Exit N75 at Eyguians and take D30.
Apr-Oct 3HEC ▨ ♠ ◔ ﬡ ♀ × ⊙ ◙ ∅ ⌸ ⌂ ⌐ ⤳ P 🗢 lau ♦ ♣ ×
⊞ Prices: pitch 75-105 (incl 3 persons)

OUNANS *Jura*
Plage Blanche 3 r de la Plage ☎84376963
In a pleasant location beside the River Loue with good recreational facilities.
1.5km S via D71 (rte de Montbarcy).
20 Mar-Oct 5HEC ▨ ◔ ﬡ ♀ × ⊙ ◙ ⌂ ⌐ ⤳ R 🗢 ⊞ lau ♦ ♣ ∅ ⌸
⤳P Prices: A23 pitch 28

PARCEY *Jura*
Bords de Loue r du Val d'Amour ☎84710382
A quiet site on the River Loue.
1.5km from the centre of the village via N5. Signposted.
Apr-15 Sep 18HEC ▨ ◔ ﬡ ♀ × ⊙ ◙ ∅ ⌐ ⤳ PR 🗢 ⊞ lau ♦ ♣ ×
Prices: A21 pitch 25

PATORNAY *Jura*
Moulin ☎84483121
Access is NE via N78, rte de Clairvaux-les-Lacs.
May-15 Sep 5HEC ▨ ♦ ﬡ ♣ ♀ × ⊙ ◙ ∅ ⤳ PR 🗢 ⊞ lau ♦ ⤳L

PLAGNE-MONTCHAVIN *Savoie*
CM ☎79078323
1 Dec-30 Sep 1HEC ▨ ◔ ﬡ ⊙ ◙ ⌸ 🗢 ⊞ lau ♦ ♣ ♀ × ∅ ⤳P ⊞
Prices: A20.50 ◙16.50 A16.50

PONTARLIER *Doubs*
Larmont r du Toulombief ☎81462333
A mountain site with good facilities in a area associated with winter sports.
All year ▨ ♠ ⤳ ﬡ ♣ ♀ × ⊙ ◙ ∅ ⌸ ⌂ 🗢 ⊞ lau ♦ × ⤳R Prices:
pitch 55-75 (incl 2 persons)

PORT-SUR-SAÔNE *Haute-Saône*
CM Maladière ☎84915132
S on the D6, between the River Saône and the Canal
15 May-15 Sep 2HEC ▨ ◔ ﬡ ⊙ ◙ ⌸ ⊞ lau ♦ ♣ ♀ × ∅ ⌸ ⤳PR
Prices: A10 V6 ◙10 A10

PRESLE *Savoie*
Combe Léat ☎79255402
A quiet mountain site.
Access via A43 and D207.
15 Jun-Aug 3.5HEC ▨ ♦ ﬡ ♀ × ⊙ ◙ ◙ ⌐ 🗢 lau ♦ ∅ ⌸ ⤳P Prices:
A15 A10 pitch 15

RENAGE *Isère*
Verdon 185 av de la Piscine ☎76914802
5km N of Tullins on D45.
Apr-15 Oct 1.5HEC ▨ ♦ ﬡ ⊙ ◙ ∅ 🗢 ⊞ lau ♦ ♣ ♀ × ⌸ ⤳P Prices:
A16 pitch 16

ROCHETTE, LA *Savoie*
Lac St-Clair Detrier ☎79257355
Jun-15 Sep 2.2HEC ▨ ◔ ﬡ ⊙ ◙ 🗢 ⊞ lau ♦ ♣ ♀ × ⌸ Prices:
A14.50 V6.50 ◙11 A11

ROSIÈRE-DE-MONTVALEZAN, LA *Savoie*
Forêt ☎79068621
A peaceful site in pleasant wooded surroundings, with good, modern facilities.
2km S via N90 towards Bourg-St-Maurice.
15 Jun-15 Sep & 15 Dec-8 May 1.5HEC ▨ ♦ ﬡ × ⊙ ◙ ⌸ ◙ 🗢
⊞ lau ♦ ♣ ∅

ROUGEMONT *Doubs*
At **BONNAL**(3.5km N on D18)
⊠Val de Bonnal ☎81869087
Quiet woodland site beside the River Ognon. Supervised swimming in lake with beach.
15 May-15 Sep 15HEC ▨ ◔ ﬡ ♣ × ⊙ ◙ ∅ ⤳ LR 🗢 ⊞ lau
Prices: A32 pitch 50

ST-AVRE *Savoie*
Bois Joli St Martin-sur-la-Chambre ☎79594230
Well shaded site with pitches and individual washing cabins.
1km N of St-Avre, off N6-E70 via La Chambre.
Apr-Sep 4HEC ▨ ♠ ♦ ﬡ ♀ × ⊙ ◙ ◙ ⌐ ⤳ P 🗢 ⊞ lau ♦ ♣ ∅ ⌸
Prices: pitch 65 (incl 2 persons)

ST-CLAIR-DU-RHÔNE *Isère*
Daxia rte du Péage ☎74563920
A riverside site with good sanitary and recreational facilities.
Access via N7/A7.
Apr-Sep 7.5HEC ▨ ◔ ﬡ ♀ × ⊙ ◙ ⌐ ⤳ LPR 🗢 Prices: A16 V9
◙21 A21

ST-CLAUDE *Jura*
Martinet ☎84450040
2km SE, beside the river
May-Sep 3HEC ▨ ◔ ﬡ ♣ ♀ × ⊙ ◙ ∅ ⤳ PR 🗢 lau

ST-DISDILLE *Haute-Savoie*
St-Disdille ☎50711411
N of N5. Signposted.
Apr-Sep 12HEC ▨ ♦ ﬡ ♣ ♀ × ⊙ ◙ ∅ 🗢 ⊞ lau ♦ ⤳LPR

ST-GERVAIS-LES-BAINS *Haute-Savoie*
Dômes de Miage rte des Contamines ☎50934596
2km S on D902.
Jun-20 Sep 2HEC ▨ ◔ ﬡ ♀ × ⊙ ◙ ∅ 🗢 ⊞ lau ♦ ♣ ⤳P Prices:
pitch 80 (incl 2 persons)

ST-INNOCENT-BRISON *Savoie*
Rolande 24 chemin des Becthets ☎79543685
Situated on gently sloping terrain.
Signposted from village centre.
May-Sep 1.5HEC ▨ ◔ ﬡ ♣ ♀ × ⊙ ◙ ∅ 🗢 ⊞ lau ♦ × ⌸ ⤳L Prices:
pitch 46.30-60 (incl 2 persons)

ST-JEAN-DE-COUZ *Savoie*
International la Bruyère ☎04657427
2km S via N6, towards Côte-Barrier
Apr-Oct 1HEC ▦ ⚲ ♠ 🐾 ⚡ ✕ ☉ 🐶 ⌿ ☇ lau ➡ ✕ ♨ ☇LS ⊞ Prices: A15
pitch 13

ST-JEAN-ST-NICOLAS *Hautes-Alpes*
CM le Châtelard Pont-du-Fossé ☎92559431
15 Jun-15 Sep 4HEC ▦ ♦ ♠ ☉ 🐶 ☇ R ☲ ⊞ lau ➡ 🐾 ⚡ ✕ ⌿ ♨
Prices: A18 V7 ⊕25 ⚑20

ST-JORIOZ *Haute-Savoie*
Europa 1444 rte d'Albertville ☎50685101
1.4km SE
15 May-15 Sep 3HEC ▦ ♪⌇ ♠ 🐾 ⚡ ✕ ☉ 🐶 ⊞ 🐶 ☇ P ☲ lau ➡ ⌿
☇L ⊞ Prices: A18-22

International du Lac d'Annecy ☎50686793
N508 towards Albertville.
Jun-15 Sep 2.5HEC ▦ ♦ ♠ 🐾 ⚡ ✕ ☉ 🐶 ⌿ 🐶 ☇ LP ☲ ⊞ lau Prices:
pitch 94 (incl 2 persons)

ST-PIERRE-DE-CHARTREUSE *Isère*
Martinière rte du Col de Porte ☎76886036
In pleasant position surrounded by mountains.
2km SW.
08 May-20 Sep & Nov-Apr 2HEC ▦ ⚲ ♠ 🐾 ⚡ ✕ ☉ 🐶 ⌿ ♨ 🐶 ☇ P
☲ ⊞ lau ➡ ✕ Prices: pitch 64-72 (incl 2 persons)

SALLE-EN-BEAUMONT, LA *Isère*
Champ-Long ☎76304181
May-15 Oct 3.8HEC ▦ ♦ ⚲ ♠ 🐾 ⚡ ✕ ☉ 🐶 ⌿ 🐶 ☇ P ☲ ⊡ ⊞ lau ➡
⌿ ♨ ☇R Prices: pitch 30 (incl 2 persons)

SÉEZ *Savoie*
Reclus rte de Tignes ☎79410105
NW on N90.
All year 1.8HEC ▦ ♦ ♠ ☉ 🐶 ⌿ 🐶 ☲ lau ➡ 🐾 ⚡ ✕ ☇P Prices:
A19 V7 ⊕11 ⚑11

SERRES *Hautes-Alpes*
Barillons ☎92670116
Well-laid out with terraces.
1km SE on N75.
May-Sep 3HEC ▦ ⚲ ♠ ⚡ ✕ ☉ 🐶 ⌿ 🐶 ☇ L ☲ ⊞ lau ➡ 🐾 ✕ Prices:
pitch 69.50 (incl 2 persons)

Domaine des 2 Soleils ☎92670133
Well-kept terraced site in Buéch Valley.
S of town off N75. Signposted.
May-Sep 26HEC ▦ ⚲ ♠ 🐾 ⚡ ✕ ☉ 🐶 ⌿ 🐶 🐶 ☇ P ☲ ⊞ lau ➡ ☇R
Prices: pitch 108-121 (incl 2 persons)

SEYSSEL *Ain*
International de Seyssel chemin de la Barotte ☎50592847
A quiet site on steep, terraced meadowland, with individual
washbasins and clean sanitary installations.
1km SW off Culoz road.
Jun-15 Sep 1.5HEC ▦ ♦ ♠ ✕ ☉ 🐶 ⌿ 🐶 🐶 ☇ P ☲ ⊞ lau ➡ 🐾
☇LR Prices: pitch 75 (incl 2 persons)

TALLOIRES *Haute-Savoie*
Lanfonnet Angon ☎50607212
1.5km SE.
May-25 Sep 1.9HEC ▦ ♦ ♠ 🐾 ⚡ ✕ ☉ 🐶 ⌿ 🐶 🐶 ☇ ⊞ lau ➡ ☇L
Prices: pitch 97.50 (incl 2 persons)

THOISSEY *Ain*
CM ☎74040425
Situated between two rivers, the Saône and the Chalaronne.
1km SW on D7.
Apr-Sep 15HEC ▦ ⋱ ⚲ ♠ ⚡ ✕ ☉ 🐶 ☇ PR ☲ lau ➡ 🐾 ⌿ ♨ ⊞
Prices: A19 pitch 14

THONON-LES-BAINS *Haute-Savoie*
Morcy ☎50704487
2.5km W of town.

Etr-15 Sep 1.7HEC ▦ ♦ ♠ 🐾 ⚡ ☉ 🐶 ⌿ ☲ lau ➡ ✕ ♨ ☇LS ⊞
Prices: A22 pitch 22

TIGNES-LES-BRÉVIÈRES *Savoie*
Escapade rte des Boisses ☎79064127
Signposted from D902.
15 Jun-18 Sep 4HEC ▦ ♦ ⚲ ♠ 🐾 ✕ ☉ 🐶 ⌿ 🐶 ☇ P ☲ ⊞ lau
Prices: A18 V8 ⊕8 ⚑8

TREPT *Isère*
3 Lac La Plaine ☎74929206
Situated at the gateway to the Alps, an undulating woody area with
small lakes.
On D517, 2.5km W.
15 Jun-15 Sep 4HEC ▦ ⚲ ♠ 🐾 ⚡ ✕ ☉ 🐶 🐶 ☇ LP ☲ ⊞ lau ➡ ✕
Prices: A25 pitch 35

VERNIOZ *Isère*
Bontemps ☎74578352
A pleasantly landscaped site beside the River Varèze.
Access via N7 and D131.
Apr-Sep 8HEC ▦ ♦ ♠ 🐾 ⚡ ✕ ☉ 🐶 ⌿ ♨ 🐶 ☇ PR ☲ ⊞ lau Prices:
A20 V10 ⊕30 ⚑30

VILLARS-LES-DOMBES *Ain*
CM Autières ☎74980021
Clean and tidy park-like site divided into plots and pitches. Part
reserved for summer campers. Clean, modern sanitary installations.
Camping Card Compulsory.
SW off N83.
20 Apr-4 Oct 4.5HEC ▦ ⚲ ♠ 🐾 ⚡ ✕ ☉ 🐶 ⌿ ☲ ⊞ lau ➡ ☇P

VOIRON *Isère*
Porte de la Chartreuse 33 av du 8 Mai 45 ☎76051420
On level terrain with some trees, divided into pitches. Much traffic
noise from nearby N75. Clean and modern sanitary installations.
Access is NW of town next to the ESSO garage.
All year 1.5HEC ▦ ♦ ⚲ ♠ ✕ ☉ 🐶 🐶 ☲ ⊞ ➡ 🐾 ♨ Prices: A20
V12 ⊕20 ⚑12

Alsace/Lorraine

In its natural border position next to Germany, Alsace enjoys a
special identity, neither German nor completely French. And, with
Lorraine, it shares some of the most turbulent chapters in French
history. They also share the impressive Vosges mountains, with
great wooded slopes, gentle pastures, fertile plains, enchanting
lakes and famous thermal spas. In the summer this region is
ablaze with colour - there are brilliant displays of wild flowers in
the Vosges, and in the towns and cities, flowers cascade from
every available ledge. Gerardmer is at the heart of the Vosges,
and La Bresse is also popular with visitors.
Nancy, the capital of Lorraine, and Metz, with its lovely old town
and fine Gothic cathedral, are great centres for the area, but
Strasbourg is a delight to discover. The waterways of the 'Petit
France' district are charming, and the splendid soaring spine of
the cathedral of Notre Dame is unforgettable.
In the countryside, vineyards surround pretty villages with half-
timbered houses and cobbled streets, and produce the fine wines
of the area, but hops are also grown in the region, and famous
beers are brewed in Strasbourg.

ANOULD *Vosges*
Acacias 191 r L-de-Vinci ☎29571106
All year 2.5HEC ▦ ♦ ♠ 🐾 ⚡ ✕ ☉ 🐶 ⌿ ♨ 🐶 🐶 ☇ P ☲ ⊡ ⊞ lau ➡
☇R Prices: A18 pitch 20

AUBURE *Haut-Rhin*
CM La Ménère ☎89739299
A peaceful site at an altitude of 800 metres.
15 May-Sep 1.5HEC ▦ ♦ ⚲ ♠ ☉ 🐶 🐶 ☲ ⊞ lau ➡ 🐾 ⚡ ✕ ♨
Prices: A12 pitch 16

BAERENTHAL *Moselle*
Ramstein Plage ☎87065073
W via r du Ramstein
Apr-Sep 6HEC ⬛ ∷ ⟷ ⋔ ⋒ ⛌ ⊙ ⊡ ⌂ ⛺ ⊞ ⌕ L ⊡ ⊞ lau ♦ ⊿ ✕ ⬝

BERNARDSWILLER *Bas-Rhin*
Chataigniers r du Stade ☎88956812
All year 4HEC ⬛ ⋒ ⊿ ✕ ⊙ ⊡ ⛺ ⛌ ⊞ A ⊞ lau ♦ ⊿ ✕ ⬝ ⌕ ⌕P

BIESHEIM *Haut-Rhin*
Ile du Rhin Zone Turistique ☎89725795
Shop only open during high season.
From Colmar take N415 towards Germany as far as the Rhine bridge.
All year 3HEC ⬛ ⋔ ⋒ ⊿ ⊙ ⊡ ⬝ ⊞ ⊞ lau ♦ ⊻ ✕ ⊿ ⌕ ⌕PR Prices:
pitch 58.30 (incl 2 persons)

BRESSE, LA *Vosges*
Belle Hutte ☎29254975
Terraced site beside the River Moselotte.
Access via D34 towards Col de la Schlucht.
All year 3HEC ⬛ ⋔ ⋒ ⊿ ⊙ ⊡ ⬝ ⬝ ⛺ ⌕ PR ⊞ lau ♦ ⊿ ✕ ⊞ Prices:
A15.50-20 V8.50-9.50 ⛺10.50-11.50 A9.50

BRUYÈRES *Vosges*
At **CHAPELLE-DEVANT-BRUYÈRES, LA**(5km SE via N423)
Pinasses 215 rte de Bruyères ☎29585110
1.2km NW on D60 towards Bruyères
Apr-10 Sep 3HEC ⬛ ♦ ⋒ ⊿ ⊻ ✕ ⊙ ⊡ ⬝ ⛺ ⛺ ⌕ P ⊞ lau

BUSSANG *Vosges*
Domaine de Champé 14 Les Champs Navés ☎29858645
In pleasant surroundings beside the River Moselle.
On N57.
Apr-Oct 1.5HEC ⬛ ⟷ ⋒ ⊙ ⊡ ⊞ lau ♦ ⊿ ✕ ⊿ ⊞ ⌕L Prices:
A11 pitch 11

CELLES-SUR-PLAINE *Vosges*
Lac Base de Loisirs, Les Lacs de Pierre-Percée ☎29411925
Set among wooded hills in an extensive natural leisure area around
the Lakes of Pierre-Percée.
Access via D392A.
Apr-Sep 5HEC ⬛ ⟷ ⋒ ⊿ ⊻ ✕ ⊙ ⊡ ⊿ ⌕ LR ⊞ ⊞ lau ♦ ✕ ⊞
Prices: A24 pitch 24

CERNAY *Haut-Rhin*
CM Acacias r R-Guibert ☎89755697
Clean, quiet site on right bank of the River Thur.
Off N83 between Colmar and Belfort.
May-Sep 4HEC ⬛ ⋒ ⊙ ⊡ ⊿ ⊞ lau ♦ ⊿ ⊻ ✕ ⌕P

COLMAR *Haut-Rhin*
Intercommunal de l'Ill ☎89411594
On meadow beside the river. Liable to flooding at certain times.
Separate sections for campers in transit.
2km E on N415.
Feb-Nov 2.2HEC ⬛ ⋒ ⊿ ⊻ ✕ ⊙ ⊡ ⊿ ⌕ R ⊞ ⊞ lau ♦ ⌕P Prices:
A14 pitch 16

CORCIEUX *Vosges*
⬝**Domaine des Bains** r J-Wiese ☎29516467
On meadow-land divided into pitches. Restricted facilities out of
season.
E of village off D8.
All year 30HEC ⬛ ∷ ⊿ ⊿ ⊻ ✕ ⊙ ⊡ ⊿ ⌕ P ⊞ lau Prices:
A30 pitch 75

CORNY-SUR-MOSELLE *Moselle*
Paquis ☎87520359
0.7km N via N57.
Mar-Sep 1.2HEC ⬛ ⋒ ⊿ ⊻ ✕ ⊙ ⊡ ⊿ ⌕ R ⊞ ⊞ ♦ ⊿ ⊻ ✕ ⬝

DABO *Moselle*
Rocher 10 pl de l'Église ☎87074452
1.5km SW via D45.

Etr-1 Nov 0.5HEC ⬛ ∷ ⊿ ⋒ ⊙ ⊡ ⊞ lau ♦ ⊿ ⊻ ✕ ⊿ ⬝ ⊞ Prices:
A11 V6 ⛺14 A6

DAMBACH-LA-VILLE *Bas-Rhin*
CM rte d'Ebersheim ☎88924860
1km E via D120.
15 May-Sep 1.8HEC ⊿ ⋒ ⊙ ⊡ ⊞ lau ♦ ⊿ ⊻ ✕ ⊞

EGUISHEIM *Haut-Rhin*
CM Aux Trois Châteaux 10 r du Bassin ☎89231939
Camping Card Compulsory.
Etr-Sep 2HEC ⬛ ⊿ ⋒ ⊙ ⊡ ⊿ ⊞ lau ♦ ⊿ ⊻ ✕ ⬝ ⌕P

FERDRUPT *Vosges*
Pommiers ☎29259835
A peaceful site at the foot of the mountains, beside the river.
May-Aug 1HEC ⬛ ⊿ ⋒ ⊙ ⊡ ⛺ ⊞ lau ♦ ⊿ ⊻ ✕ ⊿ ⌕R Prices: A10
V7 ⛺7 A7

FONTENOY-LE-CHÂTEAU *Vosges*
Fontenoy rte de St-Loup ☎29363474
Set on a hill in peaceful, wooded surroundings.
2.2km S via D40.
May-Oct 1.2HEC ⬛ ♦ ⋒ ⊿ ⊻ ✕ ⊙ ⊡ ⊿ ⛺ ⛺ ⊞ ⊞ lau ♦ ⬝ ⌕R

GEMAINGOUTTE *Vosges*
CM 'Le Violu' ☎29577070
W, beside the river, via N59.
Apr-Oct 1HEC ⬛ ⊿ ⋒ ⊙ ⊡ ⊞ lau ♦ ⊿ ⊻ ✕

GÉRARDMER *Vosges*
Ramberchamp 21 chemin du Tour du Lac ☎29630382
On S side of Lac de Gérardmer.
15 Apr-15 Sep 3.5HEC ⬛ ∷ ⊿ ⋒ ⊿ ✕ ⊙ ⊡ ⊿ ⌕ L ⊞ lau
Prices: pitch 80 (incl 2 persons)

GERSTHEIM *Bas-Rhin*
Clair Ruisseau r du Ried ☎88983004
NE on the shore of a lake, near the river.
Apr-Sep 3HEC ⬛ ⊿ ⋒ ⊙ ⊡ ⌕ L ⊞ ⊞ lau ♦ ⬝

GRANGES-SUR-VOLOGNE *Vosges*
Château Les Chappes ☎29575083
mid Jun-mid Sep 2HEC ⬛ ⊿ ⋒ ⊿ ⊙ ⊡ ⛺ ⛺ ⌕ P ⊞ lau ♦ ⊻ ✕ ⊿
⬝ ⌕R

Gina-Park ☎29514195
1km SE of town centre.
All year 4.5HEC ⬛ ♦ ⋒ ⊿ ✕ ⊙ ⊡ ⊿ ⬝ ⛺ ⛺ ⌕ LP ⊞ lau ♦ ⌕R ⊞
Prices: A17.10 pitch 18

GUEWENHEIM *Haut-Rhin*
Doller ☎89825690
Camping Card Compulsory
1km N via D34.
Apr-Oct 0.8HEC ⬛ ⊿ ⋒ ⊿ ⊻ ✕ ⊙ ⊡ ⌕ PR ⊞ lau ♦ ⊿

HARSKIRCHEN *Bas-Rhin*
Étang Zone de Loisirs, r du Canal ☎88009365
0.8km NW via D23 beside the lake.
All year 2.5HEC ⬛ ⟷ ⋒ ⊿ ✕ ⊙ ⊡ ⌕ LR ⊞ ⊞ lau ♦ ⊿ ✕ ⊿ ⬝

HEIMSBRUNN *Haut-Rhin*
Chaumière ☎89819343 or 89819321
Signposted from village centre.
All year 1.1HEC ⬛ ∷ ♦ ⋒ ⊿ ⊿ ⊙ ⊡ ⊿ ⛺ ⊞ ♦ ⬝ ⌕LR Prices:
A17 pitch 25

HOHWALD, LE *Bas-Rhin*
CM ☎88083090
W via D425
All year 2HEC ⬛ ⊿ ⋒ ⊻ ⊙ ⊡ ⊞ lau ♦ ⊿ ✕ ⊿ Prices: A13.80
pitch 8.80

KAYSERSBERG *Haut-Rhin*
CM r des Acacias ☎89471447
Between a sports ground and the River Weiss. Subdivided by low
hedges.

Camping Card Compulsory.
200m from N415. Signposted.
Apr-Sep 1.5HEC ▥ ♦ ♠ ⊙ �R ⇗ R ⊉ ⊞ lau ♦ ⅃ ♥ Ⅹ ⌀ ⚌ ⇗P
Prices: A21 V9 ⊕13 ▲13

KRUTH *Haut-Rhin*
Schlossberg Rue du Bourbach ☎89822676
In a quiet location in the heart of the Parc des Ballons with good,
modern facilities.
2.3km NW via D13b.
Etr-Sep 5.2HEC ▥ ♦ ♠ ⅃ ⊙ ⊖ ⌀ ⊖ ⇗ R ⊉ ⊞ lau ♦ ♥ Ⅹ ⚌ ⇗L
Prices: A18.50 pitch 14.50

LAUTERBOURG *Bas-Rhin*
CM des Mouettes chemin des Mouettes ☎88546860
A level site on the shores of a lake.
Access via D63 from Haguenau.
3 Mar-10 Dec 2.7HEC ▥ ⇘⇙ ♠ ♥ Ⅹ ⊙ ⌀ ⚌ ⇗ L ⊉ ⊞ ⊘ lau ♦ ⅃
Ⅹ ⇗R Prices: A19 V10 ⊕20 ▲11

LUTTENBACH *Haut-Rhin*
Amis de la Nature r du Château ☎89773860
Site on a long strip of land, divided into pitches.
From Munster follow D10 for 1km.
11 Feb-15 Nov 7HEC ▥ ⊖ ♠ ⅃ ♥ Ⅹ ⊙ ⊖ ⌀ ⇗ R ⊉ ⊞ lau ♦ ⚌
Prices: A12.50 pitch 11.50

MANDRES-AUX-QUATRE-TOURS *Meurthe-et-Moselle*
CM ☎83271331
1.5km S
Apr-Oct 4HEC ▥ ⊖ ♠ ⊙ ⊖ ⊉ ⊞

MASEVAUX *Haut-Rhin*
CM 3 r du Stade ☎89824229
Etr-Sep 3.5HEC ▥ ♦ ♠ ⊙ ⊖ ⌀ ⊉ ⊞ lau ♦ ⅃ ♥ Ⅹ ⚌

METZERAL *Haut-Rhin*
At **MITTLACH**(3km SW)
CM ☎89776377
Situated in forested area in small village, very quiet.
From Munster follow signs for Metzeral then Mittlach D10.
May-Oct ♠ ⊙ ⊖ ⌀ ⇗ R ⊉ lau

MOOSCH *Haut-Rhin*
Mine d'Argent r de la Mine d'Argent ☎89823066
1.5km SW.
May-Sep 2HEC ▥ ♦ ⊖ ♠ ⊙ ⊖ ⌀ ⚌ ⊉ ⊞ lau ♦ ⅃ ♥ Ⅹ Prices: A13
⊕13 ▲13

MORHANGE *Moselle*
Centre International de Loisirs Étang de la Mutche, Harprich
☎87862158
A well equipped site on the shore of lake Mutche, with access to
good sporting facilities.
May-Oct 7HEC ▥ ⊖ ♠ ⊙ ⊖ ⊞ ⇗ LP ⊉ lau ♦ ♥ Ⅹ ⊞

MUNSTER *Haut-Rhin*
CM Parc de la Fecht ☎89773108
Almost in town centre within park-like area surrounded by high walls
and trees.
Access on D417, 200m after entering Munster town centre by
swimming pool.
Apr-Sep 4HEC ▥ ⊖ ♠ ⅃ ♥ ⊙ ⊖ ⌀ ⇗ R ⊉ ⊞ lau ♦ Ⅹ ⇗P Prices:
A12.80 pitch 7

OBERBRONN *Bas-Rhin*
CM Eichelgarten r de Zinswiller ☎88097196
Follow signposts W from D28 (Oberbronn-Zinswiller).
All year 4HEC ▥ ⊖ ♠ ⅃ ⊙ ⊖ ⌀ ⚌ ⊞ ⊕ ⇗ P ⊉ lau ♦ ♥ Ⅹ ⊞
Prices: A14.80 pitch 10

OBERNAI *Bas-Rhin*
CM 204 rte d'Ottrott ☎88953848
Partly terraced site, situated in park.
W on D426 towards Ottrott.

Apr-Oct 2.5HEC ▥ ♦ ♠ ♠ ⊙ ⊖ ♠ ⊉ ⊞ ⊘ lau ♦ ⅃ ♥ Ⅹ ⌀ ⚌ ⇗PR
Prices: A9 V4 ⊕4 ▲4

PHALSBOURG *Moselle*
CM Vieux Château r de la Manutention ☎87241372
Site within walls of ancient Castle.
E on rte de Saverne.
Apr-Oct 1.2HEC ▥ ⊖ ♠ ⊙ ⊖ ⊉ ⊞ ♦ ⅃ ♥ Ⅹ ⌀ ⚌

RHINAU *Bas-Rhin*
Ferme des Tuileries ☎88746045
Approach from Germany via ferry across River Rhine.
Apr-Sep 1HEC ▥ ⊖ ♠ ⅃ ♥ ⊙ ⊖ ♠ ⊉ ⊞ ⊘ lau ♦ ⇗P

RIBEAUVILLE *Haut-Rhin*
Pierre de Coubertin 23 r de Landan ☎89736671
In a peaceful location. Shop open in summer only. *Camping Card
Compulsory.*
Access via ⊕106.
Mar-1 Nov 3.4HEC ▥ ♦ ♠ ⊙ ⊖ ⌀ ⊉ ⊞ lau ♦ ♥ Ⅹ ⇗P

RIQUEWIHR *Haut-Rhin*
Inter Communal ☎89479008
Extensive site overlooking vineyards. *Camping Card Compulsory.*
2km E on N83 (Colmar-Strasbourg) at Ostheim.
Apr-25 Oct 4HEC ▥ ⊖ ♠ ⊙ ⊖ ⊉ ⊞ lau ♦ ⅃ ♥ ⇗P

ROMBACH-LE-FRANC *Haut-Rhin*
Bouleaux ☎89589399
1.5km NW beside the river.
May-Sep 1HEC ▥ ⊖ ♠ ⊙ ⊖ ⇗ R ⊉ ⊞ lau ♦ ⅃ ⌀ ⚌ ⊞

ST-MAURICE-SUR-MOSELLE *Vosges*
Deux Ballons ☎29251714
1km W on N66.
Closed 2 Nov-15 Feb (ex Xmas) 3.5HEC ▥ ⊖ ♠ ⅃ ♥ ⊖ ⌀ ⊖ ⊞
⇗ P ⊉ ⊞ lau ♦ Ⅹ Prices: pitch 23 (incl 3 persons)

ST-PIERRE *Bas-Rhin*
Beau Séjour ☎8808524
4 Apr-Sep 0.9HEC ▥ ⊖ ♠ ⊙ ⊖ ⊉ ⊞ lau ♦ ⅃ ♥ Ⅹ

SAVERNE *Bas-Rhin*
CM ☎88913565
1.3km SW via D171
Apr-Sep 1.6HEC ▥ ⇘⇙ ♠ ⅃ ⊙ ⊖ ⌀ ⊉ ⊞ lau ♦ Ⅹ ⇗P

SCHIRMECK *Bas-Rhin*
Schirmeck 26 rte de Strasbourg ☎88970161
5km NE. Beside Strasbourg road and railway, on level ground.
Mar-Oct 2.5HEC ▥ ⊖ ♠ ⊙ ⊖ ⌀ ⇗ R ⊉ ⊞ lau ♦ ⅃ ♥ Ⅹ ⚌ Prices:
A15 pitch 8.50

SÉLESTAT *Bas-Rhin*
CM Cigognes r de la 1-er DFL ☎88920398
May-15 Oct 0.7HEC ▥ ⇘⇙ ♠ ⊙ ⊖ ⌀ ⊉ ⊞ lau ♦ ♥ Ⅹ ⇗P Prices:
A15 pitch 15

SEPPOIS-LE-BAS *Haut-Rhin*
CM les Lupins r de la Gare ☎89256537
Access via A36, exit 'Burnhaupt' and continue towards Dannemarie.
Apr-Oct 4HEC ▥ ⊖ ♠ ⊙ ⊖ ⌀ ⇗ P ⊉ ⊞ lau ♦ ⅃ ♥ Ⅹ ⌀ ⇗R Prices:
A20 pitch 20

SIVRY-SUR-MEUSE *Meuse*
Brouzel 26 r du Moulin ☎29858645
Apr-Oct 1.5HEC ▥ ⇘⇙ ♠ ⊙ ⊖ ⊉ ⊞ lau ♦ ⅃ ♥ Ⅹ ⌀ ⚌ ⇗R ⊞

THILLOT, LE *Vosges*
Étang de Chaume 36 r de la Chaume ☎29251030
1.3km NW via N66.
All year ▥ ⊖ ♠ ⊙ ⊖ ⊉ ⊞ lau ♦ ⅃ ♥ Ⅹ ⌀ ⚌ ⇗PR

THIONVILLE *Moselle*
CM 6 r du Parc ☎82538375
On the edge of River Moselle, adjacent to the Napoléon Park.
Apr-Sep 2HEC ▥ ⊖ ♠ ⊙ ⊖ ⊉ ⊞ lau ♦ ⅃ ♥ Ⅹ ⇗R

THOLY, LE *Vosges*
Noir Rupt ☎29618127
2km SE on D417.
15 Apr-15 Oct 3HEC ▦ 🔧🏪🚿🍽⊙🅿🏥🚐⚓ ↘ P 🏧🅿🗲 lau ♦ ✕ 🎿
↘R Prices: pitch 96.50 (incl 2 persons)

TONNOY *Meurthe-et-Moselle*
Grande Vanné ☎83266236
W via D74, beside the River Moselle
29 May-4 Sep 7HEC ▦ 🔧🏪🍽✕⊙🅿🗑🚿 ↘ R 🗲 🗲 lau ♦ 🏪

TURCKHEIM *Haut-Rhin*
CM 7 r de la Gare ☎89271808
Camping Card Compulsory.
From Colmar follow N417 to Wintzenheim, then to Turckheim. Before
bridge turn left, continue past railway station and stadium.
Apr-Oct 2.5HEC ▦ ♦🔧⊙🅿🗑 ↘ R 🗲 lau ♦ ✕ 🗲 Prices: A17.50
pitch 20

URBÈS *Haut-Rhin*
CM Benelux Bâle ☎89827876
W of rte de Bussang.
Apr-Oct 3HEC ▦ 🔧🏪🍽✕⊙🅿🗑🗲 lau ♦ 🏪🗑🚿 ↘LP Prices:
A14-15 pitch 8

VAGNEY *Vosges*
CM du Mettey ☎29248135
1.3km E on Gérardmer road.
15 Jun-15 Sep 2.5HEC ▦ ♦🔧⊙🅿🗑🗲 lau ♦🏪🍽✕🗑🚿 ↘PR
Prices: pitch 40 (incl 2 persons)

VERDUN *Meuse*
Breuils allée des Breuils ☎29861531
SW via D34. Signposted.
Apr-15 Oct 5.5HEC ▦ 🔧🏪🍽✕⊙🅿🗑🚿🚐🚐 ↘ P 🗲 🗲 lau

VILLERS-LÈS-NANCY *Meurthe-et-Moselle*
Touristique International de Nancy-Brabois av P-Muller
☎83271828
SW in Brabois park.
Apr-Oct 6HEC ▦ ♦🔧🏪🍽✕⊙🅿🗲 lau ♦🗑 ↘PR Prices: A13-
15 V7 🚐8-9 ▲7

VITTEL *Vosges*
CM r C-Bassot ☎29080271
NE via D68 rte de Domjulien.
Etr-Oct ▦ 🔧🔧🏪⊙🅿🗲 lau ♦🏪🍽✕🗑🚿 ↘P 🗲

WASSELONNE *Bas-Rhin*
CM rte de Romanswiller ☎88870008
1km W on D224.
Apr-15 Oct 2.5HEC ▦ 🔧🏪🍽✕⊙🅿🗑 ↘ P 🗲 🗲 lau ♦✕🚿

WATTWILLER *Haut-Rhin*
Sources rte des Cretes ☎89754494
Shop, bar and café only open Jul-Aug.
Apr-Sep 10HEC ▦ 🔧🔧🏪🍽✕⊙🅿🗑🚐🚐 ↘ P 🗲 🗲 lau
Prices: A27 pitch 43

WIHR-AU-VAL *Haut-Rhin*
Route Verte 13 r de la Gare ☎89711010
15 Apr-Sep 0.9HEC ▦ 🔧🏪⊙🅿🗑🗲 lau ♦🏪🍽✕ ↘R

XONRUPT/LONGEMER *Vosges*
L'Eau-Vive ☎29630737
2km SE on D67A next to Lac de Longemer.
All year 1HEC ▦ 🔧🏪🍽✕⊙🅿🗑🚿 ↘ R 🗲 🗲 lau ♦ ↘L
Prices: A14 V10 pitch 18

Jonquilles rte du lac ☎29633401
2km SE on D67A beside Lac de Longemer.
Apr-15 Oct 4HEC ▦ 🔧🏪🍽✕⊙🅿🗑 ↘ L 🗲 lau Prices: pitch
52 (incl 2 persons)

Burgundy/Champagne

The Champagne region is one of the rich greens and huge
landscapes of the Ardennes and the wide meadows of the River
Marne. Its former capital, Laon, has a rich medieval heritage and
a lovely 12th-century cathedral, while, to the south , Troyes
boasts wonderful Renaissance treasures. But the jewel of the
area is Reims, with its magnificent Gothic cathedral - an important
centre for the region and the whole of France for centuries.
The local wine of Champagne needs no introduction, and pre-
arranged visits and regular tours are available from the famous
names - Mercier, Moët, Veuve Cliquot - and there is a Champagne
Museum (Musée de Champagne) in Épernay.
The representatives of Burgundy also travel the world - names
such as Chablis, Mâcon and Nuits St Georges. A wonderful
surprise of the area, though, is the network of hundreds of miles
of navigable waterways, accessing a wealth of Romanesque
churches, abbeys, castles, and medieval fortress towns,
exquisite small villages and quiet rolling expanses of rich
pastures and vineyards - the quintessential provincial France.
Visitors should include a visit to Beaune, famous for its 14th-
century hospice.

ACCOLAY *Yonne*
Moulin Jacquot r du Moulin Jacquot ☎86815648
W, beside the Canal du Nivernais.
Apr-15 Oct 1HEC ▦ ♦🔧⊙🅿🗑 lau ♦🏪🍽✕🚿 ↘R 🗲 Prices: A7
V5 🚐5 ▲5

ANCY-LE-FRANC *Yonne*
CM rte de Cusy ☎86751321
15 Jun-15 Sep 0.6HEC ▦ ♦🔧⊙🅿🗑 lau ♦🏪🍽✕🚿 ↘R 🗲
Prices: A12 V6 🚐6 ▲6

ANDRYES *Yonne*
Bois Joli ☎86817048
0.6km SW.
Apr-Sep 5HEC ▦ ♦🔧🏪🍽✕⊙🅿🚐🚐 ↘ P 🗲 🗲 lau ♦🏪🗑🚿 ↘LR
Prices: pitch 85.50 (incl 2 persons)

ARNAY-LE-DUC *Côte-D'Or*
CM de Fouché ☎80900223
0.7km E on D17C.
All year 5HEC ▦ 🔧🏪🍽⊙🅿🗑 ↘ L 🗲 🅿 🗲 lau ♦✕🚿 Prices:
A10 V6 🚐7 ▲7

AUXERRE *Yonne*
CM 8 rte de Vaux ☎86521115
SE towards Vaux
Apr-Sep 5HEC ▦ ♦🔧🏪✕⊙🅿🗑🚿🗲🗲 lau ♦🏪✕ ↘PR Prices:
A12-14 🚐6 pitch 12

AUXONNE *Côte-D'Or*
CM Arquebuse ☎80373436
Clean, well-equipped site on right bank of River Saône near bathing
area.
From Auxonne travel W on N5 for 3km. Then turn northwards on D24
towards Athée and Pontailler-sur-Saône.
May-Sep 2HEC ▦ 🔧🏪🏪⊙🅿🗑🚿 ↘ PR 🗲 lau ♦🏪🍽✕

AVALLON *Yonne*
CM Sous Roche ☎86341039
2km SE by D944 and D427.
15 Apr-15 Oct 2HEC ▦ 🔧🏪🍽✕⊙🅿 ↘ R 🗲 🗲 lau ♦🏪🍽✕ ↘PR

BAR-SUR-AUBE *Aube*
Gravière r des Varennes ☎25271294
0.5km E of D13.
10 Apr-15 Oct 2.8HEC ▦ ♦🔧⊙🅿 ↘ R 🗲 lau ♦🏪🍽✕ ↘P

BAZOLLES *Nièvre*
Baye ☎86389033
Apr-Oct 1.5HEC ▦ 🔧🔧🏪⊙🅿🗑 ↘ L 🗲 🗲 lau ♦🏪🍽✕🗑🚿 Prices:
A10 pitch 17.50

BEAUNE *Côte-D'Or*
CM Cent Vignes 10 r A-Dubois ☎80220391
On outskirts of town. Site divided into pitches, clean, well-looked after sanitary installations. From 20 Jun-31 Aug it is advisable to arrive before 1600 hrs.
On N74 on Savigny-les-Beaune road.
15 Mar-Oct 2HEC ▦ ⊞ ♠ ♚ ☒ ⊙ ♨ ⌀ ☲ ⊞ lau ♦ ♨ ⚲LP

BOURBON-LANCY *Saône-et-Loire*
Plan d'Eau ☎85893427
May-15 Oct 1.9HEC ▦ ⤳ ♠ ♚ ☒ ⊙ ♨ ⚏ ☲ lau ♦ ♚ ☒ ⌀ ☲ ⚲LP ⊞
Prices: A13 V10.50 ♥11.50 ▲10.50

St-Prix r du St-Prix ☎85891485
By the swimming pool off the D979a.
15 Apr-Oct 2.5HEC ▦ ⊞ ♠ ♚ ☒ ⊙ ♨ ⚏ ☲ lau ♦ ☒ ☒ ⌀ ☲ ⚲LP ⊞
Prices: A13 V10.50 ♥11.50 ▲10.50

BOURBONNE-LES-BAINS *Haute-Marne*
Montmorency r du Stade ☎25900864
Apr-Oct 2.5HEC ▦ ⊞ ♠ ♚ ☒ ⊙ ♨ ⚏ ☲ ⊞ lau ♦ ⚲P Prices: A12.25 pitch 11.25

BOURG *Haute-Marne*
Croix d'Arles ☎25882402
Access via N74 or A31.
Apr-Oct 7HEC ▦ ♦ ♠ ♚ ☒ ⊙ ♨ ⚏ ⚲ P ☲ ⊞ lau Prices: A15 pitch 30

BOURG-FIDÈLE *Ardennes*
Murée rte de Rocroi ☎24542445
A lakeside site in wooded surroundings.
1km N via D22.
All year 1.3HEC ▦ ⊞ ♠ ☒ ☒ ⊙ ♨ ⚏ ⚏ ☲ lau ♦ ☒ ⌀ ☲ ⊞

CHAGNY *Saône-et-Loire*
CM Pâquier Fané ☎85872142
A clean site 600m W of the church.
Follow the D974 from town centre.
13 May-4 Sep 1.5HEC ▦ ⊞ ♠ ♚ ☒ ☒ ⊙ ♨ ⌀ ⚲ R ☲ ⊞ lau ♦ ⚲P

CHÂLONS-EN-CHAMPAGNE *Marne*
CM r de Plaisance ☎26683800
Mar-Oct 7HEC ▦ ⊞ ♦ ⊞ ♠ ☒ ⊙ ♨ ⌀ ☲ ☲ ⊞ lau ♦ ♚ ☒ Prices: A23 V14 ♥21 ▲21

CHARLEVILLE-MÉZIÈRES *Ardennes*
CM Mont Olympe r des Paquis ☎24332360
Level meadowland near the town centre and 100m from municipal indoor swimming pool.
Well signed from town centre.
Etr-15 Oct 2HEC ▦ ⊞ ♠ ♚ ☒ ☒ ⊙ ♨ ⌀ ☲ ⚲ PR ☲ ⊞ lau ♦ ☒

CHAROLLES *Saône-et-Loire*
CM rte de Viny ☎85240490
NE of town via D33 towards Viry
15 Mar-15 Oct 1.5HEC ▦ ⊞ ♠ ♚ ☒ ⊙ ♨ ⚲ PR ☲ ⊞ lau ♦ ♚ ☒ ⌀

CHÂTILLON-SUR-SEINE *Côte-D'Or*
CM espl St-Vorles ☎80910305
SE of town off rte de Langres (D928).
Apr-Sep 0.8HEC ▦ ⊞ ♠ ♚ ☒ ⊙ ♨ ⌀ ☲ ☲ ⊞ lau ♦ ♚ ☒ ⚲P Prices: A14 pitch 10

CHATONRUPT *Haute-Marne*
CM ☎25948182
Etr-Sep 1.8HEC ▦ ⊞ ⤳ ♠ ♚ ☒ ⊙ ♨ ☲ ⊞ lau ♦ ☒ ☒ ☲ Prices: A6 V5 ♥5 ▲5

CLAMECY *Nièvre*
Pont Picot rte de Chenoches ☎86270597
In a pleasant situation between the River Yonne and the Canal du Nivernais.
May-Sep 1.2HEC ▦ ⊞ ⤳ ♠ ⊙ ♨ ⚲ R ☲ lau ♦ ♚ ☒ ☒ ⌀ ☲ ⚲P ⊞
Prices: A15 pitch 11

CONFLANS-SUR-SEINE *Marne*
Vieille Seine r du Port ☎25882302
On the outskirts of the village, beside the River Seine.
Jun-Aug 3HEC ▦ ⊞ ⊞ ♠ ♠ ⊙ ♨ ♨ ▲ ⚲ R ☲ ☲ lau ♦ ♚ ☒ ⌀ ☲
Prices: A15 pitch 15-20

COSNE-SUR-LOIRE *Nièvre*
Loire & Nohain Ile de Cosne, rte de Bourges ☎86282792
Site borders River Loire.
Follow D955 W towards Sancerre.
Apr-3 Sep 4HEC ▦ ⊞ ⹅⹅⹅ ♦ ♠ ♚ ☒ ☒ ⊙ ♨ ⌀ ⚏ ☲ ⊞ ♦ ⚲P

CRÊCHES-SUR-SAÔNE *Saône-et-Loire*
CM Le Port d'Arciat ☎85371183
1.5km E via D31 beside the River Saône.
May-Sep 6HEC ▦ ⊞ ♦ ♠ ♚ ☒ ☒ ⊙ ♨ ⌀ ☲ ⚲ LR ☲ ⊞ lau Prices: A16 pitch 33

DIGOIN *Saône-et-Loire*
CM Chevrette r de la Chevrette ☎85531149
W of village on N79.
Mar-Oct 1.6HEC ▦ ⊞ ♦ ♠ ⊙ ♨ ⚏ ⚲ PR ☲ ⊞ lau ♦ ♚ ☒ ☒ ⌀ Prices: A11 pitch 23

DIJON *Côte-D'Or*
Lac 3 bd Kir ☎80435472
1.5km W on N5.
Apr-15 Oct 3HEC ▦ ⊞ ⹅⹅⹅ ♦ ⊞ ♠ ♠ ⊙ ♨ ☲ ☲ ⊞ lau ♦ ♚ ☒ ☒ ⌀ ☲

ÉCLARON-BRAUCOURT *Haute-Marne*
Presqu'île de Champaubert ☎25041320
Situated on lake peninsula.
Apr-15 Oct 3.4HEC ▦ ⊞ ♠ ♚ ☒ ☒ ⊙ ♨ ⌀ ☲ ⊞ lau ♦ ♚ ⚲L Prices: A24 pitch 22

EPINAC *Saône-et-Loire*
Pont Vert ☎85820026
S via D43 beside the River Drée.
Apr-Sep 3HEC ▦ ⊞ ♦ ♠ ♚ ☒ ☒ ⊙ ♨ ⚏ ⚲ R ☲ lau ♦ ⌀ ☲

FRONCLES *Haute-Marne*
Deux Ponts r des Ponts ☎25023350
In a peaceful location beside the River Marne.
15 Mar-15 Oct 3HEC ⊞ ♠ ⊙ ♨ ⚲ R ☲ ♦ ♚ ☒ ☒ ⊞

GIBLES *Saône-et-Loire*
Château de Montrouant Montrouant ☎85845113
1.6km NE beside the lake.
20 Jun-Aug 1HEC ▦ ⊞ ⹅⹅⹅ ♠ ♠ ♚ ☒ ☒ ⊙ ♨ ⚏ ▲ ⚲ LPR ☲ ⊞ lau ♦ ⌀ ☲

GIFFAUMONT *Marne*
Plage rte du Port ☎26726184
May-10 Sep 1.5HEC ▦ ⊞ ♠ ♚ ☒ ⊙ ♨ ⌀ ☲ ⊞ lau ♦ ♚ ☒ ☲ ⚲L

GIGNY-SUR-SAÔNE *Saône-et-Loire*
Château de l'Épervière ☎85448323
Quiet site in park surrounding 16th-century château. Close to the River Saône for fishing and sailing.
N6 to Sennecey-le-Grand, then follow signs.
12 Apr-Sep 10HEC ▦ ⊞ ♦ ♠ ♚ ☒ ☒ ⊙ ♨ ⌀ ⚏ ⚲ LP ☲ ⊞ lau ♦ ☲ ⚲R
Prices: A21-25 pitch 30-40

GRANDPRÉ *Ardennes*
CM ☎24305071
150m from village centre on D6.
Apr-Sep 2HEC ▦ ⊞ ♠ ♠ ⊙ ♨ ⚲ R ☲ ⊞ lau ♦ ♚ ☒ ☒ ⌀ ☲ Prices: A7 V4 ♥4 ▲4

GUEUGNON *Saône-et-Loire*
CM rte de Digoin, Chazey ☎85855050
A quiet site in wooded surroundings near a lake.
Jun-Sep 3HEC ▦ ⊞ ♠ ♠ ⊙ ♨ ⌀ ☲ ⚏ ⚲ L ☲ ⊞ lau ♦ ♚ ☒ Prices: A12 V7 ♥22 ▲12

ISSY-L'ÉVÊQUE *Saône-et-Loire*

CM de l'Étang Neuf ☎85249605
In a fine position beside the lake, overlooking the château.
May-15 Sep 4HEC 📷 ⚊ ♑ ⊙ ⚑ ⚐ P ⚑ ⊞ lau ➤ ⚐ ⚐
Prices: A15 pitch 15

LAIVES *Saône-et-Loire*

Lacs 'La Heronnière' Les Bois de Laives ☎85449885
Compulsory separate car park for arrivals after 2200hrs.
Access via 'Châlon Sud' autoroute exit towards Mâcon.
15 May-15 Sep 1.5HEC 📷 ⚊ ✕ ⊙ ⚐ ⊞ lau ➤ ✕ LR
Prices: A18 pitch 25

MÂCON *Saône-et-Loire*

CM ☎85381622
Divided into pitches. Water sports centre and pool nearby.
2km N on N6.
15 Mar-Oct 5HEC 📷 ⚊ ✕ ⊙ ⚐ ⊞ lau ➤ PR

MARCENAY *Côte-D'Or*

Grebes Laignes ☎80816172
22 Mar-15 Sep 2.4HEC 📷 ♑ ⊙ ⚐ L ⊞ lau Prices:
A12 V9 ⚑11 ⚑11

MAS-CABARDÈS *Aude*

Eaux Vives ☎68263105
1km E via D101, beside the river.
Apr-Sep 1HEC ♑ ⊙ ⚐ ⊞ lau ➤ ✕

MATOUR *Saône-et-Loire*

CM Le Paluet Le Paluet ☎85597058
In pleasant countryside beside the river.
Apr-Sep 2HEC ✕ ♑ ✕ ⊙ PR ⊞ lau ➤ ⚐

MESNIL-ST PÈRE *Aube*

Voie Colette Rue du Lac ☎25412715
Grassland, with trees, ornamental shrubs and flower beds. Slightly sloping, with a man-made lake nearby.
About 2km from Mesnil-St-Père; signposted from centre.
Apr-15 Oct 4HEC 📷 ♑ ✕ ⊙ ⚐ ⊞ lau ➤ ✕ L Prices: pitch 38-40 (incl 2 persons)

MEURSAULT *Côte-D'Or*

Grappe d'Or 2 rte de Volnay ☎80212248
Clean terraced site.
700m NE on D11b.
Apr-Oct 3.5HEC 📷 ♑ ✕ ⊙ ⚐ P ⊞ lau ➤ ⊞ Prices:
A18-21 V11-13 ⚑20-24 ⚑13-15

MONTAPAS *Nièvre*

CM La Chênaie ☎86583432
500m from town centre, beside the lake, via D259.
Apr-Sep 1HEC 📷 ♑ ✕ ⊙ LR ⊞ lau ➤ ✕

MONTBARD *Côte-D'Or*

CM r M-Servet ☎80922160
NW via rte de Laignes.
Feb-Oct 2.5HEC 📷 ♑ ⊙ ⚐ ⊞ lau ➤ ✕ PR ⊞
Prices: A13 pitch 15

MONTHERMÉ *Ardennes*

Base de Loisirs Départementale ☎24328161
In a pleasant wooded situation.
0.8km NE beside the River Semoy.
All year 16HEC 📷 ⊙ ⚐ lau

MONTSAUCHE *Nièvre*

Mesanges Lac des Settons, Rive Gauche ☎86845577
On the left bank of Lac des Settons. *Camping Card Recommended.*
May-15 Sep 5HEC 📷 ♑ ⊙ ⚐ ⊞ lau ➤ ✕ LPR Prices:
A20 pitch 15

Plage du Midi ☎86845197
Camping Card Compulsory.
From Salieu (on N6) follow D977. From town centre follow D193 to Les Sultons, then to site.
Etr-Sep 4HEC 📷 ♑ ✕ ⊙ ⚐ L ⊞ lau ➤ ✕

PARAY-LE-MONIAL *Saône-et-Loire*

Mambré rte du Gué-Léger ☎85888920
Well signposted from outskirts of town.
Apr-Oct 4HEC 📷 ♑ ⊙ ⚐ A P ⊞ lau ➤ R
Prices: A14-18 pitch 34-36

POUGUES-LES-EAUX *Nièvre*

CM Chanternes ☎86688618
On N7 approx. 7km N of Nevers.
Etr-Oct 1.4HEC 📷 ♑ ⊙ ⚐ lau ➤ ✕ P

PREMEAUX *Côte-D'Or*

Saule Guillaume ☎80623078
1.5km E via D109G
15 Jun-Aug 2.1HEC 📷 ♑ ⊙ ⚐ L ⊞ lau ➤ P

RADONVILLIERS *Aube*

Garillon ☎25922146
Beside the river, 250m from the lake.
Jun-15 Sep 1HEC 📷 ♑ ⊙ ⚐ lau ➤ ✕

REIMS *Marne*

Airotel de Champagne av Hoche ☎26854122
Approaching from north, turn off on outskirts of town towards Châlons-sur-Marne. Well signposted.
Etr-Sep 5HEC 📷 ♑ ✕ ⊙ ⚐ ⊞ lau Prices: A22 pitch 19

RIEL-LES-EAUX *Côte-D'Or*

Riel-les-Eaux ☎80937276
A lakeside site with fishing and boating facilities.
2.2km W via D13.
Apr-Oct 7HEC 📷 ♑ ✕ ⊙ ⚐ L ⊞ lau ➤ Prices:
A7.70 pitch 9

ROMILLY-SUR-SEINE *Aube*

Cerisiers ☎25249398
E of town, 250m from N19 Troyes road.
15 Jun-5 Sep 1.5HEC ♑ ⊙ ⚐ P ⊞ lau ➤ ✕
R

STE-MENEHOULD *Marne*

CM de la Grelette ☎26608021
E of town towards Metz, beside the River Aisne.
May-Sep 0.5HEC 📷 ♑ ⊙ ⚐ P lau ➤ ✕ ⊞

ST-HILAIRE-SOUS-ROMILLY *Aube*

Airotel La Noue des Rois ☎25244160
A quiet site in a pine forrest on the Basin d'Arcachon. Booking recommended in July and August.
2km NE.

CAMPING CARAVANNING LES GREBES ★★★
21330 MARCENAY

Tel: 03.80.81.61.72 – Fax: 03.80.81.61.99 Tel OFF
SEASON 03.80.81.43.03 (Townhall of Laignes)
Situated between LAIGNES and CHATILLON
SUR SEINE, in a well-preserved natural setting,
sheltered from motorways. Peace and rest
guaranteed. Direct access to the Lake, French
boules ground, volley, children's playground. Water
activities, horse riding, cross country bikes, fishing
nearby, walking tracks

All year 30HEC ▥ ░░ ⊕ ℮ ❢ ✕ ⊙ ❂ ♨ ⊞ ♥ ⅂ LR ☎ ▣ ⊞ ⋇ lau ♦ ▙

ST-HONORÉ *Nièvre*

Bains 15 av J-Mermoz ☎86307344
May-Sep 4HEC ▥ ⊕ ℮ ❢ ✕ ⊙ ❂ ⌀ ♨ ⅄ PR ☎ ⊞ lau ♦ ▙ ⌿ Prices:
pitch 63-90 (incl 2 persons)

ST-MARCEL *Saône-et-Loire*

Butte r J-Lenevev ☎85482686
All year 5HEC ▥ ⊕ ℮ ▙ ❢ ✕ ⊙ ❂ ⌀ ⅄ R ☎ ⊞ lau ♦ ⌿ ⅄P

ST-PÉREUSE *Nièvre*

▨**Manoir de Bezolle** ☎86844255
Situated in grounds of a manor house, at the edge of a National
Park. Well-kept site divided by hedges.
Camping Card Compulsory.
At 'X' roads of D11 and D978.
15 Mar-15 Oct 8HEC ▥ ♦ ℮ ❢ ▙ ❢ ✕ ⊙ ❂ ⌀ ♨ ⅄ P ☎ ⊞ lau Prices:
pitch 80-110 (incl 2 persons)

SAULIEU *Côte-D'Or*

CM Perron ☎80641619
1 km NW on N6.
Apr-20 Oct 8HEC ▥ ⊕ ℮ ▙ ❢ ⊙ ❂ ⌀ ♨ ⅄ P ☎ ⊞ lau ♦ ✕ Prices:
A12 pitch 20

SEDAN *Ardennes*

CM de la Prairie bd Fabert ☎24271305
Etr-15 Oct 1.5HEC ▥ ⅊⊷ ℮ ⊙ ❂ ☎ ⊞ lau ♦ ▙ ❢ ✕ ⌀ ⌿ ⅄LP
Prices: pitch 13-15

SELONGY *Côte-D'Or*

CM Les Courvelles r H-Jevain ☎80757074
May-Sep 0.4HEC ▥ ⊕ ℮ ▙ ⊙ ❂ ☎ lau ♦ ❢ ✕ ⌀ ⌿ ⅄PR ⊞

SEURRE *Côte-D'Or*

Piscine ☎80204922
From town centre follow N73 W for 600m in the direction of Beaune.
Jun-Sep ▥ ⊕ ℮ ❢ ✕ ⊙ ❂ ⌀ ☎ ⊞ lau ♦ ▙ ✕ ⅄PR Prices: A9.50
V6.50 ⊞6.50 ▲6.50

SÉZANNE *Marne*

CM rte de Launat ☎26805700
1.5km W on D239, rte de Launat.
Etr-11 Oct 1HEC ▥ ⊕ ℮ ⊙ ❂ ⅄ P ☎ lau ♦ ▙ ❢ ✕ ⌀ ⌿

SIGNY-LE-PETIT *Ardennes*

Pré Hugon Base de Loisirs ☎24535101
A pleasant site in wooded surroundings.
Access via N43.
May-15 Oct 0.8HEC ▥ ⊕ ℮ ⊙ ❂ lau ♦ ▙ ❢ ✕ ⌀ ⌿ ⅄LR ⊞

SOULAINES-DHUYS *Aube*

CM La Croix Badeau ☎25927744
May-Sep 1.5HEC ▥ ⌀ ⊕ ℮ ⊙ ❂ lau ♦ ▙ ⌀ ⌿ ⊞ Prices: A8 pitch
20

TAZILLY *Nièvre*

Château de Chigy ☎86301080
Apr-Sep 7HEC ▥ ⊕ ℮ ▙ ❢ ✕ ⊙ ❂ ⌀ ♨ ⅄ LP ☎ ⊞ lau

THONNANCE-LES-MOULINS *Haute-Marne*

▨**Forge de Ste-Marie** ☎25944200
15 May-15 Sep 32HEC ▥ ⊕ ℮ ▙ ❢ ❢ ⊙ ❂ ⌀ ⅄ PR ☎ lau ♦ ✕

TOULON-SUR-ARROUX *Saône-et-Loire*

CM du Val d'Arroux rte d'Uxeau ☎85795122
On W outskirts beside the River Arroux.
Etr-1 Nov 1.3HEC ▥ ⊕ ℮ ⊙ ❂ ⅄ R ☎ ⊞ lau ♦ ▙ ❢ ✕ ⌀ ⌿

UCHIZY *Saône-et-Loire*

National 6 ☎85405390
Site surrounded by poplar trees on banks of river.
Turn off N6 towards Saône 6km S of Tournus and continue 0.8km.
Apr-Oct 6HEC ▥ ♦ ℮ ❢ ▙ ❢ ✕ ⊙ ❂ ⌀ ⌿ ♨ ⊞ ♨ ⅄ PR ☎ ⊞ lau Prices:
A16-20.50 pitch 18-29.50

VANDENESSE-EN-AUXOIS *Côte-D'Or*

Lac de Panthier ☎80492194
5km SE from Pouilly-en-Auxois on A6.
15 May-Sep 5HEC ▥ ⊕ ℮ ▙ ❢ ✕ ⊙ ❂ ⌀ ♨ ⅄ LP ☎ ⊞ lau

Voiliers ☎80492194
In a pleasant situation beside a lake.
2.5km NE via D977.
15 Apr-30 Sep 3.5HEC ▥ ⊕ ℮ ▙ ❢ ✕ ⊙ ❂ ⌀ ⅄ LP ☎ lau Prices:
A27 pitch 40

VENAREY-LES-LAUMES *Côte-D'Or*

Alésia r Dr-Roux ☎80960776
All year 2HEC ▥ ⊕ ℮ ⊙ ❂ ☎ ♦ ▙ ❢ ✕ ⌀ ⅄L Prices: A10 V4 ⊞4
▲4

VERMENTON *Yonne*

Coulemières ☎86815302
On the N6 S of Auxerre.
10 Apr-10 Oct 1.5HEC ▥ ⊕ ℮ ❢ ⊙ ❂ ⌀ ⅄ R ☎ lau Prices: A16 V9
⊞9 ▲9

VILLENEUVE-LES-GENÊTS *Yonne*

Bois Guillaume ☎86454541
Camping Card Compulsory
2.7km NE.
All year 8HEC ▥ ⊕ ℮ ▙ ❢ ✕ ⊙ ❂ ⌀ ♨ ⊞ ♨ ⅄ P ☎ ⊞ lau ♦ ⅄R
Prices: A18 V11 ⊞11

South West/Pyrénées

One of the largest regions of France, Aquitaine stretches from
the lower plateaux of the Massif Central, west to the Atlantic and
south nearly to the foothills of the Pyrénées. This is a land of
sunshine, and the three main rivers - the Lot, the Garonne and the
Dordogne - wind through valleys and meander through orchards
and vineyards, occasionally flowing between high cliffs with
castles perched on rocky ledges. Along the Vézère valley in the
Dordogne are the impressive caves and grottos with prehistoric
remains - the remarkable Lascaux paintings can be admired in
Lascaux II - a full-scale replica of the original. On the coast in the
south of the region, holidaymakers are attracted by the
sophisticated chic of Biarritz, colourful resorts like St-Jean-de-Luz,
and Atlantic rollers offering some of the best surfing in Europe.
At the foothills of the Pyrénées is Basque country, with charming
white houses and timbered cottages, colourful cascading flowers,
and rich heritage of festivals and folklore.
Inland, popular centres include Lourdes, which has attracted
pilgrims for centuries, and the fascinating Pyrénées National Park
with its wild flora and fauna. The Renaissance city of Toulouse
has a wonderful heritage, with some of the finest examples of
Romanesque architecture in Europe. The region is internationally
famous for wonderful cuisine. Here you can find duck liver paté,
"fois gras", Armagnac, and the succulent Toulouse sausage.

ABZAC *Gironde*

Paradis rte de Perigueux ☎57490510
On meadowland near an artificial lake. Pedal boats and fishing nearby.
Drive W on N89 from the direction of Périgueux. After St-Médard-de-
Guizières turn onto D17E and follow signposts.
All year 5HEC ▥ ♦ ℮ ▙ ❢ ✕ ⊙ ❂ ⌀ ♨ ⊞ ♨ ⅄ LR ☎ ⊞ lau Prices:
A18 pitch 25

AIGUES-VIVES *Ariège*

Serre ☎61030616
Access via D625 (Lavelanet - Mirepoix), site 1km W.
All year 5HEC ▥ ❢ ℮ ⊙ ❂ ☎ ⊞ ▲ ⅄ P ☎ lau ♦ ▙ ✕ ⌀ ⌿

AIRE-SUR-L'ADOUR *Landes*

Ombrages de l'Adour ☎58717510
A clean, tidy site next to a sports stadium beside the river. Clean
sanitary installations.
May-Oct 2HEC ▥ ♦ ℮ ⊙ ❂ ☎ ▲ ⅄ R ☎ ⊞ lau ♦ ▙ ❢ ✕ ⅄P

ALBI *Tarn*

Languedoc allée du Camping Caussels ☎63603706
The site is owned by the local automobile club. It lies on terraced land in a forest next to municipal swimming pools.
Camping Card Compulsory.
From village take N99 towards Millau, then turn left onto D100 and left again into site.
Apr-Oct 1HEC ▨ ⊕ ↑ ⊙ ☺ ⊘ ⊞ lau ♦ ⅃ ♥ ✕ ↳P

AMBARÈS *Gironde*

Clos Chauvet 5 av de la Libération ☎56388108
Surrounded by vineyards.
100m from A10 via D911.
May-Oct 0.8HEC ▨ ⊕ ↑ ⊙ ☺ ⊘ ⊞ lau ♦ ⅃ ↳P

ANDERNOS-LES-BAINS *Gironde*

Fontaine-Vieille 4 bd du Cl-Wurtz ☎56820167
On level ground in sparse forest.
S of village centre.
11 May-21 Sep 12.6HEC ▨ ∷∷ ♦ ↑ ⅃ ♥ ✕ ⊙ ☺ ⊘ ⊟ ⊞ ↳ PS ⊡ ⊞ lau Prices: pitch 60-80 (incl 2 persons)
See advertisement under Colour Section

Pleine Forêt ☎56821718
Situated in a quiet location among pines.
Off D106E or D106 Andernos-les-Bains-Bordeaux road.
All year 6HEC ▨ ∷∷ ♦ ↑ ⅃ ♥ ✕ ⊙ ☺ ⊟ ⊞ ☺ ↳ P ⊡ ⊞ lau ♦ ✕ ⊘ ↳S

ANGLARS-JUILLAC *Lot*

Floiras ☎65362739
A quiet, level site beside the River Lot with good facilities for boating etc.
SW via D8.
Apr-15 Oct 1HEC ▨ ⊕ ↑ ⅃ ♥ ✕ ⊙ ☺ ⊘ ▲ ↳ R ⊡ ⊞ lau ♦ ✕
Prices: A17-19 pitch 25-30

ANGLES *Tarn*

Manoir de Boutaric rte de Lacabariede ☎63709606
Site lies in the grounds of an old Manor House.
S of village, on rte de Lacabarède.
Etr-mid Oct 3.3HEC ▨ ♦ ↑ ⅃ ♥ ✕ ⊙ ☺ ⊟ ☺ ▲ ↳ P ⊡ ⊞ lau ♦ ⅃ ⊘ ▲ ↳LR Prices: pitch 68-120 (incl 2 persons)

ANGLET *Pyrénées-Atlantiques*

Parme Quartier Brindos ☎59230300
Camping Card Compulsory
3km SW off N10
All year 3.7HEC ♦ ↑ ⅃ ♥ ✕ ⊙ ☺ ⊘ ▲ ☺ ↳ P ⊡ ⊞ lau ♦ ↳L
Prices: A22-30 V10 ⊞25-27 ▲25-27

ANGOISSE *Dorgogne*

Rouffiac en Périgord ☎53526879
May-Sep 6HEC ▨ ⊕ ↑ ⅃ ♥ ✕ ⊙ ☺ ⊘ ▲ ↳ L ⊡ lau

ARCACHON *Gironde*

Camping Club d'Arcachon av de la Galaxie, Les Abatilles ☎56832415
1.5 km S.
All year 6HEC ∷∷ ♦ ↑ ⅃ ♥ ✕ ⊙ ☺ ⊘ ▲ ☺ ☺ ↳ P ⊡ ⊞ lau ♦ ↳LS
Prices: A60-110 ⊞60-145

ARCIZANS-AVANT *Hautes-Pyrénées*

Lac ☎62970188
Set in Pyrenean landscape on outskirts of village. Lakeside site at the foot of a château.
S on N21 take D101 through St-Savin.
Jun-Sep 2.2HEC ▨ ⊕ ↑ ⅃ ⊙ ☺ ⊘ ⊡ ⊞ lau ♦ ⅃ ✕ ↳P Prices: A23 pitch 25

ARÈS *Gironde*

Abberts ☎56602680
Camping Card Compulsory.
Follow signs from D106.
10 May-Sep 2HEC ▨ ∷∷ ♦ ↑ ⅃ ♥ ✕ ⊙ ☺ ⊟ ☺ ⊡ ⊞ lau ♦ ⊘ ▲ ↳LPS

Canadienne rte de lège, 82 r du Gl-de-Gaulle ☎56602491
Shop available Jul-Aug only.
1 km N off D106.
Apr-20 Oct 2HEC ▨ ∷∷ ♦ ↑ ⅃ ♥ ✕ ⊙ ☺ ⊘ ☺ ☺ ↳ P ⊡ ⊞ lau ♦ ↳RS Prices: A23.10

Cigale Route de lège ☎56602259
Clean tidy site amongst pine trees. Grassy pitches.
0.5 km N on D106.
Apr-10 Oct 2.7HEC ♦ ↑ ⅃ ♥ ✕ ⊙ ☺ ⊟ ▲ ☺ ↳ P ⊡ ⊞ lau ♦ ↳L Prices: pitch 98 (incl 2 persons)

CM Goëlands Av de la liberation ☎56825564
1.7km SE
Apr-Sep 10HEC ▨ ∷∷ ♦ ↑ ⅃ ♥ ✕ ⊙ ☺ ⊘ ▲ ☺ ⊡ ⊞ lau Prices: pitch 67-88 (incl 2 persons)
See advertisement under Colour Section

Pasteur r du Pilote 1 ☎56603333
S of D3, 300m from the sea.
Apr-Oct 1HEC ▨ ♦ ↑ ⅃ ♥ ✕ ⊙ ☺ ☺ ☺ ↳ P ⊞ lau ♦ ✕ ↳S Prices: pitch 72-82 (incl 2 persons)

ARGELÈS-GAZOST *Hautes-Pyrénées*

At **AGOS-VIDALOS**(5km NE)

Soleil du Pibeste ☎62975323
S on N21.
All year 1.5HEC ▨ ♦ ↑ ⅃ ♥ ✕ ⊙ ☺ ⊘ ▲ ↳ P ⊡ ⊞ lau ♦ ✕ ↳R
Prices: A20-22 pitch 20-22

At **ARRAS-EN-LAVENDAN**(2km SW on N618)

Relais de l'Aubisque rte du Col de l'Aubisque ☎62970211
Etr-20 Sep 1HEC ▨ ⊕ ↑ ⅃ ⊙ ☺ ⊘ ☺ ☺ ⊡ ⊞ lau ♦ ⅃ ✕ ↳R

ARREAU *Hautes-Pyrénées*

Refuge International rte Internationale ☎62986334
Enclosed terrace site.
2km N on D929.
All year 15HEC ▨ ♦ ↑ ✕ ⊙ ☺ ⊟ ☺ ↳ PR ⊡ ⊞ lau ♦ ⅃ ✕ ⊘ ▲ ↳L

ASCAIN *Pyrénées-Atlantiques*

Nivelle rte de St-Pée-sur-Nivelle ☎59540194
2km N of town on D918 to St-Jean-de-Luz.
15 Jun-15 Sep 3HEC ▨ ♦ ↑ ⅃ ♥ ✕ ⊙ ☺ ⊟ ☺ ↳ R ⊡ ⊞ lau ♦ ⊘
Prices: A17 pitch 30

ASCARAT *Pyrénées-Atlantiques*

Europ' Camping ☎59371278
In rustic surroundings of mountains and vineyards, 300m from the River Nive.
1km W of St-Jean-Pied-de-Port on D918.
30 Mar-15 Oct 1.7HEC ▨ ⊕ ↑ ⅃ ♥ ✕ ⊙ ☺ ⊘ ↳ P ⊡ ⊞ lau ♦ ↳R
Prices: A32 pitch 46

AUREILHAN *Landes*

CM rte de Lamarque ☎58091088
Quiet site separated by a small road on the banks of Lake Aureilhan.
D626, 2km before Mimizan, on the right.
May-Sep 4.2HEC ▨ ∷∷ ♦ ↑ ⅃ ♥ ✕ ⊙ ☺ ⊘ ↳ L ⊡ ⊞ lau ♦ ✕ ▲
Prices: pitch 46-54 (incl 2 persons)

∎Parc Montana Aureilhan Promenade de l'Étang ☎58090287
Well tended site under deciduous trees providing shade, partially on open meadow.
Turn right at Labouheyre off N10 on D626 to Aureilhan. Follow signs.
May-Sep 15HEC ▨ ♦ ↑ ⅃ ♥ ✕ ⊙ ☺ ⊘ ☺ ☺ ↳ ▲ ↳ P ⊡ ⊞ lau
Prices: pitch 70-110 (incl 2 persons)

AZUR *Landes*

CM d'Azur ☎58483072
2km S, 100m from Lac de Soustons.
31 May-20 Sep 6HEC ▨ ∷∷ ⊕ ↑ ⅃ ♥ ✕ ⊙ ☺ ⊘ ▲ ☺ ☺ ↳ LS ⊡ ⊞ lau ♦ ⅃ ♥ Prices: A15.50 pitch 27.50

BAGNÈRES-DE-BIGORRE *Hautes-Pyrénées*

Bigourdan rte de Tarbes ☎62951357
2.5km NW at Pouzac
May-Sep 0.6HEC ▨ ♦ ↑ ⊙ ☺ ☺ ☺ ⊡ lau ♦ ⅃ ⊘ ▲ ⊞

Tilleuls rte de Sabassere ☎62952604
May-Sep 2.6HEC ▦ ⚑ ⋔ ⊙ ⬚ ⌀ ⚄ lau ➡ ⚏ ♟ ✕ ♨ ⇃P ⊞ Prices:
A18 pitch 22

At **TRÉBONS**(4km N on D935)

Parc des Oiseaux ☎62953026
Clean, well-kept site with large pitches.
All year 2.8HEC ▦ ⚑ ⋔ ♟ ✕ ⊙ ⬚ ⌀ ⚍ ⊞ ⊡ ▲ ⇃ R ⚄ ⊞ lau ➡ ⚏ ✕ ⇃P

BAYONNE Pyrénées-Atlantiques
Airotel la Chêneraie chemin Cazenare ☎59550131
On gently sloping field divided by hedges.
4km NE off N117 (Pau) road.
Etr-1 Oct 10HEC ▦ ➡ ⋔ ⚏ ♟ ✕ ⊙ ⬚ ⌀ ⚄ ♟ ▲ ⇃ P ⚄ ⊞ lau ➡ ⇃S
Prices: A18-23 pitch 40-75

BEAUCENS-LES-BAINS Hautes-Pyrénées
Viscos ☎62970545
1km N on D13, rte de Lourdes.
15 May-Sep 2HEC ▦ ➡ ⋔ ⚏ ⊙ ⬚ ⌀ ⚄ lau ➡ ♟ ✕ ⇃PR

BELVÈS Dordogne
🏕Hauts de Ratebout ☎53290210
An old Périgord farm, set in extensive grounds on top of a hill.
D710 to Fumel. After Vaurez-de-Belvès, take D54 to Casals.
May-13 Sep 12HEC ▦ ⚑ ⋔ ⚏ ♟ ✕ ⊙ ⬚ ⌀ ⚍ ⊡ ⇃ P ⚄ ⊞ ⚥ lau
See advertisement under Colour Section

Moulin de la Pique ☎53290115
A quiet well equipped site set out around an imposing villa and a small lake. There are fine entertainment facilities and modern sanitary installations.
500m S on D710.
May-20 Sep 12HEC ▦ ⚑ ➡ ⋔ ⚏ ♟ ✕ ⊙ ⬚ ⌀ ⊡ ▲ ⇃ LP ⚄ lau
Prices: A32 pitch 52

Nauves Bos Rouge ☎53291264
4.5km SW via D53.
May-Sep 5HEC ▦ ⚑ ⋔ ♟ ✕ ⊙ ⬚ ⊡ ⊞ ⇃ P ⚄ ⊞ lau ➡ ⚏ ⌀ ♨ ⇃LR
Prices: A22 pitch 33

BEYNAC-ET-CAZENAC Dordogne
Capeyrou ☎53295495
S beside the River Dordogne.
May-Sep 4.5HEC ▦ ➡ ⋔ ✕ ⊙ ⬚ ⇃ P ⚄ ⊞ lau ➡ ⚏ ⌀ ⇃R

BEZ, LE Tarn
Plô Lucie Mougel ☎63740082
A pleasant site in wooded surroundings.
0.9km W via D30.
15 Jun-30 Sep 2.5HEC ▦ ⚑ ⋔ ⊙ ⬚ ⚄ ⊞ lau ➡ ⚏ ♟ ✕ ♨ ⇃LPR

BIARRITZ Pyrénées-Atlantiques
Biarritz 28 r d'Harcet ☎59230012
Site lies 200m from beach; 2km from town centre on N10, follow signs 'Espagne'.
May-28 Sep 3HEC ▦ ➡ ⋔ ⚏ ♟ ✕ ⊙ ⬚ ⌀ ⇃ P ⚄ ⊞ ⚥ lau ➡ ♨ ⇃LS
Prices: pitch 72.20-102.20 (incl 2 persons)

At **ARCANGUES**(4km S on D254)
Aldabénia ☎59430730
4km from beaches.
Jun-Sep 1HEC ▦ ➡ ⋔ ⊙ ⬚ ⌀ ⊡ ▲ ⚄ ⊞ lau ➡ ♟ ✕ ♨ ⇃R

At **BIDART**(4km SW)
Berrua rte d'Arbonne ☎59549666
Level meadowland in rural surroundings. 900m to sea.
15 Apr-Sep 5HEC ▦ ⚑ ⋔ ⚏ ♟ ✕ ⊙ ⬚ ⌀ ⊡ ⇃ P ⚄ ⊞ lau ➡ ⇃LRS
Prices: pitch 68-109 (incl 2 persons)

Jean Paris Quartier M-Pierre ☎59265558
600m from beaches.
S of town, cross railway line, site on S side of N10.
Jun-Sep 1HEC ▦ ➡ ⋔ ⚏ ♟ ✕ ⊙ ⬚ ⊡ ⚄ ⊞ lau ➡ ✕ ⌀ ♨ ⇃S

Oyam Ferme Oyamburua ☎59549161
Level meadow site near farm. Views of the Pyrénées. Simple but pleasant site.
Turn off beyond the church in the direction of Arbonne, via N10, for approx 1km.
Jun-Sep 5HEC ▦ ⚑ ⋔ ♟ ✕ ⊙ ⬚ ⌀ ⊡ ⇃ P ⚄ lau ➡ ⚏ ⌀ ⇃S Prices:
pitch 50-93 (incl 2 persons)

Pavillon Royal av Prince de Galles ☎59230054
Beautiful, well-kept site, divided into pitches, most of which have open view of sea. Beside rocky beach.
2 km N.
15 May-25 Sep 5HEC ⠿ ⚑ ⋔ ⚏ ♟ ✕ ⊙ ⬚ ⌀ ⇃ PS ⚄ ⊞ ⚥ lau

Résidence des Pins rte de Biarritz ☎59230029
Terraced site with numbered pitches, 800m from sea.
2km N on N106 Biarritz road.
25 May-Sep 7HEC ▦ ➡ ⋔ ⚏ ♟ ✕ ⊙ ⬚ ⌀ ⚄ ⇃ P ⚄ ⊞ lau ➡ ♨ ⇃LS
Prices: pitch 80-120 (incl 2 persons)

🏕Ruisseau rte d'Arbonne ☎59419450
A well equipped site in wooded surroundings set out around two lakes.
2km E on D255.
15 May-20 Sep 16HEC ▦ ⚑ ⋔ ⚏ ♟ ✕ ⊙ ⬚ ⌀ ⚍ ⊡ ⊞ ⇃ LP ⚄ ⊞
lau ➡ ⇃S

Ur-Onéa r de la Chapelle ☎59265361
0.6km E
Apr-Sep 5HEC ▦ ⚑ ⋔ ⚏ ♟ ✕ ⊙ ⬚ ⌀ ⊡ ⇃ P ⚄ ⊞ lau ➡ ✕ ♨
⇃RS Prices: pitch 55-84 (incl 2 persons)

BIAS Landes
CM Le Tatiou ☎58090476
2km W towards Lespecier
Etr-Oct 10HEC ▦ ➡ ⋔ ⚏ ♟ ✕ ⊙ ⬚ ⌀ ⚍ ⊡ ⇃ P ⚄ ⊞ lau

BIRON Dordogne
Moulinal ☎53408460
In a pleasant situation beside a lake.
2km S on the Lacapelle-Biron road.
30 Apr-13 Sep 10HEC ▦ ⚑ ⋔ ⚏ ♟ ✕ ⊙ ⬚ ⌀ ⊡ ⊞ ▲ ⇃ LP ⚄ ⊞
lau Prices: A12-38

BISCARROSSE Landes
Bimbo 176 chemin de Bimbo ☎58098233
3.5km N towards Sanguinet.
All year 5HEC ▦ ➡ ⋔ ♟ ✕ ⊙ ⬚ ⌀ ⚍ ⊡ ⊞ ⇃ P ⚄ ⊞ lau ➡ ⚏ ⇃LS

Rive rte de Bordeaux ☎58781233
Level site in tall pine forest on E side of lake. Private port and beach.
N of town off D652 Sanguinet road.
Apr-Oct 15HEC ⠿ ➡ ⋔ ⚏ ♟ ✕ ⊙ ⬚ ⌀ ⚍ ⊡ ⊞ ⇃ LP ⚄ lau ➡ ⇃S ⊞
See advertisement under Colour Section

BLAYE Gironde
At **MAZION**(5.5km NE on N937)
Tilleuls ☎57421813
Camping Card Compulsory.
5.5km NE on N937.
May-Oct 0.5HEC ▦ ⚑ ⋔ ⊙ ⬚ ⚄ ⊞ lau ➡ ⚏ ♟ ✕ ⇃LPS

BOURNEL Lot-et-Garonne
Ferme de Bourgade ☎53360744
15 Apr-15 Oct 10HEC ▦ ➡ ⋔ ⬚ ⚄ ⊞ lau Prices: A10 V10 pitch 10

BRETENOUX Lot
Bourgnatelle ☎65384407
In a pleasant location beside the River Cére. Separate car park for arrivals after 22.30hrs.
May-15 Sep 6HEC ▦ ➡ ⋔ ⊙ ⬚ ⌀ ⊡ ⇃ R ⚄ ⊞ lau ➡ ⚏ ♟ ✕ ♨ ⇃P
Prices: A16.50-19.50 pitch 16-20.50

BUGUE, LE Dordogne
St-Avit Loisirs St-Avit-de-Vialard ☎53026400
A pleasant site in natural wooded surroundings.W of town via C201.
Estr-Sep 42HEC ▦ ⚑ ⋔ ⚏ ♟ ✕ ⊙ ⬚ ⌀ ⊡ ⇃ P ⚄ ⊞ lau ➡ ⇃R

At LIMEUIL(5.5km SW by D703 and D31)

Port de Limeuil alleés sur Dordogne ☎53632976
Adjacent to the confluence of the Rivers Dordogne and Vezère and facing Limeuil.
May-Sep 7HEC ▦ ░░ ♠ ♠ 📶 🛁 ❢ ✕ ⊙ 🖃 ∅ 🏕 ⤳ PR 🏊 ⊞ lau ♦ ✕ 🚿

CAHORS Lot

Rivière de Cabessut r de la Rivière ☎65300630
N of town via the Cabessut Bridge over the River Lot.
Apr-15 Oct 2HEC ▦ ♠ ♠ 📶 🛁 ❢ ✕ ⊙ 🖃 ∅ 🏕 ⤳ PR 🏊 ⊞ lau ♦ ✕ 🚿
Prices: A12 pitch 50

At ESCLAUZELS(18km SE)

Pompit ☎65315340
5km NW of Esclauzels village.
Etr-15 Sep 4.5HEC ▦ ∅ ♠ ♠ 📶 🛁 ❢ ✕ ⊙ 🖃 ∅ 🏕 ⤳ P 🏊 ⊞ lau ♦ ⤳R

CALVIAC Lot

Chênes Verts ☎53592107
May-Sep 8.5HEC ▦ ♠ ♠ 📶 🛁 ❢ ✕ ⊙ 🖃 ∅ 🏕 ⤳ P 🏊 ⊞ lau ♦ ✕ 🚿 ⤳LR

Trois Sources ☎65330301
15 May-Sep 7.5HEC ▦ ♠ ♠ 📶 🛁 ❢ ✕ ⊙ 🖃 ∅ 🏕 ⤳ LPR 🏊 ⊞ lau
Prices: A30 pitch 35

CAMBO-LES-BAINS Pyrénées-Atlantiques

Brixta Eder rte de St-Jean-de-Luz ☎59299423
Modern site with good sports facilities.
Near the junction of D932 and D10.
15 Apr-15 Oct 1HEC ▦ ∅ ♠ ♠ ⊙ 🖃 🏊 lau ♦ 🛁 ❢ ✕ ⤳LPRS ⊞

CAPBRETON Landes

Pointe ☎58721498
2km S towards Labenne on N652.
Jun-Sep 4.5HEC ░░ ♠ ♠ 📶 🛁 ❢ ✕ ⊙ 🖃 ∅ 🏊 🖃 ⊞ lau ♦ 🚿 ⤳RS

CAP FERRET Gironde

Truc Vert rte Forestière ☎56608955
In a very pleasant location on a slope in a pine wood.
On D106 in the direction of Cap Ferret to Petit Piquey. Turn right and follow signs.
15 May-Sep 11HEC ░░ ∅ ♠ 📶 🛁 ❢ ✕ ⊙ 🖃 ∅ 🚿 ⤳ S 🏊 ⊞ lau

CARLUCET Lot

Château de Lacomté ☎65387546
In wooded surroundings with good sized pitches and a variety of recreational facilities.
Feb 12HEC ▦ ∅ ♠ 📶 🛁 ❢ ✕ ⊙ 🖃 ∅ 🏕 ♠ A ⤳ P 🏊 ⊞ lau Prices: A20 pitch 40

CASTELJALOUX Lot-et-Garonne

CM de la Piscine ☎53935468
NW on D933 Marmande road.
27 Mar-30 Oct 1HEC ♠ ♠ 📶 ⊙ 🖃 ⤳ P 🏊 lau ♦ 🛁 ❢ ✕ ∅ 🚿 ⤳L ⊞
Prices: A11 pitch 10

CASTELNAUD-LA-CHAPELLE Dordogne

Maisonneuve ☎53295129
10kms S of Sarlat on D57.
Apr-Sep 6HEC ▦ ∅ ♠ 📶 🛁 ❢ ✕ ⊙ 🖃 ∅ 🏕 ⤳ PR 🏊 ⊞ lau ♦ 🚿

CAUNEILLE Landes

Sources ☎58730440
N of town, 200m from N117.
May-Sep 1.5HEC ▦ ≈✓ ♠ 🛁 ❢ ✕ ⊙ 🖃 🚿 🏕 🏕 ⤳ P 🏊 ⊞ lau ♦ ✕ ⤳LR

CAUTERETS Hautes-Pyrénées

Mamelon-Vert av du Mamelon-Vert ☎62925156
Closed Oct-10 Nov 2HEC ▦ ∅ ♠ ⊙ 🖃 🏊 🖃 ⊞ lau ♦ 🛁 ❢ ✕ ∅ 🚿 ⤳P Prices: pitch 48.30-69 (incl 3 persons)

CLAOUEY Gironde

Airotel les Viviers rte du Cap Ferret ☎56607004
Beautiful, widespread site in a forest divided by seawater channels.

On the D106, 1km S of the town.
May-Sep 33HEC ░░ ∅ ♠ ♠ 📶 🛁 ❢ ✕ ⊙ 🖃 🏕 🏕 A ⤳ S 🏊 ⊞ lau ♦ ✕ ∅
Prices: pitch 80-160 (incl 3 persons)

CONTIS-PLAGE Landes

Lous Seurrots ☎58428582
In pine forest on outskirts of village between road and stream.
Beware of current if bathing in stream.
Apr-Sep 15HEC ░░ ♠ ♠ 📶 🛁 ❢ ✕ ⊙ 🖃 ∅ 🚿 ⤳ PRS 🏊 ⊞ lau
Prices: pitch 75-119 (incl 2 persons)

CORDES Tarn

Moulin de Julien ☎63561110
900m E on D600 and D922.
Apr-Sep 6HEC ▦ ♠ 📶 🛁 ❢ ✕ ⊙ 🖃 ∅ 🏕 🏕 ⤳ P 🏊 ⊞

COUX-ET-BIGAROUQE Dordogne

Valades Les Valades ☎53291427
In wooded surroundings within a pleasant valley.
5km N of town off N703.
Apr-Oct 11HEC ▦ 📶 🛁 ❢ ✕ ⊙ 🖃 🏕 🏕 A ⤳ L 🏊 lau ♦ ✕ ∅ 🚿 ⤳PR
Prices: A20 pitch 28

DAGLAN Dordogne

Moulin de Paulhiac ☎53282088
4km N via D57 beside the Céou
20 May-15 Sep 6HEC ▦ ∅ ♠ 🛁 ❢ ✕ ⊙ 🖃 ∅ 🏕 ⤳ PR 🏊 ⊞ lau

DAX Landes

Chênes Bois-de-Boulogne ☎58900553
W of town beside River Adour.
23 Mar-early Nov 8HEC ▦ ♠ 📶 🛁 ❢ ✕ ⊙ 🖃 🏕 🏕 ⤳ P 🏊 ⊞ lau ♦ ∅ 🚿 ⤳R Prices: pitch 77-89 (incl 2 persons)

DURAS Lot-et-Garonne

Moulin de Borie Neuve St-Sernin ☎53947657
A pleasant site in the Dourdeze valley.
Access via D244 towards St-Astier-de-Duras.
15 Apr-15 Oct 1HEC ▦ ∅ ♠ ⊙ 🖃 ⤳ R 🏊 ⊞ lau ♦ 🛁 ❢ ✕ ∅ ⤳L
Prices: A13 pitch 15

DURAVEL Lot

Club de Vacances Port de Vire ☎65246506
A pleasant site with good facilities beside the River Lot.**Camping Card Compulsory**
2.3km S via D58.
26 Apr-Sep 7HEC ▦ ∅ ♠ 🛁 ❢ ✕ ⊙ 🖃 ∅ 🏕 🏕 A ⤳ PR 🏊 ⊞ lau
Prices: A30 pitch 55

DURFORT Ariège

Bourdieu ☎61673017
All year 20HEC ▦ ∅ ♠ 🛁 ❢ ✕ ⊙ 🖃 🚿 🏕 ⤳ P 🏊 ⊞ lau

ESCOT Pyrénées-Atlantiques

Mont Bleu ☎59344192
Quiet site in beautiful Pyrenean landscape.
At railway bridge take D294 for approx 6km.
All year 3.5HEC ▦ ∅ ♠ 🛁 ❢ ✕ ⊙ 🖃 🏕 🏕 ⊞ ✂ lau Prices: pitch 62 (incl 2 persons)

ÉYZIES-DE-TAYAC, LES Dordogne

At SIREUIL(7km E off D47)

Mas ☎53296806
N of D47 (Sarlat-Les Éyzies).
May-Sep 5HEC ▦ ∅ ♠ 🛁 ❢ ✕ ⊙ 🖃 ∅ 🚿 🏕 🏕 ⤳ P 🏊 ⊞ lau ♦ ⤳LR

FOIX Ariège

CM Lac de Labarre ☎61651158
On well-kept meadow.
3km N on N20.
Apr-Oct 5HEC ▦ ∅ ♠ ❢ ⊙ 🖃 ⤳ L 🏊 ⊞ ♦ ∅

FOSSAT, LE Ariège

Laillères ☎61689965
On D626.
Mar-Oct 0.3HEC ∅ ♠ ⊙ 🖃 ⤳ R 🏊 lau ♦ 🛁 ❢ ✕ ∅ 🚿 ⤳P ⊞

FRAYSSINET *Lot*
Tirelire ☎65310019
All year 2HEC ▦ ❄ ⋔ ▮ ⊙ ⊟ ⋖ R ☎ lau ➧ ⚊ ✕ ⋖P

At PONT-DE-RHODES(1km N on N20)
Plage du Relais Pont de Rhodes ☎65310016
15 Jun-5 Sep 2HEC ▦ ❄ ⋔ ▮ ✕ ⊙ ⊟ ⋖ ⊞ ⋖ PR ☎ ⊞ lau ➧ ⚊

GAUGEAC *Dordogne*
Moulin de David ☎53226525
3km from town towards Villeréal.
11 May-13 Sep 20HEC ▦ ➧ ⋔ ⚊ ▮ ✕ ⊙ ⊟ ⋖ ⏚ ⊞ ⊞ ▲ ⋖ LP ☎ ⊞
lau Prices: A19.50-32.50 pitch 24-44

GOURDON *Lot*
Paradis La Peyrugue ☎65416501
1.6km SW off N673.
15 Jun-15 Sep 2HEC ▦ ❄ ⋔ ⊙ ⊟ ⋖ ⊞ ⋖ P ☎ ⊞ lau ➧ ⚊ ▮ ✕ ⋖ ⏚
⋖L Prices: A25

At GROLÉJAC(15km N on D704)
Granges ☎53281115
Beautifully situated terraces on a hill with big pitches. The site has
been constructed around a disused railway station, incorporating the
old ticket office and the bridge into its modern design. Facilities for
sports and entertainment.
Turn off D704 in village towards Domme.
May-25 Sep 6HEC ▦ ➧ ⋔ ✕ ⊙ ⊟ ⋖ ⊞ ▲ ⋖ PR ☎ ⊞ lau ➧ ⚊ ⋖ ⋖L
Prices: pitch 137.60-172 (incl 4 persons)

At ST-MARTIAL-DE-NABIRAT(6km W)
Carbonnier ☎53284253
Off the D46.
Etr-15 Sep 8HEC ▦ ➧ ⋔ ⚊ ▮ ✕ ⊙ ⊟ ⋖ ⏚ ⊞ ⋖ LP ☎ ⊞ lau Prices:
A30 pitch 41

GOURETTE *Pyrénées-Atlantiques*
Ley ☎59051147
Terraced site with gravel and asphalt caravan pitches. TV, common
room.
From Laruns drive E to Eaux-Bonnes and drive uphill to Gourette.
1 Dec-15 May & 1 Jul-30 Aug 2HEC ⋖ ✦ ⋔ ✕ ⊙ ⊟ ⊞ ⊞ ⋖ R ☎
⊞ lau ➧ ⚊ ⋖ Prices: pitch 50 (incl 2 persons)

GRAULGES, LES *Dordogne*
Graulges ☎53607473
Off D939 between Angoulême and Périgueux.
1 Mar-Oct 8HEC ▦ ➧ ⚊ ▮ ✕ ⊙ ⊟ ⊞ ⋖ P ☎ ⊞ ➧ ⋖ ⏚ Prices:
A16 pitch 27

GRISOLLES *Tarn-et-Garonne*
Aquitaine rte de Montauban ☎63673322
1.5km N off 'X' roads N20/N113.
15 Jun-15 Oct 3HEC ▦ ➧ ⋔ ⊙ ⊟ ⊞ ⊞ ⋖ P ☎ ⊞ lau ➧ ⚊ ✕ ⋖R
Prices: A18 V18 ⊞18 ▲18

GUJAN-MESTRAS *Gironde*
Plage La Hume ☎56661215
May-Sep 3.5HEC ▦ ❄ ⋔ ▮ ✕ ⊙ ⊟ ⚊ ⊞ ☎ ⊞ lau ➧ ⚊ ✕ ⋖ ⋖S

HASPARREN *Pyrénées-Atlantiques*
Chapital rte de Cambo ☎59296294
0.5km W via D22.
Etr-Oct 2.6HEC ▦ ❄ ⋔ ⊙ ⊟ ⋖ ⊞ ⊞ ☎ ⊞ lau ➧ ⚊ ⏚ ⋖P

HAUTEFORT *Dordogne*
Moulin des Loisirs le Coucou ☎53504655
2km SW via D72 & D71, 100m from Coucou lake.
Etr-Sep 2.5HEC ▦ ➧ ⋔ ⚊ ▮ ✕ ⊙ ⊟ ⋖ ⊞ ⊞ ⋖ LP ☎ ⊞ lau ➧ ⋖ ⋖R
Prices: pitch 73.50 (incl 2 persons)

HENDAYE *Pyrénées-Atlantiques*
Acacias ☎59207876
1.8km E (rte de la Glacière).
Apr-Sep 5HEC ▦ ➧ ⋔ ✕ ⊙ ⊟ ⊞ ⋖ LP ☎ ⊞ lau ➧ ⚊ ✕ ⋖S

Airotel Eskualduna rte de la Corniche (D-912) ☎59200464
On gently sloping meadow.
2km from village on N10c.
15 Jun-Sep 8HEC ➧ ⋔ ⚊ ▮ ▮ ✕ ⊙ ⊟ ⋖ ⊞ ⊞ ⋖ R ☎ lau ➧ ✕ ⚏ ⋖PS
⊞ Prices: A27 pitch 28

HOSSEGOR *Landes*
Rey ☎58435200
Off D652.
23 Jun-Aug 10HEC ▦ ⋯⋯ ➧ ⋔ ⚊ ⊙ ⊟ ⋖ ⋖ L ☎ ⊞ lau ➧ ▮ ✕

HOURTIN *Gironde*
Acacia Ste-Helene ☎56738080
Pleasant, quiet site on the edge of a forest with good sanitary
facilities. Compulsory car park for arrivals after 2330hrs.
Off D3 towards the lake.
17 Jun-15 Sep 3.3HEC ▦ ❄ ⋔ ⚊ ⊙ ⊟ ⊞ ▲ ☎ lau ➧ ⋖L Prices:
A17 pitch 15

Mariflaude rte de Pauillac ☎56091197
Level meadowland, shaded by pines, in rural setting.
Turn onto D4 at the chemist and continue E towards Pauillac.
15 May-15 Sep 8HEC ▦ ❄ ⋔ ⚊ ▮ ✕ ⊙ ⊟ ⋖ ⊞ ⋖ P ☎ ⊞ lau
Prices: A16-20 pitch 50-60

Orée du Bois rte d'Aquitaine ☎56091588
1500m from town centre beside the lake.
Jun-15 Sep 2HEC ▦ ❄ ⋔ ⚊ ▮ ✕ ⊙ ⊟ ⋖ ⊞ ⋖ P ☎ ⊞ lau ➧ ⋖L

Ourmes av du Lac ☎56091276
On well-kept field. Boating nearby.
Follow D4 towards lake.
Apr-Sep 7HEC ➧ ⋔ ⚊ ▮ ✕ ⊙ ⊟ ⋖ ⊞ ⊞ ⋖ P ☎ ⊞ lau ➧ ⋖L Prices:
pitch 72-90 (incl 2 persons)

HOURTIN-PLAGE *Gironde*
Côte d'Argent ☎56091025
In a pine and oak forest 500m from beach with good facilities.
Access via D101 from Hourtin.
15 May-15 Sep 20HEC ⋯⋯ ➧ ⋔ ⚊ ▮ ✕ ⊙ ⊟ ⋖ ⊞ ⊞ ⊞ lau ➧ ⋖S
Prices: A25 pitch 58

HUME, LA *Gironde*
At TESTE, LA(3km SW)
Village de Loisirs Domaine de la Forge rte Sanguinet
☎56660772
Secluded site in very quiet woodland.
3km S on D652.
All year 4.5HEC ▦ ⋯⋯ ❄ ⋔ ⚊ ▮ ✕ ⊙ ⊟ ⊞ ⋖ PR ☎ ⊞ lau

LABENNE *Landes*
Savane av de l'Océan ☎59454113
On RN10.
All year 7HEC ➧ ⋔ ✕ ⊙ ⊟ ⊞ ▲ ☎ lau ➧ ⚊ ⏚ ⋖LRS ⊞
Prices: pitch 48-61 (incl 2 persons)

LABENNE-OCÉAN *Landes*
Boudigau ☎59454207
Situated in pine forest.
Turn right into site after bridge.
20 May-17 Sep 6HEC ▦ ❄ ⋔ ⚊ ▮ ✕ ⊙ ⊟ ⋖ ⊞ ⊞ ⋖ P ☎ ⊞ lau ➧
⋖S

Côte d'Argent av de l'Océan ☎59454202
Very well-managed modern site attached to holiday village.
3km W on D126.
All year 4HEC ▦ ⋯⋯ ➧ ⋔ ✕ ⊙ ⊟ ⚊ ⊞ ⊞ ⋖ P ☎ ⊞ lau ➧ ⚊ ⋖
⋖RS Prices: pitch 50-94 (incl 2 persons)

Mer rte de la Plage ☎59454209
On D126 (near de la Plage).
May-Sep 5.5HEC ▦ ⋯⋯ ➧ ⋔ ⚊ ▮ ✕ ⊙ ⊟ ⋖ ⊞ ⋖ PR ☎ ⊞ lau ➧
⋖S Prices: A12-15.50 pitch 18-53

Sylvamar av de l'Océan ☎59457516
Access via D126.
Jun-Sep 15HEC ▦ ➧ ⋔ ▮ ✕ ⊙ ⊟ ⊞ ⊞ ⋖ P lau ➧ ⚊ ⋖ ⋖RS ⊞

CAMPING LE TEDEY
★★★

Route de Longarisse - 33680 Lacanau
Tel: 05.56.03.00.15 Fax: 05.56.03.01.90

Situated in 34 acres of pine forest, peace and quiet on the edge of the Lake of Lacanau. Sandy beaches, exceptional situation for children, sailing paradise, cycling paths and fishing.

Post • change • information • shop • newspapers • swimming • windsurfing • volley-ball • ping-pong • entertainment for children • bar • cinema • music garden • supermarket • take away meals • butcher's • fishmonger's • sanitary installations for disabled • mobile homes to let.

Open: 26.4 - 21.9

Prices: pitch 60-125 (incl 2 persons)
See advertisement under Colour Section

LACANAU-OCÉAN *Gironde*
Airotel de l'Océan r du Répos ☎56032445
On rising ground in pine forest. 800m from beach.
May-Sep 9.5HEC ⁘ ♠ ⋔ ᴇ ¥ × ⊙ ⍉ ⌀ ♨ ⊞ ⍨ ⍘ P ⊡ 🄿 ⊞ lau ♦ ⍨S

Grands Pins ☎56032077
On very hilly terrain in woodland. 350m from the beach, access to which is through dunes.
Mar-Sep 11HEC ⁘ ♠ ⋔ ᴇ ¥ × ⊙ ⍉ ⌀ ♨ ⊞ ⍨ P ⍟ ⊞ lau ♦ ⍨S

At MEDOC(8km E)

Talaris rte de l'Océan ☎56030415
Separate car park for arrivals after 22.30hrs.
2km E on rte de Lacanau.
15 Jun-25 Sep 6.3HEC ⬜ ♠ ⋔ ᴇ ¥ × ⊙ ⍉ ⌀ ♨ ⊞ ⍨ P ⍟ ⊞ lau ♦ ⍨L Prices: pitch 128 (incl 2 persons)

At MOUTCHIC(5km E)

Lac ☎56030026
On D6 rte de Lacanau, 60m from lake.
Apr-15 Oct 0.7HEC ♠ ⋔ ᴇ ¥ × ⊙ ⍉ ⌀ ♨ ⍟ ⊞ lau ♦ × ⍨L
Prices: pitch 80-100 (incl 3 persons)

Tedey rte de Longarisse ☎56030015
Quiet site in pine forest, on edge of Lake Lacanau. Private bathing area.
Turn off D6 and continue along narrow track through forest for 0.5 km.
26 Apr-21 Sep 14HEC ⁘ ♠ ⋔ ᴇ ¥ × ⊙ ⍉ ⌀ ⍨ L ⍟ ⊞ lau Prices: pitch 113-133 (incl 3 persons)
See advertisement under LACANAU-OCÉAN

CAMPING et Village Vacances LE ROUMINGUE
1 KM OF SEAFRONT ON THE BASSIN D'ARCACHON

For hire: pitches, mobile homes, bungalows "grand comfort"...

(partial board free in June and Sept. in the holiday village)

IDEAL FOR CHILDREN (Secure and numerous organised activities...)

CHILDREN UP TO 14 YEARS FREE in campsite

Open all year

TEL: 05 56 82 97 48   FAX 05 56 82 96 09

LE ROUMINGUE BP 19 LANTON 33138

LACAPELLE-MARIVAL *Lot*
CM Bois de Sophie ☎65408259
1km NW via D940
May-Sep 2HEC ⬜ ♠ ⋔ ⊙ ⍉ ♨ ⊞ ⍨ P ⍟ ⊞ lau ♦ ᴇ × ⌀ ⍨ ⍨L

LANTON *Gironde*
Roumingue ☎56829748
Level terrain under a few deciduous trees partially in open meadow on the Bassin d'Arcachon.
1km NW of village towards sea.
All year 33HEC ⬜ ⁘ ⍉ ⋔ ᴇ ¥ × ⊙ ⍉ ⌀ ♨ ⊞ ⍨ S ⍟ ⊞ lau
Prices: pitch 89-105 (incl 2 persons)

LARNAGOL *Lot*
Ruisseau de Treil ☎65312339
0.6km E via D662
Etr-Nov 5HEC ⬜ ♠ ⋔ ᴇ ¥ × ⊙ ⍉ ♨ ⍨ P ⍟ lau ♦ ⌀ ⍨R Prices: A29 pitch 39

LARUNS *Pyrénées-Atlantiques*
Gaves ☎59053237
On the bank of the Gave d'Ossan. Some pitches reserved for caravans.
1km S.
All year 2HEC ⬜ ⍉ ⋔ ᴇ ⊙ ⍉ ⌀ ⍨ ♨ ⊞ ⊞ lau ♦ ᴇ × ⍨PR
Prices: A20 pitch 55

LARUSCADE *Gironde*
Relais du Chavan RN 10 ☎57686305
On well-kept meadow edged by a strip of forest. Some traffic noise.
6.5km NW on N10 near Km20.3.
15 May-Sep 3.7HEC ⬜ ⁘ ♠ ⋔ ᴇ × ⊙ ⍉ ⌀ ⍨ ♨ ⍨ P ⍟ ⊞ lau ♦ ¥ × Prices: A16 pitch 18

LECTOURE *Gers*
Lac des Trois Vallées ☎62688233
This rural site is part of a large park and lies next to a lake. It has spacious marked pitches.
3km SE on N21.
Etr-Sep 40HEC ⬛ ♠ ⋔ ᴇ ¥ × ⊙ ⍉ ⌀ ⍨ ♨ ⊞ A ⍨ L ⍟ ⊞ lau

LÉON *Landes*
Lou Puntaou ☎58487430
In oak wood with separate sections for caravans.
Turn off N652 in village and continue towards lake for 1.5km on D142.
15 Apr-Sep 14HEC ⬜ ⁘ ♠ ⋔ ᴇ ¥ × ⊙ ⍉ ⌀ ♨ ⍨ P ⍟ ⊞ lau ♦ ᴇ ⍨LR

St-Antoine St-Michel-Escalus ☎58487850
A pleasant, well equipped site beside a river in peaceful wooded surroundings.
Mar-Sep 11HEC ⬛ ♠ ⋔ ᴇ ¥ × ⊙ ⍉ ⌀ ⍨ ♨ ⊞ A ⍨ R ⊞ lau
Prices: A14.50 V11 ⍟16 A16

LESCAR *Pyrénées-Atlantiques*
Terrier av du Vert Galant ☎59810182
On meadowland split in two with pitches surrounded by hedges in foreground.

From Pau take N117 towards Bayonne for approx. 6.5km, then turn left onto D501 towards Monein to site towards bridge.
All year 5.2HEC ▥ ♨ ♠ ♠ ♀ ✗ ⊙ ☺ ∅ 🛆 🏕 🐪 ♠ ⟨ PR 🗷 🕀 lau ➡ 🛒 ⟨L Prices: A21 pitch 30

LINXE Landes

CM Le Grandjean rte de Mixe ☎58429000
A modern site situated on the edge of a forest. Ideal for family holidays.
From the Castets road, take the D42 towards Linxe.
29 Jun-14 Sep 2.7HEC ▥ ⠿⠿ ♠ ♠ ⊙ ☺ 🏕 🐪 🗷 lau ➡ 🛒 ♀ ✗ ∅ 🛆
Prices: A15 pitch 30

LIT-ET-MIXE Landes

Vignes rte de la Plage, Du Cap de L'Homy ☎58428560
In a pine forest with good sanitary and sports facilities.*Camping Card Compulsory*
3km S via D652 and D89.
Apr-Oct 15HEC ⠿⠿ ♠ ♠ 🟎 ♀ ✗ ⊙ ☺ ∅ 🛆 🏕 🐪 ⟨ P 🗷 🕀 lau
Prices: pitch 105 (incl 2 persons)

LIVERS-CAZELLES Tarn

Rédon ☎63561464
4km SE of Cordes on D600.
Apr-Nov 2HEC ▥ ⊙ ☺ ∅ 🐪 ⟨ P 🗷 🕀 lau ➡ 🛆 Prices: pitch 60 (incl 2 persons)

LOUPIAC Lot

Hirondelles ☎65376625
3km N via N20.
Apr-Oct 2.5HEC ▥ ♠ 🟎 ♀ ✗ ⊙ ☺ ∅ 🏕 🐪 ⟨ P 🗷 🕀 lau

LOURDES Hautes-Pyrénées

Arrouach 9 r des Archauges, Quartier Biscaye ☎62942575
Situated on D940 Soumoulou road.
All year 4HEC ▥ ♠ 🟎 ⊙ ☺ ∅ 🐪 🗷 🕀 lau ➡ 🛒 ♀ ✗ ⟨LR Prices: A17-18 V10-11 🚐10-11 🛆10-11

Domec rte de Julos ☎62944393
Off N21 Tarbes road N of town centre.
Etr-Oct 2HEC ♠ 🟎 ⊙ ☺ ∅ 🐪 🗷 🕀 lau ➡ 🛒 ✗ ⟨LP Prices: A12 pitch 13

LUCHON Haute-Garonne

Beauregard av de Vénasque ☎61793074
On level meadow.
Off N125.
Apr-Sep 2.5HEC ▥ ♠ 🟎 ⊙ ☺ 🐪 ⟨ R 🗷 🕀 lau ➡ 🛒 ♀ ∅ ⟨LP

Frênes Garin ☎61798844
All year 1HEC ♨ ♠ 🟎 ♀ ✗ ⊙ ☺ ∅ 🛆 🐪 🗷 lau ➡ ✗

LUZ-ST-SAUVEUR Hautes-Pyrénées

Bergons ☎62929077
600m E on D618 Barèges road.
Closed Nov-15 Dec 1HEC ▥ ♨ 🟎 ⊙ ☺ ∅ 🐪 🗷 🕀 lau ➡ 🛒 ♀ ✗ 🛆 ⟨LP Prices: A15 pitch 15

Pyrénées International rte de Lourdes ☎62928202
1.3km NW on N21.
Jun-Sep & 15 Dec-15 Apr 4HEC ♨ 🟎 ♠ ♀ ✗ ⊙ ☺ ∅ 🛆 ⟨ P 🗷 🕀 lau ➡ ⟨R

Pyrénévasion Sazos ☎62929154
All year 3HEC ♨ ⤳ 🟎 ♀ ✗ ⊙ ☺ 🏕 🐪 🗷 lau ➡ 🛒 ✗ ∅ ⟨PR

MARCILLAC-ST-QUENTIN Dordogne

Tailladis ☎53591095
2km N near D48.
15 Mar-Oct 25HEC ▥ ♠ 🟎 🛒 ✗ ⊙ ☺ ∅ 🐪 🐪 ⟨ P 🗷 🕀 lau
Prices: A25.50 pitch 35

MAREUIL Dordogne

Étang Bleu Vieux Mareuil ☎53609270
Very shaded site on level ground. Half way between Angoulême and Périgueux on D939.
Apr-Oct 9.8HEC ▥ ♠ 🟎 🛒 ♀ ✗ ⊙ ☺ ∅ 🐪 🛆 ⟨ LP 🗷 🕀 lau

MARTRES-TOLOSANE Haute-Garonne

Moulin ☎61988640
1.5km SE
15 Mar-15 Oct 0.6HEC ▥ ♠ 🟎 🛒 ♀ ✗ ⊙ ☺ 🐪 🐪 ⟨ PR 🗷 lau ➡ ⟨L
🕀 Prices: pitch 47.50-68 (incl 2 persons)

MAULÉON-LICHARRE Pyrénées-Atlantiques

Saison rte de Libarrenx ☎59281879
1.5km S on D918.
Apr-Sep 1HEC ▥ ♠ 🟎 🛒 ♀ ✗ ⊙ ☺ ∅ 🐪 ⟨ R 🗷 🕀 lau ➡ ✗ 🛆 ⟨P Prices: A17.50 pitch 19

MESSANGES Landes

Côte rte de Vieux Boucau ☎58489494
2.3km S via D652.
Apr-Sep 3HEC ▥ ♨ 🟎 🛒 ♀ ✗ ⊙ ☺ 🛆 🏕 🐪 🗷 🕀 lau ➡ 🛒 ♀ ✗ ∅ ⟨LS Prices: pitch 50-56 (incl 2 persons)

Moïsan ave de la Plage ☎58489206
15 May-Sep 6HEC ▥ ♨ 🟎 ♠ ♀ ✗ ⊙ ☺ ∅ 🛆 🏕 🐪 🗷 🕀 lau ➡ 🛒 ♀ 🛆 ⟨S Prices: pitch 45-69 (incl 2 persons)

Vieux Port rte des Lacs ☎58482200
2.5 km SW via D652.
Apr-Sep 30HEC ▥ ♨ 🟎 🛒 ♀ ✗ ⊙ ☺ ∅ 🐪 🐪 ⟨ PS 🗷 🔲 🕀 lau ➡ 🛆 ⟨LR Prices: pitch 195 (incl 3 persons)

MÉZOS Landes

Sen Yan ☎58426005
A pleasant site in exotic tropical gardens, surrounded by a pine wood.
1km E
Jun-Sep 8HEC ▥ ⠿⠿ ♠ 🟎 🛒 ♀ ✗ ⊙ ☺ ∅ 🐪 ⟨ P 🗷 🕀 lau ➡ 🛆

MIERS Lot

Pigeonnier ☎65337195
400m E via D91.
Etr-Sep 1HEC ▥ ♨ 🟎 ♀ ✗ ⊙ ☺ ∅ 🐪 🐪 ⟨ P 🗷 🕀 lau ➡ 🛒 ✗ 🛆 Prices: A16-18 pitch 18-19

MILLAC Lot

Millac Lieu dit Combe de Lafon ☎53297793
Terraced site.
Apr-Sep 2HEC ▥ ♨ ⤳ 🟎 🛒 ♀ ✗ ⊙ ☺ ∅ 🛆 🐪 ⟨ P 🗷 🕀 lau

MIMIZAN Landes

At **MIMIZAN-PLAGE**(6km E by D626)
Marina ☎58091266
In mixed woodland. 500m from beach.
Take D626 from Mimizan Plage. Well signed from paper mill.
May-Sep 9HEC ▥ ♨ 🟎 🛒 ♀ ✗ ⊙ ☺ ∅ 🐪 🐪 🛆 ⟨ P 🗷 🕀 lau ➡ ⟨RS Prices: pitch 76-165 (incl 3 persons)
See advertisement under Colour Section

MIRANDOL Tarn

Clots Les Clots ☎63769278
Situated in the Viaur valley.
5.5km N via D905, rte de Rieupeyroux.
Etr-15 Oct 3.5HEC ▥ ♠ 🟎 🛒 ♀ ✗ ⊙ ☺ ∅ 🐪 🐪 ⟨ PR 🗷 🕀 lau Prices: A23 pitch 16

MIREPOIX Gers

Mousquetaires ☎62643366
Situated on a hill in the heart of Gascony.
2km SE.
Jun-Sep 1HEC ▥ ♨ 🟎 🛒 ⊙ ☺ 🐪 🐪 🛆 ⟨ LP 🗷 🕀 lau ➡ ∅ 🛆 Prices: pitch 70 (incl 2 persons)

MOLIÈRES Dordogne

Grande Veyière ☎53632584
2.4km SE
Apr-15 Nov 4.5HEC ▥ ♨ 🟎 🛒 ♀ ✗ ⊙ ☺ 🐪 🐪 ⟨ P 🗷 lau Prices: A18.50-21.50 pitch 25-30

MOLIETS-PLAGE *Landes*
Airotel St-Martin ☎58485230
Large site on the Atlantic coast with direct access to the largest
sandy beach in the region.
Camping Card Compulsory.
Between the village and the beach.
Etr-13 Oct 18.5HEC ▨ ⠇⠇⠇ ♦ ⋒ ⚊ ▮ ✕ ⊙ ▣ ∅ ⚏ ⊞ ⌂ ▲ ⤵ PS ☝ ⊞
lau

Cigales av de l'Océan ☎58485118
On undulating ground in pine trees.
300m from beach.
15 Apr-Sep 23HEC ▨ ⠇⠇⠇ ♦ ⋒ ⚊ ▮ ✕ ⊙ ▣ ∅ ⚏ ☝ ⊞ lau ♦ ∅ ⚌
⤵RS

MONCRABEAU *Lot-et-Garonne*
CM Mouliat ☎53654279
On D219, 200m from D930.
15 Jun-15 Sep 1.3HEC ▨ ♦ ⋒ ⊙ ▣ ☝ ⊞ lau ♦ ⚊ ✕ ∅ ⚌ ⤵PR

MONTAUBAN-DE-LUCHON *Haute-Garonne*
Lanette ☎61790038
On gently sloping ground surrounded by pastures.
1.5km E of Luchon. Off D27.
All year 4.3HEC ▨ ⠇ ⋒ ⚊ ▮ ✕ ⊙ ▣ ∅ ⚌ ⌂ ⚏ ☝ ⊞ lau ♦ ⤵PR
Prices: A19 pitch 20

MONTESQUIOU *Gers*
Château le Haget ☎62709580
In grounds of Château.
May-1 Oct 12HEC ▨ ⠇ ⋒ ⚊ ▮ ✕ ⊙ ▣ ∅ ⚌ ⌂ ⚏ ▲ ⤵ P ☝ ⊞ lau

MUSSIDAN *Dordogne*
CM Le Port ☎53812009
15 Jun-15 Sep 0.5HEC ▨ ♦ ⋒ ⊙ ▣ ☝ ⊞ lau ♦ ⚊ ▮ ✕ ∅ ⚌ ⤵PR
Prices: A13.50 pitch 5.20

NAGES *Tarn*
Rieu Montagné Lac du Laouzas ☎63374052
4.5km S via D62
All year 6HEC ▨ ↝ ↜ ⋒ ⚊ ▮ ✕ ⊙ ▣ ∅ ⚌ ⌂ ⚏ ▲ ⤵ LPR ☝ ⊞ lau

NONTRON *Dordogne*
At **ABJAT**(15km NE)
Moulin de Masfrelet ☎53568270
2.4km N.
Jun-15 Sep 12HEC ▨ ♦ ⋒ ⚊ ▮ ✕ ⊙ ▣ ∅ ⚌ ⤵ LPR ☝ ⊞ lau

ONDRES *Landes*
Lou Pignada rte de la Plage ☎59453065
Turn off the N10 in the village onto rte de la Plage.
Apr-Sep 2HEC ▨ ⠇⠇⠇ ♦ ⋒ ⚊ ▮ ✕ ⊙ ▣ ∅ ⚌ ⚏ ⤵ P ☝ ⊞ lau ♦
⤵LRS

ONESSE-ET-LAHARIE *Landes*
CM Bienvenu ☎58073049
500m from village centre on D38.
15 Jun-15 Sep 1.5HEC ▨ ⠇ ⋒ ⊙ ▣ ☝ ⊞ lau ♦ ⚊ ▮ ✕ Prices:
A11.70 V7.80 ⚏11.70 ▲11.70

OUSSE *Pyrénées-Atlantiques*
Sapins ☎59817421
Access via N117, exit 'Pau' or A64, exit Soumoulou.
Apr-Oct 0.7HEC ▨ ⠇ ⋒ ✕ ⊙ ▣ ⚏ ☝ ⊞ lau ♦ ⚊ ✕ Prices: A16
pitch 22

PADIRAC *Lot*
Chênes rte du Gouffre ☎65336554
1.5km NE via D90 towards Gouffre.
May-Sep 5HEC ▨ ♦ ⋒ ⚊ ▮ ✕ ⊙ ▣ ∅ ⚌ ⌂ ⚏ ▲ ⤵ P ☝ ⊞ lau
Prices: pitch 55-90 (incl 2 persons)

PAMIERS *Ariège*
Ombrages ☎61671224
NW on D119 beside river.

All year 2.5HEC ▨ ♦ ⋒ ⚊ ▮ ✕ ⊙ ▣ ∅ ⚌ ⚏ ⤵ R ☝ ⊞ lau ♦ ⤵P
Prices: A10 V4 ⚏10 ▲10

PARENTIS-EN-BORN *Landes*
Arbre d'Or 75 rte du Lac ☎58784156
A level site in pine wood on S shore of the Étang de Biscarosse.
Turn off D652 2km S of Gastes.
All year 4.5HEC ⠇⠇⠇ ♦ ⋒ ⚊ ▮ ✕ ⊙ ▣ ∅ ⚌ ⌂ ⚏ ⤵ P ☝ ⊞ lau ♦
⤵LP

Mouteou rte de l'Étang ☎58784227
2.5km W.
15 Jun-Sep 3HEC ▨ ♦ ⋒ ⊙ ▣ ⤵ L ☝ ⊞ lau ♦ ⤵LS Prices: pitch
41.50-55.50 (incl 2 persons)

At **GASTES**(7.5km SW)
Réserve ☎58097596
3km SW via D652
15 May-17 Sep 32HEC ▨ ⠇⠇⠇ ♦ ⋒ ⚊ ▮ ✕ ⊙ ▣ ∅ ⚌ ⌂ ⚏ ⤵ LP ▲
⊞ lau Prices: pitch 76-156 (incl 2 persons)

PAUILLAC *Gironde*
CM Les Gabarreys rte de la Rivière ☎56591003
A municipal site with good sports facilities.
S of town.
28 Mar-15 Sep 1.6HEC ▨ ♦ ⋒ ⊙ ▣ ⤵ R ☝ ⚏ ⊞ lau ♦ ⚊ ▮ ✕ ∅
⚌ ⤵P Prices: pitch 60 (incl 2 persons)

PAYRAC *Lot*
Panoramic rte de Loupiac ☎65379845
All year 1.5HEC ▨ ♦ ⋒ ▮ ✕ ⊙ ▣ ∅ ⚌ ⌂ ⚏ ☝ ⊞ lau ♦ ⚊ ∅ ⤵P
Prices: A12 pitch 16

Pins rte de Cahors ☎65379632
A well-managed site, partly in forest, partly on meadowland.
Sheltered from traffic noise.
S of village off N20.
15 Apr-15 Sep 4HEC ▨ ♦ ⋒ ⚊ ▮ ✕ ⊙ ▣ ∅ ⌂ ⚏ ⤵ P ☝ ⊞ lau
Prices: A16-32 pitch 24-48

PÉRIGUEUX *Dordogne*
Barnabe-Plage Boulazac ☎53534145
Signposted on N89, 2km E of town centre.
All year 1.2HEC ▨ ♦ ⋒ ▮ ✕ ⊙ ▣ ☝ ⊞ lau ♦ ⚊ ✕ ∅ ⤵P Prices:
A15.50 V9.50 ⚏15 ▲15

At **LESPARAT**(4km E on N89)
Isle rte de Brive ☎53535775
Camping Card Compulsory3km from Périgueux in the direction of
Brive on D5.
May-Sep 3HEC ▨ ♦ ⋒ ⚊ ▮ ✕ ⊙ ▣ ∅ ⤵ PR ☝ ⊞ ♦ ✕ ⚌

PETIT-PALAIS *Gironde*
Pressoir Queyrai Petit-Palais ☎57697325
On N89 Bordeaux-Périgueux road, exit at St-Médard de Guizières &
follow signs.
May-Sep 2.5HEC ▨ ⠇ ⋒ ▮ ✕ ⊙ ▣ ⌂ ⚏ ⤵ P ☝ ⊞ ▣ ⊞ ▨ lau ♦ ⚊ ⚌
⤵R Prices: A27 pitch 29

PEZULS *Dordogne*
Forêt ☎53227169
In extensive grounds on the edge of the forest.
600m off D703. 3km from the village centre.
Apr-Oct 8HEC ▨ ♦ ⋒ ⚊ ▮ ✕ ⊙ ▣ ∅ ⚌ ⌂ ⚏ ⤵ P ☝ ⊞ lau ♦ ✕
Prices: A18.80-26.20 pitch 17.90-25.10

PONT-ST-MAMET *Dordogne*
Lestaubière ☎53829815
On wooded pasture in the grounds of Lestaubière Castle.
Off N21.
15 May-7 Sep 5HEC ▨ ⠇ ⋒ ▮ ✕ ⊙ ▣ ∅ ⤵ LP ☝ ⊞ ▨ lau ♦ ✕
Prices: A25 pitch 27.50

PRAT-BONREPAUX *Ariège*
CM Pont du Bugot ☎61966162
On D117n.
Jun-Oct 0.5HEC ▨ ⠇ ⋒ ⊙ ▣ ☝ ⊞ lau ♦ ⚊ ▮ ✕ ∅ ⚌ ⤵R

PUYBRUN *Lot*

Sole ☎65385237
On D703 leave village in the direction of Bretenoux and take the first turning after the garage.
Apr-Sep 3HEC 🎦 ♠ ☏ ♀ ✕ ⊙ 🖳 ⌀ ⬛ 🏕 🍴 P ☎ ⊞ lau ♦ 🍴 ✕ ⚡R Prices: A23 pitch 24

PUY-L'ÉVÊQUE *Lot*

At **MONTCABRIER**(7 km NW)
Moulin de Laborde ☎65246206
Surrounded by woods and hills, in a picturesque valley on the River Thèze. Situated on D673.
15 May-14 Sep 9.5HEC 🎦 ❑ ♠ 🍴 ♀ ✕ ⊙ 🖳 ⌀ LPR ☎ ⊞ ⚘ lau ♦ 🍴 Prices: A30 pitch 35

PYLA-SUR-MER *Gironde*

Dune rte de Biscarrosse ☎56227217
A beautifully situated and quiet site partly on terraced sandy fields. Opposite a dune of over 100m in height, which separates the site from the sea.
Follow the road between Pilat-Plage.
May-Sep 6HEC ⫶ ♠ 🍴 ♀ ✕ ⊙ 🖳 ⌀ 🏕 ⚡ P ☎ ⊞ lau ♦ ⚡S
Prices: pitch 90-130 (incl 2 persons)

Panorama rte de Biscarrosse, Grande dune du Pyla ☎56221044
Partially terraced site amongst dunes, on the edge of the 100m high 'Dune de Pyla'. Views of the sea from some pitches.
On the D218. Signposted.
May-Sep 15HEC ⫶ ♠ 🍴 ♀ ✕ ⊙ 🖳 ⌀ 🏕 ⚡ PS ☎ ⊞ lau Prices: A19-28 pitch 55-85

Petit Nice rte de Biscarrosse ☎56227403
Sandy terraced site, mainly suitable for tents; in parts sloping steeply in pine woodland. Paths and standings are strengthened with timber. 220 steps down to the beach.
6 km S on D218.
Apr-10 Oct 5.5HEC 🎦 ⫶ ❑ ♠ 🍴 ♀ ✕ ⊙ 🖳 ⌀ 🏕 ⚡ PS ☎ ⊞ lau Prices: A19-38 pitch 42-72

Pyla rte de Biscarrosse ☎56227456
May-Sep 8HEC ⫶ ♠ 🍴 ♀ ✕ ⊙ 🖳 ⌀ 🏕 ⚡ PS ☎ ⊞ lau

RAUZAN *Gironde*

Vieux Château ☎57841538
Situated in a peaceful valley surrounded by vineyards.
Access via D670.
All year 2.5HEC 🎦 ♠ ☏ ⊙ 🖳 ⌀ 🏕 ⚡ P ☎ ⊞ lau ♦ 🍴 Prices: A15 V10 ⊞15 ▲15

ROCAMADOUR *Lot*

Cigales ☎65336444
21 Jun-6 Sep 1.7HEC 🎦 ♠ ☏ 🍴 ♀ ✕ ⊙ 🖳 ⌀ 🏕 ⚡ P ☎ ⊞ lau ♦
Prices: pitch 80 (incl 2 persons)

Relais du Campeur l'Hospitalet ☎65336328
On D36.
Etr-Sep 1.7HEC 🎦 ❑ ♠ 🍴 ✕ ⊙ 🖳 ⌀ ⚡ P ☎ ⊞ lau ♦ 🍴 Prices: pitch 56-60 (incl 2 persons)

ROCHE-CHALAIS, LA *Dordogne*

Gerbes ☎53914065
Site on banks of River Dronne.
Off D674 in village centre. Signposted.
Apr-Oct 3HEC 🎦 ♠ ☏ ⊙ 🖳 ♦ ⚡ R ☎ ⊞ lau ♦ 🍴 ✕ ⌀ ⚡P Prices: A12 pitch 15

ROMIEU, LA *Gers*

Camp de Florence ☎62281558
Take D931 in direction Agen-Condom. 3km before Condom turn left to La Romieu.
Apr-Oct 10HEC 🎦 ❑ ♠ 🍴 ✕ ⊙ 🖳 🏕 🍴 ▲ ⚡ P ☎ ⊞ lau ♦ 🍴 ⌀
Prices: A21-32 pitch 43-53

ROQUEFORT *Landes*

CM de Nauton allées de Nauton ☎58455046
1.6km N via D932 towards Bordeaux.

ROUFFIGNAC *Dordogne*

Cantegrel ☎53054830
1.5km N via D31, rte de Thenon.
Etr-15 Oct 50HEC ❑ ♠ 🍴 ♀ ✕ ⊙ 🖳 ⌀ 🏕 🏕 🍴 ⚡ LP ☎ ⊞ lau Prices: pitch 65-105 (incl 3 persons)

SADIRAC *Gironde*

Bel Air ☎56230190
Country site.
Beside D671.
All year 2HEC 🎦 ♠ 🍴 ♀ ✕ ⊙ 🖳 ⌀ 🏕 🍴 ⚡ P ☎ ⊞ ♦ ✕ Prices: A15 pitch 27-35

ST-ANTOINE-DE-BREUILH *Dordogne*

CM St-Aulaye ☎53248280
Access via D936. Take a right turn before the village and travel 3kms in the direction of the Dordogne.
15 Jun-15 Sep 2.5HEC 🎦 ♠ 🍴 ⊙ 🖳 🏕 ☎ ⊞ ♦ ⚡R

ST-ANTONIN-NOBLE-VAL *Tarn-et-Garonne*

Trois Cantons ☎63319857
Divided into pitches, partly on sloping ground within an oak forest. Separate section for teenagers.
8.5km NW near D926. Signposted.
15 Apr-Sep 5HEC 🎦 ♠ 🍴 ♀ ✕ ⊙ 🖳 ⌀ 🏕 🍴 ⚡ P ☎ ⊞ lau Prices: A22-27 pitch 25-33

ST-BERTRAND-DE-COMMINGES *Haute-Garonne*

Es Pibous chemin de St-Just ☎61989420
May-Sep 2HEC 🎦 ♠ 🍴 ⊙ 🖳 ⌀ 🏕 🍴 ☎ lau ♦ 🍴 ✕ Prices: A13-15 pitch 15

ST-CÉRÉ *Lot*

CM de Soulhol quai A-Salesse ☎65381237
200m SE on D940.
Apr-Sep 5HEC 🎦 ♠ ☏ 🍴 ⊙ 🖳 🏕 ⚡ R ☎ ⊞ lau ♦ 🍴 ✕ ⌀ 🍴 ⚡P Prices: A17 pitch 16

ST-CIRQ *Dordogne*

Brin d'Amour ☎53541806
In a fine location overlooking the Vézère Valley with good facilities.
All year 4HEC 🎦 ♠ 🍴 ♀ ✕ ⊙ 🖳 🏕 ⚡ P ☎ ⊞ lau ♦ ⌀ 🍴
Prices: A20 pitch 30

ST-CRICQ *Gers*

Lac de Thoux ☎62657129
Apr-Oct 3HEC 🎦 ♠ 🍴 ♀ ✕ ⊙ 🖳 🏕 🍴 ⚡ L ☎ ⊞ lau pitch 57-71 (incl 2 persons)

ST-CYBRANET *Dordogne*

Bel Ombrage ☎53283414
Quiet holiday site in wooded valley.
Jun-5 Sep 6HEC 🎦 ♠ ☏ ⊙ 🖳 ⚡ PR ☎ ⊞ lau ♦ 🍴 ♀ ✕ ⌀ Prices: A25 pitch 38

ST-CYPRIEN *Dordogne*

Ferme de Campagnac Castels ☎53292603
Access from town on D25. Signposted.
Apr-Oct 0.8HEC 🎦 ♠ ☏ ⊙ 🖳 🏕 lau ♦ 🍴 ♀ ✕ ⌀ 🍴 ⊞ Prices: A8 pitch 25

CM Garrit ☎53292056
1.5km S on D48.
Apr-Oct 🎦 ❑ ♠ 🍴 ♀ ✕ ⊙ 🖳 🏕 ☎ ⊞ lau ♦ ⌀ ⚡R

Plage Vezac ☎53295083
Apr-20 Oct 2HEC 🎦 ♠ ♦ ⊙ 🖳 ⌀ ⚡ R ☎ ⊞ lau ♦ ♀ ✕ Prices: A18-19 V9-10 ⊞9-10 ▲9-10

STE-EULALIE-EN-BORN *Landes*

Bruyères chemin Laffont ☎58097336
2.5km N via D652
Etr-Sep 3HEC 🎦 ♠ ☏ 🍴 ♀ ✕ ⊙ 🖳 ⌀ 🏕 🏕 ⚡ P ☎ ⊞ lau ♦ ⚡LR
Prices: pitch 90 (incl 2 persons)

ST-ÉMILION *Gironde*
Barbanne ☎57247580
3km N via D122
Apr-Sep 10HEC 🎗 ⌓ ⋔ 🏠 ⚑ ♥ ✕ ⊙ 🖳 ∅ 🛒 ⅋ ⟍ P ⚏ ⊞ lau Prices:
A21-22 pitch 31-36

ST-GENIES *Dordogne*
Bouquerie ☎53289822
N of village on D704.
15 May-15 Sep 7HEC 🎗 ∅♣⋔🏠⚑♥✕⊙🖳∅🛒 ⟍ LP ⚏ ⊞ lau ♦ 🎂

ST-GIRONS *Ariège*
Pont du Nert rte de Lacourt ☎61665848
Grassy site between road and woodland.
Approx 3km SE at the junction of the D33 and the D3.
Jun-15 Sep 1.5HEC 🎗 ♣⋔⊙🖳⚏ lau ♦ 🏠♥✕∅🎂 ⟍R ⊞ Prices:
A14 ⊕10 ▲10

ST-JEAN-DE-LUZ *Pyrénées-Atlantiques*
International d'Erromardie ☎59263426
Site is situated by the sea and consists of several sections divided
by roads and low hedges. Take away food.
If approached from N to N10, cross railway bridge and turn
immediately right and follow signs.
15 Mar-15 Oct 2HEC 🎗 ⌓⋔🏠♥✕⊙🖳∅ ⟍ S ⊞ lau

Iratzia ☎59261489
1km NE off N10. Leave autoroute, signed St-Jean-de-Luz Nord and
follow directions for Plage d'Erromardie.
15 Mar-Sep 4HEC 🎗 ♣⋔🏠♥✕⊙🖳∅🛒⚏⊞ lau ♦ ⟍S Prices:
A19-27 V10-14 ⊕22-30

Tamaris Plage Quartier d'Acotz ☎59265590
Site divided into sections by drives and hedges.
Signposted from N10 towards the sea.
Apr-Sep 1.2HEC 🎗 ⅃⋔♥✕⊙🖳🛒⚏ lau ♦🎂∅⟍S ⊞
Prices: pitch 127-165 (incl 2 persons)

At **SOCOA**(3km SW)
Juantcho rte de la Corniche ☎59471197
2km W on D912.
May-Sep 9HEC 🎗 ⅃⋔✕⊙🖳🛒⊞✕⟍RS

ST-JEAN-PIED-DE-PORT *Pyrénées-Atlantiques*
Narbaïtz rte de Bayonne, Ascarat ☎59371013
2km NW beside the river.
Apr-Sep 3HEC 🎗 ♣⋔🏠♥✕⊙🖳∅🛒🛒⟍ PR ⚏ lau ♦🎂⊞ Prices:
pitch 64 (incl 2 persons)

ST-JULIEN-EN-BORN *Landes*
Lette Fleurie rte de Contis ☎58427409
On undulating ground in a pine wood.
Etr-Sep 12HEC 🎗 ⁙⁙⁙ ♣⋔🏠♥✕⊙🖳∅ ⟍ P ⚏ ⊞ lau Prices:
A15.50 pitch 18.90

ST-JUSTIN *Landes*
Pin rte de Roquefort ☎58448891
A quiet family site beside the lake. Bar and café open May to 15
September only.
2.3km N on D626.
Mar-Nov 3HEC 🎗 ⁙⁙⁙ ♣⋔♥✕⊙🖳∅🎂🛒▲ ⟍ P ⚏ lau ♦
🏠 Prices: A15-24 pitch 18-22

ST-LÉON-SUR-VÉZÈRE *Dordogne*
Paradis ☎53507264
Situated on the river bank in the picturesque Vézère valley.
S of village off D706 Les Éyzies road.
22 Mar-18 Oct 6HEC 🎗 ♣⋔🏠♥✕⊙🖳∅🎂 ⟍ PR ⚏ lau
Prices: A24-34.50 pitch 38.50-55

At **TURSAC**(7km SW)
Pigeonnier ☎53069690
A small, peaceful site in the heart of the Dordogne countryside.
Acces via D706.
17 Jun-25 Aug 1.1HEC 🎗 ⌓⋔♥✕⊙🖳⚏⊞ lau ♦ ⟍R Prices:
A18 pitch 20

Vézère *Périgord* ☎53069631
0.8km NE on D706.
15 May-Sep 3.5HEC 🎗 ⌓⋔🏠♥✕⊙🖳∅🛒 ⟍ P ⚏ ⊞ lau ♦ ⟍R

ST-MARTORY *Haute-Garonne*
CM rte de St-Girons ☎61902224
All year 🎗 ⌓⋔⊙🖳⚏⊞ lau ♦🏠✕ ⟍R

ST-NICOLAS-DE-LA-GRAVE *Tarn-et-Garonne*
Plan d'Eau Base de Plein Air, et de Loisirs ☎63955002 &
63955000
2.5km N via D15.
15 Jun-15 Sep 1HEC 🎗 ⌓⋔♥✕⊙🖳∅🛒 ⟍ P ⚏ ⊞

ST-PARDOUX-LA-RIVIÈRE *Dordogne*
🔖**Château le Verdoyer** ☎53569464
3km N via D96.
May-Sep 15HEC 🎗 ♣⋔🏠♥✕⊙🖳∅🎂🛒▲ ⟍ LP ⚏ ⊞ lau

ST-PAUL-LES-DAX *Landes*
Pins du Soleil ☎58913791
On a hotel complex with good modern facilities.
SW via D954.
5 Apr-1 Nov 6HEC 🎗 ♣⋔🏠♥✕⊙🖳∅🎂🛒🛒 ⟍ P ⚏ lau ♦✕
⟍R Prices: pitch 70-130 (incl 2 persons)

ST-PÉE-SUR-NIVELLE *Pyrénées-Atlantiques*
Goyetchea ☎59541959
0.8km N on rte d'Ahetze
Jun-27 Sep 3HEC 🎗 ⌓⋔🏠♥⊙🖳∅🛒🛒 ⟍ P ⚏ lau ♦✕🎂
Prices: pitch 69-86 (incl 2 persons)

At **IBARRON**(2km W)
Ibarron ☎59541043
2km W on D918.
15 May-20 Sep 2.8HEC 🎗 ♣⋔⊙🖳🛒🛒⊞ lau ♦🏠✕∅
🎂⟍LPR

ST-PIERRE-LAFEUILLE *Lot*
Quercy-Vacances ☎65368715
On N20. 12km N of Cahors.
15 May-15 Sep 3HEC 🎗 ⌓⋔🏠♥✕⊙🖳∅🛒 ⟍ P ⚏ lau
Prices: A20-25 pitch 20-40

ST-RÉMY-SUR-LIDOIRE *Dordogne*
Tuilière ☎53824729
In pleasant wooded surroundings beside a lake. Separate car park
for arrivals after 22.00hrs.
6km from Montpon on D708 towards Ste-Foy-la-Grande.
15 Apr-15 Sep 8HEC 🎗 ♣⋔🏠♥✕⊙🖳∅🎂🛒🛒 ⟍ LP ⚏ ⊞ lau
Prices: A14.40-18 pitch 19.20-24

ST-SARDOS *Tarn-et-Garonne*
Tonère ☎63643187
N, beside the lakes.
15 Jun-15 Sep 🎗 ♣⋔⊙🖳⟍ L ⚏ ⊞ lau ♦🏠♥✕∅

ST-SEURIN-DE-PRATS *Dordogne*
Plage ☎53586107
0.7kms on D11 alongside the Dordogne.
Apr-Oct 4.5HEC 🎗 ♣⋔🏠♥✕⊙🖳∅🛒⚏ ⟍ PR ⚏ lau ♦∅⟍S
Prices: A20 pitch 30

SALIGNAC *Dordogne*
'Les Peneyrals' Le Poujol, St-Crépin Carlucet ☎53288571
Quiet site among trees between the Vézère and Dordogne rivers.
10 km N of Sarlat on D60.
10 May-13 Sep 10HEC 🎗 ⌓⋔🏠♥✕⊙🖳∅🎂🛒🛒 ⟍ P ⚏ ⊞ lau
Prices: A25-33 pitch 34-45

SALLES (GIRONDE) *Gironde*
Val de l'Eyre 8 rte de Minoy ☎56884703 or 56884354
SW on D108, rte de Lugos.
Apr-Oct 13HEC ⁙⁙⁙ ⌓⋔♥✕⊙🖳∅🎂🛒🛒▲ ⟍ LR ⚏ ⊞ lau ♦🏠
⟍P

SALLES (LOT-ET-GARONNE) *Lot-et-Garonne*

Bastides ☎53408309
In peaceful wooded surroundings overlooking the Lède Valley with good sporting and entertainment facilities.
1km N via D150.
May-Sep 6HEC ▥ ⌂ ⋔ ⊾ ♥ ✕ ⊙ ➒ ∅ ⚏ ⊞ ➡ ⱦ P ☑ ⊞ lau Prices: A28 pitch 30

SARE *Pyrénées-Atlantiques*

Goyenetche rte des Grottes ☎59542171
3.5km S via D306
May-Sep 1HEC ▥ ⌂ ⋔ ⊙ ➒ ∅ ⚏ ⱦ R ☑ ⊞ lau ➡ ⊾ ♥ ✕ ⱦLPS

SARLAT-LA-CANÉDA *Dordogne*

Maillac Ste-Nathalène ☎53592212
Separate car park for arrivals after 23.00hrs.
7km NE on D47.
15 May-Sep 6HEC ▥ ⸬ ⌂ ⋔ ⊾ ♥ ✕ ⊙ ➒ ∅ ⚏ ⊞ ➡ ⱦ P ☑ ⊞ lau ➡ ⱦR Prices: A24 pitch 30

Moulin du Roch rte des Éyzies ☎53592027
Camping Card Compulsory.
10km NW via D704-D6-D47.
26 Apr-14 Sep 8HEC ▥ ⌂ ⋔ ⊾ ♥ ✕ ⊙ ➒ ∅ ⚏ ⊞ ➡ Å ⱦ P ☑ ⊞ lau Prices: pitch 70-119 (incl 2 persons)

Périères ☎53590584
Very well kept terraced site on wooded valley.
1km N of town on D47.
Etr-Sep 11HEC ▥ ⋔ ⊾ ♥ ✕ ⊙ ➒ ∅ ⚏ ⱦ P ☑ ⊞ lau Prices: pitch 146 (incl 3 persons)

At CARSAC-AILLAC(7km SE via D704a)

Aqua Viva ☎53314600
Site with numerous terraces in beautiful wooded surroundings in the heart of the Dordogne.
Along the main road Sarlat/Souillac D704A
Etr-Sep 11HEC ▥ ⸬ ⌂ ⋔ ⊾ ♥ ✕ ⊙ ➒ ∅ ⚏ ➡ Å ⱦ LP ☑ ⊞ lau Prices: A16-31 pitch 20-45

Rocher de la Cave ☎53281426
Pleasant site beside the river.
Access via D703 & D704.
May-25 Sep 4HEC ▥ ⸬ ♥ ⋔ ⊾ ♥ ✕ ⊙ ➒ ∅ ⚏ ⱦ R ☑ ⊞ lau Prices: A21 pitch 26

At PROISSANS(6km NE)

Val d'Ussel ☎95607313
Off D704 or D56.
3 May-28 Sep 7HEC ▥ ⌂ ⋔ ⊾ ⊙ ➒ ∅ ⚏ ⊞ ➡ ⱦ P ☑ ▣ lau ➡ ⱦS Prices: A20-30 pitch 22-37

SAUVETERRE-DE-BÉARN *Pyrénées-Atlantiques*

CM Gave av de la Gare ☎59385330
Turn left before bridge on St-Palais road.
All year 1.6HEC ▥ ▥ ⌂ ⋔ ⊾ ⊙ ➒ ⱦ lau ➡ ⊾ ♥ ✕ ∅ ⚏

SAUVETERRE-LA-LÉMANCE *Lot-et-Garonne*

Moulin du Périé rte de Loubejac ☎53406726
In a wooded valley.
3km E of town off D710. Follow signposts from the entrance to the village and keep to the valley road.
4 May-Sep 4.5HEC ▥ ♥ ⋔ ⊾ ♥ ✕ ⊙ ➒ ∅ ⚏ ⊞ ➡ Å ⱦ P ☑ lau ➡ ⱦLS

SEIGNOSSE *Landes*

Chevreuils ☎58433280
In a pine forest. On CD79 rte de Hossegor.
Jun-15 Sep 8HEC ▥ ⸬ ♥ ⋔ ⊾ ♥ ✕ ⊙ ➒ ∅ ⚏ ⊞ ➡ ⱦ P ☑ ⊞ lau ➡ ⱦS

CM ☎58433030
Very clean and tidy site.
Jun-Sep 16HEC ▥ ♥ ⋔ ⊾ ♥ ⊙ ➒ ∅ ⚏ ☑ ⊞ lau ➡ ✕ ⱦLPS

At SEIGNOSSE-LE-PENON(5km W)

Forêt ☎58433020
A pleasant, quiet site 300m from the sea.
13 Jun-13 Sep 11HEC ⸬ ♥ ⋔ ⊾ ♥ ✕ ⊙ ➒ ➒ ⱦ P ▣ ⊞ ⊞ ⤫ lau ➡ ⊾ ∅ ⚏ ⱦS

SEIX *Ariège*

Haut Salat ☎61668178
Very clean, well kept site beside stream. Big gravel pitches for caravans. Common room with TV.
0.8km NE on D3.
3 Jan-14 Sep & 15 Oct-21 Dec 2.5HEC ▥ ♥ ⋔ ⊾ ♥ ✕ ⊙ ➒ ∅ ⚏ ⱦ R ☑ ⊞ lau ➡ ✕ ⚏ Prices: A21 pitch 21

SIORAC-EN-PÉRIGORD *Dordogne*

At COUX-ET-BIGAROQUE(2.5 km NW by D710/D703)

Clou Meynard Haut ☎53316332
Separate section for dog owners.
Access via D703 (Le Bugue-Delve road).
Apr-Sep 3HEC ▥ ♥ ⋔ ⊾ ♥ ✕ ⊙ ➒ ∅ ⚏ ⊞ ➡ ⱦ P ☑ ⊞ lau Prices: A26 pitch 31.50

Faval ☎53316044
1km E of village on D703, near junction with D710.
Apr-Sep 3HEC ▥ ♥ ⋔ ⊾ ♥ ✕ ⊙ ➒ ∅ ⚏ ⊞ ➡ ⱦ P ☑ lau ➡ ⱦR

SORE *Landes*

CM Zone de Loisirs 'La Piscine' ☎58076006
1.2km S via D651.
15 Jun-15 Sep 1HEC ▥ ⌂ ⋔ ⊙ ➒ ⱦ PR ☑ lau ➡ ⊾ ♥ ✕ ∅ ⚏ ⊞

SOUILLAC *Lot*

CM les Ondines r des Ondines ☎65378644
Camping Card Compulsory
May-Sep ⋔ ⊙ ➒ ⱦ R ☑ ⊞ lau ➡ ⊾ ♥ ✕

Domaine de la Paille Basse ☎65378548
6.5km NW off D15 Salignac-Eyvignes road.
15 May-15 Sep 80HEC ▥ ♦ ♥ ⋔ ⊾ ♥ ✕ ⊙ ➒ ∅ ⚏ ⊞ ➡ ⱦ P ☑ ⊞ lau Prices: A32 pitch 52-64

SOULAC-SUR-MER *Gironde*

Océan L'Amélie ☎56097610
3.5km S.
Jun-15 Sep 6HEC ▥ ⸬ ⌂ ⋔ ⊾ ♥ ⊙ ➒ ∅ ⚏ ☑ ⊞ lau ➡ ⱦS Prices: pitch 64

Sables d'Argent r de l'Amélie ☎56098287
1.5km SW of village.
Etr-Sep 2.5HEC ▥ ⸬ ⌂ ⋔ ⊾ ♥ ✕ ⊙ ➒ ∅ ⚏ ⊞ ⚏ ☑ ⊞ lau ➡ ⱦS

At AMÉLIE-SUR-MER, L'(4.5km S)

Amélie-Plage ☎56098727
In hilly wooded terrain. Lovely sandy beach.
3km S on the Soulac road.
Apr-Oct 8.5HEC ▥ ♥ ⋔ ⊾ ♥ ✕ ⊙ ➒ ∅ ⚏ ⊞ ➡ ⱦ S ☑ ⊞ lau Prices: pitch 82 (incl 2 persons)

At LILIAN(4.5km S)

Pins ☎56098252
S on D101.
Jun-Sep 3HEC ▥ ⌂ ⋔ ⊾ ⊙ ➒ ∅ ⚏ ⚏ ☑ ⊞ lau ➡ ⱦS

SOUSTONS *Landes*

CM Airial ☎58411248
2km W on D652.
Etr-Sep 12HEC ▥ ♥ ⋔ ⊾ ♥ ✕ ⊙ ➒ ∅ ⱦ P ☑ ⊞ lau

TARASCON-SUR-ARIÈGE *Ariège*

Pré Lombard rte d'Ussat ☎61056194
In beautiful wooded surroundings beside the River Ariège with good, modern facilities.
1.5km SE on D23.
Closed Nov-Jan 3.5HEC ▥ ♥ ⋔ ✕ ⊙ ➒ ∅ ⚏ ⊞ ➡ Å ⱦ PR ☑ ⊞ lau ➡ ⊾ ⱦL Prices: pitch 78 (incl 2 persons)

TEILLET *Tarn*
Relais de l'Entre Deux Lacs ☎05 63557445
Shady terraced site.
All year 4HEC ▥ ♦♠♌☢✕☺◘➡♯⚡ P ☎⊞ lau ➡⚓∅⚏
Prices: pitch 71 (incl 2 persons)

TERRASSON-LA-VILLEDIEU *Dordogne*
Ile de France pl de la Vergne ☎53500882
500m E.
15 Mar-Oct 0.7HEC ▥ ♦♠☺◘☎⊞ lau ➡♌♒✕⚡P

THIVIERS *Dordogne*
CM Le Repaire ☎53526975
In a wooded valley, this well appointed family site lies in the 'Périgord
Vert' region of the Dordogne some ten minutes walk from the ancient
village of Thiviers.
May-Sep 10HEC ▥ ♌♠♒✕☺◘➡♯ LP ☎⊞ lau ➡♌✕∅⚏
♯L Prices: A20-25 pitch 30-35

TONNEINS *Lot-et-Garonne*
CM Robinson ☎05530228
500m from town centre on N113 Agen road.
Jun-Sep 0.7HEC ▥ ♦♠☺◘➡♯ R ☎ lau ➡♌♒✕⚡♯P ☎ Prices:
pitch 33 (incl 2 persons)

TOUZAC *Lot*
Ch'Timi ☎65365236
800m from Touzac on D8, beside the River Lot.
15 May-20 Sep 3HEC ▥ ♦♠♌♒✕☺◘∅⚏➡♯ P ☎⊞ lau ➡
♯R Prices: A20-22 pitch 25-32

Clos Bouyssac ☎65365221
On the fringe of a wooded hillside by the sandy shore of the River
Lot. Good for walking.
May-15 Sep 4.5HEC ▥ ♦♠♌♒✕☺◘∅⚏➡♯ PR ☎⊞ lau
Prices: A23 pitch 27

URRUGNE *Pyrénées-Atlantiques*
Larrouleta ☎59473784
Hilly meadow with young trees.
1.5 km N of Urrugne on N1 to Spain.
All year 5HEC ▥ ♦♠♌♒✕☺◘∅♯ LR ☎⊞ lau ➡⚏

VALEUIL *Dordogne*
Bas Meygnaud ☎53055844
Apr-Sep 1.7HEC ▥ ♦♠♌♒✕☺◘➡♯ P ☎⊞ lau ➡♌✕♯R
Prices: A14 V9 ⚘24 ▲22

VARILHES *Ariège*
CM Parc du Château av du 8 Mai 45 ☎61674284
N on N20.
All year ▥ ♦♠☺◘♯ PR ☎⊞ lau ➡♌♒✕∅⚏

VAYRAC *Lot*
Domaine de Bourzolles Condat ☎65321632
Off D20 between Condat and Vayrac.
15 Jun-15 Sep 4HEC ▥ ♦♠♒☺◘♯ P ☎⊞ lau

VENSAC *Gironde*
Acacias Lieu-Dit Gaudin ☎56095881
30 Jun-10 Sep 3.5HEC ▥ ♌♠✕☺◘➡♯ P ☎ lau

VERDON-SUR-MER, LE *Gironde*
Cordouan ☎56097142
Clean, pleasant meadowland with some pines and deciduous trees.
1km to sea.
N of Soulac-sur-Mer via D1.
All year 4.5HEC ▥ ♦♠♌♒✕☺◘∅⚏➡☎⊞ lau ➡✕♯S

Royannais 88 rte de Soulac ☎56096112
Level, sandy terrain under high pine and deciduous trees.
S of Le Verdon-sur-Mer in Le Royannais district on D1.
15 Jun-15 Sep 2HEC ▩ ♦♠♌♒✕☺◘∅➡⚘◘☎⊞ lau ➡♯S
Prices: pitch 48 (incl 2 persons)

VERGT-DE-BIRON *Dordogne*
Patrasses ☎53630587
3.6km S via D2E.
Jun-Sep 3HEC ▥ ♒♌♠♒✕☺◘➡♯ P ☎ Prices: pitch 60.50

VEYRINES-DE-DOMME *Dordogne*
Pastourels Le Brouillet ☎53295249
A quiet site in a pleasant rural setting near the Château des
Milandes.
3.6km via off D53 towards Belvès.
Apr-Sep 2.5HEC ▥ ▒ ♦♠♌♒☺◘∅♯ R ☎⊞ lau

VÉZAC *Dordogne*
Deux Vallées ☎53295355
A level site in a picturesque location at the rear of the disused Vézac
station.
Apr-15 Oct 2.4HEC ▥ ♦♠♌♒✕☺◘∅⚏♯ LP ☎⊞ lau ➡
♯R Prices: A12-24 pitch 16-32

VIELLE-ST-GIRONS *Landes*
Col Vert Lac de Léon ☎58429406
Quiet site on lakeside in sparse pine woodland. Small natural harbour
in the mouth of a stream.
Turn off D652 on N side of village and continue towards lake.
Etr-Nov 30HEC ▥ ♦♠♌♒✕☺◘∅⚏➡♯ LP ☎⊞ lau ➡⚏
♯S Prices: A12-25 pitch 29.50-57

Eurosol rte de la Plage ☎58479014
Jun-15 Sep 18HEC ▥ ▒ ♦♠♌♒☺◘∅⚏♯ P ☎⊞ lau
➡ ♯S Prices: A20-25 pitch 44-55

VIEUX-BOUCAU-LES-BAINS *Landes*
CM des Sablères bd du Marensin ☎58481229
Apr-15 Oct 11HEC ▥ ▒ ♦♠☺◘⊞ lau ➡♌♒✕∅⚏♯LS
Prices: A7-11 ⚘40-66 ▲35-66

VILLEFRANCHE-DU-QUEYRAN *Lot-et-Garonne*
Moulin de Campech ☎53887243
A beautiful site in a peaceful location.
Access via D11 towards Casteljaloux.
Apr-Oct 4.5HEC ▥ ♌♠♒✕☺◘➡▲♯ LPR ☎ lau ➡∅⚏
Prices: A15-21 pitch 30-43

VILLENAVE-D'ORNON *Gironde*
Gravières chemin de Macau ☎56870036
2km NE
All year 3.5HEC ▥ ♦♠♌♒✕☺◘∅⚏☎⊞ lau ➡♯P Prices:
A19 pitch 28

VILLERÉAL *Lot-et-Garonne*
⚑Château de Fonrives Rives ☎53366338
2.2km NW via D207
10 May-20 Sep 20HEC ▥ ♦♠♌♒✕☺◘∅⚏➡⚘♯ LP ☎⊞
lau Prices: A21-29 pitch 32-45

VITRAC *Dordogne*
Bouysse Caudon ☎53283305
2km E, near the River Dordogne.
Etr-Sep 3HEC ▥ ♦♠♌♒✕☺◘∅➡♯ PR ☎ lau ➡⚏⊞ Prices:
A22.10-26 pitch 26.35-31

Soleil Plage ☎53283333
4km E on D703, turn by 'Camping Clos Bernard'.
Apr-Oct 9HEC ▥ ♌♠♒✕☺◘∅➡♯ PR ☎⊞ lau Prices: A32
pitch 50

Loire/Central

The undoubted highlight of this area is the Loire, France's longest
river, which winds its unhurried way through green valleys, vine-
covered hills, meadows, and, of course, past the remarkable
châteaux and medieval citadels which are masterpieces spanning
the changing architectural style of seven centuries. The western
Loire region unites a countryside of soft hills little farms and

vineyards, and historic châteaux and abbeys with the sea. North of the river the coastline meets the Atlantic at rocky cliffs; south of the river great sandy beaches are backed by great pine woods. Still farther south, the province of Charente-Maritime boasts sunshine totals to rival the Mediterranean, and 150 miles of coastline with busy ports, family resorts - both on the mainland and off-lying islands, and harbours bustling with colourful life. La Rochelle, with its ancient harbour and fine old houses, is a popular centre. Inland, there are literally hundreds of interesting churches and abbeys, and vineyards whose grapes mature into Cognac. Inland still further, the region of Limousin is a charming backwater of rolling hills, with Limoges a fascinating porcelain centre.

AIGUILLON-SUR-MER, L' Vendée

Bel Air ☎51564405
A long, level stretch of meadowland in rural surroundings.
1.5 km NW on D44 then turn left.
May-15 Sep 6HEC ▦ ⌾ ℝ ☎ ♥ ✖ ⊙ ⊠ ∅ ☎ ⊞ A ⋟ P ☎ ⊞ lau ♦
⋟LRS Prices: pitch 105 (incl 2 persons)

AIRVAULT Deux-Sèvres

Courte Vallée ☎49647065
A new site, situated in a river valley, with large pitches.
On the outskirts of the town, 0.5km NW towards Availles.
May-Sep 3.5HEC ▦ ⌾ ℝ ♥ ✖ ⊙ ⊠ ∅ ⋟ P ⊞ lau ♦ ✖ ⋌ ⋟R
Prices: A18 pitch 36

ALLONNES Maine-et-Loire

Pô Doré Le Pô ☎41387880
In a pleasant rural setting. Separate car park for arrivals 22.00hrs.
Access via D10.
Apr-Oct 2.5HEC ▦ ⋌⋋ ℝ ♥ ✖ ⊙ ⊠ ☎ ☎ ⋟ P ⊞ lau ♦ ∅ ⋌ ⋟
Prices: pitch 55-75 (incl 2 persons) pp6.50-8.50

ANDONVILLE Loiret

Domaine de la Joullière rte de Richerelles ☎38395846
Spread over a series of small, wooded valleys with good sports and leisure facilities.
1km E on road to Richerelles.
Closed Jan 10HEC ▦ ⌾ ℝ ♥ ✖ ⊙ ⊠ ∅ ☎ ⋟ P ☎ ⊞ lau
Prices: A32 pitch 32

ANGERS Maine-et-Loire

Lac de Maine av du Lac de Maine ☎41730503
Bar and restraunt available Jul-Aug only.
Access via A11 (Angers/Nantes) at Lac de Maine exit.
10 Feb-20 Dec 4HEC ▦ ⋊⋉ ⋌⋋ ℝ ♥ ✖ ⊙ ⊠ ∅ ⋟ P ☎ ⊞ lau ♦
⋟ ⋟L Prices: pitch 57.50-72 (incl 2 persons)

ANGLES Vendée

Moncalm-Atlantique ☎51560878
Apr-Sep 10HEC ▦ ♦ ℝ ♥ ✖ ⊙ ⊠ ∅ ⋌ ☎ A ⋟ P ⊞ lau ♦
⋟R ⊞ Prices: A21-23 pitch 90-105

ANGOULINS-SUR-MER Charente-Maritime

Chirats rte de la Platèere ☎46569416
Modern site 150m from a small sandy beach. Booking advised.
7km south of La Rochelle.
Etr-15 Oct 4HEC ▦ ⋄ ⋌⋋ ℝ ♥ ✖ ⊙ ⊠ ∅ ⋟ P ⊞ lau ♦
⋟S Prices: A24-25 V10-11 ▲20-29 ▲20-29

ARDILLIÈRES Charente-Maritime

Ferme Toucherit ☎46277306
Camping Card Compulsory.
Jun-Sep 0.8HEC ▦ ℝ ⊙ ⊠ ☎ ⊞ lau ♦ ℝ ♥ ✖ ∅ ⋌ ⋟R

ARGENTAT Corrèze

Gibanel Le Gibanel ☎55281011
Pleasant site situated in grounds of a château next to a lake. Some facilities are available in high season.
S from Tulle on N120.
Jun-15 Sep 60HEC ▦ ⌾ ℝ ♥ ✖ ⊙ ⊠ ∅ ⋟ LP ☎ ⊞ lau ♦ ⋌
Prices: A26.50 pitch 29

Saulou Vergnolles ☎55281233
6km S on D116.
26 Apr-20 Sep 7HEC ▦ ♦ ℝ ⋌ ♥ ✖ ⊙ ⊠ ∅ ⊠ ⋟ PR ☎ ⊞ lau
Prices: A26 pitch 34

At MONCEAUX-SUR-DORDOGNE(3km SW)

Vaurette ☎55280967
On the banks of the River Dordogne with a beach, swimming pool & tennis court. On D12 between Argentat and Beaulieu.
May-21 Sep 4HEC ▦ ♦ ℝ ⋌ ♥ ✖ ⊙ ⊠ ∅ ⋟ PR ☎ ⊞ lau Prices:
A20-23 pitch 24-30

ARGENTON-CHÂTEAU Deux-Sèvres

CM du Lac d'Hautibus ☎49657022
0.4km S on D748.
15 Jun-15 Sep 1HEC ▦ ⌾ ℝ ⊙ ⊠ ☎ ⋌ lau ♦ ℝ ♥ ✖ ⋟P ⊞ Prices:
A10 V9 pitch 10

ASSERAC Loire-Atlantique

Traverno ☎40017335
500m from the village, towards Pont-Mahé on D82.
Jul-Sep 2HEC ▦ ⌾ ℝ ⊙ ⊠ ☎ ⋌ lau ♦ ℝ ♥ ✖ ∅ ⋌

AVRILLÉ Vendée

Forges Domaine Les Forges ☎51223885
In a pleasant position beside a lake, 300m from the town centre.
Etr-Sep 15HEC ▦ ⌾ ℝ ♥ ✖ ⊙ ⊠ ∅ ⋌ ☎ ⋟ LP ☎ lau ♦ ✖ ∅ ⋌ ⊞
Prices: pitch 50-70 (incl 2 persons)

Mancelières rte de Longeville-sur-Mer ☎51903597
Separate car park for arrivals after 23.00hrs.
1.7km S via D105 towards Longeville
May-Sep 2.6HEC ▦ ♦ ℝ ⋌ ♥ ✖ ⊙ ⊠ ∅ ☎ ⋟ P ⊞ lau Prices:
pitch 82 (incl 2 persons)

AZAY-LE-RIDEAU Indre-et-Loire

Parc du Sabot r du Stade ☎47454272
Site lies in large meadow on bank of River Indre.
Near château in town centre.
25 Mar-15 Nov 9HEC ▦ ⌾ ℝ ⊙ ⊠ ☎ ⊞ lau ♦ ℝ ♥ ✖ ∅ ⋌ ⋟PR

BARDÉCILLE Charente-Maritime

Ferme de Chez Filleux Arces-sur-Gironde ☎46908433
May-15 Sep 3HEC ▦ ⌾ ℝ ℝ ♥ ✖ ⊙ ⊠ ∅ ⋟ P ☎ ⊞ lau ♦ ✖

BATZ-SUR-MER Loire-Atlantique

Govelle 10 rte de La Govelle ☎40239163
Direct access to the sea. Supervised beach and sea-fishing nearby.
On D45 between Le Pouliguen and Batz.
Apr-Sep 0.6HEC ▦ ⋊⋉ ⌾ ℝ ♥ ✖ ⊙ ⊠ ☎ ☎ ⋟ S ☎ ⊞ lau ♦ ℝ ∅ ⋌

BAULE, LA Loire-Atlantique

Ajoncs d'Or chemin du Rocher ☎40603329
In a large wooded park, close to the beach.
Etr-Sep 5.5HEC ▦ ⌾ ℝ ♥ ✖ ⊙ ⊠ ∅ ⋌ ☎ ☎ ⋟ P ☎ ⊞ lau ♦ ⋟S
Prices: pitch 98-120 (incl 2 persons)

CM av de Diane ☎40601740
Site consists of two sections, one for caravans, one for tents, each with separate entrance. Caravan site (off av R-Flandin) is level and has good sanitary installations. Tent site (off av P-Minto) is in hilly, sandy woodland with only simple installations.
Camping Card Compulsory.
Mar-Sep 5HEC ▦ ⋊⋉ ⋄ ⌾ ♦ ℝ ℝ ♥ ✖ ⊙ ⊠ ∅ ☎ ☎ ☎ ☎ ⊠ lau ♦
⋟S

Eden St-Servais D.99 ☎40600323
In pleasant rural surroundings with good sports and sanitary facilities.
1km NW
1 Apr-Sep 4.7HEC ▦ ⌾ ℝ ♥ ✖ ⊙ ⊠ ∅ ⋌ ☎ ☎ ⋟ LP ☎ ⊞ lau ♦ ✖
∅ ⋟S

Roseraie 20 av J-Sohier ☎40604666
A well planned site in wooded surroundings with good recreational facilities.
Apr-Sep 5HEC ▦ ⌾ ℝ ♥ ✖ ⊙ ⊠ ∅ ⋌ ⋟ P ☎ ⊞ lau ♦ ⋟S

BAZOUGES-SUR-LE-LOIR *Sarthe*
CM rte de Cie-sur-Loir ☎43459580
15 May-Sep 0.8HEC ▥ ⊕♠⊙⊙♀? R ☎ lau ♦ �serX⌀ ≅ ⊞
Prices: A6.70 pitch 14.50

BEAULIEU-SUR-DORDOGNE *Corrèze*
Îles ☎55910265
On an island in the River Dordogne, within easy reach of all facilities.
May-Sep 4HEC ▥ ▚▚ ♠♀▼♀? R ☎ ⊞ lau ♦ ⌀

BESSINES-SUR-GARTEMPE *Haute-Vienne*
At **MORTEROLLES-SUR-SEMME**(4.5km N on N20)
CM ☎55766018
100m from N20; in town centre.
All year 8HEC ⊕♠⊙⊙♀☎⊞ lau ♦ ▚▼X⌀ ?R

BEYNAT *Corrèze*
Étang de Miel ☎55855066
4km E on N121 Argentat road.
Jul-Aug 9HEC ⊕♠▚▼X⊙⊙♀⌀☎♀? L ☎⊞ lau

BLÉRÉ *Indre-et-Loire*
CM r de la Gatine ☎47579260
Well-kept site beside River Cher. Two entrances.
Apr-15 Oct 4HEC ▥ ⊕♠⊙⊙♀☎☎lau ♦ ▚▼X ?P ⊞ Prices:
pitch 46.42

BLOIS *Loir-et-Cher*
CM Boire bd A-Carrel ☎54742278
1.5km E on D751.
Mar-Nov 10HEC ▥ ⊕♠⊙⊙♀☎⊞ lau ♦ ▚▼X ?LP

BONNAC-LA-CÔTE *Haute-Vienne*
▐**Château de Leychoisier** ☎55399343
Well-managed site on ground sloping gently towards the woods.
Divided into roomy pitches.
1km S off N20.
15 Apr-20 Sep 2HEC ▥ ⊕♠▚▼X⊙⊙⌀? LP ☎⊞ lau

BONNES *Vienne*
CM r de la Varenne ☎49564434
S beside the River Vienne.
15 May-Sep 30 1.2HEC ⊕♠⊙▼⊙⊙♀? R ☎⊞ lau ♦ ▚X⌀ ≅
?P

BONNY-SUR-LOIRE *Loiret*
Val ☎38315771
Woodland site situated by the side of the Loire, near the town centre
At the junction of N7 and D965.
9 Apr-15 Oct 0.8HEC ▥ ⊕♠⊙⊙♀? R ☎ lau ♦ ▚▼X ≅

BOURGES *Cher*
CM de Bourges 26 bd de l'Industrie ☎48201685
In the town near Lake Auron.
Access via A71, N144 or N76.
15 Mar-14 Nov 2.2HEC ▥ ▚▚ ⊕♠⊙⊙♀☎⊞ lau ♦ ▚▼X⌀ ≅
?LP

BOUZONVILLE-AUX-BOIS *Loiret*
Clos des Tourterelles 29 r des Rendillons ☎38330100
8km S of Pithiviers on D921.
All year 0.5HEC ⊕♠▚⊙⊙♀⌀ ≅☎☎lau ♦ ▼X

BRACIEUX *Loir-et-Cher*
CM des Châteaux rte de Blois ☎54464184
N on left bank of River Beauvron.
Apr-15 Oct 8HEC ▥ ⊕♠▚⊙⊙♀⌀? P ☎⊞ lau ♦ ▼X ≅ Prices:
A18 pitch 50

BRAIN-SUR-L'AUTHION *Maine-et-Loire*
CM Caroline ☎41804218
15 Mar-Oct 3.5HEC ▥ ⊕♠⊙⊙♀⌀☎ lau ♦ ▚▼X ≅ ?R ⊞

BRETIGNOLLES-SUR-MER *Vendée*
Dunes Plage des Dunes ☎51905532
Direct access to the beach. All plots surrounded by hedges.

2km S turn right off D38 and proceed for 1km across the dunes.
150m from beach.
Apr-30 Oct 12HEC ▚▚▚ ≠♠⊕♠▼X⊙⊙⌀ ≅☎ ? P ☎⊞ lau ♦
?S Prices: A13-25 pitch 76-122

Motine 4 r des Morinières ☎51900442
Pleasant site situated 350m from the town centre and 400m from
the beach.
Apr-Sep 1.8HEC ▥ ⊕♠▚▼X⊙⊙⌀ ≅☎ ☎⊞ lau ♦ ▚? LS
Prices: A11-17 pitch 62-82

Vagues 20 bd du Centre ☎51901948
N on D38 towards St-Gilles-Croix-de-Vie
Apr-Oct 4.5HEC ⊕♠▼⊙⊙♀? P ☎⊞ lau ♦ ▚X⌀ ≅
?LRS Prices: pitch 106-120 (incl 3 persons)

BRISSAC-QUINCÉ *Maine-et-Loire*
Domaine de l'Étang ☎41917061
A lakeside site in the heart of the Anjou countryside with good
recreational facilities.
Access via D748 towards Poitiers.
15 May-15 Sep 3.5HEC ▥ ⊕♠▚▼X⊙⊙⌀⌀ ≅? LP ☎⊞ lau
Prices: A22.50 pitch 50
See advertisement under SAUMUR

BRÛLON *Sarthe*
Brûlon-le-Lac ☎43956896
Apr-Oct 3.5HEC ⊕♠▚▼X⊙⊙⌀⌀≅☎ ? LP ☎⊞ lau

CANDÉ-SUR-BEUVRON *Loir-et-Cher*
Grande Tortue rte de Pontlevoy ☎54441520
D751, between Blois and Amboise, on the left bank of the river.
6 Apr-30 Sep 5.8HEC ⊕♠▚▼X⊙⊙⌀⌀ ≅☎☎ ? P ☎⊞ lau
Prices: pitch 53-80 (incl 2 persons)

CHALARD, LE *Haute-Vienne*
Vigeres St-Yrieix-la-Perche ☎55093722
Generally level site in peaceful surroundings in an elevated position
with fine views. English management.
Between Châlus and Le Chalard on D901.
All year 2HEC ▥ ⊕♠⊙⊙♀⌀▲ ? L ☎⊞ lau ♦ ▚▼X⌀ ?P

CHALONNES-SUR-LOIRE *Maine-et-Loire*
CM Candais ☎41780227
On the banks of the River Loire.
May-1 Oct 3HEC ▥ ≠♠▼X⊙⊙♀☎⊞ lau ♦ ▚X⌀ ≅?P Prices:
A15.80 pitch 6.10

CHARTRES *Eure-et-Loir*
CM des Bords de l'Eure r de Launay ☎37287943
Signposted towards Orléans.
21 Apr-3 Sep 3HEC ▥ ⊕♠▚⊙⊙♀☎⊞ lau ♦ ▼X ?P Prices:
pitch 47-68 (incl 2 persons)

CHARTRE-SUR-LE-LOIR, LA *Sarthe*
Vieux Moulin av des Déportés ☎43444118
15 Apr-Sep 2.4HEC ▥ ⊕♠⊙⊙♀? PR ☎⊞ lau ♦ ▚▼X⌀ ≅?LP
Prices: pitch 38-49 (incl 2 persons)

CHASSENEUIL-SUR-BONNIEURE *Charente*
CM r des Écoles ☎45395536
W of town via D27, beside the River Bonnieure.
15 Jun-15 Sep 2.1HEC ▥ ⊕♠⊙⊙♀ lau ♦ ▚▼X⌀ ?PR ⊞
Prices: A7 V4 ☎5

CHÂTEAU-DU-LOIR *Sarthe*
CM de Coemont ☎43794463
Shady site on the bank of the Loir.
15 May-15 Sep 0.6HEC ▥ ⊕♠⊙⊙♀? R ☎ lau ♦ ▚▼X⌀ ?P ⊞

CHÂTEAUDUN *Eure-et-Loir*
CM Moulin-à-Tan ☎37450534
NW via D955 beside the River Loir.
15 Mar-15 Oct 1.5HEC ▥ ≠♠▼X⊙⊙♀? R ☎⊞ lau ♦ ▼X
?P

Halfway PARIS to BORDEAUX
Motorway A10 Exit 16 Chatellerault-Nord
Outstanding environment, beside the river
Vienne, in the Chateau de Valette Park. All
facilities, water and electricity on each pitch.
Angling, swimming pool, childrens
playground. 14 mins driving distance from
FUTUROSCOPE.
Le Relais du Miel ★★★★
CHATELLERAULT

Camping-Caravaning **Tel.: 02 54 79 90 01**
LES SAULES **Fax:02 54 79 28 34**
41700 Cheverny Loire Valley
★★★★
Beautifully situated in the Loire Valley, surrounded by
15 castles. 10 ha of green Park. Bar, take-away (incl.
grill), grocery, swimming pool, paddling pool, children's
playground, mini-golf, golf course in front of site (100
ha., 18 holes), Volleyball, table tennis, small train, TV,
English spoken. During the season, organised leisure
and group excursions. Reservations possible for crafts
workshop and artistic activities. Mobile homes for hire.
Service station for motor caravans.
Open: Easter to 20 September
18km south of Blois, towards VIERZON CD 102.

CHÂTEAULONG *Vendée*
Pin Parasol Lac du Jaunay ☎51346472
In the heart of the Vendée countryside on the shore of Lac du Jaunay
with good, modern facilities.
May-Sep 4HEC ▦ ⌂ ⋒ ⚊ ⅌ ✕ ⊙ ⬛ ⬤ ≞ ⬛ ⬛ ⟍ LPR ⬚ ⊞ lau ➤ ✕
Prices: pitch 80 (incl 2 persons)

CHÂTELAILLON-PLAGE *Charente-Maritime*
Clos des Rivages av des Boucholeurs ☎46562609
Level, well-kept site.
15 Jun-10 Sep 3HEC ▦ ⌂ ⋒ ⚊ ⅌ ⊙ ⬛ ⬛ ⊞ lau ➤ ✕ ⟍PS Prices:
pitch 90 (incl 2 persons)

Deux Plages ☎46562753
May-15 Sep 4.5HEC ▦ ∷∷ ◆ ⋒ ⚊ ✕ ⊙ ⬛ ⬤ ⬛ ⊞ lau ➤ ⟍PS

CHÂTELLERAULT *Vienne*
Relais du Miel rte d' Antran ☎49020627
In the grounds of the Château de Valette, beside the River Vienne.
Access via A10 exit 16 (Châtellerault Nord).
May-Sep 7HEC ▦ ∷∷ ◆ ⌂ ⋒ ⚊ ⅌ ✕ ⊙ ⬛ ⬤ ⟍ PR ⬚ ⊞ lau ➤
⟍L Prices: pitch 130 (incl 2 persons)

CHÂTILLON-SUR-CHER *Loir-et-Cher*
'Parici' ☎54710221
Apr-Oct 1.2HEC ▦ ◆ ⋒ ⚊ ⅌ ✕ ⊙ ⬛ ⬤ ≞ ⬛ ⬛ ⟍ R ⬚ ⊞ lau
Prices: A13.30 pitch 13.30

CHÂTRES-SUR-CHER *Loir-et-Cher*
CM des Saules ☎54980455
On N76 near bridge.
May-Sep 1.8HEC ▦ ⌂ ⋒ ⊙ ⬛ ⟍ R ⬚ lau ➤ ⚊ ⅌ ✕ ⬤ ≞ ⟍P ⊞
Prices: pitch 26 (incl 2 persons)

CHAUFFOUR-SUR-VELL *Corrèze*
Feneyrolles ☎55253143 & 55840958
2.2km E.
Apr-Sep 3HEC ▦ ⬤ ◆ ⋒ ⚊ ⅌ ✕ ⊙ ⬛ ⬛ ⬤ ⟍ P ⬚ ⊞ lau ➤ ✕ ⟍R

CHEF-BOUTONNE *Deux-Sèvres*
Moulin Le Moulin de Treneuillet, rte de Niort ☎49297346
Small, secluded family site in a rural setting.
1km NE via D740.
All year 1HEC ▦ ⌂ ⋒ ⚊ ⅌ ✕ ⊙ ⬛ ⬤ ≞ ⬛ ⬛ ⚊ ⟍ P ⬚ ⊞ lau ➤ ⟍L

CHENONCEAUX *Indre-et-Loire*
Moulin Fort ☎47238622
2km SE
May-15 Sep 3HEC ▦ ⌂ ⋒ ⚊ ⅌ ✕ ⊙ ⬛ ⬤ ⟍ PR ⬚ ⊞ lau

CHÉVERNY *Loir-et-Cher*
Les Saules rte de Contres ☎54799001
Etr-20 Sep 10HEC ▦ ◆ ⋒ ⚊ ⅌ ✕ ⊙ ⬛ ⬤ ≞ ⬛ ⬛ ⟍ P ⬚ ⊞ lau ➤
⟍L

CHINON *Indre-et-Loire*
CM ☎47930835
On the banks of the river opposite the Château and off D951.
Apr-Oct 6HEC ▦ ∷∷ ⌂ ⋒ ⊙ ⬛ ⬤ ⟍ PR ⬚ ⊞ lau ➤ ⚊ ⅌ ✕ ⟍S

CHOLET *Maine-et-Loire*
Lac de Ribou av L-Mandin ☎41587474
Well set-out site bordering a lake, with fishing, boating, tennis and
volleyball.
3km from town centre.
Apr-Oct 5HEC ▦ ◆ ⋒ ⚊ ⅌ ✕ ⊙ ⬛ ⬤ ⬛ ⟍ P ⬚ lau ➤ ⟍L

CLOYES-SUR-LE-LOIR *Eure-et-Loir*
Parc des Loisirs rte du Montigny ☎37985053
On the bank of the River Loir. Extensive leisure facilities. Separate
section for teenagers. Shop only available in July and August, bar
and restaurant only May-September.
Access from Châteaudun S on N10 towards Cloyes, then right onto
Montigny-le-Gamelon road.
15 Mar-15 Nov 5HEC ▦ ⌂ ⋒ ⚊ ⅌ ✕ ⊙ ⬛ ⬤ ⟍ PR ⬚ ⊞ lau ➤ ⟍L
Prices: A25 pitch 40

COGNAC *Charente*
Cognac rte de Ste-Sévère ☎45321632
2km N on D24.
May-15 Oct 2HEC ▦ ◆ ⋒ ⚊ ⅌ ✕ ⊙ ⬛ ⟍ P ⬚ ⊞ lau Prices: pitch
70 (incl 2 persons)

CONTRES *Loir-et-Cher*
Charmoise La Charmoire ☎54795515
N956.
Etr-Oct 2HEC ▦ ⌂ ⋒ ⊙ ⬛ ⬤ ≞ ⬛ lau ➤ ⚊ ⅌ ✕ ⬤ ≞ ⟍PR ⊞

COUHÉ-VERAC *Vienne*
Peupliers ☎49592116
N of village on N10 Poitiers road.
May-Sep 8HEC ▦ ⌂ ⋒ ⚊ ⅌ ✕ ⊙ ⬛ ⬤ ⟍ PR ⬚ ⊞ lau ➤ ≞

COURÇON-D'AUNIS *Charente-Maritime*
Garenne ☎46016050
May-Oct ▦ ◆ ⋒ ⊙ ⬛ ⬤ ⊞ lau ➤ ⚊ ⅌ ✕ ≞ ⟍P

CROISIC, LE *Loire-Atlantique*
Océan ☎40230769
A quiet, well appointed site situated 150m from the sea.
1.5km NW via D45
Apr-Sep 7.5HEC ▦ ⌂ ⋒ ⚊ ⅌ ✕ ⊙ ⬛ ⬤ ≞ ⬛ ⬛ ⟍ P ⬚ ⊞ lau ➤ ⟍S
Prices: pitch 72-128 (incl 2 persons)

DISSAY *Vienne*
Bois de Chaume chemin des Meuniers ☎49623630
Situated on N10 within easy reach of the Futuroscope.
Apr-Sep 1.7HEC ▦ ⌂ ⋒ ⊙ ⬛ ⬤ ⬛ ⬛ ⚊ ⟍ P ⬚ lau ➤ ⚊ ⬤ ≞ ⊞
Prices: pitch 32 (incl 2 persons)

DISSAY-SOUS-COURCILLON *Sarthe*
CM ☎43440910
Apr-15 Oct 0.6HEC ▦ ◆ ⋒ ⊙ ⬛ ⟍ R ⬚ ⚙ lau ➤ ⚊ ⅌ ✕ ⬤ ≞

DURTAL *Maine-et-Loire*

CM 9 r du Camping ☎41763180
A pleasant site beside the River Loire.
Near the centre of the town. Access via N23 or A11.
Etr-Sep 3HEC ▦ ♣↑⊙●▨☎⊞ lau ♣ ▯▮✕◢☵ ⚲P

EGLETONS *Corrèze*

Egletons-Lac ☎55931475
A lakeside site in wooded surroundings with a fine range of
recreational facilities.
2km from Egletons towards Ussel.
All year 8.7HEC ▦ ♣▮▯✕⊙●▨◢☵☎⊞ lau ♣ ⚲LP Prices:
A17 pitch 30

EYMOUTHIERS *Charente*

Gorges du Chambon ☎45707170
3km N via D163
7HEC ⊙↑▮▮▯✕⊙●▨◢ ⚲P☎⊞ lau ♣ ☵⚲L Prices: A24-28
pitch 34-38

FAUTE-SUR-MER, LA *Vendée*

Fautais 18 rte de la Tranche ☎51564196
Situated in centre of village. Numbered pitches.
On D46.
Jul-Aug 0.9HEC ▦ ♣▮⊙●◢☎⊞ lau ♣ ▮▯✕ ⚲L

Flots Bleus av des Chardons ☎51271111
26 Apr-8 Sep 1.5HEC ▦ ⊙↑▮✕⊙●▨◢☵☎☎⊞ lau ♣ ⚲S
Prices: pitch 65-99 (incl 3 persons)

FENOUILLER, LE *Vendée*

Domaine le Pas Opton rte de Nantes ☎51551198
2km N beside the River Vie on D754.
20 May-12 Sep 6.5HEC ▦ ♣▮▮▯✕⊙●◢☎☎⚲P☎⊞⊛
lau ♣ ⚲S

FLÈCHE, LA *Sarthe*

Route d'Or allée de la Providence ☎43945590
Beside the River Loir
Closed 15 Nov-15 Feb 4.5HEC ▦ ♣▮⊙●◢⚲R☎ lau ♣ ▮▯
✕ ⚲LP ⊞

FRESNAY-SUR-SARTHE *Sarthe*

CM Sans Souci ☎43973287
Pool open weekends June and all July-Aug
1km SE on D310.
Apr-Sep 2HEC ▦ ⊰▮▮⊙●◢⚲P☎⊞ lau

GENNES *Maine-et-Loire*

Européen ☎41579163
28 Mar-Sep 9HEC ▦ ♣▮▮▯✕⊙●▨⚲P☎⊞ lau ♣◢ Prices:
pitch 80 (incl 3 persons)

Bord de l'Eau ☎41380467
N, beside the River Loire
Etr-15 Oct 2.5HEC ▦ ▧▧ ♣▮⊙●▨☎ lau ♣▮▯✕◢☵ ⚲P⊞
Prices: A11 pitch 11

GIVRAND *Vendée*

Europa Le Petit Bois ☎51553268
W from St-Gilles-Croix-de-Vie via D6 for 2.5km, then S for 0.2km.
Apr-Sep 4HEC ⊙↑▮▮▯✕⊙●▨◢☵☎⚲P☎⊞ lau ♣ ⚲LRS

GUÉMENÉ-PENFAO *Loire-Atlantique*

Hermitage 36 av du Paradis ☎40792348
Camping Card Compulsory.
1.5km E on rte de Châteaubriant.
Apr-Oct 2.5HEC ▦ ♣▮⊙●▨◢●☎⚲P☎⊞ lau ♣▮☵ ⚲R

GUÉRANDE *Loire-Atlantique*

Bréhadour ☎40249312
2km NE on D51, rte de St-Lyphard.
29 Mar-28 Sep 7HEC ▦ ⊙↑▮▮▯✕⊙●▨☎●⚲P☎ lau ♣◢
☵ ⚲P Prices: A22-27 pitch 23-39

Parc de Lévéno rte de l'Etang de Sandun ☎40247930
In a pleasant location with good facilities.

3km E via rte de Sandun.
4 May-28 Sep 12HEC ▦ ♣▮↑▮▯✕⊙●▨◢☵☎ ⚲P☎⊞ lau

Pré du Château de Careil Careil ☎40602299
Divided into pitches. Caravans only. Booking recommended for Jul &
Aug.
2km N of La Baule on D92.
Apr-24 Sep 2HEC ▦ ▧▧ ⊙↑⊙●▨ ⚲P☎⊞ lau ♣▮✕◢☵
Prices: pitch 126 (incl 2 persons)

HÉRIC *Loire-Atlantique*

Pindière ☎40576541
1km from town on D16.
All year 3HEC ▦ ⊰▮↑✕⊙●▨☎●⚲P☎⊞ lau ♣▮◢☵
Prices: A14 pitch 25

HOUMEAU, L' *Charente-Maritime*

Trépied au Plomb ☎46509082
NE via D106
20 May-25 Sep 2HEC ⊙↑⊙●▨☎⊞ lau ♣▮▯✕◢☵⚲S

INGRANDES *Vienne*

At **ST-USTRE**(2km NE)

Petit Trianon de St-Ustre ☎49026147
In beautiful park surrounding small castle, part of which is open to
the public.
Turn off N10 at signpost N of Ingrandes and continue for 1km.
15 May-Sep 7HEC ⊙↑▮⊙●▨☎●⚲P☎⊞ lau ♣ ▯✕
Prices: A35 V20 ⚟21 ▲21

JARD-SUR-MER *Vendée*

Curtys r de la Perpoise ☎51336342
May-Sep 4.4HEC ▦ ▧▨↑▮▯✕⊙●▨◢☵☎●⚲P☎ lau ♣▮ ⚲S

Écureuils r des Goffineaux ☎51334274
Quiet woodland terrain near to the sea.
Signposted.
17 May-9 Sep 4.3HEC ▦ ▧▧ ⊙↑▮▮▯✕⊙●▨◢●⚲P☎⊞⊛
lau ♣ ⚲S Prices: A27 pitch 65

Océano d'Or r G-Clemenceau ☎51336508
Apr-Sep 7.9HEC ▦ ▧▨↑▮▮▯✕⊙●▨☵●▲ ⚲P☎⊞ lau ♣
✕ ⚲S Prices: pitch 80-120 (incl 2 persons)

JARGEAU *Loiret*

Isle aux Moulins ☎38597004
On the bank of the Loire.
Mar-Nov 7HEC ▦ ▧▧ ⊙↑⊙●▨◢☎☎☎⊞ lau ♣▮▯✕☵⚲P
Prices: A13 V7 ⚟9-14.50 ▲9

JAUNAY CLAN *Vienne*

Croix du Sud rte de Neuville ☎49625814
Within easy reach of 'Futuroscope', the European Park of the Moving
Image.
Access via A10 and D62.
All year 4HEC ▦ ▧▨↑▮▮▯✕⊙●▨☎☎ ⚲P☎⊞ lau Prices:
pitch 40-65 (incl 2 persons)

JAVRON *Mayenne*

CM rte de Bagnoles-de-l'Orne ☎43034067
200m SW of town off N12. On the road to Mayenne after the little
lake take road for Bagnoles-de-l'Orne, then take first on left.
Signposted.
Jul-Aug 1.5HEC ▦ ⊙↑⊙●▨ ⚲R☎ lau ♣▮▯✕◢☵

LAGORD *Charente-Maritime*

CM Parc r du Parc ☎46676154
15 May-Sep 4HEC ⊙↑⊙●▨☎⊞ lau ♣▮▯✕◢☵

LANDEVIEILLE *Vendée*

Pong r du Stade ☎51229263
Etr-25 Sep 3HEC ▦ ♣▮↑▮▯⊙●▨◢●⚲P☎⊞ lau ♣✕

LINDOIS, LE *Charente*

Étang ☎45650267
All year 9HEC ⊙↑▮▯✕⊙●⚲L☎⊞ lau ♣▮◢☵ Prices: A22
pitch 40

LION D'ANGERS, LE *Maine-et-Loire*

CM Frénes ☎41953156
NE on N162.
15 May-Aug 2HEC lau P Prices: A10-12 pitch 11-13

LISSAC-SUR-COUZE *Corrèze*

Prairie ☎55853797
Jun-13 Sep 3HEC lau Prices: pitch 52-67 (incl 2 persons)

LONGEVILLE *Vendée*

Jarny Océan ☎51334221
Subdivided well tended meadow, with a holiday complex of the same name where shopping facilities are provided. 800m to sea via forest path.
Turn off D105 about 3km S of Longeville.
Apr-Sep 7HEC PS lau

At **CONCHES, LES**(4km S)

Dunes av de la Plage ☎51333293
Well-kept site amongst sand dunes in pine forest.
6km S of Longeville on D105.
May-Sep 5HEC P lau PRS

LUCHÉ-PRINGÉ *Sarthe*

CM de la Chabotière ☎43451000
Pleasant site with pitches surrounded by bushes between Le Lude and La Flèche.
Apr-15 Oct 1.7HEC P lau
Prices: A8.50-15 pitch 9.50

LUDE, LE *Sarthe*

CM rte du Mans ☎43946770
400m from town centre, direct from N307.
Etr-Sep 5HEC PR lau

LUSIGNAN *Vienne*

CM Vauchiron ☎49433008
500m NE on N11.
15 Apr-15 Oct 4HEC R lau Prices: A7.50 pitch 5

LUYNES *Indre-et-Loire*

CM Granges Les Granges ☎47556085
S via D49
15 May-15 Sep 0.8HEC lau P
Prices: A10 pitch 10

MAGNAC-BOURG *Haute-Vienne*

CM Écureuils rte de Limoges ☎55008028
25 kms S on N20.
Etr-Sep 1.3HEC lau Prices: A10 pitch 10

MANSIGNÉ *Sarthe*

CM de la Plage rte du Plessis ☎43461417
Etr-Oct 3.4HEC LP lau

MARANS *Charente-Maritime*

CM Le Bois Dinot rte de Nantes ☎46011051
Separate car park for arrivals after 22.00hrs.
Access via N137 (Nantes-Bordeaux).
Apr-Oct 6HEC P lau R
Prices: A15 pitch 10

MARÇON *Sarthe*

Lac des Varennes ☎43441372
15 Mar-15 Nov 5HEC LR lau
Prices: A20 pitch 17

MATHES, LES *Charente-Maritime*

Charmettes Parc d'Hotellerie, de Plein Air ☎46225096
1km SW via D141.
3 Apr-8 Oct 24HEC P lau

CAMPING **
DE MAYENNE
53100 – ☎ (33) 243 04 57 14/(33) 243 30 21 21
ON SITE

Orée du Bois La Fouasse ☎46224243
Situated in a pine and oak forest, 5 minutes from the beach.
3.5km NW.
12 May-14 Sep 6HEC P lau Prices: pitch 80-150 (incl 2 persons)

Pinède La Fouasse ☎46224513
3km NW
Apr-Sep 8HEC lau P
Prices: pitch 100-185 (incl 3 persons)

MAYENNE *Mayenne*

CM Raymond Fauque r St-Léonard ☎43045714
800m from town centre near N12.
15 Mar-Sep 1.8HEC P lau

MEMBROLLE-SUR-CHOISILLE, LA *Indre-et-Loire*

CM rte de Foudettes ☎47412040
On level meadow in sports ground beside River Choisille.
N on N138 Le Mans road.
May-Sep 1.3HEC R lau Prices: A20 pitch 13

MESLAND *Loir-et-Cher*

Parc du Val de Loire rte de Fleuray ☎54702718
In a sheltered position in the heart of the Touraine vineyards with good recreational facilities.
Camping Card Compulsory.
1.5km W between the A10 and the N152.
May-15 Sep 15HEC P lau
Prices: pitch 100-150 (incl 2 persons)
See advertisement on page114

MESQUER *Loire-Atlantique*

Beaupré rte de Kervarin, Kercabellec ☎40426748
On road between Mesquer and Quimiac. Entrance signposted.
15 Jun-15 Sep 0.6HEC lau S

Le PARC du VAL de LOIRE

★ ★ ★ ★ NN

41150 MESLAND

A PARADISE FOR CHILDREN

An ideal starting point from where to visit the famous castles of the Loire.

Mobile homes and chalets for hire.

3 swimming pools and tennis.

Tel: 02.54.70.27.18   Fax: 02.54.70.21.71

Open 1st May-15th September. Highway A10, exit 'Blois', from there follow the N152, direction Tours.

Brochure on request.

Prices: pitch 60 (incl 2 persons)

Château de Petit Bois ☎40426877
Apr-Oct 10HEC ▦ ♣ ⋒ ⅊ ✕ ⊙ ⊕ 🏠 🛖 ⌇ P 🈺 🄿 lau ♣ ∅ ⌇S ⊞
Prices: pitch 64-80 (incl 2 persons)

Praderoi alleé des Barges, Quimiac ☎40426672
70m from Lanseria Beach.
Jun-15 Sep 0.5HEC ▦ ⚐ ⋒ ⊙ ⊕ 🏠 lau ♣ ⅊ ⅄ ✕ ∅ 🚿 ⌇S ⊞
Prices: pitch 64-82 (incl 2 persons)

Welcome rue de Bel-Air ☎40425085
Separate car park for arrivals after 22.30 hrs.
1.8km NW via D352
Apr-Sep 2HEC ▦ ♣ ⋒ ⅊ ⊙ ⊕ ∅ 🚿 🏠 🏠 🈺 lau ♣ ⅊ ✕ ⌇S ⊞
Prices: pitch 69 (incl 2 persons)

MISSILLAC *Loire-Atlantique*

CM des Platanes 10 r du Château ☎40883888
1km W via D2, 50m from the lake.
Jul-Aug 2HEC ▦ ⚐ ⋒ ⊙ ⊕ 🏠 lau ♣ ⅊ ⅄ ✕ ∅ 🚿 ⊞ Prices: pitch 37
(incl 2 persons)

MONTARGIS *Loiret*

CM de la Forêt rte de Paucourt ☎38980020
1.5km NE near the station and the stadium.
Closed 15 Dec-15 Jan 5.5HEC ▦ ♣ ⋒ ⅄ ✕ ⊙ ⊕ ∅ 🚿 🈺 ⊞ lau ♣ ⅊
⌇LPR

MONTGIVRAY *Indre*

CM Solange Sand r du Pont ☎54483783
A pleasant, riverside site in the grounds of a château.
15 Mar-15 Nov 1HEC ▦ ⚐ ⋒ ⊙ ⊕ ⌇ R 🈺 ⊞ lau ♣ ⅊ ⅄ ✕

MONTLOUIS-SUR-LOIRE *Indre-et-Loire*

CM Peupliers rte de Tours ☎47458585
On level meadow.
1.5km W on N751, next to swimming pool near railway bridge.

15 Mar-15 Oct 6HEC ▦ ♣ ⋒ ✕ ⊙ ⊕ ∅ ⌇ P 🈺 ⊞ lau ♣ 🚿 ⌇R
Prices: A10 V10 ⊕10 ▲10

MONTMORILLON *Vienne*

CM Allochon av F-Tribot ☎49910233
SE via D54
All year 2HEC ▦ ♣ ⋒ ⊙ ⊕ 🈺 lau ♣ ⅊ ⅄ ✕ ⌇PR ⊞ Prices: A6.25
V3.65 ⊕3.65 ▲3.65

MONTSOREAU *Maine-et-Loire*

Isle Verte ☎41517660
On D947 between road and river.
May-Sep 2HEC ▦ ♣ ⋒ ⊙ ⊕ 🏠 🏠 🈺 ⊞ lau ♣ ⅊ ⅄ ✕ 🚿 Prices: A12 V6
pitch 7 pp5

NANTES *Loire-Atlantique*

Petit Port bd du Petit Port 21 ☎40744794
On modern well kept park by a river.
In N part of town near Parc du Petit Port. From town centre follow
Rennes road (N137) then signs to camp site.
All year 6.5HEC ▦ ♣ ⋒ ⅊ ⊙ ⊕ 🈺 ⊞ lau ♣ ⅊ ✕ 🚿 ⌇PR Prices: A18
pitch 46

NEUVILLE-SUR-SARTHE *Sarthe*

Vieux Moulin ☎0243253182
15 Apr-15 Oct 5HEC ▦ ⚐ ⋒ ⅊ ⅄ ✕ ⊙ ⊕ ∅ 🏠 ⌇ PR 🈺 ⊞ lau ♣ ✕
Prices: pitch 64 (incl 2 persons)

NIBELLE *Loiret*

Nibelle rte de Boiscommun ☎38322355
Level site in the clearing of an oak woodland.
Access via D921 turning off to Nibelle in an easterly direction.
Signposted.
Mar-Nov 6HEC ▦ ⚐ ⋒ ⅊ ⅄ ⊙ ⊕ 🚿 🏠 🏠 ⌇ P 🈺 lau ♣ ⅊ ✕ ∅ ⌇L
Prices: A50 V5 ⊕15 ▲5

NIORT *Deux-Sèvres*

Niort-Noron 21 bd S-Allende ☎49790506
Shady site by a river.
15 Apr-15 Oct 3HEC ▦ ♣ ⋒ ⅊ ⅄ ✕ ⊙ ⊕ ⌇ R 🈺 ⊞ lau ♣ ∅ 🚿

NOIRMOUTIER, ILE DE *Vendée*

BARBÂTRE

Onchères ☎51398131
In quiet setting on sand dunes.
Camping Card Compulsory.
S of village on D95.
Apr-Sep 10HEC ⬚⬚⬚ ⚐ ⋒ ⅊ ⅄ ✕ ⊙ ⊕ ∅ ⌇ S 🈺 ⊞ lau

NOTRE-DAME-DE-MONTS *Vendée*

Beauséjour ☎51588388
2km NW on D38.
Etr-Sep 1.3HEC ▦ ⚐ ⋒ ⊙ ⊕ ∅ 🏠 🏠 ⊞ lau ♣ ⅊ 🚿 ⌇S Prices: pitch
51 (incl 2 persons)

Grand Jardin Le Grand Jardin ☎51588776
0.6km N
May-20 Sep 2HEC ▦ ⚐ ⋒ ⅊ ⊙ ⊕ ∅ 🏠 🏠 ⌇ RS 🈺 ⊞ lau ♣ ⅊ ✕ 🚿
Prices: pitch 80 (incl 3 persons)

OLÉRON, ILE D' *Charente-Maritime*

BOYARDVILLE

Signol ☎46470122
W of town, leave D126 by the AVIA service station and follow signs
for 0.6km.
May-Sep 7HEC ⬚⬚⬚ ⚐ ⋒ ⅊ ⊙ ⊕ 🏠 🏠 ⌇ P 🈺 ⊞ ⌇⫽ lau ♣ ⅊ ⅄ ⌇S

CHÂTEAU-D'OLÉRON, LE

Airotel d'Oléron Domaine de Monteravail ☎46476182
Leisure centre area.
Signposted from town centre.
Etr-10 Oct 7HEC ▦ ⚐ ⋒ ⅊ ⅄ ✕ ⊙ ⊕ ∅ 🏠 🏠 ⌇ LPS 🈺 ⊞ lau

Brande rte des Huîtres ☎46476237
2.5km NW, 250m from the sea
15 Mar-15 Nov 4HEC ▦ ⚐ ⋒ ⅊ ⅄ ✕ ⊙ ⊕ ∅ 🏠 🏠 🏠 ⌇ P 🈺 ⊞ lau
♣ ⌇S Prices: pitch 70-110 (incl 2 persons)

COTINIÈRE, LA
Tamaris 72 av des Pins ☎46471051
About 150m from sea. Level site in pleasant olive grove.
W side of island. N of town.
15 Mar-15 Oct 5HEC ▥ ♠ ♠ ⚓ ✕ ☉ ⬛ ⬛ ⬛ ⟨ P ⬜ ⊞ lau ♦ 🐄 ⬇
⟨S

DOLUS-D'OLÉRON
Ostréa rte des Huîtres ☎46476236
A well equipped site in wooded surroundings close to the beach.
3.5km NE
Apr-Sep 3HEC ▥ ⫶⫶⫶ ♠ ♠ 🐄 ☉ ⬛ ⬇ ⟨ S ⬜ ⊞ lau ♦ ♥ Prices:
pitch 73-76 (incl 2 persons)

DOMINO
International Rex ☎46765597
Pleasant seaside site with good recreational facilities and access to
the beach.
May-14 Sep 10HEC ⫶⫶⫶ ⬧ ♠ 🐄 ♠ ✕ ☉ ⬛ ⬇ ⟨ PS ⬜ ⊞ lau ♦ ✕ 🏛
Prices: pitch 95-105 (incl 2 persons)

Montlabeur ☎46765222
Transport provided to beach. Water-slide.
W of town on D734.
15 May-15 Sep 7HEC ▥ ♠ 🐄 🐄 ✕ ☉ ⬛ ⬇ ⬛ ⬛ ⬜ ⊞ lau ♦ ⟨S
Prices: pitch 94 (incl 2 persons)

ST-DENIS-D'OLÉRON
Phare Ouest ☎46479000
1km NW
Apr-Oct 3HEC ▥ ⬧ 🐄 ☉ ⬛ ⬇ ⬛ ⬛ ⟨ S ⬜ ⊞ lau ♦ ♥ ✕

Soleil Levant ☎46478303
Quiet site beside sea.
1km from village adjacent to D734.
All year 7HEC ▥ ⟿ ♠ 🐄 ♥ ✕ ☉ ⬛ ⬇ 🏛 ⬛ ⬛ ⟨ S ⬜ ⊞ lau

ST-GEORGES-D'OLÉRON
Quatre Vents Le Jousselinière ☎46756547
A peaceful site with good facilities.
3km E via N739.
15 Apr-15 Sep 1.2HEC ▥ ⬧ 🐄 🐄 ☉ ⬛ ⬇ 🏛 ⬛ ⬛ ⬜ ⊞ lau ♦ ♥
✕

Suroît 1705 rte de Ponthezière, Lileau ☎46470725
5km SW of town.
Apr-Sep 4HEC ⫶⫶⫶ ⬧ ♠ 🐄 🐄 ✕ ☉ ⬛ ⬇ ⟨ S ⬜ ⊞ lau

Vérébleu La Jousselinière ☎46765770
1.7km SE via D273
6 Apr-Sep 7.5HEC ▥ ⬧ 🐄 🐄 ✕ ☉ ⬛ ⬇ 🏛 ⬛ ⟨ P ⬜ ⊞ lau ♦ 🏛

Gros Joncs ☎46765229
Quiet location on undulating land in the midst of lovely pine
woodland.
On tourist route from La Cotinière about 5km NW in the direction of
Domino, 1km SW of St-Georges-d'Oléron.
15 Mar-15 Oct 5HEC ▥ ⫶⫶⫶ ⬧ 🐄 🐄 ✕ ☉ ⬛ ⬛ ⟨ P ⬜ ⊞ lau ♦ ⬇
🏛 ⟨S Prices: pitch 65-168 (incl 2 persons)

ST-PIERRE-D'OLÉRON
Pierrière rte de St-Georges ☎46470829
NW towards St-Georges-d'Oléron
Apr-Sep 4HEC ▥ ⬧ 🐄 ♥ ✕ ☉ ⬛ ⟨ P ⊞ lau ♦ ⬇ 🏛 ⊞ Prices: pitch
119 (incl 3 persons)

Trois Masses Le Marais Doux ☎46472396
Etr-Sep 3HEC ▥ ⬧ 🐄 🐄 ✕ ☉ ⬛ ⬇ ⬛ ⬛ 🏛 ⟨ P ⬜ ⊞ lau ♦ 🏛 ⟨S
Prices: pitch 67-85 (incl 3 persons)

OLIVET Loiret
CM Olivet r du Pont Bouchet ☎38635394
Site lies partly on shaded peninsula, partly on open lawns beside
river.
2km E. Signposted from village.
Apr-15 Oct 1HEC ▥ ♠ 🐄 ☉ ⬛ ⬜ ⊞ lau ♦ ⬇ 🏛 Prices: A13 V8 🚗9
🏕9

CAMPING L'OREE ★ ★ ★ ★
5 min. from the centre of Sables d'Olonne,
1.8 km from a sandy beach and on the
edge of a wood. The ideal site for a
refreshing holiday in a tonic environment.
Swimming pools. Water-slide. Tennis.
Minigolf. Snack bar. Self-service shop.
Laundry.
F-85340 OLONNE SUR MER
Tel: 02.51.33.10.59 • Fax: 02.51.33.15.16

OLONNE-SUR-MER Vendée
Loubine 1 rte de la Mer ☎0251331292
Situated on the edge of a forest bordering the beach.N via
D87/D80.
Apr-Sep 7.5HEC ▥ ♠ 🐄 🐄 ♥ ✕ ☉ ⬛ ⬇ 🏛 ⟨ P ⬜ ⊞ ⬚ lau ♦ ⟨S
Prices: pitch 117-142 (incl 2 persons)

Moulin de la Salle r des Rabaudières ☎51959910
2.7km W
Apr-Nov 3.1HEC ▥ ♠ 🐄 🐄 ♥ ✕ ☉ ⬛ ⬇ 🏛 ⟨ PS ⬜ ⊞ lau ♦ ⟨R
Prices: pitch 75-95 (incl 2 persons)

Oreé rte des Amis de la Nature ☎51331059
3km N
Apr-Sep 5.5HEC ▥ ♠ 🐄 🐄 ♥ ✕ ☉ ⬛ ⬇ 🏛 ⬛ ⬛ 🏛 ⟨ P ⬜ ⊞ lau ♦
⟨R Prices: pitch 58-146 (incl 2 persons)

ONZAIN Loir-et-Cher
Dugny rte de Chambon-sur-Cisse ☎54207066
On a small lake, surrounded by farmland with well marked pitches
shaded by poplars.
From Onzain follow direction Chambon-sur-Cisse (CD45).
All year 8HEC ▥ ⬧ 🐄 ♥ ✕ ☉ ⬛ ⬇ 🏛 ⬛ ⬛ ⟨ P ⬜ ⊞ lau ♦ 🐄
Prices: A28-37

PALMYRE, LA Charente-Maritime
Bonne Anse Plage rte du Phare de la Coubre ☎46224090
An extensive, gently undulating site in a pine wood, 400m from the
beach.
1km from La Palmyre roundabout. Follow signs for Ronce-les-Bains.
24 May-7 Sep 17HEC ▥ ♠ 🐄 🐄 ♥ ✕ ☉ ⬛ ⬇ ⟨ P ⬜ ⊞ ⬚ lau ♦
🏛 Prices: pitch 151 (incl 3 persons)

Palmyre Loisirs 28 des Mathes ☎46236766
16HEC ▥ ⬧ 🐄 🐄 ♥ ✕ ☉ ⬛ ⬇ 🏛 ⬛ ⬛ ⟨ P ⬜ ⊞ lau ♦ ⟨S
Prices: pitch 100-160 (incl 3 persons)

Palmyr Océana 26 av des Mathes ☎46224035
Apr-Oct 17HEC ▥ ⫶⫶⫶ ⬧ 🐄 🐄 ♥ ✕ ☉ ⬛ ⬇ 🏛 ⬛ ⬛ ⟨ P ⬜ ⊞ lau ♦
⟨S

PERRIER, LE Vendée
CM de la Maison Blanche ☎51493923
17 Jun-15 Sep 3HEC ▥ ♠ 🐄 ☉ ⬛ ⬛ ⬜ ⊞ lau ♦ 🐄 ♥ ✕ ⬇ 🏛 ⊞
Prices: pitch 43 (incl 2 persons)

PEZOU Loir-et-Cher
CM "Les Ilots" rte de Renay ☎54234069
SE via D12, 50m from the River Loir
07 May-15 Sep 1HEC ▥ ♠ 🐄 ☉ ⬛ ⬜ ⊞ lau ♦ 🐄 ♥ ✕ ⬇ 🏛 Prices:
A9 pitch 10

PIERREFITTE-SUR-SAULDRE Loir-et-Cher
Sologne Parc des Alicourts Domaine des Alicourts ☎54886334
6km NE via D126 beside the lake.
May-13 Sep 25HEC ▥ ⟿ ♠ 🐄 ♥ ✕ ☉ ⬛ ⬇ ⬛ ⟨ LPR ⬜ lau Prices:
pitch 90-120 (incl 2 persons)

In Loire-Atlantique, close to the beaches, Bernadette and Didier together with the friendly team of Camping ★★★ "La Renaudière" give you a hearty welcome. Family atmosphere and recreation guaranteed for an unforgettable holiday.

Camping-Caravanning ★★★

"LA RENAUDIERE"

44770 LA PLAINE SUR MER

France

Tel: 02.40.21.50.03

Fax: 02.40.21.09.41

PIRIAC-SUR-MER *Loire-Atlantique*

Mon Calme rte de Nororet ☎40236077
On open meadow.
On D99.
May-Sep 1HEC ▦ ♣ ♠ ⊙ ☸ ∅ ☒ 🏕 ⊞ lau ♦ ☎ ♟ ✕ ♨ ⊰PS

Parc du Guibel ☎40235267
3.5km E via D52
Etr-Sep 10HEC ▦ ♣ ♠ ☎ ♟ ✕ ⊙ ☸ ∅ ☷ 🏕 ☒ ⊰ P ☒ ⊞ lau ♦ ⊰PS

Pouldroit D52 ☎40235091
300m from the sea and 600m from the village
500m E on D52.
Apr-15 Sep 7HEC ♦ ♠ ☎ ♟ ✕ ⊙ ☸ ∅ 🏕 ⊰ P ☒ ⊞ lau ♦ ☷ ⊰S
Prices: A26 pitch 24

PLAINE-SUR-MER, LA *Loire-Atlantique*

Tabardière ☎40215218
A wooded, terraced site 3km from the sea.
Situated between Pornic and La Plaine-sur-Mer off D13.
Apr-15 Oct 4HEC ▦ ♤ ♠ ☎ ♟ ✕ ⊙ ☸ ∅ 🏕 ⊰ P ☒ ⊞ lau ♦ ✕

POIRÉ-SUR-VELLUIRE, LE *Vendée*

Petits Prés ☎51523777
On S outskirts beside the River Vendée. Well signposted.
All year 2.8HEC ▦ ♤ ♠ ⊙ ☸ ♟ ▲ ⊰ R ☒ ⊞ lau ♦ ☷ ∅ ▲ Prices: A10 V6 ♲10 ▲10

PONS *Charente-Maritime*

Chardon Chardon ☎05 46940486
Quietly situated on the edge of a small village next to a farm.
From Pons take D732 westwards towards Royan. The site is 2.5km on the left. Alternatively from exit 36 of the Autoroute A10 and turn towards Pons. Site is 800m on right.
Apr-Sep 1.6HEC ▦ ♤ ♠ ⊙ ☸ ♟ ☒ lau ♦ ☷ ♟ ✕ ⊰PRS ⊞ Prices: A13 pitch 17

PORNIC *Loire-Atlantique*

Patisseau Le Patisseau ☎40821039
In wooded surroundings close to the beach with fine recreational facilities.
3km E via D751
May-14 Sep 4HEC ▦ ♤ ♠ ☷ ♟ ✕ ⊙ ☸ ∅ ☷ ▲ ⊰ P ☒ ⊞ lau ♦ ⊰L Prices: pitch 74-105 (incl 2 persons)

PORNICHET *Loire-Atlantique*

Bel Air ☎40611078
Apr-Oct 6HEC ☷ ♤ ♠ ⊙ ☸ ∅ ☷ 🏕 ☒ ⊞ lau ♦ ☷ ♟ ✕ ⊰S Prices: A22 pitch 72

Forges 98 rte de Villes Blais ☎40611884
Shop open on site in July and August only.
Access via N171.
All year 2.5HEC ▦ ♤ ♠ ☷ ⊙ ☸ ∅ ☷ 🏕 ⊰ P ☒ ⊞ lau Prices: A18-24 pitch 25-40

PORT-DE-PILES *Vienne*

Bec des Deux Eaux rte de Marigny ☎47650271
Mar-Oct 3.5HEC ▦ ♤ ♠ ☷ ♟ ✕ ⊙ ☸ ∅ 🏕 🏕 ⊰ PR ☒ lau ♦ ✕
Prices: A20 pitch 20

POUANCÉ *Maine-et-Loire*

CM Roche Martin 23 r des Étangs ☎41924397
On the edge of a lake.
On D72, in the direction of La Guerche. Site is on left, bordering Étang de St Aubin and is well signposted.
15 Apr-Sep ▦ ♤ ♠ ⊙ ☸ ∅ ▲ ☒ ⊞ lau ♦ ♟ ✕ ∅ ⊰L

PRÉFAILLES *Loire-Atlantique*

Lambertianas Vallée Mouraud, r St Dominique ☎40216105
E of town, 450m from the sea
15 Apr-15 Sep 1.7HEC ▦ ♤ ♠ ⊙ ☸ ☒ lau ♦ ☷ ♟ ✕ ∅ ⊰S ⊞

RÉ, ILE DE *Charente-Maritime*

ARS-EN-RÉ

Soleil rte de la Plage ☎46294062
On level, shaded meadow.
Signposted from the N735 shortly before reaching Ars.
All year 2HEC ▦ ♤ ♠ ☷ ♟ ✕ ⊙ ☸ ∅ ⊰ ☷ S ☒ ⊞ lau

BOIS-PLAGE-EN-RÉ, LE

Antioche ☎46092386
In quiet area among dunes.
3.5km SE of village towards the beach.
8 Apr-Sep 3HEC ▦ ♤ ♠ ☷ ♟ ✕ ⊙ ☸ ∅ ⊰ S ☒ ⊞ lau

Bonne Étoile rte de St-Martin ☎46091016
All year 3.2HEC ▦ ♤ ♠ ☷ ♟ ✕ ⊙ ☸ ∅ ☷ 🏕 ⊰ P ☒ ⊞ lau ♦ ⊰S

Camping Interlude-Gros-Jonc Plage Gros Jonc ☎46091822
17 Mar-27 Sep 6.5HEC ☷ ♤ ♠ ☷ ♟ ✕ ⊙ ☸ ∅ ☒ ⊞ lau Prices: A28-50 pitch 36-84

COUARDE-SUR-MER, LA

Océan rte d'Ars ☎46298770
In a fine position facing the sea with good modern facilities.
3km NW on N735.
Apr-Sep 7HEC ▦ ♤ ♠ ☷ ♟ ✕ ⊙ ☸ ∅ ▲ 🏕 ⊰ P ☒ ⊞ lau ♦ ⊰S
Prices: pitch 81-164 (incl 3 persons)

FLOTTE, LA

Blanche Deviation de la Flotte ☎46095243
A popular family site in a wooded location.
N on D735 towards St-Martin.
Apr-12 Nov 4HEC ☷ ⅃ ♠ ☷ ♟ ✕ ⊙ ☸ ∅ ▲ 🏕 ⊰ P ☒ ⊞ lau ♦ ⊰S
Prices: A25-38 pitch 34-66

Peupliers ☎46096235
Situated in a large, wooded park 800m from the sea with good sporting facilities.
1.3km SE
Apr-18 Sep 4.4HEC ☷ ♤ ♠ ☷ ♟ ✕ ⊙ ☸ ∅ ▲ 🏕 ⊰ P ☒ ⊞ lau ♦ ⊰S

LOIX

Ilattes Le Petit Boucheau, rte du Grouin ☎05 46290543
Access E towards Pointe du Grouin, 500m from the sea.
All year 4.5HEC ▦ ⅃ ♠ ☷ ✕ ⊙ ☸ ∅ ⊰ P ☒ ⊞ lau ♦ ☷ ∅ ▲
Prices: A25 V6-16 ♲48-143 ▲27-87

ST-CLÉMENT-DES-BALEINES

Plage ☎46294262
Meadow subdivided by hedges, close by lighthouse. Access to sea via sand dunes. Mobile shop during peak season.
NW on D735.
Etr-Sep 2.4HEC ▦ ⅃ ♠ ⊙ ☸ lau ♦ ⊰S

ST-MARTIN-DE-RÉ

CM r du Rempart ☎46092196
At foot of ramparts.
Mar-18 Oct 3HEC ▦ ♤ ♠ ♟ ✕ ⊙ ☸ ☒ lau ♦ ⊞ Prices: pitch 66-145

RONCE-LES-BAINS *Charente-Maritime*

Pignade av des Monards ☎46362525
1.5km S
May-Sep 15HEC ▦ ∷∷ ♠ ⋒ ⅊ ⋔ ✕ ⊙ ₪ ⌀ 🏤 ⋌ P ☎ ⊞ lau ♦ 🗻
⋌S Prices: pitch 58-115 (incl 2 persons)

ROSIERS, LES *Maine-et-Loire*

Val de Loire r Ste-Baudruche ☎41519433
N via D59
15 Apr-2 Oct 3.5HEC ▦ ⊶ ⋒ ⊙ ₪ 🏤 ⋌ P ☎ ⊞ lau ♦ 🗻 ⅊ ✕ ⌀ 🗻

ROYAN *Charente-Maritime*

At **MÉDIS**(4km NE)

Chênes La Verdonneric ☎46067138
Separate late arrivals car park after 22.00hrs.
2km from Royan on the Saintes-Royan road.
Apr-Oct 6.5HEC ▦ ♠ ⋒ ⅊ ✕ ⊙ ₪ ⌀ 🗻 🏤 🗻 ⋌ P ☎ ₽ ⊞ lau
Prices: pitch 69 (incl 2 persons)

At **PONTAILLAC**(2km NE on D25)

Clairfontaine allée des Peupliers ☎46390811
300m from beach.
24 May-10 Sep 5HEC ▦ ♠ ⋒ ✕ ⊙ ₪ ⌀ ☎ lau ♦ 🗻 ⅊ ✕ 🗻 ⋌LPS
Prices: pitch 149 (incl 3 persons)

SABLES-D'OLONNE, LES *Vendée*

Fosses Rouges 8 r des Fosses Rouges ☎51951795
3km SE towards La Pironnière.
All year 3.5HEC ▦ ♠ ⋒ 🗻 ⅊ ✕ ⊙ ₪ ⌀ 🗻 ▲ ⋌ P ☎ ⊞ lau ♦ ⋌LS

CM Roses r des Roses ☎51951042 or 51211650
400m from the beach
Apr-Sep 2.8HEC ▦ ♠ ⋒ 🗻 ⅊ ✕ ⊙ ₪ ⌀ 🗻 🏤 🏤 ⋌ P ☎ ⊞ lau ♦ ✕
⋌LS Prices: pitch 80-130 (incl 2 persons)

Trianon ☎51953050
A spacious site in a pleasant situation with good sporting facilities.
Access via N160 and CD80.
Etr-Sep 12HEC ▦ ⊶ ⋒ 🗻 ⅊ ✕ ⊙ ₪ ⌀ 🏤 🏤 ⋌ P ☎ ⊞ lau

SABLÉ-SUR-SARTHE *Sarthe*

Hippodrome allée du Quebec ☎43954261
Apr-Sep 3HEC ▦ ⊶ ⋒ 🗻 ⊙ ₪ ⌀ ⋌ P ☎ ⊞ lau ♦ ⅊ ✕

ST-AIGNAN-SUR-CHER *Loir-et-Cher*

CM Cochards ☎54751559
On beautiful meadowland, completely surrounded by hedges.
1km from the beach on D17 towards Selles.
Apr-Sep 4HEC ▦ ♠ ⋒ ⊙ ₪ ⌀ ▲ ⋌ R ☎ ⊞ lau ♦ ⅊ ✕ 🗻 Prices:
A14 pitch 14

ST-AMAND-MONTROND *Cher*

CM Roche chemin de la Roche ☎48960936
1.5km SW near river and canal.
Apr-Sep 4HEC ▦ ♠ ⋒ ⊙ ₪ ⌀ 🗻 ⊞ lau ♦ 🗻 ⅊ ✕ 🗻 ⋌PR

ST-ANDRÉ-DES-EAUX *Loire-Atlantique*

CM Les Chalands Fleuris r du Stade ☎40012040
A peaceful site with good facilities.
1km NE.
Apr-15 Oct 4HEC ▦ ⊶ ⋒ 🗻 ⅊ ✕ ⊙ ₪ ⌀ 🗻 🏤 🏤 ▲ ⋌ L ☎ ⊞ lau
♦ ⋌PS Prices: A19 V11 🏤32 ▲27

ST-AVERTIN *Indre-et-Loire*

CM Rives du Cher 61 rue de Rochepinard ☎47272760
N on the left bank of the River Cher
Apr-15 Oct 3HEC ▦ ⊶ ⋒ ⊙ ₪ ☎ ⊞ ♦ 🗻 ⅊ ✕ ⌀ 🗻 ⋌PR Prices: A13
pitch 13

ST-BRÉVIN-LES-PINS *Loire-Atlantique*

CM Courance 100/110 av MI-Foch ☎40272291
Camping Card Compulsory.
S off D305, in pine forest, by sea.
All year 4.6HEC ∷∷ ♠ ⋒ 🗻 ⅊ ✕ ⊙ ₪ ⌀ 🏤 ⋌ S ☎ ⊞ lau ♦ ✕ ⋌PS

Fief 57 chemin du Fief ☎40272386
A family site adjacent to a long sandy beach. The pitches are surrounded by trees and bushes and there are good modern facilities.
All year 7HEC ▦ ⊶ ⋒ 🗻 ⅊ ✕ ⊙ ₪ ⌀ 🗻 🏤 ▲ ⋌ P ☎ ⊞ lau ♦ ⋌S

ST-BRÉVIN-L'OCÉAN *Loire-Atlantique*

Village Club des Pierres Couchées L'Ermitage ☎40278564
Extensive, well screened terrain made up of 3 sites, 2 of which are open all year.
300m from the sea, 2km on D213 toward Pornic.
All year 14HEC ▦ ∷∷ ♠ ⋒ 🗻 ⅊ ✕ ⊙ ₪ 🗻 🏤 🏤 ⋌ P ⊞ lau ♦ ⋌S
Prices: pitch 116 (incl 3 persons)

ST-CYR *Vienne*

Parc de Loisirs ☎49625722
1.5km NE via D4/D82
Apr-Oct 5HEC ▦ ⊶ ⋒ 🗻 ⅊ ✕ ⊙ ₪ ⌀ 🗻 🏤 ⋌ L ☎ ⊞ lau Prices:
A15-25 pitch 30-60

STE-GEMME *Charente-Maritime*

Jamica la Sablière Ferme de Magne ☎46229099
In a pleasant situation beside a lake within a country park.
Access via A10 exit 25 (Saintes) and D728 towards Ile d'Oléron.
May-15 Oct ♠ ⋒ 🗻 ⅊ ✕ ⊙ ₪ ⌀ 🏤 ⋌ L ☎ ₽ ⊞ lau

STE-REINE-DE-BRETAGNE *Loire-Atlantique*

■Château du Deffay ☎40880057
Situated in the beautiful Parc de Brière providing fishing, walking and horse riding. Games and TV rooms.
4.5km W on D33 rte de Pontchâteau.
May-Aug 12HEC ▦ ♠ ⋒ 🗻 ⅊ ✕ ⊙ ₪ ⌀ ⋌ P ☎ ⊞ lau ♦ ⌀ 🗻 Prices:
A11-22 pitch 26-52

SAINTES *Charente-Maritime*

Au Fill de l'Eau 6 r de Courbiac ☎46930800
1km on D128.
16 May-15 Sep 7HEC ▦ ♠ ⋒ 🗻 ✕ ⊙ ₪ ⌀ 🗻 ⋌ PR ☎ ⊞ lau
Prices: A20 pitch 21

ST-FLORENT-LE-VIEIL *Maine-et-Loire*

Ile Batailleuse ☎40834501
6km SE. N of Lac du Boudon.
May-25 Sep 2.5HEC ♠ ⋒ ⊙ ₪ ⋌ R ☎ ♦ 🗻 ✕ ⋌P ⊞

ST-GAULTIER *Indre*

Village Vacances 'La Matronnerie' r de la Pierre Plate
☎54471704
All year 2.5HEC ▦ ⊶✓ ⋒ ⅊ ✕ ⊙ ₪ ⋌ P ☎ ₽ ⊞ lau ♦ 🗻 ⌀ ⋌R
Prices: pitch 68-83 (incl 2 persons)

ST-GEORGES-DE-BAILLARGEAUX *Vienne*

Futuriste ☎49524752
In an elevated position offering fine views over the Parc du Futuroscope and the Clain valley. Advance booking is advisable from June to August.
All year 2.3HEC ♠ ⋒ ⊙ ₪ ⋌ PR ☎ ⊞ lau Prices: pitch 96
(incl 3 persons)
See advertisement on page 118.

ST-GEORGES-DE-DIDONNE *Charente-Maritime*

Bois Soleil 2 av de Suzac ☎46050594
Pitches lie on different levels. Direct access to the beach.
2.5km S of town on Meschers road (D25).
Apr-Sep 8.5HEC ▦ ∷∷ ♠ ⋒ 🗻 ⅊ ✕ ⊙ ₪ ⌀ 🗻 🏤 ☎ ⊞ ⌀ lau ♦
⋌S Prices: pitch 110-140 (incl 3 persons)

Ideal Camping No 1 Suzac ☎46052904
May-15 Sep 8HEC ∷∷ ♠ ⋒ 🗻 ⅊ ✕ ⊙ ₪ 🏤 ⊞ ⊞ ⌀ lau ♦ 🗻 ⋌S
Prices: pitch 92 (incl 3 persons)

ST-GILLES-CROIX-DE-VIE *Vendée*

Pas Opton rte de Nantes ☎51551198
Well tended garden-like site in rural surroundings.
On D754 Nantes Road.
20 May-10 Sep 6.5HEC ▦ ⊶ ⋒ 🗻 ⅊ ✕ ⊙ ₪ ⌀ 🗻 ⋌ PR ☎ ⊞ ⌀ lau
Prices: pitch 91-129 (incl 2 persons)

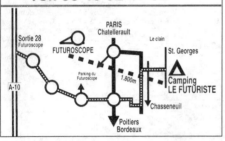
ST-HILAIRE-DE-RIEZ *Vendée*

Biches rte de Notre-Dame-de-Riez ☎51543882
2km N
15 May-15 Sep 13HEC ▦ ░░ ♦ ℝ ⅏ ☎ Ⅹ ⊙ ❷ ∅ ⍾ ⋨ P ② ⊞
lau Prices: pitch 160-185 (incl 3 persons)

Bois Tordu 84 av de la Pège ☎51543378
5.3km NW.
15 May-15 Sep 2HEC ▦ ♦ ℝ ⅏ ☎ Ⅹ ⊙ ❷ ∅ ⍾ ❷ ⋨ P ② ⊞ lau ♦
Ⅹ ⋨S Prices: pitch 165 (incl 3 persons)

Chouans 108 av de la Faye ☎51543490
2.5 km NW.
Etr-Sep 4HEC ▦ ⍾ ℝ ⅏ Ⅹ ⊙ ❷ ∅ ❷ ⋨ P ② lau ♦ ⋨S

Ecureulis 100 av de la Pège ☎51543371
In pleasant surroundings, 250m from a fine sandy beach, with good
recreational facilities.
From A11 to Nantes, then via D178 and D753 to St-Hilaire-de-Riez.
15 May-15 Sep 4HEC ░░ ⍾ ℝ ⅏ ☎ Ⅹ ⊙ ❷ ⋨ P ② ⊞ lau Prices:
pitch 135-148 (incl 2 persons)

Padrelle 1 r Prévot ☎51553203
May-Sep 1.5HEC ▦ ⍾ ℝ ⊙ ❷ ❷ ② lau ♦ ⅏ Ⅹ ∅ ⋨S Prices:
pitch 56 (incl 2 persons)

Plage 106 av de la Pège ☎51543393
On a meadow with trees. Access to beach via dunes.
5.7km NW.
15 May-15 Sep 5.5HEC ▦ ░░ ⍾ ℝ ⅏ Ⅹ ⊙ ❷ ∅ ⍾ ❷ ▲ ⋨ PS
② ⊞ lau ♦ ⅏ Prices: pitch 63 (incl 2 persons)

Prairie chemin des Roselières ☎51540856
5.5km NW, 500m from the beach
15 May-15 Sep 4HEC ♦ ℝ ⅏ ☎ Ⅹ ⊙ ❷ ∅ ⍾ ❷ ⋨ PS ② ⊞ lau
Prices: A20 V7 ♥43 ▲43

Puerta del Sol 47 r de Candale-Prolongée ☎51491010
4.5km N.

10 May-20 Sep 4HEC ▦ ♦ ℝ ⅏ ☎ Ⅹ ⊙ ❷ ❷ ⋨ P ② ⊞ lau ♦
⍾ ⋨S Prices: pitch 70-165 (incl 3 persons)

Riez à la Vie 9 av Parée Preneau ☎51543049
Flat site, divided into pitches.
3km NW.
Etr-15 Sep 2.9HEC ▦ ░░ ♦ ℝ ⅏ ☎ Ⅹ ⊙ ❷ ∅ ⍾ ❷ ⋨ P ② ⊞ lau ♦
Ⅹ ⍾ ⋨S ⊞ Prices: pitch 55-79 (incl 2 persons)

Sapinière chemin de Bellevue ☎51544574
2km NE
15 May-15 Sep 3.5HEC ▦ ░░ ♦ ℝ ⅏ Ⅹ ⊙ ❷ ∅ ❷ ⋨ P ② ⊞ lau
Prices: pitch 97 (incl 3 persons)

Sol-à-Gogo 61 av de la Pège ☎51542900
4.8km NW, directly on the beach
15 May-15 Sep 3.8HEC ▦ ⍾ ℝ ⅏ ☎ Ⅹ ⊙ ❷ ❷ ⋨ PS ② ⊞ lau ♦ ⍾
⍾ Prices: pitch 165 (incl 3 persons)

ST-JEAN-DE-MONTS *Vendée*

Abri des Pins rte de Notre-Dame-de-Monts ☎51588386
Level grassland site subdivided by hedges, bushes and trees.
4km N on D38 Notre-Dame-de-Monts road.
Jun-15 Sep 3HEC ▦ ⍾ ℝ ⅏ ☎ Ⅹ ⊙ ❷ ∅ ❷ ⋨ PS ② ⊞ lau ♦ ⍾
Prices: pitch 110-141 (incl 3 persons)

Amiaux 223 rte de Notre-Dame ☎51582222
On the edge of a forest.
3.5km NW of D38.
May-15 Sep 13HEC ▦ ░░ ∅ ⍾ ℝ ⅏ Ⅹ ⊙ ❷ ∅ ❷ ⋨ P ② ⊞ lau ♦
⋨S Prices: A16 pitch 75-120

Avenhiriers de la Calypso rte de Notre-Dame-de-Monts, Les
Tonnelles ☎51597966
Apr-Sep 4HEC ▦ ⍾ ℝ ⅏ ☎ Ⅹ ⊙ ❷ ∅ ⍾ ❷ ❷ ▲ ⋨ P ② ⊞ lau ♦
⋨S Prices: pitch 84-120 (incl 2 persons)

Bois Joly 46 r de Notre-Dame-de-Monts ☎51591163
A pleasantly landscaped, terraced site set among pine trees. Good
facilities. Close to the beach and the town centre.
Etr-28 Sep 5.5HEC ▦ ⍾ ℝ ⅏ ☎ Ⅹ ⊙ ❷ ∅ ❷ ⋨ PR ② ⊞ lau ♦ ⍾
⋨S Prices: pitch 65-115 (incl 3 persons)

Bois Masson 149 r des Sables ☎51586262
2km SE
15 Apr-Sep 7.5HEC ▦ ⍾ ℝ ⅏ ☎ Ⅹ ⊙ ❷ ∅ ⍾ ❷ ❷ ▲ ⋨ P ② ⊞
lau ♦ ⋨S

Clarys Plage av des Epines ☎51581024
15 May-15 Sep 8HEC ▦ ⍾ ℝ ⅏ ☎ Ⅹ ⊙ ❷ ∅ ❷ ⋨ P ② ⊞ lau ♦ ⍾
⋨S Prices: pitch 141 (incl 2 persons)

Sirenes av des Demoiselles ☎51580131
Camping Card Compulsory.
500m from the beach
Etr-15 Sep 15HEC ░░ ♦ ℝ ⊙ ❷ ② lau ♦ ⅏ Ⅹ ∅ ⍾ ⋨S Prices:
pitch 57 (incl 2 persons)

Forêt chemin de la Rive ☎51588463
5.5km NW
15 May-15 Sep 1HEC ▦ ░░ ⍾ ℝ ⊙ ❷ ∅ ❷ ⋨ P ② ⊞ lau ♦ ⅏ Ⅹ ⍾
⋨S ⊞ Prices: A22 pitch 75

At OROUET(6km SE)

Yole chemin des Bosses, Orouet ☎51586717
In rural surroundings 1km from a fine sandy beach.
Signposted from D38 in Orouet.
15 May-15 Sep 6HEC ▦ ░░ ⍾ ℝ ⅏ ☎ Ⅹ ⊙ ❷ ∅ ❷ ② ⊞ ⍉ lau ♦
⍾ ⋨S Prices: pitch 90-135 (incl 2 persons)

ST-JULIEN-DES-LANDES *Vendée*

Fôret ☎51466211
NE on D55, rte de Martinet.
15 May-15 Sep 5HEC ▦ ⍾ ♦ ℝ ⅏ Ⅹ ⊙ ❷ ∅ ⋨ P ② ⊞ lau ♦ ⅏

⛺Garangeoire ☎51466539
2km N of the village.
15 May-15 Sep 15HEC ▦ ⍾ ℝ ⅏ Ⅹ ⊙ ❷ ∅ ⋨ P ② ⊞ lau ♦
Prices: pitch 112-169 (incl 3 persons)

Guyonnière La Guyonnière ☎51466259
A pleasant site with pitches divided by hedges with good sanitary and recreational facilities.
2km from the town centre towards St-Gilles-Croix-de-Vie.
May-Sep 5HEC ▦ ⌂ ⋔ ▙ ⚡ ✕ ⊙ ▨ ⌀ ▟ ⬢ ▨ ⌇ P ② ⊞ lau ✦ ⋋L
Prices: A20 pitch 25

ST-LÉONARD-DE-NOBLAT *Haute-Vienne*
CM Beaufort ☎55560279
In pleasant wooded surroundings with good facilities.
Access from the D39.
15 Jun-15 Sep 2HEC ▦ ⌂ ⋔ ▙ ⚡ ⊙ ▨ ⬢ ⌇ R ② ⊞ lau

ST-MALÔ-DU-BOIS *Vendée*
Plein Air de Poupet ☎51923145
From village take D72 for 1km, then take left fork and follow signs.
Site on bank of River Sèvre Nantaise.
May-Sep 3HEC ▦ ⌂ ⋔ ⚡ ✕ ⊙ ▨ ⌇ R ② lau ✦ ▟

ST-PALAIS-SUR-MER *Charente-Maritime*
Ormeaux av de Bernezac ☎46390207
May-Sep 3.5HEC ▦ ⌂ ⋔ ⚡ ✕ ▟ ⚡ ⌇ P ② ⊞ lau ✦ ▟ ✕ ⋋S
Prices: pitch 100-135 (incl 3 persons)

Puits de l'Auture La Grande Côte ☎46232031
Situated at the edge of a forest facing the sea.
2km NW on D25 La Palmyre road.
May-Sep 5HEC ▦ ✦ ⋔ ▙ ⚡ ✕ ⊙ ▨ ⌀ ▟ ⌇ P ② ⊞ ⚡ lau ✦ ⋋S
Prices: pitch 110-155 (incl 3 persons)

ST-PRIEST-DE-GIMEL *Corrèze*
Étang-de-Ruffaud ☎55212665
On hilly wooded ground beside lake. Common room with TV.
2.5km N on D53.
15 Jun-15 Sep 5HEC ▦ ✦ ⋔ ▙ ⚡ ✕ ⊙ ▨ ⬢ ⌇ LR ② ⊞ lau

ST-VINCENT-SUR-JARD *Vendée*
'Bolée d'Air' rte du Bouil ☎51903605
2km E via D21
Apr-25 Sep 5.7HEC ▦ ↳⌂ ⋔ ▙ ⚡ ✕ ⊙ ▨ ⌀ ▟ ⬢ ▨ ▲ ⌇ P ② ⊞
lau ✦ ✕ ⋋S Prices: pitch 80-120 (incl 2 persons)

SAUMUR *Maine-et-Loire*
Chantepie ☎41679534
A pleasant site with a fine view over the River Loire.
Access via D751 towards Gennes.
15 May-15 Sep 10HEC ▦ ⌂ ⋔ ▙ ⚡ ✕ ⊙ ▨ ⚡ ⬢ ▨ ⌇ P ② ▣ ⊞
lau Prices: A20-25 pitch 48.80-60.60

Ile d'Offard r de Verden ☎41403000
On island in the middle of the Loire near municipal stadium. Some facilities are only available during the high season.
Closed 15 Dec-15 Jan 4.5HEC ▦ ⌂ ⋔ ▙ ⚡ ✕ ⊙ ▨ ⌀ ⌇ PR ② ⊞
lau Prices: A25.50 pitch 45

SILLÉ-LE-GUILLAUME *Sarthe*
Privé du Landereau ☎43201269
1.5km NW via D304
Apr-Oct 2.5HEC ▦ ⌂ ⋔ ⚡ ✕ ⊙ ▨ ⌀ ⬢ ▨ ② ⊞ lau ✦ ✕ ▟ ⋋L
Prices: A13 V5.50 ▦5.50 ▲4

SILLÉ-LE-PHILIPPE *Sarthe*
■**Château de Chanteloup** ☎43275107
Set partly in wooded cleanings and open ground. Good sanitary installations.
17km NE of Le Mans on D301.
Jun-7 Sep 20HEC ▦ ⌂ ⋔ ▙ ⚡ ✕ ⊙ ▨ ⌇ LP ② ⊞ lau Prices: A29
pitch 49

SOUTERRAINE, LA *Creuse*
Suisse Océan Le Cheix ☎55633332
1.8km E via D912 near the lake.
All year 2HEC ▦ ⌂ ⋔ ⚡ ✕ ⊙ ▨ ⬢ ▨ ② ⊞ lau ✦ ▟ ⋋L Prices:
pitch 59.50-85 (incl 2 persons)

SUÈVRES *Loir-et-Cher*
■**Château de la Grenouillère** ☎54878037
Completely divided into pitches. Castle now hotel with common room for campers. Each pitch 150sq m. Separate area for overnight campers.
3km from village towards Orléans.
15 May-15 Sep 11HEC ▦ ⌂ ⋔ ▙ ⚡ ✕ ⊙ ▨ ⌀ ⬢ ⌇ P ② ⊞ lau
Prices: pitch 120-175 (incl 2 persons)

SULLY-SUR-LOIRE *Loiret*
CM ☎38362393
Near Château, adjacent to River Loire.
100m from town.
22 Mar-31 Oct 3.4HEC ▦ ⌂ ⋔ ⊙ ▨ ② ⊞ lau ✦ ▟ ⚡ ⌀ ▨ ⌇P
Prices: A11.20 pitch 6.90

At **ST-PÈRE-SUR-LOIRE**
St-Père rte d'Orléans ☎38363594
W on D60, near the river
22 Mar-31 Oct 2.7HEC ▦ ∷ ⌂ ⋔ ⊙ ▨ ② ⊞ lau ✦ ▙ ⚡ ✕ ⌀ ▨
Prices: A12.80 pitch 12.50

TALMONT-ST-HILAIRE *Vendée*
Littoral Le Porteau ☎51220464
Situated near Port Bourgenay, 80m from the sea. Good facilities and entertainment available during the season.
Apr-Sep 8.5HEC ▦ ⌂ ⋔ ▙ ⚡ ✕ ⊙ ▨ ▨ ⌇ P ② ⊞ lau Prices: pitch
123-175 (incl 3 persons)

At **ST-HILAIRE-LA-FORÊT** (7km SE)
Batardières ☎51333385
W on D70
Jul-8 Sep 1.6HEC ▦ ⌂ ⋔ ⊙ ▨ ▨ ② lau ✦ ▙ ⚡ ✕

TOURS *Indre-et-Loire*

At **BALLAN-MIRÉ**(8.5km W D751)

Mignardière 22 av des Aubepines ☎47733100
2.5km NE.
26 Apr-30 Sep 3.5HEC ▦ ⌑⌂🔔⊙⊟∅🏠🚽⌖🛒P☎⊞lau✦🍴✕ Prices: pitch 86-100 (incl 2 persons)

TRANCHE-SUR-MER, LA *Vendée*

Bale d'Aunis 10 r du Pertuis ☎51274736
On level land on sea-shore.
300m E on D46.
Apr-Sep ▦ ⠿ ⌑⌂🔔🍴✕⊙⊟∅🏠🚽⌖PS☎⊞✻lau
Prices: pitch 80-116 (incl 2 persons)

Bel r du Bottereau ☎51304739
400m from town centre.
25 May-14 Sep 3.5HEC ▦ ✦⌂🔔🍴✕⊙⊟⌖P☎⊞✻lau✦🔔🍴✕∅🚽⌖LS Prices: pitch 108 (incl 2 persons)

Cottage Fleuri La Grière-Plage ☎51303457
2.5km E, 500m from the beach
Apr-Sep 7.5HEC ▦ ⌑⌂🔔🍴✕⊙⊟∅🏠🚽⌖PR☎⊞lau✦🔔⌖S

Repos du Pêcheur rte de la Roche ☎51303694
Situated on the banks of a canal approx 3km from the sea.
15 Jun-15 Sep 6HEC ▦ ✎⌂🔔🍴✕⊙⊟∅🚽🏠⌖P☎⊞lau

Savinière ☎51274270
Set in a beautiful natural park with good, modern facilities.
1.5km NW via D105.
Apr-Sep 2.5HEC ▦ ✦⌂🔔🍴✕⊙⊟⌖P☎⊞lau✦🔔🚽⌖S
Prices: pitch 92-104 (incl 2 persons)

TURBALLE, LA *Loire-Atlantique*

◗**Parc Ste-Brigitte** Domaine de Brèhet ☎40248891
Site in grounds of old Château. Parkland divided into pitches and surrounded by hedges.
E of village on D99 Guérande road.
11 Apr-11 Oct 10HEC ▦ ⌑⌂🔔🍴✕⊙⊟∅⌖LP☎⊞lau Prices: A25.50 pitch 27.50-57

VALENÇAY *Indre*

CM Chènes rte de Loches ☎54000392
1km W on D960
Apr-Sep 5HEC ▦ ⌑⌂⊙⊟☎⊞lau✦🔔🍴✕∅🚽⌖P

VARENNES-SUR-LOIRE *Maine-et-Loire*

◗**Étang de la Brèche** 5 Inpasse de la Breche ☎41512292
4.5km NW via N152.
15 May-14 Sep 12HEC ▦ ⠿ ✦⌂🔔🍴✕⊙⊟∅⌖P☎⊞lau
Prices: pitch 110-145 (incl 3 persons)

VEILLON, LE *Vendée*

St-Hubert av de la Plage ☎51222230
Apr-Sep 0.9HEC ▦ ✦⌂🍴✕⊙⊟∅🚽🏠☎⊞lau✦🔔✕⌖LS

VELLES *Indre*

Grands Pins Les Maisons Neuves ☎54366193
The site has individual pitches and has easy access to the countryside.
7km S of Châteauroux on N20.
All year 5HEC ▦ ⠿ ✦⌂🔔🍴✕⊙⊟🏠⌖P☎⊞lau Prices: A18 pitch 20

VENDÔME *Loir-et-Cher*

Grand Prés r G-Martel ☎54770027
Site lies on a meadow, next to a sports ground.
E of town on right bank of Loire.
15 Apr-10 Sep 3HEC ▦ ✦⌂🔔🍴🔔⊙⊟∅⌖R☎⊞lau✦✕⌖P
Prices: A14 pitch 15

VINEUIL *Loir-et-Cher*

Châteaux ☎54788205
Level site on left bank of River Loire with modern buildings. Boating.
Bathing not recommended.
From Blois drive towards St-Dye. After modern bridge continue towards 'Lac de Loire' for 1.5km.

---

7 Apr-19 Oct 30HEC ▦ ⌑⌂🔔🍴✕⊙⊟∅🏠⌖⊞lau Prices: pitch 37-70

ALENÇON *Orne*

CM de Guéramé r de Guerame ☎33263495
Situated in open country near a stream, 500m from town centre.
Access via the Boulevard Périphérique in the SW part of town.
May-Sep 1.5HEC ▦ ✦⌂⊙⊟⌖R☎⊞lau✦🔔🍴✕∅🚽⌖P
Prices: A11 V12 ▣12 ▲12

Jacques Fould av H-Chanteloup ☎33292329
On N12.
All year 1HEC ▦ ⌂⊙⊟☎⊞lau✦🔔🍴✕∅🚽⌖PR Prices: A8 V6 ▣6 ▲6

ARGENTAN *Orne*

At **MAUVAISVILLE**(2.8km SE off N158)

Val de Baize 18 r de Mauvaisville ☎33672711
All year 1HEC ▦ ⌑⌂⊙⊟⌖R☎⊞lau✦🔔🍴✕∅🚽⌖P

ARRADON *Morbihan*

Penboch ☎97447129
5 Apr-20 Sep 4HEC ▦ ⌑⌂🔔🍴⊙⊟∅🚽🏠🚽⌖P☎⊞lau✦⌖S Prices: A22 pitch 25-72

ARZANO *Finistère*

Ty Nadan rte d'Arzano ☎98717547
3km W

24 May-5 Sep 12HEC [symbols] lau Prices: A26 pitch 55

AUMALE *Seine-Maritime*
CM Grand Mail 2 le Grand Mail ☎62050022
In the town centre
May-Sep 0.5HEC [symbols] lau [symbols] PR

AVRANCHES *Manche*
At **GENÊTS**(10km W on D911)
Coques d'Or rte du Bec d'Andaine ☎33708257
1km from the sea.
Apr-Sep 4.6HEC [symbols] S Prices: A23 pitch 12

BADEN *Morbihan*
Mané Guernehué ☎97570206
In a pleasant situation at the head of the Gulf of Morbihan with good recreational facilities.
1km SW via Mériadec road.
23 Mar-Sep 5.3HEC [symbols]
Prices: A15-25 pitch 47-69

BARNEVILLE-CARTERET *Manche*
At **BARNEVILLE-PLAGE**
Pré Normand ☎33538564
On slightly hilly meadow away from traffic noise but exposed to sea winds. Vehicles allowed on beach but beware of tide.
Off D166.
Apr-30 Sep 2HEC [symbols]
S Prices: A21 pitch 23

BAYEUX *Calvados*
CM Calvados bd d'Eindhoven ☎31920843
Very clean and tidy site with tarmac drive and hardstanding for caravans. Adjoins football field.
N side of town on Boulevard Circulaire.
15 Mar-15 Nov 3.5HEC [symbols] P
Prices: A15.50 pitch 19

BEG-MEIL *Finistère*
Roche Percée ☎98949415
Camping Card Compulsory.
28 Mar-28 Sep 2HEC [symbols] X
S Prices: A18-23 pitch 55-69

BÉNODET *Finistère*
Letty ☎98570469
Site divided into sectors. Good sanitary installations, ironing rooms and games room. Good beach for children.
By the sea 1km SE.
15 Jun-6 Sep 10HEC [symbols] S lau Prices: A23 pitch 36

Mer Blanche ☎98570075
3.5km E on D44 (Fouesnant road).
All year 6.5HEC [symbols] PS lau

Plage Kéranbechenner ☎98570055
400m from the town centre and close to the beaches, with good, modern facilities.
Follow signs from town centre.
15 May-Sep 5HEC [symbols] PR lau S

Pointe St-Gilles ☎98570537
Holiday site south of village, on fields by beach. Divided into several sectors; individual pitches. Well-equipped sanitary blocks.
May-Sep 7HEC [symbols] PS lau X
Prices: A26 pitch 48

Port de Plaisance 7 rte de Quimper, Prad Puollou ☎98570238
NE off D34
Apr-Sep 5HEC [symbols] P lau S
Prices: A21-26 pitch 48-60

BÉNOUVILLE *Calvados*
Hautes Coutures rte de Ouistreham ☎31447308
Apr-Sep 8HEC [symbols] PR lau S Prices: A30 pitch 32

BERNIÈRES-SUR-SEINE *Eure*
Château-Gaillard ☎32541820
0.8km SW
Jan 24HEC [symbols] P lau

BINIC *Côtes-D'Armor*
Panoramic r Gasselin ☎96736043
On a meadow divided into pitches, on a hill above the town.
On S outskirts of village.
All year 5HEC [symbols] P lau S

BLAINVILLE-SUR-MER *Manche*
Mélette ☎33471484
1km W on D651.
15 Jun-15 Sep 6HEC [symbols] lau X PS

Senéquet ☎33472311
2km NW on D651.
Mar-early Dec 13HEC [symbols] PS lau

BLANGY-LE-CHÂTEAU *Calvados*
Brévedent ☎31647288
3km SE on D51 beside lake.
15 May-15 Sep 5HEC [symbols] LPR lau X S

Domaine du Lac rte de Mesnil-sur-Blangy ☎31646200
Apr-Oct 7HEC [symbols] lau Prices: A25 pitch 25

BLANGY-SUR-BRESLE *Seine-Maritime*
CM r des Étangs ☎35945565
300m on N28.
15 Mar-15 Oct 1HEC [symbols] lau R
Prices: A11.30 pitch 9

BLONVILLE-SUR-MER *Calvados*
Village Club le Lieu Bill rte de Beaumont-en-Auge, Le Lieu Bill ☎31879727
Apr-Sep 7HEC [symbols] P lau S
Prices: A24 pitch 35

BOURG-ACHARD *Eure*
Clos Normand 235 rte de Pont-Audemer ☎32563484
Access via N175 (Rouen-Caen).
Apr-Sep 1.5HEC [symbols] lau Prices: A18-20 V8 ☐16 ▲16

CABOURG *Calvados*
Vert Pré rte de Caen ☎31242119
2km SW on D513.
Apr-Sep 5HEC [symbols] P lau X S

CALLAC *Côtes-D'Armor*
CM Verte Vallée ☎96455850
W via D28 towards Morlaix
15 Jun-15 Sep 1HEC [symbols] lau X LR

CAMARET-SUR-MER *Finistère*
Lambézen ☎98279141
3km NE on rte de Roscanvel (D355).
Apr-Sep 2.8HEC [symbols] P lau S
Prices: A18-26 pitch 35-55

Plage de Trez Rouz ☎98279396
Etr-Sep 1HEC [symbols] lau X S Prices: A22 pitch 18

CAMPNEUSEVILLE *Seine-Maritime*
Monchy-le-Preux ☎35937703
2km N on D260.
Jun-Sep 2HEC [symbols] lau LPRS

CAMPING LE HAUT DYCK ★★★
50500 Carentan
Tel: 02.33 42 16 89

Pitches marked by trees, guarded and fenced site. Leisure room – games area – mini golf. In the heart of the Natural Park of the Marais, close to the beaches of The Landing. 14 km from the sea..

CANCALE *Ille-et-Vilaine*

Notre Dame du Verger Departoientale 201 ☎99897284
2km from Pointe-du-Grouin on D201.
Apr-Sep 2.2HEC ▥ ⊒↙♠⊙♨⊘⊞ lau ♦✕⊞ ⇌S

CARANTEC *Finistère*

Mouettes Grande Grève ☎98670246
Level site divided by low shrubs and trees.
1.5km SW on rte de St-Pol-de-Léon, towards the sea.
Etr-21 Sep 7HEC ▥ ⊒♠⊙♨⊘⇌ LP ⊞ lau ♦ ⇌S Prices:
A22-29 pitch 62-82

CARENTAN *Manche*

CM le Haut Dyck chemin du Grand-Bas Pays ☎02 33421689
Take village road off N13 towards Le Port.
All year 2.5HEC ▥ ♠⊙♨⊞ lau ♦ ♣♥✕⊘⇌PS Prices:
A12 V7 ⊕16 ▲A15

CARNAC *Morbihan*

Bruyères ☎97523057
29 Mar-20 Oct 2HEC ▥ ♦♠⊙♨⊘⊞⇌ lau ♦♥✕
⇌PS

Étang Kerlann ☎97521406
2km N at Kerlann.
Apr-Oct 2.8HEC ▥ ⊒♠⊙♨⊘⊞⇌ P ⊞ lau ♦
⇌RS Prices: A18-20 pitch 25-35

Grande Métairie rte des Alignements, de Kermario ☎02 97522401
Holiday site with modern amenities, completely divided into pitches. Country-style bar, terraced restaurant, TV. Swimming pools.
2.5km NE on D196.
22 Mar-13 Sep 15HEC ▥ ⊒♠♣✕⊙♨⊘⊞⇌ P ⊞ lau ♦
⇌S Prices: A28 pitch 116-138

Moulin de Kermaux ☎97521590
2.5km NE.
Mar-16 Sep 3HEC ▥ ♦♠♣✕⊙♨⊘⊞⇌ P ⊞ lau ♦✕⊘
⇌RS

Moustoir ☎97521618
3 km NE of Carnac.
Etr-Sep 5HEC ▥ ♦♠♣✕⊙♨⊘⊞▲⇌ P ⊞ lau ♦✕⇌RS
Prices: A19.50 pitch 48

Ombrages ☎97521652
Take rte Carnac to Auray and turn left at SHELL filling station.
15 Jun-15 Sep 1HEC ▥ ⊒♠⊙♨⊘⊞ lau ♦♥✕⇌L Prices:
A18 pitch 26

Rosnual rte d'Auray ☎97521457
1.5km from village, 2.5km from the sea.
Etr-Sep 7.8HEC ▥ ⊒♠♣✕⊙♨⊘⇌ P ⊞⊞ lau ♦⊘⇌S

Saules rte de Rosnual ☎97521498
Grassland site between road and deciduous woodland, subdivided by hedges and shrubs.
2.5km N on D119.

Apr-Sep 2.5HEC ▥ ⊒♠♣⊙♨⊘⊞⇌ P ⊞⊞ lau ♦♥✕⊞
Prices: A16-22 V6-10 ⊕22-30 ▲A22-30

At CARNAC-PLAGE(1km S)

Druides 23 chemin de Beaumer ☎97520818
Family site with well defined pitches, 400m from a fine sandy beach. SE of town centre. Approach via D781 or D119.
Jun-10 Sep 3HEC ▥ ♦♠⊙♨⊞⊘ lau ♦♣♥✕⊘⇌S Prices:
pitch 125 (incl 3 persons)

Men Dû Quartier Beaumer ☎97520423
1km from Carnac Plage via D781 and D186.
Apr-Sep 1.5HEC ▥ ♦♠✕⊙♨⊘▲⊞⊞⊞ lau ♦♣♥⇌S

CAUREL *Côtes-D'Armor*

Nautic International rte de Beau Rivage ☎96285794
A terraced site on the edge of Lake Guerlédan.
N164 in the direction of Beau Rivage.
Apr-25 Sep 3.6HEC ▥ ⊒♠♣⊙♨⊘▲⇌ LP ⊞⊞ lau ♦♥✕⊘
Prices: A21-26 pitch 35

CHAPELLE-AUX-FILZMÉENS, LA *Ille-et-Vilaine*

Camping du Logis ☎99452155
A quiet, pleasant site.
Camping Card Compulsory.
All year 20HEC ▥ ⊒♠♣✕⊙♨⊘⇌ P ⊞⊞ lau ♦ ⇌LRS

CLÉDER *Finistère*

CV Roguennic Roguennic ☎98696388
5km N on coast.
Apr-Sep 8HEC ☷ ⊒↙♠♣✕⊙♨⊘▲⇌ PS ⊞⊞ lau Prices:
pitch 32-41

CLOÎTRE-ST-THEGONNEC, LE *Finistère*

Bruyères ☎98797176
A small, secluded site in a picturesque setting within the Amorique Nature Park.
12km S of Morlaix via D769.
Jun-Sep 2.5HEC ▥ ⊒↙♠⊘⇌ R ⊞⊞ lau ♦♣♥✕▲ Prices: A14
pitch 18

COMBOURG *Ille-et-Vilaine*

Bois Coudrais Cuguen ☎99732745
A small, level site with fine views.Access via D83 (Combourg-Mont-St-Michel).
Etr-mid Oct 1HEC ▥ ⊒↙♠✕⊙♨⊞⊞⊞ lau ♦♣ Prices: A7
pitch 35

CONCARNEAU *Finistère*

Prés Verts ☎98970974
1.2km NW.
May-10 Sep 3HEC ▥ ⊒♠♣✕⊙♨⇌ PS ⊞⊞ lau ♦⊘ Prices: A38
pitch 42

COUTERNE *Orne*

Clos Normand rte de Bagnols de l'Orne ☎33379243
A pleasant site in rural surroundings in a sheltered position close to the thermal spa of Bagnoles-de-l'Orne.
Apr-Sep 1.3HEC ▥ ♦♠⊙♨⊘⊞⊞ lau ♦♣♥✕⊘▲⇌LP ⊞
Prices: pitch 37 (incl 2 persons)

CRAC'H *Morbihan*

Fort Espagnol rte de Fort Espagnol ☎97551488
Apr-15 Sep 4.5HEC ▥ ⊒♠♣✕⊙♨⊘⊞⊞▲⇌ P ⊞ lau
Prices: A25 pitch 45
See advertisement on page 123.

CRIEL-SUR-MER *Seine-Maritime*

Mouettes r de la Plage ☎35897073
Apr-Oct 1.5HEC ▥ ⊒↙♠♣✕⊙♨⊘⊞⊞ lau ♦⇌S Prices:
pitch 58 (incl 2 persons)

CROZON *Finistère*

Pen ar Menez bd de Pralognan ☎98271236
On fringe of a pinewood. Water sport facilities 5km away. Cycles for hire.
Apr-Sep 2.6HEC ▥ ♠♣✕⊙♨⊞⊞ lau ♦♣✕⊘▲⇌S ⊞

**BRETAGNE
– between AURAY and CARNAC**
Heated swimming pool – water slide – basketball –
MINICLUB for children

**Camping Caravanning
FORT ESPAGNOL ★★★
F-56950 Crac'h**

Tel: 02 97 55 14 88 • Fax: 02 97 30 01 04
For hire:
Caravans, mobile homes, chalets, canvas bungalows.
Half court tennis • recreation programme

Plage de Goulien Kernavèno ☎98271710
5km W on D308
10 Jun-20 Sep 1.8HEC ▦ 🔾 ♠ 🔽 ⊙ 🗷 🖉 🏠 🏕 🖾 ⊞ lau ➦ ⚓S
Prices: A20.50 pitch 20.50

At ST-FIACRE(5km NW)

Pieds dans l'Eau ☎98276243
Site on several meadows divided by trees. In quiet secluded situation
reaching as far as a pebbly beach. Bathing is dependent on tides.
15 Jun-15 Sep 1.8HEC ▦ ♠ 🔾 ⊙ 🗷 🔽 ⚓ S 🖾 ⊞ lau ➦ ♈ ✕ 🖉 🏕
⚓P

DEAUVILLE Calvados

At ST-ARNOULT(3km S)

Vallée rte de Beaumont ☎31885817
1km S via D27 and D275
Etr-Oct 5HEC ▦ 🔾 ♠ 🔽 🏠 ♈ ✕ ⊙ 🗷 🖉 🏠 🏕 ⚓ LPR 🖾 ⊞ lau ➦ 🏕
Prices: A31.50 pitch 35

At TOUQUES(3km SE)

Haras chemin du Calvaire ☎31884484
N on D62, to Honfleur.
All year 4HEC ▦ 🔾 ♠ 🔽 🏠 ♈ ⊙ 🗷 🖉 🏕 🖾 ⊞ lau ➦ ⚓PR

DÉVILLE-LÈS-ROUEN Seine-Maritime

CM ☎35740759
All year 1.5HEC ⁙ ♦ 🔾 ♠ 🔾 ⊙ 🗷 🖾 ⊞ lau ➦ 🔽 ♈ ✕ 🖉 🏕 ⚓PR

DIEPPE Seine-Maritime

At HAUTOT-SUR-MER(6km SW)

Source Petit-Appeville ☎35842704
15 Mar-15 Oct 2.5HEC ▦ 🔾 ♠ 🔽 ♈ ✕ ⊙ 🗷 🖉 🏠 ⚓ R 🖾 ⊞ lau ➦ ✕
Prices: A19 V6 🚐15 ▲19

DINAN Côtes-D'Armor

At TADEN(3.5km NE)

CM Hallerais ☎96391593
Beautiful clean site with level pitches on gentle slope near a country
estate. Asphalt drives. Good sanitary installations. Shop, bar and
restaurant are only open in July and August.
SW of Taden off D12.
15 Mar-Oct 8HEC ▦ 🔾 ♠ 🔽 ✕ ⊙ 🗷 🖉 🏕 ⚓ PRS 🅿 ⊞ lau Prices:
A22 pitch 65

DINARD Ille-et-Vilaine

See also **ST-LUNAIRE**

Mauny ☎99469473
Off St-Briac road (CD603).
27 Mar-27 Sep 5HEC ▦ 🔾 ♠ 🔽 ♈ ✕ ⊙ 🗷 🖉 🏕 ⚓ P 🖾 ⊞ lau ➦ ⚓S
Prices: A25 pitch 55

Prieuré 20 av Vicomte ☎99462004
SE via D114
Etr-Oct 1.4HEC ▦ 🔾 ♠ 🔽 ♈ ✕ ⊙ 🗷 🖉 🏕 🚐 ⚓ S 🖾 ⊞ lau ➦ ⚓P

DOL-DE-BRETAGNE Ille-et-Vilaine

📷Château des Ormes ☎99734959
Site in grounds of château.
7km S on N795 Rennes road.
20 May-10 Sep 150HEC ▦ ⚒ 🔾 ♠ 🔽 🏠 ♈ ✕ ⊙ 🗷 🖉 🏕 ⚓ LP 🖾
lau Prices: A29 pitch 87

CM ☎99481468
On level meadow.
SW on rte de Dinan 400m from town centre.
May-Sep 1.7HEC ▦ 🔾 ♠ ⊙ 🗷 🖾 ⊞ lau ➦ 🔽 ♈ ✕

At BAGUER-PICAN(4km E on N176)

Camping du Vieux Chêne ☎99480955
Spacious site in pleasant lakeside situation. Farm produce available.
5km E of Dol-de-Bretagne on RD576.
15 Apr-20 Sep 8HEC ▦ 🔾 ♠ 🔽 🏠 ♈ ✕ ⊙ 🗷 🖉 🏠 🏕 ⚓▲ ⚓ P 🖾 lau
Prices: A22-28 pitch 47-59

DOUARNENEZ Finistère

Kerleyou ☎98741303
Family site in wooded surroundings near the beach. Separate car
park for arrivals after 23.00hrs.
1km W on rte de Préfet-Collignon towards the sea.
Apr-Sep 3HEC ▦ ♦ 🔾 ♠ 🔽 🏠 ♈ ✕ ⊙ 🗷 🖉 🏕 lau ➦ ✕ 🏕 ⚓PS

At POULLAN-SUR-MER(5km W on D765)

Pil Koad ☎98742639
E via D7 towards Douarnenez
Apr-Sep 5.5HEC ▦ 🔾 ♠ 🔽 🏠 ♈ ✕ ⊙ 🗷 🖉 🏠 🏕 ⚓ P 🖾 ⊞ lau ➦ ⚓S
Prices: A20-28 pitch 40-70

ERDEVEN Morbihan

Sept Saints ☎97555265
2km NW via D781 rte de Plouhinec.
15 May-15 Sep 7HEC ▦ ♦ 🔾 ♠ 🔽 🏠 ♈ ✕ ⊙ 🗷 🖉 🏕 ⚓ P 🖾 ⊞ lau ➦
✕ ⚓LRS Prices: A18-26 pitch 50-72

ERQUY Côtes-D'Armor

Hautes Greés 123 r St-Michel ☎96723478
500m from the sea.
15 Apr-15 Sep 2.5HEC ▦ 🔾 ♠ 🔽 🏠 ⊙ 🗷 🏠 🏕 🚐 🖾 ⊞ lau ➦ ♈ ✕ 🖉 🏕
⚓S Prices: A17 pitch 28

Roches Caroual Village ☎96723290
3km SW
Apr-Sep 2.4HEC ▦ 🔾 ♠ 🔽 ⊙ 🗷 🖉 🏕 🏠 🏕 🖾 ⊞ lau ➦ ⚓S

St-Pabu ☎96722465
On big open meadow with several terraces in beautiful, isolated
situation by sea. Divided into pitches.
W on D786 then follow signposts from La Coutre.
Apr-5 Oct 8HEC ▦ ⚒ 🔾 ♠ 🔽 🏠 ♈ ✕ ⊙ 🗷 🖉 🏕 🏠 ⚓ S 🖾 ⊞ lau ➦ ✕
Prices: A18 pitch 36

Vieux Moulin r des Moulins ☎96723423
Clean tidy site divided into pitches and surrounded by a pine forest.
Suitable for children.
On D783.
Apr-25 Sep 3.5HEC ▦ ♦ 🔾 🔽 ♈ ✕ ⊙ 🗷 🖉 🏠 ⚓ P 🖾 ⊞ lau ➦ ⚓S
Prices: A28 pitch 47

ÉTABLES-SUR-MER Côtes-D'Armor

Abri Côtier ☎96706157
1km N of town centre on D786.
6 May-20 Sep 2HEC ▦ ♦ 🔾 ♠ 🔽 ✕ ⊙ 🗷 🖉 🏕 🏠 🏕 🚐 ⚓ P 🖾 ⊞ lau ➦
✕ ⚓S Prices: A26-28 pitch 38-42

ETRÉHAM Calvados

Reine Mathilde ☎31217655
1km W via D123
Apr-Sep 6HEC ▦ 🔾 ♠ 🔽 🏠 ♈ ✕ ⊙ 🗷 🖉 🏕 🏠 🚐 ⚓ P 🖾 ⊞ lau ➦ ⚓S

EU Seine-Maritime

CM r Mozart ☎35503017
About 7km SE of town at Incheville, on the road to Beauchamps.
Apr-Sep 2HEC ▦ 🔾 ♠ 🔽 ⊙ 🗷 🖉 🖾 ⊞ lau ➦ 🔽 ✕ ⚓LPR

FAOUËT, LE *Morbihan*

Beg Er Roch rte de Lorient ☎97231511
In pleasant surroundings on the banks of a river. A popular site with modern sanitary facilities and a wealth of opportunities for all kinds of sport.
9 Mar-15 Sep 3HEC ▦ ♁ ♠ ☉ ◘ ⌀ ♨ ♣ ♠ Å ⚓ R ☎ lau ➧ ♨ ⊞
Prices: A14-20 pitch 10-18

FORÊT-FOUESNANT, LA *Finistère*

Kérantérec ☎98569811
Well-kept terraced site, divided into sections by hedges and extending to the sea.
3km SE.
Apr-Sep 6HEC ▦ ♁ ♠ ♨ ♀ ✕ ☉ ◘ ⌀ ♨ ♣ ♠ ⚓ PR ☎ ⊞ lau ➧ ♨ ✕
Prices: A28 pitch 35

Manoir de Pen Ar Steir ☎98569775
NE off D44.
All year 3HEC ▦ ♁ ♠ ♨ ☉ ◘ ⌀ ♨ ♣ ♠ ☎ ⊞ lau ➧ ♨ ✕ ⚓S

Plage Plage de Kerleven, rte de Port la Forêt ☎98569625
2.5km SE on D783.
All year 1HEC ▦ ♒ ♠ ☉ ◘ ☎ ⊞ lau ➧ ♨ ♀ ✕ ⌀ ♨ ⚓S ⊞

Pontérec Ponterec ☎98569833
0.5km on D44 towards Bénodet.
Apr-Sep 3HEC ♁ ♠ ☉ ◘ ♨ ♣ ♠ ☎ ⊞ lau ➧ ♨ ♀ ✕ ⌀ ⚓PS

St-Laurent Kerleven ☎98569765
On rocky coast. Divided into pitches.
3.5km SE of village.
Apr-Sep 5.3HEC ▦ ♁ ♠ ♨ ♀ ✕ ☉ ◘ ♨ ♣ ⚓ PS ☎ lau ➧ ⌀ ♨ ⊞

FOUESNANT *Finistère*

Atlantique rte de Mousterlin ☎98561444
4.5km S on the road to Mousterlin.
15 May-15 Sep 9HEC ▦ ♁ ♠ ♨ ♀ ✕ ☉ ◘ ⌀ ♣ ♠ ⚓ P ☎ ⊞ ⌀ lau ➧ ⚓S

Piscine Kerleya ☎98565606
4km NW
15 May-15 Sep 3.8HEC ▦ ♁ ♠ ♨ ☉ ◘ ⌀ ♣ ♠ ⚓ P lau ➧ ⚓S
Prices: A17.50-23 pitch 36-46

FOUGÈRES *Ille-et-Vilaine*

CM Paron rte de la Chapelle Janson ☎99994081
1.5km E via D17
Mar-Nov 2.5HEC ▦ ⫶⫶ ➧ ♠ ☉ ◘ ♨ ☎ ⊞ lau ➧ ♨ ♀ ✕ ⌀ ♨ ⚓R
Prices: A11-13 pitch 11-13

GLACERIE, LA *Manche*

Clos à Froment r P & M Curie ☎33542599
A modern site near the Cherbourg ferry terminal and the Auchan hypermarket.
All year 1.7HEC ▦ ♁ ♠ ♨ ✕ ☉ ◘ ♣ ♠ ☎ ⊞ lau ➧ ♀ ✕ ⌀ ♨

GOUVILLE-SUR-MER *Manche*

Belle Étoile ☎33478687
Terraced site among sand dunes.
20m from the beach.
May-Aug 2.8HEC ▦ ♒ ♠ ♨ ♀ ✕ ☉ ◘ ⌀ ♨ ♣ ♠ ☎ ⊞ lau ➧ ⚓S

GUIDEL-PLAGES *Morbihan*

Kergal ☎97059818
3km SW
Apr-Sep 5HEC ▦ ♒ ♠ ♨ ☉ ◘ ⌀ ♣ ♠ ☎ ⊞ lau ➧ ♨ ♀ ✕ ⚓RS

GUILLIGOMARC'H *Finistère*

Bois des Ecureuils ☎98717098
Advance booking required 15 Sep-Nov & Feb-Mar.
2km W from D769 (Roscoff to Lorient).
May-Oct 1.8HEC ▦ ♁ ♠ ♠ ☉ ◘ ♨ ♣ ♠ Å ☎ ⊞ lau Prices: A13 V8 ♣13 Å13

GUILVINEC *Finistère*

Plage rte de Penmarc'h ☎98586190
On level meadow. Divided into pitches. Flat beach suitable for children.

2km W of village on the Corniche towards Penmarc'h.
May-Sep 14HEC ⫶⫶⫶ ♁ ♠ ♨ ♀ ✕ ☉ ◘ ⌀ ♨ ♣ Å ⚓ PS ☎ ⊞ lau
Prices: A20-29 pitch 50-96

HAYE-DU-PUITS, LA *Manche*

Étang des Haizes St-Symphorien-le-Valois ☎33460116
Bordering a lake, shaded by apple trees.
Access via D903 from Carentan.
All year ♁ ♠ ♨ ♀ ✕ ☉ ◘ ⌀ ♣ ⚓ LP ☎ ⊞ lau ➧ ♨ ✕ ♨ ⚓S
Prices: A23-29 pitch 34-42

HOULGATE *Calvados*

Vallée 88 r de la Vallée ☎31244069
Site with good recreational facilities, 900m from the beach.
1km S.
Apr-Sep 11HEC ▦ ♁ ♠ ♨ ☉ ◘ ⌀ ♣ ⚓ P ☎ ⊞ lau ➧ ⚓S

JULLOUVILLE *Manche*

Chaussée 1 av de la Libération ☎33618018
On large meadow, completely divided into pitches. Separated from beach and coast road by row of houses.
5 Apr-14 Sep 6HEC ▦ ♁ ♠ ♨ ♀ ✕ ☉ ◘ ⌀ ♨ ♣ ☎ ⊞ lau ➧ ✕ ⚓S
Prices: pitch 85 (incl 2 persons)

At **ST-MICHEL-DES-LOUPS**(4km SE)

Chaumière ☎33488293
4km SE on D21 via Bouillon.
Jul-Aug 4HEC ▦ ♁ ♠ ✕ ☉ ◘ ⌀ ♣ ⚓ L ☎ ⊞ lau ➧ ♨ Prices: A15-16 pitch 16

LANDAUL *Morbihan*

Pied-à-Terre Branzého ☎97246715
In a pleasant, quiet location, 15 minutes from the sea.
1km from N165. Signposted from Landaul.
Jun-Aug 1HEC ▦ ➧ ♠ ♀ ☉ ◘ ☎ ⊞ lau ➧ ⌀ ♨ Prices: A10-15 V10 ♣10 Å8

LANDÉDA _Finistère_
Abers Dunes de Ste-Marguerite ☎98049335
Very quiet beautiful site among dunes. Ideal for children.
2.5km NW on a peninsula between bays of Aber-Wrac'h and Aber
Bernoît.
May-Sep 5HEC ▦ Ҷ ⋔ ⅃⊙ ◲ ⌀ ⊞ ◲ ⅂ S ☎ ⊞ lau ➡ ⅃ ✕ Prices:
A12.80-16 pitch 19.20-24

LARMOR-PLAGE _Morbihan_
Fontaine Kerderff ☎97337128
800m from the beach, near the leisure centre.
300m from D152.
2 May-15 Sep 4HEC ▦ Ҷ ⋔ ⅃⊙ ◲ ☎ ⊞ lau ➡ ⅃ ✕ ⅃S

LESCONIL _Finistère_
Dunes ☎98878178
On slightly sloping recently landscaped ground.
Access via D53, turning S in Plobannalac. Signposted.
15 May-Sep 2.8HEC ▦ Ҷ ⋔ ⊙ ◲ ⅃ ✕ ⅃ ⌀ ⅄ ⅃S
Prices: A23.90 pitch 31.70-35.70

Grande Plage 71 r P-Langevin ☎98878827
Etr-Sep 2.4HEC ▦ Ҷ ⋔ ⊙ ◲ ⌀ ◲ ☎ ⊞ ⊞ lau ➡ ⅃ ✕ ⅄ ⅃S
Prices: A15.50-19.60 pitch 23.10-28.85

LION-SUR-MER _Calvados_
Roches av de Blagny ☎31972115
NW on D514.
Apr-Sep 1.3HEC ▦ ⅃✓ ⋔ ⅃ ⅃ ✕ ⊙ ◲ ⌀ ◲ ⅃ S ☎ ⊞ lau

LOUARGAT _Côtes-D'Armor_
At **ST-ELOI**(5km N)
▦**Cleuziou** ☎96431490
Between Guingamp and Morlaix, the site is signposted from the
church in Louargat.
17 Mar-12 Nov 7HEC ▦ Ҷ ⋔ ⅃ ✕ ⊙ ◲ ⌀ ◲ ⅃ P ☎ ⊞ lau
Prices: pitch 80-105 (incl 2 persons)

LOUVIERS _Eure_
Bel Air rte de la Haye Malherbe ☎32401077
Small site on the edge of a forest with landscaped pitches and good
facilities.
3km from the town centre via D81.
Mar-Nov 2.5HEC ▦ Ҷ ⋔ ⅃ ⅃ ⊙ ◲ ⌀ ⅄ ◲ ◲ ⅃ P ☎ ⊞ lau ➡ ⅃R
Prices: A21.50 pitch 26.50

LUC-SUR-MER _Calvados_
CM Capricieuse 2 r Brummel ☎31973443
On W outskirts, 100m from the beach.
Apr-Sep 4.5HEC ▦ ⅃✓ ⋔ ⊙ ◲ ◲ ☎ lau ➡ ⅃ ✕ ⌀ ⅃PS ⊞
See advertisement under Colour Section

MARTIGNY _Seine-Maritime_
CM ☎35856082
On the shore of a lake in pleasant surroundings 8km from Dieppe.
Access via D154.
29 Mar-12 Oct 6.8HEC ▦ Ҷ ⋔ ⅃ ⅃ ⊙ ◲ ☎ ⊞ ⌀ lau ➡ ✕ ⅃P
Prices: A12.20 V6.30 ◲22.50 ▲10.50-10

MARTRAGNY _Calvados_
▦**Château de Martragny** ☎31802140
Site in grounds of château.
From N13 take exit for Martragny. Drive through St-Léger and
campsite is on the right as you leave the village.
May-15 Sep 13HEC ▦ Ҷ ⋔ ⅃ ⅃ ⌀ ◲ ⅃ P ☎ ⊞ lau ➡ ✕ ⅃RS
Prices: A28 pitch 57

MAUPERTUS-SUR-MER _Manche_
Anse du Brick ☎33543357
Terraced site in dense wood.
200m from beach.
Apr-Sep 17HEC ▦ Ҷ ⋔ ⅃ ⊙ ◲ ⌀ ⅄ ◲ ⅃ P ☎ ⊞ lau ➡ ⅃ ✕ ⅃S
Prices: A23 pitch 35-42

MONT-ST-MICHEL, LE _Manche_
Gué de Beauvoir ☎33600923
4km S of Abbey on D776 Pontorson road.
Etr-Sep 1HEC ▦ Ҷ ⋔ ⅃ ✕ ⊙ ◲ ☎ ⊞ lau ➡ ⅃ ⌀ Prices: A14 V8
◲15 ▲10

MORGAT _Finistère_
Bouis ☎98261253
Divided into hedge-lined pitches.
Etr-Sep 3HEC ▦ Ҷ ⋔ ⅃ ⊙ ◲ ⌀ ◲ ☎ ⊞ lau ➡ ⅃ ✕ ⅃LPRS

MOYAUX _Calvados_
▦**Colombier** ☎31636308
Well-kept site on grounds of manor house.
Camping Card Compulsory.
3km NE on D143.
May-15 Sep 10HEC ▦ Ҷ ⋔ ⅃ ✕ ⊙ ◲ ⌀ ⅃ P ☎ ⊞ lau Prices:
pitch 66 (incl 3 persons)

NÉVEZ _Finistère_
Deux Fontaine Raguènes ☎98068191
Mainly level site, subdivided into several fields.
700m from Ragunes Beach.
15 May-15 Sep 4.5HEC ▦ Ҷ ⋔ ⅃ ⅃ ⊙ ◲ ⌀ ◲ ◲ ⅃ P ☎ ⊞ lau
➡ ✕ ⅃S Prices: A17-24 pitch 28-40

NOYAL-MUZILLAC _Morbihan_
Moulin de Cadillac Moulin de Cadillac ☎97670347
15 May-Sep 2HEC ▦ Ҷ ⋔ ⅃ ⊙ ◲ ⅄ ◲ ◲ ⅃ P ☎ ⊞ lau Prices:
A16 pitch 22

OUISTREHAM _Calvados_
Prairies de la Mer rte de Lion, Riva-Bella ☎31976161
Mar 15-18 Oct 8HEC ▦ Ҷ ⋔ ⊙ ◲ ◲ ◲ ☎ ⊞ lau ➡ ⅃ ✕ ⌀ ⅃S
Prices: A22 pitch 35

PÉNESTIN-SUR-MER _Morbihan_
Airotel-Inly rte de Couarne ☎99903509
2km SE via D201
15 May-15 Sep 30HEC ▦ Ҷ ⋔ ⅃ ⅃ ✕ ⊙ ◲ ⌀ ⅄ ◲ ◲ ▲ ⅃ LP ☎
⊞ lau

Cénic ☎99904565
In a forested area 2km from the sea.
Etr-Sep 7HEC ▦ Ҷ ⋔ ⅃ ⅃ ✕ ⊙ ◲ ⌀ ◲ ◲ ▲ ⅃ P ☎ ⊞ lau ➡ ✕ ⅃S
Prices: A19 pitch 30

Iles La Pointe du Bile ☎99903024
The site lies beside the beach. Paddling pool for children.
3km S on D201.
12 Apr-Sep 4.5HEC ▦ Ҷ ⋔ ⅃ ✕ ⊙ ◲ ⌀ ⅄ ◲ ⅃ S ☎ ⊞ lau
Prices: A15-25 pitch 48-80

PENTREZ-PLAGE _Finistère_
Tamaris ☎98265395
Level site divided into pitches.
200m from beach.

May-Sep 2HEC ▥ ⌕ ⋔ ⛱ ⊙ ⬟ ⬚ ⛟ ⊞ ⊡ ⊞ lau ✦ ⛉ ✕ ⦨S
Prices: A17 pitch 18

PERROS-GUIREC *Côtes-D'Armor*

Claire Fontaine Toul ar Lann ☎96230355
1.2km SW of town centre, 800m from Trestraou beach.
May-Sep 3HEC ▥ ✦⋔⛱⊙⬟⬚⛟⊡⊞ lau ✦⛱✕⛨⦨S
Prices: A29 pitch 24-34

At **LOUANNEC**(3km SE)

CM ☎96231178
Well situated site next to the sea. Take away food, games room.
1km W.
Jun-Sep 5HEC ▥ ⇌⥾⋔⛱⊙⬟⬚⛟ ⦨LS ⊡ lau ✦✕⛨⊞
Prices: A12.50-14 pitch 28.50-44.50

At **PLOUMANACH**(2km NW)

Ranolien ☎96914358
The site is divided into pitches by hedges; separate sections for caravans.
500m from the village.
3 Mar-15 Nov 16HEC ▥ ⇌⥾⋔⛱⛉✕⊙⬟⬚⛨⛟⦑P⊡⊞ lau ✦
⦨S Prices: pitch 75-130 (incl 2 persons)

PIEUX, LES *Manche*

Forgette 7 av Côte des Isles ☎33525195
S towards Barneville-Carteret via Oeteville.
6 Apr-Sep 4HEC ▥ ⌕⋔⛱⊙⬟⬚⛟⛟⊡⊞ lau ✦⛉✕⦨P

Grand Large ☎33524075
In unspoilt landscape.
3km from the town centre on D117.
5 Apr-14 Sep 4HEC ▥ ⇌⥾⋔⛱⛉✕⊙⬟⬚⛟⦑PS⊞ lau
Prices: pitch 95 (incl 2 persons)

PLÉRIN *Côtes-D'Armor*

Mouettes Les Mouettes les Rosaires ☎96745148
Camping Card Compulsory.
Jul-Sep 1HEC ▥ ⌕⥾⊙⬟⛟⊡⊞ lau ✦⛉✕⦨RS

PLEUBIAN *Côtes-D'Armor*

Port la Chaîne ☎96229238
A terraced site on the 'Wild Peninsula', overlooking the sea, with good facilities.2km N via D20.
Jun-10 Sep 5HEC ▥ ✦⥾⋔✕⊙⬟⬚⦨S⊡⊞ lau ✦⛱⛉✕
Prices: A21 pitch 36

PLEUMEUR-BODOU *Côtes-D'Armor*

Port Landrellec ☎96238779
Beautiful site by the sea with numbered pitches surrounded by hedges.
3km from Trégastel turn towards Tréburden.
Etr-Sep 2.2HEC ▥ ⌕⋔⛱⛉⊙⬟⬚⛨⦨S⊞⊞ lau ✦⛱⛉✕
Prices: A24 pitch 25

PLOBANNALEC *Finistère*

Manoir de Kerlut ☎98822389
1.6km S via D102.
15 May-15 Sep 14HEC ▥ ⌕⋔⛱⛉✕⊙⬟⬚⛨⛟⦑PS⊡ lau
✦✕ Prices: A20-29 pitch 50-96

PLOËMEL *Morbihan*

Kergo ☎97568066
2km SE via D186
15 Jun-15 Sep 2.5HEC ▥ ⌕⋔⛱⊙⬟⛟⊡ lau ✦⛉⛱⬚⦨LPRS
Prices: A20 V9 ⛟21 ⛺21

PLOËRMEL *Morbihan*

Lac rte de Taupont ☎97740122
2km from village centre, beside the lake.
May-Oct 3.5HEC ▥ ✦⋔⛱⛉⊙⬟⬚⛨⛟⦑L⊡⊞ lau Prices:
A15 pitch 20

Vallée du Ninian Le Rocher ☎97935301
May-Sep 2.7HEC ▥ ⌕⋔⛱⛉⊙⬟⛨⛟⛺⦑PR⊡⊞ lau
Prices: pitch 60 (incl 2 persons)

PLOMEUR *Finistère*

Torche Pointe de la Torche ☎98586282
3.5km W
Apr-Oct 4HEC ▥ ✦⋔⛱⛉✕⊙⬟⬚⛨⛟⦑P⊡⊞ lau ✦✕⦨S
Prices: pitch 65-92 (incl 2 persons)

PLOMODIERN *Finistère*

Iroise Plage de Pors-ar-Vag, Port du Bateau ☎98815272
5km SW, 150m from the beach
Apr-Sep 2.5HEC ▥ ⇌⥾⋔⛱⛉✕⊙⬟⬚⛨⛟⦑P⊡⊞ lau ✦✕
⦨S Prices: A19.20-24 pitch 36-45

PLONÉVEZ-PORZAY *Finistère*

International de Kervel ☎98925154
The best site in the region. Ideal for families. 800m from the sea.
SW of the village on the D107 Douarnenez road for 3km, then towards coast at 'X' roads.
May-15 Sep 7HEC ▥ ⌕⋔⛱⛉⊙⬟⬚⛨⛟⛺⦑P⊡⊞ lau ✦
⦨S Prices: A15-25 pitch 45-75

Tréguer-Plage Ste-Anne-la-Palud ☎98925352
1.3km N
Apr-Sep 6HEC ▥ ⠶ ⇌⥾⋔⛱⛉✕⊙⬟⬚⛟⦑S⊡ lau
Prices: A16 pitch 15

PLOUÉZEC *Côtes-D'Armor*

Cap Horn Port Lazo ☎96206428
2.3km NE via D77 at Port-Lazo
Apr-Sep 5HEC ▥ ⌕⋔⛱⛉✕⊙⬟⬚⛺⦑PS⊡⊞ lau Prices:
A25 pitch 39

PLOUEZOCH *Finistère*

Baie de Térénez ☎98672680
3.5km NW via D76
Apr-Sep 3HEC ▥ ⌕⋔⛱⛉✕⊙⬟⬚⛨⛟⦑P⊡⊞ lau ✦⛱⦨S
Prices: A23 pitch 35

PLOUGASNOU *Finistère*

CM Mélin-ar-Mésqueau ☎98673745
3.5km S via D46
Apr-Sep 16HEC ▥ ⌕⋔⛱⛉✕⊙⬟⦑LR⊡⊞ lau

Trégor Kerjean ☎98673764
Numbered grassy pitches. Surrounded by hedges.
All year 1HEC ▥ ✦⋔⊙⬟⬚⛟⊡⊞ lau ✦⛱⛉✕⬚ Prices: A10 pitch 8

PLOUHA *Côtes-D'Armor*

At **TRINITÉ, LA**(2km NE)

Domaine de Keravel ☎96224913
Etr-Sep 5HEC ▥ ⌕⋔⛱⛉✕⊙⬟⬚⛨⛟⦑P⊡⊞ lau ✦⦨S

PLOUHARNEL *Morbihan*

Étang de Loperhet ☎97523468
1km NW via D781
Apr-Oct 6HEC ▥ ⠶ ⌕⋔⛱✕⊙⬟⬚⛨⛟⦑P⊡ lau ✦✕⬚
⦨S⊞ Prices: A20 pitch 35

Kersily Ste-Barbe ☎97523965
Etr-Oct 3HEC ▦ ♦ ♠ 🛉 🍴 ⊕ ☉ 🗐 🚿 🏪 🚐 ⚡ P ☎ ⊞ lau Prices:
A16-22 pitch 22-30

Lande ☎97523148
20 Jun-10 Sep 1HEC ▦ 🍴 ♠ ⊙ 🗐 🚐 ⊞ lau ♦ 🛉 🍴 ✗ ∅ 🚿 ⚡S
Prices: A16-17 V6-7 ♦12 ▲12

PLOUHINEC *Morbihan*

Moténo rte du Magouer ☎97367663
On slightly sloping ground, subdivided into several fields in a rural
area.
Apr-Sep 4HEC ▦ 🍴 ♠ 🛉 🍴 ✗ ⊙ 🗐 ∅ 🚿 🏪 🚐 ⚡ P ☎ ⊞ lau ♦ ⚡S
Prices: A17-21 pitch 29-49

PLOZÉVET *Finistère*

Corniche rte de la Corniche ☎029989134
S towards the sea
May-15 Sep 2HEC ▦ 🍴 ♠ 🛉 🍴 ✗ ⊙ 🗐 ∅ 🚿 ⚡ P ☎ ⊞ lau ♦ ✗ 🚿
⚡S Prices: A23 pitch 32

PONTAUBAULT *Manche*

Vallée de la Selune 7 r du Ml-Leclerc ☎33603900
Apr-20 Oct 10.3HEC ▦ 🍴 ♠ ⊙ 🗐 🏪 🚐 ☎ lau ♦ 🍴 ✗ ∅ 🚿 ⚡LS
⊞ Prices: A15 V9 ♦11 ▲11

PONT-AVEN *Finistère*

Domaine de Ker Lann Land Rosted ☎98060273
The site covers a large area, well wooded. Good leisure facilities.
Signposted from main road.
27 Apr-28 Sep 17HEC ▦ ♦ ♠ 🛉 🍴 ✗ ⊙ 🗐 ∅ 🚿 🏪 🚐 ⚡ P ☎ ⊞ lau

PONT-L'ABBÉ *Finistère*

Écureuil ☎98870339
3.5km NE
15 Jun-15 Sep 3HEC ▦ ♠ 🍴 ✗ ⊙ 🗐 ∅ 🚿 🏪 🚐 ☎ lau ♦ ⚡P

DOMAINE DE KERLANN
★★★★
PONT AVEN

With spacious, secluded pitches measuring at least
120m² in wooded parkland, Domaine de Kerlann is
an ideal base from which to explore southern
Brittany.
Children will have a great time too, with our free
Tiger Club for 4-12 year olds.
Facilities include: Swimming pool complex,
waterslide, tennis, volleyball, bar, restaurant,
takeaway, Tiger Tots crèche for 2-4 year olds.
Open 2nd May – 26th September.
Ferry inclusive packages available.
To obtain a brochure
call 0990 143 285
quoting FMA04.

PORDIC *Côtes-D'Armor*

Madières rte de Vau Madec ☎96790248
1500m from village on St-Brieuc road (D786).
Apr-Sep 3HEC ▦ ♦ ♠ 🛉 🍴 ✗ ⊙ 🗐 🏪 ☎ ⊞ lau ♦ ⚡S Prices:
A20 pitch 16

PORTBAIL *Manche*

Vieux Fort ☎33048199
Apr-Oct 4HEC ▦ ⦂⦂⦂ ﹄﹄ ♠ ⊙ 🗐 🏪 ☎ ⊞ ⊘ lau ♦ 🍴 ✗ ⚡S

PORT-MANECH *Finistère*

St-Nicolas ☎98068975
Divided into hedge-lined pitches.
May-Sep 3HEC ▦ 🍴 ♠ ⊙ 🗐 ☎ ⊞ lau ♦ 🛉 🍴 ✗ ∅ ⚡S Prices:
A20.50 pitch 22

POULDU, LE *Finistère*

Embruns r du Philosophe Alain ☎98399107
A pleasant site with good facilities and easy access to the beach.
Separate car park for arrivals after 22.00hrs.
Apr-20 Sep 4HEC ▦ 🍴 ♠ 🛉 🍴 ✗ ⊙ 🗐 ∅ 🚿 🏪 🚐 ⚡ P ☎ 🄿 ⊞ lau ♦
✗ ⚡RS Prices: A21.50 pitch 32.50

POURVILLE-SUR-MER *Seine-Maritime*

Marqueval rte de la Mer ☎35826646
15 Mar-Sep 8HEC ▦ 🍴 ♠ 🛉 🍴 ✗ ⊙ 🗐 ∅ 🏪 🚐 ⚡ PRS ☎ ⊞ lau

QUETTEHOU *Manche*

Rivage rte du Morsalines ☎33541376
Quiet, sheltered site, 400m from the sea.
Access via D14.
Apr-Oct 1.6HEC ▦ 🍴 ♠ ⊙ 🗐 ∅ 🚿 ☎ ⊞ lau ♦ 🛉 🍴 ✗ ⚡S

QUIBERON *Morbihan*

Bois d'Amour rte de la Pointe Conguel ☎97501352
1.5 km SE at La Pointe de la Presqu'île, 100m from beach.
29 Mar-28 Sep 4.5HEC ▦ ⦂⦂⦂ ﹄﹄ ♠ ✗ ⊙ 🗐 🏪 ⚡ P ☎ lau Prices:
A18-33 pitch 35-65

Conguel ☎97501911
Directly on the beach, with fine recreational facilities.
Near the aerodrome towards Pointe de Conguel.
Apr-Oct 5HEC ▦ 🍴 ♠ 🛉 🍴 ✗ ⊙ 🗐 🏪 ⚡ PS ☎ lau ♦ ∅ 🚿 Prices:
A19-38

QUIMPER *Finistère*

▮Orangerie de Lanniron Château de Lanniron ☎98906202
2.5km from town centre via D34.
15 May-15 Sep 17HEC ▦ 🍴 ♠ 🛉 🍴 ✗ ⊙ 🗐 ∅ 🚿 🏪 🚐 ⚡ P ☎ ⊞ lau
Prices: pitch 43-47

RAGUENÈS-PLAGE *Finistère*

Airotel International Raguenès-Plage 19 r des Iles ☎98068069
On field with good views. Asphalt drives; 400m from beaches.
Leave Pont-Aven and take the road to Nevez. At Nevez follow
directions to Raguenès.
Apr-Sep 5HEC ▦ ♦ 🍴 ♠ 🛉 🍴 ✗ ⊙ 🗐 ∅ 🚿 🏪 🚐 ⚡ PS ☎ ⊞ lau
Prices: pitch 38.40-48 (incl 2 persons)

RENNES *Ille-et-Vilaine*

CM Gayeulles r du Prof-M-Audin ☎99369122
NE via N12
Apr-Sep 2HEC ▦ ﹄﹄ ♠ ⊙ 🗐 ☎ ⊞ lau ♦ 🛉 🍴 ✗ ⚡P

RIEC-SUR-BÉLON *Finistère*

Château de Bélon Port de Bélon ☎98064143
Situated in wooded parkland by the sea with facilities for sailing and
fishing.
3.5km S
Mar-15 Nov 6HEC ▦ ♦ 🍴 ♠ 🛉 🍴 🍴 ⊙ 🗐 ∅ 🏪 ⚡ S ☎ ⊞ lau ♦ ✗

ROCHE-BERNARD, LA *Morbihan*

CM Patis 3 chemin du Patis ☎99906013
On banks of River Vilaine.
100m from village centre.
Etr-Sep ▦ 🍴 ♠ ⊙ 🗐 🚐 ☎ ⊞ lau ♦ 🛉 🍴 ✗

ROSTRENEN *Côtes-D'Armor*

Fleur de Bretagne Kerandouaron ☎96291645
1.5km from Rostrenen on D764 towards Pontivy.
Apr-Sep 1HEC ▦ ⌨ ♠ ♥ ✗ ⊙ ⊖ ⚑ ⌐ P ☎ lau ⟶ ⚡ ⚙ ♨ Prices: A14
pitch 25

ST-ALBAN *Côtes-D'Armor*

St-Vrêguet St-Vrêguet ☎96329021
A peaceful site in a pleasant park with good sanitary and recreational facilities.
15 Jun-30 Sep 1HEC ▦ ⌨ ♠ ♥ ⊙ ⊖ ⚑ ⚙ ♨ ⚠ ⊞ ⊞ lau ⟶ ⚡ ✗ ↻R
Prices: A16 pitch 9

ST-AUBIN-SUR-MER *Calvados*

Côte de Nacre 17 r du Major Moulton ☎31971445
A pleasant site with good recreational facilities. Reservations recommended in high season. Separate car park for arrivals after 22.00hrs.
Apr-Sep 6HEC ▦ ᵶ⌐ ♠ ⚡ ♥ ✗ ⊙ ⊖ ⚑ ⚙ ♨ ⌐ P ☎ ⊞ lau ⟶ ↻S Prices:
pitch 28-35 (incl 6 persons)

CM Mesnil ☎35830283
2 km W on D68.
Apr-Oct 2.2HEC ▦ ⌨ ♠ ♥ ⊙ ⊖ ⚑ ⊞ ⊞ lau ⟶ ♥ ✗ ⚙ ♨ ↻S Prices:
A21.80 pitch 15.10

ST-BRIEUC *Côtes-D'Armor*

Vallées Parc de Brézillet ☎96940505
Restaurant open July and August only.
All year 3.8HEC ▦ ♠ ♠ ⚡ ♥ ✗ ⊙ ⊖ ⚑ ⚙ ⌐ ⌐ ↻ PR ☎ ⊞ lau ⟶ ⚙
Prices: A13.60-17 pitch 36-45

ST-CAST-LE-GUILDO *Côtes-D'Armor*

Château de Galinée ☎96411056
1km from CD786. Well signposted.
Etr-15 Oct 14HEC ▦ ♠ ♠ ♥ ⚡ ♥ ⊙ ⊖ ⚑ ⚙ ♨ ⌐ ⌐ ↻ P ☎ lau ⟶ ✗ ⊞
Prices: A20-26 pitch 38-55

Châtelet r des Nouettes ☎96419633
In superb landscaped surroundings overlooking the sea with good sporting facilities.
1km W, 250m from the sea.
19 Apr-15 Sep 8.4HEC ▦ ♠ ♠ ⚡ ♥ ✗ ⊙ ⊖ ⚑ ♨ ⌐ ↻ LPS ☎ ⊞ lau ⟶
⚙ Prices: A22-28 pitch 74-96

ST-COULOMB *Ille-et-Vilaine*

Chevrets La Guimorais ☎99890190
On Lupin Bay near Chevrets beach.
3km NW.
Apr-Sep 10HEC ▦ ⠿ ᵶ⌐ ♠ ♥ ⚡ ♥ ✗ ⊙ ⊖ ⚑ ⚙ ⌐ ⌐ ↻ S ☎ ⊞ lau

ST-EFFLAM *Côtes-D'Armor*

CM r de l-Carré ☎96356215
Apr-Sep 4HEC ▦ ⌨ ♠ ♥ ✗ ⊙ ⊖ ⚑ ⌐ ⌐ lau ⟶ ⚡ ✗ ⚙ ↻S Prices:
A15 V8 ⚑20 ⚠20

STE-MARIE-DU-MONT *Manche*

Utah Beach ☎33715369
6km NE via D913 and D421, 150m from the beach
Apr-Sep 3HEC ⠿ ⌨ ♠ ♥ ⚡ ♥ ✗ ⊙ ⊖ ⚑ ⚙ ♨ ⌐ ⌐ ☎ ⊞ lau ⟶ ↻S
Prices: A21 pitch 28

STE-MARINE *Finistère*

Hellès ☎98563146
400m from the beach
15 Jun-15 Sep 3HEC ▦ ⌨ ♠ ⊙ ⊖ ⚑ ⚙ ⌐ ☎ lau ⟶ ♨ ↻RS Prices:
A14 pitch 17

STE-MÈRE-ÉGLISE *Manche*

Cormoran Ravenoville-Plage ☎33413394
A quiet site with well defined pitches, 20m from the sea.
Drive towards Ravenoville Plage, then take Utah Beach road for 500m.
Apr-Sep 6.5HEC ▦ ♠ ♠ ⚡ ♥ ✗ ⊙ ⊖ ⚑ ⚙ ♨ ⌐ ↻ P ☎ lau ⟶ ↻S
Prices: A19.20-24 pitch 24-30

ST-ÉVARZEC *Finistère*

Keromen ☎98562063
Children's playground and fishing facilities on site.
Jul-Aug 2HEC ▦ ⌨ ♠ ⊙ ⚑ ☎ ⊞ lau ⟶ ⚡ ♥ ✗ ⚙ ♨

ST-GERMAIN-SUR-AY *Manche*

Aux Grands Espaces ☎33071014
On slightly sloping ground among dunes. Children's play area.
Lunchtime siesta 12.30-14.30 hrs. 500m from sea.
Leave D650 W of town and follow signs 'Plage' on D306.
May-15 Sep 15HEC ▦ ⌨ ♠ ♥ ⚡ ♥ ⊙ ⊖ ⚑ ⚙ ♨ ⚠ ↻ P ☎ ⊞ lau
⟶ ↻S Prices: A21 pitch 28

ST-GILDAS-DE-RHUYS *Morbihan*

Menhir rte de Port Crouesty ☎97452288
3.5km N.
May-15 Sep 3HEC ▦ ♠ ♠ ⚡ ♥ ✗ ⊙ ⊖ ⚑ ⚙ ⌐ ↻ P ☎ ⊞ lau ⟶ ↻S
Prices: A28 pitch 80

ST-JOUAN-DES-GUÉRÊTS *Ille-et-Vilaine*

P'tit Bois ☎99211430
A pleasant family site in quiet surroundings.
Camping Card Compulsory.
Access via N137.
May-15 Sep 6HEC ▦ ⌨ ♠ ♥ ⚡ ♥ ✗ ⊙ ⊖ ⚑ ⚙ ♨ ⌐ ⌐ ⚠ ↻ P ☎ ⊞ lau ⟶
↻RS Prices: A26 pitch 40-80

ST-LÉGER-DU-BOURG-DENIS *Seine-Maritime*

Aubette 23 r Vert Buisson ☎35084769
All year 0.8HEC ▦ ⌨ ♠ ⊙ ⊖ ⚑ ⚙ ⌐ ☎ ⊞ lau ⟶ ⚡ ♥ ✗ ↻PR Prices:
A10 pitch 16

ST-LUNAIRE *Ille-et-Vilaine*

Longchamp bd de St Cast ☎99463398
Turn off D786 towards St-Briac at end of village, site is on left.
100m from the sea.
Jun-10 Sep 5HEC ▦ ♠ ♠ ⚡ ♥ ✗ ⊙ ⊖ ⚑ ⚙ ☎ ⊞ lau ⟶ ♨ ↻S Prices:
A23 V15 ⚑25 ⚠25

Toussе ☎99466113
2km E via D786, 300m from the beach
Apr-Sep 2.6HEC ▦ ⌨ ♠ ⚡ ♥ ✗ ⊙ ⊖ ⚑ ⚙ ⌐ ⌐ ⌐ ⊞ lau ⟶ ↻PS
Prices: A19-25 V14-18 ⚑26-32 ⚠26-32

ST-MALO *Ille-et-Vilaine*

CM le Nicet av de la Varde ☎99402632
100m from the beach; direct access via staicase.
Etr-Mid Sep 2.9HEC ▦ ᵶ⌐ ♠ ⊙ ⚑ ⊞ ⊞ lau ⟶ ⚡ ↻S

Ville Huchet rte de la Passagère ☎99811183
5km S via N137.
Etr-Sep 6HEC ▦ ♠ ♠ ⚡ ♥ ✗ ⊙ ⊖ ⚑ ⚠ ☎ ⊞ lau Prices: A14-16
pitch 14-16

ST-MARCAN *Ille-et-Vilaine*

Balcon de la Baie ☎99802295
10km NW of Pontorson on D797.
15 Jun-15 Sep 2.8HEC ▦ ⌨ ♠ ♥ ⚙ ⌐ ☎ ⊞ lau ⟶ ⚡ ♥ ✗ ♨
Prices: A16 pitch 8

ST-MARTIN-EN-CAMPAGNE *Seine-Maritime*

Goelands r des Grèbes ☎35838290
Site with good recreational facilities.
NE of Dieppe, 2km from D925.
All year 3HEC ▦ ⌨ ♠ ⊙ ⊖ ⚑ ⌐ ⌐ ☎ lau ⟶ ⚡ ♥ ✗ ⚙ ♨ ↻PS ⊞

ST-MICHEL-EN-GRÈVE *Côtes-D'Armor*

Capucines ☎96357228
On D786 Lannion-Morlaix road.
8 May-8 Sep 4HEC ▦ ⌨ ♠ ♥ ⚡ ♥ ✗ ⊙ ⊖ ⚑ ⚙ ♨ ⌐ ↻ P ☎ ⊞ ⊞ ⚙ lau ⟶
↻S Prices: A24-25 pitch 50-55

ST-PAIR-SUR-MER *Manche*

▶Château de Lez-Eaux St Aubin des Preaux ☎33516609
Situated in grounds of an old Château. Bank, TV and reading room.
Fishing available.

7km SE via D973 rte d'Avranches.
Apr-15 Sep 11HEC ▦ ⌂ ╔ ♥ ╳ ⊙ ◐ ⌀ ➰ ⚡ LP ☎ ⊞ lau Prices:
pitch 140-160 (incl 2 persons)

Ecutot ☎33502629
Situated in an orchard 1km from the sea.
Apr-Sep 3.5HEC ▦ ♦ ╔ ╚ ♥ ╳ ⊙ ◐ ➰ ⚡ P ☎ ⊞ lau ♦ ╚ ⌀ ⚡S

Mariénée ☎33500571
2km from sea; situated in grounds of old farm.
2km S of town on D21.
Etr-Sep 1.2HEC ▦ ⌂ ╔ ⊙ ◐ ☎ ⊞ lau ♦ ╚ ╚ ♥ ╳ ⌀ ⚡PS

ST-PHILIBERT-SUR-MER *Morbihan*
Vieux Logis ☎97550117
Beautiful, well-kept site divided by hedges.
2km W.
Etr-Sep 2.1HEC ▦ ⌂ ╔ ⊙ ◐ ☎ ⊞ lau ♦ ╚ ╚ ♥ ╳ ⌀ ⚡PRS
Prices: A21 V9 ⊞27

ST-PIERRE-DU-VAUVRAY *Eure*
St-Pierre 1 r du Château ☎32610155
All year 3HEC ▦ ⌂ ╔ ⊙ ◐ ☎ lau ♦ ╚ ╚ ♥ ╳ ⌀ ⚡ ⚡R Prices: A18
pitch 30

ST-PIERRE-QUIBERON *Morbihan*
Park-er-Lann ☎97502493
1.5km S on D768.
May-Sep 2.5HEC ▦ ⌂ ╔ ♥ ⊙ ◐ ➰ ➰ ☎ ⊞ lau ♦ ╚ ╳ ⚡S Prices: A22
pitch 32

ST-QUAY-PORTRIEUX *Côtes-D'Armor*
Bellevue 68 bd du Littoral ☎96704184
Site adjacent to the sea.
800m from town centre.
May-15 Sep 4HEC ▦ ⥾ ╔ ╚ ⊙ ◐ ⌀ ⚡ PS ☎ ⊞ lau ♦ ╚ ♥ ╳ Prices:
A19-21 pitch 27-32

ST-THURIAL *Ille-et-Vilaine*
Ker-Landes ☎99853995
The site is situated in the middle of pine trees near an old market
town.
200m W next to the lake.
All year 2HEC ▦ ⌂ ╔ ⊙ ◐ ⌀ ☎ ➰ ⊞ lau ♦ ╚ ╚ ♥ ╳ ⚡P

SARZEAU *Morbihan*
Treste rte de la Plage du Roaliguen ☎97417960
2.5km S
29 Apr-17 Sep 2.5HEC ▦ ⌂ ╔ ╚ ♥ ⊙ ◐ ⌀ ➰ ⚡ PS ☎ ⊞ lau ♦
╳ Prices: A19 pitch 39

At **PENVINS**(7km SE D198)
Madone Penvins ☎97673330
Situated 400m from the sea. Extensive sites on edge of village near
old country road. Divided into several sections.
Jun-15 Sep 6HEC ▦ ⌂ ╔ ╚ ♥ ╳ ⊙ ◐ ➰ ☎ ⊞ lau ♦ ╳ ⌀ ⚡ ⚡S
Prices: A18 pitch 45

At **POINTE-ST-JACQUES**(5.5km S)
CM St-Jacques ☎97417929
On beach protected by dunes. Well kept site with asphalt drives.
Apr-Oct 7.5HEC ▦ ⌂ ╔ ⊙ ◐ ➰ ☎ A ⚡ S ☎ lau ♦ ╚ ╚ ♥ ╳ ⌀ ⊞

SASSETOT-LE-MAUCONDUIT *Seine-Maritime*
Trois Plages ☎35274011
1.3km S near D925
15 Apr-15 Sep 4HEC ▦ ⌂ ╔ ╚ ♥ ⊙ ◐ ⌀ ☎ ⊞ lau ♦ ♥ ╳ ⚡S

TELGRUC-SUR-MER *Finistère*
Panoramic rte de la Plage ☎98277841
Quiet terraced site with views across a wide sandy beach. Secluded
pitches.
W on D887 and then S on D208.
15 May-15 Sep 4HEC ▦ ⌂ ╔ ╚ ♥ ╳ ⊙ ◐ ⌀ ➰ ⚡ P ☎ ⊞ lau
Prices: A23 pitch 50

THEIX *Morbihan*
Rhuys Le Poteau Rouge, Atlantheix ☎97541477
Directly on the sea, with good modern facilities.
3.5km NW via N165
Apr-1 Sep 4HEC ▦ ⥾ ╔ ⊙ ◐ ➰ ➰ ⚡ P ☎ ⊞ lau ♦ ╚ ♥ ╳ ⌀ ⚡
Prices: A18-21 pitch 25-41

THURY-HARCOURT *Calvados*
CM du Bord de l'Orne r du Val-d'Orne ☎31797078
1km W on D6 and D166 near river.
Etr-15 Oct ⌂ ╔ ⊙ ◐ ⌀ ⚡ R ☎ ⊞ lau ♦ ╚ ♥ ╳

Vallée du Traspy ☎31796180
Level meadow site near a small reservoir.
11 Apr-14 Sep 1.2HEC ⌂ ╔ ⊙ ◐ ⚡ ☎ ⊞ lau ♦ ╚ ╚ ♥ ╳ ⌀ ⚡
⚡R Prices: A23 pitch 23

TINTÉNIAC *Ille-et-Vilaine*
Peupliers ☎99454975
2km SE via N137
Mar-Oct 4.5HEC ▦ ♦ ╚ ╚ ♥ ╳ ⊙ ◐ ⌀ ➰ ➰ ⚡ P ☎ ⊞ lau Prices:
A18.50 pitch 26

TOLLEVAST *Manche*
Pins ☎33430078
From Cherbourg car ferry terminal follow N13 to the Auchout
Hypermarket and then continue for 200m for site on left-hand side of
the road.
All year 6HEC ⌂ ╔ ╔ ⊙ ◐ ➰ ➰ ➰ ⤳ lau ♦ ╳ ♥ ⌀ ⚡ ⚡R
Prices: A16 pitch 18

TOURLAVILLE *Manche*
Espace Loisirs de Collignon ☎33201688
A pleasant site with good facilities, 1km from town centre.
May-Sep 4HEC ♦ ╔ ╚ ⊙ ◐ ➰ ➰ ⌀ ☎ lau ♦ ♥ ╳ ╚ ⚡PS ⊞
Prices: A18 pitch 29

TOURNIÈRES *Calvados*
Picard Holidays ☎31228244
A quiet site with pleasant, sheltered pitches conveniently situated
between Cherbourg and Caen.
Access via N13 and D15/D5.
All year 2.5HEC ⌂ ╔ ⊙ ◐ ➰ ⚡ LP ☎ ⤳ ♦ ╚ ╚ ♥ ╳ ⌀ ╚ ⊞

TRÉBEURDEN *Côtes-D'Armor*
Armor-Loisirs rte de Pors Mabo ☎96235231
Modern site with individual pitches surrounded by hedges.
Hardstandings for caravans.
500m S of the Kernévez road.
24 May-7 Sep 2.2HEC ⌂ ╔ ♥ ╳ ⊙ ◐ ⌀ ➰ ☎ ⊞ ⤳ lau ♦ ╚
⚡S Prices: A19 V11 ⊞19 ▲19

TREGUNC *Finistère*
Pendruc ☎98976628
On level grassland subdivided by hedging. Separate section for
young campers.
Access via D783 at Pont-Minaouët S in direction of Plage de Penduc.
May-Sep 3.6HEC ▦ ⌂ ╔ ╚ ⊙ ◐ ⌀ ➰ ⚡ P ☎ ⊞ lau ♦ ♥ ╳ ⚡S

Pommeraie St-Philibert ☎98500273
Apr-15 Sep 7HEC ▦ ⌂ ╔ ╚ ♥ ╳ ⊙ ◐ ╚ ➰ ➰ ⚡ P ☎ ⊞ lau ♦ ⌀
Prices: A15-23 pitch 24-37
See advertisement on page 130.

TRÉLÉVERN *Côtes-D'Armor*
Port l'Epine Pors-Garo ☎96237194
Well shaded site directly on the sea.
Apr-15 Oct 4HEC ⌂ ╔ ╚ ♥ ╳ ⊙ ◐ ⌀ ➰ ⚡ PS ☎ ⊞ lau ♦ ╚
Prices: pitch 60-90 (incl 2 persons)

TRÉPORT, LE *Seine-Maritime*
CM les Boucaniers r Mendes-France ☎35863547
Well-kept site on flat meadow on E edge of village. Sports and
games nearby.
Apr-Sep 5.5HEC ▦ ⥾ ╔ ⊙ ◐ ➰ ☎ ⊞ lau ♦ ╚ ╚ ♥ ╳ ⌀ ⚡ ⚡PRS
Prices: A13-14 pitch 12.60

Camping LA POMMERAIE ★★★
St. Philibert – F-29910 Trégunc
Tel: 02.98.50.02.73 Fax: 02.98.50.07.91

In the middle of flowers and trees, between sea and countryside, 1200 m of fine sandy beaches, Marthe and Gerard welcome you to their site from April until September. Swimming pool paddling pool – children's playground – self-service – take-away – bar, games – TV – bicycle hire – sport and music events – service station for motor caravans – Mobile homes and caravans to let – many possibilities for leisure activities close to the site – special prices off season – possibility to rent a mobile home per night off season

---

Parc International du Golf rte de Dieppe ☎35863380
In a park on the cliffs.
1km W on D940.
Apr-Sep 5HEC ▦ ⊞ ⋔ ⅃ ▼ ⨯ ⊙ ⬤ ∅ ⌂ ⊞ lau ➡ ✗ ⭨PS Prices: pitch 60-84 (incl 2 persons)

At **MESNIL-VAL**

Parc Val d'Albion 1 r de la Mer ☎35862142
Terraced site in wooded parkland next to the sea.
3 km S from Le Tréport on D126.
Jun-15 Sep 3HEC ▦ ⋔ ⊙ ⌂ ⊞ lau ➡ ⅃ ▼ ✗ ∅ ⭨S Prices: pitch 60-84 (incl 2 persons)

TRÉVOU-TRÉGUIGNEC *Côtes-D'Armor*

Mât 38 r de Trestel ☎96237152
50m from beach.
>01>Access via D38.
Jun-15 Sep 1.6HEC ▦ ⊞ ⋔ ✗ ⊙ ⬤ ∅ ⌂ ⊞ lau Prices: A23 pitch 32

TRINITÉ-SUR-MER, LA *Morbihan*

Baie Plage de Kervilen ☎97557342
Several strips of land divided by tall trees.
Signposted in the direction of Kerbihan.
15 May-15 Sep 2.4HEC ▦ ⊞ ⋔ ⅃ ▼ ⨯ ⊙ ⬤ ∅ ⭨ PS ⌂ ⊞ lau ➡ ⌁ Prices: A15-22 pitch 60-115

Kervilor ☎97557675
Camping Card Compulsory.
1.6km N
15 May-15 Sep 4.5HEC ▦ ⊞ ⋔ ⅃ ▼ ⨯ ⊙ ⬤ ∅ ⭨P ⌂ ⊞ lau ➡ ✗ ⌁ ⭨S Prices: A18-24 pitch 42-56

Plage Plage de Kervilen ☎97557328
Divided into pitches and lying behind sand dunes which shield from the wind.
1km S.
8 May-14 Sep 3HEC ▦ ⊞ ⋔ ⊙ ⬤ ⬛ ⭨ PS ⌂ ⊞ lau ➡ ⅃ ▼ ✗ ∅
Prices: A21 pitch 49-99

VEULES-LES-ROSES *Seine-Maritime*

Mouettes av J-Moulin ☎35976198
Mar-Nov 1.5HEC ▦ ⇘ ⋔ ⊙ ⬤ ⌂ ⊞ lau ➡ ⅃ ▼ ✗ ∅ ⌁ ⭨RS
Prices: A13.60 pitch 10.80

Paradis chemin de Manneville ☎35976142
mid May-mid Sep 0.9HEC ▦ ⊞ ⋔ ⊙ ⬤ ⌂ ⊞ lau ➡ ⅃ ▼ ✗ ∅ ⌁ ⭨RS
Prices: A11.25 pitch 5.90

VILLERS-SUR-MER *Calvados*

Ammonites rte de la Corniche ☎31870606
4km SW on rte de Cabourg and D163 towards Auberville.
Apr-15 Oct 2.6HEC ▦ ⣿ ⇘ ⋔ ⅃ ▼ ✗ ⊙ ⬤ ∅ ⌁ ⬛ ⬤ ⭨ PS ⌂ ⊞ lau Prices: pitch 125 (incl 2 persons)

Paris/North

The chalk cliffs and sands of the northern coast give way to the two beautiful regions of Picardy and Nord-Pas-de-Calais. Here quiet country roads meander through green wooded valleys and rolling farmland. The area has a wealth of neolithic sites, cathedrals, castles, abbeys, mansions and museums. Lille is an important centre for northern France, with its commercial and industrial interests, and has a bustling cosmopolitan centre. Amiens is the ancient capital of Picardy, and its remarkable 12th-century Cathedral of Notre Dame is one of the finest in France. The Île de France, known as the garden of Paris, is a delightful region of famous palaces, parklands, forests and attractive little towns. Visit Fontainbleau, the town of kings and emperors, with its famous palace, and the dazzling palace and grounds at Versailles.

Paris has a wealth of things to do and see - rivalling any other city in the world. Visitors can choose from the traditional rich treasures of the Louvre or the ultra modern exhibits and setting of the Pompidou Centre, immerse themselves in Parisian life along the banks of the Seine or view it from the giddy heights of Monsieur Eiffel's famous tower, discover the wonderful wide spaces of the Trocadero, the Champ de Mars and the Champs Élysées or the buzzing streets of the city's famous districts - Montmartre and Marais. And night life , too, is for all tastes, with everything from the sophisticated entertainment of the Lido, to a small quiet restaurant on the Left Bank.

ABBEVILLE *Somme*

At **PORT-LE-GRAND**(5km NW)

Airotels Château des Tilleuls ☎22240775
On gently sloping meadow surrounding a farm.
1 km SE on D940A.
Mar-Nov 4.5HEC ⊞ ⇘ ⋔ ⅃ ▼ ✗ ⊙ ⬤ ∅ ⬛ ⬤ ⡈ ⭨ P ⌂ ⊞ lau Prices: A21 V8 ⬤30 ⡈30

ARDRES *Pas-de-Calais*

At **AUTINGUES**(2km S)

St-Louis 223 r Leulène ☎21354683
Turn off N43 approx 1km SE of Ardres onto D224 and follow signs.
Mar-Oct 1.7HEC ▦ ⊞ ⋔ ⊙ ⬤ ⬤ ⡈ ⌂ ⊞ lau ➡ ∅ ⌁ ⭨LP Prices: A13 pitch 14

ATTICHY *Oise*

CM ☎44421597
On SE outskirts near the swimming pool and the river.
All year 1.5HEC ▦ ⊞ ⋔ ⊙ ⬤ ⭨ L ⌂ lau ➡ ⅃ ▼ ✗ ⭨P Prices: A8.50-13 pitch 4.25-9

AUDRUICQ *Pas-de-Calais*

CM Les Pyramides ☎21355917
A site with good sanitary and sports facilities beside the canal.
Apr-Sep ▦ ⊞ ⋔ ⊙ ⬤ ⌂ ⬤ ⊞ lau ➡ ⅃ ▼ ✗ ∅ ⌁ Prices: pitch 32 (incl 2 persons)

BEAURAINVILLE *Pas-de-Calais*

CM de la Source ☎21814071
Camping Card Compulsory.
1.5km SE via D130
All year 2.5HEC ▦ ⊞ ⋔ ⊙ ⬤ ⬛ ⬤ ⭨ R ⌂ ⊞ lau ➡ ⅃ ▼ ✗

BEAUVAIS *Oise*

Clos Normand 1 r de l'Abbaye, St-Paul ☎44822730
6km W via N31 towards Rouen.
All year 2.5HEC ▦ ⊞ ⋔ ✗ ⊙ ⬤ ∅ ⌁ ⬤ ⌂ ⊞ lau ➡ ▼

BERCK-SUR-MER *Pas-de-Calais*

Orée du Bois chemin Blanc 251, Rang-du-Fliers ☎21842851
A modern site in wooded surroundings with good sports facilities.
2km NE.
29 Mar-5 Oct 18HEC ▦ ⊞ ⋔ ▼ ✗ ⊙ ⬤ ⌁ ⬤ ⡈ ▲ ⌂ ⊞ lau ➡ ⅃ ∅
Prices: pitch 67-95 (incl 2 persons)

BERNY-RIVIÈRE *Aisne*
Croix du Vieux Pont ☎23555002
North of N31; cross River Aisne, site is 500m E of Vic-sur-Aisne on D91.
All year 19HEC ▬ 🔌 🔦 🏊 🍴 ✕ ⊙ 🅿 🗑 🛒 ⚓ ⚡ P 🔟 ⊞ lau Prices: pitch 100 (incl 2 persons)

BERTANGLES *Somme*
Château ☎22933773
Site in old orchard of Château.
Signed off Amiens-Doullens road.
25 Apr-8 Sep 0.8HEC ▬ 🔌 🔦 ⊙ 🅿 ⚓ 🔟 lau Prices: A15 V10 ⬜15 ▲15

BEUVRY *Pas-Dee-Calais*
CM r V-Dutériez ☎21650800
Apr-Oct 1HEC ▬ ➤ 🔦 ✕ ⊙ 🅿 ⚓ ⊞ lau ➤ 🏊 ✕ ∅ 🍴 ⚡P Prices: A12 pitch 16

BOUBERS-SUR-CANCHE *Pas-de-Calais*
Flore 27 rte de Frévent ☎21036576
E via D340 towards Frévent.
Apr-Oct 1HEC ▬ 🔌 🔦 ⊙ 🅿 ⚓ 🔟 ⊞ ➤ ✕ ∅ 🍴 ⚡R

BOULANCOURT *Seine-et-Marne*
Ile de Boulancourt 6 allée des Marronnièrs ☎64241338
In a convenient situation in the Essonne valley.
Access via D410.
All year 5HEC ▬ 🔌 🔦 ⊙ 🅿 🛒 🏫 ⚡ R 🔟 ⊞ lau ➤ 🏊 🍴 ✕ ∅ 🍴 ⚡P
Prices: A14 pitch 20

BRAY-DUNES *Nord*
Perroquet-Plage ☎28583737
3km NE towards La Panne.
Apr-Sep 28HEC ▬ ░ 🔌 🔦 🏊 🍴 ✕ ⊙ 🅿 ∅ 🍴 🏫 🗑 ⊞ lau
Prices: A29 V10 ⬜14 ▲10

CALAIS *Pas-de-Calais*
Peupliers 394 r du Beau Marais ☎21340356
All year 1.4HEC ▬ 🔌 🔦 🏊 ✕ ⊙ 🅿 ⚓ 🔟 ⊞ lau ➤ ✕ ∅ ⚡PRS

CAYEUX-SUR-MER *Somme*
Voyeul rte des Canadiens ☎22266084
1.5km S on D140.
Apr-15 Oct 1.7HEC ▬ 🔌 🔦 🏊 🍴 ⊙ 🅿 ∅ 🍴 🔟 ⊞ lau ➤ ✕ ⚡S Prices: A11 pitch 11

CHAMOUILLE *Aisne*
Parc de l'Ailette Parc Nautique de l'Ailette ☎23248306
On the shore of a lake within an extensive leisure park and nature reserve.
2km SE via D19.
Apr-Sep 6HEC ▬ ➤ 🔦 🏊 🍴 ⊙ 🅿 ∅ 🔟 ⊞ lau ➤ 🍴 ✕ ⚡L

CONDETTE *Pas-de-Calais*
Château 21 r Nouvelle ☎21875959
Separate car park for arrivals after 23.00hrs.
Access via D940 towards Hardelot.
Apr-Oct 1.2HEC ▬ 🔌 🔦 ⊙ 🅿 🛒 🔟 ⊞ lau ➤ 🏊 🍴 ✕ ∅ 🍴 ⚡L Prices: pitch 58-78 (incl 2 persons)

COUDEKERQUE *Nord*
Bois des Forts Chem departemetal 72 ☎28610441
0.7km NW on D72.
All year 3HEC ▬ 🔦 🍴 ✕ ⊙ 🅿 🛒 🏫 ⊞ lau ➤ 🏊 ∅ ⚡LPRS

DUNKERQUE (DUNKIRK) *Nord*
CM bd de l'Europe ☎28692668
Mar-Nov 10HEC ▬ 🔌 🔦 🍴 ✕ ⊙ 🅿 ∅ 🍴 ⚡ P 🔟 ⊞ lau ➤ 🏊 ⚡LS

ÉPERLECQUES *Pas-de-Calais*
Château de Gandspette ☎21934393
A peaceful site, surrounded by woodland.
11.5km NW on N43 and D207.
Apr-Sep 8HEC ▬ 🔌 🔦 🏊 ✕ ⊙ 🅿 ∅ ⚡ P 🔟 ⊞ lau ➤ 🏊 Prices: pitch 95 (incl 2 persons)

EPISY *Seine-et-Marne*
Peupliers rte de Sorques ☎64458000
0.9km NW via D148 beside the Loing.
All year 4HEC ▬ 🔌 🔦 ⊙ 🅿 ∅ 🍴 ⚡ R 🔟 ⊞ lau ➤ 🏊 ✕

ESCALLES *Pas-de-Calais*
Cap Blanc Nez r de la Mer ☎21852738
500m from the beach.
Apr-Nov 1.5HEC ▬ 🔌 🔦 🏊 🍴 ✕ ⊙ 🅿 ∅ 🍴 ⊞ lau ➤ ⚡S Prices: A12.50 pitch 13.50

ÉTAMPES *Essonne*
Vauvert Ormoy La Rivière ☎64942139
In a pleasant situation beside the river.
Closed 15 Dec-15 Jan 11HEC ▬ ░ ➤ 🔦 🍴 ✕ ⊙ 🅿 ∅ 🍴 ⚡ R 🔟 ⊞ lau

FELLERIES *Nord*
CM La Boisellerie r de la Place ☎27590650
15 Apr-Sep 1HEC ▬ 🔌 🔦 ⊙ 🅿 ⚓ ➤ 🏊 ✕ ∅ 🍴 ⊞ Prices: A11 V4 ⬜4 ▲4

FERTÉ-GAUCHER, LA *Seine-et-Marne*
Joël Teinturier rte de St-Martin-des-Camps ☎64202040
E via D14
All year 4HEC ▬ ➤ 🔌 🔦 ⊙ 🅿 ⚡ R 🔟 ⊞ lau ➤ 🏊 🍴 ✕ ∅ ⚡P

FERTÉ-SOUS-JOUARRE, LA *Seine-et-Marne*
Bondons 47/49 r des Bondons ☎60220098
Reserved for caravans.
2km NE via D402 & D70.
All year 10HEC ▬ ➤ 🔦 ⊙ 🅿 ⊞ lau ➤ 🏊 🍴 ✕ ⚡P

FILLIÈVRES *Pas-de-Calais*
Trois Tilleuls ☎21479415
Apr-1 Oct 2.5HEC ▬ ➤ 🔦 ⊙ 🅿 🔟 ⊞ lau ➤ 🏊 🍴 ✕ 🍴 ⚡R

FORT-MAHON-PLAGE *Somme*
Royon rte du Quend ☎22234030
Mar-Oct 4HEC ▬ 🔌 🔦 🏊 🍴 ✕ ⊙ 🅿 ∅ 🍴 🏫 🗑 ⊞ lau ➤ ✕ ⚡PS
Prices: pitch 95-105 (incl 3 persons)

FRIAUCOURT *Somme*
CM Au Chant des Oiseaux Ruelle du Grand Patis ☎22264954
In pleasant surroundings with good sanitary and sporting facilities.
NE via D63.
Apr-15 Oct 1.4HEC ▬ ➤ 🔦 ⊙ 🅿 🏫 🗑 ⊘ lau

GRAND-FORT-PHILIPPE *Nord*
CM de la Plage r Ml-Foch ☎28653195
Apr-Oct 1.5HEC ▬ 🔌 🔦 ⊙ 🅿 ⚓ lau ➤ 🏊 🍴 ✕ ∅ 🍴 ⊞

GREZ-SUR-LOING *Seine-et-Marne*
CM Près chemin des Près ☎64457275
NE towards Loing
20 Mar-11 Nov 6HEC ▬ 🔌 🔦 ⊙ 🅿 ⚓ lau ➤ 🏊 🍴 ✕ ∅ ⚡R ⊞ Prices:
A13 V8 ⬜13 ▲9

GUINES *Pas-de-Calais*
Bien Assise CD 231 ☎21352077
A nice site in the country near to a large forest and a charming little town.
Access via D231 towards Marquise.
25 Apr-25 Sep 15HEC ▬ 🔌 🔦 🏊 🍴 ✕ ⊙ 🅿 ∅ 🏫 🗑 ⚡ P 🔟 ⊞ lau
Prices: A23 pitch 56

GUISE *Aisne*
Vallée de l'Oise r du Camping ☎23611486
1km SE on D960.
Apr-20 Oct 3.5HEC ▬ 🔌 🔦 ⊙ 🅿 ∅ 🏫 🗑 🔟 ⊞ ➤ 🏊 ✕ 🍴 ⚡R

HIRSON *Aisne*
Cascade ☎23580391
1.8km N via N43 towards La Capelle.
20 Apr-20 Sep 1.6HEC ▬ 🔌 🔦 ⊙ 🅿 ∅ 🗑 ⚡ P 🔟 ⊞ lau ➤ 🍴 Prices:
A8 pitch 6

HOUDAIN *Pas-de-Calais*

Parc d'Olhain Parc d'Olhain ☎21279480
Situated in an extensive leisure park on the edge of a forest.
1.5 km S.
15 Apr-15 Sep 1HEC ▦ ᴊ↙ ♠ ☎ ♥ ⊙ 🖵 🖉 ☎ ⊞ lau ♦ ⊀P

ISQUES *Pas-de-Calais*

Cytises r de l'Église ☎0321311110
4km S of Boulogne-sur-Mer towards Abbeville, 100m from N1.,
Apr-15 Oct 2.5HEC ▦ ᴓ♠ ♥ ✕ ⊙ 🖵 🖵 ⊀ R ☎ ⊞ lau ♦ ☎ 🖉 ᴛ
Prices: A15.80-17.50 🚐15.80-17.50

LAON *Aisne*

CM allée de la Chênaie ☎23202556
Apr-Oct 3.3HEC ▦ ∷∵ ᴓ ♠ ⊙ 🖵 ☎ lau Prices: A14 pitch 8.50

LICQUES *Pas-de-Calais*

Canchy r de Canchy ☎21826341
15 Mar-Oct 1HEC ▦ ᴓ ♠ ♥ ♥ ⊙ 🖵 🖉 🖵 ⊀ R ☎ ⊞ lau ♦ ✕

LYNDE *Nord*

Becquerelle r du Becquerelle ☎28432037
Mar-Nov 1.5HEC ▦ ᴓ ♠ ♥ ⊙ 🖵 🖵 ☎ ⊞ lau ♦ 🖉 ᴛ Prices: A10 pitch 10

MAISONS-LAFFITTE *Yvelines*

Parc Montana Laffitte 1 r Johnson ☎39122191
A well-kept site in a residential area on the banks of the Seine.
Modern installations, heated in cold weather.
For access, 8 km N of St-Germain-en-Laye; alternatively follow N308
from Porte Champerret or from Colombos-Ouest exit of Autoroute
A86.
All year 7HEC ▦ ♦♠☎ 🖵 ♥ ✕ ⊙ 🖵 🖉 🖵 ᴀ ⊀ R ☎ ⊞ ⊘ lau ♦ ᴛ ⊀P
Prices: pitch 100-130 (incl 2 persons)

MAMETZ *Pas-de-Calais*

Château de Mametz 32 r du Moulin
All year 11HEC ▦ ᴓ♠ ♥ ✕ ⊙ 🖵 🖉 ᴛ ⊀ R ☎ ⊞ lau ♦ 🖵 ⊀LPS

MARNE-LA-VALLÉE *Seine-et-Marne*

🔊Davy Crockett Ranch ☎60456900
A modern site in wooded surroundings near the Disneyland Paris
complex.
Access via A4 Serris exit (no 13).
All year ♦♠☎ 🖵 ♥ ✕ ⊙ 🖵 🖉 ☎ ⊀ P ☎ ⊞ ⊘ lau

MAUBEUGE *Nord*

CM rte de Mons ☎27622548
1.5km N via N2 (Bruxelles road).
All year 2.1HEC ▦ ᴓ ♠ ⊙ 🖵 🖵 ☎ ⊞ lau ♦ 🖵 ✕ 🖉 ᴛ Prices: pitch 18

MELUN *Seine-et-Marne*

Belle Étoile Quai Joffre ☎64394812
Pleasant grassy site with two central blocks.
At La Rochette, on left bank of River Seine 1km from the town.
Apr-Oct 3.5HEC ▦ ᴓ ♠ 🖵 ♥ ✕ ⊙ 🖵 🖉 ᴛ ☎ ⊞ lau ♦ ⊀P Prices:
A22 pitch 21

MERLIMONT *Pas-de-Calais*

Parc Résidentiel du Château St-Hubert ☎21891010
3km S via D940, near Parc de Bagatelle.
Apr-11 Nov 16HEC ▦ ᴓ ♠ 🖵 ♥ ✕ ⊙ 🖵 🖉 ⊀ P ☎ ⊞ lau

MILLY-LA-FORÊT *Essonne*

Musardière rte des Grandes Vallées ☎64989191
In pleasant wooded surroundings.
4km SE via D948.
Closed 15 Dec-15 Feb 12HEC ▦ ∷∵ ᴓ ♠ ⊙ 🖵 ☎ ⊞ Prices: A25
V12 🚐26 ▲12

MONNERVILLE *Essonne*

Bois de la Justice ☎64950534
Pitches separated by trees and hedges.
N20 Orléans to Étampes.
Mar-Nov 5HEC ▦ ᴓ ♠ ♥ ⊙ 🖵 🖉 ᴛ ⊀ P ☎ ⊞ lau ♦ 🖵

MONTIGNY-LE-BRETONNEUX *Yvelines*

Parc Étang Base de Loisirs-de-St Quentin ☎30585620
In beautiful rural surroundings within a leisure centre with easy
access to Paris and Versailles.
All year 12HEC ▦ ∷∷ ♦♠☎ 🖵 ♥ ✕ ⊙ 🖵 🖉 🖵 ⊀ P ☎ ⊞ lau ♦ ⊀P

MONTREUIL-SUR-MER *Pas-de-Calais*

CM ☎21060728
N of town on N1.
All year 2HEC ▦ ᴓ ♠ ⊙ 🖵 ⊀ R ☎ ⊞ lau Prices:
pitch 24-36 (incl 2 persons)

MOYENNEVILLE *Somme*

Val de Trie Bouillancourt-sous-Miannay ☎22314888
A small site with good facilities including a lake for fishing.
1km from the D925 (Abbeville-Le Tréport).
Apr-Oct 2.6HEC ▦ ♦♠☎ 🖵 ♥ ⊙ 🖵 🖉 ⊀ P ☎ ⊞ lau ♦ ♥ ✕ 🖵 Prices:
A17-18 pitch 14-15

NEMOURS *Seine-et-Marne*

ACCCF rte nationale 7 ☎64281062
On well-kept meadow. Clean sanitary installations.
200m from N7.
Mar-Oct 4HEC ▦ ᴊ↙ ♠ ⊙ 🖵 🖉 ᴛ ⊀ R ☎ ⊞ lau ♦ 🖵 ♥ ✕

NESLES-LA-VALLÉE *Val-D'Oise*

Parc de Séjour de l'Étang 10 chemin des Belles Vues
☎34706289
Level area near a small lake.
A15 exit 10, then D927 and D79. From N1 take exit for L'Isle Adam.
Mar-Oct 6HEC ▦ ᴓ ♠ ⊙ 🖵 🖵 lau ♦ 🖵 ♥ ✕ 🖉 ᴛ ⊞ Prices: A17-24
pitch 17-24

NEUVILLE, LA *Nord*

Leu Pindu ☎20865087
N on D8.
All year 1.2HEC ▦ ♦♠☎ 🖵 ♥ ⊙ 🖵 🖵 ☎ ⊞ lau ♦ 🖵 🖉 🖵

ORVILLERS-SOREL *Oise*

Sorel ☎44850274
Divided into pitches. Local tradesmen supply provisions.
Leave A1 at N17, turn right and continue 400m.
Feb-15 Dec 3HEC ▦ ᴓ ♠ 🖵 ✕ ⊙ 🖵 🖉 ᴛ 🖵 ▲ ☎ ⊞ lau Prices:
pitch 61 (incl 2 persons)

OYE-PLAGE *Pas-de-Calais*

Oyats 272 Digue Vert ☎28646920
4.5km NW directly on the beach.
15 May-Sep 3HEC ▦ ᴓ ♠ 🖵 ✕ ⊙ 🖵 ☎ ⊞ lau Prices: A22 pitch 25

PARIS

Bois de Boulogne 2 allée du Bord de l'Eau ☎45243000
This site beside the River Seine has undergone recent renervation.
Much of its popularity stems from its location close to the city centre
and it can become crowded during high season as it is the only site
actually in Paris.
All year 7HEC ▦ ♦♠☎ 🖵 ✕ ⊙ 🖵 🖉 🖵 🖵 ☎ ⊞ lau ♦ ⊀P Prices: pitch
62-127 (incl 2 persons)
See advertisement under CHOISY-LE-ROI

At CHAMPIGNY-SUR-MARNE(12km SE)

Tremblay bd des Alliés ☎43974397
Site tends to become full during peak season. Good transportation
into city and well placed for visiting Disneyland Paris.
*Reserved mainly for International Camping Card
holders.*
Take N4 and turn left 350m after Joinville bridge.
All year 8HEC ▦ ᴓ ♠ 🖵 ✕ ⊙ 🖵 🖉 ☎ ⊞ lau ♦ 🖵 ⊀P Prices:
pitch 78-115 (incl 2 persons)
See advertisement under CHOISY-LE-ROI

At CHOISY-LE-ROI(14km SE)

Paris Sud 125 av de V-St-Georges ☎48909230
Signposted.

All year 9HEC ▦ ⬚⬚⬚⬚⬚⬚⬚⬚⬚⬚⬚⬚⬚ lau ➜ ⤸LPR Prices: pitch 90-118 (incl 2 persons)

POIX-DE-PICARDIE *Somme*

Bois des Pêcheurs ☎22901171
In a quiet riverside location with a high standard of sanitary facilities.W via D919 towards Forges-les-Eaux
Apr-Sep 2.4HEC ▦ ⬚⬚⬚⬚⬚⬚⬚⬚⬚ lau ➜ ⬚⬚⬚⤸PR

POTELLE *Nord*

Pré Vert ☎27491987
Apr-Sep 2HEC ▦ ⬚⬚⬚⬚⬚⬚⬚⬚ lau ➜✗⬚

PRESLES-VAILLY-SUR-AISNE *Aisne*

Domaine de la Nature ☎23547455
4km W via D144 near the canal and lake.
All year 3HEC ▦ ⬚⬚⬚⬚⬚⬚⬚⬚⬚⬚⬚ lau ➜⬚✗⤸LR
Prices: pitch 63-83 (incl 2 persons)

PROYART *Somme*

Loisir la Violette rte de Mericourt ☎22858136
Mar-1 Nov 1.6HEC ▦ ⬚⬚⬚⬚⬚⬚⬚⬚ lau ➜⬚✗⬚⤸P
Prices: A9 V5 ⬚6 ▲6

QUEND-PLAGE-LES-PINS *Somme*

At **MONCHAUX-LES-QUEND**(3.5km E via D102E)

Roses ☎22277617
Well-kept site with trees and hedges surrounding individual pitches. Only recommended site in area.
Turn off D940 at Quend, site 500m on left of D102.
15 Mar-Oct 9HEC ▦ ⬚⬚⬚✗⬚⬚⬚⬚⬚ lau ➜⬚⬚ Prices: pitch 70 (incl 3 persons)

RAMBOUILLET *Yvelines*

CM de l'Étang d'Or r du Château d'Eau ☎30410734
In a pleasant situation. Shop, bar etc only open Jun-Aug.

From railway station follow road SE for 1.3km passing Camping Pont Hardy.
All year 5HEC ▦ ⬚⬚⬚⬚⬚⬚⬚⬚⬚⬚ lau ➜⬚⤸P

RUE *Somme*

Garenne de Moncourt ☎22250693
On D85 towards Montreuil-sur-Mer.
All year 3HEC ▦ ⬚⬚⬚⬚⬚⤸P⬚⬚ lau ➜⬚⬚✗

ST-AMAND-LES-EAUX *Nord*

Mont des Bruyères ☎27485687
3.5km SE in the forest of St-Amand
Mar-Nov 4.5HEC ▦ ⬚⬚⬚⬚⬚⬚⬚⬚⬚⬚⬚⬚ lau ➜✗⤸PR

ST-CHÉRON *Essonne*

Parc des Roches La Petite Beauce ☎64566550
In a wooded park.
Mar-14 Oct 23HEC ▦ ⬚⬚⬚⬚✗⬚⬚⬚⤸P⬚⬚➜⬚ Prices: A31 V13 ⬚25 ▲25

ILE DE FRANCE 40 km south of Paris
Between ARPAJON and DOURDAN

CAMPING PARC DES ROCHES

91530 SAINT CHÉRON

Tel: 01 64 56 65 50   Fax: 01 64 56 54 50

Situated in a picturesque and woody setting of 23 ha,
40 km south of Paris. **Le Parc des Roches** (3 stars) is
ideally situated for visits to Paris and surroundings
(station 3 km, autoroute A6, A10 and RN20).

TENNIS • SWIMMING POOL • SOLARIUM •
BAR • RESTAURANT • LAUNDRY • SANITARY
INSTALLATIONS FOR DISABLED

Open: 1/3 – 14/12.

ST-CYR-SUR-MORIN *Seine-et-Marne*

Choisel rte de Rebais ☎60238493
In a pleasant situation. Separate carpark for arrivals after
22.00hrs.2km W via D31.
Mar-Nov 3.5HEC ▦ ⊞ ♠ ฿ ♈ ✕ ⊙ ⊘ ⊿ ⊞ ≛ ⊞ lau ♦ ฿ ✕

ST-JANS-CAPPEL *Nord*

Domaine de la Sablière Le Mont Noir ☎28494634
3.5km NE via D10 and D318.
Apr-Oct 3.6HEC ▦ ⊞ ♠ ฿ ♈ ✕ ⊙ ⊘ ⊿ ⊞ ≛ ⊞ lau ♦ ฿ ✕ ₹P

ST-LEU-D'ESSERENT *Oise*

Campix ☎44560848
In wooded surroundings, within easy reach of Chantilly.
3.5km NE via D12.
07 Mar-1 Dec 6HEC ▦ ⫶⫶⫶ ♠ ♠ ⊙ ⊘ ⊘ ⊞ lau ♦ ฿ ฿ ✕ ₹L

ST-QUENTIN *Aisne*

CM bd J-Bouin ☎23626866
A good site in pleasant wooded surroundings near the canal.
Mar-Nov 1HEC ▦ ⫶⫶⫶ ⊞ ♠ ⊘ ≛ ♦ ฿ ฿ ✕ ⊘ ⊿ ₹LPR ⊞ Prices: A7
V3.70 ♣4.60 ▲3.90

ST-VALÉRY-SUR-SOMME *Somme*

⛺Domaine du Château de Drancourt ☎22269345
In open countryside, surrounded by woods, fields and lakes
,surrounding a former hunting lodge.
3.5km S via D48
Etr-Sep 5HEC ▦ ⊞ ♠ ฿ ฿ ✕ ⊙ ⊘ ⊿ ⊿ ₹ P ≛ lau ♦ ₹L Prices:
A28 pitch 44

SALENCY *Oise*

Étang du Moulin 54 r du Moulin ☎44099981
All year 0.4HEC ▦ ⊞ ♠ ฿ ♈ ⊘ ⊿ ≛ ♦ ฿ ✕ ⊞ Prices: A8.50 V11
♣16 ▲16

SAMOIS-SUR-SEINE *Seine-et-Marne*

Samois rte du Petit Barbeau ☎64246345
Apr-Sep 3HEC ▦ ♠ ♠ ⊙ ⊘ ₹ ≛ ⊞ lau

SERAUCOURT-LE-GRAND *Aisne*

Pêche du Vivier aux Carpes 10 r C-Voyeux ☎23605102
A peaceful site bordered by lakes. Separate car park for arrivals
after 22.00hrs.A26 exit 11-left on D1 exit Essigny-D72.
All year 3HEC ▦ ⊞ ♠ ⊙ ⊘ ⊘ ⊿ ≛ ♣ ▲ ⊞ lau ♦ ฿ ฿ ✕

SERQUES *Pas-de-Calais*

Frémont rte Nationale 43 ☎21930115
1.5km SW on N43
Apr-Oct 2HEC ▦ ⤸ ⊀ ♠ ฿ ⊙ ⊘ ≛ ⊞ lau ♦ ₹R Prices: A10 V10 ♣9-
10 ▲10

SOISSONS *Aisne*

CM av du Mail ☎23745269
In pleasant surroundings with good, modern facilities.
All year 1.8HEC ▦ ⊞ ♠ ♠ ⊙ ⊘ ≛ lau ♦ ฿ ฿ ✕ ₹PR

STEENBECQUE *Nord*

Paradiso r du Bois
1.2km SE, 400m from Canal de Nieppe.
Apr-15 Oct 1.6HEC ▦ ⊞ ♠ ♠ ฿ ✕ ⊙ ⊘ ⊘ ≛ ⊞ lau ♦ ₹R

THIEMBRONNE *Pas-de-Calais*

Pommiers ☎21395019
NW on D132.
15 Mar-15 Oct 1.8HEC ▦ ⊞ ♠ ♠ ⊙ ⊘ ⊘ ⊘ ₹ P ⊡ ⊞ lau ♦ ฿ ฿ ✕
₹R Prices: pitch 49-65 (incl 2 persons)

TOLLENT *Pas-de-Calais*

Val d'Authie ☎21471427
SE via D119
All year 3.3HEC ▦ ⊞ ♠ ♠ ฿ ฿ ✕ ⊙ ⊘ ₹ P ≛ ⊞ lau ♦ ✕ ⊘ ₹R
Prices: pitch 50 (incl 2 persons)

TORCY *Seine-et-Marne*

Parc de la Colline rte de Lagny ☎60054232
An ideal base for visiting Paris (30 minutes from the centre by
Metro). Separate car park for arrivals after 22.00 hrs.
Access via exit 10 on the A104 and D10E.
All year 10HEC ▦ ⊞ ♠ ♠ ฿ ฿ ♈ ⊙ ⊘ ⊘ ⊞ ≛ ⊞ lau ♦ ฿ ฿ ✕ ₹LPR

TOUQUIN *Seine-et-Marne*

Étangs Fleuris rte de la Couture ☎64041636
Mar-Oct 5.5HEC ▦ ⊞ ♠ ฿ ♈ ✕ ⊙ ⊘ ≛ lau

TOURNEHEM *Pas-de-Calais*

Bal 500 r du Vieux Château ☎21356590
All year 1.6HEC ▦ ⊞ ♠ ♠ ฿ ฿ ✕ ⊙ ⊘ ⊿ ⊘ ≛ ⊞ lau ♦ ₹R Prices:
A18 pitch 32

VILLENNES-SUR-SEINE *Yvelines*

Club des Renardières ☎39758897
Site for caravans only, in beautiful hilly park laid out with hedges,
lawns and flower beds. Fully divided into completely separated
pitches.
Camping Card Compulsory.
Follow D113 to Maison Blanche turn right and continue 3km.
All year 6HEC ▦ ⊞ ♠ ⊙ ⊘ ₹ LPR lau ♦ ₹LPR ⊞ Prices: A14 pitch
62-75

VILLERS-HÉLON *Aisne*

Castel des Biches ☎23960499
Attractive site in grounds of an old castle.
Turn off N2 onto D2 between Soissons and Villers-Cotterêts and
continue for 7km via Longport.
All year 8HEC ▦ ⊞ ♠ ♠ ⊘ ⊘ ♣ ▲ ≛ ⊞ lau ♦ ฿ ✕ ⊘ ⊿ Prices:
pitch 70-80 (incl 2 persons)

VILLERS-SUR-AUTHIE *Somme*

Val d'Authie ☎22299247
Apr-Oct 3.5HEC ▦ ⊞ ♠ ♠ ฿ ✕ ⊙ ⊘ ⊘ ⊿ ≛ lau ♦ ฿

VILLEVAUDE *Seine-et-Marne*

Parc Montjay-la-Tour ☎60262079
Bar and restaurant facilities open summer only.
Access via A104 exit 6B, Marne-la-Vallée.
All year 10HEC ▦ ⊞ ♠ ♠ ฿ ✕ ⊙ ⊘ ≛ ⊞ lau Prices: A30 ♣60 ▲25

VIRONCHAUX *Somme*

Peupliers 221 r du Cornet ☎22235427
Apr-15 Oct 1.2HEC ▦ ⊞ ♠ ♠ ⊙ ⊘ ⊿ ≛ ⊞ lau ♦ ฿ ฿ ✕ ₹R Prices:
A11 pitch 10.50

WATTEN *Nord*

Val Joly r de l'Aa ☎21882326
Apr-Oct ▦ ⊞ ♠ ♠ ⊙ ⊘ ⊿ ₹ R ≛ ⊞ lau ♦ ฿ ✕ ⊞

Auvergne

The mountainous Massif Central characterises the Auvergne, giving an atmosphere of grandeur and tranquility to this ancient land. The rivers Dordogne and Allier begin in the region; on the banks of the Allier is the bustling town of Langeac - especially lively on market days. The rivers offer good fishing and recreational opportunities, many of these have been dammed, creating great placid lakes providing wonderful centres for watersports. A unique highlight of the area is the remarkable Parc de Volcans, where 80 extinct volcanos form a majestic line stretching some 20 miles.

South west of the Auvergne, the département of Aveyron is a little-known district with a turbulent past, and ancient abbeys, medieval citadels and fortified towns. Cordes and Villefranche-de-Rourgue are perfect 15th-century garrison towns, and Najac stands in a superb position on its 1,200ft rock. East from Aveyron is Lozère, an arid, rugged landscape. The highlight here is the well-known Gorges du Tarn, where the Tarn slices its way through the land for more than 50 miles, and twisting, narrow roads offer an unforgettable succession of spectacular views.

ALLANCHE Cantal
CM Pont Valat ☎71204587
1km S on D679 towards St-Flour.
15 Jun-15 Sep 3HEC ▦ ⌾ ⌂ ⊙ ⬛ 🅰 lau ➧ 🝙 🝘 ✕ ∅ 🝟 ⳨R ⊞
Prices: A7 pitch 4.50

ALLEYRAS Haute-Loire
CM ☎71575686
2.5km NW.
May-Sep 2HEC ▦ ⯆ ⌂ ⌂ ⊙ ⬛ 🚌 🅰 🅰 lau ➧ 🝙 🝘 ✕ 🝘 ⳨R Prices:
pitch 35 (incl 2 persons)

ANSE Rhône
Porte du Beaujolais chemin des Grandes Levées ☎74671287
A pleasant, modern site in the heart of the Beaujolais country.
Access via A6 or N6.
All year 7.5HEC ▦ ⌾ 🝙 🝘 ✕ ⊙ ⬛ ∅ 🚌 🚌 ⳨ PR 🅰 🅰 lau ➧ ✕ 🝘 Prices:
pitch 79-109 (incl 2 persons)

ARNAC Cantal
CM d'Arnac ☎71629190
On Lake Enchanet.
All year 3HEC ▦ ⌾ ⌂ ✕ ⊙ ⬛ 🝘 ⳨ LP 🅰 lau Prices: pitch
75 (incl 2 persons)

ARPAJON-SUR-CÈRE Cantal
Cère r F-Ramond ☎71645507
S towards Rodez via D920, beside the river.
Jun-Sep 2HEC ▦ ⌾ ⌂ ⊙ ⬛ ⳨ R 🅰 lau ➧ 🝙 🝘 ✕ ∅ ⊞

AUBIN Aveyron
CM ☎65630386
100m from the lake.
Apr-15 Sep 4HEC ⫶⫶⫶ ⌾ ⌂ ⊙ ⬛ 🝟 lau ➧ 🝙 🝘 ✕ 🝘 ⳨P

BELMONT-SUR-RANCE Aveyron
Val Fleuri ☎65999513
A peaceful site beside the River Rance with good, modern facilities.
Access via N9 and D999.
Jun-Sep 1.3HEC ▦ ⌾ 🝙 🝘 ✕ ⊙ ⬛ ⳨ R 🝟 lau ➧ 🝙 ∅ ⳨P
Prices: pitch 68 (incl 2 persons)

BOURBON-L'ARCHAMBAULT Allier
CM Parc Bignon ☎70670883
1km SW on N153, rte de Montluçon, turn right.
Mar-Oct 7HEC ▦ ⌾ 🝙 🝘 ✕ ⊙ ⬛ 🝟 ⳨P Prices:
A11.87-12.50 V4.75-5 ⬛6.65-7 ▲6.65-7

BOURG-ARGENTAL Loire
Astrée 'L'Allier' ☎77397297
In pleasant surroundings with good recreational facilities.
Access via N82.
15 Mar-15 Oct ▦ ⌾ ⌂ 🝙 ⌂ ⊙ ⬛ ∅ 🚌 🚌 ⳨ R 🝟 lau ➧ ✕ 🝘 ⳨P ⊞
Prices: A17 V11 ⬛14 ▲12

BRAIZE Allier
Champ de la Chapelle ☎70061545
7km SE via D28 and D978.
May-15 Sep 5.6HEC ▦ ⌾ ⌂ ✕ ⊙ ⬛ 🝟 lau ➧ 🝙 ✕

BRUSQUE Aveyron
VAL Camping Les Pibouls Domaine de Céras ☎65495066
Jun-Sep 1HEC ▦ ⌾ 🝙 🝘 ✕ ⊙ ⬛ 🚌 ⳨ LR 🝟 lau ➧ 🝙 ∅ 🝘

CANET-DE-SALARS Aveyron
Caussanel ☎65468519
N of Lac de Pareloup. Access via D911.
Apr-Oct 10HEC ▦ ⌾ ⌂ 🝙 🝘 ✕ ⊙ ⬛ ∅ 🚌 🚌 ⳨ LP 🝟 lau

CAPDENAC-GARE Aveyron
Diège Vallée de la Diège, Sonnac ☎65646125
Level, sub-divided terrain located in a narrow valley of La Diège river.
From Figeac on N140 travel 7km, in the direction of Capdenac-Gare.
Turn sharp right after the bridge and continue on D558 for about 7km in the direction of Naussac.
Apr-Oct 7HEC ▦ ⌾ ⌂ 🝙 🝘 ✕ ⊙ ⬛ ∅ 🝘 ▲ ⳨ R 🝟 lau Prices:
A18 pitch 29

CM Rives d'Olt bd P-Ramadier ☎65808887
10 Apr-Sep 1.5HEC ▦ ⌾ ⌂ ⊙ ⬛ 🚌 🝟 lau ➧ 🝙 🝘 ✕ ∅ ⳨P
Prices: A12 V7 ⬛25 ▲7

CEYRAT Puy-de-Dôme
CM av J-B-Marrou ☎73613073
On undulating meadow on partly terraced hill. Large common room with games. Supplies only available peak season.
All year 6HEC ▦ ⌾ ⌂ 🝙 🝘 ✕ ⊙ ⬛ 🚌 🝟 lau ➧ ∅

CHAMPAGNAC-LE-VIEUX Haute-Loire
Chanterelle Le Plan d'Eau ☎71763400
Situated in the heart of the Auvergne beside a wooded lake.
1km N via D5.
15 Jun-15 Sep 4HEC ▦ ➧ ⌂ ⊙ ⬛ 🚌 ▲ ⳨ L 🝟 lau ➧ 🝙 🝘 ✕ ∅ 🝘
⳨R Prices: A15 pitch 25

CHAMPS-SUR-TARENTAINE Cantal
Tarentaine ☎71787275
1km SW via D679 and D22 beside the River Tarentaine.
15 Jun-15 Sep 6HEC ▦ ⌾ ⌂ ⊙ ⬛ ⳨ R 🝟 lau ➧ 🝙 🝘 ✕ 🝘 ⳨P

CHÂTEL-DE-NEUVRE Allier
Deneuvre Les Graves ☎70420451
In pleasant surroundings beside the River Allier.
0.5km N via D9.
Apr-1 Oct 1.2HEC ▦ ⌾ ⌂ 🝙 ✕ ⊙ ⬛ ∅ 🚌 ▲ ⳨ R 🝟 lau Prices:
A18 pitch 18-25

CHÂTEL GUYON *Puy-de-Dôme*

Clos de Balanède r de la Piscine ☎73860247
A pleasant site, situated in an orchard.
Access via A71 and D685.
10 Apr-5 Oct 4HEC ▥ ♣♠☎♣✕⊙◙∅⊞◫ ♦P☎⊞ lau ♦ ♨ �≈L

CHÂTEL-MONTAGNE *Allier*

Croix Cognat ☎70593138
0.5km NW via D22 towards Vichy.
May-Oct 1HEC ▥ ♣♠☎♣✕⊙◙∅♨◙◫ ♦P☎⊞ lau ♦ ≈LR

CHAUDES-AIGUES *Cantal*

CM du Couffour ☎71235708
2km S via D921.
▥ ੫♠⊙◙☎ lau

CHOUVIGNY *Allier*

Bel Le Soult ☎70904117
3km SE via D915 beside the River Sioule.
Etr-Sep 1.5HEC ▥ ੫♠⊙◙♦P☎ lau

CONDRIEU *Rhône*

Belle Rive La Plaine ☎74595108
Bordering the Rhône.
Apr-Sep 5HEC ▥ ♣♠☎♣✕⊙◙∅♦P☎⊞ lau ♦≈L

CONQUES *Aveyron*

Beau Rivage ☎65698223
On D601n.
Apr-Oct 1HEC ▥ ♣♠☎♣✕⊙◙∅◙◫♠A♦R☎⊞ lau ♦♨ ≈LP

COURNON-D'AUVERGNE *Puy-de-Dôme*

CM Plage ☎73848130
1.5km E towards Billom
All year 5HEC ▥ ♣♠♠☎♣✕⊙◙◫♦LR☎⊞ lau ♦✕∅≈P
Prices: A16-17 pitch 23-24.50

DALLET *Puy-de-Dôme*

Ombrages rte de Pont-du-Château ☎73831097
Beside River Allier.
Jun-15 Sep 3HEC ▥ ░░ ♣♠☎♣✕⊙◙◙♦RS☎⊞⌇ lau
Prices: A25 pitch 31

DARDILLY *Rhône*

Vllle de Lyon ☎78356455
Generously arranged and equipped site divided into pitches. Ideal for overnight stays near motorway. Concrete platforms for caravans.
9km N of Lyon La Garde exit off A6.
All year 6HEC ▥ ♣♠☎♣✕⊙◙♦P☎⊞ lau ♦♨∅♨

EBREUIL *Allier*

Filature de la Sioule rte de Chouvigny ☎70907201
Beside River Sioule.
Access signposted from exit 12 on A71.
Apr-Sep 3.5HEC ▥ ♣♠☎♣✕⊙◙∅◙♦R☎⊞ lau

FERRIÈRES-ST-MARY *Cantal*

Vigeaires ☎71206147
15 Jun-Aug 1.5HEC ▥ ♣♠⊙◙♦R☎⊞ lau ♦♨♣✕∅♨

FIRMI *Aveyron*

Étang r du Camping ☎65634302
Jul-Aug 1.3HEC ▥ ੫♠⊙◙☎ lau ♦♨♣✕∅♨≈L

FLEURIE *Rhône*

CM la Grappe Fleurie ☎74698007
0.6km SE on D119 E.
15 Mar-25 Oct 2.5HEC ▥ ♣♠⊙◙☎ lau ♦♨♣✕∅♨≈LP⊞
Prices: A15-16 pitch 28

FONTANGES *Cantal*

Pierre Plate ☎71407149
Jul-Aug ▥ ੫♠⊙◙♨☎☎ lau ♦♨♣✕≈R

GOUDET *Haute-Loire*

Bord de l'Eau Plaine du chambon ☎71571682
W via D49, beside the River Loire
5 Jun-15 Sep 4HEC ▥ ੫♠♣✕⊙◙∅♦P☎⊞ lau Prices: A22 pitch 23

JABRUN *Cantal*

Tillet ☎71738080
4km SW via D921.
15 Jun-15 Sep 1.5HEC ♣♠⊙◙☎ lau ♦♣✕♨ ≈PR

JENZAT *Allier*

Champ de Sioule rte de Chantelle ☎70568635
May-Sep 1HEC ▥ ੫♠⊙◙☎ lau ♦♨♣✕∅♨≈R⊞ Prices: A10 V4 ♣4 ♠4

LACAPELLE-VIESCAMP *Cantal*

Puech des Ouilhes ☎71464238
On a wooded peninsular on Lake St-Étienne-Cantalès.
15 Jun-10 Sep 2HEC ▥ ♣♠⊙◙∅◙♦L☎⊞⌇ lau ♦♨
Prices: A17 pitch 9

LANGEAC *Haute-Loire*

Gorges d'Allier 'Le Pradeau' ☎71770501
15 Apr-Oct 12HEC ▥ ░░ ੫♠⊙◙◙A♦R☎ lau ♦♨♣✕∅♨ ≈P⊞

LAPEYROUSE *Puy-de-Dôme*

CM Les Marins ☎73520273
A modern, lakeside site with good facilities.
2km E via D998.
15 Jun-10 Sep 2HEC ▥ ੫♠♣✕⊙◙♦L☎ lau ♦✕♨≈R

LOUBEYRAT *Puy-de-Dôme*

Colombier ☎73866694
1.5km S via D16.
15 Apr-15 Oct 0.9HEC ▥ ੫♠⊙◙◙◙♦P☎⊞ lau ♦♨♣✕∅♨

MARTRES-DE-VEYRE, LES *Puy-de-Dôme*
CM la Font de Bleix r des Roches ☎73392649
SE via D225 beside the River Allier.
Jul-Aug 1.3HEC ▥ ⊰↵ ⋔ ⊙ ◒ ▥ ⋋ R ☎ lau ♦ ☍ ♥ ✕ ∅ ⊞

MASSIAC *Cantal*
CM Allagnon av de Courcelles ☎71230393
0.8km W on N122.
May-Sep 2.5HEC ▥ ♦ ⋔ ⊙ ◒ ∅ ⋋ R ☎ ⊞ lau ♦ ☍ ♥ ✕ ☷ ⋋P
Prices: A10 V7 ◙10 ▲10

MAURS *Cantal*
At **ST-CONSTANT**(4.5km SE via N663)
Moulin de Chaules rte de Calvinet ☎71491102
Terraced site in a valley by the stream of a former watermill with good, modern facilities.
3km E via D28.
20 Apr-20 Oct 3HEC ▥ ⊰ ⋔ ☍ ♥ ✕ ⊙ ◒ ∅ ☷ ⋋ PR ☎ ⊞ lau
Prices: pitch 54-67.50 (incl 2 persons)

MENDE *Lozère*
Tivoli rte des Gorges-du-Tarn ☎66650038
All year 1.8HEC ▥ ♦ ⋔ ☍ ♥ ✕ ⊙ ◒ ∅ ☷ ◙ ▥ ⋋ P ☎ ⊞ lau ♦ ✕
Prices: A21 pitch 13

MEYRUEIS *Lozère*
Ayres rte de la Brèze ☎66456051
0.5km E via D57
Apr-Sep 1.5HEC ▥ ⊰ ⋔ ♥ ✕ ⊙ ◒ ∅ ▥ ⋋ P ☎ ⊞ ⊗ lau ♦ ☍ ☷ ⋋R
Prices: A14-19 pitch 32-38

MILLAU *Aveyron*
Deux Rivières 61 av de l'Migoual ☎65600027
1.5km NE via D991, beside the River Tarn.
Apr-15 Oct 1.1HEC ▥ ⠿ ♦ ⋔ ⊙ ◒ ∅ ⋋ R ☎ ⊞ lau ♦ ☍

CM Millau Plage rte de Millau Plage ☎65601097
Beside the River Tarn.
Access via D187.
Apr-Sep 5HEC ▥ ♦ ⋔ ☍ ♥ ✕ ⊙ ◒ ∅ ⋋ R ☎ ⊞ lau Prices: pitch 62-76 (incl 2 persons)

Rivages av de l'Aigoual ☎65610107
1.7km E via D991, beside the River Dourbie
May-Sep 7HEC ▥ ⊰ ⋔ ☍ ♥ ✕ ⊙ ◒ ∅ ▥ ▲ ⋋ PR ☎ ⊞ lau ♦ ☷
Prices: pitch 81-121 (incl 2 persons)

MIREMONT *Puy-de-Dôme*
Confolant ☎73799276
7km NE via D19 and D19E.
May-15 Sep 2.5HEC ▥ ♦ ⋔ ☍ ♥ ✕ ⊙ ◒ ∅ ◙ ▥ ⋋ L ☎ ⊞ lau
Prices: A16 pitch 22

MOLOMPIZE *Cantal*
CM ☎71736006
In a wooded valley beside the River Alagnan.
0.5km NE via N122.
15 Jun-15 Sep 2HEC ▥ ⠿ ⊰ ⋔ ⊙ ◒ ⋋ R ☎ lau ♦ ☍ ♥ ✕ ∅ ☷

MONISTROL-SUR-LOIRE *Haute-Loire*
CM Beau Séjour chemin de Chaponas ☎71665390
Adjacent to N88 near the municipal swimming pool. Signposted from town centre.
Apr-Oct 1.5HEC ▥ ♦ ⋔ ⊙ ◒ ⋋ P ☎ ⊞ lau ♦ ☍ ♥ ✕ ∅ ☷ ⋋S

MONTAIGUT-LE-BLANC *Puy-de-Dôme*
CM Le Bourg ☎73967507
Jun-15 Sep 1.5HEC ▥ ♦ ⋔ ⊙ ◒ ⋋ R ☎ ⊞ lau ♦ ☍ ♥ ✕

MONT-DORE, LE *Puy-de-Dôme*
CM du L'Esquiladou rte des Cascades ☎73652374
Jul-5 Oct 2HEC ⠿ ⊰↵ ⋔ ⊙ ◒ ☎ ⊞ lau ♦ ☍ ♥ ✕ ∅ ☷ ⋋R Prices: A14 pitch 13

MORNANT *Rhône*
CM de la Trillonière bd du Gl-de-Gaulle ☎78441647

May-Sep 1.6HEC ▥ ⊰ ⋔ ⊙ ◒ ▥ ☷ ⊗ lau ♦ ☍ ♥ ✕ ∅ ⋋PR ⊞ Prices: A14-20 pitch 16

MOSTUÉJOUS *Aveyron*
Aubigue ☎65626367
1.3km SE beside the River Tarn.
Apr-Sep 1.5HEC ♦ ⋔ ☍ ♥ ✕ ⊙ ◒ ∅ ☷ ▥ ⋋ R ☎ ⊞ lau ♦ ✕

MUROL *Puy-de-Dôme*
Europe ☎73886046
25 May-10 Sep 5.5HEC ▥ ♦ ⋔ ☍ ♥ ✕ ⊙ ◒ ∅ ☷ ▥ ⋋ P ☎ lau ♦ ⋋LR ⊞ Prices: pitch 99 (incl 2 persons)

Plage ☎73886027
Busy site beside lake. Caravan section divided into pitches, terraced area for tents. Asphalt drive.
1.2km from centre of village. turn off into allée de Plage before entering village and follow signposts.
May-Sep 7HEC ▥ ♦ ⋔ ☍ ♥ ✕ ⊙ ◒ ∅ ▥ ⋋ LP ☎ ⊞ lau ♦ ☷ Prices: pitch 85-92 (incl 2 persons)

Pré-Bas Lac Chambon ☎73886304
On the side of Lake Chambon with direct access to the beach and windsurf beach.S of D996.
May-20 Sep 5.5HEC ▥ ⊰ ⋔ ✕ ⊙ ◒ ▥ ▥ ⋋ P ☎ lau ♦ ☍ ✕ ∅ ⋋R Prices: pitch 34 (incl 2 persons)

Ribeyre ☎73886429
1.2km S on rte de Jassat.
May-15 Sep 10HEC ▥ ⊰ ⋔ ☍ ♥ ✕ ⊙ ◒ ∅ ▥ ▥ ⋋ LPR ☎ lau ♦ ⊞ Prices: A24 pitch 29

NANT *Aveyron*
▮**Val de Cantobre** ☎33 0565584300
Large variety of recreational facilities.
4km N of Nant, towards Millau; next to the Dourbie river, and off D591n.
15 May-15 Sep 6.5HEC ▥ ♢ ⊰ ⋔ ☍ ♥ ✕ ⊙ ◒ ∅ ☷ ▥ ▥ ⋋ PR ☎ ⊞ lau Prices: pitch 80 (incl 2 persons)

NAUCELLE *Aveyron*
Lac de Bonnefon ☎65470067
NW of N88. Signposted.
Jun-Sep 2.5HEC ▥ ⊰ ⋔ ☍ ♥ ✕ ⊙ ◒ ▥ ▥ ⋋ P ☎ lau ♦ ∅ ☷ Prices: pitch 58 (incl 2 persons)

NAYRAC, LE *Aveyron*
CM La Planque ☎65444450
1.4km S via D97 beside the lake.
Jul-Aug 4.6HEC ▥ ⊰ ⋔ ☍ ♥ ✕ ⊙ ◒ ⋋ L ☎ ⊞ lau ♦ ☍ ♥ ✕ ⋋P Prices: A13 pitch 13

NÉBOUZAT *Puy-de-Dôme*
Domes Les Quatre rtes de Nébouzat ☎73871406
Hard-standing for caravans.
On N89.
15 May-15 Sep 1HEC ▥ ⊰ ⋔ ☍ ♥ ✕ ⊙ ◒ ∅ ▥ ▥ ⋋ P ☎ lau ♦ ♥ ✕ ⋋R Prices: A28 pitch 41.50

NEUVÉGLISE *Cantal*
Belvédère du Pont de Lanau ☎71235050
5km S on D921.
15 Jun-3 Sep 5HEC ▥ ♦ ⋔ ☍ ♥ ✕ ⊙ ◒ ∅ ▥ ▥ ⋋ P ☎ ⊞ lau ♦ ⋋LR Prices: pitch 100-160 (incl 2 persons)

OLLIERGUES *Puy-de-Dôme*
Chelles ☎73955434
5km from town centre.
Apr-Sep 3.5HEC ▥ ⊰ ♦ ⋔ ☍ ♥ ✕ ⊙ ◒ ∅ ▥ ▥ ⋋ P ☎ ⊞ lau ♦ ☷ Prices: pitch 50 (incl 2 persons)

ORCET *Puy-de-Dôme*
Clos Auroy r de la Naise ☎73842697
All year 3HEC ▥ ⊰↵ ⋔ ♥ ✕ ⊙ ◒ ∅ ▥ ⋋ PR ☎ ⊞ lau ♦ ☍ ♥
Prices: A17 pitch 30-41

ORCIVAL *Puy-de-Dôme*
Étang de Fléchat ☎73658296
A well equipped site in a pleasant location in a volcanic park beside a lake.
1.5km S via D27, then 2.5km via D74 towards Rochefort-Montagne.
Jun-15 Sep 3HEC ▦ ♦ ⋔ ⏃ X ⊙ ⬛ ∅ ⯑ ⯑ ⋔ L ☎ ⊞ ⊞ lau ♦ ⏃ ⏃

PARAY-SOUS-BRIAILLES *Allier*
CM Le Moulin du Pré ☎70450514
N via D142 beside the river.
28 Mar-Sep 1.5HEC ▦ ⊙ ⋔ ⊙ ⬛ ⋔ R ☎ lau ♦ ⏃ X ∅ ⏃ ⊞ Prices:
A7 V5 ⬛5 ▲5

POLLIONNAY *Rhône*
Col de la Luère ☎78458111
All year 5HEC ▦ ♦ ⋔ ⏃ X ⊙ ⬛ ∅ ⯑ ⋔ P ☎ ⊞ ⊞ ⊘ lau ♦ ⏃ ⋔R
Prices: A18 V13 ⬛15 ▲15

PONT-DE-SALARS *Aveyron*
Lac rte du Vibal ☎65468486
1.5km N via D523
15 Jun-5 Sep 4.8HEC ▦ ⋔ ⏃ X ⊙ ⬛ ∅ ⯑ ⋔ LP ☎ ⊞ ⊘ lau ♦ ⏃ ⏃
Prices: pitch 87 (incl 3 persons)

Terrasses du Lac rte du Vibal ☎65468818
4km N via D523
15 Jun-15 Sep 6HEC ▦ ⊙ ⋔ ⏃ X ⊙ ⬛ ∅ ⯑ ⯑ ⯑ ⋔ LP ☎ lau
Prices: pitch 65-95 (incl 2 persons)

PONTGIBAUD *Puy-de-Dôme*
CM rte de la Miouze ☎73889699
0.5km SW via D986 towards Rochefort-Montagne, beside the River Sioule.
15 Apr-15 Oct 4.5HEC ▦ ⊙ ⋔ X ⊙ ⬛ ⯑ ⋔ R ☎ ⊞ lau ♦ ⏃ X ∅
⯑ ⋔L Prices: A11-12 pitch 15-16

PRADEAUX, LES *Puy-de-Dôme*
Châteaux la Grange Fort ☎73710593
Parklike area surrounding an old château on the bank of the River Allier.
From A75 take exit 13 for Parentignat, then take D999. Signposted.
Mar-Oct 25HEC ▦ ⊙ ⋔ X ⊙ ⬛ ∅ ⯑ ⋔ PR ☎ ⊞ lau ♦ ⏃ Prices:
A17-20 ⬛34-40 ▲34-40

PUY, LE *Haute-Loire*
CM Bouthezard pl de l'Hôtel-de-Ville ☎71095509
From the town centre follow sign for Clermont-Ferrand; at traffic lights by church of St-Laurent, turn right following 'camping' signpost, site is 500m on left of road.
20 Mar-15 Oct 1.5HEC ▦ ♦ ⊙ ⊙ ⬛ ☎ ⊞ lau ♦ ⏃ X ∅ ⏃

At **BLAVOZY**(9km E)
Moulin de Barette ☎71030088
Etr-Nov 1HEC ▦ ⋎ ⋔ X ⊙ ⬛ ∅ ⯑ ⋔ PR ☎ ⊞ lau ♦ ⋔L

At **BRIVES-CHARENSAC**(4.5km E)
Audinet ☎71091018
E on N88.
May-Oct 3HEC ▦ ⊙ ⋔ ⊙ ⬛ ∅ ⏃ ⋔ R ☎ lau ♦ ⏃ X ⋔LPR

RIOM-ÈS-MONTAGNES *Cantal*
Sédour rte de Condat ☎71780571
In a pleasant situation beside the River Véronne.
Access via D678.
May-Sep ⊙ ⋔ ⊙ ⬛ ⋔ R ☎ lau ♦ ⏃ X ∅ ⏃ ⋔LP ⊞

RIVIÈRE-SUR-TARN *Aveyron*
Peyrelade rte des Gorges-du-Tarn ☎65626254
2km E via D907, beside the River Tarn.
15 May-15 Sep 4HEC ▦ ⋮⋮ ♦ ⋔ X ⊙ ⬛ ∅ ⯑ ⯑ ▲ ⋔ PR
☎ ⊞ lau Prices: A16-19.50 pitch 30-36

RODEZ *Aveyron*
CM Layoule ☎65670952
Clean, tidy site in valley below town, completely divided into pitches.
NE of town centre. Well signposted.

Jun-Sep 3HEC ▦ ⋮⋮⋮ ⊙ ⋔ ⊙ ⬛ ⯑ ☎ ⊞ lau ♦ ⏃ ⏃ X ∅ ⏃ Prices:
pitch 59 (incl 3 persons)

ROYAT *Puy-de-Dôme*
CM de l'Oclède rte de Gravenoire ☎73359705
Apr-Oct 7HEC ▦ ⋮⋮⋮ ♦ ⋔ ⏃ X ⊙ ⬛ ∅ ⏃ ☎ ⊞ lau ♦ X

RUYNES-EN-MARGERIDE *Cantal*
CM Petit Bois ☎71234226
Camping Card Compulsory.
0.5km SW on D13, rte de Garabit. Signposted.
Apr-Oct 7HEC ▦ ♦ ⋔ ⊙ ⬛ ⬛ ⋔ P ☎ ⊞ lau ♦ ⏃ ⏃ X ⋔R

SAIGNES *Cantal*
Bellevue ☎71406840
Jul-Aug 1HEC ▦ ⊙ ⋔ ⏃ ⊙ ⬛ ☎ lau ♦ ⏃ ∅ ⏃ ⋔P ⊞ Prices:
A9.50 pitch 5.80

ST-ALBAN-SUR-LIMAGNOLE *Lozère*
Galier ☎66315880
Mar-15 Nov 4HEC ▦ ⊙ ⋔ ⏃ X ⊙ ⬛ ∅ ⏃ ⯑ ⋔ PR ☎ ⊞ lau ♦ ⏃ X
Prices: A13-16 pitch 51-63

ST-AMANS-DES-COTS *Aveyron*
⬛Tours ☎65448810
6km SE via D97/D599, beside the Lake Selves
20 May-15 Sep 10HEC ▦ ⋮⋮⋮ ♦ ⋔ ⋔ X ⊙ ⬛ ∅ ⯑ ▲ ⋔ LP ☎ ⊞
lau Prices: pitch 148 (incl 3 persons)

ST-AMANT-ROCHE-SAVINE *Puy-de-Dôme*
CM Saviloisirs ☎73957345
May-Sep 0.5HEC ▦ ⊙ ⋔ ⊙ ⬛ ⏃ ⯑ ⯑ ☎ ⊞ lau ♦ ⏃ ⏃ X ⋔R
Prices: A12 V6 ⬛7 ▲5

ST-CLÉMENT-DE-VALORGUE *Puy-de-Dôme*
Narcisses ☎73954576
Jun-15 Sep 1.3HEC ▦ ♦ ⋔ ⊙ ⬛ ⬛ ▲ ⋔ R ☎ ⊞ lau ♦ ⏃ X
Prices: A12 V6 ⬛10 ▲10

STE-CATHERINE *Rhône*
CM du Châtelard ☎78818060
2km S.
Mar-Nov 4HEC ▦ ⋎ ⋔ ⊙ ⬛ ☎ ⊞ lau ♦ ⏃ ⏃ X ∅ ⋔R Prices: A11
pitch 12.50

STE-SIGOLÈNE *Haute-Loire*
Vaubarlet Vaubarlet ☎71666495
Exit for Ste-Sigolène on D44, then towards Grazac on D43.
May-Sep 3.5HEC ▦ ⊙ ⋔ ⏃ X ⊙ ⬛ ∅ ⯑ ⯑ ⯑ ▲ ⋔ PR ☎ ⊞ lau
Prices: A18 V8 pitch 25

ST-GAL-SUR-SIOULE *Puy-de-Dôme*
Pont de St-Gal ☎73974471
E via D16 towards Ebreuil, beside the River Sioule.
May-15 Sep 1HEC ▦ ♦ ⋔ ⏃ X ⊙ ⬛ ∅ ⯑ ⯑ ⋔ R ☎ ⊞ lau

ST-GENIEZ-D'OLT *Aveyron*
Marmotel ☎65704651
Grassy site on River Lot.
On D19 about 1km NW of St Geniez-d'Olt.
Jun-Sep 4HEC ▦ ♦ ⋔ ⏃ X ⊙ ⬛ ∅ ⋔ PR ☎ ⊞ lau ♦ ⏃ ⋔L Prices:
pitch 114 (incl 2 persons)

ST-GERMAIN-DE-CALBERTE *Lozère*
Garde ☎66459482
In a pleasant situation on the edge of the Cevennes National Park.
Access via A7 or A75.
Apr-Sep 1HEC ▦ ⊙ ⋔ X ⊙ ⬛ ⏃ ⋔ P ☎ ⊞ lau ♦ ⏃ X ∅ ⏃ ⋔R
Prices: A18-20 pitch 60-85

ST-GÉRONS *Cantal*
Presqu'île d'Espinet ☎71622890
8.5km SE, 300m from Lake St-Étienne-Cantalès.
15 May-15 Sep 3HEC ▦ ⊙ ⋔ ⏃ X ⊙ ⬛ ∅ ☎ ⯑ ⊞ lau ♦ ⏃ ⋔L
Prices: pitch 42 (incl 1 persons)

ST-GERVAIS-D'AUVERGNE *Puy-de-Dôme*
CM de l'Étang Philippe rte de St-Eloy-les-Mines ☎73857484
Etr-Sep 5HEC ▦ ♦ ⋔ ⊙ ☻ ▲ ⌇ L ☎ ☒ ⊞ lau ♦ ⅏ ♟ ✗ ∅ Prices:
pitch 50

ST-JACQUES-DES-BLATS *Cantal*
CM rte de la Gare ☎71470590
Jun-Sep 1HEC ▦ ⋔ ⊙ ☻ ⅊ ⌇ R ☎ ⊞ lau ♦ ⅏ ♟ ✗

ST-JODARD *Loire*
CM ☎77634242
Apr-Oct ▦ ♦ ⋔ ⊙ ☻ ☎ lau ♦ ⅏ ♟ ✗ ∅ ▲ ⌇LP

ST-JUST *Cantal*
CM ☎71737257
In the centre of the village beside the river.
Apr-Sep 2HEC ▦ ⅁ ⋔ ⊙ ☻ ☎ ⌇ PR ☎ ⊞ lau ♦ ⅏ ♟ ✗ ∅ ▲

ST-MARTIN-VALMEROUX *Cantal*
Moulin du Teinturier rte de Loupiac ☎71694312
May-Oct 5HEC ▦ ⅁ ⋔ ✗ ⊙ ☻ ▲ ⌇ R ☎ lau ♦ ⅏ ♟ ✗ ∅ ▲ ⌇P ⊞
Prices: A10.55 pitch 5.28

ST-NECTAIRE *Puy-de-Dôme*
Oasis rte des Granges ☎73885268
In wooded surroundings within the Auvergne Natural Volcanic Park.
15 Apr-Sep 2HEC ▦ ♦ ⋔ ⊙ ☻ ∅ ▲ ☻ ⌇ R ☎ ⊞ lau ♦ ⅏ ♟ ✗
Prices: A14-16 pitch 12-14.50

ST-OURS *Puy-de-Dôme*
Bel-Air ☎73887214
1km SW on D941.
Jul-Sep 2HEC ▦ ⅁ ⋔ ♟ ✗ ⊙ ☻ ☎ lau ♦ ∅ ⊞

ST-PAL-EN-CHALENÇON *Haute-Loire*
CM Ste-Reine chemin des Sources ☎71613387
Apr-Oct 0.8HEC ⅁ ⋔ ⊙ ☻ ⌇ P ☎ lau ♦ ⅏ ♟ ✗ ∅ ▲ ⊞

ST-PIERRE-COLAMINE *Puy-de-Dôme*
Ombrage ☎73967787
300m from D978.
15 Dec-30 Sep 2HEC ▦ ♦ ⋔ ⅊ ⊙ ☻ ∅ ▲ ☻ ☻ ⌇ P ☎ ⊞ lau ♦ ♟
✗ ⌇R Prices: A18 V5 ⌑13 ▲13

ST-RÉMY-SUR-DUROLLE *Puy-de-Dôme*
CM Chanterelles ☎73943171
3km NE via D201
May-Sep 6HEC ⅁ ⋔ ⊙ ☻ ∅ ☎ ⊞ lau ♦ ⅏ ♟ ✗ ⌇LP

ST-ROME-DE-TARN *Aveyron*
Cascade ☎65625659
Terraced site beside the River Tarn.
0.3km N via D993.
Apr-Sep 3HEC ▦ ⅁ ⋔ ⅊ ♟ ✗ ⊙ ☻ ∅ ▲ ☻ ⌇ PR ☎ lau ♦ ⊞
Prices: A26 pitch 75-115

ST-SALVADOU *Aveyron*
Muret ☎65818069
A modern site in peaceful, rural surroundings beside the lake.
3km SE.
Jun-Sep 2HEC ▦ ♦ ⋔ ⅊ ♟ ☻ ⊙ ☻ ∅ ☻ ⌇ L ☎ ⊞ lau ♦ ✗ ⌇R
Prices: pitch 40-49 (incl 2 persons)

SALLES-CURAN *Aveyron*
Beau Rivage Lac de Pareloup ☎65463332
3.5km N via D993n and D243.
Jun-Sep 2HEC ▦ ⅁ ⋔ ⅊ ♟ ✗ ⊙ ☻ ∅ ▲ ⌇ LP ☎ ⊞ lau ♦ ⌇R
Prices: A30-40

SEMBADEL-GARE *Haute-Loire*
Casses ☎71009062
1km W via D22.
15 Jun-Sep 2HEC ▦ ⅁ ⋔ ⊙ ☻ ☎ lau ♦ ⅏ ♟ ✗ ▲ ⌇L Prices: A12
V15 ⌑15 ▲10

SÉNERGUES *Aveyron*
Étang du Camp ☎65796225
6km SW via D242.
Jun-15 Oct 3HEC ▦ ⅁ ⋔ ⊙ ☻ ∅ ☻ ☎ ⊞ lau ♦ ⅏ ♟ ✗ Prices:
pitch 60 (incl 2 persons)

SERVERETTE *Lozère*
CM ☎66483036
0.4km S beside the River Truyère.
15 Jun-15 Sep 1HEC ▦ ⅁ ⋔ ⊙ ☻ ⌇ R ☎ lau ♦ ⅏ ♟ ✗ ⊞

SEVERAC-LE-CHÂTEAU *Aveyron*
CM av J-Moulin ☎65476482
1.2km S via N9 towards Millau.
Jun-Sep 12HEC ⅁ ⋔ ⊙ ☻ ☎ lau ♦ ⅏ ♟ ✗ ∅ ▲ ⌇PR

SINGLES *Puy-de-Dôme*
Moulin de Serre ☎73211606
1.7km S of La Guinguette via D73 beside the Burande.
15 Dec-2 Nov 3HEC ▦ ⅁ ⋔ ⅏ ♟ ✗ ⊙ ☻ ∅ ☻ ⌇ PR ☎ ⊞ lau

THÉRONDELS *Aveyron*
Source ☎65660562
In a beautiful situation beside Lake Sarrans.
end Jun-early Sep 4.5HEC ▦ ⅁ ⋔ ⅏ ♟ ✗ ⊙ ☻ ∅ ☻ ⌇ LP ☎ lau

THIZY *Rhône*
CM ☎74640529
2km S on D504, rte de Tarare. Access difficult for caravans
(gradient of 18%).
Jun-1 Sep ▦ ⅁ ⋔ ⊙ ☻ ∅ ☎ lau ♦ ✗ ⌇LP

TRIZAC *Cantal*
Pioulat ☎71786420
15 Jun-15 Sep 4.7HEC ▦ ⅊⅄ ⋔ ⊙ ☻ ☻ ⌇ LR ☎ ⊞ lau ♦ ⅏ ♟ ✗ ∅
▲ Prices: A10 V7 ⌑8 ▲8

TRUEL, LE *Aveyron*
Prade ☎65464146
In rural surroundings beside the River Tarn.
15 Jun-15 Sep 4HEC ▦ ⅁ ⋔ ⊙ ☻ ∅ ☎ lau ♦ ⅏ ♟ ✗ ▲ ⌇PR

URÇAY *Allier*
CM r de la Gare ☎70069402
Etr-Sep 0.7HEC ▦ ⁝⁝⁝ ⅁ ⋔ ⊙ ☻ ⌇ R ☎ lau ♦ ⅏ ♟ ✗ ∅ ▲ ⊞

VARENNES-SUR-ALLIER *Allier*
▦**Château de Chazeuil** ☎70450010
On well-kept meadow.
3km NW on N7.
15 Apr-15 Oct 1.5HEC ⅁ ⋔ ⊙ ☻ ⌇ P ☎ ⊞ lau ♦ ⅏ ♟ ✗ ∅ ▲
Prices: A26 V18 pitch 23

Plans d'Eau Ile de Chazeuil ☎70450155
A pleasant site in wooded surroundings near the River Allier.
3km NW via N7 and D46.
15 May-15 Sep 4HEC ▦ ⅁ ⋔ ⊙ ☻ ⌇ P ☎ ⊞ ♦ ⅏ ♟ ✗ ∅ ▲ ⌇L
Prices: A22 V15

VERRIÈRES-EN-FOREZ *Loire*
Ferme Le Soleillant Le Soleillant ☎77762273
A small terraced site within the grounds of a farm.
Access via A47.
All year 4HEC ▦ ⅁ ⋔ ⅏ ✗ ⊙ ☻ ☻ ☎ ⊞ lau ♦ ♟ ✗ ▲ ⌇R Prices:
A7.50-15 pitch 11

VICHY *Allier*
At BELLERIVE(3km W)
Acacias r C-Decloître ☎70323632
Well-managed site, sub-divided into numbered pitches by hedges.
Clean sanitary installations. Library, billiard room. Water sports are
available nearby on lake.
From Vichy turn left after bridge beside ESSO garage and follow river
for 500m.
Apr-10 Oct 2HEC ▦ ♦ ⋔ ⅏ ✗ ⊙ ☻ ∅ ☻ ⌇ LPR ☎ ⊞ lau ♦ ♟ ✗ ▲

Beau Rivage r C-Decloître ☎70322685
Neat meadowland with marked out pitches. Well kept sanitary installations. TV.
Watch for turning over bridge onto left bank of River Allier.
May-Sep 1.5HEC 🏕 ♣♠🛒⚍✕⊙🚻⌀🏕🕮🔭 PR ☎⊞ lau Prices: A21-30 pitch 21-30

VIC-SUR-CÈRE Cantal

Pommeraie ☎71475418
2km SE.
May-15 Sep 4HEC 🏕 ♣♠🛒⚍✕⊙🚻⌀🛒🏕🕮Å🔭 P ☎⊞ lau ♣
🔭R Prices: pitch 115 (incl 2 persons)

VILLEFORT Lozère

Palhère rte du Mas de la Banque ☎66468063
4km SW via D66 beside the river.
May-Sep 1HEC 🏕 ♣♠🛒✕⊙🚻🔭 PR ⬛⊞ lau

VILLEFRANCHE-DE-PANAT Aveyron

Cantarelles Alrance ☎65464035
On level grassland by Lac de Villefranche-de-Panat.
On the D25 about 3km N.
May-Sep 2.5HEC 🏕 ♠🛒✕⊙🚻⌀🏕🕮🔭 L ☎⊞ lau ♣🛒 Prices: pitch 75 (incl 2 persons)

VILLEFRANCHE-DE-ROUERGUE Aveyron

CM de Teulel ☎65451624
In a pleasant situation beside the River Aveyron.
1.5km SW via D47 rte de Montauls.
Etr-1 Oct 1.8HEC 🏕 ♣♠⊙🚻⬛☎ lau ♣🔭PR

YSSINGEAUX Haute-Loire

CM Choumouroux ☎71655344
800m S of town off the rte de Puy.
May-Sep 0.8HEC 🏕 🔭♠⊙🚻🏕☎⊞ lau ♣🛒🍴✕⌀⚍🔭P Prices: A10 pitch 14

South Coast/Riviera

Stretching along the Golfe du Lion between the Pyrénées and Provence for 150 miles, the Languedoc-Rousillon region's vast stretches of beautiful sands are backed by a gentle countryside covered in vineyards and dotted with quiet villages. Inland are attractive Roman and medieval towns - Montpellier, Bézier and the splendid Carcassonne. High on the crags of the Corbières are the remarkable medieval castles of the Cathares.
Although away from the sea, the Rhône Valley region is undoubtedly a Mediterranean land - unparalleled sunshine warms this unspoilt countryside of vineyards, pastel villages and cypressus in the valleys, against dramatic backdrops of the Provençal Alps and Cévennes, with tumbling rivers running through spectacular gorges.
South again towards the coast is Provence - a land of blue clear skies, wonderful wines and superb food. The area's many rivers begin in the Alpine foothills, and these flow south and irrigate the rich plains below, filled with wonderful fruit and herbs.
Popular with visitors since the 18th century, the chic coastal resorts of Nice, Cannes and St Tropez are ablaze with palatial hotels and celebrated restaurants and, in the summer, swarming with holidaymakers - an acknowledgement of the spectacular coastline where the Alps meet the sea. But there is still a quieter hinterland, with ancient villages perched on high peaks, spectacular deep valleys and canyons, fine lakes, and breathtaking views from high corniche roads.
The principality of Monaco, which is 350 acres in extent, is an independent enclave inside France. It consists of three adjacent towns - Monaco, the capital, la Condamine, along the harbour and Monte-Carlo, along the coast immediately to the north. It is a narrow ribbon of coastline backed by the foothills of the Alps Maritime - a wonderful natural ampitheatre overlooking the sea.

AGAY Var

Agay Soleil rte de Cannes RN 98 ☎94820079
A small site beside a sandy beach. All kinds of watersports nearby.
Between N98 and the sea.
15 Mar-15 Nov 0.7HEC 🏕 ░░░ ♣♠🛒🍴✕⊙🚻⌀🏕☎🔭 S ☎⊞ lau
♣🛒 Prices: pitch 90-115 (incl 2 persons)

🛖**Estérel** av des Joffs ☎94820328
3km from Agay-Plage towards Valescure
22 Mar-4 Oct 12.5HEC 🏕 ♣♠🛒🍴✕⊙🚻⌀🔭 P ☎⊞ lau Prices: pitch 135-150 (incl 2 persons)

Rives de l'Agay av du Gratadis ☎94820274
A level site below a country road.
Turn off N98 at Agay beach and continue for 0.5km towards Valescure.
15 Feb-4 Nov 1.4HEC 🏕 ░░░ ♣♠🛒🍴✕⊙🚻⌀🏕🕮🔭 PR ☎⊞ lau ♣🔭S Prices: pitch 80-140 (incl 2 persons)

Vallée du Paradis rte du Gratadis ☎94821600
On a large meadow and a narrow strip of land between the road and the river.
500m inland from N98.
15 Mar-15 Oct 3HEC 🏕 ♣♠🛒✕⊙🚻⌀🏕🕮🔭R ☎⊞ lau ♣🔭S Prices: pitch 75-90 (incl 3 persons)

AGDE Hérault

Domaine des 7 Fonts ☎67941462
A park-like site amongst mature pine trees 3km from sea.
Turn off road between Agde and Sète by a furniture store and the ELF petrol station. Site in 400m.
15 Apr-Sep 6HEC 🏕 ♣♠🛒🍴✕⊙🚻⌀🏕🕮🔭 PR ☎⊞ lau

Escale rte de la Tamarissière ☎67212109
A riverside site, 900m from the sea, with good recreational facilities.
Apr-Sep 3.5HEC 🏕 ♣♠🛒🍴✕⊙🚻🔭 PR ☎⊞ lau

International de l'Hérault rte de la Tamarissière ☎67941283
A grassy site on W bank of the River Hérault.
Take the exit for 'Agde' off autoroute A9, then continue via D13 and D32E.
Etr-Sep 11HEC ♣♠🛒🍴✕⊙🚻⌀🏕🕮Å🔭 P ☎⊞ lau ♣⌀ 🔭R Prices: pitch 83-125 (incl 2 persons)

Mer et Soleil rte de Rochelongue ☎67942114
15 Mar-6 Nov 7HEC 🏕 ░░░ ♣♠🛒🍴✕⊙🚻⌀🏕🕮🔭 P ☎⊞ lau ♣🔭RS Prices: pitch 55-85 (incl 2 persons)

At ROCHELONGUE-PLAGE(4km S)

Champs Blancs rte de Rochelongue ☎67942342
Quiet shady site with hedged pitches.
*Camping Card Compulsory*Situated between Agde and Cap d'Agde on route de Rochelongue.
Apr-Sep 4HEC 🏕 ♣♠🛒🍴✕⊙🚻⌀🏕🕮🔭 P ☎⊞ lau ♣🔭RS Prices: pitch 100-200 (incl 4 persons)

AIGUES MORTES *Gard*

Petite Camargue BP21 ☎66538477
A grassy site lying amongst vineyards on the D62. 3.5 km from the sea.
Access via autoroute exit Gallargues in direction of La Grande Motte.
26 Apr-20 Sep 13HEC ▦ ⌂ ℮ ⅍ ♥ ✕ ⊙ ₪ ⌀ ⌂ ⚑ ⅃ P ☎ ⊞ lau
Prices: pitch 73-160 (incl 2 persons)

AIX-EN-PROVENCE *Bouches-du-Rhône*

Arc en Ciel Pont de Trois Sautets, Route de Nice ☎42261428
A pleasant terraced site on both sides of a stream.
Near motorway exit 3 Sautets on N7 towards Toulon. 3km SE near Pont des Trois Sautets.
15 Apr-15 Oct 2.1HEC ▦ ⋮⋮⋮ ⌀ ♥ ℮ ⊙ ₪ ⌀ ⅃ PR ☎ ⊞ lau ♦ ⅍ ♥ ✕ ▥ Prices: A30 pitch 28

ALET-LES-BAINS *Aude*

Val d'Aleth chemin de la Paoulette ☎68699040
In picturesque surroundings beneath the ancient ramparts, on the banks of the River Aude. English owners.
From Carcassonne take D118 towards Quillan. Site 8km beyond Limoux.
All year ▦ ♦ ℮ ⅍ ⊙ ₪ ⌀ ▥ ⚑ ⅃ R ☎ ⊞ ♦ ♥ ✕ ⅃P Prices: pitch 52 (incl 2 persons)

ALLÈGRE *Gard*

Domaine des Fumades ☎66248078
On sloping meadow near the river. Extensive leisure facilities. Liable to flooding at certain times.
Turn off D7 (Bourgot-les-Allrègre) at TOTAL filling station and follow signs.
15 May-15 Sep 15HEC ⌀ ⌂ ♥ ⅍ ♥ ✕ ⊙ ₪ ⌀ ⌂ ⅃ PR ☎ ⊞ lau
Prices: A17-28 pitch 45-67

ANDUZE *Gard*

Arche ☎0466617408
In a beautiful situation on the River Gard with fine views of the surrounding Cevennes scenery.
Access via A7 exit Bollène and D907.
25 Mar-30 Sep 10HEC ▦ ⋮⋮⋮ ♦ ℮ ⅍ ♥ ✕ ⊙ ₪ ⌂ ⚑ ⅃ R ☎ ⊞
lau Prices: pitch 53-81 (incl 2 persons)

Castel Rose 610 chemin de Recoulin ☎66619005
1 km NW on D907.
15 Mar-Oct 6.5HEC ▦ ⋮⋮⋮ ♦ ℮ ✕ ⊙ ₪ ⚑ ⅃ R lau ♦ ⅍ ⌀ ▥
Prices: A22 pitch 19

At ATTUECH(5km SE on D907)

Fief ☎66618171
On level meadow, divided by flowerbeds and shrubs.
Turn off D982 E of Attuech and continue for 400m on partially rough track.
Etr & Jun-Sep 4.5HEC ▦ ⌂ ℮ ⅍ ♥ ✕ ⊙ ₪ ⌀ ⚑ Δ ⅃ P ☎ ⊞ lau ♦ ⅃R

At CORBÈS(5km NW on D907)

Cévennes Provence ☎66617310
Situated in a valley bordered by two rivers and offering a choice of pitches in varying levels of shade and terrain.
Near railway station.
20 Mar-Oct 30HEC ▦ ♦ ℮ ⅍ ♥ ✕ ⊙ ₪ ⌀ ▥ ⌂ ⚑ ⅃ R ☎ ⊞ lau
Prices: pitch 56-80 (incl 2 persons)

ANTHÉOR-PLAGE *Var*

Azur Rivage ☎94448312
Etr-Sep 1.2HEC ▦ ♦ ℮ ⅍ ♥ ✕ ⊙ ₪ ⌀ ▥ ⚑ ⅃ P ⊞ lau ♦ ⅃S
Prices: pitch 109 (incl 2 persons)

Viaduc bd des Lucioles ☎94448231
A quiet site 150m from a sandy beach, with good facilities.
Access via N98.
Etr-Sep 1.1HEC ▦ ♦ ℮ ⊙ ₪ ☎ ⊞ lau ♦ ⅍ ♥ ✕ ⌀ ⅃ ⅃S Prices: pitch 98-132

ANTIBES *Alpes-Maritimes*

Logis de la Brague 1221 rte de Nice ☎93335472
On a level meadow beside a small river.
On N7.
2 May-Sep 1.7HEC ▦ ⌂ ℮ ⅍ ♥ ✕ ⊙ ₪ ⌀ ⅃ RS ☎ ⊞ ♦ ▥

Prices: pitch 93-115 (incl 3 persons)

At BIOT(7km N on N7 and A8)

Airotel Parc l'Eden chemin du Val-de-Pome ☎93656370
Site on level meadowland, no tents allowed.
On D4.
Apr-Oct 2.5HEC ▦ ♦ ℮ ⅍ ♥ ✕ ⊙ ₪ ⌂ ⚑ ⅃ P ☎ ⊞ lau ♦ ⌀ ⅃S

Prés Quartier la Romaine ☎93656106
2km SE via D4
15 May-25 Sep 11.8HEC ▦ ♦ ℮ ⊙ ₪ ⌂ ☎ ⊞ lau ♦ ⅍ ♥ ✕ ⌀ ⅃S

At BRAGUE, LA(4km N on N7)

Frênes ☎93333652
Opposite Biot railway station.
15 Jun-15 Sep 2.5HEC ♦ ℮ ⅍ ♥ ✕ ⊙ ₪ ⌀ ⌂ ⚑ ⅃ S ☎ ⊞ lau
Prices: pitch 90-149 (incl 2 persons)

Pylône av du Pylône, La Brague ☎93335286
External car park from 23.00 hrs.
From N7 take D4 for Biot. First turning on left.
All year 16HEC ▦ ♦ ℮ ⅍ ♥ ✕ ⊙ ₪ ⌀ ⌂ ⚑ ⅃ P ☎ ⊞ ⊠ lau ♦ ⅃S
Prices: A25-35 V20-25 ⚑20-25 ▲20-25

ARCS, LES *Var*

Eau Vive Quartier du Pont d'Argens ☎94474066
Camping Card Compulsory.
2km S on N7.
Mar-Nov 2.5HEC ▦ ♦ ℮ ♥ ✕ ⊙ ₪ ⌂ ⚑ ⅃ PR ☎ ⊞ lau ♦ ⅍ ⌀ ▥

ARGELÈS-SUR-MER *Pyrénées-Orientales*

Criques de Porteils rte de Collioure ☎68811273
Terraced site with beautiful view of sea.
4km S on N114 turn left through railway underpass and continue for 0.3km.
Apr-Sep 5HEC ▦ ⌂ ℮ ⅍ ♥ ✕ ⊙ ₪ ⌀ ⅃ S ☎ ⊞ lau

Dauphin rte de Taxo d'Avall ☎68811754
On a long stretch of grassland shaded by poplars, 1500m from sea.
3km N of town; at Taxo d'Avall turn right onto unclass road.
25 May-Sep 7.5HEC ▦ ♦ ℮ ⅍ ♥ ✕ ⊙ ₪ ⌀ ⌂ ⅃ P ☎ ⅊ ⊞ lau ♦ ⅃RS Prices: pitch 135 (incl 2 persons)

Galets rte de Taxo d'Avall ☎68810812
Some facilities only available Jun-Sep.
4km N
22 Mar-Oct 5HEC ▦ ⌂ ℮ ⅍ ♥ ✕ ⊙ ₪ ⌀ ▥ ⚑ ⅃ P ☎ ⊞ lau ♦ ⌀ ⅃RS
Prices: A16.20-27 V4.20-7

Marsouins rte de la Plage Nord ☎68811481
2km NE towards Plage Nord.
Apr-Sep 10HEC ▦ ♦ ℮ ⅍ ♥ ✕ ⊙ ₪ ⌀ ▥ ⚑ ⅃ P ☎ ⊞ lau ♦ ⅃S
Prices: pitch 72-120 (incl 2 persons)

Massane ☎68810685
Well laid-out site in shady garden 1km from sea.
Beside D618 near the municipal sports field.
15 Mar-15 Oct 3.5HEC ♦ ℮ ⅍ ♥ ⊙ ₪ ⌀ ▥ ⚑ ⊞ lau ♦ ⅍ ✕ ⅃S
Prices: pitch 106 (incl 2 persons)

Neptune Plage Nord ☎68810047
Flat site with both sunny and shady pitches. Water-slide. Separate car park for arrivals after 23.00 hrs.
May-Sep 4.8HEC ▦ ⌂ ♦ ℮ ⅍ ♥ ✕ ⊙ ₪ ⌀ ⌂ ⚑ ⅃ PRS ☎ ⅊ ⊞ lau ♦ ⅃RS Prices: pitch 160 (incl 2 persons)

Ombrages av Gl-de-Gaulle ☎68812983
Jul-Sep 4HEC ▦ ♦ ℮ ⊙ ₪ ☎ ⊞ lau ♦ ⅍ ♥ ✕ ⅃LPRS

Pujol rte du Tamariguer ☎68810025
1km from the beach and 500m from the village.
Jun-Sep 4.5HEC ▦ ♦ ℮ ⅍ ♥ ✕ ⊙ ₪ ⌀ ⅃ P ☎ ⊞ lau ♦ ⅃S
Prices: A28 pitch 44

CM Roussillonnais bd de la Mer ☎68811042
On a long stretch of sandy terrain adjoining a fine sandy beach.
In N part of town. Well signposted.
mid Apr-mid Oct 10HEC ▦ ⠿ ⌖ ⚲ ⚑ ⚏ ♀ ✕ ⊙ ⚑ ∅ ⚏ ⚏ ⚘ S ⚐ ⊞
lau ♦ ♨ P

Sirène rte de Taxo d'Avall ☎68810461
4km NE
30 Mar-19 Sep 18HEC ▦ ⚲ ⚑ ⚏ ♀ ✕ ⊙ ⚑ ∅ ⚏ ⚘ P ⚐ ⊞ lau ♦ S

At ARGELÈS-PLAGE(2.5km E via D618)

Pins av du Tech BP46 ☎68811046
On a narrow stretch of grassland with some poplar trees.
20 May-15 Sep 4.5HEC ▦ ♦ ⚑ ⊙ ⚑ ♨ ⚐ ⊞ lau ♦ ⚏ ♀ ✕ ∅ S
Prices: pitch 70-95 (incl 2 persons)

Soleil rte du littoral, Plage Nord ☎68811448
Peaceful site in wide meadow surrounded by tall trees. Private
beach, natural harbour. Best site in region, but pitches must be
booked in advance.
Follow rte du Littoral N out of town then 1.5km towards beach.
15 May-Sep 15HEC ▦ ♦ ⚑ ⚏ ♀ ✕ ⊙ ⚑ ∅ ♨ ⚏ ▲ ⚘ PRS ⚐ ⊞
⚙ lau Prices: A39 pitch 56

ARLES Bouches-du-Rhône

Rosiers Pont de Crau ☎90960212
Access via autoroute exit 'Arles Sud' or N443.
Etr-15 Oct 3.5HEC ▦ ⚲ ⚑ ⚏ ♀ ✕ ⊙ ⚑ ∅ ⚏ ⚏ ▲ ⚘ P ⚐ ⊞ lau
Prices: A16 V5 ⚏15 ▲15

ARLES-SUR-TECH Pyrénées-Orientales

Riuferrer ☎68391106
Quiet holiday site on gently sloping ground in pleasant area. Clean
sanitary installations. Separate area reserved for overnight stops.
Bar, ice for iceboxes and nearby municipal swimming pool are
available in summer only.
Signposted from N115.
All year 4HEC ⠿ ♦ ♦ ⚑ ♀ ⚏ ⊙ ⚑ ∅ ♨ ⚐ ⊞ lau ♦ ⚏ ✕ PR Prices:
A16-21 pitch 18-21

ARPAILLARGUES Gard

Mas de Rey Mas de Rey ☎66221827
Apr-15 Oct 3HEC ▦ ♦ ⚑ ⚏ ♀ ✕ ⊙ ⚑ ∅ ⚏ ⚘ P ⚐ ⊞ lau ♦ ♨
Prices: pitch 67-89 (incl 2 persons)

AUBIGNAN Vaucluse

Intercommunal du Brégoux chemin du Vas ☎90626250
A level site with good views of Mt.Ventoux.
On southern outskirts of town turn off D7 onto D55 and continue
towards Caromb for 0.5km.
15 May-Oct 4HEC ▦ ♦ ⚑ ⊙ ⚑ ⚐ ⊞ lau ♦ ⚏ ✕ ∅ ♨ LPRS

AUPS Var

International ☎94700680
0.5km W via D60 towards Fox-Amphoux
Apr-Sep 4HEC ⚲ ⚑ ✕ ✕ ⊙ ⚑ ⚏ ⚏ ⚘ P ⚐ ⊞ ♦ ⚏ ✕ ∅ ♨ Prices:
A22 pitch 17

INTERNATIONAL CAMPING

83630 AUPS (Var)

Route de Fox-Amphoux

Tel: 04.94.70.06.80 & 04.94.70.06.47

Fax: 04.94.70.10.51

Open: 1/4 – 30/9

Family site, 40,000m², 5 min from the town centre
and 15 min from the Lake Ste Croix and the Grand
Canyon du Verdon. SWIMMING POOL – TENNIS –
SHADED – NICE ATMOSPHERE – SOUNDPROOF
DISCOTHEQUE – CARAVAN HIRE AND STORAGE.

RESERVATIONS POSSIBLE

AVIGNON Vaucluse

Bagatelle Ile de la Barthelasse ☎90863039
Pleasant site with tall trees on the Isle of Barthelasse. All pitches are
numbered; on hard standing and divided by hedges. Separate
section for young people.
Travel alongside the old town wall and the Rhône onto the Rhône
bridge (Nîmes road). About halfway along turn right and follow signs.
All year 4HEC ▦ ♦ ⚑ ⚏ ♀ ✕ ⊙ ⚑ ∅ ⚐ ⊞ lau ♦ P

CM Pont St-Bénézet Ile de la Barthelasse ☎90826350
On island opposite bridge with fine views of town. Several tiled
sanitary blocks with individual wash cabins. Individual pitches.
Common room with TV, souvenir shop, car wash. Several playing
fields for volleyball and basketball. Definite divisions for tents and
caravans.
NW of the town on the right bank of the Rhône, 370m upstream from
bridge on right. (N100 leading to Nîmes).
Mar-Oct 9HEC ♦ ⚑ ⚏ ♀ ✕ ⊙ ⚑ ∅ ⚐ ⊞ lau ♦ P Prices: A18-25
⚏22-25 ▲16-18

AXAT Aude

Crémade ☎68205064
A shady, peaceful site, ideal for water sports.
May-Sep 3HEC ♦ ⚑ ⚏ ♀ ✕ ⊙ ⚑ ∅ ⚏ ⚏ ⚐ ⊞ lau

Moulin du Pont d'Alies ☎68205327
Junction of D117 and D118, 800m from Axat.
All year 2HEC ▦ ♦ ⚑ ⚏ ♀ ✕ ⊙ ⚑ ∅ ♨ ⚘ PR ⚐ ⊞ lau Prices:
A15-18 pitch 31-38

BANDOL Var

Vallongue ☎94294955
Terraced site, parts of which have lovely sea views.
Camping Card Compulsory.
Apr-Sep 1.5HEC ♦ ⚲ ⚑ ⊙ ⚑ ⚏ ⊞ lau ♦ ⚏ ∅ ♨

BARCARÈS, LE Pyrénées-Orientales

Bousigues av des Corbières ☎68861619
Quiet site standing about 1km from the sea.From D83 take exit 10.
Apr-1 Nov 3HEC ▦ ♦ ⚑ ⚏ ⊙ ⚑ ∅ ⚏ ⚏ ⚘ P ⚐ ⊞ lau ♦ S
Prices: pitch 48.50-97 (incl 2 persons)

California rte de St-Laurent ☎68861608
1.5km SW via D90
18 Apr-26 Sep 5HEC ▦ ♦ ⚲ ⚑ ⚏ ♀ ✕ ⊙ ⚑ ∅ ⚏ ⚏ ⚘ P ⚐ ⊞
lau ♦ LRS Prices: pitch 102 (incl 2 persons)

Europe ☎68861536
Via D90 2km SW, 200m from Agly and 500m from the sea.
All year 6HEC ▦ ♦ ⚑ ⚏ ♀ ✕ ⊙ ⚑ ∅ ⚏ ⚏ ⚘ P ⚐ ⊞ lau ♦ RS

Presqu'île ☎68861280
2km on rte de Leucate, turn right.
Apr-Oct 3HEC ⠿ ♦ ⚑ ⚏ ♀ ✕ ⊙ ⚑ ∅ ⚏ ⚏ ⚘ LP ⚐ ⊞ lau ♦ S

Sable d'Or r des Palombes ☎68861841
Off D627 between Le Barcarès and Port Barcarès.
All year 4HEC ▦ ♦ ⚑ ⚏ ♀ ✕ ⊙ ⚑ ∅ ⚏ ⚘ LPS ⚐ ⊞ lau

BAR-SUR-LOUP, LE Alpes-Maritimes

Gorges du Loup 965 chemin des Vergers ☎93424506
Terraced site divided into pitches, in an olive grove. Very steep
entrance.
Access from Grasse on D2085 towards Le Pré du Lac (NE), then
turn left on D2210 in the direction of Vence.
Apr-Sep 2HEC ▦ ♦ ⚑ ⚏ ♀ ✕ ⊙ ⚑ ∅ ⚏ ⚘ P ⊞ lau ♦ R Prices:
pitch 90-160 (incl 2 persons)

BEAUCHASTEL Ardèche

CM Voiliers La Voulte-Rhône ☎75622404
900m S of N86.
All year 1.5HEC ▦ ♦ ⚑ ✕ ⊙ ⚑ ⚘ P ⊞ lau ♦ ⚏ ♀ ∅ ♨ R ⊞

BELGENTIER Var

Tomasses Quartier les Tomasses ☎94489270
1.5km SE towards Toulon. Leave autoroute A6 at exit 'St-Maximin'
and continue via D554.
Apr-Sep 2.3HEC ▦ ⚲ ⚑ ⚏ ♀ ✕ ⊙ ⚑ ∅ ⚏ ⚘ PR ⚐ ⊞ lau

BESSÈGES *Gard*

At **PEYREMALE**(3km W)

Drouilhèdes ☎66250480
2km W on D17 rte de Génolhac, and continue 1km on D386.
Mar-Sep 2HEC ▥ ♦♠☎♀✕☉ ▣ ∅ ♨ ♣ ₹ R ☎⊞ lau ♦ 볶
Prices: pitch 85 (incl 2 persons)

BOISSERON *Gard*

Boisseron Domaine de Gajan ☎66809430
Mar-Oct 3HEC ♦♠☎♀✕☉ ▣ ∅ 볶 ♣ ♣ ₹ P ☎⊞ lau ♦ ₹R

BOISSON *Gard*

◨**Château de Boisson** ☎66248221
Camping Card Compulsory.
D7 in direction Fumades. Boisson is 10km on the right and the
campsite is signposted.
May-Oct 7HEC ▥ ⁖⁖⁖ ♦♠☎♀✕☉ ▣ ∅ ♣ ♣ ₹ P ☎⊗ lau ♦
₹R Prices: A35 pitch 55

BOLLÈNE *Vaucluse*

Barry ☎90301320
Well-kept site near ruins of Barry.
Signposted from Bollène via D26.
All year 3HEC ▥ ♦♠☎♀✕☉ ▣ ∅ 볶 ♣ ₹ P ☎⊞ lau ♦ ₹LR

Simioune ☎90304462
Follow signs from Bollène exit on A7.
All year 1.5HEC ⁖⁖⁖ ♦♠☎♀✕☉ ▣ ♣ ₹ P ☎⊞ lau ♦ ₹R

BORMES-LES-MIMOSAS *Var*

Clau Mar Jo 895 chemin de Benat ☎94715339
Apr-Sep 1HEC ♦♠☎♀ ☉ ▣ ♣ ♣ ⊞ lau ♦ ☎♣ ∅ 볶 Prices: pitch
98 (incl 2 persons)

Manjastre 1789 rte de Martegasse ☎94710328
5km NW via N98 on road to La Môle/Cogolin.
All year 3.5HEC ▥ ♦♠☎♀✕☉ ▣ ∅ ♣ ₹ P ☎⊞ lau ♦ ₹LS
Prices: A27 pitch 35

At **FAVIÈRE, LA**(3km S)

Domaine La Favière ☎94710312
In a very attractive setting with a long sandy beach and numbered
pitches. Fine views of sea. Sport facilities.
Camping Card Compulsory.
0.5km E of Bormes-Cap Bénat road.
15 Mar-Oct 45HEC ▥ ⁖⁖⁖ ♦♦♠☎♀✕☉ ▣ ∅ 볶 ₹ S ☎⊞ lau ♦
⊞ Prices: A27 pitch 83

BOULOU, LE *Pyrénées-Orientales*

Mas Llinas ☎68832546
3km N via N9
All year 4HEC ▥ ♦☉♠☎✕☉ ▣ ∅ ♣ ♣ ₹ P ☎⊞ lau Prices:
pitch 64 (incl 2 persons)

BOULOURIS-SUR-MER *Var*

Ile d'Or ☎94955213
Mar-Oct 10HEC ♦♠☎♀✕☉ ▣ ∅ ₹ S ☎⊞ lau

Val Fleury ☎94952152
Terraced site with tarred drives.
Off N98 at Km 93.1.
All year 1HEC ♦♠♀✕☉ ▣ ♣ ♣ ☎⊞ lau ♦ ☎ ∅ ₹PS Prices: pitch
120-200 (incl 4 persons)

BOURDEAUX *Drôme*

At **POËT-CÉLARD, LE**(3km NW)

Couspeau Quartier Bellevue ☎75533014
1.3km SE via D328A
May-Sep 3HEC ▥ ☉♠☎♀✕☉ ▣ ∅ 볶 ♣ ♣ ♠ ₹ P ☎⊞ lau
Prices: pitch 72-100 (incl 2 persons)

BOURG-MADAME *Pyrénées-Orientales*

Ségre 8 av du Puymorens ☎68046587
100m N on N20.
Closed Oct 1HEC ▥ ♦♠☎☉ ▣ ♣ ₹ R ☎⊞ lau ♦ ☎♀✕∅볶 ₹PR
⊞

BOURG-ST-ANDÉOL *Ardèche*

Lion ☎75545320
Large well-shaped park in wooded terrain, beside River Rhône.
N86 in direction of Viviers, through the centre of town.
Apr-15 Sep 8HEC ▥ ♦♠☎♀✕☉ ▣ ∅ ♣ ♣ ₹ PR ☎⊞ lau Prices:
pitch 57-82 (incl 2 persons)

BRISSAC *Hérault*

Val d'Hérault St-Étienne d'Issensac ☎67737229
A terraced site in a quiet location. Bar and restaurant facilities
available July and August only.
4km S via D4.
15 Mar-30 Oct 3.4HEC ⁖⁖⁖ ♦♠☎♀✕☉ ▣ ∅ ♣ ₹ R ☎ lau ♦
⊞ Prices: A17 V10 ♣43 ▲43

BROUSSES-ET-VILLARET *Aude*

Martinet Rouge ☎68265198
A pleasant, well equipped site on gently sloping terrain. Terraced,
with well marked pitches.
Access via D48.
Apr-Oct 2.6HEC ▥ ♦♠☎☉ ▣ ∅ 볶 ♣ ♣ ₹ P ☎⊞ lau ♦ ✕ ₹R
Prices: pitch 58 (incl 2 persons)

CADENET *Vaucluse*

Val de Durance Les Routes ☎90683775
29 Mar-12 Oct 3.5HEC ▥ ☉♠☎♀✕☉ ▣ ♣ ▲ ₹ LP ☎ lau
Prices: A22-27 pitch 23-39

CAGNES-SUR-MER *Alpes-Maritimes*

Colombier 35 chemin de Ste-Colombe ☎93731277
Apr-Sep 0.6HEC ▥ ♦♠☎♀✕☉ ▣ ∅ ₹ P ☎⊞⊗ lau ♦☎♣✕볶
₹RS Prices: pitch 68-135 (incl 2 persons)

Country Club Cocagne Camp'otel rte de Vence, chemin du Pain
de Sucre ☎92135777
A small luxurious family site with numbered pitches divided by
hedges. There is a tractor to help vehicles climb the entrance ramp.
N of Cagnes-sur-Mer on D36.
3HEC ⁖⁖⁖ ☉♥♠☎♀✕☉ ▣ ♣ ₹ P ☎⊞ lau ♦ ∅ 볶 Prices: pitch
125-290 (incl 2 persons)

Rivière val de Cagnes, 168 Chemin des Saffes ☎93206227
4km N beside River Cagne.
All year 1.2HEC ♦♠☎♀✕☉ ▣ ∅ ♣ ₹ PR ☎⊞ lau ♦ 볶 ₹LS

Todos 159 Vallon-des-Vaux L93312005
In a beautiful Mediterranean setting. A large section has been
reserved for young people and there is a disco in this area.
Access via N7 towards Nice.
15 Mar-31 Oct 2HEC ▥ ♦♠☎♀✕☉ ▣ ∅ ♣ ♣ ₹ P ☎⊞ lau ♦
₹S Prices: pitch 59.90 (incl 2 persons)
See advertisement on page 144.

At **CROS-DE-CAGNES**(2km S)

Panoramer 30 Chemin des Gros Buaux ☎93311615
Pleasant terraced site with sea view. Separate sections for tents and
caravans.

LE TODOS ★★

meeting point for the European youth. Vallon des Vaux
(Val Fleuri), 06800 Cagnes sur Mer
N8 exit Cagnes sur Mer. Follow N7 direction Nice. Follow arrows
- swimming pool on site
- a very beautiful site with typical, shady vegetation of the
  Mediterranean Sea.
- Caravans, bungalows and chalets with heating to let.
- Reservations possible.
- **A large part of the site has been reserved for the
  young people with dance-evenings and meals with
  special prices for young people.**
- Restaurant, pizzeria.
- Volleyball, table tennis and French boules.
- Tennis 300m.
- Green Park planned for 1997.
- **Open: 1.3 - 30.10**
- **Tel: 04.93.31.20.05 Fax: 04.92.12.81.66**

2km N of town.
Etr-Sep 1.4HEC ▦ ⠿ ♦ ⋔ ☎ ▼ ✕ ⊙ ☺ ∅ ☎ ⊞ lau ♦ ☎ ♨ ⌇S
Prices: pitch 130-150 (incl 3 persons)

CAMURAC Aude

Sapins ☎68203811
Good views.
1.5km from village.
All year 2HEC ▦ ♁ ⋔ ▼ ✕ ⊙ ☺ ☎ ▲ ⌇ P ⊞ lau ♦ ☎ ∅ ♨ ⌇LRS

CANET-PLAGE Pyrénées-Orientales

Domino r des Palmiers ☎68802725
Apr-Sep 6.8HEC ▦ ⠿ ♦ ⋔ ☎ ▼ ✕ ⊙ ☺ ☎ ☎ ⊞ lau ♦ ∅ ⌇S
Prices: A25 pitch 75

At **CANET-VILLAGE**(2km W)

Brasilia Voie de la Gauste, Zone Technique du Port ☎68802382
Near beach. Divided into pitches. Sanitary installations not up to high
standard of rest of site.
Turn off main road in village and continue towards beach for 2km.
10 Apr-5 Oct 15HEC ▦ ♦ ⋔ ☎ ▼ ✕ ⊙ ☺ ∅ ☎ ▲ ⌇ PRS ☎ ⊞ lau ♦
♨

Peupliers Voie de la Crouste ☎68803587
Quiet site divided into pitches.
15 Jun-15 Sep 4HEC ▦ ♦ ⋔ ☎ ▼ ✕ ⊙ ☺ ∅ ♨ ☎ ⌇ PS ☎ ⊞ lau
Prices: A25 pitch 65

Ma Prairie ☎68732617
Grassland site in a hollow surrounded by vineyards.
Access from D11 in the direction of Elne off N617 Perpignan-Canet-
Plage road.
May-Sep 4HEC ▦ ♦ ⋔ ☎ ▼ ✕ ⊙ ☺ ☎ ▲ ⌇ P ☎ ⊞ lau ♦ ⌇RS

CANNES Alpes-Maritimes

At **CANNET, LE**

Grand Saule 24 bd J-Moulin ☎93905510
Separate sections for families and groups of young people.
Apr-Sep 1HEC ▦ ♦ ⋔ ☎ ▼ ⊙ ☺ ☎ ⌇ P ☎ ⊞ lau ♦ ☎ ∅ ♨ ⌇LS
Prices: pitch 87-124 (incl 2 persons)

Ranch chemin St-Joseph, L'Aubarède ☎93460011
Apr-30 Oct 2HEC ⠿ ♁ ⋔ ☎ ⊙ ☺ ☎ ☎ ⌇ P ☎ ⊞ lau ♦ ▼ ✕ ⌇S
Prices: pitch 90-125 (incl 2 persons)

CARCASSONNE Aude

Breil d'Aude rte de Limoux, Preixan ☎68268818
1.5km N via D118.
15 Apr-30 Sep 11HEC ▦ ♦ ⋔ ☎ ▼ ✕ ⊙ ☺ ☎ ☎ ☎ ⌇ LPR ☎ ⊞
lau ♦ ∅ Prices: pitch 85-102 (incl 2 persons)

At **PENNAUTIER**(4km NW off N113)

Lavandières N113 ☎68254166
Apr-Oct 1HEC ▦ ♦ ⋔ ☎ ✕ ⊙ ☺ ☎ ☎ ⊞ lau ♦ ☎ ∅ ♨ ⌇LPR

CARPENTRAS Vaucluse

Lou Comtadou 881 av P-de-Coubertin ☎90670316
Near the Carpentras swimming pool in pleasant surroundings with
good, modern facilities.
Apr-Oct 2HEC ▦ ♦ ⋔ ☎ ▼ ✕ ⊙ ☺ ☎ ☎ ☎ ▲ ☎ ⊞ lau ♦ ♨ ⌇P
Prices: A18-22 pitch 90-95

CARQUEIRANNE Var

◼Beau-Vezé rte de la Moutonne ☎94576530
2.5km NW via N559 and then D76 between Hyères and Toulon.
Jun-15 Sep 7HEC ♦ ⋔ ☎ ▼ ✕ ⊙ ☺ ▲ ♨ ⌇ P ☎ ⊞ lau

CASTELLANE Alpes-de-Haute-Provence

International Plan de la Palud ☎92836667
Signposted.
15 Apr-15 Sep 6HEC ▦ ♁ ⋔ ☎ ▼ ✕ ⊙ ☺ ☎ ☎ ☎ ⌇ P ☎ ⊞ lau ♦ ∅
⌇R Prices: pitch 80-100 (incl 2 persons)

Nôtre Dame ☎92836302
In meadowland with deciduous and fruit trees.
200m W on D952.
Apr-20 Oct 0.6HEC ▦ ♦ ⋔ ☎ ▼ ⊙ ☺ ☎ ☎ ☎ ▲ ☎ ⊞ lau ♦ ✕ ♨
⌇PR Prices: pitch 57 (incl 2 persons)

◼Verdon Domain de la Salaou, rte de Moustiers/Ste-Marie
☎92836129
Well-maintained site on meadowland on banks of River Verdon.
Divided into pitches (100-150 sqm). Rooms in rustic style.
Reservations recommended Jul-Aug.
Below the D952 towards the Gorges du Verdon.
15 May-15 Sep 14HEC ▦ ♦ ⋔ ☎ ▼ ✕ ⊙ ☺ ☎ ▲ ☎ ☎ ⌇ PR ☎ ⊞
lau Prices: pitch 90-178 (incl 3 persons)

At **CHASTEUIL**(9km W on D952)

Gorges du Verdon ☎92836364
Situated on bank of the Verdon, surrounded by mountains and at an
altitude of 660 metres. Fully divided into pitches split into two by
road. Bathing in river not advised due to strong current.
0.5km S of village.
27 Apr-30 Sep 4HEC ▦ ♦ ⋔ ☎ ▼ ✕ ⊙ ☺ ☎ ☎ ⌇ PR ☎ ⊞ lau
Prices: pitch 69-102 (incl 2 persons)

At **GARDE-CASTELLANE**(7.5km SE)

Clavet rte de Grasse Napoléon ☎92836896
Site of woods and grassland with mountain views.
15 May-15 Sep 7HEC ▦ ♦ ⋔ ☎ ▼ ✕ ⊙ ☺ ∅ ☎ ☎ ▲ ⌇ P ☎ ⊞ lau
Prices: pitch 60-98 (incl 2 persons)

CAVAILLON Vaucluse

Durance Digue des Grands Jardins ☎90711178
2km S.
All year 4HEC ▦ ♦ ⋔ ☎ ▼ ✕ ⊙ ☺ ☎ ☎ ☎ ⊞ lau ♦ ☎ ▼ ✕ ♨ ⌇LPRS

CAVALAIRE-SUR-MER Var

Cros de Mouton ☎94641087
Terraced site with individual pitches, separated for caravans and
tents. Good view of sea, 1.5km distance.
Turn off N559 in town centre and continue inland for 1.5km.
15 Mar-Oct 4.3HEC ♦ ♦ ⋔ ☎ ▼ ⊙ ☺ ∅ ♨ ☎ ☎ ⌇ P ☎ ⊞ lau ♦
⌇S Prices: A30-32 pitch 30-34

Pinède chemin des Mannes ☎94641114
400m from sea.
10 Mar-15 Oct 2HEC ♦ ⋔ ☎ ⊙ ☺ ∅ ☎ ⊞ lau ♦ ▼ ✕ ⌇S

Roux r Pardigon ☎94640547
23 Mar-30 Sep 5HEC ▦ ♦ ⋔ ☎ ▼ ✕ ⊙ ☺ ∅ ☎ ☎ ⊞ lau ♦ ⌇S

CENDRAS Gard

Croix Clémentine ☎66865269
An extensive, partly terraced site, in wooded surroundings.
Signposted W of town towards La Baume via D160.
Apr-22 Sep 12HEC ▦ ♦ ⋔ ☎ ▼ ✕ ⊙ ☺ ∅ ☎ ☎ ⌇ P ☎ ⊞ lau ♦
⌇R Prices: pitch 64-104 (incl 2 persons)

CHABEUIL *Drôme*
Grand Lierne ☎75598314
On the edge of the Vercors Regional Park.
Access via A7 exit 'Valence Sud' towards Chabeuil, then follow signs for site.
May-15 Sep 3.6HEC ▦ ♦ ⋔ ⋒ ♋ ⚑ ✕ ⊙ ☒ ∅ ≞ ⊞ ⊡ ▲ ⋆ P ⚐ ⊞ ∅
lau ♦ ⋆L Prices: A30 pitch 45-80

CHAPELLE-EN-VERCORS, LA *Drôme*
Bruyères ☎75482146
All year 1HEC ▦ ⋒ ⋔ ⊙ ☒ ☒ ▲ ⚐ ⊞ ♦ ⋒ ♋ ✕ ∅ ≞ ⋆P

CHÂTEAU-ARNOUX *Alpes-de-Haute-Provence*
Salettes ☎92640240
Some facilities (shop, café etc) available in summer only.
1km E beside the river.
All year 4HEC ▦ ♦ ⋒ ♋ ✕ ⊙ ☒ ☒ ⋆ P ⚐ ⊞ lau Prices: A22 pitch 22

CHÂTEAUNEUF-DU-RHÔNE *Drôme*
CM ☎75908096
N end of village.
Jun-Sep 0.6HEC ▦ ⋒ ⋔ ⊙ ☒ ⋆ P ⚐ ⊞ lau ♦ ⋆ Prices:
A8.50 V5.50 ☒5.50 ▲5.50

CHAUZON *Ardèche*
Digue ☎75396357
1km E, 100m from the River Ardèche
20 Mar-Sep 3HEC ▦ ♦ ⋒ ⋔ ♋ ✕ ⊙ ☒ ∅ ≞ ☒ ♋ ⋆ PR ⚐ ⊞ lau
Prices: pitch 73-87 (incl 2 persons)

CIOTAT, LA *Bouches-du-Rhône*
Oliviers rte de Toulon ☎42831504
Terraced site between the N559 and the railway line from Nice.
Turn inland off the N559 at Km34, some 5km E of the centre of the town and drive for 150m.
Mar-Sep 10HEC ▦ ♦ ⋒ ⋔ ♋ ✕ ⊙ ☒ ∅ ≞ ☒ ⋆ P ⚐ ⊞ lau ♦ ⋆S
Prices: A27 pitch 35

St Jean 30 av de St-Jean ☎42831301
Site on the right side of the coast road.
Between D559 and sea behind the motel in NE part of town.
May-Oct 0.9HEC ♦ ⋒ ⋔ ♋ ✕ ⊙ ☒ ∅ ⊞ ☒ ⊞ lau ♦ ⋆S

Soleil rte de Marseille ☎42715532
Divided into pitches.
15 Mar-15 OCT 0.5HEC ▦ ♦ ⋒ ⋔ ♋ ✕ ⊙ ☒ ☒ ☒ ⚐ ⊞ lau ♦ ⋆ ∅ ≞
⋆PS Prices: A23-24 pitch 23-25

COGOLIN *Var*
Argentière chemin de l'Argentière ☎94545786
Landscaped, partly terraced site.
1500m NW along D48 rte de St-Maur.
15 Apr-Sep 8HEC ▦ ⋒ ⋔ ♋ ✕ ⊙ ☒ ∅ ≞ ☒ ⋆ P ⊞ lau

COLLE-SUR-LOUP, LA *Alpes-Maritimes*
Pinèdes rte du Pont de Pierre ☎93329894
Well-kept campsite on steep slope with woodland providing shade.
By the motorway A8 exit 'Cagnes-sur-Mer' turn right off D6 towards La Colle-sur-Loup.
Mar-Oct 3.8HEC ▦ ♦ ⋒ ⋔ ♋ ✕ ⊙ ☒ ∅ ≞ ☒ ☒ ⋆ PR ⚐ ⊞ lau
Prices: A19-24 V12-15 ☒39-43 ▲31-37

Vallon Rouge rte Greolières ☎93328612
Forest-like area, divided into pitches.
3km W of town, 100m to right of D6 towards Gréolières.
Apr-Sep 3HEC ▦ ♦ ⋒ ⋔ ♋ ✕ ⊙ ☒ ∅ ≞ ☒ ☒ ⋆ PR ⚐ ⊞ lau Prices: pitch 60-120 (incl 2 persons)

COURONNE, LA *Bouches-du-Rhône*
Mas Plage de Ste-Croix ☎42807034
On sparse, stony grassland on a plateau with a fine view of the bay, and access to a sandy beach.
Access from D49.
Apr-Sep 6HEC ♦ ⋒ ⋔ ♋ ✕ ⊙ ☒ ∅ ≞ ☒ ☒ ⋆ PS ⚐ lau Prices:
A25.20-31.50 V21 ☒31.50 ▲31.50

CRAU, LA *Var*
Bois de Mont-Redon 480 chemin du Mont-Redon ☎94667334
3km NE via D29
15 Jun-15 Sep 5HEC ▦ ♦ ⋒ ⋔ ♋ ✕ ⊙ ☒ ∅ ⋆ P ⚐ ⊞ lau Prices:
pitch 112 (incl 3 persons)

CRESPIAN *Gard*
Mas de Reilhe ☎66778212
Individual pitches with hedges and trees dividing them. Recreational facilities.
On N110.
Jun-14 Sep 3HEC ▦ ♦ ⋒ ⋔ ♋ ✕ ⊙ ☒ ∅ ⋆ P ⚐ lau ♦ ⊞ Prices:
A31 pitch 50

DIE *Drôme*
Pinède Quartier du Pont-Neuf ☎75221777
W via D93 beside the River Drôme
Apr-15 Sep 8HEC ▦ ♦ ⋒ ⋔ ♋ ✕ ⊙ ☒ ∅ ≞ ▲ ⋆ PR ⚐ ⊞ lau
Prices: pitch 60-94 (incl 2 persons)

DIEULEFIT *Drôme*
Source du Jabron Comps ☎75906130
A terraced site in a pleasant location beside the River Jabron.
N of town on D538.
May-Sep 6HEC ▦ ♦ ⋒ ⋔ ♋ ✕ ⊙ ☒ ∅ ≞ ☒ ☒ ⋆ PR ⚐ ⊞ lau ♦ ⋆ ≞
⋆LS

ENTRECHAUX *Vaucluse*
Bon Crouzet rte de St-Marcelin ☎0490460161
Apr-Sep 1.4HEC ▦ ⋒ ⋔ ♋ ✕ ⊙ ☒ ∅ ≞ ▲ ⋆ R ⚐ ⊞ lau ♦ ✕ ∅ ≞
⋆P

ESPARRON-DE-VERDON *Alpes-de-Haute-Provence*
Soleil ☎92771378
In wooded surroundings beside Lake Esparron with well defined pitches.
Etr-Sep 2HEC ▦ ♦ ♦ ⋒ ⋔ ♋ ✕ ⊙ ☒ ∅ ⋆ L ☒ ⊞ ∅ lau

FONTES *Hérault*
Clairettes ☎67250131
D9 10km N of Pézenas, access via Adissan D128.
May-Oct 1.6HEC ♦ ⋒ ⋔ ♋ ✕ ⊙ ☒ ∅ ≞ ☒ ☒ ⋆ P ⚐ ⊞ lau

FONTVIEILLE *Bouches-du-Rhône*
CM Pins r Michelet ☎90547869
1km from village via D17.
Apr-14 Oct 3.5HEC ▦ ♦ ♦ ⋒ ⊙ ☒ ☒ ⊞ lau ♦ ⋒ ♋ ✕ ∅ ≞ ⋆P

FOS-SUR-MER *Bouches-du-Rhône*
Estagnon Plage St-Gervais ☎42050119
Level, rather dusty site. Public beach on other side of road.
Camping Card Compulsory.
Situated S of an industrial zone-Quartier St-Gervais.
May-Sep 2HEC ▦ ⋒ ⋔ ♋ ✕ ⊙ ☒ ∅ ≞ ☒ ☒ ⋆ S ⚐ lau

CAMPING CARAVANNING DE MONTOUREY

(**** applied for)
Route de Bagnols en Forêt,
Chemin du Reyran, 83600 FREJUS (Var)
MORE SPACE: sites of 150 sqm
MORE QUIETNESS: 4 ha of well shaded grass ground
MORE RELAXATION: 2 swimming pools, bar, restaurant, dancing,
organised leisure, tennis. Mobile homes, caravans and tents for hire
INTERNATIONAL RECEPTION SERVICE
Open: 1.4 – 30.9
Reservations: Tel: 0 4 .94.53.26.41
Fax: 04.94.53.26.75

FRÉJUS *Var*

Dattier rte de Bagnols-en-Forêt ☎94408893
Laid out in terraces with a view of the Esterel mountains.
Access from A8 via RN7, then CD4.
Etr-Sep 4HEC ▦ ♣ ♠ ▨ ▼ ✕ ⊙ ❾ ⊘ ❼ ❿ ⅃ P ⌂ ⊞ lau ♦ ⚱

Fréjus rte de Bagnols-en-Forêt ☎94408803
Camping Card recommended. Access via N7 and D4.
Closed 15 Dec-16 Jan 4HEC ▦ ♁ ♠ ▨ ▼ ✕ ⊙ ❾ ⊘ ⚱ ⛺ A ⅃ PS ⌂ ⊞ lau

Holiday Green rte de Bagnols-en-Forêt ☎94408820
6km N via D4.
22 Mar-24 Oct 15HEC ▦ ♠ ♠ ▨ ▼ ✕ ⊙ ❾ ⊘ ⅃ P ⌂ ⊞ lau Prices:
A26-40 pitch 74-105

Montourey rte de Bagnols-en-Forêt, chemin du Reyran, St-Jean-les-Cais ☎94532641
2km N.
Mar-Sep 5HEC ♁ ♠ ▨ ▼ ✕ ⊙ ❾ ⊘ ⚱ ⛺ ⅃ P ⌂ ⊞ lau ♦ ⅃LS

Pierre Verte rte de Bagnols-en-Forêt ☎94408830
Access on A8 from Puget-sur-Argens.
Apr-Oct 28HEC ▦ ♦ ♠ ♠ ▨ ▼ ✕ ⊙ ❾ ⊘ ⚱ ⛺ ❿ ⅃ P ⌂ ❒ ⊞ lau
Prices: pitch 96 (incl 2 persons)

Pins Parasols rte de Bagnols-en-Forêt ☎94408843
4km N via D4.
Apr-Sep 4.5HEC ▦ ♁ ♠ ▨ ▼ ✕ ⊙ ❾ ⊘ ⅃ P ⌂ ⊞ lau Prices: pitch
125 (incl 2 persons)

FRONTIGNAN *Hérault*

Soleil ☎67430202
Family site bordering the beach.
NE via D60.
May-Sep 1.5HEC ♁ ♠ ▨ ✕ ⊙ ❾ ⚱ ⛺ ❿ ⅃ PS ⌂ ❒ ⊞ lau

Tamaris ☎67434477
From N112 take D129 and D60/D50 for 6km.
24 May-15 Sep 4.5HEC ♁ ♠ ▨ ▼ ✕ ⊙ ❾ ⊘ ⚱ ⛺ ❿ ⅃ PS ⌂ ⊞ lau
Prices: pitch 100-175 (incl 2 persons)

GALLARGUES-LE-MONTUEUX *Gard*

Amandiers ☎66352802
8 May-7 Sep 3HEC ▦ ♁ ♠ ▨ ▼ ✕ ⊙ ❾ ⊘ ⛺ ❿ ⅃ P ⌂ ⊞ lau ♦
✕ ⅃R Prices: pitch 55-68 (incl 2 persons)

GALLICIAN *Gard*

Mourgues ☎66733088
Situated in an old vineyard with some vines retained to separate
pitches. Views overlooking the Camargues
On the N572 between St-Gilles and Vauvert at the junction with the
road to Gallician.
Apr-15 Sep 2HEC ▦ ♦ ♁ ♠ ▨ ▼ ⊙ ❾ ⊘ ❿ ⅃ P ⌂ ⊞ lau ♦ ✕ ⊘ ⚱ ⅃P

GASSIN *Var*

Moulin de Verdagne ☎94797821
All year 5.5HEC ▦ ♦ ♠ ▨ ▼ ✕ ⊙ ❾ ⊘ ⛺ ❿ A ⅃ P ⌂ ⊞ lau Prices:
A16-21 pitch 34-47

Parc Montana Gassin rte du Bourrian ☎94552020
Park-like site on slopes of a hill.
2.5km E of N559. Access from main road at Km84.5 and 84.9 on
D89.
Closed 15 Nov-15 Dec 32HEC ▦ ♦ ♠ ▨ ▼ ✕ ⊙ ❾ ⊘ ⚱ ❿ ⅃ P ⌂ ⊞
lau Prices: A15-26 pitch 49-90

GIENS *Var*

Cigales pl de la Badine ☎94582106
A well-kept site with numbered pitches. Special places for caravans.
0.3km E of D97.
24 Apr-5 Oct 1.8HEC ▦ ▨▨▨ ♦ ♠ ▨ ▼ ⊙ ❾ ❿ ⌂ ⊞ lau ♦ ✕ ⊘ ⚱
⅃S Prices: pitch 68-130 (incl 2 persons)

GILETTE *Alpes-Maritimes*

Moulin Noù Pont C-Albert, rte de Carros ☎93089240
On the D2209, 1.8km SW of the Pont-Charles-Albert
Apr-Sep 3HEC ▦ ♦ ♁ ♠ ▨ ▼ ✕ ⊙ ❾ ⊘ ⚱ ❿ ⅃ PR ⌂ ⊞ lau Prices:
pitch 70-100 (incl 2 persons)

GRANDE-MOTTE, LA *Hérault*

Garden 44 pl des Tamaris ☎67565009
Completely divided into pitches separated by hedges and
surrounded by a wall. 0.3km from beach.
Access from D62. Site by crossroads towards Palavas/Grand Travers.
Mar-Oct 3HEC ▦ ▨▨▨ ♦ ♠ ▨ ✕ ⊙ ❾ ⊘ ⚱ ❿ ⅃ P ⌂ lau ♦ ⅃S

Lous Pibols ☎67565008
Well-organised. Divided into level pitches.
W on D59, 0.4km from sea.
Apr-Sep 3HEC ▨▨▨ ♦ ♠ ▨ ⊙ ❾ ⊘ ⚱ A ⅃ P ⌂ ⊞ lau ♦ ✕ ⅃LS
Prices: pitch 140-174 (incl 3 persons)

GRASSE *Alpes-Maritimes*

Paoute 160 rte de Cannes ☎93091142
15 Apr-Oct 2.5HEC ▦ ♦ ♠ ▨ ▼ ✕ ⊙ ❾ ⊘ ⚱ ❿ ⅃ P ⌂ ❒ ⊞ lau
Prices: pitch 90 (incl 2 persons)

At OPIO(8km E via D2085 & D3)

Caravan Inn 18 rte de Cannes ☎93773200
Terraced rustic site for caravans only. Occupied largely by static
caravans. Steep approach to site (15%) - free towage available.
1.5km S of Opio on D3.
Etr-15 Sep 5HEC ▦ ♠ ▨ ✕ ⊙ ❾ ⊘ ⚱ ❿ ⅃ P ⌂ ⊞ lau ♦ ▨
Prices: A17.40 pitch 158.30-197.70

GRAU-DE-VENDRES *Hérault*

Foulègues ☎67373365
Camping Card Compulsory.
Signposted.
Jun-Sep 4HEC ▦ ▨▨▨ ♁ ♠ ▨ ▼ ✕ ⊙ ❾ ⊘ ⛺ ❿ ⅃ PRS ⌂ ⊞ lau

GRAU-DU-ROI, LE *Gard*

Abri de Camargue rte du Phare de l'Espiguette ☎66515483
A pleasant site near the beach on the edge of the Camargue with
well-marked pitches and modern installations.

2.5km S on L'Espiguette road.
29 Mar-19 Oct 4HEC 🛏 ♠ ♠ ⚡ 🍴 ✕ ⊙ 🚻 ⌀ ♨ 🚿 ⤳ P 🅿 ⊞ lau ♦
⤳S Prices: pitch 115-250 (incl 2 persons)

Bon Séjour ☎66514711
Clean, tidy, well-kept site.
3km E of village off road to lighthouse.
Apr-Sep 5HEC 🛏 ♠ ♠ ⚡ 🍴 ✕ ⊙ 🚻 ⌀ ♨ 🚿 ⤳ L 🅿 ⊞ lau

Eden Port-Camargue ☎66514981
Quiet site on both sides of access road. 300m from beach.
On D626 towards Espiguette.
29 Mar-4 Oct 5.3HEC 🛏 ♠ ♠ ⚡ 🍴 ✕ ⊙ 🚻 ⌀ ♨ 🚿 P 🅿 ⊞ lau ♦ ⤳S
Prices: pitch 110-179 (incl 2 persons)

Elysée Résidence rte de l'Espiguette ☎66535400
22 May-5 Oct 32HEC 🛏 ░░░ ♠ ♠ ⚡ 🍴 ✕ ⊙ 🚻 ⌀ ♨ 🚿 ⤳ LP 🅿 lau
♦ ⤳S ⊞ Prices: pitch 50-150 (incl 2 persons)

Jardins de Tivoli rte de l'Éspiguette ☎66518296
Apr-Sep 7HEC 🛏 ♠ ♠ ⚡ 🍴 ✕ ⊙ 🚻 ⌀ ♨ 🚿 ⤳ P 🅿 ⊞ lau ♦ ⤳S
Prices: pitch 120 (incl 2 persons)

Mouettes av J-Jaurès ☎66514400
Camping Card Compulsory.
1.2km SE.
Apr-Sep 1HEC 🛏 ░░░ ♠ ♠ ⚡ 🍴 ✕ ⊙ 🚻 ⌀ ♨ 🚿 ⤳ 🅿 ⊞ lau ♦ ⤳LPS
Prices: pitch 58-130 (incl 3 persons)

Salonique rte du Phare de l'Espiguette ☎66531163
26 Apr-21 Sep 3.5HEC 🛏 ░░░ ♠ ♠ ⚡ 🍴 ✕ ⊙ 🚻 ⌀ ♨ 🚿 ⤳ P 🅿 ⊞
lau ♦ ⤳S Prices: pitch 78-137 (incl 2 persons)

GRIGNAN *Drôme*

Truffières Lieu-dit Nachony ☎75469362
A family site opposite the Château Grignan within easy reach of local
tourist attractions.
Apr-30 Sep 1HEC 🛏 ♠ ♠ ⚡ 🍴 ✕ ⊙ 🚻 ♨ 🚿 ⤳ P 🅿 ⊞ lau ♦ ♠ ⌀ ⤳LR
Prices: pitch 70-85 (incl 2 persons)

GRIMAUD *Var*

At **PORT-GRIMAUD**(4km E)

Plage ☎94563115
Wide area of land near Km59.6 on N98 on both sides of road beside
sea. Partly terraced and divided into pitches.
15 Mar-Sep 18HEC 🛏 ░░░ ♠ ♠ ⚡ 🍴 ✕ ⊙ 🚻 ⌀ ⤳ S 🅿 ⊞ lau ♦ 🚿
Prices: pitch 100 (incl 2 persons)

HYÈRES *Var*

At **AYGUADE-CEINTURON**(4km SE)

Ceinturon II ☎94663966
A popular site on level meadowland divided into pitches. Some
individual washing cubicles.
4km SE of Hyères on D42.
Jun-Aug 4.8HEC 🛏 ♠ ♠ ⚡ 🍴 ✕ ⊙ 🚻 ⌀ 🅿 ⊞ lau ♦ ⤳S Prices:
A23.50 pitch 24.90-33.60

Ceinturon III ☎94663265
Well-kept and divided into numbered pitches. Individual washing
cubicles.
4km SE of Hyères on D42.
Apr-Sep 3HEC 🛏 ♠ ♠ ⚡ 🍴 ✕ ⊙ 🚻 ⌀ ♨ ⤳ S 🅿 🅿 lau ♦ 🚿
Prices: A25 pitch 31

At **HYÈRES-PLAGE**(4km SE)

Pins Maritimes 1633 bd de la Marine ☎94663357
Situated in a pine wood close to the beach.
Turn off D42 between Hyères-Plage and L'Ayguade and continue
inland for 200m.
Apr-Sep 37HEC 🛏 ♠ ♠ ⚡ 🍴 ✕ ⊙ 🚻 ⌀ ♨ ♨ 🚿 ⊞ lau ♦ ⤳S Prices:
A28 V15 🚐15 ▲15

ISLE-SUR-LA-SORGUE, L' *Vaucluse*

CM Sorguette rte d'Apt ☎90380571
In tranquil wooded surroundings beside the River Sorguette with
good sports and entertainment facilities.
Access via N100 towards Apt.

---

15 Mar-24 Oct 2.5HEC 🛏 ♠ ♠ ⚡ 🍴 ✕ ⊙ 🚻 ⌀ ♨ ♨ 🚿 ⤳ R 🅿 ⊞ lau
♦ ⤳P Prices: A25 pitch 22

LAGORCE *Ardèche*

Domaine de Chaussy ☎75939966
On D559 near Ruoms.
Etr-Sep 18.5HEC 🛏 ♠ ♠ ⚡ 🍴 ✕ ⊙ 🚻 ⌀ ♨ ▲ ⤳ P 🅿 🅿 ⊞ lau
Prices: pitch 110-136

LAROQUE-DES-ALBÈRES *Pyrénées-Orientales*

Planes rte de Villelongue ☎68892136
15 Jun-Aug 2.5HEC 🛏 ♠ ♠ ⚡ ⊙ 🚻 ⌀ ⤳ P 🅿 ⊞ lau ♦ ♠ ⚡ ✕ ♨
⤳LRS Prices: pitch 36 (incl 2 persons)

LATTES *Hérault*

See also MONTPELLIER

Lac des Rêves rte de Pérols ☎67502600
Individual pitches. Alongside lake.
On the road between Pérols and Lattes.
30 Mar-28 Sep 33HEC 🛏 ⤳ ♠ ♠ ⚡ 🍴 ✕ ⊙ 🚻 ♨ 🚿 ⤳ P 🅿 ⊞ 🏊
lau

LAURENS *Hérault*

Oliveraie chemin de Bédarieux ☎67902436
D909 from Bédarieux. 900m from village centre.
All year 7HEC 🛏 ♠ ♠ ⊙ 🚻 ♨ 🚿 lau

LÉZIGNAN-CORBIÈRES *Aude*

CM Pinède ☎68270508
Well-kept terraced site with numbered pitches and tarred drives,
decorated with bushes and flower beds. Shop available July and
August only.
Signposted from N113.
All year 3.5HEC ♠ ♠ ✕ ⊙ 🚻 ⌀ ♨ ♨ 🚿 ⤳ P 🅿 lau ♦ 🍴 ⤳L ⊞
Prices: A16-18 pitch 34

LONDE-LES-MAURES, LA *Var*

Forge ☎94668265
Level meadow with good sanitary facilities.
Camping Card Compulsory.
Turn off N98 into village, at traffic lights turn N for 1km to site on
outskirts of village.
Jun-Sep 1.2HEC 🛏 ⤳ ♠ ⊙ 🚻 ⌀ ♨ 🚿 ⊞ lau ♦ ♠ 🍴 ✕

Moulières ☎94668238
Well tended level meadowland in quiet location. 1km from the sea.
Camping Card Compulsory.
On western outskirts towards the coast.
Jun-15 Sep 3.1HEC 🛏 ♠ ♠ ⚡ 🍴 ✕ ⊙ 🚻 ⌀ ♨ 🚿 ⊞ lau ♦ ⤳S Prices:
pitch 99-120 (incl 3 persons)

Pansard ☎94668322
Beautiful, wide piece of land in a pine forest beside the beach.
Turn off N98.
Apr-Sep 6HEC 🛏 ♠ ♠ ⚡ 🍴 ✕ ⊙ 🚻 ⌀ ♨ 🚿 ⤳ S 🅿 🏊 lau ♦ ⊞
Prices: A25 pitch 104 (incl 3 persons)

Pascalinette ☎94668272
Jun-Sep 5HEC 🛏 ♠ ♠ ⚡ 🍴 ✕ ⊙ 🚻 ⌀ ♨ 🚿 ♨ 🅿 lau

Val Rose rte du Lavandou ☎94668136
4km NE on N98.
Apr-Oct 2.4HEC 🛏 ♠ ♠ ⚡ 🍴 ✕ ⊙ 🚻 ♨ 🚿 ⤳ P 🅿 lau ♦ ⤳L Prices:
pitch 75-95 (incl 2 persons)

LUNEL *Hérault*

Bon Port rte de la Petite Camargue ☎67711565
Access via D24.
Mar-Oct 5HEC 🛏 ♠ ♠ ⚡ 🍴 ✕ ⊙ 🚻 ⌀ ♨ 🚿 ⤳ P 🅿 lau ♦ ⤳R

Mas de l'Isle 85 chemin du Clapas ☎67832652
1.5km SE via D34 near junction with the D61.
15 May-15 Sep 3HEC 🛏 ♠ ♠ ⚡ ⊙ 🚻 ♨ 🚿 🅿 ⊞ lau ♦ ♠ ✕ ⌀ ♨ ⤳P
Prices: A18 pitch 30

MALLEMORT *Bouches-du-Rhône*

Durance et Luberon Domaine du Vergon ☎90591336
2.5 km on D23c, 200m from Canal.

May-14 Sep 4HEC ▥ ⌕ ⋔ ⊙ ⊕ ▲ ⋌ P ☎ ⊞ lau Prices: A22-27 pitch 23-39

MANDELIEU Alpes-Maritimes
Cigales bd de la Mer ☎93492353
S on N7.
All year 2HEC ▥ ♠ ⋔ ⟟ ✕ ⊙ ⊟ ∅ ⊞ ⊡ ☎ ⊞ lau ♦ ⚑ ⋌S Prices: A20 V20 ⊕45-120 ▲30-120

Plateau des Chasses Rue Jean Monnet ☎93492593
Terraced land, on hill in a park.
Turn off N7 at Km 4.2 and continue uphill for 1.2km.
Apr-Sep 4HEC ▥ ♠ ⋔ ⟟ ✕ ⊙ ⊟ ⊟ ⊞ ⋌ P ☎ ⊞ lau ♦ ⋌RS Prices: A20 pitch 121-132

MARSEILLAN-PLAGE Hérault
Charlemagne av du Camping ☎67219249
200m from the beach in quiet, wooded surroundings with good sanitary and sporting facilities.
22 Mar-4 Oct 6.6HEC ▥ ░░░ ♠ ⋔ ⚑ ⟟ ✕ ⊙ ⊟ ∅ ⊞ ⊡ ⋌ PS ☎ ⊞ lau Prices: pitch 85-180 (incl 3 persons)

Languedoc-Camping 117 chemin du Pairollet ☎67219255
20 Mar-Oct 1.5HEC ▥ ░░░ ♠ ⋔ ⚑ ✕ ⊙ ⊟ ⊞ ⊟ ⋌ S ☎ ⊡ ▯ lau ♦ ∅ Prices: pitch 75-145 (incl 2 persons)

Plage 69 chemin du Pairollet ☎67219254
A family site with direct access to a sandy beach.
20 Mar-20 Oct 1.3HEC ░░░ ♠ ⋔ ⟟ ✕ ⊙ ⊟ ∅ ⋌ S ☎ lau ♦ ⚑ ⛺ ⊞ Prices: pitch 75-140 (incl 2 persons)

MAUREILLAS Pyrénées-Orientales
Val Roma Park ☎68831972
2.5km NE on N9.
All year 3HEC ▥ ♠ ⋔ ⚑ ⟟ ✕ ⊙ ⊟ ∅ ⊞ ⊟ ▲ ⋌ PR ☎ ⊞ lau

MENTON Alpes-Maritimes
Fleur de Mai 67 rte du Val de Gorbio ☎93572236
Terraced site in a peaceful situation by a stream in the heart of the Côte-d'Azur.
Exit from D23 at the Parc de la Madone.
Apr-Sep 2HEC ▥ ⌕ ⋔ ⊙ ⊟ ⊡ ⊞ lau ♦ ⚑ ⟟ ✕ ∅ ⋌S Prices: pitch 78-113 (incl 2 persons)

MÉOUNES-LES-MONTRIEUX Var
Aux Tonneaux ☎94339834
Site in wooded area, divided into pitches.
200m S of village off N554.
All year 2.7HEC ▥ ⌕ ⋔ ✕ ⊙ ⊟ ∅ ⊞ ⊟ ⋌ PR ☎ ⊞ lau ♦ ⚑ ⟟

MONDRAGON Vaucluse
CM La Pinède Quartier Les Massanes ☎90408298
1km SW via N7.
All year 3HEC ▥ ░░░ ♠ ⋔ ⊙ ⊟ ☎ lau ♦ ⚑ ⟟ ✕ ∅ ⛺ ⊞

MONTBLANC Hérault
Rebau ☎67985078
Divided into pitches and surrounded by vineyards.
From Pézenas follow N113; in La Bégude de Jordy turn off main road and drive 2km on D18 towards Montblanc.
Mar-30 Oct 3HEC ♠ ⋔ ⟟ ⊙ ⊟ ∅ ⊞ ⊟ ⋌ P ☎ ⊞ lau ♦ ⚑ ✕ ⛺ Prices: pitch 80-85 (incl 2 persons)

MONTCLAR Aude
Au Pin d'Arnauteille Domaine d'Arnauteille ☎68268453
2.2km SE via D43
Apr-1 Oct 7HEC ▥ ⌕ ⋔ ⚑ ⟟ ✕ ⊙ ⊟ ∅ ⊞ ⊟ ⊞ ▲ ⋌ P ☎ ⊞ lau Prices: A18-21 V11-13 ⊕21-25 ▲21-25

MONTÉLIMAR Drôme
Deux Saisons ☎75018899
From bank of River Roubion.
From town centre follow D540 across Pont de la Libération; then first turning right into chemin des Alexis.
Mar-Nov 1.5HEC ▥ ░░░ ♠ ⋔ ✕ ⊙ ⊟ ∅ ⊞ ⊡ ⊞ lau ♦ ⚑ ⛺ ⋌LPR Prices: A20 pitch 20

MONTPELLIER Hérault
See also LATTES
Floréal r de la 1ère Écluse, ZA Parc St Hubert, La Céreirède ☎67929305
On level ground surrounded by vineyards.
500m off Autoroute A9, exit Montpellier-Sud. From town centre follow road for Palavas (D986).
Apr-Oct 1.5HEC ▥ ♠ ⋔ ⚑ ⟟ ✕ ⊙ ⊟ ⊞ ⊟ ⊞ ⊞ lau ♦ ✕ ⋌PR Prices: pitch 75 (incl 2 persons)

MONTPEZAT Alpes-de-Haute-Provence
Coteau de la Marine ☎92775333
A pleasant wooded site, providing easy access to the Verdon Gorges.
May-Sep 10HEC ∅ ♠ ⋔ ⚑ ⟟ ✕ ⊙ ⊟ ∅ ⊞ ⊞ ⊟ ⋌ LPR ☎ ⊞ lau Prices: pitch 70-145 (incl 3 persons)

MONTRÉAL Ardèche
Moulinage rte des Défilés de Ruoms ☎75368620
Apr-Sep 3.5HEC ▥ ⌕ ⋔ ⟟ ✕ ⊙ ⊟ ∅ ⊞ ⊞ ⊞ ▲ ⋌ PR ☎ ⊞ lau ♦ ⚑

MOURIÈS Bouches-du-Rhône
Devenson ☎90475201
Terraced site amongst pine and olive trees in Provençal countryside.
Turn off N113 at La Samatane and continue N towards Mouriès. Site is in N part of village.
Etr-15 Sep 3.5HEC ∅ ♠ ⋔ ⊙ ⊟ ∅ ⊟ ⋌ P ☎ ⊞ lau Prices: A25 pitch 30

MOUSTIERS-STE-MARIE Alpes-de-Haute-Provence
St-Jean ☎92746695
12 Apr-22 Sep 1.6HEC ▥ ♠ ⋔ ✕ ⊙ ⊟ ⊟ ⋌ R ☎ ⊞ lau ♦ ⚑ ⟟ ✕ ⛺

Vieux Colombier Quartier St-Michel ☎92746189
A family site near the entrance to the Gorges du Verdon at an altitude of 630 metres.
0.8km S via D952 towards Castellane.
Apr-Sep 2.7HEC ▥ ⌕ ⋔ ⟟ ✕ ⊙ ⊟ ☎ ⊞ lau ♦ ⚑ ⛺ Prices: A18 pitch 20

MUY, LE Var
Cigales ☎94451208
Hilly terrain with Mediterranean pine trees, many terraces and some large boulders.
Exit 'Draguignan' off A8 onto N7. 0.8km to site. Well signposted.
Apr-15 Oct 10HEC ▥ ♠ ⋔ ⚑ ⟟ ✕ ⊙ ⊟ ∅ ⊞ ⋌ P ☎ lau ♦ ⚑ ⛺ Prices: A18-27 pitch 18-23

Sellig 41 chemin des Valettes ☎94451171
1.5km W on N7.
All year 1.9HEC ▥ ♠ ⋔ ⚑ ⟟ ✕ ⊙ ⊟ ∅ ⊞ ⊞ ⊟ ⋌ P ☎ ⊞ lau

NANS-LES-PINS Var
Ste-Baume ☎94789268
0.9km N via D80
3 May-7 Sep 7HEC ∅ ♠ ⋔ ⚑ ⟟ ✕ ⊙ ⊟ ∅ ⊞ ⊞ ▲ ⋌ P ☎ ⊞ lau ♦ ✕ Prices: pitch 79-129 (incl 2 persons)

NAPOULE, LA Alpes-Maritimes
Azur-Vacances bd du Bon Puits ☎93499112
Site with many long terraces, on edge of mountain slope in mixed woodland.
Turn inland 200m after fork at railway station and continue 600m.
Apr-Sep 10HEC ▥ ♠ ⋔ ⚑ ⟟ ✕ ⊙ ⊟ ∅ ⊞ ⊞ lau ♦ ⛺ ⋌PRS Prices: pitch 82 (incl 2 persons)

NARBONNE Aude
Relais de Nautique Anse des Galères, La Nautique ☎68904819
Situated on the salt water lake 'Étang de Bages et de Sigean', this site is particularly well appointed, each pitch having its own washing and toilet facilities. There are good recreational facilities and advance booking is recommended.
Access via Narbonne Sud exit on A9.
Mar-Nov 16HEC ▥ ⌕ ⋔ ⚑ ⟟ ✕ ⊙ ⊟ ∅ ⊞ ⊞ ⊟ ⋌ LP ☎ ⊞ lau Prices: pitch 88-125 (incl 3 persons)

At **NARBONNE-PLAGE**(15km E D168)
CM de la Côte des Roses rte de Gruissan ☎68498365
3 km SW.
Apr-Sep 16HEC ▥ ⊕ ♠ ⬧ ⚱ ♀ ✗ ⊙ ▯ ∅ 🛒 ⚱ ⅂ S ☎ ⊞ lau Prices: pitch
51-87 (incl 2 persons)

CM Falaise ☎68498077
W of Narbonne Plage, 400m from beach.
Apr-Sep 7HEC ▥ ⊕ ♠ ⚱ ♀ ✗ ⊙ ▯ ∅ ⚱ ☎ ⊞ lau ♦ ⅂S

NÉBIAS *Aude*
Fontaulié-Sud ☎68201762
0.6km S via D117.
Etr-Oct 3.5HEC ▥ ⊕ ♠ ⚱ ♀ ✗ ⊙ ▯ ∅ ⚱ 🛒 ♀ ⅂ P ☎ ⊞ lau
Prices: A18 pitch 16

NÎMES *Gard*
Domaine de la Bastide rte de Generac ☎66380921
Shop open summer only.5km S of town centre on D13.
All year 4.7HEC ▥ ⊕ ♠ ⚱ ♀ ✗ ⊙ ▯ ∅ ⚱ 🛒 ♀ ☎ ⊞ lau ♦ ⅂P
Prices: pitch 57.50-74 (incl 2 persons)

NIOZELLES *Alpes-de-Haute-Provence*
Moulin de Ventre ☎92786331
2.5km E via N100
Apr-25 Sep 2.8HEC ▥ ⊕ ♠ ✗ ⊙ ▯ ∅ 🛒 ♀ ⅂ LP ☎ ⊞ lau
Prices: pitch 85-105 (incl 2 persons)

NYONS *Drôme*
CM av de la Digue ☎75262239
Situated on bank of river on level meadow with fruit trees. Sports
ground and golf course in town.
May-Nov 1.6HEC ▥ ⊕ ♠ ⊙ ▯ ☎ ▯ ⊞ lau ♦ ⚱ ♀ ✗ ⚱ ⅂PR
Prices: pitch 41 (incl 3 persons)

Sagittaire ☎75276439
Well-kept site divided by hedges.
S of town on D538 road to Vaison-la-Romaine.
All year 13HEC ▥ ♦ ♠ ⚱ ♀ ✗ ⊙ ▯ ∅ 🛒 ♀ ⅂ LR ☎ ⊞ lau Prices:
pitch 105 (incl 3 persons)

OLLIÈRES-SUR-EYRIEUX, LES *Ardèche*
🏕**Domaine des Plantas** ☎75662153
Games room, discotheque and other leisure activities.
15 Apr-Sep 6.5HEC ▥ ♦ ♠ ⚱ ♀ ✗ ⊙ ▯ ∅ 🛒 ♀ ⅂ R ☎ ⊞ lau
Prices: pitch 107 (incl 2 persons)

ORANGE *Vaucluse*
Jonquier r A-Carrel ☎90341983
On the NW outskirts
Apr-Oct 5HEC ▥ ⊕ ♠ ⚱ ♀ ✗ ⊙ ▯ ∅ 🛒 ♀ ⅂ P ☎ ⊞ lau ♦ ✗
Prices: A28 pitch 30

ORGON *Bouches-du-Rhône*
Vallée Heureuse ☎90730278
A quiet transit site in a rocky valley.
1.5km from the village on the N7. Access is past a non-working
quarry.
11 Jun-31 Aug 8HEC ◊ ♦ ♠ ♀ ✗ ⊙ ▯ ∅ ⅂ P ☎ lau ♦ ⚱ ✗ ⚱ ⅂L ⊞
Prices: A17 pitch 20

PALAVAS-LES-FLOTS *Hérault*
Roquilles 267 bis av St-Maurice ☎67680347
An attractive site 50m from the sea.
15 Apr-25 Sep 15HEC ▥ ⸬ ⁙ ⊕ ♠ ⚱ ♀ ✗ ⊙ ▯ ∅ 🛒 ♀ ⅂ P ☎
⊞ ∅ lau ♦ ✗ ⅂S

PEYREMALE-SUR-CÈZE *Gard*
Droulhèdes ☎66250480
In a beautiful location beside the River Cèze surrounded by pine and
chestnut trees.
Access via A6 and D17.
Mar-Sep 2HEC ▥ ♦ ♠ ⚱ ♀ ✗ ⊙ ▯ ∅ 🛒 ♀ ⅂ R ☎ ⊞ lau ♦ ⚱
Prices: pitch 85 (incl 2 persons)

PONT-D'HÉRAULT *Gard*
Magnanarelles Le Rey ☎67824013
0.3km W via D999, beside the river
All year 2HEC ▥ ♦ ♠ ⚱ ♀ ✗ ⊙ ▯ ∅ 🛒 ♀ ⅂ PR ☎ ⊞ lau Prices:
A20.50 pitch 30

PONT-DU-GARD *Gard*
International des Gorges du Gardon rte de Uzès ☎66228181
1km from aqueduct on D981 Uzès road.
15 Mar-15 Oct 3HEC ▥ ⸬ ♦ ♠ ⚱ ♀ ✗ ⊙ ▯ ∅ 🛒 ♀ ⅂ PR ☎ ⊞
lau Prices: pitch 100 (incl 4 persons)

PORTIRAGNES-PLAGE *Hérault*
Mimosas ☎67909292
Leave A9 at exit Béziers Est and continue towards coast via N112
and D37.
May-15 Sep 7HEC ▥ ⊕ ♠ ⚱ ♀ ✗ ⊙ ▯ ∅ 🛒 ♀ ⅂ S ☎ ⊞ lau
Prices: pitch 125 (incl 2 persons)

Sablons rte de Portiragnes ☎67909055
Large site subdivided into fields by fences. Beside beach. Night club
and discothèque.
0.5km N on D37.
Apr-Sep 12HEC ♦ ♠ ⚱ ♀ ✗ ⊙ ▯ ∅ 🛒 ♀ ⅂ LPRS ☎ ⊞ lau

PRADET, LE *Var*
Mauvallon chemin de la Gavaresse ☎94213173
A well-kept site amidst young trees divided into pitches.
Turn off the N559 in Le Pradet and take the D86 for 2.5km towards
sea.
Apr-Sep 1HEC ▥ ♦ ♠ ⊙ ▯ ∅ ⊞ lau ♦ ⚱ ♀ ✗ ⚱ ⅂S Prices: A17-
20 pitch 23-41

Pin de Galle Quartier San Peyre ☎94212606
On the Toulon road on the outskirts of Pradet.
All year 1HEC ▥ ♦ ♠ ⚱ ♀ ✗ ⊙ ▯ ∅ 🛒 ♀ ⚱ ⊞ lau ♦ ∅ ⚱ ⅂S
Prices: A20 pitch 25

PRAMOUSQUIER *Var*
Pramousquier ☎94058395
2km E via D559
May-Sep 3HEC ♦ ♠ ⚱ ♀ ✗ ⊙ ▯ ∅ 🛒 ⚱ ☎ ⊞ lau ♦ ⅂S Prices: A22-
26.50 pitch 29-32.50

PRIVAS *Ardèche*
CM Espace Ouvèze bd de Paste ☎75640580
Etr-15 Oct Closed 13-21 May & 16-24 Sep 3.5HEC ♦ ♠ ⊙ ▯ ∅
☎ lau ♦ ⚱ ♀ ✗ ⚱ ⅂P Prices: pitch 35.50-50 (incl 2 persons)

PUGET-SUR-ARGENS *Var*
Aubrèdes ☎94455146
Situated on undulating meadowland.
Leave autoroute A8 at exit Puget-sur-Argens, then site is 850m. If
approaching from Fréjus on N7 turn left before Puget, cross
motorway and follow road towards Lagourin.
Apr-Sep 3.8HEC ▥ ♦ ♠ ⚱ ♀ ✗ ⊙ ▯ ∅ 🛒 ♀ ⅂ P ☎ ⊞ lau ♦ ⚱
Prices: A16-23 V11-15 ▯12-20

Bastiane ☎94455131
Hilly site divided into numbered pitches in pine and oak wood.
Individual washing cubicles. Meals to take away. Separate car park
for arrivals after 23.00hrs.
Access from A8.
16 Nov-14 Feb 4HEC ▥ ⓓ ♦ ⋔ ⓔ ♨ ⵏ ✕ ⊙ ⬛ ⓪ ⬚ ⬛ ⬚ P ⬚ ⊞ lau
Prices: A32 pitch 21-33

QUILLAN *Aude*

Sapinette 2 r René Delpech ☎68201352
Access W via D79, rte de Ginoles.
All year 1.8HEC ▥ ⳾ ⮂ ⋔ ⊙ ⬛ ⓪ ⬚ ⊞ lau ♦ ⓔ ⵏ ✕ ⵏ ⵏPR

RAMATUELLE *Var*

Croix du Sud rte des Plages ☎94798084
Terraced site in beautiful pine forest divided into pitches with view of
sea. Minimum stay 3 days.
3km NE of town, 80m N of D93.
Apr-Oct 2.5HEC ▥ ♦ ⋔ ⓔ ♨ ⵏ ✕ ⊙ ⬛ ⓪ ⬚ ⬚ ⊞ lau ♦ ⵏS
Prices: A25-30 pitch 36-43

Tournels rte de Camarat ☎94559090
Lovely views to Pampelonne Bay from part of this site. 1km to
beach.
Access from D93 Croix-Valmer/St-Tropez road, follow the signs to
'Cap Camarat'.
Closed 10 Jan-10 Feb 20HEC ♦ ⋔ ✕ ⊙ ⬛ ⓪ ⬚ ⵏ P ⬚ ⊞ lau
♦ ⓔ ⵏS Prices: A26-36 pitch 42-81

REMOULINS *Gard*

Soubeyranne rte de Beaucaire ☎66370321
S on D986.
May-15 Sep 6HEC ▥ ♦ ⋔ ⓔ ♨ ⵏ ✕ ⊙ ⬛ ⓪ ⬚ ⬚ ⵏ P ⬚ ⊞ lau ♦ ⵏR
Prices: pitch 86-134 (incl 2 persons)

Sousta av du Pont-du-Gard ☎66371280
2km NW
All year 12HEC ⸬ ♦ ⋔ ⓔ ♨ ⵏ ✕ ⊙ ⬛ ⓪ ⬚ A ⵏ PR ⬚ ⊞ lau Prices:
pitch 64-82 (incl 2 persons)

RIA *Pyrénées-Orientales*

Bellevue ☎68964896
Beautifully situated terraced site. Very well kept. Beside former
vineyard.
2km S on N116, take road to Sirach, turn right and continue 600m
up drive which is difficult for caravans.
14 Apr-30 Sep 2.5HEC ▥ ♦ ⋔ ⓔ ♨ ⓔ ⊙ ⬛ ⬚ ⬚ ⬚ ⊞ lau ♦ ⓔ ✕
Prices: A16 pitch 18

ROQUEBRUNE-SUR-ARGENS *Var*

Domaine de la Bergerie Valleé du Fournel ☎94829011
In a pleasant location with fine recreational facilities:
Access via A8 exit Le Muy N7 and D7.
Apr-Sep 60HEC ▥ ⓓ ⋔ ⓔ ♨ ⵏ ✕ ⊙ ⬛ ⓪ ⬚ ⬚ ⵏ LP ⬚ ⊞ lau
Prices: pitch 95-131

Lei Suves Quartier du Blavet ☎94454395
4km N via N7.
15 Mar-15 Oct 7HEC ▥ ♦ ⋔ ⓔ ♨ ⵏ ✕ ⊙ ⬛ ⓪ ⬚ A ⬚ ⬚ ⵏ P ⬚ ⊞ lau
Prices: pp27.50-34.50

Moulin des Iscles ☎94457074
On bank of River Argens.
Apr-Oct 1.2HEC ▥ ♦ ⋔ ⓔ ♨ ⵏ ✕ ⊙ ⬛ ⓪ ⬚ ⵏ R ⬚ ⊞ lau ♦ ⵏL
Prices: pitch 100 (incl 3 persons)

Pêcheurs ☎94457125
0.5km NW via D7, near the lake
May-Sep 4HEC ▥ ♦ ⓔ ♨ ⵏ ✕ ⊙ ⬛ ⓪ ⬚ ⵏ LPR ⬚ ⊞ lau Prices:
pitch 130-145 (incl 3 persons)

ROQUE-D'ANTHÉRON, LA *Bouches-du-Rhône*

Domaine les Iscles ☎42504425
1.8km N via D67c.
Mar-15 Nov 10HEC ▥ ⓓ ♦ ⓔ ♨ ⵏ ✕ ⊙ ⬛ ⓪ ⬚ ⵏ LPR ⬚ ⊞ lau
Prices: A16-26 pitch 22-62

Silvacane av de la Libération ☎42504054
Level gravelled ground with 100 sq m pitches. Heated common
room with TV. Water sports centre and stables nearby. Site in wood
on slopes of hill.
All year 3.5HEC ♦ ⋔ ⓔ ♨ ⵏ ✕ ⊙ ⬛ ⓪ ⬚ ⵏ P ⬚ ⊞ lau ♦ ✕ ⵏLR
Prices: A16-26 pitch 22-62

ROQUETTE-SUR-SIAGNE, LA *Alpes-Maritimes*

Panoramic Quartier St-Jean ☎92190777
All year 1HEC ▥ ♦ ⋔ ⓔ ♨ ⵏ ✕ ⊙ ⬛ ⓪ ⬚ A ⬚ ⬚ ⵏ P ⬚ ⊞ lau ♦ ⓔ
Prices: pitch 90 (incl 2 persons)

St-Louis bd de la République ☎93422667
Well equipped site in a pleasant rural setting , backed by hills.
On D9, 800m from Pégomas towards La Bocca.
Apr-1 Oct 5HEC ▥ ♦ ⋔ ⓔ ♨ ⵏ ✕ ⊙ ⬛ ⓪ ⬚ ⵏ P ⬚ ⊞ lau ♦ ⵏR

RUOMS *Ardèche*

▨Bastide ☎75396472
4km SW on the banks of the Ardèche.
15 Mar-15 Sep 6HEC ⓓ ⋔ ⓔ ♨ ⵏ ✕ ⊙ ⬛ ⓪ ⬚ A ⬚ ⬚ ⵏ PR ⬚ ⊞ lau
Prices: pitch 104-174 (incl 2 persons)

Ternis rte de Lagorce ☎75939315
A terraced site in a delightful setting in the southern Ardèche region,
with good recreational facilities. Separate car park for arrivals
between 22.00 and 08.00hrs.
Access via D559 towards Lagorce.
Etr-20 Sep 6HEC ▥ ♦ ⋔ ⓔ ♨ ⵏ ✕ ⊙ ⬛ ⓪ ⬚ ⬚ ⵏ P ⬚ ⊞ lau

At **SAMPZON**(6km S)

Aloha-Plage ☎75396762
50m from the River Ardèche.
Apr-Sep 3HEC ▥ ♦ ⋔ ⓔ ♨ ⵏ ✕ ⊙ ⬛ ⓪ ⬚ A ⬚ ⬚ ⵏ R ⬚ ⊞ lau ♦ ⓔ

Soleil Vivarais ☎75396756
On several levels beside River Ardèche. Good base for canoeing.
From Vallon drive towards Ruoms on D579 for 5km and cross bridge
over River Ardèche.
21 Mar-Sep 8HEC ▥ ♦ ⋔ ⓔ ♨ ⵏ ✕ ⊙ ⬛ ⓪ ⬚ ⬚ A ⵏ PR ⬚ ⊞ lau
Prices: pitch 107-163 (incl 2 persons)

SAILLAGOUSE *Pyrénées-Orientales*

Cerdan ☎04 68047046
On meadow with some terraces. Hot meals served during peak
season.
Closed Oct 0.8HEC ▥ ⓓ ⋔ ⊙ ⬛ ⓪ ⬚ A ⬚ ⊞ lau ♦ ⓔ ♨ ✕ ⵏPR
Prices: pitch 63 (incl 2 persons)

ST-ALBAN-AURIOLLES *Ardèche*

Ranc Davaine ☎753960055
Well equipped, mainly level site.
2.3km SW via D58.
22 Mar-15 Sep 10HEC ▥ ⸬ ♦ ⋔ ⓔ ♨ ⵏ ✕ ⊙ ⬛ ⓪ ⬚ A ⵏ PR ⬚ ⊞
lau Prices: pitch 85-138 (incl 2 persons)

ST-AMBROIX *Gard*

Beau-Rivage Le Moulinet ☎66241017
In a fine location between the sea and the Cevennes mountains
beside the River Cèze.
3.5km SE on D37.
Apr-Sep 3.5HEC ♦ ⓔ ♨ ⊙ ⬛ ⓪ ⵏ R ⬚ ⊞ lau ♦ A Prices: A21.50
pitch 22

Clos ☎66241008
Beside the River Cèze.Access to the right of the church square.
Apr-Oct 1.8HEC ▥ ⓓ ⋔ ⓔ ✕ ⊙ ⬛ ⓪ ⬚ ⬚ A ⵏ PR ⬚ ⊞ lau ♦ ⓔ

ST-ANDIOL *Bouches-du-Rhône*

St-Andiol ☎90950113
Well situated village centre. Divided into pitches.
All year 1HEC ▥ ♦ ⋔ ⓔ ⊙ ⬛ ⓪ ⬚ ⵏ P ⬚ ⊞ lau ♦ ✕ Prices: A19
pitch 24

Ideally located in the heart of the Côte d'Azur, exceptional site with friendly atmosphere on the banks of the Argens river with direct access to the fine sandy beaches (there is one for naturist). Bar, restaurant, take away food, swimming-pool which is heated in cool weather.
Entertainment: discotheque, giant barbecues, cabarets, concerts, excursions and a miniclub for children.
Mobile home and caravans available for hire.

Camping Caravanning Le Pont d'Argens
RN 98 Fréjus Saint Aygulf – FRANCE
Tél: 04 94 51 14 97 – Fax: 04 94 51 29 44

ST-AYGULF *Var*
Étoile d'Argens ☎94810141
Private harbour on River Argens and boat coach to beach.
5km NW, beside the River Argens
Apr-Sep 11HEC ▥ ♦ ⋔ ⓡ ⚑ ♥ ✕ ⊙ ❑ ∅ ⌳ ☎ ⋋ P ⓔ ⊞ lau Prices: pitch 184-202 (incl 3 persons)

Paradis des Campeurs La Gaillarde Plage ☎94969355
2.5km towards Gaillarde-Plage.
20 Mar-1 Oct 1.6HEC ▥ ⌿⋋ ⋔ ⓡ ⚑ ♥ ✕ ⊙ ❑ ∅ ⌳ ☎ ⋋ S ⓔ lau ♦ ⊞
Prices: pitch 77-144 (incl 3 persons)

Pont d'Argens N98 ☎94511497
A pleasant site with good facilities beside the river.
Apr-15 Oct 7HEC ♦ ⋔ ⓡ ⚑ ♥ ✕ ⊙ ❑ ∅ ☎ ⋋ PR ⓔ lau ♦ ⋋S
Prices: pitch 85-130 (incl 2 persons)

St-Aygulf 270 av Salvarelli ☎94176249
Access to beach via underpass.
Inland from N98 at Km881.3 N of town. Entrance on right of av Salvarelli.
Apr-Oct 22HEC ▥ ⠿ ♦ ⋔ ⓡ ⚑ ♥ ✕ ⊙ ❑ ∅ ⌳ ☎ ⋋ LS ⓔ lau
Prices: A18-33 V8-14 ⌸22-38

STE-MARIE *Pyrénées-Orientales*
At **TORREILLES**(4km NW on D11)
Dunes de Torreilles ☎68283829
At the sea, with direct access to beach.
15 Mar-15 Oct 16HEC ⠿ ♦ ⋔ ⓡ ⚑ ♥ ✕ ⊙ ❑ ∅ ⌳ ☎ ⋋ PS ⓔ ⊞ lau
♦ ⋋R Prices: pitch 78-200 (incl 6 persons)

Mar-I-Sol Plage de Torreilles ☎68280407
350m from the beach
All year 9HEC ▥ ⠿ ⚙ ⋔ ⚑ ♥ ✕ ⊙ ❑ ∅ ⌳ ☎ ☎ ⋋ PS ⓔ ⊞ lau

Trivoly bd des Plages ☎68282028
Access via autoroute exit 'Perpignan Nord' towards Le Barcarès.
Apr-Sep 6HEC ▥ ⚙ ⋔ ♥ ✕ ⊙ ❑ ∅ ⌳ ☎ ⋋ P ⓔ ⊞ lau ♦ ⚑ ⋋RS

STES-MARIES-DE-LA-MER *Bouches-du-Rhône*
CM Brise r M-Carrière ☎90978467
NE via D85A, near the beach
All year 25HEC ⠿ ⌿⋋ ⋔ ♥ ✕ ⊙ ❑ ∅ ⋋ PS ⓔ lau ♦ ⚑ ✕

Clos-du-Rhône rte d'Aigues-Mortes ☎90978599
2km W via D38, near the beach
May-Sep 7HEC ⚙ ⋔ ⚑ ♥ ✕ ⊙ ❑ ∅ ⌳ ☎ ⋋ PS ⓔ ⊞ lau

ST-JEAN-PLA-DE-CORTS *Pyrénées-Orientales*
Deux Rivières rte de Maureillas ☎68832320
0.5km SE via D13, beside the River Tech
May-15 Sep 8.5HEC ▥ ⠿ ♦ ⋔ ⓡ ⚑ ♥ ✕ ⊙ ❑ ∅ ⌳ ☎ ⋋ PR ⓔ ⊞
lau ♦ ⌳ ⋋L

ST-LAURENT-DU-VAR *Alpes-Maritimes*
Magali 1814 rte de la Baronne ☎93315700
Level meadowland site.

Leave A8 at 'St-Laurent-du-Var' exit, cross industrial zone turn left for 100m, then right and continue for 2km.
Feb-Oct 1.2HEC ▥ ⚙ ⋔ ⓡ ♥ ✕ ⊙ ❑ ∅ ☎ ☎ ⋋ P ⓔ ⊞ lau ♦ ♥ ⚑ ✕
Prices: pitch 95-149 (incl 4 persons)

ST-LAURENT-DU-VERDON *Alpes-de-Haute-Provence*
Farigoulette Lac de St Laurent ☎92744162
1.5km NE near Verdon
15 May-15 Sep 14HEC ♦ ♦ ⋔ ⓡ ⚑ ♥ ✕ ⊙ ❑ ∅ ⌳ ⋋ LP ⓔ ⊞ lau
Prices: pitch 78 (incl 2 persons)

ST-MARTIN-DE-LONDRES *Hérault*
Pic St-Loup rte du Pic St-Loup ☎67550053
E via D122
Apr-Sep 3HEC ▥ ⚙ ⋔ ⓡ ⚑ ♥ ✕ ⊙ ❑ ∅ ☎ ⋋ P ⓔ lau ♦ ⊞

ST-MAXIMIN-LA-STE-BAUME *Var*
Provençal rte de Mazaugues ☎94781697
Bar, café and swimming pool are open Jul-Aug only.
2.5km S via D64.
Apr-Sep 5HEC ▥ ⚙ ♦ ⋔ ⓡ ♥ ✕ ⊙ ❑ ∅ ⌳ ☎ ⋋ P ⓔ ⊞ lau ♦ ⊞
Prices: A22 pitch 26

ST-PAUL-EN-FORÊT *Var*
Parc ☎94761535
Quiet, fairly isolated site surrounded by woodland.
3km N on D4.
All year 5HEC ▥ ♦ ⋔ ⓡ ⚑ ♥ ✕ ⊙ ❑ ∅ ⌳ ☎ ⋋ P ⓔ ⊡ ⊞ lau ♦ ⋋L

ST-PAUL-LES-ROMANS *Drôme*
CM de Romans ☎75723527
Shady pitches separated by hedges.
May-Sep 1HEC ▥ ♦ ⋔ ⊙ ❑ ☎ ⓔ lau ♦ ⚑ ♥ ✕ ∅ ⊞ Prices: A10.40
V6.50 ⌸13.10 ▲13.10

ST-RAPHAËL *Var*
Douce Quiétude bd J-Baudino ☎94443000
Meadowland site in quiet location in attractively hilly countryside.

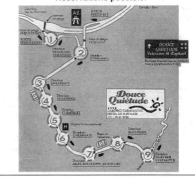

Camping • Caravanning
DOUCE QUIETUDE
83700 SAINT RAPHAEL
Tel: 04.94.44.30.00 • Fax: 04.94.44.30.30
Open: Easter - 30.9. 10 ha in the middle of the countryside
5 km from the beaches of St. Raphael and Agay.
Shopping centre, Restaurant, Bar Meals to take away, 3 Swimming pools, organised leisure, games room, tennis, children's playground, telephone cabin, sanitary installations, with every comfort and hot water. All pitches have telephone and TV (17 channels) hook-ups. Mobile Homes and Bungalows for hire.
Reservations possible.

Approach from Agay Plage past Esterel Camping in direction of Valescure.
Apr-Sep 1OHEC ▥ ⚲ ⋔ ⛵ ⚑ ♀ ✗ ⊙ ▣ ⌀ ♨ ♠ ⊞ ⊟ ⇥ P ⚐ ⊞ lau

Royal Camp Long ☎94820020
Level site divided by walls and hedges. Ideal bathing for children. Bar and hall next to site.
On N98 towards Cannes.
15 Mar-20 Oct 0.6HEC ▥ ♠ ⋔ ⛵ ♀ ✗ ⊙ ▣ ⌀ ♨ ⇥ S ⚐ ⊞ ♨ lau
Prices: pitch 125 (incl 3 persons)

ST-REMÈZE *Ardèche*

Domaine de Briange rte de Gras ☎75041131
In a wooded location close to the Gorges de l'Ardèche.
25 Jun-1 Sep 4HEC ▥ ♠ ⋔ ⛵ ♀ ✗ ⊙ ▣ ⇥ P ⚐ ♨ lau ♠ ⋔ ✗ ⌀ ♨
⇥R ⊞ Prices: pitch 72 (incl 2 persons)

ST-RÉMY-DE-PROVENCE *Bouches-du-Rhône*

Pégomas ☎90920121
Well-tended grassland with trees and bushes. Divided into several fields by high cedars providing shade.
500m E of village. Well signposted.
Mar-Oct 2HEC ▥ ♠ ⋔ ✗ ⊙ ▣ ⌀ ♨ ♠ ⇥ P ⚐ ⊞ lau ♠ ⋔ ✗

ST-SAUVEUR-DE-MONTAGUT *Ardèche*

Ardechois Le Chambon, Gluiras ☎75666187
In the grounds of a restored 18th-century farm.
8.5km W on D102, beside the River Glueyre.
29 Mar-25 Sep 5HEC ▥ ⚲ ⋔ ⛵ ♀ ✗ ⊙ ▣ ⌀ ♨ ⇥ PR ⚐ ⊞ lau
Prices: pitch 80-98 (incl 2 persons)

ST-SORLIN-EN-VALLOIRE *Drôme*

Château de la Pérouze ☎75317021
2.5km SE via D1.
15 Jun-15 Sep 14HEC ▥ ♠ ⋔ ✗ ⊙ ▣ ⌀ ♨ ⇥ LP ⚐ ⊞ ♨ lau ♠ ⋔
✗ ⇥R Prices: A25 ⛺25 ▲25

ST-THIBÉRY *Hérault*

Tane ☎67778429
Jun-Sep 3HEC ▥ ⚲ ⋔ ♀ ✗ ⊙ ▣ ♠ ⇥ P ⚐ ⊞ lau ♠ ⋔ ⇥R

ST-VALLIER-DE-THIEY *Alpes-Maritimes*

Parc des Arboins RN85 ☎93426389
Pleasantly situated terraced site on hillside with some oak trees.
Entrance at Km V36 on N85.
All year 4HEC ▥ ♠ ⋔ ⛵ ♀ ✗ ⊙ ▣ ⌀ ♠ ♨ ⇥ P ⚐ ⊞ lau Prices:
pitch 125 (incl 3 persons)

SALAVAS *Ardèche*

Chauvieux ☎75880537
NE off D579.
May-15 Sep 1.8HEC ▥ ⚲ ⋔ ⛵ ♀ ✗ ⊙ ▣ ⌀ ♨ ⊞ lau ♠ ✗ ⇥R
Prices: pitch 90 (incl 2 persons)

Péquelet ☎75880449
Beside the River Ardèche
Apr-Oct 2HEC ▥ ♠ ⋔ ⛵ ♀ ✗ ⊙ ▣ ⌀ ♠ ⇥ R ⚐ lau ♠ ✗ ⊞

SALERNES *Var*

Arnauds Quartier des Arnauds ☎94675195
Level site situated alongside a river and a lake.
Access via D560. Site entrance just beyond the village.
May-Sep 1.3HEC ▥ ⚲ ⋔ ⛵ ✗ ⊙ ▣ ♠ ⇥ PR ⚐ ⊞ lau ♠ ⋔ ✗ ⌀

SALINS-D'HYÈRES, LES *Var*

Port Pothuau ☎94664117
Completely divided into pitches.
6km E of Hyères on N98 and D12.
Etr-Oct 6HEC ▥ ♠ ⋔ ⛵ ♀ ✗ ⊙ ▣ ⌀ ♨ ♠ ♠ ⇥ P ⚐ ⊞ lau ♠ ⇥S

SALON-DE-PROVENCE *Bouches-du-Rhône*

Nostradamus rte d'Eyguières ☎90560836
In pleasant, wooded surroundings with good sporting facilities.5km W on D17 towards Eyguières and Arles.
All year 2.2HEC ▥ ♠ ⋔ ⛵ ♀ ✗ ⊙ ▣ ⌀ ♠ ♠ ⇥ PR ⚐ ⊞ lau Prices:
pitch 72 (incl 2 persons)

SANARY-SUR-MER *Var*

Girelles chemin de Beaucours ☎94741318
Camping Card Compulsory.
3km NW via D539, beside the sea
Etr-Sep 2HEC ♠ ⋔ ⛵ ♀ ✗ ⊙ ▣ ⌀ ⇥ S ⚐ ⊞ lau Prices: A27 pitch 48

Mogador ☎94745316
Situated 800m from the sea. The site, divided into pitches by hedges, is well managed and very well kept.
2km NW on N559 turn off at KM15 and take next left.
Etr-5 Oct 2.7HEC ▥ ♠ ⋔ ⛵ ♀ ✗ ⊙ ▣ ⌀ ♠ ♠ ⇥ P ⚐ ⚐ ⊞ ♨ lau ♠
⇥S Prices: A21 pitch 45

Pierredon chemin de Pierredon ☎94742502
Wooded site.
Apr-Sep 4HEC ▥ ⚲ ⋔ ⛵ ✗ ⊙ ▣ ⌀ ♠ ▲ ⇥ P ⚐ ⊞ lau ♠ ⇥S

SAUVE *Gard*

Domaine de Bagard ☎66775599
1.2km SE via D999
Apr-Sep 16HEC ▥ ♠ ⋔ ⛵ ♀ ✗ ⊙ ▣ ⌀ ♨ ♠ ♠ ⇥ P ⚐ ⊞ lau Prices:
pitch 165 (incl 2 persons)

SAUVIAN *Hérault*

Gabinelle ☎67395087
A modern site in pleasant wooded surroundings with good facilities.
Leave Sauvian in the direction of Valras Plage on D19.
15 Jun-15 Sep 3HEC ▥ ⚲ ⋔ ⛵ ✗ ⊙ ▣ ♠ ⇥ P ⚐ ⊞ lau ♠ ⋔ ✗ ⌀ ♨
Prices: pitch 94 (incl 3 persons)

SÉRIGNAN-PLAGE *Hérault*

Camargue ☎67321964
Situated in the edge of a wide sandy beach.
Arp-15 Oct 3.5HEC ▥ ⚲ ⋔ ⛵ ♀ ✗ ⊙ ▣ ⌀ ♨ ♠ ♠ ⇥ LPS ⚐ ⊞ lau

Clos Virgile ☎67322064
Situated 400m from the beach, the site is level meadowland with big pitches and has two clean, well kept sanitary blocks.
May-Sep 5HEC ▥ ♠ ⋔ ⛵ ♀ ✗ ⊙ ▣ ⌀ ♨ ⇥ P ⚐ ⊞ lau ♠ ⇥S
Prices: pitch 88-140 (incl 2 persons)

Grand Large ☎67397130
Situated by the sea with private access to the beach. Good facilities.
Entertainment during high season.
8 Apr-Sep 6HEC ▥ ⚲ ⠿⠿ ⚲ ⋔ ⛵ ♀ ✗ ⊙ ▣ ⌀ ♨ ⇥ PRS ⚐ ⊞ lau

Sérignan-Plage ☎67323533
On a fine sandy beach, this is a family site with good recreational facilities.
Access via A9 exit Béziers Est.
15 Apr-15 Sep 9HEC ▥ ⠿⠿ ♠ ⋔ ⛵ ♀ ✗ ⊙ ▣ ⌀ ♨ ♠ ▲ ⇥ PS ⚐ ⊞
lau Prices: A55-138 pitch 55-138

SIX-FOURS-LES-PLAGES *Var*

Héliosports La Font de Fillol ☎94256276
Between the town centre and the beach
1km W
25 Mar-15 Oct 5.3HEC ▥ ♠ ⋔ ⊙ ▣ ⚐ lau ♠ ⋔ ♀ ✗ ⌀ ♨ ⇥PS ⊞
Prices: pitch 75 (incl 3 persons)

International St-Jean 1155 av de la Collégiale ☎94875151
Site with pitches, separated by hedges and reeds. Well managed, and lies just below the Fort Six-Fours.
Access from N559 and D63 via chemin de St-Jean.
All year 4HEC ▥ ♠ ⋔ ⛵ ✗ ⊙ ▣ ⌀ ♠ ♠ ⇥ P ⚐ ⊞ lau ♠ ⇥S
Prices: pitch 17-96 (incl 3 persons)

Playes 419 r Grand ☎94255757
Terraced site on north side of town. Trees abound in this excellent location.
Access from N559 and D63 via chemin de St-Jean.
All year 1.5HEC ▥ ⚲ ⋔ ⛵ ♀ ✗ ⊙ ▣ ⌀ ♠ ⊞ lau ♠ ✗ ⇥S
Prices: pitch 89 (incl 3 persons)

SOSPEL *Alpes-Maritimes*
Domaine St-Madeleine rte de Moulinet ☎93041048
4.5km NW via D2566
Apr-30 Oct 3.5HEC ▦ ⓐ ♠ ♥ ⊙ ⊘ ∅ ⊞ ⊕ ⱦ P ☲ ⊞ lau Prices:
pitch 75 (incl 2 persons)

TAIN-L'HERMITAGE *Drôme*
CM Lucs 24 av Prés-Roosevelt ☎75083282
Good overnight stopping place but some traffic noise.
S of town near N7. Turn towards River Rhône at ESSO garage.
15 Mar-Oct 2HEC ▦ ∷ ⓐ ♠ ⊙ ⊞ ☲ ⊞ lau ♠ ♥ ♥ Ⅹ ∅ ⇗ ⱦP
Prices: pitch 74 (incl 2 persons)

TARASCON *Bouches-du-Rhône*
St-Gabriel rte de Fontvieille ☎90911983
Apr-Sep 1HEC ♠ ♠ ♥ ♥ Ⅹ ⊙ ⊞ ⊞ lau ♠ Ⅹ ⱦL

Tartarin rte de Vallabrèques ☎90910146
Site lies on E bank of River Rhône.
Follow signs for 'Vallabrèques'.
15 Mar-Sep 0.7HEC ▦ ♠ ♠ ♥ Ⅹ ⊙ ⊞ ☲ ⊞ lau ♠ ♥ Ⅹ ∅ ⱦPR

THOR, LE *Vaucluse*
Jantou ☎90339007
In wooded surroundings beside a river. Separate car park for arrivals
after 22.00hrs.
Access via N100.
Apr-Oct 6HEC ▦ ♠ ♠ ♥ Ⅹ ⊙ ⊞ ∅ ⇗ ⊞ ⊞ ⱦ PR ☲ ⊞ lau ♠ ∅ ⇗
ⱦL Prices: A18.90-24.50 pitch 22.75-29.50

TOURNON-SUR-RHÔNE *Ardèche*
CM 1 Promenade Roche de France ☎0475080528
Well laid-out site in town centre beside River Rhône.
NW on N86.
15 Mar-25 Oct 1.1HEC ▦ ♠ ♠ ⊙ ⊞ ∅ ☲ ⊞ lau ♠ ♥ Ⅹ ⇗ ⱦPR
Prices: A17 V11 ⊞11 ▲11

Manoir rte de Lamastre ☎75080250
Etr-1 Oct 2HEC ▦ ∷ ♠ ♠ ♥ Ⅹ ⊙ ⊞ ∅ ⇗ ⊞ ⱦ PR ☲ lau
Prices: pitch 59-69 (incl 2 persons)

TOURRETTE-SUR-LOUP *Alpes-Maritimes*
Camassade 523 rte de Pie Lombard ☎93593154
Quiet site under oak trees and pines with several terraces.
From Vence turn left immediately beyond Tourette.
All year 1.8HEC ▦ ⓐ ♠ ♠ ♥ ⊙ ⊞ ∅ ⊞ ⊞ ⱦ P ⊞ lau ♠ ♥ Ⅹ
Prices: pitch 66-90 (incl 2 persons)

UCEL *Ardèche*
Domaine de Gil rte de Vals ☎75946363
Pleasantly situated on the banks of the River Ardèche.
N of Aubenas off N104.
1 May-15 Sep 8HEC ▦ ♠ ♠ ♥ Ⅹ ⊙ ⊞ ∅ ⇗ ⊞ ⱦ R ☲ ⊞ lau
Prices: pitch 70-97 (incl 2 persons)

UR *Pyrénées-Orientales*
Gare d'Ur rte d'Espagne ☎68048095
Closed Oct 1HEC ▦ ♠ ♠ ⊙ ⊞ ∅ ⊞ ⊞ ♠ ♥ Ⅹ ⱦR Prices: A16
V15 ⊞15 ▲15

UZÈS *Gard*
At **ST-QUENTIN-LA-POTERIE**(4km NE)
Moulin Neuf ☎66221721
Quiet site on extensive meadowland within an estate.
4 km NE on D982.
Etr-21 Sep 5HEC ▦ ♠ ♠ ♥ Ⅹ ⊙ ⊞ ∅ ⊞ ⱦ P ☲ ⊞ lau Prices:
pitch 83 (incl 2 persons)

VAISON-LA-ROMAINE *Vaucluse*
International Carpe Diem rte de St-Narcellin ☎90360202
15 Mar-15 Nov 10HEC ▦ ⓐ ♠ ♥ Ⅹ ⊙ ⊞ ⇗ ⊞ ⊞ ▲ ⱦ P ☲ ⊞ lau
♠ ∅ Prices: pitch 28-94 (incl 3 persons)

Théâtre Romain Quartier des Arts, chemin du Brusquet
☎90287866
15 Mar-Oct 1HEC ▦ ♠ ♠ ⊙ ⊞ ⱦ P ☲ ⊞ ⊞ lau ♠ ♥ Ⅹ ∅ ⇗ ⱦR
Prices: A20 ⊞25-40 ▲25-40

VALENCE *Drôme*
CM chemin de l'Epervière ☎75423200
Bordering the Rhône.
Access via exit Valence Sud off A7.
All year 3.5HEC ∷ ⓐ ♠ ♥ Ⅹ ⊙ ⊞ ⱦ P ☲ ⊞ lau ♠ ♥ ∅ ⇗ ⱦR
Prices: pitch 56-72 (incl 2 persons)

VALLABRÈGUES *Gard*
Lou Vincen ☎66592129
Mar-Oct 1.4HEC ▦ ♠ ♠ ♥ ⊙ ⊞ ∅ ⱦ P ☲ ⊞ lau ♠ ♥ Ⅹ ⇗ ⱦLR
Prices: A20-21 pitch 23-24

VALLON-PONT-D'ARC *Ardèche*
Ardechois ☎75880663
In a pleasant situation in the Ardèche Gorge. Good access for
caravans and plentiful sporting facilities.
From Vallon take D290 towards St-Martin. Signposted.
Etr-20 Sep 5HEC ▦ ♠ ♠ ♥ Ⅹ ⊙ ⊞ ∅ ⊞ ⱦ PR ☲ ⊞ lau ♠ ⇗
Prices: pitch 96-136 (incl 2 persons)
See advertisement under Colour Section

Mondial rte des Gorges ☎75880044
Modernised site on the bank of the Ardèche with good sanitary
arrangements.
Access from Vallon-Pont-d'Arc D290. 800m towards Gorge
d'Ardèche.
15 Mar-15 Oct 4.2HEC ▦ ♠ ♠ ♥ Ⅹ ⊙ ⊞ ∅ ⇗ ⊞ ▲ ⱦ PR ☲ ⊞
⊗ lau Prices: pitch 75-129 (incl 2 persons)
See advertisement under Colour Section

Plage Fleurie Les Mazes ☎75880115
Holiday site in unspoilt village beside river.
Take D579 towards Ruoms, turn left after 2.5km towards Les
Mazes.
Etr-Sep 12HEC ▦ ♠ ♠ ♥ Ⅹ ⊙ ⊞ ∅ ⱦ R ☲ ⊞ ⊞ lau

PARC BELLE-VUE
F-34350 Valras-Plage
Tel. & Fax 04.67.37.33.94

Large selection of accommodation to let. 400 mobile
homes and bungalows.

Tariff per week (FF)	high season	low season
Mobile home Comfort	4p.2.800	1.050
Mobile home Comfort	6p.3.380	1.360
Bungalows	4p.3.275	1.245
Bungalows	6p.3.640	1.580

Leisure programme, swimming pool, tennis, minigolf,
archery, volleyball etc... Ask for our free brochure and
tariffs without obligation, indicating the composition of
the family and the period.

VALRAS-PLAGE *Hérault*

Lou Village ☎67373379
Situated along a sandy beach, bordered by sand-dunes.
2km SW, 100m from the beach
27 Apr-27 Sep 6HEC ⚶ ♦ ♠ ♠ ♣ ♀ ✕ ⊙ ⚑ ∅ ♨ ⚏ ♣ ¾ PS ☎ ⊞ lau
Prices: pitch 125 (incl 2 persons)

Occitane BP 29 ☎67395906
Site on rising ground to the north of town.
Access from autoroute exit 'Béziers-Est' towards Valras.
17 May-13 Sep 6HEC ⚑ ♠ ♠ ♣ ♀ ✕ ⊙ ⚑ ∅ ♣ ▲ ¾ P ☎ ⊞ lau ♦
♨ ¾S Prices: pitch 78-115 (incl 2 persons)

Vagues ☎67373312
Etr-Sep 7.5HEC ⚶ ⚑ ♠ ♣ ♀ ✕ ⊙ ⚑ ∅ ♨ ⚏ ♣ ¾ P ☎ ⊞ lau ♦ ¾S
Prices: pitch 68-185

Yole ☎67373387
Very comfortable site divided into pitches. Good sanitary installations
with individual washing cubicles. Hot water tap. Sailing boats for hire.
Riding stables in village. Reservation recommemded in July and
August.
SW of D37E towards Vendres.
3 May-20 Sep 20HEC ▦ ⚶ ♦ ♠ ♠ ♣ ♀ ✕ ⊙ ⚑ ∅ ♨ ⚏ ♣ ¾ P ☎ ⊞
lau ♦ ¾S Prices: pitch 102-158 (incl 2 persons)

VAUVERT *Gard*

Tourrades chemin des Canaux, CD 135 ☎66888020
3km W via N572 and D135.
All year 7HEC ⚑ ♠ ♠ ♣ ♀ ✕ ⊙ ⚑ ♨ ⚏ ♣ ¾ P ☎ ⊞ lau ♦ ⊞

VEDÈNE *Vaucluse*

Flory rte d'Entraigues ☎90310051
Well-kept site on hill.
From motorway, do not head for Vedène but follow D942 for 800m.
15 Mar-15 Oct 6.5HEC ♦ ♠ ♣ ♀ ✕ ⊙ ⚑ ∅ ♨ ⚏ ♣ ¾ P ☎ ⊞ lau
Prices: pitch 75.60-79.50

VENCE *Alpes-Maritimes*

Domaine de la Bergerie rte de la Sine ☎93580936
Well-kept site on hilly land. Pitches near to a wood. Some facilities
are only available in high season.
3km W on D2210.
25 Mar-15 Oct 13HEC ▦ ♦ ♠ ♠ ♣ ♀ ✕ ⊙ ⚑ ∅ ♨ ⚏ ♣ ¾ P ☎ ⊞ lau
Prices: pitch 50.50-94.50 (incl 2 persons)

VERCHENY *Drôme*

Acacias ☎75217251
Pleasant site beside the River Drôme.
Access via D93.
Apr-Sep 3HEC ▦ ♦ ♠ ♠ ♣ ♀ ✕ ⊙ ⚑ ∅ ♨ ⚏ ♣ ¾ R ☎ �℗ ⊞ lau Prices:
pitch 50-60 (incl 2 persons)

VÉREILLES *Hérault*

Sieste ☎67237296
Jun-15 Sep 2HEC ▦ ⚶ ♦ ♠ ♠ ♣ ♀ ✕ ⊙ ⚑ ∅ ♨ ⚏ ♣ ¾ PR ☎ ⊞ lau
Prices: pitch 60 (incl 2 persons)

VIAS *Hérault*

Air Marin ☎67216490
15 May-Sep 7HEC ▦ ♦ ♠ ♠ ♣ ♀ ✕ ⊙ ⚑ ∅ ♨ ⚏ ♣ ¾ PR ☎ ⊞ lau ♦
¾S Prices: pitch 128 (incl 2 persons)

Bourricot ☎67216427
3km S on D137; at Vias look for Farinette-Plage and in 100m before
beach turn right.
22 May-18 Sep 2HEC ▦ ♦ ♠ ♠ ♣ ♀ ✕ ⊙ ⚑ ∅ ♨ ¾ R ☎ ⊞ lau ♦ ¾S

Carabasse rte de la Mer ☎67216401
Clean modern well-kept site.
2km S.
15 May-17 Sep 20HEC ▦ ♦ ♠ ♠ ♣ ♀ ✕ ⊙ ⚑ ∅ ♨ ⚏ ♣ ¾ P ☎ ⊞ lau ♦
¾S Prices: pitch 82.50-165 (incl 2 persons)

Farret ☎67216445
On level meadow beside flat sandy beach, ideal for children.
22 May-Sep 7HEC ⚶ ♦ ♠ ♠ ♣ ♀ ✕ ⊙ ⚑ ∅ ♨ ⚏ ♣ ¾ PS ☎ ⊞
lau ♦ ¾R Prices: pitch 155 (incl 2 persons)

Gai Soleil Côte Ouest ☎67216477
On level land near sea. Divided into pitches.
Cross Canal du Midi, S of town, then turn W.
All year 5HEC ▦ ♦ ♠ ♠ ♣ ♀ ✕ ⊙ ⚑ ∅ ♨ ⚏ ♣ ▲ ¾ P ☎ ⊞ lau ♦
¾RS Prices: pitch 72-95 (incl 2 persons)

Hélios Vias-Plage ☎67216366
On level ground divided into pitches.
On D137 S of village signposted 'Farinette'.
26 May-Sep 2.5HEC ▦ ⚶ ⚑ ♠ ♠ ♣ ♀ ✕ ⊙ ⚑ ∅ ♨ ⚏ ♣ ¾ lau ♦
✕ ¾RS

Méditerranée Plage ☎67909907
15 May-Sep 10HEC ▦ ⚶ ⚑ ♠ ♠ ♣ ♀ ✕ ⊙ ⚑ ∅ ♨ ⚏ ♣ ¾ S ☎ ⊞
lau

Napoléon Vias Plage ☎67216437
Etr-Sep 3HEC ⚶ ♦ ♠ ♠ ♣ ♀ ✕ ⊙ ⚑ ∅ ♨ ⚏ ♣ ▲ ¾ P ☎ ⊞ lau
♦ ¾RS Prices: pitch 98-140 (incl 2 persons)

Ondines ☎67216359
May-Sep 4.4HEC ▦ ♦ ♠ ♠ ♣ ♀ ✕ ⊙ ⚑ ∅ ♨ ⚏ ♣ ¾ P ☎ ♦ ∅ ¾S
Prices: pitch 113 (incl 2 persons)

VIC-LA-GARDIOLE *Hérault*

Europe ☎67781150
A pleasant site in peaceful surroundings.
1.5km W via D114.
May-Sep 5HEC ▦ ⚑ ♠ ♠ ♣ ♀ ✕ ⊙ ⚑ ∅ ♨ ⚏ ♣ ¾ P ☎ ⊞ lau ♦ ¾L
Prices: pitch 40-130 (incl 2 persons)

VIGAN, LE *Gard*

Val de l'Arre rte de Ganges ☎67810277
2.5km E on D999.
Apr-Sep 4HEC ▦ ♦ ♠ ♠ ♣ ♀ ✕ ⊙ ⚑ ∅ ♨ ⚏ ♣ ¾ PR ☎ ⊞ lau Prices:
pitch 74 (incl 2 persons)

VILLARS-COLMARS *Alpes-de-Haute-Provence*

Haut-Verdon ☎92834009
On D908 bordering river.
29 Jun-Aug 3.5HEC ♦ ♠ ♠ ♣ ♀ ✕ ⊙ ⚑ ∅ ♨ ¾ P ☎ ⊞ lau Prices:
A25 pitch 50

VILLEMOUSTAUSSOU *Aude*

Pinhiers chemin du Pont Neuf ☎68478190
A61 in the direction of Mazamet.
Apr-Sep 2HEC ⚑ ♠ ♠ ♣ ♀ ✕ ⊙ ⚑ ⚏ ♣ ¾ P ☎ lau ♦ ✕ ∅ ♨ Prices:
A16.50-18 pitch 18.50-20

VILLENEUVE-LOUBET-PLAGE *Alpes-Maritimes*

Hippodrôme 6 av des Rives ☎93200200
Divided into two by a busy road. 0.3km from the sea.
Turn right off the N7 at ATLAS furniture store.
All year 7.8HEC ♦ ♠ ♠ ♣ ♀ ⊙ ⚑ ⚏ ☎ ⊞ lau ♦ ♣ ✕ ∅ ♨ ¾S Prices:
A19 V9 ⚘60-112 ▲47-110

Panorama 766 Bretelle Autoroute A8 ☎93209153
Small terraced site mainly for tents 0.8km from the sea.
About 500m from the Nice-Cannes Autoroute.
All year 1HEC ♦ ♠ ♠ ♣ ♀ ✕ ⊙ ⚑ ∅ ♨ ⚏ ☎ ⊞ lau ♦ ♣ ¾S Prices:
pitch 28-40 (incl 2 persons)

Parc des Maurettes 730 av du Dr-Lefebvre ☎93209191
Terraced site in a pine forest.
Access via A8: From Cannes take exit 'Villeneuve-Loubet-Plage', then
N7 towards Antibes for 1km. From Nice, take Villeneuve exit and A8
for 2km.
10 Jan-15 Nov 2HEC ▦ ♦ ♠ ♣ ♀ ✕ ⊙ ⚑ ∅ ♨ ⚏ ℗ ⊞ lau ♦ ♣ ¾PS
Prices: pitch 72-120 (incl 2 persons)

Parc Montana Loubet La Tour de la Madone, La Vanade
☎93209611
Parkland dominated by an 11th-century monastery.
2km W on D2085
18 Mar-14 Oct 8HEC ▦ ♦ ⚑ ♠ ♣ ♀ ✕ ⊙ ⚑ ∅ ♨ ⚏ ♣ ¾ P ☎ ⊞ lau
♦ ¾R

Vieille Ferme 296 bd des Groules ☎93334144
Site lies in Vaugrenier Park. Level meadow, terraced site for tents.
900m from sea.
All year 2.8HEC ▥ ♠ ⚘ ⋔ ⅏ ⊙ ⬛ ⌀ ⬛ ⬛ ⤳ P ⚐ ⊞ lau � ☀ ✕ ⤳S
Prices: pitch 78-146 (incl 3 persons)

VILLEROUGE-LA-CRÉMADE *Aude*

Pinada ☎68436193
In pleasant rural surroundings on edge of forest.
600m NW on D106.
15 May-Sep 4.3HEC ▥ ⋮⋮ ♠ ⋔ ⚐ ⊙ ⬛ ⌀ ⬛ ⬛ ⤳ P ⚐ ⊞ lau ➤
✕

VILLES-SUR-AUZON *Vaucluse*

Verguettes rte de Carpentras ☎90618818
W via D942
15 May-Sep 2HEC ▥ ⚘ ⋔ ☀ ✕ ⊙ ⬛ ⤳ P ⚐ lau ➤ ☰ ⌀

VIOLS-LE-FORT *Hérault*

Cantagrils ☎67550188
4.5km S on D127
Apr-15 Oct 14HEC ♠ ⋔ ⋔ ☰ ☀ ✕ ⊙ ⬛ ⌀ ⬛ ⬛ ⤳ P ⚐ lau

VIVIERS *Ardèche*

Centre de Vacances d'Imbours ☎75543806
15 Jun-5 Sep 10HEC ▥ ♠ ⋔ ☰ ☀ ✕ ⊙ ⬛ ⌀ ⬛ ⬛ ⤳ P ⚐ ⊞ lau Prices:
A30 pitch 63

Rochecondrie Loisirs RN 86 ☎75527466
N of town on N86.
Apr-Oct 3.8HEC ▥ ♠ ⋔ ☀ ✕ ⊙ ⬛ ⬛ ⤳ PR ⚐ ⊞ lau ➤ ☰ ✕ ⌀ ⛾
Prices: pitch 86 (incl 2 persons)

VOGÜE *Ardèche*

Domaine du Cros d'Auzon ☎75377586
2.5km via D579 bordering the river.
Etr-15 Sep 20HEC ▥ ⋮⋮ ♠ ⋔ ☰ ☀ ✕ ⊙ ⬛ ⌀ ⬛ ⬛ ▲ ⤳ PR ⚐ ⊞
lau Prices: pitch 98 (incl 2 persons)

VOLONNE *Alpes-de-Haute-Provence*

Hippocampe rte Napoléon ☎92335000
Several strips of land, interspersed with trees, and running down the
edge of lake. Surrounded by fields and gardens.
On S edge of town. 2km E of N85.
Apr-Sep 8HEC ▥ ⚘ ⋔ ☰ ☀ ✕ ⊙ ⬛ ⌀ ⬛ ⬛ ▲ ⤳ LP ⚐ ⊞ lau Prices:
pitch 58-115 (incl 2 persons)

Corsica

Corsica is a wonderful blend of green mountains, deep valleys,
and spectacular pink granite peaks where rain and melting snow
merge into torrents that rush down the hillsides. In the spring the
mountains are ablaze with wild flowers and the maquis - the
abundance of which gives the island its name 'the scented isle'.
This southernmost outpost of France, some 100 miles south
of Toulon in the Mediterranean. Beaches abound, and all kinds of
watersports are available in season, but in this relatively
undiscovered place it is still possible to find a quiet beach on a
summer day.
Corsica's capital is Ajaccio, birthplace of Napoleon, and today a
cosmopolitan centre with its busy harbour and broad boulevards
with smart shops. From Ajaccio there is a railway to Bastia, in the
north. This is a beautiful three-hour trip, and ideal for drivers
reluctant to venture onto more tortuous minor roads.

CORSE (CORSICA)

ALÉRIA *Haute-Corse*

Marina d'Aléria Plage de Padu-lone ☎95570142
3km E of Cateraggio via RN200
Apr-Oct 10HEC ⋮⋮ ♠ ⋔ ☰ ☀ ✕ ⊙ ⬛ ⌀ ⬛ ⤳ RS ⚐ lau ➤ ⊞ Prices:
A28-36 V10-12 ⊞11-13 ▲8-10

BONIFACIO *Corse-du-Sud*

Rondinara Suartone ☎95704315
Midway between Porto-Vecchio and Bonifacio on N198 in the
direction of Suartone-La Rondinara.
Jun-Sep 5HEC ⋮⋮ ♠ ⚘ ⋔ ☰ ☀ ✕ ⊙ ⬛ ⌀ ⬛ ⤳ P ⚐ ⊞ lau ➤ ⤳S

CALVI *Haute-Corse*

Dolce Vita Ponte Bambino ☎95650599
4km SW of Calvi between N197 to L'Ile Rousse and the sea.
May-Sep 6HEC ▥ ♠ ⋔ ☰ ☀ ✕ ⊙ ⬛ ⌀ ⬛ ⤳ RS ⚐ lau

CARGESE *Corse-du-Sud*

Torraccia ☎95264239
4km N on N199.
15 May-Sep 3.5HEC ♠ ⋔ ☰ ☀ ✕ ⊙ ⬛ ⌀ ⬛ ⚐ ⊞ lau ➤ ✕ ⤳S
Prices: A30-32 V12-13 ⊞12-13 ▲12-13

CENTURI *Haute-Corse*

Isulottu ☎95356281
16 Dec-14 Jan 3HEC ▥ ♠ ⋔ ☰ ☀ ✕ ⊙ ⬛ ⌀ ⊞ lau ➤ ⤳S

CLOS-DU-MOUFLON *Haute-Corse*

Mouflon ☎95650353
Terraced site, divided into pitches. Very steep access via partly
asphalted, winding road with gradient of 20%. **Tents and motorised
caravans only.**
15km from Calvi on D81 on the coastal road, in the direction of Porto.
6 Jun-25 Sep 2.5HEC ♠ ⚘ ⋔ ☰ ☀ ✕ ⊙ ⌀ ⤳ S ⚐ ⊞ lau ➤ ☰

FARINOLE, MARINE DE *Haute-Corse*

A Stella ☎95371437
On D80 beside the sea
Jun-15 Oct 5HEC ▥ ⚘ ⋔ ☰ ☀ ✕ ⊙ ⬛ ⬛ ⤳ S ⚐ ⊞ lau

GALÉRIA *Haute-Corse*

Deux Torrents ☎95620067
5km E on D51 towards Calenzana.
15 Jun-15 Sep 6.3HEC ▥ ♠ ⋔ ☰ ☀ ✕ ⊙ ⬛ ⌀ ⛾ ⬛ ⚐ lau Prices:
A26 V13 ⊞22 ▲13

GHISONACCIA *Haute-Corse*

Arinella-Bianca Arinella-Bianca ☎95560478
In wooded surroundings, directly on the beach.
Etr-Oct 12HEC ▥ ♠ ⋔ ☰ ☀ ✕ ⊙ ⬛ ⌀ ⬛ ⬛ ▲ ⤳ PRS ⚐ ⊞ lau

LOZARI *Haute-Corse*

Clos des Chênes rte de Belgodère ☎95601513
In a delightful wooded setting, 1km from a fine sandy beach.
1.5km S via N197 towards Belgodère
Apr-Sep 5.5HEC ▥ ♠ ⋔ ☰ ☀ ✕ ⊙ ⬛ ⌀ ⛾ ⬛ ⬛ ▲ ⤳ P ⚐ ⊞ lau ➤
⤳S Prices: A30-33 V11 ⊞19 ▲16

LUMIO *Haute-Corse*

Panoramic rte de Belgodère D71 ☎95607313
Very clean and tidy site divided into pitches.
From Calvi, 12km on N197, 200m from main road.
Jun-15 Sep 6HEC ▥ ♠ ⋔ ☰ ☀ ✕ ⊙ ⬛ ⌀ ⬛ ⤳ P ⚐ ⊞ lau ➤ ⤳S

OLMETO-PLAGE *Corse-du-Sud*

Esplanade ☎95760503
All year 5HEC ▥ ♠ ⋔ ☰ ☀ ✕ ⊙ ⬛ ⌀ ⬛ ⬛ ⤳ S ⚐ ⊞ lau

PIANOTTOLI *Corse-du-Sud*

Kevano Plage Plage de Kevano ☎95718322
Apr-Sep 6HEC ▥ ♠ ⚘ ⋔ ☰ ☀ ✕ ⊙ ⬛ ⬛ ⬛ ⊞ lau ➤ ⤳S

PISCIATELLO *Corse-du-Sud*

Benista ☎95251930
Apr-Oct 5HEC ▥ ♠ ⋔ ☰ ☀ ✕ ⊙ ⬛ ⌀ ⛾ ⬛ ⬛ ⤳ R ⚐ ⊞ lau ➤ ⤳S
Prices: pitch 75-95 (incl 2 persons)

PORTO-VECCHIO *Corse-du-Sud*

Pirellu rte de Palomlaggia ☎95702344
S of Porto-Vecchio, take road for Bonifacio. After Pont du Stabiacco
take first road on the left.
May-Sep 5HEC ⚘ ⋔ ☰ ☀ ✕ ⊙ ⬛ ⌀ ⛾ ⬛ ⬛ ⤳ P ⚐ ⌀ lau Prices: A28-
30 V12-13 ⊞18-20 ▲12-13

Vetta La Trinité ☎95700986
5.5km N on N198.
Jun-Sep 8HEC ▥ ♠ ♠ ⚍ ⟟ ✕ ⊙ ⬚ ⌀ ♨ ♨ ↖ P ☎ ⊞ lau

ST-FLORENT *Haute-Corse*

U Pezzo chemin de la Plage ☎95370165
Pleasant site; partly level, partly terraced under eucalyptus trees.
Private access to large beach.
S of town on road to beach.
15 Apr-15 Oct 2HEC ▥ ♠ ♠ ⚍ ⟟ ✕ ⊙ ⬚ ⌀ ♨ ↖ S ☎ ⊞ lau

SOTTA *Corse-du-Sud*

U Moru Figari ☎95712340
4km SW via D859.
Mar-Oct 6HEC ▥ ♠ ⚍ ⟟ ✕ ⊙ ⬚ ⌀ ♨ ⚠ ☎ ⊞ lau ↖ ⚌ ↖S

TIUCCIA *Corse-du-Sud*

Couchants rte de Casaglione ☎95522660
3km from the sea.
All year 5HEC ▥ ⚭ ♠ ⚍ ⟟ ✕ ⊙ ⬚ ⌀ ⟰ ♨ ♨ ⚠ ☎ ⊞ lau Prices: A23
V10 ♨15 ⚠10

U Sommalu rte de Casaglione ☎95522421
2.5km N via D81 and D25.
15 Mar-Sep 6HEC ▥ ♠ ♠ ⚍ ⟟ ✕ ⊙ ⬚ ⌀ ♨ ♨ ⚠ ☎ lau ↖ ⚌ ↖RS
⊞ Prices: A22-25 V14-16 ♨20-22 ⚠12-14

VICO *Corse-du-Sud*

Sposata Col Stantaine ☎95266155
On partly terraced, partly sloping ground.
1km SW on N195.
Apr-Sept 2.5HEC ▥ ♠ ♠ ⚍ ⟟ ✕ ⊙ ⬚ ⌀ ♨ ☎ ⊞ lau ↖ ⚌ ↖LRS

GERMANY

Germany, with its fairytale castles and ancient towns, is a country offering legend and tradition amongst its many attractions.

Germany is bordered by nine countries: Austria, Belgium, Czech Republic, Denmark, France, Luxembourg, Netherlands, Poland and Switzerland. It is a country of forests, rivers and mountains. The Rhine Valley boasts magnificent cliffs and woods whilst the Black Forest has some fine valley scenery with countless waterfalls and gorges.

The climate is temperate and variable but Germany enjoys hotter summers than Britain.

Off-site camping Permission to camp off an official campsite must be obtained from the landowner or local police. Overnight parking at parking places is tolerated for one night, unless otherwise indicated, provided nearby campsites and hotels are fully booked. However, caravans must remain connected to the towing vehicle. Make sure you do not contravene local regulations.

HOW TO GET THERE

For western Germany use the Channel Tunnel, or one of the short Channel crossings and travel via Belgium. For northern Germany take a direct ferry from Harwich to **Hamburg** (20hrs) or Newcastle to Hamburg (23hrs) or one of the Channel crossings to the Netherlands. For southern Germany use the Channel Tunnel, or one of the short Channel crossings and drive through northern France entering Germany near **Strasbourg**; this is also the route if using one of the longer Channel crossings to Caen, Cherbourg, Dieppe or Le Havre. For details of the *AA European Routes Service* please consult the Contents Page.

FACTS AND FIGURES

Capital: Berlin
Language: German
IDD code: 49. To call the UK dial 00 44.
Currency: Deutsche Mark (*DM* 1 = 100 Pfennigs). At the time of going to press £1 = 2.25*DM*.
Local time: GMT + 1 (summer GMT + 2)
Emergency services: Police and Ambulance 110; Fire 112.
Business hours-
Banks: 0830-1230 & 1330-1530 Mon-Wed and Fri, 0830-1230 & 1330-1730 Thur. These are approximate, there are no uniform banking hours.
Shops: 0900-1800 or 1830 Mon-Wed, 0900-2030 Thur and 0830 - 1400 Sat (later if first Sat in month).

These opening hours apply to city shops.
Average daily temperatures: Munich

Jan 2°C	Sep 15°C
Jul 18°C	May 13°C
Mar 4°C	Nov 3°C

Tourist Information: German National Tourist Office
UK 65 Curzon Street London W1Y 8NE
☎0171 493 0080 (0891 600100 premium rate information line)
USA 747 Third Ave New York, NY 10017
☎(212) 308-3300.
Camping card: generally recommended; some reductions on site fees.

Distance

From the Continental Channel ports, Köln (Cologne) is about 419km (260 miles) and within a comfortable day's drive; routes to southern and eastern Germany usually require one or two overnight stops.

MOTORING & GENERAL INFORMATION

The information given here is specific to Germany. It **must** be read in conjunction with the European ABC at the front of the book, which covers those regulations which are common to many countries.

British Embassy/Consulates*

At the time of writing the British Embassy is located at 53113 Bonn, Friedrich-Ebert-Allee 77, ☎(0228) 9167-0; it has no Consular Section. The British Embassy Office is located at 0-10117 Berlin, Unter den Linden 32/34 ☎ (030) 201 840. There are British Consulates in Dusseldorf, Frankfurt/Main, Hamburg, München(Munich) and Stuttgart; there are British Consulates with Honorary Consuls in Bremen, Hannover, Kiel and Nürnberg (Nuremberg).

Children in cars
Child under 12 and/or 1.5metres in height not permitted to travel as front or rear seat passenger unless using suitable restraint system, if fitted.

Currency
There are no restrictions on the amount of foreign or German currency that a *bona fide* tourist can import or export.

Banks and post offices provide exchange facilities for currency, Eurocheques and Travellers Cheques.

Dimensions and weight restrictions
Private **cars** and **trailers** or **caravans** are restricted to the following dimensions - height, 4 metres; width, 2.50metres; length, 12 metres. The maximum permitted overall length of vehicle/trailer or caravan combinations is 18 metres. A fully-laden trailer without an adequate braking system must not weigh more than 37.5kg plus 50% of the weight of the towing vehicle. A fully-laden trailer with an adequate braking system must not weigh more than the towing vehicle.

Driving licence*
A valid UK or Republic of Ireland licence is acceptable in Germany. The minimum age at which visitors from UK or Republic of Ireland may use a temporarily imported car or motorcycle is 17 years.
First-aid kit*
The German authorities recommend that visiting motorists equip their vehicles with a first-aid kit.

Foodstuffs*
There are no limits on the importation of foodstuffs obtained duty and tax paid within the EC. Up to 500g of coffee (200g of coffee extract) and 100g of tea (40g of tea extract) purchased duty free or outside the EC may be imported free of duty and tax. However, coffee bought duty free or outside the EC cannot be

imported by visitors under 15 years of age. Visitors may also import up to 1kg of fresh meat and meat products and up to 30kg of game and poultry per person, but meat and meat products from Brazil, Portugal, Spain, Turkey, former USSR and all countries in Africa and Asia are strictly prohibited.
Lights*
The German authorities recommend that visiting motorists equip their vehicles with a spare set of vehicle bulbs.

Motoring clubs*
The principal German motoring clubs are the **Allgemeiner Deutscher Automobil Club e.V.** (ADAC) which has its headquarters at 81373 München, Am Westpark 8 ☎(089) 7676-0 and the **Deutscher Touring Automobil Club e.V.** (DTC) whose headquarters are 81247 München, Amalienburgstrasse 23 ☎(089)891133-0. The ADAC has offices in the larger towns, and office hours are 09.00-18.00hrs Mon-Fri. The ADAC also has offices at major frontier crossings.

Roads
The *Bundesstrassen,* or state roads, vary in quality. In the north and west, and in the touring areas of the Rhine Valley, Black Forest, and Bavaria, the roads are good and well-graded. Germany has a comprehensive motorway *(Autobahn)* network which dominates the road system and takes most of the long distance traffic. Emergency telephones are sited every 2km, the direction of the nearest telephone is indicated by the point of the black triangle on posts alongside the motorway. Traffic at weekends increases considerably during the school holidays, which are from July to mid September. In order to ease congestion, heavy lorries are prohibited on all roads at weekends from approximately mid June to the end of August and generally on all Sundays and Public holidays.

Speed limits*
Car
Built-up areas 50kph (31mph)
Other roads 100kph (62mph)
Motorways/dual carriageways †130kph (80mph)

Car/caravan/trailer

Built-up areas 50kph (31mph)
Other roads 80kph (49mph)
Motorways/dual-carriageways 80kph (49mph)
†If signposted, otherwise *recommended* maximum speed.

Notes i In bad weather 50kph (31mph) on all roads when visibility reduced to 50 metres (55yrds).

ii Outside special built-up areas, motor vehicles to which a special speed limit applies, as well as vehicles with trailers with a combined length of more than 7 metres (23ft), must keep sufficient distance from the preceding vehicle so that an overtaking vehicle may pull in. Anyone driving so slowly that a line of vehicles has formed behind must permit the following vehicles to pass, by stopping at a suitable place if necessary.

Warning triangle

The use of a warning triangle is compulsory in the event of accident or breakdown. The triangle must be placed on the road behind the vehicle to warn following traffic of any obstruction: 100 metres (110yds) on ordinary roads and 200 metres (220yds) on motorways. Vehicles over 2,500kg (2 tons, 9cwt, 24lb) must also carry a yellow flashing light.

*Additional information will be found in the Continental ABC at the front of the book.

A-Z DIRECTORY

Prices are in German Marks (Deutschmarks)
Abbreviations: Abbreviations: pl Platz pl Platz str S trasse str Strasse
Each placename preceded by 'Bad' is listed under the name that
follows it.

South East

The highest peak in Germany can be found in the Alps along the
southern border of Bavaria. Superb walks and easy climbs bring
rewarding views of lush meadows and secluded lakes, and there
are some rare and wonderful species of Alpine fauna to be seen.
Bavaria is also a land of spruce, pine, and deciduous forests
impressively strewn with massive boulders and rock labyrinths
which are perfect for climbing, exploring and caving. Many areas
are also excellent for winter sports.
The Octoberfest and the Wagner festival are both held in this
region; other attractions include medieval tournaments, Alpine
horn-blowing, and Schuhplatter dancing.
To the south of the region, Munich is a most beautiful city famed
for art and learning, with an atmosphere and charm of its own.
Further north, be sure to visit Passau, which possesses the
largest church organ in the world, and the former Imperial city of
Regensburg.

AACH BEI OBERSTAUFEN Bayern

Aach ☎08386 363
A terraced site with beautiful views of the mountains. Sauna,
solarium, games room.
From Oberstaufen follow B308 for 7km towards the Austrian border.
All year 2HEC ▦ ⬦ ⌾ ⋒ ⒮ ⍩ ✕ ⊖ ⍾ ⌀ ⌸ ⍭ ⍨ PR ⒫ ⊞ lau Prices:
A7 ⊕10-14 ▲6-12

AITRANG Bayern

Elbsee 3 ☎08343 248
On the E shore of the lake with good bathing facilities. Section
reserved for campers with dogs.
Take B12 from Marktoberdorf travel for 11km then turn N to Aitrang.
Closed 4 Nov-13 Dec 3.5HEC ▦ ⌾ ⋒ ⊖ ⍾ ⌀ ⌸ ⍭ ⒫ ⊞ lau ✦ ⍩
✕ ⍨L Prices: A6 V3 ⊕14 ▲14

ARLACHING Bayern

Kupferschmiede Trostberger Str 4 ☎08667 446
On meadowland. Partially gravel.
On Seebruck-Traunstein road.
Apr-Sep 2HEC ⌾ ⋒ ⒮ ⍩ ✕ ⊖ ⍾ ⌸ ⍭ L ⒲ lau ✦ ⌀ Prices: A8.90
pitch 9.90

AUGSBURG Bayern

Augusta Mühlhauser Str 546 ☎0821 707575
Hard standings for caravans. Separate section for residential
caravans.
Leave E11 by Augsburg-Ost exit. Continue N towards Neuburg and
turn right after 400m.
All year 5.5HEC ▦ ⌾ ⋒ ⒮ ⍩ ✕ ⊖ ⍾ ⌀ ⌸ ⍭ ⍭ ▲ ⍨ L ⒲ ✦ ⍩ ✕

BAMBERG Bayern

At **BUG**(5km S)

Insel ☎0951 56320
The site lies on the bank of the River Regnitz, S of Bamberg.
If approaching from the S, leave motorway at Bamberg exit, take
B505 and then B4 towards Bamberg. If approaching from N, drive
through Bamberg on B4 and leave it at Nürnberg exit.
All year 5HEC ▦ ⌾ ⋒ ⒮ ⍩ ✕ ⊖ ⍾ ⌀ ⍭ R ⒲ ⊞ lau Prices: A6.50
pitch 12

BEILNGRIES Bayern

Altmühl ☎08461 8406
Modern, well-tended municipal site on grassland with trees in the
Altmühl.
Access via A9/E6 (München-Nürnberg) road exit Altmühltal about
18km NE turn right, off B299 towards Landshut.
All year 2.8HEC ▦ ⌾ ⋒ ⒮ ⍩ ✕ ⊖ ⍾ ⌀ ⌸ ⍭ PR ⒲ ⊞ lau ✦ ⍨P

BERCHTESGADEN Bayern

Allwegiehen ☎08652 2396
A terraced site at the foot of the Untersalzberg Mountain surrounded
by bushy woods. There is also a steep and narrow asphalt access
road with passing places. A truck is available for towing caravans.
The camp is closed between 12.30 and 14.30 hrs and from 21.00
hrs.
For access, take the B305, and drive approx. 3.5km towards
Schellenberg.
All year 3HEC ▦ ▦ ⁖⁖⁖ ⬦ ⌾ ⋒ ⒮ ⍩ ✕ ⊖ ⍾ ⌀ ⍭ ⍨ P ⒲ ⊞ ⍒ Prices:
A7.80 pitch 11.50

BERGEN Bayern

Wagnerhof Campingstr 11 ☎08662 8557
Level site.
Camping Card Compulsory.
Access from München-Salzburg motorway, Bergen exit. Turn right at
sawmill just before entering town.
All year 2.8HEC ▦ ⬦ ⭢⭣ ⋒ ⒮ ⍩ ✕ ⊖ ⍾ ⌀ ⌸ ⒲ lau ✦ ✕ ⍨P

BERNAU-AM-CHIEMSEE Bayern

At **FELDEN**(3km N)

Chiemsee-Süd ☎08051 7540 & 7175
Level meadowland shaded by trees, on lake shore.
Leave the A8/E11 (München-Salzburg) at exit Felden, continue W
towards lake.
15 Apr-15 Oct 2HEC ▦ ⌾ ⋒ ⒮ ✕ ⊖ ⍾ ⌀ ⌸ ⍭ L ⒲ ⊞ lau ✦ ⍨P
Prices: A6.50 pitch 10-12

BRUNNEN FORGGENSEE Bayern

Brunnen Seestr 81 ☎08362 8273
Situated on E shore of Lake Forggensee.
From Füssen follow B17 to Schwangau, then continue N on minor
road.
15 Nov-15 Dec 2HEC ▦ ▦ ⁖⁖⁖ ⬦ ✦ ⋒ ⒮ ⍩ ✕ ⊖ ⍾ ⌀ ⍭ ⍨ L ⒲ ⊞ lau
Prices: A10-10.50 pitch 8-10

CHIEMING Bayern

Chieming Möwenplatz Haupstr 3 ☎08664 361 & 653
Small site on shore of lake, with gravelly terrain.
Camping Card Compulsory.
5km S of Chieming.
Apr-Sep 0.8HEC ▦ ⌾ ⋒ ⒮ ✕ ⊖ ⍾ ⍭ L ⒲ ⊞ lau ✦ ⍩ ✕ ⌀ ⍭L

DIESSEN Bayern

St-Alban ☎08807 7305
Clean site next to St-Alban, lakeside with private bathing beach and
reserved section for residential campers. Good sanitary installations
also used by the public.
From München follow B12 towards Landsberg/Lech. Near
Greifenberg turn left, proceed via Utting to St-Alban.
Apr-Oct 3.8HEC ▦ ⌾ ⋒ ⒮ ✕ ⊖ ⍾ ⌀ ⍭ L ⒲ ⊞ ✦ ⌀ Prices: A6 pitch
15.50

DINKELSBÜHL Bayern

Romantische Strasse ☎09851 7817
Terraced site with some hedges and trees. Separate field for young
people. Good sporting facilities.
Signposted.
All year 9HEC ⌾ ⋒ ⒮ ⍩ ✕ ⊖ ⍾ ⌀ ⍭ L ⒲ ⒲ ⊞ lau

EGGLFING *Bayern*

Max ☎08537 356
On meadow divided into pitches and 1km from spa baths at Bad Füssing.
Take B12 to Tutling and then turn off towards Egglfing and the national frontier.
Closed 15 Jan-15 Feb 2.5HEC ▥ ⊶ ⋔ ℥ ✕ ⊙ ⊡ ⌀ ♨ ♠ ♥ ☎ ⊞ lau ➡ ⇗R

ERLANGEN *Bayern*

Naturfreunde Wohrmühle 6 ☎09131 28499
Site lies on meadowland on an island in the River Regnitz.
Well signposted from outskirts of town.
All year 10HEC ▥ ⊶ ⋔ ✕ ⊙ ⊡ ⌀ ♨ ☎ ⊞ ➡ ⇗PR

Rangau Campingstr 44 ☎09135 8866
Long stretch of land behind the sportsground and next to the Dechsendorfer Weiher Lake in nature reserve.
Leave motorway (A3/E5 Nürnberg-Würzburg) at exit Erlangen-West.
Apr-Sep 1.8HEC ▥ ⊶ ⋔ ✕ ⊙ ⊡ ♨ ⊞ lau ➡ ⇗ Prices: A6.50 pitch 8

ESCHERNDORF *Bayern*

Escherndorf-Main Gaststatte ☎09381 2889
Site lies on meadowland by the River Main, next to the ferry station (River Ferry Northeim). Lunchtime siesta 13.00-15.00 hrs.
Site can be reached from motorway A7/E70 via exit Würzburg Estenfeld and follow road E towards 'Volkach'.
Apr-Oct 1.5HEC ▥ ⊶ ⋔ ℥ ✕ ⊙ ⊡ ⌀ ⇗ R ☎ ➡ ⇗P

ESTENFELD *Bayern*

Estenfeld Maidbronner Str 38 ☎09305 228
On meadowland next to sportsground.
From motorway A7/E70 leave at exit 'Würzburg/Estenfeld' and continue S on B19 for 1km.
Mar-23 Dec 0.5HEC ▥ ⊶ ⋔ ℥ ✕ ⊙ ⊡ ♨ ☎ ⊞ lau ➡ ✕ ⌀
Prices: A7 pitch 6-12

FEILNBACH, BAD *Bayern*

Tenda Reithof 2 ☎08066 533
Well organised site on level grassland with pitches laid out in circles and hardstandings for tourers near the entrance.
Leave München-Salzburg motorway (A8/E11) at 'Bad Aibling' exit and continue S for 4km on unclass road.
All year 14HEC ▥ ⊶ ⋔ ℥ ✕ ⊙ ⊡ ♨ ⇗ P ☎

FICHTELBERG *Bayern*

Fichtelsee ☎09272 801
Gently sloping meadow amid pleasant woodland 100m from Lake Fichtelsee.
From A9/E6 Bad Berneck exit, take B303 to the Fichtelsee Leisure Centre turning.
6 Nov-15 Dec 2.6HEC ▥ ⊶ ⋔ ⊙ ⊡ ⌀ ☎ ⊞ lau ➡ ✕ ⇗LP
Prices: A9 pitch 10

FINSTERAU *Bayern*

Nationalpark-Ost ☎08557 768
Terraced site on edge of extensive woodland area at entrance to National Park.
N of Freyung towards the frontier.
15 May-15 Oct 3HEC ▥ ⊶ ⋔ ℥ ✕ ⊙ ⊡ ♨ ☎ ⊞ lau ➡ ♠ ⌀ Prices: A6 pitch 7.50

FISCHBACH AM INN *Bayern*

Inntal ☎08034 2869
On level grassland near a small forest lake.
Off B15 S of town.
All year 1.7HEC ▥ ⊶ ⋔ ✕ ⊙ ⊡ ⌀ ⇗ L ⊞ ➡ ℥ ✕ ⇗R

FRICKENHAUSEN *Bayern*

AZUR-Knaus Park Frickenhausen ☎09331 3171
On level meadow in a small poplar wood beside River Main.
Lunchtime siesta 13.00-15.00 hrs.
On N bank of Main 0.5km E of Oshsenfurt.
All year 4HEC ▥ ⊶ ⋔ ℥ ✕ ⊙ ⊡ ⌀ ♨ ♠ ⇗ P ☎ ⊞ lau ➡ ⇗P

FÜRTH IM WALD *Bayern*

SC Einberg Daberger Str ☎09973 1811
Municipal site in Dabergerstr, near swimming pool.
NE of Cham on B20.
Mar-Oct 2HEC ▥ ⊶ ⋔ ⊙ ⊡ ⇗ R ☎ ⊞ lau ➡ ℥ ✕ ⌀ ♨ ⇗P Prices: A4 V3.50 ⊡4 ⚑3

GADEN *Bayern*

Schwanenplatz Schwanenpl 1 ☎08681 281
Site lies on a meadow, divided into sections beside one of Bavaria's warmest lakes, Waginger See.
For access drive from Traunstein to Waging, then turn right in direction Freilassing 2km, then left to lake.
10 May-20 Sep 3.8HEC ▥ ♠ ⋔ ℥ ✕ ⊙ ⊡ ♨ ⇗ L ☎ ⊞ ⊡ ⋇ Prices: A9-10 pitch 10-16

GARMISCH-PARTENKIRCHEN *Bayern*

Zugspitze Griesener Str 4 ☎08821 3180
In beautiful setting at the foot of the Zugspitze between the road and the Loisach.
On the B24 towards the Austrian frontier.
All year 3HEC ▥ ⁛ ⊶ ⋔ ℥ ✕ ⊙ ⊡ ⌀ ♨ ♠ ♥ ⇗ R ☎ lau Prices: A7.50 pitch 10

GEMÜNDEN AM MAIN *Bayern*

Saaleinsel Duivenallee 7 ☎09351 8574
This municipal site lies a short distance off the main road bordering the River Fränkische Saale. It is in the grounds of a sports field and has a swimming pool. Individual washing cubicles with curtains for the ladies.
Access signposted off main B26 road.
Apr-15 Oct 5.1HEC ▥ ⋇ ⋔ ⊙ ⊡ ♨ ♠ ⇗ PR ☎ ⊞ ➡ ℥ ♥ ⌀

GEMÜNDEN-HOFSTETTEN *Bayern*

Schönrain ☎09351 8645
Slightly sloping, partly terraced meadowland E of River Main. Lunchtime siesta 13.00-15.00 hrs.
From Gemünden/Main along the left bank of the River Main about 3km downstream. Turn left off B26 through Hofstetten to site.
27 Mar-Sep 7HEC ▥ ⊶ ⋔ ℥ ✕ ⊙ ⊡ ♨ ♠ ♥ ⇗ P ☎ ⊞ lau Prices: A7.50 pitch 10

GOTTSDORF *Bayern*

AZUR-Ferienzentrum Bayerwald ☎08593 880
Extensive terrain in quiet location.
Access via A3 (Regensburg-Passau) and B388.
All year 12HEC ▥ ⊶ ⋔ ℥ ✕ ⊙ ⊡ ⌀ ♨ ☎ ⊞ lau ➡ ⇗LP

GRIESBACH, BAD *Bayern*

Kur-Und Feriencamping Dreiquellenbad ☎08532 96130
1km S of Griesbach Spa, on the Karpfham-Schwaim road.
All year 2.5HEC ▥ ♠ ⋔ ℥ ✕ ⊙ ⊡ ♨ ♥ ☎ ⊞ lau Prices: A8.50 pitch 9

HANAU *Bayern*

At BRUCHKÖBEL

SC Bärensee ☎06181 12306
Lakeside site with touring and residential sections. Lunchtime siesta 13.00-15.00 hrs.
Take B40 to NE of town as far as the Eriensee turning, then follow signposts.
Mar-Oct 38HEC ▥ ⊶ ⋔ ℥ ✕ ⊙ ⊡ ⌀ ♨ ⇗ L ☎ ⊞ lau ➡ ⇗P

At KAHL AM MAIN(9km SE)

Kahl am Main Königsberger Str ☎06188 94467
Extensive site on the lakeshore with public swimming facilities.
Take B8 to Kahl, then turn off at ARAL petrol station.
Apr-Sep 22HEC ▥ ⋇ ⊶ ⋔ ℥ ✕ ⊙ ⊡ ⌀ ♨ ⇗ L ☎ ⊞ lau ➡ ⇗PR Prices: A5 pitch 5

HASLACH *Bayern*

Feriencenter Wertacher Hof ☎08361 770
Well-kept site on Lake Grüntensee.
Access road near the Wertach-Haslach railway station.

All year 3.5HEC ▦ ♨ ᵛ ↑ 〒 ⅄ ✕ ⊙ ☺ ∅ ♨ ⌁ ⅃ lau ♦ ⊞ Prices: A9 ⚑10 ▲10

HERSBRUCK *Bayern*

At **HOHENSTADT**(6km E)

Pegnitz Eschenbacher Weg 4 ☎09154 1500
A quiet holiday site in set among wooded hills near the River Pegnitz. About 6km E of Hersbruck.
Closed Jan 1HEC ▦ ᵛ ↑ 〒 ⅄ ⊙ ☺ ∅ ⌁ ⅃ R ☎ ⊞ lau ♦ ⅃
Prices: A5.20 pitch 11.60

HOFHEIM *Bayern*

Brugger am Riegsee ☎08847 728
A lakeside site in a rural setting with good, modern facilities.
20 Oct-14 Dec 6HEC ▦ ♨ ᵛ ↑ 〒 ⅄ ✕ ⊙ ☺ ∅ ⌁ ⅃ L ☎ ⊞ lau
Prices: A8 pitch 14

HOHENWARTH *Bayern*

Fritz-Berger-Comfort ☎09946 367
Meadowland in the valley of the Weissens Regens with views of the mountain range and town above.
Access from Cham on the B85 S to Miltach and continue via Kotzing to Hohenwarth.
All year 12HEC ▦ ᵛ ↑ 〒 ⅄ ✕ ⊙ ☺ ∅ ⌁ ⅃ LP ☎

HOPFEN AM SEE *Bayern*

Hopfensee ☎08362 917710
In quiet situation beside lake. Private beach. Ski-ing lessons.
4km N of Füssen.
Closed 3 Nov-18 Dec 7HEC ▦ ♨ ᵛ ↑ 〒 ⅄ ✕ ⊙ ☺ ⌁ ⅃ LP ☎ ⊞ lau
Prices: A13-14 pitch 19-20.50

ILLERTISSEN *Bayern*

Illertissen ☎07303 7888
Partially terraced site with plenty of trees.
Turn off towards Dietenheim at the ARAL filling station and continue along road for 1.5km. Site on left hand side of road.
Apr-15 Oct 3HEC ▦ ᵛ ↑ 〒 ⅄ ✕ ⊙ ☺ ∅ ⌁ ⅃ P ☎ ⊞ lau

IMMENSTADT *Bayern*

At **MISSEN**(9km NW)

Wiederhofen ☎08320 481
In lovely mountainous area.
Access from Immenstadt direction, Isny to Missen. Turn left along winding road to Wiederhofen, left again and continue 1.5km downhill.
Mar-Sep 1.2HEC ▦ ᵛ ↑ ✕ ⊙ ☺ ∅ ⌁ ⊞ ⊞ lau ♦ ⅃ ⅃P

INGOLSTADT *Bayern*

AZUR Camping Ingolstadt ☎0841 9611616
Near to Auwaldsee, this site lies in a beautiful setting beside the München-Ingolstadt motorway.
Access via the Ingolstadt-Süd exit off the A9/E6 (Müchen-Nürnberg motorway).
All year 10HEC ▦ ᵛ ↑ 〒 ⅄ ✕ ⊙ ☺ ∅ ⌁ ⅃ L ☎ ⊞ lau ♦ ⅃P Prices: A7-9 pitch 10-12

ISSIGAU *Bayern*

Schloss Issigau Altes Schloss 3 ☎09293 7173
About 5km W off A9/E6 (München-Berlin) road via the Berg/Bad Steben exit.
15 Mar-Oct 2HEC ▦ ᵛ ↑ 〒 ⅄ ✕ ⊙ ☺ ⌁ ⚑ ☎ ⊞ lau ♦ ⅃ ⅃R Prices: A6.50 pitch 7-8

JODITZ *Bayern*

Auensee ☎09295 381
Municipal site on partly terraced meadowland above lake.
Leave München-Berlin motorway at Berg-Bad Steben exit and drive E for 4km.
All year 2.5HEC ▦ ᵛ ↑ ↑ ✕ ⊙ ☺ ∅ ⌁ ⅃ L ☎ ⊞ lau ♦ ⅃ 〒 ✕

KIPFENBERG *Bayern*

AZUR-Camping Altmühltal Am Festpl 3 ☎08465 905167
All year 5.5HEC ▦ ♦ ↑ ⊙ ☺ ⅃ R ☎ ⊞ lau ♦ ⅃ ✕ ⌁ ⅃P Prices: A8-10 V3-4 ⚑11-13 ▲3-4

KIRCHZELL *Bayern*

AZUR-Camping Odenwald ☎09373 566
In natural terraced meadowland in wooded hilly country. No admission after 21.30 hrs. Lunchtime siesta 13.00-15.00 hrs.
From Amorbach follow the Eberbach road for 5km. Site 1km from town.
All year 7HEC ▦ ᵛ ↑ 〒 ⅄ ✕ ⊙ ☺ ∅ ⌁ ⚑ ⅃ P ☎ ⊞ lau ♦ ⊞ Prices: A8-10 pitch 11-13

KISSINGEN, BAD *Bayern*

Bad Kissingen Euerdorfer Str 1 ☎0971 5211
In park beside River Saale. Lunchtime siesta 13.00-15.00 hrs.
Access near the southern bridge over the Saale.
Apr-15 Oct 1.8HEC ▦ ᵛ ↑ ⅄ ✕ ⊙ ☺ ∅ ⌁ ☎ ⊞ lau ♦ ⅃P Prices: A10.50 pitch 11

KLINGENBRUNN *Bayern*

NationalPark ☎08553 727
For access, leave the B85, which turns from Cham to Passau, approx. 12km SE of Regen near Kirchdorf turn off E and drive about 6km towards Klingenbrunn.
All year 5HEC ▦ ♦ ↑ 〒 ⅄ ✕ ⊙ ☺ ⌁ ⚑ ☎ ⊞ lau ♦ ∅ Prices: A7.50 V1.50 ⚑6 ▲6

KÖNIGSDORF *Bayern*

Königsdorf ☎08171 81580
Unspoilt site in natural setting in meadowland. A number of individual pitches for tourers. Lunchtime siesta 12.30-14.30 hrs.
Off B11, 2km N of town just beyond the edge of the forest.
All year 8.6HEC ▦ ᵛ ↑ 〒 ⅄ ✕ ⊙ ☺ ∅ ⌁ ⅃ L ☎ ⊞ Prices: A7-8 V3-4 ⚑4-5 ▲3-4

KÖNIGSSEE *Bayern*

Mühlleiten ☎08652 4584
All year 1.5HEC ▦ ᵛ ↑ 〒 ⅄ ✕ ⊙ ☺ ⌁ ☎ ⊞ lau ♦ ✕ ⅃LPR Prices: A8 pitch 10

KRUN *Bayern*

Tennsee ☎08825 170
Closed 17 Nov-13 Dec 5.2HEC ▦ ▒▒▒ ᵛ ↑ 〒 ⅄ ✕ ⊙ ☺ ∅ ⌁ ☎ ⊞ lau ♦ ⅃L Prices: A12-13 pitch 14.50-24

KÜHNHAUSEN *Bayern*

Stadler Strandbadstr 10 ☎08686 8037
Level meadow on lake with private beach.
2m E shore of Lake Waginger.
Apr-Sep 1HEC ▦ ᵛ ↑ ⊙ ☺ ⅃ L ☎ ⊞ lau ♦ ⅃ ✕ ∅ Prices: A8 V3 ⚑8-10 ▲5-8

LACKENHÄUSER *Bayern*

AZUR-Knaus-Camping-Park ☎08583 311
Extensive site with woodland parks, waterfalls. Siesta 13.00-15.00 hrs. Many health resort facilities. Garden chess. Curling.
All year 19HEC ▦ ᵛ ↑ 〒 ⅄ ✕ ⊙ ☺ ∅ ⌁ ⚑ ⅃ LP ☎ ⊞ lau

LANDSBERG *Bayern*

Romantik am Lech ☎08191 47505
Level site with some terraces on right bank of the Lech. Lunchtime siesta 13.00-15.00 hrs.
Camping Card Compulsory.
S towards Gut Pössing.
All year 6.5HEC ▦ ▒▒▒ ♨ ᵛ ↑ 〒 ⅄ ✕ ⊙ ☺ ∅ ⌁ ☎ ⊞ lau ♦ 〒 ✕ ⅃R Prices: A8 pitch 17

LANGLAU *Bayern*

Langlau Seestr 30, Kleiner Brombachsee ☎09834 96969
On the shores of the Kleiner Brombachsee.
From Gunzevhausen 10km in the direction of Pleinfield.
Mar-15 Nov 12.4HEC ▦ ᵛ ↑ 〒 ⅄ ✕ ⊙ ☺ ∅ ⌁ ☎ ⊞ lau ♦ ⅃L ⊞ Prices: A9 pitch 11.50

LECHBRUCK *Bayern*

DCC Stadt Essen Oberer Lechsee ☎08862 8426
Terraced site, very tidy and well maintained on Oberen Lech lake.

Separate section for dog owners. Closed 13.00-15.00 hrs and
22.00-07.00 hrs.
Signposted from town centre.
All year 16HEC ▦ ⌖ ⋒ ⛾ ✕ ⊙ ☒ ⌀ ⋜ L ☎ ⊞ lau ➡ ⋜P Prices: A8
pitch 20

LINDAU IM BODENSEE *Bayern*

At OBERREITNAU(5km N)

Gitzenweiler Hof ☎08382 5475
A large site, partly divided into pitches and lying on rather hilly
ground. Small lake and facilities for boating.
For access, turn off the B12 which runs from Lindau to Munich,
approx 5km N of Lindau and drive W through Rehlings, and a further
1.5km to the site.
All year 13.5HEC ▦ ⌖ ⋒ ⛾ ✕ ⊙ ☒ ⌀ ⚐ ⋜ P ☎ ⊞ lau

At ZECH(4km SE)

Lindau-Zech Fraunhoferstr 20 ☎08382 72236
Site lies on meadowland with trees, reaching down to the lake. Very
large sanitary blocks. Common room, reading room, field for ball
games and a separate common room for young people.
From Lindau, take the B31 towards Bregenz and turn right
(signposted) just before the level crossing. The site is 500m further
down the road.
Apr-15 Oct 5HEC ▦ ∷⋰ ➡ ⋒ ⛾ ⛾ ✕ ⊙ ☒ ⋜ L ☎ ⊞ ⚿ lau ➡ ⋜P

MEMMINGEN *Bayern*

At BUXHEIM(5km NW)

See International Am Weiherhaus 7 ☎08331 71800
Terraced site beyond public bathing area.
Leave Um-Kempten motorway at Memminger Kreuz then right to
Buxheim.
May-Sep 4.2HEC ▦ ⌀ ➡ ⋒ ⛾ ⛾ ✕ ⊙ ☒ ⌀ ⚐ ⋜ L ☎ ⊞ lau ➡ ⌀
Prices: A7 pitch 13

MITTENWALD *Bayern*

Isarhorn ☎08823 5216
In a loop of the River Isar with many pines. Lunchtime siesta 13.00-
15.00 hrs.
3km N to the W of B2 (Garmisch-Partenkirchen-Mittenwald road).
All year 7.5HEC ▦ ⌀ ➡ ⋒ ⛾ ⊙ ☒ ⌀ ⋜ R ☎ ➡ ⛾ ✕ ⊞ Prices: A8
pitch 12

MÖRSLINGEN *Bayern*

Mörslingen ☎09074 4024
Camping Card Compulsory.
6km N of Dillengen.
All year 1HEC ▦ ➡ ⋒ ⊙ ☒ ⚐ ⚐ ⋜ L ☎ ⊞ lau Prices: A8 pitch
15

MÜHLHAUSEN BEI AUGSBURG *Bayern*

Lech Seeweg 6 ☎08207 2200
On level grassland with own swimming facilities on lakeside.
4km N in direction of Neuburg.
Mar-25 Oct 5HEC ▦ ⌖ ⋒ ⛾ ✕ ⊙ ☒ ⌀ ⚐ ⚐ ⋜ L ☎ ⊞ lau ➡ ⛾
Prices: A6.50 V2 ⚐12 ▲5

Ludwigshof am See Augsburger Str 36 ☎08027 1077
Clean site with small lake away from motorway, near restaurant of
the same name. Separate section for residential pitches.
1.5km from Augsburg Ost exit towards Neuberg.
Apr-Oct 14HEC ▦ ➡ ⋒ ⛾ ✕ ⊙ ☒ ⌀ ⚐ ⋜ L ☎ ⊞ ⚿ lau ➡ ⋜P

MÜNCHEN (MUNICH) *Bayern*

Langwieder See Eschenriederstr 119 ☎089 8641566
Site in well-tended grassland totally enclosed by a very high hedge
about 50m from lakeshore.
Follow München-Augsburg motorway for 5km then leave at exit for
Rasthaus Langwiedersee.
Apr-15 Oct 0.8HEC ▦ ⌖ ⋒ ⛾ ✕ ⊙ ☒ ⌀ ⚐ ⋜ L ☎ ⊞ ⚿ lau

At OBERMENZING

München-Obermenzing Lochhausener Str 59 ☎089 8112235
Park-like site near motorway. Shop closed in winter and no campers
accepted after 31 Oct.

Waldcamping München-Obermenzing

To reach the site follow motorway signs for Stuttgart – coming
from Salzburg direction follow Lindau signs and leave
motorway at Pasing exit.
Set in a large park of 50,000 sq.m 900m from the end of the
motorway Stuttgart-München.
130 spaces for caravans each with own electricity supply and
separated by hedges. Individual washing cubicles, free hot
water for washing, hot showers, washing machine, dryer.
heated washrooms, self-service shop.
Opportunities for swimming 2.5km from site.
Locked from 22.00 hrs. Good connections to city centre by bus,
tram or urban railway.
Open from 15.3-31.10.
Farmer: A. Blenck Telephone 089/8 11 22 35 Fax 089/8 14 48 07

Camping Card or Identification papers Compulsory.
Approx 1km from the end of Stuttgart-München motorway.
15 Mar-Oct 5.5HEC ▦ ⌖ ⋒ ⛾ ✕ ⊙ ☒ ⌀ ⚐ ⚐ ☎ ⊞ lau ➡ ✕ ⚐
⋜L Prices: A7 V5 ⚐8 ▲7.50

At THALKIRCHEN

SC München-Thalkirchen Zentrallandstr 49 ☎089 7231707
15 Mar-Oct 4.5HEC ⌀ ⌖ ⋒ ⛾ ✕ ⊙ ☒ ⌀ ▲ ☎ ⊞ lau ➡ ⋜P

MÜNCHSTEINACH *Bayern*
Münchsteinach ☎09166 750
Level, long stretch of grassland with isolated bushes and trees.
Lunchtime siesta 13.00-15.00 hrs. Pool also open to public.
All year 4HEC ▦ ⌖ ⋒ ⊙ ☒ ⌀ ⌀ ⋜ P ☎ ⊞ lau ➡ ⛾ ⛾

MURNAU *Bayern*

Halbinsel Burg ☎08841 9870
In pleasant situation beside Lake Staffel.
1.5km SW of Seehausen.
May-15 Oct 2HEC ▦ ➡ ⋒ ⛾ ⛾ ✕ ⊙ ☒ ⌀ ⋜ L ☎ ⚿ lau

NEBELBERG *Bayern*

Waldhof ☎09922 1024
Partially terraced site on the Schwarzachbach.
Turn off the B85 to Regen then N to Langdorf and continue NE.
All year 1HEC ▦ ⌖ ⋒ ⛾ ✕ ⊙ ☒ ⚐ ⚐ ▲ ⋜ L ☎ ⊞ ➡ ⋜R

NEUBÄU *Bayern*

Seecamping Seestr 4 ☎09469 331
Meadowland site along lakeshore.
Access from Schwandorf on the B85 in direction of Cham.
Closed Nov 5HEC ▦ ⌖ ⋒ ⛾ ⛾ ✕ ⊙ ☒ ⌀ ⋜ L ☎ ⊞ lau

NEUSTADT *Bayern*

Main-Spessart-Camping-International ☎09393 639
Beautifully situated site along the River Main. Watersports, including
water skiing. Lunchtime siesta 12.00-14.00 hrs.

Access from Frankfurt-Würzburg motorway A3/E5, leave at Marktheidenfeld exit, and follow road towards Lohr.
Apr-Sep 5.6HEC ▥ ⬢ ♠ ↖ ➋ ✕ ☉ ◘ ⌀ ⌀ ↝ PR ☎ ➡ ✕ Prices: A7.50 pitch 9.50

NÜRNBERG (NUREMBERG) *Bayern*
SC Volkspark Dutzendteich Hans-Kalb-Str 56 ☎0911 811122
Well-kept municipal site in beautiful situation in a forest between a stadium with a swimming pool and the Trade Fair Centre.
Leave A9 München motorway at Nürnberg-Fischbach exit, and continue towards the stadium.
May-Sep 2.7HEC ▥ ⬢ ♠ ↖ ✕ ☉ ◘ ⌀ ⊞ lau ↝ ↝P Prices: A8 V5 ⊞10 ▲5

OBERAMMERGAU *Bayern*
Oberammergau Ettaler Str 56b ☎08822 94105
All year 2HEC ▥ ♦ ⬢↙ ♠ ↖ ▾ ✕ ☉ ◘ ⌀ ➈ ▲ ☎ ⊞ lau ➡ ↝PR Prices: A6-9 pitch 7-10

OBERNDORF *Bayern*
Donau-Lech ☎09002 4044
Apr-Oct 5HEC ▥ ♠ ↖ ▾ ✕ ☉ ◘ ⌀ ⌀ ☎ ↝ L ☎ ⊞ lau

OBERSTDORF *Bayern*
Oberstdorf ☎08322 4022 & 6525
Level grassland site with fine mountain views.
800m N of town centre near railway line.
All year 16HEC ▥ ♦ ⬢ ♠ ↖ ✕ ☉ ◘ ⌀ ➈ ☎ ⊞ lau ➡ ↖ ↝P Prices: A11.10-12.10 V4 ⊞8-10 ▲4-9

OBERWÖSSEN *Bayern*
Litzelau ☎08640 8704
Almost level meadowland surrounded by forested slopes.
Take B305 from Bernau exit on München-Salzburg motorway and continue through Marquartstein and Unterwössen.
All year 4HEC ▥ ⬢ ♠ ↖ ↖ ✕ ☉ ◘ ⌀ ☎ ↝ R ☎ ⊞ lau ➡ ↝LP Prices: A7 ⊞12 ▲6.50

OCHSENFURT *Bayern*
Polisina Marktbreiter Str 265 ☎09331 8440
Terraced site at edge of wood.
From town centre follow road towards Markbreit and in 2km turn off under railway and continue uphill.
All year 2.5HEC ▥ ⬢ ♠ ☉ ◘ ➡ ↖ ✕ ➋ ↝P Prices: A6 pitch 8-10

PASSAU *Bayern*
Dreiflüsse ☎08546 633
A well equipped site in pleasant wooded surroundings.
From A3 exit 'Passau-Nord' follow signposts.
Apr-Oct 5HEC ▥ ⠿ ➡ ♠ ↖ ✕ ☉ ◘ ⌀ ☎ ☎ ➈ ↝ P ☎ ⊞ lau Prices: A6-7 V5-9 ⊞9-11 ▲9-11

PFAFFENHOFEN *Bayern*
SC Warmbad Hauptpl 1 ☎08441 83543
The municipal site lies on the northern outskirts of the town beside the River Lim.
Take the München-Nürnberg motorway, and leave at Pfaffenhofen exit, or take the B13 which runs from München to Ingolstadt.
May-Sep 0.9HEC ▥ ⬢ ♠ ↖ ☉ ◘ ↝ P ☎ ⊞ lau ➡ ↖ ✕ Prices: A11 pitch 12

PFRAUNDORF *Bayern*
Kratzmühle ☎08461 525
Terraced site, divided into pitches, on a wooded hillside overlooking the River Altmühl.
In village turn off to Kratzmühle.
All year 9.6HEC ▥ ⬢ ♠ ↖ ✕ ☉ ◘ ⌀ ➈ ☎ ↝ R ☎ ⊞ lau ➡ ↝L Prices: A9 pitch 8-14

PIDING *Bayern*
Staufeneck ☎08651 2134
In beautiful and quiet situation beside River Saalach.
Leave motorway A8/E11 (München-Salzburg) via exit Bad Reichenall road for 2.5km and then turn right.
Apr-Oct 2.7HEC ▥ ⬢ ♠ ↖ ☉ ◘ ☎ ⊞ lau ➡ ✕ ✕ ⌀ ➈ ↝R Prices: A8 pitch 8

PIELENHOFEN *Bayern*
Naabtal ☎09409 373
The site is well-situated beside the River Nab, and has a special section for overnight visitors.
Access from the Nittendorf turn off from A3/E5 Nürnberg-Regensburg N via Etterzhausen.
All year 6HEC ▥ ⬢ ♠ ↖ ▾ ✕ ☉ ◘ ⌀ ➈ ☎ ↝ R ☎ ⊞ lau Prices: A8 pitch 9

POTTENSTEIN *Bayern*
Bärenschlucht ☎09243 206
The site lies on unspoilt meadowland in the narrow Püttlach valley and is surrounded by the rocky hills of the Fränkische Schweiz range.
From the München-Berlin motorway leave at the Pegnitz exit and drive W for 10km on the B470 towards Forchheim.
All year 5HEC ▥ ⬢ ♠ ↖ ✕ ☉ ◘ ⌀ ➈ ➡ ↝ R ☎ ⊞ lau ➡ ↝LP

REGENSBURG *Bayern*
AZUR-Regensburg Weinweg 40 ☎0941 270025
The municipal site lies on the western outskirts of the town, and the right bank of the Danube. Has a special section reserved for caravans.
Access via the western by-pass, and over the Pfaffenstein Bridge.
All year 2.6HEC ▥ ⬢ ♠ ↖ ✕ ☉ ◘ ⌀ ☎ lau ➡ ↝LPR Prices: A8-10 V3-4 ⊞11-13 ▲3-4

ROSSHAUPTEN *Bayern*
Warsitzka ☎08367 406
A well-kept site with good installations.
Fron Füssen follow road B16 for 10km towards Rosshaupten. About 2km before the village and before the bridge turn right.
All year 2.5HEC ▥ ⬢ ♠ ↖ ▾ ✕ ☉ ◘ ⌀ ↝ LR ☎ ⊞ lau Prices: A8.50-9 pitch 10-13.50

ROTHENBURG OB DER TAUBER *Bayern*
Tauber-Idyll Detwang 28A ☎09861 3177
The well-kept site lies on a meadow scattered with trees and bushes, on the outskirts of the N suburb of Detwang and next to the River Tauber.
Access from all main roads is well signposted. The best route is from Nordinger Str (B25) heading W along the River Tauber in the direction of Bad Mergentheim.
22 Mar-Oct 0.5HEC ▥ ⬢ ♠ ☉ ◘ ⌀ ☎ ⊞ lau ➡ ✕ ↝R Prices: A6.50 V3 ⊞5 ▲5

Tauber-Romantik Detwang 39 ☎09861 6191
Apr-Oct 1.2HEC ▥ ➡ ♠ ↖ ▾ ✕ ☉ ◘ ⌀ ☎ lau ➡ ↝R ⊞ Prices: A7.50 pitch 5.50

ROTTENBUCH *Bayern*
Terrassencamping am Richterbichl ☎08867 1500
Several pleasant terraces with good views.
On S outskirts on B23.
All year 1.2HEC ▥ ⬢ ♠ ☉ ◘ ⌀ ➈ ↝ L ☎ lau ➡ ✕ ↝R ⊞ Prices: A8.50 pitch 8

RUHPOLDING *Bayern*
Ortnerhof Ort 5 ☎08663 1764
Well-kept site at the foot of the Rauschberg Mountain, opposite the cable-car station.
Off Deutsche Alpenstr.
All year 2.4HEC ▦ ⌗ ⌂ ⛄ ✕ ⊙ ⌀ ⌀ ☎ ⊞ ⌁ lau ➡ ♨ Prices: A8-8.50 V2-2.50 ♣3.50-4 ▲4-3.50

SCHECHEN *Bayern*
Erlensee ☎08039 1695
The site lies on the shores of an artificial lake.
If approaching from Rosenheim, take the B15 approx 10km N of Rosenheim towards Wasserburg and turn right upon entering Schechen.
All year 6HEC ▦ ⌗ ⌂ ⛄ ♨ ✕ ⊙ ⌀ ⌀ ⛵ ⌁ ⌁ L ☎ ⊞ lau ➡ ♨ Prices: A7 V3.50 ♣8.50 ▲5-8.50

SCHWANGAU *Bayern*
At **BANNWALDSEE**(4km N)
Bannwaldsee ☎08362 81001
Meadow gently sloping towards lake.
Turn off the B17 about 4km NE of Schwangau, in westerly direction towards lake.
All year 12HEC ▦ ⌗ ⦂⦂⦂ ⌂ ♦ ⌂ ⛄ ♨ ✕ ⊙ ⌀ ⌀ ⛵ ⌁ L ☎ ⊞

SEEFELD *Bayern*
Strandbad Pilsensee Graf Toerringstr 11 ☎08152 7232 or 7233
S towards Pilsensee.
All year 10HEC ▦ ⌗ ⌂ ⛄ ♨ ✕ ⊙ ⌀ ⌀ ⛵ ⌁ L ☎ ⊞ lau ➡ ✕
Prices: A7-8 pitch 11-12

SOMMERACH AM MAIN *Bayern*
Katzenkopf am See ☎09381 9215
Apr-20 Oct 4HEC ▦ ⌗ ⌂ ⛄ ♨ ✕ ⊙ ⌀ ⌀ ⛵ ⌁ LR ☎ ⊞ lau Prices: A7.50-8 pitch 9-11

SONTHOFEN *Bayern*
Iller Sinwagstr 2 ☎08321 2350
Site lies on the shore of the River Iller (too dangerous for swimming) near a swimming pool.
1km on the B19 towards Oberstdorf, before the bridge over the River Iller.
Closed Nov-20 Dec 1.6HEC ▦ ⌗ ⌂ ✕ ⊙ ⌀ ⌀ ⛵ ⌁ R ☎ ⊞ lau ➡ ♨ ✕ ⌁LP Prices: pitch 30-35

SOYEN *Bayern*
Soyen-See Seestr 28 ☎08071 3860
Partly terraced site on eastern shore of Lake Soyen. Several pitches for tourers near entrance.
From B15 between Wasserburg and Haag.
Apr-Oct 10HEC ▦ ⌗ ⌂ ⛄ ♨ ⌀ ⌁ L ☎

STADTSTEINACH *Bayern*
AZUR-Stadtsteinach Badstr 5 ☎09225 95401
Terraced site on SE facing slope with a view over the town and surrounding hills. Lunchtime siesta 13.00-15.00 hrs.
Access via Badstr.
All year 5HEC ▦ ⌀ ⌗ ⌂ ♦ ⌂ ⛄ ✕ ⊙ ⌀ ⌀ ⛵ ⌁ P ☎ ⊞ lau Prices: A7-9 V3-4 ♣10-12 ▲3-4

TETTENHAUSEN *Bayern*
Gut Horn ☎08681 227
Quiet site, divided into pitches on lake shore, sheltered by forest. Lunchtime siesta 13.00-14.00 hrs.
SE on Waginsersee.
All year 5HEC ▦ ⌗ ⌂ ⛄ ✕ ⊙ ⌀ ⌀ ⛵ ⌁ ⛵ L ☎ ⊞ lau Prices: A8.50 pitch 9

TITTMONING *Bayern*
Seebauer ☎08683 541
On meadow with a few terraces. Near a farm, beside a lake.
3km NW towards Burghausen.
All year 2.3HEC ▦ ♦ ⌂ ⛄ ✕ ⊙ ⌀ ⌀ ⌁ LP ☎ ⊞ lau ➡ ⌁R Prices: A7-9 pitch 8-10

TRAUSNITZ *Bayern*
Trausnitz ☎09655 1304
All year 3.5HEC ▦ ⌗ ⌂ ⛄ ♨ ✕ ⊙ ⌀ ⌀ ⛵ ⌁ LR ☎ ⊞ lau ➡ ⌁P

TÜCHERSFELD *Bayern*
Fränkische Schweiz Tüchersfeld 57 ☎09242 1788
Access from motorway A9/E6, leave at exit 'Pegnitz' then 12km W on B470 towards Forchheim.
Apr-15 Oct 2HEC ▦ ⌗ ⌂ ⛄ ♨ ✕ ⊙ ⌀ ⌀ ⛵ ☎ ⊞ lau ➡ ✕ Prices: A7.10-7.60 V4.25-4.85 ♣7.25-9.95 ▲6.45-8.45

UFFENHEIM *Bayern*
Uffenheim ☎09842 1568
Access from Würzburg, follow B13 SE. On entering Uffenheim turn right, then 500m to site.
May-15 Sep 0.5HEC ▦ ⌗ ⌂ ⛄ ✕ ⊙ ⌀ ⛵ P ☎ ⊞ lau ➡ ♨ ♨ ✕

VELBURG *Bayern*
Hauenstein ☎09182 454
A well-appointed site, lies on several terraces and is completely divided into individual pitches. All with electric points.
From motorway A3 Nürnberg-Regensburg leave at exit Velberg, then continue through village towards the S following signs Naturbad.
All year 5HEC ▦ ⌗ ⌂ ⛄ ✕ ⊙ ⌀ ⌀ ☎ ⊞ lau ➡ ⌁P Prices: A8.50 V4 ♣7 ▲6

VIECHTACH *Bayern*
AZUR-Knaus-Camping-Park ☎09942 1095
Site on slightly undulating meadow, divided by rows of trees. The site has modern installations.
For access, take the B85 which runs from the junction with the road towards Freibad Viechtach, and follow the signposts.
Closed 6 Nov-14 Dec 9HEC ▦ ⌗ ⌂ ⛄ ✕ ⊙ ⌀ ⌀ ♣ ☎ ⊞ lau

WAGING *Bayern*
Strandcamping Am See 1 ☎08681 552
Extensive, level grassland site divided in two by access road to neighbouring sailing club. The site lies near the Strandbad and Kurhaus bathing area and spa, and the Casino. There is a Kneipp (hydrotherapeutic) pool in the camp.
Follow the signposts leading to the Strandbad bathing area.
Apr-Sep 15HEC ▦ ♦ ⌂ ⛄ ♨ ✕ ⊙ ⌀ ⌀ ⛵ ♣ L ☎ ⊞ lau ➡ ⊞ Prices: A8.80-10.30 pitch 10-19

WAISCHENFELD *Bayern*
Steinerner Beutel ☎09202 359
The site lies on a meadow beside the River Wiesent. The camp has a footbridge leading to the heated swimming pool across the river.
Camping Card Compulsory.
Leave the motorway A9/E6 (Munich/Berlin) at either Bayreuth-Nord or Sud exit and follow B22 westwards to Donndorf-Eckersdorf. The turn off to Obernsees and via Truppach and Munkenfels to site.
All year 2.2HEC ▦ ⌗ ⌂ ⛄ ⊙ ⌀ ☎ ⊞ lau ➡ ⌁PR

WALTENHOFEN *Bayern*
Insel-Camping am See ☎08379 881
All year 1.5HEC ▦ ⌗ ⌂ ⛄ ✕ ⊙ ⌀ ⌀ ⛵ L ☎ ⊞ lau Prices: A7 pitch 8-10

WEILER-SIMMERBERG *Bayern*
Alpenblick Schreckenmanklitz 18 ☎08381 3447
Clean facilities on this site belonging to the Deutsche Alpenstrasse.
Access from the B308 in Weiler. Signposted.
Etr-4 Nov 2.2HEC ▦ ⌗ ⌂ ♨ ✕ ⊙ ⌀ ⌀ ⛵ ☎ ⊞ ⌁ lau ➡ ♨ ✕ Prices: A8 pitch 11

WEISSACH *Bayern*
Wallberg Rainerweg 10 ☎08022 5371
The well-kept site lies on a level meadow with a few trees beside a stream.
For access take the B318 from Gmund to Tegernsee, drive through Bad Wiessee, and on to Wiessach, approx 9km further on.
All year 3HEC ▦ ⌗ ⌂ ⛄ ✕ ⊙ ⌀ ⌀ ♣ ⛵ L ☎ ⊞ lau ➡ ♨ ⌁P Prices: A8-8.80 V4 ♣10-12 ▲8

WEISSENSTADT Bayern
Weissenstädter See Badestr 91 ☎09253 288
This municipal site is in close proximity to a swimming pool and a
lake, so offering numerous sports facilities.
1km NW of the town.
All year 1.7HEC ▦ ⚶♪♥✗⊙☻∅ ⱦ LP 초 lau ♦ ⚘

WEMDING Bayern
AZUR Waldsee Wemding ☎09092 90101
All year 9HEC ▦ ♨⚶♪⚘✗⊙☻∅☻ ⱦ L ▣ ⊞ lau ♦ ⚘ ♨P
Prices: A8-10 V3-4 ☷11-13 ▲3-4

WERTACH Bayern
Grüntensee Grüntenseestr 41 ☎08365 375
A modern site beside Lake Grünten.
If approaching from Kempten, turn right entering Nesselwerg, and
follow the signposts.
All year 5HEC ▦ ♨⚶♪♥✗⊙☻∅⚘ⱦ L 초 ⊞ lau

WINKL BEI BISCHOFSWIESEN Bayern
Winkllandthal ☎08652 8164
In meadow between the B20 and edge of woodland.
From Bad Reichenhall to Berchtesgaden about 8km.
All year 2.5HEC ▦ ∷ ♨⚶♪⚘♥✗⊙☻∅⚘▲ⱦ R 초 ⊞ lau
♦ ✗ Prices: A7 V3 ☷7 ▲7

WÖRISHOFEN, BAD Bayern
Kur Gottlieb-Daimler-Str 5 ☎08247 5446
Level grassy site.
Site lies at the N end of Kniepp-Spa Wörishofen.
15 Apr-15 Oct 10HEC ▦ ♦♪♥✗⊙☻∅☷ 초 ⊞ lau ♦ ⚘♨P

ZWIESEL Bayern
AZUR-Ferienzentrum Bayerischer Wald Waldesruhweg 34
☎09922 802595
A modern site. Clean sanitary installations.
All year 16HEC ▦ ⚶♪♥✗⊙☻∅⚘ 초 ⊞ lau ♦ ♨P Prices: A8-
10 V3-4 ☷11-13 ▲3-4

South West

A rich variety of scenery both charming and grandiose, has led
this magnificent area of Germany to become one of the most
popular holiday regions.
In the far south, Lake Constance is a majestic expanse of water,
ideal for watersports, fringed with historic towns and attractive
villages.
The Black Forest is a perennial delight with its vast coniferous
woodlands, rushing mountain streams, and glacier-cut valleys.
Spectacular views are to be had from the popular Black Forest
Ridgeway.
The Neckarland-Schwaben covers the rest of the region and is
an exciting area to explore. There are castles and palaces,
bustling towns and fascinating museums. At its core is Stuttgart,
beautifully situated in a basin enclosed by forest-covered hills,
orchards and vineyards that extend widely into the city.
This undisputed cultural and commercial centre of the state, is a
city of technical progress, while five castles remind us of its
princely past.

ABTSGMÜND Baden-Württemberg
At **POMMERTSWEILER**(6km N)
Hammerschmiede-See Hammerschmiede 6 ☎07963 1205 &
415
A terraced site in a wooded setting beside the lake. Partly divided
into pitches with concrete paths.
From Abtsgmünd travel for 3km then turn N to Pommertsweiler, site
signposted.
All year 4HEC ▦ ⚶♪⚘✗⊙☻∅☷ⱦ L 초 ⊞ lau

ACHERN Baden-Württemberg
SC am Achernsee ☎07841 25253
All year 6.5HEC ▦ ⚶♪⚘✗⊙☻∅⚘ⱦ L 초 ⊞ lau

ALPIRSBACH Baden-Württemberg
Wolpert ☎07444 6313
On level land beside the River Kinzig.
1km N of town below B294.
20 May-20 Sep 1HEC ▦ ⚶♪♥⊙☻∅☷⊞ lau ♦ ♥✗☷

ALTENSTEIG Baden-Württemberg
Schwarzwald ☎07453 8415
Parkland site of motor sport club Altensteig beside the River Nagold.
Separate section for dog owners.
On road to Garrweiler 1km from Altensteig.
All year 3.3HEC ▦ ⚶♪♥✗⊙☻∅☷ⱦ R 초 ⊞ lau ♦ ♨P
Prices: A7 pitch 8.50

ALTNEUDORF Baden-Württemberg
Steinachperle ☎06228 467
The site lies in the narrow shady valley of the River Steinach.
Lunchtime siesta 13.00-15.00 hrs.
The entrance to the camp lies next to the Gasthaus zum Pflug, on
the outskirts of Altneudorf.
Apr-Sep 3.5HEC ▦ ⚶♪♥✗⊙☻∅☷ 초 ⊞ lau Prices: A6-7 pitch
7-8

BADENWEILER Baden-Württemberg
Badenweiler Weilertalstr 73 ☎07632 1550
All year 1.6HEC ▦ ⚶♪⚘♥⊙☻∅☷ 초 ⊞ lau ♦ ✗ ♨P Prices:
A9.90 pitch 12.90

BUCHHORN BEI ÖHRINGEN Baden-Württemberg
Seewiese Seestr 11 ☎07941 61568
7km S of Öhringen via Pfedelbach.
All year 5.1HEC ▦ ⚶♪♥⚘♥✗⊙☻∅☷☻ⱦ L 초 ⊞ lau Prices:
A8 V5 ☷5-7 ▲3-5

BÜHL Baden-Württemberg
Adam Campingstr 1 ☎07223 23194
On level grassland, by lake.
1km from the Bühl exit of the A5/E4-E11 (Karlsruhe-Basel) in
direction of Lichtenau.
All year 15HEC ▦ ⚶♪⚘✗⊙☻∅☷⚘ⱦ L ▣ ⊞ lau Prices:
A7.50-11 ☷8-11 ▲6.50-11

CREGLINGEN Baden-Württemberg
AZUR Camping Romantische Strasse ☎07933 20289
A site completely divided into pitches, lying on the S outskirts of
Münster. Children's playground. Individual washing cubicles.
If approaching from Bad Mergentheim or from Rothenburg/Tauber,
take the ' Romantic road' up to Creglingen. Then turn S and drive
3km up to Münster.
All year 6HEC ▦ ⚶♪♥✗⊙☻∅ ⱦ P 초 ⊞ lau ♦ ♨L Prices: A7-9
V3-4 ☷10-12 ▲3-4

DINGELSDORF Baden-Württemberg
Fliesshorn ☎07533 5262
At a farm, on meadowland with fine trees.
In town turn off Stadd-Dettingen road and follow signs to NW for
1.3km.
Apr-Sep 5HEC ▦ ⚶♪♥✗⊙☻∅⚘⊞ lau ♦ ♨LS

DONAUESCHINGEN Baden-Württemberg
Riedsee ☎0771 5511
Level meadow on lakeside.
Turn off A81 exit 'Geisingen' and continue 13km on B31 towards
Pfohren, then turn left and continue for 1km.
All year 8HEC ▦ ⚶♪♥✗⊙☻∅⚘ⱦ LS 초 ⊞ lau

DÜRRHEIM, BAD Baden-Württemberg
Sunthauersee ☎07706 712
Apr-Sep 9HEC ▦ ♦♪♥⊙☻∅⚘ⱦ 초 ⊞ lau ♦ ⚘♥✗⊞ Prices: A7
pitch 15

EBERBACH *Baden-Württemberg*
Eberbach ☎06271 1071
On slightly sloping meadow on left bank of the river. Separate field for young people. Some traffic noise and liable to flooding when river is high. Lunchtime siesta 13.00-15.00 hrs.
For access head for the sportsground after crossing bridge from town centre.
Apr-15 Oct ▦ ⌔⌂☂✕⊝◒☎⟀ lau ✦☂⌀⌘ ⋞P

ERPFINGEN *Baden-Württemberg*
AZUR Schwäbische Alb (Rosencamping) ☎07128 466
Extensive site on a hill.
Access from Reutlingen on B312 in south easterly direction to Grooengstingen, then S on Schwabische Albstr (B313) for 3.5km to Haid , then turn right to Erpfingen. Site on W outskirts.
All year 9HEC ▦ ⋎⌂⌔✕⊝◒⌀⌘ ⋞P ⟀⊞ lau Prices: A8-10 V3-4 ⊞11-13 ▲3-4

ETTENHEIM *Baden-Württemberg*
Oase ☎07822 9881
25 Mar-5 Oct 6HEC ▦ ◊⌔⌂⌔✕⊝◒⌀⌘⟀⊞ lau ✦ ⋞P Prices: A7-9 pitch 10

FREIBURG IM BREISGAU *Baden-Württemberg*
Breisgau Seestr 20 ☎07665 2346
Extensive level grassland site on outskirts of town. Section reserved for campers with dogs.
500m E of autobahn exit 'Freiburg Nord'.
All year 6.5HEC ▦ ⌔⌂⌔✕⊝◒⌀⌀⋞ L ⟀ lau Prices: A7.90 pitch 9

Ferien & Kurbad Mösle-Park Waldseestr 77 ☎0761 72938
On outskirts of town near 'Busse's Waldschänke' inn.
Turn right after town hall across railway and follow Waldseestr towards Littenweiler.
23 Mar-25 Oct 0.7HEC ▦ ✦⌂⌔☂✕⊝◒⌀⌘⟀⊞ lau Prices: A8 pitch 9

FREUDENSTADT *Baden-Württemberg*
Langenwald Strassburgerstr 167 ☎07441 2862
The site consists of several sections and lies next to a former mill beside the River Forbach.
4km W of Freudenstadt below the B28 (Freudenstadt-Strasbourg).
Apr-Oct 3HEC ▦ ⌔⌂⌔☂✕⊝◒⌀⌀⋞ R ⟀ lau ✦ ✕ Prices: A8 pitch 10

GAMMELSBACH *Baden-Württemberg*
Freienstein Neckartalstr 172 ☎06068 1306
The site lies just off the B45 in a landscaped preservation area. It is terraced and divided into pitches. Lunchtime siesta 13.00-15.00 hrs.
Apr-Sep 5HEC ▦ ⌔⌂⊝◒⌀⟀ lau ✦ ✕ Prices: A6.50 pitch 7.50

HALLWANGEN *Baden-Württemberg*
Königskanzel ☎07443 6730
In an elvated position in the centre of the Black Forest.
Via B28 from Freudenstadt.
Closed 11 Nov-19 Dec 4HEC ▦ ⌔⌂⌔☂✕⊝◒⌀⌀⋞P⟀⊞ lau ✦ ✕ Prices: A7.50-8.50 pitch 10

HAUSEN *Baden-Württemberg*
Wagenburg Kirchstr 24 ☎07579 559
On meadowland between the railway bank and the Danube. Entrance through subway.
4 Apr-4 Oct 1.2HEC ▦ ⌔⌂⊝◒⌀⋞ R lau ✦☂☂✕⌀⊞ Prices: A6.80 pitch 4.50-10.50

HERBOLZHEIM *Baden-Württemberg*
Herbolzheim Im Laue 1 ☎07643 1460
Etr-15 Oct 2HEC ▦ ⌔⌂☂✕⊝◒⌀⌀ lau ✦ ⋞P ⊞

HÖFEN AN DER ENZ *Baden-Württemberg*
Quellgrund ☎07081 6984
Well maintained municipal site on grassland between the B294 and the River Enz.

Access from Pforzheim on the B294 in SW direction to the 'Quelle' inn with entrance to ARAL petrol station at entrance to Höfen, then turn right.
All year 3.8HEC ▦ ⌔⌂☂⊝◒⌀⟀ lau ✦ ✕ ⌀ ⋞P ⊞ Prices: A6.50 ☎7.50 ▲7.50

HORB *Baden-Württemberg*
Schüttehof ☎07451 3951
Situated on flat mountain top.
Access from Horb in direction of Freudenstadt. 1.5km beyond the town boundary turn towards stables and site, and onward for 1km.
All year 6HEC ▦ ⋎⋎⌔⌂☂✕⊝◒⌀⌀⋞ P ⟀⊞ lau

HORN BODENSEE *Baden-Württemberg*
Horn ☎07735 685
A large and well-managed municipal site with a pleasant beach. In Horn turn off the Radolfszell-Stein am Rhein road and towards the lake.
Apr-10 Oct 10HEC ▦ ⌔⌂☂✕⊝◒⌀⌘⋞ LP ⊞⊞⌘ lau ✦ ⋞L

KARLSRUHE *Baden-Württemberg*
At **DURLACH**(8km SE)
AZUR Türmbergblick Tiegener Str 40 ☎0721 497236
On level ground amongst orchards. Lunchtime siesta 12.30-15.00 hrs.
Access via Karlsruhe-Dürlach exit on A5/E4. Signposted.
All year 3.5HEC ▦ ✦⌂☂✕⊝◒⌀⊞⊞ lau ✦ ⋞P Prices: A7.80-8.80 V3-3.50 ☎10.60-11.60 ▲5.80-6.80

KEHL *Baden-Württemberg*
Kehl-Strassburg ☎07851 2603
Park-like site divided into separate sections for young campers, transit and holiday campers. Lunchtime siesta 13.00-15.00 hrs. Turn left at the Rhine dam on the outskirts of the town.
15 Mar-Oct 2.3HEC ▦ ⌔⌂☂✕⊝◒⌀⌀⟀⊞✦ ⋞PR

KIRCHBERG *Baden-Württemberg*
Christophorus ☎07354 663
Completely enclosed, clean site.
Leave motorway A7 (Ulm-Memmingen) at exit Illereichen Allenstadt to town centre, then towards the railway station.
All year 9.2HEC ▦ ⌔⌂☂✕⊝◒⌀⌀⋞ LP ⟀⊞

KIRCHZARTEN *Baden-Württemberg*
Kirchzarten ☎07661 39375
Extensive site with trees providing shade.
About 8km E of Freiburg im Breisgau off the B31.
All year 5.6HEC ▦ ⌔⌂☂✕⊝◒⌀⌀⋞ P ⟀⊞⌘ lau Prices: A7.50-12 pitch 9-11
See advertisement on page 168.

KRESSBRONN *Baden-Württemberg*
Gohren am See ☎07543 8656
A large site beside the lake. It has an older section divided by many hedges reserved for residential campers, and a newer section with fewer bushes.
3km from Kressbronn. Well signposted from B31.
21 Mar-19 Oct 40HEC ▦ ⌔⌂☂☂✕⊝◒⌀⌀⋞ L ⟀⊞ lau Prices: A9 pitch 9

LAICHINGEN *Baden-Württemberg*
Heidehof Blaubeurer str 50 ☎07333 6408
Well-cared for site on hillside with some high firs. Asphalt roads. Separate section outside enclosure for overnight campers.
Leave Ulm-Stuttgart motorway at Merkingen exit, then continue S via Machtolsheim to camp 2km S.
All year 25HEC ▦ ⌔⌂☂✕⊝◒⌀⌀⋞ P ⟀⊞ lau Prices: A8 pitch 10

LAUTERBURG *Baden-Württemberg*
Hirtenteich ☎07365 296
This site lies on gently sloping terrain, near the Hirtenteich recreation area.

CAMP SITE

SOUTHERN BLACK FOREST

Comfortable holiday site in the southern Black Forest near Freiburg. New toilet facilities, 380 sites for visiting holiday-makers. Heated outdoor pool 23°C from 15.5-15.9 on the site itself. Wide range of facilities for sports and games. Walk in the magnificent countryside. Trips to the higher parts of the Black Forest, Switzerland and France.

**79199 Kirchzarten
Tel: 07661/39375
Fax 07661/61624**

Turn off the B29 (Aalen-Schwäbisch Gmünd) in Essingen and drive S for a pprox. 5km.
All year 2.5HEC ▦ ⊕ ⋔ ⅌ ✕ ⊙ ⊟ ⊘ ♨ ⇥ ⌇ P ⊛ ⊞ lau Prices: A6 pitch 8-9

At **BARTHOLOMÄ**(3km S)
Feriendorf Arnalienhof Haflinger Str 15 ☎07173 7542
Level site on high plateau of eastern Alps, partially surrounded by tall trees.
All year 4HEC ▦ ⊕ ⋔ ⊙ ⊟ ⊘ ♨ ⊛ ⊟ ⊞ lau ♦ ⅀ ✕ ⌇P

LENGFURT Baden-Württemberg
Main-Spessart-Park ☎09395 1079
Site lies partly on terraced meadowland and partly on the E slopes of the Main Valley. Lunchtime siesta 13.00-15.00 hrs, Possibilities for water sports, nearby private mooring on the River Main.
From Frankfurt-Würzburg motorway A3/E5 leave at exit Markheidenfeld. N to Altfeld then E for 6km to Lengfurt. Site lies at NW edge of village.
All year 10HEC ⊕ ⋔ ✕ ⊙ ⊟ ⊘ ⊛ ⊞ ⊞ lau ♦ ⌇PR Prices: A7 V3 ₪5.50 ▲5.50

LENZKIRCH Baden-Württemberg
Kreuzhof Bonndorfer Str 65 ☎07653 700
Grassland near former farm below the Rogg Brewery on the B315.
Access from Freiburg on the B31 to Titisee, continue on the B317 towards Schaffhausen junction then take the B315 via Lenzkirch, site is some 2km from centre.
All year 1HEC ▦ ♦ ⋔ ⅀ ⅌ ✕ ⊙ ⊟ ⊘ ⌇ P ⊞ ⊞ lau Prices: A7.30-7.80 pitch 10-11

LIEBELSBERG Baden-Württemberg
Erbenwald Neubulach 3 ☎07053 7382
Pleasant site on edge of wood.
Approach via Calw on the B463 for about 6km travelling S, then turn right and shortly before Neubulach continue N about 2km.

All year 6.5HEC ▦ ⊕ ⋔ ⅀ ⅌ ✕ ⊙ ⊟ ⊘ ♨ ⊞ ⌇ P ⊛ ⊞ lau Prices: A7 pitch 9

LIEBENZELL, BAD Baden-Württemberg
Bad-Liebenzell Kurhausdamm 2 ☎07052 40460
Municipal site with trees near tennis courts. Divided by hedges and internal asphalt roads.
Approach from Pforzheim on the B463 about 19km S. Turn left 500m before Bad Liebenzell to site on the banks of the Nagold.
All year 3HEC ⊕ ⋔ ⅀ ✕ ⊙ ⊟ ⊘ ⌇ P ⊛ ⊞ ⊗ lau ♦ ✕

LÖRRACH Baden-Württemberg
Grütt Grüttweg 8 ☎07621 82588
Level, grassy site near frontier.
From motorway exit Lörrach on B316 then via Freiburger Str and bridge over the Wiesse and turn left after 100m.
15 Mar-Oct 23.4HEC ▦ ⊕ ⋔ ✕ ⊙ ⊟ ⊘ ⊛ lau ♦ ⅀ ⅌ ✕ ⌇PR ⊞ Prices: A6.50 V2 ₪5-7 ▲3-5

LÖWENSTEIN Baden-Württemberg
Heilbronn am Breitenauer See ☎07130 8558
Exit at Weinsberg/Elhofen from A81/E41 (Stuttgart-Würzburg) and take B39 to Obersulm.
All year 10HEC ▦ ⇢⅃ ⋔ ⅀ ✕ ⊙ ⊟ ⊘ ♨ ⌇ L ⊛ lau ♦ ⊞ Prices: A9 pitch 11

LUDWIGSHAFEN AM BODENSEE Baden-Württemberg
See Ende ☎07773 5366
Meadowland with tall trees W of town, between railway and lake.
Access via Stuttgart-Singen-Lindau motorway. In Ludwigshafen turn off in direction of Radolfzell.
May-Sep 2.6HEC ▦ ⊕ ⋔ ⅀ ✕ ⊙ ⊟ ⊘ ♨ ⌇ L ⊛ ⊞ ⊗ lau Prices: A10 V6.50 ₪6 ▲6

MANNHEIM Baden-Württemberg
At **NECKARAU**(5.5km S)
Strandbad ☎0621 856240
A minicipal site in the grounds of a park beside the Rhine. At high water the site can get flooded.
From motorway exit 'Mannheim' to Neckarau, via the Freudenheim Bridge, then drive through Morchfeldstr, Friedrichstr, Rheingoldstr, Franzosenweg and Strandbadweg to the camp.
Apr-15 Oct 0.9HEC ⊕ ⋔ ⊙ ⊟ ⊘ ♨ ⊞ ▲ ⌇ R ⊞ ♦ ⅀ ⅌ ✕ ⌇LP

MARKDORF Baden-Württemberg
Wirthshof ☎07544 2325
15 Mar-Oct 6.5HEC ▦ ⊕ ⋔ ⅀ ✕ ⊙ ⊟ ⊘ ⌇ P ⊛ ⊞ ⊗ lau Prices: A7-9 pitch 15

MERGENTHEIM, BAD Baden-Württemberg
Willingertal ☎07931 2177
Site lies on a meadow between high green bank and wooded hillside.
From Bad Mergentheim follow B19 S towards Stuttgart, then left towards Wachbach after 2km. then left to Gastätte.
All year 15HEC ▦ ⇢⅃ ⋔ ⅀ ✕ ⊙ ⊟ ⊘ ♨ ⊞ ⊞ ▲ ⊛ ⊞ lau ♦ ⌇P

MÖRTELSTEIN Baden-Württemberg
Germania ☎06262 1795
Site is in Mörtelstein, 5km W of Obrigheim. Site lies between the left bank of the River Neckar and a wooded hillside.
Follow road B292 W towards 'Sinsheim' to just beyond Obergheim, then N on a narrow, steep road into the Neckar Valley.
Apr-Sep 0.8HEC ▦ ⊕ ⋔ ✕ ⊙ ⊟ ⊘ ⊞ ⌇ R ⊞ lau ♦ ⅀ ⅌ ✕ Prices: A5 V3 ₪5 ▲4

MÜNSTERTAL Baden-Württemberg
Münstertal ☎07636 353
Level, grassy site in pleasant situation with fine views. Lunchtime siesta 13.00-15.00 hrs.
Leave Karlsruhe-Basel motorway at Bad Kroningen exit and continue SE via Stauffen to W outskirts of Untermünstertal.
All year 3.9HEC ▦ ⊕ ⋔ ✕ ⊙ ⊟ ⊘ ♨ ⌇ P ⊛ ⊞ lau

MURRHARDT *Baden-Württemberg*

At **FORNSBACH**(6km E)

Waldsee ☎07192 6436
The site lies near Lake Waldsee. Asphalt paths and pitches, with gravel surface.
Drive through Murrhardt towards Fornsbach and the camp, which is on the eastern shore of the lake.
All year 2HEC ▦ ⌕ ⋒ 🏊 ✕ ⊙ ❷ ⌀ ♨ 🕭 ⅂ LP ☝ ⊞ lau Prices: A5-6 V3.50-5 ⬢4-5 ▲4-5

NECKARGEMÜND *Baden-Württemberg*

Dilsberg ☎06223 72585
Beside the Lido
From Neckargemünd towards Rainbach-Dilsberg turn left about 300m after Rainbach to site. Difficult access for caravans due to narrow road through village and 17% gradient.
Apr-Sep 3HEC ▦ ⌕ ⋒ 🏊 ✕ ⊙ ❷ ⌀ ♨ 🕭 R ☝ ⊞

Friedensbrücke ☎06223 2178
Campsite lies on the left bank of the River Neckar below the Frieden's bridge.
Mar-Sep 3HEC ▦ ⌕ ⋒ 🏊 ✕ ⊙ ❷ ⌀ ♨ 🕭 PR ☝ ⊞ lau

NECKARZIMMERN *Baden-Württemberg*

Cimbria ☎06261 2562
Site lies on level meadowland on the bank of the River Neckar.
Access to the site is signposted from road B27.
Apr-Oct 3HEC ▦ ⌕ ⋒ ✕ ⊙ ❷ ⌀ ♨ 🕭 ⬢ ⅂ P ⊞ lau ➡ 🏊 ⅂R ⊞ Prices: A7.50 pitch 9

NEUENBURG *Baden-Württemberg*

Dreiländer Camping und Freizeitpark Oberer Wald
☎07631 7719
An excellent site, very extensive, providing many entirely separate pitches.
Access via Karlsruhe-Basel motorway A5/E4, take the Müllheim/Neuenburg exit, then about 3km to site.
All year 12.8HEC ▦ ⌕ ⋒ 🏊 ✕ ⊙ ❷ ⌀ ♨ 🕭 ⅂ P ☝ ⊞ lau ➡ ⅂L Prices: A8.50 V6.50 ⬢8.50 ▲5.50-8.50

NUSSDORF *Baden-Württemberg*

Denz-Köhne ☎07551 4121
Narrow stretch of land, partly sloping, between the old lakeside road and the shore.
4km from Überlingen.
Apr-7 Oct 1HEC ▦ ⌕ ⋒ 🏊 ⅃ ⊙ ❷ ⌀ ♨ 🕭 ⅂ L ☝ ⊞ lau ➡ ✕

Nell Überlinger See ☎07551 4254
Site with orchard between farm of same name and the lakeside promenade. Small private beach.
Under railway bridge, then turn right.
Apr-15 Oct 0.8HEC ▦ ⌕ ⋒ ⊙ ❷ ⌀ ♨ 🕭 ⊞ ⅀ lau ➡ 🏊 ⅃ ✕ ⌀ ♨ ⅂LP Prices: A7 V5 ⬢10 ▲10

OSTRINGEN *Baden-Württemberg*

Kraichgau Camping Wackerhof ☎07259 361
A modern terraced site. Lunchtime siesta 13.00-15.00 hrs (except Saturdays).
From motorway A5 exit 'Kronau/Bad Schönborn' follow road B292 to Östringen.
15 Mar-15 Oct 3HEC ▦ ⋒ ⊙ ❷ ⌀ ♨ 🕭 lau Prices: A4.80 pitch 5.50

PFORZHEIM *Baden-Württemberg*

International Schwarzwald Freibadweg 4 ☎07234 6517
Site on edge of wood with southerly aspect. Separate fields for residential, overnight and holiday campers.
S through Huchenfeld from Pforzheim to Schellbron (15km).
All year 5HEC ▦ ⌕ ⋒ 🏊 ✕ ⊙ ❷ ⌀ ♨ ⬢ ☝ ⊞ ⅀ lau ➡ ⅂P Prices: A7 pitch 9.50

RHEINMÜNSTER *Baden-Württemberg*

At **STOLLHOFEN**

Freizeitcenter-Oberrhein ☎07227 2500
Modern leisure complex next to Rhine.

All year 36HEC ▦ ⌕ ⋒ 🏊 ⅃ ✕ ⊙ ❷ ⌀ ♨ ⬢ ⅂ L ☝ ⊞ lau Prices: A8-13 pitch 8-12

ROSENBERG *Baden-Württemberg*

Hüttenhof Hüttenhof 1 ☎07963 203
Flat meadow on incline in quiet woodland area, next to large farm.
From Ellwangen 3km N towards Crailsheim, turn W towards Adelmannsfelden and continue for 8km to turn off to N at Gaishardt.
All year 3HEC ▦ ⌕ ⋒ 🏊 ⊙ ❷ ⌀ ♨ 🕭 ⅂ ☝ ⊞ lau ➡ 🏊 ✕ Prices: A6 pitch 7

SCHAPBACH *Baden-Württemberg*

Alisehof ☎07839 203
The site lies on well-kept ground with several terraces and is separated from the road by the River Wolfach.
In Wolfach turn off the B924 at the Kinzigbrücke and drive N for about 8km to Schapbach. Site is 1km N of village.
All year 3HEC ▦ ⌕ ⋒ 🏊 ⊙ ❷ ⌀ ♨ 🕭 R ☝ ⊞ ➡ ✕ ⅂P Prices: A7.50-8.50 pitch 8-9

SCHILTACH *Baden-Württemberg*

Schiltach ☎07836 7289
The site lies on meadowland on the banks of the River Kinzig and is well placed for excursions.
May-Sep 3.6HEC ▦ ⌕ ⋒ 🏊 ✕ ⊙ ❷ ⌀ ♨ 🕭 R ☝ ⊞ ⅀ lau Prices: A5 V4 ⬢5 ▲5

SCHÖMBERG *Baden-Württemberg*

Höhen-Camping-Langenbrand ☎07084 6131
All year 1.6HEC ▦ ⌕ ⋒ ⊙ ❷ ⌀ ♨ ☝ ⊞ lau ➡ 🏊 ⅃ ✕ ⅂P Prices: A8 pitch 8-10

SCHWÄBISCH GMÜND *Baden-Württemberg*

At **RECHBERG**(6km S)

Schurrenhof ☎07165 8190
The site lies in a beautiful setting on the edge of a forest, and has a lovely view of the surrounding countryside.
Drive S on the B29 from Schwäbisch Gmünd, through Strassdorf and Rechberg, and towards Reichenbach on the B10. Then turn towards Schurrenhof.
All year 2.8HEC ▦ ⌕ ⋒ 🏊 ✕ ⊙ ❷ ⌀ ♨ 🕭 ⅂ P ☝ ⊞ ⅀ lau

SCHWÄBISCH HALL *Baden-Württemberg*

Steinbacher See Mühlsteige 26 ☎0791 2984
A modern site situated in the beautiful Kocher Valley. There are good sporting facilities and many places of interest nearby in the medieval town.
Access via B14/19 to Steinbach.
Apr-15 Oct 1.4HEC ▦ ⌕ ⋒ 🏊 ⊙ ❷ ⌀ ♨ lau ➡ 🏊 ✕ ⌀ ♨ ⅂P ⊞ Prices: A7 pitch 9

STAMMHEIM *Baden-Württemberg*

Obere Mühle ☎07051 4844
The site is divided into two sections by the access road, and sub-divided into pitches.
Off B296 almost 3km S of Calw.
All year 2.5HEC ▦ ⌕ ⋒ 🏊 ✕ ⊙ ❷ ⌀ ♨ ⬢ ☝ ⊞ lau ➡ ⅂P Prices: A8.50 pitch 9

STAUFEN *Baden-Württemberg*

Belchenblick Münstertaler Str 43 ☎07633 7045
Well kept site on level ground.
Access from motorway exit Bad Krozingen/Staufen and continue 4km SE.
All year 2.5HEC ▦ ⌕ ⋒ 🏊 ⅃ ✕ ⊙ ❷ ⌀ ▲ ♨ PR ☝ ⊞ lau ➡ ✕ Prices: A10.50-13.50 pitch 10.50

STEINACH *Baden-Württemberg*

Kinzigtal ☎07832 8122
Site on level meadowland with tall trees, situated next to the municipal heated swimming pool.
Signposted from Steinach.
15 Mar-Oct 4HEC ▦ ⌕ ⋒ 🏊 ✕ ⊙ ❷ ⌀ ♨ ⅂ P ☝ ⊞ lau

STUTTGART Baden-Württemberg

Canstatter Wasen Mercedesstr 40 ☎0711 556696
Level site with tall poplar trees alongside the River Neckar.
Lunchtime siesta 12.30-14.00 hrs.
Access from Bad Cannstatt near sports stadium.
All year 1.7HEC ⬛ ♠ ⋒ ✕ ⊙ 🖵 ∅ 🏛 ⊞ lau ➡ ⚡P

SULZBURG Baden-Württemberg

Alte Sägemuhle ☎07634 8550
Quiet holiday site in beautiful situation, surrounded by woodland.
Partly terraced the site is divided into two sections by the approach road.
From autobahn exit 'Bad Krozingen' and B3 to Heitersheim. Here turn E for site in 6km.
All year 2.5HEC ⬛ ♠ ⋒ ⊙ 🖵 ∅ 🏛 ⚡ P 🏛 ⊞ ➡ ✕ Prices: A8 pitch 6-10

TITISEE-NEUSTADT Baden-Württemberg

Bankenhof ☎07652 1351
From Titisee village follow signs 'Camping platz'. Access road to site closed 22.00-06.00 hrs.
All year 3.5HEC ⬛ ∷ ♠ ⋒ ⚡ ✕ ⊙ 🖵 ∅ 🏛 ⚡ R ⊞ lau ➡ ⚡LP Prices: A6-7.70 pitch 10-13

Bühlhof Bühlhofweg 13 ☎07652 1606
In pleasant situation on hillside above lake. Lunchtime siesta 13.00-14.30 hrs.
Well signposted.
Closed Nov-15 Dec 6HEC ⬛ ♠ ⋒ ✕ ⊙ 🖵 ∅ 🏛 🅿 ⊞ lau ➡ ⚡ ⚡LP

Sandbank ☎07651 8243 & 8166
On terrain rising from lakeside, upper part terraced, landscaped with trees.
Access from Titisee, N bank of lake, turn into old Feldbergstr. At SW end of lake turn left and continue along narrow private road through Camping 'Bankenhof' (closed 22.00-06.00 hrs) to the site about 700m on SE bank of lake.
Apr-20 Oct 2HEC ⬛ ∷ ♠ ⋒ ⚡ ⊙ 🖵 ∅ ⚡ L 🏛 ⊞ lau Prices: A6-8 pitch 9.50-12

Wellerhof ☎07652 1468
Mainly level site with trees, bordering on lake shore for about 400m.
Signposted from Titisee.
15 May-Sep 2HEC ⬛ ∷ ♠ ⋒ ⚡ ⊙ 🖵 ∅ ⚡ L 🏛 ⊞ lau ➡ ⚡P

TODTNAU Baden-Württemberg

Hochschwarzwald ☎07671 1288
Terraced site, partially grassland, by ski-lift.
6km NW of Todtnau.
All year 2.5HEC ⬛ ♠ ⋒ ⚡ ✕ ⊙ 🖵 ∅ 🏛 ⊞ lau Prices: A6.50-7 pitch 8.50-9

TÜBINGEN Baden-Württemberg

Tübingen ☎07071 43145
A quiet site, well situated on the left bank of the River Neckar.
For access from the town centre, cross the Neckar bridge, then turn right and drive S through Uhlandstr or Bahnhofstr to next bridge.
Cross bridge and drive upstream to the Rappenberghalde hill.
Apr-Oct 1HEC ⬛ ♠ ⋒ ⚡ ✕ ⊙ 🖵 ∅ ⚡ R lau ➡ ⚡LP Prices: A9.50 V3 ⚡7 ▲5.50-7

ÜBERLINGEN Baden-Württemberg

West Bahnhofstr 57 ☎07551 64583
The site lies on the western outskirts of the town, between the railway line and the road on one side, and the concrete shore wall on the other. It is divided into several sections by low wooden barriers and has a very small beach. No individual youths under 18.
Apr-10 Oct 3HEC ⬛ ♠ ⋒ ⚡ ✕ ⊙ 🖵 ∅ 🏛 ⚡ L 🏛 lau ➡ ⚡ ⊞ Prices: A9.50-10 pitch 17-19

UHLDINGEN Baden-Württemberg

At **SEEFELDEN**(1km W)

Seeperle ☎07556 5454
This site has some large trees along the shore of the lake. 50m-long

boat landing stage. It is one of the few camps that does not reserve its best pitches for residential campers.
Turn off B31 at Oberuhldingen and head towards Seefelden. Site 1km.
Apr-Oct 0.7HEC ⬛ ∷ ♠ ⋒ ⚡ ⊙ 🖵 ∅ ⚡ L 🏛 ⊞ ➡ ⚡ ✕ ⚡P Prices: A9.80 V6.50 ⚡12.50-16 ▲9-16

WALDBRONN Baden-Württemberg

Albgau Herrenalbstr 2 ☎07243 61069
Extenisve meadowland adjacent to the little Alb river.
Near the Neurod Inn and the infrequent Ettingen-Herrenalb railway.
Closed 15 Oct-15 Nov 3.6HEC ⬛ ♠ ⋒ ⚡ ✕ ⊙ 🖵 ∅ 🏛 ⊞ lau ➡ ✕

WALDKIRCH Baden-Württemberg

Elztalblick ☎07681 7433
Leave autobahn at 'Waldkirch/Ost' exit and follow signs for 3km.
Mar-15 Nov 1.5HEC ⬛ ♠ ⋒ ⚡ ✕ ⊙ 🖵 ∅ 🏛 ⊞ lau

WERTHEIM Baden-Württemberg

Wertheim-Recra An den Christwiesen 35 ☎09342 83111
Site lies on a level, long stretch of meadowland on the banks of the River Main next to a swimming pool. Lunchtime siesta 12.00-14.00 hrs.
Follow road towards 'Miltenberg', and in 1km turn right at the ARAL petrol station and head towards the site.
All year 7HEC ⬛ ♠ ⋒ ⚡ ✕ ⊙ 🖵 ∅ 🏛 ⚡ R 🏛 ⊞ lau Prices: A8-10 V3-4 ⚡11-13 ▲3-4

At **BETTINGEN**(5km E)

Wertheim-Bettingen Geiselbrunnweg 31, Wertheim ☎09342 7077
Motorway Frankfurt-Würzburg, exit Wertheim/Lengfurt, 1km.
Apr-Oct 7.5HEC ⬛ ♠ ⋒ ⚡ ✕ ⊙ 🖵 ∅ 🏛 ⊞ lau Prices: A6 V3 ⚡4 ▲4

WILDBAD IM SCHWARZWALD Baden-Württemberg

AZUR-Camping Schwarzwald ☎07055 1795
Long narrow site with some terraces, set between the River Enz and the wooded hillside. Separate section for young campers.
Access is from Pforzheim along B294 via Calmbach southwards.
All year 2.5HEC ⬛ ♠ ⋒ ⚡ ⊙ 🖵 ∅ ⚡ P 🏛 ⊞ lau

Kleinenzhof ☎07081 3435
All year 6HEC ⬛ ♠ ⋒ ⚡ ✕ ⊙ 🖵 ∅ 🏛 ⚡ R 🏛 ⊞ lau Prices: A7.50 pitch 9.60

Berlin and Eastern Provinces

This unique city has always been popular, but it surely must now be the most exciting city to visit in the world.
The splendid palaces and monuments are the city's architectural legacies of a rich and colourful history, of many periods and many noble families, of events that have rocked the world and made Berlin a focal point of political and cultural life.
No longer divided, the city offers many contrasts; stroll along the 'Unter den Linden' for an impression of "old" Berlin; visit the 'Kurfstendamm' which packs no fewer than 1,000 shops, boutiques, restaurants and galleries, into an elegant half-mile; relax in the delightful havens of parks, forests and lakes, which make up one third of the city.
Berlin is alive, bursting with a vibrant energy that never dies down; the nightlife offers everything from grand opera to erotic nightclubs, and stays open longer than you can stay up.

ALTENBERG Sachsen

Kleiner Galgenteich ☎035056 5007
Leave E55 at exit Dresden-Nord and continue towards the Czech border via B170/E55.
All year 8HEC ⬛ ⚡ ⋒ ✕ ⊙ 🖵 ∅ ⚡ LP 🏛 ⊞ lau

BERLIN

At KLADOW

DCC Else-Eckert-Platz Krampnitzer Weg 111-117 ☎030 3652797
All year 7.8HEC ⬛ ⁘ ⌖ ⌂ ℝ ⅃ ✕ ⊙ ₪ 📶 ⊞ ☎ lau ♦ ⌀ ⊰L ⊞
Prices: A9.50 pitch 7-12.50

At SCHMÖCKWITZ

Krosssinsee Wernsdorfer Str 45 ☎4930 6758687
All year 7HEC ⬛ ♦ ℝ ⌖ ✕ ⊙ ₪ 📶 ⊰ L ☎ ⊞ lau

At WANNSEE

Kohlhasenbrück Neue Kreisstr 36 ☎4930 8051737
Very pleasantly situated site on shore of Lake Griebnitz, owned by Deutscher Camping Club. Bathing area.
From Wannsee railway station, drive through Königstr, past Rathaus, through Chausseestr, Kohlhasenbrückerstr, and Kreisstr.
Mar-Oct 65HEC ⬛ ⌖ ℝ ✕ ⊙ ₪ ⊰ R ⊞ lau ♦ ⅃ ⌀ 📶 ⊞ Prices: A9.50 V4 🚐12.50 ▲12.50

BODSTEDT Mecklenburg-Vorpommern

Bodstedt Damm 1 ☎038231 4226
May-Sep 3.5HEC ⬛ ⌖ ℝ ⅃ ✕ ⊙ ₪ ⌀ 📶 📶 ▲ ⊰ P ⊞ ⊞ lau ♦ ⅃ ⊰LS

BREITENBACH Thüringen

AZUR-Camping Am Waldbad ☎036841 41153
Access via B247.
All year 4.5HEC ⬛ ⌖ ℝ ⌖ ⊙ ₪ 📶 ⊞ ⊞ lau ♦ ✕ 📶 ⊰PR Prices: A6-7 V3-4 🚐8-9 ▲3-4

CAPUTH Brandenburg

Himmelreich Wentorfinsel, Geltow ☎033209 70475
All year 6HEC ⬛ ⁘ ⌖ ℝ ⅃ ✕ ⊙ ₪ ⌀ 📶 ⊰ LR ☎ ⊞ lau Prices: A6 V3 🚐10 ▲3

CATTERFELD Thüringen

Paulfeld ☎036253 5171
Take E40 Frankfurt-Dresden and exit at Waltershausen.
All year 7HEC ⬛ ⌖ ℝ ⌖ ✕ ⊙ ₪ 📶 ⊰ L ☎ ⊞ lau

COLDITZ Sachsen

Waldbad ☎034381 43122
Apr-Sep 1.5HEC ⬛ ⌖ ℝ ⌖ ✕ ⊙ ₪ 📶 ⊰ P ☎ ⊞ lau ♦ ✕ Prices: A5 V5 🚐10 ▲8-11

DEUTSCHBASELITZ Sachsen

Waldbad Deutschbaselitz Teichstr 30 ☎03578 301489
The site may close for a short time in the winter and the shop and café are only open between May and September.
All year 5HEC ⬛ ⌖ ℝ ⌖ ✕ ⊙ ₪ 📶 ⊰ L ☎ Prices: A6-7 pitch 8-9

DRESDEN Sachsen

Wostra Trieskestr 100 ☎0351 2013254
Café open May-Sep only.
Apr-Oct 1.8HEC ⬛ ⌖ ℝ ✕ ⊙ 📶 📶 🚐 ⊰ LP ☎ ⊞ lau ♦ ⅃ ✕

FALKENBERG Brandenburg

Erholungsgebiet Kiebitz ☎035365 2135
Access via E55 Duben exit, then B87/B101 towards Herzberg.
Apr-Oct 5.5HEC ⬛ ⌖ ℝ ⅃ ✕ ⊙ ₪ ⊰ L ☎ lau ♦ ⌀ ⊞ Prices: A3.45-5.75 V4.60 🚐4.60-6.90 ▲4.60-5.75

FÜRSTENBERG Brandenburg

Röblinsee Röblinsee Nord ☎033093 38278
All year 1.2HEC ⬛ ♦ ℝ ⌖ ✕ ⊙ ₪ 📶 ⊰ P ☎ ⊞ lau ♦ ⅃ ✕ ⌀

GEORGENTHAL Thüringen

Georgenthal ☎036253 41314
Apr-Oct 1HEC ⬛ ⌀ ⌖ ℝ ✕ ⊙ ₪ ⌀ 📶 ⊰ P lau ♦ ⅃ ⅃ 📶 ⊞ Prices: A6.50 V2.50 🚐8 ▲4.50-5

HÖFCHEN Sachsen

Höfchen an der Talsperre 3 ☎034327 3153
May-Oct ⌖ ℝ ⌖ ✕ ⊙ ₪ ⌀ 📶 ⊰ L 🔲

HOHENFELDEN Thüringen

Stausee ☎036450 2081
Shop open May-Sep only.
All year 22.5HEC ⬛ ⌖ ℝ ⌖ ✕ ⊙ ₪ ⊰ L ☎

KELBRA Thüringen

Stausee Kelbra Lange Str 150 ☎034651 6310
All year 8HEC ⬛ ⌖ ℝ ⌖ ✕ ⊙ ₪ 📶 📶 ⊰ L ☎ ⊞ lau

KLEINMACHNOW Brandenburg

Yacht-Caravan-Club Bäkehang 9a ☎033203 79684
A riverside site with an hotel SW of town off A115.
All year 22HEC ⬛ ⌖ ℝ ℝ ⅃ ✕ ⊙ ₪ ⌀ ⊰ R ☎ ⊞ lau Prices: A8 V4 🚐5 ▲4.50

KÖNIGSTEIN Sachsen

Königstein Schandauer Str 23 ☎035021 68224
Federal road B172 within Königstein near Dresden.
Apr-Oct 2.5HEC ⬛ ⌖ ℝ ℝ ⅃ ✕ ⊙ ₪ 📶 📶 🚐 lau ♦ ⊰P ⊞ Prices: A7 V6 🚐6 ▲4-6

LEHNIN Brandenburg

Seeblick am Klostersee ☎03382 700274
50 miles from Berlin on E30.
Apr-Sep 1.5HEC ⬛ ⌖ ℝ ⌖ ⊙ ₪ ⊰ L ☎ ⊞ ♦ ⌀ Prices: A6 V3 🚐6 ▲4

MÖHLAU Sachsen Anhalt

Möhlauer See ☎034953 88344
Apr-Sep 5HEC ⬛ ♦ ℝ ✕ ⊙ ₪ 📶 🚐 ⊰ L 🔲 ⊞ ♦ ⌖ ✕

NIESKY Sachsen

Tonschächte ☎03588 5771
May-Sep 15HEC ⬛ ⌖ ℝ ℝ ⅃ ✕ ⊙ ₪ 📶 ⊰ L ☎ lau ♦ ⌀ ⊞ Prices: A5-6.50 V3 🚐5-7 ▲5-7

PLÖTZKY Sachsen

Waldsee ☎039200 50155
All year 8HEC ⬛ ⌖ ℝ ⊙ ₪ 📶 ☎ lau ♦ ⅃ ⅃ ⊰L ⊞

POTSDAM Brandenburg

Sanssouci-Gaisberg An der Pirscheide, Templiner See 41 ☎03327 55680
Apr-Oct 6HEC ⬛ ⁘ ⌖ ℝ ✕ ⊙ ₪ ⌀ 📶 ⊰ LS ☎ Prices: pitch 12 (incl 2 persons)

PRORA/RÜGEN Mecklenburg-Vorpommern

Meier ☎038393 2085
Apr-Oct 2.5HEC ⬛ ⌖ ℝ ✕ ⊙ ₪ 📶 ⊰ S ☎ lau ♦ ⅃ ⅃ ⌀ 📶 ⊰P ⊞

REICHENBERG Sachsen

Sonnenlehn Dresdner Str 115 ☎0351 4727788
Arp-Oct 20HEC ⬛ ♦ ⌖ ✕ ⊙ ₪ ⌀ 📶 ⊰ L ☎ ⊞ lau Prices: A7 V3 🚐9 ▲5

SIETOW Mecklenburg-Vorpommern

Sietower Bucht Dorfstr 21 ☎039931 52068
All year 0.9HEC ⬛ ⌖ ℝ ✕ ⊙ ₪ ⌀ lau ♦ ✕ ⊰L ⊞

SUHRENDORF Mecklenburg-Vorpommern

Suhrendorf ☎038305 82234
All year 9HEC ⬛ ⌖ ℝ ℝ ⅃ ✕ ⊙ ₪ 📶 🚐 ⊰ S ⊞ lau Prices: A7 V3.50 🚐12-16 ▲7-11

WAREN Mecklenburg-Vorpommern

AZUR-Ferienpark Ecktannen Fontanestr ☎03991 2607
Access via A19/E55 (Berlin-Rostock).
All year 17HEC ⬛ ⌖ ℝ ℝ ⅃ ✕ ⊙ ₪ 📶 🚐 ☎ lau ♦ ✕ ⊰L Prices: A8-10 V3-4 🚐11-13 ▲3-4 pitch 0.60-0.60

ZINNOWITZ Mecklenburg-Vorpommern

Pommerland ☎038377 40348 & 40177
In wooded surroundings on the north sea coast.
Access via B111.
All year 7.7HEC ⬛ ⁘ ⌖ ℝ ℝ ⅃ ✕ ⊙ ₪ ⌀ 📶 📶 ⊰ S ☎ ⊞ lau ♦ ⊰P

Central

The centre of Germany incorporates an enormous range of different landscapes - from the heavily-wooded Saarland, to the gorge-like valleys of the Rhine, to the vine-covered slopes of the Moselle. There are castles perched above steeply scarped banks, and ancient but thriving towns nestling in open valleys, combining scenic beauty with architectural masterpieces and an historic past.

Contained within this region is Bonn, birthplace of Beethoven, now a busy commercial and political centre, and Cologne, a fine modern town centred around a majestic Gothic cathedral.

Trier is Germany's oldest city and one of the largest wine-producing communities in the region. Discover the vast network of cellars extending beneath the streets and passages - a city in itself!

One of the most important commercial and economic centres in Germany, by virtue of its central situation, is Frankfurt, birthplace of Goethe, and now home to over 5,000 animals in its famous zoo.

AACHEN Nordrhein-Westfalen

Passtrasse Pass Str.79 ☎0241 158502
Municipal site in town centre near the Kurplatz. Becomes very full during the peak season.
Apr-Oct 1HEC ▦ ⌂ ◖ ⚑ ♥ ✗ ⊙ ⚑ ▲ ☲ ⊞ lau ♦ ✗ ∅ ♨ ₹P

ASBACHERHÜTTE Rheinland-Pfalz

Harfenmühle ☎06786 7076
A quiet site, beautifully situated in Fischbach Valley. Level grassland, partly terraced.
3km NW of the B327 towards Kempfeld.
All year 6.2HEC ▦ ♦ ⌂ ◖ ⚑ ♥ ✗ ⊙ ⚑ ∅ ♨ ₹ L ☲ ⊞ lau Prices: A6.50 pitch 9

ATTENDORN Nordrhein-Westfalen

Biggesee-Waldenburg ☎02722 95500
Generously terraced recreational site on the northern shore of the Bigge Reservoir, with adjoining public bathing area. Private sunbathing area. Lunchtime siesta 13.00-15.00 hrs.
From Attendorn follow road towards Heldren. Shortly after the railway turn right and follow the signs to the site, about 1.5km on.
All year 6.5HEC ▦ ⌂ ◖ ⊙ ⚑ ∅ ₹ L ☲ ⊞ lau ♦ ♥ ✗ ₹P Prices: A5.50-6.50 pitch 18-24

Hof Biggen Finnentroper Str 131 ☎02722 9553-0
Well-equipped terraced site, surrounded by woodlands. Lunchtime siesta 13.00-15.00 hrs.
Follow Atterdorn road to Ahauser Reservoir. Entrance near 'Haus am See' inn.
All year 18HEC ▦ ♦ ⌂ ◖ ⚑ ♥ ✗ ⊙ ⚑ ∅ ♨ ☲ lau ♦ ₹R ⊞ Prices: A6.75-8.75 V3.15-4.50 ⚑6.15-8.75 ▲6.15-8.75

BACHARACH Rheinland-Pfalz

Sonnenstrand Strandbadweg 9 ☎06743 1752
A beautifully situated site on grassland beside the Rhine with some high trees.
The turn off from B9 into the site can be difficult for caravans coming from the north, due to one way traffic.
Apr-Oct 1.3HEC ▦ ∷∷∷ ⌂ ◖ ♥ ✗ ⊙ ⚑ ∅ ☲ ⊞ lau ♦ ₹R

BALHORN Hessen

Erzeberg ☎05625 5274
Site lies on meadowland on slightly sloping ground above the village. Lunchtime siesta 13.00-15.00 hrs.
On B450 between Istha and Fritzlar.
All year 5HEC ▦ ♦ ◖ ⚑ ♥ ✗ ⊙ ⚑ ∅ ⚑ ₹ P ☲ lau ♦ ♨ ⊞ Prices: A6 pitch 12

BARNTRUP Nordrhein-Westfalen

Schwimmbad Fischteiche 4 ☎05263 2221
This well-kept site lies next to an open-air swimming pool, which is covered over in autumn and winter.

Barntrup lies B66, near to junction with B1. Approach signposted from Barntrup.
All year 2.4HEC ▦ ⌂ ◖ ⚑ ⊙ ⚑ ∅ ⚑ ▲ ₹ P ☲ ⊞ lau ♦ ✗

BERNKASTEL-KUES Rheinland-Pfalz

Kueser Werth Am Hafen 2 ☎06531 8200
Grassy site near Mosel and boating marina, with view of Castle Landshut.
On S outskirts of town.
Apr-Oct 2.2HEC ▦ ⌂ ◖ ⚑ ♥ ✗ ⊙ ⚑ ∅ ♨ ₹ R ☲ ⊞ lau Prices: A7 V3 ⚑8 ▲5-8

Schenk ☎06531 8176
Etr-Oct 1HEC ▦ ⌖♥ ◖ ⚑ ♥ ⚑ ₹ P lau ♦ ✗ Prices: A7 pitch 8

BIRKENFELD Rheinland-Pfalz

Waldwiesen ☎06782 5215
Leave the B41 E of Birkenfeld. Signposted.
15 Apr-15 Oct 4.5HEC ▦ ⌂ ♦ ◖ ⊙ ⚑ ∅ ▲ ⚑ ⚑ ₹ P ☲ ⚑ ⊞ lau ♦ ♨ ♥ ✗ Prices: A9 pitch 12

BOLLENDORF Rheinland-Pfalz

Altschmiede ☎06526 375
The site lies at a farm, on a long stretch of meadowland next to the River Sauer. It is situated partly on level ground and partly on slightly sloping ground.
From Bitburg on road B257 to Echternacherbrück, then for 7km in NW direction to Bollendorf. At end of village take road towards 'Köperich', 1.5km to site. Final section is narrow.
Apr-Oct 3HEC ▦ ⌂ ◖ ⚑ ♥ ⊙ ⚑ ₹ R ☲ lau ♦ ∅

BÖMIGHAUSEN Hessen

Barenberg ☎05632 1044
Beautifully terraced site at Neerdar reservoir.
Access from B251 between Korbach and Brilon.
All year 1HEC ▦ ⌂ ◖ ⚑ ⊙ ⚑ ∅ ₹ LR ☲ lau Prices: A5 pitch 5

BORLEFZEN Nordrhein-Westfalen

Borlefzen ☎05733 80008
Apr-Oct 40HEC ▦ ⌂ ◖ ⚑ ✗ ⊙ ⚑ ∅ ♨ ₹ LR ☲ ⊞ lau Prices: A9 pitch 11

BRAUNFELS Hessen

Braunfels Am Weiherstieg 2 ☎06442 4366
A terraced site surrounded by a forest of pine and deciduous trees. Separate meadow for touring campers. Lunchtime siesta 12.30-14.30 hrs.
Access from Köln-Frankfurt motorway, exit 'Limburg', then B49 towards town.
All year ▦ ♦ ⌂ ◖ ♥ ⊙ ⚑ ⚑ ☲ lau ♦ ♨ ₹P

BREISIG, BAD Rheinland-Pfalz

Rheineck ☎02633 95645
A quiet, well-kept site on a level meadow in Vinxtbach Valley.
From Koblenz follow B9 NW to Bad Breisig, then turn left, cross railway and continue for 400m.
All year 5HEC ▦ ⌂ ◖ ⚑ ♥ ⊙ ⚑ ∅ ♨ ☲ ⊞ lau ♦ ✗ ₹R Prices: A7 V6 ⚑7 ▲5

BRITTEN Saarland

AZUR Hochwald (Reiterhof Girtenmühle) ☎06872 3879
The site lies on a slightly sloping, open meadowland, set around the main building. The lower section is bordered by the Loscheimer Bach (Brook).
1km off the main B268.
All year 5HEC ▦ ⌂ ◖ ✗ ⊙ ⚑ ∅ ♨ ₹ P ☲ ⊞ lau ♦ ♨ ₹P

BULLAY Rheinland-Pfalz

Bären-Camp Am Moselufer 1/3 ☎06542 900097
On level meadow on right bank of the Mosel, next to the football ground. Fine view.
Access via B49 Cochem-Alf, then over the bridge and through the village. Signposted.
Etr-4 Nov 1.8HEC ▦ ⌂ ◖ ⚑ ♥ ✗ ⊙ ⚑ ∅ ♨ ₹ R ☲ ⊞ lau ♦ ₹P Prices: A6.57-7.50 V5-5 ⚑5-5 ▲5

BURGEN *Rheinland-Pfalz*

Burgen ☎02605 2396
A well maintained site with individual pitches set on level meadow with trees by the River Mosel. Site is broken up by shrubs and flower beds.
On the B49 (Kloblenz-Treis).
7 Apr-22 Oct 4HEC ▦ ⌂ ⋔ ⚲ ⚑ ⊙ ◨ ⌀ ⩞ ⚬ PR ☎ ⊞ lau ➧ ✗

COBLENCE

See **KOBLENZ**

COCHEM *Rheinland-Pfalz*

Freizeitzentrum Stationstr ☎02671 4409
Site lies on level meadowland with trees. On right bank of the Mosel, downstream from the swimming pool and sports ground.
In town cross the Mosel bridge, turn sharp right, follow signs 'Wellenbad' along riverside road for 1km.
end Mar-Oct 2.8HEC ▦ ⌂ ⋔ ⚲ ⚑ ✗ ⊙ ◨ ⌀ ⩞ ⚬ R ☎ ⊞ lau ➧ ✗
⚬LP Prices: A6 pitch 5-11

At LANDKERN(7km N)

Altes Forsthaus Haupstr 2 ☎02671 8701
The partly terraced site lies near woodland in the valley below Landkern.
From motorway A48 (Eifel motorway) leave at exit Kaisersesch, go S to Landkern, then follow signs to site.
All year 1OHEC ▦ ⌂ ⋔ ✗ ⊙ ◨ ⌀ ⚬ P ☎ ⊞ lau ➧ ⚲ ✗ Prices:
A6 V3 ⚗5-11 ⚑5-11

COLOGNE

See **KÖLN**

DAHN *Rheinland-Pfalz*

Büttelwoog ☎06391 5622
Site lies in a magnificent pine forest, partly surrounded by steep hills and rocks. Section reserved for young people with tents. Lunchtime siesta 12.00-14.00 hrs.
From Pirmasens follow B10 up to Hinterweidenthal then S on B427 to Dahn.
All year 6HEC ▦ ⋮⋮⋮ ⌂ ⋔ ⚲ ⚑ ✗ ⊙ ◨ ⌀ ⩞ ☎ ⊞ lau ➧ ⚬P
Prices: A9 pitch 10

DIEMELSEE-HERINGHAUSEN *Nordrhein-Westfalen*

AZUR-Camping Hohes Rad ☎05633 99099
Access via B251 (Korbach-Beilon).
All year 2.8HEC ⨝⌙ ⌂ ⋔ ⚲ ✗ ⊙ ◨ ⌀ ⩞ ☎ lau ➧ ✗ ⚬LP ⊞ Prices:
A8-10 V3-4 pitch 11-13

Seeblick Arnold ☎05633 388
The fenced-in site lies next to the Diemel-Stausee (reservoir) at the Craststätte Seeblick.
From Brilon follow road B7 eastwards to Messinghausen, here turn off main road and follow road to Diemel-Stausee (8km).
All year ▦ ⌂ ⋔ ✗ ⊙ ◨ ⌀ ⩞ ☎ ⊞ lau ➧ ⚲ ⚬LP

DIEZ *Rheinland-Pfalz*

Ochsenwiese ☎06432 2122
On a meadow on the left bank of the River Lahn, below Schloss Oranienstein.
From N leave motorway A3 at Diez exit (from S at Limburg-Nord exit) then continue on B54 approx. 7km.
Apr-Oct 7HEC ▦ ⨝⌙ ⌂ ⋔ ⚲ ⚑ ✗ ⊙ ◨ ⌀ ⩞ ⚗ ⚬ R ☎ lau ➧ ⚬LP ⊞
Prices: A4.40 V4.40 ⚗5.50 ⚑3-5.50

DORSEL AN DER AHR *Rheinland-Pfalz*

Stahlhütte ☎02693 438
Site with individual pitches, on meadowland with trees near River Ahr.
Off B258 (Aachen-Koblenz) road.
All year 5HEC ▦ ⌂ ⋔ ⚲ ✗ ⊙ ◨ ⌀ ⩞ ⚬ R ☎ ⊞ ⚏ lau Prices:
A7.50 ⚗15 ⚑13

DORTMUND *Nordrhein-Westfalen*

Hohensyburg Syburger Dorfstr 69 ☎0231 774374
Terraced site on hilly grassland near Weitkamp inn.
Access via B54.

CAMPING HOHENSYBURG

Weitkamp
D-44265 Dortmund-Hohensyburg
Tel: & Fax: 0231/77 43 74
– Near the new casino
– Easy access, road has been widened
Terraced design with all connection facilities – also available to touring vans. Modern washing facilities.
An attractive and quiet location on the Ruhr and Lake Hengstey.
Gateway to the Sauerland. Attractive bridleways and footpaths lead to places of historic interest and excellent day trip opportunities close by.
Access: Cologne-Bremen motorway (Hansa route) to the Hagen-Nord exit, A1 then to Hohensyburg.
A45 Dortmund-Frankfurt motorway (Sauerland route) to Dortmund-Süd and then the B54 to Hohensyburg.
B1 to Dortmund-Mitte exit and then the B54 to Hohensyburg.

All year 11.5HEC ▦ ⨝⌙ ⌂ ⋔ ⚲ ⚑ ✗ ⊙ ◨ ⌀ ⩞ ⚬ LR ☎ ⊞ lau Prices:
A8 V6 ⚗10 ⚑9

DREIEICH-OFFENTHAL *Hessen*

Offenthal Bahnhofstr 77 ☎06074 5629
Camping Card compulsory Exit B486 at Dreieich-Offenthal in direction of Dietzenbach.
Apr-Oct 3HEC ▦ ⌂ ⋔ ⚲ ⊙ ◨ ⌀ ⩞ ⚬ P ☎ ⊞ ⚏ lau ➧ ✗

DROLSHAGEN *Nordrhein-Westfalen*

Gut Kalberschnacke ☎02763 7501
Terraced site above Bigge-Lister Reservoir in wooded area.
Turn off A45 (E41) autobahn at Wegringhausen exit and continue NE for approx. 4km.
All year 13HEC ⨝⌙ ⌂ ⋔ ✗ ⊙ ◨ ⌀ ⩞ ⩞ lau ➧ ⚬L Prices: A6.80-8.50 V2.80-3.50 ⚗9.60-12 ⚑7.20-9

DÜLMEN *Nordrhein-Westfalen*

Tannenwiese Borkenbergestr 217 ☎02594 4795
The site lies on meadowland in a well wooded country area, near the gliderdrome. Lunchtime siesta 12.30-14.30 hrs.
Take the B51 from Recklinghausen towards Münster as far as Hausdülmen, then follow signpost 'Segelflugplatz Borkenberge'.
Mar-Oct 3.7HEC ⌂ ⋔ ⊙ ◨ ⌀ ⩞ ☎ ⊞ ➧ ⚲ ✗

DÜRKHEIM, BAD *Rheinland-Pfalz*

AZUR-Knaus ☎06322 61356
Lakeside site on level meadow between vineyards, adjoining a sportsfield. Lunchtime siesta 12.00-15.00 hrs.
Access from E outskirts of town. Turn N at railway viaduct, near JET petrol station.
5 Feb-19 Nov ▦ ⌂ ⋔ ⚲ ✗ ⊙ ◨ ⌀ ⩞ ⚬ L ⊞ ⊞ ⚏ lau

DÜSSELDORF *Nordrhein-Westfalen*

Unterbacher See Kleiner Torfbruch 31 ☎0211 899-2038
Site on sloping grassland.
From Düsseldorf B326 to 'Erkrath' exit. Turn left by Unterbacher lake.
Etr-1 Sep 5HEC ▦ ⌂ ⋔ ⊙ ◨ ⚬ L ⊞ ⊞ ⚏ ➧ ⚲

EMS, BAD *Rheinland-Pfalz*

Bad Ems ☎02603 4679
Level grassy site with isolated trees by the River Lahn.
On E outskirts on B260.
Apr-Oct 16HEC ⌂ ⋔ ⚲ ⚑ ✗ ⊙ ◨ ⌀ ⚍ ⚬ PR ⊞ lau Prices:
A7.50 pitch 8

ESCHWEGE *Hessen*

Fluss und Mineralbad Torwiese 4-5 ☎05651 3871
In grounds of mineral swimming pool at the foot of the Leuchtberg with Bismarck Tower.
From B27 E take B452 or B249 to Eschwege then follow signs.
Apr-Sep 1HEC ▦ ⌂ ⋔ ⊙ ◨ ⌀ ⚬ PR ☎ ⊞ ⚏ ➧ ⚲ ⚲ ✗ ⩞

ESSEN *Nordrhein-Westfalen*

At **WERDEN**(10km S)

Essen-Werden Im Löwental 67 ☎0201 492978
Several fields divided by bushes and surrounded by thick hedges.
Lunchtime siesta 13.00-15.00 hrs.
From centre of Essen towards Werden, then turn towards railway station and follow signposts.
All year 4HEC ⬛ 🏕🏕🏕⊙🏕🏕🏕 R ⊞ ⌇ lau ➧ ⌇P Prices: A7.50 pitch 15

FREILINGEN *Rheinland-Pfalz*

At **MAXSAIN**(4km SW)

Klingelwiese ☎02626 5043
On a meadow beside a woodland lake.
Leave A3/E5 motorway (Köln-Frankfurt) at 'Ransbach/Baumbach' exit and continue via Mogendorf and Selters to Maxsain. Site lies 2km further on.
All year 15HEC ⬛ 🏕🏕🏕⊙🏕🏕⊞➧⌇L

FULDATAL-KNICKHAGEN *Hessen*

Fulda-Freizeitzentrum ☎05607 340
All year 3.2HEC ⬛ 🏕🏕🏕🏕🏕🏕🏕 ⌇ P ⊞ lau Prices: A6 pitch 9

FÜRTH IM ODENWALD *Hessen*

Tiefertzwinkel Am Schwimmbad ☎06253 5804
Pleasantly landscaped site in beautiful setting next to the municipal open-air swimming pool. Lunchtime siesta 13.00-15.00 hrs.
Feb-Nov 5HEC ⬛ 🏕🏕🏕🏕×⊙🏕🏕🏕 ⌇ lau ➧🏕×⌇P ⊞
Prices: A5.60 ❑10 ▲7

GEMÜNDEN *Rheinland-Pfalz*

Aumühle Auestr 26 ☎06453 7286
Well-kept meadowland site next to the municipal 'Freibad' (swimming pool) in the valley of the River Wohra. Lunchtime siesta 13.00-15.00 hrs.
From Road B3 (Marburg-Fritzlar) turn N in Halsdorf.
All year 1HEC ⬛ 🏕🏕🏕⊙🏕🏕 R ⊞➧🏕×🏕🏕⌇P ⊞

GERBACH *Rheinland-Pfalz*

AZUR-Camping Pfalz ☎06361 8287
Lunchtime siesta 13.00-15.00 hrs.
Access from A8/E12 motorway at junction Enkenbach-Hochspeyer. Then N on B48 via Rockenhausen and at Dielkirchen continue E for 4.5km to Gerbach.
All year 8.5HEC ⬛ 🏕🏕🏕🏕×⊙🏕🏕🏕🏕▲⌇P ⊞ lau

GILLENFELD *Rheinland-Pfalz*

Feriedorf Pulvermaar ☎06573 9135
Partly terraced municipal site on a slightly sloping meadow at Pulver Maar, surrounded by woods.
From motorway A48 (Eifel autobahn) leave at exit Mehren/Daun, continue S o n B421 and take the first turning into Gillenfeld. On near side of village turn off towards Pulver Maar.
All year 4HEC ⬛ 🏕🏕🏕×⊙🏕🏕🏕⊞ lau ➧🏕 Prices: A4.50-6 V2-4 ❑14-16 ▲11-14

GROSS-GERAU *Hessen*

Niederwaldsee ☎06152 2981
Clean and well laid out site in bird reserve beside Lake Niederwald.
Lunchtimes siesta 13.00-15.00 hrs.
Off B44.
All year 12HEC ⬛ 🏕🏕🏕🏕🏕×⊙🏕🏕🏕⊞ lau

GRÜNBERG *Hessen*

Spitzer Stein Alsfelderstr ☎06401 804
Beautifully situated site at a forest swimming pool.
From the Frankfurt-Kassel motorway (A5) leave at Homberg junction. Campsite is 8km s.
All year 4HEC ⬛ 🏕🏕🏕🏕🏕⊙🏕🏕🏕⊞ lau ➧🏕🏕×🏕⌇P

GRUNDMÜHLE BEI QUENTEL *Hessen*

Grundmühle Quentel ☎05602 3659
A forest camp site with a sunny location. Lunchtime siesta 13.00-15.00 hrs.

From Melsungen follow road B83 to Röhrenfurth. Here turn right towards 'Furstenhagen' and follow road via Eiterhagen to Quentel.
All year 18HEC ⬛ 🏕🏕🏕🏕🏕🏕🏕⌇ P ⊞🏕➧🏕🏕× Prices: A5.50 pitch 7.50

GULDENTAL *Rheinland-Pfalz*

Guldental ☎06707 633
Site lies in a valley of the Guldenbach Valley. Some terraces are reserved for tourers and there is a lake suitable for bathing.
Camping Card Compulsory.
From Bad Kreuznach N on road B48 to Langenlonsheim, and on nearside turn left to Guldental.
All year 5HEC ⬛ 🏕🏕🏕🏕×⊙🏕🏕🏕🏕⊞ lau ➧⌇P

HALDERN *Nordrhein-Westfalen*

Strandhaus Sonsfeld ☎02857 2247
On meadowland at the 'Hagener-Meer' next to B8 and railway line.
All year 1.5HEC ⬛ 🏕🏕🏕🏕⊙🏕🏕 R ⊞🏕➧🏕🏕 Prices: A4 V4 ❑4 ▲4

HAMMER *Nordrhein-Westfalen*

Hammer ☎02473 8115
In a quiet secluded valley.
Apr-Sep ⬛ 🏕🏕🏕×⊙🏕⌇ R ⊞🏕 lau ➧×

HAUSBAY *Rheinland-Pfalz*

At **PFALZFELD-HAUSBAY**

Schinderhannes ☎06746 1674
Terraced site on S facing slope, broken up by trees and shrubs beside a small lake. Separate section for young people. Lunchtime siesta 13.00-15.00 hrs.
E of B327. 29km S of Koblenz.
All year 30HEC 🏕🏕🏕🏕🏕⊙🏕🏕🏕⌇ L ⊞ lau Prices: A7 pitch 12

HEIMBACH *Nordrhein-Westfalen*

Rurthal-Burg Blens ☎02446 3377
Site with individual pitches on meadowland beside the River Ruhr.
From Düren follow road S via Nideggen and Abenden to Blens, then cross bridge and turn left.
All year 7HEC ⬛ 🏕🏕🏕⊙🏕🏕🏕🏕⌇ P ⊞ lau ➧× Prices: A6.10 V5 ❑5.80 ▲5

HEIMERTSHAUSEN *Hessen*

Heimertshausen Ehringshauser Str ☎06635 206
Near swimming pool in extensive, grassy, wooded valley. Lunchtime siesta 13.00-15.00 hrs.
From Kassel-Frankfurt motorway take Alsfeld-West exit, then continue via Romrod and Zell.
Apr-Sep 3.6HEC ⬛ 🏕🏕🏕🏕×⊙🏕🏕🏕🏕⊞ lau ➧⌇P Prices: A5 pitch 10

HELLENTHAL *Nordrhein-Westfalen*

Hellenthal ☎02482 1500
On extensive meadowland.
0.5km S of town.
All year 6HEC ⬛ 🏕🏕🏕🏕×⊙🏕🏕🏕⌇ P ⊞ lau ➧🏕 Prices: A6 pitch 15

HERINGEN *Hessen*

Werra ☎06624 9330
Municipal site on slightly sloping ground at the swimming pool.
Lunchtime siesta 13.00-15.00 hrs.
All year 13.5HEC ⬛ 🏕🏕🏕⊙🏕⌇ P ⊞ lau ➧🏕×🏕 Prices: A4-5.50 V4 ❑4 ▲4

HIRSCHHORN AM NECKAR *Hessen*

Odenwald ☎06272 809
Extensive site in wooded valley. Divided by River Ülfenbach and hedges.
Turn off B37 towards Wald-Michelbach and continue for 1.5km.
Apr-15 Oct 7HEC ⬛ 🏕🏕🏕🏕×⊙🏕🏕⌇ P ⊞ lau

HOFGEISMAR *Hessen*

Parkschwimmbad Schöneberger Str 16 ☎05671 1215
Municipal site, subdivided by hedges. Next to a swimming pool.

Lunchtime siesta 13.00-15.00 hrs. Mobile shop.
All year 1.5HEC ▥ ⊶ ⋒ ✕ ⊙ ☻ ▦ ᐞ P ☎ ⊞ lau ➡ ⍑ ✕ ⌀ Prices:
A5.50 ⊕7 ▲4

At **LIEBENAU-ZWERGEN**(9km W)

Ponyhof Terrassen-Camping Wärmetal ☎05676 1509
A terraced, south facing site, with magnificent scenery. 300m from a
swimming pool.
Access from B83, at Hofgeismar turn W towards Liebenau,
alternatively from B7 turn N at Obemeiser towards Liebenau.
All year 8HEC ▥ ⊶ ⋒ ⍑ ✕ ⊙ ☻ ⌀ ☻ ☻ ᐞ R ☎ ⊞ lau ➡ ᐞP

HONNEF, BAD Nordrhein-Westfalen

At **HONNEF-HIMBERG, BAD**(7km E)

Jillieshof ☎02224 972066
All year 4HEC ▥ ⊶ ⋒ ⍑ ⊙ ☻ ⌀ ᐞ P Prices: A9 V4 ⊕8 ▲4

HORN-BAD MEINBERG Nordrhein-Westfalen

Eggewald Kempener Str 33 ☎05255 236
Site lies in well wooded countryside.
Access via road B1. In Horn-Bad Meinberg turn off main road at the
Waldschlosschen and follow the 'Altenbeken' road for about 8km up
to Kempen.
All year 2HEC ▥ ▲ ⊶ ⋒ ⍑ ⊙ ☻ ▦ ᐞ P ☎ ⊞ lau ➡ ✕

IDSTEIN Hessen

AZUR-Camping Idstein ☎06126 91299
Access via A3 (Frankfurt-Limburg).
All year 2.6HEC ▥ ⊶ ⋒ ⍑ ✕ ⊙ ☻ ⌀ ᐞ P ☎ ⊞ lau ➡ ✕ Prices: A8-
10 V3-4 ⊕11-13 ▲3-4

INGENHEIM Rheinland-Pfalz

SC Klingbachtal ☎06349 6278
Municipal site lies on level meadowland at the edge of the village,
next to the sports ground.
8km S of Landau via B38. Final approach well signposted.
Apr-Oct 1.5HEC ▥ ⊶ ⋒ ✕ ⊙ ☻ ⌀ ▦ ☎ ⊞ lau ➡ ⍑ ⍣ ✕ ᐞP Prices:
A5 V4 ⊕8 ▲6-8

IRREL Rheinland-Pfalz

Nimseck ☎06525 314
Site on long grassy strip in wooded valley on the bank of River Nims.
Approach from Bitburg via B257/E42 in SW direction. At the turn-off
from the bypass to Irrel, turn left.
Apr-Oct 7HEC ▥ ⊶ ⋒ ⍑ ✕ ⊙ ☻ ⌀ ▦ ☎ ⊞ ➡ ᐞPR

KALLETAL-VARENHOLZ Nordrhein-Westfalen

Ost/Weser/Freizeit-Zentrum ☎05755 444
Extensive site in Weser recreation area near River Weser N of
Schloss Varenholz. Separate field and common room for young
campers.
Leave A2/E8 motorway at Exter exit then continue via Vlotho
towards Rintein.
All year 12HEC ▥ ⊶ ⋒ ⍑ ⊙ ☻ ⌀ ▦ ᐞ L ☎ ⊞ ⍥ lau

KELL Rheinland-Pfalz

Freibad Hochwald ☎06589 1695
On meadow on slightly sloping wooded hillside, near a public open-
air swimming pool.
Advance booking necessary in high season.
2km from B407 towards Trier.
May-Sep 2.5HEC ▥ ⊶ ⋒ ✕ ⊙ ☻ ᐞ P ☎ ⊞ ➡ ⍑ ✕ ⌀ ▦

KERNBACH Hessen

Kernbach ☎06420 7494
Site lies on level meadowland at the River Lahn. Lunchtime siesta
13.00-14.30 hrs.
From Marburg on B3 N to Cölbe, then follow road B62 W to
Kernbach, and t hen turn left to site. Alternative approach from
Marburg via Marbach (Behringwerke) and Caldern to Kernbach.
Etr-Oct 2.6HEC ▥ ⍒ ⋒ ⊙ ☻ ᐞ P ☎ ⊞ lau ➡ ⍑

KIRCHHEIM Hessen

Seepark Kirchheim ☎06628 1525
This terraced site, with individual pitches, is part of an extensive and

well equipped leisure and recreation centre.
All year 10HEC ▥ ⊶ ⋒ ⍑ ⍣ ✕ ⊙ ☻ ⌀ ☻ ☻ ᐞ LP ☎ ⊞ lau

KOBLENZ (COBLENCE) Rheinland-Pfalz

At **WINNINGEN**(9km SW)

Ziehfurt Fährstr 35 ☎02606 357 & 1800
Site lies on level wooded meadowland.
From Koblenz follow road B416 for 11km towards Trièr. Access to
site at the Schwimmbad (swimming pool).
May-Sep 7HEC ▥ ⊶ ⋒ ⍑ ⍣ ✕ ⊙ ☻ ⌀ ᐞ R ☎ ⊞ lau ➡ ᐞP Prices:
A8 pitch 8

KÖLN (COLOGNE) Nordrhein-Westfalen

At **RODENKIRCHEN**

Berger Ueferstr 71 ☎0221 9355240
All year 6HEC ▥ ⊶ ⋒ ⍑ ⍣ ✕ ⊙ ☻ ⌀ ▦ ᐞ R ☎ ⊞ lau ➡ ✕ ᐞP
Prices: A7 V4 ⊕8 ▲4

KÖNEN Rheinland-Pfalz

Horsch Könenerstr 36 ☎06501 17571
Apr-Oct ▥ ⊶ ⋒ ⍑ ⍣ ✕ ⊙ ☻ ⌀ ▦ ᐞ R ☎ ⊞ ➡ ᐞP Prices: pitch 25
(incl 2 persons)

KÖNIGSTEIN IM TAUNUS Hessen

At **EPPSTEIN**(8km SW)

Hubertushof Bezirksstr 2 ☎01778 456700
In the Taunus landscape preservation area.
Follow B455 from Königstein.
All year 3HEC ▥ ⊶ ⋒ ⍑ ⊙ ☻ ⌀ ☎ ⊞ lau ➡ ⍑ ⍣ ✕ Prices: A9 pitch
10

KÖNIGSWINTER Nordrhein-Westfalen

Holstein Pleiserhohenstr 12 ☎02244 3222
All year 2.5HEC ▥ ⊶ ⋒ ⍑ ⍣ ⊙ ☻ ᐞ P ☎ ⊞ ⍥ ➡ ✕ ⌀

KRÖV Rheinland-Pfalz

Kröver-Berg ☎06541 2081
All year 2HEC ▥ ⊶ ⋒ ✕ ⊙ ☻ ⌀ ⊞ lau ➡ ⍑ ⍣ Prices: pitch 20 (incl
2 persons)

LADBERGEN Nordrhein-Westfalen

Waldsee Waldseestr 81 ☎05485 1816
Site lies at the inn, near the bathing area of the lake.
2km N. From motorway leave at 'Ladbergen' exit following road
towards Saerbeck/Emsdetten and after 100m turn right.
All year 6HEC ▥ ⊶ ⋒ ⍑ ✕ ⊙ ☻ ⌀ ☻ ᐞ L ☎ ⊞ lau ➡ ⌀ Prices:
A5 pitch 7

LAHNSTEIN Rheinland-Pfalz

Burg Lahneck ☎02621 2765
Level grassland site with sunny aspect and terraces which provide
shade. Situated next to Lahneck Castle. Pleasant view of the Rhine
Valley.
From Koblenz (8km distance) follow road B42. In Lahnstein, leave
main road and follow signs (Burg Lahneck), 1.5km to site.
Apr-Oct 1.8HEC ▥ ⊶ ⋒ ⍑ ⍣ ✕ ⊙ ☻ ⌀ ☎ ⊞ lau ➡ ᐞP Prices:
A9.50 V6 ⊕9.50 ▲7-9.50

LANGENSELBOLD Hessen

GC Kinzigsee ☎06184 3589
Lakeside site on level meadowland. Lunchtime siesta 13.00-15.00
hrs.
A66 between Hanau and Gelnhausen.
Apr-Sep 6HEC ▥ ⍒ ⋒ ⍑ ✕ ⊙ ☻ ⌀ ᐞ L ☎ ⊞ lau

LEBACH Saarland

Lebach Dillingerstr 81 ☎06881 2764
Local authority site. Grassland, slightly sloping on edge of wood.
Take B269, 750m from sports field.
All year 3.2HEC ▥ ⊶ ⋒ ⍑ ✕ ⊙ ☻ ᐞ P lau ➡ ⍑

LEIWEN Rheinland-Pfalz

AEGON-Ferienpark Sonnenberg ☎06507 93690
Extensive terraced site in one of the largest wine growing areas of
this district. Lies above the River Mosel.

Access from main B53 (Mosel Valley road) cross the River Mosel at Thornich then via Leiwen to site.
All year 25HEC ▥ ♨ ♦ ♠ ♠ ⚍ ♥ ✕ ⊙ ▨ ∅ ☲ ☎ ⚞ P ☎ ⊞ lau Prices: pitch 41-52 (incl 5 persons)

LEMGO *Nordrhein-Westfalen*

Alten Hansestadt Regenstorstr ☎05261 14858
The site lies by the swimming pool.
All year 2HEC ▥ ♨ ♠ ⊙ ▨ ∅ ☲ ☎ ⚞ R ☎ ⊞ lau ♦ ☲ ♥ ✕ ⚞P
Prices: A7 V6 ⚐6 ▲3-9

LIBLAR *Nordrhein-Westfalen*

Liblarer See ☎02235 3899
This site lies at Lake Liblar, with its own bathing area.
Camping Card Compulsory.
Access SW from Cologne on the B265 (for approx 15km) 1km before Liblar turn left towards the lake.
All year 9.5HEC ♒✓♨ ♠ ☲ ♥ ✕ ⊙ ▨ ∅ ☲ ⚞ L ☎ ⊞ lau

LICHTENBERG *Hessen*

Odenwald Idyll Fischbachtal ☎06166 8577
In quiet and beautiful setting. Lunchtime siesta 13.00-15.00 hrs.
Access from Darmstadt amd Gross-Bieberau.
Apr-15 Oct 3.5HEC ▥ ♨ ♠ ✕ ⊙ ▨ ☲ ⚞ P ☎ ⊞ Prices: A5 ⚐8 ▲5

LINDENFELS *Hessen*

Terrassencamping Schlierbach Am Zentbuckel 11 ☎06255 630
Site is fenced and lies on sloping terrain. Lunchtime siesta 13.00-15.00 hrs.
From Bensheim-Michelstadt road B47, turn off in Lindenfels and go SW to Schlierbach.
Apr-Oct 4.2HEC ▥ ♨ ♠ ☲ ♥ ▨ ∅ ☲ ☎ ♦ ♥ ✕ ⚞P ⊞ Prices: A5.20-6.50 pitch 6.80-8.50

LINGERHAHN *Rheinland-Pfalz*

Mühlenteich ☎06746 533
Site lies on slightly sloping meadowland, divided into sections by a group of trees. Isolated situation at the edge of woodland and adjoining the forest swimming pool (free entry for campers). Lunchtime siesta 13.00-15.00 hrs. Trout fishing.
Access is from Koblenz-Bingen motorway A61 via exit 'Pfalzfeld' - or for caravans, an easier approach would be via exit 'Laudert'.
All year 15HEC ▥ ♦ ♠ ☲ ♥ ✕ ⊙ ▨ ∅ ☲ ☎ ⊞ lau

LORCH *Hessen*

Suleika ☎06726 9464
Well laid out terraced site in Rhine Valley. Separate car park for users of the smaller pitches.
From Assmannshausen take B42 for 3km towards Lorch then turn right into the Bodental - access to site through railway underpass. Approach for larger caravans - turn right 1km before Lorch.
Mar-Oct 4HEC ▥ ♨ ♠ ☲ ♥ ✕ ⊙ ▨ ∅ ☲ ☎ P ⊞ lau ♦ ⚞P Prices: A8 V2.50 ⚐8 ▲5-8

LOSHEIM *Saarland*

AZUR-Camping Reiterhof Girtenmühle ☎06872 9024-0
Access via B268 (Trier-Losheim).
All year 5HEC ▥ ♠ ✕ ⊙ ▨ ∅ ☲ ⊞ lau ♦ ⚞LP

MAINZ-KOSTHEIM *Hessen*

Mainz-Wiesbaden Maarau ☎06134 4383
Shop closed in April.
15 Mar-Oct 2HEC ▥ ♦ ♠ ✕ ⊙ ▨ ☲ lau ♦ ☲ ✕ ∅ ⚞R

MARBURG AN DER LAHN *Hessen*

GC Lahnaue Tro je damm 47 ☎06421 21331
Municipal site on level meadowland next to the 'Sommerbad' (swimming pool) in the W part of this 'Town on the River Lahn'.
Apr-15 Nov 1HEC ▥ ♨ ♠ ☲ ✕ ⊙ ▨ ∅ ☲ ⚞ R ☎ lau ♦ ⚞P

MEERBUSCH *Nordrhein-Westfalen*

AZUR-Camping Meerbusch Zur Rheinfähre 21 ☎02150 911817
Access via A57 (Neuss-Krefeld).
Apr-Sep 6HEC ♒✓♨ ♠ ☲ ♥ ✕ ⊙ ▨ ∅ ☲ ⚞ R ☎ ⊞ lau Prices: A8-10 V3-4 ⚐11-13 ▲3-4

MEHLEM *Nordrhein-Westfalen*

Genienau ☎0228 344949
The site lies opposite the Drachenfels.
All year 1.8HEC ▥ ♦ ♠ ♥ ⊙ ▨ ☲ ⊞ lau ♦ ☲ ✕ ∅ ☲ Prices: A8 V3 ⚐5-8 ▲5-8

MEINHARD *Hessen*

Werra-Meissner-Kreis ☎05651 6200
Apr-Oct 7HEC ▥ ♨ ♠ ♥ ✕ ⊙ ▨ ⚞ L ▨ ⊞ ∅ lau ♦ ☲ Prices: A5 ⚐10 ▲10

MESCHEDE *Nordrhein-Westfalen*

Sauerland-Camp Hennesee ☎0291 99950
In pleasant wooded surroundings beside the Hennesee. Shop and café only open during high season.
S via B55.
All year 13HEC ▥ ♦ ♠ ☲ ♥ ✕ ⊙ ▨ ∅ ☲ ⚞ P ☎ ⊞ lau ♦ ⚞L

MICHELSTADT *Hessen*

Odenwaldparadies ☎06061 74152
Site is partly fenced in and lies next to the station and swimming pool in the NE part of town.
Site is well signposted from the by-pass road of Michelstadt.
May-Sep 1.2HEC ▥ ♒✓♨ ♠ ✕ ⊙ ▨ ∅ ☲ ☲ ∅ ♦ ⚞P

MITTELHOF *Rheinland-Pfalz*

Eichenwald ☎02742 931915
In oakwood, mainly divided into pitches.
Camping Card Compulsory.
From Siegen follow B62 towards Wissen. Turning to site approximately 4km NE of Wissen.
All year 10HEC ▥ ♨ ♠ ☲ ♥ ✕ ⊙ ▨ ∅ ☲ ⚞ LPR ☎ ⊞ lau ♦ Prices: A5-5.50 V6-7 ▲4-4.50

MONTABAUR *Rheinland-Pfalz*

At **GIROD**(4km E)

Eisenbachtal ☎06485 766
Situated in the 'Nassau Nature Park'.
From motorway exit 40 'Montabaur' turn right, before Montabaur follow sign 5km towards Limburg. From motorway exit 41 'Wallmerod/Diez' 5km towards Montabaur.
All year 4HEC ▥ ♨ ♠ ☲ ♥ ✕ ⊙ ▨ ∅ ☲ ☲ ⊞ lau Prices: A8 pitch 10

MÖRFELDEN-WALLDORF *Hessen*

Arndt Mörfelden ☎06105 22289
Well laid out site in two sections near motorway. Lunchtime siesta 13.00-15.00 hrs.
Well signposted 0.3km from Langen/Mörfelden exit on A5/E4 Frankfurt-Darmstadt motorway.
All year 4HEC ▥ ♨ ♠ ☲ ♥ ✕ ⊙ ▨ ∅ ☲ ☲ lau ♦ ☲ ✕ ⚞L ⊞

MÜLHEIM *Rheinland-Pfalz*

AZUR Camping Mülheim ☎06534 940157
Near M?heim-Lieser bridge over the Mosel.
Camping Card Compulsory.
Access from Bernkastel, 5.5km along B53 towards Trier.
Mar-Nov 1.5HEC ▥ ♨ ♠ ♥ ✕ ⊙ ▨ ⚞ R ☲ ⊞ lau ♦ ☲ ∅ ☲ Prices: A7-9 V3-4 ⚐10-12 ▲3-4

MÜLHEIM AN DER RUHR *Nordrhein-Westfalen*

Entenfangsee ☎0203 760111
Extensive site near lake. Touring pitches near railway line. Adventure playground. Lunchtime siesta 13.00-15.00 hrs.
From motorway exit Duisburg-Wedau, continue towards Bissingheim to lake.
All year 85HEC ▥ ♨ ♠ ☲ ♥ ✕ ⊙ ▨ ∅ ☲ ☲ ⊞ lau ♦ ⚞L

MÜLLENBACH *Rheinland-Pfalz*

Nürburgring ☎02692 224
All year 30HEC ▥ ⁑⁑⁑ ♨ ♠ ☲ ✕ ⊙ ▨ ∅ ☲ ⚐ ☲ ⊞ lau

NEHREN *Rheinland-Pfalz*

Nehren ☎02673 4612
On level terrain beside the River Moselle. Separate section for teenagers. Lunchtime siesta 13.00-15.00 hrs. Liable to flood at

certain times of the year.
Turn off the B49 Cochem-Alf road in Nehren.
Apr-10 Oct 0.5HEC ▦ ⚓ ⋔ ⚡ ✕ ⊙ ⚑ ⚎ ⋏ R ☎ ⊞ lau ➧ ⚡ ⌀ Prices: pitch 28 (incl 2 persons)

NEUERBURG *Rheinland-Pfalz*

Neuerburg ☎06564 2660
Site divided by hedges, close to an open-air pool with a smaller lake for inflatable boats.
Access via the B50 (Bitburg-Vianden). At Sinspett turn N and continue to site on N outskirts (7km).
All year 1.5HEC ▦ ⚓ ⋔ ⚡ ✕ ⊙ ⚑ ⌀ ⚎ ⋏ PRS ☎ ⌀ lau ➧ ⚡

NIEDENSTEIN *Hessen*

At **KIRCHBERG**(4.5km S)

Wiesenthalsmühle ☎05624 363
Grassy site, fenced off in woodland area, close to inn of same name.
From Fritzlar take B450 N to Riede. turn right and continue for 2km towards Kirchberg, then branch left for 1.5km.
All year 5HEC ⚓ ⋔ ⚡ ✕ ⊙ ⚑ ⚎ ⋏ P ⚑ ⊞ lau

NIEDERBERGHEIM *Nordrhein-Westfalen*

Niederbergheim Sauerlandstr 168 ☎02925 1842
Site lies on a meadow surrounded by woodland to the E of the Möhne Dam.
From the Möhne Dam follow the B516 E to Niederbergheim, here turn S towards Hirschberg. 2km to site.
All year 2.2HEC ▦ ⚓ ⋔ ⚡ ⊙ ⚑ ⚎ ☎ ⊞ lau ➧ ⚡ ✕

NIEDEREISENHAUSEN *Hessen*

Hinterland Ouotshauser Weg 32, Steffenberg ☎06464 7564
Lunchtime siesta 13.00-14.30 hrs.
Follow signs to 'Schwimmbad'.
All year 2HEC ▦ ➧ ⋔ ✕ ⊙ ⚑ ⚎ ⚑ ☎ ⊞ lau ➧ ⚡ ⋏P Prices: A6 pitch 6.50

NIEDERKRÜCHTEN *Nordrhein-Westfalen*

Lelefeld Lelefeld 4 ☎02163 81203
In a quiet, wooded, location on the outskirts of the village.
Signposted from Elmpt.
All year 1.5HEC ▦ ⚓ ⋔ ⊙ ⚡ ⊞ lau ➧ ✕ ⋏LPR Prices: A5 V2 ⚑6 ⚎6

NIEDERWÖRRESBACH *Rheinland-Pfalz*

Fischbachtal ☎06785 7372
On level grassland in Fischbach valley. Lunctime siesta 12.00-14.00 hrs.
6km N of Fischbach towards Herrsteig.
All year 1.8HEC ▦ ⚓ ⋔ ⚡ ✕ ⊙ ⚑ ⌀ ☎ ⊞ lau ➧ ⋏P Prices: A5 pitch 10

OBERLAHR *Rheinland-Pfalz*

Lahrer Herrlichkeit In der Huth ☎02685 7326 & 8282
Holiday site with leisure park in wooded surroundings. Lunchtime siesta 13.00-15.00 hrs.
From motorway A3 (Frankfurt-Köln) leave at exit 'Neuwied/Altenkirchen' then 5km on B256 towards Altenkirchen.
All year 8HEC ⚓ ⋔ ⚡ ✕ ⊙ ⚑ ⌀ ⚎ ⚑ ☎ lau ➧ ⚡ ✕ ⋏PR

OBERSGEGEN *Rheinland-Pfalz*

Reles-Mühle Kapellenstr 3 ☎06566 8741
In rural surroundings next to a farmhouse, set on a level meadow at a brook with trees and bushes.
From Bitburg on road B50 towards Vianden. Site lies near the Luxembourg frontier.
All year 2HEC ▦ ⚓ ⋔ ⊙ ⚑ ⚎ ⋏ R ☎ ⚑ ⊞ lau ➧ ⚡ ✕ ⌀ ⚎ ⋏P Prices: A4 pitch 8

OBERWEIS *Rheinland-Pfalz*

SC Oberweis ☎06527 426
Local authority site on long, level stretch of meadow beside River Prüm and sports ground.
From Bitburg take B50 towards Vianden (Luxembourg).
15 Mar-15 Oct 3HEC ▦ ⚓ ⋔ ⚡ ⊙ ⚑ ⌀ ⚑ ☎ ⊞ lau ➧ ✕ ⚡ ⋏PR

OLPE *Nordrhein-Westfalen*

At **KESSENHAMMER**

Biggesee-Kessenhammer ☎02761 94420
Long, narrow partly terraced site in quiet woodland setting on E shore of Bigge-Reservoir. Lunchtime siesta 13.00-15.00 hrs.
A45 exit Olpe continue B54 to Olpe eastwards on B55 and turn off at exit Rhode.
All year 5.7HEC ▦ ⚓ ⋔ ⚡ ✕ ⊙ ⚑ ⌀ ⋏ L ☎ ⊞ lau ➧ ✕ Prices: A5.50-6.50 pitch 17-23

At **SONDERN**

Biggesee-Sondern Sonderner Kopf 3 ☎02761 944111
Exit Olpe A45 in direction Attendorn. In 6km turn off for Erholungsanlage Biggesee-Sondern.
All year 6HEC ▦ ⚓ ⋔ ⚡ ✕ ⊙ ⚑ ⌀ ⋏ L ☎ ⊞ lau ➧ ✕ Prices: A5.50-6.50 pitch 18.50-24.50

OLSBERG *Nordrhein-Westfalen*

At **BRUCHHAUSEN**(7km SE)

Bruchhauser Steine Am Medebach 96 ☎02962 3000
The site lies on meadowland next to a brook. Lunchtime siesta 13.00-14.30 hrs.
From Meschede follow road B7 for 13 km eastwards, the turn off the 'Bigge' and continue via 'Olsberg' and 'Bruchhausen' and finally follow signs to 'Skighebiet Sternrodt'.
All year 2HEC ▦ ⚓ ⋔ ⊙ ⚑ ⌀ ⚑ ⚎ ☎ ⊞ lau ➧ ⚡ ✕

OSTRHAUDERFEHN *Nordrhein-Westfalen*

AZUR-Camping Idasee ☎04952 994297
Access via B27 (Cloppenburg-Aurich).
All year 5HEC ▦ ⚓ ⋔ ⊙ ⚑ ⌀ ⚑ ⋏ L ☎ ⊞ lau Prices: A7-9 V3-4 ⚑10-12 ⚎3-4

POMMERN *Rheinland-Pfalz*

Pommern Moselweinstr ☎02672 2461
The site lies on level meadowland on the left bank of the River Mosel. fine views along the valley.
About 8km E of Cochem and just outside Pommern on the B49.
Etr-Oct 4HEC ▦ ✁ ⚓ ⋔ ⚡ ✕ ⊙ ⚑ ⌀ ⚑ ⋏ PR ☎ ⊞ lau

PORTA WESTFALICA *Nordrhein-Westfalen*

Grosser Weserbogen ☎05731 6188
From A2 (travelling towards Dortmund), take exit Porta Westfalica-Minden.
All year 50HEC ▦ ⚓ ⋔ ⚡ ✕ ⊙ ⚑ ⌀ ⋏ L ☎ ⊞ ⌀ lau Prices: A7.50-8.50 V3-4 ⚑6-7 ⚎6-7

PRÜM *Rheinland-Pfalz*

Waldcampingplatz ☎06551 2481
Site lies on both side of the River Prüm and is surrounded by woods. Divided into three sections of level meadowland.
Situated at the NW of Prüm.
All year 3.5HEC ▦ ⚓ ⋔ ⚡ ✕ ⊙ ⚑ ⌀ ⚎ ☎ ⊞ lau ➧ ✕ ⋏P

REINSFELD *Rheinland-Pfalz*

AZUR Camping Hunsrück ☎06503 95123

Access via the B52 or B407.
All year 20HEC ▦ ⚓ ⋔ ⚡ ✕ ⊙ ⚑ ⌀ ⚎ ⋏ P ☎ ⊞ lau Prices: A8-10 V3-4 ⚑11-13

ROTENBURG-FULDA *Hessen*

SC Campingweg ☎06623 5556
SE of town on River Fulda, follow 'DCC' signs.
Apr-Oct 0.9HEC ▦ ⚓ ⋔ ⚡ ✕ ⊙ ⚑ ☎ ⊞ lau ➧ ⚡ ✕ ⌀ ⚎ ⋏P

At **LICHERODE**(10km NW)

Alte Mühle Alheim 3, Rotenburg-Fulda ☎05664 8141
In beautiful wooded valley. Lunchtime siesta 13.00-15.00 hrs.
From motorway A7/E4 (Kassel-Frankfurt) take 'Raststätte-Hasselbirg' exit, follow road towards Wichte then turn off towards Licherode.
Mar-Oct 2HEC ▦ ⚓ ⋔ ⚡ ✕ ⊙ ⚑ ⌀ ⚎ ⋏ LP ☎ ⊞ lau

ROTHEMANN *Hessen*
Rothemann Maulkuppenstr 17 ☎06659 2285
A small, well-kept site surrounded by a hedge, lies next to the main Fulda road.
From Fulda follow road B27 for 10km towards Bad Br?kenau; can also be reached from the Kassel-W?zburg motorway leaving exit Fulda Süd, then 3km along B27 towards Bad Br?kenau.
Apr-Oct 0.6HEC ▥ ⌾ ⋒ ⛟ ⊙ ⊠ ⊘ ≞ ⋌ P ⊡ ⊞ ✦ ✕ Prices: A6.50 V4 ⊞4 ▲3.50

RÜDESHEIM *Hessen*
Landgut Ebental 'Ponyland' ☎06722 2518
On meadowland surrounded by woodlands. Ponies and carriages for hire. Private sports plane for pleasure flights.
N towards Presberg. Steep approach road to Ebental. Signposted.
15 May-15 Nov 2HEC ▥ ⌾ ⋒ ⊙ ⊠ ⊘ ≞ ≞ ⊡ ⊞ lau ✦ ⛟ ⛟

Rhein ☎06722 2528 & 2582
Near the open-air swimming pool and the River Rhine.
May-3 Oct 2.9HEC ▥ ⌾ ⋒ ⛟ ✕ ⊙ ⊠ ⊘ ≞ ⊞4 ⊡⊗ lau ✦ ✕ ⋌P ⊞
Prices: A6.40 V5.40 ⊞7 ▲6.10-8.10

RUNKEL AN DER LAHN *Hessen*
Runkel Auf der Bleiche ☎06482 911022
On road from Limburg.
Apr-Sep 2HEC ▥ ⌾ ⋒ ⛟ ✕ ⊙ ⊠ ⊘ ≞ ▲ ⋌ R ⊡ ⊞ ✦ ⛟ ✕ Prices: A5 V3 ⊞5 ▲3

SAARBURG *Rheinland-Pfalz*
Landal Greenpark Warsberg ☎06581 91460
Open site in quiet situation on top of a hill. Chairlift (700m) leads down to the town.
At N end of the town leave the B51 'Trier' road and follow signs ' Ferienpark Warsberg' 3km uphill on good road.
21 Mar-3 Nov 11HEC ▥ ⌾ ⋒ ⛟ ⛟ ✕ ⊙ ⊠ ⊘ ≞ ⊞ ⋌ P ⊡ ⊞ lau
Prices: pitch 32-47 (incl 5 persons)

Leukbachtal ☎06581 2228
Municipal site on level meadows on both sides of the Leuk-Bach (brook).
Leave Saarburg on road B51 towards Trassen, then after crossroads, turn left off the B51.
Etr-15 Oct 3.5HEC ▥ ⌾ ⋒ ⛟ ✕ ⊙ ⊠ ⊘ ≞ ⋌LP ⊞
Prices: A6.50 V8 ⊞8

Waldfrieden Im Fichtenhain 4 ☎06581 2255
Site lies next to the Café Waldfrieden on unspoilt, slightly rising meadowland in woods.
S of town leave B51 or B407 and follow road towards Nennig (Luxembourg). 200m to site.
Mar-Oct 1.2HEC ▥ ⌾ ⋒ ⛟ ✕ ⊙ ⊠ ⊘ ≞ ⊡ ⊞ lau ✦ ⛟ ✕ ⋌P Prices: A4 V3 ⊞8-11 ▲6-8

SAARLOUIS *Saarland*
AZUR-Camping Saarlouis St-Nazairer Alle 23 ☎06831 3691
A municipal site, divided into pitches, and set on level meadowland with tall trees. Lunchtime siesta 13.00-14.30 hrs.
Turn off road B51 in suburb of Roden, cross new bridge over the River Saar and continue to site, beyond sports hall.
All year 2HEC ▥ ⇥ ⋒ ✕ ⊙ ⊠ ⊘ ≞ ⊡ ⊞ lau ✦ ⋌P Prices: A7-9 pitch 10-12

ST GOAR *Rheinland-Pfalz*
Friedenau Gruendelbach 103 ☎06741 368
On level, narrow stretch of meadowland at Gasthaus Friedenau.
Leave B9 in St-Goar and continue through railway underpass towards Emmelshausen for approx 1km.
Apr-Nov 0.8HEC ▥ ✦ ⋒ ⛟ ✕ ⊙ ⊠ ⊘ ≞ ⋌ R ⊡ ⊞ lau ✦ ⋌P Prices: A6.50-7.50 V4.50 ⊞4.50 ▲3-4.50

ST GOARSHAUSEN *Rheinland-Pfalz*
Loreleystadt ☎06771 2592
Municipal site on level meadow beside the Rhine. Near a sportsfield and opposite Rheinfels Castle.
Access via B42.

15 Mar-Oct 1.5HEC ▥ ⌾ ⋒ ⛟ ⛟ ⊙ ⊠ ⊘ ≞ ⋌ R ⊡ ⊞ lau ✦ ✕
Prices: A8 V4 ⊞6 ▲5-8

SCHACHEN *Hessen*
Hochrhön ☎06654 7836
Lies 1.5km from the Kneipp (hydrotherapeutic) Spa area of Gersfeld.
2km N of Gersfeld.
All year 3HEC ▥ ⌾ ⋒ ⊙ ⊠ ⊘ ≞ ⊞ ⊞ lau ✦ ⛟ ⛟ ✕ Prices: A6 pitch 8

SCHALKENMEHREN *Rheinland-Pfalz*
Camp am Maar Maarstr 22 ☎06592 551
Terraced lakeside site on meadowland at the Schalkenmehrener Maar (water-filled crater). Towing help for caravans.
From A48 (Eifelautobahn) leave at 'Mehren/Daun' exit and follow B42 to Mehren. Turn off to the SW.
All year 1HEC ▥ ✦ ⋒ ⛟ ✕ ⊙ ⊠ ⊘ ≞ ⋌ L ⊡ ✦ ⋌P ⊞ Prices: A5 ⊞15-18 ▲10-18

SCHLEIDEN *Nordrhein-Westfalen*
Schleiden Im Wiesengrund 39 ☎02445 7030
Site lies on hilly, well-wooded country.
On the B258 to Monschau, 1km to site.
All year 4.4HEC ▥ ⌾ ⋒ ✕ ⊙ ⊠ ⊘ ≞ ⊡ ⊗ lau ✦ ⛟ ✕ ⋌P
Prices: A6 V3 ⊞7.50 ▲6-8

SCHLÜCHTERN *Hessen*
At **HUTTEN**(8km E)
Hutten Heiligenborn ☎06661 2424
Site lies at Heiligenborn and has a pleasant southerly aspect.
Lunchtime siesta 13.00-15.00 hrs.
Approach from Fulda on B40 towards Frankfurt to Flieden for 19km, then turn left via Rückers to Hutten (8km).
All year 3.5HEC ▥ ⌾ ⋒ ✕ ⊙ ⊠ ⊘ ≞ ⊡ ⊞ lau ✦ ⋌P Prices: A6.20 pitch 6-8

SCHÖNENBERG *Saarland*
Ohmbachsee ☎06373 4001
Terraced site on sloping ground above E bank of the Ohmbachsee. Separate field for young people. Lunchtime siesta 13.00-15.00 hrs. Signposted.
All year 7.8HEC ▥ ⌾ ⋒ ⛟ ✕ ⊙ ⊠ ⊘ ≞ ⊞ ⋌ P ⊡ ⊞ lau ✦ ⋌L
Prices: A8.50 pitch 15

SCHOTTEN *Hessen*
Nidda-Stausee Vogelsbergstr 184 ☎06044 1418
Access via B455.
All year 3.8HEC ▥ ⌾ ⋒ ⛟ ✕ ⊙ ⊠ ⊘ ≞ ⋌ L ⊡ ⊞ lau

SCHWEICH *Rheinland-Pfalz*
Schweich ☎06502 91300
On level meadowland on the Mosel, next to a marina.
Access via A48 (Eifelautobhan) exit 'Schweich' in direction of Trier.
Continue through Schweich, turning left just before the Mosel bridge.
15 Apr-15 Oct 3.5HEC ▥ ⌾ ⋒ ⛟ ✕ ⊙ ⊠ ⊘ ≞ ⋌ R ⊡ lau ✦ ⋌P ⊞
Prices: A6.50 V2 ⊞8 ▲4.50-8

SECK *Rheinland-Pfalz*
Weiherhof ☎02664 8555
Site lies on level meadowland next to a small lake in a wooded nature reserve. Special section reserved for young people. Many bathers at weekends.
Take the B255 from Rennerod and drive to Hellenbahn-Schellenberg. Then turn S and continue for approx 2km.
All year 10HEC ▥ ⌾ ⋒ ⛟ ✕ ⊙ ⊠ ⊘ ≞ ⋌ L ⊡ ⊞ lau

SENHEIM *Rheinland-Pfalz*
Internationaler Holländischer Hof ☎02673 4660
On level meadowland, divided into pitches beside the River Mosel which has boatmooring facilities.
Access from Cochem on the B49 in direction of Zell as far as Senhals, then over the bridge and turn left.
15 Apr-15 Oct 3.5HEC ▥ ⌾ ⋒ ⛟ ✕ ⊙ ⊠ ⊘ ≞ ⋌ R ⊡ ⊞ ⊗ lau
Prices: A6 pitch 11

SENSWEILER MÜHLE *Rheinland-Pfalz*

Bauernhof Bundestr 422 ☎06786 2395
On extenisve grassland beside the Idar, partially terraced, in rural area near a farm. Views of wooded range of hills. Next to Camping Oberes Idartal. Separate section for young groups.
From Idar-Oberstein follow road B422 for about 10km to the NW.
Site lies between Katzenloch and Allenbach.
Apr-Oct 2HEC ▦ � ♠ ♃ 🛏 ⚡ 🗙 ⊙ 🚻 🚮 ☎ ⊞ lau ➧ 🛒

Oberes Idartal ☎06786 2114
Site lies on a farm by the Idar, set on several small meadows and partly on terraced terrain next to Camping Sensweiler Mühel.
Blockhouse with facilities for spit-roasting.
From Idar-Oberstein follow road B422 for about 10km to the NW.
site lies between Katzenloch and Allenbach.
All year 2.8HEC ▦ ♥ ♠♥ 🛏 ⊙ 🚻 🚮 ☎ 🚮 ⇥ R ☎ ⊞ lau ➧ 🛒 🗙

SOLINGEN *Nordrhein-Westfalen*

At **GLÜDER**

Waldcamping Glüder ☎0212 242120
Site on level terrain surrounded by woodland on banks of the River Wupper.
Access via Köln-Kamen Autobahn exit Burscheid, via Hilgen and Witzhelden to Glüder or from Solingen on B299/B224 in direction of Witzhelden via Burg Hohenscheid.
All year 2HEC ▦ ♥ ♠ 🛏 🗙 ⊙ 🚻 🚮 ☎ ⊞ lau Prices: A7 pitch 12

STADTKYLL *Rheinland-Pfalz*

AEGON Ferienpark Wirfttal ☎06597 92920
Extensive, level grassland beside the upper of two small reservoirs, approx 1km outside the town.
Access S from Euskirchen on the A1, through Blankenheim and towards Stadtkyll.
All year 2HEC ▦ ꝛ♥ ♠ 🛏 ♃ 🗙 ⊙ 🚻 🚮 ☎ ⇥ P ⊞ lau Prices: pitch 26-48 (incl 5 persons)

STEINEN *Rheinland-Pfalz*

Hofgut Schönerlen ☎02666 207
Beautiful and quiet site at Lake Hausweiher, has a special section reserved for residential campers. Young campers under 18 years old not accepted unless with adults.
Take the B8 Limburg-Altenkirchen road. In Steinen turn left to the site.
All year 15HEC ▦ ♠♥ 🛏 ⊙ 🚻 🚮 ⇥ L ☎ ⊞ ⊗ lau ➧ 🗙 Prices: A8 pitch 10

STUKENBROCK *Nordrhein-Westfalen*

Furlbach Am Furlbach 33 ☎05257 3373
Extensive site, partly on level, open meadow and partly in woodland. Separate section for dog owners. Old barn is used as a common room for young campers. Lunchtime siesta 12.30-14.30 hrs.
From the Dortmund-Hannover motorway (A2/E73) leave at exit 'Bielefeld/Sennenstadt' then follow the B68 for about 12km towards Paderborn. At Km44.2 turn off main road then 400m to site.
Apr-Oct 9HEC ♥ ♠♥ 🗙 ⊙ 🚻 🚮 ☎ ⊞ lau ➧ 🛒 🗙 ⊘ Prices: A7 V4.50 🚐6 ▲5-6

TANN *Hessen*

Ulstertal Dippach 4 ☎06682 8292
Terraced site on slightly sloping meadowland.
Leave the Bischofsheim-Tann road B278 in Wendershausen and go SE to Dippach.
All year 2.4HEC ▦ ♥ 🗙 ⊙ 🚻 🚮 ☎ 🚮 ⊞ lau ➧ 🛒 Prices: A6.50-7.50 pitch 6-7

TECKLENBURG *Nordrhein-Westfalen*

At **LEEDEN**(12km E, also E of motorway)

Truma-Campingpark ☎05405 1007
Site lies on undulating meadowland, with asphalted roads. Four separate buildings. Separate section for dog owners. Lunchtime siesta 13.00-15.00 hrs.
From A1-E3 Bremen-Münster motorway leave at Lengerich/Tecklenburg exit, then via Lengerich to Leeden (10km).
All year 30HEC ▦ ♥ ♠ 🗙 ⊙ 🚻 🚮 ☎ ⊞ lau

TREIS-KARDEN *Rheinland-Pfalz*

Mosel-Islands ☎02672 2613
An extensive, level site on a grassy island in the Mosel next to a yacht marina.
Turn off the B49 in Treis onto the southern coastal road.
Apr-Oct 4.5HEC ▦ ♥ ♠ ⊙ 🚻 🚮 ⇥ R ☎ lau ➧ 🛒 🛒 🗙 ⇥P ⊞ Prices: A6 V5 🚐9.50 ▲4.50

TRENDELBURG *Hessen*

Trendelburg ☎05675 301
Site located at the foot of the castle, subdivided on the banks of the River Diemel. Covered tennis court.
Access from Kessel N via Hofgeismar (B83) to Trendelburg cross the bridge and turn right, down to site.
All year 1.5HEC ▦ ♥ ♠ 🛏 🛒 ⊙ 🚻 🚮 🚮 ⇥ PR ☎ lau Prices: A5.20 V2 🚐5 ▲5

TRIER *Rheinland-Pfalz*

Monaise ☎0651 86210
Municipal site on level meadow under high trees in former Schloss Park on banks of the Mosel.
From town follow B49 along left bank of the Mosel 5km up river towards Zewen.
Apr-Oct 3.5HEC ▦ ♥ ♠ 🛒 🗙 ⊙ 🚻 🚮 ☎ ⊞ lau

Trier-City Luxemburger Str 81 ☎0651 86921
Level site owned by the Rowing Club Treviris, on left bank of the Mosel divided by an asphalt road.
It lies between the Romer bridge and Adenauer bridge on road towards Luxembourg.
Apr-Oct 1.5HEC ▦ ♠ ♠ 🗙 ⊙ 🚻 🚮 ▲ ⇥ R ☎ ➧ ⊘ 🚮 Prices: A7 V4 🚐8 ▲4

TRIPPSTADT *Rheinland-Pfalz*

Sägmühle Sägmühle 1 ☎06306 1215
The site lies in a wooded valley beside the Sagmühle Lake (Saw Mill Lake). It consists of several unconnected sections, some of them terraced. Lunchtime siesta 12.30-14.00 hrs.
14km S of Kaiserslautern.
All year 10HEC ▦ ♥ ♠ 🛒 🗙 ⊙ 🚻 🚮 🚮 ⇥ L ☎ lau ➧ 🛒 ⊞ Prices: A9 pitch 7

UTSCHEID *Rheinland-Pfalz*

Michelbach ☎06564 2097
A municipal site at the Michelbach, surrounded by meadows and woods, 500 individual pitches.
From the B50 Bittburg-Vianden road turn N in Sinspelt. Then continue via Niederraden to Utscheid.
All year 1.5HEC ♠ 🗙 ⊙ 🚻 🚮 lau ➧ 🛒 🛒 ⊘ 🚮 ⇥LPR ⊞

VINKRATH BEI GREFRATH *Nordrhein-Westfalen*

SC Waldfrieden ☎02158 3855
Site within nature reserve.
From Grefrath N towards Wankum after 3km. Turn right.
Apr-15 Oct 4.5HEC ▦ ♥ ♠ 🗙 ⊙ 🚻 🚮 ☎ ⊞ ⊗ lau ➧ 🛒 🛒 ⇥LP

VORDERWEIDENTHAL *Rheinland-Pfalz*

Bethof Am Bethof 1 ☎06398 993011
Terraced site at the 'Naturefreudhaus' (hostel belonging to Friends of Nature). Separate tent area for the young.
Camping Card Compulsory.
From Bad Bergzabern follow road B427 for 7km westwards, after Birkenhördt turn right, then 1.5km to site.
Apr-Oct 2HEC ▦ ⫶⫶⫶ ♥ ♠ 🗙 ⊙ 🚻 🚮 ☎ ⊞

WALDECK *Hessen*

Hohe Pappel ☎05634 484
The site, on some terraced individual pitches, lies on the northern shore of the Eder-Stausee (reservoir), on the Schied peninsula.
From Korbach follow road B251 to Sachsenhausen, then turn S via Nieder-Werbe to Halbinsel Scheid.
15 Mar-Oct 1HEC ▦ ♥ ♠ ⊙ 🚻 🚮 ⇥ L ☎ ⊞ ⊗ lau ➧ 🛒 🛒 🗙 ⇥L

WALD-MICHELBACH *Hessen*

Schöner-Odenwald ☎06207 2237
The site is split in two sections and lies partly on sloping ground, bordered by woodland. Lunchtime siesta 13.00-15.00 hrs.
From Beerfelden on road 45 turn W, then via Affolterbach to Wald-Michelbach. Alternatively, from Mörlenbach on road B38 turn SE to Wald-Michelbach. The turn off for the site lies in the village centre.
All year 2.5HEC 🔌 ♠ 🖫 ✕ ⊙ 🔊 ⌀ 🚙 ⊞ lau ➡ ⭢P

WARBURG *Nordrhein-Westfalen*

Eversburg ☎05641 8668
Site lies next to restaurant of the same name on the SE outskirts of the town.
All year 1.5HEC ▥ 🔌 ♠ 🖫 ♀ ✕ ⊙ 🔊 ⌀ ⊞ ⊞ lau ➡ 🚙 ⭢R Prices: A8 V3 ♨12 ▲6-12

WASSERFALL *Nordrhein-Westfalen*

Wasserfall Aurorastr 9 ☎02905 332
Terraced site, surrounded by woodland, next to leisure centre 'Fort Fun'. Little room for touring campers during the winter.
About 10km E of Meschedes, between Bestwig and Nuttlar, turn S off the B7. Driver past Gevelinghausen and up to Wasserfall.
All year 1HEC ▥ 🔌 ♠ 🖫 ✕ ⊙ 🔊 🚙 ▲ 🔥 🔊 🄿 ⊞

WAXWEILER *Rheinland-Pfalz*

AEGON-Ferienpark Im Prümtal ☎06554 427
Site lies on level terrain and is divided into pitches, with a separate field on the opposite side of the River Prüm. Near swimming pool. Lunchtime siesta between 13.00-15.00 hrs.
From N end of Waxweiler, turn off towards the River Prüm.
31 Mar-5 Nov 3HEC ▥ 🔌 ♠ 🖫 ⊙ 🔊 ⌀ 🚙 🔥 ⭢ P 🄿 ⊞ lau ➡ 🖫 ✕ ⭢P

WEHLEN *Rheinland-Pfalz*

Schenk Hauptstr 165 ☎06531 8176
A site in the Mosel valley, partly set on terraces. The site approach can be difficult for caravans due to the steep gradient.
From Bernkastel-Kues follow B53 for 4km NW towards 'Koblenz' reaching Wehlen turn right.
Etr-Oct 1HEC ▥ 🔌 ♠ 🔥 ⊙ 🔊 🔥 ⭢ PR 🄿 lau ➡ 🚙 ⌀ ⊞ Prices: A8 pitch 8

WEILBURG *Hessen*

At **ODERSBACH**

Odersbach Runkler Str 50 ☎06471 7620
In attractive setting beside the River Lahn, next to a public swimming pool. Lunchtime siesta 12.00-14.00 hrs.
On S outskirts of town.
Apr-Oct 5HEC 🔌 ♠ ✕ ⊙ 🔊 ⌀ 🔥 ⭢ PR 🄿 ⊞ lau ➡ 🚙 🖫 ✕ Prices: A5.50 V4 ♨4.50 ▲3

WINTERBERG *Nordrhein-Westfalen*

At **NIEDERSFELD**(8.5km N)

Vossmecke ☎02985 8418
All year 4.5HEC ♨ ⌇⭠ ♠ 🖫 ✕ ⊙ 🔊 ⌀ 🚙 🄿 lau ➡ ⊞ Prices: pitch 23-29.10 (incl 2 persons)

WISSEL *Nordrhein-Westfalen*

Wisseler See Am See 10 ☎02824 6613
Well-kept municipal site with modern equipment beside Lake Wissel. There is a separate car park next to the open-air swimming pool. The pool belongs to the camp. The washrooms are closed during lunchtimes and at night.
From Kieve, take the B57 towards Xanten. After about 9km, turn left and drive a further 3km towards Wissel.
All year 30HEC ▥ 🔌 ♠ 🔥 🖫 ✕ ⊙ 🔊 ⌀ 🚙 ⭢ L 🄿 ⊞ ⌇ lau Prices: A8 V2 ♨10 ▲10

WOLFSTEIN *Rheinland-Pfalz*

AZUR Camping Königsberg ☎06304 7543
Municipal site, beside small River Lauter next to open air swimming pool.
Site lies at S end of Wolfstein to the right of B270 from Kaiserslautern.
All year 1.4HEC ▥ 🔌 ♠ 🖫 ♀ ✕ ⊙ 🔊 ⌀ ⭢ R 🄿 lau ➡ 🚙 ⌀ ⭢P ⊞

ZERF *Rheinland-Pfalz*

Rübezahl ☎06587 814
Meadowland site in natural grounds on wooded hillside.
Leave Zerf S on B268 towards Saarbrücken then turn towards Oberzerf 2.5km to site from turning. From Saarburg, follow B407 beyond Vierherrenhorn, turn right and follow track for 60m.
All year 3HEC 🔌 ♠ ⊙ 🔊 ⌀ 🔥 ⭢ P 🄿 ⊞ lau ➡ 🚙 🖫 ✕ Prices: A6 pitch 7

ZWESTEN *Hessen*

Waldcamping Hinter dem Wasser ☎05626 379
Site in bend of River Schwalm. Lunchtime siesta 13.00-15.00 hrs. For touring campers there is also an overflow site outside the actual campsite.
Access from Kassel in SW direction via Fritzlar to Zwesten.
All year 3.2HEC ▥ ➡ ♠ 🖫 ✕ ⊙ 🔊 🚙 🔥 ⭢ PR 🄿 ⊞ lau ➡ 🚙 Prices: A5 pitch 7

North

The northern finger of Germany has the bracing North Sea to the west, with a landscape of dykes, green beaches and pretty offshore islands. The gentle Baltic is to the east, and its coast is one continuous succession of delightful resorts. Excellent natural harbours have been formed by "forden" cut deep into the land between the ridges of wooded hills. Inland, there are tranquil lakes, stately homes and nature reserves.
The north of Germany is a land of mountains and plains, of estuaries and inlets, of forests and heaths. Delightful undulating landscape is scattered with fascinating towns and cities; Hamburg, whose beautiful skyline is characterised by the towers of its principal churches; Bremen, with its many parks and gardens, its fairytale streets and passages, and its cosy atmosphere; Hannover, whose flower-filled Royal Gardens at Herrenhausen have been a major attraction since 1666.

ALTENAU *Niedersachsen*

Okertalsperre Kornhardtweg 1 ☎05328 702
On a long stretch of grassland at the S end of the Oker Reservoir. Lunchtime siesta 13.00-15.00 hrs.
Signposted from B498 (Oker-Altenau road).
All year 4HEC 🔌 🔌 ♠ 🖫 ✕ ⊙ 🔊 ⌀ 🚙 ▲ ⭢ L 🄿 ⊞ ⌇ lau Prices: A6 pitch 11

APEN-NORDLOH *Niedersachsen*

Nordloh Schanzenweg 4 ☎04499 2625
All year 8HEC ▥ ⌇⭠ ♠ ✕ ⊙ 🔊 ⌀ ⭢ L 🄿 ⊞ lau ➡ 🚙 🖫 ✕ Prices: A2 ♨14 ▲11

BASSUM *Niedersachsen*

At **GROSS-RINGMAR**

Gross-Ringmar Dorfstr 15 ☎04241 5292
On level meadow with trees. Situated approx. 200m from the edge of the village.

Turn off B51 approx. 3km SW of Bassum.
All year 10HEC ▦ ⊕ ᴿ ᴛ ✕ ⊙ ⊕ ₐ ↺ LP 🅿 ⊞ lau

BLECKEDE *Niedersachsen*

Alt-Garge (ADAC) Am Waldbad 23 ☎05854 311
A modern site surrounded by tall trees, lying at the SE end of Alt-Garge next to a heated swimming pool in the woods. The camp has its own gas-filling station. Archery butts. Lunchtime siesta 13.00-14.30 hrs.
5km SE of Bleckede.
All year 6HEC ▦ ∷ ⊕ ᴿ ᴛ ⊙ ⊕ ₐ 🅿 ⊞ lau ✕ ↺P Prices: pitch 24-27 (incl 2 persons)

BODENWERDER *Niedersachsen*

Himmelspforte Zigelerweg 1 ☎05533 4938
Site on grassland, with a fruit orchard, next to River Weser. Good possibilites for water sport. Separate section and common room for young campers.
Cross River Weser and turn right towards Rühle. Site is in about 2km.
All year 6HEC ▦ ⊕ ᴿ ᴛ ✕ ⊙ ⊕ ₐ ↺ R 🅿 ⊞ ↺P

Rühler Schweiz ☎05533 2827
This site lies on well-kept meadowland by the River Weser.
From the Weser Bridge in Bodenwerder and follow road for 4km towards Rühle.
All year 6HEC ▦ ⊁ ⊕ ᴿ ᴛ ✕ ⊙ ⊕ ₐ ↺ PR 🅿 ⊞ lau

BOTHEL *Niedersachsen*

Hanseat ☎04266 355
All year 4HEC ▦ ⊁ ⊕ ᴿ ᴛ ✕ ⊙ ⊕ ₐ ⊞ lau ✦ ↺P

BRAUNLAGE *Niedersachsen*

Ferien vom Ich ☎05520 413
Quiet site, partly on different levels, near woodland inn.
2km from town centre on B27 towards Lauterberg.
All year 5.5HEC ▦ ⊕ ᴿ ✕ ⊙ ⊕ ₐ ⊞ 🅿 ⊞ lau ✦ ↺P

At **ZORGE**(14km S)

Waldwinkel ☎05586 1048
A site on different levels, surrounded by high trees, 200m from an open-air woodland pool in Kunzen Valley.
All year 1.5HEC ▦ ♨ ⊕ ᴿ ᴛ ⊙ ⊕ ₐ ⊞ 🅿 ⊞ ✦ ✕ ↺P Prices: A7 pitch 9

BREMEN *Bremen*

Freie Hansestadt Bremen Am Stadtwaldsee 1 ☎0421 212002
Situated in a Nature Reserve 700m from lake.
Access from autobahn A27 exit University Bremen.
Mar-Oct 5.8HEC ▦ ⊕ ᴿ ᴛ ✕ ⊙ ⊕ ₐ ⊞ lau ✦ ↺LP Prices: A7.50 V2.50 ♥11 ▲7.50-11

BRIETLINGEN-REIHERSEE *Niedersachsen*

Reihersee 1 Alte Salzstr 8 ☎04133 3671 & 3577
Divided into pitches by hedges and pine trees. Private bathing area.
At car park, 2km beyond Brietlingen, turn E towards Reihersee and continue for 800m.
All year 6.2HEC ▦ ⊕ ᴿ ✕ ⊙ ⊕ ₐ ↺ LR 🅿 ⊞ ✦ ᴛ

BÜCHEN *Schleswig-Holstein*

Waldschwimmbad ☎04155 5360
On gently sloping grassland. Lunchtime siesta 13.00-15.00 hrs.
From Lauenburg or Mölln follow road to Büchen then follow signposts to site.
All year 1.6HEC ▦ ⊕ ᴿ ᴛ ✕ ⊙ ⊕ ₐ ⊞ ⊞ lau ✦ ᴛ ✕ ↺P Prices: A6 ♥10 ▲5

BURG (ISLAND OF FEHMARN) *Schleswig-Holstein*

At **KLAUSDORF**(5km NW)

Klausdorf ☎04371 2549
A grassy site with sea views. Divided into pitches. Sandy beach. Lunchtime siesta 12.30-14.30 hrs.
From Burg turn off the main road 2.5km before Klausdorf onto a narrow asphalt road.
15 Apr-15 Oct 12HEC ▦ ✦ ᴿ ᴛ ✕ ⊙ ⊕ ₐ ⊕ ᴛ S 🅿 ⊞ lau ✦ ↺L

BURGWEDEL *Niedersachsen*

Erholungsgebiet Springhorstsee ☎05139 3232
All year 25HEC ▦ ⊕ ᴿ ✕ ⊙ ⊕ ⊞ ⊕ ↺ LP 🅿 🅿 ⊞ lau ✦ ₐ Prices: A6 pitch 6

BUSUM *Schleswig-Holstein*

Nordsee Nordseestr 90 ☎04834 2515
Situated immediately behind the high dyke. The site is divided into two and surrounded by tall bushes. Lunchtime siesta 12.30-14.00 hrs.
Mar-Oct 3HEC ▦ ⊕ ᴿ ᴛ ✕ ⊙ ⊕ ₐ ⊞ ⊕ 🅿 ⊞ lau ✦ ↺PS Prices: A10 V11-12 ♥13

CLAUSTHAL-ZELLERFELD *Niedersachsen*

Prahljust ☎05323 1300
The site lies on slightly sloping grassland in an area of woodland and lakes.
Follow road B242 SE from outskirts 2km in direction of Braunlage, then turn right to site in 1.5km.
All year 13HEC ▦ ⊕ ᴿ ᴛ ✕ ⊙ ⊕ ₐ ↺ LP 🅿 lau Prices: A6.70-8 V3.50-4.10 ♥3.40-4.10 ▲3.50

Waldweben Spiegelthalerstr 31 ☎05323 81712
Holiday village with individual pitches in open meadow and coniferous woodland by three small lakes.
Signposted from B241 in direction of Goslar.
All year 4.5HEC ▦ ♨ ⊕ ᴿ ᴛ ✕ ⊙ ⊕ ₐ ⊞ 🅿 ✦ ↺LP ⊞ Prices: A5 V4 ♥4 ▲4

DAHRENHORST *Niedersachsen*

Irenensee ☎05173 98120
A lakeside site on meadowland, partly surrounded by woods, with separate section for tourers, statics and residentials. Lunchtime siesta 13.00-15.00 hrs.
From Burgdorf follow road B188 for about 15km towards Uetze.
All year 12HEC ▦ ⊕ ᴿ ✕ ⊙ ⊕ ₐ ⊞ ⊕ ᴛ L ⊞ ⊞ lau

DÄNSCHENDORF (ISLAND OF FEHMARN) *Schleswig-Holstein*

Fehmarnbelt ☎04372 445
The site lies at the north tip of the island.
Access via the B207/E47, turn left after the Fehmarnsund Bridge and drive through Landkirchen, Lemkendorf, Dänschendorf and Altenteil up to the dyke.
Apr-Sep 7.5HEC ▦ ⊁ ᴿ ᴛ ✕ ⊙ ⊕ ₐ ⊕ ᴛ S 🅿 ⊞ lau

DETERN *Niedersachsen*

Jümmesee ☎04957 1808
Access via B72 (Aurich-Cloppenburg).
Apr-Oct 18HEC ▦ ⊕ ᴿ ✕ ⊙ ⊕ ₐ ⊞ ᴛ LR 🅿 ⊞ lau ✦ ⊘ Prices: A8 ♥9

DORUM *Schleswig-Holstein*

AZUR-Camping Dorumer Tief ☎04741 5020
Access via A27 (Bremerhaven-Cuxhaven).
Apr-Sep 7HEC ▦ ⊁ ᴿ ᴛ ✕ ⊙ ⊕ ₐ ⊞ ᴛ PS 🅿 ⊞ lau Prices: A6-7 V3-4 ♥8-9 ▲3-4

DRANSFELD *Niedersachsen*

Hohen Hagen ☎05502 2147
Well laid out municipal site. Lunchtime siesta 13.00-15.00 hrs.
S of town off Hohen Hagen road.
All year 5HEC ▦ ⊁ ⊕ ᴿ ᴛ ᴛ ✕ ⊙ ⊕ ₐ ⊞ ⊕ ⊞ lau ✦ ↺P

EGESTORF *Niedersachsen*

AZUR-Camping Lüneburger Heide ☎04175 666
Modern site on wooded heathland on the edge of the Lüneburger Heath Nature Reserve 2km S of town on slightly sloping terrain with asphalt internal roads.
Access via Hamburg-Hannover motorway A7/E4 Egestorf or Evendorf exits.
All year 22HEC ∷ ⊕ ᴿ ᴛ ᴛ ✕ ⊙ ⊕ ₐ ⊞ ᴛ P 🅿 ⊞ lau Prices: A8-10 V3-4 pitch 11.60-13.60

EHLERSHAUSEN *Niedersachsen*

Waldsee Rotweg 3 ☎05085 7115
Apr-Oct 10HEC ▦ ⊕ ᴿ ⊙ ⊕ ₐ ᴛ L ⊞ lau ✦ ᴛ ✕

EIMKE *Niedersachsen*

Eimke Im Extertal ☎05262 3307
Extensive, partly terraced site on slightly sloping meadowland with two ponds.
Camping Card Compulsory.
From Dortmund-Hannover motorway (A2/E8) take 'Bad Eilsen' exit and follow B238 S. 1km beyond Rinteln, turn left and continue for 18km along External-Barntrup road.
All year 5HEC ▥ ⌧ ⧊ ⚐ ♀ ✗ ⊙ ⚑ ∅ ⋌ L ⊡ ⊞ lau Prices: A5 pitch 7-10

ELISABETH SOPHIENKOOG (ISLAND OF NORDSTRAND)
Schleswig-Holstein

Elisabeth-Sophienkoog ☎04842 8534
On meadowland behind the North Sea dyke. Lunchtime siesta 12.00-14.00 hrs.
Access via Husum to Island of Nordstrand.
Apr-Oct 1.7HEC ▥ ⤳ ⌧ ⚐ ♀ ✗ ⊙ ⚑ ∅ ⋌ S ⊡ ⊞ lau Prices: A6.50 V4 ⚘7.50 ▲5

ENGEHAUSEN *Niedersachsen*

AZUR-Camping Allertal Marschweg 1 ☎05071 912292
Useful as a transit site, lying only 500m from Autobahn A7/E4.
Situated on the Aller and surrounded by pine trees.
For access, leave autobahn A7 at service area Allertal and follow road towards Celle.
All year 8HEC ▥ ⌧ ⚐ ✗ ⊙ ⚑ ∅ ⋌ R ⊡ lau Prices: A7-9 V3-4 ⚘10-12 ▲3-4

ESENS-BENSERSIEL *Niedersachsen*

Bensersiel Kirchpl ☎04971 4906
Well-managed, extensive leisure centre with harbour, good fish restaurant and reading room. Swimming pools have sea water and artificial waves.
Take B210 NE from Aurich to Ogenbargenn then via Esens.
May-15 Sep 9HEC ▥ ⦂⦂⦂ ⤳ ⚐ ⛝ ♀ ✗ ⊙ ⚑ ☎ ⋌ S ⊡ ⊞ ⤫ lau ♦ ∅ ⩜ ⋌P

EUTIN-FISSAU *Schleswig-Holstein*

Prinzenholz Prinzenholzweg 20 ☎04521 5281
Terraced lakeside site divided by trees and bushes. Mobile shop.
N of town take Malente road and turn right after 2km.
Etr-Oct 2.2HEC ▥ ⚐ ⌧ ⚐ ⊙ ⚑ ∅ ⚘ ⋌ L ⊡ lau ♦ ✗ ⋌P ⊞
Prices: A8.50 V2.50 ⚘11 ▲10

FALSHÖFT *Schleswig-Holstein*

Seehof ☎04643 693
A partly sheltered site beside the Baltic Sea, near a lighthouse.
Leave B199 at Gelting and travel N for 5km.
Apr-Oct 2HEC ▥ ⤳ ⌧ ⚐ ⊙ ⚑ ⊡ ⊞ lau ♦ ✗ ⋌S

FEHMARN (ISLAND OF)

See **BURG, DÄNSCHENDORF, FEHMARNSUND, MEESCHENDORF, WULFEN**

FEHMARNSUND (ISLAND OF FEHMARN) *Schleswig-Holstein*

Miramar ☎04371 3220 & 2221
A family site on meadowland situated at the southern end of the island.
Turn off the B207/E4 at the first turning after the Sundbrücke (bridge) and drive towards Svendorf.
All year 13HEC ▥ ⚐ ⌧ ⚐ ♀ ✗ ⊙ ⚑ ∅ ⚘ ⋌ L ⊡ lau

GANDERSHEIM, BAD *Niedersachsen*

DCC Kur-Campingpark Braunschweiger Str 12 ☎05382 1595
On level meadow, divided in two by a brook beside a public park.
Good sporting facilities. Separate section for young people.
Access from Hannover-Kassel motorway via exit Soesen.
All year 9HEC ▥ ⚐ ⌧ ⚐ ⊙ ⚑ ⩜ ⊡ ⊞ lau ♦ ✗ ⋌P Prices: A7.50 pitch 12.50-16.50

GARTOW *Niedersachsen*

Gartow am See Springstr 14 ☎05846 2151
Situated in woodland with adjoining meadow.*Camping Card Compulsory*

NE on A493 from Lüchow.
All year 14HEC ▥ ⚐ ⌧ ⚐ ♀ ⊙ ⋌ P ⊡ lau ♦ ⩜ ⋌LR ⊞

GIFHORN *Niedersachsen*

At **RÖTGESBÜTTEL**(8km S)

Glockenheide ☎05304 1581
Tranquil site in heathland. Lunchtime siesta 13.00-15.00 hrs.
Camping Card Compulsory.
In Rötgesbüttel turn left, then turn left again after level crossing.
All year 5HEC ▥ ⚐ ⌧ ⚐ ♀ ✗ ⊙ ⚑ ⩜ ⊡ ⊞ ♦ ⩜

GLÜCKSBURG *Schleswig-Holstein*

AZUR-Camping Glücksburg Am Kurstrand Holnis ☎04631 622071
25 Mar-26 Oct 6HEC ▥ ⤳ ⌧ ⚐ ✗ ⊙ ⚑ ⩜ ⊡ ⊞ lau ♦ ⩜ Prices: A7-9 V3-4 ⚘10-12 ▲3-4

Schwennau Stoebe ☎04631 2670
A watercourse divides the site into two sections which are linked by a bridge.
In town centre make for Postplatz, then Hindenburgplatz, Collenburger Strasse. Schwennau-Strasse direct onto the site which lies adjacent to the Flensburger Förde.
All year 1HEC ▥ ⤳ ⚐ ✗ ⊙ ⚑ ⩜ ⋌ RS ⊡ lau ♦ ⩜ ♀ ⋌PS Prices: A6 pitch 6-10

GOSLAR *Niedersachsen*

Sennhütte Clausthastr 28 ☎05321 22498
In woodland adjacent to the Hotel Sennhütte.
3km S on B241 Clausthal-Zellerfeld road.
All year 3HEC ▥ ◊ ⚐ ⌧ ⚐ ✗ ⊙ ⚑ ⩜ ⊡ ⊞ lau ♦ ⋌LP

At **HAHNENKLEE**(13km S on road B241 at turn-off to Hahnenklee)

Kreuzeck Goslar 2 ☎05325 2570
In the forest beside a lake. Terraces and a separate section for dog-owners.
Beside Café am Kreuzeck at the junction of the B241 and the Hahnenklee road.
All year 5HEC ▥ ⦂⦂⦂ ◊ ⚐ ⌧ ⚐ ✗ ⊙ ⚑ ⩜ ☎ ⋌ LP ⊡ lau

At **WOLFSHAGEN**(11km W on unclass road off B82)

SC Krähenberg Langelsheim ☎05326 4088
Situated in a quiet valley.
S off the B82 between Langelsheim and Astfeld.
All year 6.5HEC ▥ ⚐ ⌧ ⚐ ✗ ⊙ ⚑ ⋌ P ⊡ ⊞

GRUBE *Schleswig-Holstein*

Rosenfelder Strand Textil Segeberger Str 17 ☎04365 412
Excellently managed family site beside the sea with a 1km long beach. Divided into separate fields by rows of bushes. Children's playground in woodland between site and sea. Strict observance of lunchtime siesta 13.00-15.00 hrs.
Take the B207/E4 from Lübeck and drive N to Lensahn, then E to Grube.
15 Apr-15 Oct 20HEC ▥ ⚐ ⌧ ⚐ ✗ ⊙ ⚑ ⩜ ⚘ ⋌ S ⊡ ⊞ ⤫ Prices: A6 pitch 16

HADDEBY *Schleswig-Holstein*

Haithabu ☎04621 32450
Clean, tidy site beside River Schlei.
From Schleswig follow B76 towards Eckernförde.
Mar-Oct 4.4HEC ▥ ⚐ ⌧ ⚐ ♀ ✗ ⊙ ⚑ ⩜ ⩜ ⚘ ⋌ LRS ⊡ ⊞ lau Prices: A6 V4 ⚘15 ▲11

HADEMSTORF *Niedersachsen*

Waldhaus Allertal ☎05071 1872
Apr-Sep 1.8HEC ▥ ♦ ⌧ ⚐ ♀ ✗ ⊙ ⚑ ⩜ ⊡ lau ♦ ⋌R

HAMBURG *Hamburg*

Anders Kieler Str 650 ☎040 5704498
Useful transit site on a level meadow.
All year 2HEC ▥ ⚐ ⌧ ⊙ ⚑ ⩜ ⚘ ⊡ lau ♦ ♀ ✗ ⋌P

HAMELN *Niedersachsen*
Waldbad Pfedeweg 2 ☎05158 2774
A grassy terraced site on the edge of woodland beside a public swimming pool.
Camping Card Compulsory.
Follow 'swimming pool' signs from Havelstorf.
Apr-Oct 2.8HEC ▦ ⌨ ⋔ ✗ ⊙ ◪ ⏃ ⊞ ▦ ▦ lau ➤ ⅏ ⚡P

HANNOVER *Niedersachsen*
At **GARBSEN**(10km W)
Blauer See ☎05137 8996-0
On a small lake beside the Garbsen service area on Hannover-Bielefeld motorway A2/E8.
All year 22HEC ▦ ⌨ ♦ ⋔ ⋎ ✗ ⊙ ◪ ⌀ ◪ ⚡ LR ⊞ ▦ lau ➤ ⚡P
Prices: A9-9.90 V3 ◪5-5.90 ▲3-3.90

At **ISERNHAGEN**(16km NE)
Parksee Lohne ☎05139 88260
Recreation area by a lake. On the flight approach path for Hannover Langenhagen airport. Separate section for tourers.
From motorway exit 'Kirchorst' follow Altwarmbüchen road to Isernhagen.
All year 16HEC ▦ ⌨ ⋔ ✗ ⊙ ◪ ⌀ ⚡ L ⊞ lau ➤ ⅏ ⚡ ▦ Prices: A7 pitch 13

HARDEGSEN *Niedersachsen*
Ferienpark Solling ☎05505 2272
Terraced site in forested area. Separate field for touring pitches.
Lunchtime siesta 13.00-15.00 hrs.
In town take 'Waldgebiet Gladeberg' road.
All year 2.7HEC ▦ ⌨ ⋔ ✗ ⊙ ◪ ⏃ ◪ ⊞ ⊞ lau ➤ ⅏ ✗ ⌀ ⚡P Prices: A6 V4 ◪4 ▲4

HARZBURG, BAD *Niedersachsen*
Wolfstein ☎05322 3585
Long, terraced site on edge of woodland.
500m from town on B6 towards Eckertal.
All year 20HEC ⋔ ⅏ ♀ ✗ ⊙ ◪ ⌀ ⏃ ⊞ ⊞ lau

At **ORSTEIL GOTTINGERODE**
Freizeit Oase Harz Camp Kreisshr 66 ☎05322 81215
On outskirts of village next to main road. Terraced site with separate touring field. Lunchtime siesta 13.00-15.00 hrs.
On the B6 between Bad Harzburg and Goslar.
All year 8HEC ▦ ⌨ ⋔ ✗ ⊙ ◪ ⌀ ⚡ P ⊞ ⊞ lau Prices: A7 pitch 9

HASELÜNNE *Niedersachsen*
Haseufer Andruper Str 1 ☎05961 1331
Beside the River Hase in an attractive area E of the town.
Camping Card Compulsory.
Signposted from Andrup.
Closed Nov-15 Dec 10HEC ▦ ♦ ⋔ ⅏ ♀ ✗ ⊙ ◪ ⌀ ⚡ L ⊞ ⊞ lau ➤ ⚡PRS

HATTEN *Niedersachsen*
Freizeitzentrum Hatten Kreyenweg 8 ☎04482 677
All year 4.5HEC ▦ ⌨ ⋔ ⅏ ✗ ⊙ ◪ ⌀ ⚡ P ⊞ ⊗ lau

HATTORF *Niedersachsen*
Oderbrücke ☎05521 4359
On the B27 towards Herzberg.
All year 2.5HEC ▦ ⌨ ⋔ ⅏ ✗ ⊙ ◪ ⌀ ⏃ ⚡ R ⊞ lau ➤ ⊞ Prices: A6 ◪8 ▲8

HEIKENDORF *Schleswig-Holstein*
Möltenort ☎0431 241316
Terraced site by the Kieler Förde. 15km NE of Kiel to W of road B502.
Approach to site is via a narrow, winding road.
Apr-Oct 2HEC ▦ ⋎ ⋔ ⅏ ⊙ ◪ ⏃ ⚡ S ⊞ ⊞ lau ➤ ⅏ ✗

HELMSTEDT *Niedersachsen*
Waldwinkel Maschweg 46 ☎05351 37161
In an orchard next to the Gasthaus Waldwinkel.
Signposted from autobahn exit 'Helmstedt'.
All year 10HEC ▦ ♦ ⋔ ⅏ ✗ ⊙ ◪ ◪ ⊞ ⊞ lau ➤ ⚡P

HEMELN *Niedersachsen*
Hemeln ☎05544 1414
Well-kept site on N outskirts of village, beside the River Weser.
From Autobahn A7 take the Gothenburg exit & follow B3 to Dransfeld then follow signposts.
All year 1.4HEC ▦ ⌨ ⋔ ✗ ⊙ ◪ ⏃ ◪ ◪ ⚡ R ⊞ ⊞ ➤ ⚡P Prices: A6 V3.50 ◪5.50 ▲4-10

At **REINHARDSHAGEN-VAAKE**(2km W)
Ahletal ☎05544 408
Well kept municipal site about 500m from River Weser, adjacent to a leisure centre with an indoor swimming pool. Lunchtime siesta 13.00-15.00 hrs.
From autobahn Kassel-Hannover leave at 'Hann-Münden' exit. Then follow B80 N along W bank of Weser to Reinhardshagen-Vaake then turn left.
All year 3.7HEC ▦ ♦ ⋔ ✗ ⊙ ◪ ⌀ ⏃ ⚡ P ⊞ lau ➤ ✗

HERMANNSBURG *Niedersachsen*
Örtzetal ☎05052 3072 & 1555
Site lies on meadows on the E bank of the River Örtze, set in unspoilt woodlands of the Lüneburg Heath. Boat landing stage. Lunchtime siesta 13.00-15.00 hrs.
From the B3 Celle-Soltau road turn off in Bergen and follow road NE towards Hermannsburg, then continue towards Eschwege.
15 Mar-Oct 4HEC ▦ ░░ ⌨ ⋔ ⅏ ✗ ⊙ ◪ ◪ ◪ ⚡ R ⊞ ⊞ lau ➤ ⅏ ♀ ⚡P

HOLLE *Niedersachsen*
At **DERNEBURG**(2km NW on unclass road)
Seecamp-Derneburg ☎05062 565
A terraced lakeside site on a hill slope with a southerly aspect.
Separate towing field. Useful transit site near autobahn.
From the motorway, leave at exit 'Derneburg' and continue to road B6.
Apr-15 Sep 7.8HEC ▦ ⌨ ⋔ ✗ ⊙ ◪ ⏃ ◪ ⚡ L ⊞ ⊞ lau ➤ ⚡R

KLEINWAABS *Schleswig-Holstein*
Ostsee Heide ☎04352 2530
Divided into pitches and pleasantly landscaped. Large games room for teenagers. Lunchtime siesta 13.00-14.30 hrs.
15 Mar-Oct 20HEC ▦ ⌨ ⋔ ⅏ ✗ ⊙ ◪ ⌀ ⏃ ◪ ◪ ⚡ P ⊞ ⊞ lau ➤ ⚡S

KLINT-BEI-HECHTHAUSEN *Niedersachsen*
Geesthof Geesthofer Weg 37 ☎04774 512
On dry meadowland next to the River Oste, in quiet setting with trees. Lunchtime siesta 13.00-15.00 hrs.
In Hechthausen leave road B73 and drive W towards 'Lamstedt' for about 3 km.
All year 10HEC ▦ ♦ ⋔ ⅏ ♀ ✗ ⊙ ◪ ⌀ ⏃ ◪ ◪ ⚡ PR ⊞ ⊞ lau ➤ ⅏ Prices: A5-8 ◪10-15 ▲8-9

LANGBALLIGAU *Schleswig-Holstein*
Langballigau ☎04636 308
Level grassland site between the Baltic road inland lake.
Leave B199 Flensburg to Kappeln road at Langballig and travel N for 3km.
Apr-Oct 5HEC ▦ ⋎ ⋔ ⅏ ♀ ✗ ⊙ ◪ ⌀ ⏃ ◪ ⊞ ⊞ lau ➤ ⚡S

LANGHOLZ ÜBER ECKERNFÖRDE *Schleswig-Holstein*
Langholz Fischerstr 9 ☎04352 2542
A holiday site surrounded by a belt of trees situated at a wide natural beach, at the mouth of the Eckernförde Bay.
Camping Card Compulsory.
From the Eckernförde take the B203 towards the NE to the turn off for Langholz, then right and continue 3km to site.
Apr-Sep 2HEC ▦ ⋎ ⋔ ⅏ ✗ ⊙ ◪ ◪ ◪ ⚡ S ⊞ ⊞ lau

LAUTERBERG, BAD *Niedersachsen*
Wiesenbeker Teich ☎05524 2510
In wooded surroundings on the Wiesenbeker Teich.
All year 5.2HEC ▦ ⋎ ⋔ ⅏ ✗ ⊙ ◪ ⏃ ⚡ LP ⊞ ⊞ ➤ ⅏ ⌀ Prices: A7.50 V2 ◪8 ▲8

LEER *Niedersachsen*

At **BINGUM MARINA**

Marina Bingum Marinastr ☎0491 64447
Camping Card Compulsory.
On B75, over Ems bridge, 200m W of river.
All year ▥ ⌾♠⌷⚑✕⊙♨⌀⍾↺R ☺⊞ lau

LOOSE *Schleswig-Holstein*

Gut Ludwigsburg ☎04358 1068
This partly wooded holiday site lies between an inland lake and the
sea. 100m long private beach. It is divided into pitches.
From Eckernförde, head towards Klein-Wabbs up to Gut
Ludwigsburg, then follow a dirt track for 2km.
Apr-Sep 10HEC ⌾♠⌷⚑✕⊙♨⌀⍾⌷↺L☺⊞ lau ♦↺S

LÜBECK *Schleswig-Holstein*

At **RATEKAU**(10km N)

Waldklause Badenstr ☎04504 3833
Divided by trees and shrubs. Noise from E4 (B207) partially
absorbed by wood and motel.
Access from Lübeck-Puttgarden motorway exit Ratekau.
Apr-Oct 10HEC ▥ ⌾♠⌷⊙♨☺⊞ lau ♦⚑✕

LÜNEBURG *Niedersachsen*

Rote Schleuse ☎04131 791500
In woodland clearing. Lunchtime siesta 13.00-15.00 hrs.
S of town off B4. Signposted.
Mar-Oct 2HEC ⌾♠⌷⚑✕⊙♨⌷☺⊞ lau ♦✕↺R Prices: A5
V4 ♨5.50 ▲3

LÜRSCHAU BEI SCHLESWIG *Schleswig-Holstein*

Lürschau am See ☎04621 41846
N of Schleswig off B76.
All year 1.5HEC ▥ ⌾♠⚑✕⊙♨☎↺LPS☺⊞ lau ♦⚑

MALENTE-GREMSMÜHLEN *Schleswig-Holstein*

Schwentine Wiesenweg 14 ☎04523 4327
A park-like setting with trees and bushes, at a river within the village
of Malente.
A17 18km NW of Eutin.
Apr-19 Oct 2.5HEC ▥ ⌾♠⌷⊙♨⌷↺R☺⊞❄ lau ♦⌀↺LP
Prices: A7.50 pitch 10-12

MEESCHENDORF (ISLAND OF FEHMARN) *Schleswig-Holstein*

Südstrand ☎04371 2189
Site stretches up to public footpath along the beach. Narrow, difficult
approach road.
From town, head towards Südstrand.
Apr-Sep 10HEC ▥ ↳♠✕⊙♨⌀⌷↺S☺⊞ lau

MELBECK *Niedersachsen*

Melbeck ☎04134 7311
Extensive site in woodland on the banks of the Ilmenau. Centre of
site free of trees and reserved for tourers.
On B4, 9km Lüneburg.
All year 20HEC ▥ ⌾♠✕⊙♨⌀↺R☺ lau Prices: A6 V6 ♨6 ▲6

MEPPEN *Niedersachsen*

Bleiche an der Bleiche ☎05931 16411
Level, grassy terrain between open air and indoor pool next to the
River Ems. Lunchtime siesta 13.00-15.00 hrs.
From Lingen N on road B70, alongside the Dortmund-Ems canal.
Apr-Sep 1.2HEC ▥ ⌾♠✕⊙♨↺P☺⊞ lau ♦⚑✕

MÜNDEN *Niedersachsen*

Zella Im Werratal Zella im Werratal ☎05541 31310
Beautiful site on left bank of the River Werra near motel and
restaurant of the same name.
7 km from town towards Laubach.
Apr-10 Sep 2HEC ▥ ↳♠✕⊙♨⌷☺⊞

NEUSTADT *Schleswig-Holstein*

Strande Pelzerhakenerstr ☎04561 4188
The site is divided into small sections and slopes down to the sea.
Narrow sandy beach.

Access from Neustadt towards Pelzerhaken, first site on the right
after leaving Neustadt.
Apr-Sep 4.5HEC ▥ ⌾♠⌷⚑✕⊙♨⌷⚑↺S☺⊞ lau ♦✕⌀
Prices: A7 pitch 10-14

Südstrand ☎04561 7238
Pleasant, well cared for site on grassland, sloping down a broad
stretch of sandy beach.
Access from Neustadt 2km towards Pelzerhaken, 3rd site on right.
Apr-Sep 10HEC ▥ ⌾♠⌷⊙♨⌀⌷↺S☺⊞❄ lau ♦⚑✕

NORDSTRAND (ISLAND OF)

See **ELISABETH SOPHIENKOOG**

NORTHEIM *Niedersachsen*

Sultmer Berg Sultmerberg 3 ☎05551 51559
Grassland site with views of surrounding hills. Lunchtime siesta
13.00-15.00 hrs.
Follow B3 from town centre.
All year 5HEC ▥ ⌾♠⌷⊙♨⌀⌷☺⊞ lau ♦⌀ Prices: A6.50-7
V4-6 ♨8-12 ▲4.50-6.50

OEHE-DRAECHT *Schleswig-Holstein*

Oehe-Draecht ☎04642 6124 & 6029
Grassy site, divided into pitches, on sandy ground behind a sea
dyke.
From Kappeln follow B199, turn towards Hasselberg and follow
signs 'Strand'.
Apr-Sep 6HEC ▥ ⌀⋯ ⌷↳♠⌷⚑✕⊙♨⌀⌷⚑☺⊞ lau ♦↺S
Prices: A5 pitch 12

OSNABRÜCK *Niedersachsen*

Niedersachsenhof Nordstr 109 ☎0541 77226
The site lies on a gently sloping meadow bordering a forest, near a
converted farmhouse with an inn.
On outskirts of town 5km from town centre NW on B51/65 towards
Bremen, turn right and continue 300m.
All year 3HEC ▥ ⌾♠⌷⊙♨⌀⌷☺⊞ lau ♦⚑ Prices: A6
pitch 11

OSTERODE *Niedersachsen*

Sösestausee ☎05522 3319
Terraced site on edge of woodland and by reservoir.
Follow road B498 from Osterode towards Altenau and after 3km turn
right to the site.
All year 4.5HEC ▥ ⌾♠⌷⊙♨⌀⌷↺LR☺⊞ lau ♦✕ Prices: A6
pitch 9

OTTERNDORF *Niedersachsen*

See Achtern Diek Deichstr 14 ☎04751 2933
Apr-Oct 1.3HEC ▥ ⌾♠⊙♨☺⊞ lau ♦⚑⚑⌀↺LPRS Prices:
A6 V3 ♨9 ▲4

PEINE *Niedersachsen*

At **HÄMELERWALD**(8km NW)

Waldsee ☎05175 05175
Near a woodland lake and a railway line. Lunchtime siesta 13.00-
15.00 hrs.
From motorway A2/E8 (Hannover-Braunschweig) leave at exit
'Hämelerwald' and follow road S.
All year 5HEC ▥ ⌀⋯♠⌷⚑✕⊙♨⌀⌷↺L☺⚑⊞ lau ♦⚑

PLÖN *Schleswig-Holstein*

Spitzenort Ascheberger Str 76 ☎04522 2769
A pleasantly situated site with hedges on the shore of Lake Plön.
Surrounded by the lake on three sides, it is ideal for water sports.
Access from Plön on B430 towards Neumünster.
Apr-15 Oct 4.5HEC ▥ ⌾♠⌷✕⊙♨⌀⌷↺L☺⊞ lau

PYRMONT, BAD *Niedersachsen*

Bad Pyrmont Im Schellental 1-3 ☎05281 8772
Site partially flat grassland, partially terraced with large building in
the middle. Some tall trees, many bushes and flowers.
E from town centre to Dak-Kurcenter, then turn left towards
Friedensthal.
All year 5HEC ▥ ⌾♠⌷⚑✕⊙♨⌀⌷☺⊞ lau ♦↺P

At **LÜDGE-ELBRINXEN**(3km S)

Eichwald Obere Dorfstr 80 ☎05283 335
Pleasantly situated grassy site near woodland and pool.
S of Lüdge in direction of Rischenau to Elbrinxen.
All year 8HEC ▦ ⌖ ⌂ ⚑ ♨ ✕ ⊙ ⚑ ⌀ ᴀ ☎ ⊞ lau ➧ ⤴P

RINTELN Niedersachsen

Doktor-See Hartler Str 6/7 ☎05751 2611
In a beautiful situation by a recreation area and beside the Doktor
See bathing beach. Section for touring campers. Lunchtime siesta
13.00-15.00 hrs.
In town turn down stream at the River Weser bridge and continue
along the left bank for 1.5km.
All year 152HEC ▦ ➧ ⌂ ⚑ ♨ ✕ ⊙ ⚑ ⌀ ᴀ ☎ ⤴ L ☎ ⊞ lau Prices:
A9 pitch 8

ST ANDREASBERG Niedersachsen

Erikabrücke ☎05582 1431
Open site next to B27 NE of Oderstausee. Off B27 from Bad
Lauterberg towards Braunlage.
All year 8.5HEC ▦ ⠿ ♨ ⌂ ⚑ ♨ ✕ ⊙ ⚑ ⌀ ᴀ ⤴ L ☎ lau
Prices: A7 V3 ♻7 ▲7

SALZHEMMENDORF Niedersachsen

Ferienland Humboldtsee ☎05186 348
Extensive, partially terraced site with lake suitable for bathing.
Separate touring field. Lunchtime siesta 13.00-15.00 hrs.
Camping Card Compulsory.
Access from Hameln on B1 to Hemmendorf. Turn right via
Salzhemmendorf to Thüste. Then right again to Wellensen.
May-Sep 15HEC ⌂ ⌂ ⚑ ✕ ⊙ ⚑ ᴀ ⤴ L ☎ ⊞ lau ➧ ⤴P

SCHOBÜLL Schleswig-Holstein

Seeblick ☎04841 3321
Beautifully situated beside the sea and divided into two sections.
Turn off the B5 on the northern outskirts of Husum, and drive
towards Insel Nordstrand for 4km up to Schobüll.
Apr-15 Oct 3.4HEC ▦ ➧ ⌂ ⚑ ✕ ⊙ ⚑ ⌀ ⚑ ☎ ⊞ lau ➧ ⚑ ▼ ✕ ⤴P

SCHÖNBERG Schleswig-Holstein

At **KALIFORNIEN**(5km N)

California Deichweg 46-47 ☎04344 9591
Family site behind the dyke, divided by numerous hedges.
Access through Schönberg, follow road to Kalifornien, then left at the
dyke. Turn left and continue by rough track for 800m to site.
Apr-Sep 8HEC ▦ ⌂ ⌂ ⚑ ▼ ✕ ⊙ ⚑ ᴀ ⚑ ⤴ S ☎ ⊞ ⚒ Prices:
A5.50-7 pitch 11-18

SOLTAU Niedersachsen

Scandinavia-Paradies ☎05191 2293
Heathland site in pine forest. Useful transit site 1km from motorway
(from which there is some noise). Separate section for young
campers. Lunchtime siesta 13.00-15.00 hrs.
Access from the Soltau Ost (East) motorway exit then 1km on the
B209/71 towards Lüneberg.
All year 24HEC ▦ ⠿ ⌂ ⌂ ⚑ ✕ ⊙ ⚑ ⌀ ⤴ LP ☎ ⚑ Prices: A4-6
pitch 11-26

STELLE Niedersachsen

Steller See Zum Steller See 15 ☎04206 6490
Delmenhorst-Ost eixt off motorway. Site 300m.
Apr-Sep 15HEC ▦ ⌂ ⚑ ▼ ✕ ⊙ ⚑ ᴀ ⚑ ⤴ LP ☎ ⊞ lau Prices:
A7 V2 ♻6 ▲6

SUDERBURG Niedersachsen

At **HÖSSERINGEN**(5km SW)

Hardausee ☎05826 7676
Grassland site without firm internal roads. Statics have individual
pitches and outbuildings. Separate fields for tourers.
Approach from Uelzen S on B4. In 9km turn right, continue via
Suderburg to site on the right just before Hösseringen.
All year 10HEC ▦ ➧ ⌂ ⚑ ✕ ⊙ ⚑ ᴀ ☎ lau ➧ ⤴L

SÜSSAU Schleswig-Holstein

Minigolf ☎04365 284
The site lies on bushy meadowland behind a dyke next to the
Süssauer beach.
Access from Neustadt N to Lensahn, then E to Goube, and then to
Süssau. From there, follow the signposts to the site, 1km away.
Apr-Sep 3HEC ▦ ➧ ⌂ ⚑ ♨ ᴀ ⤴ S ☎ ⊞ lau ➧ ⚑ ▼ ✕ ⌀

TARMSTEDT Niedersachsen

Rethbergsee ☎04283 422
Level site on a grand scale. Lunchtime siesta 13.00-15.00 hrs.
About halfway between Bremen-Lilienthal and Zeven.
All year 15HEC ▦ ⌂ ⌂ ⚑ ▼ ✕ ⊙ ⚑ ⌀ ᴀ ⤴ L ☎ ⊞ Prices: A7 pitch 7

TELLINGSTEDT Schleswig-Holstein

Tellingstedt Teichstr ☎04838 657
Divided by a row of high shrubs.
Off B203 towards the swimming pool.
May-15 Sep 1.2HEC ⌂ ⌂ ⚑ ✕ ⊙ ⚑ ⤴ P ☎ ⊞ lau ➧ ⚑ ▼ ✕

TINNUM (ISLAND OF SYLT) Schleswig-Holstein

Südhörn ☎04651 3607
Well-kept site divided into pitches.
Well signposted from railway unloading ramp. No road connections
between the island and the mainland-rail from Niebüll to Westerland.
All year 2HEC ▦ ⠿ ⌂ ✕ ⊙ ⚑ ᴀ ⚑ ⚑ ➧ ▼ ✕ ⌀ ⤴PS ⊞
Prices: A8 V3 ♻15-20 ▲10-20

TÖNNING Schleswig-Holstein

Lilienhof Katinger Landstr 5 ☎04861 439
Well-maintained site in the woodland grounds of an old manor house
next to a quiet country road.
Leave B202 at far end of Tönning, then 2km W towards Welt.
All year 2HEC ▦ ⌂ ⚑ ▼ ✕ ⊙ ⚑ ⚑ ⚑ ☎ ⊞ lau ➧ ⚑ ⌀ Prices: A7
V3 ♻11 ▲7-9

USLAR Niedersachsen

At **DELLIEHAUSEN SOLLING**(8km NE)

Bergsee Bergseestr 1 ☎05573 1217
Well-kept site on meadow beside lake, in Solling nature reserve.
Separate section for young campers. Lunchtime siesta 13.00-15.00
hrs. Mobile shop.
Access from motorway exit Nörten-Hardenberg, take the B446 and
then the B421 via Hardegsen to Volpriehausen, then right to
Delliehausen (2.5km).
All year 1HEC ▦ ⌂ ⊙ ⚑ ⌀ ᴀ ⤴ LP ⚑ ⊞ lau ➧ ⚑ ▼ ✕

WALKENRIED Niedersachsen

AZUR-Knaus Ellricher Str 7 ☎05525 778
All year 6HEC ▦ ⌂ ⚑ ✕ ⊙ ⚑ ⌀ ⤴ P ☎ ⊞ ⚒ lau ➧ ⤴P

WEENER Niedersachsen

Weener Am Erholungsgebiet 4 ☎04951 1740
A municpal site, pleasantly landscaped and set inside a leisure
centre with swimming pool and harbour. Lunchtime siesta 13.00-
15.00 hrs.
From the main road B75 (E35) from Leer towards the Dutch frontier
and turn off in the centre of Weener and follow signs to site.
Apr-Oct 3.2HEC ⌂ ⌂ ⊙ ⚑ ᴀ ⤴ P ☎ ⊞ lau ➧ ⚑ ▼ ✕ ⌀ Prices:
A4.50-6 ♻6-7.50 ▲3-4

WIETZENDORF Niedersachsen

Südsee Soltau-Süd ☎05196 98016
This site is beautifully situated in a forest beside lake.
Leave the Hannover-Hamburg motorway at the Soltau-Süd exit, and
take the B3 for 2km towards Bergen. At the underpass in Bokel, turn
left and drive on for approx 4km towards Wietzendorf.
All year 53HEC ▦ ⌂ ⌂ ⚑ ▼ ✕ ⊙ ⚑ ⌀ ᴀ ⚑ ⚑ ⤴ LP ☎ ⊞ lau
Prices: pitch 27-49.50 (incl 2 persons)

WILSUM Niedersachsen

AZUR-Ferienpark Wilsumer Berge ☎05945 1029
Parts of the site adjoin a large lake. The separate section for touring
campers has its own sanitary building.
From Nordhorn follow road B403 via Uelsen to Wilsum. On nearside

of Wilsum turn right.
All year 88HEC ▬ ⁚⁚⁚ ⋺ ℾ ㏑ ♥ × ⊙ ▨ ∅ ㅂ ♘ ⋋ L ⊞ ⊞ lau
Prices: A8-10 V3-4 ♛11-13 ▲3-4

WINGST *Niedersachsen*

AZUR-Knaus Camping-Park Wingst ☎04778 7044

This modern comfortable site extends over several terraces, above a
small artificial lake on the northern edge of an extensive forested
area. Lunchtime siesta 13.00-15.00 hrs. Municipal recreation centre
across the road.
Turn off the B73 between Stade and Cuxhaven, about 3km S of
Cadenberge.
All year ▬ ⋺ ℾ ㏑ ♥ × ⊙ ▨ ∅ ㅂ ♘ ⋋ P ⊞ ⊞ lau

WINSEN-ALLER *Niedersachsen*

AZUR Camping auf der Hude ☎05143 2444

Site lies on meadowland at the River Aller. Watersports available.
Lunchtime siesta 13.00-15.00 hrs.
From Celle go NW to Winsen.
All year 12HEC ⋺ ℾ ㏑ ♥ × ⊙ ▨ ∅ ⋋ R ⊞ ⊞ lau ♦ ⋋P

WITTENBORN *Schleswig-Holstein*

Weisser Brunnen ☎04554 1757 & 1413

A lakeside site consisting of several sections, hilly in parts, next to
Lake Mözen. A public road, leading to the lake, passes through part
of the site.
Turn off B206 at Km23.6 towards lake.
Apr-Oct 7.5HEC ▬ ⋺ ℾ ㏑ ♥ × ⊙ ▨ ∅ ⋋ L ⊞ ⊞ lau Prices:
A7 pitch 12

WITZENHAUSEN *Niedersachsen*

Werratal Am Sande 11 ☎05542 1465

The site lies on meadow between the outskirts of Witzenhausen and
the banks of the Werra.

For access, leave Hannover-Kassel motorway at Werratal. 10km on
B80 to Witzenhausen. From market place follow signs.
All year 2.5HEC ▬ ♦ ℾ ㏑ ♥ ⊙ ▨ ∅ ㅂ ♘ ♘ ⋋ R ⊞ ⊞ lau ♦ × ⋋P
Prices: A6 pitch 6-8

WOLTERDINGEN *Niedersachsen*

Auf dem Simpel ☎05191 3651

The site lies in the Lüneberg Heath area in a very quiet setting of the
main road. Densely wooded terrain. Separate section for touring
campers. Lunchtime siesta 13.00-15.00 hrs.
From Soltau head N on the B3 for about 4km towards 'Hamburg'. At
the junction for Wolterdingen turn right and continue towards
'Harber'. Approach road is signposted.
All year 4HEC ⁚⁚⁚ ℾ ㏑ ♥ × ⊙ ▨ ㅂ ⋋ P ⊞ ⊞ lau ♦ ×

WULFEN (ISLAND OF FEHMARN) *Schleswig-Holstein*

Wulfener Hals ☎04371 8628-0

Meadowland site beside the Baltic Sea and an inland lake (Burger
Binnensee). 1700m long private beach.
Turn off B20/E4 (Vogelfluglinie) after the 'Sundbrücke' and follow
roads towards 'Avendorf', then 'Wulfen' and 'Wulfener Hals'.
All year 34HEC ⋺ ℾ ㏑ ♥ × ⊙ ▨ ∅ ㅂ ♘ ♘ ⋋ S ⊞ ⊞ lau Prices:
A6.60-9.80 pitch 13-29

ZEVEN *Niedersachsen*

Sonnenkamp Zeven ☎04281 2876

The site lies mainly on open terrain, on the outskirts of town,
opposite the swimming pool. For touring campers there is an open
meadow near the entrance. Lunchtime siesta 13.00-15.00 hrs.
From Zeven town centre follow road for 'Friebad' (swimming pool).
May-Sep 8HEC ▬ ℾ ㏑ × ⊙ ▨ ㅂ ⊞ ⊞ lau ♦ ⋋P

ITALY

Italy, with its many beautiful cities and rich architectural heritage, is bordered by four countries: from west to east, France, Switzerland, Austria and Slovenia.

The approaches are all dominated by mountains. The lakes of the north present a striking contrast with the sun-parched lands of the south and there is some beautiful countryside in the central Appenines. There are fine, sandy beaches on both the Tyrrhenian and Adriatic coasts.

The north has a typically Continental climate whilst the south has a temperate Mediterranean climate with extremely hot summers. The language is Italian, a direct development of Latin. There are several dialect forms such as Sicilian and Sardinian, but the accepted standard derives from the vernacular spoken in Florence 700 years ago. German is spoken, to a small extent, near the Austrian frontier.

The International Reservation Centre in Calenzano (near Florence) *Federcampeggio* provides a campsite information and reservation service ☎(055) 882391.

The *Assessorati Regionali per il Turismo* (ART) and the *Ente Provinciale per il Turismo* (EPT) have regional and provincial information offices and can provide details of campsites within their locality. In northern Italy, especially by the lakes and along the Adriatic coast, sites tend to become very crowded and it is advisable to book in advance during the season which extends from May to the end of August.

Off-site camping is permitted provided the landowner's permission has been obtained, but is strictly prohibited in State forests and national parks. In built-up areas, if parking is allowed, the towing vehicle must remain connected to the trailer or caravan and the corner steadies must not be used.

FACTS AND FIGURES

Capital: Roma (Rome)
Language: Italian
IDD code: 39. To call the UK dial 00 44
Currency: Italian lira (*Lit*). At the time of going to press 1 = *Lit*2,550.
Local time: GMT + 1 (summer GMT + 2)
Emergency Services: Police and Ambulance 113, Fire 115 (Carabinieri 112)
Business hours-
Banks: Mon-Fri 08.30-13.30 and 15.30-16.30
Shops: Mon-Sat 08.30-13.30 and 15.30-19.30

Average daily temperatures:
Roma

Jan 8°C	Jul 25°C
Mar 11°C	Sep 21°C
May 18°C	Nov 12°C

Tourist Information: Italian State Tourist Office (ENIT)
UK 1 Princes Street London W1R 8AY
☎ 0171-408 1254
USA 630 Fifth Avenue, Suite 1545 New York, NY 10111
☎(212) 245 4822
Camping card: Not generally compulsory, but required on some sites. Reductions available.

HOW TO GET THERE

Although there are several ways of getting to Italy, entry will most probably be by way of France and Switzerland. Some passes, which are closed in winter, are served by road or rail-tunnels (please consult the Contents Page). For details of the *AA European Routes Service* please consult the Contents Page.

Distance

From the Channel ports Milano (Milan) is about 1100km (684 miles) requiring one or two overnight stops. Roma (Rome) is about 580km (360 miles) further south.

Car-sleeper services operate during the summer from Calais, 's-Hertogenbosch or Paris to Milano; Calais to Bologna; and Paris to Rimini.

MOTORING & GENERAL INFORMATION

The information given here is specific to Italy. It **must** be read in conjunction with the European ABC at the front of the book, which covers those regulations which are common to many countries.

Boats*

Third party insurance is compulsory in Italian waters for motorboats; an Italian translation of the insurance certificate must be carried.

British Embassy/Consulates*

The British Embassy together with its consular section is located at 00187 Roma, Via XX Settembre 80A ☎(06) 4825441 and 4825551. There are British Consulates in Firenze (Florence), Genova (Genoa), Milano (Milan), and Napoli (Naples); there are British Consulates with honorary Consuls in Bari, Brindisi, Cagliari, Genova (Genoa), Messina, Palermo, Trieste, Torino (Turin) and Venezia (Venice)..

Children in cars*

Child under 4 not permitted to travel as front or rear seat passenger unless using suitable restraint system. Child between 4 and 12 travelling in front seat must use suitable restraint system.

Currency

A visitor may *import* and *export* Italian and foreign currency up to *Lit* 20,000,000 without formality. However, if you wish to export any amount in excess of this it must have been declared on arrival on Form V2 within the preceding 6 months. This form is then shown to the Customs when leaving Italy.

Dimensions and weight restrictions

Private *cars* and towed *trailers* or *caravans* are restricted to the following dimensions - car height, 4 metres: width, 2.50 metres: length (including tow-bar), with one axle 6 metres, with two or more axles,12 metres. Caravan/trailer height, must not exceed 1.8 times the distance between the wheels of the vehicle; width 2.30 metres; length (including tow-bar) with one axle 6.50 metres, with two axles 8 metres. The maximum permitted overall length of vehicle/trailer or caravan combination is 18.75 metres.

Trailers with an unladen weight of over 750kg or 50% of the weight of the towing vehicle must have service brakes on all wheels.

Driving Licence*

A valid UK or Republic of Ireland EC model licence is acceptable in Italy. The minimum age at which visitors from UK or Republic of Ireland may use a temporarily imported car is 18 years. The minimum age for using a temporarily imported motorcycle of up to 125cc, not transporting a passenger, is 16 years; to carry a passenger, or use a motorcycle over 125cc, the minimum age is 18 years.

Note The Italian translation or 'Declaration', formerly issued to accompany older all-green UK licences (in Northern Ireland any licence issued before 1 April 1991) is no longer valid. If time allows, they should be changed for a new format licence. Alternatively, an International Driving Permit to accompany the older licence should be obtained.

Fiscal receipt

In Italy, the law provides for a special numbered fiscal receipt (*ricevuta fiscale*) to be issued after paying for a wide range of goods and services including meals and accommodation. This receipt indicates the cost of the various goods and services obtained, and the total charge after adding VAT. Tourists should ensure that this receipt is issued, as spot checks are made by the authorities, and both the proprietor and consumer are liable to an on-the-spot fine if the receipt cannot be produced.

Foodstuffs*

There are no limits on the importation of foodstuffs obtained duty and tax paid within the EC. Up to 500g of coffee (200g of coffee extract) and 100g of tea (40g of tea extract) purchased duty-free or outside the EC may be imported free of duty and tax. However, coffee bought duty-free or outside the EC cannot be imported by visitors under 15 years of age.

Lights*

Full-beam headlights can be used only outside cities and towns. Dipped headlights are compulsory when passing through tunnels, even if they are well-lit. The

Italian authorities recommend that visiting motorists equip their vehicles with a spare set of vehicle bulbs.

Motoring clubs*

There are two motoring organisations in Italy. The **Touring Club Italiano** (TCI) which has its head office at 20122 Milano, 10 Corso Italia ☎(02) 85261 and the **Automobile Club d'Italia** (ACI) whose head office is at 00185 Roma, 8 Via Marsala ☎(06) 4477. Both clubs have branch offices in most leading cities and towns.

Roads

Main and secondary roads are generally good, and there are an exceptional number of by-passes. Mountain roads are usually well engineered; for details of mountain passes consult the contents page.

Italy has some 4,000 miles of motorway (*autostrada*) with tolls payable on most sections. Emergency telephones are located every 2km on most motorways; there are two call buttons one for technical assistance and one for Red Cross services.

Speed limits*

The speed limit in *built-up areas* is 50kph (31mph); *outside built-up areas* the speed limit is 90kph (55mph) on ordinary roads, 110kph (68mph) on main roads and 130kph (80mph) on motorways. Motorcycles under 150cc are not allowed on motorways.

For cars towing a caravan or trailer the speed limits are 70kph (43mph) outside built-up areas and 80kph (49mph) on motorways.

Warning triangle*

The use of a warning triangle is compulsory in the event of accident or breakdown. It should be used to give advance warning of any stationary vehicle which is parked on a road in fog, near a bend or on a hill at night when the rear lights have failed. The triangle must be placed on the road not less than 50 metres (55yds) behind the vehicle. Motorists who fail to do this are liable to an administrative fine of between *Lit* 25,000 and 100,000.

*Additional information will be found in the Continental ABC at the front of the book.

A-Z DIRECTORY

Prices are in Italian Lire Abbreviations: pza piazza.
Each placename preceded by 'Lido', 'Lido di', 'Marina' or 'Marina di' is listed under the name that follows it.

North West/Alps & Lakes

The Gran Paradiso mountains on the French border, and the Matterhorn and Monte Rosa to the north on the Swiss border, give a dramatic glacier-topped backdrop to the steep-sided valleys and the distinctively Italian Lakes, below where decorated villas and medieval castles border the lakes, and palm trees and magnolias grow. The mountains provide winter skiing, and walking in the summer, and wood and stone chalets contribute to the Alpine landscape. On the lakes, boats take you from harbour to harbour, yet within an hour you can be in Lombardy's capital, Milan. Turin, to the west, is an elegant town with its Piazza San Carlo and many cafés. Nearby, in the Alba region, the vineyards produce the distinguished Barolo red wine and sparkling Asti Spumante.
To the north and eastwards in the Dolomites, roads are good in the summer and the scenery is dramatic with fortresses dominating high peaks. Through wooded countryside is the border town of Bolzano where you will hear German spoken (this was once the South Tyrol) and may be served sausage and sauerkraut and locally produced Reisling wine.

ANFO Brescia
Palafitte via Calcaterra ☎0365 809051
Pleasant site divided into plots, sloping towards the lake where there are some trees.
Access as for Pilù, then turn right.
22 Apr-18 Sep 2HEC ▦ ♦♠♋⛱▾✕⊙◨◍◫▱⛰ ⅃LP ⓢ lau ♦✕▱
⊞ Prices: A6000-7500 ⌑9000-13500

Pilù via Venturi 4 ☎0365 809037
Well-maintained, slightly sloping site subdivided by trees and rows of shrubs on pebble beach from which it is separated by narrow public footpath.
On southern outskirts; well signed.
Nov 20HEC ▦ ♦♠♋⛱▾✕⊙◨◍◫▱⛰ ⅃LPR ⓢ⊞ lau ♦✕
Prices: A4500-8000 pitch 7500-140000

ANGERA Varese
Città di Angera via Bruschera 99 ☎0331 930736
Signposted
2 Feb-Dec 8HEC ▦ ♦♠♋⛱▾✕⊙◨◍◫▱⛰ ⅃LP ⓢ⊞ lau Prices:
A8000-11000 pitch 14000-17000

ARONA Novara
At **DORMELLETTO**(5km S)
Lago Azzurro via E-Fermi 2 ☎0322 497197
A lakeside site in beautiful surroundings with fine sporting facilities.
S of Arona off SS Sempione 33.
All year 2.5HEC ▦ ░∴ ♦♠♋⛱▾✕⊙◨◍▱⛰ ⅃LP ⓢ⊞✾ lau
Prices: A7000 pitch 10500

Lago Maggiore via L-da-Vinci 7 ☎0322 497193
Well-maintained site divided into plots, pleasantly landscaped by the lakeside.
Access from SS33, well signposted.
Apr-Sep 5HEC ▦ ♦♠♋⛱▾✕⊙◨◍◫▱⛰ ⅃P ⓢ⊞ lau ♦⅃L
Prices: A7000-9000 pitch 10000-14000

Lido Holiday Inn via M-Polo 1 ☎039 497047
Site on bank of the lake, with some trees.
Turn off the SS33 at Km60/VII and the IP petrol station.
Apr-Sep 3.5HEC ▦ ⓐ♠♋⛱▾✕⊙◨◍◫▱⛰ ⅃LP ⓢ lau Prices:
A8000-9000 pitch 11000-13500

Smeraldo via Cavour 103 ☎0322 497031
Well-landscaped site, divided into plots and situated in woodland by lakeside.
Access from SS33.
Mar-Oct 24HEC ▦ ♦♠♋⛱▾✕⊙◨◍◫▱⛰ ⅃L ⓢ⊞ lau Prices:
A7500-8600 pitch 12700-14500

ARVIER Aosta
Arvier via St Antoine 6 ☎0165 99088
20 Jun-Aug 1HEC ▦ ⓐ♠♋⊙◨◫▱⅃P ⓢ♦▾✕◍⊞ Prices: A7700
V4200 ⌑6500 ▲6500

ASTI Asti
Umberto Cagni strada Valmanera 152 ☎0141 271238
Apr-Sep 13HEC ▦ ♦♠♋⛱▾✕⊙◨◍▱⛰◍⊞

BASTIA MONDOVI Cuneo
Cascina via Pieve 27 ☎0174 60181
Closed Sep 4HEC ▦ ⓐ♠♋⛱▾✕⊙◨◍◫▱⅃PR ▣ lau ♦✕

BAVENO Novara
Lido Bruno via Piase 66 ☎0323 924775
Etr-Oct 1.5HEC ▦ ⓐ♠♋⛱▾✕⊙◨◍◫▱⛰ ⅃L ⓢ⊞ lau ♦⅃P

BELLAGIO Como
Azienda Agricola Clarke via Valassina 170/c ☎031 951325
A small, secluded site situated on a horsebreeding farm on the shores of Lake Bellagio.

international camping

22100 como (Italia)
tel. (031) 52.14.35 (summer)
tel. (02) 89513430 (winter)
Quiet position • Swimming pool • Pizzeria • Bar • Self
Service • Showers, warm and cold water • Bungalow •
5 minutes from the City • Nearest the Motor-Highway
Milan • Como • Chiasso

Apr-Oct 0.5HEC ⬛ ⬛⬛⬛⬛⬛⬛⬛⬛⬛⬛⬛⬛⬛⬛⬛⬛ Prices: pitch
12000 (incl 2 persons)

BOLZANO-BOZEN *Bolzano*
Moosbauer Moritzingerweg 83 ☎0471 918492
All year 1HEC ⬛ ⬛⬛⬛⬛⬛⬛⬛⬛⬛⬛⬛⬛⬛ P ⬛ lau ✦ ⬛ Prices:
A7500-9000 pitch 15000-18000

BRESCIA *Como*
International via Cecilio ☎031 521435
On a level meadow near the motorway. Lunchtime siesta 13.00-
15.30 hrs.
Off A9 Como-Milan motorway.
15 Apr-15 Oct 1.8HEC ⬛ ✦⬛⬛⬛⬛⬛⬛⬛⬛⬛⬛⬛⬛⬛⬛ P ⬛⬛ lau

BRESSANONE-BRIXEN *Bolzano*
Löwenhof Brennsrstr 60 ☎0472 836216
25 Dec-30 Oct 0.5HEC ⬛ ✦⬛⬛⬛⬛⬛⬛⬛⬛⬛⬛⬛ PR ⬛⬛ lau
Prices: A9000-11500 pitch 8000-15000

BUISSON *Aosta*
Cervino ☎0166 545111
All year 6HEC ⬛ ⬛⬛⬛⬛⬛⬛⬛⬛⬛⬛⬛ R lau ✦ ⬛ Prices:
A6200-8800 V3600-4800 ✿6000-8000 ▲6000-8000

CALCERANICA *Trento*
Al Pescatore ☎0461 723062
The site consists of several sections of meadowland, inland from the
lake shore road to Lago di Caldonazzo. Well maintained with private
beach.
Jun-15 Sep 3.8HEC ⬛ ⬛⬛⬛⬛⬛⬛⬛⬛⬛⬛ L ⬛ lau

Fleiola via Trento 20 ☎0461 723153
Site is divided into sectors beside lake.
Apr-7 Oct 12HEC ⬛ ✦⬛⬛⬛⬛⬛⬛⬛⬛⬛⬛⬛⬛ L ⬛ lau ✦⬛⬛ ⬛
⬛ Prices: A4500-9000 pitch 6000-12000

Riviera viale Venezia 10 ☎0461 724464
All year 1.5HEC ⬛ ✦⬛⬛⬛⬛⬛⬛⬛⬛ L ⬛ lau ✦ ⬛ Prices: A6500-
8000 pitch 8900-11500

CALDONAZZO *Trento*
Mario via Lungolago 4 ☎0461 723341
May-Sep ⬛ ✦⬛⬛⬛⬛⬛⬛⬛⬛⬛⬛⬛ L ⬛⬛⬛ lau

CAMPITELLO DI FASSA *Trento*
Miravalle via Camping 13 ☎0462 62002
Camping Card Compulsory.
Signposted.
Dec-Apr & Jun-Sep 2HEC ⬛ ⬛⬛⬛⬛⬛⬛⬛⬛⬛⬛⬛⬛ R ⬛⬛ lau ✦
⬛⬛⬛ ⬛P

CAMPODOLCINO *Sondrio*
Campodolcino ☎0343 50097
All year 2HEC ⬛ ⬛⬛⬛⬛⬛⬛⬛⬛⬛ ⬛ lau ✦⬛ ⬛R ⬛

CANAZEI *Trento*
Marmolada ☎0462 61660
Grassland site extending to the river, part of it in spruce woodland.
Located on S outskirts on the right of the road to Alba Penia.
All year 3HEC ⬛ ⬛⬛⬛⬛⬛⬛⬛⬛⬛⬛⬛⬛⬛ lau ✦ ⬛ ⬛ ⬛ Prices:
A11000 pitch 13000

CANNOBIO *Novara*
International Paradis via Casali Darbedo 12 ☎0323 71227
A level site on the bank of a lake.
Access from the SS34 at Km35/V.
25 Mar-15 Oct 1.2HEC ⬛ ✦⬛⬛⬛⬛⬛⬛⬛⬛⬛⬛⬛⬛ L ⬛⬛ lau ✦
⬛

Residence Campagna via Casali Darbedo 20/22 ☎0323 70100
Turn off SS34 to Locarno at Km35/V on N outskirts of village. W of
lake on road 21.
15 Mar-20 Oct 1.2HEC ⬛ ✦⬛⬛⬛⬛⬛⬛⬛⬛⬛⬛⬛⬛⬛ lau
Prices: A9000-11000 V7500-8500 ✿7500-8500 ▲7500-8500

Valle Romantica ☎0323 71249
A pleasant site with trees, shrubs and flowers. Internal roads are
asphalted and a mountain stream provides bathing facilities.
1.5km w off road to Malesco.
15 Mar-Sep 5HEC ⬛ ✦⬛⬛⬛⬛⬛⬛⬛⬛⬛⬛⬛⬛ PR ⬛⬛ lau ✦ ⬛
⬛L Prices: A10000-11000 pitch 16000-18000

CASTELLETTO TICINO *Novara*
Italia Lido via Cicognola 88 ☎0331 923032
Signposted from SS33.
Mar-30 Oct 2.5HEC ⬛ ✦⬛⬛⬛⬛⬛⬛⬛⬛⬛⬛⬛⬛⬛ L ⬛ lau Prices:
A7000-8000 pitch 8000-10000

CHIUSA-KLAUSEN *Bolzano*
Gamp Griesbruck 10 ☎0472 847425
The site lies next to the Gasthof Gamp, between the Brenner railway
line and the motorway bridge, which passes high above the camp.
Access from the motorway exit and the SS12 is well signposted.
All year 0.8HEC ⬛ ⬛⬛⬛⬛⬛⬛⬛⬛⬛⬛⬛ P ⬛ lau ✦ ⬛

CHIUSO *Como*
Rivabella via Alla Spiaggia 35 ☎0341 421143
Signposted from SS639.
25 Apr-Sep 2HEC ⬛ ✦⬛⬛⬛⬛⬛⬛⬛⬛⬛⬛ L ⬛ lau ✦ ⬛ ⬛P ⬛
Prices: A6000-7000 pitch 11000-13000

COLFOSCO *Bolzano*
Colfosco via Sonegau ☎0471 836515
Jun-Oct 2.5HEC ⬛ ⬛⬛⬛ ⬛⬛⬛⬛⬛⬛⬛⬛⬛⬛⬛⬛⬛ R ⬛ lau ✦
⬛ ⬛ Prices: A8000-10000 V8000-10000 ✿15000-60000 ▲7000-
20000

COLOMBARE *Brescia*
Sirmione ☎030 919045
From SS11 drive towards Sirmione and turn right after approx.
0.4km.
15 Mar-15 Oct 3.5HEC ⬛ ⬛⬛⬛⬛⬛⬛⬛⬛⬛⬛⬛⬛ L ⬛ lau ✦ ⬛⬛ ⬛
⬛ Prices: A8000-9000 pitch 15000-20000

CUNEO *Cuneo*
Turistico Comunale Bisalta San Rocco Castagnaretta ☎0171
491334
All year 4HEC ⬛ ✦⬛⬛⬛⬛⬛⬛⬛⬛⬛⬛ P ⬛ lau ✦ ⬛ ⬛

DESENZANO DEL GARDA *Brescia*
Vò via Vò 9 ☎030 9121325
Situated on Lake Garda, 1500m from Desenzano, surrounded by
meadows and woods.
Camping Card Compulsory.
Apr-Sep 5HEC ⬛ ⬛⬛⬛⬛⬛⬛⬛⬛⬛ LP ⬛⬛ lau ✦ ⬛ ⬛ ⬛
Prices: A6000-8000 pitch 12000-18000

DIMARO *Trento*
Dolomiti di Brenta via Gole 105 ☎0463 974332
Turn off SS42, at Km173.5

Jun-Sep & 7 Dec-15 Apr 3HEC ▥ ⌗ ⋔ ⚲ ☻ ♥ ✗ ⊙ ⊡ ⌀ ♨ ♠ ⚲ P ☎
⊞ ⚙ lau Prices: A7000-10500 pitch 12000-18500

DOBBIACO-TOBLACH *Bolzano*

Olympia ☎0474 72147
The extensive site lies next to Hotel Olympia. Part of the camp lies in
a wood of tall pine trees.
At Km56/V on the SS49 through the Puster Valley.
All year 4HEC ▥ ⌗ ⋔ ⚲ ☻ ♥ ✗ ⊙ ⊡ ⌀ ♠ ⚲ PR ☎ lau ♥ ⚲L

DOMASO *Como*

Gardenia via Case Sparse 138 ☎0344 96262
N at Case Sparse
Apr-Sep 2HEC ▥ ⌗ ⋔ ⚲ ☻ ♥ ✗ ⊙ ⊡ ⌀ ♨ ♠ ⚲ L ☎ ⊞ ⚙ lau

EDOLO *Brescia*

Adamello ☎0364 71694
1.5km W of SS39.
All year 1.2HEC ▥ ♥ ⋔ ⚲ ♥ ✗ ⊙ ⊡ ⌀ ♨ ♠ A ☎ lau ♥ ✗ ⚲PR
Prices: A8000 pitch 19000

FERIOLO *Novara*

Orchidea via Repubblica dell' Ossola ☎0323 28257
Near a lake visible from SS33.
Mar-Oct 4HEC ▥ ♥ ⋔ ⚲ ♥ ✗ ⊙ ⊡ ⌀ ♠ ♨ ⚲ L ☎ lau ♥ ⊞ Prices:
A6000-8500 pitch 10500-15000

FONDOTOCE *Novara*

Continental Lido via 42 Martiri 156 ☎0323 496300
By Lake Mergozzo and 1km from Lake Maggiore.
On right hand side of road from Verbania Fondotoce to Gravellona.
30 Mar-22 Sep 8HEC ▥ ∷ ⌗ ⋔ ⚲ ♥ ✗ ⊙ ⊡ ♠ ♨ A ⚲ L ☎
lau ♥ ♨

Lido Toce ☎0323 496220
On E shore of lake.
May-Sep 2HEC ▥ ∷ ⌗ ⋔ ⚲ ♥ ⊙ ⊡ ⚲ LR ☎ ⊞ lau ♥ ⌀ Prices:
A6800-8000 V5000-6000 ♣6500-8000 ▲6500-8000

Village Isolino via Per Feriolo 25 ☎0323 496080
22 Mar-21 Sep 12HEC ▥ ♥ ⋔ ⚲ ♥ ✗ ⊙ ⊡ ⌀ ♨ ♠ ♣ A ⚲ L ☎ ⊞
lau ♥ ⚲R Prices: A6400-8500 pitch 11200-15000

FUCINE DI OSSANA *Trento*

Cevedale ☎0463 751630
4km W of Savona.
All year 3HEC ▥ ⌗ ⋔ ⚲ ♥ ✗ ⊙ ⊡ ♠ ⚲ R ☎ ⊞ ⚙ lau ♥ ⌀ Prices:
A8000-12000 pitch 11000-16000

IDRO *Brescia*

AZUR Idro Rio Vantone ☎0365 83125
The site lies at the mouth of the river of same name beside Lake
Idro. Subdivided into pitches (separate pitches for youths) on grass
and woodland at the foot of strange rock formations.
Approach from Idro direction of Vantone, well signed from there.
All year 4.5HEC ▥ ⌗ ⋔ ⚲ ♥ ✗ ⊙ ⊡ ⌀ ♠ ⚲ L ☎ ⊞ lau Prices:
A5500-10000 pitch 6500-14000

Vantone Pineta ☎0365 83347
On eastern shore of lake. Grassland enclosed by rush and willow
fencing. Part of site in small woodland on bank of stream.
Approach from Idro and follow signs for Camping Rio Vantone.
31 Mar-Oct 2HEC ▥ ♥ ⋔ ⚲ ♥ ✗ ⊙ ⊡ ⚲ LP ☎ lau ♥ ⌀ ♨ ⊞ Prices:
A6000-7500 pitch 9000-13500

ISEO *Brescia*

Punta d'Oro via Antonioli 51/53 ☎030 980084
Apr-15 Oct 0.6HEC ▥ ♥ ⋔ ⚲ ♥ ✗ ⊙ ⊡ ♠ ⚲ L ☎ ⊡ lau ♥ ✗ ⌀ ♨
⚲P ⊞ Prices: A5000-7000 pitch 13000-16000

Quai via Antonioli 73 ☎030 981161
W of town. Signposted.
10 Apr-22 Sep 1.3HEC ▥ ♥ ⋔ ✗ ⊙ ⊡ ♠ ⚲ L ☎ ⊞ ⚙ lau ♥ ⚲ ⌀
⚲P Prices: A6000-8000 pitch 11000-14000

Sassabanek via Colombera 2 ☎030 980300
Apr-Oct 3HEC ▥ ♥ ⋔ ⚲ ♥ ✗ ⊙ ⊡ ⌀ ♨ ♠ ⚲ LP ⊡ ⊞ ⚙ lau Prices:
A6400-9300 pitch 11800-19000

Sole via per Rovato 26 ☎030 980288
W of town. Signposted.
May-Sep 6.5HEC ♥ ⋔ ✗ ⊙ ⊡ ♠ ⌀ ♠ ♣ A ⚲ LP ⊡ ⊞ lau ♥ ⚲

KALTERN *Bolzano*

St Josef am Kalterer See Welnstr 75 ☎0471 960170
Signposted from the Kalten-Tramin road.
15 Mar-5 Nov 1.4HEC ▥ ∷ ⌗ ⋔ ⚲ ♥ ✗ ⊙ ⊡ ⚲ L ☎ ⊞ lau ♥ ♨
Prices: A7000-8800 V5000-6000 ♣5500-7000 ▲5000-6500

LAIVES-LEIFERS *Bolzano*

Steiner ☎0471 950105
The site lies behind the Gasthof Steiner, the AGIP petrol station and a
bungalow estate.
Off the SS12 on the northern outskirts of the village.
Apr-4 Nov 2.5HEC ▥ ♠ ♥ ⋔ ⚲ ♥ ✗ ⊙ ⊡ ⌀ ♠ ⚲ P ☎ ⊞ lau ♥ ♨

LATSCH *Bolzano*

Latsch an der Etsch Reichstr 4 ☎0473 623217
All year 1.5HEC ▥ ♥ ⋔ ⚲ ♥ ✗ ⊙ ⊡ ⌀ ♨ ♠ ⚲ PR ☎ ⊞ lau Prices:
A7500-8000 pitch 14000-16000

LEVICO TERME *Trento*

Due Laghi Loc Costa 3 ☎0461 512707
23 May-14 Sep 2.5HEC ▥ ⌗ ⋔ ⚲ ♥ ✗ ⊙ ⊡ ⌀ ⚲ LP ☎ ⊞ lau
Prices: A11000 pitch 16000

Jolly Loc Pleina ☎0461 706934 & 234351
The site is divided into plots and lies 200 metres from the lake with
three inside swimming pools.
15 May-15 Sep 2HEC ▥ ⌗ ⋔ ⚲ ♥ ✗ ⊙ ⊡ ⌀ ♠ ♠ ⚲ P ☎ ⊞ lau ♥
✗ ⚲L

Levico ☎0461 706491
Site is by a lake with a private beach.
Signposted from the Levico/Caldonazzo exit on SS47.
Apr-Sep 4HEC ▥ ♥ ⋔ ⚲ ♥ ⊙ ⊡ ⌀ ♨ ⚲ LR ☎ ⊞ lau ♥ ✗ ⚲P

LILLAZ *Aosta*

Salasses ☎0165 74252
Pleasant site surrounded by mountains, grassland and conifers. The
site lies at the end of the Val di Cogne.
Entrance to site before Camping al Sole.
All year 1.5HEC ▥ ⌗ ⋔ ⚲ ♥ ✗ ⊙ ⊡ ⌀ ♨ ♠ ⚲ R ☎ ⊡ lau ♥ ⌀ ♨
Prices: A6500 V4000 ♣6000 ▲6000-5000

LIMONE PIEMONTE *Cuneo*

Luis Matlas ☎0171 927565
This tidy site offers winter facilities and skiing lessons are provided
by the owner. Fishing is also available.
It lies to the north of the town, off the Limone-Nice road.
Closed 1-15 Sep 1.5HEC ▥ ♠ ♣ ⋔ ⚲ ♥ ✗ ⊙ ⊡ ⌀ ♨ ☎ lau ♥ ♨ ✗
⚲R ⊞

LIMONE SUL GARDA *Brescia*

Nanzel via IV Novembre 3 ☎0365 954155
Well managed site, with low terraces in olive grove.
Access from Km101.2 (Hotel Giorgiol).
Mar-Oct 0.7HEC ▥ ⌗ ⋔ ⚲ ♥ ✗ ⊙ ⊡ ⌀ ⚲ L lau ♥ ♨ ⊞ Prices:
A7500 pitch 12500

LINFANO D'ARCO *Trento*

Bellavista via Gardesana 31 ☎0464 505644
Apr-20 Oct 1HEC ▥ ♥ ⋔ ⚲ ♥ ✗ ⊙ ⊡ ⚲ L ☎ lau ♥ ✗

MACCAGNO *Varese*

AZUR-Lago Maggiore ☎0332 560203
By the lake.
In village turn off SS394 at Km43/III towards lake and after 500 m
turn right.
15 Mar-15 Nov 1.5HEC ▥ ⌗ ⋔ ⚲ ♥ ✗ ⊙ ⊡ ⌀ ♠ ⚲ L ☎ ⊞ lau ♥ ✗
Prices: A5500-10000 pitch 6500-14000

Lido via 6 Pietraperzia 13 ☎0332 560250
23 Mar-5 Oct 7.5HEC ▥ ⌗ ⋔ ⚲ ♥ ✗ ⊙ ⊡ ⚲ L ☎ ⚙ lau ♥ ✗ ⚲R ⊞
Prices: A6500-8000 pitch 9000-13000

MADERNO *Brescia*
Riviera SAS via Promontoorio 59 ☎0365 643039
Apr-Sep 3.8HEC ▥ ♦ⓇⓁⓎ✕⊙ ⍉ ⌀ㄥ ⇲ LR ☎⊞ lau

MAGGIORE (LAGO)
See **ARONA, BAVENO, CANNOBIO, FONDOTOCE, MACCAGNO**

MANERBA DEL GARDA *Brescia*
Rio Ferienglück via del Rio 37 ☎0365 551450
Follow SS572 Desenzano-Salo road, turn off between Km8 and 9,
site 4km N.
Apr-Sep 5HEC ▥ ♦ⓇⓁⓎ✕⊙ ⍉ ⌀ 🕮 ⍢ ⇲ L ☎⊞ lau
Prices: A7000-9000 V7000-9000 ⌖7000-10000 ▲7000-9000

Rocca via Cavalle 22 ☎0365 551738
Apr-Sep 5HEC ▥ ♦ⓇⓁⓎ✕⊙ ⍉ ⌀ ㄥ 🕮 ⇲ LP ☎⊞♦✕ ⌀ Prices:
A5500-9000 pitch 14000-18500

San Biagio via Cavalle 19 ☎0365 551046
Signposted from SS572.
Apr-Sep ▥ ♦ⓇⓁⓎ✕⊙ ⍉ ⌀ ㄥ ⇲ L ☎⊞ lau

Zocco via del Zocco 43 ☎0365 551605
The site consists of several, terraced sections. The section below
the maintenance/supply building lies on a sloping olive grove and is
somewhat obstructed by bungalows.
500m S of Gardonicino di Manerbe.
Etr-29 Sep 5HEC ▥ ♦ⓇⓁⓎ✕⊙ ⍉ ⌀ 🕮 ⍢ ⇲ L ☎⊞ lau ♦ ㄥ
Prices: A7000-8000 pitch 15000-17100

MOLINA DI LEDRO *Trento*
International Camping Al Sole via Maffei ☎0464 508496
May-Sep 2HEC ▥ ⌀ ⍾ⓇⓁⓎ✕⊙ ⍉ ⌀ ⇲ L ☎⊞♦ ㄥ

MOLVENO *Trento*
Spiaggia-Lago di Molveno via Lungolago 27 ☎0461 586978
In a picturesque setting on the lake shore, at the foot of the Brenta
Dolomites. Signposted from SS421.
All year 3.5HEC ▥ ♦ⓇⓁⓎ✕⊙ ⍉ ㄥ ⇲ L ☎ lau ♦ ⇲PR ⊞ Prices:
A6000-11000 pitch 10000-17000

MONIGA DEL GARDA *Brescia*
Fontanelle via del Magone 13 ☎0365 502079
Apr-Sep 4.5HEC ▥ ♦ⓇⓁⓎ✕⊙ ⍉ ⌀ ㄥ ▲ ⇲ LP ☎⊞ lau ♦ ㄥ
Prices: A7500-9000 pitch 15000-18000
See advertisement under Colour Section
San Michele via San Michele 8 ☎0365 502026
Apr-Sep 2.8HEC ▥ ♦ⓇⓁⓎ✕⊙ ⍉ 🕮 ⇲ LP ☎⊞ lau ♦ ⌀ ㄥ
Prices: A6000-8000 pitch 16000-19500

Sereno via San Sivino ☎0365 502080 & 502220
Well-maintained and appointed site with good lakeside and swimming
facilities.
Turn off SS572D-S at Km13/VII or (better for caravans) 13/IV.
Apr-Sep 4HEC ▥ ⌀ ⍾ⓇⓁⓎ✕⊙ ⍉ ⌀ 🕮 ⇲ LP ☎⊞ lau

NATURNO-NATURNS *Bolzano*
Wald Dornsbergweg 8 ☎0473 667298
The site lies on gently rising ground, in a forest of pine and
deciduous trees.
For access, turn off the SS38 near the Gasthof Alderwirt in the
village, and drive 0.8km S over the railway line.
15 Mar-Oct 1.5HEC ▥ ⌀ ⍾ⓇⓁ⊙ ⍉ ㄥ ⇲ P ☎⊞ lau ♦✕Ⓛ⌀ ⇲R

NOVATE MEZZOLA *Sondrio*
El Ranchero via Nazionale 3 ☎0343 44169
Apr-Sep 1HEC ▥ ⌀ ⍾Ⓡ ✕⊙ ⍉ 🕮 ⇲ LR ☎⊞♦ ⌀ㄥ✕ ⇲P ⊞
Prices: A7000 V5000 ⌖7000-10000 ▲7000-10000

ORA-AUER *Bolzano*
Wasserfall ☎0471 810519
Sloping site in front of the Gasthaus Wasserfall, between wooded
rocky hills and the River Schwarzbach.
For access turn off Fleimstralstrasse (SS48) E of the bridge over the
River Schwarzbach and drive N for 300m.
Apr-5 Nov 1HEC ▥ ⋮⋮⋮ ⌀ ⍾♦Ⓡ⊙ ⍉ ⌀ ⇲ P ☎⊞⍲ lau ♦ ㄥ Ⓛ✕

ORTA SAN GIULIO *Novara*
Cusio Lago d'Orta ☎0322 90290
Mar-Dec 2HEC ▥ ⌀ⓇⓁⓎ✕⊙ ⍉ ⍉ ⇲ P ☎ lau ♦ ㄥ ⇲L

PADENGHE *Brescia*
Cá via S.Cassiano 12 ☎030 9907006
The site lies in a park-like setting on terraced ground.
For access, turn off the road along the lake, 1.5km N turn for
Padenghe, and drive down a very steep road towards the lake.
Mar-Oct 2HEC ▥ ♦ⓇⓁⓎ✕⊙ ⍉ ⌀ ㄥ 🕮 ⇲ L ☎ lau
Prices: A6000-9300 V5500-8800 ⌖5500-8800 ▲5500-8800

Campagnola via Marconi 99 ☎030 9907523
In a beautiful position on the shores of Lake Garda with good,
modern facilities.
4km from Desenzano on the road to Salo.
May-Sep 5HEC ▥ ♦ⓇⓁⓎ✕⊙ ⍉ ⌀ ⇲ LP ☎⊞⍫ lau Prices:
A3000-12000 pitch 8000-44000

PEIO *Trento*
Val di Sole Loc Dossi di Cavia ☎0463 753177
The site lies on terraced slopes at the foot of the Ortier mountain
range.
400m off SP87.
Closed May & Oct 4.5HEC ▥ ⌀ ⍾ⓇⓁⓎ✕⊙ ⍉ ⌀ ㄥ ☎ ⊞ lau ♦
✕

PERA DI FASSA *Trento*
Soal via Dolomiti 32 ☎0462 764519
All year ▥ ⋮⋮⋮ ⌀ ⍾ⓇⓁⓎ✕⊙ ⍉ ⌀ ㄥ ⇲ R ☎ lau ♦ ⊞ Prices:
A9500-11500 pitch 13000-15000

PERGINE *Trento*
Punta Indiani Lago di Caldonazzo ☎0461 531262
15 May-Sep 1.5HEC ▥ ♦Ⓡ⊙ ⍉ ⇲ L ☎⍫ ♦ ㄥ ⓁⓎ ⌀ ㄥ

San Cristoforo via dei Pescatori ☎0461 512707
23 May-15 Sep 2.5HEC ▥ ♦ⓇⓁⓎ✕⊙ ⍉ ⌀ ⇲ PR ☎⊞ lau ♦
⇲L

PETTENASCO *Novara*
Punta di Crabbia via Crabbia 2/A ☎0323 89117
All year 2HEC ▥ ♦ⓇⓁⓎ✕⊙ ⍉ ⇲ L lau ♦✕ Prices: A7000
pitch 8500

PIETRAMURATA *Trento*
Daino ☎0464 507131
May-Nov 1.6HEC ▥ ♦ⓇⓁⓎ✕⊙ ⍉ ⌀ ⇲ P ☎⊞ lau ♦ ㄥ ㄥ ⇲R

PIEVE DI MANERBA *Brescia*
Faro via Repubblica 52 ☎0365 651704
15 Apr-15 Sep 1HEC ▥ ♦Ⓡ✕⊙ ⍉ ⍉ ▲ ⇲ P ☎♦ⓁⓎ✕⌀ ㄥ ⇲L
⊞ Prices: A6000-7000 pitch 15000

PISOGNE *Brescia*
Eden via Piangrande 3 ☎0364 880500
The site lies on eastern lake shore with tall trees and a level beach.
Turn off SS510 at Km37/VII, over railway line and towards lake.
Apr-Oct 2HEC ▥ ♦ⓇⓁⓎ✕⊙ ⍉ 🕮 ⇲ L ☎ lau ♦ ㄥ ⌀ ㄥ Prices:
A6300-7000 pitch 17500

PONTE TRESA *Varese*
Trelago via Trelago 20 ☎0332 716583
5 Apr-8 Sep 3.1HEC ▥ ⌀ ⍾ⓇⓁⓎ✕⊙ ⍉ ⌀ ㄥ 🕮 🕮 ⇲ LP ☎⊞
lau ♦✕ Prices: A6000 pitch 9000

PORLEZZA *Como*
Paradiso ☎0344 61027
The site lies in meadowland on the north eastern lake shore.
S from SS340.
Apr-Sep 5HEC ▥ ♦ⓇⓁⓎ✕⊙ ⍉ ⌀ ⇲ LPR ☎♦✕

PORTESE *Brescia*
Eden via Preone 45 ☎0365 62093
Site with good facilities on the shore of Lake Garda.
Apr-Sep 4.4HEC ▥ ♦ⓇⓁⓎ✕⊙ ⍉ ⌀ ㄥ 🕮 ⇲ LP ☎ lau ♦ ⊞
Prices: A7000-9500 pitch 14000-19000

POZZA DI FASSA *Trento*

Rosengarten via Avisio 15 ☎0462 763305
Signposted from SS48.
Closed May & Oct 3.5HEC ▦ ⌕ ⋔ ⛺ ✕ ⊙ ⊞ ⌀ ♨ ⛽ ⊞ ⊡ ⌕ R ☎ ⊞
lau ♦ ⛄ ✕ ⌕L Prices: A12000-14000 pitch 13000-16000

Vidor via Valle S Nicolo ☎0462 63247
Signposted from SS48.
All year 1.7HEC ▦ ⤳ ⋔ ⛺ ⛱ ✕ ⊙ ⊞ ⌀ ♨ ⊞ ⊡ lau ♦ ✕ Prices:
A8000-10000 pitch 12000-13000

PRAD AM STILFSERJOCH *Bolzano*

Kiefernhain ☎0473 616422
Apr-Oct 3HEC ▦ ⠸⠸ ♦ ⋔ ⛺ ✕ ⊙ ⊞ ⌕ PR ☎ ♦ ⛄ ♨ ⌕L ⊞

PRATO ALLO STELVIO *Bolzano*

Sägomühle via delle Spine ☎0473 616078
Closed 10 Nov-10 Dec 1.2HEC ▦ ⌕ ⋔ ⛺ ✕ ⊙ ⊞ ⌀ ♨ ⛽ ⊞ ⌕ P ☎
⊞ lau ♦ ⌀ ⌕LR Prices: A6000-7500 pitch 13500-14000

RASUN *Bolzano*

Corones ☎0474 496490
A modern site in an ideal mountain location with good sporting
facilities.
Closed 6 Apr-10 May 2.5HEC ⠸⠸ ⤳ ⋔ ⛺ ⛱ ✕ ⊙ ⊞ ⌀ ♨ ⛽ ⌕ P ☎
Prices: pitch 28800-37200 (incl 2 persons)

RHÊMES ST GEORGES *Aosta*

Val di Rhêmes ☎0165 907648
Jun-10 Sep 18HEC ▦ ⌕ ⋔ ⛺ ⛱ ✕ ⊙ ⌀ ♨ ⛽ ⊞ ⛽ ⊡ ⌕ R ☎ ⊞ lau

RIVA DEL GARDA *Trento*

Bavaria viale Rovereto 100 ☎0464 552524
On SS240 towards Rovereto.
Apr-Oct 0.6HEC ▦ ⠸⠸ ⌕ ⋔ ⛺ ✕ ⊙ ⊞ ♨ ⌕ L ☎ ♦ ⛄ ♨ ⛽ ⊞
Prices: A9000 pitch 10000

Monte Brione via Brione 32 ☎0464 520885
A new site at the foot of a hill covered with olive trees with good
sports facilities.
Etr-Sep 3.3HEC ▦ ⌕ ⋔ ⛺ ⛱ ✕ ⊙ ⊞ ⌕ P ☎ ⊞ lau ♦ ✕ ♨ ⌕L
Prices: A11000 pitch 17000

RIVOLTELLA *Brescia*

San Francesco strada Vicinale San Francesco ☎030 9110245
This well-kept site is divided into many sections by drives, vineyards
and orchards and has a private gravel beach.
At Km268 on SSN11.
Jun-Sep 8.5HEC ▦ ⋔ ⛺ ⛱ ✕ ⊙ ⊞ ⌀ ♨ ⛽ ⊞ ⌕ L ☎ ⊞ lau

ST-ANSELME *Aosta*

Village la Grolla Challand ☎0125 929587
Access via SS506 Km116.
All year 1.3HEC ▦ ⌕ ⋔ ⛺ ✕ ⊙ ⊞ ⌕ R lau ♦ ⛄ ✕ ⌀ ⊞

SALLE, LA *Aosta*

Green Park ☎0165 861300
All year 6HEC ▦ ♦ ⋔ ⛺ ⛱ ✕ ⊙ ⊞ ⌀ ⌕ P ⊞ ⊞ lau ♦ ⌕R

SAN ANTONIO DI MAVIGNOLA *Trento*

Faé ☎0465 507178
Situated in famous winter skiing region of Madonna di Campiglio.
Good base for climbing in Brenta mountain range. On four gravel
terraces, and alpine meadow in hollow next to SS239. *Camping
Card Compulsory.*
15 Jun-Sep & Dec-Apr 2.2HEC ▦ ⌕ ⋔ ⛺ ✕ ⊙ ⊞ ⌀ ♨ ⊞ ⊞ lau ♦
⛄ ✕ Prices: A10000 pitch 12000

SAN FELICE DEL BENACO *Brescia*

Europa-Silvella via Silvella ☎0365 651095
One site separated in two parts by the joint approach road. The
beach is situated about 80m below.
Signposted.
19 Apr-30 Sep 7.4HEC ▦ ♦ ⋔ ⛺ ⛱ ✕ ⊙ ⊞ ⌀ ♨ ⛽ ⌕ LP ☎ ⊞ lau
Prices: A6500-10000 pitch 17000-25000

Fornella ☎0365 62294
A quiet site in an ideal location on the shore of Lake Garda.
Signposted from SS572 (Salo-Desenzano).
May-25 Sep 7.4HEC ▦ ⌕ ⋔ ⛺ ⛱ ✕ ⊙ ⊞ ⌀ ♨ ⛽ ⛽ ⌕ LP ⊞ lau ♦
♨ Prices: A7500-9500 pitch 15500-19000
See advertisement under Colour Section

Gardiola via Gardiola 36 ☎0365 559240
Apr-Sep 9HEC ▦ ⤳ ⋔ ⛺ ⛱ ✕ ⊙ ⊞ ⌀ ♨ ⛽ ⌕ L ⊞ lau ♦ ⛄ ✕ ⌀ ♨
Prices: A5500-9800 pitch 13000-215000

Ideal Molino ☎0365 62023
Situated right beside Lake Garda amid beautiful scenery. Charming
and quiet site 1km from S. Felice. On the beach there is a pier and
boat moorings. Pedal boats can be hired for lake trips.
15 Mar-Sep 2HEC ▦ ♦ ⋔ ⛺ ⛱ ✕ ⊙ ⊞ ⛽ ⛽ ⌕ L ☎ ♦ lau ♦ ⌀ ♨

Weekend via Vallone della Selva 10 ☎0365 43712
A quiet family site with modern facilities, situated in a olive grove
overlooking Lake Garda.
May-29 Sep 5HEC ▦ ♦ ⋔ ⛺ ⛱ ✕ ⊙ ⊞ ⌀ ♨ ⛽ ⛽ ⌕ A ⌕ P ⊞ lau ♦
⌕L Prices: A7500-10000 pitch 15000-22000

SAN LORENZEN *Bolzano*

Wildberg ☎0474 74080
All year 1HEC ▦ ⤳ ⋔ ⛺ ⊙ ⊞ ⛽ ⛽ ⌕ ⌕ PR ☎ lau ♦ ⛄ ✕ ⌀

SAN MARTINO DI CASTROZZA *Trento*

Sass Maor via Laghetto 48 ☎0439 68347
A Winter Sports site in a beautiful mountain setting.
All year 2.1HEC ▦ ♦ ⋔ ⛺ ⛱ ✕ ⊙ ⊞ ⌀ ♨ ⌕ R ☎ ♨ lau ♦ ⌕L ⊞
Prices: A100000-15000 pitch 15000-25000

SAN PIETRO DI CORTENO GOLGI *Brescia*

Villaggio Aprica via Nazionale 507 ☎0342 710001
On SS39 (Aprica-Edolo).
All year 2.1HEC ▦ ⌕ ⋔ ⛺ ⛱ ✕ ⊙ ⊞ ⌀ ♨ ⛽ ⛽ ⌕ R ☎ lau ♦ ⌕LP ⊞
Prices: A5000-8000 pitch 11000-18000

SAN SIGMUND *Bolzano*

Gisser ☎0474 565305
By the bank of a stream, surrounded by meadows and woodland.
Access via SS49
May-10 Oct 2HEC ▦ ♦ ⋔ ⛺ ✕ ⊙ ⊞ ⌕ PR ☎ ⊞ lau ♦ ⛄ ⌀ ♨ ⌕L

SARRE *Aosta*

International Touring ☎0165 257061 & 35187
4km W of Aosta on SS26.
15 May-Sep 6HEC ▦ ♦ ⋔ ⛺ ⛱ ✕ ⊙ ⊞ ⌀ ♨ ⛽ ⛽ ⌕ PR ☎ ⊞ lau
Prices: A6900-7200 V3900-4100 ⚌5900-6200 ▲5900-6200

Monte Bianco ☎0165 257523
Apr-Sep 7.5HEC ▦ ♦ ⋔ ⊙ ⊞ ⌕ R ☎ ♦ ⛄ ✕ ⌀ ♨ Prices: A6300-
6700 V3400-3600 ⚌5200-5600 ▲5200-5600

Camping "AU LAC DE COMO"

I-22010 Sorico (CO) • Tel: 0344/84035-84716
Fax: 84802 • Mobile phone 0335/216421

Spend your holiday by the lake on the site's
own sunny private beach, children's play area,
restaurant, bar and supermarket.
Swim, sail, water ski, wind surf, hunt, fish,
parascend for pleasure or fitness and enjoy the
open air in the woods and mountains.

SORICO *Como*
Au Lac De Como via C-Battisti 18 ☎0344 84035
The well-kept site lies on the right of the River Mera as it flows into
Lake Como.
Turn off the SS340d at Km25 near TOTAL petrol station and drive
200m towards the lake.
All year 2HEC ▦ ♦ ♠ ዿ ♥ ✕ ⊕ ♨ ⌀ ⇌ ♨ ⊞ ♥ ⇌ LR ☎ ⊞ lau Prices:
A5000-10000 pitch 7000-20000

TORBOLE *Trento*
Europa via Sarca Vecchio 21 ☎0464 505888
20 Mar-1 Nov 1.6HEC ▦ ♦ ♠ ⊕ ♨ ♨ ⇌ ♨ ⊞ ⊞ ⊘ ♦ ⇌ ♥ ✕ ⌀ ⇌
⇌R

Porto ☎0464 505891
A new site with modern facilities, situated in a quiet position near the
lake.
Apr-2 Nov 1HEC ▦ ♦ ♥ ♥ ✕ ⊕ ♨ ☎ lau ♦ ⇌ ✕ ⌀ ⇌LR

TORRE DANIELE *Torino*
Mombarone via Nazionale 54 ☎0125 757907
13km N of Ivrea on SS26. Very close to River.
All year 1.2HEC ▦ ♦ ♥ ♥ ✕ ⊕ ♨ ⇌ ♨ ⇌ PR ☎ lau ♦ ⇌ ✕ ⌀
Prices: A4000 V2000 ⇌4000 ▲3500

TOSCOLANO MADERNO *Brescia*
Chiaro di Luna via Statale 218 ☎0365 641179
Apr-Sep 9HEC ♦ ♠ ♥ ♥ ✕ ⊕ ♨ ♨ ⇌ ♨ ⇌ L ☐ lau ♦ ✕

VALNONTEY *Aosta*
Lo Stambecco ☎0165 74152
Jun-20 Sep 1.6HEC ▦ ♦ ♥ ♥ ⊕ ♨ ⇌ ♨ ⇌ R ☎ lau ♦ ✕ ⊞ Prices:
A7000 V3500 ⇌6500 ▲6500

VIPITENO *Bolzano*
Sadobre Autoporto ☎0472 721500
All year 1.5HEC ♨ ♠ ♥ ♥ ✕ ⊕ ♨ ⇌ ♦ ⌀ ⇌LPR ⊞

VIVERONE *Vercelli*
Rocca via Lungo Lago 35 ☎0161 987479
Apr-Sep 1HEC ♦ ♠ ♥ ♥ ✕ ⊕ ♨ ♨ ▲ ⇌ LP ☎ ⊞ lau

VOLS *Bolzano*
Seiseralm ☎0471 706459
All year 2.5HEC ▦ ♨ ♨ ♠ ♥ ♥ ✕ ⊕ ♨ ⌀ ⇌ ♨ ☎ lau ♦ ⇌L Prices:
A7500-10000 pitch 10000-13000

Venice/North
Venice dominates this region. It is an ancient centre of arts and
trade and is unique in having waterways as roads and many
architectural splendours, as well as producing fine glass and lace
and, due to the revival of the carnival, masks.
Venetian influence is apparent in towns like Udine with its Piazza
della Libertà surrounded by Renaissance buildings or at Treviso,
with its own canal system, and where concerts and theatre
performances are held in the main square. Echoes of Rome can
be found in Palladio's architecture in Vicenza or in Verona where
the amphitheatre is the setting for the July-September opera
season.
Art lovers can enjoy Giotto's frescoes and Donatello's sculptures
in the university town of Padua, and at Rovigo are paintings by
Bellini and Tiepolo.
Trieste, on the Yugoslav border is the major port and contains
handsome 19th-century architecture and there are attractive
villages like Bellini on the southern edge of the Dolomites built
overlooking two rivers. Vineyards and wineries (Soave and
Valpolicella) welcome tourists.

ARSIE *Belluno*
Gajole Loc Soravigo ☎0439 58505
Access from SS50 bis.
Apr-Sep 1.1HEC ▦ ♨ ♠ ♥ ♥ ✕ ⊕ ♨ ☎ lau ♦ ✕ ⌀ ⇌ ⇌L

ASIAGO *Vicenza*
Ekar ☎0424 455157
Jun-Sep & 15 Nov-15 Apr 3.5HEC ▦ ♦ ♠ ♥ ♥ ✕ ⊕ ♨ ⌀ ⇌ ☎ ⊞ lau
Prices: A9000 pitch 13000

AURISINA *Trieste*
Imperial Aurisina Cave 55 ☎040 200459
Access via SS14 in Sistiana-Aurisina direction.
25 May-15 Sep 1.5HEC ▦ ♦ ♠ ♥ ⊕ ♨ ⌀ ♨ ⇌ P ☎ ⊞ ♦ ♥ ✕
Prices: A5500-8500 V5500-7000 ⇌5500-7000 ▲5500-7000

BARDOLINO *Verona*
Continental ☎045 7210192
Apr-Sep 3.5HEC ▦ ♦ ♠ ♥ ♥ ✕ ⊕ ♨ ⌀ ♨ ⇌ L ☎ lau Prices:
A6000-8500 pitch 11500-18000

Rocca ☎045 7211111
Subdivided site in slightly sloping grassland broken up by rows of
trees. Separated from the lake by a public path (no cars). Part of site
on the other side of the main road is terraced amongst vines and
olives with lovely view of lake.
Below the SS249 at Km40/IV
May-Sep 8HEC ▦ ♦ ♠ ♥ ♥ ✕ ⊕ ♨ ♨ ⇌ LP ☎ lau Prices:
A6500-9500 pitch 12000-19000

Serenella ☎045 7211333
Apr-Sep 5HEC ▦ ♦ ♠ ♥ ♥ ✕ ⊕ ♨ ⌀ ♨ ♨ ⇌ LP ☎ ⊞ ⊘ lau

BIBIONE *Venezia*
Villagio Turistico Internazionale via Colonie ☎0431 439191
Mostly sandy terrain under pine trees. Some meadowland with a few
deciduous trees. Wide sandy beach. Tennis court.
Access is well signed along approach.
May-26 Sep 13HEC ⠿⠿⠿ ♨ ♦ ♠ ♥ ♥ ✕ ⊕ ♨ ⌀ ♨ ⇌ PS ☎ ⊞ lau

BRENZONE *Verona*
Primavera via Benaco 5 ☎045 7420421
10 Apr-Sep 0.8HEC ▦ ♦ ♠ ♥ ♥ ✕ ⊕ ♨ ⌀ ♨ ⇌ L ☎ lau ♦ ✕ ⌀ ⊞
Prices: A7500-8500 pitch 12500-14500

CA'NOGHERA *Venezia*
Alba d'Oro via Triestina 214/B ☎041 5415102
Access from SS14.
Apr-Sep 6HEC ▦ ♦ ♠ ♥ ♥ ✕ ⊕ ♨ ♨ ⇌ PR ☎ ⊞ lau

CAORLE *Venezia*
Falconera ☎0421 84282
Level sandy site partially on sandy meadowland under tall poplars on the
Porto di Falconera.
E on riverside road to Pizzeria Capri, then turn seawards.
May-15 Sep 2.9HEC ▦ ⠿⠿⠿ ♦ ♠ ♥ ♥ ✕ ⊕ ♨ ⌀ ♨ ♨ ♦ ⇌S ⊞

Jolly via dei Cacciatori 5 ☎0421 81586
15 May-15 Sep 7.5HEC ▦ ⠿⠿⠿ ♦ ♠ ♥ ♥ ✕ ⊕ ♨ ⌀ ♨ ♨ ⇌ S ☎ ⊘
♦ ⇌P ⊞

San Francesco via Selva Rosata ☎0421 299333
This generously laid-out site, on level lawns with shady poplars, lies in the midst of a holiday village.
Follow signs from Caorle for access.
May-Sep 32HEC ▦ ░░ ♦♠⌂♨✕⊙♥∅▲⌖♥⇗PS☎lau
Prices: A5000-15000 pitch 10000-35000

CASSONE *Verona*

Bellavista ☎045 7420244
In a fine position in an olive grove overlooking Lake Garda with modern sanitary installations. Access to the lake is by an underpass and good watersports facilities are available.
All year 27HEC ▦ ♦♠⌂♨✕⊙♥∅▲⌖♥⇗L☎⊞❀lau♦
⇗PR Prices: A8000 pitch 15000-18000

CASTELLETTO DI BRENZONE *Verona*

Maior Loc Croce ☎045 7430333
A comfortable, modern site in a pleasant, quiet location.
Etr-5 Oct 0.8HEC ▦ ♦♠⌂♨✕⊙♥∅▲⌖☎lau♦✕⇗L⊞
Prices: A7000-8500 pitch 13000-17000

San Zeno via A-Vespucci 91 ☎045 7430231
May-Sep 1.3HEC ▦ ♦♠⌂♨✕⊙♥∅☎⊞♦✕∅⇗L

CAVALLINO *Venezia*

Cavallino via delle Batterie 164 ☎041 966133
30 Apr-Sep 8HEC ░░ ♦♠⌂♨✕⊙♥∅▲⌖⇗PS☎⊞lau
Prices: A5200-9800 pitch 11500-24800

Europa via Fausta 332 ☎041 968069
On grassland reaching to the sea, with some poplars. Lunchtime siesta 13.00-15.00 hrs.
Well signposted on Punta Sabbioni road.
Apr-Sep 10.7HEC ▦ ♦♠⌂♨✕⊙♥∅▲⌖⇗S☎⊞lau
Prices: A3900-8000 pitch 9900-19800

Italy via Fausta 272 ☎041 968090
Small family-type campsite 6km from Lido di Jesolo on a peninsula.
Venice can be reached by public ferry.
Etr-Sep 3.9HEC ♦♠⌂♨✕⊙♥∅▲⌖⇗PS☎❀♦⊞
Prices: A6000-10000 pitch 10000-26000

Joker via Fausta 318 ☎041 5370766
Between coastal road and the sandy beach with tall poplars. Partially subdivided.
May-Sep 4.4HEC ▦ ♦♠⌂♨✕⊙♥∅▲⌖♠⇗PS☎⊞❀lau

Residence via F-Baracca 47 ☎041 968027
Well laid out site on level grassland, by a sandy beach, between Jesolo and Cavallino. Lunchtime siesta 13.00-15.00 hrs. Signposted.
24 Apr-24 Sep 7HEC♦♠⌂♨✕⊙♥∅▲⌖⇗PS☎⊞❀lau
Prices: A5500-10500 pitch 12000-24000

Sant'Angelo via F-Baracca 63 ☎041 968882
May-Sep 17HEC ▦ ♦♠⌂♨✕⊙♥∅▲⌖⇗PS☎⊞❀lau

Silva via F-Baracca 53 ☎041 968087
The site lies on sand and grassland and is located between road and beach, divided by a vineyard. The section of site near the beach is quiet.
May-15 Sep 3.3HEC ▦ ♦♠⌂♨✕⊙♥∅⌖⇗S☎⊞lau Prices:
A6000-9000 pitch 11000-16000

Union-Lido via Fausta 258 ☎041 968080
This site lies on a long stretch of land next to a 1km-long beach. Separate section for tents and caravans. *Minimum stay during peak period is one week.*
May-Sep 60HEC ▦ ♦♠⌂♨✕⊙♥∅▲⌖⇗PS☎⊞❀lau
Prices: A9000-12600 pitch 15500-31000

Villa al Mare via del Faro 12 ☎041 968066
Level site divided into plots on a peninsula behind the lighthouse.
Direct access to a long, sandy beach.
May-20 Sep 2HEC ▦ ♦♠⌂♨✕⊙♥∅▲⌖⇗S☎⊞❀lau
Prices: A5000-9500 pitch 11000-23000

CHIOGGIA *Venezia*

Miramare via A-Barbarigo 103 ☎041 490610
Longish site reaching as far as the beach, clean and well-maintained.
Access from Strada Romeo (SS309) in direction of Chioggia Sottomarina, turn right on reaching beach and continue 500m.
May-20 Sep 4HEC ▦ ░░ ♦♠⌂♨✕⊙♥∅▲⌖⇗PS☎⊞❀lau
Prices: A6000-10000 pitch 10000-18000

Villaggio Turistico Isamar via Isamar 9, Isolaverde ☎041 498100
The site lies on level grassland at the mouth of the River Etsch.
Shade is provided by high poplars. Good beach.
Access via the SS309. Caravans are advised to approach via Km84/VII near the Brenta village.
9 May-26 Sep 30HEC ▦ ♦♠⌂♨✕⊙♥∅▲⌖⇗PS☎⊞lau♦
⇗R Prices: A5000-14000 pitch 13000-33000

CHIOGGIA SOTTOMARINA *Venezia*

Atlanta via A-Barbarigo 302 ☎041 491311
May-13 Sep 4.3HEC ▦ ♦♠⌂♨✕⊙♥∅⌖⇗PS☎⊞❀lau♦▲
⇗R

Oasi via A-Barbarigo ☎041 490801
A well equipped site situated on a wooded peninsula near the mouth of the Brenta River with a wide private beach.
Apr-21 Sep 25HEC ▦ ░░ ♦♠⌂♨✕⊙♥∅▲⌖⇗PRS☎⊞
lau♦⊞ Prices: A6000-10000 pitch 10000-18000

CISANO *Verona*

Cisano via Peschiera ☎045 6229098
Quiet, partly terraced site beside Lake Garda with good watersports facilities.
AFFI exit on Brenner-Verona motorway, access 4km further.
23 Mar-1 Oct 14HEC ▦ ♦♠⌂♨✕⊙♥∅♠♥⇗LP☎⊞❀lau

San Vito via Pralesi 3 ☎045 6229026
23 Mar-Sep 5HEC ▦ ♦♠⌂♨✕⊙♥∅♠♥⇗LP☎⊞❀lau

CORTINA D'AMPEZZO *Belluno*

Cortina via Campo 2 ☎0436 867575
This site lies amongst pine trees, several hundred metres away from the edge of town, off the Dolomite road towards Belluno.
Turn off road and drive 1km to the campsite which is situated by a small river.
All year 4.5HEC ▦ ░░ ♦♠⌂♨✕⊙♥∅⌖♥⇗PR☎lau

Dolomiti via Campo di Sotto ☎0436 2485
The site is beautifully situated on grassland with pine trees in a hollow, not far from the Olympic ski-jump.
For access, follow the directions for Camping Cortina. The camp is then 500m further on 2.7km S of Cortina.
Jun-15 Sep 5.4HEC ▦ ♠⌂♨✕⊙♥∅⌖♥⇗P☎⊞lau Prices:
A7000-13000 pitch 9000-17000

Olympia Fiames 1 ☎0436 5057
A very beautiful site set in the centre of the centre of the magnificent Dolomite landscape.
It lies N of town off the SS51.
All year 4HEC ▦ ♠⌂♨✕⊙♥∅♠♥⇗R☎lau

Rocchetta via Campo 1 ☎0436 5063
In beautiful wooded surroundings.
Access S from Cortina via SS51.
Jun-20 Sep 2.3HEC ▦ ♠⌂♨✕⊙♥∅▲☎lau♦✕⇗L Prices:
A7000-13000 pitch 9000-17000

DUINO-AURISINA *Trieste*

At SISTIANA

Marepineta ☎040 299264
A modern site. On SS14 near the harbour and beach. Highway A4 Venice-Trieste, exit Duino 1km on left.
May-Sep 10.8HEC♦♠⌂♨✕⊙♥∅♠♥⇗P☎⊞❀lau♦∅▲
⇗S Prices: A7000-9800 pitch 13000-20000

ERACLEA MARE *Venezia*

Porto Felice viale dei Fiori 15 ☎0421 66411
6 May-18 Sep 1.6HEC ▦ ♦♠⌂♨✕⊙♥∅▲⌖⇗PS☎🅿⊞❀
lau♦⇗R⊞

FUSINA VENEZIA *Venezia*
Fusina via Moranzani 79 ☎041 5470055
All year 5HEC ▦ ♣♠♟♖♚♥✕⊙ ⬛☐▥♠☎♠Å☎⊞ lau Prices:
A10000 pitch 20000

GEMONA DEL FRIÚLI *Udine*
Ai Pioppi via del Bersaglio 44 ☎0432 981276
Quiet, well equipped site in a pleasant mountain setting.
1km from town centre via N13.
15 Mar-Oct 1HEC ▦ ♣♠♟♖♚♥✕⊙ ⬛☐▥♠☎☎ lau ♣♟✕⊞ Prices:
A6000-7000 V5000 ♠7000-9000 Å5000-6000

GRADO *Gorizia*
Europa ☎0431 80877
In level terrain under half grown poplars. Partially in shade in pine
forest.
On road to Monfalcone.
19 Apr-21 Sep 22HEC ▦ ░░░ ♣♠♟♖♚♥✕⊙ ⬛☐▥♠☎☎♟ PS ☎⊞
lau Prices: A6000-12000 pitch 10000-22000

Tenuta Primero Loc Primero ☎0431 81523
The site lies in extensive level grassland between the road and the
dam, which is 2m high along the narrow and level beach. Tennis
court.
Access from Monfalcone road. Signposted.
7 May-15 Sep 20HEC ▦ ♣♠♟♖♚♥✕⊙ ⬛☐▥♠☎♟ PS ☎⊞✂
lau Prices: A10000-13000 pitch 18000-23000

IÉSOLO
See **JÉSOLO, LIDO DI**

JÉSOLO, LIDO DI *Venezia*
At **JÉSOLO PINETA**(6km E)
Malibu Beach viale Oriente 78 ☎0421 362212
From Venezia via coast road to Cortellazzo.
15 May-14 Sep 10HEC ▦ ░░░ ♣♠♟♖♚♥✕⊙ ⬛☐♠☎♟ PS ☎⊞
✂ lau Prices: A7500-125000 pitch 17500-28000

Waikiki viale Oriente 144 ☎0421 980186
15 May-7 Sep 5.2HEC ▦ ░░░ ♣♠♟♖♚♥✕⊙ ⬛☐▥♠☎♟ PS ☎ lau ♣
⊞ Prices: A6200-11500 ♠10500-24000 Å8500-20000

At **PORTO DI PIAVE VECCHIA**(8km S)
Jesolo International via dei Mille 89 ☎0421 971826
Site on sandy beach side of coast road.
W opposite lighthouse.
May-Sep 11HEC ▦ ░░░ ♣♠♟♖♚♥✕⊙ ⬛☐▥♠☎♟ S ☎⊞✂ lau ♣
♟PR Prices: A5500-11000 V2500-5000 ♠8500-11000 Å7500-
17000

LAZISE *Verona*
Ideal Loc Vanon ☎045 7580077
On the shore of Lake Garda with asphalt roads and access to a safe,
flat beach.
Etr-Sep 12.5HEC ▦ ♣♠♟♖♚♥✕⊙ ⬛☐▥♠☎☎♟ LP ☎⊞✂ lau ♣
▥

Parc Loc Sentieri ☎045 7580127
Well-kept, lakeside site off main road.
If approaching from Garda, the site is on S side of Lazise just after
turning for Verona.
20 Mar-Oct 4.5HEC ▦ ♣♠♟♖♚♥✕⊙ ⬛☐▥♠☎☎♟ L ☎⊞ lau ♣♥▥

Quercia ☎045 6470577
The site is divided into many large sections by tarred drives and lies
on terraced ground that slopes gently down to the lake. There is a
large private beach.
For access, turn off the main road SS49 at Km31/8 and drive for
400m.
Apr-Sep 1.8HEC ▦ ♠♟♖♚♥✕⊙ ⬛☐▥♠☎♟ LP ☎⊞ lau

LIDO DI JÉSOLO
See **JÉSOLO, LIDO DI**

LIGNANO SABBIADORO *Udine*
Sabbiadoro via Sabbiadoro 8 ☎0431 71455
May-Sep 13HEC ▦ ░░░ ♣♠♟♖♚♥✕⊙ ⬛☐▥♠☎☎♟ P ☎⊞ lau ♣
♟S Prices: A5900-10000 pitch 9600-17000

MALCESINE *Verona*
Claudia via Molini 2 ☎045 7400786
Apr-20 Oct 1HEC ▦ ♠♟♖♚♥✕⊙ ⬛☐♠☎ ☎♣✕ ♟L

MALGA CIAPELA *Belluno*
Malga Ciapela Marmolada ☎0437 722064
A terraced site in tranquil wooded surroundings at the foot on Mt.
Marmolada.
Jun-22 Sep & Dec-25 Apr 3HEC ▦ ♦♟♖♚♥⊙ ⬛☐▥♠☎♟ R ☎ lau
♣✕⊞ Prices: A8000-10000 pitch 9000-12000

MARGHERA *Venezia*
Jolly delle Querce via A-de-Marchi 7 ☎041 920312
The site lies on meadowland scattered with poplars.
For access, turn off into the Autostrada in Venezia in the direction of
Chioggia on the SS309 and continue for 200m.
Apr-Oct 3.6HEC ▦ ♣♠♟♖♚♥✕⊙ ⬛☐▥♠☎☎ ☎⊞ lau

MASARÉ *Belluno*
Alleghe ☎0437 723737
Several terraces on a wooded incline below a road.
16 Jun-Sep & Dec-1 May 2HEC ░░░ ♠♟♖♚✕⊙ ⬛☐▥♠☐ lau ♣♟✕
♟LR Prices: A9000-10000 pitch 10000-12000

MONFALCONE *Gorizia*
Isola Panzano Lido via Bagni 171 ☎0481 411202
15 May-15 Sep 13HEC ▦ ♣♠♟♖♚♥✕⊙ ⬛☐▥♠☎☎♟ S ☎⊞ lau
Prices: A7000-9000 pitch 13500-15500

MONTEGROTTO TERME *Padova*
Sporting Center ☎049 793400
5 Mar-10 Nov 6.5HEC ▦ ♣♠♟♖♚♥✕⊙ ⬛☐♠☎♟ P ☎⊞ lau ♣♟▥
Prices: A8000-1100 pitch 15000-21000

ORIAGO *Venezia*
Serenissima ☎041 920286
Etr-10 Nov 2HEC ▦ ♣♠♟♖♚♥✕⊙ ⬛☐▥♠☎♟ R ☎ lau ♣⊞
Prices: A9000 pitch 15000-18000

PACENGO *Verona*
Lido via Peschiera 2 ☎045 7590611
Apr-Sep 10HEC ♣♠♟♖♚♥✕⊙ ⬛☐▥♠☎♟ LP ☎⊞ lau

PALAFAVERA *Belluno*
Palafavera ☎0437 788506
1 Dec-1 Jun 5HEC ▦ ♠♟♖♚♥✕⊙ ⬛☐▥♠☎♟ R ☎✂ lau ♣⊞
Prices: A8000-10000 pitch 10000-12000

PESCHIERA DEL GARDA *Verona*
Bella Italia via Bella Italia 2 ☎045 6400688
Extensive lakeside site.

Turn off Brescia road between Km276.2 and Km275.8 and head towards lake.
15 Mar-5 Oct 20HEC ▥ ♠♠🛁🍴✕⊙🚗⌗🏕🚐 ⁇ LP ⚑⊞♨ lau
♣ ⁇R Prices: A6000-9500 pitch 14000-21000

Bergamini via Bergamini 51 ☎045 7550283
Apr-15 Sep 1.4HEC ♣♠♠🛁🍴✕⊙🚗⌗🏕 ⁇ LP ⚑ lau ♣✕⌀
Prices: A8000-12000 pitch 15000-25000

Garda via Marzan ☎045 7550540 & 7551899
A quiet, pleasant site with beach access on the shore of Lake Garda. Near the town centre, 2km from Milan/Venice motorway exit.
Apr-Sep 20HEC ▥ ♣♠♠🛁🍴✕⊙🚗⌗🏕🚐 ⁇ LP ⚑⊞♨ lau ♣📯
Prices: A6000-9000 pitch 12000-19000

San Benedetto via Bergamini 14 ☎045 7550544
Apr-Sep 220HEC ▥ ♣♠🛁🍴✕⊙🚗⌗🏕▲ ⁇ L ⚑⊞ lau ♣⌀📯 ⁇R

PORTO SANTA MARGHERITA *Venezia*

Pra'delle Torri ☎0421 299063
Extensive site on flat ground.
3km W at edge of beach.
May-29 Sep 53HEC ▥ ♣♠♠🛁🍴✕⊙🚗⌗🏕🚐 ⁇ PS ⚑⊞♨ lau
Prices: A4800-11000 pitch 8000-29000

PUNTA SABBIONI *Venezia*

Marina di Venezia via Montello 6 ☎041 5300955
Extensive, well-organised and well maintained holiday centre, extremely well appointed, with ample shade by trees. A section of the site is designated for dog owners, caravans and tents.
Access from the coastal road, turn seawards about 500m before the end then continue along narrow asphalt road. Well signposted approach.
Apr-Oct 80HEC ▥ ♣♠♠🛁🍴✕⊙🚗⌗🏕▲ ⁇ PS ⚑⊞ lau ♣📯
Prices: A6000-10000 pitch 17000-29000

Miramare Lungomare D-Alighieri 29 ☎041 966150
In a magnificent location overlooking the lagoon.
20 Mar-3 Nov 1.8HEC ▥ ♣♠♠🛁🍴✕⊙🚗⌗🏕 ⚑♨ lau ♣📯⊞
Prices: A5300-8000 pitch 11200-17600

ROSOLINA MARE *Rovigo*

Margherita via Foci Adige 10 ☎0426 68212
25 Apr-30 Sep 7HEC ▥ ∴ ♣♠♠🛁🍴✕⊙🚗📯 ⁇ PS ⚑ lau ♣
⌀ ⁇R ⊞ Prices: A6000-1000 pitch 8000-15000

Rosapineta Strada Nord 24 ☎0426 68033
The site lies in the grounds of an extensive holiday camp. Pitches for caravans and tents are separate.
Take Strada Romea towards Ravenna and drive to the bridge over the River Adige. Continue for 800m, then turn off, cross bridge and head towards Rosolina Mare and Rosapineta (approx 8km).
10 May-21 Sep 22HEC ▥ ∴ ♣♠🛁🍴✕⊙🚗⌗🏕🚐 ⁇ PS ⚑
⊞ lau ♣ ⁇R Prices: A5300-7800 🚐9800-13800 ▲6500-9100

TREPORTI *Venezia*

Cá Pasquali via Poerio 33 ☎041 966110
Sandy, meadowland site with poplar and pine trees.
Access from Cavallino-Punta Sabbioni coast road, along an asphalt road for 400m.
May-20 Sep 9HEC ▥ ∴ ♣♠♠🛁🍴✕⊙🚗⌗🏕🚐▲ ⁇ PS ⚑
⊞ ♨ lau Prices: A5500-8800 🚐11500-27000 ▲11500-27000

Cá Savio via Cà Savio ☎041 966017
A level site along the edge of the sea with private, sandy beach. Separate pitches for caravans and tents.
From Cá Savio, at traffic lights, turn towards the sea and continue for 500m to the beach.
May-Sep 268HEC ▥ ♣♠♠🛁🍴✕⊙🚗⌗🏕🚐 ⁇ PS ⚑⊞♨ lau

Fiori via V-Pisani 52 ☎041 966448
The site stretches over a wide area of sand dunes and pine trees with separate sections for caravans and tents.
24 Apr-6 Oct 10HEC ▥ ∴ ♣♠♠🛁🍴✕⊙🚗🏕🚐 ⁇ PS ⚑⊞♨
lau ♣⌀📯 ⁇R Prices: A6500-12700 pitch 13200-29800

Camping "ROMEO e GIULIETTA"
Via Bresciana 54 • I-37139 Verona
Telephone: (045) 8510243
Open from 1.3/30.11. *Coolbox ice for sale*

From the Brenner motorway: Verona-Nord exit towards Borgo Trento, about 2km on the SS 11 towards the town centre, site is on the left.

Swimming pool. Bar. Market. Play area. Thickly wooded. Camper service. Public bus to the town centre. Comfortable campsite. Ideal for visitors attending the Opera and Ballet festivals in the Arena **(including ticket reservations with or without transfer).**

Mediterráneo via delle Batterie 38 ☎041 966721
Slightly hilly grassland site with trees and sunshade roofs. Lunchtime siesta 13.00-15.00 hrs.
Camping Card Compulsory.
Well signposted.
1 May-Sep 17HEC ▥ ♣♠♠🛁🍴✕⊙🚗⌀🏕🚐 ⁇ PS ⚑⊞♨ lau

Scarpiland via A-Poerio 14 ☎041 966488
May-Sep 4.5HEC ▥ ♣♠♠🛁🍴✕⊙🚗⌀🏕🚐 ⁇ S ⚑⊞ lau
Prices: A4500-8000 pitch 9000-17000

VERONA *Verona*

Romeo & Giulietta ☎045 8510243
Comfortable site in wooded surroundings. Shop open June to September only.
Access via A22 exit 'Verona Nord' towards Borgo Trento.
Mar-Nov 3.5HEC ▥ ♣♠🛁⊙🚗⌀ ⁇ P ⚑ lau ♣✕

VICENZA *Vicenza*

Vicenza Strada Pelosa 239 ☎0444 582311
A modern, well-equipped site.
Access via A4 exit 'Vicenza-Est'.
22 Mar-Sep 3HEC ▥ ♣♠🍴✕⊙🚗📯▲ ⚑ lau ♣🛁✕⌀ ⁇R ⊞
Prices: A7000-8500 pitch 18000-24200

ZOLDO ALTO *Belluno*

Pala Favera ☎0437 788506 & 789161
Site with some woodland, at the foot of Monte Pelmo.
Dec-Apr & Jun-Sep 5HEC ▥ ♨♣♠🛁🍴✕⊙🚗⌀🏕 ⁇ R ⊞♨ lau
♣ ⊞ Prices: A8000-10000 pitch 10000-12000

North West/Med Coast

Liguria is known as the Italian Riviera, having many small harbours and a large and prosperous port, Genoa. Inland, the slopes of the Alps and Apennines, covered in lavender and herbs, provide the sheltering warmth in which carnations and chrysanthemums are grown as a major industry.
Tuscany stretches down the north western coast with medieval hill towns, towers and cultural centres such as Florence and Sienna, a medieval town famous for its fan shaped square Piazza del Campo and the Palio horse races run twice a year.
Landscapes vary from oak and chestnut woods near the Apennines, tall cypresses and farmhouses, vineyards (red Chianti is produced here), olive groves, and the rugged hills of the Carrara marble. Jousting and archery competitions take place between rival towns and festivals are occasions for pageantry. Elba, off the Tuscan coast, is a thriving holiday island with resorts around the coast, and inland you can find some attractive old villages with narrow alleyways or take the cable car from the village of Marciano to the top of Monte Capanne.

ALBENGA Savona
Bella Vista Campochiesa, Reg Campore 23 ☎0182 540213
1km from Km613.5 on SS1.
Apr-Sep 0.8HEC ▦ ◗ ⋒ ⛺ ♥ ✕ ⊙ ◙ ♨ ⬛ ◱ ⊞ lau ➧ ✕ ⇗PS

Green Village viale Che Guevara ☎0182 559248
Site facing the Mediterranean sea among eucalyptus and pine trees
with a private beach.
Signposted
Apr-Sep & 22 Dec-7 Jan 2HEC ▦ ♦ ⋒ ⛺ ♥ ✕ ⊙ ◙ ◱ ☎ lau ➧ ✕ ∅
⊯ ⇗PRS ⊞ Prices: pitch 35000-64000 (incl 3 persons)

Roma Regione Foce ☎0182 52317
The site is divided into pitches and laid out with many flower beds.
N of bridge over Centa, turn left.
Apr-Sep 0.8HEC ▦ ♦ ⋒ ⛺ ♥ ✕ ⊙ ◙ ♨ ⬛ ◱ ⇗ S ☎ lau ➧ ∅ ⇗PR ⊞

ALBINIA Grosseto
Acapulco via Aurelia ☎0564 870165
Set on hilly terrain in pine woodland.
Take coast road from via Aurelia at Km155.
15 May-15 Sep 2HEC ⋮⋮ ♦ ⋒ ⛺ ♥ ✕ ⊙ ◙ ♨ ♨ ⬛ ◱ ⇗ S ₧ ⊞ ⊛ lau
Prices: A6000-10500 pitch 95000-17000

Hawaii ☎0564 870164
The site lies in a pine forest on rather hilly ground.
Turn off via Aurelia at Km154/V and drive towards the sea.
22 Apr-30 Sep 4HEC ▦ ♦ ⋒ ⛺ ♥ ✕ ⊙ ◙ ♨ ♨ ⬛ ◱ ⇗ S ₧ ⊞ ⊛ lau
Prices: A6000-11000 pitch 9500-17000

International Argentario ☎0564 870302
Set in a pine forest on the shores of the Bay of Porto S Stefano.
Mooring facilities.
Etr-Sep 10HEC ♦ ⋒ ⛺ ♥ ✕ ⊙ ◙ ♨ ⬛ ◱ ⇗ S ₧ ⊞ ⊛ lau
See advertisement under Colour Section

BIBBONA, MARINA DI Livorno
See also FORTE DI BIBBONA
Capannino via cavalleggeri sud 26 ☎0586 600252
Well tended park site in pine woodland with private beach.
On via Aurelia by Km272/VII turn towards sea.
May-Sep 3HEC ▦ ⋮⋮ ♦ ⋒ ⛺ ♥ ✕ ⊙ ◙ ♨ ⬛ ◱ ⇗ S ₧ ⊞ ⊛ lau ➧ ✕ ∅
⇗P Prices: A7000-11000 pitch 12500-15500

Casa di Caccia via del Mare 40, La Califorina ☎0586 600000
19 Mar-15 Oct 3.5HEC ⋮⋮ ♦ ⋒ ⛺ ♥ ✕ ⊙ ◙ ♨ ⬛ ◱ ⇗ S ☎ ⊞ ⊛
lau Prices: A7000-13000 V5000-5500 ◱11000-15000 ▲11000-
15000

Free Beach via Cavalleggeri Nord 88 ☎0586 600388
Situated 300m from the sea through pine woods.
Etr-Sep 9HEC ▦ ⋮⋮ ◗ ⋒ ⛺ ♥ ✕ ⊙ ◙ ♨ ⇗ LP ₧ lau ➧ ⇗S

BOGLIASCO Genova
Genova Est via Marconi, Localitá Cassa ☎010 3472053
Feb-Nov 1.2HEC ▦ ♦ ⋒ ⛺ ♥ ✕ ⊙ ◙ ♨ ⬛ ◱ ▲ lau ➧ ⋒ ⇗S ⊞
Prices: A7500 V4500 ◱9000 ▲7500

BOTTAI Firenze
Internationale Firenze via S Cristoforo 2 ☎055 2374704
Apr-15 Oct 6HEC ▦ ◗ ⋒ ⛺ ♥ ✕ ⊙ ◙ ♨ ⬛ ◱ ⇗ P ₧ ⊞ lau
Prices: A10000 pitch 20000

CALENZANO Firenze
Autosole via V-Emanuele 11 ☎055 8825576
All year 2.2HEC ▦ ♦ ⋒ ⛺ ♥ ✕ ⊙ ◙ ♨ ◱ ⇗ P ☎ ⊞ lau ➧ ⋒ Prices:
A9500-10500 pitch 14500-16500

CAPANNOLE Arezzo
Chiocciola via G-Cesare 14 ☎055 995776
15 Mar-Oct 2HEC ▦ ♦ ⋒ ⛺ ♥ ✕ ⊙ ◙ ♨ ∅ ⬛ ◱ ⇗ P ₧ ⊞ lau ➧ ✕ ⇗R
Prices: A10000 ◱12000 ▲10000

CASALE MARITTIMO Pisa
Valle Gaia via Cecinese 87 ☎0586 681236
Site amongst pines and olive trees in a quiet rural location.
In Southern Cecina heading south from Livorno take the
autostrada/superstrada then take 2nd exit for Cecina (Casale

Marittimo - ignore first signpost for Cecina S Pietro). Camp is
signposted. Site about 9km from the coast.
22 Mar-18 Oct 4HEC ▦ ◗ ⋒ ⛺ ♥ ✕ ⊙ ◙ ♨ ⬛ ◱ ⇗ P ☎ ⊞ lau
Prices: A7900-10200 pitch 13300-19900

CASCIANO DI MURLO Siena
Soline ☎0577 817410
Terraced hilly site surrounded by woodland.
Take the left turning at Fontazzi and ascend hill.
All year 6HEC ▦ ◗ ⋒ ⛺ ♥ ✕ ⊙ ◙ ♨ ⬛ ◱ ▲ ⇗ P ☎ ⊞ lau
Prices: A9500 V3000 ◱10000 ▲7500-9000

CASTAGNETO CARDUCCI Livorno
Climatico Le Pianacce via Bolgherese ☎0565 763667
Terraced site on slopes of mountain in tyrpical Tuscany landscape,
enhanced by site landscaping. Pleasant climate due to height.
Turn off via Aurelia at Km344/VIII in direction of Castagneto
Carducci/Sassetta. In 3.2km to left in direction of Bolgheri, in 500m
turn right towards mountains.
15 Mar-15 Oct 9HEC ▦ ♦ ⋒ ⛺ ♥ ✕ ⊙ ◙ ♨ ∅ ⬛ ◱ ⇗ P ☎ ⊞ lau ➧ ⋒
Prices: A6500-10500 pitch 11000-180000

CASTEL DEL PIANO Grosseto
Amiata via Roma 15 ☎0564 955107
A grassland site with a separate section for dog owners.
On the outskirts of Castel del Piano, on the national road (SS) 323,
towards Arcidosso.
All year 4.2HEC ▦ ◗ ⋒ ⛺ ♥ ✕ ⊙ ◙ ♨ ∅ ⬛ ◱ ⊞ lau ➧ ⇗P Prices:
A6600-9900 pitch 6600-9900

CASTIGLIONE DELLA PESCAIA Grosseto
Santa Pomata Strada della Rocchette ☎0564 941037
Site in hilly woodland terrain with some pitches amongst bushes. Flat
clean sandy beach.
Turn off the SS322 at Km20, then in direction of Le Rocchette
4.5km NW and continue towards the sea for 1km to site on left.
Etr-20 Oct 6HEC ▦ ⋮⋮ ♦ ⋒ ⛺ ♥ ✕ ⊙ ◙ ♨ ⬛ ◱ ⇗ S ₧ ⊞ lau
Prices: A7000-12000 pitch 10000-18000

CÉCINA, MARINA DI Livorno
Tamerici ☎0586 620629
Camping Card Compulsory
All year 8.7HEC ▦ ♦ ⋒ ⛺ ♥ ✕ ⊙ ◙ ♨ ∅ ⬛ ◱ ⊞ ⊛ lau ➧ ⇗PRS
Prices: A8000-12000 V3500-5500 ◱10000-14500 ▲10000-
14500

CERIALE Savona
Baciccia via Torino 19 ☎0182 990743
An orderly site, lying inland off the via Aurelia.
Entrance 100m W of Km612/V.
All year 1.2HEC ▦ ♦ ⋒ ⛺ ♥ ✕ ⊙ ◙ ♨ ∅ ⬛ ◱ ⇗ P ☎ ⊞ lau ➧ ✕
⇗S

CERVO Imperia
Lino ☎183 400087
A seaside site shaded by grape vines, which is clean and well
managed. There is a knee-deep lagoon suitable for children.

Turn off via Aurelia at Km637/V near the railway underpass and follow via Nazionale Sauro towards sea.
14 Mar-15 Oct 1.1HEC ▦ ⋙ ♦ ⋒ ⛴ ⵀ ⅄ ⊙ ⊘ ∅ ┉ ⊞ ⟲ S ⊞ lau ➡ ✗
Prices: pitch 33000-60000 (incl 2 persons)

DEIVA MARINA *La Spezia*

Costabella ☎0817 825343
Etr-Sep 1.5HEC ▦ ♦ ⋒ ⛴ ⵀ ⅄ ✗ ⊙ ⊘ ∅ ┉ lau ➡ ⟲S ⊞ Prices:
A8500-11500 V2500 ⊞8500-14000 ▲6500-11500

Villaggio Turistico Arenella Arenella ☎0187 825259
In a beautiful, quiet valley 1.5km from the sea with good facilities.
Access via A12 (Genoa-La Spezia).
Closed Nov 1.6HEC ▦ ♦ ⋒ ⛴ ⵀ ⅄ ✗ ⊙ ⊘ ∅ ┉ ⊞ ⊞ ⟲ lau ➡ ⟲S ⊞
Prices: A9000-10000 ⊞9000-10000 ▲7000-10000

ELBA, ISOLA D' *Livorno*

MORCONE

Croce del Sud de Vago Giovanna ☎0565 968640
Apr-15 Oct 1HEC ▦ ⋒ ⋒ ⛴ ⵀ ⅄ ✗ ⊙ ⊘ ∅ ┉ ⊞ lau ➡ ⟲S

NISPORTO

Sole e Mare ☎0565 934907
Apr-10 Oct 1.5HEC ▦ ♦ ⋒ ⛴ ⵀ ⅄ ✗ ⊙ ⊘ ∅ ┉ ⊞ ⊞ ⟲ S ⊞ lau ➡ ⟲P

ORTANO

Canapai ☎0565 939165
Camping Card Compulsory.
15 May-Sep 3.7HEC ♦ ⋒ ⋒ ⛴ ⵀ ⅄ ✗ ⊙ ⊘ ∅ ⊞ ⊞ ⊞ ➡ ⟲S

OTTONE

Rosselba le Palme ☎0565 933101
24 Apr-Sep 30HEC ▦ ♦ ⋒ ⛴ ⵀ ⅄ ✗ ⊙ ⊘ ∅ ┉ ⊞ ⊞ lau ➡ ⟲S

PORTO AZZURRO

Reale ☎0565 95678
Apr-Sep 2.5HEC ▦ ♦ ⋒ ⛴ ⵀ ⅄ ✗ ⊙ ⊘ ∅ ┉ ⊞ ⟲ S ⊞ lau Prices:
A10000-14000 V3000-4000 ⊞12000-18000 ▲12000-18000

PORTOFERRAIO

Acquaviva Acquqviva ☎0565 930674
Etr-Sep 1.7HEC ▦ ⋙ ♦ ⋒ ⛴ ⵀ ⅄ ✗ ⊙ ⊘ ∅ ⊞ ⟲ S ⊞ lau ➡ ✗ ┉
Prices: A10000-18500 V3000-4000 ⊞11000-20500 ▲11000-20500

Enfola Enfola ☎0565 939001
Apr-Sep 1OHEC ▦ ⋒ ⋒ ⛴ ⵀ ⅄ ✗ ⊙ ⊘ ∅ ∅ ┉ ⊞ ⟲ S ⊞ lau ➡ ⊞
Prices: A10000-18500 V4000 ⊞13500-20000 ▲10000-19000

Scaglieri via Biodola 1, casella postale 158 ☎0565 969940
Apr-Oct 2HEC ⋙ ♦ ⋒ ⛴ ⵀ ⅄ ✗ ⊙ ⊘ ∅ ⊞ ⊞ ⊞ lau ➡ ⟲PS Prices:
A11000-19000 V4500 ⊞16000-20000 ▲11000-19000

FIÉSOLE *Firenze*

Panoramico via Peramonda 1 ☎055 599069
All year 5.5HEC ▦ ♦ ⋒ ⛴ ⵀ ⅄ ✗ ⊙ ⊘ ∅ ┉ ⊞ ⊞ ⟲ lau ➡ ┉ Prices:
A11000 pitch 19000

FIGLINE VALDARNO *Firenze*

Norcenni Girasole via Norcenni 7 ☎055 959666
Terraced site on partial slope. Separate section for young people.
3km W of village. Take Valdarno motorway exit and drive N for 15km.
All year 11HEC ▦ ⊚ ♦ ⋒ ⛴ ⵀ ⅄ ✗ ⊙ ⊘ ∅ ┉ ⊞ ⟲ P ⊞ ⊞ lau

FIRENZE (FLORENCE) *Firenze*

See also Troghi

At MARCIALLA

Toscana Colliverdi via Marcialla 108, Certaldo ☎0571 669334
A sloping, terraced site with good facilities, surrounded by vineyards and olive groves.
Access via 'Firenze-Certosa' exit on Autostrada del Sole or 'Tavarnelle Valpesa' exit on Autostrada del Palio.
Apr-Sep 2.4HEC ▦ ⊚ ⋒ ⊙ ⊞ ⊞ lau ➡ ⛴ ⅄ ✗ ∅ Prices: A7500 pitch 16000

FLORENCE

See FIRENZE

FORTE DI BIBBONA *Livorno*

See also BIBBONA, MARINA DI

Capanne via Aurelia ☎0586 600064
Site is situated on level tidy grassland amongst trees.
Access from Km273 via Aurelia travelling inland.
May-15 Sep 6HEC ▦ ♦ ⋒ ⛴ ⵀ ⅄ ✗ ⊙ ⊘ ∅ ┉ ⊞ ⟲ P ⊞ lau ➡ ⟲S
Prices: A5600-9800 ⊞10500-13000 ▲10500-13000

Esperidi ☎0586 600196
Site stretching to the sea with pines and other coniferous trees.
Turn off via Aurelia, at Km727.7.
Apr-Sep 11HEC ▦ ♦ ⋒ ⛴ ⵀ ⅄ ✗ ⊙ ⊘ ∅ ⟲ S ⊞ ⊞ ⊞ lau

Forte via dei Platani 58 ☎0586 600155
Level site, grassy, sandy terrain.
Apr-Sep 8HEC ▦ ♦ ⋒ ⛴ ⵀ ⅄ ✗ ⊙ ⊘ ∅ ┉ ⊞ ⟲ P ⊞ ⊞ lau ➡ ⟲S

GROSSETO, MARINA DI *Grosseto*

Rosmarina via delle Colonie 37 ☎0564 36319
A modern site situated in a pine wood and close to the sea.
10 May-21 Sep 1.4HEC ⋙ ♦ ⋒ ⛴ ⵀ ⅄ ✗ ⊙ ⊘ ∅ ┉ ⟲ S ⊞ lau ➡
⊞ Prices: A8000-12000 pitch 11000-17000

IMPERIA *Imperia*

Eucalyptus ☎0183 61534
All year 1HEC ▦ ⊚ ⊘ ⋒ ⊙ ⊞ ➡ ⛴ ✗ ⟲S

LERICI *La Spezia*

Maralunga via Carpanini 61, Maralunga ☎0187 966589
Jun-Sep 1HEC ⋙ ♦ ⋒ ⛴ ⵀ ⅄ ✗ ⊙ ⊘ ∅ ⟲ S ⊞ ⊞ ➡ ✗ ┉ Prices:
A9000-12500 V8500 ⊞14000-17000 ▲8500-16000

MASSA, MARINA DI *Massa Carrara*

Giardino viale delle Pinete 382 ☎0585 869291

Camping le Capanne covering an area of 60,000 sq m is set in the heart of the magnificent Tuscan landscape with its wide range of places to visit and about 2000m from a sandy beach. The campsite is equipped with the latest washing and toilet facilities. We can also offer bungalows (fully equipped with showers & W.C.), spacious sites for tents and caravans, a wide range of sports facilities (boccie, table tennis, volleyball etc.) tennis courts and swimming pool (including lessons). Restaurant, bar and pizzeria.

To reach us take exit "BIBBONA-LA CALIFORNIA" from the Aurelia motorway and proceed in direction Rome.

CAMPING LE CAPANNE
I-57020 BIBBONA (LIVORNO)
Via Aurelia km. 273
Tel: 0039 (586) 600064

Site in pine woodland and on two meadows, shade provided by roof matting.
On the island side of the SS328 to Pisa.
Apr-Sep 3HEC ▦ ♠ ♠ ⚓ ♀ ✕ ⊙ ⚑ ▵ ⊞ ⚌ ⚐ ⊞ ⊞ ⊘ lau ➤ ⚜S

MONTECATINI TERME *Pistoia*
Belsito via delle Vigne ☎0572 67396
All year 6.4HEC ⚐ ♠ ⚓ ♀ ✕ ⊙ ⚑ ⚋ ▵ ⚌ ⚐ ⚑ Å ⚜ ✕ P ⊟ ⊞ ➤ ⚜LR

MONTE DI FO *Firenze*
Sergente ☎055 8423018
All year 1HEC ▦ ♠ ♠ ⚓ ♀ ✕ ⊙ ⚑ ⚋ ⚌ ⚐ ⚑ ⊞ lau Prices:
A8500 pitch 15000

MONTERIGGIONI *Siena*
Piscina Luxor Quies Loc Trasqua ☎0577 743047
Lies on a flat-topped hill, partly in an oak wood, partly in meadowland.
Turn off via Cassia (SS2) at Km239/II or Km238/IX and continue for further 2.5km, crossing railway line. Approach to site via very steep and winding road.
Jun-7 Sep 4.5HEC ▦ ♠ ♠ ⚓ ♀ ✕ ⊙ ⚑ ⚋ ⚜ P ⚐ ⊞ Prices: A9500
V4300 ⚑5200 Å4600

MONTESCUDÁIO *Livorno*
Montescudáio via del Poggetto ☎0586 683477
This modern site is situated on a hill and is completely divided into individual pitches, some of which are naturally screened. Children under 2 years are not accepted.
From Cecinia (on SS1, via Aurelia) follow road to Guardistallo for 2.5km.
10 May-28 Sep 25HEC ▦ ♠ ♠ ⚓ ♀ ✕ ⊙ ⚑ ⚋ ▵ ⚌ ⚐ ⊘ lau ➤
⚜S Prices: A7400-9500 pitch 16000-22000

MONTICELLO AMIATA *Grosseto*
Lucherino Lucherino ☎0564 992975
A peaceful site 735m above sea level on the slopes of Mount Amiata.
Access via SS223 to Paganico then follow signs to Monte Amiata.
15 Jun-15 Sep 2HEC ▦ ♠ ♠ ⚓ ♀ ✕ ⊙ ⚑ ⚋ ⚜ P ⚐ ⊞ ➤ lau ➤ ⚐ ▵
Prices: A8000-9000 ⚑9000-10000 Å7000-9000

PEGLI *Genova*
Villa Doria via al Campeggio 15n ☎010 6969600
Quiet site in pleasant wooded surroundings.
Access via SS1. Signposted.
All year 0.5HEC ♠ ♠ ⚓ ♀ ✕ ⊙ ⚑ ⚌ ⚑ ➤ ✕ ⚜S ⊞ Prices:
A7000 pitch 12000-16000

PISA *Pisa*
Torre Pendente viale della Cascine 86 ☎050 561704
Pleasant, modern site in a rural setting. 1km walk to the Leaning Tower.
18 Mar-15 Oct 2.5HEC ▦ ♠ ♠ ⚓ ♀ ✕ ⊙ ⚑ ⚋ ⚑ Å ⚐ ⊞ lau ➤ ▵
Prices: A9500-10000 V5000 ⚑8000 Å7000

POPULÓNIA *Livorno*
Sant'Albinia via della Principessa ☎0565 29389
A good overnight stopping place with plenty of facilities. Ideally placed for the ferry ports.
10km N of Piombino on the San Vincenzo road.
May-15 Sep 3HEC ▦ ♠ ♠ ⚓ ♀ ✕ ⊙ ⚑ ⚌ Å ⚜ S ⊟ ⊞ ⊘ lau
Prices: A6700-9800 V2900-4000 ⚑8000-12000 Å7000-9000

RIOTORTO *Livorno*
Orizzonte Perelli ☎0565 28007
In a fine coastal position overlooking the island of Elba.
All year 10HEC ▦ ♠ ♠ ⚓ ♀ ✕ ⊙ ⚑ ⚋ ⚌ ⚑ ⊟ ⊞ lau ➤ ⚜PS Prices:
A5000-17000 pitch 13000-21000

SAN BARONTO *Firenze*
Barco Reale via Nardini 11-13 ☎0573 88332
Apr-Sep 8.5HEC ▦ ♠ ♠ ⚓ ♀ ✕ ⊙ ⚑ ⚋ ▵ ⚌ ⚑ ⚜ P ⚐ ⊞ lau
Prices: A9000 V4700 ⚑10000 Å8000

SAN GIMIGNANO *Siena*
Boschetto di Piemma Santa Lucia ☎0577 940352
Apr-15 Oct 1.5HEC ▦ ♠ ♠ ⚓ ♀ ✕ ⊙ ⚑ ⚋ ⚑ ⚜ P ⊟ ⊞ ➤ ▵ Prices:
A7500 V3500 ⚑7500 Å700

SAN PIERO A SIEVE *Firenze*
Mugello Verde via Masso Rondinaio 2 ☎055 848511
Terraced site in wooded surroundings. Lunchtime siesta 14.00-16.00 hrs.
Leave motorway at exit 18 and follow signs.
All year 12HEC ▦ ♠ ♠ ⚓ ♀ ✕ ⊙ ⚑ ⚋ ▵ ⚑ ⚜ P ⚐ ⊞ lau ➤ ⚜R

SAN REMO *Imperia*
Villaggio dei Fiori via Tiro a Volo 3 ☎0184 660635
All year 2.3HEC ▦ ♠ ♠ ⚓ ♀ ✕ ⊙ ⚑ ⚑ ⚜ PS ⚐ ⊞ ⊘ lau ➤ ⚐ ⚋ ▵

SAN VINCENZO *Livorno*
Park Albatros ☎0565 701018
The site lies amongst beautiful, tall pine trees. 1km from sea.
Turn off SP23 beyond San Vincenzo at Km7/III and drive 600m inland.
5 Apr-9 Sep 11.4HEC ▦ ♠ ♠ ⚓ ♀ ✕ ⊙ ⚑ ⚋ ⚌ Å ⚐ ⊞ ⊘ lau ➤
⚜S

SARTEANO *Siena*
Bagno Santo via del Bagno Santo 29 ☎0578 265531
24 Mar-Sep 15HEC ▦ ⠿ ♠ ♠ ⚓ ♀ ✕ ⊙ ⚑ ⚑ ⚜ P ⚐ ⊞ ⊘ lau ➤ ⚐
⚋ ▵ Prices: A12000-15000 V4500-5500 ⚑11500-15000 Å11500-15000

Delle Piscine ☎0578 26971
The site lies 8 km S of Chianciano Terme; 6 km from Chiusi/Chianciano Terme motorway (A1) exit.
Apr-Sep 15HEC ⚐ ♠ ♠ ✕ ⊙ ⚑ ⚑ ⚜ P ⚐ ⊞ ⊘ lau Prices:
A14500 pitch 19500

SARZANA *La Spezia*
Iron Gate via XXV Aprile 54 ☎0187 676370
All year 120HEC ▦ ♠ ⚓ ♀ ✕ ⊙ ⚑ ⚋ ▵ ⚌ ⚜ PR ⚐ ⊘ ➤ ⚜S

SESTRI LEVANTE *Genova*
Fossa Lupara via Costa 31 ☎0185 43992
All year 1.3HEC ▦ ♠ ♠ ⚓ ♀ ✕ ⊙ ⚑ ⚋ ▵ ⚐ ⊞ lau ➤ ⚜S

SIENA *Siena*
Montagnola Sovicille ☎0577 314473
Quiet site in an oak wood.
Etr-Sep 2.5HEC ▦ ⠿ ♠ ♠ ⚓ ♀ ✕ ⊙ ⚑ ⚋ ▵ ⚌ ⚐ ➤ ✕ ⊞ Prices:
A9000 pitch 9000

Siena Colleverde Strada di Scacciapensieri 47 ☎0577 280044
21 Mar-10 Nov 4.5HEC ▦ ♠ ♠ ⚓ ♀ ✕ ⊙ ⚑ ⚋ ⚜ P ⚐ lau ➤ ⊞
Prices: A11000-13000 pitch 14000-18000

STELLA SAN GIOVANNI *Savona*
Stella Riobasco ☎019 703269
Apr-Sep 3.2HEC ▦ ♠ ♠ ✕ ⊙ ⚑ ⚋ ▵ ⚜ PR ⚐ lau ➤ ⚐ ⚋ ⚜S ⊞
Prices: pitch 32000-41000 (incl 3 persons)

TALAMONE Grosseto

International Camping Talamone ☎0564 887026
Some facilities may not be available before April and vehicles must
use a separate car park during the high season.
Etr-Sep 5HEC ▥ ♨ ♩✔ ♠ ♠ ✗ ⊙ ♠ ⅂ P ♦ ⅂S

TORRE DEL LAGO PUCCINI Lucca

Burlamacco via le Marconi Int ☎0584 359544
Apr-Sep 4HEC ▥ ♦ ♠ ♠ ⅂ ✗ ⊙ ♠ ∅ ♨ ♠ ♠ A ⅂ P ▣ ✋ ♦ ⅂S ⊞
Prices: A5800-9800 V4000 ♠10500-18000

Europa ☎0584 350707
Site in pine and poplar woodland.
On the land side of the viale dei Tigli, coming from Viareggio.
Apr-Sep 5.5HEC ▥ ♦ ♠ ♠ ⅂ ✗ ⊙ ♠ ∅ ♨ ♠ ⅂ S ② ⊞ ✋ ♦ ⅂LPR
Prices: A6000-10000 pitch 11000-16000

Italia ☎0584 359828
This site is divided into pitches and lies in meadowland planted with
poplar trees.
Inland from the Viareggio road (viale dei Tigli).
23 Apr-14 Sep 9HEC ▥ ♦ ♠ ♠ ⅂ ✗ ⊙ ♠ ∅ ♨ ♠ ♠ ▣ ⊞ ✋ lau ♦
✗ ⅂LS Prices: A6000-10000 pitch 11000-16000

Tigli ☎0584 341278
Camping Card Compulsory.
Apr-Sep 9HEC ▥ ♦ ♠ ♠ ⅂ ✗ ⊙ ♠ ∅ ♨ ♠ ② ⊞ ♦ ⅂LPS Prices:
A8800 pitch 12000

TROGHI Firenze

Il Poggetto Il Poggetto 143 ☎055 8307323
A modern site with good facilities.
5km from exit 'Incisa Valdarno' on the A1.
All year 4.5HEC ▥ ♦ ♠ ♠ ⅂ ✗ ⊙ ♠ ∅ ♨ ♠ A ⅂ P ② ⊞ lau
Prices: A9000-10000 pitch 16000-17500

VADA Livorno

Flori ☎0586 770096
Level grassland surrounded by fields. Shade provided by roof
matting.
Access from the SS1 S of Vada, after 1.5km turn right and continue
for 500m.
29 Mar-Sep 15HEC ♦ ♠ ♠ ⅂ ✗ ⊙ ♠ ∅ ♨ ♠ ⅂ P ② ⊞ lau ♦ ⅂S
Prices: A7500-10000 V2300-3500 ♠12000-16000 ▲12000-
16000

Rada Etrusca via Cavalleggeri 77 ☎0586 788344
25 Apr-Sep 4.5HEC ▥ ♦ ♠ ♠ ⅂ ✗ ⊙ ♠ ∅ ♨ ♠ ⅂ S ▣ ⊞ ✋ lau

VIAREGGIO Lucca

Paradiso via dei Tigli ☎0584 392005
Site with tall pine trees and firm terrain.
2.5km S off via Aurelia at Km354/V onto via Comparini towards the
sea to site in 600m.
May-15 Sep 4.8HEC ▥ ♦ ♠ ♠ ⅂ ✗ ⊙ ♠ ∅ ♨ ♠ ⅂PS

Pineta via dei Lecci ☎0584 383397
May-20 Sep 3.2HEC ▥ ♦ ♠ ♠ ⅂ ✗ ⊙ ♠ ∅ ♨ ♠ ▣ ⊞ lau ♦ ⅂PS
Prices: A7500-11000 pitch 12000-16000

Viareggio via Comparini/viale dei Tigli ☎0584 391012
The site lies in a poplar wood.
1.5km S of town. At Km354/V head towards coast.
25 Apr-15 Sep 1.8HEC ▥ ♦ ♠ ♠ ⅂ ✗ ⊙ ♠ ∅ ♨ ⅂ S ② ⊞ ✋ lau ♦
⅂L Prices: A6000-10000 ♠14000-16000 ▲11000-16000

VOLTERRA Pisa

Balze via di Mandringa 15 ☎0588 87880
Mar-Oct 3.2HEC ▥ ♨ ♠ ♠ ♠ ⅂ ✗ ⊙ ♠ ∅ ⅂ P ② ♦ ✗ ♨ ⊞

ZINOLA Savona

Buggi International via N S del Monte 15 ☎019 860120
All year 3HEC ▥ ♦ ♠ ♠ ⅂ ✗ ⊙ ♠ ♠ ② lau ♦ ∅ ♨ ⅂PS ⊞
Prices: A8500 V7500 ♠10000 ▲8000

North East/Adriatic

This area covers some very dissimilar regions east of the
Apennine mountains on whose slopes the glaciers glint for much
of the year. Fish from the Adriatic make specialities like the fish
soup *brodetto* worth trying. Inland you may like to try Bologna's
Mortadella sausage and the Lambrusco Frizzante wine. Emilia
Romagna's varied geography - mountains, the river Po and the
sea - allows winter skiing, and walking in pine forests in summer.
Art lovers can see the mosaics in Ravenna, or Corrigio's
paintings in Parma, a town which is famous for its dried ham and
cheese.
In the rugged Marches you can find the splendid Renaissance
palace of Urbino or perhaps visit the hill town of Maceratas which
has a Roman arena where concerts and dramas are held, or go
to Ascoli Piceno, enclosed by two rivers and with a delightful
town centre.
The Abruzzo in the centre of Italy is dramatic with high mountains,
and a National Park where bears, chamois and wolves live.
Attractive towns like L'Aquila dominated by its castle, contrast
with the flourishing seaside resorts such as Pescara.

ALBA ADRIATICA Teramo

At **TORTORETO, LIDO**(4km S)

Salinello c da Piane a Mare ☎0861 786306
Well-tended meadowland site with numerous rows of poplars. Private
beach, siesta 13.30-16.00 hrs.
On southern outskirts, signposted from Km405 of the SS16.
15 May-28 Sep 15HEC ▥ ♦ ♠ ♠ ⅂ ✗ ⊙ ♠ ∅ ♨ ♠ ⅂ P ② ⊞ ✋
lau ♦ ⅂S Prices: A4000-9500 pitch 12000-23000

AQUILA, L' L'Aquila

Funivia del Gran Sasso Fonte Cerreto ☎0862 606163
Etr, 15 May-24 Sep 1HEC ▥ ♦ ♠ ♠ ⅂ ✗ ⊙ ♠ ♠ A ▣ ♦ ⊞
Prices: A6000-7000 V2000 ♠9000-10000 ▲5000-6000

ASSISI Perugia

Internationale via San Giovanni, Campiglione 110 ☎075 813710
Etr-Oct 3HEC ▥ ♨ ♠ ♠ ⅂ ✗ ⊙ ♠ ♨ ♠ A ② ⊞ ♦ ∅ Prices: A8000
V3000 ♠9000 ▲7000

BARREA L'Aquila

Grenziana Parco Nazionale d'Abruzzo, Tre Croci ☎0864 88101
In picturesque wooded surroundings on the shore of a lake.
All year 2HEC ▥ ♨ ♠ ♠ ⅂ ✗ ⊙ ♠ ∅ ♠ A ② lau ♦ ✗ ♨ ⊞ Prices:
A8000 V5000 ♠12000 ▲11000-12000

BELLARIA Forli

Happy via Panzini 228 ☎0541 346102
Apr-Sep 4HEC ▥ ∷∷ ♨ ♠ ♠ ⅂ ✗ ⊙ ♠ ∅ ♨ ♠ ⅂ PS ② lau ♦ ⅂L
⊞ Prices: A7500-12000 pitch 15000-25000

BOLOGNA Bologna

Citta di Bologna via Romita 12/IVA ☎051 325016
All year 6.3HEC ▥ ♨ ♠ ♠ ⅂ ✗ ⊙ ♠ ♠ ② ⊞ lau ♦ ✗ ∅ ♨ Prices:
A5500-7500 pitch 12000

BORGHETTO Perugia

Badiaccia strada Umbro Casentinese, Bivio Borghetto
☎075 9659097
Apr-Sep 5.5HEC ▥ ♦ ♠ ♠ ⅂ ✗ ⊙ ♠ ∅ ♠ ♠ ⅂ LP ▣ ⊞ lau ♦ ♨ A
Prices: A9000-9500 V3000 ♠9000-10000 ▲8000-9000

BRUCIATA Modena

Modena via Cave di Ramo 111 ☎059 332252
Apr-Sep 1HEC ▥ ♦ ♠ ♠ ⅂ ✗ ⊙ ♠ ∅ ⅂ P ② ⊞ lau ♦ ⅂R Prices:
A8000 pitch 13000-16000

CASALBORDINO, MARINA DI Chieti

Santo Stefano ☎0873 918118
Level terrain, below road, within agricultural area, adjoining railway
line. Open air disco. Lunchtime siesta 14.00-16.00 hrs.
Camping Card Compulsory.

Exit off Vastro-Nord of A14 and continue north via SS16 to Km498.
All year 2HEC ▦ ♠♠☎☎♥✕☉♥⌀☷☎⚡ S ⚉⚘ lau ♦ ⊞

CASAL BORSETTI Ravenna

Adria via Spallazzi N30 ☎0544 445217
The site lies in a field behind the Ristorante Lugo.
Turn off the motorway at the Ravenna exit or take the SS309
(Romea) Km13 N of Ravenna.
May-20 Sep 4.4HEC ▦ ♠♠☎☎♥✕☉♥⌀☷☎ ⚡ PS ⚉⊞ lau

Reno via Spaccazzi 11 ☎0544 445020
Meadowland in sparse pine woodland and separated from the sea by
dunes.
Turn off SS309 at Km8 or 14.
Apr-Sep 33HEC ▦ ♠♠☎☎♥✕☉♥⌀☷☎⚉⊞ lau ♦ ⚡S Prices:
A7000-8500 pitch 12000-14000

CASTIGLIONE DEL LAGO Perugia

Listro via Lungolago ☎075 951193 & 96581
Apr-Sep 2HEC ▦ ♠♠☎☉♥☷⚡ L ⚉⚘♦♥✕⚡P⊞

CERVIA Ravenna

Adriatico via Pinarella 90 ☎0544 71537
Level meadowland site with plenty of shade, pleasantly landscaped
with olives, willows, elms and maples.
Located shortly before Pinarella di Cervia. Access by via Cadultí per
le Liberta (SS16) 600m from sea.
10 May-14 Sep 3.4HEC ▦ ♠♠☎☎♥✕☉♥⌀☷⚡ P ⚉⊞ lau ♦
⚡S Prices: A5400-7900 pitch 13100-15200

CESENATICO Forli

Cesenatico via Mazzini 182 ☎0547 81344
The site stretches over an area of land belonging to the Azienda di
Soggiomo e Turismo.
1.5km N at Km178 turn off the SS16 towards the sea.
29 Mar-21 Sep 19HEC ▦ ∴∴ ♠♠☎☎♥✕☉♥⚡ S ⚉⊞ lau ♦
⌀⚡P Prices: A6000-10500 pitch 17000-23500

Zadina via Mazzini 184 ☎0547 82310
Very pleasant terrain in dunes on two sides of a canal.
23 Apr-16 Sep 10HEC ∴∴ ♠♠☎☎♥✕☉♥⌀☷⚡ S ⚉⊞ lau

CIVITANOVA MARCHE Macerata

Nuove Giare via Castelletta 34 ☎0733 70440
15 May-15 Sep 6HEC ▦ ♠♠☎♥✕☉♥⌀☷☎⚡ PS ⚉⊞ lau

CUPRAMARITTIMA Ascoli Piceno

Calypso via Boccabianca 8 ☎0735 778686
Apr-Sep 26HEC ▦ ♠♠☎☎♥✕☉♥⌀☷⚡ PS ⊞ lau Prices:
A5500-10500 pitch 11000-20000

DANTE, LIDO DI Ravenna

Classe viale Catone ☎0544 492005
Level meadowland in grounds of former farm.
Access from the SS16 turning towards the sea at Km154/V and
continue 9km to site.
10 May-30 Sep 7.1HEC ▦ ♠♠☎☎♥✕☉♥⌀☷☎⚡A ⚡ PS ⚉
⊞ lau Prices: A7000-9000 V5000 ⚑12000-15500 ▲9000-10000

ESTENSI, LIDO DEGLI Ferrara

International Mare Pineta via delle Acace 67
☎0533 330194 & 330110
Extensive site on slightly hilly ground under pines and decidous
trees, providing shade. Near the beach and has numerous mobile
homes.
2km SE of Port Garibaldi.
24 Apr-22 Sep 16HEC ▦ ∴∴ ♠♠☎☎♥✕☉♥⌀☷☎⚡ PS ⚉
lau Prices: A6500-11300 pitch 11600-18400
See advertisement under Colour Section

FANO Pesaro & Urbino

Mare Blu ☎0721 884201
Apr-Sep 2HEC ▦ ♠♠☎☎♥✕☉♥⌀☷⚡ S ⚉⊞⚘ lau ♦ ⚡PR

FERRARA Ferrara

Estense via Gramicia ☎0532 752396
Mar-30 Oct 3.3HEC ▦ ♠♠♥☎☎⚡PR ⚉ lau ♦ ☎♥✕⌀☷⚡P⊞
Prices: A3000-5000 pitch 8000-12000

FIORENZUOLA DI FOCARA Pesaro & Urbino

Panorama Strada Panoramica ☎0721 208145
May-Sep 2.2HEC ▦ ♠♠☎☎♥✕☉♥⌀☷☎⚡ PS ⚉⊞ lau
Prices: A6500-10000 V3500-4500 ⚑8500-12000 ▲8500-12000

GATTEO MARE Forli

Rose via Adriatica 29 ☎0547 86213
In a peaceful setting close to the sea and the town centre. Turn off
SS16, at Km186.
May-25 Sep 5HEC ▦ ∴∴ ♠♠☎☎♥✕☉♥⌀☷☎⚡ PS ⚉⊞
lau Prices: A5700-10700 pitch 13000-20000

MAGIONE Perugia

Villaggio Italgest via Martiri di Cefalonia ☎075 848238
Situated by a lake and surrounded by woodland. There are good,
modern facilities and all kinds of recreation are available.
Apr-Sep 3.5HEC ▦ ♠♠☎☎♥✕☉♥☷☎⚡A ⚡ LP ⚉⊞ lau ♦ ⌀
Prices: A8000-9500 V2500-3500 ⚑8500-10000 ▲7000-9000

MARCELLI DI NUMANA Ancona

Conero Azzurro via Litoranea ☎071 7390507
May-15 Sep 5HEC ▦ ♠♠☎☎♥✕☉♥⌀☷☎⚡ PS ⚉⊞ lau
Prices: A8000-11000 V4000-5000 ⚑13000-16000 ▲13000-
16000

MAROTTA Pesaro & Urbino

Gabbiano via Faa' di Bruno 95 ☎0721 96691
May-Sep 2HEC ▦ ♠♠☎☎♥✕☉♥⌀☷⚡ P ⚉⚘ lau ♦ ⚡S ⊞
Prices: A7000-8500 pitch 16000-19000

MARTINISCURO Teramo

Duca Amedeo Lungomare Europa 158 ☎0861 797376
By the sea.
May-20 Sep 1.6HEC ▦ ♠♠☎☎♥✕☉♥⌀☷☎⚡ S ⚉⊞ lau ♦ ☎
✕ Prices: A4500-9000 pitch 13000-22000

MILANO MARITTIMA Ravenna

Romagna viale Matteoti 190 ☎0544 949326
Level and flat site with young trees.
Access via the SS16 (Strada Adriatica) turn off beyond Milano
Marittima and follow signs.
25 Apr-15 Sep 4HEC ▦ ∴∴ ♠♠☎☎♥✕☉♥⌀☷⚡ S ⚉⚘ lau ♦ ⊞
Prices: A6000-9000 ⚑12000-17000 ▲12000-15000

MONTENERO, MARINA DI Campobasso

Costa Verde ☎0873 803144
This seaside site lies E of San Salvo Marino.
Camping Card Compulsory.
Leave the coast road, SS16, at Km525/VII and continue by a farm
road for 300m to the site.
May-15 Sep 1HEC ▦ ♠♠☎☎♥✕☉♥⌀☷☎⚡A ⚡ RS ⚉⊞⚘

NAZIONI, LIDO DELLE Ferrara

Tahiti viale Libia 133 ☎0533 379500
Pleasantly laid out site 650m from sea. Has own private beach
accessible via a miniature railway. Lunchtime siesta 13.30-15.30 hrs.
Turn off SS309 near Km32.5 then 2km to site. Signposted.
10 May-21 Sep 8HEC ▦ ∴∴ ♠♠☎☎♥✕☉♥⌀☷☎ ⚡
P ⚉⊞⚘ lau ♦ ⚡S
Prices: A6800-11000 pitch 12800-20900

OLMO Perugia

Rocolo strada Trinita Fontana 1-N ☎075 5178550
15 Jun-15 Sep 2.4HEC ▦ ♠♠☎☎♥✕☉♥⚑☷A ⚉♦⌀☷⚡LP
Prices: A8000-8500 V3000-3500 ⚑8500-9500 ▲6000-7000

ORVIETO Terni

Orvieto Lago di Corbara ☎0744 950240
Turn off SS448 at Km3.770.
Etr-Sep 1.6HEC ▦ ♠♠☎☎♥✕☉♥⌀☎☎A ⚡ LP ⚉⊞ lau

PARMA Parma

Cittadella ☎0521 961434
Camping Card Compulsory.
Apr-Oct 0.4HEC ▦ ♠♠☎♥☉♥⚉⚉♠☎♥✕ Prices: A9500 V8000
⚑8000 ▲8000

PASSIGNANO *Perugia*
Kursaal viale Europa 41 ☎075 828085
The site is situated between the road and the lake, near the villa of the same name.
Access from SS75, Arezzo to Perugia road, from Km35.2.
Apr-Oct 3HEC ▦ ♦♠️🐾♟️♥️✕⊙◉∅🏕️⚡ LP ፻⊞ lau ♦ ♨ Prices:
A9000-10000 pitch 14000-18000

PASSIGNANO SUL TRASIMENO *Perugia*
Europa Loc San Donato ☎075 827405
Situated by Lake Trasimeno with private beach.
From the motorway take exit Passignano Est and campsite is signposted.
Etr-05 Oct 3HEC ▦ ♦♠️🐾♟️♥️✕⊙◉∅♨🏕️♥️⚡△♟️ L ፻⊞ lau
Prices: A7500-8000 V3500-4000 ◗8000-8500 ▲6500-7000

PESARO *Pesaro & Urbino*
Marinella via Adriatica 244 ☎0721 55795
Access is through railway underpass from Km244 of SS16.
Apr-Sep 1.5HEC ▦ ⊕♠️🐾♟️♥️✕⊙◉∅♨🏕️⚡ S ፻⊞ lau
Prices: A8500-12000 V4000-6000 ◗8500-12500 ▲8000-10000

PETROGNANO *Perugia*
Il Girasole ☎0743 51335
S of Spoleto via SS3 towards Montefalco.
25 Mar-Sep 4HEC ▦ ♦♠️♟️♥️✕⊙◉∅♨🏕️△♟️
P ፻⊞⌀ lau ♦ ♨∅

PIEVEPELAGO *Modena*
Fra Dolcino ☎0536 71229
All year 4HEC ▦ ♦♠️🐾♟️♥️✕⊙◉∅♨🏕️⚡፻⊞ lau ♦ ♟️PR

Rio Verde via M-de-Canossa 34 ☎0536 72204
All year ▦ ⊕♠️♟️✕⊙◉♨🏕️♟️ R ℗ lau♦♨∅♨♟️P ⊞

PINARELLA *Ravenna*
Pinarella viale Abruzzi 52 ☎0544 987408
Subdivided terrain surrounded by houses. Partially shaded, some young plants. Private beach.
May-15 Sep 1.8HEC ▦ ♦♠️🐾♟️♥️✕⊙◉፻⊞⌀ lau ♦♨✕∅♟️S
Prices: A5100-7500 ◗11500-13500

Safari viale Titano 130 ☎0544 987356
The site is divided into several sections. Only families are accepted.
9 May-13 Sep 2.5HEC ▦ ♦♠️🐾♟️♥️✕⊙◉♨🏕️፻⊞⌀ lau♦✕
♟️S

PINETO *Teramo*
Heliopolis via Villa Fumosa ☎085 9492720
Apr-Sep 1.2HEC ▦ ♦♠️🐾♟️♥️✕⊙◉∅♨🏕️⚡♟️PS ℗ lau

International Loc Torre Cerrano ☎085 930639 & 9354262
Site on level terrain with young poplars. Sunshade roofing on the beach.
Turn off SS16 at Km431.2 and continue under railway underpass.
Adjoining railway line.
May-Sep 1.5HEC ▦ ♦♠️🐾♟️♥️✕⊙◉∅♨🏕️⚡♟️ S ℗⊞⌀ lau
Prices: A6000-9000 pitch 13000-22000

Pineto Beach ☎085 9492724
A well equipped site in wooded surroundings with direct access to the beach.
At Km425 on SS16 'Adriatica'.
Jun-Sep 2HEC ▦ ♦♠️🐾♟️♥️✕⊙◉∅♨🏕️♟️S ℗⊞

POMPOSA *Ferrara*
International Tre Moschettieri ☎0533 380076
Camp site set beneath pine trees next to sea.
Signposted from SS309.
23 Apr-21 Sep 11HEC ▦ ♦♠️🐾♟️♥️✕⊙◉∅♨🏕️⚡♟️PS ፻ lau♦♟️L
⊞ Prices: A4500-9000 pitch 10000-16000

Vigna sul Mar via Capanno Garibaldi 20 ☎0533 380216
Well tended meadowland under poplars. Well signposted from entrance to Lido.
Private beach of 1km beyond the dunes.
May-20 Sep 12HEC ▦ ♦♠️🐾♟️♥️✕⊙◉♨🏕️⚡♟️P ፻⊞ lau♦∅

PORTO RECANATI *Macerata*
Bellamare ☎071 976628
On the S side of the mouth of the Musone.
Access from the Autostrada exit Ancona Sud via the SS16 turn to S bank at Km324.
May-Sep 5HEC ▦ ⊕♠️🐾♟️♥️✕⊙◉∅♨🏕️♟️PS ፻⊞⌀ lau

PORTO SANT'ELPÍDIO *Ascoli Piceno*
Risacca ☎0734 991423
Clean, well-kept site on level meadowland, with some trees surrounded by fields.
Turn off main SS16 N of village, follow road seawards under railway (narrow underpass maximum height 3m), then 1.2km along field paths to site. Caravan access is 400m further S along SS16, then under railway and along field paths to site.
May-Sep 8HEC ▦ ♦♠️🐾♟️♥️✕⊙◉∅♨🏕️⚡♟️PS ℗⊞⌀ lau
Prices: A5200-11400 pitch 10600-25000

PUNTA MARINA *Ravenna*
At **ADRIANO, LIDO**(4.5km S)
Adriano via dei Campeggi 7 ☎0544 437230
300m from the sea. A pleasantly landscaped site amidst the dunes of the Punta Marina.
On SS309 via Lido Adriano to Punta Marina.
25 Apr-24 Sep 14HEC ▦ ♦♠️🐾♟️♥️✕⊙◉∅♨🏕️🏕️♟️P ፻⊞
lau♦♟️S

Coop 3 via dei Campeggi 8 ☎0544 437353
300m to the sea. Level site under isolated high pines and poplars.
Across flat dunes to the beach.
Signposted.
25 Apr-14 Sep 7HEC ▦ ♦♠️🐾♟️♥️✕⊙◉♨🏕️⚡፻⊞♦∅♟️PS
Prices: A5300-9000 pitch 11000-17000

RAVENNA, MARINA DI *Ravenna*
International Piomboni viale Della Pace 421 ☎0544 530230
Site on slightly undulating mainly grassy terrain with pines and poplars. Separate section for tents. Lunchtime siesta 14.00-15.30 hrs.
Access is 1km S from town centre off coast road.
May-15 Sep 5HEC ▦ ♦♠️🐾♟️♥️✕⊙◉∅♨🏕️♟️ S ፻⊞ lau
Prices: A6000-8300 pitch 11000-14000

RICCIONE *Forli*
Alberello via Torino 80 ☎0541 615402
May-20 Sep 40HEC ▦ ♦♠️🐾♟️♥️✕⊙◉∅♨♟️ S ፻⊞⌀ lau
Prices: A5300-10000 pitch 11500-17500

Fontanelle via Torino 56 ☎0541 615449
On southern outskirts separated from beach by coast road.
Underpass to public beach.
Camping Card Compulsory.
Turn off SS16 between Km216 and 217.
Etr-20 Sep 6HEC ▦ ♦♠️🐾♟️♥️✕⊙◉∅♨🏕️♟️ S ፻ lau ♦⊞

Riccione via Marsala ☎0541 690160
About 300m from sea. Extensive flat meadowland, with poplars of medium height.
From SS16 turn seawards on the S outskirts of the town and continue for 200m. Alternative access from coast road, turn inland on S outskirts at sign and continue for 700m.
May-Sep 6.5HEC ▦ ♦♠️🐾♟️♥️✕⊙◉♨🏕️♟️PS ፻⊞ lau

ROSETO DEGLI ABRUZZI *Teramo*
Eurcamping-Roseto Lungomare Trieste Sud 90 ☎085 8993179
A meadow site at the S end of the beach road.
Leave the SS16 within the town, then continue for 500m to the site.
All year 5HEC ▦ ♦♠️🐾♟️♥️✕⊙◉∅♨🏕️♟️PS ℗⊞ lau Prices:
A5900-9100 V3800-6500 ◗5100-10000 ▲4900-9400

Gilda viale Makarska ☎085 8941023
Jun-Aug 1.5HEC ▦ ♦♠️🐾♟️♥️✕⊙◉∅♨🏕️♟️ S ፻⊞ lau♦♟️P

SALSOMAGGIORE TERME *Parma*
Arizona via Tabiano 40 ☎0524 565648
Apr-15 Oct 12HEC ▦ ♦♠️🐾♟️♥️✕⊙◉∅♨⚡♟️ P ℗ lau Prices:
A7500-1000 pitch 12000-15000

SAN MARINO
Centro Turistico San Marino Strada San Michele 50
☎0549 903964
In a quiet, wooded location close to the centre of the Republic of San Marino.
Access via 'Rimini Sud' exit on the A14.
All year 12HEC ▦ ⊕ ∩ ⚞ ⚡ ✕ ⊙ ❾ ∅ ♨ 📶 🚑 🏠 ⚄ ⫠ ₹ P ⊡ lau ➠ ⊞
Prices: A7500-11000 V3000-6000 ⊞6500-11000 ▲6000-11000

SAN MÁURO MARE Forli
Green ☎0541 346929
Site lies in well-kept grassland with poplars and plane trees by the railway.
Camping Card Compulsory.
About 300m from the sea.
Apr-Nov 1.2HEC ░░░ ◆ ∩ ⚞ ⊙ ❾ ∅ 🏠 ⊞ lau ➠ ⚡ ✕ ₹S

At SAVIGNANO SUL RUBICONE
Rubicone via M-Destra 1 ☎0541 346377
An extensive, level site divided into two sections by a narrow canal. It extends to the beach.
Situated about 0.8km from the road fork at Km187/0 off SS16 (Strada Adriatica).
May-Sep 13HEC ▦ ◆ ∩ ⚞ ⚡ ✕ ⊙ ❾ ∅ 🏠 ₹ PS ⊡ ⊞ ⊿ lau ➠ 🚑
Prices: A7800-1250 pitch 16000-22500

SAN PIERO IN BAGNO Forli
Altosavio strada Provinciale per Alfero, 37c ☎0543 917670
25 Apr-Sep 1.3HEC ▦ ◆ ∩ ⚞ ✕ ⊙ ❾ ∅ lau ➠ ⚞ ✕ ∅ 🚑 ₹LS ⊞
Prices: A6000-7000 pitch 12000

SASSO MARCONI Bologna
Piccolo Paradiso ☎051 842680
Pleasant site with plenty of trees.
Leave A1 autostrada (Milano-Roma) at town exit and continue towards Vado for 2km. Signposted.
All year 6.5HEC ▦ ◆ ∩ ⚞ ⚡ ✕ ⊙ ❾ ∅ 🚑 ⊡ 🏠 ⚄ lau ➠ ✕ ₹LPR
Prices: A6200-8800 pitch 14000-19000

SCACCHI, LIDO DEGLI Ferrara
Florenz via alpi Centrali 199 ☎(0533) 380193
Site with sand dunes extending to the sea.
Turn off the Strada Romea in the direction of Lido Degli Scacchi, and continue along an asphalt road to the sandy beach.
26 Apr-20 Sep 60HEC ▦ ░░░ ⊕ ∩ ⚞ ⚡ ✕ ⊙ ❾ ∅ 🏠 🚑 ⚄ ₹ S ⊡ ⊞ lau Prices: A6000-10000 pitch 13000-16000

SENIGALLIA Ancona
Summerland via Podesti 236 ☎071 7926816
3km on SS16.
Jun-15 Sep 4.5HEC ▦ ◆ ∩ ⚞ ⚡ ✕ ⊙ ❾ ∅ 🚑 ⊡ ⊞ lau ➠ ₹PS

SIROLO Ancona
Green Garden via Peschiera 3 ☎0471 9331317
15 May-15 Sep 22HEC ▦ ◆ ∩ ⚞ ⚡ ✕ ⊙ ❾ ⚄ ₹ PS ⊡ ➠ ∅ 🚑 ⊞

SPINA, LIDO DI Ferrara
Spina via del Campeggio 99 ☎0533 330179
Widespread site on level meadowland and on slightly hilly sand dune terrain. Separate section for dog owners.
Off SS309. Signposted.
19 Apr-21 Sep 24HEC ▦ ◆ ∩ ⚞ ⚡ ✕ ⊙ ❾ ∅ ▲ ₹ PS ⊡ lau ➠ ⊞
Prices: A5000-8700 pitch 8100-15500

SPOLETO Perugia
Il Girasole Petrognano ☎0743 51583
Closed Jan-10 Feb 1.8HEC ▦ ◆ ∩ ⚞ ⚡ ✕ ⊙ ❾ 🏠 🚑 ⊞ lau ➠ ∅ 🚑
Prices: A7000-9000 V3000-4000 ⊞8000-10000 ▲6000-8000

Monteluco S.Pietro ☎0743 220358
A modern site situated on the slopes of Monteluco.
Apr-Sep 6HEC ♨ ◆ ∩ ⚡ ✕ ⊙ ❾ 🚑 ⊡ ➠ ⚞ ∅ 🚑 ⊞ Prices: A8000-9000 V3000-4000 ⊞7000-8000 ▲7000-8000

TORINO DI SANGRO MARINA Chieti
Belvedere ☎0873 911381
Jun-15 Sep 1.5HEC ▦ ⊕ ∩ ⚞ ⚡ ✕ ⊙ ❾ ∅ 🚑 ⚄ ₹ S ⊡ ➠ ✕ ₹PR ⊞

VASTO Chieti
Europa ☎0873 801988
Site on level terrain by the road with poplars.
At Km522 of road SS16.
May-Sep 2.3HEC ▦ ∩ ⚞ ⚡ ✕ ⊙ ❾ ∅ ♨ 🏠 ⚄ ⊡ lau ➠ ₹S

Grotta del Saraceno via Osca 6, loc Vignola ☎0873 310213
Site in olive grove on steep coastal cliffs with lovely views. Steep path to beach. Siesta 14.00-16.00 hrs.
Turn off SS16 at Km512.200.
15 Jun-15 Sep 12HEC ▦ ◆ ∩ ⚞ ⚡ ✕ ⊙ ❾ ♨ 🚑 ⚄ ₹ S lau ➠ ∅ ⊞
Prices: A4500-8500 pitch 7000-17000

Pioppeto ☎0873 801466
Camping Card Compulsory.
May-Sep 1HEC ░░░ ◆ ∩ ⚞ ⚡ ✕ ⊙ ❾ ₹ S ⊡ ➠ ∅ ♨ ⊞ Prices: A7500-9500 V5500-7000 ⊞10000-12500 ▲10000-12500

VILLALAGO L'Aquila
I Lupi ☎0864 740100
All year 7HEC ▦ ⊕ ∩ ⚞ ⊙ ❾ 🏠 ⚄ ⊡ ➠ ∅ ♨ ₹LP Prices: A7000 pitch 13000

Rome

Rome has affected western culture and attitudes for more than 2,000 years. The city is uniquely beautiful; from the famous Colosseum (a third of which is still intact) to the elegantly proportioned piazzas and churches, there are historic buildings which provide dramatic examples of changing architectural ideals. Of the 22 bridges which span the Tiber, some date from the first century BC.

Situated on the famous seven hills, the city is the focus of the province of Latium, which has been described as 'the cradle of Roman civilization'. Stretching from the Apennines to the Tyrrhenian sea, it is characterised by magnificent and beautiful scenery, especially in the volcanic regions, where long extinct volcanoes form the lakes of Albano, Bracciano, Bolsena and Vico. Viterbo, in the northern hills, is a large town with many fine examples of religious architecture, including the 13th-century Papal Palace. Rieti's Civic Museum houses an extensive collection of Roman artifacts, while Frosinone commands breathtaking views of surrounding countryside. The Latin Lido features sheltered harbours and sandy beaches.

ANGUILLARA-SABAZIA Roma
Parco del Lago ☎06 99802003
Alongside Lake Bracciano, off the Trevignano road.
Apr-Sep 3HEC ▦ ◆ ∩ ⚞ ⚡ ✕ ⊙ ❾ ∅ 🚑 🏠 ⚄ ₹ L ⊡ ⊘ lau ➠ ⊞
Prices: A7500-8500 pitch 8000-13000

BOLSENA Viterbo
Amalasunta via del Lago 77 ☎0761 825294
Apr-Sep 3HEC ▦ ◆ ∩ ⚞ ⚡ ✕ ⊙ ❾ ∅ 🚑 ₹ L ⊡ ⊞

Lido via Cassia ☎0761 799258
A lakeside family site with good modern facilities.
Access via motorway exit 'Orvieto'.
Apr-Sep 10HEC ▦ ◆ ∩ ⚞ ⚡ ✕ ⊙ ❾ ∅ 🚑 ₹ L ⊡ ⊘ lau ➠ ⊞
Prices: A8000-11500 pitch 8500-12000

BRACCIANO Roma
Porticciolo via del Porticciolo ☎06 99803060
Apr-Sep 2.8HEC ▦ ◆ ∩ ⚞ ⚡ ✕ ⊙ ❾ 🏠 🚑 ⚄ ₹ L ⊡ lau Prices: A8000 V2500 ⊞7000 ▲5000-7000

FORMIA Latina
Gianola via delle Vigne ☎0771 720223
Situated in a narrow grassland area near a little stream and trees amidst agricultural land. Pleasantly sandy beach edged by rocks.
Access via Roma-Napoli road, from S Croce 800m.
Apr-Sep 4HEC ▦ ░░░ ◆ ∩ ⚞ ⚡ ✕ ⊙ ❾ ∅ 🏠 🚑 ⚄ ▲ ₹ RS ⊡ ➠ ⊞
Prices: pitch 19000-44000 (incl 2 persons)

MINTURNO, MARINA DI *Latina*
Golden Garden via Dunale 74 ☎0771 681425
Secluded quiet site within agricultural area by the sea.
Camping Card Compulsory.
Access from the SS7 across river bridge (Garigliano) and continue
4.6km changing direction. Last km sandy field track.
All year 2.3HEC ▦ ♦⋔�ில🌳♥✕⊙♥∅🚿⚫⚑ ↺ S 🅿 ⊞ lau

MONTALTO DI CASTRO, MARINA DI *Viterbo*
Internazionale Pionier Etrusco via Vulsinia ☎0766 802199
Camping Card Compulsory.
All year 3HEC ⠿⠿⠿ ♦⋔🌳✕⊙♥∅🚿⚫⚑ ↺ RS 🅿 ⊿ lau ♦🌳✕ ↺P
⊞ Prices: pitch 35000-40000 (incl 2 persons)

PESCIA ROMANA, MARINA DI *Viterbo*
Gli Amici ☎0766 830250
A quiet, pleasantly situated site behind dunes. Clean wide beach.
Turn off via Aurelia seawards at Km118.5. After 4.3km turn right and
continue on sandy tracks 900m.
All year 2.6HEC ▦ ♦⋔🌳🌳✕⊙♥∅🚿♥🅿 lau ♦ ↺PS

ROMA (ROME) *Roma*
Flaminio via Flaminia Nuova 821 ☎06 3332604
An exstensive site, which lies in a quiet valley on narrow terraces on
a hill.
From ring road follow via Flaminia, SS3, for 2.5km towards city
centre.
All year 8.3HEC ▦ ♦⋔🌳🌳✕⊙♥∅🚿⚫⚑ ↺ P ⊡ ♦ ↺R ⊞
Prices: A12000-13000 V5500-6000 ♥7500-8000 ▲6000-7000

Happy via Prato della Corte 1915 ☎06 33626401
Conveniently placed in northern area of town. Modern installations,
electricity and hot water free throughout.
Exit No.5 "Grande Raccordo Anulare" (ring road).
15 Mar-Oct 3.6HEC ▦ ♦⋔🌳🌳✕⊙♥∅♥ ↺ P ⊡ ⊞ lau Prices:
A8800-10200 V4500-5100 ♥6900-8000 ▲4500-5100

The site, in the shade of the Macchia Mediterrania,
immediately adjacent to the crystal-clear sea with a
marvellous beach of fine sand stretching as far as the
eye can see.
Nearby are the nature reserves of Burano, Ortbetello
(WWF) and the Maremma National Park, the remains
of the Etruscan culture of Vulci and Tarquinia,
Argentario and the islands, Montecristo, Giglio and
Giannutri – all in a radius of about 30 kilometres and
therefore within easy reach for excursions.
Bar, foodstore and restaurant, pizzeria, one and two-
room bungalows with toilet, cooking area and
veranda. Caravans with own toilet, cooking area and
veranda
Sites with or without toilets. Dogs are very welcome.
Sites can be reserved.
On the beach: canoes, water bikes and pedal boats.
Entertainment in high season, archery, swimming and
canoe courses.
**Club degli Amici Camping Village
01010 Pescia Romana (VT)
For reservations:
Tel. and Fax 0766/830250
Tel. 0564/870068
Fax 0564/870470**

Roma via Aurelia 831 ☎06 6623018
The site lies on terraces on a hill near the AGIP Motel. All kinds of
excursions can be arranged.
From ring road follow SS1 (via Aurelia) for 1.5km towards town
centre turn off to site at Km8/11.
All year 3HEC ▦ ♦⋔🌳🌳✕⊙♥∅🚿⚫⊞ lau Prices: A11000-
11700 V5500-5900 ♥9500-10000 ▲5500-5900

Seven Hills via Cassia 1216 ☎06 30310826
A fine, partly terraced site in beautiful rural surroundings yet ideally
situated for access to the city by bus or underground.2.5km NE of
the outer ring road via exit '3'.
All year 5.5HEC ▦ ♦⋔🌳🌳✕⊙♥∅🚿⚫▲ ↺ P ⊡ lau Prices:
A11000 V6000 ♥10000 ▲8000

Tiber via Tiberina ☎06 33612314
On level grassland, shaded by poplars beside the Tiber.
N of city. Signposted from ringroad. Access from via exit '3' or
from S follow signs 'Prima Porta'.
Mar-10 Nov 5HEC ▦ ♦⋔🌳🌳✕⊙♥∅🚿⚫⚑▲ ↺ PR ⊡ ⊞ lau
Prices: A9500-10000 V4500-4800 ♥8000-8500 ▲4800-6500
See advertisement on page 207.

SALTO DI FONDI *Latina*
Fondi Holiday Camp via Flacce ☎0771 555009
Apr-20 Sep 4HEC ▦ ♦⋔🌳🌳✕⊙♥∅🚿⚫ ↺ PS 🅿 ⊞ ⊿ lau

SPERLONGA *Latina*
Nord-Sud via Flacca ☎0771 54255
1km from town towards Gaeta.
May-13 Oct 4.5HEC ▦ ♀♦⋔🌳🌳✕⊙♥∅🚿⚫⊿ lau ♦ ↺S

TERRACINA *Latina*
Badino Porto Badino ☎0773 764430
Apr-Sep 2HEC ⠿⠿⠿ ♀⋔🌳✕⊙♥♥⚫♥▲ ↺ S 🅿 ♦🌳✕∅🚿⊞
Prices: A7000-11500 pitch 12000-21500

An island of tranquillity outside the gates of the capital (peace). The TIBER campsite is located on the banks of the Tevere and is open from 01.03 to 10.11. Bar – Restaurant – Pizzeria – Supermarket – Swimming-pool – Playground for children – Sightseeing tours – Automatic washing machine. Rooms and caravans to let and accommodation for groups. Centre of Rome 20 minutes by public transport. **From the North: from A1, direction ROME NORTH exit FIANO ROMANO than on the Tiberina Road towards Rome. From Gran Raccordo Anulare: Exit Nr. 6 FLAMINIA – PRIMA PORTA than follows the signs to via Tiberina. Via Tiberina Km. 1,400. Tel. 06/33610733. Fax: 33612314 I-00188 PRIMA PORTA ROMA, ITALY**

South

The area known as the Mezzogiorno, takes in Campania and the 'toe and heel' provinces of Calabria (the toe), Basilicata, and Apulia (the heel).

From Naples, a port set in a beautiful bay with volcanic Vesuvius behind it, you travel south to an area in which you look back in time and where the language is different from northern Italian. Apulia is mountainous but has fertile plains producing olives, wines and tobacco. In the university town of Lecce you can see the exuberant 'Lecce Baroque' ornate stone carving while in Alberobella you find the circular 'trulli' houses made of drystone with cone shaped roofs. Equally intriguing is the abandoned city at Matera where semi-cave dwellings made of tufa used to house hundreds of families.

Baby octopus and other fish are part of a healthy diet of seafood, vegetables and pulses. Travel though the poorest region of Italy, Basilicata, before arriving in Calabria - also mountainous, with skiing in winter, but with 372 miles of coastline. Reggio di Calabria, right on the toe, has a mild climate in which exotic plants like the bergamot orange flourish.

ACCIAROLI Salerno

Ondina ☎0974 904040
Delightful seaside site, full of flowers. Lunchtime siesta 14.00-16.00 hrs.
Turn off towards the sea at Km35/VII.
Apr-Oct 3HEC ▥ ♦ ♠ ⚊ ⚓ ♥ ✕ ⊙ ᠗ ⌀ ᨖ ☎ ⁁ S ☒ ⊞ Prices:
A6500-10500 pitch 14500-18000

BAIA DOMIZIA Caserta

Baia Domizia ☎0823 930164
Part of this extensive seaside site is laid out with flower beds. No radios allowed.

Turn off the SS7 (qtr) at Km6/V, then 3km seawards.
May-Sep 30HEC ▥ ⠿ ♦ ♠ ⚊ ⚓ ♥ ✕ ⊙ ᠗ ⌀ ᨖ ☎ ♥ ⁁ PS ☒ ⊞ ⚛ lau
Prices: A5600-12600 V3000-5000 ☞8400-17600 ▲8400-17600

BATTIPAGLIA Salerno

Lido Mediterraneo via Litoranea ☎0828 624097
In a pinewood with direct access to a private beach.
15 Apr-10 Oct 1.5HEC ▥ ♦ ♠ ⚊ ⚓ ♥ ✕ ⊙ ᠗ ᨖ ☎ ⁁ S ☒ ♦ ✕ ⊞

BRANCALEONE Reggio di Calabria

Villaggio Africa via S Giorgio ☎0964 933164
All year 1.7HEC ♨ ♦ ♠ ⚊ ⚓ ♥ ✕ ⊙ ᠗ ᨖ ☎ ⁁ S ☒ ♦ ⌀ ⊞

BRIATICO Catanzaro

Dolomiti ☎0963 391355
The site is in a delightful setting on two terraces planted with olive trees. It lies by the road and 150m from the sea.
Turn off road 522 between Km17 and Km18 and head towards the sea.
May-Sep 18HEC ▥ ♦ ♠ ⚊ ⚓ ♥ ✕ ⊙ ᠗ ⌀ ᨖ ☎ ⁁ S ☒ ⊞ lau
Prices: A8000-13500 V4000-6000 ☞9000-13500 ▲5000-9000

CAMEROTA, MARINA DI Salerno

Happy ☎0974 932326
The site lies on a park-like hill sloping down to the sea and is scattered with olive trees.
1km N of village just off the coast road.
Jun-Sep 12HEC ▥ ♦ ♠ ⚊ ⚓ ♥ ✕ ⊙ ᠗ ᨖ ☎ ⁁ S ☒ ⊞ Prices:
A12000-24000 ☞12000-24000 ▲12000-24000

Isola ☎0974 932230
Lies on several terraces in an olive grove. Pleasant bathing area with sandy beach.
Entrance is just off Palinuro-Marina coast road (SS562) 1km N of village near ESSO petrol station.
May-Oct 2.5HEC ▥ ♦ ♠ ⚊ ⚓ ♥ ✕ ⊙ ᠗ ⌀ ᨖ ☎ ♥ ♦ ⁁ S ⊞

Risacca via delle Barche 11 ☎0974 932415
20 May-15 Sep 2HEC ▥ ⠿ ♦ ♠ ⚊ ⚓ ♥ ✕ ⊙ ᠗ ⌀ ᨖ ☎ ⁁ S ☒ ⊞

CAMPORA SAN GIOVANNI Cosenza

Principessa ☎0982 46903
Modern motel with camp site annexed to it, lying 150m from the sea and a fine sandy beach.
2km S and inland from Campora on SS18.
All year 30HEC ▥ ⠿ ♦ ♠ ⚊ ⚓ ♥ ✕ ⊙ ᠗ ⌀ ᨖ ☎ ⁁ PS ☒ ⊞ lau

CAPO VATICANO Catanzaro

Gabbiano San Nicolo di Ricadi ☎0963 663159
Apr-Oct 1.8HEC ▥ ♦ ♠ ⚊ ⚓ ♥ ✕ ⊙ ᠗ ⌀ ᨖ ☎ ▲ ⁁ S ☒ ⊞ lau

Quattro Scogli San Nicolo di Ricadi ☎0963 663126 & 663115
The site is in a quiet sandy bay surrounded by rocks.
Drive from San Nicolo di Ricardi to Capo Vaticano.
Apr-Oct 1HEC ▥ ⠿ ♦ ♠ ⚊ ⚓ ♥ ✕ ⊙ ᠗ ⌀ ᨖ ☎ ⁁ S ☒ ⊞ Prices:
A9000-12000 V4000-6000 ☞12000-13000 ▲8000-10000

CAROVIGNO Brindisi

At SPECCHIOLLA, LIDO

Pineta al Mare ☎0831 987821
Site in pine woodland with sandy beach and some rocks.
E of Bari-Brindisi road at Km21.5.
All year 5.5HEC ▥ ♦ ♠ ⚊ ⚓ ♥ ✕ ⊙ ᠗ ᨖ ☎ ⁁ S ☒ ☒ ⊞ lau Prices:
A8500-12000 V3000-4500 ☞10000-12000 ▲10000-12000

CIRÒ MARINA Catanzaro

Punta Alice ☎0962 31160
The site lies on meadowland amidst lush Mediterranean vegetation and borders a fine gravel beach, some 50m wide.
2km from town. From SS106 (Strada Ionica) turn off at Km290 seaward to Cira Marina. Pass through village and follow beach road for 1.5m towards the lighthouse.
Apr-Sep 5.5HEC ▥ ♦ ♠ ⚊ ⚓ ♥ ✕ ⊙ ᠗ ⌀ ᨖ ☎ ⁁ S ☒ ⊞ lau

Villaggio Torrenova via Torrenova ☎0962 31482
Dogs only allowed May, Jun & Sep.
May-Sep 1.2HEC ⠿ ♦ ♠ ⚊ ⚓ ♥ ✕ ⊙ ᠗ ⌀ ᨖ ☎ ⁁ S ☒ ⊞ lau ♦
⁁L Prices: pitch 45000 (incl 2 persons)

CORIGLIANO CÁLABRO *Cosenza*
Thurium ☎0983 851955
Jun-15 Sep 14HEC ░░░ ⊑ ♠ ⋔ ⚑ ⚏ ⚊ ✕ ⊙ ⊟ ∅ ⚌ 🏠 ⚑ ⤴ S ⚐ ⊟ ⊞
lau Prices: A5000-11500 V2000-5500 🚐5000-12000
▲3500-9500

EBOLI *Salerno*
Paestum ☎0828 691003
Sandy, meadowland site in tall poplar wood by river mouth. Steps
and bus service to private beach, 600m from site.
Access from the Litoranea at Km20 from the road fork to Santa
Cecilia and continue for 0.3km. Signposted.
Apr-15 Sep 8HEC ▦ ░░░ ♠ ⋔ ⚏ ⚊ ✕ ⊙ ⊟ ∅ ⚌ 🏠 ⚑ ⤴ P ⚐ ⊞ ⊘
lau ● ⤴PR

GAGLIANO DEL CAPO *Lecce*
Village St Maria di Leuca ☎0833 548157
All year 3HEC ▦ ♠ ⋔ ⚏ ⚊ ✕ ⊙ ⊟ ∅ ⚌ ⤴ P ⚐ ⊞

GALLIPOLI *Lecce*
Baia di Gallipoli ☎0832 315542 or 358957
Camping Card Compulsory.
May-Sep 11HEC ▦ ♠ ⋔ ⚏ ⚊ ✕ ⊙ ⊟ ∅ ⚌ 🏠 ⚑ ⤴ P ⚐ ⊞ ● ⤴S

Vecchia Torre ☎0833 209083
This well-kept and clean site lies amidst sand dunes in a pine wood.
Small size pitches.
5km N of Gallipoli and 200m S of Hotel Rivabella at seaward side of
coast road.
15 May-Sep 8HEC ░░░ ♠ ⋔ ⚏ ⚊ ✕ ⊙ ⊟ ∅ 🏠 ⚑ ⚐ ⊞ ⊘ lau ● ⤴S

GIOVINAZZO *Bari*
Campofreddo ☎080 8942112
Site in level terrain by the sea, mainly under sunshade roofing. Siesta
14.00-16.00 hrs.
Turn off the SS16, 20km N of Bari at Km784,300.
May-Sep 34HEC ⚑ ♠ ⋔ ⚏ ⚊ ✕ ⊙ ⊟ 🏠 ⚐ ⊞ ⊘ lau ● ✕ ⤴S

GUARDAVALLE, MARINA DI *Catanzaro*
Dello Ionio via Nazionale ☎0967 86002
Jun-15 Sep 5HEC ▦ ♠ ⋔ ⚏ ⚊ ✕ ⊙ ⊟ ∅ ⚌ 🏠 ⚑ ⤴ S ⚐ ⊞ lau
Prices: A6000-10000 pitch 8000-11500

LÁURA *Salerno*
Hera Argiva ☎0828 851193
Site in sandy terrain in eucalyptus grove by the sea.
Signposted from Km88/VII SS18.
Apr-Sep 40HEC ░░░ ♠ ⋔ ⚏ ⚊ ✕ ⊙ ⊟ ∅ 🏠 ⤴ S ⚐ ⊞ lau

LEPRANO, MARINA DI *Taranto*
Porto Pirrone Litoranea Salentina Km12 ☎099 5334844
Jun-Sep 3.2HEC ░░░ ♠ ⋔ ⚏ ⚊ ✕ ⊙ ⊟ ∅ ⚌ ⤴ S ⚐ ⊘ Prices:
A6000-9000 V3000-4500 🚐6000-9000

MÁCCHIA *Foggia*
Monaco ☎0884 530280
Jun-Aug 5.3HEC ▦ ♠ ⋔ ⚏ ⚊ ✕ ⊙ ⊟ ∅ 🏠 ⚑ ⤴ PS ⚐ ⊘ lau
Prices: A5000-10000 pitch 8000-12000

MASSA LUBRENSE *Napoli*
Villa Lubrense via Partenope 31 ☎081 5339781
All year 2.5HEC ▦ ♠ ⋔ ⚏ ⚊ ✕ ⊙ ⊟ ∅ 🏠 ⚑ ⤴ PS ⚐ ⊞

MATTINATA *Foggia*
Degli Ulivi ☎0884 550118
This well-kept grassland site lies in an old olive grove, facing a
picturesque bay.
Camping Card Compulsory.
Off SS89, 0.6km N of turning to Mattinata.
Jun-Sep 2.1HEC ▦ ♠ ⋔ ⚏ ⚊ ✕ ⊙ ⊟ ⚌ 🏠 ⚑ ⤴ PS lau ● ✕ ⊞
Prices: pitch 7000-17000

Villaggio Turistico San Lorenzo ☎0884 4152
The site is situated above the coast road in direction of Viesta.
Bungalows for hire.
Camping Card Compulsory.
All year 5HEC ▦ ♠ ⋔ ⚏ ⚊ ✕ ⊙ ⊟ 🏠 ⚑ ⤴ PS ⚐ ⊞ lau ● ∅ ⊞

METAPONTO, LIDO DI *Matera*
Camel Camping Club viale Magna Grecia
☎0835 741926/7
All year 3.5HEC ◊ ♠ ⋔ ⚏ ⚊ ✕ ⊙ ⊟ ∅ ⚌ ⚑ ⤴ PS ⚐ ● ⤴LR ⊞
Prices: A6000-14000 V3000-7500 🚐6000-14500
▲6000-14500

NICÓTERA MARINA *Catanzaro*
Sabbia d'Oro ☎0963 886395
Lies on level ground amidst farmland 100m from a beautiful lonely
beach.
Turn off SS18 at Km453/VII and continue 15km.
Jun-Sep 2.7HEC ♠ ⋔ ⚏ ⚊ ✕ ⊙ ⊟ ∅ ⚌ 🏠 ⚑ ▲ ⤴ S ⚐ ⊞ lau
Prices: pitch 20000-24000 (incl 2 persons)

OTRANTO *Lecce*
Mulino d'Acqua via S Stefano ☎0836 802191
Camping Card Compulsory
15 Jun-15 Sep 10HEC ▦ ♠ ⋔ ⚏ ⚊ ✕ ⊙ ⊟ ∅ ⚌ 🏠 ⚑ ⤴ PS ⚐ ⊘
lau ● ⊞ Prices: pitch 10500-14500 (incl 4 persons)

PAESTUM *Salerno*
Vilaggio del Pini ☎0828 811030 & 811323
The site lies on hilly ground in a pine forest beside clean and sandy
beach.
Camping Card Compulsory.
Turn off via Tirrenia at Km95/1X and continue 1km.
All year 3HEC ▦ ░░░ ⊑ ♠ ⋔ ⚏ ⚊ ✕ ⊙ ⊟ ∅ ⚌ 🏠 ⚑ ⤴ PRS ⚐ ⊞ lau

PALINURO *Salerno*
Arco Naturale Club via Molpa 1 ☎0974 931157
Jun-15 Sep 10HEC ▦ ♠ ⋔ ⚏ ⚊ ✕ ⊙ ⊟ ∅ 🏠 ⤴ PRS ⊟ ⊞ lau

PALMI *Reggio di Calabria*
San Fantino via S-Fantino ☎0966 479430
Site on several terraces with lovely views of the bay of Lido di Palmi.
200m to the beach. Siesta 13.00-16.00 hrs.
Turn off road SS18 seawards N of Palmi.
All year 4HEC ♠ ⋔ ⚏ ⚊ ✕ ⊙ ⊟ ∅ ⚌ 🏠 ⚑ ⚐ ⚑ lau ● ⤴PS ⊞

PESCHICI *Foggia*
Centro Turistico San Nicola Loc San Nicola ☎0884 964024
Terraced site in lovely situation by the sea, in a bay enclosed by
rocks. Can become overcrowded.
Turn off coast road Peschici-Vieste, follow signs along winding road
to site in 1km.
Apr-15 Oct 12HEC ▦ ♠ ⋔ ⚏ ⚊ ✕ ⊙ ⊟ ∅ ⚌ 🏠 ⤴ S ⚐ ⊞ lau Prices:
A6500-14000 V4700-8500 🚐8500-17000 ▲6500-14000

Internazionale Manacore ☎0884 911020
Meadowland with a few terraces in attractive bay, surrounded by
wooded hills.
Turn off the coastal road (Peschici-Vieste) towards ths sea in a wide
U bend.
Apr-20 Oct 20HEC ░░░ ♠ ⋔ ⚏ ⚊ ✕ ⊙ ⊟ ∅ ⚌ 🏠 ⤴ S ⊟ ⊞

Parco degli Ulivi ☎0884 963404
29 May-25 Sep 12HEC ▦ ♠ ⋔ ⚏ ⚊ ✕ ⊙ ⊟ ∅ ⚌ 🏠 ⚑ ⤴ P ⊟ ⊞
● ⤴S

PIZZO, MARINA DI *Catanzaro*
Pinetamare ☎0963 534871
N of town.
2 Jun-29 Sep 11HEC ░░░ ♠ ⋔ ⚏ ⚊ ✕ ⊟ ∅ ⚌ 🏠 ⤴ PS ⚐ ⊞ ⊘ lau

POMPEI *Napoli*
Spartacus via Plinio ☎081 5369519
Site is on a level meadow with orange trees.
Lies near the motorway exit, Pompei and access is from the main
Napoli road, opposite Scavi di Pompei near an IP petrol station.
All year 1.1HEC ▦ ♠ ⋔ ⚏ ⚊ ✕ ⊙ ⊟ ∅ ⚌ 🏠 ⚑ ⚐ lau ● ⤴P ⊞
Prices: A7000-9000 V3000 🚐5000-6000 ▲3000

POZZUOLI *Napoli*
Vulcano Solfatara via Solfatara 161 ☎081 5267413
Clean and orderly site situated in a deciduous forest near the crater
of the extinct Solfatara volcano.

Leave Nuova via Domiziana (SS7 qtr) at Km60/1 (at about 6km short of Napoli) and turn inland through stone gate.
Apr-Oct 3HEC ▥ ♣⋔ℙⅇ♀Ⅹ⊙◍∅≛☎⚑Åⅈℙ☒⊞ lau ♦ ⅈS
Prices: A10000-12000 V6500-9000 ⚑11000-13000
▲6000-8000

At VARCATURO, MARINA DI(12km N)

Partenope ☎081 5091076
Partially undulating terrain in woodland of medium height.
Turn seawards for 300m at Km45/ll of the SS7 (via Domiziana).
May-Sep 6HEC ▥ ♣⋔ℙⅇ♀Ⅹ⊙◍∅≛☎ⅈ RS ☒⊞ ⚿ lau
Prices: A10000-12000 pitch 13000-17000

PRAIA A MARE *Cosenza*

Internazionale sul Mare ☎0985 72211
In a beautiful location on the Gulf of Policastro with fine recreational facilities.
Access via A3 to Falerna and then SS18.
15 Jun-15 Sep 4HEC ▥ ♣♣⋔ℙⅇ♀Ⅹ⊙◍∅≛☎⚑
Å ⅈS ☒⊞

RODI GARGANICO *Foggia*

Ripa via Ripa ☎0884 965367
14 Jun-13 Sep 6HEC ▥ ♣⋔ℙⅇ♀Ⅹ⊙◍≛☎ ⅈ PS ℙ lau ♦⊞
Prices: A12000-15000 pitch 15000-20000

ROSSANO SCALO *Cosenza*

Marina di Rossano Contrada Leuca ☎0983 512069
In wooded surroundings close to the beach, with good, modern facilities.
Access via N106.
Apr-Sep 7HEC ▥ ♣⋔ℙⅇ♀Ⅹ⊙◍∅☎⚑ⅈ PS lau ♦∅≛⊞
Prices: A6000-10000 pitch 23000-38000

SALVE, MARINA DI *Lecce*

Ionian Club ☎0833 741379
May-Oct 6HEC ▥ ♣⋔ℙⅇ♀Ⅹ⊙◍∅≛☎⚑Åⅈ
ℙ☒⊞♦ ⅈS

SAN MENÁIO *Foggia*

Valle d'Oro via Degli Ulivi ☎0884 991580
Site in olive grove surrounded by wooded hills with some terraces.
Turn off the SS89 onto SS528 and to site at Km1.800. 2km from the sea.
Jun-Sep 3HEC ▥ ♣⋔ℙⅇ♀Ⅹ⊙◍≛∅ⅈS⊞ Prices:
A3000-8000 ⚑5000-10000 ▲5000-10000

SAN NICOLO DI RICADI *Catanzaro*

Agrumeto ☎0963 663175
The access road leads over a dusty field track, then on to a steep ramp with large, wide bends. Because the trees are very close together, the pitches are rather narrow. Lying in a lemon grove beside the sea, this site looks more like a garden. Beautiful beach. Excursions by boat can be arranged.
Apr-Sep 3.7HEC ▥ ♣⋔ℙⅇ♀Ⅹ⊙◍∅ⅈS☒⊞ lau
Prices: A5900-8900 V4000-6000 ⚑6700-9900 ▲6700-9900

SANTA CESÁREA TERME *Lecce*

Scogliera ☎0836 944216
1km S on SS173.
All year 8HEC ⣿ ♣⋔ℙⅇ♀Ⅹ⊙◍∅☎⚑ⅈℙ♦ⅩⅈS⊞

SANTA MARIA DI CASTELLABATE *Salerno*

Trezene ☎0974 965027
The site is partly divided into pitches and consists of two sections lying either side of the access road. Pitches between road and fine sandy beach are reserved for touring campers.
Apr-Oct 2.7HEC ▥ ♣⋔ℙⅇ♀Ⅹ⊙◍☎ⅈS☒⊞ lau ♦∅⊞

SOLE, LIDO DEL *Foggia*

Lido del Mare c da Pantanello 27 ☎0884 97039
31 May-27 Sep 2.2HEC ▥ ⣿ ♣⋔ℙⅇ♀Ⅹ⊙◍≛☎⚑ⅈS☒ lau
♦▥Ⅹ∅⊞ Prices: A5500-13000 V1800-6500 ⚑6000-13000
▲6000-13000

SORRENTO *Napoli*

Campogaio via Capo 39 ☎081 8073579
Lies on terraces scattered with olive trees.
2km from town centre and 400m beyond the turning from the SS145 on road towards Massa Lubrense and 50m from sea.
Apr-15 Oct 10HEC ▥ ♦⋔ℙⅇ♀Ⅹ⊙◍∅☎⚑ⅈS☒⊞ lau
Prices: A10000-13000 V6000-7000 ⚑11000-14000 ▲7500-9500

International Camping Nube d'Argento via Capo 21 ☎081 8781344
The site lies on narrow terraces just off a steep concrete road between the beach and the outskirts of the town.
Access is rather difficult for caravans.
All year 1.5HEC ▥ ♦⋔ℙⅇ♀Ⅹ⊙◍☎⚑ⅈℙ☒⊞♦ ⅈS
Prices: A11000-14000 V5000-6000 ⚑11000-14000
▲6000-13000

Santa Fortunata via Capo ☎081 8073579
Extensive site lying on terraces in a shady olive grove with many small secluded pitches.**Camping Card Compulsory**
1km from town and 50m from sea.
Apr-Sep 12HEC ▥ ♦⋔ℙⅇ♀Ⅹ⊙◍∅≛☎⚑Åⅈ PS ☒⊞ lau

TORRE RINALDA *Lecce*

Torre Rinalda Lit Salentina 152 ☎0832 652161
On an extensive level meadow, separated from the sea by dunes. Discotheque. Lunchtime siesta 13.30-16.00 hrs.
Camping Card Compulsory.
Access via SS613 (Brindisi-Lecce) exit Trepuzzi then coastal road for 1.5km.
All year 23HEC ▥ ♦⋔ℙⅇ♀Ⅹ⊙◍∅☎⚑ⅈ PS ℙ⊞ lau

UGENTO *Lecce*

Riva di Ugento ☎0833 933600
20 May-Sep 33HEC ▥ ♦⋔ℙⅇ♀Ⅹ⊙◍≛☎⚑ⅈ PS ☒ℙ⊞⚿ lau

VICO EQUENSE *Napoli*

Sant' Antonio via Marina d'Equa 21 ☎081 8028570
Camping Card Compulsory.
15 Mar-15 Oct 1HEC ▥ ♦⋔ℙⅇ♀Ⅹ⊙◍∅☎⚑ⅈ PS ☒⊞⚿ lau
Prices: A9000-11000 V5000 ⚑9000-11000 ▲7000-9000

Seiano Spiaggia Marina Aequa, Casella Postale 38 ☎081 8028560
About 20m from the sea.
Apr-Sep 2.2HEC ▥ ♦⋔ℙⅇ♀Ⅹ⊙◍∅≛☒⊞ lau ♦Ⅹ ⅈPS
Prices: A8200-9500 V3500-4600 ⚑7900-9000 ▲7100-8200

VIESTE *Foggia*

Baia dei Lambardi Santa Maria di Merino ☎0884 706480
Apr-Sep 2.5HEC ▥ ⣿ ♦⋔ℙⅇ♀Ⅹ⊙◍∅≛☎ⅈS ℙ

Baia Turchese ☎0884 708587
1km N of Vieste on Strada Panoramica towards Peschici.
May-Sep 4HEC ▥ ♦⋔ℙⅇ♀Ⅹ⊙◍≛☎ⅈS☒⊞⚿ lau Prices:
A4000-9000 V3000 ⚑5000-13000 ▲5000-13000

Capo Vieste ☎0884 706326
The site lies on a large area of unspoilt land, planted with a few rows of poplar and pine trees. It is by the sea and has a large bathing area.
Off coastal road to Peschici about 7km beyond Vieste.
15 Mar-30 Oct 6HEC ▥ ⣿ ⏚♦⋔ℙⅇ♀Ⅹ⊙◍∅≛☎⚑ⅈS ℙ
⊞ lau

Castello Lungomare E-Mattei 77 ☎0884 707415
Etr-Sep 2.5HEC ▥ ♦⋔ℙⅇ♀Ⅹ⊙◍∅ⅈS☒⚿ lau ♦⊞
Prices: A12000-23000

Porticello ☎0884 706125
The site lies in a long, sandy bay which is bordered on one side by rocks.
Camping Card Compulsory.
5km on coast road to Peschici and then turn right.
May-Sep 2.7HEC ▥ ⣿ ⏚⋔ℙⅇ♀Ⅹ⊙◍∅≛☎ⅈℙ☒♦ ⅈS

Umbramare Santa Maria di Merino ☎0884 706174
On A14 leave at Poggio Imperiale and take route via Rodi Gargánico
and Peschici.
All year 1.3HEC ▥ ∷ ♣♠☎⚊♥✗⊙❷∅♨⯑ ‹ S ▣⊞⊛♥♨
Prices: A7500-13500 pitch 13000-20000

Vieste Marina ☎0884 706471
Level site adjacent to the coast road.
5km N of Vieste, signposted.
Jun-Sep 5HEC ▥ ♥♠☎⚊♥✗⊙❷⯑‹ P ☎♥∅♨ ‹S Prices:
A5100-12500 V2900-5300 ☎8000-16500

Village Punta Lunga ☎0884 706031
A terraced site including two sandy bathing bays, a rocky peninsula
and the village of Vieste.
2km N of Vieste, signposted from coast road.
21 Mar-12 Oct 6HEC ▥ ∷ ♣♠☎⚊♥✗⊙❷∅⯑‹ S ▣⊞⊛
lau ♥♨ Prices: A5500-14000 V4500 ☎7000-16000 ▲6000-14000

ZAPPONETA Foggia
Ippocampo ☎0884 371121
In grounds of a holiday village.
15 Jun- 15 Sep 6.4HEC ∷ ⌖♠♥✗⊙❷☎♨▲‹ S ☎♥♠✗
♨‹P ⊞

The Islands

Sardinia and Sicily are virtually the same size but Sardinia's
population is 1.5 million compared with Sicily's 5 million.
Sardinia's mountains are less dramatic, much of the coast is
deserted and the people with their distinctive dialect, clothes and
folklore, seem far removed from the 20th century. The Costa
Smeralda on the north-east coast is luxuriously developed but
elsewhere on the coast tourism is increasing only slowly, and
inland, the old town of Nuoro set high on a 1500ft granite hill,
remains mysterious. Cagliari is the capital, a modern city, whilst
Oristano is the provincial capital with old streets and lively
atmosphere.
Where Sardinia is an island on which to relax, in Sicily there is
much to see: classical sites at Taormina, Syracuse or Agrigento;
busy cities like Palermo and Catánia and the dramatic, erupting
volcano Etna in whose foothills oranges and lemons grow
profusely. There is also poverty and the occasional outburst from
the Mafia. The best beaches and clearest waters are around the
Aolian islands to the north, but Sicily is not primarily a seaside
resort island. Seafood, vegetables and fresh fruit are in
abundance, not forgetting of course, the inimitable ice-cream.

SARDEGNA (SARDINIA)

AGLIENTU Sassari
Baia Blu la Tortuga Pineta di Vignola Mare ☎079 602060
Site in pine forest by the sea.
Apr-Sep 1.7HEC ∷ ♣♠☎⚊♥✗⊙❷∅♨▲⯑‹ S ☎⊞ lau
Prices: A7000-11000 pitch 9000-23000

ARBATAX Nuoro
Telis ☎0782 667261
All year 3HEC ▥ ♠☎⚊♥✗⊙❷∅♨▲⯑‹ S ☎⊞ lau

BARI SARDO Nuoro
Domus de Janas Torri di Bari ☎0782 29361
All year 2.5HEC ▥ ♣♠☎⚊♥✗⊙❷∅♨▲⯑‹ RS ☎ lau

CAGLIARI

At SANT'ANTIOCO
Tonnara Loc Calasapone ☎0781 809058
Situated in the centre of Calasapone Bay with enclosed plots, good
sporting facilities and access to a sandy beach.
Apr-Oct 7HEC ▥ ∷ ⌖♠☎⚊♥✗⊙❷∅♨☎⯑‹ S ▣ lau
Prices: A10000-17000 V2500-5000

CANNIGIONE DI ARZACHENA Sassari
Isuledda ☎0789 86003
Near the sea on the beautiful Costa Smeralda with good, modern
sanitary installations and plentiful sports and entertainment facilities.
27 Mar-15 Oct 15HEC ▥ ∷ ♣♠☎⚊♥✗⊙❷∅♨☎⯑‹ S ☎⊞
⊛ lau Prices: A7000-15000 V3500-6000 ☎8000-23000
▲8000-23000

LOTZORAI Nuoro
Cernie ☎0782 669472
All year 3.5HEC ∷ ♣♠☎⚊♥✗⊙❷∅♨▲⯑‹ S lau ♥⊞

PLATAMONA LIDO Sassari
Cristina ☎079 310230
Jun-Sep 10HEC ∷ ♣♠☎⚊♥✗⊙❷∅♨▲⯑‹ PS ☎ lau ♥⊞

PORTO ROTONDO Sassari
Cugnana Loc Cugnana ☎0789 33184
15 May-Sep 5HEC ▥ ⌖♠☎⚊♥✗⊙❷∅♨☎⯑‹ PR ☎♥‹S ☎
Prices: A10000-18000 V4000-5000

SANTA LUCIA Nuoro
Cala-Pineta ☎0784 819184
Jun-15 Sep 5HEC ▥ ♣♠☎⚊♥✗⊙❷∅♨☎⯑ ‹ S ☎ lau Prices:
A6000-11000 pitch 9000-15000

Selema ☎0784 819068
Camping Card Compulsory
15 May-15 Oct 7.5HEC ▥ ∷ ♣♠☎⚊♥✗⊙❷∅♨☎⯑‹ RS ☎
lau ♥⊞ Prices: A15000-20000 pitch 10000-17500

SAN TEODORO Nuoro
San Teodoro la Cinta via Tirreno ☎0784 865777
15 May-15 Oct 3HEC ▥ ⌖♠☎⚊♥✗⊙❷∅♨☎⯑‹ S ☎⊞⊛ lau
♥✗

TEULADA Cagliari
Porto Tramatzu ☎070 9271022
SS195 from Cagliari.
Apr-Oct 3.5HEC ∷ ⌖♠☎⚊♥✗⊙❷‹ S ☎⊞ lau Prices:
A8000-11000 pitch 14000-17000

TORRE SALINAS Cagliari
Torre Salinas ☎070 999032
Apr-15 Oct 1.5HEC ∷ ♣♠☎⚊♥✗⊙❷☎▲⯑ S ☎ lau Prices:
A6500-11500 pitch 11500-16500

VALLEDORIA Sassari
Foce via Ampurias ☎079 582109
15 May-Sep 18HEC ▥ ∷ ♣♠☎⚊♥✗⊙❷∅♨☎⯑‹ PRS ☎
lau ♥⊞ Prices: A11500-16000 V3000-4500

Valledoria ☎079 584070
Jun-Sep 10HEC ∷ ♣♠☎⚊♥✗⊙❷∅♨☎⯑‹ S ☎⊛ lau ♥⊞
Prices: A11500-16000 V3000-4500

VILLASIMIUS Cagliari
Spiaggia del Riso ☎070 797150
3km S.
Apr-Oct 6HEC ∷ ♣♠☎⚊♥✗⊙❷∅♨⯑‹ S lau

SICILIA (SICILY)

ACIREALE

At CARRUBA(10.2km N)
Praiola ☎095 964366
In idyllic location, very quiet.
5km S of Riposto by the sea between orchards. 6km from A18 exit
Giarre.
15 Mar-Sep 22HEC ♨♣♠☎⚊✗⊙❷∅♨☎☎▲⯑‹ S ☎ lau Prices:
A7500-9000 pitch 17000-19000

AVOLA Siracusa
Pantanello Lungomare di Avola ☎0931 823275
All year 7.5HEC ▥ ♣♠⚊⊙❷☎▲⯑⊞ lau ♥☎⚊♥✗∅♨‹S
Prices: A7000 V3000 ☎9000 ▲7000

Sabbia d'Oro ☎0931 822415
All year 2HEC ▥ ♠ ⋔ ⅃ ⚑ ✗ ⊙ ⬛ ⊟ ⊞ ﹢ S ▣ lau

BUONFORNELLO Palermo
Himera ☎091 8140175
All year ♠ ⋔ ⅃ ⚑ ✗ ⊙ ⬛ ∅ ﹡ ⊟ ⊞ ﹢ PRS ☎ ▣ ⊞ lau

CASTEL DI TUSA Messina
Scoglio ☎0921 334345
A terraced site. No shade on the gravel beach.
Camping Card Compulsory.
Turn off SS113 st Km164, 2km W of Castel di Tusa.
May-Sep 1.5HEC ▥ ♠ ⋔ ⅃ ⚑ ✗ ⊙ ⬛ ∅ ﹡ ⊟ ﹢ S ☎ ⊞

CATANIA Catania
Ionio via Villini a Mare 2 ☎095 491139
On a clifftop plateau. Access to beach via steps. Lunchtime siesta 14.00-17.00 hrs.
Turn off SS14 N of town towards sea.
All year 1.2HEC ▥ ♠ ⋔ ⅃ ⚑ ✗ ⊙ ⬛ ∅ ﹡ ⊟ ⊞ ﹢ S ▣ ⊞ lau
Prices: A6600-9000 V4000-5000 ⊟9000-10400 ▲9000-10400

CEFALÚ Palermo
Plaja degli Uccelli ☎0921 999068
Apr-10 Oct 1.9HEC ▥ ∷∴ ♠ ⋔ ⅃ ⚑ ✗ ⊙ ⬛ ∅ ﹡ ⊟ ﹢ S ☎ ⊞

FINALE DI POLLINA Palermo
Rais Gerbi ☎0921 26570
Take the SS113 Messina-Palermo road to Km172.9.
May-Oct 4.5HEC ∷∴ ♦ ♠ ⋔ ⅃ ⚑ ✗ ⊙ ⬛ ∅ ﹡ ⊟ ▲ ﹢ PS ☎ ⊞

FONDACHELLO Catania
Mokambo ☎095 938731
Level terrain, thickly wooded in parts not directly next to the sea.
For access leave A18 (Messina-Catania) at Giarre exit, through Giarre and via Máscali to Fondachello on coast.
Apr-Sep 2.8HEC ∷∴ ♠ ⋔ ⅃ ✗ ⊙ ⬛ ∅ ﹡ ⊟ ﹢ S ☎ ⊞ lau

FÚRNARI MARINA Messina
Village Bazia Contrada Bazia ☎0941 800130
May-Sep 4HEC ∷∴ ♠ ⋔ ⅃ ⚑ ✗ ⊙ ⬛ ∅ ﹡ ⊟ ﹢ PS ▣ ⊘ Prices:
A7750-9700 V2650-3300 ⊟8650-10800 ▲6950-10800

GIARRE
At **MILO**(11km E)
Mareneve ETNA ☎095 7082163
Site in hilly terrain with lovely view of the sea.
Camping Card Compulsory.
Approach from the A18 exit Giarre direction Venerina and Milo about 10km.
All year 2HEC ▥ ♠ ⋔ ⅃ ✗ ⊙ ⬛ ∅ ﹡ ⊟ ﹢ P ☎ ⊞ lau

ÍSOLA DELLE FÉMMINE Palermo
La Playa viale Marino 55 ☎091 8677001
By the sea .
A29 Palermo to Trapani and SS113.
Apr-30 Oct 2.2HEC ∷∴ ♠ ⋔ ⅃ ✗ ⊙ ⬛ ∅ ﹡ ⊟ ﹢ S ☎ lau ﹢ ✗
⊞ Prices: A6500 pitch 10000-13000

MENFI Agrigento
Palma via delle Palme n 29 ☎0925 72232
Camping Card Compulsory.
6km S.
All year 1.4HEC ▥ ♠ ⋔ ⅃ ✗ ⊙ ⬛ ∅ ﹡ ⊟ ﹢ RS ☎ lau

MILAZZO Messina
Sayonara via Riviera di Ponente, Contrada Grunda ☎090 9283647
Closed Nov 25HEC ▥ ∷∴ ♠ ⋔ ⅃ ✗ ⊙ ⬛ ∅ ﹡ ⊟ ﹢ S ▣ ﹢ ⊞

NICOLOSI Catania
Etna via Goethe ☎095 914309
All year 29HEC ∷∴ ♠ ⋔ ⅃ ✗ ⊙ ⬛ ﹡ ⊟ ☎ lau ﹢ ⋆ ⊞

OLIVERI Messina
Marinello Contrada Marinello ☎0941 313000
Apr-Oct 3.2HEC ∷∴ ♠ ⋔ ⅃ ✗ ⊙ ⬛ ∅ ﹡ ⊟ ﹢ S ▣ lau ﹢ ﹢ ⊞
Prices: A6500-9000 pitch 18000-24000

PACHINO
At **PORTOPALO**(6.6km SE)
Capo Paissero ☎0931 842333
Site slightly sloping towards the sea with view of fishing harbour of Portopalo. Discotheque.
Turn S on 115 in Noto or Ioispica in direction of Pachino.
All year 3.5HEC ▥ ♠ ⋔ ⅃ ✗ ⊙ ⬛ ﹡ ⊟ ▣ ⊞ lau ﹢ ✗ ⋆S

PALAZZOLO ACREIDE Siracusa
Torre Torre Tudica ☎0931 32694
All year 2HEC ♠ ⋔ ⅃ ✗ ⊙ ⬛ ﹡ ﹢ PR ☎ ﹢ ﹡ ∅ ⊞

PALERMO Palermo
Internazionale Trinacria via Barcarello ☎091 530590
Lying on level ground near a large rock, the site is separated from a rocky beach by an asphalt road.
12km NW of Palermo. Turn off SS113 at Km273/1 and drive 1km towards the sea.
All year 4.5HEC ▥ ⊿ ⋔ ⅃ ✗ ⊙ ⬛ ∅ ﹡ ⊟ ⊞ ⊘ lau ﹢ ⋆S

Punta Braccetto Ragusa
Eurocamping ☎0932 918126
Jun-Sep 1.4HEC ∷∴ ♦ ♠ ⋔ ⊙ ﹡ S ☎ ⊘ ﹢ ⅃ ✗ ⋆P ⊞

Rocca dei Tramonti ☎0932 918054
The site lies in a quiet setting on rather barren land near a beautiful sandy bay surrounded by cliffs.
Camping Card Compulsory.
From Marina di Ragusa 10km W on coast road to Punta Braccetto.
Etr-15 Oct 3HEC ▥ ♠ ⋔ ⅃ ✗ ⊙ ⬛ ∅ ﹡ ⊟ ▲ ﹢ S ☎ ⊞

RAGUSA, MARINA DI Ragusa
Baia del Sole Lungomare A-Doria ☎0932 239844 & 230344
Well tended level site. Pitches provided with roofs of straw matting.
All year 5HEC ▥ ♠ ⋔ ⅃ ✗ ⊙ ⬛ ∅ ﹡ ⊟ ﹢ PS ☎ ⊞ lau

SAN GIORGIO Messina
Cicero via Cicero ☎941 39551
15 May-Sep 2.5HEC ▥ ∷∴ ♠ ⋔ ⅃ ✗ ⊙ ⬛ ∅ ﹡ ⊟ ﹢ S ▣ ⊞ lau

SANT' ALESSIO SICULO Messina
Focetta Sicula via Torrente Agrò ☎095 751657
A well equipped site with a private beach in a quiet location.
From Messina take autostrada to 'Roccalumera' exit, then SS114 towards Sant' Alessio and follow signs.
All year 1.2HEC ▥ ♠ ⋔ ⅃ ✗ ⊙ ⬛ ∅ ﹡ ⊟ ☎ ⊞ lau Prices:
A6300-8700 V3800-4800 ⊟8500-9900 ▲8500-9900

SANT' ANTONIO DI BARCELLONA Messina
Centro Vacanze Cantoni ☎090 9710165
May-Sep 1HEC ∷∴ ♦ ♠ ⋔ ✗ ⊙ ⬛ ﹡ ⊟ ﹢ PS ▣ ⊞ lau

SCOPELLO Trapani
Baia di Guidaloca via Modena ☎0924 541262
Apr-Sep 3HEC ▥ ♠ ⋔ ⅃ ✗ ⊙ ⬛ ﹡ ﹢ ⋆S

SECCAGRANDE Agrigento
Kameni Camping Village ☎0925 69212
All year 4HEC ▥ ♠ ⋔ ⅃ ✗ ⊙ ⬛ ∅ ▲ ﹢ PS ☎ lau ﹢ ﹡ ∅ ﹡ ⊞
Prices: A6000-9000 V4000 ⊟9000-12000 ▲5000-8000

TAORMINA
At **CALATABIANO**(5.2km SW)
Castello San Marco ☎095 641181
In lemon grove by an old castle, 9km S of Taormina.
Turn off SS114 between Calatabiano and Fiumefreddo in direction of the sea and continue for 1km.
All year 3.5HEC ▥ ♠ ⋔ ⅃ ✗ ⊙ ⬛ ∅ ﹡ ⊟ ☎ ⊞ lau ﹢ ⋆S

LUXEMBOURG

Luxembourg, the tiny Grand Duchy only 999 square miles in size, offers a wide range of facilities to the visitor.

Entirely landlocked it is bordered by three countries: Belgium, France and Germany. One third of the country is occupied by the hills and forests of the Ardennes, while the rest is taken up by the wooded farmland and, in the south-east, the rich wine-growing valley of the Moselle. The Grand Duchy enjoys a temperate climate, the summer often extending from May to late October. The official languages are French and German, but most of the people speak Luxembourgeois as an everyday language. Tourists will find, however, that English is also widely spoken and understood.

There are over 100 officially recognised campsites throughout the country. Most of them are open from April to October, but some function throughout the year. A booklet containing details of campsites is obtainable from the National Tourist Office (B.P.1001, L-1010 Luxembourg). All campsites open to the public must be authorised by the Minister of Tourism.

Off-site camping Caravans may only be parked on campsites. Non-coupled caravans may not be parked on the public highway or used as living accommodation. Casual camping with a tent is permitted, but permission must be obtained from the landowner. The owner is not allowed to give permission for more than 2 tents to be erected on his/her land. Casual camping is not allowed on the banks of Esch-sur-Sûre.

FACTS AND FIGURES

Capital: Luxembourg City
Language: Luxembourgeois, French and German
IDD code: 352. To call the UK dial 00 44
Currency: Luxembourg Franc (*LFr*1 = 100 centimes). At the time of going to press 1 = *LFr*46.40 The Belgian Franc is also accepted in Luxembourg.
Local time: GMT + 1 (summer GMT + 2)
Emergency Services: Fire and ambulance 112; police 113
Business hours-
Banks: Mon-Fri 09.00-12.00 and 13.30-16.30

Shops: Mon-Sat 09.00-18.00
Average daily temperatures: Luxembourg City

Jan 1°C	Jul 19°C
Mar 6°C	Sep 15°C
May 13°C	Nov 5°C

Tourist Information: Luxembourg National Tourist Office
UK 122 Regent Street London W1R 5FE
☎ 0171-434 2800
USA 801 Second Avenue New York, NY 10017
☎ (212) 370 9850
Camping card: Recommended. Few reductions offered.

HOW TO GET THERE

Luxembourg is easily approached through either Belgium or France. Apart from crossing by the Channel Tunnel, the usual Continental Channel ports for this journey are Boulogne, Calais or Dunkerque (Dunkirk) in France, and Oostende (Ostende) or Zeebrugge in Belgium. For details of the *AA European Routes Service* please consult the Contents Page.

Distance

Luxembourg City is just over 330km (205 miles) from the Belgian ports, or about 420km (260 miles) from the French ports, and is, therefore, within a day's drive of the Channel coast.
See Belgium for location map.

Motoring & General Information

The information given here is specific to Luxembourg.

It **must** be read in conjunction with the Continental ABC at the front of the book, which covers those regulations which are common to many countries.

British Embassy/Consulate*

The British Embassy together with its consular section is located at L-2450 Luxembourg, 14 Boulevard Roosevelt ☎229864/65/66

Children in cars

Child under 12 and/or 1.5 metres in height not permitted to travel as front seat passenger unless using suitable restraint system. Child in rear must use child seat or restraint if fitted.

Currency

There are no restrictions on the amount of foreign or local currency which can be taken into or out of the country, but because of the limited market for Luxembourg notes in other countries, it is advisable to change them into Belgian or other foreign notes before leaving.

Dimensions and weight restrictions

Private **cars** and towed **trailers** or **caravans** are restricted to the following dimensions - height, 4 metres; width, 2.50 metres; length, 12 metres. The maximum permitted overall length of vehicle/trailer or caravan combination is 25 metres.

The weight of a caravan must not exceed 75% of the weight of the towing vehicle.

Driving licence*

A valid UK or Republic of Ireland licence is acceptable in Luxembourg. The minimum age at which visitors from UK or Republic of Ireland may use a temporarily imported car or motorcycle is 17 years.

Foodstuffs*

There are no limits on the importation of foodstuffs

obtained duty and tax paid within the EC. Up to 500g of coffee (200g of coffee extract) and 100g of tea (40g of tea extract) purchased duty-free or outside the EC may be imported free of duty and tax. However, coffee bought duty-free or outside the EC cannot be imported by visitors under 15 years of age.

Motoring club*

The **Automobile Club du Grand-Duché de Luxembourg** (ACL) has its head office at 8007 Bertrange, 54 route de Longwy ☎450045-1. ACL office hours are 08.30-12.00hrs and 13.30-18.00hrs from Monday to Friday; closed Saturday and Sunday.

Roads

There is a comprehensive system of good main and secondary roads. Luxembourg has 58 miles of toll-free motorway.

Speed limits*

Car
Built-up areas 50kph (31mph)
Other roads 90kph (55mph)
Motorways 120kph (74mph)
Car/caravan/trailer
Built-up areas 50kph (31mph)
Other roads 75kph (46mph)
Motorways 90kph (56mph)
All lower signposted speed limits must be adhered to.

Warning triangle*

The use of a warning triangle is compulsory in the event of accident or breakdown. The triangle must be placed on the road about 100 metres (110yds) behind the vehicle to warn following traffic of any obstruction.

*Additional information will be found in the Continental ABC at the front of the book.

A-Z DIRECTORY

Prices are in Belgian Francs Abbreviations: r rue rte route

BERDORF

Parc Martbusch 3 Baim Maartbesch ☎79545
All year 3HEC ▦ ⬡ ⋔ �< ✕ ⊙ ⬕ ∅ ♨ ☎ ⚘ P ☎ lau

BOUS/REMICH

Source rte de Luxembourg 47 ☎698332
Mar-Oct 0.5HEC ▦ ⤳⬦ ⋔ ⊙ ⬕ ∅ ☎ ⊞

CLERVAUX

Official de Clervaux 33 r Klatzewee ☎920042
Situated next to the sports stadium, between the La Clervé stream
and the railway in a forested area. Trains only run during the day and
there is little noise. Separate field for tents.
0.5km SW from the village.
21 Mar-10 Nov 3HEC ▦ ✦⋔🐾⊙⬕∅♨☎⚘P☎⊞ lau ✦ ♨
✕ Prices: A140 pitch 140

CONSDORF

Bel Air Burgkapp 15 r Burgkapp ☎790353
The site is divided into pitches and lies on level meadowland in the
forest area of 'Petite Suisse Luxembourgeoise'.
On W outskirts of village. Turn right off E42. 6km S of Echternach.
28 Apr-31 Aug 2.3HEC ▦ ✦⋔⊙⬕∅⚘P☎⊞ lau ✦🐾✕♨
Prices: A150 pitch 150

DIEKIRCH

Bleesbruck ☎803134
A modern site in tranquil wooded surroundings.
Apr-1 Nov 5HEC ▦ ✦⋔🐾✕⊙⬕∅♨☎⚘R☎⊞ lau ✦✕

Op der Sauer rte de Gilsdorf ☎808590
500m from town centre on Gilsdorf road near the sports stadium.
All year 5HEC ▦ ⬡⋔✕⊙⬕∅♨☎☎⊞ lau ✦⚘PR Prices:
A120 pitch 120

DILLINGEN

Benelux 1-3 chemin de la Forêt ☎86267
A terraced, grassland site partially in an orchard and divided into
pitches.
Off N10, turn right before reaching the church.
15 Apr-11 Nov 1.7HEC ▦ ⬡⋔⊙⬕∅♨☎☎⊞ lau ✦🐾✕⚘R
Prices: A117-130 pitch 126-140

Wies-Neu 12 r de la Sûre ☎86110
Apr-Oct 3.2HEC ▦ ⬡⋔🐾⊙⬕∅♨☎⚘R☎⊞ lau ✦♨✕ Prices:
A110 pitch 130

ECHTERNACH

Alferweiher Alferweiher 1 ☎72271
From Echternach take route for Wasserbillig and follow signs.
May-15 Sep 4HEC ▦ ⬡⋔🐾✕⊙⬕∅♨P☎⊞ lau ✦♨✕⚔⚘L

Official 5 rte de Diekirch ☎720272
Take E42 to Echternach.
15 Mar-15 Oct 7HEC ▦ ✦⋔⊙⬕☎☎⚘☎⊞ lau ✦🐾♨✕∅⚔
⚘LPR Prices: A120 ☎120 ▲120

ENSCHERANGE

Val d'Or ☎920691
Quiet family site in a beautiful natural setting beside a small river.
Camping Card Compulsory
All year 4HEC ▦ ⤳⬦ ⋔✕✕⊙⬕☎♨☎☎▲⚘R☎⊞✦🐾 Prices:
A120 pitch 140

ESCH-SUR-ALZETTE

Gaalgebierg ☎541069
A level park-like site with lovely trees on a hillock.
SE along N6 from the town centre in the direction of Dudelange as
far as the motorway underpass. Then turn right and follow the steep
climb uphill.

All year 2.5HEC ▦ ⬡⋔🐾♨✕⊙⬕∅♨☎☎⊞ lau Prices: A130
pitch 130

HALLER

Relax r Henerecht 6 ☎86748
All year 2.3HEC ▦ ⤳⬦⬡⋔♨✕⊙⬕☎⚘P☎⊞ lau ✦🐾

HEIDERSCHEID

Fuussekaul rte de Bastogne 2 ☎89659
A level grassland site with a large subdivision of pitches on a plateau
adjoining a woodland area.
Turn off the N15 (Ettelbruck-Wiltz/Bastogne) S of Heiderscheid in a
westerly direction.
All year 30HEC ▦ ⬡⋔🐾♨✕⊙⬕∅♨☎☎⚔⚘▲⚘P☎⊞ lau ✦⚘R
Prices: A180 pitch 320

INGLEDORF

Gritt r du Pont ☎802018
On southern bank of River Sûre between Ettelbruck and Diekirch. In
beautiful country setting ideal for fishing.
Apr-Oct 5HEC ▦ ⬡⋔⊙⬕♨⚘R☎⊞✦🐾⚔♨ Prices: pitch 600
(incl 2 persons)

KOCKELSCHEUER

Kockelscheuer 22 rte de Bettembourg ☎471815
Etr-Oct 4HEC ▦ ⬡⋔🐾⊙⬕∅♨☎⚔☎⊞ lau ✦✕ Prices: A110 pitch
120

LAROCHETTE

Kengert ☎352 87186
On gently sloping meadow.
Take the N8 towards Mersch, then the CR119 towards Nommern
and turn right after approx 2km.
07 Feb-8 Nov 4HEC ▦ ✦⋔🐾♨✕⊙⬕∅♨⚘P☎⊞ lau Prices:
pitch 290-350

MERSCH

Krounebierg r de la Piscine 12 ☎329756
A clean, well-kept site on five terraces, split into sections by hedges.
Approx 0.5km W of village church.
Apr-Sep 5HEC ▦ ⬡⋔🐾♨✕⊙⬕∅♨⚘P☎ lau Prices: pitch
705-925 (incl 2 persons)

NOMMERN

Belle Vue 3 r Principale ☎878068
Camping Card Compulsory.
20 Apr-25 Oct 2HEC ▦ ✦⋔🐾♨✕⊙⬕∅♨☎⚔⚘P☎☎⊞ lau
✦✕ Prices: pitch 325-790 (incl 4 persons)

Europe Nommerlayen ☎878078
A terraced site in wooded surroundings.
Etr-7 Nov 15HEC ▦ ⬡⋔🐾♨✕⊙⬕∅♨⚔⚘P☎⊞ lau Prices:
pitch 650-1590
See advertisement on page 215.

OBEREISENBACH

Kohnenhof 1 Maison ☎00352 929464
Quiet site in a rural setting in the River Our valley.
Apr-Nov 8HEC ▦ ⬡⋔🐾♨✕⊙⬕∅♨⚔⚘R☎⊞ lau Prices:
A125 pitch 250

REISDORF

Rivière rte de la Sûre ☎86398
The entire site is divided into pitches and lies on a field near the
church.
Between the River Sûre/Sauer and Km9.5 off the N19, 10km E of
Diekirch.
Mar-Sep 1.7HEC ▦ ⬡⋔🐾♨✕⊙⬕∅♨☎⚘R☎⊞ lau ✦🐾

europacamping "Nommerlayen"

Luxurious terrace-camping with views onto the Ardennes. In midst of beautiful scenery, surrounded by 1.000 ha of woods with over 100 km of foot-path.

Luxurious campsite with individual pitches with an average size of 100 m², all with electricity, water and sewage connections and night lamp. Toilet room for handicapped, special sanitary facilities for babies and kids. Swimming pool (50 x 10 m) and paddling pool (Ø 35 m) with high waves track (free), water playground, very large playground for all ages, football, basket and volleyball field, table tennis, bowling, billards and snooker. Full leisure programme in high season, different programme daily. Football, festive nights and evening shows. **In off season:** scenery at its best, personal attention, considerable discount, relaxation, leisure programme when required.

Europacamping Nommerlayen • Robert Miny • L-7465 Nommern
Tel. +352-878078 and 878093

ROSPORT

Barrage rte d'Echternach ☎730160
Situated by Lake Sûre on the German border.
Main road from Echternach to Wasserbillig.
Mar-Oct 3.2HEC ▥ ⌂ ⋒ ⊝ ⊡ ⋋ LPR ☎ ⊞ lau ♦ ⚎ ⛾ ✕ ∅ ≞ Prices: A120 pitch 150

STEINFORT

Steinfort 72 rte de Luxembourg ☎398827
All year 2.5HEC ▥ ⌂ ⋒ ⚎ ⛾ ✕ ⊝ ⊡ ∅ ≞ ⚍ ⛿ ⋋ P ☎ ⊞ lau
Prices: A85-95 pitch 216-240

VIANDEN

Deich ☎84375
Etr-Oct 3HEC ▥ ⌂ ⋒ ⊝ ⊡ ⋋ R ☎ ⊞ lau ♦ ⚎ ⛾ ✕ ∅ ≞ ⋋P Prices: A130 pitch 130

Moulin rte de Bettel ☎84501
On Bettel-Vianden road beside the river.
10 May-2 Sep 2.8HEC ▥ ♦ ⋒ ⚎ ⊝ ⊡ ⋋ R ☎ ⊞ lau ♦ ∅ ≞ ⋋P

At **WALSDORF** (2km SW)

Romantique Tandelerbaach ☎84464
A terraced grassland site.
W of Diekirch-Vianden road, access from the N17 and CR354.
Apr-Oct 6HEC ⌂ ⋒ ⚎ ⛾ ✕ ⊝ ⊡ ∅ ⚍ ☎ ⊞ lau ♦ ⋋PR

NETHERLANDS

The Netherlands is bordered by two countries, Belgium and Germany.

A fifth of this flat, level country criss-crossed by rivers and canals lies below sea-level. The areas reclaimed from the sea, known as *polders*, are extremely fertile. The landscape is broken up by the forests of Arnhem, the bulbfields in the west, the lakes in the central and northern areas, and the coastal dunes which are the most impressive in Europe.

The climate is generally mild and tends to be damp. The summers are moderate with changeable weather and are seldom excessively hot. The language, Netherlandish or Dutch, is fairly guttural and closely allied to the low German dialect. Other dialect forms exist throughout the Netherlands.

There are some 900 officially recognised and classifed campsites throughout the Netherlands. It is not generally possible to book sites in advance. Coastal sites tend to be crowded in June, July and August when many of the Dutch take their holidays. Local tourist information offices (VVV) can provide detailed information about sites in their area. The camping season is generally from April to September, but some sites are open all year.

Off-site camping is not possible outside organised sites. Overnight stops are not permitted.

HOW TO GET THERE

There are direct ferry services to the Netherlands: Harwich to the Hoek van (Hook of) Holland (6hrs 30mins day, 8hrs 30mins night); *Sheerness to Vlissingen (7hrs 30mins day, 9hrs 30mins night); Hull

to Rotterdam-Europoort (13hrs 30mins); Newcastle to Amsterdam (14hrs - terminal is actually Ijmuiden 30 km away - summer only service). Alternatively, use the Channel Tunnel, or take one of the short Channel crossings and drive through France and Belgium. For details of the *AA European Routes Service* please consult the Contents Page.

• Eurolink ferries are currently taking bookings up to 7 April 1997.

Distance

From Calais to Den Haag (The Hague) is just over 340km (211 miles) (within a day's drive).

MOTORING & GENERAL INFORMATION

The information given here is specific to The Netherlands. It **must** be read in conjunction with the European ABC at the front of the book, which covers those regulations which are common to many countries.

British Embassy/Consulate*

The British Embassy is located at 2514 ED Den Haag, Lange Voorhout 10 ☎(070) 4270427, but the Embassy has no consular section. The British Consulate is located at 1075 AE Amsterdam, Koningslaan 44 ☎(020) 6764343.

Children in cars

Child under 12 and/or 1.5 metres* in height cannot travel as front seat passenger unless using a suitable restraint. Child under 3 in the rear does not have to wear a seat belt but must use child seat or restraint if fitted; child over 3 and under 12 must wear seat belt in the absence of such equipment.
*A child of 10 at least 1.6 metres in height may sit in the front wearing normal seat belts.

Currency

There are no restrictions limiting the import of currency. All imported currency may be freely exported, as well as any currency exchanged in, or drawn on, an account established in the Netherlands.

Dimensions and weight restrictions

Private **cars** and towed **trailers** or **caravans** are restricted to the following dimensions - height, 4 metres; width†, 2.55 metres.; length†† 12 metres. The maximum permitted overall length of vehicle/trailer or caravan combination is 18 metres. The maximum weight of caravan/luggage trailers will be determined by the instructions of the manufacturer of the towing vehicle and/or the manufacturer of the caravan/luggage trailer.
  †Some very small roads have a maximum width restriction of 2.20 metres.
  ††Trailers with single axle up to 3,500kg (empty weight and carrying capacity) is 8 metres.

Driving licence*

A valid UK or Republic of Ireland licence is acceptable in the Netherlands. The minimum age at which visitors from UK or Republic of Ireland may use a temporarily imported car or motorcycle is 18 years.

Firearms

Dutch laws concerning the possession of firearms are the most stringent in Europe. Any person crossing the frontier with any type of firearm will be arrested. The law applies also to any object which, on superficial inspection, shows any resemblance to real firearms (*eg* plastic imitations). If you wish to carry firearms, real or imitation, of any description into the Netherlands, seek the advice of the Netherlands Consulate.

Foodstuffs*

There are no limits on the importation of foodstuffs obtained duty and tax paid within the EC. Up to 500g of coffee (200g of coffee extract) and 100g of tea (40g of tea extract) purchased duty-free or outside the EC may be imported free of duty and tax. However, coffee bought duty-free or outside the EC cannot be imported by visitors under 15 years of age. The importation of unpreserved meat products is forbidden.

Motoring club*

The **Koninklijke Nederlandse Toeristenbond** (ANWB) has its headquarters at 2596 EC 's-Gravenhage, Wassenaarseweg 220, and offices in numerous provincial towns. They will assist motoring tourists generally, and supply road and touring information. Offices are usually open between 08.45 and 16.45hrs Monday to Friday 08.45 and 12.00hrs on Saturday. Traffic information for the Netherlands can be obtained from the ANWB on ☎(06) 9622; this costs *Fls*0.5 per minute but only Dutch is spoken.

Roads

Main roads usually have only two lanes, but are well-surfaced. The best way to see the countryside is to tour along minor roads, often alongside canals.

  The Netherlands has a network of motorways (*autosnelweg*) carrying most inter-city and long distance traffic. Yellow ANWB emergency telephone pillars are located every 2km along highways.

Speed limits*

Car

Built-up areas 50kph (31mph)

Other roads 80kph (49mph)

Motorways 100kph (62mph) or 120kph (74mph)

Car/caravan/trailer

Built-up areas 50kph (31mph)

Other roads 80kph (49mph)

Motorways 80kph (49mph)

The minimum speed on motorways for cars and vehicles towing a caravan or trailer is 80kph (49mph).

Warning triangle*

In the event of accident or breakdown a motorist must use either a warning triangle or hazard warning lights to warn approaching traffic of any obstruction. However, a warning triangle is recommended as hazard warning lights may be damaged or inoperative.

*Additional information will be found in the Continental ABC at the front of the book.

A-Z DIRECTORY

Prices are in Dutch Florins (Guiden or Guilder) Abbreviations: Str Straat.
Each name preceded by 'Den' is listed under the name that follows it. **Most telephone area codes and some numbers are changing during the currency of this guide. It is advisable to check the current situation before phoning the Netherlands.**

North

The Dutch have been doing battle with the sea for centuries. It is part of their history, an essential element in the country's security and prosperity, and a large influence on the people's make-up. It is a battle the people have, for the most part, won. Where there once was nothing but water, we now find one of the most fertile countries in Europe; vast polders with peacefully grazing Frisian cattle, drainage mills along the canals, and drawbridges leading to farmhouses.
The West Frisian islands extend along the coast like a string of pearls, sheltering the mainland from the unpredictable and stormy North Sea, offering visitors long white beaches and many nature parks.
On the mainland, visit Dokkum, the small walled town where St Boniface was murdered in 754; Noordbergum, where clogm akers demonstrate their skills; Hindeloopen, famed for painted furniture; and Leeuwarden, the home of Mata Hari - whose statue stands on the Korfmakerspijp - and of the Princesshof, which houses a unique ceramic museum.

AMELAND (ISLAND OF)

See **NES**

AMEN *Drenthe*
Reservaat Diana Heide 53 Amen ☎0592 389297
An ideal site for relaxation, which lies away from the traffic amongst forest and heathland.
If approaching from Assen along the E35, drive through Amen and on towards Hooghalen.
15 Mar-Oct 30HEC ▦ ░░░ ⌕ ⋔ ⛭ ⚡ ✕ ⊙ ⬚ ⊘ ♨ ▲ ⤸ LP ⊕ 🄿
⊞ lau Prices: A5.25 ⚌12.50 ▲12.50

ANNEN *Drenthe*
Hondsrug Annerweg 3 ☎0592 271292
Apr-Oct 18HEC ▦ ░░░ ⅃⅄ ⋔ ⛭ ✕ ⊙ ⬚ ♨ ⤸ P ⊕ ⊞ lau
Prices: pitch 30-44

ASSEN *Drenthe*
Witterzomer Witterzomer 7 ☎0592 393535
A large site with asphalt internal roads, lying in mixed woodland near nature reserve. Separate sections for dog owners. Individual washing facilities for the disabled.
Turn off the E35 at Assen W exit into Europaweg Zuid and continue for 100m, then turn right. Continue through Witten and follow signs.
All year 75HEC ▦ ⌕ ⋔ ⛭ ✕ ⊙ ⬚ ⊘ ⊞ ▲ ⤸ LP ⊕ 🄿 lau ♦ ♨
Prices: A4-6 V9 ⚌9 ▲4-6

BORGER *Drenthe*
Hunzedal De Drift 3 ☎0599 234698
The site is clean, well-kept and lies NE of the village.
For access, turn off the road towards Buinen, drive 200m E of the bridge over the Buinen-Schoondoord canal, then head S for a further 1km.
28 Mar-24 Oct 30HEC ▦ ⌕ ⋔ ⛭ ⚡ ✕ ⊙ ⬚ ⊘ ⊞ ⤸ LP ⊕ 🄿 ⊞ lau ♦ ♨ Prices: pitch 37.50-65

DELFZIJL *Groningen*
Delfzijl Kustweg 13 ☎05960 12870
On coast.
Apr-Sep 2HEC ▦ ♦ ⋔ ⛭ ⚡ ⊙ ⬚ ⬚ ⤸ PS ♦ ⛭ ✕

DIEVER *Drenthe*
Hoeve aan de Weg Bosweg 12 ☎0521 387269
Camping Card Compulsory.
Apr-Oct 4.5HEC ▦ ⌕ ⋔ ⛭ ⚡ ✕ ⊙ ⬚ ⊘ ♨ ⬚ ▲ ⤸ P ⊕ 🄿 ⊞ lau ♦ ⤸L Prices: A5 pitch 13.50

At **DIEVERBRUG**(2km SE)
Ellert en Brammert Groningerweg 13 ☎05219 1207
On hilly ground in a forest of conifers and deciduous trees.
0.2km W of Km22.4 off the E35.
Apr-Oct 28HEC ▦ ░░░ ⌕ ⋔ ⛭ ⚡ ✕ ⊙ ⬚ ⊘ ♨ ⬚ ⊕ 🄿 ⊞ lau ♦ ⤸P

DWINGELOO *Drenthe*
Noordster Noordster 105 ☎05219 7238
3km S on E35.
All year 40HEC ▦ ♦ ⋔ ⛭ ⚡ ✕ ⊙ ⬚ ⊘ ♨ ⬚ ⤸ P ⊕ ⊞ lau ♦ ✕

EMMEN *Drenthe*
Emmen Angelsloerdijk 31 ☎0591 612080
On several pitches of well-kept meadowland, near an indoor swimming pool.
Camping Carnet Compulsory.
From village drive towards Angelso for 1.5km, then follow signposts.
All year 6HEC ▦ ⌕ ⋔ ⛭ ⚡ ✕ ⊙ ⬚ ⊘ ♨ ⬚ ⬚ ⊕ 🄿 ⊞ lau ♦ ⤸P
Prices: A5 pitch 3

EXLOO *Drenthe*

Hunzebergen Valtherweg 36 ☎05919 49116
2.5km SE.
Apr-Oct 45HEC ▥ ⚗♠☎⚓⊙ �"𝄐 ≜☎ ₹ LP ☎⊞ lau

FORMERUM (ISLAND OF TERSCHELLING) *Friesland*

Nieuw Formerum Formerum 13 ☎0562 448977
Apr-Sep 7HEC ▥ ⚗♠⊙☎🄿☎⊞⊗ lau ♦☎♀✗🖉≜ ₹S

GASSELTE *Drenthe*

Berken Borgerweg 23 ☎599 564255
Part of this site lies in wooded surroundings.
0.5km SW.
Apr-25 Oct 3.5HEC ▥ ⚗♠⊙ 🖉𝄐≜☎⊞ lau ♦☎♀✗ Prices:
pitch 25-28 (incl 2 persons)

Hoefslag Achter de Brinken 14 ☎05999 64343
Camping Card Compulsory.
E of town.
Apr-23 Oct 8HEC ▥ ⚗♠☎♀✗⊙ 🖉𝄐≜☎⊞ ₹ P ⊞ lau

GROLLOO *Drenthe*

Berenkuil De Pol 15 ☎0592 501242
Partly in a forest and partly on heathland.
On the western outskirts of the village towards Hooghalen. Drive a
further 0.8km along a road which narrows at the end.
Apr-Sep 39HEC ▥ ⚗♠✗⊙🖉𝄐≜ ₹ LP 🄿 ⊞ lau ♦☎

GRONINGEN *Groningen*

Stadspark Campinglaan 6 ☎050 5251624
A well-kept site on patches of grass between rows of bushes and
groups of pine and deciduous trees. Some of its pitches are
naturally screened.
Camping Card Compulsory.
For access from the SW outskirts of the town, take the road towards
Peize and Roden.
15 Mar-15 Oct 7.2HEC ▥ ⚗♠☎♀✗⊙🖉𝄐≜☎⊞ lau ♦✗ ₹P

HARKSTEDE *Groningen*

Grunopark Mooldweg 163 ☎050 416371
All year 23HEC ▥ ⚗♠☎♀✗⊙🖉𝄐≜☎♀ ₹ L ☎⊞ lau Prices:
A4.50 V4.50 ♨6 ▲3

HARLINGEN *Friesland*

Zeehoeve ☎05178 413465
A well-kept meadow site which is divided into large sections by rows
of bushes.
It lies 1km S of Harlingen near a dyke.
Apr-Sep 10HEC ▥ ⚗♦♠☎♀⊙🖉𝄐♀ ₹ S ☎⊞ lau ♦☎

HEE (ISLAND OF TERSCHELLING) *Friesland*

Kooi ☎05620 2743
Apr-10 Sep 9HEC ▥ ⚗♠♀✗⊙☎🄿☎⊞ lau ♦☎✗🖉≜ ₹L Prices:
A6.50 V3.25 ♨6.50 ▲4-6.50

HINDELOOPEN *Friesland*

Hindeloopen Westerdijk 9 ☎0514 521452
A peaceful site on the Ysselmeer with fishing and watersports
facilities.
1km S.
Apr-1 Nov 16HEC ▥ ⚗♦♠☎♀✗⊙🖉𝄐♀ ₹ L ☎🄿⊞ lau Prices:
pitch 24 (incl 2 persons)

KOUDUM *Friesland*

Nautic Park "De Kuilart" Kuilart 1 ☎0514 521606
A camping and watersports centre on the shores of 'De Fluessen'
lake.
Access via N359.
21 Mar-Oct 30HEC ▥ ⚗♠☎♀✗⊙🖉𝄐≜☎♀ ₹LP☎⊞⊗
lau Prices: pitch 37.50-44.50 (incl 2 persons)

LAUWERSOOG *Groningen*

Lauwersoog Strandweg 7 ☎5193 49133
In a pleasant situation on the shores of Lauwersmeer. A good
excursion centre with fine water sports facilities.

Camping Card Compulsory.
All year 11HEC ▥ ⚗♠☎♀✗⊙🖉𝄐≜☎♀ ₹ LS 🄿⊞ lau
Prices: pitch 22.50-27.50 (incl 2 persons)

MAKKUM *Friesland*

Holle Poarte Holle Poarte 2 ☎515 231344
A modern site with fine water sports facilities on the Ijsselmeer.
All year 36HEC ▥ ⠿⠿⠿ ⚗♠☎♀✗⊙🖉𝄐≜☎♀ ₹ L ☎⊞ lau
Prices: pitch 20-40

NES (ISLAND OF AMELAND) *Ameland*

Duinoord J-van Eijckweg 4 ☎05191 42070
Take ferry at Holward, site left off road towards beach.
Apr-Nov 17HEC ▥ ⚗♦♠☎♀✗⊙🖉𝄐▲🄿⊞⊗ lau ♦ ₹PS

ONNEN *Groningen*

Fruitberg Dorpsweg 67 ☎050 4061282
S of the village, and right of the Haren-Zuidlaren road.
15 Mar-Oct 5.5HEC ▥ ⚗♠♀⊙🖉𝄐≜♀ ₹ P ☎🄿⊞ lau ♦☎
Prices: A5 V4 ♨4

OPENDE *Friesland*

'T Strandheem Parkweg 2 ☎0594 659555
Apr-Oct 15HEC ▥ ⚗♠☎♀✗⊙🖉𝄐≜☎♀▲ ₹ LP☎⊞ lau
Prices: pitch 27.50 (incl 2 persons)

RODEN *Drenthe*

Cnossen Leekstermeer Meenweg 13 ☎05945 12073
On the S shores of the Leekstemeer.
For access, turn off the N13 about 1.6km SE of Leek (towards
Roden) and drive NE. Then take a narrow paved road, and continue
for a further 2.7km.
Apr-Nov 3.8HEC ▥ ⚗♦♠✗⊙🖉𝄐☎⊞ lau ♦ ₹L

RUINEN *Drenthe*

Wiltzangh Witteveen 2 ☎0552 471227
N of the village in the middle of a coniferous and deciduous forest,
and within the grounds of a big holiday village. Advance booking is
necessary for the peak season.
For access, drive from Ruinen towards Ansen for 3km, then turn and
head N.
Apr-Oct 13HEC ▥ ⚗♠☎✗⊙🖉𝄐☎ ₹ P ☎🄿⊞ lau ♦☎♀✗
Prices: pitch 23-33

SONDEL *Friesland*

Sondel Beuckeswijkstr 26 ☎05140 2300
In a dense wood.
Just off the Sondel-Rijs road.
29 Mar-Oct 6HEC ⚗♠☎✗⊙☎ ₹ LPRS ☎🄿⊞⊗ lau ♦☎🖉
𝄐 Prices: pitch 20.20 (incl 2 persons)

TERSCHELLING (ISLAND OF)

See **FORMERUM, HEE & WEST TERSCHELLING**

WATEREN *Drenthe*

Olde Lanschap Schurerslaan 4 ☎0521 387244
A spacious family site near the outskirts of a National Park.
Apr-Oct 13HEC ▥ ⚗♠☎♀✗⊙🖉𝄐≜☎ ₹ LP ☎🄿⊞ lau Prices:
A4.50 pitch 14.95

WEDDE *Groningen*

Wedderbergen Molenweg 2 ☎0597 561673
On meadowland divided by deciduous trees and bush hedges.
On the E outskirts of the village take a narrow asphalt road, and
drive N for 3.2km. Then take Spanjaardsweg and Molenweg to the
camp.
All year 40HEC ▥ ⚗♠☎♀✗⊙🖉𝄐≜ ₹ L ☎⊞ lau Prices: A7-9
V3-5 ♨10-12 ▲3-5

WESTERBROEK *Groningen*

Groningen International Woortmansdijk 1 ☎05904 1433
A pleasant site on the outskirts of Groningen.
From Groningen take A7 to Hoogezand and follow signs.
All year 3HEC ▥ ⚗♠☎♀✗⊙🖉𝄐≜☎⊞ lau

WEST TERSCHELLING (ISLAND OF TERSCHELLING) *Friesland*
Cnossen Hoofdweg 8 ☎0562 442321
Several patches of meadowland, left of the road towards Formerum, and right of the forest.
For access, take the ferry from Harlingen.
Mar-Nov 2.5HEC ▦ ⌕ ⋔ ⧖ ⚡ ✕ ⊖ ⚑ ⌀ ⛟ ⚑ ▲ ▣ ⊞ ➡ ⌇LP
Prices: A6.25 V3 ⊕8 ▲5-8

Central

In the heart of the Netherlands lies the country's largest nature reserve - the Hogwe Veluwe National Park. In addition to its many rare species, there are numerous museums and galleries, including the National Kröller-Müller Museum which houses a wonderful Van Gogh collection.
The Noord-Holland is *the* flower province of the Netherlands, with fields of daffodils, tulips, hyacinths and crocuses. Beautiful canals run through its capital, Amsterdam, with richly ornamental mansions on their banks. The most attractive and compact shopping centre in Holland, it is said you can buy anything in Amsterdam!
In winter, the region of Overijsell is a paradise for those who enjoy long-distance skiing "langlauf". Alternatively, a visit in July to Dedomsvaart during its week-long festival will show you the largest open-air dinner and the largest shovel-board in the world.
Utrecht is truly unique; it combines a rich past and a dynamic present. It is the home of the tallest and finest church tower in Holland - the 'Dom'. Breathtaking views will reward those who climb its 465 steps.

AALSMEER Noord-Holland
Amsterdamse Bos Kleine Noorddijk 1 ☎020 6416868
The site is in a park-like setting in the Amsterdam wood. The camp is near the Airport flight path and is subject to noise depending on the wind direction.
If approaching from The Hague along the motorway, turn at the northern edge of the airport, and head towards Amstelveen. Then follow directions for Aalsmeer. Alternatively, if approaching from Utrecht, leave the motorway at the Amstelveen exit, and drive towards Aalsmeer, passing through Bovenkerk.
Apr-Oct 6.8HEC ▦ ⌕ ⋔ ⚡ ✕ ⊖ ⚑ ⌀ ⛟ ⚑ ▣ ⊞ lau ➡ ⌇LP
Prices: A8.25 V4.25 ⊕6.25 ▲5.25

ALKMAAR Noord-Holland
Alkmaar Bergerweg 201 ☎072 116924
The site is well-kept and divided into many sections by rows of trees and bushes.
Camping Card Compulsory.
Lies on the NW outskirts of the town, off the Bergen road.
Jul-Sep 2.5HEC ▦ ⌕ ⋔ ⚡ ⊖ ⚑ ⚑ ▣ ⊞ lau ➡ ⚡ ✕ ⌀ ⌇LPS
Prices: A7 V4 ⊕10 ▲7

AMSTERDAM Noord-Holland
See also AALSMEER & GAASPERPLAS
Vliegenbos Meeuwenlaan 138 ☎0031 20 6368855
This is a tent site for young people.
From main railway station through tunnel, then right and right again at traffic lights, then follow signposts.
Apr-Sep 3HEC ▦ ⌕ ⋔ ⚡ ✕ ⊖ ⚑ ⌀ ⛟ ▣ ⊞ ⌀ lau ➡ ⌇P

ANDIJK Noord-Holland
Vakantiedorp Het Grootslag Proefpolder 4 ☎050 262627
Apr-Oct 5HEC ▦ ⌴ ⋔ ⚡ ✕ ⊖ ⚑ ⌀ ⛟ ⌇ ▣ lau ➡ ⌇L

APPELTERN Gelderland
Het Groene Eiland Lutenkampstr 2 ☎0487 562130
15 Mar-Oct 16HEC ▦ ⌕ ⋔ ⚡ ✕ ⊖ ⚑ ⌀ ⌇ ⌇ LR ▣ ⊞ lau Prices:
A4.50 V2.50 ⊕16.50 ▲8

ARNHEM Gelderland
Arnhem Kemperbegerweg 771 ☎026 4431600
The site lies on grassland and is surrounded by trees.

NW of town and S of E36.
Mar-Oct 36HEC ▦ ⌕ ⋔ ⚡ ✕ ⊖ ⚑ ⌀ ⌇ ⛟ ▣ ⊞ lau ➡ ⌇P Prices: pitch 22 (incl 2 persons)

Hooge Veluwe Koningsweg 14 ☎085 432272
Camping Card Compulsory.
From Apeldoorn exit on E36 drive NW towards Hooge Veluwe.
Apr-29 Oct 18HEC ▦ ⌕ ⋔ ⚡ ✕ ⊖ ⚑ ⌀ ⛟ ⚑ ⌇ P ▣ ⊞ lau

Warnsborn Bakenbergseweg 257 ☎085 423469
The site is surrounded by woodland and lies on slightly sloping meadowland. Near zoo and open-air museum.
Near the E36 motorway NW of town in the direction of Utrecht. 200m S of SHELL filling station, continue in W direction for 0.7km.
Apr-Nov 3.5HEC ▦ ⌕ ⋔ ⊖ ⚑ ⌀ ⛟ ⚑ ⚑ ▣ ⊞ lau ➡ ⚡ ✕ ⌇P

BABBERICH Gelderland
Rivo Torto Beekseweg 8 ☎0316 247332
3km W on E36.
Apr-Oct 7HEC ▦ ⌕ ⋔ ⊖ ⚑ ⌀ ⌇ ▣ ⊞ lau ➡ ✕ ⌇LPR Prices: A3.50 V5 ⊕10.50 ▲7.50

BEEKBERGEN Gelderland
Bosgraaf Kanaal Zuid 444 ☎055 5051359
Situated on hilly grassland and woodland, but the woodland pitches are mainly used by residential caravans.
For access from the N50, Arnhem-Apeldoorn road, turn N in West Hoeve onto the Loenen road, then follow signs for 2km.
Apr-Oct 20HEC ▦ ⌕ ⋔ ⚡ ⚡ ⊖ ⚑ ⌀ ⌇ ⛟ ⚑ ⌇ P ▣ ⊞ ▣ ⌀ lau ➡ ✕ Prices: pitch 30.50 (incl 2 persons)

Groot Panorama Groot Panorama 36 ☎05766 2707
All year 3HEC ▦ ⌕ ⋔ ⊖ ⚑ ⌀ ⛟ ⚑ ⌇ ▣ ⊞ lau

Lange Bosk Hoge Bergweg 16 ☎05765 1252
On level ground in a spruce forest. Divided into pitches.
Turn off the Beekbergen-Loenen road at Km4.3 and drive N. Site about 3.5km from town.
Apr-1 Nov 37.5HEC ▦ ⌕ ⋔ ⚡ ✕ ⊖ ⚑ ⌀ ⛟ ⌇ P ▣ ⊞ lau ➡ ⌇L

BERKHOUT Noord-Holland
Westerkogge Kerkebuurt 202 ☎02295 1208
Apr-1 Oct 11HEC ▦ ⌕ ⋔ ⚡ ⊖ ⚑ ⌀ ⌇ ⛟ ⚑ ⌇ P ▣ ⊞ lau

BILTHOVEN Utrecht
Biltse Duinen Burg v.d Borchlaan 7 ☎030 2286777
Family site in wooded surroundings with asphalt drives.
Signposted from town centre.
Apr-1 Oct 20HEC ⌇⌇⌇ ⌴ ⋔ ✕ ⊖ ⚑ ⌀ ⌇ P ▣ ⊞ ▣ ⌀ lau ➡ ⚑
Prices: pitch 21-28 (incl 2 persons)

BLOKZIJL Overijssel
Tussen de Diepen Duinigermeerweg 1A ☎0527 291565
Secluded site surrounded by water. Fishing, water-sports and sailing.
Apr-Oct 5HEC ▦ ⌕ ⋔ ✕ ⊖ ⚑ ⌀ ⚑ ⌇ R ▣ ⊞ lau ➡ ⚑ ⌀ ⌇P Prices: A6 V2.50 ⊕5.75 ▲5.75

BUURSE Overijssel
't Hazenbos Oude Buursedijk 1 ☎053 5696338
On several meadows, partially surrounded by trees.
All year 8HEC ▦ ⌕ ⋔ ⚡ ⊖ ⚑ ⌀ ⌇ ▣ ⊞ lau ➡ ⚑ ✕ Prices: A4.65 V3.65 ⊕4.65 ▲3.85-4.65

CALLANTSOOG Noord-Holland
Recreatiecentrum de Nollen Westerweg 8 ☎0224 581281
E of town towards N9.
Apr-Nov 9HEC ▦ ⌕ ⋔ ⚡ ✕ ⊖ ⚑ ⌀ ⛟ ⚑ ⌇ S ▣ ⊞ lau ➡ ⌇P
Prices: pitch 24.75-27.50

Tempelhof Westerweg 2 ☎02248 581522
Apr-Nov 13HEC ▦ ⌕ ⋔ ⚡ ✕ ⊖ ⚑ ⌇ PS ▣ ▣ ⊞ lau ➡ ⌀ ⌇LR
Prices: pitch 32.80-41 (incl 3 persons)

COCKSDORP, DE (ISLAND OF TEXEL) Noord-Holland
Krim Roggeslootweg 6 ☎0222 390111
All year 31HEC ▦ ⌕ ⋔ ⚡ ✕ ⊖ ⚑ ⌀ ⌇ ⛟ ⚑ ▲ ⌇ P ▣ ⊞ lau
Prices: pitch 30.30 (incl 3 persons)

Sluftervallei Krimweg 102 ☎0222 316214
On sand-dunes. It is advisable to book in advance during the peak season.
From the ferry landing stage, drive to the N tip of the island. Just before entering the village, turn left and head towards Vuurtoren (lighthouse). Turn left again after several hundred metres. The road leads directly to the site.
Etr-Oct 10HEC ⬛ ∷⁖ ᴝↄ ᘕ ⌦ ᴪ ♥ ✕ ⊙ ᗯ ⬤ ≗ 🔥 ⺇ P ☂ ⊞ lau ➧ ⬤ ⛺
⬗S Prices: pitch 34-44 (incl 5 persons)

DALFSEN *Overijssel*

Buitenplaats Gerner Haersolteweg 9-17 ☎0529 431181
Camping Card Compulsory.
Turn off at Dalfsen and take second road on the left.
All year 14HEC ⬛ ᴝↄ ᘕ ⌦ ᴪ ♥ ✕ ⊙ ᗯ ⬤ ≗ 🔥 ▲ ⺇ LP ⊡ ⊞ lau
Prices: pitch 24-33 (incl 2 persons)

DELDEN *Overijssel*

Park Camping International De Mors 6 ☎074 3763420
On two grassy terraces at the edge of a wood, to the SE of town.
Take A1 and exit at Hengelo-Zuid.
15 Mar-Oct 5HEC ⬛ ᴝↄ ᘕ ⌦ ᴪ ✕ ⊙ ᗯ ⬤ ≗ ☂ ⊞ ⊗ lau ➧ ⬤ ⺇P
Prices: A5.50 V5.50 ⍟5.50 ▲5.50

DENEKAMP *Overijssel*

Papillon Kanaalweg 30 ☎05413 51670
Predominantly a chalet site on meadowland in a tall coniferous and deciduous forest, about 2km N of Denekamp. It has a few naturally screened pitches.
For access, turn off the E72 towards Nordhorn (Germany), about 0.3km N of the signposts for Almelo-Nordhorn canal, and drive NE for 1.5km.
All year 11HEC ⬛ ᴝↄ ᘕ ⌦ ᴪ ♥ ✕ ⊙ ᗯ ⬤ ≗ 🔥 ⛺ ▲ ⺇ P ☂ ⊞ lau ➧ ✕

DIEPENHEIM *Overijssel*

Molnhofte Nyhofweg 5 ☎0547 351514
E of town.
All year 5HEC ⬛ ᴝↄ ᘕ ⌦ ᴪ ✕ ⊙ ᗯ ⬤ ≗ ⺇ P ☂ ⊡ ⊞ Prices: A5.05
V3 ⍟5 ▲5

DOESBURG *Gelderland.*

Ijsselstrand Eekstr 18 ☎313 472797
On level meadow with trees and hedges beside the River Ijssel.
Separate field for young people. Water sports.
NE across river. Signposted.
All year 45HEC ⬛ ᴝↄ ᘕ ⌦ ᴪ ♥ ✕ ⊙ ᗯ ⬤ ≗ 🔥 ⛺ ⺇ LR ☂ ⊞ lau

DOETINCHEM *Gelderland*

Wrange Rekhemseweg 144 ☎0314 324852
On the eastern outskirts of the town. It is set in meadowland and surrounded by bushes and deciduous trees.
200m E of link road between roads to Varsseveld and Terborg.
Apr-Nov 10HEC ⬛ ᴝↄ ᘕ ⌦ ᴪ ✕ ⊙ ᗯ ⬤ ≗ 🔥 ⛺ ⺇ P ⊡ ⊞ lau
Prices: A5 V5 ⍟5 ▲5

DOORN *Utrecht*

Bonte Vlucht Leersumsestraatweg 23 ☎0343 512476
3km E.
Apr-Oct 17HEC ⬛ ∷⁖ ᴝↄ ᘕ ⌦ ᴪ ✕ ⊙ ᗯ ⬤ ≗ ⊡ ⊞ ⊗ lau

Het Grote Bos Hydeparklaan 24 ☎0343 513644
Well layed out site on wooded grassland. Varied leisure activities for children and adults.
Camping Card Compulsory
About 1km NW of Doorn.
All year 80HEC ⬛ ♥ ᘕ ⌦ ᴪ ✕ ⊙ ᗯ ⬤ ≗ 🔥 ⛺ ⊞ lau Prices: pitch 43-47 (incl 2 persons)

DRONTEN *Gelderland*

At **BIDDINGHUIZEN**(9km S)

Flevostrand Strandweg 1 ☎0320 288480
Plots of grassland separated by close belts of shrubs. Own marina.
On the Polder, 5km S of Biddinghuizen turn right near the Veluwemeer.
Apr-Nov 25HEC ⬛ ᴝↄ ᘕ ⌦ ᴪ ♥ ✕ ⊙ ᗯ ⬤ ≗ 🔥 ⺇ LP ⊡ ⊞ lau Prices: pitch 46.25-57.50 (incl 4 persons)

Riviera Park Spijkweg 15 ☎0321 331344
Situated on grassland near a forest of deciduous trees and surrounded by shrubs.
On the Polder beside the Veluwemeer, 5km S of Biddinghuizen turn left.
21 Mar-29 Oct 63HEC ⬛ ᴝↄ ᘕ ⌦ ᴪ ✕ ⊙ ᗯ ⬤ ≗ 🔥 ⛺ ⺇ LP ⊡ ⊞ lau
Prices: pitch 49.50-64.50 (incl 4 persons)

EDAM *Noord-Holland*

Strandbad Zeevangszeedijk 7a ☎0299 371994
Apr-Sep 4HEC ⬛ ᴝↄ ᘕ ⌦ ᴪ ✕ ⊙ ᗯ ⬤ ≗ 🔥 ⺇ L ☂ ⊞ ⊗ lau ➧ ⺇P
Prices: A4.35 V4.50 ⍟7 ▲5

EERBEEK *Gelderland*

Coldenhove Boshoffweg 6 ☎0313 659101
In woodland.
From Apeldoorn-Dieren road, drive 2km SW, then NW for 1km.
All year 74HEC ⬛ ᴝↄ ᘕ ⌦ ᴪ ✕ ⊙ ᗯ ⬤ ≗ 🔥 ⛺ ⺇ P ☂ ⊡ ⊞ ⊗ lau
Prices: pitch 42-54 (incl 2 persons)

Robertsoord Doonweg 4 ☎0313 651346
1km SE.
All year 2.5HEC ⬛ ᴝↄ ᘕ ⌦ ᴪ ✕ ⊙ ᗯ ⬤ ≗ 🔥 ⛺ ☂ ⊞ lau ➧ ⬤ Prices: A3
V3 ⍟8 ▲8

EMST *Gelderland*

Wildhoeve Hanendorperweg 102 ☎05787 1324
3.5km W. Signposted.
Apr-Oct 11HEC ⬛ ᴝↄ ᘕ ⌦ ᴪ ✕ ⊙ ᗯ ⬤ ≗ 🔥 ⛺ ⺇ P ⊡ ⊞ ⊗ lau

ENSCHEDE *Overijssel*

Klein-Zandvoort Keppelerdijk 200 ☎053 4611372
E towards Glanerbrug.
All year 10HEC ⬛ ᴝↄ ᘕ ⌦ ᴪ ✕ ⊙ ᗯ ⬤ ≗ 🔥 ⺇ P ☂ ⊡ ⊞ lau Prices:
pitch 29 (incl 2 persons)

ERMELO *Gelderland*

Haeghehorst Fazantlaan 4 ☎0341 553185
Well equipped site in pleasant wooded surroundings.
Camping Card Compulsory.
Access via A28/E35 towards Amersfoort, then N303.
All year 9.8HEC ⬛ ᴝↄ ᘕ ⌦ ᴪ ✕ ⊙ ᗯ ⬤ ≗ 🔥 ⛺ ⺇ P ☂ ⊡ ⊞ ⊗ lau Prices: pitch 32-53 (incl 2 persons)

GAASPERPLAS *Noord-Holland*

Gaasper Loosdrechtdreef 7 ☎020 6967326
Situated on the edge of a wooded park within easy reach of Amsterdam.
Camping Card Compulsory.
From A9 take Gaasperplas exit before city centre and follow camping signs.
15 Mar-Dec 5.5HEC ⬛ ᴝↄ ᘕ ⌦ ᴪ ✕ ⊙ ᗯ ⬤ ≗ 🔥 ☂ ⊞ lau ➧ ✕ ⺇LP
Prices: A6 V5.50 ⍟8 ▲6-8

GAASPER CAMPING AMSTERDAM

Gaasper Camping Amsterdam
Loosdrechtdreef 7,
NL-1108 AZ Amsterdam
Tel: +31 20 696 73 26
Fax: +31 20 696 93 69
Just 20 minutes from the centre of Amsterdam there is a unique region of natural beauty, the "Gaasperpark" on the Gaasperplas. Within easy reach of a tube-station one of the finest camp sites of the Dutch capital is found: Gaasper Camping Amsterdam, situated on the verge of a park, with many trees and flowers.

GROET Noord-Holland

Groede Hargerweg 8 ☎072 5091555
The site consists of a meadow enclosed by hedges.
15 Apr-15 Sep 3HEC ▥ ⌕ ⋒ ⚏ ⊙ ⊟ ⌀ ▣ ⊞ ⊗ ◆ ⇃S Prices: A6
⊞13.50 ▲13.50

GROOTE KEETEN Noord-Holland

Callassande Voorweg 5A ☎02248 1663
Apr-Oct 1.5HEC ▥ ⌕ ⋒ ⚏ ⚑ × ⊙ ⊟ ⚏ ⇃ P ⊞ lau ◆ × ⌀ ⚍ ⇃S
Prices: A5.50 V5 ⊞24 ▲19

HAAKSBERGEN Overijssel

Scholtenhagen Scholtenhagenweg 30 ☎05427 22384
The internal site roads are asphalt.
Turn off by-pass W of town and drive towards Eilbergen for 0.7km,
then turn right and follow Zwemmbad signposts.
Apr-Oct 10HEC ▥ ⌕ ⋒ ⚏ × ⊙ ⊟ ⌀ ⚑ ⊞ ⊞ lau ◆ ⇃P

't Stien'nboer Scholtenhagenweg 42 ☎053 5722610
Apr-Oct 10.5HEC ▥ ⌕ ⋒ × ⊙ ⊟ ⌀ ⊞ ⚑ ⇃ P ⊞ ▣ ⊞ lau ◆ ⚏ ⚍
Prices: pitch 14.95-23 (incl 2 persons)

HALFWEG Noord-Holland

Houtrak Zuickerweg 2 ☎020 4972796
Grassy site on several levels subdivided by trees, hedges and
shrubs. Separate section for young campers.
Camping Card Compulsory.
Signposted from Spaarwonde exit on A5.
Apr-Sep 13HEC ▥ ◆ ⋒ ⚏ × ⊙ ⊟ ⌀ ⚍ ⚑ ▲ ⇃ L ⊞ ⊞ lau Prices:
A8 V5 ⊞8 ▲6-8

HATTEM Gelderland

Grandgoed Molecaten Koeweg 1 ☎038 4447044
Trailer caravans not admitted.
31 Mar-Sep 4HEC ⋒ × ⊙ ⊟ ⌀ ⇃ P ▣ ⊞ lau

Leemkule Leemkuilen 6 ☎038 4441945
2.5km SW.
All year 26HEC ▥ ◆ ⋒ ⚏ × ⊙ ⊟ ⌀ ⚑ ⇃ P ▣ ⊞ ⊗ lau Prices:
pitch 37 (incl 2 persons)

HEILOO Noord-Holland

Heiloo De Omloop 24 ☎072 5331950
One of the best sites in the area. It is divided into many large
squares by hedges.
Apr-Oct 4HEC ▥ ↳↲ ⋒ ⚑ × ⊙ ⊟ ⌀ ⚍ ⚑ ⊞ ▣ ⊞ ⊗ lau ◆ ⚏ ⇃LPS
Prices: A1.90 ◆17.25-23.50 ▲14.25-18.75

Klein Varnebroek De Omloop 22 ☎072 5331627
A grassy family campsite surrounded by trees.
25 Mar-Oct 4.2HEC ▥ ⌕ ⋒ ⚏ × ⊙ ⊟ ⌀ ⚑ ▣ ⊞ ⊗ lau ◆ ⇃P
Prices: pitch 40 (incl 4 persons)

HELDER, DEN Noord-Holland

Donkere Duinen Jan Verfailleweg 616 ☎0223 614731
800m towards the beach. Follow signs 'Nieuw-Den Helder' Strand.
Etr-15 Sep 7HEC ▥ ⌕ ⋒ ⊙ ⊟ ⌀ ⚍ ⇃ P ⊞ ⊞ lau ◆ ⚏ ⚏ × ⇃S
Prices: A6.85 pitch 15.75

Noorder Sandt Noorder Sandt 2, Julianadorp aan Zee ☎0223
641266
A flat, well-maintained site on meadowland, with good sanitary
blocks.
Access from the Den Helder to Callantsoog coastal road.
15 Mar-15 Sep 9.8HEC ▥ ⌕ ⋒ × ⊙ ⊟ ⌀ ⚍ ⚑ ⇃ P ⊞ ⊞ lau ◆ ⚏ ⚏
× ⇃S

HENGELO Gelderland

Kom-Es-An Handwijzersdijk 4 ☎0575 467242
NE of village in wooded area in the direction of Ruurlo.
Apr-Oct 10.5HEC ▥ ⌕ ⋒ ⚏ × ⊙ ⊟ ⌀ ⚍ ⚑ ⇃ P ⊞ ▣ ⊞ lau Prices:
A4 pitch 11

HENGELO Overijssel

Zwaaikom Kettingbrugweg 60 ☎074 916560
SE towards Enschede between canal and road.
15 Apr-15 Sep 4HEC ▥ ⌕ ⋒ ⚏ ⚏ × ⊙ ⊟ ⌀ ⚏ ⇃ P ⊞ ⊞ ⊗

HEUMEN Gelderland

Heumens Bos Vosseneindseweg 46 ☎024 3581481
NW of village, 100m N of the Wijchen road.
Apr-Oct 16HEC ▥ ⌕ ⋒ ⚏ ⚏ × ⊙ ⊟ ⌀ ⚍ ⚑ ⚑ ⇃ P ⊞ lau ◆ ⇃L
Prices: A6 V10 ◆10 ▲6

HOENDERLOO Gelderland

Pampel Woeste Hoefweg 33-35 ☎055 3781760
All year 14.5HEC ▥ ∷∷ ⌕ ⋒ ⚏ ⚏ × ⊙ ⊟ ⌀ ⚍ ⇃ P ⚏ ▣ ⊞ lau
Prices: A7.50 pitch 10

't Veluws Hof Krimweg 154 ☎055 3781777
W of N93.
All year 16HEC ▥ ◆ ⋒ ⚏ ⚏ × ⊙ ⊟ ⌀ ⚍ ⚑ ⚑ ⇃ P ⊞ ⊞ lau

HOLTEN Overijssel

Prins Wildweg 2 ☎0548 512272
A holiday complex operated by the Dutch ENNIA Company, in an
area of attraction to the rambler. Swimming pool on edge of site.
Access from the E8 Deventer-Almelo road. Take the Holten/Rijssen
exit then turn off.
Apr-Sep 4HEC ▥ ⌕ ⋒ ⚏ ⚏ × ⊙ ⊟ ⌀ ⚏ ▲ ⇃ P ⊞ ⊞ lau

HOORN, DEN (ISLAND OF TEXEL) Noord-Holland

Loodsmansduin Rommelpot 19 ☎0222 319203
Extensive site, numerous large and small hollows between dunes,
connected by paved paths. Several sanitary blocks. At the highest
part there is a bungalow village in amongst a shopping and
administrative complex. A section is reserved for naturists and there
is a naturists beach 2km away.
From the ferry drive N towards Den Burg, then turn left at
crossroads towards Den Hoorn.
Apr-26 Oct 38HEC ▥ ↳↲ ⋒ ⚏ ⚏ × ⊙ ⊟ ⌀ ⌀ ⇃ P ⊞ lau ◆ ⇃S
Prices: A6.50 V2.75 ⊞9.50 ▲9.50

KESTEREN Gelderland

Lede en Oudewaard Hogedijkseweg 40 ☎0488 481477
On level meadowland surrounded by bushy hedges and divided into
individual pitches. 100m from private beach and pool.
2km N of village, turn W off main Rhenen-Kesteren road, and
continue for 2.7km.
All year 30HEC ▥ ⌕ ⋒ ⚏ ⚏ × ⊙ ⊟ ⌀ ⌀ ⚑ ⇃ L ⊞ ⊞ lau Prices:
pitch 27.50 (incl 2 persons)

KOOG, DE (ISLAND OF TEXEL) Noord-Holland

Kogerstrand Badweg 33 ☎0222 3117208
Apr-Sep 50HEC ∷∷ ↳↲ ⋒ ⋒ ⌀ ⌀ ⇃ S ▣ ⊞ lau ◆ ⚏ ⚏ × ⚍ ⇃P

Shelter Boodklaan 93 ☎0222 317475
15 Mar-15 Oct 1.1HEC ▥ ↳↲ ⋒ ⊙ ⊟ ⊞ ⊞ lau ◆ ⚏ ⚏ × ⌀ ⚍ ⇃S
Prices: A4.85 V2.40 ⊞13.50 ▲9.85

LATHUM Gelderland

Honingraat Marsweg 2 ☎0313 633211
Site with modern facilities on an arm of the Ijssel with good boating
facilities and its own marina.
For access, turn off Arnhem-Doesburg road and pass through the
village to the site in 1.5km.
mid Mar-mid Oct 17HEC ▥ ↳↲ ⋒ ⚏ ⚏ × ⊙ ⊟ ⚏ ⇃ LP ▣ ⊞ lau ◆ ⌀

Mars Marsweg 6 ☎0313 631131
Divided into pitches on level meadowland beside a dammed tributary
of River Ijssel.
Turn off Arnhem-Doesberg road N of village and continue W for
1.7km.
Apr-Sep 10HEC ▥ ↳↲ ⋒ ⚏ ⚏ × ⊙ ⊟ ⚍ ⇃ L ⊞ ⊞ lau Prices: A5.25
V2.25 ⊞4.75 ▲4.75

LOCHEM Gelderland

Ruighenrode Vordenseweg 8 ☎0573 289400
Site among mixed woodland with tall spruce.
2km SW of town. For access, turn off the road to Zutphen at
Km10.4 in S direction on the Vorden road for the site.
All year 58HEC ▥ ⋒ ⚏ ⚏ × ⊙ ⊟ ⌀ ⌀ ⚑ ⚑ ⇃ LP ⊞ ⊞ lau ◆ ⚍

LUTTENBERG *Overijssel*
Luttenberg Heuvelweg 9 ☎0572 301405
Camping Card Compulsory.
Apr-Sep 12HEC ▥ ⇘⇙ ⋔ ⅃ ⅄ ✕ ⊙ ▣ ⌀ ♨ ⊞ ♥ ♯ P ☒ ▣ ⊞ lau
Prices: A6 V5 ☗5 ▲5

MAARN *Utrecht*
Laag-Kanje Laan van Laag-Kanje 1 ☎0343 441348
Situated 500m from the lake.
2km NE.
Apr-Sep 30HEC ▥ ⅃ ⋔ ⅃ ⅄ ✕ ⊙ ▣ ⌀ ♨ ⊞ ⊘ lau ♥ ♯L Prices:
A5.25 V2.95 ☗9 ▲6.50-9

MARKELO *Overijssel*
Hessenheem Potdijk 8 ☎0547 621200
Situated near a swimming pool.
3km NE.
All year 31HEC ▥ ∷∷ ♦ ⋔ ⅃ ⅄ ✕ ⊙ ▣ ⌀ ♨ ⊞ ♯ P ☒ ⊞ lau

MIJNDEN *Utrecht*
Mijnden Bloklaan 22a ☎0294 233165
Apr-Sep 25HEC ▥ ⇘⇙ ⋔ ⅃ ⅄ ✕ ⊙ ▣ ⌀ ♨ ♯ LP ☒ ⊞ lau Prices:
pitch 26-33 (incl 2 persons)

NEEDE *Gelderland*
Eversman Bliksteeg 1 ☎0545 291906
Situated in a quiet position, surrounded by trees.
W of town.
Apr-Oct 4HEC ▥ ⅃ ⋔ ⅃ ⅄ ✕ ⊙ ▣ ♨ ♯ P ☒ ⊞ lau ♥ ♯ ⌀ Prices: A6
V5 ☗5 ▲5

NIJMEGEN *Gelderland*
Kwakkenberg Luciaweg 10 ☎080 232443
On gently sloping meadowland between rows of deciduous trees and
groups of bushes.
Situated on E outskirts of town and reached by turning off N53 (
Nijmegen-Klef/Kleve) and drive S.
Apr-Sep 5HEC ▥ ♦ ⋔ ⅃ ⅄ ✕ ⊙ ▣ ⌀ ♦ ♯P

NOORD SCHARWOUDE *Noord-Holland*
Molengroet Molengroet 1 ☎02269 3444
Site with modern facilities within easy reach of the beach and the
'Geestmerambacht' water park.
Signposted on N245.
All year 11HEC ▥ ♦ ⋔ ⅃ ⅄ ✕ ⊙ ▣ ⌀ ♨ ♯ L ☒ ⊞ lau ♥ ♯LPS

NUNSPEET *Gelderland*
Vossenberg Groenlaantje 25 ☎03412 252458
Apr-1 Nov 3.6HEC ▥ ⅃ ⋔ ⅄ ✕ ⊙ ▣ ⌀ ♨ ♯ ☒ ⊞ ⊘ ♦ ♯LP

OMMEN *Overijssel*
Calluna Stouweweg 3 ☎05291 55553
NW on left off road to Zwolle.
Apr-Nov 25HEC ▥ ⅃ ⋔ ⅃ ⅄ ✕ ⊙ ▣ ⌀ ♨ ♯ LP ☒ ⊞

OTTERLO *Gelderland*
Beek en Hei Heldeweg 4 ☎0318 591483
Camping Card Compulsory.
All year 3HEC ▥ ⅃ ⋔ ⊙ ▣ ♨ ▣ ⊞ lau ♥ ⅃ ⅄ ✕ ⌀ ♨ ♯L

PETTEN *Noord-Holland*
Corfwater Korfwaterweg 1a ☎02268 1981
15 Apr-Oct 5.5HEC ∷∷ ⅃⇙ ⋔ ⊙ ▣ ♯ S ▣ ⊞ ⊘ lau ♥ ⅃ ⅄ ✕ ⌀ ♨
♯P

PUTTEN *Gelderland*
Strand Nulde Strandboulevard 27 ☎03418 61304
Camping Crad Compulsory.
31 Mar-31 Oct 6HEC ▥ ∷∷ ⅃ ⋔ ⅃ ⅄ ✕ ⊙ ▣ ⌀ ♯ L ▣ ⊞ lau
Prices: pitch 32.50-49.50 (incl 4 persons)

RHENEN *Utrecht*
Thymse Berg Nieuwe Veenendaalseweg 229 ☎0317 612384
N of town.
Apr-Oct 10HEC ▥ ⅃ ⋔ ⅃ ⅄ ✕ ⊙ ▣ ⌀ ♨ ♯ P ▣ ⊞ ⊘ lau ♥ ♨ ♯R
Prices: pitch 22.50-29 (incl 2 persons)

RUURLO *Gelderland*
't Sikkeler Sikkelerweg 8 ☎0573 461221
4km SW.
All year 7HEC ▥ ⅃ ⋔ ⅃ ⅄ ✕ ⊙ ▣ ⌀ ♨ ⊞ ⊞ lau Prices: pitch 22
(incl 2 persons)

ST MAARTENSZEE *Noord-Holland*
St Maartenszee Westerduinweg 30 ☎02246 561401
Completely surrounded and divided into pitches by hedges, lying on
meadowland on the edge of a wide belt of sand dunes.
For access, turn off the Alkmaar to Den Helder road at St
Maartensvlotburg and drive towards the sea. Take the road over the
dunes and follow it for about 1.5km, then turn right and continue for
a further 300m.
22 Mar-22 Sep 5HEC ▥ ⅃ ⋔ ⅃ ⅄ ✕ ⊙ ▣ ⌀ ♨ ⊞ ☒ ⊞ ⊘ lau ♥
♯LS Prices: A6.55 pitch 15.75-40

SOEST *Utrecht*
King's Home Birkstr 136 ☎033 4619118
All year 5HEC ▥ ⅃ ⋔ ⅃ ⅄ ✕ ⊙ ▣ ⌀ ♨ ▣ ⊞ lau ♥ ♨ ♯P Prices:
A5 V5 ☗10 ▲5-10

STEENWIJK *Overijssel*
Kom Bultweg 25 ☎0521 513736
Split into two sections, lying near a country house, and is surrounded
by a beautiful oak forest.
The access road off the Steenwijk-Frederiksoord road is easy to
miss.
Apr-Oct 12HEC ▥ ⅃ ⋔ ⅃ ⅄ ✕ ⊙ ▣ ⌀ ♨ ⊞ ♯ P ▣ ⊞ lau Prices:
pitch 24.75-30.75 (incl 2 persons)

TEXEL (ISLAND OF)
See **COCKSDORP, DE, HOORN, DEN & KOOG, DE**

UITDAM *Noord-Holland*
Uitdam Zeedijk 2 ☎020 4031433
Camping Card Compulsory.
Apr-Oct 22HEC ▥ ⅃⇙ ⋔ ⅃ ⅄ ✕ ⊙ ▣ ⌀ ♨ ♯ L ☒ ⊞ lau Prices:
A6 V6 ☗6 ▲4-6

URK *Flevoland*
Vormt Vormtweg 9 ☎0527 681785
Camping Card Compulsory.
Apr-Oct 12HEC ▥ ♦ ⋔ ⅃ ⅄ ✕ ⊙ ▣ ⌀ ♨ ☒ ▣ ⊞ lau Prices: A5
V3.25 ☗5.50 ▲2.75-5.50

UTRECHT *Utrecht*
Berekuil Arienslaan 5 ☎030 713870
On N outskirts near motorway to Hilversum.
All year 4.5HEC ▥ ⅃ ⋔ ⅃ ⅄ ✕ ⊙ ▣ ⌀ ♨ ⊞ ♯ P ▣ ⊞ lau

VAASSEN *Gelderland*
Bosrand Elspeterweg 45 ☎05788 71343
In castle grounds.
All year 3HEC ▥ ⅃ ⋔ ⅄ ✕ ⊙ ▣ ⌀ ♨ ♯ P ☒ ⊞ lau ♥ ♨ Prices:
A6 ☗9 ▲9

VELSEN-ZUID *Noord-Holland*
Weltevreden ☎023 383726
Camping Card Compulsory.
Apr-Oct 10HEC ▥ ♦ ⋔ ⅃ ⅄ ✕ ⊙ ▣ ⌀ ♨ ⊞ ♯ ▲ ♯ LP ☒ ▣ ⊞ lau
♥ ✕ ♯S Prices: A7.50-8.30 ☗8.70

VOGELENZANG *Noord-Holland*
Vogelenzang Tweede Doodweg 17 ☎023 5847014
1km W.
Etr-15 Sep 22HEC ▥ ⅃ ⋔ ⅃ ⅄ ✕ ⊙ ▣ ⌀ ♨ ♯ P ☒ ⊞ ⊘ lau
Prices: A6 pitch 10-18

VOORTHUIZEN *Gelderland*
Zanderij Hoge Boeschoterweg 96 ☎03429 1343
Apr-Oct 13HEC ▥ ♦ ⋔ ⅃ ⅄ ✕ ⊙ ▣ ⌀ ♨ ♯ P ☒ ⊞ ⊘ lau

WEZEP Gelderland
Heidehoek Heidehoeksweg 7 ☎038 3761382
0.5km W of railway station.
Apr-Oct 15HEC ▦ ⌀ ♠ ⚍ ♈ ✕ ⊙ ➊ ⌀ ♨ ⚐ ⊞ lau ♦ ⚡P Prices:
pitch 17-29 (incl 2 persons)

WIJDENES Noord-Holland
Het Hof Zuideruitweg 64 ☎0229 501435
23 Mar-26 Oct 4HEC ▦ ⌀ ⋔ ⚍ ♈ ✕ ⊙ ➊ ⌀ ♨ ⚡ LP ⊡ ⊞ lau
Prices: A5 pitch 12.50

WINTERSWIJK Gelderland
Twee Bruggen Meenkmolenweg 11 ☎0543 565366
A family site in pleasant wooded surroundings with good, modern
facilities.
All year 30HEC ▦ ⌀ ⋔ ⚍ ♈ ✕ ⊙ ➊ ⌀ ♨ ⚐ ⚡ PR ⊡ ⊞ lau ♦ ⚡L
Prices: pitch 31.50 (incl 2 persons)

ZEEWOLDE Flevoland
RCN Zeewolde Dasselaarweg 1 ☎03424 1246
Apr-Oct 42HEC ▦ ⌀ ⋔ ⚍ ♈ ✕ ⊙ ➊ ⌀ ⚡ L ⊡ ⊞ lau

South

The south of the Netherlands is the home of the traditional Delft
china and Gouda cheese, and is also the location of a project
which is the first of its kind in the world: the building of a
moveable marine floodgate across the outlet of the
Oostenschelde River.
One of the oldest cities in Holland, and the provincial capital of
Limburg, is Maastricht. Shaped through the ages by art and
culture, the city has a rich heritage and a wealth of historic
monuments.
The region also includes two prominent and very different cities.
The Hague, with its favourable reputation as the City of Arts, has
parliamentary buildings and stately palaces, wide streets and
spacious squares, giving an impression of distinction and
elegance.
The world's premier harbour has expanded to become the
dynamic metropolis of Rotterdam; a city full of vitality and
conviviality with a variety of architecture ranging from snug
Delfshaven to the futuristic pencil flats and cube houses.

AFFERDEN Limburg
Klein Canada Dorpstr 1 ☎08853 1223
All year 10HEC ▦ ⌀ ⋔ ⚍ ♈ ✕ ⊙ ➊ ⌀ ♨ ⚡ P ⊡ ⊞ lau

ARCEN Limburg
Maasvallei Dorperheideweg 34 ☎473 1564
Off the N271
All year 11HEC ▦ ⌀ ⋔ ⚍ ♈ ✕ ⊙ ➊ ⌀ ♨ ⚐ ⚡ LP ⊡ ⊡ ⊞ ⌘
Prices: pitch 38

ARNEMUIDEN Zeeland
Witte Raaf Muidenweg 3 ☎0118 601212
A modern well-maintained site in meadowland, divided into sections
by rows of shrubs, ideal for sailing and motor boat enthusiasts with
yacht marina.
Situated on the Veersmeer, N of the Goes-Vlissingen motorway, from
Arnemuiden exit follow signs for about 5km.
Apr-Sep 20HEC ▦ ⌀ ⋔ ⚍ ♈ ✕ ⊙ ➊ ⌀ ♨ ⚑ ⚏ ⚡ L ⊡ ⊞ ⌘ lau

ASSELT Limburg
Maasterras Eind 4 ☎0475 501207
Well-kept site on terrace. Private beach.
W of Swalmen-2.3km W of the TEXACO petrol station on the N273.
15 Mar-15 Oct 5HEC ▦ ⌀ ⋔ ♈ ✕ ⊙ ➊ ⌀ ⊡ ⊞ lau ♦ ⌀ ♨

BAARLAND Zeeland
Scheldeoord Landingsweg 1 ☎01193 9226
S of town on the coast.
All year 16HEC ▦ ⌀ ⋔ ⚍ ♈ ✕ ⊙ ➊ ⌀ ♨ ⚑ ⚏ ⚡ PS ⊞ lau

BAARLE NASSAU Noord-Brabant
Heimolen Heimolen 6 ☎507 9425
1.5km SW.
All year 15HEC ⣿⣿ ♦ ⋔ ⚍ ♈ ✕ ⊙ ➊ ⌀ ♨ ⚑ ⚏ ⚐ ⊡ ⊞ lau Prices: A4
V2.50 ⚑5.50 ▲3-5.50

BARENDRECHT Zuid-Holland
Jachthaven de Oude Maas Achterzeedijk 1a ☎078 6772445
On the banks of the Oude Maas, the site is particularly suitable for
families and hikers.
All year 12HEC ▦ ♦ ⋔ ⚍ ♈ ✕ ⊙ ➊ ⌀ ♨ ⚑ ⚏ ⚡ P ⊡ ⊡ ⊞ lau Prices:
A5.90 V5.90 ⚑5.90 ▲5.90

BERG EN TERBLIJT Limburg
Oriëntal Rijksweg 6 ☎043 6040075
On Maastricht-Valkenburg road 3km from Maastricht.
25 Apr-26 Oct 4.5HEC ▦ ⌀ ⋔ ⚍ ♈ ✕ ⊙ ➊ ⌀ ♨ ⚏ ⚡ P ⊡ ⊡ ⊞ lau
♦ ✕ Prices: A6 pitch 28-34 (incl 2 persons)

BERGEYK Noord-Brabant
Paal De Paaldreef 14 ☎0497 571977
Campsite especially catering for families with children.
Camping Card Compulsory
Signposted.
28 Mar-26 Oct 31HEC ▦ ⌀ ⋔ ⚍ ♈ ✕ ⊙ ➊ ⌀ ♨ ⚡ P ⊡ ⊞ lau
Prices: pitch 42 (incl 2 persons)

BLADEL Noord-Brabant
Achterste Hoef Troprijt 10 ☎04977 81579
S of town.
Apr-29 Oct 15HEC ▦ ⌀ ⋔ ⚍ ♈ ✕ ⊙ ➊ ⌀ ♨ ⚡ P ⊡ ⊞ lau

BOXTEL Noord-Brabant
Dennenoord Dennendreef 5 ☎0411 601280
Level, grassy site with hedging and groups of trees. Leisure
activities organised for adults and young people. Soundproof disco.
Turn off the N2 at Esch in direction of Osterwijk. Follow signs.
Apr-1 Oct 7HEC ▦ ⌀ ⋔ ⚍ ♈ ✕ ⊙ ➊ ⌀ ♨ ⚡ P ⊡ ⊞ lau Prices: pitch
25

BRESKENS Zeeland
Napoleon Hoeve Zandertje 30 ☎0117 383838
A family site with access to the beach.
All year 13HEC ▦ ⌀ ⋔ ⚍ ♈ ✕ ⊙ ➊ ⌀ ♨ ⚑ ⚏ ⚡ P ⊡ ⊡ ⊞ lau ♦
⚡S Prices: pitch 57 (incl 5 persons)

Schoneveld Schoneveld 1 ☎0117 383220
Camping Card Compulsory.
3km S at the beach.
All year 14HEC ▦ ⌀ ⋔ ⚍ ♈ ✕ ⊙ ➊ ⌀ ♨ ⚑ ⚏ ▲ ⚡ PS ⊞ lau
Prices: pitch 39-57 (incl 3 persons)

BRIELLE Zuid-Holland
Krabbeplaat Oude Veerdam 4 ☎0181 412363
On level ground scattered with trees and groups of bushes. It has
asphalt drives. Nearest campsite to the coast and ferries.
Apr-1 Oct 20HEC ▦ ⌀ ⋓ ⋔ ⚍ ♈ ✕ ⊙ ➊ ⌀ ⚡ L ⊡ ⊞ ⌘ lau Prices:
pitch 20-26.25 (incl 2 persons)

BROEKHUIZENVORST Limburg
Kasteel Ooyen Blitterswijkseweg 2 ☎077 4631307
20 Mar-1 Nov 16HEC ▦ ⌀ ⋔ ⚍ ♈ ✕ ⊙ ➊ ⌀ ⚑ ⚏ ⚡ P ⊡ ⊞ lau ♦ ⚡R
Prices: A9 pitch 24.36-34 (incl 2 persons)

BROUWERSHAVEN Zeeland
Osse Blankersweg 4 ☎0111 691513
An attractive site with good watersports facilities.
Apr-Oct 8.5HEC ▦ ⌀ ⋔ ⚍ ♈ ✕ ⊙ ➊ ⌀ ♨ ⚑ ⚏ ⚡ LPS ⊡ ⊞ lau ♦ ⚍ ✕

BURGH-HAAMSTEDE Zeeland
Zeelandcamping Duinoord Steenweg 16 ☎0111 651964
All year 4.1HEC ▦ ⌀ ⋔ ⚍ ⊙ ➊ ⌀ ♨ ⊡ ⊡ ⊞ lau ♦ ⚍ ✕ ⚡S Prices:
pitch 29-41 (incl 2 persons)

CROMVOIRT *Noord-Brabant*
Vondst Pepereind 13 ☎04118 1431
1km SE.
All year 8HEC 🏕 ⌂ ♠ ♣ ⚑ ♥ × ⊙ ⚑ ⌂ ▵ ⚑ ⚑ ⟡ P ☎ 🖂 lau ➡ ⟡L

DELFT *Zuid-Holland*
Delftse Hout Korftlaan 5 ☎015 2130040
1 mile E of A13. Take exit 9 (Delft/Pijnacker) towards city centre
then right at first traffic lights. After three quarters of a mile turn
right onto Korftlaan and follow signs through the tunnel under the
A13.
Camping Card Compulsory.
All year 5.5HEC 🏕 ⌂ ♠ ♣ ♥ × ⊙ ⚑ ⌂ ⚑ ⚑ ⟡ P ☎ 🖂 lau ➡ ⟡L
Prices: pitch 32-35 (incl 2 persons)
See advertisement under ROCKANJE

DOMBURG *Zeeland*
Domburg Schelpweg 7 ☎0118 583210
On meadowland divided into several sections, with asphalt drives. It
is on the inland side of the road, along the dyke, with a belt of shrubs
dividing it from the road. 2 tennis courts, small golf course, a
children's swimming pool and play garden.
500m on main road to Westkapelle.
All year 8HEC 🏕 ⌂ ♠ ♣ ♥ × ⊙ ⚑ ⌂ ⚑ ⚑ ⟡ P 🖂 🖂 ✿ lau ➡ ⟡S

DORDRECHT *Zuid-Holland*
Bruggehof Rijksstraatweg 186 ☎078 183241
Near Moerdijkbrug.
Apr-15 Oct 21HEC 🏕 ⌂ ♠ ♣ ♥ × ⊙ ⚑ ⌂ ⟡ P ☎ 🖂 lau

ECHT *Limburg*
Marisheem Brugweg 89 ☎04754 481458
The site is well-kept and lies E of the village.
From town drive approx 2.2km towards Echterbosch and the border,
then turn left.
Apr-Oct 12HEC 🏕 ⌂ ♠ ♣ ♥ × ⊙ ⚑ ⌂ ⚑ ⟡ P ☎ 🖂 🖂 ✿ lau
Prices: A7.85 V8 ⚑8

EERSEL *Noord-Brabant*
Ter Spegelt Postelseweg 88 ☎0497 512016
A large family-orientated site with good recreational facilities.
22 Mar-27 Oct 63HEC 🏕 ⌂ ♠ ♣ ♥ × ⊙ ⚑ ⌂ ▵ ⚑ ⚑ ⟡ LP 🖂 🖂
✿ lau Prices: pitch 45-60 (incl 2 persons)

FLUSHING
See **VLISSINGEN**

'S-GRAVENZANDE *Zuid-Holland*
Jagtveld Nieuwlandsedijk 41 ☎0174 413479
Apr-Sep 3.3HEC 🏕 ✂ ♠ ♣ ♥ × ⊙ ⚑ ⌂ ▵ ⟡ S ☎ 🖂 ✿ lau Prices:
A4.25 V2.75 ⚑12-16 ▲12

GROEDE *Zeeland*
Groede Zeeweg 1 ☎0117 371384
Apr-Oct 16HEC 🏕 ⌂ ♠ ♣ ♥ × ⊙ ⚑ ⌂ ⚑ 🖂 🖂 lau ➡ ⟡PS Prices:
A4 pitch 20

HAAG, DEN (THE HAGUE) *Zuid-Holland*
Ockenburg Wijndaelerweg 25 ☎070 3252364
Site lies on the SW of town and 500m from beach. Divided into
sections by trees with modern installations and good facilities.
For access follow signs towards Kijkduin.
4 Apr-24 Oct 46HEC ⁙ ⌂ ♠ ♣ ♥ × ⊙ ⚑ ⌂ ▵ ☎ 🖂 ✿ lau ➡ ▵
⟡PS

HANK *Noord-Brabant*
Brabantse Biesbosch Kurenpolderweg 31 ☎0162 402787
Site in a nature park.
Take A27 and exit at Hank. Signposted.
Apr-Sep 102HEC 🏕 ♠ ♣ ♥ × ⊙ ⚑ ⌂ ▵ ⚑ ▲ ⟡ L ☎ 🖂 ✿ lau

HELLEVOETSLUIS *Zuid-Holland*
'T Weergors Zuiddyk 2 ☎0181 312430
Apr-Oct 9.7HEC 🏕 ⌂ ♠ ♣ ♥ × ⊙ ⚑ ⌂ ▵ ⚑ ☎ 🖂 lau Prices: A5
V2.50 ⚑8 ▲8

HENGSTDIJK *Zeeland*
Vogel Vogelweg 4 ☎0114 681625
All year 65HEC 🏕 ⌂ ♠ ♣ ♥ × ⊙ ⚑ ⌂ ⚑ ⚑ ⟡ L 🖂 🖂 lau
Prices: pitch 20-45 (incl 2 persons)

HERKENBOSCH *Limburg*
Vrijetijdspark Elfenmeer Meinweg 1 ☎0475 531689
Hilly, well-maintained site in pine forest beside a small lake.
NE off Roermond road.
Apr-18 Oct 30HEC 🏕 ⌂ ♠ ⊙ ⚑ ⚑ ⟡ P ☎ 🖂 lau ➡ ♣ ♥ × ⌂

HERPEN *Noord-Brabant*
Herperduin Schaykseweg 12 ☎08867 1383
Situated in extensive woodland.
Access from the 'S-Hertogenbosch-Nijmegen motorway. Take the
Ravenstein exit and continue towards Herpen, then in direction
Bergheim/Oss.
Apr-20 Oct 9HEC 🏕 ⌂ ♠ ♣ ♥ × ⊙ ⚑ ⌂ ⟡ LP ☎ 🖂 ✿ lau

HILVARENBEEK *Noord-Brabant*
Beekse Bergen Beekse Bergen 1 ☎013 5360032
Situated in a holiday centre in the Brabant afforestation on the edge
of a safari park. Lake suitable for swimming. Various other facilities.
10km N of Tilburg.
20 Mar-26 Oct 46HEC 🏕 ⌂ ♠ ♣ ♥ × ⊙ ⚑ ⌂ ▵ ⚑ ▲ ⟡ LP ☎ 🖂
lau Prices: A7 pitch 17.50-31

HOEK *Zeeland*
Braakman Middenweg 1 ☎01152 1730
On meadowland between a wood and shrubs.
About 4km W of town and 40m N of expressway to Breskens.
All year 2HEC 🏕 ⌂ ♠ ♣ ♥ × ⊙ ⚑ ⌂ ▵ ⚑ ▲ ⟡ L 🖂 🖂 lau ➡
⟡S Prices: pitch 22-55

HOEK VAN HOLLAND *Zuid-Holland*
Hoek van Holland Wierstr 101 ☎01747 82550
On grass, surrounded by bushes and paved drives.
If approaching from the N, turn off the E36 and drive to the beach.
Apr-Nov 5.5HEC 🏕 ✂ ♠ ♣ ♥ × ⊙ ⚑ ⌂ ⚑ 🖂 🖂 ✿ lau ➡ ⟡S
Prices: pitch 19.75-39.75

HOEVEN *Noord-Brabant*
Bosbad Hoeven Oude Antwerpse Postbaan 81b ☎0165 502570
Between Breda and Roosendaal W of Etten-Leur.
Apr-28 Oct 35HEC ⁙ ⌂ ♠ ♣ ♥ × ⊙ ⚑ ⌂ ⚑ ⟡ P ☎ 🖂 ✿ lau Prices:
pitch 30.90 (incl 2 persons)

HOOGERHEIDE *Noord-Brabant*
FamilyLand Groene Papegaai 19 ☎164 613155
In pleasant wooded surroundings, the site, as its name suggests has
fine facilities for both adults and children with all kinds of sports and
entertainments available.
2km from junction of A30 and A58.
All year 25HEC 🏕 ⌂ ♠ ♥ × ⊙ ⚑ ⌂ ▵ ⚑ ⟡ P ☎ 🖂 lau ➡ ♣ ⟡L
Prices: A8.05 pitch 10

KAMPERLAND *Zeeland*
Roompot Mariapolderseweg 1 ☎01107 4000
A level, well-maintained site with a private beach.
Turn off Kamperland-Wissenkerke road and drive N for 0.5km.
All year 33HEC 🏕 ⌂ ♠ ♣ ♥ × ⊙ ⚑ ⌂ ⚑ ⚑ ⟡ PS 🖂 lau

Schotsman Schotsmanweg 1 ☎0113 371751
On a large, level meadow beside the Veerse Meer, next to a Nature
Reserve. Water sports.
Signposted.
22 Mar-25 Oct 28HEC 🏕 ♠ ♣ ♥ × ⊙ ⚑ ⌂ ▵ ⚑ ⚑ ⟡ L 🖂 🖂 ✿
lau ➡ ⟡S Prices: pitch 43-54 (incl 2 persons)

KATWIJK AAN ZEE *Zuid-Holland*
Noordduinen Campingweg 1 ☎0171 4025295
Family site set among sand dunes close to the sea.
Access via Hoorneslaan.
22 Mar-25 Oct 11HEC 🏕 ⌂ ♠ ♣ ♥ × ⊙ ⚑ ⌂ ⟡ S ☎ 🖂 🖂 ✿ lau ➡
▵ Prices: pitch 33-41
See advertisement under ROCKANJE

★★★★★
VAKANTIECENTRUM
de hertenwei
WELLENSEIND 7-9
NL-5094 EG LAGE, MIERDE.
Tel: 013-5091295

Located 2km North of Lage Mierde, on the Tilburg-Reusel road (road No. N.269). Pleasantly wooded site. Ideal starting point for Efteling, Beekse Bergen, Theme Park "Land van Ooit" and Belgium. Modern, heated sanitary blocks with hot water and hot showers. Heated pool and paddling pool. Indoor pool with hot whirlpool, sauna, solarium, bar, supermarket, snackbar, washing machines, tennis-courts, children's play area. Restaurant and disco. Please ask for our brochure.

KORTGENE Zeeland
Paardekreek Havenweg 1 ☎0113 302051
A municipal site next to the Veerse Meer canal.
For access, turn off the Zierikzee-Goes trunk road at the CHEVRON petrol station and drive towards Kortgene, continue through the village and drive SW.
Apr-30 Oct 10HEC ▦ 🔧↑🔥💈🍴✕⊙🖭⌀🏛🛱 ⁀ LP 🖽 lau Prices: pitch 25-36 (incl 3 persons)

KOUDEKERKE Zeeland
Dishoek Dishoek 2 ☎118 551348
W on Vlissingen-Dibhoek road.
22 Mar-26 Oct 2.3HEC ▦ 🔧↑🔥💈🍴✕⊙🖭⌀🏛⚓🖽 lau ➡🔥✕ ⁀S Prices: pitch 32-44.50 (incl 2 persons)

Duinzicht Strandweg 7 ☎0118 551397
1.5km SW of Koudekerke.
Apr-Sep 6HEC ▦ 🔧↑🔥💈⊙🖭⌀🏛⚓🖽➡💈✕ ⁀S

LAGE MIERDE Noord-Brabant
Vakantiecentrum de Hertenwei Wellenseind 7-9 ☎013 5091295
Pleasant wooded site with modern facilities.**Camping Card Compulsory.**
2km N on N269 (Tilburg-Reusel).
All year 20HEC ▦ 🔧↑🔥💈🍴✕⊙🖭⌀🏛⚓ ⁀P 🖽 lau Prices: pitch 34.50-54.50 (incl 4 persons)

LUYKSGESTEL Noord-Brabant
Zwarte Bergen Zwarte Bergen Dreef 1 ☎0497 541373
The site is isolated and very quiet, and lies in a pine forest.
From Eindhoven through Valkenswaard and Bergiejkl. Signposted.
All year 25.5HEC ▦ 🔧↑🔥💈🍴✕⊙🖭⌀🏛⚓🛱 ⁀P 🖽 lau

MAASBREE Limburg
BreeBronne Lange Heide ☎077 4652360
On the E3 just before Venlo, on the border with Germany.
Apr-Sep 16HEC ▦ 🔧↑🔥💈🍴✕⊙🖭⌀🏛 ⁀ LP 🖽 lau Prices: pitch 39.75-49.75 (incl 4 persons)

MAASTRICHT Limburg
Dousberg Dousbergweg 102 ☎043 432171
A modern site with good facilities.
From the Eindhoven-Liège motorway follow sings for Hasselt, then pick up local signs to the site.
26 Mar-1 Nov 10HEC ▦ 🔧↑🔥💈✕⊙🖭⌀🏛🖽 lau➡ ⁀P Prices: A7 V4 ⚓7.50 🔺7.50

MIDDELBURG Zeeland
Middelburg Koninginnelaan 55 ☎0118 625395
On meadowlands surrounded by trees and bushes.
On W outskirts of town.
Apr-15 Oct 2.4HEC ▦ 🔧↑🔥✕⊙🖭⌀🏛⚓🖱🖽 lau➡💈✕ ⁀P Prices: A5.80 V4.75 ⚓5.25 🔺4.75

MIERLO Noord-Brabant
Wolfsven Patrijslaan 4 ☎0492 661661
Large campsite with wooded areas and several lakes. Asphalt drives.
All year 80HEC ▦ ⠿ 🔧↑🔥💈🍴✕⊙🖭⌀🏛⚓ ⁀ LP 🖽🖽➿ lau
Prices: pitch 25.75-32.75 (incl 2 persons)

NIEUWVLIET Zeeland
International St-Bavodk 2d ☎0117 371233
On N outskirts, near a windmill on the road leading to the dyke.
Apr-Oct 5.9HEC ▦ 🔧↑🔥✕⊙🖭⌀🏛⚓ ⁀S 🖽 lau ➡💈🔥 ⁀P
Prices: pitch 30 (incl 2 persons)

Pannenschuur Zeedijk 19 ☎0117 372300
A modern site with good facilities. Close to the beach.NW of town.
Signposted.
All year 14HEC ▦ 🔧↑🔥💈🍴✕⊙🖭⌀🏛⚓🛱 ⁀ PS 🖱🖽 lau
Prices: A5.50 pitch 28

NOORDWIJK AAN ZEE Zuid-Holland
Carlton Kraaierslaan 13 ☎0253 272783
Camping Card Compulsory.
23 Mar-1 Nov 2HEC ▦ ↑⊙🖭⌀🛱 ⁀ P 🖱 lau ➡💈✕⌀ ⁀S Prices: A7.50 ⚓10.75 🔺7.25

Jan de Wit Kapelleboslaan 10 ☎252 372405
15 Mar-1 Nov 5HEC ▦ 🔧↑🔥💈✕⊙🖭⌀🏛⚓🛱🖱🖽➿ lau ➡ ⁀LS Prices: A9 ⚓10 🔺8.50

At **NOORDWIJKERHOUT**(5km NE)
Club Soleil Kraaierslaan 7 ☎0252 374225
Camping Card Compulsory.
Signposted.
28 Mar-Nov 5.5HEC ▦ 🔧↑🔥💈🍴✕⊙🖭⌀🏛⚓🛱 ⁀P 🖱🖽➡ ⁀S Prices: pitch 47.60-64 (incl 4 persons)

OISTERWIJK Noord-Brabant
Reebok Duinenweg 4 ☎013 5282309
Situated in a large pine forest, hardly fenced off and impossible to overlook. In attractive surroundings with numerous small lakes.
SE of town.
Apr-Oct 8HEC ▦ 🔧↑🔥💈✕⊙🖭⌀🏛⚓🛱🖽 lau ➡ ⁀LP Prices: A4.50 V4.50 ⚓5.50 🔺4.50

OOSTERHOUT Noord-Brabant
Katjeskelder Bredaseweg ☎0162 453539
Apr-1 Nov 25HEC ▦ 🔧↑🔥💈✕⊙🖭⌀🏛⚓🛱 ⁀P 🖱🖱🖽 lau
Prices: pitch 40-55 (incl 4 persons)

OOSTKAPELLE Zeeland
Dennenbos Duinweg 64 ☎0118 581310
15 Mar-5 Nov 2.5HEC ▦ 🔧↑🔥⊙🖭⌀🏛⚓🛱 ⁀P 🖱🖽➿ lau ➡💈✕ ⁀S Prices: pitch 29.95-36.50 (incl 4 persons)

In de Bongerd Brouwerijstr 13 ☎0118 581510
Well-kept in a meadow with hedges and apple trees.
500m S.

20 Mar-26 Oct 7.4HEC ▥ ⊕ ⋒ ☪ ✗ ⊙ ☻ ⊘ ♨ ☷ ⊹ P ☎ �ℙ ⊞ lau ➧
☘ ✗ ⅂S Prices: A6.50 pitch 101

Ons Buiten Aagtekerkeseweg 2a ☎0118 581813
From church drive S towards Grijpskerke, turn W and continue
400m.
21 Mar-Oct 7.7HEC ▥ ⊕ ⋒ ☪ ☘ ✗ ⊙ ☻ ⊘ ♨ ⅂ P ☎ ⊞ ⍟ lau ➧ ☷
⅂S Prices: pitch 27 (incl 2 persons)
See advertisement on page 226.

Pekelinge Landmetersweg 1 ☎0118 582820
The on-site facilities have seasonal opening.
Apr-Oct 12HEC ⊕ ⋒ ☘ ☪ ✗ ⊙ ☻ ⊘ ⅂ P ℙ ⊞ ⍟ lau ➧ ⊘ ⅂S

OOSTVOORNE Zuid-Holland

Kruininger Gors Gorspl 2 ☎0181 482711
A small site, divided by hedges, close to the lake.
Access via N15.
Apr-1 Oct 1.1HEC ▥ ⅃↙ ⋒ ☘ ☪ ✗ ⊙ ☻ ⊘ ☷ ℙ ⊞ ⍟ lau ➧ ⅂L
Prices: pitch 25 (incl 2 persons)

OUDDORP Zuid-Holland

Groene Welde Oude Nieuwlandseweg 11 ☎01878 1747
On flat grassland surrounded by trees.
On outskirts. Signposted.
Apr-Oct 12HEC ▥ ⊕ ⋒ ☘ ☪ ☪ ✗ ⊙ ☻ ⊘ ♨ ℙ ⊞ lau ➧ ✗ ⅂S

Klepperstee Klepperstee ☎01878 1511
On level meadow divided by hedges and trees.
Access via N57 (Rotterdam-Vlissingen) exit Ouddorp.
Apr-Nov 38HEC ⠿ ⅃↙ ⋒ ☘ ☪ ☪ ✗ ⊙ ☻ ⊘ ☷ ☻ ♨ ⅂ P ⊞ ⍟ lau ➧
⅂LS

PLASMOLEN Limburg

Eldorado Witteweg 18 ☎08896 1914
Camping Card Compulsory.
S of N271.
Apr-Oct 6HEC ▥ ⊕ ⋒ ☘ ☪ ☪ ✗ ⊙ ☻ ⊘ ☷ ⅂ LP ☎ ℙ ⊞ lau Prices:
A5.50 V4 ♨7.50 ▲7.50

RENESSE Zeeland

Brem Hoogenboomlaan 11 ☎0111 461403
Well-kept site belonging to a trade union, but also accepting tourists.
The last camping site in Hoogenboomlaan with numbered sections. It
is advisable to reserve pitches between 21 Jun and 9 Aug.
Apr-25 Oct 12HEC ▥ ⊕ ⋒ ☪ ✗ ⊙ ☻ ⊘ ☻ ♨ ⅂ P ℙ ⊞ ⍟ lau ➧ ☘
⊘

International Scharendijkseweg 8 ☎0111 461391
On grassland, between rows of tall shrubs and trees. Between dyke
road and main road to Scharendijk on E outskirts of village.
Mar-Nov 3HEC ⊕ ⋒ ☘ ☪ ☪ ⊙ ☻ ⊘ ⊘ ☎ ℙ ⊞ lau ➧ ✗ ⅂S Prices:
A6.50 V5 ♨6.50 ▲6.50

Vakantiepark 'Schouwen' Hoogenboomlaan 28 ☎0111 461231
Mar-Oct 9HEC ▥ ⊕ ⋒ ☘ ☪ ✗ ⊙ ☻ ⊘ ☷ ♨ ⅂ PS ☎ ⊞ ⍟ lau

RETRANCHEMENT Zeeland

De Zwinhoeve Duinweg 1 ☎0117 392120
In a beautiful position backed by sandunes with easy access to the
fine beaches of the Zeeuws-Vlaanderen coast.
All year 9HEC ▥ ⊕ ⋒ ☘ ☪ ✗ ⊙ ☻ ⊘ ♨ ⅂ S ☎ ⊞ lau ➧ ⅂P Prices:
A7.35 ♨10 ▲10

RIJEN Noord-Brabant

D'n Mastendol Oosterhoutseweg 7-13 ☎0161 222664
SW of town.
Apr-Oct 10.5HEC ▥ ⊕ ⋒ ☘ ☪ ✗ ⊙ ☻ ⊘ ☷ ⅂ P ☎ ⊞ lau ➧ ✗ ⊘ ⅂L
Prices: A6.25 V3.75 ♨3.75 ▲3.75

RIJNSBURG Zuid-Holland

Koningshof Elsgeesterweg 8 ☎0171 4026051
Modern site on level meadow near the flower fields.
1km N. Signposted
All year 8.5HEC ▥ ⊕ ⋒ ☘ ☪ ✗ ⊙ ☻ ⊘ ☻ ♨ ▲ ⅂ P ☎ ⊞ lau ➧
⅂S Prices: pitch 34-35 (incl 2 persons)
See advertisement under ROCKANJE

ROCKANJE Zuid-Holland

Itersoncamping C-G-Kleyburgweg 3 ☎0181 401200
A small site close to a North Sea beach, divided by hedges. **Motor
caravans and tents only.**
Access via N15.
28 Mar-Sep 8HEC ▥ ⊕ ⋒ ☘ ☪ ✗ ⊙ ☻ ⊘ ⅂ S ℙ ⊞ ⍟ lau Prices:
pitch 25 (incl 2 persons)

Rondeweibos Schapengorsedijk 19 ☎0181 401944
15 Mar-Oct 32HEC ▥ ⊕ ⋒ ☘ ☪ ✗ ⊙ ☻ ⊘ ☷ ♨ ☎ ⊞ lau ➧ ⅂P
Prices: A6 V4 ♨9 ▲9

Waterboscamping Duinrand 11 ☎0181 401900
A small, pleasant site near the beach. **Motor caravans and tents
only.**
Access via N15.
28 Mar-Sep] 11HEC ▥ ⊕ ⋒ ☘ ☪ ✗ ⊙ ☻ ⊘ ⅂ S ☎ ⊞ ⍟ lau Prices:
pitch 21 (incl 2 persons)

ROELOFARENDSVEEN Zuid-Holland

Braassem Galgekade 2A ☎01713 12091
Off highway A4/E10. (Amsterdam-Leiden). Follow signs for
Braassemer Meer from Roelofarendsveen exit.
Apr-Sep 2HEC ▥ ⅃↙ ⋒ ⊙ ☻ ☻ ♨ ⅂ LP ℙ ⊞ lau ➧ ☘ ☪ ⊘ ☷

ROERMOND Limburg

Hatenboer Hatenboer 51 ☎0031 4750
Situated in a beautiful area with access to all watersports.
Camping Card Compulsory
Leave A68 (Roermond-Eindhoven) at 'Hatenboer' exit.
Apr-Oct 10HEC ▥ ⊕ ⋒ ☘ ☪ ✗ ⊙ ☻ ⅂ L ☎ ℙ ⊞ lau ➧ ☘ ⊘ ☷ ⅂PR
Prices: A5.50 V5 ▲5.50

Marina Oolderhuuske Oolderhuuske 1 ☎4758 588686
27 Mar-31 Oct 6HEC ▥ ⅃↙ ⋒ ☘ ☪ ✗ ⊙ ☻ ⊘ ☻ ⅂ LR ☎ ℙ ⊞ lau
Prices: pitch 25-30 (incl 3 persons)

ROOSENDAAL *Noord-Brabant*

Zonneland Tufvaartsestr 6 ☎01656 365429
S of town towards the Belgian border.
Mar-15 Oct 14HEC ▦ ♠ 🏠 🍴 ⊙ ⊕ ↘ P ⚐ ⊞ ⚲ lau Prices: A4 V4 ⊞5 ▲5

ROTTERDAM *Zuid-Holland*

Rotterdam Kanaalweg 84 ☎010 4153440
Leave motorway by-pass (roads E10/E36) at exit Rotterdam-Centrum, then follow signs.
All year 4HEC ▦ ⊶ 🏠 🍴 ✕ ⊙ ⊟ ⊘ ≛ ⊞ ⊞ ⊞ lau ➡ 🚲 ↘P Prices: A8.25 V5 ⊞9 ▲6

ST ANTHONIS *Noord-Brabant*

Ullingse Bergen Bosweg 36 ☎0485 381700
W of town.
Apr-Oct 11HEC ▦ ⊶ 🏠 🍴 🍴 ✕ ⊙ ⊟ ⊘ ≛ ⊞ ↘ P ⚐ ⊞ ⚲ lau ➡ ⊞
Prices: pitch 24-31.50 (incl 2 persons)

ST OEDENRODE *Noord-Brabant*

Kienehoef Zwembadweg 37 ☎0413 472877
NW towards Boxtel.
Apr-Oct 11HEC ▦ ⊶ 🏠 🍴 ✕ ⊙ ⊟ ⊘ ≛ ⊞ ↘ P ⚐ ⊞ ⚲ lau ➡ ↘R

SCHAESBERG *Limburg*

Bousberg Boomweg 10 ☎045 311213
NW towards Kakert.
Apr-Oct 7HEC ▦ ⊶ 🏠 🍴 🍴 ✕ ⊙ ⊟ ⊘ ≛ ⊞ ⊞ ↘ P ⚐ ⊞ lau ➡ ✕

SEVENUM *Limburg*

Schatberg Midden Peelweg 5 ☎077 4677777
SW towards Eindhoven.
All year 86HEC ▦ ⊶ 🏠 🍴 🍴 ✕ ⊙ ⊟ ⊘ ≛ ⊞ ⊞ ▲ ↘ LP ⚐ ⚑ ⊞ ⚲ lau Prices: pitch 25-44.50 (incl 2 persons)

SLUIS *Zeeland*

Meldoorn Hoogstr 68 ☎0117 461662

In a meadow surrounded by rows of deciduous trees.
Camping Card Compulsory.
N on the road to Zuidzande.
22 Mar-20 Oct 5.5HEC ▦ ⊶ 🏠 🍴 🍴 ✕ ⊙ ⊟ ⊘ ≛ ⊞ ⊞ lau ➡ 🚲

SOERENDONK *Limburg*

Soerendonk Strijperdijk 9 ☎495 591652
A spacious site in wooded surroundings close to the Belgian border. There are good recreational facilities and good fishing is available in the lake.
Apr-1 Oct 18HEC ▦ ⠿ ⊶ 🏠 🍴 ✕ ⊙ ⊟ ⊘ ≛ ⊞ ↘ P ⚐ ⊞ lau
Prices: pitch 10-22

STRAMPROY *Limburg*

't Vosseven Lochstr 26 ☎04956 1560
Turn right at the church and continue for 5km.
Apr-Oct 10.6HEC ▦ ⊶ 🏠 🍴 ✕ ⊙ ⊟ ⊞ ↘ P ⚑ ⊞ lau

SUSTEREN *Limburg*

Hommelheide Hommelweg 2 ☎04499 2900
All year 42HEC ▦ ⊶ 🏠 🍴 🍴 ✕ ⊙ ⊟ ⊘ ≛ ⊞ ⚑ ↘ L ⚐ ⊞ lau

VALKENBURG *Limburg*

Europa Couberg 29 ☎043 6013097
SW of town.
Apr-Oct 13HEC ▦ ⊶ 🏠 🍴 🍴 ✕ ⊙ ⊟ ⊘ ≛ ⊞ ↘ P ⚐ lau

VENLO *Limburg*

Ons Buiten St-Urbansweg 120-122 ☎077 3515821
Camping Card compulsory.
All year 12HEC ▦ ⊶ 🏠 🍴 ✕ ⊙ ⊟ ⊘ ≛ ↘ P ⚐ ⊞ lau ➡ ↘R Prices: A5 pitch 8

VENRAY *Limburg*

Oude Barrier Maasheseweg 93 ☎04780 82305
NE of town.
Apr-Sep 9.8HEC ▦ ⊶ 🏠 🍴 ✕ ⊙ ⊟ ⊘ ↘ P ⚐ ⊞ lau

VESSEM *Noord-Brabant*

Eurocamping Vessem BV Zwembadweg 1 ☎04979 1214
Apr-Sep 50HEC ▦ ⚲ ⋔ ⛴ ♣ ⊙ ⊟ ⌀ ᴧ ⌁ P ☎ ⊞ lau ➧ ✕

VLISSINGEN (FLUSHING) *Zeeland*

Lange Pacht Boksweg 1 ☎01184 60447
Apr-Sep 1.2HEC ▦ ⚲ ⋔ ⊙ ⊟ ⊡ ➧ ⛴ ✕ ⟍S

Nolle Woelderenlaan 1 ☎01184 14371
The site consists of five sections near two tennis courts.
15 Mar-2 Jan 1.2HEC ▦ ⣿ ⚲ ⚲ ⋔ ⛴ ⊙ ⊟ ⌀ ⛫ ⊡ ⊞ lau ➧ ♟ ✕
⟍S

VROUWENPOLDER *Zeeland*

Oranjezon Koningin Emmaweg 16a ☎0118 591549
Well-kept between tall, thick hedges and bushes. SW of the village.
Camping Card Compulsory.
For access drive towards Oostkapelle for approx 2.5km, then turn N
and continue for 300m.
Apr-Oct 5.3HEC ▦ ⚲ ⋔ ⛴ ♟ ✕ ⊙ ⊟ ⌀ ᴧ ⛫ ⟍ P ☎ ⊞ lau ➧ ⟍S
Prices: pitch 30-50 (incl 4 persons)

WASSENAAR *Zuid-Holland*

Duinrell Duinrell 5 ☎0175 155255
Very well maintained site with additional recreation centre which is
free for campers. NW in area of same name. Some noise from
aircraft. Toilets for invalids. Area restricted to cars. Naturist beach
nearby.
Camping Card Compulsory.
Turn off A44 (Den Haag-Leiden) at traffic lights in Wassenaar dorp'
and camping signs.
All year 110HEC ▦ ⚲ ⋔ ⛴ ♟ ✕ ⊙ ⊟ ⌀ ⛫ ⟍ P ☎ ⊡ ⊞ lau ➧ ᴧ
Prices: A17.50 V7.50 ⛟2.50 ▲2.50
See advertisement on page 228.

WEERT *Limburg*

Ijzeren Man Herenvennenweg 60 ☎04950 33202
Well-kept with asphalt drives, in a big nature reserve with zoo, heath
and forest.
Off E9.
Apr-Oct 9.8HEC ▦ ⚲ ⋔ ⛴ ♟ ✕ ⊙ ⊟ ⌀ ᴧ ⛫ ⟍ LP ☎ ⊞ lau

WEMELDINGE *Zeeland*

Linda Oostkanaalweg 4 ☎0113 621259
On meadowland surrounded by rows of tall shrubs.
Turn opposite bridge in town and continue 100m, over bridge to
camp.
Apr-Oct 5HEC ▦ ᴗ⟍ ⋔ ⛴ ♟ ✕ ⊙ ⊟ ⌀ ᴧ ⛫ ⛫ ⊡ ⊞ lau ➧ ⟍S
Prices: A6.50 V5 ⛟5 ▲5

WESTKAPELLE *Zeeland*

Boomgaard Domineeshofweg 1 ☎01187 1377
A flat grassy site.
For access turn off the Middleburg road on the S outskirts of the
town, then follow signs.
19 Mar-30 Oct 8HEC ▦ ⚲ ⋔ ⛴ ♟ ✕ ⊙ ⊟ ⌀ ᴧ ⛫ ⛫ ☎ ⊞ lau ➧ ⟍S

ZEVENHUIZEN *Zuid-Holland*

Zevenhuizen Tweemanspolder 8 ☎0180 631654
Situated NW of the village, this site is surrounded by a wide belt of
bushes.
On NW outskirts follow signs . Site on right of the road beyond a car
park.
Apr-Oct 6HEC ▦ ⚲ ⋔ ⛴ ♟ ✕ ⊙ ⊟ ⌀ ᴧ ⛫ ⟍ PS ⊡ ⊞ lau ➧ ✕
Prices: A7.75 V5 ⛟5.25 ▲4

ZOUTELANDE *Zeeland*

Meerpaal Duinweg 133 ☎01186 561300
On meadowland hidden behind bushy hedges at the end of a cul-de-
sac.
1km SE.
20 Mar-26 Oct 1.8HEC ▦ ᴗ⟍ ⋔ ⛴ ⌀ ⊙ ⊟ ⌀ ᴧ ⛫ ⟍ S ⊡ ⊞ ⟲ lau
➧ ♟ ✕ Prices: A7.75 V6.30 ⛟12.30 ▲12.30

Weltevreden Melseweg 1 ☎0118 561321
30 Mar-26 Oct 2.5HEC ▦ ⚲ ⋔ ⊙ ⊟ ⌀ ⛫ ⟍ S ⊡ ⊞ ⟲ lau ➧
♟ ✕ Prices: pitch 38.50 (incl 4 persons)

PORTUGAL

A relatively small country lying in the south western corner of the Iberian peninsula, Portugal's only land frontier is the Spanish border in the east.

The country is, perhaps, best known for its five hundred miles of coastline. The Algarve in the extreme south is one of the finest stretches of coastline in Europe, with unique caves and a remoteness which has been conserved despite the development of the area. Inland, the cool valleys and pastures of the Tagus contrast sharply with the wooded mountain slopes of the Minho area in the north.

Generally the country enjoys a mild climate with the Algarve being very hot in the summer. The language is Portuguese, which was developed from Latin and closely resembles Spanish, although English is often spoken in the Algarve.

Portugal has about 184 campsites most of which are on the coast. There are about 21 *Orbitur* parks in the country which are privately owned and of a high standard, as indeed are the municipal parks. Orbitur parks are open throughout the year and most of them offer fully-equipped bungalows which accommodate four people. A booklet containing details of officially classified parks is produced by the Direcção Geral de Turismo, Palácio Foz, Praça dos Restauradores, Lisboa ☎(01) 363314. The Oporto office is at Praça D João I-25-4 ☎(02) 27556 and the Coimbra office is at Largo da Portagem. Otherwise ask for Comissao Municipal de Turismo, Junta de Turismo or Câmara Municipal.

Off-site camping. It is prohibited to camp outside organised campsites. However, when stopping in a motorway rest or service area with a caravan, it is permitted to cook a meal.

FACTS AND FIGURES

Capital: Lisbon
Language: Portuguese
IDD code: 351. To call the UK dial 00 44
Currency: Escudo (*ESc*1 = 100 centavos). At the time of going to press £1 = *ESc*237.40.
Local time: GMT(summer GMT+1)
Emergency Services: Police, Fire and Ambulance 115
Business hours-
Banks: Mon-Fri 08.30-15.00
Shops: Mon-Fri 09.00-13.00-and 15.00-19.00, Sat 09.00-13.00 (and 15.00-19.00 Dec); shopping centres Mon-Sun 10.00-24.00

Average daily temperature:
Lisbon

Jan 11°C	Jul 21°C
Mar 13°C	Sep 20°C
May 17°C	Nov 14°C

Tourist Information: Portuguese National Tourist Office
UK 22-25A Sackville Street London W1X 1DE
☎ 0171-494 1441
USA 548 Fifth Avenue New York, NY 10036
☎ (212) 354 4403
Camping card: Compulsory at Federação Portuguesa de Campismo parks and camping clubs offering special prices. Recommended elsewhere.

HOW TO GET THERE

You can ship your vehicle to Spain, using either the Plymouth to Santander service (24hrs) - Portsmouth to Santander in winter (30hrs) - or the Portsmouth to Bilbao service (30hrs) and then travel onwards by road. For details of the *AA European Routes Services* please consult the Contents Page.

Distance

From Santander to Lisboa (Lisbon) is about 920km (570 miles), normally requiring one or two overnight stops. Using the Channel ports, or the Channel tunnel, driving through France and Spain (enter Spain on the Biarritz to San Sebastian (Donostia) road at the western end of the Pyrénées).

From the Channel ports to Lisboa (Lisbon) is about 2,157km (1,340 miles). This will require 3 or 4 overnight stops.

Car sleeper trains

Services are available from Calais to Biarritz, or Paris to Madrid.

See Spain for location map

MOTORING & GENERAL INFORMATION

The information given here is specific to Portugal. It **must** be read in conjunction with the European ABC at the front of the book, which covers those regulations which are common to many countries. **Note** Portuguese law requires that everyone carries photographic proof of identity at all times.

British Embassy/Consulates*

The British Embassy is located at 1200 Lisboa, 33 rua de Sâo Bernardo☎(01) 3924000; consular section ☎(01) 3954082. There is a British Consulate in Porto (Oporto) and one with an Honorary Consul in Portimão.

Children in cars

Child under 3 cannot travel as front seat passenger unless seated in approved child seat; child over 3 and under 12 must use approved restraint system unless the car is a two seater.

Currency

Visitors may import up to *ESc*100,000 in Portuguese currency and unlimited amounts of foreign currency, but amounts of foreign currency in excess of *ESc*500,000 must be declared on arrival. However, visitors entering Portugal must be in posession of a minimum amount of Portuguese or foreign currency equivalent to *ESc*20,000 plus *ESc*6,000 for each day of their stay. Any amount of foreign currency may be exported provided it was declared on entry, but no more than *ESc* 100,000 in Portuguese currency may be exported. During the summer, currency exchange facilities are usually provided throughout the day in main tourist resorts, at frontier posts, airports and in some hotels.

Dimensions and weight restrictions

Private **cars** and towed **trailers** or **caravans** are restricted to the following dimensions - height, 4 metres; width, 2.50 metres; length, 12 metres. The maximum permitted overall length of vehicle/trailer or caravan combination is 18 metres.

There are no weight restrictions governing the temporary importation of trailers into Portugal. However, it is recommended that the following be adhered to: weight (unladen), up to 750kg if the towing vehicle's engine is 2,500cc or less; up to 1,500kg if the towing vehicle's engine is between 2,500cc and 3,500cc; up to 2,500kg if the towing vehicle's engine is more than 3,500cc.

Driving licence*

A valid UK or Republic of Ireland licence is acceptable in Portugal. The minimum age at which a visitor may use a temporarily imported motorcycle (over 50cc) or car is 18 years*. See also Speed limits below.

Foodstuffs*

There are no limits on the importation of foodstuffs obtained duty and tax paid within the EC. Up to 500g of coffee (200g of coffee extract) and 100g of tea (40g of tea extract) purchased duty-free or outside the EC may be imported free of duty and tax. However, coffee bought duty-free or outside the EC cannot be imported by visitors under 15 years of age.

Motoring club*

The **Automóvel Club de Portugal** (ACP) which has its headquarters at Lisboa 1250 rua Rosa Araüjo 24 ☎(01) 3563931 has offices in a number of provincial towns. ACP offices are normally open 09.00-16.45hrs Monday to Friday (to 17.30hrs rom 1 April to 30 September); English and French are spoken. Offices are closed on Saturday and Sunday.

Roads

Main roads and most of the important secondary roads are good, as are the mountain roads to the north-east.

Portugal has about 378 miles of motorway (*auto-estrada*)) with tolls payable on most sections. Emergency telephones are located every 2km on most motorways.

Speed limits*

Car

Built-up areas 50kph (31mph)

Other roads 90kph (55mph) or 100kph (62mph)

Motorways min† 40kph (24mph)

max 120kph (74mph)

Car/caravan/trailer

Built-up areas 50kph (31mph)

Other roads 70kph (43mph) or 80kph (49mph)

Motorways min† 40kph (24mph)

max 100kph (62mph)

†Minimum speeds on motorways apply, except where otherwise signposted.

Visiting motorists to Portugal who have held a full driving licence for less than one year are restricted to driving at a top speed of 90kph (55mph). They must also display a yellow disc bearing the figure '90' at the rear of their vehicle (obtainable from any vehicle accessory shop in Portugal). Leaflets giving details in English are handed to visitors at entry point.

Warning triangle*

The use of a warning triangle is compulsory in the event of accident or breakdown. The triangle must be placed on the road 30 metres (33yds) behind the vehicle and must be clearly visible from 100 metres (110yds).

*Additional information will be found in the Continental ABC at the front of the book.

A-Z DIRECTORY

Prices are in Portuguese Escudos Abbreviation: r rua

South

Bordered by the Atlantic coast on two sides, by mountains in the north and by Spain in the east, the Algarve enjoys one of the most settled climates in the world. Though poorer than the rest of Portugal in art and architecture, the region is rich in subtropical vegetation; almond and orange groves, cotton plantations, and fields of rice and sugar cane.

Beyond the mountains in the north, the land is predominantly agricultural, with low rolling hills stretching beyond the horizon. Cork oaks are grown to provide much-needed shade, making an important contribution to the region's economy.

Water is also a major source of income in the south; inland, the salt-pans of the Sado river maintain the pretty towns of narrow twisting lanes and whitewashed houses. On the coast, towns such as Faro, Lagos, and Cape St. Vincent, glory in a history of trade, shipbuilding, sea battles and exploration.

ALBUFEIRA *Algarve*

Albufeira ☎089 587627

Signposted from N125

All year 15HEC ▦ ⟨symbols⟩ ⟨lau⟩ ⟨symbols⟩

ALCANTARILHA *Algarve*

Turismovel - Parque Campismo de Canelas ☎082 312612

All year 6.5HEC ⟨symbols⟩ Prices: A225-450 V320-360 ⟨symbol⟩450-580 ▲420-550

ALVITO *Baixo Alentejo*

Markádia Barragem de Odivelas ☎084 76141

Open savannah terrain.

Leave N121 (Beja-Lisboa) at Ferrera do Alentejo and continue N towards Torrão. From Odivelas follow signposts.

All year 10HEC ⟨symbols⟩ Prices: A340-680 V340-680 ⟨symbol⟩340-680 ▲340-680

BEJA *Baixo Alentejo*

CM de Beja av Vasco da Gama ☎084 24328

All year 1.2HEC ⟨symbols⟩ Prices: pitch 158-315

PORTIMÃO *Algarve*

Da Dourada Alvor ☎82 458002

All year 4HEC ▦ ⟨symbols⟩ Prices: A250-500 V200-400 ⟨symbol⟩275-550 ▲250-500

PRAIA DA LUZ *Algarve*

At VALVERDE

Orbitur Praia da Luz ☎082 789211

Well-equipped site with children's playground and tennis courts. Off N125 Lagos-Cape St Vincent road. 4km from Lagos.

All year 9HEC ▦ ⟨symbols⟩ Prices: A660 V550 ⟨symbol⟩680-750 ▲560-660

QUARTEIRA *Algarve*

Orbitur Barros da Fonte Santa ☎089 302826

A terraced site at the top of a hill.

Off M125 in Almoncil and follow signs to Quarteira. About 500m before reaching the sea turn left into the camp.

All year 9.8HEC ⟨symbols⟩ Prices: A660 V550 ⟨symbol⟩680-750 ▲560-660

SAGRES *Algarve*

Parque de Campismo de Sagres Cerro das Moitas ☎082 64351

Closed Dec-2 Jan 6HEC ⟨symbols⟩ Prices: A400-600 V250-450 ⟨symbol⟩600-700 ▲400-600

SÃO MIGUEL *Baixo Alentejo*

São Miguel ☎082 94145

A well equipped site within a Nature Protected Area. 1.5km from Odemira.

Closed Nov 4HEC ⟨symbols⟩

SINES *Baixo Alentejo*

S Torpes ☎069 632105

Jun-Sep 7HEC ⟨symbols⟩

Sines r di Farol ☎069 862531
Closed 16 Dec-14 Jan 4.5HEC ▥ ♠ ℝ ⅋ ⅏ ✕ ⊙ ☯ ⌀ ☵ ☍ ☲ ⊞ lau
♦ ⅃S Prices: A360-450 V330-410 ☗400-500 ▲360-450

S. Tonnes S. Tonnes ☎069 632105
In a pine wood on the Cabo de Sines peninsula, to the N of the town.
Follow signs for Algarve/ S. Tonnes.
30 Jun-Sep 3.5HEC ▥ ♠ ℝ ⅋ ⅏ ✕ ⊙ ☯ ⌀ ☵ ☍ ▲ ⊞ lau ♦ ⅃S

VILA DO BISPO Algarve

At **PRAIA DE SALEMA**(7.5km SE)

Quinta dos Carriços Praia da Salema ☎082 65201
All year 20HEC ▥ ♠ ℝ ⅋ ⅏ ✕ ⊙ ☯ ⌀ ☷ ☍ ☲ ⊞ lau ♦ ⅃S
Prices: A620 V620 ☗860 ▲620-800

VILA NOVA DE MILFONTES Baixo Alentejo

Parque de Campismo de Milfontes ☎083 96104
All year 6HEC ♠ ℝ ⅋ ⅏ ✕ ⊙ ☯ ⌀ ☵ ☷ ☍ ☲ lau ♦ ⅃RS ⊞ Prices:
A300-540 V180-370 ☗285-490 ▲220-410

North

Northern Portugal offers medieval castles perched on mountain
crags, grey stone villages, and purple vineyards whose grapes
produce the popular Vinho Verde, Mateus Rosé and Portugal's
most famous product - port wine. There are magnificent forests,
spectacular lakes, long sandy beaches sheltered by pinewoods,
and villages hidden by the springtime blossom of almond and
chestnut trees.
A region of ancient human settlement, even the smallest towns
are rich in architectural treasures, from palaces of the
Renaissance period to prehistoric rock engravings. The region
also boasts a wealth of traditional crafts of a variety and colour
to match the splendid local costumes worn for the many religious
festivals and "romarias" celebrated with enormous enthusiasm
and energy throughout the year.
The capital of the region, Oporto, is Portugal's second largest
city and also its most untypical - a lively port, a university town
and a hub of industry and commerce in one.

CAMINHA Minho
Orbitur Mata do Caminha ☎058 921295
On undulating sandy ground with trees.
Turn off N13 at Km89.7 and drive W, along the Rio Minho for about
800m, then turn left.
All year 2.5HEC ▥ ░ ⅍ ℝ ⅋ ✕ ⊙ ☯ ⌀ ⅃ S ☲ lau Prices: A550
V470 ☗540-630 ▲450-550

CAMPO DO GERES Minho
Cerdeira ☎053 351005
Camping Card Compulsory.
All year 4.6HEC ▥ ░ ♠ ℝ ⅋ ⅏ ✕ ⊙ ☯ ⌀ ☷ ☍ ☲ ⊞ ⅏ lau ♦ ☷ ⅃LR
Prices: A500-600 V450-550 ☗800-10000 ▲500-900

MATOSINHOS Douro Litoral

At **ANGEIRAS**(12km N)

Orbitur Lavra ☎02 9270571
A modern, well-kept site in a pine wood on a hill overlooking the sea.
W of the N13 at the X-roads at Km12.1, E of Vila do Pinheiro and
towards the sea for 5km.
All year 7.7HEC ♠ ℝ ⅋ ⅏ ✕ ⊙ ☯ ⌀ ⅃ S ☲ lau ♦ ☷ Prices: A550
V470 ☗540-630 ▲450-550

PÓVOA DE VARZIM Douro Litoral
Rio Alto Estela-Rio Alto ☎052 615699
Situated near dunes 150m from the sea.
All year 9HEC ▥ ░ ⅍ ⅍ ℝ ⅋ ⅏ ✕ ⊙ ☯ ⅃ P ☲ ⊞ lau ♦ ⌀ ⅃S
Prices: A460-550 V450-550 ☗865-940 ▲365-400

VIANA DO CASTELO Minho
Orbitur Matado Cabedelo ☎058 322167
Closed 16 Nov-15 Jan 2.5HEC ▥ ░ ♠ ℝ ⅋ ⅏ ✕ ⊙ ☯ ⌀ ☵ ☍ ☲
lau ♦ ⅃PS Prices: A550 V470 ☗540-630 ▲450-550

VILA REAL Tras-Os-Montes Alto Douro
Parque Campismo de Vila Real r Dr-Monuel Cardona
☎059 24724
In the E part of town off N2 by GALP petrol station. Site in 300m
near new school.
Closed Jan 3HEC ▥ ░ ⅍ ℝ ⅋ ✕ ⊙ ☯ ⌀ ☲ ⊞ lau ♦ ☷ ⅃PR

Central

This is a vast and wonderful region of infinite variety; to the west,
the popular Costa da Prata; the beautiful park-like landscape in
the south; the dramatic mountains in the north and east; and the
cattle-herding country in the centre, where the fighting bulls
graze along the River Tejo, watched by mounted cattle herders in
colourful local costume.
The highest town in Portugal is Guarda, the ideal base from
which to explore the magnificent Serra da Estrala. Further west
is the romantic town of Coimbra, whose university is amongst
the oldest in the world and until 1911, was the only one in the
country.
Portugal's capital, Lisbon, has the attraction of combining the
charm of the past with the excitement of a progressive capital
city. It is also the heart of the production of the famous Azulejos -
the glazed ornamental tiles which are Portugal's favourite form
of architectural decoration.

ABRANTES Ribatejo
Castelo do Bode Martinchel ☎041 99244
Closed Dec-1 Jan 1.5HEC ▥ ♠ ℝ ⅋ ⅏ ✕ ⊙ ☯ ⌀ ⅃ L ☲ ⊞ ⅏ lau ♦ ☷
✕ ⅃R

ALCOBAÇA Estremadura
CM ☎062 42265
Terraced hill site with tall eucalyptus trees overlooking the town.
Divided into pitches and partly bordered by hedges and flower beds.
Turn off by-pass (N8) in NE outskirts at large roundabout and turn
towards hills at covered market.
All year 11HEC ▨░ ░ ⅍ ⊙ ☯ ☍ ☲ ⊞ lau ♦ ☷ ⅋ ✕ ⅃S

ARGANIL Beira Litoral
Orbitur Saraedo ☎035 25706
In a pleasant situation among pine trees, close to the River Alva.
On N342-4.
All year 2HEC ▥ ░ ░ ⅍ ℝ ⅋ ⅏ ✕ ⊙ ☯ ⌀ ☍ ⅃ R ☲ lau Prices: A380
V330 ☗350-420 ▲320-380

CALDAS DA RAINHA Estremadura
Orbitur Parc Rainha D Leonor ☎062 832367
Long narrow site on wooded hill.
300m from N8 on S outskirts.
16 Jan-15 Nov 2.4HEC ▨░ ░ ░ ⅍ ℝ ⅋ ⅏ ✕ ⊙ ☯ ⌀ ☲ lau ♦ ☷ ⅃P
Prices: A480 V430 ☗500-550 ▲400-490

CASTRO DAIRE Beira Alta
Orbitur ☎032 32803
Jun-Sep 2HEC ▥ ░ ⅍ ℝ ⅋ ✕ ⊙ ☯ ⌀ ☍ ☲ ⊞ lau Prices: A480 V430
☗500-550 ▲400-490

COIMBRA Beira Litoral
CM de Coimbra Praça 25 de Abril ☎039 701497
Camping Gaz available summer only.
All year 1.1HEC ▥ ♠ ℝ ⅋ ⅏ ✕ ⊙ ☯ ⌀ ☍ ☲ ⊞ lau ♦ ✕ ☷ ⅃PR

COSTA DA CAPARICA Estremadura
Orbitur ☎01 2903894
Afer crossing the 'Ponte Sul' on the road to Caparica, turn right at
first traffic light. Campsite is 1km on left.
All year 5.5HEC ▨░ ░ ♠ ℝ ⅋ ✕ ⊙ ☯ ⌀ ☷ ☍ ☲ ⊞ lau ♦ ⅃PS Prices:
A620 V550 ☗660-750 ▲560-620

ÉVORA Alto Alentejo
Orbitur ☎066 25190
2km S right of road near Km94.5.

All year 3.8HEC ▦ ⚐ ⋔ ♥ ⤬ ⊙ ⊟ ⌀ ⚏ ⤳ P ☎ ⊞ lau Prices: A550 V470 ⬤540-630 ▲450-630

ÉVORA DE ALCOBAÇA *Estremadura*
Rural de Silveira Capuchos ☎062 509573
3km from Alcobaça on N86.
Jun-Sep 0.5HEC ♦ ⋔ ♥ ⤬ ⊙ ⊟ ☎ ⊞ lau ♦ ⤳ ⌀ ⚏ ⤳S Prices:
A400 V250 ⬤500-650 ▲300-700

FIGUEIRA DA FOZ *Beira Litoral*
Foz do Mondego Cabedelo, Gala ☎033 31542
Closed Dec 4HEC ⠿ ⤳⤢ ⋔ ⬛ ⋔ ♥ ⤬ ⊙ ⊟ ⌀ ⤳ RS ☎ ⊞ ⚡ lau

Orbitur Gala ☎033 31492
In an enclosed area within a municipal park on top of Guarda Hill.
At Km177, on the NW outskirts of the town, turn left off the N16
Porto road and drive uphill for about 500m.
16 Jan-15 Nov 6HEC ▦ ♦ ⋔ ♥ ⤬ ⊙ ⊟ ⌀ ☎ ☎ ⊞ lau ♦ ⤳S Prices:
A550 V470 ⬤540-630 ▲450-630

GUARDA *Beira Alta*
Orbitur ☎071 211406
16 Jan-15 Nov 1.8HEC ⠿ ♦ ⚐ ⋔ ♥ ⤬ ⊙ ⊟ ⌀ ⚏ ☎ lau Prices:
A550 V470 ⬤540-630 ▲450-550

GUINCHO *Estremadura*
Orbitur Crismina ☎01 4870450
On hilly ground amidst a pine wood in the Parque du Guincho, near
the Boca do Inferno.
4km W of Cascais at Km98, turn right and follow road no 247-6 for
1km.
All year 6.9HEC ▦ ⠿ ♦ ⋔ ♥ ⤬ ⊙ ⊟ ⌀ ☎ ☎ ⊞ lau ♦ ⤳PS Prices:
A620 V550 ⬤660-750 ▲560-620

LISBOA (LISBON) *Estremadura*
CM Monsanto Estrada da Circunvalação ☎01 702061
Park like site on flat hill. Metalled interior roads and pitches.
Turn off motorway at KmV2/111 towards Estoril and follow signs.
All year 38HEC ▦ ♦ ⋔ ♥ ⤬ ⊙ ⊟ ⌀ ⤳ P ☎ ⊞ lau

LOURIÇAL *Beira Litoral*
De Klomp Casas Brancas ☎036 952551
In pleasant wooded surroundings.
Access via N109 or A1.
All year 1.8HEC ▦ ♦ ⋔ ⊙ ⊟ ☎ ☎ ⬤ ☎ lau ♦ ⬛ ⋔ ⤬ ⌀ ⊞ Prices:
A350 V200 ⬤300 ▲300

MONTARGIL *Alto Alentejo*
Orbitur Barragem de Montargil ☎042 91207
All year 5.9HEC ⠿ ⚐ ⋔ ♥ ⤬ ⊙ ⊟ ⌀ ⤳ L ☎ ⊞ lau Prices: A550
V470 ⬤540-630 ▲450-550

NAZARÉ *Estremadura*
Orbitur Valado Valado ☎062 561111
300m E of village, S of road 8-4 Nazaré-Alcobaça.
16 Jan-15 Nov 6.7HEC ▦ ⚐ ⋔ ♥ ⤬ ⊙ ⊟ ⌀ ⚏ ☎ ⊞ lau ♦ ⤳S
Prices: A550 V470 ⬤540-630 ▲450-550

Vale Paraiso Estrada National N242 ☎062 561800
All year 8HEC ▦ ♦ ⋔ ⬛ ⤬ ⊙ ⊟ ⌀ ⤳ A ⤳ P ☎ ⊞ lau ♦ ⤳LS Prices:
A336-560 V276-460 ⬤354-590 ▲294-490

PALHEIROS DE MIRA *Beira Litoral*
Orbitur ☎031 471234
Site lies in a dense forest.
N off the N334 at KM2, towards Videira, opposite a road fork.
16 Jan-15 Nov 3HEC ♦ ⋔ ♥ ⤬ ⊙ ⊟ ⌀ ☎ ☎ ⊞ lau ♦ ⤳LP Prices:
A550 V470 ⬤540-630 ▲450-550

PENICHE *Estremadura*
CM ☎062 789529
On a sandy hillock, partly wooded 0.5km from sea.
2km E.
All year 12HEC ⠿ ⤳⤢ ⋔ ♥ ⤬ ⊙ ⊟ ⌀ ☎ ⊞ lau ♦ ⚏ ⤳PS Prices:
A250 V250 ⬤410 ▲250-370

Peniche Praia ☎062 783460
All year 1.5HEC ▦ ⠿ ⤳⤢ ⋔ ⬛ ⋔ ♥ ⤬ ⊙ ⊟ ☎ ☎ ⊞ lau ♦ ⤬ ⌀ ⚏
⤳PS Prices: A235-390 V200-330 ⬤270-450 ▲235-390

PORTALEGRE *Alto Alentejo*
Orbitur Quinta da Saude ☎045 22848
Closed 16 Nov-15 Jan 2.8HEC ⠿ ♦ ⋔ ⤬ ⊙ ⊟ ☎ ⊞ lau
Prices: A480 V430 ⬤500-550 ▲400-490

PRAIA DE PEDRÓGÃO *Beira Litoral*
Parque Municipal de Campismo ☎044 695403
Camping Card Compulsory.
15 Feb-15 Dec 9HEC ▦ ⚐ ⋔ ⬛ ⋔ ♥ ⤬ ⊙ ⊟ ⌀ ⤳ S ⬤ ⊞ ⚡

SALVATERRA DE MAGOS *Ribatejo*
Parque de Campismo de Escaroupim Mata Florestal de
Escaroupim ☎063 55484
Closed Dec-1 Jan 4HEC ⠿ ♦ ⋔ ♥ ⤬ ⊙ ⊟ ⌀ ⤳ P ☎ ⊞ ⚡ lau

SÃO JACINTO *Beira Litoral*
Orbitur ☎034 48284
In a dense pine wood seawards from the uneven, paved road from
Ovar which runs alongside the lagoon.
1.5km from the sea.
16 Jan-15 Nov 1.5HEC ▦ ⠿ ♦ ⋔ ♥ ⤬ ⊙ ⊟ ⌀ ☎ ☎ ⊞ lau ♦
⤳PS Prices: A550 V470 ⬤540-630 ▲450-630

SÃO PEDRO DE MOEL *Estremadura*
Orbitur ☎044 599168
On a hill amidst pine trees.
Off road No 242-2 from Marinha Grande at the roundabout near the
SHELL petrol station on the E outskirts of the village and drive N for
100m.
All year 7HEC ▦ ⠿ ♦ ⋔ ♥ ⤬ ⊙ ⊟ ⌀ ⤳ S ☎ ⊞ lau ♦ ⤳P
Prices: A550 V470 ⬤540-630 ▲450-550

VAGOS *Beira Litoral*
Vagueira ☎034 797618
All year 12HEC ⠿ ♦ ⋔ ♥ ⬛ ⋔ ♥ ⤬ ⊙ ⊟ ⌀ ☎ ⊞ lau ♦ ⤳LPRS

VISEU *Beira Alta*
Orbitur Mata do Fontelo ☎032 26146
Closed 16 Nov-15 Jan 2.2HEC ▦ ♦ ⚐ ⋔ ♥ ⤬ ⊙ ⊟ ⌀ ⚏ ☎ ⊞ ♦ ⤳P
Prices: A550 V470 ⬤540-630 ▲450-550

SPAIN & ANDORRA

Rich in history and natural beauty, Spain is bordered by two countries, France in the north and Portugal in the west.

Central Spain is mountainous and barren while the coastline is mostly extremely rocky. Some of the most popular holiday areas in Europe are in Spain, the best known being the Costa Brava, the Costa Blanca, the Costa Dorada and the Costa del Sol. All these regions offer fine, sandy and safe beaches. Spain has a varied climate; temperate in the north, dry and hot in the south and in the Balearic Islands. Languages spoken are Spanish, Catalan, Basque and Galician. Spanish has developed from Castilian and there are many local dialects spoken thoughout the provinces.

Sites are numerous on the Costa Brava and elsewhere along the coast, but there are not many inland. They are officially classified according to the facilities and services provided and their classification should be displayed at the site entrance and on any literature. If you intend visiting sites at popular resorts along the coast between late spring and mid-October, it is not generally possible to book in advance. The best advice is to arrive before midday when the new charge begins. Late spring is recommended, as the intense heat of mid-summer is avoided and sites and roads are less congested. Opening dates vary considerably and some sites are open all year. Information about campsites and a detailed guide book are available from the Spanish National Tourist Office (see *Tourist Information*) and local tourist information offices.

Hire of equipment is not generally possible, but some campsites have bungalow accommodation.

Off-site camping is generally prohibited. Permission to camp off an official campsite must be

obtained from the landowner or local police. **Camp fires are absolutely forbidden.** Free camping near to beaches, rivers, towns or established campsites is forbidden.

HOW TO GET THERE

You can ship your vehicle direct to Spain using either the Plymouth to Santander service (24hrs) Portsmouth to Santander in winter (30hrs) - or the Portsmouth to Bilbao service (30hrs). Using the Channel Tunnel, or the Channel ports, approach Spain through France; pass either end of the Pyrenean mountains: **For central and southern Spain** take the Biarritz to San Sebastian (Donostia) road or motorway at the western end; **For the Costa Brava and beyond** take the Perpignan to Barcelona road, or motorway, at the eastern end of the mountains. **For Andorra** from France via Pas de la Casa (6860ft) then over the Envalira Pass (7897ft). Between

---

FACTS AND FIGURES

Capital: Madrid

Language: Spanish (Castilian), Catalan, Galician, Basque

IDD code: 34. To call the UK dial 07* 44
(* wait for second dialling tone)

Currency: Spanish peseta (*Ptas*1 = 100 centimos). At the time of going to press 1 = *Ptas*195.30.

Local time: GMT + 1 (summer GMT + 2)

Emergency Services: Madrid and Barcelona Police 091; Fire 080; Ambulance 092; in other towns call the operator.

Business hours:

Banks: Mon-Fri 09.00-14.00, Sat 09.00-13.00.

Shops: Mon-Sat 09.00-13.00 and 16.30-19.30.

Average daily temperatures:
Madrid

Jan 4°C	Jul 24°C
Mar 9°C	Sep 19°C
May 16°C	Nov 8°C

Tourist Information:

UK Spanish National Tourist Office Metro House, 57-58 St James's Street London SW1A 1LD
☎ 0171-499 0901

USA National Tourist Office of Spain 665 Fifth Avenue, New York NY 10022
☎ (212) 759 8822

Camping card:
Not compulsory, but recommended

November and April the roads through the central Pyrénées may sometimes be closed. From Spain, the approach via La Seu d'Urgell is always open. For details of the *AA European Routes Service* please consult the Contents Page.

Distance
From Calais to Madrid is about 1,600km (994 miles), usually requiring two or three overnight stops.

Car sleeper trains
Calais to Narbonne; Calais to Biarritz; Paris to Madrid.

MOTORING & GENERAL INFORMATION
The information given here is specific to Spain and/or Andorra. It **must** be read in conjunction with the European ABC at the front of the book, which covers those regulations which are common to many countries.

Bail Bond
An accident in Spain can have serious consequences, including the impounding of car and property, and a Bail Bond is advisable. It provides a written guarantee that a cash deposit of usually up to £1500 will be paid to the Spanish court as surety for bail and for any fine which may be imposed. However, the Bond is not insurance cover as such, insofar as the insurers must be reimbursed. Bail Bonds are usually available from vehicle insurers. Alternatively, a Bail Bond is supplied free of charge with AA Five Star Europe.

British Embassy/Consulates*
The British Embassy is located at Madrid 28010, Calle de Fernando el Santo 16 ☎(91) 3190200 (12 lines); consular section, 28004 Madrid, Centro Colón Marqués de la Ensenada 16 ☎(91) 3085201. There are British Consulates in Alicante, Barcelona, Bilbao, Malaga, Seville and Palma (Majorca); there are British Consulates with Honorary Consuls in Santander, Tarragona and Vigo. There is a British Vice-Consulate in Ibiza and a British Vice-Consulate with Honorary Vice-Consul in Menorca.

Children in cars
Child under 12 not permitted to travel as front seat passengers unless using suitable restraint system.

Currency
Visitors may import unlimited amounts of Spanish and foreign currency. Spanish currency up to Ptas 1,000,000 or its equivalent in foreign currency, or any amount declared on arrival, may be exported.

Dimensions and weight restrictions
Private **cars** and towed **trailers** or **caravans** are restricted to the following dimensions - height, 4 metres; width 2.50 metres; length 12 metres. The maximum permitted overall length of private vehicle/trailer or caravan combinations is 12 metres. Trailers with an unladen weight exceeding 750kg must have an independent braking system.

Driving licence
A valid UK or Republic of Ireland EC model licence is acceptable in Spain. The minimum age at which visitors from UK or Republic of Ireland may use a temporarily imported motorcycle (over 75cc) or car is 18 years.
The holder of an older all-green UK licence (in Northern Ireland any licence issued before 1 April 1991) should consider exchanging it for a new-style licence if time allows to avoid any local difficulties. Alternatively these older licences may be accompanied by an International Driving Permit (IDP).**Note** The licence of a Spanish driver who needs glasses to drive is endorsed accordingly. Such drivers must carry a spare pair of glasses in their vehicle. It is strongly recommended that visiting motorists do the same to avoid any misunderstandings with the local authorities.

Foodstuffs*
There are no limits on the importation of foodstuffs obtained duty and tax paid within the EC. Up to 500g of coffee (200g of coffee extract) and 100g of tea (40g of tea extract) purchased duty-free or outside the EC may be imported free of duty and tax. However, coffee bought duty-free or outside the EC cannot be imported by visitors under 15 years of age.

Lights*

Visiting motorists must equip their vehicles with a spare set of vehicle bulbs.

Motoring club*

The **Real Automóvil Club de España** (RACE), which has its headquarters at 28003 Madrid, Calle José Abascal 10 ☎(91) 4473200, is associated with local clubs in a number of provincial towns. The office hours of RACE in Madrid are 08.30-17.30hrs Mon-Thu and 08.30-14.30hrs Fri during the summer (15 Jun-15 Sep) and, for the rest of the year, 08.30-17.30hrs Mon-Fri.

Roads, including holiday traffic

The surfaces of the main roads vary, but on the whole are good. The roads are winding in many places, and at times it is not advisable to exceed 30-35mph. Secondary roads are often rough and winding. Holiday traffic, particularly on the coast road to Barcelona and Tarragona and in the San Sebastian-Donostia area, causes congestion which may be severe at weekends.

In the *Basque* and *Catalan* areas some place names appear on signposts as alternative spellings *eg* San Sebastian-Donostia and Gerona-Girona. The current AA directories and maps show both names.

Spain has some 2,500 miles of dual carriageways, of which over 1,200 miles are motorway toll roads (*autopista*) and the rest are free (*autovías*). Emergency telephones are located every 2km on both.

Speed limits*

Car
Built-up areas 50kph (31mph)
Other roads †90kph (55mph)
††100kph (62mph)
Motorways 120kph (74mph)
Car/caravan/trailer
Built-up areas 50kph (31mph)
Other roads †70kph (43mph) or
††80kph (49mph)
Motorways 80kph (49mph)
†On ordinary roads
††On roads with more than one lane in each direction, a special lane for slow-moving vehicles or wide lanes.

Warning triangles*

In the event of accident or breakdown, the use of two warning triangles is compulsory for vehicles weighing more than 3,500kg (3 tons, 8cwt, 100lbs) and passenger vehicles with more than nine seats (including the driver's). The triangles must be placed on the road in front of and behind the vehicle at a distance of 30 metres (33yds) and be visible from at least 100 metres (110yds). It is strongly recommended that other vehicles carry a warning triangle for use in an emergency to avoid any misunderstandings with the local authorities.

Note A warning triangle is not required for two-wheeled vehicles.

ANDORRA

Andorra is an independent Principality located high in the Pyrenees between France and Spain.

Covering 180 square miles, it has a population of 60,000 and is administered by its own government and independent Legislative Assembly. The constitutional heads of state are its traditional co-princes, the President of France and the Bishop of Seu d'Urgell. Catalan is the official language, but French and Spanish are widely spoken. General regulations for France and Spain apply to Andorra with the following exceptions.

British Consulate*
Andorra comes within the consular district of the British Consul-General at Barcelona.

FACTS AND FIGURES

Capital: Andorra la Vella
Language: Catalan, Spanish and French
IDD Code: 376. To call the UK dial 0*44 (* wait for second dialling tone)
Currency: French Franc (*Fr*1 = 100 centimes) and Spanish Peseta (*Ptas*1 = 100 centimos).
Local time: GMT + 1 (summer GMT + 2)
Emergency services: Fire & Ambulance 118; Police 110
Business hours: variable
Banks: Mon-Fri 09.00-13.00/15.00-17.00 Sat 09.00-12.00

Shops: Daily 09.00-20.00
Average daily temperatures:
Andorra la Vella
Jan 3°C   Jul 19°C
Mar 9°C   Sep 16°C
May 11°C   Nov 6°C
Tourist Information:
UK Andorran Delegation
63 Westover Road
London SW18 2RF
☎ 0181-874 4806 (am if telephoning; personal visit by appointment only)
Camping card: Recommended.

Children in cars
Child under 10 not permitted as front-seat passenger.

Dimensions
The maximum height for vehicles going through tunnels is 3.5 metres.

Driving licence*
A valid UK or Republic of Ireland driving licence is acceptable. The minimum age at which a visitor may use a temporarily imported car or motorcycle is 18 years.

Motoring club*
The **Automobil Club d'Andorra** (ACA) has its head office at Andorra la Vella, Carrer Babot Camp 13 ☎820890.

Roads
The three main roads in Andorra are prefixed 'N' and numbered; side roads are prefixed 'V'. Andorra has no motorways.

Speed limits*
Car, car/caravan combinations
Built-up areas 40kph (24mph)
Other roads 90kph (55mph)
Some villages have a speed limit of 20kph (12mph).

Warning triangle*
The use of a warning triangle is compulsory in the event of an accident or breakdown.

*Additional information will be found in the Continental ABC at the front of the book.

A-Z DIRECTORY

Prices are in Spanish Pesetas Abbreviations: ctra carretera Gl Generalissimo.
Each name preceded by 'El' 'La' or 'Las' is listed under the name that follows it.

North East Coast

The brava, or 'wild' coast, and resorts such as Tossa and Lloret de Mar, have long been a favourite with sun-seekers. Low season can be a perfect time to visit the beautiful coastline, and art lovers are drawn year-long to Figueres' Salvador Dali Museum and historic Girona's impressive cathedral, interesting monuments and medieval Jewish quarter.
On the Mediterranean to the south lies Barcelona, capital of Catalonia. Catalonians are proud of their heritage and language. Host of the 1992 Olympics, this bustling, vital seaport has many faces: literary capital of Spain, shopper's paradise and beach town. Walk along its famous boulevards, the Ramblas, or visit Gaudi's monumental Church of the Holy Family - symbol of the city and its region. The site of the Olympic stadium at Montjuic also boasts several museums and shares spectacular views with its neighbouring hilltop, Tibidabo. The fiesta in September is a colourful carnival famed for its enormous papier-maché figures, its street celebrations and bullfights, and the local sardana dancing.

ARENYS DE MAR Barcelona
Carlitos ctra NII ☎93 7921355
May-Sep 3.5HEC ☼ ♣ ♠ 🏠 ♀ ✗ ⊙ 🅟 🔺 🛁 🐕 ⚡ P 🔳 ⊞ lau ♦ ≜ ⚡S Prices: A450-495 V450-495 ⚏450-495 ▲450-495

BAGUR
See **BEGUR**

BEGUR Girona
Begur ☎972 623201
A terraced site in a dip.
1.4km SE of town and right of the road to Palafrugell, 400m after the turn towards Fornells and Aiguablava.
27 Apr-1 Sep 4HEC ▦ ☼ ♣ ♠ 🏠 ♀ ✗ ⊙ 🅟 🔺 🐕 ⚡ P 🔳 ⊞ lau ♦ ⚡S Prices: A450-560 V450-560 ⚏450-560 ▲450-560

Maset Playa de sa Riera ☎972 623023
A well-kept terraced site, divided into pitches in a beautiful valley.
2km N of Begur. If entering from the W, turn left just before reaching the town.
22 Mar-25 Sep 1.2HEC ▦ ♣ ♠ 🏠 ♀ ✗ ⊙ 🅟 🔺 ⚡ P 🔳 ⊞ ⚙ lau ♦ ⚡S Prices: A530-670 V530-670 ⚏650-840 ▲550-710

BLANES Girona
Bella Terra av Villa de Madrid ☎972 331955
Apr-Sep 8HEC ☼ ♣ ♠ 🏠 ♀ ✗ ⊙ 🅟 🔺 🐕 ⚡ PS 🔳 ⊞ lau

Blanes ☎972 331591
In a pine forest bordering the beach.
On left of the Paseo Villa de Madrid coast road towards town.
15 Apr-Sep 2HEC ☼ ♣ ♠ 🏠 ♀ ✗ ⊙ 🅟 🔺 ⚡ S 🔳 ⊞ lau Prices: A575 pitch 1675

Masia Apdo 95 ☎972 331013
50m inland from Paseo Villa de Madrid coast road.
May-Sep 9HEC ▦ ♣ ♠ 🏠 ♀ ✗ ⊙ 🅟 🔺 🛁 🐕 ⚡ P 🔳 ⊞ lau ♦ ⚡RS ⊞ Prices: A435-575 pitch 1375-1850

Pinar av Villa de Madrid ☎72 331083
Divided into two by the coastal road. Partially meadow under poplars.
1km on Paseo Villa de Madrid coast road.

May-Sep 4HEC ▦ ☼ ♣ ♠ 🏠 ♀ ✗ ⊙ 🅟 🔺 🐕 ⚡ S 🔳 ⊞ lau Prices: A430-570 pitch 1370-1650

S'Abanell av Villa Madrid s/n ☎972 331809
Within a pine wood, a section of which is inland and open to the public.
On either side of the Avenida Villa de Madrid road. Off coast road S of Blanes.
All year 3HEC ☼ ♣ ♠ 🏠 ♀ ✗ ⊙ 🅟 🔺 🏠 ⚡ S 🔳 ⊞ lau Prices: A350-575 pitch 1175-1675

Vora Mar av de Madrid ☎972 330349
Level site with pine trees on sandy beach.
1.5km from Blanes on seaward side of the Paseo Villa de Madrid coast road.
Mar-Sep 2.4HEC ♣ ♠ ⊙ 🅟 🔺 🐕 ⚡ R 🔳 ⊞ lau ♦ ≜ ♀ ✗ ⚡LPS

CABRERA DE MAR Barcelona
Costa de Oro ☎93 7591234
Quiet site bordered by cultivated fields. The beach is reached via a railway underpass.
Lies at Km650 of the N11, on the seaward side, between the road and the railway embankment.
15 May-11 Sep 2HEC ☼ ♣ ♠ ✗ ⊙ 🅟 🔺 ⚡ S 🔳 ⊞ ⚙ lau ♦ ≜ 🔺 ⊞

CALELLA DE LA COSTA Barcelona
Botanic Bona Vista ☎93 7692488
Totally subdivided and well tended terraced site on a hillside, beautifully landscaped. Internal roads steep. Access to beach via pedestrian underpass.
Camping Card Compulsory.
Turn off the N11 at Km665.
All year 3.4HEC ☼ ♣ ♠ ⊙ 🅟 🔺 🔳 ⊞ lau ♦ ≜ ♀ ✗ ⚡PS Prices: A475 V475 ⚏475 ▲475

Far ☎93 7690967
Terraced site on a hillock under deciduous trees with lovely view of Calella and out to sea. Steep internal roads.
For access, travel S before reaching a major left hand bend at Km666 to the right of the N11.
Apr-Sep 2.5HEC ☼ ♣ ♠ 🏠 ♀ ✗ ⊙ 🅟 🔺 🔳 ⊞ lau ♦ 🛁 ⚡PS Prices: A505 V505 ⚏505 ▲505

CASTELL D'ARO Girona
Castell d'Aro ☎972 819699
May-Sep 8HEC ▦ ☼ ♣ ♠ 🏠 ♀ ✗ ⊙ 🅟 🔺 ⚡ P 🔳 ⊞ lau ♦ ⚡RS Prices: A440-545 V440-545 ⚏440-545 ▲440-545

CASTELLÓ D'EMPURIES Girona
Castell-Mar Platja de la Rubina ☎972 450822
10 May-28 Sep 4HEC ▦ ☼ ♣ ♠ 🏠 ♀ ✗ ⊙ 🅟 🔺 🐕 🔺 ⚡ P 🔳 ⊞ lau ♦ ⚡S Prices: A195-325 pitch 2000-3330

Laguna ☎972 450553
Flat grassland site by the sea.
Turn right at Km11 Figueres-Roses road in direction of Sant Pere Pescador and continue, last 4km poorly surfaced lane.
15 Mar-20 Oct 15.6HEC ☼ ♣ ♠ 🏠 ♀ ✗ ⊙ 🅟 🔺 🐕 ⚡ PRS 🔳 ⊞ lau Prices: A503-781 V503-781 ⚏503-781 ▲503-781

Mas-Nou ☎972 454175
Exit from the Figueres-Roses road at Km38.
22 Mar-Sep 7.8HEC ▦ ♣ ♠ 🏠 ✗ ⊙ 🅟 🔺 🐕 ⚡ P 🔳 ⊞ lau ♦ 🛁 Prices: A502-684 V502-684 ⚏502-684 ▲502-684

Nautic Almanta ☎972 454477
Level meadowland, no shade, good facilities, reaching as far as the sea. Alongside the River Fluvia which has been made into a canal. Boating is possible in the canal which flows into the sea.
Turn S at Km11 on C260, approx, halfway along the road and turn E along the track and continue 2.2km.

10 May-28 Sep 22HEC ▦ ⚒ ♠ ℝ ⅊ ⅊ ✕ ⊙ ⊕ ⌀ ⌂ 𝐀 ⥿ PRS ⌲ ⊞ lau
Prices: A300-315 pitch 1640-3180

ESCALA, L' *Girona*
Escala ☎972 770084
Level site, partially under pines.
Within village on the left of the road towards Riells.
22 Mar-8 Sep 1.8HEC ▦ ♠ ℝ ⅊ ⅊ ✕ ⊙ ⊕ ⌀ ⌂ ⌲ ♦ ⥿S Prices:
A350 pitch 1375-2125

Maite Playa Riells ☎972 770544
An extensive site, lying inland, but near the sea, at a small lake.
Partly on a hillock under pine trees.
The access is well signed from the outskirts of L'Escala on the road
towards Cala Montgo.
Jun-15 Sep 6HEC ♦ ℝ ℝ ⅊ ⅊ ✕ ⊙ ⊕ ⌀ ⥿ S ⌲ ⊞ Prices: A525
pitch 420

ESTARTIT, L' *Girona*
Castell Montgri ☎972 758630
On a large terraced meadow in pine woodlands.
100m N of GE road from Torroella de Montgri and about 0.5km
before L'Estartit on a hillock.
10 May-12 Oct 25HEC ▦ ♦ ℝ ℝ ⅊ ⅊ ✕ ⊙ ⊕ ⌀ ⌂ ⌂ 𝐀 ⥿ P ⌲ ⊞
lau ♦ ⥿S Prices: A195-325 pitch 2155-3590
See advertisement under Colour Section

Estartit Cap Villa Primavera 12 ☎972 758909
In a valley on sloping ground which is rather steep in places. Some
terraces, shaded by pine trees.
It is located about 200m from the church and the road from
Torroella de Montgri.
Apr-Sep 2.5HEC ⋰⋰ ♦ ℝ ℝ ⅊ ⅊ ✕ ⊙ ⊕ ⌀ ⌂ ⥿ P ⌲ ⊞ lau ♦ ⥿RS
Prices: A389-556 V389-556 ⌸412-588 𝐀355-508

Medes ☎972 751805
Quiet holiday site in rural surroundings with clearly marked pitches
and good modern facilities.
Turn right off GE641 from Torroella di Montgri by Km5 and continue
for 1.5km .
All year 2.6HEC ▦ ⚒ ♠ ℝ ⅊ ⅊ ✕ ⊙ ⊕ ⌀ ⥿ P ⌲ ⊞ ⊞ ⊘ lau Prices:
A556 V1177

Molino ☎972 758629
Divided into several sections of open meadowland near the beach on
grassland with young poplars. The reconstructed mill is a landmark.
Approaching from Torroella de Montgri turn right on entering
L'Estartit and follow signs.
May-Sep 10HEC ▦ ⚒ ♠ ℝ ℝ ⅊ ⅊ ✕ ⊙ ⊕ ⌀ ⥿ S ⌲ ⊞ lau ♦ ⥿LR
Prices: A475 V475 ⌸475 𝐀475

GAVÁ *Barcelona*
Albatros ☎93 6330695
In a shady pine wood divided into pitches on partly level, partly
uneven terrain by the sea.
For access, turn off the C246, dual carriageway at Km15 and drive
towards the sea.
May-27 Sep 15HEC ⋰⋰ ♦ ℝ ℝ ⅊ ⅊ ✕ ⊙ ⊕ ⌀ ⌂ ⥿ PS ⌲ ⊞ lau

Tortuga Ligera ☎93 6580504
Apr-Sep 22HEC ▦ ⋰⋰ ♦ ℝ ℝ ⅊ ⅊ ✕ ⊙ ⊕ ⌀ ⌂ ⌂ ⌂ ⥿ PS ⌲ ⊞ lau
Prices: A583-615 pitch 1471-2675

GUILS DE CERDANYA *Girona*
Pirineus ctra de Guils de Cerdanya, Km 2 ☎972 881062
20 Jun-14 Sep 5HEC ▦ ♦ ℝ ℝ ⅊ ⅊ ✕ ⊙ ⊕ ⌀ ⥿ P ⌲ ⊞ ⊘ lau ♦ ⥿R
Prices: A642 pitch 2033

LLANÇÁ *Girona*
Ombra ☎972 380335
All year 1.1HEC ℝ ℝ ⅊ ⅊ ⊙ ⊕ ⌀ ⌀ 𝐀 ⌲ ⊞ lau ♦ ⥿S ⊞

LLORET DE MAR *Girona*
Lloret ctra Vieja de Vidreras ☎972 365483
500m from the sea.
Jun-Sep 2.3HEC ⋰⋰ ⚒ ℝ ℝ ⅊ ⅊ ✕ ⊙ ⊕ ⌀ ⥿ P ⌲ ⊞ lau ♦ ℝ ⅊ ✕ ⌀ ⥿
⥿S ⊞

MALGRAT DE MAR *Barcelona*
Naciones ☎93 7654153
Level site divided by a small stream. Partially dusty, another part in
meadow under high poplars.
Approach road passes through Camping Malgrat de Mar.
Apr-Sep 9.6HEC ▦ ⚒ ♠ ℝ ℝ ⅊ ⅊ ✕ ⊙ ⊕ ⌀ ⥿ S ⌲ ⊞ lau ♦ ⛺

MASNOU, EL *Barcelona*
Masnou carreteta Nacional 11 ☎93 5551503
Inland from the N11 at Km633.
All year 2HEC ▦ ♦ ℝ ℝ ⅊ ⅊ ✕ ⊙ ⊕ ⌀ ⌂ ⌂ ⌂ ⥿ P ⌲ ⊞ lau ♦ ⥿S
Prices: A615 pitch 615

PALAFRUGELL *Girona*
At LLAFRANC
Kim's ☎972 301156
Terraced site with winding drives, lying on the wooded slopes of a
narrow valley leading to the sea.
For access, turn right off the Palafrugell-Tamariu road, follow a wide
tarred road for 1km, past the El Paranso Hotel and head towards
Llafranc. 0.4km from sea.
May-Sep 5.3HEC ▦ ⋰⋰ ⚒ ♠ ℝ ℝ ⅊ ⅊ ✕ ⊙ ⊕ ⌀ ⌂ ⌂ ⥿ P ⌲ ⊞ lau
♦ ⥿S Prices: A475-650 V450-650 ⌸540-790 𝐀540-750

At MONTRÁS(3km SW)
Relax-Ge ☎972 301549
Level meadow under poplars and olive trees.
Turn off the C255 at Km38.7. 4km to the sea.
Jun-1 Sep 2.7HEC ▦ ♦ ℝ ℝ ⅊ ⅊ ✕ ⊙ ⊕ ⌂ ⥿ P ⌲ ⊞ lau Prices:
A482 pitch 1284

At PLAYA DE ENSUEÑOS
Tamariu ☎972 620422
Terraced site with mixture of high young pines.
Turn towards site at beach parking area and continue 300m.
May-Sep 2HEC ▦ ♦ ℝ ℝ ⅊ ⅊ ✕ ⊙ ⊕ ⌀ ⥿ PS ⌲ ⊞ lau

PALAMÓS *Girona*
Castell Park ☎972 315263
Level and gently sloping meadow with poplars and pine woodland on
a hill.
At Km40 about 100m to the right of the C255 to Palamós and 3km
S of Montras.
Apr-Sep 4.5HEC ▦ ♦ ℝ ℝ ⅊ ⅊ ✕ ⊙ ⊕ ⌀ ⥿ P ⌲ ⊞ lau ♦ ⥿S
Prices: A395-500 ⌸450-550 𝐀410-510

Coma Cami Vell de la Fosca 2 ☎972 314638
Sloping terraced terrain with young deciduous trees and isolated
pines. 0.8km from the sea.
In N outskirts turn seawards off the C255 near the RENAULT garage.
Apr-Sep 4.2HEC ▦ ♦ ℝ ℝ ⅊ ⅊ ✕ ⊙ ⊕ ⌀ ⌂ 𝐀 ⥿ P ⌲ ⊞ lau ♦ ⥿S

Internacional Palamós Playa de la Fosca ☎972 314736
Signposted.
Apr-12 Oct 5.3HEC ♦ ℝ ℝ ⅊ ⅊ ✕ ⊙ ⊕ ⌀ 𝐀 ⌲ ⊞ lau ♦ ⌀ ⥿S

Palamós ctra la Fosca 12 ☎972 314296
By the sea.
22 Mar-Sep 5.5HEC ▥ ⠸⠿ ♠ℝ⚡⚡✕☉⌑∅⛺⚑ₜPS✓⊞
lau Prices: A535 pitch 1177-1980

Vilarromá calle del Mar ☎972 314375
Clean and tidy site, almost completely divided into pitches.
Turn off on the eastern outskirts of Palamós near big petrol station.
May-25 Sep 1.8HEC ⠸⠿ ♠ℝ⚡⚡✕☉⌑∅⛺⚑✓⊞ lau ♠ ₜS
Prices: A578-631 V578-631 ⊞578-738 ▲578-738

At **CALONGE**(5km W)

Cala Gogo ☎972 651564
Terraced site in tall pine woodland and poplars with some good views of the sea. Underpass across to section of site with private beach. Some internal dusty roads
Access from Palamós 4 km S on coastal road C253, entrance to site on right shortly after Km47.
Apr-Sep 16HEC ▥ ♠ℝ⚡⚡✕☉⌑∅⛺⚑▲ₜPS✓⊞ lau
Prices: A476-733 V492-813 ⊞637-1161 ▲519-979

Internacional de Calonge ☎972 651233
Set on a pine covered hill overlooking the sea within easy reach of a sandy beach.
Apr-Oct 11HEC ⠸⠿ ♠ℝ⚡⚡✕☉⌑∅⛺▲ₜPS✓⊞ lau Prices:
A444-717 V481-797 ⊞610-851 ▲578-851

PALS *Girona*

Cypsela ☎972 667696
Well-kept grassy site in a pine wood.
For access, turn sea N of Pals and follow road towards Playa de Pals, then turn left after Km3.
15 May-28 Sep 20HEC ⠸⠿ ♠ℝ⚡⚡✕☉⌑∅⛺ₜP✓◪⊞⌀
lau ♠ ⚑ ₜS Prices: A599-749 pitch 1969-2461

Mas Patoxas ctra de Pala Frugell, a Torroella Km5 ☎972 636928
Apr-Sep 5.5HEC ▥ ⚡ℝ⚡⚡✕☉⌑∅⚑▲⛺▲ₜP✓⊞ lau
Prices: A400-650 pitch 1300-1850

At PLAYA DE PALS

Playa Brava ☎972 636894
On level terrain adjoining pine woodlands, golf course, rivers and sea.
From N end of village of Pals turn towards sea and Playa de Pals.
15 May-24 Sep 11HEC ▦ ♦ ⚑ ☒ ☘ ♀ ✕ ⊙ ☒ ⌀ ₹ PRS ☎ ⊞ ⚡ lau
Prices: A193-278 pitch 2210-3157

PINEDA DE MAR *Barcelona*

Camell Los Naranjos 12 ☎93 7671520
Surrounded by deciduous trees next to a small wood owned by the Taurus Hotel.
Turn off the N11 at Km670 and drive along av de los Naranjos in direction of sea.
Mar-Sep 2.2HEC ☒☒ ♦ ⌂ ☒ ☘ ♀ ✕ ⊙ ☒ ⌀ ₹ PS ☎ ⊞ lau ♦ ☰ Prices:
A525 pitch 1300

Enmar ☎08397 7671730
Leave autopista at exit 9 (Lloret and Malgrat) and continue towards Pineda de Mar.
Mar-Oct 2.5HEC ☒☒ ⌆ ⌂ ☒ ☘ ♀ ✕ ⊙ ☒ ⌀ ⌀ ₹ PS ☎ ⊞ lau

PLATJA D'ARO, LA *Girona*

Valldaro ☎72 817515
Extensive level meadowland under poplars, pines and eucalyptus trees. Some large pitches without shade.
Site lies on the left of the GE662 towards Castell and Santa Cristina d 'Aro at Km4.
Apr-Sep 18HEC ▦ ♦ ⌂ ☒ ☘ ♀ ✕ ⊙ ☒ ⌀ ☎ ☰ ₹ P ☎ ⊞ lau ♦ ₹S
Prices: A535 pitch 1498-2675

PUERTO DE LA SELVA *Girona*

Port de la Selva ☎972 387287
Level, grassland site with young poplar trees.
1.5km from the village, in a valley off the Puerto de la Selva to Cadaques road.
Jun-Sep 3HEC ♦ ⌂ ☒ ☘ ♀ ✕ ⊙ ☒ ⌀ ₹ P ☎ ⊞ lau ♦ ₹S

PUIGCERDÀ *Girona*

Stel ctra Puigcerdà-Llivia ☎972 882361
Modern campsite in the Pyrenees on level land. First class sanitary installations.
20 Jun-Sep 7HEC ▦ ⌆ ⌂ ☒ ☘ ♀ ✕ ⊙ ☒ ⌀ ⌀ ₹ P ☎ ⊞ lau ♦ ₹LR
Prices: A642 pitch 2000

RIPOLL *Girona*

Solana del Ter ☎972 701062
May-Oct 8.5HEC ▦ ⌆ ⌂ ☒ ♀ ✕ ⊙ ☒ ₹ P ☎ ⊞ lau ♦ ☒ ⌀ Prices:
A600 pitch 1100

SANT ANTONI DE CALONGE *Girona*

Costa Brava ☎972 650222
Level site with tall pine woodland partially subdivided under deciduous trees.
From Calonge de les Gavarres turn off C253 S of Calonge. Site lies behind the hotel.
Jun-Sep 2.4HEC ▦ ♦ ⌂ ☒ ☘ ♀ ✕ ⊙ ☒ ₹ P ☎ ⊞ lau ♦ ⌀ ₹S

Euro ☎72 650879
May-Sep 13HEC ▦ ♦ ⌂ ☒ ☘ ♀ ✕ ⊙ ☒ ₹ PS ☎ ⊞ lau ♦ ⌀ Prices:
A289-375 pitch 2033-3173

Treumal ☎972 651095
Entrance on Sant Feli…-Platja d'Aro-Palamós road.
22 Mar-12 Oct 6HEC ▦ ☒☒ ♦ ⌂ ☒ ☘ ♀ ✕ ⊙ ☒ ⌀ ⌀ ₹ PS ☎ ⊞ lau
Prices: A429-715 V468-780 ☎660-1110 ▲588-980

SANTA SUSANA *Barcelona*

Bon Répos ☎93 7678475
In pine woodland between railway and the beach with some sunshade roofing.
Turn off the N11 at Km681 and approach via the underpass (height 2.5m) just before reaching the beach.
All year 6HEC ▦ ☒☒ ⌆ ♦ ⌂ ☒ ☘ ♀ ✕ ⊙ ☒ ⌀ ☎ ₹ PS ☎ ⊞ lau
Prices: A630 pitch 2300

SANT CEBRIÁ DE VALLALTA *Barcelona*

Verneda av Maresme ☎93 7630657
Inland and among tall trees.
Leave the N11 Girona-Barcelona road at the far end of Sant Pol de Mar, turn inland at Km670. Continue for 2km to edge of the village and short of the bridge over the River Vallala turn right.
Apr-Sep 1.6HEC ☒☒ ♦ ⌂ ☒ ☘ ♀ ✕ ⊙ ☒ ⌀ ₹ P ☎ ⊞ lau ♦ ☰ Prices:
A460 V460 ☎460 ▲460

SANT FELIU DE GUIXOLS *Girona*

Sant Pol ctra Palamos ☎972 321019
In wooded surroundings near the beach with good facilities.
800m from the town centre towards Palamos.
24 May-Sep 1.5HEC ▦ ♦ ⌂ ☒ ☘ ♀ ✕ ⊙ ☒ ☎ ₹ P ☎ lau ♦ ☒ ✕ ⌀ ₹S
Prices: A685-725 pitch 700-800

SANT PERE PESCADOR *Girona*

Amfora Mas Sopas ☎972 520540
A pleasant site, directly on the beach, with good modern sanitary facilities. There are plentiful leisure facilities and English is spoken.
8 May-Sep 8.1HEC ▦ ♦ ⌂ ☒ ☘ ♀ ✕ ⊙ ☒ ☎ ☎ ₹ PRS ☎ ⊞ lau
Prices: A400 pitch 1590-2975

Aquarius ☎972 520003
Level meadowland. Partially in shade, quiet well organised site by the lovely sandy beach of Bahia de Rosas.
Travel in direction of L'Escala and turn towards the beach following signs.
14 Mar-25 Oct 6HEC ▦ ⌆ ⌂ ☒ ☘ ♀ ✕ ⊙ ☒ ⌀ ₹ S ☎ ⊞ lau Prices:
A470-850 V470-850 ☎470-850 ▲470-850

Ballena Alegre 2 ☎93 520302
Extensive site near wide sandy beach with dunes. Large shopping complex. Washing and sanitary facilities have recently undergone extensive modernisation.
Access from L'Escala to San Martin de Ampurias, then onward to site in 2km .
All year 24HEC ▦ ⌆ ⌂ ☒ ☘ ♀ ✕ ⊙ ☒ ⌀ ☎ ☎ lau ♦ ₹PRS Prices:
pitch 1700-3500 (incl 3 persons)
See advertisement under Colour Section

Dunas ☎972 520400
Level extensive grassland site with young poplars, some of medium height on the beach, totally subdivided.
It lies 5km SE of village. If approaching from L'Escala follow an asphalt road to San Martin, then follow a dusty earth track for 2.5km.
10 May-26 Sep 24HEC ▦ ⌆ ⌂ ☒ ☘ ♀ ✕ ⊙ ☒ ⌀ ☰ ▲ ₹ PRS ☎ ⊞ lau
Prices: A350 pitch 1400-3200

Palmeras ctra de la Platja ☎972 520506
On level grassland with plenty of shade. Recently installed modern sanitary blocks and heated swimming pool.
Off the road from Sant Pere Pescador to the beach about 200m from the sea.
Apr-15 Oct 3HEC ▦ ♦ ⌂ ☒ ☘ ♀ ✕ ⊙ ☒ ⌀ ₹ PS ☎ ⊞ lau Prices:
A300-400 pitch 1225-1800

SITGES *Barcelona*

Roca ☎93 8940043
On three terraces with a view of Sitges. Shade is provided by pines and deciduous trees. Separate section for young people. 1km from the sea.
Camping Card Compulsory.
Turn off the C246 (Barcelona-Tarragona) in the direction of Sant Pere de Ribes/San Pedro de Ribas. In 15m turn right to site.
Apr-Sep 2HEC ☒☒ ♦ ⌂ ☒ ☘ ♀ ✕ ⊙ ☒ ⌀ ☎ ⊞ lau ♦ ✕ ₹PS

TARADELL *Barcelona*

Vall Cami de la Vallmissand ☎93 8126336
In the mountains near the Guilleries-Montseny, with good recreational facilities.
All year 8HEC ▦ ☒☒ ⌆ ⌂ ☒ ☘ ♀ ✕ ⊙ ☒ ⌀ ☰ ☎ ₹ P ☎ ⊞ lau ♦ ₹L
Prices: pitch 1500-1800

TORROELLA DE MONTGRI *Girona*

Delfin Verde ☎972 758450
On undulating ground with some pine trees, and an open meadow beside the long sandy beach.
Turn left off the road to Begur approx 2km S of Torroella de Montgri, and head towards Maspinell following a wide asphalt road 4.8km towards the sea.
22 Mar-21 Sep 35HEC ▥ ⊕ ⋔ ⚑ ⚑ ⋣ × ⊙ ⚑ ⌀ ⚑ ⋨ PS ⚿ ⊞ lau ◆ ⋨R Prices: A325 pitch 1550-3350

Sirena ☎972 758542
Level site with some grass near the sea.
Approaching from Toroella de Montgri turn right about 400m from 'Estartit' sign at Km1 and continue 300m.
May-Oct 2HEC ▥ ⊕ ⋔ ⚑ ⚑ ⋣ × ⊙ ⚑ ⌀ ⚑ ⋨ PS ⚿ ⊞ lau ◆ ⋨S

TOSSA DE MAR *Girona*

Cala Llevadó ☎972 340314
Magnificent terraced site with hairpin roads overlooking three bays, all suitable for bathing. Narrow, winding drives which are quite steep in parts. Separate section for caravans.
Take the coast road for about 4km towards Lloret de Mar and turn towards the sea.
May-Sep 14HEC ⠿⠿ ◆ ⋔ ⚑ ⚑ ⋣ × ⊙ ⚑ ⚑ ⚑ ▲ ⋨ PS ⚿ ⊞ lau Prices: A555-790 V555-790 ⚑630-860 ▲555-790

Can Marti ☎972 340851
Pleasant, unspoilt site in a partly wooded location. Good modern facilities. English spoken.
1km from the sea.
May-Sep 10HEC ▥ ◆ ⋔ ⚑ ⚑ ⋣ × ⊙ ⚑ ⌀ ⋨ P ⊞ lau ◆ ⋨S Prices: A575-725 ⚑625-750 ▲625-750

Tossa ctra Llagostera ☎972 340547
On a meadow in a quiet, isolated valley, in a deciduous forest. 3km from the sea.
3km SW near the GE681 (Tossa de Mar-Llagostera), in 600m to site along an unmade road.
Apr-Sep 9.5HEC ⠿⠿ ◆ ⋔ ⚑ ⚑ ⋣ × ⊙ ⚑ ⌀ ⚑ ⚑ ⋨ PS ⚿ ⊞ lau

VILADECANS *Barcelona*

Ballena Alegre I ☎93 6330642
Apr-Sep 10HEC ▥ ⊕ ⋔ ⚑ ⚑ ⋣ × ⊙ ⚑ ⌀ ⚑ ⋨ PS ⚿ ⊞ lau Prices: A575 V750 ⚑750 ▲750
See advertisement under Colour Section

Toro Bravo Autovia de Castelldefels, Km11 ☎93 6373462
Level site in extensive pine woodland area by the sea. To the left of the access road on the banks of a stagnant canal about 1km long is a leisure and sports complex with many facilities including evening entertainment in the season.
Leave the C246 (Barcelona-Castelldeféls), at Km11 and continue towards the sea for 1km.
All year 30HEC ▥ ◆ ⋔ ⚑ ⚑ ⋣ × ⊙ ⚑ ⌀ ⚑ ⚑ ⋨ PS ⚿ ⊞ lau Prices: A600-650 ⚑650-700 ▲650-700

VILALLONGA DE TER *Girona*

Conca de Ter ctra Camprodon-Setcases ☎972 740629
All year 1.2HEC ▥ ◆ ⋔ ⚑ ⚑ ⋣ × ⊙ ⚑ ⌀ ⚑ ⋨ PR ⚿ ⊞ lau Prices: A550 pitch 1495

VILANOVA I LA GELTRÚ *Barcelona*

Vilanova Park ☎93 8933402
All year 50HEC ▥ ⊙ ◆ ⋔ ⚑ ⚑ ⋣ × ⊙ ⚑ ⌀ ⚑ ⚑ ⚑ ⋨ P ⚿ ⊞ lau Prices: A830 V830 ⚑830 ▲830
See advertisement under Colour Section

Central

The La Mancha plains and Don Quixote's windmills, massive mountain ranges, pastures, wheatfields, vineyards, and ancient forests are some of the regions's contrasts.
Here are St Teresa's walled city of Avila, Cáceres' exceptional old quarter, Guadalajara's outstanding Renaissance palace,

---

Salamanca, with its university and beautiful square and Segovia's dramatic Roman aqueduct and 14th-century palace.
Architectural and artistic riches continue with Cuenca's hanging houses and Teruel, part of which, like Toledo, belongs to the Heritage of Mankind. The framed walled city of Toledo, with its mosque, synagogue and medieval cathedral, has its associations with El Cid and contains El Greco's house and museum.
Spain's vital capital, Madrid, is home to the Prado and numerous other museums, a colourful old town, lovely parks, squares and palaces, while a short drive away lie the Sierra of Guadarrama with its forests, wild animals and birds of prey and the Pedriza del Manzanares' geological wonderland.

ALBA DE TORMES *Salamanca*

Tormes av Dehesa Boyal ☎923 160998
Camping Card Compulsory.
All year 2.2HEC ▥ ⊕ ⋔ ⚑ ⚑ ⋣ × ⊙ ⚑ ⋨ R ⚿ ⊞ lau ◆ ⚑ × ⌀ ⚑ ⋨P Prices: A350 V350 ⚑375 ▲350-375

ALDEANUEVA DE LA VERA *Cáceres*

Yuste ☎927 560910
Meadowland with dense woodland on a hill above two valleys.
300m S of C501 at Km47.1.
Apr-Sep 3HEC ▥ ◆ ⋔ ⚑ ⚑ ⋣ × ⊙ ⚑ ⌀ ⋨ P ⊞ lau ◆ ⋨R

ARANJUEZ *Madrid*

Soto del Castillo ctra de Andalucia 1 ☎91 8911395
Site developed into two parts with trees and lawns in large castle park.
Turn off NIV at Km46. In the village 200m beyond FIRESTONE petrol station turn sharp NE and continue for 1km.
Apr-Sep 3.3HEC ▥ ◆ ⋔ ⚑ ⚑ ⋣ × ⊙ ⚑ ⌀ ⚑ ⋨ PR ⚿ ⊞ lau Prices: A525-575 V425-475 ⚑600-650 ▲450-500

BURGO DE OSMA, EL *Soria*

Pedriza ☎975 340806
In an orchard on rising ground.
Turn off N122 (Soria-Aranda de Duero), turn left in town and follow signs.
Jun-Oct 3HEC ▥ ⊙ ◆ ⋔ ⚑ ⋣ × ⊙ ⚑ ⌀ ⚿ ⊞ lau ◆ ⚑ × ⋨PR ⊞

CUENCA *Cuenca*

Cuenca ctra Cuidad Bucautada Km 8 ☎969 231656
15 Mar-15 Dec 23HEC ▥ ⊕ ⋔ ⚑ ⚑ ⋣ × ⊙ ⚑ ⌀ ⚑ ⋨ P ⚿ ⊞ lau ◆ ⋨LR Prices: A524 V481 ⚑588 ▲481

FUENTE DE SAN ESTEBAN, LA *Salamanca*

Cruce ☎923 440130
Useful transit site.
On N620 at Km291.
15 Jun-15 Sep 0.5HEC ▥ ⊕ ⋔ ⚑ ⚑ ⋣ × ⊙ ⚑ ⌀ ⚑ ⋨ P ⚿ ⊞ lau Prices: A375 V375 ⚑450 ▲300

GARGANTILLA DE LOZOYA *Madrid*

Monte Holiday ☎91 8695065
Turn off N1 (Burgos-Madrid) at Km69 towards Cotos and continue for 10km.
All year 30HEC ▥ ⊙ ◆ ⋔ ⚑ ⚑ ⋣ × ⊙ ⚑ ⌀ ⋨ P ⚿ ⊞ lau ◆ ⋨LR Prices: A535 V535 ⚑535 ▲535

GETAFE *Madrid*

Alpha ☎91 6958069
All year 4.8HEC ⠿⠿ ◆ ⋔ ⚑ ⚑ ⋣ × ⊙ ⚑ ⌀ ⚑ ⋨ P ⚿ ⊞ lau Prices: A615 pitch 685

MADRID *Madrid*

Arco Iris ☎91 6160387
From M40 (Madrid ring road) take exit 36 to Boadilla del Monte and continue towards Villaviciosa to Km12.
All year 4HEC ▥ ⠿⠿ ◆ ⋔ ⚑ ⚑ ⋣ × ⊙ ⚑ ⌀ ⚑ ⚑ ⋨ LP ⚿ ⊞ lau Prices: A600 ⚑625

Osuna av de Logrono ☎91 7410510
On long stretch of land, shade being provided by pines, acacias and maple. Some noise from airfield, road and railway.
If approaching from the town centre take N11 road and drive towards Barajas for about 7.5km. At Km1 in 300m and after railway underpass turn right.
All year 23HEC ▦ ♦ ♠ ⚑ ⚎ ♥ ✗ ⊙ ▣ ∅ ☎ ⊞ lau ♦ ✗ ∅ ≞
Prices: A600 V600 ♣525-600

MALPARTIDA DE PLASENCIA Cáceres
Parque Natural de Monfrague ctra Trujillo ☎927 459220
All year 7HEC ▦ ⁚⁚⁚ ⚑ ♠ ⚎ ⚎ ✗ ⊙ ▣ ∅ ≞ ⚑ Ａ ⚑ P ⊞ ⊞ lau
Prices: A480 V480 ♣480 Ａ480

MÉRIDA Badajoz
Lago de Proserpina Apdo 121 ☎924 313236
Apr-15 Sep 5.5HEC ▦ ⁚⁚⁚ ⚑ ♦ ♠ ⚎ ⚎ ✗ ⊙ ▣ ∅ ⚑ L ⊞ lau ♦ ✗
⚑P Prices: A400 ♣400 Ａ400

SANTA MARTA DE TORMES Salamanca
Regio ctra Salamanca/Madrid Km4 ☎923 138888
Divided into several fields.
100m from the N501 (Salamanca-Avila) behind Hotel Jardin-Regio.
All year 3HEC ⚑ ♠ ⚎ ⚎ ✗ ⊙ ▣ ∅ ⚑ P ⊞ ⊞ lau ♦ ✗ ≞ Prices:
A260-425 ♣260-425 Ａ260-425

SEGOVIA Segovia
Acueducto ☎921 425000
SE next to N601 at Km112
Apr-Sep 3HEC ▦ ♦ ♠ ⚎ ⚎ ♥ ✗ ⊙ ▣ ∅ ☎ ⚑ P ⊞ ⊞ lau ♦ ✗ ⚑R
Prices: A450 pitch 1500

TOLEDO Toledo
Greco ☎925 220090
Few shady terraces on slope leading down to the River Tajo. On SW outskirts of town.
Approaching from the town centre take the C401, Carretera Comarcal and drive SW for about 2km. Turn right at Km28 and drive 300m towards Puebla de Montalban.
All year 2.5HEC ⁚⁚⁚ ⚑ ♠ ⚎ ⚎ ✗ ⊙ ▣ ∅ ⚑ PR ⊞ ⊞ lau Prices: A550 V550 ♣625 Ａ570

South East Coast

The Costa Blanca is a household name; Benidorm a tourist mecca. South of Alicante, tourism is less developed and, inland, there are lemon and orange groves and picturesque mountain towns.
A busy port and relatively unspoiled, Alicante has a cathedral and museum of 20th-century art, and there are tremendous views from its fascinating castle. Roman remains surround Tarragona, whose medieval walled city has a Gothic cathedral, interesting palace and architectural museum. Journey out to the Monastery of Poblet inside its three perimeter walls and the Abbey of Santa Creus, burial place of the kings of Aragon.
Valencia, home of paella, is Spain's third largest city with a countryside criss-crossed by ancient irrigation channels. Numerous historic buildings include a cathedral with the legendary Holy Grail, beautiful bridges and gardens and many museums. The Fallas - a fortnight of celebrations - take place in mid-March. Inland, Requena has a moorish castle, medieval walls and the house of El Cid.

ALCANAR Tarragona
Mare Nostrum ☎977 737179
Gently sloping towards the sea with pines, olive and deciduous trees.
Turn towards the sea off the N340 at Km58.3.
All year 1.4HEC ▦ ♦ ♠ ⚎ ⚎ ✗ ⊙ ▣ ∅ ⚑ S ⊞ ⊞ lau ♦ ✗

ALCOCEBER Castellón
Playa Tropicana ☎964 412463
On a 500m long sandy beach 3km from the village.

For access, leave motorway at exit 44, then drive 3km N on the CN340 and turn towards the sea at Km1018.
15 Mar-Oct 3.1HEC ▦ ♦ ♠ ⚎ ⚎ ♥ ✗ ⊙ ▣ ∅ ☎ ⚑ PS ⊞ ⊞ ∅ lau

Ribamar Partida Ribamar s/n ☎964 414165
Quiet wooded site between sea and mountains. Individual pitches.
22 Mar-28 Sep 2.2HEC ♦ ⚑ ♠ ⚎ ♥ ✗ ⊙ ▣ ∅ ⚑ P ⊞ ⊞ lau ♦ ⚑S
Prices: A338-530 V338-530 ♣411-642 Ａ411-642

ALTEA Alicante
Cap Blanch Playa del Albir 25 ☎96 5845946
A new site on Albir beach.
All year 4HEC ♦ ♦ ♠ ⚎ ♥ ✗ ⊙ ▣ ☎ ⊞ ⊞ lau ♦ ⚑ ∅ ≞ ⚑S Prices:
A600 pitch 24000

AMETLLA DE MAR, L' Tarragona
Nautic c Libertad ☎977 456110
Terraced with pines, palms and olives and has uneven stony ground. Has own beach.
Turn right off N340 (Tarragona-Valencia) at Km20.1, take TV3025 and continue to railway station via flyover and level crossing. Turn right and take third road on left. Access road has 10% gradient.
15 Mar-15 Oct 8HEC ▦ ⁚⁚⁚ ♦ ♠ ⚎ ⚎ ✗ ⊙ ▣ ∅ ☎ ⚑ A ⚑ LPS ⊞
⊞ lau

BENICARLÓ Castellón
Alegria del Mar ctra Valencia/Barcelona 340, KM 136 ☎964 470871
All year 0.7HEC ▦ ⚑ ♠ ⚎ ✗ ⊙ ▣ ∅ ⚑ PRS ⊞ ⊞ lau Prices:
A200-400 ♣200-400 Ａ200-400

BENICASIM Castellón
Bonterra av Barcelona 47 ☎964 300007
Between the railway line and avenida de Barcelona with a number of deciduous trees.
300m N towards Las Villas de Benicasim.
Etr-Sep 5HEC ▦ ⁚⁚⁚ ⚑ ♠ ⚎ ♥ ✗ ⊙ ▣ ∅ ☎ ⚑ P ⊞ ⊞ lau ♦ ⚑S
Prices: A210-420 pitch 1760-2200

BENIDORM Alicante
Arena Blanca av Rincon de Loix Sin ☎96 5861889
All year 2.5HEC ▦ ♦ ♠ ⚎ ⚎ ✗ ⊙ ▣ ∅ ≞ ♣ A ⚑ PS ⊞ ⊞ lau
Prices: pitch 850-1500 (incl 2 persons)

Armanello av de la Comunidad Valencia ☎96 5853100
Divided by bushes with large pitches on terraces under olive and palm trees next to a small orange grove.
For access turn off the N332 at Km123.1 N of the town.
All year 16HEC ▦ ♦ ♠ ⚎ ⚎ ✗ ⊙ ▣ ∅ ≞ ♣ A ⚑ PS ⊞ ⊞ lau
Prices: A500 pitch 1500

Benisol av de la Comunidad ☎96 5851673
All year 7HEC ⁚⁚⁚ ⚑ ♠ ⚎ ✗ ⊙ ▣ ∅ ☎ ♣ ⚑ P ⊞ ⊞ lau
Prices: pitch 475-500

BENISA Alicante
Fanadix ctra Calpe-Moraira Km 5 ☎96 5747307
Terraced site completely divided into pitches.
10km E & 400m from the sea. Access off AV-1445.
Apr-Sep 15.7HEC ⁚⁚⁚ ♦ ♠ ⚎ ♥ ✗ ⊙ ▣ ∅ ⚑ P ⊞ ⊞ lau ♦ ≞ ≞ ⚑S

CALPE Alicante
Viña de Calpe ☎96 5831551
Level site with sunshade roofing.
1.5km towards Benisa and turn inland towards Cometa.
All year 2HEC ♠ ⚎ ✗ ⊙ ▣ ☎ ⚑ P ⊞ ▣ ⊞ ∅ lau ♦ ∅ ⚑S

CAMBRILS Tarragona
Playa Cambrils ☎977 361490
Divided into pitches, lying on both sides of the coast road.
Drive 2km N of the town towards Salou and W of the bridge over the river.
15 Mar-12 Oct 12HEC ⁚⁚⁚ ♦ ♠ ⚎ ⚎ ♥ ✗ ⊙ ▣ ∅ ☎ ♣ ⚑ PS ⊞ ⊞ lau
Prices: A423-620 V423-620 ♣423-620 Ａ423-620

CAMPELLO *Alicante*
Costa Blanca c Convento s/n, Nacional 332 Km121.5 ☎96 5630670
On most level ground scattered with old olive and eucalyptus trees. The Alicante-Denia railway line runs behind the camp.
For access turn off the N332 at Km94.2 next to the big petrol station, and drive along a narrow gravel track towards the sea for 0.5km.
15 Apr-15 Sep 1.1HEC ⫶⫶⫶ ♣ ⋔ ⛺ ⵌ ✗ ⊙ ⚑ ⊘ 🛖 ⬤ ▲ ⋜ ⫚ P ☎ ⊞ lau ♦ ⋜S Prices: A350-500 V350-500 ⬤500-700 ▲300-400

CUNIT *Tarragona*
Mar de Cunit Playa Cunit ☎977 674058
Jun-Sep 2HEC ⫶⫶⫶ ⤓⥁ ⋔ ⛺ ⵌ ✗ ⊙ ⚑ ⊘ 🛖 ⋜ S ☎ ⊞ lau ♦ ⊞

DAIMUS *Valencia*
Aventura ctra Platja Daimus ☎96 2818330
In wooded surroundings on a safe, sandy beach.
Mar-Sep 1.8HEC ⫶⫶⫶ ♣ ⋔ ⛺ ⵌ ✗ ⊙ ⚑ ⊘ 🛖 ⋜ P ☎ ⊞ lau ♦ ⋜S
Prices: A471-610 pitch 1500-2000

DENIA *Alicante*
Marinas Les Bovetes, Nord-A / 1 Los Angeles ☎03700 5781446
For access turn off the N332 in Vergel and drive E on the Denia road for 4km . Turn N, cross the P1324, turn right near the beach and continue for 200m.
Apr-Sep 1.3HEC ⫶⫶⫶ ⚙ ♣ ⋔ ⛺ ⵌ ✗ ⊙ ⚑ ⊘ 🛖 ⊞ lau ♦ ⛺ ⋜P Prices: A370-500 pitch 945-1450

ELCHE *Alicante*
Palmeral Prolongacion Curtidores s/n ☎96 5422766
Long narrow site in a palm forest. It has many pitches in recesses between groups of trees.
Camping Card Compulsory.
Off the N340 and continue for 200m. Signposted.
All year 18HEC ▦ ⚙ ⋔ ⛺ ⵌ ✗ ⊙ ⚑ ⊘ ⋜ P ☎ ⊞ lau

GUARDAMAR DEL SEGURA *Alicante*
Mare Nostrum ☎96 5728073
Partially terraced meadow with some shade from roofing.
Turn towards the sea off the N332 Alicante-Cartagena road at about Km38.5.
Apr-15 Sep 20HEC ⚙ ⚙ ⋔ ⛺ ⵌ ✗ ⊙ ⚑ ⊘ ⋜ P ☎ ⊞ lau ♦ ⋜S

Palm Mar ☎96 5728856
Jun-Sep 2HEC ⫶⫶⫶ ♣ ⋔ ⛺ ⵌ ✗ ⊙ ⚑ ⊘ ⋜ S ☎ ⊞ lau ♦ ✗ ⋜P Prices: A530 pitch 1390

HOSPITALET DE L'INFANT, L' *Tarragona*
El Templo del Sol Platja del Torn ☎977 810486
A new site with modern sanitary installations and good recreational facilities on a 1.5km long beach.**This is a naturist site and only families or holders of an International Naturism Carnet are allowed.**
Access via A3 (Barcelona-Valencia), 4km from exit 38 towards the sea.
▦ ⚙ ⋔ ⛺ ✗ ⊙ ⚑ ⋜ S lau

Masia Playa de la Almadraba ☎77 820588
All year 2.6HEC ⫶⫶⫶ ⚙ ⋔ ⛺ ⵌ ✗ ⊙ ⚑ ⊘ 🛖 ⋜ S ☎ ⊞ lau

JARACO *Valencia*
San Vincente Playa Xeraio ☎96 2888188
Level subdivided site with some trees.
On leaving Jaraco at Km332 turn off at Km304 (Valencia-Alicante) in the direction of Playa to the site in 3.5km.
All year 5HEC ⚙ ♣ ⋔ ⛺ ⵌ ✗ ⊙ ⚑ 🛖 ☎ ⊞ lau ♦ ⛺ ⊘ ⥁ ⋜PRS
Prices: A400-490 ⬤600-665 ▲400-490

MARINA, LA *Alicante*
International la Marina ☎6 5419051
All year 6HEC ⫶⫶⫶ ⚙ ⋔ ⛺ ⵌ ✗ ⊙ ⚑ ⊘ 🛖 ⥁ 🛖 ⬤ ⋜ PS ☎ ⊞ lau Prices: A182-535 pitch 691-2033

MIRAMAR PLAYA *Valencia*
Coelius av del Mar ☎96 2819574

A fine camp site 500m from the Miramar beach with good, modern facilities.
Access via N430.
Apr-Sep 1.7HEC ⫶⫶⫶ ⚙ ♣ ⋔ ⛺ ⵌ ✗ ⊙ ⚑ 🛖 ⬤ ⋜ P ☎ ⊞ lau ♦ ⊘ ⋜S Prices: A425-575 V425-575 ⬤800 ▲5750-800

MONT-ROIG DEL CAMP *Tarragona*
Marius ☎977 810684
Pitches are planted with flowers and shrubs. Separate section for dog owners.
For access, leave the N340, Tarragona to Valencia road, at Km1137 and drive through a 4.9m-wide railway underpass with a clearance of 3.65m, then head towards the beach.
Apr-Oct 4HEC ▦ ♣ ⋔ ⛺ ⵌ ✗ ⊙ ⚑ ⊘ ⊞ lau ♦ ⋜S Prices: A300-600 pitch 1100-2000

Oasis Mar ☎977 837395
Completely divided into pitches, about 5km S of Cambrils. Shade is provided by trees.
For access, leave N340 at Km226.7 and turn seawards, then continue on an unsurfaced road for 500m.
All year 2.5HEC ▦ ♣ ⋔ ⛺ ⵌ ✗ ⊙ ⚑ ⊘ ⋜ S ☎ ⊞ lau

Playa Montroig ☎977 810637
An ideal holiday centre for the whole family with sanitary installations of the highest quality. Situated on a fine sandy beach and surrounded by tropical gardens, this award winning site offers a wide range of sporting and recreational facilities and is noted for its helpful and friendly staff.
Turn left off the N340 at Km1136. Use motorway exit 37 or 38.
Mar-Oct 30HEC ▦ ♣ ⋔ ⛺ ⵌ ✗ ⊙ ⚑ ⊘ ⋜ PS ☎ ⊞ ⬳ lau Prices: pitch 1900-3700 (incl 2 persons)

MORAIRA *Alicante*
Moraira Camino Paellero 50 ☎96 5745249
0.3km from the sea in a pine forest. On several terraces and divided into pitches.
1km S on AP1347, turn W and continue up a hill for 500m.
All year 11HEC ⫶⫶⫶ ⚙ ⋔ ⛺ ⵌ ✗ ⊙ ⚑ ⊘ 🛖 ⬤ ▲ ⋜ P ☎ ⊞ lau ♦ ⋜S Prices: A220-550 V220-550 ⬤220-650 ▲220-550

MUCHAMIEL *Alicante*
Muchamiel ctra Veneteta 7 ☎96 5950126
Jul-Sep 1.7HEC ⫶⫶⫶ ♣ ⋔ ⛺ ⵌ ✗ ⊙ ⚑ ⊘ ⋜ P ☎ ⊞ lau ♦ ⛺ ✗

NULES *Castellón*
Huertas ☎964 675009
Clean, well-kept site, completely divided into pitches. Few trees but equipped with straw mat roofs. Dancing every Saturday and Sunday.
Turn off N340 at Km47.1 and drive towards sea for 5.3km. Site about 20m from the sea.
Jun-15 Sep 2HEC ▦ ⫶⫶⫶ ⚙ ♣ ⋔ ⛺ ⵌ ✗ ⊙ ⚑ ⊘ 🛖 ⋜ PS ☎ ⊞ lau

OLIVA *Valencia*
Azul Partida Rabdells ☎96 2854106
Apr-Oct 2.5HEC ⫶⫶⫶ ♣ ⋔ ⛺ ⵌ ✗ ⊙ ⚑ ⊘ ⥁ 🛖 ⬤ ⋜ S ☎ ⊞ lau ♦ ⋜PR Prices: A500 V550 ⬤750 ▲700

Euro Camping ☎96 2854098
On a wide sandy beach between orange groves and well shaded with poplar and eucalyptus trees.
For access turn off the N332 at Km184.9, 600m from Oliva. Following signs for camp drive towards the sea for 3.3km. The access road has narrow stretches and some blind corners so beware of oncoming traffic.
Mar-Oct 4.5HEC ⫶⫶⫶ ⚙ ♣ ⋔ ⛺ ⵌ ✗ ⊙ ⚑ ⊘ 🛖 ▲ ⋜ S ☎ ⊞ lau ♦ ⋜R Prices: A575 pitch 1475-1930
See advertisement under Colour Section

Ferienplatz Olé ☎96 2851180
An extensive site with some pitches amongst dunes.
Turn off the N332 at Km209.9 about 5km S of Oliva. In about 3km continue to site on access road partially asphalt, through an orchard.
Apr-Sep 5HEC ⫶⫶⫶ ♣ ⋔ ⛺ ⵌ ✗ ⊙ ⚑ ⊘ ⥁ 🛖 ⋜ RS ☎ ⊞ lau

Kiko Playa de Oliva ☎96 2850905
Family holiday camp, divided into pitches, lying between marshland and vineyard. The sea can be reached by crossing a dyke and there are sunshade roofs.
Access from motorway A7 exit 61 and continue via CN332 towards Oliva.
All year 3HEC ⚏ ♠♠♣♥✗⊙♠∅≞♠≺ S ☎⊞ lau ♦ ≺PR
Prices: A663 pitch 2247

OROPESA DEL MAR *Castellón*

Alondra Camino Latall ☎964 310686
All year ≺♠♠♣♥✗⊙♠≺ PS ☎⊞ lau ♦ ∅

Didota av de la Didota ☎964 319551
Mar-Oct 1.7HEC ⚏ ♠♠♣♥✗⊙♠≺ PS ☎⊞ lau

PEÑISCOLA *Castellón*

Camping Eden ☎964 480562
All year 5HEC ⚏ ≺♠♣♥✗⊙♠∅≞♠♥★≺ PS ☎⊞ lau

PUEBLA DE FARNALS *Valencia*

Brasa ☎96 1460388
Level meadowland site with poplars near village centre.
For access leave motorway Barcelona-Valencia at exit 3, towards Playa Puebla de Farnals.
All year 3.9HEC ⚏ ≺♠♣♥✗⊙♠∅≺ PS ☎⊞ lau ♦ ♣
Prices: A425 ♠575 ▲525

RODA DE BERÁ *Tarragona*

Stel ☎977 802002
Via motorway (A7) exit 31.
Apr-Sep 10.5HEC ⚏ ♠♠♣♥✗⊙♠∅≺ P ☎⊞ lau ♦ ≞ ≺S

SALOU *Tarragona*

Cambrils Park ☎977 351031
May-Sep 17HEC ⚏ ≺♠♣♥✗⊙♠∅≺ P ☎⊞ ≪ lau ♦ ≺S
Prices: A600 pitch 2600-2900

Pineda de Salou Playa de la Pineda ☎977 372176
Mar-3 Nov 4HEC ⚏ ♠♠♣♥✗⊙♠∅≺ LP ☎⊞ lau ♦ ≺S

Sanguli ☎977 381641
A large, family site in pleasant wooded surroundings, 50 metres from the beach, with extensive sports and entertainment facilities.
SW outskirts, 200m inland from coast road to Cambrils
15 Mar-Oct 23HEC ⚏ ⚏ ≺♠♣♥✗⊙♠∅≞♠≺ PS ☎⊞ ≪ lau Prices: pitch 690-1730
See advertisement on page 247.

Siesta c Norte 37 ☎977 380852
Divided into pitches and planted with young deciduous trees and old olive trees. Sunshade roofs.
If approaching from Tarragona, turn right off the main road on outskirts of Salou and drive a further 150m to the camp. The site is between the railway and road 0.4km from the sea.
18 Mar-Oct 5HEC ⚏ ≺♠♣♥✗⊙♠∅♠♥≺ P ☎⊞ lau ♦ ≞ ≺S

Union c/ Pompeu Fabra 31 ☎977 384816
May-Oct 3.8HEC ⚏ ≺♠♣♥✗⊙♠∅♠▲≺ P ☎⊞ lau ♦ ≺S
Prices: A460-625 V460-625 ♠550-800 ▲460-625

SANTA OLIVA *Tarragona*

Santa Oliva Jaume Balmes 122 ☎977 661252
At Km3 on Vendrell-Santa Oliva road.
All year 1.9HEC ⚏ ♠♠♣♥✗⊙♠∅♠♠≺ P ☎⊞ lau ♦ ♣✗
Prices: A500 V500 ♠500 ▲500

TAMARIT *Tarragona*

Caledonia ☎977 694009
All year 3.5HEC ⚏ ≺♠♣♥✗⊙♠∅≺ P ☎⊞ lau ♦ ≺S

Trillas Platja Tamarit ☎977 650249
About 50m from the sea. On several terraces planted with olive trees next to a farm.
For access, turn off the N340 at Km1.172, about 8km N of

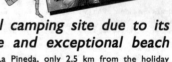

Tarragona. Follow road and cross a narrow railway bridge. (Beware of oncoming traffic).
22 Mar-Sep 4.5HEC ▦ ♣♠♜☘♥✕☉🅿⊘ ⚡ ⅃ S ⊞ lau ♣ ♨
Prices: A440-575 pitch 880-1150

TARRAGONA *Tarragona*
Gaya El Cattlar ☎977 653070
On level grassland with single poplars on the River Gaya.
Turn N inland at Km259.7 off the N340 (Barcelona-Tarragona).
Continue on metalled road in 7.5km via T202 and T203 to just before the Gaia river bridge at El Cattlar. To via site via unmade road to right in 0.2km.
May-Sep 1HEC ░░░ ♣♜☘✕☉🅿⊘ ⚡ PR ⊞ lau

Tamarit-Park Platja Tamarit ☎977 650128
Well-kept site at the sea beneath Tamarit Castle. One section lies under tall shady trees, and a new section lies in a meadow with some trees.
Turn off N340 and Km259.3 about 8km N of Tarragona and drive 800m seaward along a narrow track.
Apr-Sep 10HEC ▦ ░░░ ♣♜☘✕☉🅿⊘ ⚡ S ⊞ lau

TORREBLANCA *Castellón*
Mon Rossi Carrasa Mon Rossi, Torrenostra ☎964 420296
All year 0.7HEC ♣♠♜☘✕☉🅿⊘ ⚡ ♠ A ⚡ P ⊞ lau ♣♠♨ ⚡S
Prices: A450 pitch 375-450

VALENCIA *Valencia*
Saler ☎96 1830023
Amongst pines providing shade with its own entrance to sandy beach in 300m. The site has recently undergone many improvements and has modern sanitery and recreational facilities.
Access from Valencia via coastal road towards Cullera as far as El Saler, then turn left at SE end of village and turn right.
All year 9.5HEC ▦ ░░░ ♣♜☘☘✕☉🅿⊘♨ ⚡ LP ⊞ lau ♣ ⚡S
Prices: A495-525 pitch 1900-2015

VENDRELL, EL *Tarragona*
Franca's ☎77 680725
Slopes gently towards the sea, between the beach and the railway line which separates the two sections. These are connected by a pedestrian underpass.
Lies about 100m away from the N340 on the seaward side at Km273.
Apr-Sep 3.5HEC ░░░ ♣♠♜☘☘✕☉🅿⊘ ⚡ S ⊞ lau

San Salvador ☎77 680804
On two large grassy terraces and has some sunshade roofs. Near the sea in the centre of the town.
Access via A7 exit 31 (Barcelona-Tarragona). Site in centre of Comarruga-Sant Salvador.
8 Apr-Sep 3HEC ▦ ░░░ ♣♜☘☘✕☉🅿⊘♨ ⊞ lau ♣ ⚡S

Vendrell Coma-ruga -Sant Salvador ☎77 694009
21 Mar-Sep 7.5HEC ▦ ░░░ ♣♜☘☘✕☉🅿⊘♨ ⚡ S ⊞ lau
Prices: A674 V674 ⛺674 ▲674

VERGEL *Alicante*
Llanos ☎96 6474488
In a field next to an orange grove and shaded by tall trees.
Turn off N332 between Km203 and Km204 and continue on gravel road for 200m.
Jun-15 Sep 2HEC ▦ ♣♜☘☘✕☉🅿⊘♨ ⚡ P ⊞ lau ♣ ⚡S

VILANOVA DE PRADES *Tarragona*
Serra de Prades Sant Antoni ☎977 869050
A fine site close to the beach and within easy reach of Barcelona and the Port Aventura theme park.
All year 50HEC ▦ ░░░ ♠♣♜☘☘✕☉🅿⊘♨⛺♨ ⚡ P ⊞ lau
Prices: A589 V589 ⛺589 ▲589

VILLAJOYOSA *Alicante*
Camping la Cala-Garoa Cala de Finestrat ☎96 5851461
On level ground on the seaward side of the N332. Large pitches, asphalt interior roads. Different types of trees provide shade.
On N332 at Km143.
All year 3.3HEC ▦ ♜☘☘✕☉🅿⊘⛺ ⚡ P ⊞ lau ♣ ⚡S

Hércules ☎96 5891343
Section near sea is well shaded. Asphalt interior road, separate section for caravans with numbered pitches.
Turn E off N332 near Km141 then turn S.
All year 6.3HEC ░░░ ♠♣♜☘☘✕☉🅿⊘♨⛺♨ ⚡ PS ⊞ lau
Prices: A540 V540 ⛺540 ▲540

Sertorium N332.PK 141 ☎96 5891599
On level ground on the seaward side of the N332. Small stony beach, suitable for non-swimmers.
On N332 at Km141.
All year 6.9HEC ♠♣♜☘☘✕☉🅿⊘♨⛺ ⚡ PS ⊞ lau Prices: A539 pitch 1617

VINAROZ *Castellón*
Garoa-Sol de Riu Playa ☎964 454917
All year 5.5HEC ▦ ♠♣♜☘☘✕☉🅿⊘ ⚡ PS ⊞ lau Prices: pitch 1100-1500

North Coast

The region varies from the beaches of the Cantabrian coast to mountain gorges, and attracts sun-lovers as well as hikers, fishermen and outdoor enthusiasts. Of the two coastal provinces, Cantabria has dairy farms and a huge hunting reserve; its capital, Santander, has a cathedral and spectacular beaches, with superb views from the Magdalene peninsular. The Altamira caves, with wall-paintings, are nearby. Asturias has a more rugged countryside. Its capital, Oviedo, is a cathedral city with fine buildings in the old quarter.

On the Pilgrim Way to Compostela lies Lugo, with its cathedral and picturesque old quarter of ancient streets and wrought-iron balconies. Walk around the city's perimeter on top of encircling walls dating from Roman times.

Famous in both Spanish and British history is Corunna. Now a bustling seaside resort and good touring centre, this old town saw the departure of the ill-fated Spanish Armada and has the tomb of Sir John Moore, killed in the Napoleonic Wars. There is also a Roman lighthouse. North east of Corunna is Ferrol, Franco's birthplace.

BARREIROS *Lugo*
Gaivota Playa de Benquerencia ☎982 124451
Site leads down to a sandy beach with windsurfing. The main buildings have been designed and built by the owner, who is a painter.
15 Jun-15 Sep 1HEC ▦ ♠♜☘☘✕☉🅿⊘♨⛺ A ⚡ S ⊞ lau ♣ ✕ ⚡P Prices: A400 V400 ⛺500 ▲350

BERGONDO *La Coruña*
Santa Marta ☎981 791628
Apr-Sep 28.5HEC ▦ ♠♜☘☘✕☉🅿⊘♨⛺ A ⚡ P ⊞ lau ♣ ⚡RS

CADAVEDO *Asturias*
Regalina ctra de la Playa ☎98 5645056
The site has mountain and sea views.
Jun-12 Oct 1HEC ▦ ♠♜☘☘✕☉🅿⊘♨⛺ A ⊞ lau ♣ ♜☘✕ ⚡S
Prices: A400 V400 ⛺500 ▲425

CÓBRECES *Cantabria*
Cóbreces Playa de Cóbreces ☎942 725120
50m from the beach.
15 Jun-15 Sep 1.5HEC ▦ ♜☘☘✕☉🅿⊘ ⚡ S ⊞ lau Prices: A450 pitch 1400

COMILLAS *Cantabria*
Comillas ☎42 720074
Level grassland site to the right of the road to the beach.
E on C6316 at Km23.
Jun-Sep 3HEC ▦ ♣♜☘☘✕☉🅿⊘ ⊞ lau ♣ ⚡S

CUDILLERO *Asturias*
Amuravela El Pito ☎985 590995
Etr & Jun-15 Sep 2.8HEC ▦ ⟓ ⋒ ⋐ ⚡ ✗ ⊙ ⊟ ∅ ⊞ ▲ ⟍ P ☒ ⊞ lau
➡ ⛺ ⟍RS Prices: A508 V508 ⊞588 ▲481-535

FOZ *Lugo*
San Rafael Playa de Peizas ☎982 132218
Camping Card Compulsory.
May-Sep 1HEC ▦ ⟓ ⋒ ⋐ ⚡ ✗ ⊙ ⊟ ∅ ⟍ S ☒ ⊞ lau ➡ ⟍R Prices:
A475 V475 ⊞595 ▲495

FRANCA, LA *Asturias*
Las Hortensais Playa de la Franca, ctra CN 634-Km 286 ☎98
5412145
Jun-Sep 2.8HEC ▦ ⟓ ⋒ ⋐ ⚡ ✗ ⊙ ⊟ ∅ ⟍ S ☒ ⊞ lau ➡ ⛺ Prices:
A525 V495 ⊞675 ▲520

ISLARES *Cantabria*
Playa Arenillas ☎942 863152
In meadowland with some pine trees.
On N634 at Km155.8 turn N and continue 100m. The entrance is
rather steep.
Apr-Sep 3HEC ▦ ⟓ ⋒ ⋐ ⚡ ✗ ⊙ ⊟ ∅ ☒ ⊞ ⊞ lau ➡ ⟍S Prices:
A510 pitch 1300

LAREDO *Cantabria*
Carlos V pl de Carlos V ☎942 605593
Camp surrounded by walls and buildings on W outskirts of Laredo.
Turn off N634 at Km171.6 into an avenue and drive towards the
sea. Turn left before reaching the beach and drive around the
roundabout on the plaza Carlos V.
May-Sep 1HEC ⁖⁖⁖ ➡ ⋒ ⋐ ⚡ ✗ ⊙ ⊟ ∅ ⛺ ☒ ⊞ lau ➡ ✗ ⟍S Prices:
A500 V500 ⊞450 ▲450

LLANES *Asturias*
Barcenas Antigua CN 634 ☎98 5402887
Jun-Sep 2.2HEC ▦ ⟓ ⋒ ⋐ ⚡ ✗ ⊙ ⊟ ∅ ⊞ ▲ ☒ ⊞ ⊞ lau ➡ ✗ ⟍S
Prices: A455 V430 ⊞695 ▲640

Brao ☎98 5400014
Humpy hillside side on three terraces totally enclosed by 2m-high
wall.
0.5km from the sea. At Km96.2 on N634 turn N for 1.8km and turn
towards Cue for 200m.
Jun-Sep 27HEC ▦ ➡ ⋒ ⋐ ✗ ⊙ ⊟ ∅ ☒ ⊞ lau ➡ ⟍S Prices: A470
V470 ⊞620 ▲470

Palacio de Garaña ☎98 5410075
May-15 Sep 2HEC ▦ ⟓⟍ ⋒ ⋐ ⚡ ✗ ⊙ ⊟ ∅ ⛺ ⟍ P ☒ ⊞ lau ➡ ⟍S
Prices: A585 V550 ⊞750 ▲595

LUARCA *Asturias*
Cantiles ☎98 5640938
Meadowland beautifully situated high above the cliffs with little shade
form bushes. Footpath to bay 70m below.
At Km308.5 turn off the N634 from Oviedo, turn towards Faro de
Luarca beyond the Firestone filling station. In Villar de Luarca turn
right and onwards 1km to site.
Jul-Sep 2.3HEC ▦ ⟓ ⋒ ⋐ ⚡ ✗ ⊙ ⊟ ∅ ⟍ S ☒ ⊞ lau ➡ ⟍PR

MOTRICO (MUTRIKU) *Guipúzcoa*
Aitzeta ☎943 603356
On two sloping meadows, partially terraced. Lovely view of the sea
1km away.
0.5km NE on C6212 turn at KmSS5.1.
All year 1.5HEC ▦ ➡ ⋒ ⋐ ⚡ ✗ ⊙ ⊟ ∅ ⟍ PS ☒ ⊞ lau ➡ ✗ Prices:
A400 V400 ⊞500 ▲400-500

NOJA *Cantabria*
Playa Joyel Playa de Ris ☎42 630081
Etr-Sep 25HEC ▦ ⟓ ⋒ ⋐ ⚡ ✗ ⊙ ⊟ ∅ ⟍ PS ☒ ⊞ ⊞ lau ➡ ▲
Prices: A425-700 pitch 1450-1550

ORIO *Guipúzcoa*
CM Playa de Orio ☎943 834801
On two flat terraces along cliffs and surrounded by hedges.

Turn off the N634 San Sebastian-Bilbao road at about Km12.5 in
Orio. Shortly before the bridge over the River Orio turn towards the
sea and continue for 1.5km.
Closed Nov & Dec 5.4HEC ▦ ⟓⟍ ⋒ ⋐ ⚡ ✗ ⊙ ⊟ ∅ ⟍ P ☒ ⊞ ⊞ lau
➡ ⟍RS Prices: A260-520 pitch 1590-3175

PECHÓN *Cantabria*
Arenas ☎942 717188
On numerous terraces between rocks, reaching down to the sea.
Turn off N634 E of Unquera at Km74 towards sea and take road
towards S.
Jun-Sep 10HEC ▦ ⟓ ⋒ ⋐ ⚡ ✗ ⊙ ⊟ ∅ ⊞ ⟍ LRS ☒ ⊞ lau

PERLORA-CANDAS *Asturias*
Perlora ☎98 5870048
On top of a large hill on a peninsula with a few terraced pitches.
Access 7km W of Gijon, turn off N632 in direction Luanco and
continue for 5km.
All year 1.4HEC ▦ ⟓⟍ ⋒ ⋐ ⚡ ✗ ⊙ ⊟ ∅ ⟍ S ☒ ⊞ lau ➡ ⛺ Prices:
A460 V400 ⊞450 ▲400

REINANTE *Lugo*
Reinante ☎982 134005
Longish site beyond a range of dunes on lovely sandy beach.
Camping Carnet Compulsory.
On N634 at Km391.7.
All year 2.5HEC ▦ ⟓ ⋒ ⋐ ⚡ ✗ ⊙ ⊟ ∅ ⊞ ⟍ LR ☒ ⊞ ⊞ lau ➡ ⟍S
Prices: A350-400 V300-350 ⊞350-400 ▲300-450

SAN SEBASTIAN (DONOSTIA) *Guipúzcoa*

At **IGUELDO**
Garoa Camping Igueldo ☎943 214502
Terraced site on Monte Igualdo divided by hedges.
Follow signs Monte Igualdo from town, and beach road, about
4.5km.
All year 3HEC ▦ ⟓ ⋒ ⋐ ⚡ ✗ ⊙ ⊟ ∅ ☒ ⊞ lau Prices: pitch 1300-
3100 (incl 4 persons)

SANTIAGO DE COMPOSTELA La Coruña
As Cancelas r do 25 de Xulls 35 ☎981 580266
All year 1.8HEC ▦ ♠♠♥♣♀✕⊙☺∅☺♠▲⚡ P ☎⊞ lau Prices:
A482-600 V482-642 ☻482-663 ▲482-642
See advertisement on page 249.

SANTILLANA DEL MAR Cantabria
Santillana ☎942 818250
Slightly sloping meadow with bushes on a hillock within the area of a restaurant adjoining a swimming pool.
Access from Santander via C6316 turn off shortly after the Santillana sign and continue up the hill.
All year 50HEC ♠♠♥♣♀✕⊙☺∅☺♠⚡ P ☎⊞ lau Prices:
A460-560 V435-535 ☻595-695 ▲435-535

VALDOVIÑO La Coruña
Valdoviño ☎981 487076
Six gently sloping fields partly in shade. Located behind Cafeteria Andy and block of flats with several villas beyond.
Turn off the C646 towards Cedeira seawards and continue 700m to site.
Apr-Sep 18HEC ▦ ♠♠♥♣♀✕⊙☺∅▲☺⚡ S ☎⊞ lau ➡ ⚡LPR
Prices: A550-560 V590-600 ☻600-620 ▲590-600

VEGA DE LIÉBANA Cantabria
Molino ☎942 736009
In an orchard by river about 300m outside town.
Jun-Sep 1HEC ♠♠♥♣♀✕⊙☺∅⚡ PR ☎⊞ lau ➡✕

VIDIAGO Asturias
Paz Playa de Vidiago ☎98 5411012
From N634 turn off at Km292 between Buelna and Vidiago towards the sea.
Jun-17 Sep 10HEC ▦ ♨♒♠♥♣♀✕⊙☺∅♨ S ☎⊞ lau ➡ ♨

VILLAR DE LUARCA Asturias
Los Cantiles ☎98 5640938
Access via N634.
All year 2.3HEC ▦ ♒♠♥♣♀✕⊙☺∅☺♠☎⊞ lau ➡ ⚡PS
Prices: A428 V428 ☻535 ▲455

VIVEIRO Lugo
Vivero ☎982 560004
In tall woodland near beach road and sea.
Turn off the C642 Barreois-Ortueire road at Km443.1 and follow signs.
Jun-Sep 1.6HEC ♠♠♥♣♀✕⊙☺∅☺⊞ lau ➡✕ ⚡S

ZARAUZ (ZARAUTZ) Guipúzcoa
Talai Mendi ☎943 830042
In meadowland on hillside divided by interior roads without shade.
0.5km from the sea.
On outskirts of town at FIRESTONE filling station at Km17.5 on N634 turn towards the sea and continue for 350m along narrow asphalt road.
Jul-10 Sep 4HEC ▦ ♒♠♥♣♀✕⊙☺∅☺⊞ lau ➡ ⚡S Prices: A450 pitch 2465

Zarauz ☎943 831238
Site with terraces separated by hedges.
1.8km from the N634 San Sebastian-Bilbao road. Asphalt access road from Km15.5.
All year 4HEC ▦ ♒♠♥♣♀✕⊙☺∅♠☎⊞ lau ➡ ⚡S Prices: A500 V500 ☻525 ▲525

North East
Medieval villages, green valleys, forests, and arid gorges are some of this region's varied attractions. Tranquil Burgos, with its pleasant river setting and old centre, was Franco's capital during the Civil War. The principal city of Castille has a magnificent Gothic cathedral which reflects its importance on the Pilgrim Way to Compostela and contains the tomb of the legendary El Cid.

The city of Saragossa lies in a fertile pocket. Its basilica contains a national shrine to the Virgin of the Pillar. The province of the same name contains Spain's largest natural inland lake and is a great attraction for ornithologists.
Beautiful scenery surrounds the pleasant cathedral city of Huesca. Nearby Loarre Castle is a wonderful medieval fortress; superb views can be had from its rocky heights and the amazing grotto site of the Monastery of San Juan de la Peña.
Lush valleys and Pyrennean crags are just two faces of Navarre. Its ancient capital, Pamplona, is notorious for the Running of the Bulls each morning during its week-long fiesta celebrations in July. Wine lovers will be attracted to La Rioja - an area renowned for its fine wines.

ARANDA DE DUERO Burgos
Costaján ☎947 502070
Turn off N1 (Burgos-Madrid) at Km162.1 N of town.
All year 1.8HEC ░░░ ♠♠♥♣♀✕⊙☺∅☺♠⚡ P ☎⊞ lau Prices:
A481-533 V481-533 ☻481-533 ▲481-533

BELLVER DE CERDANYA Lleida
Solana del Segre ☎973 510310
On the River Segre, known for its trout fishing.
15 Sep-11 Oct 6.5HEC ▦ ♠♠♥♣♀✕⊙☺∅▲☺⚡ PR ☎⊞ lau
Prices: A575 V575 ☻575 ▲575

BIESCAS Huesca
Edelweiss ctra de Ordesa a Francia ☎974 485084
In meadow with deciduous trees on a hill in a pleasant situation.
Turn right off C138 at Km97.
15 Jun-15 Sep 30HEC ▦ ♠♠♥♣♀✕⊙☺∅☺⚡ PR
Prices: A525 V550 ☻550 ▲550

BONANSA Huesca
Baliera Cruce crta Castejon Desos ☎974 554016
All year 5HEC ▦ ♠♠♥♣♀✕⊙☺∅☺⚡ PR ☎⊞ lau Prices: A550 V550 ☻550 ▲550

BORDETA, LA Lleida
Bedurá-Park ctra N230, Km 174,5 ☎973 648293
May-Sep 5HEC ▦ ♠♠♥♣♀✕⊙☺∅☺♠☺⚡ LPR ☎⊞⊞ lau
Prices: A550 pitch 1200-1500

Prado Verde ☎973 640241
Level meadowland on River Garona with sparse trees and sheltered by high hedges from traffic noise.
On the N230, Puente de Rey (French border)-Lleida road, at Km199 behind PIRELLI GENERAL filling station.
All year 1.5HEC ▦ ♠♠♥♣♀✕⊙☺∅⚡ LPR ☎⊞ lau Prices:
A500-550 V500-550 ☻500-550 ▲500-525

CALATAYUD Zaragoza
Calatayud ctra Madrid-Barcelona ☎976 880592
15 Mar-15 Oct 1.7HEC ▦ ♒♠♥♣♀✕⊙☺∅⚡ P ☎⊞ lau ➡✕
Prices: A455 V465 ☻465 ▲455

CASTAÑARES DE RIOJA La Rioja
Rioja ctra Haro a Sto Domingo de la, Calzada ☎941 300174
A well appointed site on the banks of the River Oja with a private beach.
21 Jun-21 Sep 10HEC ▦ ♨♠♠♥♣♀✕⊙☺∅⚡ PR ☎⊞ lau ➡ ⚡PR

ESPOT Lleida
Sol I Neu ctra d'Espot ☎973 624001
Jun-Sep 1.5HEC ▦ ♠♠♥♣♀✕⊙☺∅⚡ P ☎⊞ lau ➡✕ Prices:
A525 V525 ☻525 ▲525

ESTELLA Navarra
Lizarra Ordoiz ☎948 551733
Jul-Aug 45HEC ▦ ♒♠♥♣♀✕⊙☺∅☺♠▲⚡ P ☎⊞ lau

GUINGUETA, LA Lleida
Vall d'Aneu ☎973 626083
In meadowland on rising ground on both sides of the road, partially in shade. No shade on terrace between road and lake.
On outskirts of town near the by-pass, C147.
Etr & May-Sep 0.5HEC ▥ ♦ ♠ � ♀ ✕ ⊙ ⊠ ⌀ ⌇ P ⌹ ⊞ lau ♦ ⚤ ✕ ⚲ ⌇L Prices: A475 V475 ⊞475 ▲475

HECHO Huesca
Selva de Osa Selva de Osa ☎974 375168
On meadowland, partly covered with pines and deciduous trees and between a dirt track and a mountain stream.
12.5km towards Espata.
15 Jun-15 Sep 2HEC ⌇ ♠ ⚲ ♀ ✕ ⊙ ⊠ ⌀ ⌇ R ⌹ ⊞ lau Prices: A550 V620 ⊞700 ▲525

HUESCA Huesca
San Jorge Ricardo del Arco ☎974 227416
Site with sports field surrounded by high walls. Subdivided by hedges, sparse woodland.
From town centre, about 1.5km along M123 towards Zaragoza direction and follow signs.
Apr-15 Oct 0.7HEC ▥ ⌇ ♠ ♀ ✕ ⊠ ⌇ P ⌹ ⊞ lau ♦ ⚤ ⌀ Prices: A508 ⊞535 ▲508

JACA Huesca
At GUASA
Peña Oroel ctra Jaca-Sabiñanigo ☎974 360215
Grassland site with rows of high poplars.
At Km13.8 of the C134 Jaca-Sabiñanigo road.
15 Jun-15 Sep 50HEC ▥ ♦ ♠ ⚲ ♀ ✕ ⊙ ⊠ ⌀ ⌇ P ⌹ ⊞ lau Prices: A525 V550 ⊞550 ▲550

LABUERDA Huesca
Peña Montañesa ctra Ainsa-Bielsa ☎974 500730
All year 10HEC ▥ ♦ ♠ ⚲ ♀ ✕ ⊙ ⊠ ⌀ ⊠ ⌇ PR ⌹ ⊞ lau ♦ ⌇LR
Prices: A650 pitch 1850

MENDIGORRIA Navarra
El Molino ctra N111 ☎948 340604
All year 15HEC ▥ ♦ ♠ ⚲ ♀ ✕ ⊙ ⊠ ⌀ ⊠ ⌇ ⚤ ⌇ PR ⌹ ⊞ lau ♦ ⚤ ⌇R

NÁJERA La Rioja
Ruedo Paseo San Julian 24 ☎941 360102
Amongst poplars and the area of the bullring, almost no shade.
Turn off the N120 Logroño-Burgos road in Nájera and then continue along the river banks just before the stone bridge across the River Majerilla, then turn left.
Apr-Oct 0.5HEC ▥ ♦ ♠ ⚲ ♀ ✕ ⊙ ⊠ ⌀ ⌹ lau ♦ ⚤ ⌇PR Prices: A550 ⊞550 ▲550

NUEVALOS Zaragoza
Lago Park ctra Alhama de Aragón-Nuevalos ☎976 849038
NE towards Alhama de Aragon.
Apr-Sep 3HEC ▥ ∴ ♦ ♠ ⚲ ♀ ✕ ⊙ ⊠ ⌀ ⌇ P ⌹ ⊞ lau ♦ ⌇LR
Prices: A600 V650 ⊞650 ▲650

ORICAIN Navarra
Ezcaba ctra Francia-Irun km7 ☎948 331665
Gently sloping meadowland and a few terraces on a flat topped hill.
N of Pamplona. Turn off N121 at Km7.3 and drive towards Berriosuso. Turn right and drive uphill after crossing the bridge over the River Ulzama.
All year 2.2HEC ▥ ⌇ ♠ ⚲ ♀ ✕ ⊙ ⊠ ⌀ ⌀ ▲ ⌇ ⌹ ⊞ lau ♦ ⌇R
Prices: A500 V500 ⊞700 ▲500

PANCORBO Burgos
Desfiladero ☎947 354027
Off N1 at Km305.2.
All year 13HEC ▥ ♦ ∆ ♠ ⚲ ♀ ✕ ⊙ ⊠ ⌀ ⊠ ⊠ ⌇ PR ⌹ ⊞ lau

PUEBLA DE CASTRO, LA Huesca
Lago de Barasona ☎974 545148
Apr-Sep 3HEC ▥ ♦ ♠ ⚲ ♀ ✕ ⊙ ⊠ ⌀ ⌇ LP ⌹ ⊞ lau ♦ ⌇R

RIBERA DE CARDÓS Lleida
Cardós ☎973 623112
Long stretch of meadowland divided by four rows of poplars.
Camping Card Compulsory.
Near the electricity plant in Llavorsi turn NE onto the Ribera road and follow it for 9km. Entrance near hostel Soly Neu.
Apr-Sep 2.2HEC ▥ ∴∴ ♦ ♠ ⚲ ♀ ✕ ⊙ ⊠ ⌀ ⊠ ⌇ PR ⌹ ⊞ lau ♦ ⌇PR

SANTO DOMINGO DE LA CALZADA La Rioja
Bañares ☎941 342804
All year 9HEC ▥ ♦ ♠ ⚲ ♀ ✕ ⊙ ⊠ ⌀ ⌇ P ⌹ ⊞ lau Prices: A575 V575 ⊞575 ▲575

SOLSONA Lleida
Solsonès ☎973 482861
Camping Card Compulsory.
All year 3HEC ▥ ♦ ♠ ⚲ ♀ ✕ ⊙ ⊠ ⌀ ⚤ ⊠ ▲ ⌇ P ⌹ ⊞ lau ♦ ⌇LR
Prices: A599 V599 ⊞599 ▲599

TIERMAS Zaragoza
Mar del Pirineo ☎948 887009
On broad terraces sloping down to the banks of the Embalse de Yese. Roofing provides shade for tents and cars.
Situated on the N240 Huesca-Pamplona road at Km317.7.
Etr & May-Sep 3HEC ▥ ⌇ ♠ ⚲ ♀ ✕ ⊙ ⊠ ⌇ LP ⌹ ⊞ lau

TORLA Huesca
Ordesa ctra de Ordesa ☎974 486146
On three terraces between well-kept hedges.
2km N of the village at Km96 and N of the C138.
Closed Nov-Xmas 3.5HEC ▥ ♦ ♠ ⚲ ♀ ✕ ⊙ ⊠ ⌀ ⌇ P ⌹ ⊞ lau ♦ ⌇R

North West
In this region of contrasts are beautiful green valleys, rugged mountains still roamed by bears and wolves, a wealth of historic monuments, fine resorts such as Bayona, and quiet fishing villages. This is Galicia, a land of mild climate mostly bordered by the Atlantic - a celtic land with strong traditions, local costume, bagpipes and drums.
The regional capital, Santiago de Compostela, was once the most visited city in Europe, ranking alongside Rome and Jerusalem. The pilgrimage tradition lives on in its cathedral - one of the finest in the world - and the architecture it inspired on the Pilgrim Way.
This legacy has left a wealth of historic monuments, such as the magnificent cathedral at Léon, with its wonderful stained glass. Mountains form the backdrop to Orense, with its fine cathedral and interesting museums, while a green valley is the setting for Pontevedra. Here, in the old town, lie a fascinating museum and cathedral, and houses bearing armorial badges and narrow streets, just as they were hundreds of years ago.

BAIONA Pontevedra
Baiona Playa ctra Vigo-Baionna ☎986 350035
On a long sandy peninsula on the Galicia coast with direct access to the beach. The site has good, modern facilities including facilities for a variety of watersports.
Jun-Sep 4HEC ▥ ♦ ♠ ⚲ ♀ ✕ ⊙ ⊠ ⌀ ⊠ ⌇ PS ⌹ ⊞ lau Prices: A452-695 V501-770 ⊞452-696 ▲459-706

CUBILLAS DE SANTA MARTA Valladolid
Cubillas ☎983 585002
Meadowland with young trees, subdivided by hedges.
Entrance on the right of the N620 from Burgos between Km100 & 101.
All year 4HEC ▥ ⌇ ♠ ⚲ ♀ ✕ ⊙ ⊠ ⌀ ⚤ ⊠ ▲ ⌇ P ⌹ ⊞ lau ♦ ⌇R

LEIRO *Orense*
Leiro ☎988 488036
On level meadow in a pine forest in a valley by a stream, behind the football ground.
Closed Nov 1.8HEC ▦ ◕ ⋔ ⚊ ⚌ ▼ ✕ ⊙ ⚑ ⌀ ⚏ ⌇ R ☎ ⊞ lau Prices: A475 V500 ⛽500 ▲400

NIGRÁN *Pontevedra*
Playa America ☎986 365404
Jun-15 Sep 4HEC ▦ ◆ ⋔ ⚊ ▼ ✕ ⊙ ⚑ ⌀ ⚌ ⚏ ⌇ PS ☎ ⊞ lau ◆ ⌇LR
Prices: A500-550 V500-550 ⛽515-570 ▲515-570

PORTONOVO *Pontevedra*
Paxariñas ☎986 723055
Slightly sloping towards a bay, in amongst dunes, with high pines and young deciduous trees. Lovely beach.
Camping Card Compulsory.
All year 2HEC ▦ ◆ ⋔ ⚊ ▼ ✕ ⊙ ⚑ ⌀ ▲ ☎ ⊞ lau ◆ ⌇S Prices: A525 V500 ⛽550 ▲550

SANTA MARINA DE VALDEON *Léon*
El Cares ☎987 742676
N off N621 from Portilla de la Reina.
Apr-15 Oct 1.5HEC ▦ ◆ ⋔ ⚊ ▼ ✕ ⊙ ⚑ ⌀ ⚏ ▲ ⌇ R ☎ ⊞ lau Prices: A482 V482 ⛽535 ▲481-535

SAN VICENTE DO MAR *Pontevedra*
Siglo XXI ☎986 738100
Jun-Sep 1.6HEC ▦ ◆ ⋔ ⚊ ▼ ✕ ⊙ ⚑ ⌀ ⌇ PS ☎ ⊞ lau Prices: A650-685 pitch 1500-2300

SIMANCAS *Valladolid*
Plantió ☎983 590082
In a poplar wood, on the river bank.
On outskirts turn off N620 at Km132.2 and continue 500m on narrow asphalt road and a long single track stone bridge over the River Pisverga.
15 Jun-22 Sep 1.5HEC ▦ ▒▒ ◆ ⋔ ⚊ ▼ ✕ ⊙ ⚑ ⌀ ▲ ⌇ PR ☎ ⊞ lau ◆ ⚌ Prices: A425 ⛽450 ▲425

TORDESILLAS *Valladolid*
Astral Camino de Pollos 8 ☎983 770953
Apr-Sep 3HEC ▒▒ ◕ ⋔ ⚊ ▼ ✕ ⊙ ⚑ ⚏ ▲ ⌇ P ☎ ⊞ lau ◆ ⌇R
Prices: A401-498 V348-428 ⛽401-498 ▲401-498

VALENCIA DE DON JUAN *Léon*
Pico Verde C/Santas Martas 18 ☎987 750525
Turn E off the N630 (Léon-Madrid) at Km32.2 and continue for 4km.
15 Jun-13 Sep 2.7HEC ▦ ◆ ⋔ ⚊ ▼ ✕ ⊙ ⚑ ⌀ ⌇ P ☎ ⊞ lau ◆ ⌇R
Prices: A430 V430 ⛽430 ▲400

VILLAMEJIL *Léon*
Rio Tuerto ☎908 226998
Jun-Aug 0.6HEC ▦ ◆ ⋔ ▼ ✕ ⊙ ⚑ ⌀ ▲ ⌇ R ☎ ⊞ lau ◆ ⚊ ✕ Prices: A360 V375 ⛽425 ▲425

South

Forbidding crags, dry river beds, spectacular snow-capped mountains, terraced olive groves, flamenco and some of Spain's finest historic cities, draw the visitor to the Andalusian south , a region with attractions as varied as itself.
The amazing backdrop of the Sierra Nevada towers over lovely Granada and its palace-fortress, the Alhambra. The Moorish heritage of ancient Córdoba is proclaimed by its astonishing mosque-cathedral - one of the glories of Spain. Inside the dazzlingly beautiful mosque's forest of archways and columns, sits a Gothic cathedral. The wonderful gardens of a 14th-century castle are nearby.
Bullfights and carnival are part of the excitement of Cádiz. In Seville, Easter week sees the procession of penitents while, in May, colourful celebrations drawing vast numbers from throughout Spain, mark the El Rocío pilgrimage.

The isolation of much of Andalusia contrasts with the better-known hectic charms of the coast, which draws sun-seekers and pleasure-lovers to the resorts of Marbella, Málaga and many more.

ADRA *Almeria*
Las Gaviotas ☎950 400660
2km W on N340 (Almeria-Málaga)
Jul-15 Sep 2HEC ▒▒ ◕ ◆ ⋔ ⚊ ▼ ✕ ⊙ ⚑ ⌀ ⚌ ⚏ ⌇ PS ☎ ⊞ lau ◆
⌇R Prices: A481 V481 ⛽508 ▲481

Habana ☎950 522127
2km W at Km58.3 on N340 (Almeria-Málaga).
All year 2HEC ◕ ⋔ ⚊ ▼ ✕ ⊙ ⚑ ⌀ ▲ ⌇ S ☎ ⊞ lau Prices: A400 V400 ⛽400 ▲400

AGUILAS *Murcia*
Calarreona ctra de Aguilas a Vera ☎968 413704
A quiet site, 50m from the sea.
Near Km4 on N332 (Aguilas-Murcia).
Jun-15 Sep 3.6HEC ▒▒ ◕ ⋔ ⚊ ▼ ✕ ⊙ ⚑ ⌀ ⌇ S ☎ ⊞ lau Prices: A445 V445 ⛽445 ▲445

ALCALA DE GUADAIRA *Sevilla*
Los Naranjos ☎954 5630354
All year 16HEC ◕ ⋔ ⚊ ▼ ✕ ⊙ ⚑ ⚏ ⚌ ▲ ⌇ P ☎ ⊞ lau ◆ ⌀ ⚊

ALCAZARES, LOS *Murcia*
Cartagonova ☎968 575100
On CN332 between Los Alcazares and La Union.
Jul-Sep 1.5HEC ▒▒ ◆ ⋔ ⚊ ▼ ⊙ ⚑ ⌀ ⚏ ⌇ LPS ☎ ⊞ lau ◆ ✕ Prices: A439 V439 ⛽503 ▲503

ALJARAQUE *Huelva*
Las Vegas ☎959 318141
From Huelva cross the bridge over the River Odiel and continue for 8km towards Punta Umbria. Signposted
All year 3HEC ▒▒ ◆ ⋔ ⚊ ▼ ✕ ⊙ ⚑ ⌀ ⌇ PRS ☎ ⊞ lau

BAÑOS DE FORTUNA *Murcia*
Fuente ☎968 685454
Take C3223 from Fortuna à Pinoso to Balncario de Fortuna. Signposted.
Jun-15 Sep 0.9HEC ▦ ⚊⌇ ⋔ ▼ ✕ ⊙ ⚑ ⚌ ☎ ⊞ lau ◆ ⚊ ⌀ ⌇P
Prices: A300-350 pitch 950-1100

Las Palmeras ☎968 685123
Camping Card Compulsory.
All year ▒▒ ⚊⌇ ◕ ⋔ ⚊ ▼ ✕ ⊙ ⚑ ⌀ ⚌ ⌇ P ☎ ⊞ lau Prices: A250 ⛽250 ▲250

BOLNUEVO *Murcia*
Garoa Camping Playa de Mazarrón ☎968 150660
On level ground divided by a footpath and partly bordered by palm trees.
Turn W off N332 in Puerto de Mazarrón at approx Km111 and head towards Bolnuevo. Then take the MU road and drive 4.6km to site entrance which is 1km E of Punta Bela.
All year 8HEC ▒▒ ◔ ◆ ⋔ ⚊ ▼ ✕ ⊙ ⚑ ⌀ ⌇ S ☎ ⊞ lau
Prices: pitch 975-1500

CARCHUNA *Granada*
Don Cactus ☎958 623109
Modern site adjoining the beach. Dogs not allowed in July and August.
At Km343 on N340 (Carchuna-Motril).
All year 4HEC ▒▒ ◆ ⋔ ⚊ ▼ ✕ ⊙ ⚑ ⌀ ⌇ S ☎ ⊞ lau ◆ ⌇P Prices: A500 pitch 940

CARLOTA, LA *Cordoba*
Carlos III ☎957 300697
In wooded surroundings with modern facilities.
Access via 'La Carlota' exit on NIV.
All year 5HEC ▒▒ ◆ ⋔ ⚊ ▼ ✕ ⊙ ⚑ ⚏ ⚌ ⌇ P ☎ ⊞ lau ◆ ⚊ ⌇L
Prices: A508 V508 ⛽535 ▲508

CASTILLO DE BAÑOS *Granada*
Castillo de Baños ☎958 829528
Well equipped site next to the beach.
At Km360 on N340 (Castillo de Baños-La Mamola).
15 Jun-15 Sep 2.8HEC ⠿ ♦ ⋔ ⅀ ☩ ✕ ⊙ ⊟ ⌀ ☷ ⟨ PS ⚐ ⊞ lau
Prices: A475 pitch 900

CONIL DE LA FRONTERA *Cádiz*
Cala del Aceite Roche Viejo ☎956 440972
All year 30HEC ⠿ ⋬ ⋔ ⅀ ☩ ✕ ⊙ ⊟ ⌀ ☎ ☷ ⚐ ⊞ lau ➡ ⟨RS

Fuente del Gallo Fuente del Gallo ☎956 440137
300m from the beach.
Signposted from N340, Km21.6.
15 Mar-5 Oct 2.5HEC ⠿ ♦ ⋔ ⅀ ☩ ✕ ⊙ ⊟ ⌀ ☍ ⟨ S ⚐ ⊞ lau
Prices: A510 V420 ⊞480 ▲420

Roche ctra Pago del Zorro ☎956 442216
All year 2.9HEC ⠿ ⠿ ♦ ⋔ ⅀ ☩ ✕ ⊙ ⊟ ⌀ ▲ ⟨ PS ⚐ ⊞ lau

EJIDO, EL *Almeria*
Mar Azul Playa de San Miguel ☎950 497505
Sports and recreational facilities available.
6km from village.
All year 22HEC ⠿ ♦ ⋔ ⅀ ☩ ✕ ⊙ ⊟ ⌀ ☎ ⟨ PS ⚐ ⊞ lau

ESTEPONA *Málaga*
Parque Tropical ☎95 2793618
A modern site situated at the foot of the Sierra Bermeja mountains,
five minutes walk from the sea.
Access via N340 at Km162.
All year 1.2HEC ⌀ ⋬ ⋔ ⅀ ☩ ✕ ⊙ ⊟ ⌀ ⟨ PS ⚐ ⊞ lau Prices: A348-
482 V348-482 ⊞482-535 ▲482-535

FUENGIROLA *Málaga*
Calazul Mijas Costa ☎95 2493219
Exit from C340 at Km200.
All year 4HEC ⠿ ⠿ ⋬ ⋔ ⅀ ☩ ✕ ⊙ ⊟ ⌀ ⚐ ⊞ lau ➡ ⟨S Prices:
A325-500 V325-500 ⊞325-850 ▲325-850

GALLARDOS, LOS *Almeria*
Gallardos ☎950 528324
Level site with individual pitches, 10 minutes from the sea and the
old Moorish village of Mojacar. English management.
500m from km 525 on CN340.
All year 3.5HEC ⠿ ⋬ ⋔ ⅀ ☩ ✕ ⊙ ⊟ ⌀ ☷ ☎ ⟨ P ⚐ ⊞ lau Prices:
A185-450 V185-450 ⊞185-450 ▲185-450

GRANADA *Granada*
Sierra Nevada ctra de Jaen 107 ☎958 150062
Almost level grassy site, in numerous sections, within motel
complex.
Mar-Oct 3.2HEC ⠿ ♦ ⋔ ⅀ ☩ ✕ ⊙ ⊟ ⌀ ☎ ⟨ P ⚐ ⊞ lau

GUIJAROSSA, LA *Cordoba*
Campiña ☎957 315158
In a quiet location.
Access via N4 turn off at Km424 or Km441 and follow signs to
Santaella and campsite.
All year 0.7HEC ⠿ ⋬ ⋔ ⅀ ☩ ✕ ⊙ ⊟ ⌀ ☎ ▲ ⟨ P ⚐ ⊞ lau Prices:
A455 V455 ⊞481 ▲428

ISLA PLANA *Murcia*
Madrilles ctra de la Azohia Km45 ☎68 152151
All year 5HEC ⠿ ⠿ ⋬ ⋔ ⅀ ☩ ✕ ⊙ ⊟ ⌀ ⟨ P ⚐ ⊞ ⊗ lau ➡ ✕
⟨S Prices: pitch 476

MARBELLA *Málaga*
Buganvilla ☎95 2831974
Camping Card Compulsory.
All year 4HEC ⠿ ⠿ ⋬ ⋔ ⅀ ☩ ✕ ⊙ ⊟ ⌀ ☷ ☎ ⟨ PS ⚐ ⊞ lau
Prices: A375-490 ⊞425-800 ▲425

Marbella Playa ☎952 833998
On beach with large sports area.
Access is via N340 Cádiz-Málaga Km200.
All year 5.5HEC ⠿ ⠿ ⋬ ♦ ⋔ ⅀ ☩ ✕ ⊙ ⊟ ⌀ ⟨ P ⚐ ⊞ lau ➡ ⟨S

MAZAGÓN *Huelva*

Mazagón cuesta de la Barca s/n ☎959 376208
Undulating terrain amongst dunes in sparse pine forest. Long sandy beach.
Turn off the N431 Sevilla-Huelva road just before San Juan del Puerto in direction of Moguer and continue S via Palso de la Frontera.
All year 8HEC ⬛ ⣿⣿ ⌂ ⋔ 🛒 🍽 ✕ ⊙ ⛺ ⌀ ≈ S ☎ ⊞ lau Prices: A475 V475 ⌷475 ▲475

PUERTO DE SANTA MARÍA, EL *Cádiz*

Playa Las Dunas de San Anton ps Maritimo de la Puntilla ☎9566 872210
All year 13.2HEC ⣿⣿ ◆ ⋔ 🛒 🍽 ✕ ⊙ ⛺ ⌀ 🚿 ⌷ ≈ 🌳 P ☎ ⊞ lau ➡ ≈LRS Prices: A572-515 V492-444 ⌷621-556 ▲621-556

PUNTA UMBRIA *Huelva*

Derena Mar ☎959 312004
All year 12.5HEC ⣿⣿ ◆ ⋔ 🛒 🍽 ✕ ⊙ ⛺ ⌀ ▲ ☎ ⊞ lau ➡ ≈LS

RONDA *Málaga*

El Sur ctra de Algeciras ☎095 2875939
All year 4HEC ⬛ ⣿⣿ ⌂ ⋔ 🛒 🍽 ✕ ⊙ ⛺ ⌀ 🚿 ≈ P ☎ ⊞ lau Prices: A455 V430 ⌷430 ▲430

ROQUETAS-DE-MAR *Almeria*

Roquetas Los Parrales ☎95 343809
Access by road No 340. 1.7km from Km428.6.
All year 8HEC ⣿⣿ ⌂ ⋔ 🛒 🍽 ✕ ⊙ ⛺ ⌀ 🚿 ≈ PS ☎ ⊞ lau Prices: A490 V490 ⌷490 ▲490

SAN ROQUE *Cádiz*

Motel San Roque ☎956 780100
All year 4HEC ⬛ ◆ ⋔ 🛒 🍽 ✕ ⊙ ⛺ 🚿 ▲ ≈ P ☎ ⊞ lau ➡ ≈S Prices: A375 V321 ⌷481 ▲455

SANTA ELENA *Jaén*

El Estanque ☎953 623093
15 May-15 Sep 1.5HEC ⣿⣿ ⌂ ⋔ 🛒 🍽 ✕ ⊙ ⛺ ☎ ⊞ lau ➡ 🛒 ≈LPR

SEVILLA (SEVILLE) *Sevilla*

Sevilla ☎954 514379
Level site near airfield, road and railway.
About 2km from airfield, 100m from the NIV (Madrid-Sevilla) at Km533.8.
15 Apr-15 Sep 2.5HEC ⣿⣿ ⌂ ⋔ 🛒 🍽 ✕ ⊙ ⛺ ⌀ 🚿 ≈ P ☎ ⊞ lau Prices: A460 V460 ⌷450 ▲430

TARAMAY *Granada*

Paraiso ☎958 632370
All year 0.7HEC ⣿⣿ ◆ ⋔ 🛒 🍽 ✕ ⊙ ⛺ ⌀ ≈ S ☎ ⊞ lau ➡ ≈P

TARIFA *Cádiz*

Paloma ☎956 684203
All year 4.9HEC ⬛ ⌂ ⋔ 🛒 🍽 ✕ ⊙ ⛺ ⌀ 🚿 ≈ P ☎ ⊞ lau ➡ ≈RS Prices: A369-615 ⌷305-508 ▲273-455

Rió Jara ☎956 680570
Extensive site on meadowland with good tree coverage. Long sandy beach.
On the N340 Málaga-Cádiz road at Km79.7 turn towards the sea.
All year 3.5HEC ⬛ ◆ ⋔ 🛒 🍽 ✕ ⊙ ⛺ ⌀ ☎ ⊞ lau ➡ ≈RS Prices: A575 ⌷475 ▲425

CAMPING TORRE DEL MAR
Paseo Maritimo s/n • E-29740 Torre del Mar (Prov. Málaga)

1st category holiday site, right on a beautiful beach of the Costa del Sol and not far from Torre del Mar. Restaurant with terrace and typical regional restaurant, swimming-pool and paddling-pool with aquatic toboggan, clean and modern sanitary installations, free hot water in showers. Satellite dish. No long-term campers. Special prices in low season (1.10.-31.3): up to 9 days 20%, up to 19 days 40%, 30 days or more 50%. Special fees in low season for pensioners.

Tarifa ☎956 684778
Terraced sites.
All year 3.2HEC ⣿⣿ ◆ ⋔ 🛒 🍽 ✕ ⊙ ⛺ ⌀ ≈ S ☎ ⊞ lau Prices: A575 V425 ⌷475 ▲425

At TORRE DE LA PEÑA(7km NW)

Torre de la Peña ☎956 684903
Terraced, on both sides of through road. Upper terraces are considerably quieter. Roofing provides shade. View of the sea, Tarifa and on clear days N Africa (Tangier).
Entrance on the N340 Cádiz-Málaga, at Km76.5 turn inland by the old square tower.
All year 3HEC ⬛ ⣿⣿ ⌂ ◆ ⋔ 🛒 🍽 ✕ ⊙ ⛺ ⌀ 🚿 ≈ S ☎ ⊞ lau Prices: A590 V430 ⌷430 ▲430

TORRE DEL MAR *Málaga*

Torre del Mar ☎95 2540224
A fine site on a beautiful beach, with good facilities. Shop open June-September only.
SW of town. Access via N340 (Almeria-Málaga).
All year 2.4HEC ⬛ ◆ ⋔ 🛒 🍽 ✕ ⊙ ⛺ ⌀ ≈ P ☎ ⊞ lau ➡ ≈S Prices: A550 V550 ⌷585 ▲550

VEJER DE LA FRONTERA *Cádiz*

Vejer ctra National (N340) ☎956 450098
15 Jun-15 Sep 0.8HEC ⣿⣿ ◆ ⋔ 🛒 🍽 ✕ ⊙ ⛺ ⌀ ≈ P ☎ ⊞ lau ➡ ✕ Prices: pitch 1175-1275

ANDORRA

Prices are in French Francs or Spanish Pesetas.

SANT JULIÀ DE LÒRIA

Huguet ctra de Fontaneda ☎843718
On level strip of meadowland with rows of fruit and deciduous trees.
Off La Seu d'Urgell road N1, S of village and drive W across river.
All year 1.5HEC ⬛ ⌂ ◆ ⋔ 🍽 ✕ ⊙ ⛺ ≈ R ☎ ⊞ lau ➡ 🛒 ✕ ⌀ 🚿 ≈P Prices: A475 V475 ⌷475 ▲475

SWITZERLAND

Bordered by France in the west, Germany in the north, Austria in the east, and Italy in the south, Switzerland is considered by many to be one of the most beautiful countries in Europe.

It has the highest mountains in Europe and some of the most awe-inspiring waterfalls and lakes, features that are offset by picturesque villages set amid green pastures and an abundance of Alpine flowers covering the valleys and lower mountain slopes during the spring. The highest peaks are Monte Rosa (15,217ft) on the Italian border, the Matterhorn (14,782ft), and the Jungfrau (13,669ft). Some of the most beautiful areas are the Via Mala Gorge, the Falls of the Rhine near Schaffhausen, the Rhône Glacier, and the lakes of Luzern and Thun.

The Alps cause many climatic variations throughout Switzerland, but generally the climate is said to be the healthiest in the world. In the higher Alpine regions temperatures tend to be low, whereas the lower land of the northern area has higher temperatures and hot summers. French is spoken in the western cantons (regions), Swiss-German dialects (although German is understood) in the central and northern cantons and Italian in Ticino. Romansch is spoken in Grisons.

Switzerland has 350 campsites, 76 of them are run by the Touring Club Suisse (TCS) who publish details of classified sites annually. Information can also be obtained from tourist offices, which are to be found in most provincial towns and resorts. The season extends from April or May to September or October, although some sites are open all year, particularly at winter sports resorts.

Off-site camping regulations differ from canton (region) to canton. However, overnight parking may be tolerated in rest areas of some motorways, but at all times the high standard of hygiene regulations must be observed. Make sure you do not contravene local laws. It is recommended that an official site should be used for this purpose.

HOW TO GET THERE

From Britain, Switzerland is usually approached via France. For details of the *AA European Routes Service* please consult the Contents Page.

Distance

From the Channel ports to Bern is approximately 810km (503 miles), a distance which will normally require only one overnight stop.

If you intend to use Swiss motorways, you will be liable for a tax of *SFr* 40 - see 'Motorway tax' below for full details.

FACTS AND FIGURES

Capital: Bern (Berne)

Language: German, French, Italian, Romansh

IDD code: 41. To call the UK dial 00 44

Currency: Swiss Franc (*SFr*1 = 100 centimes). At the time of going to press 1 = *SFr*1.82.

Local time: GMT + 1 (summer GMT + 2)

Emergency Services: Police 117; Fire 118; Ambulance 117 or 144 (dependant on the telephone zone).

Business Hours-

Banks: Mon-Fri 08.30-16.30 (in towns)

Shops: Mon-Fri 08.30-12.00 and 14.00-18.30; Sat 08.30-12.00 and 14.00-16.00/17.00 (shops remain open all day in cities).

Average daily temperatures:
Zurich

Jan 0°C	Jul 19°C
Mar 5°C	Sep 15°C
May 9°C	Nov 5°C

Tourist Information: Swiss National Tourist Office

UK Swiss Centre, Swiss Court London W1V 8EE
☎ 0171-734 1921

USA 608 Fifth Avenue New York, NY 10020
☎ (212) 757 5944

Camping card: recommended. Some reductions available.

MOTORING & GENERAL INFORMATION

The information given here is specific to Switzerland. It **must** be read in conjunction with the European ABC at the front of the book, which covers those regulations which are common to many countries.

Boats*

Third party insurance is compulsory for craft used on the Swiss lakes.

British Embassy/Consulates*

The British Embassy together with its consular section is located at 3005 Berne, Thunstrasse 50 ☎(031) 352 5021/6. There are British Consulates in Genève (Geneva) and Zürch, and Honorary Consuls in Lugano, Montreux, Vevey (St Légier) and Valay (Muraz/Sierre).

Children in cars

Children under 12 may not travel as front or rear seat passengers unless using seat belts or a child restraint system appropriate to the size of the child.

Currency

There are no restrictions on the import or export of foreign or Swiss currency. In addition to banks there are exchange offices at the border, railway stations in large towns, airports and in travel agencies and hotels which are usually open 08.00-20.00hrs.

Dimensions and weight restrictions

Private cars and towed trailers or caravans are restricted to the following dimensions - **car** height, 4 metres; width, 2.50 metres; length, 12 metres. **Trailer/caravan** height, 4 metres; width, 2.50 metres; length, 12 metres (including tow bar). The maximum permitted overall length of vehicle/trailer or caravan combination is 18.35 metres.
Note It is dangerous or forbidden to use a vehicle towing a trailer or caravan on some mountain roads; motorists should ensure that roads on which they are about to travel are suitable for the conveyance of vehicle/trailer or caravan combinations.

The fully-laden weight of trailers which do not have an independent braking system should not exceed 50% of the unladen weight of the towing vehicle, but trailers which have an independent braking system can weigh up to 100% of the unladen weight of the towing vehicle.

Driving licence*

A valid UK or Republic of Ireland licence is acceptable in Switzerland. The minimum age at which visitors from UK or Republic of Ireland may use a temporarily imported car is 18 years and a temporarily imported motorcycle of between 50-125cc (not exceeding 40kph) 16 years, exceeding 125cc 18 years.

Foodstuffs*

Travellers over 15 years of age may import provisions for 1 day but a maximum of 500g of butter and a maximum of 2.5kg of meat and meat products, made up of no more than 500g of meat and/or no more than 1kg of meat products such as ham, sausages, canned/tinned meat and/or no more than 2.5kg of rabbit, poultry, game, fish and shellfish. The import of meat and meat products (except tins or preserves) of all animals from Africa, Asia (except Japan), Turkey and the former USSR is forbidden, as is the import of pork meat and pork products from Spain, Portugal, Sardinia, Bosnia Herzegovina and Macedonia (FYROM).

Lights*

Driving on sidelights only is prohibited. Spotlights are forbidden. Fog lamps in front must be in pairs. Dipped headlights must be used in cities and towns. Dipped headlights are compulsory in tunnels, whether they are lit or not, and failure to observe this regulation can lead to a fine. Switerland has a *'tunnel'* road sign (a rectangular blue panel showing the entrance of the tunnel), which serves to remind drivers to turn on their dipped headlights. In open country, headlights must be dipped as follows: at least 200 metres (220yds) in front of any pedestrian or oncoming vehicle (including trains parallel to the road); when requested to do so by the driver of an oncoming vehicle flashing lights; or when reversing, travelling in lines of traffic or stopping. Parking lights must be used when waiting at level crossings, or near roadworks. They must also be used in badly-lit areas when visibility is poor. It is recommended that *motorcyclists* use dipped headlights during the day.

Motoring club*

The **Touring Club Suisse** (TCS) has branch offices in all important towns, and has its head office at 1211 Genève 3, rue Pierre-Fatio 9 ☎(022) 7371212. The TCS will extend a courtesy service to all motorists but their major services will have to be paid for. The opening hours of TCS offices vary according to location and time of year, but generally they are 08.00/09.00-11.45/12.30hrs and 13.30/14.00-17.00/18.30hrs Monday to Friday and 08.00/09.00-11.45/12.00hrs Saturday (summer only).

Motorway tax

The Swiss authorities levy an annual motorway tax. A vehicle sticker, costing SFr40 for vehicles up to 3.5 tonnes maximum total weight and known locally as a *vignette*, must be displayed by vehicles using Swiss motorways including motorcycles, trailers and caravans. Motorists may purchase the stickers from the AA or at the Swiss frontier. Vehicles over 3.5 tonnes maximum total weight are taxed on all roads in Switzerland; a licence for one day, 10 days, one month and one year periods can be obtained. There are no stickers, and the tax must be paid at the Swiss frontier.

Roads

The road surfaces are generally good, but some main roads are narrow in places. Traffic congestion may be severe at the beginning and end of the German school holidays.

On any stretch of mountain road, the driver of a private car may be asked by the driver of a postal bus which is painted yellow, to reverse, or otherwise manoeuvre to allow the postal bus to pass. Postal bus drivers often sound a distinctive three note horn; no other vehicles may use this type of horn in Switzerland.

Switzerland has about 1,000 miles of motorway (*autobahn* or *autoroute*). Tolls are not payable but see *Motorway Tax* above. Emergency telephones, which connect you to the motorway control police, are located every 2km.

Speed limits*

Car

Built-up areas 50kph (31mph)
Other roads 80kph (49mph)
semi-motorways 100kph (62mph)
Motorways 120kph (74mph)

Car/caravan/trailer

Built-up areas 50kph (31mph)
Other roads, including semi-motorways 80kph (49mph)†
Motorways 80kph (49mph)

These limits do not apply if another limit is indicated by signs, or if the vehicle is subject to a lower general speed limit.

†If the weight of the caravan or luggage trailer exceeds 1,000kg, a speed limit of 60kph (37mph) applies on roads outside built-up areas and semi-motorways, but 80kph (49mph) is still permissible on motorways.

Warning triangle/Hazard warning lights*

The use of a warning triangle is compulsory in the event of accident or breakdown. The triangle must be placed on the road at least 50 metres (55yds) behind the vehicle on ordinary roads, and at least 100 metres (109yds) on motorways. If the vehicle is in an emergency lane, the triangle must be placed on the right of the emergency lane. Hazard warning lights may be used in conjunction with the triangle on ordinary roads, but on motorways and semi-motorways they must be switched off as soon as the warning triangle is erected. If this is not done, the police may impose an on-the-spot fine (see *Police Fines* in the Continental ABC).

*Additional information will be found in the Continental ABC at the front of the book.

A-Z DIRECTORY

Prices are in Swiss Francs Abbreviations str strasse TCS Touring Club Suisse.
Each name preceded by 'Bad', 'La', 'Le' or 'Les' is listed under the name that follows it.

North

Basel owes its prosperity to its key geographical position - at the junction of the borders of France, Germany and Switzerland, and at the point on the Rhine where it becomes navigable. It has evolved into an important business and industrial centre. The old town has a great Gothic cathedral - with a fine view from the top of the towers, and a remarkable collection of art in the Fine Arts Museum, "Kunstmuseum". The town also has an extensive Zoological Garden, with an emphasis on breeding threatened species. The countryside of this area is one of medieval castles, quaint villages, thermal spas, dense forests, lush meadows and sparkling lakes. But above the charming Baroque town of Solothurn is the last ridge of the Jura - the giddy crests of the Weissenstein, from where, at over 4,000ft, there is an outstanding view over Berne and the lakes of Neuchâtel, Murten and Biel.

GRENCHEN Solothurn

At **STAAD**

Strausak (TCS) ☎065 521133
12 Apr-Sep 1HEC ▦ ⌐ ⋔ ⋔ ⋔ ⋔ ✕ ⊙ ⊕ ⋋ LR ⊡ ⊞ ♦ ⋋P

KÜNTEN Aargau

Sulz ☎056 4964879
Situated by a river.
From motorway N1 turn off at Baden in the direction of Bremgarten.
15 Mar-Oct 2.5HEC ▦ ⌐ ⋔ ⋔ ✕ ⊙ ⊕ ⌀ ⋋ PR ⊡ ⊞ lau

LÄUFELFINGEN Basel

Läufelfingen ☎062 2991189
On road from Basel to Olten.
Apr-Oct 0.5HEC ▦ ⌐ ⋔ ⊙ ⊕ ⋔ ⊞ ⊞ Prices: A4 V3 ⋔4.50 ▲3-4

MÖHLIN Aargau

Bachtalen (TCS) ☎061 8515095
2km N.
3 Apr-6 Oct 1.3HEC ▦ ⋗⋌ ⋔ ⊙ ⊕ ⋋ R ⊡ ⊞ lau ♦ ⋔ ⋔ ✕ ⌀ Prices:
A4.40-5.40 ⋔9-13 ▲4.30-5.30

Waldhort Basel

at the motorway Basle-Delémont (exit Reinach-Nord), about 4 miles outside the city

Quiet and well equipped site: hot showers, shop, kitchen commodities. Swimming pool 10 x 4m. Good base for the -worthwhile-visit of Basle: cathedral, museums, fairs, Goetheanum, zoo, etc.

Information: Camping-Caravanning club beider Basel, P.O.B. 78, CH-4027 Basel

REINACH Basel

Waldhort Heideweg 16 ☎061 7116429
15 Mar-18 Oct 2.9HEC ▦ ⌐ ⋔ ⋔ ✕ ⊙ ⊕ ⌀ ≞ ⋋ P ⊞ ⊞ lau ♦ ✕
Prices: A6.50 V3.50 ⋔6-8 ▲4-6

ZURZACH Aargau

Oberfeld ☎56 2492575
Apr-Oct 2HEC ▦ ♦ ⋔ ⋔ ✕ ⊙ ⊕ ⌀ ⋔ ⊞ ⊞ lau ♦ ⋋PR Prices: A5
V1.80 ⋔8-15.50 ▲2.50-7

North East

At the northern gateway to Switzerland, the town of Schaffhausen falls in terraces from the 16th-century Munot Castle, and is the traditional starting point for a visit to the Rhine Falls, "Rheinfall". The most powerfull waterfall in Europe, the Rhine makes a spectacular 70ft drop - one of the most famous sights in Europe. St Gallen is popular with visitors; the twin domed towers of the cathedral overlook the attractive old town. The cathedral's plain exterior belies a wonderfully rich Baroque interior, with mural paintings covering the central dome and nave, and there is a remarkable chancel with a huge high altar.
The largest city in Switzerland, cosmopolitan Zürich hums around the Bahnhofstrasse - a fine, wide, tree-lined boulevard of glittering shops and modern offices and banks. For more sedate pursuits visit the quays along the banks of Lake Zürich - lined with immaculate gardens and lawns, visit the old quarters with their cobbled streets, or take a boat trip on the lake. The Swiss National Museum, "Schweizerisches Landesmuseum" is a treasure-house of Swiss civilisation from prehistoric times to the present.
The countryside of the region provides good walking, and the mountains and hills are dotted with attractive farms. Picturesque villages contain traditional colourful houses, and sparkling lakes adorn the valleys.
Between the borders of Switzerland and Austria is the principality of Leichtenstein, with its extensive tourist attractions, but retaining its own individual charm and appeal. The capital and main centre is Vaduz, overlooked by its 14th- century castle.

ALTNAU Thurgau

Ruderbaum ☎071 6951885
By Lake Bodensee between Constance and Romanshorn.
Apr-Oct 6.5HEC ▦ ⌐ ⋔ ⊙ ⊕ ⌀ ≞ ⋋ L ⊞ ⊞ lau ♦ ⋔ ⋔ ✕ Prices:
A5.50-6.50 V3.50 ⋔8 ▲7

ALT ST JOHANN St-Gallen

3 Eidgenossen (TCS) ☎071 9991274
All year 0.5HEC ▦ ⌐ ⋔ ✕ ⊙ ⊕ ⌀ ⊡ ⊞ lau ♦ ⋋R Prices: A4 ⋔12
▲10

APPENZELL Appenzell

Kau Appenzell ☎071 7875030
Camping Card Compulsory.
All year 2HEC ▦ ⋗⋌ ⋔ ⋔ ✕ ⊙ ⊕ ≞ ⊞ ⊞ ⊞ ✖ lau

EGNACH Thurgau

Wiedehorn ☎071 661006
Etr-Sep 2.5HEC ▦ ⋗⋌ ⋔ ⋔ ✕ ⊙ ⊕ ⌀ ⊡ ⊞ ♦ ⋋L

ESCHENZ Thurgau

Hüttenberg ☎052 7412337
Terraced site lying above village.
1km SW.
All year 5HEC ▦ ⌐ ⋔ ⋔ ⊙ ⊕ ⌀ ≞ ⋋ P ⊞ ⊞ lau ♦ ⋔ ✕ ⋋LR ⊞

GOLDINGEN *St-Gallen*
Atzmännig ☎055 2841235
All year 1.5HEC ▦ ⅃⅄ ⋔ ✕ ⊙ ⬛ ☎ ⊞ lau ✦ ⅃ ⅄ Prices: A5.50
pitch 6.50

KRUMMENAU *St-Gallen*
Adler ☎074 41030
On edge of village.
All year 0.8HEC ▦ ⅃⅄ ⋔ ⅃ ✕ ⊙ ⬛ ⊞ lau

LEUTSWIL BEI BISCHOFFZELL *Thurgau*
Sitterbrücke ☎071 4226398
Signposted from Bischoffzell on the Konstanz-St Gallen road.
Apr-Sep 1HEC ▦ ⅄ ⋔ ⊙ ⬛ ⌀ ⌸ ☎ lau ✦ ✕ ⅃R Prices: A5 V2
⬛6.50 ▲3.50-6.50

MAMMERN *Thurgau*
Guldifuss Guldifusstr 1 ☎052 7411320
Mar-Dec ▦ ⅄ ⋔ ✕ ⊙ ⬛ ⌀ ⌸ ⅃ L ⬛ lau ✦ ⅃ Prices: A8 V4 ⬛4 ▲4

OTTENBACH *Zürich*
Reussbrücke (TCS) ☎01 7612022
By river of same name.
Access from Zürich via road 126 in SW direction, via Affoltern to
Ottenbach.
7 Apr-8 Oct 1.5HEC ▦ ⅄ ⋔ ⅃ ✕ ⊙ ⬛ ⌀ ⌸ ⅃ R ☎ ⊞ lau ✦ ⅃ ✕

ST GALLEN *St-Gallen*
Leebrücke (TCS) ☎071 384969
29 Apr-1 Oct 1.5HEC ▦ ⅃⅄ ⋔ ⅃ ⅄ ✕ ⊙ ⬛ ⌀ ⌸ ⅃ R ⬛ ⊞ lau ✦ ⅃P

ST MARGRETHEN *St-Gallen*
Bruggerhorn ☎071 712201
Apr-Oct ▦ ⅄ ⋔ ⅃ ✕ ⊙ ⬛ ⌀ ⅃ LP ☎ ⊞ ⩘ lau

SCHÖNENGRUND *Appenzell*
Schönengrund ☎071 3611268
All year 1.2HEC ⅄ ⋔ ⊙ ⬛ ⌀ ☎ ⊞ lau ✦ ⅃ ✕ ⊞ Prices: A5.30 V3
⬛3 ▲3

SIHLWALD *Zürich*
Sihlwald Tahletenstr ☎01 7200498
May-Sep 1.2HEC ▦ ⅃⅄ ⋔ ⅃ ✕ ⊙ ⬛ ⌀ ⌸ ⅃ R ☎ ⊞ ✦ ✕

STEIN AM RHEIN *Schaffhausen*
Grenzstein Öhningerstr 75 ☎052 7415141
1.8km E.
All year 1.1HEC ▦ ⦂⦂⦂ ⅄ ⋔ ⅃ ⅄ ✕ ⊙ ⬛ ⌀ ⌸ ⬛ ⅃ P ☎ ⊞ lau

WAGENHAUSEN *Schaffhausen*
Wagenhausen Hauptstr 82 ☎052 7414271
In a delightful wooded location beside the River Rhein.
Apr-Oct 4.5HEC ⅄ ⋔ ⅃ ⅄ ✕ ⊙ ⬛ ⌀ ⌸ ⅃ PR ☎ ⊞ lau ✦ ⅃L
Prices: A7 ⬛12 ▲11

WALENSTADT *St-Gallen*
See-Camping ☎081 7351212
Camping Card Compulsory.
mid May-mid Sep 2.2HEC ⅄ ⋔ ⅃ ⊙ ⬛ ⅃ L ⬛ ⩘ lau ✦ ⅃ ✕ ⌀ ⌸
⊞ Prices: A7 ⬛5-7 ▲4-8

WILDBERG *Zürich*
Weid ☎052 453388
On a terraced meadow in a very peaceful situation surrounded by
woods.
In Winterthur, follow Tösstal signs, then turn right after spinning-mill
in Turbenthal.
All year 5.4HEC ▦ ⅄ ⋔ ⅃ ⅄ ✕ ⊙ ⬛ ⌀ ⌸ ⊞ lau ✦ ⅃LPR Prices:
A5 pitch 10-13

WINTERTHUR *Zürich*
Schützenhaus Rosenberg Eichliwaldstr 4 ☎052 2125260
To the left of the Schaffhausen road, near the Schützenhaus
restaurant.
All year 0.8HEC ▦ ⅄ ⅃ ⋔ ⊙ ⬛ ⌀ ☎ ⊞ lau ✦ ⅃ ⅄ ✕ ⅃P

Zürich-Seebucht
Seestrasse 559 – Phone 01-4821612

- One of the most attractively located town sites on a lake.
- New modern facilities.
- Visit us out of season. Good choice for pitches then.
- Only 4 km from the town centre (direct bus connection).

Herr Urs Glättli
Seestr. 559, 8037 Zürich

ZÜRICH *Zürich*
Seebucht Seestr 559 ☎01 4821612
Beautiful park-like site between the shore road and the lake.
1km S.
May-Sep 2.5HEC ▦ ⦂⦂⦂ ♦ ⋔ ⅃ ⅄ ✕ ⊙ ⬛ ⌀ ⬛ ▲ ⅃ LP ⬛ ⊞ lau
✦ ⅃LP

North West/Central

This region extends from the French border in the northwest, to
Adermatt in the canton of Uri, in the heart of the St Gothard
Massif at the crossroads of the Alps. The Province of Jura makes
a lovely transition from the Saône plain to the Germanic 'middle
country' - it is a gentle land of peaceful pastures and low houses,
and is a favourite with cross-country skiers in winter. Neuchâtel,
capital of its own canton, stands in a delightful position between
the lake of Neuchâtel and the mountains, and has a picturesque
old town. The lake offers good facilities for watersports and
cruising, and a nearby funicular railway serves Chaumont, from
where there is a vast panorama of the Bernese Alps and the
Mont Blanc Massif.
Bern is a delight, with pretty arcaded buildings lining the streets
of the old town, and a lovely setting facing the Alps. Lucerne has
a superb site at the northwestern end of Lake Lucerne, and
cruises on the lake offer breathtaking changing panoramas. The
Transport Museum in Lucerne contains a fascinating story of the
development of Swiss transport.
But the highlight of the central region must be the Alps, with the
Jungfrau Massif reaching heights of over 13,600ft. Of course
during the winter this is a paradise for winter sports, but during
the summer there is good access to the most well-known peaks
by road, rail or cable-car, with dizzy heights and spectacular
views.

AESCHI Bern

Panorama ☎033 6544377
400m SE of Camping Club Bern.
15 May-Sep 1HEC ▥ ⊕ ⋒ ⅀ ⊙ ⊟ ⊞ ⅂ PR ⌂ lau ✦ ⅄ ✕ ⊞ Prices:
A4.80-5 V2.50 ◚8-9

ALTDORF Uri

Moosbad Flüelerstr ☎041 8708541
All year 0.9HEC ▥ ⍥ ⅊ ⋒ ⅀ ⊙ ⊟ ⌀ ⅀ ⊞ ⅂ P ⌂ ⊞ lau ✦ ⅄ ✕
⅂LPR

BERN (BERNE) Bern

At **WABERN**

SC Eichholz Strandweg 49 ☎031 9612602
In municipal parkland. Separate section for caravans.
Approach via Gossetstr and track beside river.
May-29 Sep 4HEC ▥ ✦ ⋒ ✕ ⊙ ⊟ ⌀ ⊟ ⅂ R ⊡ ⊞ lau ✦ ⅀ ⅂P

BRENZIKOFEN Bern

Wydeli (TCS) Wydeli 60 ☎031 7711141
8km N of Thun.
Jun-Aug 1.5HEC ▥ ⅊ ⋒ ✕ ⊙ ⊟ ⌀ ⅀ ⅂ PR ⊡ ⊞ lau ✦ ⅀ Prices:
A5.30-5.90 pitch 12-14

BRUNNEN Schwyz

Hopfreben ☎043 311873
On the right bank of the Muotta stream 100m before it flows into the
lake.
1km W.
May-Sep 1.5HEC ▥ ⋒ ⅄ ✕ ⊙ ⊟ ⌀ ⅀ ⅂ LP ⊞ ⊞ Prices: A5.50
pitch 10-18

BURGDORF Bern

Waldegg (TCS) ☎034 227943
On Oberburg road, turn left at petrol station.
Apr-Sep 0.8HEC ▥ ⠿ ⅊ ⠿ ⋒ ⊙ ⊟ ⅂ R ⌂ ⊞ ✦ ⅀ ⅄ ✕

CHAUX-DE-FONDS, LA Neuchâtel

Bois du Couvent ☎079 2405039
Partly on uneven ground.
Take turning off Neuchâtel road near the Zappella and Moeschler
factory and drive for 200m.
15 Jul-15 Aug 2.5HEC ▥ ⊕ ⋒ ⅀ ⅄ ✕ ⊙ ⊟ ⌀ ⊟ ⊟ ⅂ P ⌂ ⊞ lau
Prices: pitch 13-17 (incl 2 persons)

COLOMBIER Neuchâtel

Paradis-Plage ☎038 412446
Mar-Oct 4HEC ▥ ✦ ⋒ ⅀ ⅄ ✕ ⊙ ⊟ ⌀ ⅀ ⅂ L ⊟ ⊞ Prices: A5.50 V1-
2 ◚7-12 ▲7-12

ENGELBERG Obwalden

Eienwäldli Wasserfallstr 108 ☎041 6371949
1.5km SW behind restaurant Einwäldi.
Closed Nov 4HEC ▥ ⍥ ⋒ ⅀ ⅄ ✕ ⊙ ⊟ ⌀ ⅀ ⅂ PR ⌂ ⊞ lau Prices:
A5-6 V2 ◚10 ▲6-10

ERLACH Bern

Mon Plaisir ☎032 881358
Well equipped site beside the lake.
All year 0.6HEC ▥ ⊕ ⋒ ⅀ ✕ ⊙ ⊟ ⌀ ⅀ ⊟ ⊟ ⅂ L ⊡ ⊞ lau ✦ ✕
Prices: A9-12 pitch 34-46

FLÜELEN Uri

Urnersee ☎041 8709222
15 Apr-Oct 4HEC ▥ ⊕ ⋒ ⅀ ⅄ ✕ ⊙ ⊟ ⅀ ⅂ LR ⌂ ⊞ ✦ ⌀ ⅂P
Prices: A8 V6 ◚7-10 ▲5-6

FRUTIGEN Bern

Grassi ☎033 711149
Scattered with fruit trees beside a farm on the right bank of the River
Engstilgern.
From the Hauptstr, turn right at the Simplon Hotel.
All year 1.5HEC ▥ ⊕ ⋒ ⅀ ⊙ ⊟ ⌀ ⅀ ⊟ ⊞ lau ✦ ⅄ ✕ ⅂P

Camping FRUTIGEN

- Located off the road, alongside the Enstligen
  stream, surrounded by high pine trees, this is
  the location for the quiet and well equipped tent
  site in the summer holiday resort of Frutigen.
- Inexhaustible choice of excursions.
- Favourable starting point for the popular upland
  walks on the north and south approaches of the
  Lötschberg railway.

Winter Camping Ski-ing resort of Adelboden,
Kandersteg, Elsigenalp. Swiss Ski School only 10-
12km distant. Inf. W. Glausen, CH-3741 Frutigen.

GAMPELEN Bern

Fanel (TCS) ☎032 3132333
On the shore of Lake Neuchâtel.
26 Mar-5 Oct 11.5HEC ▥ ⊕ ⋒ ⅀ ⅄ ✕ ⊙ ⊟ ⅀ ⅂ L ⌂ ⊞ lau
Prices: A4.40-6.20 pitch 10-15
See advertisement under FRUTIGEN

GOLDAU Schwyz

Bernerhöhe ☎041 821887
On the edge of a forest with a beautiful view of Lake Lauerz.
Separate field for tents.
1.5km SE and turn left.
All year 2.5HEC ▥ ⊕ ⋒ ⅀ ⊙ ⊟ ⊟ ⌂ ⊞ ⍷ lau ✦ ⅄ ✕ ⅂L Prices:
A5.30 V1 ◚3 ▲3

Buosingen ☎041 8553898
All year 1.5HEC ▥ ⊕ ⋒ ⅀ ✕ ⊙ ⊟ ⌀ ⅀ ⊟ ⊟ ⌂ lau ✦ ⅄ ✕ ⅂LP
Prices: A2.50 V1.50 ◚1.50 ▲1.50

GRINDELWALD Bern

Aspen Aspen-Itramen ☎036 8531124
Sunny hill terraces.
May-Oct 2.5HEC ▥ ⊕ ⋒ ✕ ⊙ ⊟ ⌀ ⅀ ⌂ ⊞ Prices: A6 pitch 10-18

Eigernord 27 ☎036 534227
1.2HEC ▥ ⊕ ⋒ ⅀ ⅄ ✕ ⊙ ⊟ ⌀ ⅀ ⌂ ⊞ lau ✦ ⅂P

GSTAAD Bern

Bellerive ☎033 4746330
All year 0.8HEC ▥ ⊕ ⋒ ✕ ⊙ ⊟ ⅀ ⊟ ⊟ ⅂ R ⊟ lau ✦ ⅂P Prices:
A6.40-7.50 V2.20 ◚11-13 ▲11-13

INNERTKIRCHEN Bern

Aareschlucht Hauptstr 6/11 ☎033 9715332
All year 0.5HEC ▥ ⊕ ⋒ ⊙ ⊟ ⅀ ⊟ ⊟ lau ✦ ⅄ ✕ ⅂LPR Prices:
A4.90 pitch 6-13

Grund ☎036 714409
Next to a farm on southern outskirts of village.
Turn S off main road in centre of village at hotel Urweider. Drive for
0.3km, turn right.
All year 80HEC ▥ ⊕ ⋒ ⊙ ⊟ ⊟ ▲ ⌂ ⊞ lau ✦ ⅀ ⅄ ✕ ⌀ ⅂R
Prices: A3.50-3.90 pitch 13-15
See advertisement on page 261.

INTERLAKEN Bern

Alpenblick Seestr 135, Neuhaus ☎036 227757
On the left bank of the River Lombach upstream from the bridge in a
meadow bordering a forest opposite the Neuhaus Motel and the
Strandbad Restaurant.
8km N.
All year 2.4HEC ▥ ⊕ ⋒ ⊙ ⊟ ⌀ ⅀ ⌂ ⊞ lau ✦ ✕ ⅀ ⅂LPR Prices: A5-
5.50 V4 ◚10-16 ▲9-16

Hobby 3 ☎033 229652
Access via N8 (Spiez-Interlaken) towards Gunten/Beatenberg.
Apr-15 Oct 1.2HEC ▥ ⊕ ⋒ ⊙ ⊟ ⌀ ⅀ ⌂ ⊞ lau ✦ ⅄ ✕ ⅀ ⅂LPR
Prices: A5-6 pitch 10-25

Snow-capped mountains
clean lakes
active holidays

Quality at reasonable prices

Fifty Bernese Oberland campsites welcome
you to enjoyable holidays in marvellous
Alpine scenery.

For a brochure and
reservation form write to: **i** Bernese Oberland Tourism BOT
CH-3800 Interlaken

Jungfrau Steindlerstr 60 ☎036 227107
Has a beautiful view of the Eiger, the Monch and the Jungfrau.
Turn right at Unterseen, drive through the Schulhaus and Steinler Str
to site.
Mar-Oct 2HEC ▦ ♦ ⋔ ⅀ ♥ ✕ ☉ ♀ ♨ ⌑ ⁁ P ☒ ⊞ lau ♦ ⁁LR

Jungfraublick Gsteigstr 80 ☎036 8224414
Take Autobahn N8 through tunnel, leave at Lauterbrunnen-
Grindelwald exit, site on left, 300m from N8 sliproad.
May-25 Sep 1.4HEC ▦ ⇘⇙ ⋔ ⊙ ☉ ♀ ♨ ☒ ⊞ lau ♦ ♥ ✕ ⌒ Prices:
A5.20-6 pitch 10-28

Lazy Rancho ☎033 8228716
A family campsite.
Motorway N8: exit Unterseen, turn toward Gunten. After 2km turn
right, then at Landhotel Golf turn left.
Apr-15 Oct 1.6HEC ▦ ⋔ ⅀ ♥ ☉ ♀ ♨ ⁁ P ☒ ⊞ lau ♦ ♥ ✕ ⁁LR
Prices: A5-6.20 pitch 6-25

Manor Farm ☎036 222264
From motorway N8 (Bern-Speiz-Interlaken-Brienz), exit
Gunten/Beatenberg; follow signposts.
All year 7HEC ▦ ♀ ⋔ ⅀ ✕ ♥ ☉ ♀ ♨ ⌑ ⊞ ♀ ▲ ⁁ LR ☒ ▣ ⊞ lau

Sackgut (TCS) ☎036 8224434
Between a hill and the River Aare.
From Brienz turn left before Interlaken opposite the Ost railway
station.
May-6 Oct 1.2HEC ▦ ♀ ⋔ ⅀ ✕ ♥ ☉ ♀ ♨ ☒ ⊞ lau ♦ ⁁P

KANDERSTEG Bern

Rendez-Vous ☎033 751534
750m E of town.
All year 0.5HEC ▦ ⇘⇙ ⋔ ⅀ ✕ ♥ ☉ ♀ ♨ ⊞ lau ♦ ♥ ⁁P Prices: A5
V3 ⊞8-16 ▲6-12

LANDERON, LE Neuchâtel
Peches Case postale 136 ☎038 7512900
Apr-Sep 1HEC ▦ ♀ ⋔ ⅀ ⊙ ♀ ♨ ☒ lau ♦ ✕ ⁁LPR Prices: A6
V3.50 ⊞8.50 ▲5.50-7.50

LAUTERBRUNNEN Bern
Jungfrau ☎036 552010
Widespread site in meadowland crossed by a stream. Partly divided
into pitches.
100m before the church turn right, drive a further 400m.
All year 5HEC ▦ ♀ ⋔ ⅀ ✕ ☉ ♀ ♨ ⌑ ⊞ ♀ ▲ ☒ ⊞ lau ♦ ♥ ⁁P
See advertisement under Colour Section

Schützenbach (TCS) ☎036 551268
About 300m from the lake.
S of village to the left of road leading to Stechelberg opposite B50.
0.8km SE towards Stechelberg.
All year 2.5HEC ▦ ♀ ⋔ ⅀ ♥ ✕ ☉ ♀ ♨ ⌑ ⊞ ♀ ▲ ☒ ⊞ lau ♦ ⁁P

LOCLE, LE Neuchâtel
Communal (TCS) ☎032 9317493
3 May-19 Oct 1.2HEC ▦ ⋔ ✕ ♥ ☉ ♀ ♨ ⁁ P ☒ ⊞ lau ♦ ✕
Prices: A4.30-6 ⊞9.50-15 ▲5.30-15

LUCERNE
See **LUZERN**

LUNGERN Obwalden
Obsee ☎041 6781748
Beside lake.
1km W.
All year 1.5HEC ▦ ♀ ⋔ ⅀ ✕ ☉ ♀ ♨ ⁁ LR ☒ ⊞ lau Prices: A5 V3
⊞7 ▲7

LÜTSCHENTAL Bern
Dany's Camp ☎036 531824
15 May-Sep 4HEC ▦ ♦ ⋔ ☉ ♀ ♨ ☒ ⊞ lau ♦ ♥ ⅀ ♥ ✕

LUZERN (LUCERNE) Luzern
At **HORW**
Steinibachried (TCS) ☎041 4601466
In gently sloping meadow next to the football ground and the beach,
separated from the lake by a wide belt of reeds.
3.2km S of Luzern.
26 Mar-5 Oct 2HEC ▦ ♀ ⋔ ⅀ ✕ ♥ ☉ ♀ ♨ ⌑ ▣ ⊞ lau ♦ ✕ ⁁L
Prices: A4.60-6.40 pitch 10.50-16

MAUENSEE Luzern
Sursee Waldheim ☎041 9211161
Next to Waldheim Country Estate.
0.8km W of Sursee, 100m from Sursee-Basel road.
Apr-Oct 1.7HEC ▦ ♀ ⋔ ⅀ ✕ ☉ ♀ ♨ ⌑ ☒ ⊞ lau Prices: A5.50 V3
⊞3 ▲3

MOSEN Luzern
Seeblick ☎041 851666
In two strips of land on edge of lake, divided by paths into several
squares.
N on the N26.
Apr-Oct 3HEC ▦ ⇘⇙ ⋔ ☉ ♀ ♨ ⁁ L ☒ ⊞ lau ♦ ✕

NOTTWIL Luzern
St Margrethen ☎045 541404
Natural meadowland under fruit trees, with own access to lakeside.
Turn off road to Sursee 400m NW of Nottwil and drive towards lake
for 100m.
Apr-Oct 1HEC ▦ ♀ ⋔ ⅀ ♥ ☉ ♀ ♨ ⁁ L ☒ ⊞ ♦ ✕ ⁁L

PRÊLES Bern
Prêles ☎032 951716
Turn off the main Biel-Neuchâtel road at Twann and follow signs for
Prêles. Pass through village, site on left.
All year 6HEC ▦ ♀ ⋔ ⅀ ✕ ☉ ♀ ♨ ⁁ P ☒ ⊞ Prices: A6 V2
⊞11

SAANEN *Bern*

Beim Kappeli (TCS) ☎033 7446191
In a long meadow between railway and River Saane.
1km SE.
Closed 29 Oct-2 Dec 0.8HEC ▦ ⌂ ♩ ⊙ ☺ ⌀ ♨ ☎ ⊞ lau ♦ ✕ ⇂P
Prices: A4.40-4.80 pitch 8.50-14

SACHSELN *Obwalden*

Ewil ☎041 6663270
On Lake Sarnersee.
Apr-Sep 1.5HEC ▦ ⌂ ♩ ⅀ ⊙ ☺ ⌀ ⇂ L ☎ ⊞ lau ♦ ✕ ⇂R Prices: A5-
6 V2 ⬤5 ▲2-4

SARNER SEE

See **SACHSELN**

SEMPACH *Luzern*

Seeland (TCS) ☎041 4601466
Rectangular, level site on SW shore of lake.
700m S on Luzern road by lake.
26 Mar-5 Oct 5.2HEC ▦ ⌂ ♩ ♩ ⅀ ✕ ⊙ ⌀ ☎ ⊞ lau Prices: A4.60-
6.20 ⬤12-16 ▲5.20-16

STECHELBERG *Bern*

Breithorn ☎036 8551225
3km S of Lauterbrunnen.
All year 1HEC ▦ ⌂ ♩ ⅀ ⊙ ☺ ⌀ ♨ ☎ ⊞ lau ♦ ✕

UNTERAEGERI *Zug*

ZKZS Unteraegeri Wilbrunnenstr 81 ☎042 723928
All year 6HEC ▦ ⌂ ♩ ⅀ ⊙ ☺ ⌀ ⇂ L ☎ ⊞ ⌀ lau ♦ ⇂P

VITZNAU *Luzern*

Vitznau ☎041 3971280
Well tended terraced site, in lovely countryside with fine views of
lake.
Approaching from N, turn towards mountain at church and follow
signs.
27 Mar-5 Oct 1.8HEC ▦ ♦ ♩ ⅀ ⊙ ☺ ⌀ ♨ ⇂ P ☎ ⊞ lau ♦ ✕ ⇂L
Prices: A7-8.50 pitch 13-17

VORDERTHAL *Schwyz*

Wägital Steinweid ☎055 691259
In a beautiful circular valley high up in mountains.
12km SW of Lachen.
Mar-Oct 0.8HEC ⌂ ♩ ⊙ ☺ ⌀ ⇂ R ▣ ⊞ lau ♦ ⅀ ✕ ⇂LP

WILDERSWIL *Bern*

Oberei ☎036 221335
Etr-15 Oct 0.5HEC ▦ ⌂ ♩ ⅀ ⊙ ☺ ⌀ ♨ ☎ ⊞ lau ♦ ⅀ ✕ ⇂PR
Prices: A4.50-4.90 pitch 8.50-16

ZUG *Zug*

Innere Lorzenallmend (TCS) Chamer Fussweg 36 ☎041
7418422
Pleasantly situated with beautiful view of Lake Zug and surrounding
mountains. Much traffic on railway which passes the site.
1km NW by lake.
27 Apr-Sep 1.1HEC ▦ ⌂ ♩ ⅀ ✕ ⊙ ☺ ⌀ ♨ ⇂ L ▣ ⊞ lau ♦ ⅀ ✕
Prices: A5-6 V2-3 ⬤10-17 ▲6.50-12

ZWEISIMMEN *Bern*

Fankhauser ☎030 21356
All year 12HEC ▦ ♦ ⌂ ♩ ⊙ ☺ ⌀ ♨ ☎ ⊞ lau ♦ ⅀ ⅀ ✕ ⇂LPR

Vermeille ☎030 21940
Well laid-out site along the River Simme.
1km N towards Lake Thun.
All year 1.3HEC ♦ ♦ ♩ ⅀ ⊙ ☺ ⌀ ☎ lau ♦ ✕ ⇂P ⊞

East

The cantons of Glarus and Grisona make up this region of eastern
Switzerland. The town of Glarus still maintains the practice of

---

direct democracy, when every spring all active citizens fill the
great Zaunplatz, and in a highly ceremonial meeting decide all
issues affecting the community by a show of hands.
Grisons, astride the Alps, is truly Switzerland's holiday corner.
Superb road, railway and cable-car networks, run with usual
Swiss efficiency, access the wonderful winter sports regions and
well-equipped resorts - the elegant Arosa, Davos, Chur, Flims, the
famous royal retreat of Klosters and glittering St Moritz. This
efficient transport makes the area a summer paradise for walkers
and hikers - there are over 3,000 miles of unsignposted cross-
country footpaths. Many areas of superb natural beauty are
protected by law - the largest is the 65-square-mile Swiss National
Park, reached from Zernez, where authorised roads and paths
(and guided walks in season), give glimpses of a flora and fauna
completely protected from man.

ANDEER *Graubünden*

Sut Baselgia (TCS) ☎081 611453
N towards Chur.
Nov 1.2HEC ▦ ⌀⌂ ⌂ ♩ ⊙ ☺ ⌀ ♨ ☎ ⊞ lau ♦ ⅀ ✕ ⇂PR

AROSA *Graubünden*

Arosa ☎081 311745
All year 0.6HEC ▦ ⌂ ♩ ⊙ ☺ ☎ ♦ ⅀ ⅀ ✕ ⌀ ⇂LP ⊞ Prices: A7-8 V3
⬤8 ▲5

CHUR (COIRE) *Graubünden*

Camp Au (TCS) Felsenaustr 61 ☎081 242283
Take exit Chur-Süd from N13.2km NW of town centre on bank of
Rhein. Access is via outskirts of town.
All year 2.6HEC ▦ ⌂ ♩ ⅀ ✕ ⊙ ☺ ⌀ ♨ ☎ ⊞ lau ♦ ⇂P

LENZ *Graubünden*

St Cassian ☎081 3842472
All year 25HEC ▦ ♦ ♩ ⅀ ✕ ⊙ ☺ ⌀ ♨ ☎ lau ♦ ⅀ ⅀ ⇂LP ⊞ Prices:
A6.50-7 V2.50 ⬤8.50 ▲5.50-8.50

MÜSTAIR *Graubünden*

Clenga ☎082 85410
Next to small river near the Italian frontier.
15 May-20 Oct 1HEC ▦ ⌂ ♩ ⅀ ✕ ⊙ ☺ ⌀ ⬤ ☎ ⊞ lau ♦ ✕ ⇂P

PONTRESINA *Graubünden*

Plauns (TCS) ☎081 8426285
Beautiful situation at foot of Pit Palü.
Access from road towards Bernina pass about 4.5km beyond
Pontresina. Turn off main road 29 towards Hotel Morteratsch then
0.5km to site.
25 May-15 Oct 4HEC ▦ ⚬⚬⚬ ♦ ♩ ⌂ ♩ ⅀ ✕ ⊙ ☺ ⌀ ♨ ⬤ ☎ ⊞ lau
Prices: A7.50 pitch 9-14

POSCHIAVO *Graubünden*

Boomerang ☎082 50713
In a quiet setting.
2km SE.
All year 1.5HEC ▦ ⌂ ♩ ⊙ ☺ ⌀ ☎ ⊞ lau ♦ ⅀

SAMEDAN *Graubünden*

Punt Muragl (TCS) ☎081 8428197
Near Bernina railway halt, to the right of the fork of the two roads
Samedan and Celerina/Schlarigna to Pontresina.
1 Dec-15 Apr & 1 Jun-30 Sep 2HEC ▦ ⌂ ♩ ⅀ ⅀ ✕ ⊙ ☺ ⌀ ♨ ☎ ⊞
lau ♦ ✕ Prices: A4.20-7.30 pitch 10.50-15

SANTA MARIA *Graubünden*

Pè da Munt ☎082 85727 & 081 8587133
Jun-20 Oct 1.2HEC ♦ ⌀⌂ ⌂ ♩ ⊙ ☺ ⇂ R ☎ ♦ ⅀ ⅀ ✕ ⌀ ⊞

SPLÜGEN *Graubünden*

Sand ☎081 621476
On left bank of River Hinterrhein.
Turn off the main trunk road in the village and follow signposts.
All year 0.8HEC ▦ ⌂ ♩ ⅀ ⊙ ☺ ⌀ ♨ ⇂ R ▣ ♦ ⅀ ✕

STRADA IM ENGADIN *Graubünden*

Arina ☎081 8863212
At the foot of a mountain, SW of village.
15 May-Sep 0.6HEC ▨ ⚅ ⋔ ⊙ ◘ ⚲ P ☒ ⊞ lau ♦ ⚏ ✕ �⚞R

SUR EN *Graubünden*

Sur En ☎081 8663544
All year 2.5HEC ▨ ⚆⚘ ♦ ⋔ ⚏ ⚍ ✕ ⊙ ◘ ⚲ ♨ ⚤ ⚞ R ▣ ⊞ lau

SUSCH *Graubünden*

Muglinas ☎081 8622744
200m W.
Jun-Sep 1HEC ▨ ⚅ ⋔ ⊙ ◘ ☒ ♦ ⚏ ⚍ ✕ ⚲ ♨

THUSIS *Graubünden*

Rheinau (TCS) ☎081 6512472
May-Sep 4.5HEC ▨ ⚅ ⋔ ⚍ ✕ ⊙ ◘ ⚲ ♨ ⊞ lau ♦ ⚏ ♨ ⚞PR Prices:
A4.50-5.10 pitch 8.50-13

TSCHIERV *Graubünden*

Sternen (TCS) ☎082 85551
In village behind the Sternen Hotel.
Between Ofen Pass and Santa Maria.
All year 2HEC ▨ ⚅ ⋔ ⚍ ⚏ ✕ ⊙ ◘ ⚲ ♨ ⚞ PR ☒ ⊞ lau ♦ ⚞P Prices:
A4.50-5 V3 ◘8 ⚠3

VICOSOPRANO *Graubünden*

Mulina ☎081 8221035
May-Oct 1HEC ▨ ⚅ ⋔ ⊙ ◘ ⚲ ⚞ LR ☒ ♦ ⚏ ⚍ ✕ ⚲ ♨ ⊞ Prices: A5.90
V4.50 ◘9-11 ⚠4.50

ZERNEZ *Graubünden*

Cul ☎081 8561462
Off road 27 W of Zernez.
May-15 Oct 3.6HEC ▨ ⚅ ⋔ ⚍ ⚏ ✕ ⊙ ◘ ⚲ ♨ ⚞ R ⊞ ⊞ lau ♦ ⚞P
Prices: A6.50 pitch 12

South

Here, in the canton of Ticino, the German and Italian cultures mingle in a land where Alpine mountains and valleys fall towards the great lakes and the plain of Lombardy. The province is a climatic oasis: the Alpine chain protects it from strong winds, and even in winter there is a comparatively high number of sunny days. Alpine and Mediterranean plant species flourish side by side, giving Ticino a unique flora.

In this area of outstanding beauty, Lugano remains a favourite with visitors. The town has a traditional atmosphere, with attractive lanes and shopping arcades, spacious parks and lakeside promenades. Excursions from Lugano lead to high mountains and some of the best views in the country - Mount San Salvatore, Mount Bré and Mount Generoso. Locarno, a lovely town on the shores of Lake Maggiore, is also popular, and the exceptionally mild southern climate produces lush vegetation and a wonderfully colourful display of flowers in early spring.

ACQUACALDA *Ticino*

Ai Cembri Lukmanierstr ☎091 8722610
Jun-Oct 5HEC ▨ ⚅ ⋔ ✕ ⊙ ◘ ⚲ ⚞ R ☒ ⊞ ⚝ lau

AGNO *Ticino*

Eurocampo ☎091 6052114
Part of site is near its own sandy beach and is divided by groups of trees.
600m E on road from Lugano to Ponte Tresa. Entrance opposite Aeroport sign and Alfa Romeo building.
Apr-Oct 6HEC ▨ ♦ ⚅ ⚏ ⚍ ✕ ⊙ ◘ ⚲ ⚞ LR ☒ ⊞ lau

Golfo del Sole via Rivera 6 ☎091 6054802
By lake. Separate play area for children.
Apr-Oct 0.7HEC ▨ ⚆ ⚅ ⋔ ⚏ ⚍ ✕ ⊙ ◘ ⚲ ♨ ⚞ L ▣ ⊞ lau ♦ ✕ ⚞P
Prices: A7 V2 ◘9-15 ⚠7-13

AVEGNO *Ticino*

Piccolo Paradiso ☎093 811581
In the Maggia Valley between the main road and River Maggia.
6km NW from Locarno on the Maggia Valley road.
Mar-Oct 4HEC ▨ ⚅ ⚏ ⚍ ✕ ⊙ ◘ ⚲ ♨ ⚞ R ▣ ⊞ lau ♦ ⚞P

CHIGGIOGNA *Ticino*

Gottardo ☎091 8661562
Open meadowland on mountain slope partly on natural terraces.
1km S of Faido, 20m above N2.
All year 0.8HEC ▨ ⚅ ⋔ ⚏ ⚍ ✕ ⊙ ◘ ⚲ ♨ ⚞ PR ☒ ⊞ lau Prices: A7-8.50 pitch 5-14

CLARO *Ticino*

Censo ☎091 8631753
Below a woodland slope.
Off the N2 (E9).
Apr-Sep 2HEC ▨ ♦ ⚅ ⚏ ⚍ ✕ ⊙ ◘ ⚲ ♨ ⚞ PR ☒ ⊞ lau

CUGNASCO *Ticino*

Park-Camping Riarena ☎091 8591688
Beautiful park-like site.
1.5km NW. Turn off road 13 at BP filling station 9km NE of Locarno and continue 0.5km.
Apr-20 Oct 3.2HEC ▨ ⁖⁖⁖ ♦ ⚅ ⚏ ⚍ ✕ ⊙ ◘ ⚲ ♨ ⚤ ⚞ P ☒ ⊞ lau
Prices: A7-8 V2-3 ◘11-15 ⚠11-15

GORDEVIO *Ticino*

Bellariva ☎093 871444
In quiet location between the road and the left bank of the River Maggia.
Apr-Oct 2.5HEC ▨ ⚅ ⋔ ⊙ ◘ ⚲ ⚞ PR ☒ ⊞ lau ♦ ⚏ ✕

LOCARNO *Ticino*

Delta via G-Respini ☎091 7516081
A beautiful, well-equipped and well-organised site at Lake Maggiore.
2km away from the city.
Mar-Oct 6HEC ▨ ⚅ ⋔ ⚏ ⚍ ✕ ⊙ ◘ ⚲ ♨ ⚞ LR ☒ ⊞ ⚝ lau ♦ ⚍ ⚞P Prices: A9-12 pitch 20-30

At LOSONE(4km W)

Zandone ☎093 356563
A level site amidst deciduous forest behind an extensive military area.
Situated between the Losone-Golino road and the River Melezza.
Apr-Oct 2.1HEC ▨ ⚅ ⋔ ⚏ ⊙ ◘ ⚲ ⚤ ♨ ⚞ R ☒ ⊞ ♦ ⚏ ✕ ⚞P

MELANO *Ticino*

Pedemonte ☎091 6498333
Between railway and lake with own private beach.
Turn off road no.2 in S outskirts of Maroggia towards lake.
Apr-Oct 2HEC ▨ ⚅ ⋔ ⚏ ✕ ⊙ ◘ ⚲ ⚞ L ☒ ⊞ lau

MOLINAZZO DI MONTÉGGIO *Ticino*

Tresiana ☎091 6083342
Meadowland with trees on riverbank.
O1>Turn right after bridge in Ponte Tresa, then 5km to site.
15 Apr-Oct 1.5HEC ▨ ⚅ ⋔ ⚏ ⚍ ✕ ⊙ ◘ ⚲ ⚤ ⚠ ⚞ PR ☒ ⊞ lau ♦ ⚏ ✕
Prices: A6 V2.50 ◘10-13.50 ⚠4.50-13.50

PRIMADENGO *Ticino*

Piantett ☎094 381043
All year 2.3HEC ▨ ⚅ ⋔ ⚏ ✕ ⊙ ◘ ⚲ ♨ ⚤ ⚤ ⚞ P ☒ ⊞

ROVEREDO *Ticino*

Vera ☎091 8271857
10km N of Bellinzona near N13 exit 'Chur-Bellinzona'.
All year 4HEC ▨ ⚅ ⋔ ⚏ ✕ ⊙ ◘ ⚲ ♨ ⚞ PR ☒ lau ♦ ⚏ ⚍ ⊞ Prices: A6-8 pitch 10-22

TENERO *Ticino*

Campofelice ☎093 671417
Beautifully situated and extensive site completely divided into pitches, and crossed by asphalt drives.
1.9km S. Signposted.
Apr-22 Oct 15HEC ▨ ⚅ ⋔ ⚏ ⚍ ✕ ⊙ ◘ ⚲ ♨ ⚤ ⚞ LR ☒ ⊞ ⚝ lau ♦ ⚞P Prices: pitch 33-71 (incl 2 persons)

Lido Mappo via Mappo ☎091 7451437
Beautifully situated, well appointed site on lakeside. Teenagers not accepted on their own. Minimum stay, 1 week in Jul-Aug.
700m SW. Signposted.
14 Mar-26 Oct 6.5HEC ▦ ♦♠🕿🍽✕⊙◙⌀🛒⚡ ⚘L 🏛⊞❄ lau ♦ ⚡PR⊞ Prices: pitch 32-65 (incl 2 persons)

Miralago ☎093 671255
Situated in pleasant position by the lake. Caravans only.
Access from main road TL 21 to via Pressighe to via Roncaccio.
All year 2HEC ▦ ⚙♠♠🕿✕⊙◙⌀🛒⚡ LP 🏛⊞ lau

Tamaro via Mappo ☎091 7452161
Partly on sandy shore.
Camping Card Compulsory.
Signposted.
21 Mar-19 Oct 6HEC ▦ ⚘⚙♠🕿🍽✕⊙◙⌀🛒⚡🛒⚡L 🏛⊞❄ lau ♦ ⚡PR Prices: pitch 30-42 (incl 2 persons)

Verbano ☎093 671020
Site in two sections, of which one is on the lakeside. The larger section has access to the lake about 150m distance.
Signposted.
Apr-Oct 2.6HEC ▦ ⚙♠🕿⊙◙⚡⚡LR⊞ lau ♦🍽✕

South West

Vaud, Fribourg, Valais and Geneva are the cantons in this south-west region. All these provinces have resorts at every altitude to welcome both summer and winter visitors - the mountains and glaciers are easily accessed in winter for skiers, and in summer mountain huts, chalets, and hotels provide facilities for walkers and hikers.
Valais has been a trading crossroads since Roman times, with its passes at St Bernard and Simplon. The Rhône, with its tributaries, cuts a lovely swathe through Valais on its way to the jewel of the south west - Lake Geneva. Resorts dot the lake shores - small towns like Crans, Nyon and Vevey, popular Montreux, cosmopolitan Lausanne, and, of course, the country's great international centre, Geneva. Art, culture and education are great traditions here, and there is a wealth of attractions for tourists - excellent shopping centres, renowned restaurants, an attractive old town, fascinating museums, and miles of attractive promenades along the shores of the lake with wonderful views of the mountains.

AGARN Valais
Gemmi ☎4127 631154
Exit from N9 at Agarn. Signposted
26 Apr-12 Oct 1HEC ▦ ⚙♠🕿🍽✕⊙◙⌀🛒🏛⊞ lau ♦✕⚡P Prices: A6-7 pitch 10-18

AIGLE Vaud
Glariers (TCS) ☎025 262660
Near railway line and the avenue des Glariers.
800m NE off the N9 near SHELL/MIGROL petrol station.
3 Apr-29 Sep 1HEC ▦ ⚘⚙♠🕿🍽✕⊙◙⌀🛒🏛 lau ♦✕⚡P

AROLLA Valais
Petit Praz ☎027 832163
In an imposing mountain setting.
Jun-Sep 0.6HEC ▦ ⚙♠⊙◙

AVENCHES Vaud
Plage ☎037 751750
Apr-Sep 8HEC ▦ ▓▓▓ ⚙♠🕿✕⊙◙⌀⚡L🏛⊞ lau

BALLENS Vaud
Bois Gentil ☎021 8095120
200m S of station.
Apr-15 Oct 2.5HEC ▦ ⚙♠🕿⊙◙⌀⚡P🏛⊞ Prices: A5-6.50 V2 ⊞6.50 ▲5

BOUVERET, LE Valais
Rive Bleue ☎025 812161
Beside lake with a natural sandy beach and good, modern facilities.
Turn off the N37 to Monthey in the SW district of Bouveret and drive NE for about 0.8km.
Apr-Sep 3HEC ▦ ⚙♠🕿🍽✕⊙◙⌀🛒🚐◙⊞ lau ♦⚡LP

BULLET Vaud
Cluds C.P 515 ☎024 611440
In beautiful mountain setting among pine trees with a private beach on Lake Neuchâtel.
1.5km NE.
All year 1.2HEC ▦ ⚙♠✕⊙◙⌀🛒◙⊞ ♦🛒 Prices: A5.35 V3.20 ⊞5.35-10.70 ▲4.25-10.70

CHÂTEAU-D'OEX Vaud
Berceau (TCS) La Place ☎029 47788
On level strip of grass between the mountain and the river bank.
1km SE at junction of roads 77 and 76.
All year 1HEC ▦ ⚙♠🕿🍽✕⊙◙⌀⚡PR🏛⊞ lau

CHÂTEL-ST-DENIS Fribourg
Bivouac rtes des Paccots ☎021 9487849
Turn E in Châtel-St Denis and continue for 2km.
All year 2HEC ▦ ⚙♠🕿🍽✕⊙◙⌀🛒▲⚡P🏛⊞ lau ♦⚡R Prices: A6 pitch 15

CHESSEL Vaud
Grands Bois ☎025 814225
All year 3.5HEC ▦ ⚙♠⊙◙🛒⚡P🏛 lau ♦🛒🍽✕

CUDREFIN Vaud
Chablais ☎037 773277
15 Mar-Oct 228HEC ▦ ⚙♠⊙◙⚡L◙ lau ♦🛒🍽✕⌀⚡R⊞

CULLY Vaud
Moratel ☎021 7991914
E on main Lausanne-Vevey road.
Mar-Sep 3HEC ▦ ⚙♠✕⊙◙⌀🏛⊞ lau ♦🍽⚡L

DÜDINGEN Fribourg
Schiffenensee ☎037 433486
Leave the N12 (Bern-Fribourg) at Düdingen and go N towards Murten.
Apr-Oct 9HEC ▦ ⚙♠🕿🍽✕⊙◙⌀⚡LP🏛⊞ lau

EPAGNY-GRUYÈRES Fribourg
Sapins ☎029 29575
1km N on the edge of a forest.
30 May-Sep 2.2HEC ▦ ⚙♠🕿🍽✕⊙◙⌀🛒🚐◙⊞ lau ♦⚡LPR Prices: A6 V2 ⊞6 ▲6

EVOLÈNE Valais
Evolène ☎027 831144
200m from town
All year 0.9HEC ▦ ⚘⚙♠⊙◙⌀🛒🏛⊞ lau ♦🛒🍽✕⚡R

FOREL Vaud
Forel ☎021 7811464
Leave the N9 at Chexbres in the direction of Forel and take left turning to Savigny.
All year 4HEC ▦ ⚙♠🕿🍽✕⊙◙⌀🛒⚡P🏛⊞ lau Prices: A4.50-6.50 V2.50-3.50 ⊞6.50-8.50 ▲4.50-6.50

FOULY, LA Valais
Glaciers ☎026 831735
At end of village.
20 May-Sep 7HEC ▦ ▓▓▓ ♦⚙♠⊙◙⌀🛒🏛⊞ lau ♦🛒✕ Prices: A5.50 pitch 10-16

GENÈVE (GENEVA) Genève
At **VÉSENAZ**(6km NE)
Pointe á la Bise (TCS) ☎022 7521296
Small pool for children. On shores of lake.
NE between Vésenaz and Bellerive.
3 Apr-27 Oct 3.2HEC ▦ ♦♠🛒🍽✕⊙◙⌀🛒⚡L🏛⊞ Prices: A5-6 V6.50-7 ⊞6.50-12 ▲6.50-9

GRANDSON *Vaud*
Pécos C.P. 515 ☎024 244969
400m SW of railway station between railway and lake.
Apr-Sep 2HEC ▦ ⅃⌇ ⋒ ᵬ ⅃ ✕ ⊙ ➋ ∅ ᄆ ⚏ ⋜ L ⊡ ⊞ ⅋ lau
Prices: A5.35 V3.20 ⊞5.35-10.70 ▲4.25-10.70

GUMEFENS *Fribourg*
Lac ☎029 52162
On the borders of the lake.
15 May-15 Sep 1.2HEC ▦ ⅃⌇ ⋒ ᵬ ⅃ ✕ ⊙ ➋ ∅ ⋜ L ⊡ ⅋ lau
Prices: A6.40 V2.20 ⊞6.50-8.50 ▲6.50-8.50

LAUSANNE *Vaud*
At **OUCHY**
Vidy chemin du Camping 3 ☎021 6242031
All year 4.5HEC ᵬ ⋒ ᵬ ✕ ⊙ ➋ ∅ ᄆ ⋜ L ⊡ ⊞ lau ➡ ⋜P
Prices: A6.50 V2 ⊞12 ▲7

LEUKERBAD *Valais*
Sport-Arena Leukerbad ☎027 4701037
On road N of Leuk.
May-Oct 1.6HEC ▦ ⋒ ✕ ⊙ ➋ ⊡ ⊞ lau Prices: A7 V4 ⊞4 ▲4

LEYSIN *Vaud*
Semiramis ☎025 341148
After entering the village turn left at SHELL filling station and
continue for 400m.
All year 11.7HEC ▦ ᵬ ⋒ ᵬ ✕ ⊙ ➋ ∅ ᄆ ⊡ ⊞ lau ➡ ⅃ ✕ ⋜P

MORGES *Vaud*
Petit Bois (TCS) ☎021 8011270
Follow Geneva road from town. Site by lakeside.
26 Mar-19 Oct 3.2HEC ▦ ⅃⌇ ⋒ ᵬ ⅃ ✕ ⊙ ➋ ∅ ᄆ ⊡ ⊞ lau ➡ ⋜LP
Prices: A4.80-6.20 pitch 13-17

MORGINS *Valais*
Morgins (TCS) ☎025 772361
A terraced site below pine forest.
Turn left at end of village towards Pas de Morgins near Swiss Customs.
All year 1.3HEC ▦ ⅃⌇ ⋒ ⊙ ➋ ⅌ ⊡ lau ➡ ⅃ ✕ ∅ ᄆ ⋜PR

PAYERNE *Vaud*
Piscine de Payerne ☎037 614322
Apr-Sep 8HEC ▦ ᵬ ⋒ ᵬ ✕ ⊙ ➋ ∅ ᄆ ⋜ P ⊡ ⊞ lau ➡ ⅃

RARON *Valais*
Santa Monica ☎027 9342424
All year 4HEC ▦ ᵬ ⋒ ✕ ⊙ ➋ ∅ ᄆ ⋜ PR ⊡ lau ➡ ⅃ Prices: A6
pitch 12

Simplonblick ☎027 9341274
300m W of Turtig.
Apr-Oct 6HEC ▦ ᵬ ⋒ ᵬ ⅃ ✕ ⊙ ➋ ∅ ᄆ ⋜ P ⊡ ᄆ lau ➡ ᵬ Prices:
A4.50-6.50 pitch 12.50

RECKINGEN *Valais*
Ellbogen (TCS) ☎028 731355
400m S on bank of Rhône.
13 May-13 Oct 1.3HEC ⅃⌇ ⋒ ᵬ ✕ ⊙ ➋ ∅ ᄆ ⊡ ⊞ lau ➡ ⋜P

RIED-BRIG *Valais*
Tropic ☎028 232537
To the left of Simplon road near entrance to village. 3km above Brig.
May-15 Sep 1.5HEC ▦ ᵬ ⋒ ᵬ ⅃ ✕ ⊙ ➋ ∅ ᄆ ⚏ ⊡ ⊞ lau Prices:
A4.50 V3.50 ⊞5-6 ▲4-7

RÖCHE *Vaud*
Clos de la George (TCS) Les Ecots ☎025 265828
4.5km from Aigle.
All year 2.6HEC ᵬ ⋒ ᵬ ⅃ ✕ ⊙ ➋ ∅ ᄆ ᄆ ⚏ ▲ ⋜ P ⊡ ⊞ lau

SAAS-GRUND *Valais*
Kapellenweg ☎028 572989
Turn right over bridge towards Saas-Almagell.
All year 1.5HEC ▦ ᵬ ⋒ ⊙ ➋ ∅ ᄆ ᄆ ⚏ ⊡ lau ➡ ⅃ ✕ ⋜PR Prices:
pitch 20-25 (incl 2 persons)

SALGESCH *Valais*
Swiss Plage ☎027 4556608
Etr-Oct 10HEC ▦ ᵬ ⋒ ᵬ ⅃ ✕ ⊙ ➋ ∅ ᄆ ᄆ ⋜ LR ⊡ lau ➡ ⋜P ⊞
Prices: A6.60 pitch 14

SEMBRANCHER *Valais*
Prairie (TCS) ☎026 852206
12km from Martigny and 500m from town.
All year 12HEC ▦ ⅃⌇ ⋒ ᵬ ⅃ ✕ ⊙ ➋ ∅ ᄆ ⊡ lau

SIERRE (SIDERS) *Valais*
Bois de Finges (TCS) ☎027 550284
Very beautiful site.
Camping Carnet Compulsory.
Access difficult for caravans.
May-Sep 7HEC ▦ ᵬ ⋒ ᵬ ⅃ ✕ ⊙ ➋ ∅ ⋜ PR ⊡ lau ➡ ✕ ᄆ ⋜L
Prices: A4.80-5.60 pitch 10.50-16

SORENS *Fribourg*
Forêt ☎029 51882
Turn right off the N12 in Gumefens and drive on to the village.
All year 4HEC ▦ ᵬ ⋒ ᵬ ⅃ ✕ ⊙ ➋ ∅ ᄆ ᄆ ⋜ P ⊡ lau

STABLBACH BEI VISP *Valais*
Staldbach ☎028 462855
Feb-Dec 1.4HEC ▦ ᵬ ⋒ ᵬ ⅃ ✕ ⊙ ➋ ᄆ ⚏ ⋜ PR ⊡ ⊞ ⅋ lau ➡ ∅ ᄆ

STEG *Valais*
Lötschberg ☎028 421859
May-Sep 1.3HEC ▦ ᵬ ⋒ ᵬ ✕ ⊙ ➋ ∅ ⋜ P ⊡ ⊞ lau Prices: A4.80
V1.60 ⊞4.80 ▲4.80

SUSTEN *Valais*
Bella Tola (TCS) ☎027 4733641
In a quiet position. Easy access for caravans. 2km from village.
15 May-28 Sep 3.6HEC ▦ ᵬ ⋒ ᵬ ⅃ ✕ ⊙ ➋ ∅ ᄆ ⋜ P ⊡ ⊞ lau
Prices: A7-9.50 pitch 7.50-25

Rhodania Kantonstr ☎027 4731312
All year 0.3HEC ➡ ᵬ ✕ ⊙ ➋ ⋜ R ⊡ ➡ ᵬ ∅ ⋜LPR ⊞ Prices: A5
V2 ⊞4.50 ▲3.50

ULRICHEN *Valais*
Nufenen ☎027 9731437
1km SE to right of road to Nufenen Pass.
Jun-Sep 8HEC ▦ ➡ ᵬ ᵬ ⊙ ➋ ⋜ R ⊡ ⊞ lau ➡ ✕
Prices: A6 V3 ⊞4 ▲3.50

VALLORBE *Vaud*
Pré sous Ville (TCS) ☎021 8432309
On left bank of River Orbe.
May-Oct 0.8HEC ▦ ᵬ ⋒ ⊙ ➋ ∅ ⋜ P ⊡ ⊞ lau ➡ ᵬ ⅃ ⋜R
Prices: A6 V8-9.50 ⊞8-9.50 ▲3.50-6

VERS-L'ÉGLISE *Vaud*
Murée (TCS) ☎021 8011908
Partially terraced site by a stream.
Signposted on the right at the entry to the village.
All year 1.1HEC ⅃⌇ ᵬ ⋒ ⊙ ➋ ∅ ᄆ ⋜ R ⊡ lau ➡ ✕

VETROZ *Valais*
Botza (TCS) ☎027 361940
All year 3HEC ▦ ᵬ ⋒ ᵬ ✕ ⊙ ➋ ∅ ᄆ ⚏ ⋜ P ⊡ ⊞ ➡ ᄆ
Prices: A5.60-6.90 pitch 11-14

VEX *Valais*
Val d'Hérens ☎027 271985
Near main road, about 500m from village.
All year 1HEC ▦ ➡ ᵬ ⋒ ⊙ ➋ ∅ ᄆ ⚏ ⊡ ⊞ lau ➡ ᵬ ✕

YVONAND *Vaud*
Pointe d'Yvonand ☎024 311655
6km NE of Yverdon bordering Lake Neuchâtel with private beach
1km away, boat moorings, private jetty and boat hire.
3km W. Signposted.
Apr-Sep 5HEC ▦ ➡ ᵬ ᵬ ⅃ ✕ ⊙ ➋ ∅ ᄆ ⚏ ⋜ L ⊡ ⊞ ⅋ lau
Prices: A5.35 V3.20 ⊞5.35-10.70 ▲4.25-10.70

COUNTRY MAP SECTION

AUSTRIA

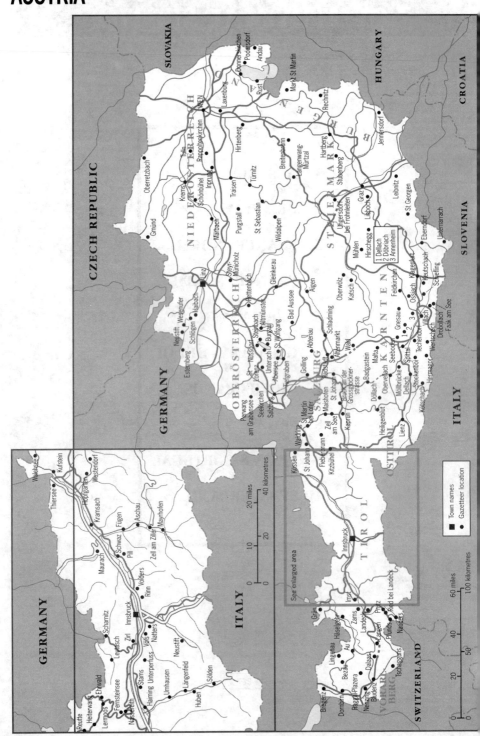

1

BELGIUM

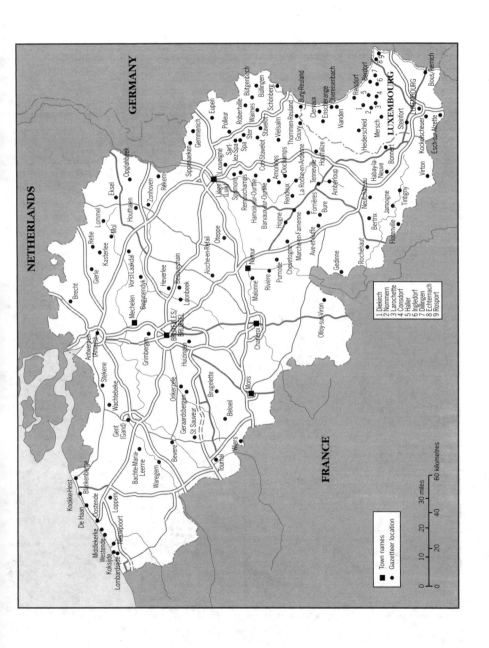

FRANCE

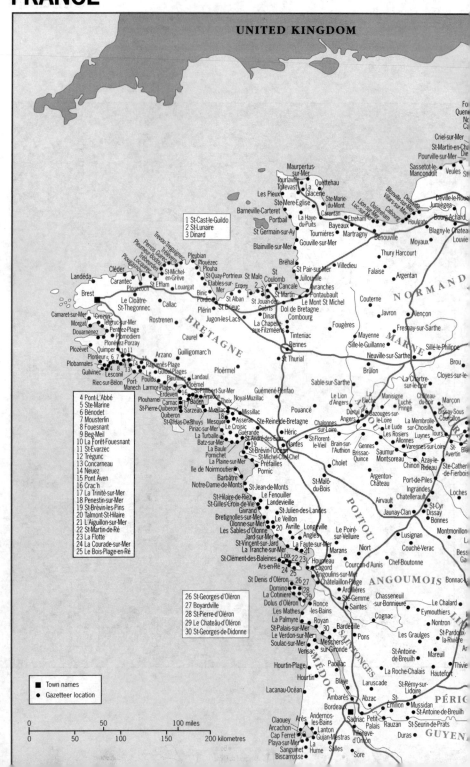

UNITED KINGDOM

NORMAND

MARNE

BRETAGNE

POITOU

ANGOUMOIS

SAINTONGE

MÉDOC

GUYEN

PÉRIG

LIN

1 St-Cast-le-Guildo
2 St-Lunaire
3 Dinard

4 Pont-L'Abbé
5 Ste-Marine
6 Bénodet
7 Mousterlin
8 Fouesnant
9 Beg-Meil
10 La Forêt-Fouesnant
11 St-Evarzec
12 Trégunc
13 Concarneau
14 Neuez
15 Pont Aven
16 Crac'h
17 La Trinité-sur-Mer
18 Penestin-sur-Mer
19 St-Brévin-les-Pins
20 Talmont-St-Hilaire
21 l'Aiguillon-sur-Mer
22 St-Martin-de-Ré
23 La Flotte
24 La Couarde-sur-Mer
25 Le Bois-Plage-en-Ré

26 St-Georges-d'Oléron
27 Boyardville
28 St-Pierre-d'Oléron
29 Le Chateau-d'Oléron
30 St-Georges-de-Didonne

■ Town names
● Gazetteer location

0   50   100 miles
0   50   100   150   200 kilometres

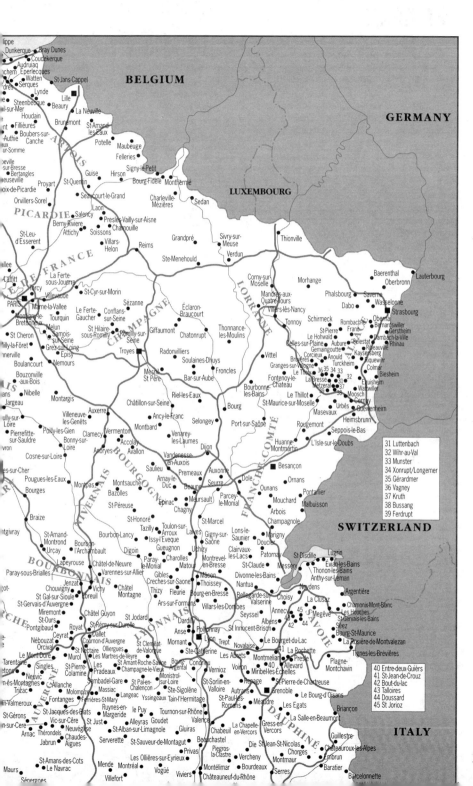

3

FRANCE

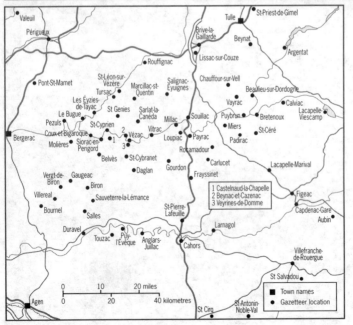

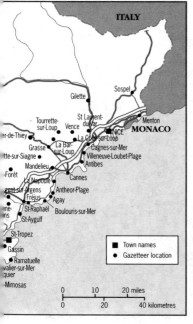

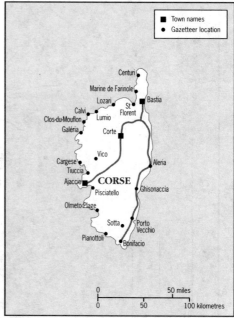

GERMANY

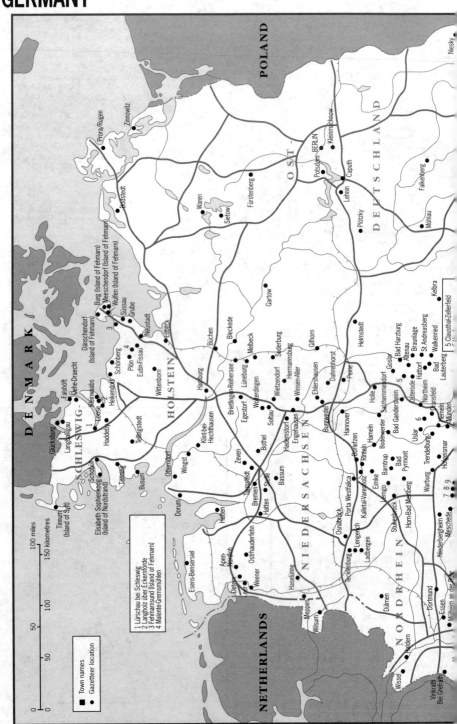

5

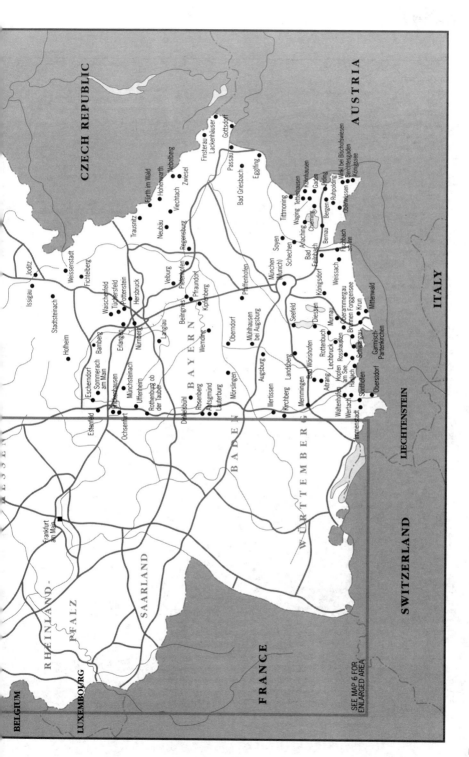

5

GERMANY

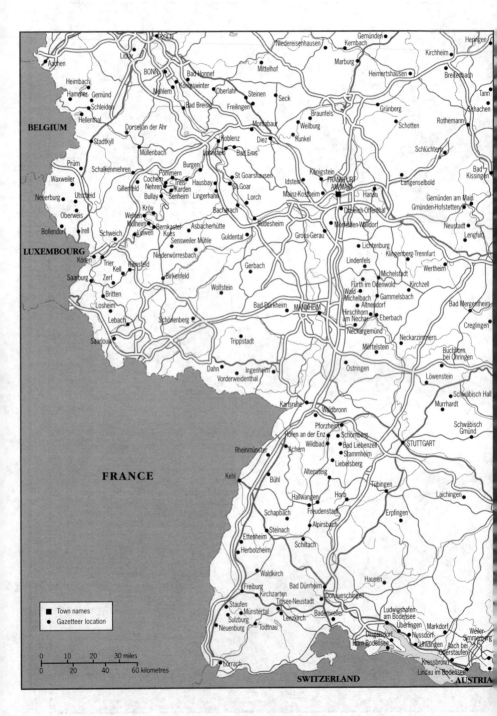

NETHERLANDS

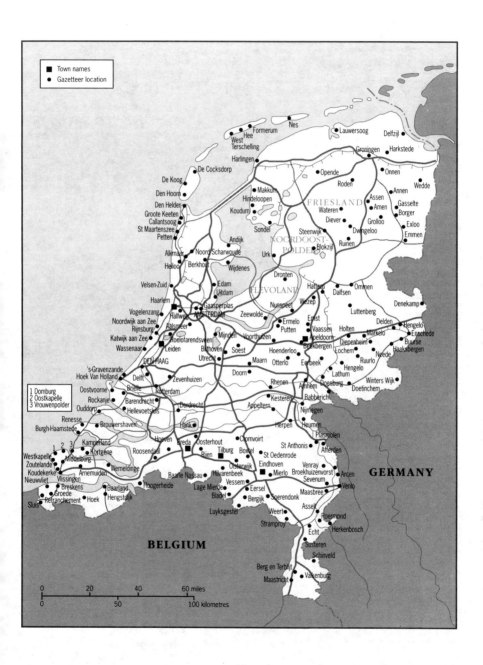

Town names
Gazetteer location

1 Domburg
2 Oostkapelle
3 Vrouwenpolder

FRIESLAND
NOORDOOST-POLDER
FLEVOLAND
GERMANY
BELGIUM

Formerum Nes Lauwersoog Delfzijl
Hee West Groningen Harkstede
Terschelling Harlingen Opende Onnen
De Cocksdorp Roden Annen Wedde
De Koog Makkum Wateren Assen Gasselte
Den Hoorn Hindeloopen Diever Amen Borger
Den Helder Koudum Grolloo Exloo
Groote Keeten Sondel Steenwijk Dwingeloo Emmen
Callantsoog Andijk Blokzijl Ruinen
St Maartenszee Noord Scharwoude Urk Dronten
Petten Alkmaar Berkhout Wijdenes Hatten Ommen
Helloo Edam Dalfsen Denekamp
Velsen-Zuid Uitdam Nunspeet Wezep Luttenberg
Haarlem Gaasperplas Zeewolde Ernst Delden Hengelo
Vogelenzang Halfweg AMSTERDAM Ermelo Vaassen Holten Markelo Enschede
Noordwijk aan Zee Aalsmeer Putten Apeldoorn Diepenheim Buurse
Rijnsburg Mijnden Voorthuizen Beekbergen Lochem Haaksbergen
Katwijk aan Zee Roelofarendsveen Hoenderloo Neede
Wassenaar Leiden Blithoven Soest Eerbeek Hengelo Ruurlo
DEN HAAG Utrecht Maarn Otterlo Lathum Winters Wijk
's-Gravenzande Doorn Rhenen Arnhem Doesburg Doetinchem
Hoek Van Holland Delft Zevenhuizen Babberich
Oostvoorne Brielle Rotterdam Kesteren Nijmegen
Rockanje Barendrecht Appeltern
Ouddorp Hellevoetsluis Dordrecht Herpen Heumen
Renesse Brouwershaven Hank Plasmolen
Burgh-Haamstede Hoeven Breda Oosterhout Clomvoirt St Anthonis Afferden
Kamperland Roosendaal Rijen Tilburg Boxtel St Oedenrode
Westkapelle Kortgene Oosterhout Oisterwijk Eindhoven Venray Arden
Zoutelande Middelburg Werneldinge Mierlo Broekhuizenvorst Venlo
Koudekerke Arnemuiden Baarle Nassau Hilvarenbeek Sevenum
Nieuwvliet Vlissingen Hoogerheide Vessem Maasbree
Breskens Baarland Lage Mierde Eersel Soerendonk Asset
Groede Hengstdijk Bladel Bergijk Weert Roermond
Sluis Retranchement Hoek Luyksgestel Echt Herkenbosch
Stramproy Susteren Schinveld
Berg en Terblijt Valkenburg
Maastricht

0   20   40   60 miles
0   50   100 kilometres

7

ITALY

8

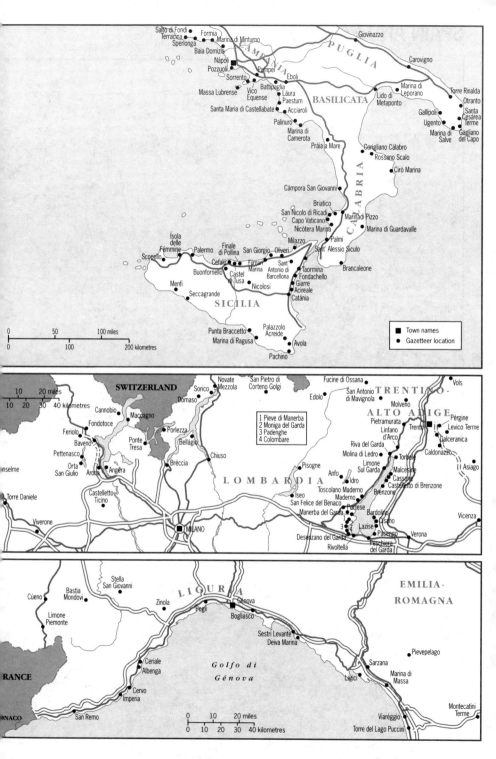

SPAIN AND PORTUGAL

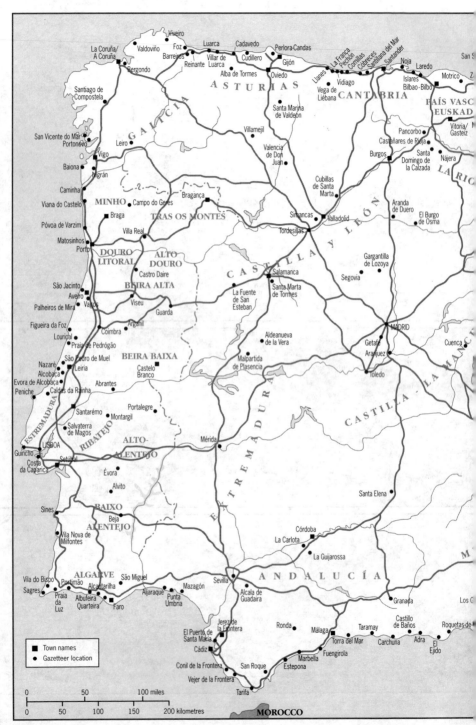

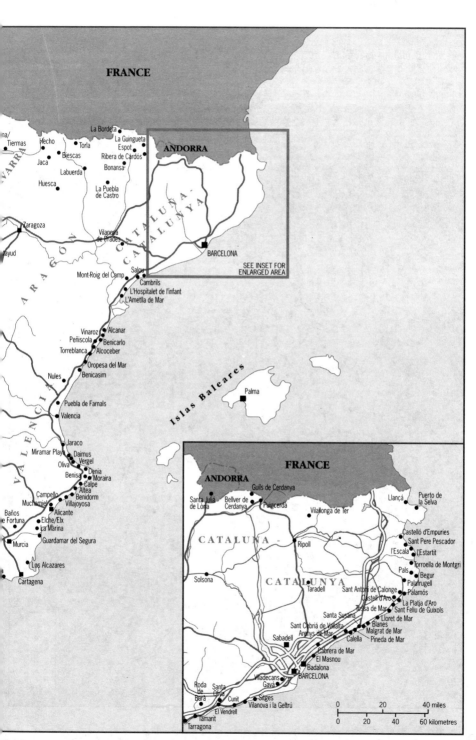

FRANCE

La Bordeta
Tiermas
Hecho
Torla
La Guingueta
Espot
ANDORRA
na/
Biescas
Ribera de Cardós
Jaca
Bonansa
Labuerda
Huesca
La Puebla
de Castro

Zaragoza
Vilanova
de Prades
BARCELONA

ayud
Salou
SEE INSET FOR
ENLARGED AREA
Mont-Roig del Camp
Cambrils
L'Hospitalet de l'Infant
L'Ametlla de Mar

Vinaroz
Alcanar
Peñiscola
Benicarlo
Torreblanca
Alcoceber
Oropesa del Mar
Nules
Benicasim

Islas Baleares

Puebla de Farnals
Palma
Valencia

Jaraco
Miramar Playa
Daimus
Oliva
Vergel
Benisa
Denia
Moraira
Calpe
Campello
Altea
Muchamiel
Benidorm
Villajoyosa
Baños
Alicante
e Fortuna
Elche/Elx
La Marina
Murcia
Guardamar del Segura

Los Alcazares
Cartagena

FRANCE

ANDORRA
Guils de Cerdanya
Santa Juliá
de Lòria
Bellver de
Cerdanya
Puigcerdà
Llançà
Puerto de
la Selva
Vilallonga de Ter

CATALUÑA -
Ripoll
l'Escala
Castelló d'Empuries
Sant Pere Pescador
l'Estartit
Pals
Torroella de Montgri
Solsona
CATALUNYA
Begur
Taradell
Sant Antoni de Calonge
Palafrugell
Palamós
Castell d'Aro
La Platja d'Aro
Tossa de Mar
Sant Feliu de Guixols
Santa Susana
Lloret de Mar
Sant Cebriá de Vallalta
Blanes
Sabadell
Arenys de Mar
Malgrat de Mar
Calella
Pineda de Mar
Cabrera de Mar
El Masnou
Badalona
Roda
Santa
Viladecans
BARCELONA
de
Oliva
Gavá
Bara
Cunit
Sitges
El Vendrell
Vilanova i la Geltrú
Tamarit
Tarragona

0   20   40 miles
0   20   40   60 kilometres

9

SWITZERLAND

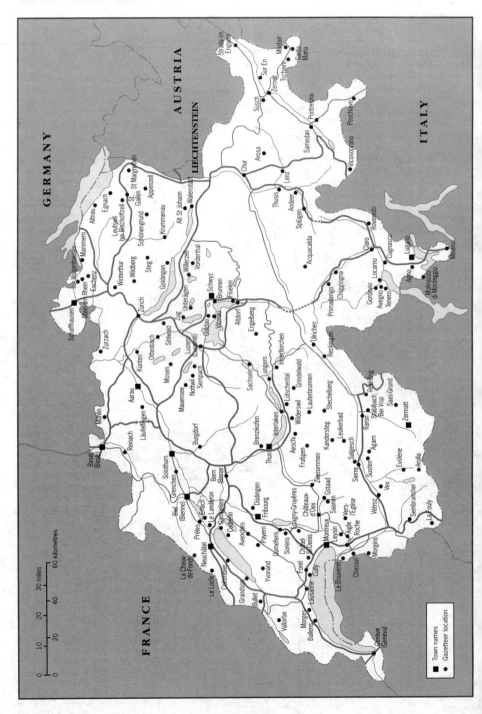

10

MAJOR ROADS AND RAIL TUNNELS

• ROAD TUNNELS •

See Lights in the ABC. There are also minimum and maximum speed limits in operation in the road tunnels.

During the winter wheel chains may occasionally be required on the approaches to some tunnels. However, they are not allowed to be used in tunnels and laybys are available for the removal and refitting of wheel chains. Charges listed below should be used as a guide only.

BIELSA France-Spain

The trans-Pyrenean tunnel is 3km (2 miles) long, and runs nearly 1830 metres (6000ft) above sea level between Aragnouet and Bielsa. Under normal weather conditions the Bielsa is open 24hrs a day; it is not recommended for caravans.

CADI Spain

The tunnel is 5km (3 miles) long and runs about 1220 metres (4000ft) above sea level under the Sierra del Cadi mountain range between the villages of Bellver de Cerdanya and Baga, and to the west of the Toses (Tosas) Pass.

Charges	(in Pesetas)
Motorcycles	1070
Cars	1330
Car/caravan	2900

FREJUS France-Italy

This tunnel is over 1220 metres (4000ft) above sea level and runs between Modane and Bardonecchia. The tunnel is 12.8km (8 miles) long, 4.5 metres (14ft 9in) high, and the single carriageway is 9 metres (29ft 6in) wide. The minimum speed is 60kph (37mph) and the maximum 80kph (49mph).

Charges	(in French francs)
Motorcycles	92
Cars wheelbase less than 2.30 metres (7ft 6.5in)	92
Wheelbase from 2.30 metres to	

2.63 metres (7ft 6.5in to 8ft 7.5in)	139
Charges	**(in Pesetas)**
Wheelbase from 2.63 metres to	
3.30 metres (8ft 7.5in to 10ft 10in)	181
Car/caravan	181
Wheelbase over 3.30 metres (10ft 10in)	444
Vehicles with three axles	677
With four or more axles	895

MONT BLANC Chamonix (France)-Courmayeur (Italy)

The tunnel is over 1220 metres (4000ft) above sea level and is 11.6km (7 miles) long and the single carriageway is 7 metres (23ft) wide. The permitted dimensions of vehicles are: height 4.30 metres (14ft 1in); length 20 metres (65ft 7in); width 2.80 metres (9ft 2in). Larger vehicles, up to 4.70 metres (15ft 5in) high, by special arrangement. The minimum speed is 50kph (31mph) and the maximum 80kph (49mph). Do not stop, overtake, sound your horn or make U-turns. Use only side/rear lights not headlights and keep 100 metres (110yds) distance between vehicles.

Make sure you have sufficient petrol for the journey, 30km (19 miles). There are break-down bays with telephones. From November to March, wheel chains may occasionally be required on the approaches to the tunnel.

Charges	(in French francs)
Motorcycles	90
Cars wheelbase less than 2.30 metres (7ft 6.5in)	90
Wheelbase from 2.30 metres but less than	
2.63 metres (7ft 6.5in to 8ft 7.5in)	140
Wheelbase from 2.63 metres to a maximum of	
3.30 metres (8ft 7.5in to 10ft 10in)	185
Car/caravan	185
Wheelbase over 3.30 metres (10ft 10in)	455
Vehicles with three axles	690
With four or more axles	920

GRAND ST BERNARD Switzerland - Italy

The tunnel is over 1830 metres (6000ft) above sea level. Although there are covered approaches, wheel chains may be needed to reach it in winter. The Customs, passport control and toll offices are at the entrance. The tunnel is 5.9km (3.6 miles) long. The permitted maximum dimensions of vehicles are: height 4 metres (13ft 1in), width 2.5 metres (8ft 2.5in). The minimum speed is 40kph (24mph) and the maximum 80kph (49mph). Do not stop or overtake. There are breakdown bays with telephones on either side.

Charges	(in Swiss francs)
Motorcycles	27
Cars	27
Car/caravan	27
Minibus, camper van (2 axles)	56.50
Vehicles with three axles	90
with four axles	134
with five or more axles	139

ST GOTTHARD Switzerland

The world's longest road tunnel at 16.3km (10 miles) is about 1159 metres (3800ft) above sea level; it runs under the St Gotthard Pass from Göschenen, on the northern side in the Alps, to Airolo in the Ticino. The tunnel is 4.5 metres (14ft 9in) high, and the single carriageway is 7.5 metres (25ft) wide. The maximum speed is 80kph (49mph). Forming part of the Swiss motorway network, the tunnel is subject to the annual motorway tax, and the tax disc must be displayed (see Switzerland - Motorway tax).

SAN BERNARDINO Switzerland

This tunnel is over 1525 metres (5000ft) above sea level. It is 6.6km (4 miles) long, 4.8 metres (15ft 9in) high; the carriageway is 7 metres (23ft) wide. Do not stop or overtake in the tunnel. Keep 100 metres (110yds) between vehicles. There are breakdown bays with telephones.

Forming part of the Swiss national motorways network, the tunnel is subject to the annual Swiss motorway tax, and the tax disc must be displayed (see Switzerland - Motorway tax).

ARLBERG Austria

This tunnel is 14km (8.75 miles) long and runs at about 1220 metres (4000ft) above sea level, to the south of and parallel to the Arlberg Pass.

Charges	(in Austrian schillings)
Motorcycles	100
Cars	190
Caravans	80

BOSRUCK Austria

This tunnel is 742 metres (2434ft) above sea level. It is 5.8km (3.6 miles) long and runs between Spital am Pyhrn and Selzthal, to the east of the Pyhrn Pass. The maximum speed is 80kph (49mph). Do not overtake. Use of dipped headlights compulsory; there are occasional emergency laybys with telephones. With the Gleinalm Tunnel (see below) it forms an important part of the A9 Pyhrn Autobahn between Linz and Graz, now being built in stages

Charges	(in Austrian schillings)
Motorcycles	60
Cars	70
Car/caravan	100

FELBERTAUERN Austria

This tunnel is over 1525 metres (5000ft) above sea level; it runs between Mittersill and Matrei, west of and parallel to the Grossglockner Pass. The tunnel is 5.3km (3.25 miles) long, 4.5 metres (14ft 9in) high, and the two-lane carriageway is 7 metres (23ft) wide. From November to April, wheel chains may be needed on the approach to the tunnel.

Charges	(in Austrian schillings)
Motorcycles	100
Cars summer rate (May-Oct)	190
winter rate (Nov-Apr)	110
Car/caravan summer rate (May-Oct)	230
winter rate (Nov-Apr)	150

GLEINALM Austria

This tunnel is 817 metres (2680ft) above sea

level; it is 8.3km (5 miles) long and runs between St Michael and Friesach, near Graz. The tunnel forms part of the A9 Pyhrn Autobahn, which will in due course, run from Linz, via Graz, to Slovenia.

Charges	(in Austrian schillings)
Motorcycles	100
Cars	130
Car/caravan	160

KARAWANKEN Austria-Slovenia

This motorway tunnel under the Karawanken mountain range was opened in 1991. About 610 metres (2000ft) above sea level and nearly 8km (5 miles) long, it runs between Rosenbach in Austria and Jesenice in Slovenia.

Charges	(in Austrian schillings)
Motorcycles	90
Cars	90
Car/caravan	135

TAUERN AUTOBAHN (Katschberg and Radstädter) Austria

Two tunnels, the Katschberg and the Radstädter Tauern, form the key elements of this toll motorway between Salzburg and Carinthia.

The Katschberg tunnel is 1110 metres (3642ft) above sea level. It is 5.4km (3.5 miles) long, 4.5 metres (14ft 9in) high, and the single carriageway is 7.5 metres (25ft) wide.

The Radstädter Tauern tunnel is 1340 metres (4396ft) above sea level and runs to the east of and parallel to the Tauern railway tunnel (see below). The tunnel is 6.4km (4 miles) long, 4.5 metres (14ft 9in) high and the single carriageway is 7.5m (25ft) wide.

Charges	(in Austrian schillings)
for the whole toll section between Flachau and Rennweg:	
Motorcycles	100
Cars summer rate (May-Oct)	190
winter rate (Nov-Apr)	120
Car/caravan summer rate (May-Oct)	230
winter rate (Nov-Apr)	160

● RAIL TUNNELS ●

CHANNEL TUNNEL See the Continental ABC

SWITZERLAND

Vehicles are conveyed throughout the year through the Lötschberg tunnel (Kandersteg-Goppenstein). Services are frequent with no advance booking necessary; the actual transit time is 15-20 minutes for each tunnel but loading and unloading formalities can take some time.

A full timetable and tariff list which is available from the Swiss National Tourist Office (see Switzerland - Tourist information for address) or at most Swiss frontier crossings.

ALBULA TUNNEL Switzerland

Thusis (723 metres, 2372ft) - Samedan (1722 metres, 5650ft)

The railway tunnel is 5.9km (3.5 miles) long. Motor vehicles can be conveyed through the tunnel, but you are recommended to give notice. Thusis telephone 081 811113 and Samedan telephone 082 65404. Journey duration 90 minutes.

Services
9 trains daily going south; 6 trains daily going north

Charges	(in Swiss francs; likely to increase)
Cars (including driver)	100
Additional passengers	24
Car/caravan	270

FURKA TUNNEL Switzerland

Oberwald (1367 metres, 4482ft)-Realp (1539 metres, 5046ft)

The railway tunnel is 15.4km (9.5 miles) long. Journey duration 15 minutes.

Services
Hourly from 06.50-21.00 hrs

Charges	(in Swiss Francs)
Cars (including passengers)	34
Car/caravan	68

OBERALP RAILWAY Switzerland

Andermatt (1444 metres, 4737ft)-Sedrun

(1441 metres, 4728ft). Journey duration 50 minutes.

Booking
Advance booking is necessary; Andermatt telephone 044 67220, Sedrun tel 086 91137.

Services
2-4 trains daily, winter only (from October-April).

Charges	(in Swiss francs)
Cars (including driver)	73
Additional passengers	11
Car/caravan	146

TAUERN TUNNEL Austria
Bockstein (1131 metres, 3711ft)(near Badgastein)-Mallnitz, 8.5km (5.5 miles) long. Maximum dimensions for caravans and trailers: height 8ft 10.5in, width 8ft 2.5in.

Booking
Advance booking is unnecessary (except for request trains), but motorists must report at least 30 minutes before the train is due to depart. Drivers must drive their vehicles on and off the wagon.

Services
At summer weekends, trains run approximately every half-hour in both directions, 06.30-22.30hrs; and every half-hour during the night. During the rest of the year, there is an hourly service from 06.30-22.30hrs (23.30hrs on Friday and Saturday from 7 July-9 September). Journey duration 12 minutes.

Charges	(in Austrian schillings)
Motorcycles (with or without sidecar)	100
Cars (including passengers)	190
Caravans	80

SPECIMEN BOOKING LETTERS FOR RESERVATIONS

Please use blcok captals and enclose an International Reply Coupon, obtainable from post offices. Be sure to fill in your own name and address, including the post code and the country.

ENGLISH
Dear Sir,
I intend to stay at your site for ....days, arriving on.............(date and month) and departing on....................(date and month).

We are a party of ....people, including....adults and ....children (aged...........) and shall require a pitch for ....tent(s) and/or parking space for our car/caravan/caravan trailer.

We should like to hire a tent/caravan/bungalow.

Please quote full charges when replying and advised on the deposit require, which will be forwarded without delay.

FRENCH
Monsieur,
Je me propose de séjourner à votre terraine de camping pour ....jours, depuis le..... jusqu'au..........

Nous sommes........personnes en tout, y compris ....adultes et ....enfants (âgés de......) et nous aurons besoin d'un emplacement pour ....tente(s), et/ou un parking pour notre voiture/caravane/remorque.

Nous voudrions louer une tente/caravane/bungalow.

Veuillez me donner dans votre réponse une idée de vos prix, m'indiquant en même temps le montant qu'il faut payer en avance, ce qui vous sera envoyé sans délai.

GERMAN
Sehr geehrter Herr!
Ich beabsichtige, mich auf Ihrem Campingplatz ....Tage aufzuhalten, und zwar vom.....bis zum......

Wir sind im ganzen ....Personen, ...Erwachsene und ....Kinder (in Alter von......), und benötigen Platz für Zelt(e) und/oder unseren Wagen/Wohnwagen/Wohnwagenanhänger.

Wir möchten ein Zelt/Wohnwagen/Bungalow mieten.

Bitte, geben Sie mir in Ihrem Antwortschreiben die vollen Preise bekannt, und ebenso die Höhe der von mir zu leistenden Anzahlung, die Ihnen alsdann unverzüglich überwiesen wird.

ITALIAN
Egregio Signore,
Ho intenzione di remanere presso di voi per .....giorni. Arriverò il.....e partirò il......

Siamo un gruppo di.......persone in totale, compreso ......adulti e ......bambini (de età.....) e vorrremo un posto per ......tenda(tende) e/o spazio per parcheggiare la nostra vetture/carovana/roulette.

Desideriamo affittare una tenda/carovana/bungalow.

Vi preghiamo di quotare i prezzi completi quando ci risponderete, e darci informazioni sul deposito richiesto, che vi sarà rimesso senza ritardo.

SPANISH
Muy señor mio,
Desearia me reservara espacio por ......dias, a partir del.......hasta el......

Nuestro grupo comprende .....personas todo comprendido, ...adultos y ....niños (.......de años de edad). Necesitarimos un espacio por......tienda(s) y/o espacio para apacar nuestro choche/caravana/remolque.

Deseariamos alquilar una tienda de campana/caravan/bungalow.

Le ruego nos comunique los precios y nos informe sobre el depósito que debemos remitirle.

USING THE TELEPHONE ABROAD

• LOCAL AND INTERNATIONAL CALLS •

It is no more difficult to use the telephone abroad than it is at home. It only appears to be so because of unfamiliar language and equipment. The following chart may help with elementary principles when making local calls from public callboxes, but try to get help if you encounter language difficulties.

International Direct Dial (IDD) calls can be made from many public callboxes abroad, avoiding surcharges imposed by most hotels.

Types of callboxes from which IDD calls can be made are identified in the chart. You will need to dial the international code, international country code (for the UK it is 44), the telephone dialling code (omitting the initial 'O'), followed by the number. For example to call the AA, Basingstoke 01256 20123 from Italy dial 00 44 1256 20123. Use higher-denomination coins for IDD calls to ensure reasonable periods of conversation before the coin expiry warning. The equivalent of £2 should allow for a reasonable amount of time.

Cardphones are in general use; the phonecards to operate them may be purchased from a post office or shop in the vicinity, unless stated otherwise.

* Where asterisk shown wait for second dialling tone.

Country	Insert coin/card before or after lifting receiver	Dialling tone	Making local and national calls
AUSTRIA	After (instructions in English in many callboxes)		
BELGIUM	After	Same as UK	Precede number with relevant area code where necessary
FRANCE	After	Continuous tone	10 digit numbers have been introduced throughout France). This change took place at the end of 1996. Please see the note on p. 59.
GERMANY	After	Continuous tone	Precede number with relevant area code when necessary
ITALY	Before		Precede number with relevant area code when necessary
LUXEMBOURG	After	Same as UK	There are no area codes
NETHERLANDS	After (instructions in English in all callboxes)		
PORTUGAL	After	Same as UK	Precede number with relevant area code when necessary
SPAIN	After	(instructions in English in many callboxes)	Do not press button to left of the dial or you may lose your money
SWITZERLAND	After	Continuous tone	Precede number with relevant area code when necessary

Some useful premium rate numbers for help and advice on motoring abroad

Hints & Advice

Austria	0336 401 866
Belgium	0336 401 867
France	0336 401 869
Germany	0336 401 870
Italy	0336 401 874
Luxembourg	0336 401 875
Netherlands	0336 401 876
Portugal	0336 401 878

Spain	0336 401 879
Switzerland	0336 401 881

Weather Forecasts

Channel Crossings	0336 401 361
City by City Six Day	0336 411212

Other Useful Information

French Motorway Tools	0336 401 884
European Fuel Prices	0336 401 883

Port Information

Hampshire/Dorset Ports	0336 401 891
Kent Ports	0336 401 890

Calls are charged at 50p per minute daytime, 45p per minute evenings and weekends. Prices are correct at time of going to press.

Coins needed to operate callbox (local calls)	Higher value coins accepted	International callbox identification	What to dial for the UK	What to dial for the Irish Republic
3 coin slot ASch 1, 5, or 10 4 coin slot Asch 1, 5, 10, or 20. Also cardphones, the phonecards may be purchased from post offices and tobacconists (ASch 50, 100, or 200)	ASch10 or 20	Payphones with 3/4 coin slots. Cardphones, credit card phones at airports and on railway platforms	00 44	00 353
BFr5 or BFr20 (BFr 50 in some booths). Phonecard - only booths increasing.	BFr5 or 20 (BFr 50 in some booths).	Payphones identified with European flags. Cardphones	00 44	00 353
Fr1 for payphone, phonecard (telecarte) for cardphones. Payphones disappearing, phonecards may be purchased from airports, post offices, railway stations, tobacconists - look for 'Telecarte en vente ici'. French phonecards may be purchased in the UK from Voyages Vacances, Linen Hall, 162 Regent Street W1R 5TB telephone 0171-287 3171	Fr0.5,1, 2 or 5 (FR10 only in small payphones in café, hotel etc)	All payphones. Cardphones	00 44	00 44
3 x 10 pfennig (increase likely). Payphones being replaced by cardphones	DM1 or DM5	Payphones and cardphones marked 'International'	00 44	00 353
Public callboxes may only be operated with phonecards		All public callboxes	00 44	00 353
Public callboxes may only be operated with phonecards		Roadside callboxes	00 44	00 353
25 cents x 2. Few payphones remain, largely replaced by cardphones	1, 2.5 or 5 guilders	All payphones. Cardphones	00 44	00 353
ESc5, 10, 20 or 50	ESc50	Payphones with notice in English. Cardphones	00 44	00 353
Ptas 5,25 or 100. Many callboxes accept both phonecards and coins. Cards worth Ptas 1,000/2,000 may be purchased from tobacconists (Estanco) NOT post offices	Ptas 200 or 500	International calls can be made from almost all public callboxes	07 *44	07 *353
20 centimes x 3	SFr1 or 5	All phones including cardphones	00 44	00 353

* Where asterisk shown wait for second dialling tone.

PLACE INDEX

Salve, Marina di 209
San Antonio di Mavignola 194
San Baronto 201
San Felice del Benaco 194
San Gimignano 201
San Giorgio 211
San Lorenzen 194
San Marino 205
San Martino di Castrozza 194
San Máuro Mare 205
San Menáio 209
San Nicolo di Ricadi 209
San Piero a Sieve 201
San Piero in Bagno 205
San Pietro di Corteno Gogli 194
San Remo 201
San Sigmund 194
Santa Cesárea Terme 209
Santa Lucia 210
Santa Maria di Castellabate 209
Sant'Alessio Siculo 211
Sant'Antioco 210
Sant'Antonio di Barcellona 211
San Teodoro 210
San Vincenzo 201
Sardegna (Sardinia) 210
Sarre 194
Sarteano 201
Sarzana 201
Sasso Marconi 205
Savignano sul Rubicone 205
Scacchi, Lido degli 205
Scopello 211
Seccagrande 211
Senigallia 205
Sestri Levante 201
Siena 201
Sirolo 205
Sistiana 196
Sole, Lido del 209
Sorico 195
Sorrento 209
Specchiolla, Lido 207
Sperlonga 206
Spina, Lido di 205
Spoleto 205
Stella San Giovanni 201

Talamone 202
Taormina 211
Terracina 207

Teulada 210
Torbole 195
Torino di Sangro Marina 205
Torre Daniele 195
Torre del Lago Puccini 202
Torre Rinalda 209
Torre Salinas 210
Tortoreto, Lido 202
Toscolano Maderno 195
Treporti 198
Troghi 202

Ugento 209

Vada 202
Valledoria 210
Valnontey 195
Varcaturo, Marina di 209
Vasto 205
Verona 198
Viareggio 202
Vicenza 198
Vico Equense 209
Vieste 209
Villalago 205
Villasimius 210
Vipiteno 195
Viverone 195
Vols 195
Volterra 202

Zapponeta 210
Zinola 202
Zoldo Alto 198

LUXEMBOURG

Berdorf 214
Bous/Remich 214
Clervaux 214
Consdorf 214
Diekirch 214
Dillingen 214
Echternach 214
Enscherange 214
Esch-sur-Alzette 214
Haller 214
Heiderscheid 214
Ingeldorf 214
Kockelscheuer 214
Larochette 214
Mersch 214
Nommern 214
Obereisenbach 214
Reisdorf 214
Rosport 215

Steinfort 215
Vianden 215
Walsdorf 215

NETHERLANDS

Aalsmeer 220
Afferden 224
Alkmaar 220
Ameland, Island of 218
Amen 218
Amsterdam 220
Andijk 220
Annen 218
Appeltern 220
Arcen 224
Arnemuiden 224
Arnhem 220
Asselt 224
Assen 218

Baarland 224
Baarle Nassau 224
Babberich 220
Barendrecht 224
Beekbergen 220
Berg en Terblijt 224
Bergeyk 224
Berkhout 220
Biddinghuizen 221
Bilthoven 220
Bladel 224
Blokzijl 220
Borger 218
Boxtel 224
Breskens 224
Brielle 224
Broekhuizenvorst 224
Brouwershaven 224
Burgh-Haamstede 224
Buurse 220

Callantsoog 220
Cocksdorp, De 220
Cromvoirt 225

Dalfsen 221
Delden 221
Delft 225
Delfzijl 218
Denekamp 221
Diepenheim 221
Diever 218
Dieverbrug 218
Doesburg 221
Doetinchem 221

Domburg 225
Doorn 221
Dordrecht 225
Dronten 221
Dwingeloo 218

Echt 225
Edam 221
Eerbeek 221
Eersel 225
Emmen 218
Emst 221
Enschede 221
Ermelo 221
Exloo 219

Flushing see Vlissingen
Formerum 219

Gaasperplas 221
Gasselte 219
s'-Gravenzande 225
Groede 225
Groet 222
Grolloo 219
Groningen 219
Groote Keeten 222

Haag, Den (The Hague) 225
Haaksbergen 222
Halfweg 222
Hank 225
Harkstede 219
Harlingen 219
Hattem 222
Hee 219
Heiloo 222
Helder, Den 222
Hellevoetsluis 225
Hengelo (Gelderland) 222
Hengelo (Overijssel) 222
Hengstdijk 225
Herkenbosch 225
Herpen 225
Heumen 222
Hilvarenbeek 225
Hindeloopen 219
Hoek 225
Hoek van Holland 225
Hoenderloo 222
Hoeven 225
Holten 222
Hoogerheide 225
Hoorn, Den 222

Kamperland 225